FEDERAL COURTS

Aspen Casebook Series

FEDERAL COURTS

Context, Cases, and Problems

Second Edition

Michael P. Allen
Stetson University College of Law

Michael Finch
Stetson University College of Law

Caprice L. Roberts
Savannah Law School

Wolters Kluwer

Published by Wolters Kluwer in New York.

Wolters Kluwer serves customers worldwide with CCH, Aspen Publishers, and Kluwer Law International products. (www.wolterskluwerlb.com)

To contact Customer Service, e-mail customer.service@wolterskluwer.com, call 1-800-234-1660, fax 1-800-901-9075, or mail correspondence to:

Wolters Kluwer
Attn: Order Department
PO Box 990
Frederick, MD 21705

Printed in the United States of America.

4 5 6 7 8 9 0

ISBN 978-1-4548-2266-0

Library of Congress Cataloging-in-Publication Data

Allen, Michael, 1967- author.
Federal courts: context, cases, and problems / Michael P. Allen, Stetson University College of Law; Michael Finch, Stetson University College of Law; Caprice L. Roberts, West Virginia University College of Law. — Second edition.
pages cm
Includes bibliographical references and index.
ISBN 978-1-4548-2266-0 (alk. paper)
1. Courts — United States. I. Finch, Michael, 1952- author. II. Roberts, Caprice L., author. III. Title.
KF8719.A835 2015
347.73′2 — dc23

2014047976

About Wolters Kluwer Law & Business

Wolters Kluwer Law & Business is a leading global provider of intelligent information and digital solutions for legal and business professionals in key specialty areas, and respected educational resources for professors and law students. Wolters Kluwer Law & Business connects legal and business professionals as well as those in the education market with timely, specialized authoritative content and information-enabled solutions to support success through productivity, accuracy and mobility.

Serving customers worldwide, Wolters Kluwer Law & Business products include those under the Aspen Publishers, CCH, Kluwer Law International, Loislaw, ftwilliam.com and MediRegs family of products.

CCH products have been a trusted resource since 1913, and are highly regarded resources for legal, securities, antitrust and trade regulation, government contracting, banking, pension, payroll, employment and labor, and healthcare reimbursement and compliance professionals.

Aspen Publishers products provide essential information to attorneys, business professionals and law students. Written by preeminent authorities, the product line offers analytical and practical information in a range of specialty practice areas from securities law and intellectual property to mergers and acquisitions and pension/benefits. Aspen's trusted legal education resources provide professors and students with high-quality, up-to-date and effective resources for successful instruction and study in all areas of the law.

Kluwer Law International products provide the global business community with reliable international legal information in English. Legal practitioners, corporate counsel and business executives around the world rely on Kluwer Law journals, looseleafs, books, and electronic products for comprehensive information in many areas of international legal practice.

Loislaw is a comprehensive online legal research product providing legal content to law firm practitioners of various specializations. Loislaw provides attorneys with the ability to quickly and efficiently find the necessary legal information they need, when and where they need it, by facilitating access to primary law as well as state-specific law, records, forms and treatises.

ftwilliam.com offers employee benefits professionals the highest quality plan documents (retirement, welfare and non-qualified) and government forms (5500/PBGC, 1099 and IRS) software at highly competitive prices.

MediRegs products provide integrated health care compliance content and software solutions for professionals in healthcare, higher education and life sciences, including professionals in accounting, law and consulting.

Wolters Kluwer Law & Business, a division of Wolters Kluwer, is headquartered in New York. Wolters Kluwer is a market-leading global information services company focused on professionals.

For Debbie, Ben, and Noah

—MPA

For Lora, Chloe, and Lily

—MF

For Rosemarie Falzone
(May 10, 1936–May 11, 2011)

—CLR

SUMMARY OF CONTENTS

CONTENTS

PREFACE

We believe that Federal Courts is one of the most challenging courses in the law school curriculum. It draws on principles from Constitutional Law, Civil Procedure, Remedies, and Administrative Law to name just a few law school courses. Moreover, the course requires a strong understanding of American history as well as philosophical underpinnings of government under the United States Constitution.

At the same time, Federal Courts is also an immensely practical course. For example, if one intends to actually enforce the constitutional rights afforded clients, an understanding of 42 U.S.C. § 1983 (Chapter 9) is usually indispensible. Similarly, if one intends to pursue a career as a state prosecutor, a public defender, or private criminal defense lawyer, the law of federal habeas corpus (Chapter 13) is critical to effective litigation in the criminal justice system. And for those who intend to engage in general civil litigation in federal courts, an understanding of subjects like justiciability (Chapter 2), subject matter jurisdiction (Chapters 5, 6, and 7), and abstention (Chapter 10) is vital to one's ability to secure access to the courts.

One of our principal goals in writing this textbook was to preserve the theoretical richness of the material while providing opportunities for students to put that information into practice. For these reasons, we have used a variety of methods to explore the material in each chapter. Most chapters begin with a "Reference Problem" designed to preview many of the issues that will be explored in the pages that follow. While students will not be ready to fully resolve the problem as they begin the chapter, the problem introduces the issues that follow and gives students an appreciation for their practical importance. Once students have completed their study of the chapter materials, students can return to the Reference Problem and assess their understanding.

Each chapter presents an overview of the relevant area of law. This narrative section is designed to allow students to see the forest before exploring the individual trees. In other words, it provides the broader context for the specific doctrines explored.

Our presentation of the chapter materials differs from that used in most legal textbooks. After reproducing the principal cases, we offer narrative text and questions and avoid use of numbered notes. We also periodically use charts, graphs, and other visual aids to offer working summaries of the material previously discussed. These aids are not meant to take the place of a student's own synthesis of the material, which is critical to the learning process. We believe, however, that a tentative structuring of the complex doctrines addressed in Federal Courts will enhance student synthesis. That said, we recognize that your professor may have a different approach to the material, one that improves on the structures we have suggested.

Finally, each chapter includes intermittent problems that require students to apply the material just studied. These problems provide the opportunity to consolidate your understanding of a topic before moving on to a new topic. We conclude each chapter with a separate section providing yet more problems for review and discussion.

In sum, this text focuses on the *use* of the doctrines studied. If our approach assists you in your exploration of Federal Courts, we will consider it a success.

Michael P. Allen
Michael Finch
Caprice L. Roberts

December 2014

ACKNOWLEDGMENTS

This textbook, now in its second edition, would not have been possible without the assistance and understanding of a great many people. We collectively extend our thanks to the wonderful people at Wolters Kluwer/Aspen Publishers, including Steve Erlich, Carol McGeehan, Rick Mixter, Eric Holt, and Dana Wilson. The project would never have come to be if not for their faith in us and their excellent guidance. We would also not be in a position to see this second edition in print without their collective support in our vision.

We also thank Stetson University College of Law, West Virginia University College of Law, and Savannah Law School for the support each institution has provided to this project from its inception through this current edition. Numerous people at each College have been instrumental in assisting us. Space does not allow us to mention all of them. However, we would be remiss if we did not single out the following people for their help: Stetson University College of Law former Dean Darby Dickerson and current Dean Chris Pietruszkiewicz; members of the Stetson's Faculty Support Office (formerly led by Ms. Louise Petren and now in the capable hands of Ms. Shannon Edgar); Stetson graduates Jason P. Stearns, Scott Stevenson, and Paul Crochet for their excellent research assistance and valuable comments; Savannah Law School forthcoming graduate Cameron Crandell Kuhlman for thoughtful suggestions and Professor Judd F. Sneirson for chart assistance under pressure; West Virginia University College of Law former Dean Joyce E. McConnell and former Dean John W. Fisher II; West Virginia graduates Paul Hudson Jones II, Matthew Lincoln Clark, Allen Porter Mendenhall, and Natalie S. Wright for their helpful suggestions; West Virginia Faculty Assistant Bertha Romine; and professors Gerald G. Ashdown, Laura S. Fitzgerald Cooper, Michael R. Dimino, Scott Dodson, Sr., Susan S. Kuo, Marcia L. McCormick, Philip A. Pucillo, Joan M. Shaughnessy, Stephen I. Vladeck, and other federal courts professors who provided thoughtful and insightful reviews through the anonymous Aspen review process. We also want to thank all the faculty members who have shown faith in us by adopting the casebook. Your comments have been helpful beyond our ability to convey. As with our first edition, any errors are, of course, our own.

We also recognize that we could not have completed the project, including all our updates over the years and this second edition, without the support and understanding of our families. They put up with long nights, obsession over details, and, we confess, an occasional bit of short temper. What is more, they did all of this in good spirits. Specifically, Professor Allen thanks his wife Debbie and his sons Ben and Noah. Professor Finch thanks his wife, Lora, and his daughters, Chloe and Lily. Professor Roberts thanks Andrew McCanse Wright and Garrett Robert Wright. She also thanks the Honorable Julia Smith Gibbons and the Honorable Ronald Lee Gilman for the opportunity to experience the federal judiciary in action.

Finally, we want to acknowledge all the students we have had in our careers. In many ways, our vision for this textbook has been shaped with those students—and those to come—in mind. Our experiences in the classroom helped us immeasurably as we engaged in this endeavor.

Michael P. Allen
Michael Finch
Caprice L. Roberts

December 2014

FEDERAL COURTS

CHAPTER
1

The Federal Court System: Structure and Themes

A. THE FEDERAL COURT SYSTEM IN HISTORICAL PERSPECTIVE

1. The Federal Courts in the Constitutional Generation

The federal courts of the United States, although thought to comprise "the least dangerous branch"[1] of the federal government, represent a significant and

1. Alexander Hamilton, The Federalist No. 78, at 465-66 (Clinton Russiter ed., 1961) ("It proves incontestably that the judiciary is beyond comparison the weakest of the three departments of

indelible component of America's constitutional democracy. The executive, legislative, and judicial branches embody our tripartite system of federal government. The federal judiciary is a separate and coequal branch that serves as a critical check on powers exercised by the executive and legislative branches.

The breadth and depth of federal court power are more than a check. They permit resolution of a wide array of disputes under federal law and under state law. For example, the primary bodies of the federal judiciary— the United States Supreme Court, the federal courts of appeals, and the federal district courts— collectively considered approximately 439,854 cases, according to the Court's 2013 year-end report.[2] While the federal judiciary continues to grow in size and import, its recipe for success lies in its design, its balance with the other branches, and its exercise of restraint.

a. The Articles of Confederation

Before the Constitution, the Articles of Confederation governed the new republic. Many of the same men who drafted the Constitution were also involved in the drafting of the Articles of Confederation in 1777. They feared a strong central government with too much power. The Articles of Confederation represented a limited attempt to form a national government, but they lacked sufficient structure or enforcement mechanisms to handle the significant challenges emerging in the young nation.[3] For example, defiant states disregarded recommendations of the Confederation Congress with impunity.[4] The Articles formed neither an executive branch nor a system of national courts.[5] Most power was vested in individual states.

Under the Articles of Confederation, the national government's minor judicial power was vested in Congress.[6] Specifically, Congress had the power of "appointing courts for the trial of piracies and felonies committed on the high seas and establishing courts for receiving and determining finally appeals in all cases of captures." Congress never established the supremacy of these national admiralty courts, however, as several states either restricted litigants' right to appeal to the national courts or refused to enforce the decrees they issued.[7]

---

power"; reassuring that the judicial branch would be "least dangerous to the political rights of the constitution") (citing Charles de Secondat, Baron de Montesquieu, The Spirit of the Laws (1748)); *see also* Alexander M. Bickel, The Least Dangerous Branch–The Supreme Court at the Bar of Politics (1962).

2. Chief Justice John G. Roberts, *2013 Year-End Report on the Federal Judiciary*. This figure includes 77 cases argued from the 7,509 filings in the 2012 Term of the Supreme Court; 56,475 filed in the federal appellate courts in fiscal year 2013; and 284,604 civil filings and 91,266 criminal cases in the federal district courts.

3. Richard H. Fallon, Jr., John F. Manning, Daniel J. Meltzer, & David L. Shapiro, Hart & Wechsler's The Federal Courts and the Federal System 2 (6th ed. 2009) [hereinafter Fallon et al., Hart & Wechsler's The Federal Courts].

4. *Id.*

5. *Id.*

6. State courts exercised trial jurisdiction in admiralty disputes, while Congress exercised some form of appellate jurisdiction over state court admiralty disputes through the appointment of congressional committees that functioned as appellate "courts." *See* Wythe Holt, *"To Establish Justice": Politics, the Judiciary Act of 1789, and the Invention of the Federal Courts, 1989 Duke L.J. 1421,* 1427-29.

7. *See id.* at 1428.

b. Establishing a National Court and Discretion for Congress to Create Lower Federal Courts

The delegates to the Constitutional Convention of 1787 wanted a national, independent judiciary. Before 1787, American leaders agreed that the Articles of Confederation required enhancement.[8] To those favoring national representative institutions over the passions of local politics, "a new, national constitution was necessary to restore a regime of virtuous government—or, failing that, a scheme that would protect individual rights and the public good by ensuring that faction would be checked by faction and ambition set against ambition."[9]

Yet early American leaders were unsure exactly how to form the federal judiciary. Many of the details of the judiciary's organization would not become clear until the First Congress convened in 1789. But before Congress could implement federal judicial power through the Judiciary Act of 1789, the Framers first had to forge the governing framework for the federal judiciary in the Constitution. Remarkably, the structure of the federal judiciary in Article III of the Constitution endures without change.[10]

The touchstone of the American federal judiciary is Article III of the United States Constitution. It both establishes the federal judiciary and outlines its power. Section 1 of Article III first provides the contours of the federal courts:

> The judicial Power of the United States, shall be vested in one Supreme Court, and in such inferior Courts as the Congress may from time to time ordain and establish. . . .

This provision establishes the federal judicial system by mandating that the national judicial power "shall be vested." Significantly, this national judicial power would resolve disputes involving states and individuals.[11] The remainder of the quoted passage from section 1 *establishes* the United States Supreme Court and *permits* the creation of lower federal courts. This combination represents the Framers' compromise, which established a national court while permitting state courts to exercise jurisdiction over disputes arising under federal law. Accordingly, section 1 leaves discretion to Congress regarding the possibility of creating inferior federal courts.

Section 1 also sets forth the parameters of judges' tenure:

> The Judges, both of the supreme and inferior Courts, shall hold their Offices during good Behaviour, and shall, at stated Times, receive for their Services, a Compensation, which shall not be diminished during their Continuance in Office.

To support the independence of the federal judiciary, Article III provides that all federal judges shall maintain their office "during good Behaviour," with

8. *Id.*

9. FALLON ET AL., HART & WECHSLER'S THE FEDERAL COURTS, *supra* note 3, at 3 (citing THE FEDERALIST, Nos. 10 & 51 (James Madison)).

10. The Article III template remains, but federal court power has changed in numerous ways, for example, the Eleventh Amendment.

11. *Id.* at 3-4 (noting that "perhaps the most crucial decision of the Constitutional Convention was that a federal government should be established with powers to act directly on individuals, not just on the member states" and "that there should be a federal judicial power operating, like the legislative and executive powers, upon both states and individuals"); *see also* U.S. Const. art. III, § 2.

salaries that cannot be decreased during their time in office. This good-behavior clause establishes that all federal judges have life tenure—removable only through impeachment by the House of Representatives and conviction by Senate trial of "high crimes and misdemeanors."

The Framers also set forth foundational, structural protection of judicial independence in Articles I (the legislative branch) and II (the executive branch) of the Constitution. They resolved that it was essential for federal jurists to be appointed by the President and confirmed by the Senate rather than be popularly elected. This remains a critical distinction between the federal judiciary and many state judiciaries.

Section 2 of Article III sets forth the nature of federal jurisdiction:

> The judicial Power shall extend to all Cases, in Law and Equity, arising under this Constitution, the Laws of the United States, and Treaties made, or which shall be made, under their Authority;–to all Cases affecting Ambassadors, other public Ministers and Consuls;–to all Cases of admiralty and maritime Jurisdiction;–to Controversies to which the United States shall be a Party;–to Controversies between two or more States;–between a State and Citizens of another State;–between Citizens of different States;–between Citizens of the same State claiming Lands under Grants of different States, and between a State, or the Citizens thereof, and foreign States, Citizens or Subjects.
>
> In all Cases affecting Ambassadors, other Public Ministers and Consuls, and those in which a State shall be Party, the supreme Court shall have original Jurisdiction. In all the other Cases before mentioned, the supreme Court shall have appellate Jurisdiction, both as to Law and Fact, with such Exceptions, and under such Regulations as the Congress shall make.

Clause 1 of section 2 states nine categories of cases included in the federal judicial power. The "arising under" jurisdiction over the Constitution, federal laws, and treaties is an essential ingredient to the creation and maintenance of a national body of law, but note that this section does *not* make such jurisdiction exclusive to federal courts. The Framers also wanted national protection for Ambassadors and other noted public officials; thus, they included such related cases as part of the federal judicial power. They maintained national authority over admiralty and maritime matters, which existed under the Articles of Confederation. The Framers believed that the United States should not be forced to proceed in state courts, so they included in the federal judicial power cases where the United States was a party. Before the Constitution, "border disputes had plagued the new states."[12] To foster national peace,[13] the Framers included national judicial power over controversies between states. Regarding jurisdiction over actions between a state and a citizen of another state, few breadcrumbs exist regarding the genesis of this provision but "concern about prejudices seems the only possible explanation."[14] In authorizing jurisdiction over suits between citizens of different states, the Framers expressed concerns about state court prejudice against noncitizens and the impact this might have on the nation's

12. *Id.* at 16.

13. *Id.* ("Though not specifically mentioned [during the Convention debates], a jurisdiction in controversies between states could be viewed as implicit in the . . . 'national peace and harmony' provision" of the plan submitted by Governor Edmund Randolph of Virginia).

14. *Id.* at 17.

developing economy.[15] Similar concerns appear to have influenced extension of federal judicial power to cases between a state (or its citizens) and "foreign" states (or its citizens or subjects).

Clause 2 of section 2 describes the original and appellate jurisdiction of the Supreme Court. The Constitution limits the original jurisdiction to all actions concerning "Ambassadors, other Public Ministers and Consuls, and those in which the State shall be a Party," leaving all other matters within the federal judicial power as part of the appellate jurisdiction of the Supreme Court. Although the Supreme Court's appellate jurisdiction extends to "Law and Fact" of all the matters listed in the nine categories of Clause 1, the final caveat shows Congress' significant control over this jurisdiction — "with such Exceptions, and under such Regulations as the Congress shall make."

How did the Framers settle on this pivotal language, and what were their intentions regarding the meaning of such provisions? Keep reading.

c. A Limited Historical Record of the Framers' "Original Intentions"

Constitutional Convention proposals for a national judiciary Edmund Randolph proposed the "Virginia Plan" drafted by James Madison. Under the Plan, Madison suggested that the federal legislature be given the power to create one or more supreme courts. These courts, possibly possessing different jurisdiction, would hear appeals of cases of national interest. He offered that Congress also be given authority to create inferior federal courts to serve as trial courts for such national matters. The Virginia Plan detailed that the federal legislature should appoint the judges who would then hold office during good behavior with a fixed salary that Congress could not increase or diminish during their tenure.

The Plan proposed a "council of revision" comprised of the President and a suitable number of federal judges. Significantly, the proposed council would review state and federal laws and veto laws viewed as violating, or even simply harmful, to the Constitution.

The delegates to the Constitutional Convention agreed early that there should be one supreme court. They then engaged in lengthy, rousing debates regarding judicial selection methods, judicial term of office, judicial salaries, the appropriate body for exercising judicial review of state and federal laws, and the relationship between federal and state courts.

Regarding judicial selection, the delegates ultimately agreed that the Executive should appoint federal judges with the advice and consent of the Senate. Before reaching this decision in the final weeks of the Convention, a variety of competing arguments unfolded. Certain delegates, such as James Wilson of Pennsylvania, argued that the Executive should solely possess the power of appointment. More delegates preferred legislative appointment or simply Senate appointment. Nathanial Gorham of Massachusetts recommended that federal judges be appointed by the Executive with the advice and consent of a subset of the legislative branch, as set forth in the Massachusetts constitution. He believed that any poor choice in an individual judicial appointment would rest with the Executive via public censure for mistakes.

15. The ongoing dispute concerning the Framers' specific intent in authorizing diversity jurisdiction is explored in Chapter 6.

With respect to judicial tenure, the delegates settled on tenure during good behavior. The thorny corollary issues centered on the substantive standard for good behavior and who would enforce the standard against failing judges. Fearing that judges would be overly influenced by political pressures, the Framers permitted removal of judges solely upon impeachment by the House of Representatives for "high crimes and misdemeanors" and subsequent conviction in a Senate trial.

A fixed, protected salary was a consensus staple to an independent judiciary. Some delegates believed the salary should neither be increased nor decreased during the judge's service. Delegates, such as Charles Cotesworth Pinckney of South Carolina, contended that the finest caliber potential judges would not serve without attractive salaries. Madison worried that judges would then curry favor to the legislative branch in order to receive raises, so he suggested triggering possible increases to an objective criterion like the price of a common commodity. In the end, the bulk of delegates agreed on no diminishment, but wanted the option for salary increases to remain viable.

Madison's proposal for the council of revision stimulated the longest debate at the Convention. It ultimately failed. Many delegates believed the council, comprised of the Executive and certain judges, would violate the separation of powers. Even more importantly, many delegates viewed the council as superfluous because they anticipated, or assumed, that the federal judiciary would exercise the power of judicial review to invalidate laws contrary to the Constitution. This assumption may explain why the Constitution has no explicit provision addressing judicial review.

The Convention delegates heavily debated the organization and jurisdiction of the federal judiciary. The delegates agreed to establish one national court, the Supreme Court. They outlined the jurisdiction of the Supreme Court and the potential jurisdiction of lower federal courts—as set forth in section 2 of Article III discussed above.

The delegates were split on the establishment of lower federal courts.[16] The delegates rejected a proposal to create such courts. Many delegates believed in the strength and appropriateness of state courts as trial courts for questions arising under federal laws or the Constitution. Based on a compromise offered by Madison, the delegates agreed to give Congress the prerogative to establish inferior federal courts. By implication, state courts retained jurisdiction over most legal disputes outlined in Article III.

d. Public Debates After the Constitutional Convention

On September 17, 1787, the delegates to the Constitutional Convention presented the proposed Constitution to the states for ratification. Intense debate followed with the ultimate fate of the document remaining unclear. The critics, the "Anti-Federalists," feared that the proposed federal judiciary would abuse and encroach upon states' rights. A public dialogue ensued between the Anti-Federalists and the supporters of the Constitution, the "Federalists." Both of these groups included divergent views within their ranks. The main themes from

16. The delegates agreed to guarantee the jury trial in criminal cases, but rejected similar language for civil cases.

each camp, however, provide relevant context for the primary battles over the national judiciary.

i. Anti-Federalists' Critiques

Many Anti-Federalists worried that the proposed national judiciary represented expansive power of the national government that would devour the states. They feared that the broad jurisdiction of the federal judiciary would extend the scope as far as the federal judges and lawyers desired. In public letters signed anonymously under the penname Brutus, the Anti-Federalist author maintained:

> The powers of these courts are very extensive; and their jurisdiction comprehends all civil causes, except such as arise between citizens of the same state; and it extends to all cases in law and equity arising under the constitution. . . . It is easy to see, that in the common course of things, *these courts will eclipse the dignity, and take away from the respectability, of the state courts.* These courts will be, in themselves, totally independent of the states, deriving their authority from the United States, and receiving from them fixed salaries; and in the course of human events it is to be expected, that *they will swallow up all the powers of the courts in their respective states.*[17]

In another letter, an Anti-Federalist voice warned against the "altogether unprecedented" judicial power vested in the federal judiciary. Specifically, this Anti-Federalist feared the independence of the federal judges:

> They are to be rendered totally independent, both of the people and the legislature, both with respect to their offices and salaries. No errors they may commit can be corrected by any power above them, if any such power there be, nor can they be removed from office for making ever so many erroneous adjudications.[18]

The Constitution's omission of any right to a jury trial in the federal courts spurred further criticism by Anti-Federalists. Another critic insisted:

> The jury trial, especially politically considered, is by far the most important feature in the judicial department in a free country, and the right in question is far the most valuable part, and the last that ought to be yielded, of this trial. . . . If the conduct of judges shall be severe and arbitrary, and tend to subvert the laws, and change the forms of government, the jury may check them, by deciding against their opinions and determinations, in similar cases.[19]

ii. Federalists' Responses

Federalist Alexander Hamilton provided the richest defense of judicial independence and the federal judiciary more generally. In Federalist No. 78, Hamilton quoted Montesquieu to defend the critical independence of the judiciary: "'there is no liberty, if the power of judging be not separated from the legislative

17. N.Y. J., Oct. 18, 1787 (emphasis added).
18. N.Y. J., Jan. 31, 1788.
19. Herbert J. Storing, The Complete Anti-Federalist 319-20 (1981).

and executive powers.'" Hamilton emphasized: "The complete independence of the courts of justice is peculiarly essential in a limited Constitution." In order to preserve the limited Constitution, he maintained that it is the judiciary "whose duty it must be to declare all acts contrary to the manifest tenor of the Constitution void."

Hamilton believed that the Constitution, once ratified by the states, would represent the supreme expression of the people's will. Then it would be the federal judiciary's obligation to defend the popular will—the Constitution—against contrary federal legislation. According to Hamilton, life tenure and protected salaries for federal judges were necessary for maintaining judicial independence. Only then could federal judges effectively protect the Constitution from encroachments by other branches of government without fear of reprisal.

Regarding the breadth of federal jurisdiction, Hamilton defended the scope of jurisdiction as necessary to maintain (i) the supremacy of federal law, (ii) equal rights for citizens in every state, and (iii) the government's capacity to handle foreign nations. Hamilton also reassured critics that selection of the most qualified citizens to serve as federal judges would protect traditional liberties. Also, Hamilton emphasized that Congress would order the federal judicial system to ensure the sanctity of traditional liberties including the right to trial by jury.

e. Ratification

Many critics, including some who ultimately supported ratification, continued to fear that the Constitution's proposed federal judicial structure failed to erect proper safeguards for traditional legal rights and procedures. Under Article VII, nine states were necessary for successful ratification of the Constitution. New Hampshire became the ninth state to ratify on June 21, 1788, whereupon the Constitution became effective in those nine states, replacing the Articles of Confederation. Operations under the new Constitution began on March 4, 1789.

Certain states passed resolutions proposing amendments to the Constitution. Such amendments included the addition of the jury trial right in civil cases and limitations on the scope of federal court jurisdiction. The Bill of Rights, the first ten amendments to the Constitution, became part of the Constitution at the end of 1791. Many of the amendments included limitations on national government power, including the Seventh Amendment's right to a trial by jury in certain civil cases.

f. Judicial Federalism and the Continued Existence of State Courts

Article III of the Constitution establishes federal judicial power. It does not create exclusive jurisdiction regarding the nine categories, however. The Articles of Confederation provided significant powers to the states and very little judicial power to the national government. In contrast, Article III of the Constitution focuses attention on creating federal judicial power. Yet the Framers were cognizant of the continued confidence in and desire for powerful state courts. Accordingly, jurisdiction is overlapping between federal and state courts (unless Congress statutorily creates exclusive jurisdiction in federal courts). The roots of this dual jurisdiction lie in the strongly held view that state courts could adequately handle and resolve legal issues, including those arising under federal laws or the United States Constitution. In fact, the federal courts lacked general authority to adjudicate disputes arising under federal law until 1875.[20]

Recall that state courts in America chose to adhere to the tradition of English common law and typically adopted that common law through "reception" statutes. Further, state courts retained the final power to interpret their own state law. Yet federal courts could be given the power, through diversity jurisdiction, to share in the interpretation and enforcement of state law. As discussed in Chapter 6, cases founded on diversity jurisdiction were the most important part of the federal courts' docket during the first 80 years the courts operated.

g. The Judiciary Act of 1789

The Constitution does not establish the inferior federal courts, so federal trial court jurisdiction would not exist until Congress created such courts and granted them jurisdiction. It did so when it first met and passed the Judiciary Act of 1789. Many of the Framers were members of this first Congress, and the constitutional ratification debates influenced the shaping of the federal judiciary in the Judiciary Act. Through compromise, the Judiciary Act created a three-tier federal court structure—the United States Supreme Court, federal circuit courts, and federal district courts. Notably, Congress established federal courts but permitted state courts concurrent jurisdiction over those disputes within the new federal courts' jurisdiction (e.g., diversity cases). For certain federal-question cases of Article III such as federal crimes and admiralty, Congress provided exclusive jurisdiction to federal courts.

Article III did not require Congress to create lower federal courts. Congress opted to exercise this power in 1789 and never looked back. The lower federal courts have existed since 1789 and proliferated in unforeseen ways in the years that followed. Yet as seen, Congress chose not to vest lower federal courts with the full jurisdiction possible under Article III. Even today Congress has not vested full Article III jurisdiction.[21]

Under the Judiciary Act of 1789, district court original jurisdiction covered admiralty cases and minor criminal matters and civil cases. Each state possessed at least one federal district court. The procedures of the federal courts generally followed the rules of the state in which the federal district or circuit court met. The Judiciary Act also established removal jurisdiction—not mentioned in the Constitution—permitting parties to remove certain actions from state to federal court.

Circuit courts constituted the next level of the federal judiciary. Congress did not designate that permanent judges would fill the circuit courts. Instead, Congress designated that the circuit courts would hold two sessions a year administered by two Supreme Court justices and one district court judge. Congress amended the Judiciary Act in 1793 to assign one Supreme Court justice and

20. Congress created federal question jurisdiction in the Judiciary Act of 1801, but it was repealed the following year and not restored until the Judiciary Act of 1875.

21. For example, Congress requires that most suits based on diversity jurisdiction satisfy an amount-in-controversy requirement, even though not required by Article III.

one district court judge to serve in each circuit court. This burdensome, controversial, and widely criticized feature of utilizing Supreme Court justices to "ride circuit" continued for more than 100 years. Congress viewed it as essential that Supreme Court justices stay connected to the citizenry by riding circuit in the regions across the country (then three circuit courts for the country). Circuit court jurisdiction included most federal crimes, disputes between citizens of different states if the case's worth exceeded $500, actions involving the United States if the amount in controversy exceeded $500, and some appeals from the district courts. Had Congress not authorized these courts to exercise diversity jurisdiction, they "would have had very little to do."[22]

Regarding the Supreme Court, recall that Article III established the Supreme Court without requiring congressional action. The Judiciary Act provided for six justices to preside in the Court. The Act echoed the original jurisdiction outlined in Article III and provided that the Court could hear appeals from the circuit court in civil actions valued over $2,000. Congress did not authorize the Court to review criminal convictions. The Judiciary Act authorized judicial review of the highest state courts' final decisions, but *only if* the state ruling was against a person raising a federal law claim.

2. *The Development and Growth of the Federal Court System*

Many facets of the original organizational structure from the Judiciary Act remain intact, but few could have foreseen how federal courts would develop over the course of time. Federal courts have expanded in number, jurisdiction, and import.

Below the Supreme Court are thirteen judicial circuits. Twelve regional circuits cover ninety-four judicial districts. The thirteenth judicial circuit is the Court of Appeals for the Federal Circuit, which possesses nationwide jurisdiction to hear appeals in specialized cases such as those arising under patent law and matters decided by the Court of International Trade and the Court of Federal Claims.

Each circuit has a federal court of appeals. These federal appellate courts hear appeals from the district courts located within the circuit. They also hear appeals from federal administrative agency decisions. The First Circuit is the smallest court; it has six judges. The Ninth Circuit is the largest court; it has twenty-nine judges.

A list of states comprising each circuit is set forth in 28 U.S.C. § 41, and the number of judgeships in each circuit in 28 U.S.C. § 44. For a map of the division of the federal circuits, see http://www.uscourts.gov/courtlinks/.

Below the federal circuit courts are a growing number of federal district courts in ninety-four judicial districts. These federal district courts are the trial courts. There is at least one district in each state, the District of Columbia, and Puerto Rico. Additionally, three United States' territories — the Virgin Islands, Guam, and the Northern Mariana Islands — have district courts that hear federal cases, including bankruptcy matters. Some states, like Alaska, possess only one judicial district. Others have multiple judicial districts that cover the state. For example, the state of Tennessee houses three districts: the Eastern District, the Middle

22. Henry Friendly, Federal Jurisdiction: A General View 141 (1973).

District, and the Western District of Tennessee. The number of judgeships for each district is set forth in 28 U.S.C. § 133.

Within each federal district is a federal bankruptcy court. These courts, whose judges serve limited terms and lack the "tenure" accorded judges in the district courts, have exclusive jurisdiction over bankruptcy cases. Accordingly, state courts cannot hear bankruptcy cases.

Two special federal trial courts possess nationwide jurisdiction over certain cases. First, the Court of International Trade handles issues involving international trade and customs. Second, the United States Court of Federal Claims addresses most claims for money damages against the United States, federal contracts disputes, unlawful takings of private property by the United States, and other claims against the federal government.

Growth in numbers — Courts, judges, and cases In 2012, the total number of authorized federal judgeships for the inferior federal courts was 1,206. This number includes 179 judges on the courts of appeals, 677 judges on the district courts (excluding magistrate judges), and 350 bankruptcy judges.[23]

In all of the courts of appeals except the Federal Circuit, litigants filed 57,501 cases in 2012; this figure represents an increase from the 50,072 cases filed in 1995, though the caseload is less than the 2005 load of 68,473 cases.[24] In the district courts, parties filed 278,442 civil cases in 2012.[25] In the same year, 71,303 criminal cases were filed in the district courts.[26]

As depicted in the following two charts, the range of subjects addressed by civil cases in the federal trial courts covered the gamut, including contracts, real estate, torts, and statutory actions.[27] The actions under statutes included antitrust, bankruptcy, banking, civil rights, environmental, deportation, prisoner petitions, forfeiture, labor, protected property rights, securities, social security, RICO, state reapportionment, tax suits, freedom of information, constitutionality of state statutes, and other statutory actions.[28] In 2012, for example, civil actions filed in federal district courts included 28,713 contracts cases; 12,960 real property cases; 61,306 tort cases; and 175,463 cases arising under statutes.[29] Within the category of statutory actions, prisoner petitions and civil rights cases constitute the largest components, 54,300 and 37,705 cases, respectively.[30] Each breakdown presents an interesting visual snapshot of the federal civil trial court docket for 2012.

23. *See* Table 1.1, Total Judicial Officers. Courts of Appeals, District Courts, Bankruptcy Courts, derived from Annual Report of the Director, http://www.uscourts.gov/statistics/judicialfactsandfigures.aspx.

24. *See* Table 2.1, U.S. Courts of Appeals (Excludes Federal Circuit). Appeals Filed, Terminated, Pending — Summary. This table may be accessed from "2012 Judicial Facts and Figures," http://www.uscourts.gov/Statistics/JudicialFactsAndFigures/judicial-facts-figures-2012.aspx.

25. *See* Table 4.1, U.S. District Courts — Civil Cases Filed, Terminated, Pending.

26. *See* Table 5.1, U.S. District Courts — Criminal Cases and Defendants Filed, Terminated, Pending (Includes Transfers).

27. *See* Table 4.4, U.S. District Courts — Civil Cases Filed by Nature of Suit.

28. *Id.*

29. *Id.*

30. *Id.*

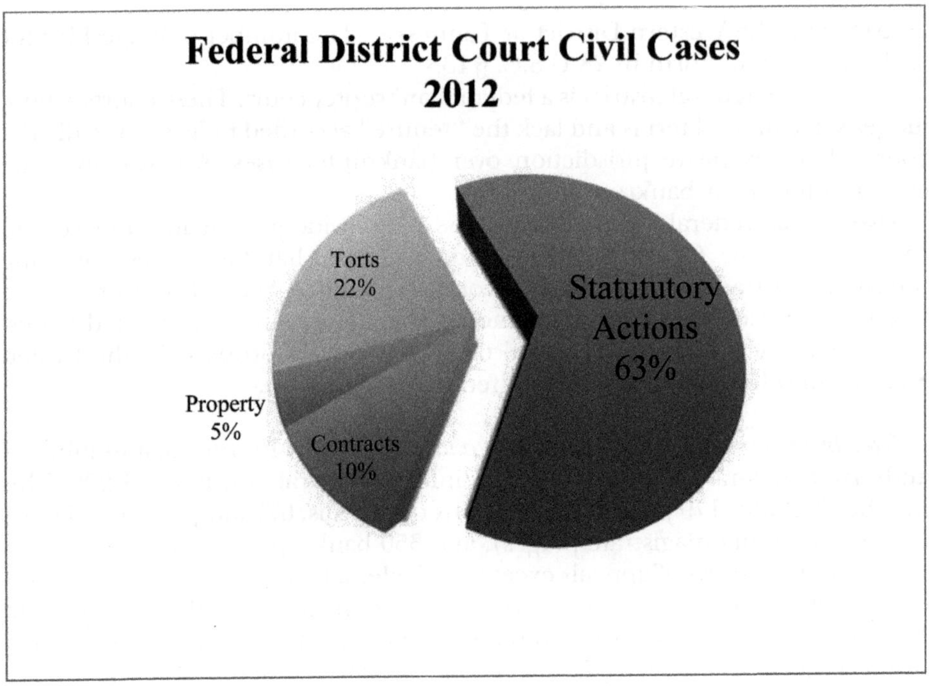

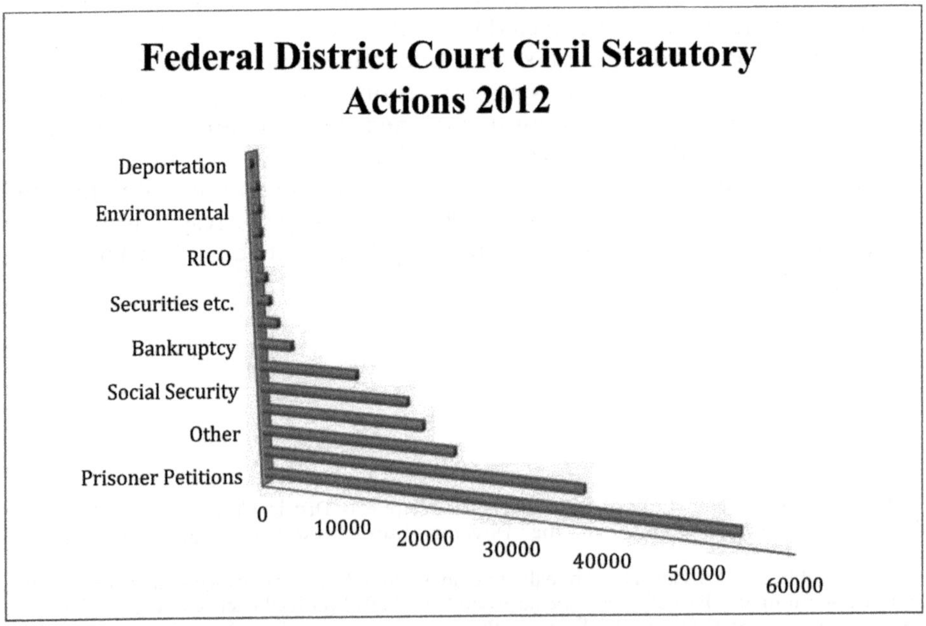

For extensive statistics on the "Judicial Business of the United States Courts 2012," see http://www.uscourts.gov/Statistics/JudicialBusiness/2012.aspx.

B. THE FEDERAL COURTS TODAY (AND TOMORROW)

The federal court system today is robust in its presence and effect. The concept of "federal courts" is much broader today than envisioned during the constitutional generation. Because the Framers drafted the Constitution in 1789 "for a small, rural nation," it is a formidable undertaking to apply it "to today's massive federal government."[31] All three branches of government have blossomed and decentralized.[32] In light of growth, decentralization, and docket expansion, the federal judicial branch faces complex challenges. For example, "[t]he Supreme Court, at the apex of a constantly growing pyramid of lower federal courts that finally decide most federal questions, struggles to manage the articulation of national law."[33]

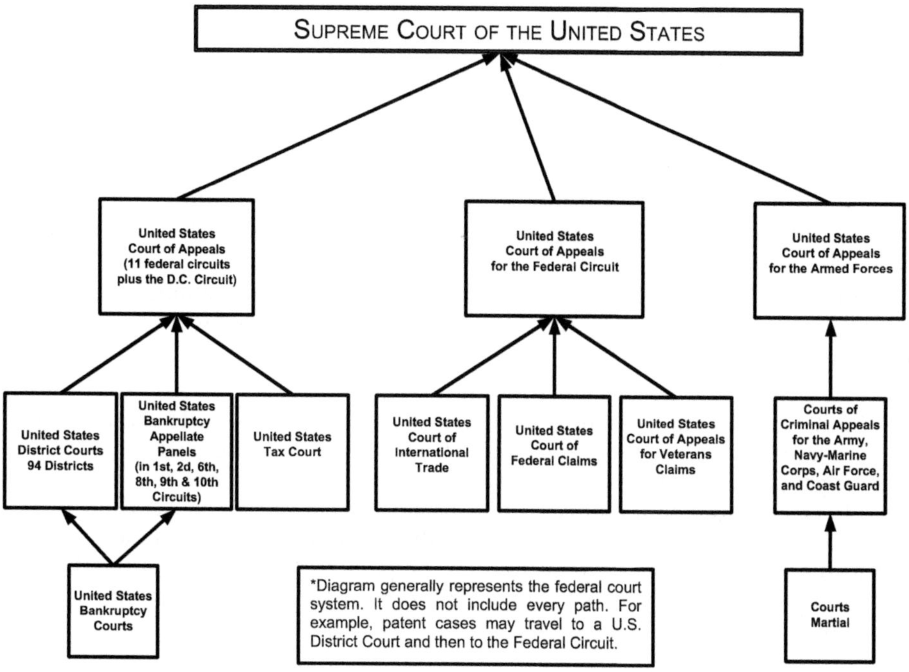

Federal Court System*

Also relevant to the federal court structure are many non–Article III judicial actors, including administrative law judges, magistrate judges, and bankruptcy judges. Also, Congress has established Article I "legislative" courts, which possess limited judicial power in certain specialized areas such as the United States Court of Appeals for Veterans Claims, the United States Court of Appeals for the

31. PETER M. SHANE & HAROLD H. BRUFF, SEPARATION OF POWERS LAW—CASES AND MATERIALS 26 (3d ed. 2011).
32. *Id.*
33. *Id.*

Armed Forces, and the United States Tax Court. See Chapter 4 (exploring jurisdiction allocated to non–Article III tribunals).

1. *The Evolving Judicial Role*

Federal trial court dockets continue to grow, which affects the judicial role. In 1982, Professor Judith Resnik explored the ongoing transition of judicial role from the classic dispassionate and disengaged judges to judges who utilize a "more active, 'managerial' stance."[34] Professor Resnik described the morphing role of federal judges in particular, but noted "similar changes are underway in many state courts."[35] She emphasized that federal "judges are not only adjudicating the merits of issues presented to them by litigants, but also are meeting with parties in chambers to encourage settlement of disputes and to supervise case preparation."[36] The incorporation of case management functions had resulted in federal judges "playing a critical role in shaping and influencing results" both pre- and post-trial.

This managerial role has continued.[37] It creates greater burdens on court time, but also provides enhanced judicial power. As Professor Resnik warned, judicial restraints are "conspicuously absent" because judges engage in managerial activities way beyond "public view, off the record, with no obligation to provide written, reasoned opinions, and out of reach of appellate review."[38] Vexing issues remain with respect to the complex and ever-evolving role of the federal judiciary.

Professors Peter Shane and Harold Bruff have recently commented on the "air of crisis" surrounding the federal courts as largely stemming from the evolving nature of the federal appellate courts:

> The 191 circuit judges now receive about 60,000 appeals per year. The caseload has risen faster than the number of judges — from 1960 to 1987, the caseload per judge nearly tripled. To handle the flood, these courts now decide almost half their cases without oral argument and rely upon growing numbers of law clerks and staff attorneys. Able judges complain about the increasingly bureaucratic routine, which leaves little time for reflection on the path of the law. As with the district courts, courts of appeal lack the discretion to turn away cases they do not wish to decide.[39]

Despite the "flood" of appeals that prevent "reflection on the path of the law," the thirteen courts of appeals "are now almost always the final deciders of federal law."[40] In a tenfold decrease from 1924, the Supreme Court reviews only a tiny portion of appellate decisions: one in one hundred.[41] With its

34. Judith Resnik, *Managerial Judges*, 96 Harv. L. Rev. 374 (1982).
35. *Id.* at 376 n.4.
36. *Id.* at 376-77.
37. For example, federal rules now require that federal judges take an active role in managing litigation, including issuing case management and scheduling orders that control the subsequent course of litigation. *See* Fed. R. Civ. P. 16(b), 26(f).
38. Resnik, *supra* note 34, at 378.
39. Shane & Bruff, *supra* note 31, at 33.
40. *Id.*
41. *Id.*

now largely discretionary jurisdiction, the Supreme Court grants only 3 to 4 percent of petitions for certiorari. Four of the nine Supreme Court Justices must vote in favor of granting certiorari to hear a case.

2. *Improving Federal Court Systems Through Judicial Independence*

Healthy court systems strive to promote the rule of law. Judicial reform efforts seek to ensure greater equality and justice by first strengthening judicial independence. Independence requires structural protection from encroachments of other government branches, as well as safeguards for fostering unbiased judicial decisionmaking. Scholars and practitioners at international institutions devote research and technical training toward building judicial independence abroad. In addition to balance-of-power considerations, non-governmental forces threaten judges' lives and impartiality. In 2007, Pakistani President Pervez Musharraf fired dozens of senior judges, resulting in serious separation-of-powers battles that destabilized Pakistan's democracy and triggered massive riots and deaths. Likewise, paramilitary groups in southern Mexico intimidated and assassinated judges to protect their criminal enterprises.[42] The murder of the husband and mother of Judge Joan H. Lefkow of the United States District Court for the Northern District of Illinois showed that American federal judges are also vulnerable to violence. In response, Congress gave the Administrative Office of the United States Courts a budget to install a security system in a judge's home and an in-house United States Marshal detail during prominent trials.

What is the best system to foster justice and the rule of law? The means and models used in recent rule-of-law efforts are under scrutiny. Every judiciary needs independence from the executive and legislature, and emerging democracies require both funds and technical assistance to strengthen their judiciaries. At times, countries like the United States that offer financial and people support dominate the reform agenda. Such reforms are not without skeptics, however: "Judicial reform projects are suspect when they are accompanied by an attitude that only models from the United States can fix what is wrong. . . ."[43] The World Bank believes that "wholesale importation of other legal systems may not be appropriate" and that "legal reform should come from within the country itself."[44] Many countries welcome such reforms, however. They utilize judicial exchange programs in order to gain the greatest benefits from democratic countries with advanced independent federal judiciaries. As global importation of the American federal court system continues, it is all the more important for attorneys to understand and seek to enhance the American federal judicial system.

42. Luz Estella Nagle, *Latin America in the Twenty-First Century: Article, The Cinderella of Government: Judicial Reform in Latin America*, 30 Cal. W. Int'l L.J. 345, 367 (2000).

43. *Id.* at 373-77.

44. Stephen Zamora, *Introduction: Judicial Review in Latin America*, 7 Sw. J.L. & Trade Am. 227, 232 (Fall 2002).

C. RECURRING THEMES AND QUESTIONS

Federal courts' jurisprudence features certain recurring themes. For example, you can view almost every federal courts issue that follows in this casebook from the perspective of both separation of powers and federalism. Accordingly, these prevalent concepts serve well as organizing principles for the study of federal courts. Other themes such as the parity debate concerning the relative competence of state and federal courts resonate as well.

1. *Federalism*

Federalism represents a vertical concern about the relationship between the federal and state governments. With respect to the judiciary, federalism concerns arise when a federal court acts in a manner that may encroach on state government or a state interest. The Supreme Court outlined the contours of federalism concerns in *Younger v. Harris*, 401 U.S. 37, 44-45 (1971), which held that a federal court may not enjoin a pending, good-faith state criminal proceeding (i.e., "*Younger* Abstention"). Justice Black emphasized the import and nuances of federalism:

> [There is] an even more vital consideration, the notion of "comity," that is, a proper respect for state functions, a recognition of the fact that the entire country is made up of a Union of separate state governments, and a continuance of the belief that the National Government will fare best if the States and their institutions are left free to perform their separate functions in their separate ways. This, perhaps for lack of a better and clearer way to describe it, is referred to by many as "Our Federalism," and one familiar with the profound debates that ushered our Federal Constitution into existence is bound to respect those who remain loyal to the ideals and dreams of "Our Federalism." The concept does not mean blind deference to "States' Rights" any more than it means centralization of control over every important issue in our National Government and its courts. The Framers rejected both these courses. What the concept does represent is a system in which there is sensitivity to the legitimate interests of both State and National Governments, and in which the National Government, anxious though it may be to vindicate and protect federal rights and federal interests, always endeavors to do so in ways that will not unduly interfere with the legitimate activities of the States. It should never be forgotten that this slogan, "Our Federalism," born in the early struggling days of our Union of States, occupies a highly important place in our Nation's history and its future.

Accordingly, the federal judiciary must take great care to balance its interest in developing and enforcing national law with a respect for state prerogatives.

A potential benefit of protecting state freedom stems from Justice Brandeis's observation:

> It is one of the happy incidents of the federal system that a single courageous State may, if its citizens choose, serve as a laboratory; and try novel social and economic experiments without risk to the rest of the country.[45]

45. *New State Ice Co. v. Liebmann*, 285 U.S. 262, 311 (1932) (Brandeis, J., dissenting).

Thus, the federal system may wish to encourage state creativity and experimentation regarding thorny issues. The federal judiciary must remain, however, a bulwark against tyranny of the majority and protect constitutional rights of the individual. As experimentation flourishes, there may be need for intervention by the federal judiciary. Consequently, respect for "Our Federalism" must always be balanced against the imperative of restraining unconstitutional state action.

2. *Separation of Powers*

Separation of powers represents a horizontal concern about the relationship between coordinate branches of government. Accordingly, on the federal level, separation-of-powers issues arise when the act of any one of the three federal branches (legislative, executive, or judicial) affects one or more of the remaining branches.

The very structure of the Constitution, separately conferring authority on the three branches in Articles I, II, and III, embodies this separation of powers. The Framers remained faithful to "the political maxim, that the legislative, executive, and judiciary departments ought to be separate and distinct."[46] Madison expounded on the sentiments of Montesquieu: "where the *whole* power of one department is exercised by the same hands which possess the *whole* power of another department, the fundamental principles of a free constitution, are subverted."[47]

The separation of powers is not a rigid, clean separation. Rather, the Constitution permits blended powers in order to facilitate the necessary checks and balances among branches. Justice Robert H. Jackson's famous concurrence in *Youngstown Sheet & Tube Co. v. Sawyer*, 343 U.S. 579 (1952), describes a "zone of twilight" in which branches possess concurrent authority. Separation-of-powers tensions are a regular part of the federal government. Differing opinions exist regarding whether the tension is healthy.

When federal courts invalidate federal law or executive action they may exacerbate separation-of-powers tensions. Yet such judicial rulings represent the judicial branch's own "check" on unlawful usurpations of power by another branch. What are the limits on the federal judiciary's power to override another branch? When should the judiciary decline the exercise of such power in order to protect the delicate separation-of-powers balance?

3. *Parity*

The parity debate centers on the relative performance of federal and state courts. Is one judicial system more competent than the other? Are federal courts more hospitable to the enforcement of federal law? The Framers maintained that state courts could adequately and fairly decide matters arising under federal law, and for almost a century Congress did not confer "arising under" jurisdiction on federal courts. Yet today many contend that federal courts are

46. The Federalist No. 47, at 323 (James Madison) (Jacob E. Cooke ed., 1961).
47. *Id.* at 326.

qualitatively better than state courts. Consider what criteria should be used in determining parity. Is "parity" something that can actually be measured?[48]

When is parity an issue? In cases falling outside the federal courts' jurisdiction, the question of parity never arises. Similarly, when Congress confers exclusive jurisdiction on the federal courts, as with patent and copyright cases, the issue of parity is irrelevant. Parity is quite relevant, however, to Congress' decision whether to grant exclusive jurisdiction. The parity issue arises when state and federal courts share jurisdiction over aspects of a controversy. For example, when state and federal courts have concurrent jurisdiction over a controversy, litigants often have a choice of forum. Strategy dictates a determination of which forum, state or federal, is more advantageous. The parity issue also arises when a federal court is asked to resolve an issue of federal law that might also be presented in a pending state court action. For example, a federal court might be asked to declare the unconstitutionality of a state criminal law under which the federal plaintiff is currently being prosecuted in state court. If the federal court believes in the parity of state courts, it may be more inclined to abstain and let plaintiff present her federal issue for resolution in state court.

Parity can raise delicate issues, since discussions about the relative competence of state court judges may be impolitic. Of course, reasonable minds may disagree. Yet the issue of parity may not be avoidable. Professor Burt Neuborne argues that "the assumption of parity is, at best, a dangerous myth, fostering forum allocation decisions which channel constitutional adjudication under the illusion that state courts will vindicate federally secured constitutional rights as forcefully as would the lower federal courts."[49] Not all agree on whether federal courts are, in fact, "better," yet the perception of real differences remains. As you analyze limitations on federal court jurisdiction placed by Congress or the federal courts, consider whether an adequate substitute forum exists within state courts.

4. *Judicial Review in the Context of Limited Jurisdiction*

The first case we examine in this text presents a foundational mega-theme — the power of judicial review. The power is an awesome one, but it exists within the confines of the federal court system's limited jurisdiction. Further, Article III never explicitly grants federal courts the power to invalidate federal or state laws or Executive actions as contrary to the Constitution. This power creates genuine interbranch tension, especially given that the federal judiciary is not a representative body and thus is most distant from popular will.[50] Yet judicial review is central to the American conception of the federal judiciary's function. Judicial review is essential to the proper functioning of government within our constitutional democracy. This power is so entrenched that it is rarely questioned. The power of judicial review is often identified with the seminal case of *Marbury v. Madison* and its progeny.

48. *See* Erwin Chemerinsky, *Ending the Parity Debate*, 71 B.U. L. Rev. 593 (1991) (reasoning that the parity debate cannot be empirically resolved because there is no consensus on a baseline for comparison).

49. Burt Neuborne, *The Myth of Parity*, 90 Harv. L. Rev. 1105 (1977).

50. The federal courts are only connected indirectly to the people's will via their choice of the President and Senators who in turn appoint and confirm federal judges.

Revisit Chief Justice Marshall's unanimous opinion in *Marbury* with an eye toward: separation-of-powers tensions, rights without remedies, and the proper role of the federal judiciary. As you review *Marbury*, keep in mind the political intrigue of the time.[51] The following summary signals some of the key players and their political moves, but the full context is worthy of your independent study.

Center stage was the heated presidential battle between incumbent President John Adams, a Federalist, and ultimate challenger Thomas Jefferson. President Adams and his predecessor appointed federal judges "who uniformly shared their conservative philosophy."[52] Jefferson's party, the Democratic-Republican party, feared that an isolated federal judiciary "insulated from democratic accountability and armed with the power to make law" would trump the people's will.[53] In an extremely close election, the Democratic-Republican party prevailed. Under then-governing rules, electors cast votes and the candidate receiving the most votes became President while the second highest vote recipient became Vice President.[54] The electors voted equally for Jefferson and his running mate, Aaron Burr of New York.[55] In the face of this tie, the lameduck House of Representatives, dominated by the Federalist Party of Adams and Alexander Hamilton, controlled the ultimate outcome.[56] A dangerous deal loomed in which the House would choose Burr as President—defying the popular will—if he agreed to support the Federalists.[57]

Although this controversial plan did not come to fruition, the air of crisis provided the cover under which defeated President Adams and the Federalists proceeded to bolster the federal judicial branch with their supporters.[58] For example, to replace the resigned Chief Justice of the Supreme Court, Adams appointed "his most trusted cabinet officer, forty-five year old John Marshall of Virginia," despite his having "no prior judicial experience."[59] Marshall was "an uncommonly able lawyer, with an affable disposition that helped him build coalitions and disarm critics," although he did "not get along with his distant cousin, Thomas Jefferson, who had just defeated Adams for the presidency."[60] The Senate confirmed Marshall one week after his January 20, 1801, nomination, yet curiously Marshall remained in his prior office, Acting Secretary of State, for the five-week duration of Adam's presidency.[61] Ironically, as Acting Secretary, Marshall would affix the Great Seal on Adams's final commissions, but would "make a mistake"—failing to deliver many of the commissions—"which precipitated the most famous constitutional decision of his career."[62]

With this rich and controversial political backdrop in mind, analyze *Marbury*.

51. For a full elucidation of *Marbury*, read William W. Van Alstyne, *A Critical Guide to* Marbury v. Madison, 18 Duke L.J. 1 (1969). *See also* Michael W. McConnell, *The Story of* Marbury v. Madison: *Making Defeat Look Like Victory*, in Constitutional Law Stories 13-31 (Michael C. Dorf ed., 2004).
52. McConnell, *supra* note 51, at 13.
53. *Id.* at 14.
54. *Id.*
55. *Id.*
56. *Id.*
57. *Id.*
58. *Id.*
59. *Id.*
60. *Id.* at 15.
61. *Id.*
62. *Id.* at 15, 17.

MARBURY v. MADISON

5 U.S. (1 Cranch) 137 (1803)

MR. CHIEF JUSTICE MARSHALL delivered the opinion of the Court.

[Mr. Marbury filed a motion in the Supreme Court for a mandamus that would direct the secretary of state, James Madison, "to deliver to William Marbury his commission as a justice of the peace for the county of Washington, in the district of Columbia." The Court first considered whether Mr. Marbury had a right to the commission.

Congress passed an act in February 1801 regarding Washington, D.C., which provided "that there shall be appointed . . . such number of discreet persons to be justices of the peace as the president of the United States shall, from time to time, think expedient, to continue in office for five years." Pursuant to this Act, President John Adams signed a commission, affixed with the United States seal, for William Marbury as a justice of the peace. The commission never reached Mr. Marbury. According to the Court, if Mr. Marbury was appointed to the office, he was entitled to the office for five years.]

The 2d section of the 2d article of the constitution, declares, that, "the president shall nominate, and, by and with the advice and consent of the senate, shall appoint ambassadors, other public ministers and consuls, and all other officers of the United States, whose appointments are not otherwise provided for."

The third section declares, that "he shall commission all the officers of the United States."

An act of congress directs the secretary of state to keep the seal of the United States, "to make out and record, and affix the said seal to all civil commissions to officers of the United States, to be appointed by the President, by and with the consent of the senate, or by the President alone; provided that the said seal shall not be affixed to any commission before the same shall have been signed by the President of the United States."

These are the clauses of the constitution and laws of the United States, which affect this part of the case. They seem to contemplate three distinct operations:

1st. The nomination. This is the sole act of the President, and is completely voluntary.

2d. The appointment. This is also the act of the President, and is also a voluntary act, though it can only be performed by and with the advice and consent of the senate.

3d. The commission. To grant a commission to a person appointed, might perhaps be deemed a duty enjoined by the constitution. "He shall," says that instrument, "commission all the officers of the United States."

* * * *

This is an appointment made by the President, by and with the advice and consent of the senate, and is evidenced by no act but the commission itself. In such a case therefore the commission and the appointment seem inseparable; it being almost impossible to shew an appointment otherwise than by proving the existence of a commission; still the commission is not necessarily the appointment; though conclusive evidence of it.

* * * *

The discretion of the executive is to be exercised until the appointment has been made. But having once made the appointment, his power over the office is terminated in all cases, where, by law, the officer is not removable by him. The right to the office is *then* in the person appointed, and he has the absolute, unconditional, power of accepting or rejecting it.

Mr. Marbury, then, since his commission was signed by the President, and sealed by the secretary of state, was appointed; and as the law creating the office, gave the officer a right to hold for five years, independent of the executive, the appointment was not revocable; but vested in the officer legal rights, which are protected by the laws of this country.

To withhold his commission, therefore, is an act deemed by the court not warranted by law, but violative of a vested legal right.

This brings us to the second inquiry; which is,

2dly. If he has a right, and that right has been violated, do the laws of this country afford him a remedy?

The very essence of civil liberty certainly consists in the right of every individual to claim the protection of the laws, whenever he receives an injury. One of the first duties of government is to afford that protection. In Great Britain the king himself is sued in the respectful form of a petition, and he never fails to comply with the judgment of his court.

[According to Blackstone,] "it is a general and indisputable rule, that where there is a legal right, there is also a legal remedy by suit or action at law, whenever that right is invaded."

[F]or it is a settled and invariable principle in the laws of England, that every right, when withheld, must have a remedy, and every injury its proper redress."

The government of the United States has been emphatically termed a government of laws, and not of men. It will certainly cease to deserve this high appellation, if the laws furnish no remedy for the violation of a vested legal right.

* * * *

It follows then that the question, whether the legality of an act of the head of a department be examinable in a court of justice or not, must always depend on the nature of that act.

If some acts be examinable, and others not, there must be some rule of law to guide the court in the exercise of its jurisdiction.

In some instances there may be difficulty in applying the rule to particular cases; but there cannot, it is believed, be much difficulty in laying down the rule.

By the constitution of the United States, the President is invested with certain important political powers, in the exercise of which he is to use his own discretion, and is accountable only to his country in his political character, and to his own conscience. To aid him in the performance of these duties, he is authorized to appoint certain officers, who act by his authority and in conformity with his orders.

In such cases, their acts are his acts; and whatever opinion may be entertained of the manner in which executive discretion may be used, still there exists, and can exist, no power to control that discretion. The subjects are political. They respect the nation, not individual rights, and being entrusted to the executive, the decision of the executive is conclusive. . . . This officer, as his duties were prescribed by that act, is to conform precisely to the will of the President. He is the mere organ by whom that will is communicated. The acts of such an officer, as an officer, can never be examinable by the courts.

But when the legislature proceeds to impose on that officer other duties; when he is directed peremptorily to perform certain acts; when the rights of individuals are dependent on the performance of those acts; he is so far the officer of the law; is amenable to the laws for his conduct; and cannot at his discretion sport away the vested rights of others.

The conclusion from this reasoning is, that where the heads of departments are the political or confidential agents of the executive, merely to execute the will of the President, or rather to act in cases in which the executive possesses a constitutional or legal discretion, nothing can be more perfectly clear than that their acts are only politically examinable. But where a specific duty is assigned by law, and individual rights depend upon the performance of that duty, it seems equally clear that the individual who considers himself injured, has a right to resort to the laws of his country for a remedy.

* * * *

The question whether a right has vested or not, is, in its nature, judicial, and must be tried by the judicial authority. If, for example, Mr. Marbury had taken the oaths of a magistrate, and proceeded to act as one; in consequence of which a suit had been instituted against him, in which his defense had depended on his being a magistrate; the validity of his appointment must have been determined by judicial authority.

So, if he conceives that, by virtue of his appointment, he has a legal right, either to the commission which has been made out for him, or to a copy of that commission, it is equally a question examinable in a court, and the decision of the court upon it must depend on the opinion entertained of his appointment.

That question has been discussed, and the opinion is, that the latest point of time which can be taken as that at which the appointment was complete, and evidenced, was when, after the signature of the president, the seal of the United States was affixed to the commission.

It is then the opinion of the court,

1st. That by signing the commission of Mr. Marbury, the president of the United States appointed him a justice of peace, for the county of Washington in the district of Columbia; and that the seal of the United States, affixed thereto by the secretary of state, is conclusive testimony of the verity of the signature, and of the completion of the appointment; and that the appointment conferred on him a legal right to the office for the space of five years.

2dly. That, having this legal title to the office, he has a consequent right to the commission; a refusal to deliver which, is a plain violation of that right, for which the laws of his country afford him a remedy.

It remains to be inquired whether,

3dly. He is entitled to the remedy for which he applies. . . .

* * * *

Blackstone . . . defines a mandamus to be, "a command issuing in the king's name from the court of king's bench, and directed to any person, corporation, or inferior court of judicature within the king's dominions, requiring them to do some particular thing therein specified, which appertains to their office and duty, and which the court of king's bench has previously determined, or at least supposes, to be consonant to right and justice."

Lord Mansfield [states that whenever] "there is a right to execute an office . . . (more especially if it be in a matter of public concern, or attended with profit) and a person is kept out of possession . . . and has no other specific legal remedy, this court ought to assist by mandamus, upon reasons of justice, as the writ expresses, and upon reasons of public policy, to preserve peace, order and good government." In the same case he says, "this writ ought to be used upon all occasions where the law has established no specific remedy, and where in justice and good government there ought to be one."

* * * *

This writ, if awarded, would be directed to an officer of government, and its mandate to him would be, to use the words of Blackstone, "to do a particular thing therein specified, which appertains to his office and duty and which the court has previously determined, or at least supposes, to be consonant to right and justice." Or, in the words of Lord Mansfield, the applicant, in this case, has a right to execute an office of public concern, and is kept out of possession of that right.

These circumstances certainly concur in this case.

Still, to render the mandamus a proper remedy, the officer to whom it is to be directed, must be one to whom, on legal principles, such writ may be directed; and the person applying for it must be without any other specific and legal remedy.

1st. With respect to the officer to whom it would be directed. The intimate political relation, subsisting between the president of the United States and the heads of departments, necessarily renders any legal investigation of the acts of one of those high officers peculiarly irksome, as well as delicate; and excites some hesitation with respect to the propriety of entering into such investigation. Impressions are often received without much reflection or examination, and it is not wonderful that in such a case as this, the assertion, by an individual, of his legal claims in a court of justice; to which claims it is the duty of that court to attend; should at first view be considered by some, as an attempt to intrude into the cabinet, and to intermeddle with the prerogatives of the executive.

It is scarcely necessary for the court to disclaim all pretensions to such a jurisdiction. An extravagance, so absurd and excessive, could not have been entertained for a moment. The province of the court is, solely, to decide on the rights of individuals, not to enquire how the executive, or executive officers, perform duties in which they have discretion. Questions, in their nature political, or which are, by the constitution and laws, submitted to the executive, can never be made in this court.

But, if this be not such a question; if so far from being an intrusion into the secrets of the cabinet, it respects a paper, which, according to law, is upon record, and to a copy of which the law gives a right, on the payment of ten cents; if it be no intermeddling with a subject, over which the executive can be considered as having exercised any control; what is there in the exalted station of the officer, which shall bar a citizen from asserting, in a court of justice, his legal rights, or shall forbid a court to listen to the claim; or to issue a mandamus, directing the performance of a duty, not depending on executive discretion, but on particular acts of congress and the general principles of law?

If one of the heads of departments commits any illegal act, under color of his office, by which an individual sustains an injury, it cannot be pretended that his office alone exempts him from being sued in the ordinary mode of proceeding, and being compelled to obey the judgment of the law. How then can his office exempt him from this particular mode of deciding on the legality of his conduct, if the case be such a case as would, were any other individual the party complained of, authorize the process?

It is not by the office of the person to whom the writ is directed, but the nature of the thing to be done that the propriety or impropriety of issuing a mandamus, is to be determined. . . .

* * * *

It is true that the mandamus, now moved for, is not for the performance of an act expressly enjoined by statute.

It is to deliver a commission; on which subject the acts of Congress are silent. This difference is not considered as affecting the case. It has already been stated that the applicant has, to that commission, a vested legal right, of which the executive cannot deprive him. He has been appointed to an office, from which he is not removable, at the will of the executive; and being so appointed, he has a right to the commission which the secretary has received from the president for his use. The act of congress does not indeed order the secretary of state to send it to him, but it is placed in his hands for the person entitled to it; and cannot be more lawfully withheld by him, than by any other person.

* * * *

This, then, is a plain case for a mandamus, either to deliver the commission, or a copy of it from the record; and it only remains to be inquired,

Whether it can issue from this court.

The act to establish the judicial courts of the United States authorizes the supreme court "to issue writs of mandamus, in cases warranted by the principles and usages of law, to any courts appointed, or persons holding office, under the authority of the United States."

The secretary of state, being a person holding an office under the authority of the United States, is precisely within the letter of the description; and if this court is not authorized to issue a writ of mandamus to such an officer, it must be because the law is unconstitutional, and therefore absolutely incapable of conferring the authority, and assigning the duties which its words purport to confer and assign.

The constitution vests the whole judicial power of the United States in one supreme court, and such inferior courts as congress shall, from time to time, ordain and establish. This power is expressly extended to all cases arising under the laws of the United States; and consequently, in some form, may be exercised over the present case; because the right claimed is given by a law of the United States.

In the distribution of this power it is declared that "the supreme court shall have original jurisdiction in all cases affecting ambassadors, other public ministers and consuls, and those in which a state shall be a party. In all other cases, the supreme court shall have appellate jurisdiction."

It has been insisted, at the bar, that as the original grant of jurisdiction, to the supreme and inferior courts, is general, and the clause, assigning original jurisdiction to the supreme court, contains no negative or restrictive words; the power remains to the legislature, to assign original jurisdiction to that court in other cases than those specified in the article which has been recited; provided those cases belong to the judicial power of the United States.

If it had been intended to leave it in the discretion of the legislature to apportion the judicial power between the supreme and inferior courts according to the will of that body, it would certainly have been useless to have proceeded further than to have defined the judicial power, and the tribunals in which it should be vested. The subsequent part of the section is mere surplusage, is entirely without meaning, if such is to be the construction. If congress remains at liberty to give this court appellate jurisdiction, where the constitution has declared their jurisdiction shall be original; and original jurisdiction where the constitution has declared it shall be appellate; the distribution of jurisdiction, made in the constitution, is form without substance.

Affirmative words are often, in their operation, negative of other objects than those affirmed; and in this case, a negative or exclusive sense must be given to them or they have no operation at all.

It cannot be presumed that any clause in the constitution is intended to be without effect; and therefore such a construction is inadmissible, unless the words require it.

If the solicitude of the convention, respecting our peace with foreign powers, induced a provision that the supreme court should take original jurisdiction in cases which might be supposed to affect them; yet the clause would have proceeded no further than to provide for such cases, if no further restriction on the powers of congress had been intended. That they should have appellate jurisdiction in all other cases, with such exceptions as congress might make, is no restriction; unless the words be deemed exclusive of original jurisdiction.

When an instrument organizing fundamentally a judicial system, divides it into one supreme, and so many inferior courts as the legislature may ordain and establish; then enumerates its powers, and proceeds so far to distribute them, as to define the jurisdiction of the supreme court by declaring the cases in which it shall take original jurisdiction, and that in others it shall take appellate jurisdiction; the plain import of the words seems to be, that in one class of cases its jurisdiction is original, and not appellate; in the other it is appellate, and not original. If any other construction would render the clause inoperative, that is an additional reason for rejecting such other construction, and for adhering to their obvious meaning.

To enable this court then to issue a mandamus, it must be shewn to be an exercise of appellate jurisdiction, or to be necessary to enable them to exercise appellate jurisdiction.

It has been stated at the bar that the appellate jurisdiction may be exercised in a variety of forms, and that if it be the will of the legislature that a mandamus should be used for that purpose, that will must be obeyed. This is true, yet the jurisdiction must be appellate, not original.

It is the essential criterion of appellate jurisdiction, that it revises and corrects the proceedings in a cause already instituted, and does not create that cause. Although, therefore, a mandamus may be directed to courts, yet to issue such a writ to an officer for the delivery of a paper, is in effect the same as to sustain an original action for that paper, and therefore seems not to belong to appellate, but to original jurisdiction. Neither is it necessary in such a case as this, to enable the court to exercise its appellate jurisdiction.

The authority, therefore, given to the supreme court, by the act establishing the judicial courts of the United States, to issue writs of mandamus to public officers, appears not to be warranted by the constitution; and it becomes necessary to enquire whether a jurisdiction, so conferred, can be exercised.

The question, whether an act, repugnant to the constitution, can become the law of the land, is a question deeply interesting to the United States; but, happily, not of an intricacy proportioned to its interest. It seems only necessary to recognize certain principles, supposed to have been long and well established, to decide it.

That the people have an original right to establish, for their future government, such principles as, in their opinion, shall most conduce to their own happiness, is the basis, on which the whole American fabric has been erected. The exercise of this original right is a very great exertion; nor can it, nor ought it to be frequently repeated. The principles, therefore, so established, are deemed fundamental. And as the authority, from which they proceed, is supreme, and can seldom act, they are designed to be permanent.

This original and supreme will organizes the government, and assigns, to different departments, their respective powers. It may either stop here; or establish certain limits not to be transcended by those departments.

The government of the United States is of the latter description. The powers of the legislature are defined, and limited; and that those limits may not be mistaken, or forgotten, the constitution is written. To what purpose are powers limited, and to what purpose is that limitation committed to writing, if these limits may, at any time, be passed by those intended to be restrained? The distinction, between a government with limited and unlimited powers, is abolished, if those limits do not confine the persons on whom they are imposed, and if acts prohibited and acts allowed, are of equal obligation. It is a proposition too plain to be contested, that the constitution controls any legislative act repugnant to it; or, that the legislature may alter the constitution by an ordinary act.

Between these alternatives there is no middle ground. The constitution is either a superior, paramount law, unchangeable by ordinary means, or it is on a level with ordinary legislative acts, and like other acts, is alterable when the legislature shall please to alter it.

If the former part of the alternative be true, then a legislative act contrary to the constitution is not law: if the latter part be true, then written constitutions are absurd attempts, on the part of the people, to limit a power, in its own nature illimitable.

Certainly all those who have framed written constitutions contemplate them as forming the fundamental and paramount law of the nation, and consequently the theory of every such government must be, that an act of the legislature, repugnant to the constitution, is void.

This theory is essentially attached to a written constitution, and is consequently to be considered, by this court, as one of the fundamental principles of our society. It is not therefore to be lost sight of in the further consideration of this subject.

If an act of the legislature, repugnant to the constitution, is void, does it, notwithstanding its invalidity, bind the courts, and oblige them to give it effect? Or, in other words, though it be not law, does it constitute a rule as operative as if it was a law? This would be to overthrow in fact what was established in theory; and would seem, at first view, an absurdity too gross to be insisted on. It shall, however, receive a more attentive consideration.

It is emphatically the province and duty of the judicial department to say what the law is. Those who apply the rule to particular cases, must of necessity expound and interpret that rule. If two laws conflict with each other, the courts must decide on the operation of each.

So if a law be in opposition to the constitution; if both the law and the constitution apply to a particular case, so that the court must either decide that case conformably to the law, disregarding the constitution; or conformably to the constitution, disregarding the law; the court must determine which of these conflicting rules governs the case. This is of the very essence of judicial duty.

If then the courts are to regard the constitution; and the constitution is superior to any ordinary act of the legislature; the constitution, and not such ordinary act, must govern the case to which they both apply.

Those then who controvert the principle that the constitution is to be considered, in court, as a paramount law, are reduced to the necessity of maintaining that courts must close their eyes on the constitution, and see only the law.

This doctrine would subvert the very foundation of all written constitutions. It would declare that an act, which, according to the principles and theory of our government, is entirely void; is yet, in practice, completely obligatory. It would declare, that if the legislature shall do what is expressly forbidden, such act, notwithstanding the express prohibition, is in reality effectual. It would be giving to the legislature a practical and real omnipotence, with the same breath which professes to restrict their powers within narrow limits. It is prescribing limits, and declaring that those limits may be passed at pleasure.

That it thus reduces to nothing what we have deemed the greatest improvement on political institutions — a written constitution — would of itself be sufficient, in America, where written constitutions have been viewed with so much reverence, for rejecting the construction. But the peculiar expressions of the constitution of the United States furnish additional arguments in favour of its rejection.

The judicial power of the United States is extended to all cases arising under the constitution.

Could it be the intention of those who gave this power, to say that, in using it, the constitution should not be looked into? That a case arising under the constitution should be decided without examining the instrument under which it arises?

This is too extravagant to be maintained.

In some cases then, the constitution must be looked into by the judges. And if they can open it at all, what part of it are they forbidden to read, or to obey?

* * * *

[I]t is apparent, that the framers of the constitution contemplated that instrument, as a rule for the government of *courts*, as well as of the legislature.

Why otherwise does it direct the judges to take an oath to support it? This oath certainly applies, in an especial manner, to their conduct in their official character. How immoral to impose it on them, if they were to be used as the instruments, and the knowing instruments, for violating what they swear to support?

The oath of office, too, imposed by the legislature, is completely demonstrative of the legislative opinion on this subject. It is in these words, "I do solemnly swear that I will administer justice without respect to persons, and do equal right to the poor and to the rich; and that I will faithfully and impartially discharge all the duties incumbent on me as according to the best of my abilities and understanding, agreeably to *the constitution,* and laws of the United States."

Why does a judge swear to discharge his duties agreeably to the constitution of the United States, if that constitution forms no rule for his government? If it is closed upon him, and cannot be inspected by him?

If such be the real state of things, this is worse than solemn mockery. To prescribe, or to take this oath, becomes equally a crime.

It is also not entirely unworthy of observation, that in declaring what shall be the *supreme* law of the land, the *constitution* itself is first mentioned; and not the laws of the United States generally, but those only which shall be made in *pursuance* of the constitution, have that rank.

Thus, the particular phraseology of the constitution of the United States confirms and strengthens the principle, supposed to be essential to all written constitutions, that a law repugnant to the constitution is void; and that *courts,* as well as other departments, are bound by that instrument.

The rule must be discharged.

DISCUSSION AND QUESTIONS

As you reflect on *Marbury*, consider the following questions:

- Does the Constitution directly support the power of judicial review? By its structure? Do you think the Framers assumed the power of judicial review inherently existed?
- How does Chief Justice Marshall describe the contours of the judicial review power? How does he justify placing this significant power in the federal judiciary? Does the Court's rationale persuade you?
- How did Chief Justice Marshall navigate the separation-of-powers tension with Congress and the Executive?
- Should Marshall have recused himself from the case?
  - The modern recusal standard requires that "[a]ny justice, judge, or magistrate of the United States shall disqualify himself in any proceeding in which his impartiality might reasonably be questioned." 28 U.S.C. § 455. Other mandatory recusal situations include, inter alia, personal bias concerning a party, certain financial interests in the outcome, and familial relationships to actors in the case.
- A traditional maxim of law flows that "for every wrong, there is a remedy." Does *Marbury* fulfill that maxim? Could Mr. Marbury refile the case in another court?
- What is the modern relevance of *Marbury*? Has the Supreme Court fully utilized the judicial review power as envisioned by *Marbury*?
- Articulate the elements of judicial power and judicial restraint in the reasoning and in the result of the opinion.
  - In what ways does the opinion enhance the federal judiciary's role vis-à-vis other branches?
  - Was it wise for the Court to refrain from granting the relief sought?
  - If the Court had granted mandamus relief, would its power have been strengthened or weakened?
- If *Marbury* provides the significant power of judicial review, what limits should exist for federal court review? [Chapter 2 explores many constitutional and prudential limits on the power of judicial review.]
- Ultimately, the Supreme Court ruled that it lacked the power to resolve the case because it lacked original jurisdiction under the Constitution to entertain an action seeking issuance of a writ of mandamus against a federal officer. If the Court is right, what precedential value should its other decisions in the case have? In other words, if the Court lacked the power to rule on the case, was it necessary for the Court to determine the merits of whether Mr. Marbury possessed a substantive right to the commission or a remedy for the vindication of that right?
- The Court also seems to foreclose the possibility that the legislature could augment the Supreme Court's original jurisdiction. Is that holding necessary to the outcome of the case? Should it constitute binding precedent?

CHAPTER
2

Justiciability and the Judicial Function

A. A REFERENCE PROBLEM

This chapter explores the nature of the judicial function. Specifically, we focus on when the federal judiciary has the power to hear a case. Simply put, who may come before the court, when, and what types of disputes may the federal courts resolve? This chapter focuses your sights on the appropriate role of federal courts in our constitutional design. The following Reference Problem foreshadows a number of the concepts we examine.

* * * *

In the aftermath of the terrorist attacks of September 11, 2001, the President of the United States initiated a counterterrorism program operated by the National Security Agency (NSA). Nothing was publicly known about the program until a print news story uncovered and publicized that the program included wiretapping without warrants of telephone and email communications between any United States citizen and foreign nationals potentially associated with the terrorist group al Qaeda. United States telephone companies and Internet service providers cooperated with the program. The Administration admitted the existence of a warrantless wiretapping operation but refused to divulge any further information about the program.

A civil liberties organization filed a lawsuit in federal district court on behalf of lawyers, academics, and journalists who frequently communicate overseas with foreign nationals—some of whom the NSA likely deems as having potential al Qaeda affiliations. Plaintiffs assert a "well-founded belief" that the NSA is tapping these communications.

Plaintiffs sued the NSA and others for declaratory and injunctive relief, alleging irreparable harm incurred, including cessation of necessary professional communications out of fear of leaking confidential and privileged information and increased expenses due to necessitated in-person communications. According to plaintiffs, the warrantless wiretapping violates the First and Fourth Amendments, the Separation of Powers, the Administrative Procedure Act, Title III of the Omnibus Crime Control and Safe Streets Act, and the Foreign Intelligence Surveillance Act (FISA).

The NSA challenged jurisdiction and claimed that the relevant evidence constituted privileged national security documents. It asserted that the state secrets doctrine, as enunciated in *United States v. Reynolds*, 345 U.S. 1 (1953), commanded the nondisclosure of such evidence. As an executive agency, the NSA invoked the state secrets doctrine to bar discovery and admission of the sensitive evidence.

On dueling motions for summary judgment, the federal district court found jurisdiction proper. The court grounded standing on the public fact that the NSA program involved warrantless wiretapping of telephone and email communications where at least one party is suspected to be an al Qaeda affiliate. Further, the court ruled that these facts warranted summary judgment in plaintiffs' favor. Accordingly, the court granted injunctive and declaratory relief.

The federal appellate court stayed the injunction pending appeal. Thereafter, a FISA judge authorized wiretapping of international communications into or out of the United States as long as the government has probable cause that one participant is associated with al Qaeda. Ultimately, the appellate court, in a 2-1 decision, reversed the district court and dismissed the case for lack of jurisdiction. The United States Supreme Court granted *certiorari.*

How should the Supreme Court rule regarding whether plaintiffs present justiciable claims?

* * * *

As you reflect on your response, consider these supplemental questions that the problem may also trigger:

- Does the lawsuit ask the federal court to render advice based on a hypothetical rather than resolve a concrete dispute? Note: It is impermissible for federal courts to issue advisory opinions.
- Is the claim a live controversy between adversarial parties?
- Are these the "right" plaintiffs to bring this challenge? Can you think of a more appropriate set of plaintiffs?
- Do plaintiffs exhibit constitutional and prudential standing?

- Should these plaintiffs be granted access to the federal courts to have their claims heard and resolved?
- Must there be standing for every plaintiff on each claim?
- How do the jurisdictional requirements differ between constitutional versus statutory challenges?
- Could Congress grant standing to such plaintiffs?
- What is the nature of the injury?
    - Is it current or future? Is it real or hypothetical? Is it tangible or speculative? Is it a "general grievance" or a particularized harm? Is it imminent or remote?
    - What is the relief sought? Is it connected to the injury?
- Is the matter any less worthy for access to federal court because plaintiffs seek purely "equitable" remedies, for example, injunctions, rather than "legal" relief such as money damages?
- Does the federal court have the ability to redress the alleged harms? How?

- Is this lawsuit ripe for review? Consider whether it is premature, ripe, or stale.
    - Is it dispositive that the FISA judge approved the procedure—does it render the claim moot? Is the alleged harm "capable of repetition yet evading review"?
    - Does it matter that plaintiffs do not know, and cannot know, for certain that they have been subject to wiretapping?
- If these claims lack justiciability, is the NSA warrantless wiretapping operation thus unreviewable in federal court? Is it reviewable anywhere by anyone? Does national security post-9/11 justify such a result regardless of the ordinary desire to provide relief?
- Are there separation-of-powers concerns regarding the political nature of the program and potential tension between the judicial and executive branches that militate in favor of the federal judiciary's staying its hand?
- Does the fact that the nation is engaged in a "War on Terror" make it more likely that the Court should decline to address plaintiffs' claims? Or, on the other hand, should the "war" make it *more appropriate* for the courts to become engaged?

You may not be able to answer comprehensively yet, but you should strengthen your analysis after consideration of the materials presented in this chapter.

B. CONTEXT AND BACKGROUND

This chapter builds upon the foundational premises of Chapter 1 by focusing our interest on the exact nature of the judicial function under the Constitution. This section reviews, largely in descriptive text, basic information about justiciability doctrines to which students have been exposed in other courses. The remainder of the chapter seeks to examine these doctrines in-depth and will raise more advanced issues concerning the role of federal courts in the United States constitutional system.

The judicial function encompasses powers and limits. It operates within the structures of federalism and separation of powers. The federal judiciary serves dual purposes: it resolves individual disputes while constituting a coequal branch of government. Whether you apply the party-centered or government-structure view of federal courts will often affect your perspective on the application of many of the doctrines you will encounter in this chapter.

In order to understand and appreciate the nature of the judicial function, we must explore the scope of the judiciary's authority. The United States Constitution empowers federal courts to engage in judicial review. Recall *Marbury v. Madison*'s declaration: "It is emphatically the province and duty of the judicial department to say what the law is." Accordingly, federal courts may review the acts of other branches of government, interpret the law, and invalidate governmental acts violative of the Constitution. This awesome judicial power may place the judiciary in direct tension with the executive or legislative branch. Also, if a federal court invalidates a state law, federalism strains arise between the federal judiciary and state authorities. Thus, the judiciary must proceed cautiously in order to avoid violating the delicate separation-of-powers equilibrium between the branches and the federalism balance with the states. Constitutional and prudential limits exist to help protect against encroachments into the core domains of other branches and extensions beyond the federal courts' proper judicial function in our constitutional democracy.

In particular, this chapter examines the myriad doctrines of limitation on federal court power—advisory opinions, standing, ripeness, mootness, and political questions. These distinct, yet related, doctrines comprise what is known as *justiciability*. The heart of the justiciability inquiry is: what renders a case able to be heard and resolved in federal court? In processing this query, we should focus on the distinctions between what the Constitution dictates and what additional voluntary standards the judiciary adds in order to proceed prudently. In other words, if a doctrine of limitation arises, ask whether the federal judiciary *may* constitutionally hear and resolve the matter, yet *ought* to refrain from deciding the case, or whether the Constitution denies federal courts the *power* to hear the case. The framing of a limit as constitutional versus prudential is pivotal because Congress has the power to instruct federal courts to ignore prudential, but not constitutional, requirements. *See, e.g., Raines v. Byrd*, 521 U.S. 811, 820 n.3 (1997).

As we explore the justiciability principles, remember that the federal courts determine these justiciability issues, which raises a "fox guarding the henhouse" issue: Are these doctrines *really* limitations on the power of federal courts when, after all, the federal courts decide the limits of their own power? The justiciability doctrines do not remain purely static despite constitutional roots because the doctrines are the result of Supreme Court jurisprudence. Thus, we should critically explore the Supreme Court's interpretation of constitutional requirements and the policy justifications for any limitations applied.

Bear in mind that even if a controversy satisfies justiciability concerns, a federal court may still dismiss the case based on other hurdles such as Eleventh Amendment sovereignty principles or an abstention doctrine. Justiciability hurdles can be formidable obstacles for plaintiffs who desire the federal courthouse doors to swing open and remain open until the dispute reaches resolution.

When the federal courthouse door closes, state courthouse doors may remain open. Thus, the relative quality of justice meted out by federal and state courts often becomes critical to the consequences of federal justiciability doctrines. Put another way, if state courts are your only forum, are they as good as federal courts?

C. THE LAW AND PROBLEMS

1. *The Prohibition on Advisory Opinions*

Pursuant to Article III, section 2, of the Constitution, the federal judiciary has power to hear "Cases" and "Controversies." Accordingly, judicial interpretation of this clause has resulted in a long-standing prohibition on the federal courts: they cannot issue advisory opinions. The prohibition helps reserve federal judicial decisionmaking for actual controversies between disputing parties. This Article III–rooted command thus dictates that federal courts not render advice on theoretical matters. Note that some state courts may issue advisory opinions in limited circumstances such as constitutional queries referred from a lower federal court or another branch of government. For a federal court to find a justiciable, rather than advisory, claim, two conditions must exist: (1) an actual controversy between adverse parties and (2) a substantial likelihood that a federal court ruling in favor of the claimant would have some effect. *See Muskrat v. United States*, 219 U.S. 346 (1911); *Hayburn's Case*, 2 U.S. (2 Dall.) 409 (1792).

Explore the advisory opinion prohibition by considering Problem 2-1.

PROBLEM 2-1

To Declare, Yes; To Advise, No.

Secretary of State Rachel Case sent a letter to the United States Supreme Court. The letter asked the Supreme Court to answer a lengthy list of vexing questions about the legality of the Administration's actions regarding immigration enforcement. Case informed the Justices that the President would greatly appreciate the Court's guidance on this pressing national security matter given that very few analogies exist in precedent. The President's cabinet approved the letter and its long list of questions because it believed the Court would offer its wisdom to clarify this critical issue.

You are a law clerk to the Chief Justice. The Justices are privately in disagreement about the propriety of their response to the request. The Chief Justice has asked you to provide analysis of the following: (i) Is the Court obligated to provide guidance when another branch of government seeks it?; (ii) May the Court provide answers if the Justices would like to declare the Court's position and potentially avoid greater controversies to follow?; (iii) Would any answer at all constitute an advisory opinion?; and (iv) Must the Court decline any substantive response because the request seeks an advisory opinion, and, if so, on what grounds?

The Supreme Court encountered a request of this very nature from Thomas Jefferson when he served as Secretary of State to President George Washington. Based on your analysis of Problem 2-1, how do you think the Supreme Court responded to Jefferson's detailed request regarding America's position of neutrality in the war between France and England? Given that the prohibition on advisory opinions is the most straightforward of all the justiciability doctrines,

Problem 2-1 may have posed little difficulty. Yet identifying what constitutes an advisory opinion is not always so simple.

For example, how should we assess a Supreme Court opinion in which justiciability is met, but the Court offers *obiter dictum*, which in Latin means "said by the way"? We often discuss the concept of *dictum* as a portion of a court's opinion that is not necessary to its holding. Isn't *dictum*, then, a prohibited miniature advisory opinion housed within a valid opinion? What about alternative holdings? What if a federal court fails to conduct statutory interpretation that would avoid unnecessary interpretation of a federal constitutional provision?[1] How should we view a federal court's assumption of "hypothetical jurisdiction" in order to reach the merits when it could easily resolve the matter and the prevailing party would be the same if the court denied jurisdiction? Justice Scalia authored an opinion of the Court maintaining that such an "advisory opinion" is impermissible because Article III jurisdiction, including standing, must be satisfied at the outset. *See Steel Co. v. Citizens for a Better Env't*, 523 U.S. 83 (1998).

A thorny issue may arise when distinguishing a valid request for a declaratory judgment versus an improper request for an advisory opinion. The Federal Declaratory Judgment Act permits federal courts to "declare the rights and other legal relations of any interested party seeking such declaration, whether or not further relief is or could be sought" provided the matter is "a case of actual controversy within its jurisdiction." 28 U.S.C. § 2201(a). An issue seeking purely an advisory opinion does not pose "a case of actual controversy." Declaratory judgment jurisprudence emphasizes whether either party could validly bring an action for coercive relief such as money damages. If so, then it is likely, if not certain, that an actual controversy is present and declaratory relief available. *See Aetna Life Ins. Co. v. Haworth*, 300 U.S. 227 (1937); RICHARD H. FALLON, JOHN F. MANNING, DANIEL J. MELTZER, & DAVID L. SHAPIRO, HART & WECHSLER'S THE FEDERAL COURTS AND THE FEDERAL SYSTEM 56-57 (6th ed. 2009). An attempt to isolate particular issues, however, rather than seek a declaration regarding the entire controversy may prove to be an improper advisory opinion. *See Calderon v. Ashmus*, 523 U.S. 740 (1998).

With the foundational prohibition against advisory opinions in mind, now progress into the murkier waters of the standing doctrine.

2. *Standing*

Plaintiffs seek access to federal courts for the airing and resolution of their claims. Although the formal notion of standing is only a mid-twentieth-century development, it has a long historical development. Standing now raises a complex and significant hurdle for plaintiffs seeking to enter federal court. The proliferation of administrative agencies and the expansion of substantive constitutional rights contributed to the perceived need to establish "who, if anyone, should be able to sue to ensure governmental compliance with statutory

1. Pursuant to the canon of constitutional avoidance, "where an otherwise acceptable construction of a statute would raise serious constitutional problems, the Court will construe the statute to avoid such problems unless such construction is plainly contrary to the intent of Congress." *Edward J. DeBartolo Corp. v. Florida Gulf Coast Bldg. & Constr. Trades Council*, 485 U.S. 568, 575 (1988); *see also Gonzales v. Carhart*, 127 S. Ct. 1610, 1631 (2007) ("[E]very reasonable construction must be resorted to, in order to save a statute from unconstitutionality.") (citations and quotations omitted).

and constitutional provisions intended to protect broadly shared interests of large numbers of citizens." FALLON ET AL., HART & WECHSLER'S THE FEDERAL COURTS, *supra*, at 114.

a. The Constitutional and Prudential Parameters of Standing

The law of standing remains unsettled in many facets. The historical roots and progression demonstrate the Supreme Court's participation in the conception of its own role and the role of federal courts generally. Study of standing principles requires an appreciation of how the federal judiciary has carefully safeguarded its own authority over the years.

Certain foundational principles do exist. From a vast and intricate body of standing jurisprudence, we encounter the "irreducible constitutional minimum" for Article III standing. Any plaintiff seeking to litigate in federal court must demonstrate:[2]

(i) Injury in fact	→ Has plaintiff personally suffered some actual injury?
(ii) Causation	→ Is the injury "fairly traceable" to the challenged action?
(iii) Redressability	→ Will a favorable decision redress the injury?

A labyrinth of case law expounds these three threshold standing requirements. Keep in mind that the party invoking federal court jurisdiction has the burden to satisfy the standing components. "Injury in fact" means a "concrete and particularized" harm to a protected interest where that harm is "actual or imminent, not 'conjectural' or hypothetical." *Lujan v. Defenders of Wildlife*, 504 U.S. 555, 560 (1992). In other words, plaintiff must establish:

> A "personal stake in the outcome." . . . Abstract injury is not enough. The plaintiff must show that he "has sustained or is immediately in danger of sustaining some direct injury" as the result of the challenged official conduct and that the injury or threat of injury must be both "real and immediate," not "conjectural" or "hypothetical."

Id. at 579 (Kennedy, J., concurring) (citing *Los Angeles v. Lyons*, 461 U.S. 95, 101-02 (1983)).

Should Article III standing exist for a class of plaintiffs seeking medical monitoring for increased risk of future disease due to exposure to perfluorooctanoic acid? Yes, according to a federal district court that raised the issue of standing *sua sponte*. *Rhodes v. E.I. du Pont de Nemours & Co.*, 657 F. Supp. 2d 751 (S.D. W. Va. 2009). The court found that plaintiffs' "significantly increased risk of future disease" constituted Article III injury in fact: "The plaintiff's interest in safe drinking water is certainly an 'important interest,' and even if they may not currently be able to show a large impairment of that interest, they have a 'direct stake' in this issue as residents of the [Parkersburg Water District] and former, and perhaps future, consumers of its water." *Id.* at 759-60. The Fourth Circuit,

2. *See, e.g.*, *Lujan v. Defenders of Wildlife*, 504 U.S. 555 (1992); *Valley Forge Christian Coll. v. Americans United for Separation of Church & State*, 454 U.S. 464 (1982); *Simon v. E. Ky. Welfare Rights Org.*, 426 U.S. 26 (1976); *Friends of the Earth Inc. v. Laidlaw Envtl. Servs., Inc.*, 528 U.S. 167 (2000).

however, dismissed in part the plaintiff's appeal, concluding that, "when a putative class plaintiff voluntarily dismisses the individual claims underlying a request for class certification, as happened in this case, there is no longer a 'self-interested party advocating' for class treatment in the manner necessary to satisfy Article III standing requirements." 636 F.3d 88, 100 (4th Cir. 2011).

In a battle over regulation of genetically modified Roundup Ready Alfalfa, the Supreme Court found both sides satisfied standing requirements: (i) Petitioners (the Government, Monsanto, and Forage Genetics International) possessed standing by alleging injury from their inability to sell or license the genetically modified alfalfa to prospective customers until the relevant agency completes the required environmental impact statement, and (ii) Respondents (conventional alfalfa seed farms and concerned environmental groups) have standing to seek injunctive relief based on their allegation of a substantial risk of gene flow crop contamination injury, which has an environmental as well as an economic component sufficient to satisfy prudential zone of interests concerns. *Monsanto Co. v. Geertson Seed Farms*, 561 U.S. 139, 149-50, 154 (2010). On the merits, the Court ruled that the district court abused its discretion in enjoining the agency from implementing a partial deregulation of genetically modified alfalfa and in forbidding the potential planting in conjunction with the terms of that deregulation. *Id.* at 165. In dissent, Justice Stevens maintained that the Court may have misconstrued the district court's injunctive relief, but regardless, the relief was not an abuse of discretion given the court's consideration of the voluminous record and the court's detailed findings. *Id.* at 167 (Stevens, J., dissenting). The future no doubt holds continued efforts to litigate alleged environmental harms and coordinate challenges to Article III standing.

By securing the federal forum for only those who have a concrete stake in a real dispute, the standing doctrine "confines the Judicial Branch to its proper, limited role in the constitutional framework of Government." *Lujan*, 504 U.S. at 581. Thus, the standing doctrine serves separation-of-powers goals. Poignantly, Justice Kennedy emphasized the purpose of standing in shaping the appropriate role of the federal judiciary:

> An independent judiciary is held to account through its open proceedings and its reasoned judgments. In this process it is essential for the public to know what persons or groups are invoking the judicial power, the reasons that they have brought suit, and whether their claims are vindicated or denied. The concrete injury requirement helps assure that there can be an answer to these questions; and . . . that is part of the constitutional design.

Id. Failure to satisfy the injury prong will result in dismissal of plaintiff's federal case.

If plaintiff shows injury in fact, then she must still establish causation and redressability. For causation, examine the connection between the alleged injury and defendant's challenged behavior. Is the injury "fairly traceable" to defendant's conduct? Did defendant's alleged action cause plaintiff's injury? Would plaintiff continue to enjoy her interest but for defendant's conduct? For redressability, consider whether a federal court's grant of plaintiff's requested remedy would address the alleged harm.

Federal courts generally combine analysis of the causation and redressability elements. An exception to joint treatment, however, is *Allen v. Wright*, 468 U.S. 737 (1984), in which the parents of black public school children failed to satisfy the injury and causation prongs. The parents alleged that the black children suffered stigma as a result of the government's according tax-exempt status to private discriminatory schools. According to the Supreme Court, the alleged injury failed concreteness while also being indirect and caused by independent third parties not in front of the court. The Court assumed that the requested relief would have a significant effect on public school desegregation but dismissed jurisdiction based on plaintiffs' failure to show a concrete injury caused by the IRS's challenged conduct. Compare *Duke Power Co. v. Carolina Environmental Study Group, Inc.*, 438 U.S. 59 (1978), in which the Supreme Court held jurisdiction proper where plaintiffs, some of whom lived nearby a planned nuclear power plant, challenged a federal law limiting liability for nuclear mishaps. Despite no accident's having occurred, the *Duke Power* Court found that plaintiffs showed a present injury, including increased pollution of resident lakes from power plant facilities, caused by defendant's challenged behavior. Are you persuaded that distinct treatment makes sense for these two cases?

EXPLORING DOCTRINE

Balancing Litigant Access with Proper Federal Court Role

What principles do you think the federal judiciary seeks to serve by applying standing requirements? Separation-of-powers interests include maintaining appropriate boundaries on the federal judicial function. How is this goal served by requiring actual disputes with concrete injuries that are caused by defendant's conduct and redressable through plaintiff's requested relief? Does this justify restrictive standing interpretations, or is there a risk of manipulation of the standing doctrine by the federal judiciary based on its motivations to resolve or avoid the substantive merits?

In addition to injury, causation, and redressability, a plaintiff may have to satisfy prudential standing concerns such as demonstrating she is not a third party to the controversy and that the grievance is personalized rather than generalized. *See Fed. Election Comm'n v. Akins*, 524 U.S. 11 (1998). Ordinarily, an organization may sue only if it has itself suffered an injury. Yet, the organization may possibly satisfy standing in order to represent third parties who encounter barriers to effective vindication of their rights. While an organization will not be able to establish standing based on its concern about an issue, if its members have been affected in a tangible way by the challenged conduct, then the organization might have standing to represent their interests. *Hunt v. Washington State Apple Advertising Commission*, 432 U.S. 333 (1977), articulates a three-part test for an organization to determine if it has sufficient standing to represent its members' interests: (1) its members would have had standing in their own right, (2) the interests at stake in the litigation are germane to the organization's purpose, and (3) neither the claim asserted nor the relief requested requires individual members' participation in the lawsuit. *See id.* at 343.

Other exceptions to prudential concerns may allow certain third parties to sue, permitting third-party standing or *jus tertii* standing. For example, a third party may satisfy standing to pursue an "overbreadth" challenge where the individual's speech may not be protected under the First Amendment, but the statute will sweep broadly to restrict others' protected speech. *See Secretary of State of Md. v. J.H. Munson Co.*, 467 U.S. 947 (1984).

The Court addressed an interesting prudential standing argument in *Bond v. United States*, 564 U.S. ____, 131 S. Ct. 2355 (2011). The plaintiff, who was indicted under a federal statute for using a chemical to harm her husband's lover, challenged that federal statute on the grounds that it interfered with powers reserved to the states under the Tenth Amendment. Amicus maintained that federal courts should not hear plaintiff's claim based on the prudential rule that a party "'generally must assert his own legal rights and interests, and cannot rest his claim to relief on the legal rights or interests of third parties.'" 131 S. Ct. at 2363 (quoting *Warth v. Seldin*, 422 U.S. 490, 499, 500 (1975)). According to amicus only the states possessed standing to argue that the federal government interfered with their sovereignty in violation of the Tenth Amendment. The Court disagreed and held that plaintiff possessed both constitutional and prudential standing. Justice Kennedy took the occasion to opine on the connections among individual liberty, federalism, the separation of powers, and standing:

> Federalism is more than an exercise in setting the boundary between different institutions of government for their own integrity. State sovereignty is not just an end in itself: Rather, federalism secures to citizens the liberties that derive from the diffusion of sovereign power. . . . Federalism secures the freedom of the individual. . . . True, of course, these objects cannot be vindicated by the Judiciary in the absence of a proper case or controversy; but the individual liberty secured by federalism is not simply derivative of the rights of the States. . . . Just as it is appropriate for an individual, in a proper case, to invoke separation-of-powers or checks-and-balances constraints, so too may a litigant, in a proper case, challenge a law as enacted in contravention of constitutional principles of federalism.

Id. at 2364-65.

The prudential standing doctrine is in serious doubt given the Supreme Court's reasoning in *Lexmark International, Inc. v. Static Control Components, Inc.*, 134 S. Ct. 1377 (2014). The Court, per Justice Scalia, clarified that a request to dismiss a claim on prudential grounds when an Article III case or controversy exists "is in some tension with our recent reaffirmation of the principle that a federal court's obligation to hear and decide cases within its jurisdiction is virtually unflagging.'" *Id.* at 1386 (internal quotations omitted) (citing *Sprint Commc'ns, Inc. v. Jacobs*, 571 U.S. ____, 134 S. Ct. 584, 591 (2013); *see* Chapter 10 (exploring *Jacobs* in the abstention context)). According to the Court, the issue of whether plaintiff falls within the zone of interests protected—in this case under the Lanham Act—should be resolved pursuant to statutory interpretation rather than an impermissible judicial determination to "limit a cause of action that Congress has created merely because 'prudence' dictates." *Id.* at 1388. This logic injects Justice Scalia's separation-of-powers jurisprudence in lieu of classic prudential standing analysis.

Whether the zone-of-interests issue is purely prudential or a matter of statutory interpretation remains to be seen. Prudential requirements historically have arisen where plaintiffs pursue a statutory-based claim and thus must show they are "within the zone of interests" of the relevant statute. *See, e.g., Bennett v. Spear*, 520 U.S. 154 (1997). The definition of "within the zone of interests," however, includes those who are "*arguably* within the zone of interests" rather than only those who are actually in the zone. *See Data Processing Serv. Orgs., Inc. v. Camp*, 397 U.S. 150 (1970) (emphasis added). Congress may create legal rights via statute—for example, taxpayer and "citizen suit" standing—even where Article III standing is otherwise lacking. Congressional ability to confer standing is not boundless, however. Plaintiff must still have suffered an injury. Simple conference on statutory standing is insufficient by itself. Rather, Congress should articulate language that "at the very least identif[ies] the injury it seeks to vindicate and relate[s] the injury to the class of persons entitled to bring suit." *Lujan*, 504 U.S. at 580 (Kennedy, J., concurring). Thus, Congress may overcome obstacles to congressionally created citizen standing by carefully crafting statutory language and establishing clear legislative history.

Statute-based standing and Article III's injury-in-fact requirement have generated substantial confusion in federal courts. The Court granted certiorari, but then ultimately dismissed certiorari as improvidently granted, to determine whether standing exists for a private individual who lacks actual injury but alleges violation of a federal statute conferring an individual's right of recovery. *First Am. Fin. Corp. v. Edwards*, Docket No. 10-708. The federal circuits remain split on the issue. In *Edwards*, plaintiff is a consumer who purchased a home and at her closing bought title insurance at the state-regulated rate. Plaintiff seeks to represent a nationwide class; she raises no complaint about the price or quality but alleges a violation of the Real Estate Settlement Procedures Act's (RESPA's) referral-payment prohibition. She seeks to recover three times all settlement service charges. Should plaintiff survive a standing challenge? The Ninth Circuit held that, given RESPA conferred standing and provided for the trebling remedy, plaintiff possessed standing despite lack of actual injury. Stay tuned to see whether the Supreme Court takes up other cases to render clarification on statute-based claims and injury-in-fact requirements for standing.

Now explore *Clapper v. Amnesty International USA*, in which the Court considers Article III standing to challenge federal wiretapping procedures where there is no proffered evidence that the United States would imminently acquire plaintiffs' international communications using the statutorily prescribed surveillance or that the injunction sought would redress the alleged injuries.

CLAPPER v. AMNESTY INTERNATIONAL USA

133 S. Ct. 1138 (2013)

JUSTICE ALITO delivered the opinion of the Court.

Section 702 of the Foreign Intelligence Surveillance Act of 1978 allows the Attorney General and the Director of National Intelligence to acquire foreign intelligence information by jointly authorizing the surveillance of individuals who are not "United States persons" and are reasonably believed to be located outside the United States. Before doing so, the Attorney General and the Director of National Intelligence normally must obtain the Foreign Intelligence Surveillance Court's approval. Respondents are United States persons whose work, they allege, requires them to engage in sensitive international communications with individuals who they believe are likely targets of surveillance under § 1881a. Respondents seek a declaration that § 1881a is unconstitutional, as well as an injunction against § 1881a-authorized surveillance. The question before us is whether respondents have Article III standing to seek this prospective relief.

Respondents assert that they can establish injury in fact because there is an objectively reasonable likelihood that their communications will be acquired under § 1881a at some point in the future. But respondents' theory of *future* injury is too speculative to satisfy the well-established requirement that threatened injury must be "certainly impending." And even if respondents could demonstrate that the threatened injury is certainly impending, they still would not be able to establish that this injury is fairly traceable to § 1881a. As an alternative argument, respondents contend that they are suffering *present* injury because the risk of § 1881a-authorized surveillance already has forced them to take costly and burdensome measures to protect the confidentiality of their international communications. But respondents cannot manufacture standing by choosing to make expenditures based on hypothetical future harm that is not certainly impending. We therefore hold that respondents lack Article III standing.

I

A

In 1978, after years of debate, Congress enacted the Foreign Intelligence Surveillance Act (FISA) to authorize and regulate certain governmental electronic surveillance of communications for foreign intelligence purposes. . . .

In constructing such a framework for foreign intelligence surveillance, Congress created two specialized courts: [(i) the Foreign Intelligence Surveillance Court (FISC) and (ii) the Foreign Intelligence Surveillance Court of Review].

In the wake of the September 11th attacks, President George W. Bush authorized the National Security Agency (NSA) to conduct warrantless wiretapping of telephone and e-mail communications where one party to the communication was located outside the United States and a participant in "the call was reasonably believed to be a member or agent of al Qaeda or an affiliated terrorist organization." . . .

[T]he FISA Amendments Act of 2008 (FISA Amendments Act) . . . left much of FISA intact, but it "established a new and independent source of intelligence collection authority, beyond that granted in traditional FISA." . . . Unlike traditional FISA surveillance, § 1881a does not require the Government to demonstrate probable cause that the target of the electronic surveillance is a foreign power or agent of a foreign power. And, unlike traditional FISA, § 1881a does not require the Government to specify the nature and location of each of the particular facilities or places at which the electronic surveillance will occur.

The present case involves a constitutional challenge to § 1881a. Surveillance under § 1881a is subject to statutory conditions, judicial authorization, congressional supervision, and compliance with the Fourth Amendment. . . .

Section 1881a mandates that the Government obtain the Foreign Intelligence Surveillance Court's approval of "targeting" procedures, "minimization" procedures, and a governmental certification regarding proposed surveillance. [The Court detailed the certification requirements and the FISC's role in assessing the same.]

B

Respondents are attorneys and human rights, labor, legal, and media organizations whose work allegedly requires them to engage in sensitive and sometimes privileged telephone and e-mail communications with colleagues, clients, sources, and other individuals located abroad. Respondents believe that some of the people with whom they exchange foreign intelligence information are likely targets of surveillance under § 1881a. Specifically, respondents claim that they communicate by telephone and e-mail with people the Government "believes or believed to be associated with terrorist organizations," "people located in geographic areas that are a special focus" of the Government's counterterrorism or diplomatic efforts, and activists who oppose governments that are supported by the United States Government.

Respondents claim that § 1881a compromises their ability to locate witnesses, cultivate sources, obtain information, and communicate confidential information to their clients. Respondents also assert that they "have ceased engaging" in certain telephone and e-mail conversations. According to respondents, the threat of surveillance will compel them to travel abroad in order to have in-person conversations. In addition, respondents declare that they have undertaken "costly and burdensome measures" to protect the confidentiality of sensitive communications.

C

On the day when the FISA Amendments Act was enacted, respondents filed this action seeking (1) a declaration that § 1881a, on its face, violates the Fourth Amendment, the First Amendment, Article III, and separation-of-powers principles and (2) a permanent injunction against the use of § 1881a. Respondents assert what they characterize as two separate theories of Article III standing. First, they claim that there is an objectively reasonable likelihood that their communications will be acquired under § 1881a at some point in the future, thus causing them injury. Second, respondents maintain that the risk of surveillance under § 1881a is so substantial that they have been forced to take costly and burdensome measures to protect the confidentiality of their international communications; in their view, the costs they have incurred constitute present injury that is fairly traceable to § 1881a.

[T]he District Court held that respondents do not have standing. On appeal, however, a panel of the Second Circuit reversed. The panel agreed with respondents' argument that they have standing due to the objectively reasonable likelihood that their communications will be intercepted at some time in the future. In addition, the panel held that respondents have established that they are suffering "*present* injuries in fact—economic and professional harms—stemming from a reasonable fear of *future* harmful government conduct." The Second Circuit denied rehearing en banc by an equally divided vote.

Because of the importance of the issue and the novel view of standing adopted by the Court of Appeals, we granted certiorari, and we now reverse.

II

Article III of the Constitution limits federal courts' jurisdiction to certain "Cases" and "Controversies." As we have explained, "[n]o principle is more fundamental to the judiciary's proper role in our system of government than the constitutional limitation of federal-court jurisdiction to actual cases or controversies." "One element of the case-or-controversy requirement" is that plaintiffs "must establish that they have standing to sue."

The law of Article III standing, which is built on separation-of-powers principles, serves to prevent the judicial process from being used to usurp the powers of the political branches. In keeping with the purpose of this doctrine, "[o]ur standing inquiry has been especially rigorous when reaching the merits of the dispute would force us to decide whether an action taken by one of the other two branches of the Federal Government was unconstitutional." "Relaxation of standing requirements is directly related to the expansion of judicial power," and we have often found a lack of standing in cases in which the Judiciary has been requested to review actions of the political branches in the fields of intelligence gathering and foreign affairs, *see, e.g., Richardson* (plaintiff lacked standing to challenge the constitutionality of a statute permitting the Central Intelligence Agency to account for its expenditures solely on the certificate of the CIA Director); *Schlesinger* (plaintiffs lacked standing to challenge the Armed Forces Reserve membership of Members of Congress); *Laird v. Tatum* (plaintiffs lacked standing to challenge an Army intelligence-gathering program).

To establish Article III standing, an injury must be "concrete, particularized, and actual or imminent; fairly traceable to the challenged action; and redressable by a favorable ruling." "Although imminence is concededly a somewhat elastic concept, it cannot be stretched beyond its purpose, which is to ensure that the alleged injury is not too speculative for Article III purposes — that the injury is *certainly* impending." Thus, we have repeatedly reiterated that "threatened injury must be *certainly impending* to constitute injury in fact," and that "[a]llegations of *possible* future injury" are not sufficient.

III

A

Respondents assert that they can establish injury in fact that is fairly traceable to § 1881a because there is an objectively reasonable likelihood that their communications with their foreign contacts will be intercepted under § 1881a at some point in the future. This argument fails. As an initial matter, the Second Circuit's "objectively reasonable likelihood" standard is inconsistent with our requirement that "threatened injury must be certainly impending to constitute injury in fact." Furthermore, respondents' argument rests on their highly speculative fear that: (1) the Government will decide to target the communications of non-U.S. persons with whom they communicate; (2) in doing so, the Government will choose to invoke its authority under § 1881a rather than utilizing another method of surveillance; (3) the Article III judges who serve on the Foreign Intelligence Surveillance Court will conclude that the Government's proposed surveillance procedures satisfy § 1881a's many safeguards and are consistent with the Fourth Amendment; (4) the Government will succeed in intercepting the communications of respondents' contacts; and (5) respondents will be parties to the particular communications that the Government intercepts. As discussed below, respondents' theory of standing, which relies on a highly attenuated chain of possibilities, does not satisfy the requirement that threatened injury must be certainly impending. . . .

First, it is speculative whether the Government will imminently target communications to which respondents are parties. Section 1881a expressly provides that respondents, who are U.S. persons, cannot be targeted for surveillance under § 1881a. Accordingly, it is no surprise that respondents fail to offer any evidence that their communications have been monitored under § 1881a, a failure that substantially undermines their standing theory. See *ACLU v. NASA*, 493 F.3d 644, 655–56, 673–74 (6th Cir. 2007) (Batchelder, J.) (concluding that plaintiffs who lacked evidence that their communications had been intercepted did not have standing to challenge alleged NSA surveillance). Indeed, respondents do not even allege that the Government has sought the FISC's approval for surveillance of their communications. Accordingly, respondents' theory necessarily rests on their assertion that the Government will target *other individuals*—namely, their foreign contacts.

Yet respondents have no actual knowledge of the Government's § 1881a targeting practices. Instead, respondents merely speculate and make assumptions about whether their communications with their foreign contacts will be acquired under § 1881a. For example, journalist Christopher Hedges states: "I have no choice but to *assume* that any of my international communications *may* be subject to government surveillance, and I have to make decisions . . . in light of that *assumption*." Similarly, attorney Scott McKay asserts that, "[b]ecause of the [FISA Amendments Act], we now have to *assume* that every one of our international communications *may* be monitored by the government." "The party invoking federal jurisdiction bears the burden of establishing" standing—and, at the summary judgment stage, such a party "can no longer rest on . . . 'mere allegations,' but must 'set forth' by affidavit or other evidence 'specific facts.'" Respondents, however, have set forth no specific facts demonstrating that the communications of their foreign contacts will be targeted. Moreover, because § 1881a at most *authorizes*—but does not *mandate* or *direct*—the surveillance that respondents fear, respondents' allegations are necessarily conjectural. Simply put, respondents can only speculate as to how the Attorney General and the Director of National Intelligence will exercise their discretion in determining which communications to target.[3]

Second, even if respondents could demonstrate that the targeting of their foreign contacts is imminent, respondents can only speculate as to whether the Government will seek to use § 1881a-authorized surveillance (rather than other methods) to do so. The Government has numerous other methods of conducting surveillance, none of which is challenged here. . . .

Third, even if respondents could show that the Government will seek the Foreign Intelligence Surveillance Court's authorization to acquire the communications of respondents' foreign contacts under § 1881a, respondents can only speculate as to whether that court will authorize such surveillance. In the past, we have been reluctant to endorse standing theories that require guesswork as to how independent decisionmakers will exercise their judgment. . . .

3. [Footnote 4 in Court's opinion.] It was suggested at oral argument that the Government could help resolve the standing inquiry by disclosing to a court, perhaps through an *in camera* proceeding, (1) whether it is intercepting respondents' communications and (2) what targeting or minimization procedures it is using. This suggestion is puzzling. As an initial matter, it is *respondents'* burden to prove their standing by pointing to specific facts not the Government's burden to disprove standing by revealing details of its surveillance priorities. Moreover, this type of hypothetical disclosure proceeding would allow a terrorist (or his attorney) to determine whether he is currently under U.S. surveillance simply by filing a lawsuit challenging the Government's surveillance program. Even if the terrorist's attorney were to comply with a protective order prohibiting him from sharing the Government's disclosures with his client, the court's post disclosure decision about whether to dismiss the suit for lack of standing would surely signal to the terrorist whether his name was on the list of surveillance targets.

Fourth, even if the Government were to obtain the Foreign Intelligence Surveillance Court's approval to target respondents' foreign contacts under § 1881a, it is unclear whether the Government would succeed in acquiring the communications of respondents' foreign contacts. And fifth, even if the Government were to conduct surveillance of respondents' foreign contacts, respondents can only speculate as to whether *their own communications* with their foreign contacts would be incidentally acquired.

In sum, respondents' speculative chain of possibilities does not establish that injury based on potential future surveillance is certainly impending or is fairly traceable to § 1881a.[4]

B

Respondents' alternative argument—namely, that they can establish standing based on the measures that they have undertaken to avoid § 1881a-authorized surveillance—fares no better. Respondents assert that they are suffering ongoing injuries that are fairly traceable to § 1881a because the risk of surveillance under § 1881a requires them to take costly and burdensome measures to protect the confidentiality of their communications. Respondents claim, for instance, that the threat of surveillance sometimes compels them to avoid certain e-mail and phone conversations, to "tal[k] in generalities rather than specifics," or to travel so that they can have in-person conversations. The Second Circuit panel concluded that, because respondents are already suffering such ongoing injuries, the likelihood of interception under § 1881a is relevant only to the question whether respondents' ongoing injuries are "fairly traceable" to § 1881a. Analyzing the "fairly traceable" element of standing under a relaxed reasonableness standard, the Second Circuit then held that "plaintiffs have established that they suffered *present* injuries in fact—economic and professional harms—stemming from a reasonable fear of *future* harmful government conduct."

The Second Circuit's analysis improperly allowed respondents to establish standing by asserting that they suffer present costs and burdens that are based on a fear of surveillance, so long as that fear is not "fanciful, paranoid, or otherwise unreasonable." This improperly waters down the fundamental requirements of Article III. Respondents' contention that they have standing because they incurred certain costs as a reasonable reaction to a risk of harm is unavailing—because the harm respondents seek to avoid is not certainly impending. In other words, respondents cannot manufacture standing merely by inflicting harm on themselves based on their fears of hypothetical future harm that is not certainly impending. Any ongoing injuries that respondents are suffering are not fairly traceable to § 1881a.

If the law were otherwise, an enterprising plaintiff would be able to secure a lower standard for Article III standing simply by making an expenditure based

4. [Footnote 5 in Court's opinion.] Our cases do not uniformly require plaintiffs to demonstrate that it is literally certain that the harms they identify will come about. In some instances, we have found standing based on a "substantial risk" that the harm will occur, which may prompt plaintiffs to reasonably incur costs to mitigate or avoid that harm. But to the extent that the "substantial risk" standard is relevant and is distinct from the "clearly impending" requirement, respondents fall short of even that standard, in light of the attenuated chain of inferences necessary to find harm here. In addition, plaintiffs bear the burden of pleading and proving concrete facts showing that the defendant's actual action has caused the substantial risk of harm. Plaintiffs cannot rely on speculation about "'the unfettered choices made by independent actors not before the court.'"

on a nonparanoid fear. As Judge Raggi accurately noted, under the Second Circuit panel's reasoning, respondents could, "for the price of a plane ticket, . . . transform their standing burden from one requiring a showing of actual or imminent . . . interception to one requiring a showing that their subjective fear of such interception is not fanciful, irrational, or clearly unreasonable." Thus, allowing respondents to bring this action based on costs they incurred in response to a speculative threat would be tantamount to accepting a repackaged version of respondents' first failed theory of standing. . . .

For the reasons discussed above, respondents' self-inflicted injuries are not fairly traceable to the Government's purported activities under § 1881a, and their subjective fear of surveillance does not give rise to standing.

IV

A

Respondents incorrectly maintain that "[t]he kinds of injuries incurred here — injuries incurred because of [respondents'] reasonable efforts to avoid greater injuries that are otherwise likely to flow from the conduct they challenge — are the same kinds of injuries that this Court held to support standing in cases such as" *Laidlaw* . . . and *Monsanto.* [N]one of these cases holds or even suggests that plaintiffs can establish standing simply by claiming that they experienced a "chilling effect" that resulted from a governmental policy that does not regulate, constrain, or compel any action on their part. Moreover, each of these cases was very different from the present case.

In *Laidlaw,* plaintiffs' standing was based on "the proposition that a company's continuous and pervasive illegal discharges of pollutants into a river would cause nearby residents to curtail their recreational use of that waterway and would subject them to other economic and aesthetic harms." Because the unlawful discharges of pollutants were "concededly ongoing," the only issue was whether "nearby residents" — who were members of the organizational plaintiffs — acted reasonably in refraining from using the polluted area. *Laidlaw* is therefore quite unlike the present case, in which it is not "concede[d]" that respondents would be subject to unlawful surveillance but for their decision to take preventive measures. *Laidlaw* would resemble this case only if (1) it were undisputed that the Government was using § 1881a-authorized surveillance to acquire respondents' communications and (2) the sole dispute concerned the reasonableness of respondents' preventive measures. . . .

Monsanto . . . is likewise inapposite. In *Monsanto,* conventional alfalfa farmers had standing to seek injunctive relief because the agency's decision to deregulate a variety of genetically engineered alfalfa gave rise to a "significant risk of gene flow to non-genetically-engineered varieties of alfalfa." The standing analysis in that case hinged on evidence that genetically engineered alfalfa "'seed fields [we]re currently being planted in all the major alfalfa seed production areas'"; the bees that pollinate alfalfa "'have a range of at least two to ten miles'"; and the alfalfa seed farms were concentrated in an area well within the bees' pollination range. Unlike the conventional alfalfa farmers in *Monsanto,* however, respondents in the present case present no concrete evidence to substantiate their fears, but instead rest on mere conjecture about possible governmental actions.

B

[The Court roundly rejected respondents' assertion that no one would have standing if they lack it. Further, the Court denied that its holding would insulate § 1881a from judicial review given Congress' comprehensive legislative scheme.]

We hold that respondents lack Article III standing because they cannot demonstrate that the future injury they purportedly fear is certainly impending and because they cannot manufacture standing by incurring costs in anticipation of non-imminent harm. . . .

It is so ordered.

JUSTICE BREYER, with whom JUSTICE GINSBURG, JUSTICE SOTOMAYOR, and JUSTICE KAGAN join, dissenting.

The plaintiffs' standing depends upon the likelihood that the Government will harm them by intercepting at least some of their private, foreign, telephone, or e-mail conversations. In my view, this harm is not "speculative." Indeed it is as likely to take place as are most future events that commonsense inference and ordinary knowledge of human nature tell us will happen. This Court has often found the occurrence of similar future events sufficiently certain to support standing. I dissent from the Court's contrary conclusion.

I

Article III specifies that the "judicial Power" of the United States extends only to actual "Cases" and "Controversies." It thereby helps to ensure that the legal questions presented to the federal courts will not take the form of abstract intellectual problems resolved in the "rarified atmosphere of a debating society" but instead those questions will be presented "in a concrete factual context conducive to a realistic appreciation of the consequences of judicial action."

The Court has recognized that the precise boundaries of the "case or controversy" requirement are matters of "degree . . . not discernible by any precise test." . . .

No one here denies that the Government's interception of a private telephone or e-mail conversation amounts to an injury that is "concrete and particularized." Moreover, the plaintiffs, respondents here, seek as relief a judgment declaring unconstitutional (and enjoining enforcement of) a statutory provision authorizing those interceptions; and, such a judgment would redress the injury by preventing it. Thus, the basic question is whether the injury, *i.e.*, the interception, is "actual or imminent."

II

A

. . . . The addition of § 1881a in 2008 changed [Foreign Intelligence Surveillance Act of 1978] in three important ways. First, it eliminated the requirement that the Government describe to the court each specific target and identify each facility at which its surveillance would be directed, thus permitting surveillance on a programmatic, not necessarily individualized, basis. Second, it eliminated the requirement that a target be a "foreign power or an agent of a foreign power." Third, it diminished the court's authority to insist upon, and eliminated its authority to supervise, instance-specific privacy-intrusion minimization procedures (though the Government still must use court-approved general minimization procedures). Thus, using the authority of § 1881a, the Government can obtain court approval for its surveillance of electronic communications between places within the United States and targets in foreign territories by showing the court (1) that "a significant purpose of the acquisition is to obtain foreign intelligence information," and (2) that it will use general targeting and privacy-intrusion minimization procedures of a kind that the court had previously approved.

B

It is similarly important to understand the kinds of communications in which the plaintiffs say they engage and which they believe the Government will intercept. Plaintiff Scott McKay, for example, says in an affidavit (1) that he is a lawyer; (2) that he represented "Mr. Sami Omar Al-Hussayen, who was acquitted in June 2004 on terrorism charges"; (3) that he continues to represent "Mr. Al-Hussayen, who, in addition to facing criminal charges after September 11, was named as a defendant in several civil cases"; (4) that he represents Khalid Sheik Mohammed, a detainee, "before the Military Commissions at Guantánamo Bay, Cuba"; (5) that in representing these clients he "communicate[s] by telephone and email with people outside the United States, including Mr. Al-Hussayen himself," "experts, investigators, attorneys, family members . . . and others who are located abroad"; and (6) that prior to 2008 "the U.S. government had intercepted some 10,000 telephone calls and 20,000 email communications involving [his client] Al-Hussayen."

Another plaintiff, Sylvia Royce, says in her affidavit (1) that she is an attorney; (2) that she "represent[s] Mohammedou Ould Salahi, a prisoner who has been held at Guantánamo Bay as an enemy combatant"; (3) that, "[i]n connection with [her] representation of Mr. Salahi, [she] receive[s] calls from time to time from Mr. Salahi's brother, . . . a university student in Germany"; and (4) that she has been told that the Government has threatened Salahi "that his family members would be arrested and mistreated if he did not cooperate."

The plaintiffs have noted that McKay no longer represents Mohammed and Royce no longer represents Ould Salahi. But these changes are irrelevant, for we assess standing as of the time a suit is filed, and in any event McKay himself continues to represent Al Hussayen, his partner now represents Mohammed, and Royce continues to represent individuals held in the custody of the U.S. military overseas.

A third plaintiff, Joanne Mariner, says in her affidavit (1) that she is a human rights researcher, (2) that "some of the work [she] do[es] involves trying to track down people who were rendered by the CIA to countries in which they were tortured"; (3) that many of those people "the CIA has said are (or were) associated with terrorist organizations"; and (4) that, to do this research, she "communicate[s] by telephone and e-mail with . . . former detainees, lawyers for detainees, relatives of detainees, political activists, journalists, and fixers" "all over the world, including in Jordan, Egypt, Pakistan, Afghanistan, [and] the Gaza Strip."

Other plaintiffs, including lawyers, journalists, and human rights researchers, say in affidavits (1) that they have jobs that require them to gather information from foreigners located abroad; (2) that they regularly communicate electronically (*e.g.*, by telephone or e-mail) with foreigners located abroad; and (3) that in these communications they exchange "foreign intelligence information" as the Act defines it.

III

Several considerations, based upon the record along with commonsense inferences, convince me that there is a very high likelihood that Government, *acting under the authority of § 1881a*, will intercept at least some of the communications just described. First, the plaintiffs have engaged, and continue to engage, in electronic communications of a kind that the 2008 amendment, but not the prior Act, authorizes the Government to intercept. These communications include discussions with family members of those detained at Guantanamo, friends and acquaintances of those persons, and investigators, experts and others with knowledge of circumstances related to terrorist activities. These persons are foreigners located outside the United States. They are not "foreign power[s]" or "agent[s] of . . . foreign power [s]." And the plaintiffs state that they exchange with these persons "foreign intelligence information," defined to include information that "relates to" "international terrorism" and "the national defense or the security of the United States."

Second, the plaintiffs have a strong *motive* to engage in, and the Government has a strong *motive* to listen to, conversations of the kind described. A lawyer representing a client normally seeks to learn the circumstances surrounding the crime (or the civil wrong) of which the client is accused. . . . Journalists and human rights workers have strong similar motives to conduct conversations of this kind.

At the same time, the Government has a strong motive to conduct surveillance of conversations that contain material of this kind. The Government, after all, seeks to learn as much as it can reasonably learn about suspected terrorists (such as those detained at Guantanamo), as well as about their contacts and activities, along with those of friends and family members. . . .

Third, the Government's *past behavior* shows that it has sought, and hence will in all likelihood continue to seek, information about alleged terrorists and detainees through means that include surveillance of electronic communications. . . .

Fourth, the Government has the *capacity* to conduct electronic surveillance of the kind at issue. . . .

Of course, to exercise this capacity the Government must have intelligence court authorization. But the Government rarely files requests that fail to meet the statutory criteria. . . .

The upshot is that (1) similarity of content, (2) strong motives, (3) prior behavior, and (4) capacity all point to a very strong likelihood that the Government will intercept at least some of the plaintiffs' communications, including some that the 2008 amendment, § 1881a, but not the pre–2008 Act, authorizes the Government to intercept. . . .

The majority is wrong when it describes the harm threatened plaintiffs as "speculative."

IV

A

The majority more plausibly says that the plaintiffs have failed to show that the threatened harm is "*certainly impending.*" But, as the majority appears to concede, *certainty* is not, and never has been, the touchstone of standing. The future is inherently uncertain. Yet federal courts frequently entertain actions for injunctions and for declaratory relief aimed at preventing future activities that are reasonably likely or highly likely, but not absolutely certain, to take place. And that degree of certainty is all that is needed to support standing here.

The Court's use of the term "certainly impending" is not to the contrary. Sometimes the Court has used the phrase "certainly impending" as if the phrase described a *sufficient*, rather than a *necessary*, condition for jurisdiction. On other occasions, it has used the phrase as if it concerned *when*, not *whether*, an alleged injury would occur. Thus, in *Lujan*, the Court considered a threatened future injury that consisted of harm that plaintiffs would suffer when they "soon" visited a government project area that (they claimed) would suffer environmental damage. The Court wrote that a "mere profession of an intent, some day, to return" to the project area did not show the harm was "*imminent*," for "soon" might mean nothing more than "in this lifetime." Similarly, in *McConnell v. Federal Election Comm'n*, the Court denied standing because the Senator's future injury (stemming from a campaign finance law) would not affect him until his reelection. That fact, the Court said, made the injury "too remote temporally to satisfy Article III standing."

On still other occasions, recognizing that "'imminence' is concededly a somewhat elastic concept," the Court has referred to, or used (sometimes along with "certainly impending") other phrases such as "reasonable probability" that suggest less than absolute, or literal certainty [(citing a string of precedent, noting the following other phrases: "a *realistic danger* of sustaining a direct injury"; "that . . . the defendant's allegedly wrongful behavior will likely occur or continue"; "reasonable probability"; "substantial risk"; "realistic and impending threat of direct injury"; "genuine threat of enforcement"; "substantially likely"; "sufficient likelihood of economic injury"; "realistic danger"; "quite realistic" threat; and "likely")]. Taken together the case law uses the word "certainly" as if it emphasizes, rather than literally defines, the immediately following term "impending."

B

1

More important, the Court's holdings in standing cases show that standing exists here. The Court has often *found* standing where the occurrence of the relevant injury was far *less* certain than here. Consider a few, fairly typical, cases. Consider *Pennell*. A city ordinance forbade landlords to raise the rent charged to a tenant by more than 8 percent where doing so would work an unreasonably severe hardship on that tenant. A group of landlords sought a judgment declaring the ordinance unconstitutional. The Court held that, to have standing, the landlords had to demonstrate a "'*realistic danger of sustaining a direct injury* as a result of the statute's operation.'" It found that the landlords had done so by showing a likelihood of enforcement and a "probability," that the ordinance would make the landlords charge lower rents—even though the landlords had not shown (1) that they intended to raise the relevant rents to the point of causing unreasonably severe hardship; (2) that the tenants would challenge those increases; or (3) that the city's hearing examiners and arbitrators would find against the landlords. Here, even more so than in *Pennell*, there is a "*realistic danger*" that the relevant harm will occur.

Or, consider *Blum*. A group of nursing home residents receiving Medicaid benefits challenged the constitutionality (on procedural grounds) of a regulation that permitted their nursing home to transfer them to a less desirable home. Although a Medicaid committee had recommended transfers, Medicaid-initiated transfer had been enjoined and the nursing home itself had not threatened to transfer the plaintiffs. But the Court found "standing" because "the threat of transfers" was "not 'imaginary or speculative'" but "quite realistic," hence "sufficiently substantial." The plaintiffs' injury here is not imaginary or speculative, but "quite realistic."

Or, consider *Davis.* The plaintiff, a candidate for the United States House of Representatives, self-financed his campaigns. He challenged the constitutionality of an election law that relaxed the limits on an opponent's contributions when a self-financed candidate's spending itself exceeded certain other limits. His opponent, in fact, had decided not to take advantage of the increased contribution limits that the statute would have allowed. But the Court nonetheless found standing because there was a "realistic and impending threat," not a certainty, that the candidate's opponent would do so at the time the plaintiff filed the complaint. The threat facing the plaintiffs here is as "realistic and impending."

Or, consider *MedImmune.* The plaintiff, a patent licensee, sought a declaratory judgment that the patent was invalid. But, the plaintiff did not face an imminent threat of suit because it continued making royalty payments to the patent holder. In explaining why the plaintiff had standing, we (1) assumed that if the plaintiff stopped making royalty payments it would have standing (despite the fact that the patent holder might not bring suit), (2) rejected the Federal Circuit's "reasonable apprehension of *imminent* suit" requirement, and (3) instead suggested that a "genuine threat of enforcement" was likely sufficient. A "genuine threat" is present here.

Moreover, courts have often found *probabilistic* injuries sufficient to support standing. In *Duke Power*, for example, the plaintiffs, a group of individuals living near a proposed nuclear powerplant, challenged the constitutionality of the Price-Anderson Act, a statute that limited the plant's liability in the case of a nuclear accident. The plaintiffs said that, without the Act, the defendants would not build a nuclear plant. And the building of the plant would harm them, in part, by emitting "non-natural radiation into [their] environment." The Court found standing in part due to "our generalized concern about exposure to radiation and the apprehension flowing from the *uncertainty* about the health and genetic consequences of even small emissions."

[The dissent set forth lower court cases finding standing based on "increased *risk* of:" "wildfires"; "developing skin cancer"; "nonrecovery inherent in the reduction of collateral securing a debt of uncertain amount"; "harm caused by implantation of defective medical device"; "Employee Retirement Income Security Act beneficiary will not be covered due to increased amount of discretion given to ERISA administrator."]

How could the law be otherwise? Suppose that a federal court faced a claim by homeowners that (allegedly) unlawful dam-building practices created a high risk that their homes would be flooded. Would the court deny them standing on the ground that the risk of flood was only 60, rather than 90, percent? . . .

2

In some standing cases, the Court has found that a reasonable probability of *future* injury comes accompanied with *present* injury that takes the form of reasonable efforts to mitigate the threatened effects of the future injury or to prevent it from occurring. Thus, in *Monsanto Co.*, plaintiffs, a group of conventional alfalfa growers, challenged an agency decision to deregulate genetically engineered alfalfa. They claimed that deregulation would harm them because their neighbors would plant the genetically engineered seed, bees would obtain pollen from the neighbors' plants, and the bees would then (harmfully) contaminate their own conventional alfalfa with the genetically modified gene. The lower courts had found a "reasonable probability" that this injury would occur.

Without expressing views about that probability, we found standing because the plaintiffs would suffer present harm by trying to combat the threat. The plaintiffs, for example, "would have to conduct testing to find out whether and to what extent their crops have been contaminated." And they would have to take "measures to minimize the likelihood of potential contamination and to ensure an adequate supply of non-genetically-engineered alfalfa." We held that these "harms, which [the plaintiffs] will suffer even if their crops are not actually infected with" the genetically modified gene, "are sufficiently concrete to satisfy the injury-in-fact prong of the constitutional standing analysis."

Virtually identical circumstances are present here. Plaintiff McKay, for example, points out that, when he communicates abroad about, or in the interests of, a client (*e.g.*, a client accused of terrorism), he must "make an assessment" whether his "client's interests would be compromised" should the Government "acquire the communications." If so, he must either forgo the communication or travel abroad. ("I have had to take measures to protect the confidentiality of information that I believe is particularly sensitive," including "travel that is both time-consuming and expensive").

Since travel is expensive, since forgoing communication can compromise the client's interests, since McKay's assessment itself takes time and effort, this case does not differ significantly from *Monsanto*. And that is so whether we consider the plaintiffs' present necessary expenditure of time and effort as a separate concrete, particularized, imminent harm, or consider it as additional evidence that the future harm (an interception) is likely to occur. See also *Friends of the Earth, Inc.*, 528 U.S. at 183–84, (holding that plaintiffs who curtailed their recreational activities on a river due to reasonable concerns about the effect of pollutant discharges into that river had standing).

3

The majority cannot find support in cases that use the words "certainly impending" to *deny* standing. While I do not claim to have read every standing case, I have examined quite a few, and not yet found any such case. The majority refers to *Whitmore v. Arkansas*. But in that case the Court denied standing to a prisoner who challenged the validity of a death sentence given to a *different* prisoner who refused to challenge his own sentence. The plaintiff feared that in the absence of an appeal, his fellow prisoner's death sentence would be missing from the State's death penalty database and thereby skew the database against him, making it less likely his challenges to his own death penalty would succeed. The Court found no standing. . . .

In *Lujan*, the case that may come closest to supporting the majority, the Court also found no standing. But, as I pointed out, *Lujan* is a case where the Court considered *when*, not *whether*, the threatened harm would occur. The relevant injury there consisted of a visit by environmental group's members to a project site where they would find (unlawful) environmental depredation. The Court pointed out that members had alleged that they would visit the project sites "soon." But it wrote that "soon" might refer to almost any time in the future.

By way of contrast, the ongoing threat of terrorism means that here the relevant interceptions will likely take place imminently, if not now.

The Court has, of course, denied standing in other cases. But they involve injuries *less* likely, not more likely, to occur than here. In a recent case, *Summers v. Earth Island Institute,* for example, the plaintiffs challenged a regulation exempting certain timber sales from public comment and administrative appeal. The plaintiffs claimed that the regulations injured them by interfering with their esthetic enjoyment and recreational use of the forests. The Court found this harm too unlikely to occur to support standing. The Court noted that one plaintiff had not pointed to a specific affected forest that he would visit. The Court concluded that "[t]here may be a chance, but . . . *hardly a likelihood,*" that the plaintiff's "wanderings will bring him to a parcel about to be affected by a project unlawfully subject to the regulations."

4

In sum, as the Court concedes, the word "certainly" in the phrase "certainly impending" does not refer to absolute certainty. As our case law demonstrates, what the Constitution requires is something more akin to "reasonable probability" or "high probability." The use of some such standard is all that is necessary here to ensure the actual concrete injury that the Constitution demands. [T]he standard is readily met in this case. . . .

While I express no view on the merits of the plaintiffs' constitutional claims, I do believe that at least some of the plaintiffs have standing to make those claims. I dissent, with respect, from the majority's contrary conclusion.

* * * *

Standing has remained prominent in the Court's agenda. Two such cases garnered significant public attention regarding marriage equality: *Hollingsworth v. Perry* and *United States v. Windsor,* both excerpted below. In *Perry,* the Court found standing lacking for supporters who wished to defend California's Proposition 8 where defendant government officials decided not to appeal. Yet the Court in *Windsor* held standing existed where the United States chose not to defend section 3 of the Defense of Marriage Act (DOMA). Are these cases reconcilable? After examining the reasoning of both cases, where do we stand on standing?

HOLLINGSWORTH v. PERRY

133 S. Ct. 2652 (2013)

CHIEF JUSTICE ROBERTS delivered the opinion of the Court.

The public is currently engaged in an active political debate over whether same-sex couples should be allowed to marry. That question has also given rise to litigation. In this case, petitioners, who oppose same-sex marriage, ask us to decide whether the Equal Protection Clause "prohibits the State of California from defining marriage as the union of a man and a woman." Respondents, same-sex couples who wish to marry, view the issue in somewhat different terms: For them, it is whether California—having previously recognized the right of same-sex couples to marry—may reverse that decision through a referendum.

Federal courts have authority under the Constitution to answer such questions only if necessary to do so in the course of deciding an actual "case" or "controversy." As used in the Constitution, those words do not include every sort of dispute, but only those "historically viewed as capable of resolution through the judicial process." This is an essential limit on our power: It ensures that we act *as judges,* and do not engage in policymaking properly left to elected representatives.

For there to be such a case or controversy, it is not enough that the party invoking the power of the court have a keen interest in the issue. That party must also have "standing," which requires, among other things, that it have suffered a concrete and particularized injury. Because we find that petitioners do not have standing, we have no authority to decide this case on the merits, and neither did the Ninth Circuit.

* * * *

II

Article III of the Constitution confines the judicial power of federal courts to deciding actual "Cases" or "Controversies." One essential aspect of this requirement is that any person invoking the power of a federal court must demonstrate standing to do so. This requires the litigant to prove that he has suffered a concrete and particularized injury that is fairly traceable to the challenged conduct, and is likely to be redressed by a favorable judicial decision. In other words, for a federal court to have authority under the Constitution to settle a dispute, the party before it must seek a remedy for a personal and tangible harm. "The presence of a disagreement, however sharp and acrimonious it may be, is insufficient by itself to meet Art. III's requirements."

The doctrine of standing, we recently explained [in *Clapper*], "serves to prevent the judicial process from being used to usurp the powers of the political branches." In light of this "overriding and time-honored concern about keeping the Judiciary's power within its proper constitutional sphere, we must put aside the natural urge to proceed directly to the merits of [an] important dispute and to 'settle' it for the sake of convenience and efficiency." [*Raines v. Byrd.*]

Most standing cases consider whether a plaintiff has satisfied the requirement when filing suit, but Article III demands that an "actual controversy" persist throughout all stages of litigation. That means that standing "must be met by persons seeking appellate review, just as it must be met by persons appearing in courts of first instance." We therefore must decide whether petitioners had standing to appeal the District Court's order.

Respondents initiated this case in the District Court against the California officials responsible for enforcing Proposition 8. The parties do not contest that respondents had Article III standing to do so. Each couple expressed a desire to marry and obtain "official sanction" from the State, which was unavailable to them given the declaration in Proposition 8 that "marriage" in California is solely between a man and a woman.

After the District Court declared Proposition 8 unconstitutional and enjoined the state officials named as defendants from enforcing it, however, the inquiry under Article III changed. Respondents no longer had any injury to redress—they had won—and the state officials chose not to appeal.

The only individuals who sought to appeal that order were petitioners, who had intervened in the District Court. But the District Court had not ordered them to do or refrain from doing anything. To have standing, a litigant must seek relief for an injury that affects him in a "personal and individual way." He must possess a "direct stake in the outcome" of the case. Here, however, petitioners had no "direct stake" in the outcome of their appeal. Their only interest in having the District Court order reversed was to vindicate the constitutional validity of a generally applicable California law.

We have repeatedly held that such a "generalized grievance," no matter how sincere, is insufficient to confer standing. A litigant "raising only a generally available grievance about government—claiming only harm to his and every citizen's interest in proper application of the Constitution and laws, and seeking relief that no more directly and tangibly benefits him than it does the public at large—does not state an Article III case or controversy."

Petitioners argue that the California Constitution and its election laws give them a "'unique,' 'special,' and 'distinct' role in the initiative process—one 'involving both authority and responsibilities that differ from other supporters of the measure.' True enough—but only when it comes to the process of enacting the law. Upon submitting the proposed initiative to the attorney general, petitioners became the official "proponents" of Proposition 8. As such, they were responsible for collecting the signatures required to qualify the measure for the ballot. . . .

But once Proposition 8 was approved by the voters, the measure became "a duly enacted constitutional amendment or statute." Petitioners have no role—special or otherwise—in the enforcement of Proposition 8. They therefore have no "personal stake" in defending its enforcement that is distinguishable from the general interest of every citizen of California.

Article III standing "is not to be placed in the hands of 'concerned bystanders,' who will use it simply as a 'vehicle for the vindication of value interests.'" No matter how deeply committed petitioners may be to upholding Proposition 8 or how "zealous [their] advocacy," that is not a "particularized" interest sufficient to create a case or controversy under Article III.

III

A

Without a judicially cognizable interest of their own, petitioners attempt to invoke that of someone else. They assert that even if *they* have no cognizable interest in appealing the District Court's judgment, the State of California does, and they may assert that interest on the State's behalf. It is, however, a "fundamental restriction on our authority" that "[i]n the ordinary course, a litigant must assert his or her own legal rights and interests, and cannot rest a claim to relief on the legal rights or interests of third parties." [E]ven when we have allowed litigants to assert the interests of others [per "limited exceptions"], the litigants themselves still "must have suffered an injury in fact, thus giving [them] a sufficiently concrete interest in the outcome of the issue in dispute."

In *Diamond*, for example, we refused to allow Diamond, a pediatrician engaged in private practice in Illinois, to defend the constitutionality of the State's abortion law. In that case, a group of physicians filed a constitutional challenge to the Illinois statute in federal court. The State initially defended the law, and Diamond, a professed "conscientious object[or] to abortions," intervened to defend it alongside the State.

After the Seventh Circuit affirmed a permanent injunction against enforcing several provisions of the law, the State chose not to pursue an appeal to this Court. But when Diamond did, the state attorney general filed a "'letter of interest,'" explaining that the State's interest in the proceeding was "'essentially coterminous with the position on the issues set forth by [Diamond].'" That was not enough, we held, to allow the appeal to proceed. As the Court explained, "[e]ven if there were circumstances in which a private party would have standing to defend the constitutionality of a challenged statute, this [was] not one of them," because Diamond was not able to assert an injury in fact of his own. And without "any judicially cognizable interest," Diamond could not "maintain the litigation abandoned by the State."

For the reasons we have explained, petitioners have likewise not suffered an injury in fact, and therefore would ordinarily have no standing to assert the State's interests.

B

Petitioners contend that this case is different, because the California Supreme Court has determined that they are "authorized under California law to appear and assert the state's interest" in the validity of Proposition 8. The court below agreed[.] As petitioners put it, they "need no more show a personal injury, separate from the State's indisputable interest in the validity of its law, than would California's Attorney General or did the legislative leaders held to have standing in *Karcher v. May*. . . ."

The point of *Karcher* is not that a State could authorize *private parties* to represent its interests; Karcher and Orechio were permitted to proceed only because they were state officers, acting in an official capacity. As soon as they lost that capacity, they lost standing. Petitioners here hold no office and have always participated in this litigation solely as private parties. . . .

C

Both petitioners and respondents seek support from dicta in *Arizonans for Official English v. Arizona*, 520 U.S. 43.The plaintiff in *Arizonans for Official English* filed a constitutional challenge to an Arizona ballot initiative declaring English "'the official language of the State of Arizona.'" After the District Court declared the initiative unconstitutional, Arizona's Governor announced that she would not pursue an appeal. Instead, the principal sponsor of the ballot initiative—the Arizonans for Official English Committee—sought to defend the measure in the Ninth Circuit. Analogizing the sponsors to the Arizona Legislature, the Ninth Circuit held that the Committee was "qualified to defend [the initiative] on appeal," and affirmed the District Court.

Before finding the case mooted by other events, this Court expressed "grave doubts" about the Ninth Circuit's standing analysis. We reiterated that . . . the litigant [must] possess 'a direct stake in the outcome.'" We recognized that a legislator authorized by state law to represent the State's interest may satisfy standing requirements, as in *Karcher*, but noted that the Arizona committee and its members were "not elected representatives, and we [we]re aware of no Arizona law appointing initiative sponsors as agents of the people of Arizona to defend, in lieu of public officials, the constitutionality of initiatives made law of the State."

Petitioners argue that, by virtue of the California Supreme Court's decision, they *are* authorized to act "'as agents of the people' of California." But that Court never described petitioners as "agents of the people," or of anyone else. Nor did the Ninth Circuit. The Ninth Circuit asked—and the California Supreme Court answered—only whether petitioners had "the authority to assert the State's interest in the initiative's validity." All that the California Supreme Court decision stands for is that, so far as California is concerned, petitioners may argue in defense of Proposition 8. This "does not mean that the proponents become de facto public officials"; the authority they enjoy is "simply the authority to participate as parties in a court action and to assert legal arguments in defense of the state's interest in the validity of the initiative measure." That interest is by definition a generalized one, and it is precisely because proponents assert such an interest that they lack standing under our precedents. . . .

[The Court determined that petitioners fell far short of showing an agency relationship per the requirements of the *Restatement of Agency*, including the principal's right to control agent action and the agent's fiduciary obligation to the principal. The petitioners utterly failed, according to the Court, because they "answer to no one; they decide for themselves, with no review, what arguments to make and how to make them"; they "owe nothing of the sort [of a fiduciary obligation] to the people of California."]

Neither the California Supreme Court nor the Ninth Circuit ever described the proponents as agents of the State, and they plainly do not qualify as such.

IV

The dissent eloquently recounts the California Supreme Court's reasons for deciding that state law authorizes petitioners to defend Proposition 8. We do not "disrespect[ ]" or "disparage[ ]" those reasons. Nor do we question California's sovereign right to maintain an initiative process, or the right of initiative proponents to defend their initiatives in California courts, where Article III does not apply. But . . . standing in federal court is a question of federal law, not state law. And no matter its reasons, the fact that a State thinks a private party should have standing to seek relief for a generalized grievance cannot override our settled law to the contrary.

The Article III requirement that a party invoking the jurisdiction of a federal court seek relief for a personal, particularized injury serves vital interests going to the role of the Judiciary in our system of separated powers. "Refusing to entertain generalized grievances ensures that . . . courts exercise power that is judicial in nature," and ensures that the Federal Judiciary respects "the proper—and properly limited—role of the courts in a democratic society[.]" States cannot alter that role simply by issuing to private parties who otherwise lack standing a ticket to the federal courthouse. . . .

We have never before upheld the standing of a private party to defend the constitutionality of a state statute when state officials have chosen not to. We decline to do so for the first time here.

Because petitioners [lacked] standing to appeal[, t]he judgment of the Ninth Circuit is vacated, and the case is remanded with instructions to dismiss the appeal for lack of jurisdiction.

It is so ordered.

JUSTICE KENNEDY, with whom JUSTICE THOMAS, JUSTICE ALITO, and JUSTICE SOTOMAYOR join, dissenting.

[The dissent recognizes that standing is a matter of federal law but clarifies that this case required "a threshold determination of state law" regarding "how California defines and elaborates the status and authority of an initiative's proponents who seek to intervene in court to defend the initiative after its adoption by the electorate" — all issues the Supreme Court of California already unanimously and thoroughly resolved.]

Under California law, a proponent has the authority to appear in court and assert the State's interest in defending an enacted initiative when the public officials charged with that duty refuse to do so. The State deems such an appearance essential to the integrity of its initiative process. Yet the Court today concludes that this state-defined status and this state-conferred right fall short of meeting federal requirements because the proponents cannot point to a formal delegation of authority that tracks the requirements of the Restatement of Agency. But the State Supreme Court's definition of proponents' powers is binding on this Court. And that definition is fully sufficient to establish the standing and adversity that are requisites for justiciability under Article III of the United States Constitution.

In my view Article III does not require California, when deciding who may appear in court to defend an initiative on its behalf, to comply with the Restatement of Agency or with this Court's view of how a State should make its laws or structure its government. The Court's reasoning does not take into account the fundamental principles or the practical dynamics of the initiative system in California, which uses this mechanism to control and to bypass public officials — the same officials who would not defend the initiative, an injury the Court now leaves unremedied. The Court's decision also has implications for the 26 other States that use an initiative or popular referendum system and which, like California, may choose to have initiative proponents stand in for the State when public officials decline to defend an initiative in litigation. In my submission, the Article III requirement for a justiciable case or controversy does not prevent proponents from having their day in court. . . .

I

As the Court explains, the State of California sustained a concrete injury, sufficient to satisfy the requirements of Article III, when a United States District Court nullified a portion of its State Constitution. To determine whether justiciability continues in appellate proceedings after the State Executive acquiesced in the District Court's adverse judgment, it is necessary to ascertain what persons, if any, have "authority under state law to represent the State's interests" in federal court. . . .

This Court, in determining the substance of state law, is "bound by a state court's construction of a state statute." And the Supreme Court of California, in response to the certified question submitted to it in this case, has determined that State Elections Code provisions directed to initiative proponents do inform and instruct state law respecting the rights and status of proponents in postelection judicial proceedings. Here, in reliance on these statutes and the California Constitution, the State Supreme Court has held that proponents do have authority "under California law to appear and assert the state's interest in the initiative's validity and appeal a judgment invalidating the measure when the public officials who ordinarily defend the measure or appeal such a judgment decline to do so."

The reasons the Supreme Court of California gave for its holding have special relevance in the context of determining whether proponents have the authority to seek a federal-court remedy for the State's concrete, substantial, and continuing injury. As a class, official proponents are a small, identifiable group. Because many of their decisions must be unanimous . . . they are necessarily few in number. Their identities are public. Their commitment is substantial. They know and understand the purpose and operation of the proposed law. . . . Having gone to great lengths to convince voters to enact an initiative, they have a stake in the outcome and the necessary commitment to provide zealous advocacy.

Thus, in California, proponents play a "unique role . . . in the initiative process." They "have a unique relationship to the voter-approved measure that makes them especially likely to be reliable and vigorous advocates for the measure and to be so viewed by those whose votes secured the initiative's enactment into law." Proponents' authority under state law is not a contrivance. It is not a fictional construct. It is the product of the California Constitution and the California Elections Code. There is no basis for this Court to set aside the California Supreme Court's determination of state law[, which is also consistent with recent decisions from other States.]

For these and other reasons, the Supreme Court of California held that the California Elections Code and Article II, § 8, of the California Constitution afford proponents "the authority . . . to assert the state's interest in the validity of the initiative" when State officials decline to do so. The court repeated this unanimous holding more than a half-dozen times and in no uncertain terms. That should suffice to resolve the central issue on which the federal question turns.

II

A

The Court concludes that proponents lack sufficient ties to the state government. It notes that they "are not elected," "answer to no one," and lack "'a fiduciary obligation.'" But what the Court deems deficiencies in the proponents' connection to the State government, the State Supreme Court saw as essential qualifications to defend the initiative system. The very object of the initiative system is to establish a lawmaking process that does not depend upon state officials. In California, the popular initiative is necessary to implement "the theory that all power of government ultimately resides in the people." The right to adopt initiatives has been described by the California courts as "one of the most precious rights of [the State's] democratic process." That historic role for the initiative system "grew out of dissatisfaction with the then governing public officials and a widespread belief that the people had lost control of the political process." The initiative's "primary purpose," then, "was to afford the people the ability to propose and to adopt constitutional amendments or statutory provisions that their elected public officials had refused or declined to adopt."

The California Supreme Court has determined that this purpose is undermined if the very officials the initiative process seeks to circumvent are the only parties who can defend an enacted initiative when it is challenged in a legal proceeding. . . . As a consequence, California finds it necessary to vest the responsibility and right to defend a voter-approved initiative in the initiative's proponents when the State Executive declines to do so.

Yet today the Court demands that the State follow the *Restatement of Agency*. There are reasons, however, why California might conclude that a conventional agency relationship is inconsistent with the history, design, and purpose of the initiative process. The State may not wish to associate itself with proponents or their views outside of the "extremely narrow and limited" context of this litigation, or to bear the cost of proponents' legal fees. The State may also wish to avoid the odd conflict of having a formal agent of the State (the initiative's proponent) arguing in favor of a law's validity while state officials (*e.g.*, the attorney general) contend in the same proceeding that it should be found invalid.

Furthermore, it is not clear who the principal in an agency relationship would be. . . .

And if the Court's concern is that the proponents are unaccountable, that fear is neither well founded nor sufficient to overcome the contrary judgment of the State Supreme Court. . . .

B

Contrary to the Court's suggestion, this Court's precedents do not indicate that a formal agency relationship is necessary. [Unlike the state officer in *Karcher*,] proponents' authority under California law is not contingent on office-holder status, so their standing is unaffected by the fact that they "hold no office" in California's Government.

Arizonans for Official English v. Arizona is consistent with the premises of this dissent, not with the rationale of the Court's opinion. . . . The Court did use the word "agents"; but, read in context, it is evident that the Court's intention was not to demand a formal agency relationship in compliance with the *Restatement*. Rather, the Court used the term as shorthand for a party whom "state law authorizes" to "represent the State's interests" in court. . . .

The Court of Appeals, [and the Supreme Court of California], was mindful of this requirement. Although that panel divided on the proper resolution of the merits of this case, it was unanimous in concluding that proponents satisfy the requirements of Article III. Its central premise, ignored by the Court today, was that the "State's highest court [had] held that California law provides precisely what the *Arizonans* Court found lacking in Arizona law: it confers on the official proponents of an initiative the authority to assert the State's interests in defending the constitutionality of that initiative, where state officials who would ordinarily assume that responsibility choose not to do so." The Court of Appeals and the State Supreme Court did not ignore *Arizonans for Official English*; they were faithful to it.

C

[The dissent notes friction with traditional sanctioned representative-party litigation, including criminal court appointed private attorneys to investigate and prosecute criminal contempt, *qui tam* suits, "next friends" litigation on behalf of a real party in interest, and shareholder-derivative actions.

Accordingly, the Court "unsettles" this foundation, rendering "the District Court's judgment, and its accompanying statewide injunction, effectively immune from appellate review."]

III

There is much irony in the Court's approach to justiciability in this case. A prime purpose of justiciability is to ensure vigorous advocacy, yet the Court insists upon litigation conducted by state officials whose preference is to lose the case. The doctrine is meant to ensure that courts are responsible and constrained in their power, but the Court's opinion today means that a single district court can make a decision with far-reaching effects that cannot be reviewed. And rather than honor the principle that justiciability exists to allow disputes of public policy to be resolved by the political process rather than the courts, here the Court refuses to allow a State's authorized representatives to defend the outcome of a democratic election.

The Court's opinion disrespects and disparages both the political process in California and the well-stated opinion of the California Supreme Court in this case. The California Supreme Court, not this Court, expresses concern for vigorous representation; the California Supreme Court, not this Court, recognizes the necessity to avoid conflicts of interest; the California Supreme Court, not this Court, comprehends the real interest at stake in this litigation and identifies the most proper party to defend that interest. The California Supreme Court's opinion reflects a better understanding of the dynamics and principles of Article III than does this Court's opinion.

Of course, the Court must be cautious before entering a realm of controversy where the legal community and society at large are still formulating ideas and approaches to a most difficult subject. But it is shortsighted to misconstrue principles of justiciability to avoid that subject. As the California Supreme Court recognized, "the question before us involves a fundamental procedural issue that may arise with respect to *any* initiative measure, without regard to its subject matter." If a federal court must rule on a constitutional point that either confirms or rejects the will of the people expressed in an initiative, that is when it is most necessary, not least necessary, to insist on rules that ensure the most committed and vigorous adversary arguments to inform the rulings of the courts. . . .

In the end, what the Court fails to grasp or accept is the basic premise of the initiative process. And it is this. The essence of democracy is that the right to make law rests in the people and flows to the government, not the other way around. Freedom resides first in the people without need of a grant from government. The California initiative process embodies these principles and has done so for over a century. "Through the structure of its government, and the character of those who exercise government authority, a State defines itself as sovereign." In California and the 26 other States that permit initiatives and popular referendums, the people have exercised their own inherent sovereign right to govern themselves. The Court today frustrates that choice by nullifying, for failure to comply with the Restatement of Agency, a State Supreme Court decision holding that state law authorizes an enacted initiative's proponents to defend the law if and when the State's usual legal advocates decline to do so. The

Court's opinion fails to abide by precedent and misapplies basic principles of justiciability. Those errors necessitate this respectful dissent.

UNITED STATES v. WINDSOR

133 S. Ct. 2675 (2013)

JUSTICE KENNEDY delivered the opinion of the Court.

Two women then residents in New York were married in a lawful ceremony in Ontario, Canada, in 2007. Edith Windsor and Thea Spyer returned to their home in New York City. When Spyer died in 2009, she left her entire estate to Windsor. Windsor sought to claim the estate tax exemption for surviving spouses. She was barred from doing so, however, by a federal law, the Defense of Marriage Act, which excludes a same-sex partner from the definition of "spouse" as that term is used in federal statutes. Windsor paid the taxes but filed suit to challenge the constitutionality of this provision. The United States District Court and the Court of Appeals ruled that this portion of the statute is unconstitutional and ordered the United States to pay Windsor a refund. This Court granted certiorari and now affirms the judgment in Windsor's favor.

I

In 1996, as some States were beginning to consider the concept of same-sex marriage, see, *e.g., Baehr v. Lewin,* 74 Haw. 530, 852 P.2d 44 (1993), and before any State had acted to permit it, Congress enacted the Defense of Marriage Act (DOMA), 110 Stat. 2419. DOMA contains two operative sections: Section 2, which has not been challenged here, allows States to refuse to recognize same-sex marriages performed under the laws of other States. See 28 U.S.C. § 1738C.

Section 3 is at issue here. It amends the Dictionary Act in Title 1, § 7, of the United States Code to provide a federal definition of "marriage" and "spouse." Section 3 of DOMA provides as follows:

> In determining the meaning of any Act of Congress, or of any ruling, regulation, or interpretation of the various administrative bureaus and agencies of the United States, the word "marriage" means only a legal union between one man and one woman as husband and wife, and the word "spouse" refers only to a person of the opposite sex who is a husband or a wife.

The definitional provision does not by its terms forbid States from enacting laws permitting same-sex marriages or civil unions or providing state benefits to residents in that status. The enactment's comprehensive definition of marriage for purposes of all federal statutes and other regulations or directives covered by its terms, however, does control over 1,000 federal laws in which marital or spousal status is addressed as a matter of federal law. *See* GAO, D. Shah, Defense of Marriage Act: Update to Prior Report 1.

Edith Windsor and Thea Spyer met in New York City in 1963 and began a long-term relationship. Windsor and Spyer registered as domestic partners when New York City gave that right to same-sex couples in 1993. Concerned about Spyer's health, the couple made the 2007 trip to Canada for their marriage, but they continued to reside in New York City. The State of New York deems their Ontario marriage to be a valid one.

Spyer died in February 2009, and left her entire estate to Windsor. Because DOMA denies federal recognition to same-sex spouses, Windsor did not qualify for the marital exemption from the federal estate tax, which excludes from taxation "any interest in property which passes or has passed from the decedent to his surviving spouse." Windsor paid $363,053 in estate taxes and sought a refund.

The Internal Revenue Service denied the refund, concluding that, under DOMA, Windsor was not a "surviving spouse." Windsor commenced this refund suit in the United States District Court for the Southern District of New York. She contended that DOMA violates the guarantee of equal protection, as applied to the Federal Government through the Fifth Amendment.

While the tax refund suit was pending, the Attorney General of the United States notified the Speaker of the House of Representatives, that the Department of Justice would no longer defend the constitutionality of DOMA's § 3. Noting that "the Department has previously defended DOMA against . . . challenges involving legally married same-sex couples," the Attorney General informed Congress that "the President has concluded that given a number of factors, including a documented history of discrimination, classifications based on sexual orientation should be subject to a heightened standard of scrutiny." The Department of Justice has submitted many § 530D letters over the years refusing to defend laws it deems unconstitutional, when, for instance, a federal court has rejected the Government's defense of a statute and has issued a judgment against it. This case is unusual, however, because the § 530D letter was not preceded by an adverse judgment. The letter instead reflected the Executive's own conclusion, relying on a definition still being debated and considered in the courts, that heightened equal protection scrutiny should apply to laws that classify on the basis of sexual orientation.

Although "the President . . . instructed the Department not to defend the statute in *Windsor*," he also decided "that Section 3 will continue to be enforced by the Executive Branch" and that the United States had an "interest in providing Congress a full and fair opportunity to participate in the litigation of those cases." The stated rationale for this dual-track procedure (determination of unconstitutionality coupled with ongoing enforcement) was to "recogniz[e] the judiciary as the final arbiter of the constitutional claims raised."

In response to the notice from the Attorney General, the Bipartisan Legal Advisory Group (BLAG) of the House of Representatives voted to intervene in the litigation to defend the constitutionality of § 3 of DOMA. The Department of Justice did not oppose limited intervention by BLAG. The District Court denied BLAG's motion to enter the suit as of right, on the rationale that the United States already was represented by the Department of Justice. The District Court, however, did grant intervention by BLAG as an interested party. *See* Fed. Rule Civ. Proc. 24(a)(2).

On the merits of the tax refund suit, the District Court ruled against the United States. It held that § 3 of DOMA is unconstitutional and ordered the Treasury to refund the tax with interest. Both the Justice Department and BLAG filed notices of appeal, and the Solicitor General filed a petition for certiorari before judgment. Before this Court acted on the petition, the Court of Appeals for the Second Circuit affirmed the District Court's judgment. It applied heightened scrutiny to classifications based on sexual orientation, as both the

Department and Windsor had urged. The United States has not complied with the judgment. Windsor has not received her refund, and the Executive Branch continues to enforce § 3 of DOMA.

In granting certiorari on the question of the constitutionality of § 3 of DOMA, the Court requested argument on two additional questions: whether the United States' agreement with Windsor's legal position precludes further review and whether BLAG has standing to appeal the case. All parties agree that the Court has jurisdiction to decide this case; and, with the case in that framework, the Court appointed Professor Vicki Jackson as *amicus curiae* to argue the position that the Court lacks jurisdiction to hear the dispute. She has ably discharged her duties. . . .

II

It is appropriate to begin by addressing whether either the Government or BLAG, or both of them, were entitled to appeal to the Court of Appeals and later to seek certiorari and appear as parties here.

There is no dispute that when this case was in the District Court it presented a concrete disagreement between opposing parties, a dispute suitable for judicial resolution. "[A] taxpayer has standing to challenge the collection of a specific tax assessment as unconstitutional; being forced to pay such a tax causes a real and immediate economic injury to the individual taxpayer." *Hein v. Freedom From Religion Foundation, Inc.*, 551 U.S. 587, 599 (2007) (plurality opinion). Windsor suffered a redressable injury when she was required to pay estate taxes from which, in her view, she was exempt but for the alleged invalidity of § 3 of DOMA.

The decision of the Executive not to defend the constitutionality of § 3 in court while continuing to deny refunds and to assess deficiencies does introduce a complication. Even though the Executive's current position was announced before the District Court entered its judgment, the Government's agreement with Windsor's position would not have deprived the District Court of jurisdiction to entertain and resolve the refund suit; for her injury (failure to obtain a refund allegedly required by law) was concrete, persisting, and unredressed. The Government's position — agreeing with Windsor's legal contention but refusing to give it effect — meant that there was a justiciable controversy between the parties, despite what the claimant would find to be an inconsistency in that stance. Windsor, the Government, BLAG, and the *amicus* appear to agree upon that point. The disagreement is over the standing of the parties, or aspiring parties, to take an appeal in the Court of Appeals and to appear as parties in further proceedings in this Court.

The *amicus*' position is that, given the Government's concession that § 3 is unconstitutional, once the District Court ordered the refund the case should have ended; and the *amicus* argues the Court of Appeals should have dismissed the appeal. The *amicus* submits that once the President agreed with Windsor's legal position and the District Court issued its judgment, the parties were no longer adverse. From this standpoint the United States was a prevailing party below, just as Windsor was. Accordingly, the *amicus* reasons, it is inappropriate for this Court to grant certiorari and proceed to rule on the merits; for the United States seeks no redress from the judgment entered against it.

This position, however, elides the distinction between two principles: the jurisdictional requirements of Article III and the prudential limits on its exercise.

The latter are "essentially matters of judicial self-governance." The Court has kept these two strands separate: "Article III standing, which enforces the Constitution's case-or-controversy requirement, see *Lujan v. Defenders of Wildlife,* 504 U.S. 555, 559–562 (1992); and prudential standing, which embodies 'judicially self-imposed limits on the exercise of federal jurisdiction,' *Allen* [*v. Wright,*] 468 U.S. [737,] 751, [(1984)]." *Elk Grove Unified School Dist. v. Newdow,* 542 U.S. 1, 11–12 (2004).

The requirements of Article III standing are familiar:

> First, the plaintiff must have suffered an "injury in fact"—an invasion of a legally protected interest which is (a) concrete and particularized, and (b) "actual or imminent, not 'conjectural or hypothetical.'" Second, there must be a causal connection between the injury and the conduct complained of—the injury has to be "fairly . . . trace[able] to the challenged action of the defendant, and not . . . th[e] result [of] the independent action of some third party not before the court." Third, it must be "likely," as opposed to merely "speculative," that the injury will be "redressed by a favorable decision." *Lujan.*

Rules of prudential standing, by contrast, are more flexible "rule[s] . . . of federal appellate practice," designed to protect the courts from "decid[ing] abstract questions of wide public significance even [when] other governmental institutions may be more competent to address the questions and even though judicial intervention may be unnecessary to protect individual rights."

In this case the United States retains a stake sufficient to support Article III jurisdiction on appeal and in proceedings before this Court. The judgment in question orders the United States to pay Windsor the refund she seeks. An order directing the Treasury to pay money is "a real and immediate economic injury," *Hein,* indeed as real and immediate as an order directing an individual to pay a tax. That the Executive may welcome this order to pay the refund if it is accompanied by the constitutional ruling it wants does not eliminate the injury to the national Treasury if payment is made, or to the taxpayer if it is not. The judgment orders the United States to pay money that it would not disburse but for the court's order. The Government of the United States has a valid legal argument that it is injured even if the Executive disagrees with § 3 of DOMA, which results in Windsor's liability for the tax. Windsor's ongoing claim for funds that the United States refuses to pay thus establishes a controversy sufficient for Article III jurisdiction. It would be a different case if the Executive had taken the further step of paying Windsor the refund to which she was entitled under the District Court's ruling.

This Court confronted a comparable case in *INS v. Chadha,* 462 U.S. 919 (1983). A statute by its terms allowed one House of Congress to order the Immigration and Naturalization Service (INS) to deport the respondent Chadha. There, as here, the Executive determined that the statute was unconstitutional, and "the INS presented the Executive's views on the constitutionality of the House action to the Court of Appeals." The INS, however, continued to abide by the statute, and "the INS brief to the Court of Appeals did not alter the agency's decision to comply with the House action ordering deportation of Chadha." This Court held "that the INS was sufficiently aggrieved by the Court of Appeals decision prohibiting it from taking action it would otherwise take," regardless of whether the agency welcomed the judgment. The necessity of a "case or controversy" to satisfy Article III was defined as a requirement that the Court's "'decision will have real meaning: if we rule for Chadha, he will not be deported; if we uphold [the statute], the INS will execute its order and deport him.'" This conclusion was not dictum. It was a necessary predicate to the Court's holding that "prior to Congress' intervention, there was adequate Art. III adverseness." The holdings of cases are instructive, and the words of *Chadha* make clear its holding that the refusal of the Executive to provide the relief sought suffices to preserve a justiciable dispute as required by Article III. In short, even where "the Government largely agree[s] with the opposing party on the merits of the controversy," there is sufficient adverseness and an "adequate basis for jurisdiction in the fact that the Government intended to enforce the challenged law against that party."

It is true that "[a] party who receives all that he has sought generally is not aggrieved by the judgment affording the relief and cannot appeal from it." *Roper, supra,* at 333, *see also Camreta v. Greene,* 563 U.S. _____, 131 S.Ct. 2020, 2030 (2011) ("As a matter of practice and prudence, we have generally declined to consider cases at the request of a prevailing party, even when the Constitution allowed us to do so"). But this rule "does not have its source in the jurisdictional limitations of Art. III. In an appropriate case, appeal may be permitted . . . at the behest of the party who has prevailed on the merits, so long as that party retains a stake in the appeal satisfying the requirements of Art. III." *Roper.*

While these principles suffice to show that this case presents a justiciable controversy under Article III, the prudential problems inherent in the Executive's unusual position require some further discussion. The Executive's agreement with Windsor's legal argument raises the risk that instead of a "'real, earnest and vital controversy,'" the Court faces a "friendly, non-adversary, proceeding . . . [in which] 'a party beaten in the legislature [seeks to] transfer to the courts an inquiry as to the constitutionality of the legislative act.'" *Ashwander v. TVA,* 297 U.S. 288, 346 (1936) (Brandeis, J., concurring). Even when Article III permits the exercise of federal jurisdiction, prudential considerations demand that the Court insist upon "that concrete adverseness which sharpens the presentation of issues upon which the court so largely depends for illumination of difficult constitutional questions." *Baker v. Carr,* 369 U.S. 186, 204 (1962).

There are, of course, reasons to hear a case and issue a ruling even when one party is reluctant to prevail in its position. Unlike Article III requirements—which must be satisfied by the parties before judicial consideration is appropriate—the relevant prudential factors that counsel against hearing this case are subject to "countervailing considerations [that] may outweigh the concerns underlying the usual reluctance to exert judicial power." *Warth,* 422 U.S., at 500–501. One consideration is the extent to which adversarial presentation of the issues is assured by the participation of *amici curiae* prepared to defend with vigor the constitutionality of the legislative act. With respect to this prudential aspect of standing as well, the *Chadha* Court encountered a similar situation. It noted that "there may be prudential, as opposed to Art. III, concerns about sanctioning the adjudication of [this case] in the absence of any participant supporting the validity of [the statute]. The Court of Appeals properly dispelled any such concerns by inviting and accepting briefs from both Houses of Congress." *Chadha* was not an anomaly in this respect. The Court adopts the practice of entertaining arguments made by an *amicus* when the Solicitor General confesses error with respect to a judgment below, even if the confession is in effect an admission that an Act of Congress is unconstitutional.

In the case now before the Court the attorneys for BLAG present a substantial argument for the constitutionality of § 3 of DOMA. BLAG's sharp adversarial presentation of the issues satisfies the prudential concerns that otherwise might counsel against hearing an appeal from a decision with which the principal parties agree. Were this Court to hold that prudential rules require it to dismiss the case, and, in consequence, that the Court of Appeals erred in failing to dismiss it as well, extensive litigation would ensue. The district courts in 94 districts throughout the Nation would be without precedential guidance not only in tax refund suits but also in cases involving the whole of DOMA's sweep involving over 1,000 federal statutes and a myriad of federal regulations. For instance, the opinion of the Court of Appeals for the First Circuit, addressing the validity of DOMA in a case involving regulations of the Department of Health and Human Services, likely would be vacated with instructions to dismiss, its ruling and guidance also then erased. See *Massachusetts v. United States Dept. of Health and Human Servs.*, 682 F.3d 1 (C.A.1 2012). Rights and privileges of hundreds of thousands of persons would be adversely affected, pending a case in which all prudential concerns about justiciability are absent. That numerical prediction may not be certain, but it is certain that the cost in judicial resources and expense of litigation for all persons adversely affected would be immense. True, the very extent of DOMA's mandate means that at some point a case likely would arise without the prudential concerns raised here; but the costs, uncertainties, and alleged harm and injuries likely would continue for a time measured in years before the issue is resolved. In these unusual and urgent circumstances, the very term "prudential" counsels that it is a proper exercise of the Court's responsibility to take jurisdiction. For these reasons, the prudential and Article III requirements are met here; and, as a consequence, the Court need not decide whether BLAG would have standing to challenge the District Court's ruling and its affirmance in the Court of Appeals on BLAG's own authority.

The Court's conclusion that this petition may be heard on the merits does not imply that no difficulties would ensue if this were a common practice in ordinary cases. The Executive's failure to defend the constitutionality of an Act of Congress based on a constitutional theory not yet established in judicial decisions has created a procedural dilemma. On the one hand, as noted, the Government's agreement with Windsor raises questions about the propriety of entertaining a suit in which it seeks affirmance of an order invalidating a federal law and ordering the United States to pay money. On the other hand, if the Executive's agreement with a plaintiff that a law is unconstitutional is enough to preclude judicial review, then the Supreme Court's primary role in determining the constitutionality of a law that has inflicted real injury on a plaintiff who has brought a justiciable legal claim would become only secondary to the President's. This would undermine the clear dictate of the separation-of-powers principle that "when an Act of Congress is alleged to conflict with the Constitution, '[i]t is emphatically the province and duty of the judicial department to say what the law is.'" *Zivotofsky v. Clinton*, 566 U.S. ____, 132 S.Ct. 1421, 1427–1428 (2012) (quoting *Marbury v. Madison*, 1 Cranch 137, 177 (1803)). Similarly, with respect to the legislative power, when Congress has passed a statute and a President has signed it, it poses grave challenges to the separation of powers for the Executive at a particular moment to be able to nullify Congress' enactment solely on its own initiative and without any determination from the Court.

The Court's jurisdictional holding, it must be underscored, does not mean the arguments for dismissing this dispute on prudential grounds lack substance.

Yet the difficulty the Executive faces should be acknowledged. When the Executive makes a principled determination that a statute is unconstitutional, it faces a difficult choice. Still, there is no suggestion here that it is appropriate for the Executive as a matter of course to challenge statutes in the judicial forum rather than making the case to Congress for their amendment or repeal. The integrity of the political process would be at risk if difficult constitutional issues were simply referred to the Court as a routine exercise. But this case is not routine. And the capable defense of the law by BLAG ensures that these prudential issues do not cloud the merits question, which is one of immediate importance to the Federal Government and to hundreds of thousands of persons. These circumstances support the Court's decision to proceed to the merits.

III

[T]he Federal Government, through our history, has deferred to state-law policy decisions with respect to domestic relations. . . . In order to respect this principle, the federal courts, as a general rule, do not adjudicate issues of marital status even when there might otherwise be a basis for federal jurisdiction. Federal courts will not hear divorce and custody cases even if they arise in diversity because of "the virtually exclusive primacy . . . of the States in the regulation of domestic relations." . . .

The judgment of the Court of Appeals for the Second Circuit is affirmed.

It is so ordered.

CHIEF JUSTICE ROBERTS, dissenting.

I agree with Justice Scalia that this Court lacks jurisdiction to review the decisions of the courts below. . . .

We may in the future have to resolve challenges to state marriage definitions affecting same-sex couples. That issue, however, is not before us in this case, and we hold today that we lack jurisdiction to consider it in the particular context of *Hollingsworth v. Perry*, 133 S.Ct. 1521. I write only to highlight the limits of the majority's holding and reasoning today, lest its opinion be taken to resolve not only a question that I believe is not properly before us — DOMA's constitutionality — but also a question that all agree, and the Court explicitly acknowledges, is not at issue.

JUSTICE SCALIA, with whom JUSTICE THOMAS joins, and with whom THE CHIEF JUSTICE joins as to Part I, dissenting.

This case is about power in several respects. It is about the power of our people to govern themselves, and the power of this Court to pronounce the law. Today's opinion aggrandizes the latter, with the predictable consequence of diminishing the former. We have no power to decide this case. And even if we did, we have no power under the Constitution to invalidate this democratically adopted legislation. The Court's errors on both points spring forth from the same diseased root: an exalted conception of the role of this institution in America.

I

A

The Court is eager — *hungry* — to tell everyone its view of the legal question at the heart of this case. Standing in the way is an obstacle, a technicality of little interest to anyone but the people of We the People, who created it as a barrier against judges' intrusion into their lives. They gave judges, in Article III, only the "judicial Power," a power to decide not abstract questions but real, concrete "Cases" and "Controversies." Yet the plaintiff and the Government agree entirely on what should happen in this lawsuit. They agree that the court below got it right; and they agreed in the court below that the court below that one got it right as well. What, then, are we *doing* here?

The answer lies at the heart of the jurisdictional portion of today's opinion, where a single sentence lays bare the majority's vision of our role. The Court says that we have the power to decide this case because if we did not, then our "primary role in determining the constitutionality of a law" (at least one that "has inflicted real injury on a plaintiff") would "become only secondary to the President's." But wait, the reader wonders—Windsor won below, and so *cured* her injury, and the President was glad to see it. True, says the majority, but judicial review must march on regardless, lest we "undermine the clear dictate of the separation-of-powers principle that when an Act of Congress is alleged to conflict with the Constitution, it is emphatically the province and duty of the judicial department to say what the law is."

That is jaw-dropping. It is an assertion of judicial supremacy over the people's Representatives in Congress and the Executive. It envisions a Supreme Court standing (or rather enthroned) at the apex of government, empowered to decide all constitutional questions, always and everywhere "primary" in its role.

This image of the Court would have been unrecognizable to those who wrote and ratified our national charter. They knew well the dangers of "primary" power, and so created branches of government that would be "perfectly coordinate by the terms of their common commission," none of which branches could "pretend to an exclusive or superior right of settling the boundaries between their respective powers." The Federalist, No. 49, p. 314 (C. Rossiter ed. 1961) (J. Madison). The people did this to protect themselves. They did it to guard their right to self-rule against the black-robed supremacy that today's majority finds so attractive. So it was that Madison could confidently state, with no fear of contradiction, that there was nothing of "greater intrinsic value" or "stamped with the authority of more enlightened patrons of liberty" than a government of separate and coordinate powers. *Id.*, No. 47, at 301.

For this reason we are quite forbidden to say what the law is whenever (as today's opinion asserts) "'an Act of Congress is alleged to conflict with the Constitution.'" We can do so only when that allegation will determine the outcome of a lawsuit, and is contradicted by the other party. The "judicial Power" is not, as the majority believes, the power "'to say what the law is,'" giving the Supreme Court the "primary role in determining the constitutionality of laws." The majority must have in mind one of the foreign constitutions that pronounces such primacy for its constitutional court and allows that primacy to be exercised in contexts other than a lawsuit. See, *e.g.*, Basic Law for the Federal Republic of Germany, Art. 93. The judicial power as Americans have understood it (and their English ancestors before them) is the power to adjudicate, with conclusive effect, disputed government claims (civil or criminal) against private persons, and disputed claims by private persons against the government or other private persons. Sometimes (though not always) the parties before the court disagree not with regard to the facts of their case (or not *only* with regard to the facts) but with regard to the applicable law—in which event (and *only* in which event) it becomes the "'province and duty of the judicial department to say what the law is.'"

In other words, declaring the compatibility of state or federal laws with the Constitution is not only not the "primary role" of this Court, it is not a separate, free-standing role *at all*. We perform that role incidentally—by accident, as it were—when that is necessary to resolve the dispute before us. Then, and only then, does it become "'the province and duty of the judicial department to say what the law is.'" That is why, in 1793, we politely declined the Washington Administration's request to "say what the law is" on a particular treaty matter that was not the subject of a concrete legal controversy. 3 Correspondence and Public Papers of John Jay 486–489 (H. Johnston ed. 1893). And that is why, as our opinions have said, some questions of law will *never* be presented to this Court, because there will never be anyone with standing to bring a lawsuit. As Justice Brandeis put it, we cannot "pass upon the constitutionality of legislation in a friendly, non-adversary, proceeding"; absent a "'real, earnest and vital controversy between individuals,'" we have neither any work to do nor any power to do it. *Ashwander v. TVA*, 297 U.S. 288, 346 (1936) (concurring opinion). Our authority begins and ends with the need to adjudge the rights of an injured party who stands before us seeking redress. *Lujan.*

That is completely absent here. Windsor's injury was cured by the judgment in her favor. And while, in ordinary circumstances, the United States is injured by a directive to pay a tax refund, this suit is far from ordinary. Whatever injury the United States has suffered will surely not be redressed by the action that it, as a litigant, asks us to take. The final sentence of the Solicitor General's brief on the merits reads: "For the foregoing reasons, the judgment of the court of appeals *should be affirmed.*" That will not cure the Government's injury, but carve it into stone. One could spend many fruitless afternoons ransacking our library for any other petitioner's brief seeking an affirmance of the judgment against it.[5] What the petitioner United States asks us to do in the case before us is exactly what the respondent Windsor asks us to do: not to provide relief from the judgment below but to say that that judgment was correct. And the same was true in the Court of Appeals: Neither party sought to undo the judgment for Windsor, and so that court should have dismissed the appeal (just as we should dismiss) for lack of jurisdiction. Since both parties agreed with the judgment of the District Court for the Southern District of New York, the suit should have ended there. The further proceedings have been a contrivance, having no object in mind except to elevate a District Court judgment that has no precedential effect in other courts, to one that has precedential effect throughout the Second Circuit, and then (in this Court) precedential effect throughout the United States.

We have never before agreed to speak—to "say what the law is"—where there is no controversy before us. In the more than two centuries that this Court has existed as an institution, we have never suggested that we have the power to decide a question when every party agrees with both its nominal opponent *and the court below* on that question's answer. The United States reluctantly conceded that at oral argument.

5. [Footnote 1 in Justice Scalia's dissent.] For an even more advanced scavenger hunt, one might search the annals of Anglo-American law for another "Motion to Dismiss" like the one the United States filed in District Court: It argued that the court should agree "with Plaintiff and the United States" and "*not* dismiss" the complaint. (Emphasis mine.) Then, having gotten exactly what it asked for, the United States promptly appealed.

The closest we have ever come to what the Court blesses today was our opinion in *INS v. Chadha*. But in that case, two parties to the litigation disagreed with the position of the United States and with the court below: the House and Senate, which had intervened in the case. Because *Chadha* concerned the validity of a mode of congressional action — the one-house legislative veto — the House and Senate were threatened with destruction of what they claimed to be one of their institutional powers. The Executive choosing not to defend that power,[6] we permitted the House and Senate to intervene. Nothing like that is present here.

To be sure, the Court in *Chadha* said that statutory aggrieved-party status was "not altered by the fact that the Executive may agree with the holding that the statute in question is unconstitutional." But in a footnote to that statement, the Court acknowledged Article III's separate requirement of a "justiciable case or controversy," and stated that *this* requirement was satisfied "because of the presence of the two Houses of Congress as adverse parties." Later in its opinion, the *Chadha* Court remarked that the United States' announced intention to enforce the statute also sufficed to permit judicial review, even absent congressional participation. That remark is true, as a description of the judicial review conducted in the Court of Appeals, where the Houses of Congress had not intervened. (The case originated in the Court of Appeals, since it sought review of agency action under 8 U.S.C. § 1105a(a)). There, absent a judgment setting aside the INS order, Chadha faced deportation. This passage of our opinion seems to be addressing that initial standing in the Court of Appeals, as indicated by its quotation from the lower court's opinion. But if it was addressing standing to pursue the appeal, the remark was both the purest dictum (as congressional intervention at that point made the required adverseness "beyond doubt,") and quite incorrect. When a private party has a judicial decree safely in hand to prevent his injury, additional judicial action requires that a party injured by the decree *seek to undo it*. In *Chadha*, the intervening House and Senate fulfilled that requirement. Here no one does.

The majority's discussion of the requirements of Article III bears no resemblance to our jurisprudence. It accuses the *amicus* (appointed to argue against our jurisdiction) of "elid[ing] the distinction between . . . the jurisdictional requirements of Article III and the prudential limits on its exercise." It then proceeds to call the requirement of adverseness a "prudential" aspect of standing. *Of standing*. That is incomprehensible. A plaintiff (or appellant) can have all the standing in the world — satisfying all three standing requirements of *Lujan* that the majority so carefully quotes — and yet no Article III controversy may be before the court. Article III requires not just a plaintiff (or appellant) who has standing to complain but *an opposing party* who denies the validity of the complaint. It is not the *amicus* that has done the eliding of distinctions, but the majority, calling the quite separate Article III requirement of adverseness between the parties an element (which it then pronounces a "prudential" element) of standing. The question here is not whether, as the majority puts it, "the

6. [Footnote 2 in Justice Scalia's dissent.] There the Justice Department's refusal to defend the legislation was in accord with its longstanding (and entirely reasonable) practice of declining to defend legislation that in its view infringes upon Presidential powers. There is no justification for the Justice Department's abandoning the law in the present case. The majority opinion makes a point of scolding the President for his "failure to defend the constitutionality of an Act of Congress based on a constitutional theory not yet established in judicial decisions." But the rebuke is tongue-in-cheek, for the majority gladly gives the President what he wants. Contrary to all precedent, it decides this case (and even decides it the way the President wishes) *despite* his abandonment of the defense and the consequent absence of a case or controversy.

United States retains a stake sufficient to support Article III jurisdiction," the question is whether there is any controversy (which requires *contradiction*) between the United States and Ms. Windsor. There is not.

I find it wryly amusing that the majority seeks to dismiss the requirement of party-adverseness as nothing more than a "prudential" aspect of the sole Article III requirement of standing. (Relegating a jurisdictional requirement to "prudential" status is a wondrous device, enabling courts to ignore the requirement whenever they believe it "prudent"—which is to say, a good idea.) Half a century ago, a Court similarly bent upon announcing its view regarding the constitutionality of a federal statute achieved that goal by effecting a remarkably similar *but completely opposite* distortion of the principles limiting our jurisdiction. The Court's notorious opinion in *Flast v. Cohen*, 392 U.S. 83, 98–101 (1968), held that *standing* was merely an element (which it pronounced to be a "prudential" element) of the sole Article III requirement of *adverseness*. We have been living with the chaos created by that power-grabbing decision ever since, see *Hein*, as we will have to live with the chaos created by this one. . . .

It may be argued that if what we say is true some Presidential determinations that statutes are unconstitutional will not be subject to our review. That is as it should be, when both the President and the plaintiff agree that the statute is unconstitutional. Where the Executive is enforcing an unconstitutional law, suit will of course lie; but if, in that suit, the Executive admits the unconstitutionality of the law, the litigation should end in an order or a consent decree enjoining enforcement. This suit saw the light of day only because the President enforced the Act (and thus gave Windsor standing to sue) even though he believed it unconstitutional. He could have equally chosen (more appropriately, some would say) neither to enforce nor to defend the statute he believed to be unconstitutional, see Presidential Authority to Decline to Execute Unconstitutional Statutes, 18 Op. Off. Legal Counsel 199 (Nov. 2, 1994)—in which event Windsor would not have been injured, the District Court could not have refereed this friendly scrimmage, and the Executive's determination of unconstitutionality would have escaped this Court's desire to blurt out its view of the law. The matter would have been left, as so many matters ought to be left, to a tug of war between the President and the Congress, which has innumerable means (up to and including impeachment) of compelling the President to enforce the laws it has written. Or the President could have evaded presentation of the constitutional issue to this Court simply by declining to appeal the District Court and Court of Appeals dispositions he agreed with. Be sure of this much: If a President wants to insulate his judgment of unconstitutionality from our review, he can. What the views urged in this dissent produce is not insulation from judicial review but insulation from Executive contrivance.

The majority brandishes the famous sentence from *Marbury v. Madison*, 1 Cranch 137, 177 (1803), that "[i]t is emphatically the province and duty of the judicial department to say what the law is." But that sentence neither says nor implies that it is *always* the province and duty of the Court to say what the law is—much less that its responsibility in that regard is a "primary" one. The very next sentence of Chief Justice Marshall's opinion makes the crucial qualification that today's majority ignores: "*Those who apply the rule to particular cases*, must of necessity expound and interpret that rule." Only when a "particular case" is before us—that is, a controversy that it is our business to resolve under Article III—do we have the province and duty to pronounce the law. For the views of our early Court more precisely addressing the question before us here, the majority ought instead to have consulted the opinion of Chief Justice Taney in *Lord v. Veazie,* 8 How. 251 (1850):

> The objection in the case before us is . . . that the plaintiff and defendant have the same interest, and that interest adverse and in conflict with the interest of third persons, whose rights would be seriously affected if the question of law was decided in the manner that both of the parties to this suit desire it to be.
>
> A judgment entered under such circumstances, and for such purposes, is a mere form. The whole proceeding was in contempt of the court, and highly reprehensible. . . . A judgment in form, thus procured, in the eye of the law is no judgment of the court. It is a nullity, and no writ of error will lie upon it. This writ is, therefore, dismissed.

There is, in the words of *Marbury,* no "necessity [to] expound and interpret" the law in this case; just a desire to place this Court at the center of the Nation's life.

B

A few words in response to the theory of jurisdiction set forth in Justice Alito's dissent: Though less far reaching in its consequences than the majority's conversion of constitutionally required adverseness into a discretionary element of standing, the theory of that dissent similarly elevates the Court to the "primary" determiner of constitutional questions involving the separation of powers, and, to boot, increases the power of the most dangerous branch: the "legislative department," which by its nature "draw[s] all power into its impetuous vortex." The Federalist, No. 48, at 309 (J. Madison). Heretofore in our national history, the President's failure to "take Care that the Laws be faithfully executed," U.S. Const., Art. II, § 3, could only be brought before a judicial tribunal by someone whose concrete interests were harmed by that alleged failure. Justice Alito would create a system in which Congress can hale the Executive before the courts not only to vindicate its own institutional powers to act, but to correct a perceived inadequacy in the execution of its laws.[7] This would lay to rest Tocqueville's praise of our judicial system as one which "intimately bind[s] the case made for the law with the case made for one man," one in which legislation is "no longer exposed to the daily aggression of the parties," and in which "[t]he political question that [the judge] must resolve is linked to the interest" of private litigants. A. de Tocqueville, Democracy in America 97 (H. Mansfield & D. Winthrop eds. 2000). That would be replaced by a system in which Congress and the

7. [Footnote 3 in Justice Scalia's dissent.] Justice Alito attempts to limit his argument by claiming that Congress is injured (and can therefore appeal) when its statute is held unconstitutional without Presidential defense, but is *not* injured when its statute is held unconstitutional *despite* Presidential defense. I do not understand that line. The injury to Congress is the same whether the President has defended the statute or not. And if the injury is threatened, why should Congress not be able to participate in the suit from the beginning, just as the President can? And if having a statute declared unconstitutional (and therefore inoperative) by a court is an injury, why is it not an injury when a statute is declared unconstitutional by the President and rendered inoperative by his consequent failure to enforce it? Or when the President simply declines to enforce it without opining on its constitutionality? If it is the *inoperativeness* that constitutes the injury—the "impairment of [the legislative] function," as Justice Alito puts it—it should make no difference which of the other two branches inflicts it, and whether the Constitution is the pretext. A principled and predictable system of jurisprudence cannot rest upon a shifting concept of injury, designed to support standing when we would like it. If this Court agreed with Justice Alito's distinction, its opinion in *Raines v. Byrd,* 521 U.S. 811 (1997), which involved an original suit by Members of Congress challenging an assertedly unconstitutional law, would have been written quite differently; and Justice Alito's distinguishing of that case on grounds quite irrelevant to his theory of standing would have been unnecessary.

Executive can pop immediately into court, in their institutional capacity, whenever the President refuses to implement a statute he believes to be unconstitutional, and whenever he implements a law in a manner that is not to Congress' liking.

Justice Alito's notion of standing will likewise enormously shrink the area to which "judicial censure, exercised by the courts on legislation, cannot extend," For example, a bare majority of both Houses could bring into court the assertion that the Executive's implementation of welfare programs is too generous—a failure that no other litigant would have standing to complain about. Moreover, as we indicated in *Raines v. Byrd*, 521 U.S. 811, 828 (1997), if Congress can sue the Executive for the erroneous application of the law that "injures" its power to legislate, surely the Executive can sue Congress for its erroneous adoption of an unconstitutional law that "injures" the Executive's power to administer—or perhaps for its protracted failure to act on one of his nominations. The opportunities for dragging the courts into disputes hitherto left for political resolution are endless.

Justice Alito's dissent is correct that *Raines* did not formally decide this issue, but its reasoning does. The opinion spends three pages discussing famous, decades-long disputes between the President and Congress—regarding congressional power to forbid the Presidential removal of executive officers, regarding the legislative veto, regarding congressional appointment of executive officers, and regarding the pocket veto—that would surely have been promptly resolved by a Congress-vs.-the-President lawsuit if the impairment of a branch's powers alone conferred standing to commence litigation. But it does not, and never has; the "enormous power that the judiciary would acquire" from the ability to adjudicate such suits "would have made a mockery of [Hamilton's] quotation of Montesquieu to the effect that 'of the three powers above mentioned . . . the JUDICIARY is next to nothing.'" *Barnes v. Kline*, 759 F.2d 21, 58 (C.A.D.C.1985) (Bork, J., dissenting) (quoting The Federalist No. 78 (A. Hamilton)).

To be sure, if Congress cannot invoke our authority in the way that Justice Alito proposes, then its only recourse is to confront the President directly. Unimaginable evil this is not. Our system is *designed* for confrontation. That is what "[a]mbition . . . counteract[ing] ambition," The Federalist, No. 51, at 322 (J. Madison), is all about. If majorities in both Houses of Congress care enough about the matter, they have available innumerable ways to compel executive action without a lawsuit—from refusing to confirm Presidential appointees to the elimination of funding. (Nothing says "enforce the Act" quite like ". . . or you will have money for little else.") But the condition is crucial; Congress must care enough to act against the President itself, not merely enough to instruct its lawyers to ask *us* to do so. Placing the Constitution's entirely anticipated political arm wrestling into permanent judicial receivership does not do the system a favor. And by the way, if the President loses the lawsuit but does not faithfully implement the Court's decree, just as he did not faithfully implement Congress' statute, what then? Only Congress can bring him to heel by . . . what do you think? Yes: a direct confrontation with the President.

II

For the reasons above, I think that this Court has, and the Court of Appeals had, no power to decide this suit. We should vacate the decision below and remand to the Court of Appeals for the Second Circuit, with instructions to dismiss the appeal. Given that the majority has volunteered its view of the merits, however, I proceed to discuss that as well.

A

. . . In the majority's telling, this story is black-and-white: Hate your neighbor or come along with us. The truth is more complicated. It is hard to admit that one's political opponents are not monsters, especially in a struggle like this one, and the challenge in the end proves more than today's Court can handle. Too bad. A reminder that disagreement over something so fundamental as marriage can still be politically legitimate would have been a fit task for what in earlier times was called the judicial temperament. We might have covered ourselves with honor today, by promising all sides of this debate that it was theirs to settle and that we would respect their resolution. We might have let the People decide.

But that the majority will not do. Some will rejoice in today's decision, and some will despair at it; that is the nature of a controversy that matters so much to so many. But the Court has cheated both sides, robbing the winners of an honest victory, and the losers of the peace that comes from a fair defeat. We owed both of them better. I dissent.

Justice Alito, with whom Justice Thomas joins as to Parts II and III, dissenting. . . .

I turn first to the question of standing. In my view, the United States clearly is not a proper petitioner in this case. The United States does not ask us to overturn the judgment of the court below or to alter that judgment in any way. Quite to the contrary, the United States argues emphatically in favor of the correctness of that judgment. We have never before reviewed a decision at the sole behest of a party that took such a position, and to do so would be to render an advisory opinion, in violation of Article III's dictates. For the reasons given in Justice Scalia's dissent, I do not find the Court's arguments to the contrary to be persuasive.

Whether the Bipartisan Legal Advisory Group of the House of Representatives (BLAG) has standing to petition is a much more difficult question. It is also a significantly closer question than whether the intervenors in *Hollingsworth v. Perry*—which the Court also decides today—have standing to appeal. It is remarkable that the Court has simultaneously decided that the United States, which "receive[d] all that [it] ha[d] sought" below, *Deposit Guaranty Nat. Bank v. Roper*, 445 U.S. 326, 333 (1980), is a proper petitioner in this case but that the intervenors in *Hollingsworth*, who represent the party that lost in the lower court, are not. In my view, both the *Hollingsworth* intervenors and BLAG have standing.[8]

8. [Footnote 1 in Justice Alito's dissent.] Our precedents make clear that, in order to support our jurisdiction, BLAG must demonstrate that it had Article III standing in its own right, quite apart from its status as an intervenor. See *Diamond v. Charles*, 476 U.S. 54, 68, 106 S. Ct. 1697, 90 L.Ed.2d 48 (1986) ("Although intervenors are considered parties entitled, among other things, to seek review by this Court, an intervenor's right to continue a suit in the absence of the party on whose side intervention was permitted is contingent upon a showing by the intervenor that he fulfills the requirements of Art. III" (citation omitted)); *Arizonans for Official English v. Arizona*, 520 U.S. 43, 64, 117 S. Ct. 1055, 137 L.Ed.2d 170 (1997) ("Standing to defend on appeal in the place of an original defendant, no less than standing to sue, demands that the litigant possess a direct stake in the outcome" (internal quotation marks omitted)); *id.* at 65, 117 S. Ct. 1055 ("An intervenor cannot step into the shoes of the original party unless the intervenor independently fulfills the requirements of Article III").

A party invoking the Court's authority has a sufficient stake to permit it to appeal when it has "'suffered an injury in fact' that is caused by 'the conduct complained of' and that 'will be redressed by a favorable decision.'" *Camreta v.* Greene, 131 S.Ct. 2020, 2028 (2011) (quoting *Lujan*). In the present case, the House of Representatives, which has authorized BLAG to represent its interests in this matter,[9] suffered just such an injury.

In *INS v. Chadha*, 462 U.S. 919 (1983), the Court held that the two Houses of Congress were "proper parties" to file a petition in defense of the constitutionality of the one-house veto statute. Accordingly, the Court granted and decided petitions by both the Senate and the House, in addition to the Executive's petition. . . . In discussing Article III standing, the Court suggested that Congress suffered a similar injury whenever federal legislation it had passed was struck down, noting that it had "long held that Congress is the proper party to defend the validity of a statute when an agency of government, as a defendant charged with enforcing the statute, agrees with plaintiffs that the statute is inapplicable or unconstitutional."

The United States attempts to distinguish *Chadha* on the ground that it "involved an unusual statute that vested the House and the Senate themselves each with special procedural rights—namely, the right effectively to veto Executive action." Brief for United States (jurisdiction) 36. But that is a distinction without a difference: just as the Court of Appeals decision that the *Chadha* Court affirmed impaired Congress' power by striking down the one-house veto, so the Second Circuit's decision here impairs Congress' legislative power by striking down an Act of Congress. The United States has not explained why the fact that the impairment at issue in *Chadha* was "special" or "procedural" has any relevance to whether Congress suffered an injury. Indeed, because legislating is Congress' central function, any impairment of that function is a more grievous injury than the impairment of a procedural add-on. . . .

Both the United States and the Court-appointed *amicus* err in arguing that *Raines v. Byrd*, 521 U.S. 811 (1997), is to the contrary. In that case, the Court held that Members of Congress who had voted "nay" to the Line Item Veto Act did not have standing to challenge that statute in federal court. *Raines* is inapposite for two reasons. First, *Raines* dealt with individual Members of Congress and specifically pointed to the individual Members' lack of institutional endorsement as a sign of their standing problem: "We attach some importance to the fact that appellees have not been authorized to represent their respective Houses of Congress in this action, and indeed both Houses actively oppose their suit." *Id.* at 829 (citing cases to the effect that "members of collegial bodies do not have standing to perfect an appeal the body itself has declined to take.").

Second, the Members in *Raines*—unlike the state senators in *Coleman*—were not the pivotal figures whose votes would have caused the Act to fail absent some challenged action. Indeed, it is telling that *Raines* characterized *Coleman* as standing "for the proposition that legislators whose votes would have been sufficient to defeat (or enact) a specific legislative Act have standing to sue if that legislative action goes into effect (or does not go into effect), on the ground that their votes have been completely nullified." Here, by contrast, passage by the

9. [Footnote 2 in Justice Alito's dissent.] H. Res. 5, 113th Cong., 1st Sess., § 4(a)(1)(B) (2013) ("[BLAG] continues to speak for, and articulates the institutional position of, the House in all litigation matters in which it appears, including in Windsor v. United States").

House was needed for DOMA to become law. U.S. Const., Art. I, § 7 (bicameralism and presentment requirements for legislation).

I appreciate the argument that the Constitution confers on the President alone the authority to defend federal law in litigation, but in my view, as I have explained, that argument is contrary to the Court's holding in *Chadha*, and it is certainly contrary to the *Chadha* Court's endorsement of the principle that "Congress is the proper party to defend the validity of a statute" when the Executive refuses to do so on constitutional grounds. Accordingly, in the narrow category of cases in which a court strikes down an Act of Congress and the Executive declines to defend the Act, Congress both has standing to defend the undefended statute and is a proper party to do so. . . .

For these reasons, I would hold that § 3 of DOMA does not violate the Fifth Amendment. I respectfully dissent.

****

Standing jurisprudence continues to grow in sometimes unpredictable directions. Situations that appear to raise a simple set of facts may raise controversial and confusing rulings on standing. Try your standing instincts with the following problem.

PROBLEM 2-2

The Environmental Standing Limbo—How Low Can You Go?

Evaluate the relative strengths and weaknesses of the following with respect to the standing doctrine and specifically the presence of a cognizable injury.

(a) A group of law students sue in order to protect the environment. Under the Administrative Procedure Act, the students seek federal judicial review of an Interstate Commerce Commission determination to increase railroad freight rates. The students contend that the decision would diminish the use of recycled goods because of the enhanced shipping costs, thereby causing greater use of natural resources and more mining and pollution. A further result, according to the students, is that they will experience less enjoyment of local forests, streams, and mountains.

(b) Wildlife Organization files a federal lawsuit challenging a governmental policy decreasing environmental protection of particular federal lands and creating the possibility of development of thousands of acres. Increased mining operations ensued on certain federal lands. Sarah and Dane, members of the organization, allege that additional mining would ruin the region's land and that they had used land in the vicinity.

(c) Earth Club, representing citizens from across the United States devoted to protecting the environment, bring a federal action to stop the construction of a ski resort in Salmon Valley in Oregon. The Interior Department authorized the construction. The Earth Club seeks review of the Department's decision pursuant to the Administrative Procedure Act. It is not clear whether any members of Earth Club have ever been to Salmon Valley, but the complaint asserts their mission to preserve the Valley and other national parks, refuges, and forests.

(d) Save Our Planet Organization brings a federal lawsuit under a provision of the Clean Water Act. They challenge the discharge of mercury that damages an area they have used and enjoyed recreationally. The suit seeks civil money penalties payable to the government pursuant to the Act. Without defendants' pollution, members of Save Our Planet claim they would use the affected river.

(e) Organizations promoting wildlife preservation sue the Secretary of the Interior in federal court seeking declaratory and injunctive relief regarding the invalidity of a new regulation that under-regulates threats to wildlife with respect to government-funded activities abroad. Two organizational members, Nancy and Morgan, allege they have traveled internationally to visit specific habitats of endangered species prior to the threatened projects. Further, they intend to return, although they have no set plans to do so. The relevant statute does not discuss whether any person would be injured by a violation of the Endangered Species Act, but it explicitly provides any person a right to sue a governmental authority for an injunction to halt a violation of the Act.

(f) Earth Organization sues the United States Forest Service for failure to provide the requisite notice and comment pursuant to administrative statute. The federal district court finds for the plaintiff and approves a nationwide injunction against the Forest Service. Earth Organization voluntarily settles a portion of the lawsuit dealing with members' interests in a timber sale and does not allege that its members plan to visit the sites where the challenged regulations are being applied.

Problem 2-2 demonstrates the import of subtle nuances in facts when making standing determinations under Supreme Court precedent. Each of the hypothetical patterns in Problem 2-2 presents a concise sketch crafted from an actual Supreme Court case. Having conducted your own analysis of the five fact patterns in Problem 2-2, would you be surprised to learn that of the plaintiffs from the actual cases, only two survived standing scrutiny? Review the problem again to discern if you can determine which two scenarios appear the strongest. What other factual allegations do you think are missing in the Court's eyes? A determination of a lack of standing leaves observers to wonder, why did the plaintiffs simply not allege the essential element the Court found missing? Remember that hindsight is 20/20 and the precise parameters of the standing doctrine involve ongoing interpretations as new challenges arise. Also, note that reasonable minds may strongly disagree about the presence or absence of sufficient standing allegations.

Now, compare your analysis of these fact patterns with the results in their case inspirations: (a) *United States v. Students Challenging Regulatory Agency Procedures (SCRAP)*, 412 U.S. 669 (1973); (b) *Lujan v. National Wildlife Federation*, 497 U.S. 871 (1990); (c) *Sierra Club v. Morton*, 405 U.S. 727 (1972); (d) *Friends of the Earth v. Laidlaw Environmental Services, Inc.*, 528 U.S. 167 (2000); (e) *Lujan v. Defenders of Wildlife*, 504 U.S. 555 (1992);(f) *Summers v. Earth Island Institute*, 555 U.S. 488 (2009).

b. Focus: Traditional Standing versus Special Solicitude Standing for States

In *Massachusetts v. Environmental Protection Agency*, 127 S. Ct. 1438 (2007), the Supreme Court addressed the global warming controversy, despite four Justices urging that standing was lacking. Specifically, the majority opinion found standing on behalf of the state of Massachusetts for its challenge to the Environmental Protection Agency's failure to regulate emissions of greenhouse gases from new cars. The Court methodically examined the three elements of standing and also emphasized the special import of *parens patriae* suits—suits in which states sue on behalf of their citizens.

i. Reaching the Merits of a Controversy

The majority opinion in *Massachusetts v. EPA* noted that one of the lower court judges sidestepped a final determination on standing and instead proceeded to the merits. Justice Scalia, in dissent, warned against federal courts' undertaking hypothetical jurisdiction. Does proceeding to the merits streamline the process and make sense given the justification that the standing and merits analyses overlap? The Supreme Court majority ultimately renders the opposite view on the merits than the lower court. Do you think the majority's interest in resolving the merits in favor of the plaintiffs, or any interest of dissent in avoiding a substantive determination, influenced the respective standing analyses? As a general matter, is it possible to conduct justiciability analysis distinctly from merits analysis?

To what extent do you think the Court could be affected by a surge of interest in global warming? Remember that federal judges have a duty to remain impartial and independent decisionmakers. Yet judges are human and do not realistically decide cases without some awareness of the context and consequences. To what extent must a federal district court focus purely on the precise nature of the adversarial claim before it in order to comport with its Article III role? Consider more generally whether context beyond the adversarial parties at issue should have any bearing on a federal court's determination that it is the right time to resolve a controversy.

The Court continues to exhibit conflict over the existence of standing to challenge environmental regulations. In *American Electric Power Co. v. Connecticut*, 564 U.S. ____, 131 S. Ct. 2527 (2011), an equally divided Court affirmed a finding of jurisdiction: "at least some plaintiffs have Article III standing under *Massachusetts*, which permitted a State to challenge EPA's refusal to regulate greenhouse gas emissions. . . ." *Id.* at 2535. Meanwhile, four members of the Court would adhere to the *Massachusetts* dissent or distinguish *Massachusetts* and rule that none of the plaintiffs exhibit Article III standing. The plaintiffs included several states, the city of New York, and three private land trusts; all of them alleged federal common-law public nuisance claims against carbon-dioxide emitters (four private power companies and the federal Tennessee Valley Authority). Although the divided Court affirmed plaintiffs' standing to proceed in federal court, the Court ultimately held the Clean Air Act and the EPA action the Act authorizes displaced plaintiffs' federal common-law claims.

ii. Generalized versus Particularized Grievances

Judge Sentelle's separate concurring opinion in the *Massachusetts* lower appellate court emphasized that plaintiffs lack standing given that their global warming injuries are "harmful to humanity at large" rather than "particularized." In a dissenting opinion in the lower court, Judge Tatel asserted that Massachusetts met all of the standing elements. Specifically, Judge Tatel viewed plaintiffs' allegations as a "far cry" from generalized in that EPA's failure to regulate greenhouse gas emissions included a "substantial probability" that the projected emissions would contribute to the sea's rising levels and thus result in serious erosion of Massachusetts's coastal property. Judge Tatel also contended that Massachusetts satisfied redressability because possible EPA regulations of American car emissions could "delay and moderate many of the adverse impacts of global warming." On the merits, Judge Tatel maintained that EPA's refusal was unjustified.

Before the Supreme Court, the EPA asserted that standing poses "an insuperable jurisdictional obstacle." The Court rejected this contention and reiterated the standing mandates as articulated by Justice Kennedy in his *Lujan* concurrence—presence of an actual or imminent, particularized concrete injury that is fairly traceable to the challenged conduct and redressable via a favorable judicial decision. According to the Court, however, a plaintiff suing pursuant to a congressionally created "procedural right to protect his concrete interests . . . can assert that right without meeting all the normal standards of redressability and immediacy." As standing jurisprudence permits, the Court then focused on one plaintiff to establish standing—the state of Massachusetts suing on behalf of its citizens. At length, the Court emphasized "the special position and interests" of a sovereign state litigant as opposed to a private citizen as in *Lujan*. The Court reasoned that Massachusetts can satisfy standing "if there is some possibility that the requested relief will prompt the injury-causing party to reconsider the decision that allegedly harmed the litigant." Does "some possibility" sound in line with governing interpretations of Article III standing?

The *Massachusetts* Court noted that the EPA, rather than individual states, possessed the relevant rulemaking authority regarding regulation of pollution emissions, and as Congress has set forth, affected parties may challenge EPA denials of rulemaking petitions as arbitrary. "[I]t is clear," according to the Court, that the allegations present a "risk of harm" to Massachusetts that is "actual" and "imminent," and that the requested judicial remedy poses a "substantial likelihood" to trigger "EPA to take steps to reduce that risk." Are you convinced that Massachusetts offers more than a generalized grievance? If the Court did not give "special" consideration to Massachusetts suing in its sovereign representative capacity, could Massachusetts meet the traditional standing requirements as Justice Kennedy articulated in his *Lujan* concurrence?

Evaluate the consequences of nonjusticiability, including what recourse petitioners have in the face of the alleged injury. Consider whether it is relevant, as a policy matter, that the purported injury connects to an underlying harm that petitioners no doubt assert is an escalating environmental crisis. Is there an alternative forum? Is action by another branch the next necessary step to any resolution?

iii. Some Federalism Concerns

Consider what role state sovereignty plays in this analysis. Does it reinforce the authority of federal courts in this case? Bear this question in mind as you study Chapter 8's exploration of the limits on federal power imposed by the Eleventh Amendment. Do you agree with the logic that "special solicitude" does, or should, exist on behalf of a state bringing a *parens patriae* action? Do diluted standing requirements erode the proper role of Article III courts? What significance does this case pose in standing jurisprudence and the future of standing litigation? Be sure to reexamine whether Massachusetts's factual allegations can meet traditional injury in fact, causation, and redressability. Is a state's assertion of an interest in protecting its shoreline tangibly different from an individual seeking to protect the same area (where it is not the individual's personal property)? Recall the litigants in Problem 2-2. Were they better or worse suited than a state to bring environmental challenges? This complex arena raises serious questions about who should help enforce the law, when, and what role the federal judiciary should play in the face of slow, inadequate, or even illegal, actions of another branch of government.

c. Classic Standing Analysis Revisited

REVIEW AND CONSOLIDATION

The Constitutional and Prudential Bounds of the Standing Doctrine

- Standing is jurisdictional. It helps define the role of federal courts in our constitutional design. Accordingly, all lawsuits filed in federal court must satisfy standing requirements. A federal judge may raise standing *sua sponte* during any juncture in the federal court process.
- Congress cannot override constitutional standing requirements. Article III standing mandates that a litigant show she suffers, or imminently will suffer, an actual injury that is (i) fairly traceable to defendant's conduct, and (ii) redressable via her requested relief from the federal court.
- Prudential standing requests that plaintiff (i) assert his own rights rather than a third party's; (ii) not pursue a generalized grievance; and (iii) be within the zone of interests of the relevant statute.
- *Note*: regarding the prohibition on generalized grievances, such as citizen suits and taxpayer standing, the Supreme Court has alternated between prudential and constitutional classification. Reexamine the status after you complete the standing materials and decide which categorization is correct.
- Congress may trump prudential standing considerations. Congress should do so with carefully crafted statutory language that redefines the nature of an injury that Congress seeks to protect via citizen suits.

Clapper turned on the imminence requirement. The dissent in *Massachusetts v. EPA* also argued that plaintiff failed to show that global warming posed an "imminent" or "immediate" threat to its interests. Consider the imminence requirement as you apply classic standing strictures in Problem 2-3.

PROBLEM 2-3

Injured — Is There a Likelihood of Future Injury?

The Chicago Police Department stops David for a malfunctioning light on his car. David is a black adult male. The officers conduct a pat-down search and force David's hands onto his head. David complains about pain caused by the key ring he holds. Within seconds, the officers choke David into unconsciousness. David awakens, facedown on the ground, spitting up blood and dirt to find he has urinated and defecated during the chokehold. The officers issue David a traffic citation and release him.

The Chicago Police Department maintains a policy authorizing chokeholds where necessary to stop a target's use of deadly force. Its police officers have used chokeholds with frequency and have caused several deaths.

During David's stop, he offered no resistance. David fears the police will choke him again. Accordingly, David files a lawsuit in federal district court seeking injunctive and declaratory relief based on an unconstitutional use of force via the chokehold.

Evaluate whether David presents a cognizable case or controversy under Article III. Is your analysis affected by the governing standard that additionally applies in cases seeking equitable injunctive relief: plaintiffs must establish the likelihood of substantial and immediate irreparable injury and that legal remedies, such as money damages, are inadequate?

Test your understanding with these follow-up questions: (1) How would you evaluate his standing if he pursues money damages for inflicted injuries from the chokehold?; (2) What if the chokehold had killed David and his father sues fearing that David's brother, a minor, would be subjected to an unconstitutional chokehold?; and (3) If David's case is nonjusticiable, what additional facts would be persuasive in gaining David access to a federal forum?

EXPLORING DOCTRINE

From Federal Court to State Court

If the door to federal court closes for failure to satisfy Article III's requirements, is the federal judiciary effectively channeling such claims into state court? Is there any reason why a state court could not adequately hear and resolve such claims? Consider whether the federal court's dismissal of such claims may demonstrate respect toward state courts and the state's executive authority.

d. Focus: Generalized Grievance Prohibition and Standing as a Citizen and Taxpayer

Given that a litigant must have an actual or imminent particularized injury rather than a generalized grievance, can an individual raise a federal legal challenge pursuant to the individual's interest as a taxpayer and citizen? The Supreme Court has crafted a narrow path for "*taxpayer standing*" and citizen standing. The Court follows the prohibition on generalized grievances and thus does not ordinarily permit taxpayer and citizen suits. Regarding taxpayer standing, the Court opened the door in *Flast v. Cohen*, 392 U.S. 83 (1968), in which the Court validated a taxpayer's standing to challenge government spending allegedly violative of the First Amendment Establishment Clause. Later Supreme Court rulings circumscribed taxpayer and citizen standing,[10] yet the route to federal court *appears* to remain within certain bounds.

Of essential importance, *Flast* handles the generalized grievances prohibition as *prudential*.[11] Also, the majority endorsed a taxpayer's standing only where "a logical nexus" exists "between the status asserted and the claim sought to be adjudicated." *Id.* at 102. In other words, the taxpayer must show that the challenged enactment violates specific constitutional limitations imposed on Congress' taxing and spending power and not merely that the enactment exceeds Congress' broader delegated powers. What rationales can you articulate in support of, and then against, standing based on status as a taxpayer, even assuming the logical nexus is met? As you will see in the following case, the Supreme Court continues to grapple with whether, and to what extent, the taxpayer avenue should remain viable as a route to federal court. Recall that *Massachusetts v. EPA* suggests that "case" and "controversy" are situational concepts, or, in other words, what constitutes a case for one purpose might not for another. Use this case to explore both the constitutional and prudential standing limits. Remember to examine whether the Court appears to treat the prohibition of generalized grievance as prudential or constitutional.

HEIN v. FREEDOM FROM RELIGION FOUNDATION, INC.

551 U.S. 587 (2007)

JUSTICE ALITO announced the judgment of the Court and delivered an opinion in which THE CHIEF JUSTICE and JUSTICE KENNEDY join.

This is a lawsuit in which it was claimed that conferences held as part of the President's Faith-Based and Community Initiatives program violated the Establishment Clause of the First Amendment because, among other things, President Bush and former Secretary of Education Paige gave speeches that used

10. *See, e.g., United States v. Richardson*, 418 U.S. 166 (1974) (denying standing to plaintiff who asserted taxpayer and citizen standing because allegations posed a prohibited generalized grievance about government action). On similar grounds, the Supreme Court also denied standing in *Schlesinger v. Reservists Committee to Stop the War*, 418 U.S. 208 (1974), and notably remarked that the fact that no one would possess standing does not warrant finding standing based on a generalized grievance. In contrast to *Flast*, the Supreme Court denied taxpayer standing despite a parallel Establishment Clause theory; the Court distinguished *Flast* because the instant plaintiffs differed in two respects that the Court deemed pivotal: that plaintiffs (i) objected to conduct of the Department of Health, Education and Welfare rather than a congressional statute, and (ii) targeted governmental conduct under Congress's power over government property rather than a spending program. *See Valley Forge, supra*, at 479-80.

11. *See also Warth v. Seldin*, 422 U.S. 490, 499 (1979) (providing that jurisdiction should ordinarily be declined, under prudential principles, "when the asserted harm is a 'generalized grievance' shared in substantially equal measure by all or a large class of citizens"). *But cf. Fed. Election Comm'n v. Akins*, 524 U.S. 11, 23 (1998) ("Whether styled as a constitutional or prudential limit on standing, the Court has sometimes determined that where large numbers of Americans suffer alike, the political process, rather than the judicial process, may provide the more appropriate remedy for a widely shared grievance.").

"religious imagery" and praised the efficacy of faith-based programs in delivering social services. The plaintiffs contend that they meet the standing requirements of Article III of the Constitution because they pay federal taxes.

It has long been established, however, that the payment of taxes is generally not enough to establish standing to challenge an action taken by the Federal Government. In light of the size of the federal budget, it is a complete fiction to argue that an unconstitutional federal expenditure causes an individual federal taxpayer any measurable economic harm. And if every federal taxpayer could sue to challenge any Government expenditure, the federal courts would cease to function as courts of law and would be cast in the role of general complaint bureaus.

In *Flast* v. *Cohen*, 392 U. S. 83 (1968), we recognized a narrow exception to the general rule against federal taxpayer standing. Under *Flast*, a plaintiff asserting an Establishment Clause claim has standing to challenge a law authorizing the use of federal funds in a way that allegedly violates the Establishment Clause. In the present case, Congress did not specifically authorize the use of federal funds to pay for the conferences or speeches that the plaintiffs challenged. Instead, the conferences and speeches were paid for out of general Executive Branch appropriations. The Court of Appeals, however, held that the plaintiffs have standing as taxpayers because the conferences were paid for with money appropriated by Congress.

The question that is presented here is whether this broad reading of *Flast* is correct. We hold that it is not. We therefore reverse the decision of the Court of Appeals.

* * * *

II

A

. . . The requisite elements of Article III standing are well established: "A plaintiff must allege personal injury fairly traceable to the defendant's allegedly unlawful conduct and likely to be redressed by the requested relief." *Allen v. Wright.*

The constitutionally mandated standing inquiry is especially important in a case like this one, in which taxpayers seek "to challenge laws of general application where their own injury is not distinct from that suffered in general by other taxpayers or citizens." This is because "[t]he judicial power of the United States defined by Art. III is not an unconditioned authority to determine the constitutionality of legislative or executive acts." *Valley Forge.* The federal courts are not empowered to seek out and strike down any governmental act that they deem to be repugnant to the Constitution. Rather, federal courts sit "solely, to decide on the rights of individuals," *Marbury v. Madison,* and must "'refrai[n] from passing upon the constitutionality of an act . . . unless obliged to do so in the proper performance of our judicial function, when the question is raised by a party whose interests entitle him to raise it.'" *Valley Forge.* . . .

B

As a general matter, the interest of a federal taxpayer in seeing that Treasury funds are spent in accordance with the Constitution does not give rise to the kind of redressable "personal injury" required for Article III standing. Of course, a taxpayer has standing to challenge the *collection* of a specific tax assessment as unconstitutional; being forced to pay such a tax causes a real and immediate economic injury to the individual taxpayer. But that is not the interest on which respondents assert standing here. Rather, their claim is that, having paid lawfully collected taxes into the Federal Treasury at some point, they have a continuing, legally cognizable interest in ensuring that those funds are not *used* by the Government in a way that violates the Constitution.

We have consistently held that this type of interest is too generalized and attenuated to support Article III standing. . . .

Because the interests of the taxpayer are, in essence, the interests of the public-at-large, deciding a constitutional claim based solely on taxpayer standing "would be not to decide a judicial controversy, but to assume a position of authority over the governmental acts of another and co-equal department, an authority which plainly we do not possess."

"[T]he interests of a taxpayer in the moneys of the federal treasury are too indeterminable, remote, uncertain and indirect to furnish a basis for an appeal to the preventive powers of the Court over their manner of expenditure." We therefore rejected a state taxpayer's claim of standing to challenge a state law authorizing public school teachers to read from the Bible because "the grievance which [the plaintiff] sought to litigate . . . is not a direct dollars-and-cents injury but is a religious difference." In so doing, we gave effect to the basic constitutional principle that

> a plaintiff raising only a generally available grievance about government—claiming only harm to his and every citizen's interest in proper application of the Constitution and laws, and seeking relief that no more directly and tangibly benefits him than it does the public at large—does not state an Article III case or controversy.

Lujan v. Defenders of Wildlife, 504 U.S. 555, 573-574 (1992).

C

In *Flast*, the Court carved out a narrow exception to the general constitutional prohibition against taxpayer standing. The taxpayer-plaintiff in that case challenged the distribution of federal funds to religious schools under the Elementary and Secondary Education Act of 1965, alleging that such aid violated the Establishment Clause. The Court set out a two-part test for determining whether a federal taxpayer has standing to challenge an allegedly unconstitutional expenditure:

> First, the taxpayer must establish a logical link between that status and the type of legislative enactment attacked. Thus, a taxpayer will be a proper party to allege the unconstitutionality only of exercises of congressional power under the taxing and spending clause of Art. I, § 8, of the Constitution. It will not be sufficient to allege an incidental expenditure of tax funds in the administration of an essentially regulatory statute. . . . Secondly, the taxpayer must establish a nexus between that status and the precise nature of the constitutional infringement alleged. Under this requirement, the taxpayer must show that the challenged enactment exceeds specific constitutional limitations imposed upon the exercise of the congressional taxing and spending power and not simply that the enactment is generally beyond the powers delegated to Congress by Art. I, § 8.

The Court held that the taxpayer-plaintiff in *Flast* had satisfied both prongs of this test: The plaintiff's "constitutional challenge [was] made to an exercise by Congress of its power under Art. I, § 8, to spend for the general welfare," and she alleged a violation of the Establishment clause, which "operates as a specific constitutional limitation upon the exercise by Congress of the taxing and spending power conferred by Art. I, § 8."

III

A

Respondents argue that this case falls within the *Flast* exception, which they read to cover any "expenditure of government funds in violation of the Establishment Clause." But this broad reading fails to observe "the rigor with which the *Flast* exception to the *Frothingham* principle ought to be applied."

The expenditures at issue in *Flast* were made pursuant to an express congressional mandate and a specific congressional appropriation. The plaintiff in that case challenged disbursements made under the Elementary and Secondary Education Act of 1965. That Act expressly appropriated the sum of $100 million for fiscal year 1966, and authorized the disbursement of those funds to local educational agencies for the education of low-income students. The Act mandated that local educational agencies receiving such funds "ma[k]e provision for including special educational services and arrangements (such as dual enrollment, educational radio and television, and mobile educational services and equipment)" in which students enrolled in private elementary and secondary schools could participate. In addition, recipient agencies were required to ensure that "library resources, textbooks, and other instructional materials" funded through the grants "be provided on an equitable basis for the use of children and teachers in private elementary and secondary schools."

* * * *

Given that the alleged Establishment Clause violation in *Flast* was funded by a specific congressional appropriation and was undertaken pursuant to an express congressional mandate, the Court concluded that the taxpayer plaintiffs had established the requisite "logical link between [their taxpayer] status and the type of legislative enactment attacked." In the Court's words, "[t]heir constitutional challenge [was] made to an exercise by Congress of its power under Art. I, § 8, to spend for the general welfare." But as this Court later noted, *Flast* "limited taxpayer standing to challenges directed 'only [at] exercises of congressional power'" under the Taxing and Spending Clause.

B

The link between congressional action and constitutional violation that supported taxpayer standing in *Flast* is missing here. . . . [T]he expenditures at issue here were not made pursuant to any Act of Congress. Rather, Congress provided general appropriations to the Executive Branch to fund its day-to-day activities. These appropriations did not expressly authorize, direct, or even mention the expenditures of which respondents complain. Those expenditures resulted from executive discretion, not congressional action.

* * * *

Respondents attempt to paint their lawsuit as a[n] as-applied challenge, but this effort is unavailing for the simple reason that they can cite no statute whose application they challenge. The best they can do is to point to unspecified, lump-sum "Congressional budget appropriations" for the general use of the Executive Branch — the allocation of which "is a[n] administrative decision traditionally regarded as committed to agency discretion." . . .

Because the expenditures that respondents challenge were not expressly authorized or mandated by any specific congressional enactment, respondents' lawsuit is not directed at an exercise of congressional power, and thus lacks the requisite "logical nexus" between taxpayer status "and the type of legislative enactment attacked."

* * * *

[IV]

[A]

2

While respondents argue that Executive Branch expenditures in support of religion are no different from legislative extractions, *Flast* itself rejected this equivalence: "It will not be sufficient to allege an incidental expenditure of tax funds in the administration of an essentially regulatory statute."

Because almost all Executive Branch activity is ultimately funded by some congressional appropriation, extending the *Flast* exception to purely executive expenditures would effectively subject every federal action — be it a conference, proclamation or speech — to Establishment Clause challenge by any taxpayer in federal court. . . .

It would also raise serious separation-of-powers concerns. As we have recognized, *Flast* itself gave too little weight to these concerns. By framing the standing question solely in terms of whether the dispute would be presented in an adversary context and in a form traditionally viewed as capable of judicial resolution, *Flast* "failed to recognize that this doctrine has a separation-of-powers component, which keeps courts within certain traditional bounds vis-à-vis the other branches, concrete adverseness or not." Respondents' position, if adopted, would repeat and compound this mistake.

The constitutional requirements for federal-court jurisdiction — including the standing requirements and Article III — "are an essential ingredient of separation and equilibration of powers." "Relaxation of standing requirements is directly related to the expansion of judicial power," and lowering the taxpayer standing bar to permit challenges of purely executive actions "would significantly alter the allocation of power at the national level, with a shift away from a democratic form of government." The rule respondents propose would enlist the federal courts to superintend, at the behest of any federal taxpayer, the speeches, statements, and myriad daily activities of the President, his staff, and other Executive Branch officials. This would "be quite at odds with . . . *Flast*'s own promise that it would not transform federal courts into forums for taxpayers' 'generalized grievances'" about the conduct of government and would "open the Judiciary to an arguable charge of providing 'government by injunction.'" It would deputize federal courts as "'virtually continuing monitors of the wisdom and soundness of Executive action,'" and that, most emphatically, "'is not the role of the judiciary.'"

* * * *

B

Respondents set out a parade of horribles that they claim could occur if *Flast* is not extended to discretionary Executive Branch expenditures. For example, they say, a federal agency could use its discretionary funds to build a house of worship or to hire clergy of one denomination and send them out to spread their faith. Or an agency could use its funds to make bulk purchases of Stars of David, crucifixes, or depictions of the star and crescent for use in its offices or for distribution to the employees or the general public. Of course, none of these things has happened, even though *Flast* has not previously been expanded in the way that respondents urge. In the unlikely event that any of these executive actions did take place, Congress could quickly step in. And respondents make no effort to show that these improbable abuses could not be challenged in federal court by plaintiffs who would possess standing based on grounds other than taxpayer standing.

C

Over the years, *Flast* has been defended by some and criticized by others. But the present case does not require us to reconsider that precedent. The Court of Appeals did not apply *Flast*; it extended *Flast*. It is a necessary concomitant of the doctrine of *stare decisis* that a precedent is not always expanded to the limit of its logic. That was the approach that then-Justice Rehnquist took in his opinion for the Court in *Valley Forge*, and it is the approach we take here. We do not extend *Flast*, but we also do not overrule it. We leave *Flast* as we found it.

Justice Scalia says that we must either overrule *Flast* or extend it to the limits of its logic. His position is not "[in]sane," inconsistent with the "rule of law," or "utterly meaningless." But it is wrong. Justice Scalia does not seriously dispute either (1) that *Flast* itself spoke in terms of "legislative enactment[s]" and "exercises of congressional power," or (2) that in the four decades since *Flast* was decided, we have never extended its narrow exception to a purely discretionary Executive Branch expenditure. We need go no further to decide this case. Relying on the provision of the Constitution that limits our role to resolving the "Cases" and "Controversies" before us, we decide only the case at hand. . . .

For these reasons, the judgment of the Court of Appeals for the Seventh Circuit is reversed.

It is so ordered.

[In Justice Kennedy's concurring opinion, he underscores the importance of the need for a narrow reading of *Flast* in order to maintain the proper limits on judicial power vis-à-vis the other branches.]

JUSTICE SCALIA, with whom JUSTICE THOMAS joins, concurring in the judgment.

Today's opinion is, in one significant respect, entirely consistent with our previous cases addressing taxpayer standing to raise Establishment Clause challenges to government expenditures. Unfortunately, the consistency lies in the creation of utterly meaningless distinctions which separate the case at hand from the precedents that have come out differently, but which cannot possibly be (in any sane world) the reason it comes out differently. If this Court is to decide cases by rule of law rather than show of hands, we must surrender to logic and choose sides: Either *Flast v. Cohen* should be applied to (at a minimum) *all* challenges to the governmental expenditure of general tax revenues in a manner alleged to violate a constitutional provision specifically limiting the taxing and spending power, or *Flast* should be repudiated. For me, the choice is easy. *Flast* is wholly irreconcilable with the Article III restrictions on federal-court jurisdiction that this Court has repeatedly confirmed are embodied in the doctrine of standing.

I

A

There is a simple reason why our taxpayer-standing cases involving Establishment Clause challenges to government expenditures are notoriously inconsistent: We have inconsistently described the first element of the "irreducible constitutional minimum of standing," which minimum consists of (1) a "concrete and particularized" "'injury in fact'" that is (2) fairly traceable to the defendant's alleged unlawful conduct and (3) likely to be redressed by a favorable decision. See *Lujan v. Defenders of Wildlife.* We have alternately relied on two entirely distinct conceptions of injury in fact, which for convenience I will call "Wallet Injury" and "Psychic Injury."

Wallet Injury is the type of concrete and particularized injury one would expect to be asserted in a *taxpayer* suit, namely, a claim that the plaintiff's tax liability is higher than it would be, but for the allegedly unlawful government action. The stumbling block for suits challenging government expenditures based on this conventional type of injury is quite predictable. The plaintiff cannot satisfy the traceability and redressability prongs of standing. It is uncertain what the plaintiff's tax bill would have been had the allegedly forbidden expenditure not been made, and it is even more speculative whether the government will, in response to an adverse court decision, lower taxes rather than spend the funds in some other manner.

Psychic Injury, on the other hand, has nothing to do with the plaintiff's tax liability. Instead, the injury consists of the taxpayer's *mental displeasure* that money extracted from him is being spent in an unlawful manner. This shift in focus eliminates traceability and redressability problems. Psychic Injury is directly traceable to the improper *use* of taxpayer funds, and it is redressed when the improper use is enjoined, regardless of whether that injunction affects the taxpayer's purse. *Flast* and the cases following its teaching have invoked a peculiarly restricted version of Psychic Injury, permitting taxpayer displeasure over unconstitutional spending to support standing *only if* the constitutional provision allegedly violated is a specific limitation on the taxing and spending power. Restricted or not, this conceptualizing of injury in fact in purely mental terms conflicts squarely with the familiar proposition that a plaintiff lacks a concrete and particularized injury when his only complaint is the generalized grievance that the law is being violated. As were affirmed unanimously just this Term: "'We have consistently held that a plaintiff raising only a generally available grievance about government—claiming only harm to his and every citizen's interest in proper application of the Constitution and laws, and seeking relief that no more directly and tangibly benefits him than it does the public at large—does not state an Article III case or controversy.'"

As the . . . review of our cases demonstrates, we initially denied taxpayer standing based on Wallet Injury, but then found standing in some later cases based on the limited version of Psychic Injury described above. The basic logical flaw in our cases is thus twofold: We have never explained why Psychic Injury was insufficient in the cases in which standing was denied, and we have never explained why Psychic Injury, however limited, is cognizable under Article III.

* * * *

[B.2]

In *Flast v. Cohen*, taxpayers challenged the Elementary and Secondary Education Act of 1965, alleging that funds expended pursuant to the Act were being used to support parochial schools. They argued that either the Act itself proscribed such expenditures or that the Act violated the Establishment Clause. The Court held that the taxpayers had standing. Purportedly in order to determine whether taxpayers have the "personal stake and interest" necessary to satisfy Article III, a two-pronged nexus test was invented.

The first prong required the taxpayer to "establish a logical link between [taxpayer] status and the type of legislative enactment." The Court described what that meant as follows:

> [A] taxpayer will be a proper party to allege the unconstitutionality only of exercises of congressional power under the taxing and spending clause of Art. I, § 8, of the Constitution. It will not be sufficient to allege an incidental expenditure of tax funds in the administration of an essentially regulatory statute. . . .

The second prong required the taxpayer to "establish a nexus between [taxpayer] status and the precise nature of the constitutional infringement alleged." The Court elaborated that this required "the taxpayer [to] show that the challenged enactment exceeds specific constitutional limitations imposed upon the exercise of the congressional taxing and spending power and not simply that the enactment is generally beyond the powers delegated to Congress by Art. I, § 8." The Court held that the Establishment Clause was the type of specific limitation on the taxing and spending power that it had in mind because "one of the specific evils feared by" the Framers of that Clause was that the taxing and spending power would be used to favor one religion over another or to support religion generally.

Because both prongs of its newly minted two-part test were satisfied, *Flast* held that the taxpayers had standing. Wallet Injury could not possibly have been the basis for this conclusion. . . . Thus, *Flast* relied on Psychic Injury to support standing, describing the "injury" as the taxpayer's allegation that "his tax money is being extracted and spent in violation of specific constitutional protections against such abuses of legislative power."

* * * *

[Relevant precedent] reveals is that there are only two logical routes available to this Court. We must initially decide whether Psychic Injury is consistent with Article III. If it is, we should apply *Flast* to *all* challenges to government expenditures in violation of constitutional provisions that specifically limit the taxing and spending power; if it is not, we should overturn *Flast.*

II

A

The plurality today avails itself of neither principled option. Instead, essentially accepting the Solicitor General's primary submission, it limits *Flast* to challenges to expenditures that are "expressly authorized or mandated by . . . specific congressional enactment." It offers no intellectual justification for this limitation, except that "[i]t is a necessary concomitant of the doctrine of *stare decisis* that a precedent is not always expanded to the limit of its logic." That is true enough, but since courts purport to be engaged in *reasoned* decisionmaking, it is *only* true when (1) the precedent's logic is seen to require narrowing or readjustment in light of relevant distinctions that the new fact situation brings to the fore; or (2) its logic is fundamentally flawed, and so deserves to be limited to the facts that begot it. Today's plurality claims neither of these justifications. As to the first, the plurality offers no explanation of why the factual differences between this case and *Flast* are *material.* It virtually admits that express congressional allocation *vel non* has nothing to do with whether the plaintiffs have alleged an injury in fact that is fairly traceable and likely to be redressed. As the dissent correctly contends and I shall not belabor, *Flast* is *indistinguishable* from this case for purposes of Article III. Whether the challenged government expenditure is expressly allocated by a specific congressional enactment *has absolutely no relevance* to the Article III criteria of injury in fact, traceability, and redressability.

Yet the plurality is also unwilling to acknowledge that the logic of *Flast* (its Psychic Injury rationale) is simply wrong, and *for that reason* should not be extended to other cases. Despite the lack of acknowledgment, however, that is the only plausible explanation for the plurality's indifference to whether the "distinguishing" fact is legally material, and for its determination to limit *Flast* to its "'*resul[t].*'"[12] Why, then, pick a distinguishing fact that may breathe life into *Flast* in future cases, preserving the disreputable disarray of our Establishment Clause standing jurisprudence? Why not hold that only taxpayers raising Establishment Clause challenges to expenditures pursuant to the Elementary and Secondary Education Act of 1965 have standing? That, I suppose, would be too obvious a repudiation of *Flast,* and thus an impediment to the plurality's pose of minimalism.

Because the express-allocation line has no mooring to our tripartite test for Article III standing, it invites demonstrably absurd results. For example, the plurality would deny standing to a taxpayer challenging the President's disbursement to a religious organization of a discrete appropriation that Congress had not explicitly allocated to that purpose, even if everyone knew that Congress and

12. [Footnote 3 in Justice Scalia's concurring opinion.] This explanation does not suffice with regard to Justice Kennedy, who, unlike the other Members of the plurality, openly and avowedly contends both that *Flast* was correctly decided and that respondents should nevertheless lose this case. He thus has the distinction of being the only Justice who affirms both propositions. I cannot begin to comprehend how the amorphous separation-of-powers concerns that motivate him bear upon whether the express-allocation requirement is grounded in the Article III criteria of injury in fact, traceability, or redressability.

the President had informally negotiated that the entire sum would be spent in that precise manner. . . . Indeed, taking the plurality at its word, Congress could insulate the President from *all Flast*-based suits by codifying the truism that no appropriation can be spent by the Executive Branch in a manner that violates the Establishment Clause.

* * * *

B

While I have been critical of the Members of the plurality, I by no means wish to give the impression that respondents' legal position is any more coherent. Respondents argue that *Flast* did not turn on whether Congress has expressly allocated the funds to the allegedly unconstitutional use, and their case plainly rests on Psychic Injury. They repeatedly emphasize that the injury in *Flast* was merely the governmental extraction and spending of tax money in aid of religion. Respondents refuse to admit that their argument logically implies, for the reasons already discussed, that *every* expenditure of tax revenues that is alleged to violate the Establishment Clause is subject to suit under *Flast.*

* * * *

The logical consequence of respondents' position finds no support in this Court's precedents or our Nation's history. Any taxpayer would be able to sue whenever tax funds were used in alleged violation of the Establishment Clause. So, for example, any taxpayer could challenge the fact that the Marshal of our Court is paid, in part, to call the courtroom to order by proclaiming "God Save the United States and this Honorable Court." As much as respondents wish to deny that this is what *Flast* logically entails, it blinks reality to conclude otherwise. . . .

C

. . . . Either *Flast* was correct, and must be accorded the wide application that it logically dictates, or it was not, and must be abandoned in its entirety. I turn, finally, to that question.

III

* * * *

Flast's crabbed (and judge-empowering) understanding of the role Article III standing plays in preserving our system of separated powers has been repudiated:

> To permit a complainant who has no concrete injury to require a court to rule on important constitutional issues in the abstract would create the potential for abuse of the judicial process, distort the role of the Judiciary in its relationship to the Executive and the Legislature and open the Judiciary to an arguable charge of providing "government by injunction."

We twice have noted explicitly that *Flast* failed to recognize the vital separation-of-powers aspect of Article III standing. And once a proper understanding of the relationship of standing to the separation of powers is brought to bear, Psychic

Injury, even as limited in *Flast*, is revealed for what it is: a contradiction of the basic propositions that the function of the judicial power "is, solely, to decide on the rights of individuals," *Marbury v. Madison*, and that generalized grievances affecting the public at large have their remedy in the political process.

* * * *

[W]hat experience has shown is that *Flast*'s lack of a logical theoretical underpinning has rendered our taxpayer-standing doctrine such a jurisprudential disaster that our appellate judges do not know what to make of it. And of course the case has engendered no reliance interests, not only because one does not arrange his affairs with an eye to standing, but also because there is no relying on the random and irrational. I can think of few cases less warranting of *stare decisis* respect. It is time—it is past time—to call an end. *Flast* should be overruled.

JUSTICE SOUTER, with whom JUSTICE STEVENS, JUSTICE GINSBURG, and JUSTICE BREYER join, dissenting.

* * * *

The plurality points to the separation of powers to explain its distinction between legislative and executive spending decisions, but there is no difference on that point of view between a Judicial Branch review of an executive decision and a judicial evaluation of a congressional one. We owe respect to each of the other branches, no more to the former than to the latter, and no one has suggested that the Establishment Clause lacks applicability to executive uses of money. It would surely violate the Establishment Clause for the Department of Health and Human Services to draw on a general appropriation to build a chapel for weekly church services (no less than if a statute required it), and for good reason: if the Executive could accomplish through the exercise of discretion exactly what Congress cannot do through legislation, Establishment Clause protection would melt away.[13]

* * * *

II

While *Flast* standing to assert the right of conscience is in a class by itself, it would be a mistake to think that case is unique in recognizing standing in a plaintiff without injury to flesh or purse. Cognizable harm takes account of the nature of the interest protected, which is the reason that "the constitutional component of standing doctrine incorporates concepts concededly not susceptible of precise definition," leaving it impossible "to make application of the

13. [Footnote 1 in Justice Souter's dissenting opinion.] The plurality warns that a parade of horribles would result if there were standing to challenge executive action, because all federal activities are "ultimately funded by some congressional appropriation." But even if there is Article III standing in all of the cases posited by the plurality (and the Court of Appeals thought that at least sometimes there is not), that does not mean taxpayers will prevail in such suits. If these claims are frivolous on the merits, I fail to see the harm in dismissing them for failure to state a claim instead of for lack of jurisdiction. To the degree the claims are meritorious, fear that there will be many of them does not provide a compelling reason, much less a reason grounded in Article III, to keep them from being heard.

constitutional standing requirement a mechanical exercise." The question, ultimately, has to be whether the injury alleged is "too abstract, or otherwise not appropriate, to be considered judicially cognizable."

In the case of economic or physical harms, of course, the "injury in fact" question is straightforward. But once one strays from these obvious cases, the enquiry can turn subtle. Are esthetic harms sufficient for Article III standing? What about being forced to compete on an uneven playing field based on race (without showing that an economic loss resulted), or living in a racially gerrymandered electoral district? These injuries are no more concrete than seeing one's tax dollars spent on religion, but we have recognized each one as enough for standing. This is not to say that any sort of alleged injury will satisfy Article III, but only that intangible harms must be evaluated case by case.

Thus, *Flast* speaks for this Court's recognition (shared by a majority of the Court today) that when the Government spends money for religious purposes a taxpayer's injury is serious and concrete enough to be "judicially cognizable." The judgment of sufficient injury takes account of the Madisonian relationship of tax money and conscience, but it equally reflects the Founders' pragmatic "conviction that individual religious liberty could be achieved best under a government which was stripped of all power to tax, to support, or otherwise to assist any or all religions," and the realization continuing to the modern day that favoritism for religion "sends the . . . message to . . . nonadherents "that they are outsiders, not full members of the political community.""[14]

Because the taxpayers in this case have alleged the type of injury this Court has seen as sufficient for standing, I would affirm.

DISCUSSION AND QUESTIONS

After the plurality decision in *Hein*, where do we stand on the prudential versus constitutional distinction regarding prohibitions on citizen and taxpayer standing? (A citizen suit arises when a private citizen sues to enforce a statute or regulation). *Flast* and *Warth* work under a prudential paradigm, yet in *Lujan*, the Supreme Court treats the bar on citizen suits as constitutional. Accordingly, congressional statutes attempting to set forth citizen standing for federal lawsuits must continue to meet Article III injury in fact. Recall that if the prohibition on citizen and taxpayer standing is constitutional, Congress cannot statutorily override the Article III requirements. Rather, if the prohibition is constitutional and thus stems from Article III, it confines the proper parameters of the federal court's jurisdiction. Citizens, although otherwise lacking an actual injury, may be successful, however, in establishing such harm where Congress has carefully articulated a statutory injury and the citizens are within the scope of that statute.

Should citizen suits and taxpayer suits be treated the same regarding classification as constitutional versus prudential? The *Hein* Court faced an opportunity to distinguish taxpayer standing from citizen suits and to continue to view the

14. [Footnote 5 in Justice Souter's dissenting opinion.] There will not always be competitors for the funds who would make better plaintiffs (and indeed there appears to be no such competitor here), so after accepting the importance of the injury there is no reason to refuse standing as a prudential matter.

prohibition on taxpayer standing as prudential in line with *Flast.* Did Justice Alito choose this path? What support does the plurality opinion provide for its declaration of constitutional treatment, and what are the implications of this determination? Does Justice Kennedy concur with this aspect of the plurality opinion? With respect to this critical classification, do Justices Scalia and Thomas agree with the plurality's assertion?

The plurality opinion takes great pains to ensure that it acts according to minimalist principles and thus it opts *not* to overrule *Flast.* Instead, the plurality claims to enforce tight boundaries around the interpretation of *Flast* so as not to extend the reasoning to *Hein.* The plurality's approach tightly cabins taxpayer standing in an effort to maintain the federal judiciary's appropriate role. Does the opinion succeed in its goal?

The Court continues to narrow the interpretation of the *Flast* exception. In *Arizona Christian School Tuition Organization v. Winn,* 563 U.S. ____, 131 S. Ct. 1436, (2011), a 5-4 opinion, the Court determined that the *Flast* exception did not apply to tax credits. Justice Kennedy, speaking for the Court, distinguished tax credits from governmental expenditures and reasoned that a "tax credit is not tantamount to a religious tax or to a tithe and does not visit the injury identified in *Flast.* It follows that respondents have neither alleged an injury for standing purposes under general rules nor met the *Flast* exception. Finding standing under these circumstances would be more than the extension of *Flast* 'to the limits of its logic.'" 131 S. Ct. at 1447 (quoting *Hein*).

Justice Kagan issued a strong dissent. The dissent charged, "[T]his Court and others have exercised jurisdiction to decide taxpayer-initiated challenges not materially different from this one." *Id.* at 1450 (Kagan, J., dissenting). Justice Kagan criticized the Court's "arbitrary distinction" and warned that the door to the federal courthouse might be closed to all taxpayers challenging the government's financial support of religion:

> Today's opinion thus enables the government to end-run *Flast*'s guarantee of access to the Judiciary. From now on, the government need follow just one simple rule — subsidize through the tax system — to preclude taxpayer challenges to state funding of religion.
>
> And that result — the effective demise of taxpayer standing — will diminish the Establishment Clause's force and meaning.

Id. at 1450-51. The dissent noted that the Court has confronted identical circumstances five times and resolved the cases without questioning standing. *Id.* at 1452-53. According to the dissent, the majority, without reason or logic, offers a "one-step instruction — to any government that wishes to insulate its financing of religious activity from legal challenge." *Id.* at 1462. The dissent warns that, if the government uses a tax expenditure device, *Flast* will not help, standing will not lie, and regardless how "blatantly the government may violate the Establishment Clause, taxpayers cannot gain access to the federal courts." *Id.*

Justice Scalia reluctantly concurred but maintained that "a principled reading of Article III" demonstrates that "*Flast* is an anomaly in [the Court's] jurisprudence, irreconcilable with the Article III restrictions on federal judicial power. . . ." *Id.* at 1450 (Scalia, J., concurring). As such, Justice Scalia again called for *Flast* to be overruled.

EXPLORING DOCTRINE

Must the Court Overrule *Flast*?

Justice Scalia argues that the plurality radically misfires, procedurally and substantively, on its insistence in keeping *Flast* alive. Given the plurality's classification of the prohibition on citizen and taxpayer standing as constitutional, should it have discontinued the taxpayer standing exception and instead overruled *Flast*? Justice Scalia forcefully asserts, "*Flast* is wholly irreconcilable with the Article III restrictions on federal-court jurisdiction that this Court has repeatedly confirmed are embodied in the doctrine of standing." If so, must the Court overrule *Flast*?

Evaluate which opinion presents the strongest path to serve separation-of-powers interests. The following selected excerpts should help you begin the relevant analysis. The plurality opines:

> The federal courts are not empowered to seek out and strike down any governmental act that they deem to be repugnant to the Constitution. Rather, federal courts sit "solely, to decide on the rights of individuals," *Marbury v. Madison*, and must "'refrai[n] from passing upon the constitutionality of an act . . . unless obliged to do so in the proper performance of our judicial function, when the question is raised by a party whose interests entitle him to raise it.

With direct regard to separation-of-powers principles, the plurality remarks on the broader path not chosen: "The rule respondents propose would enlist the federal courts to superintend, at the behest of any federal taxpayer, the speeches, statements, and myriad daily activities of the President, his staff, and other Executive Branch officials." Consider the contours of what the plurality implies here. Is this a fair characterization of respondent's position? If so, is the plurality correct that the Court has no business, given its constitutional role, going down that road? Further, should the Court follow Justice Scalia's position and get off the taxpayer standing road entirely?

Justice Kennedy echoes the separation-of-powers import in the Constitution's design with respect to the federal judiciary's role under Article III, but then he states that "these principles, in some cases, must accommodate the First Amendment's Establishment Clause." How do we attain the balance Justice Kennedy commends? Justice Scalia demands full repudiation of "*Flast's* crabbed (and judge-empowering) understanding of the role Article III standing plays in preserving our system of separated powers." What does Justice Scalia mean? Despite the plurality's upholding *Flast*, would the plurality agree with Justice Scalia's underlying assertion? Do you agree? The dissent maintains: "We owe respect to each of the other branches, no more to the [executive] than to the [legislative], and no one has suggested that the Establishment Clause lacks applicability to executive uses of money." Through these varying interpretations, how do the separation-of-powers principles fare?

Despite *Hein*'s following of *Lujan* with respect to viewing the prohibition on taxpayer suits as similarly constitutional as the bar on citizen suits, recall that Congress retains power to confer standing as long as the statutory language provides a sufficient basis to find that injury is created on behalf of the relevant litigants who are within the scope of the statute. Explore this opening in Problem 2-4.

PROBLEM 2-4

Do Any Hopes Remain for Generalized Grievances?

A group of voters brings a federal court challenge of a Federal Election Commission (the "Commission") determination that the American Pacific-Islander Committee (APIC) is not a "political committee" under relevant federal campaign laws. Under the campaign law, "political committee" means "any committee, club, association or other group of persons which receives more than $1,000 in contributions or expends more than $1,000 in any given year." The law covers, however, only contributions or expenditures that are made "for the purpose of influencing any election for Federal office." The Commission administers and enforces rules to serve the federal campaign law's goal of remedying actual or perceived corruption in the political process.

The group of voters is not connected to APIC; rather, the group generally opposes views promoted by APIC. Regarding injury, the group of voters alleges it suffers the inability to obtain information that the campaign law, under the group's interpretation, requires. By not deeming APIC a political committee, the Commission has refused to require public disclosures regarding membership, contributions, and expenditures that the campaign law would otherwise mandate. In the relevant campaign law statute, Congress provides that "any person who believes a violation of this Act . . . has occurred, may file a complaint with the Commission" and, in the event of the Commission's dismissal of such complaint, "the aggrieved party may file a petition in federal district court seeking review of that dismissal." The Commission dismissed the voters' complaint.

Evaluate whether the group of voters possess standing to challenge the Commission's denial in federal court. Analyze specifically whether the group exhibits constitutional and prudential standing.

EXPLORING DOCTRINE

What Is the Proper Role of the Federal Judiciary?

Does the *constitutional* prohibition against generalized grievances via citizen suits still exist? To what extent is the bar nullified when the Supreme Court allows Congress to supply Article III standing? Congress would use citizen-suit provisions to create new rights and violations constituting sufficient injury, even though society generally experiences the harm. Should federal courts cling more tightly to particularized harms and redressing such injuries? Or should they embrace citizen suits that foster the judiciary's role as the protector of the Constitution?

3. *Ripeness*

While standing doctrine focuses its inquiry on "who" may bring a suit, ripeness doctrine shifts the focus to "when" a suit may be brought. When is a claim ready for judicial resolution in federal court? The ripeness doctrine speaks to this timing question. Similarly, the mootness doctrine discussed in the next section also focuses on timing. Ripeness asks whether it is too early. Mootness asks whether it is too late. A litigant must still satisfy standing, but ripeness requires that the lawsuit not occur prior to the proper moment. Before this moment, the lawsuit is premature. The federal judiciary fears inappropriate consideration of speculative claims. Accordingly, the ripeness doctrine centers on whether the harm has occurred yet.

In *United Public Workers of America v. Mitchell*, 330 U.S. 75 (1947), the Supreme Court found ripeness lacking where a union challenged the constitutionality of the Hatch Act's regulation of political activities of federal employees. The union members at issue had not violated the challenged provisions of the Hatch Act. In its reasoning, the Court reiterated the prohibition on advisory opinions and the Article III requirement of concrete issues in actual controversies. In declining to find the case ripe for review, the Court emphasized:

> The power of courts, and ultimately of this Court, to pass upon the constitutionality of acts of Congress arises only when the interests of litigants require the use of this judicial authority for their protection against actual interference. A hypothetical threat is not enough. We can only speculate as to the kinds of political activity the appellants desire to engage in. . . . It would not accord with judicial responsibility to adjudge, in a matter involving constitutionality, between the freedom of the individual and the requirements of public order except when definite rights appear upon the one side and definite prejudicial interferences upon the other.

Id. at 89-90. To satisfy ripeness concerns, what would you have advised union members to do prior to filing the instant lawsuit? Consider the legal, ethical, and practical implications of the Court's holding.

As you examine the following important ripeness case, note that the Supreme Court generally focuses on two key factors in rendering a ripeness determination: (1) the *hardship* to the parties if the federal court refuses to consider the case and (2) the *fitness* of the issues for judicial review. Under the hardship factor, the federal court evaluates whether the seriousness of the hardship warrants a finding of ripeness so the court may consider the case. The fitness concern flows from a practical judicial need to have a sufficient record for judicial review and resolution; the more purely legal the claim, and the less factual, the more likely the federal court will deem the case ripe.

ABBOTT LABORATORIES v. GARDNER

387 U.S. 136 (1967)

JUSTICE HARLAN delivered the opinion of the Court.

In 1962 Congress amended the Federal Food, Drug, and Cosmetic Act to require manufacturers of prescription drugs to print the "established name" of the drug "prominently and in type at least half as large as that used thereon for any proprietary name or designation for such drug," on labels and other printed material. . . . The underlying purpose of the 1962 amendment was to bring to the attention of doctors and patients the fact that many of the drugs sold under familiar trade names are actually identical to drugs sold under their "established" or less familiar trade names at significantly lower prices. The Commissioner of Food and Drugs, exercising authority delegated to him by the Secretary, published proposed regulations designed to implement the statute. After inviting and considering comments submitted by interested parties the Commissioner promulgated the following regulation for the "efficient enforcement" of the Act:

> If the label or labeling of a prescription drug bears a proprietary name or designation for the drug or any ingredient thereof, the established name, if such there be, corresponding to such proprietary name or designation, shall accompany each appearance of such proprietary name or designation.

A similar rule was made applicable to advertisements for prescription drugs.

The present action was brought by a group of 37 individual drug manufacturers and by the Pharmaceutical Manufacturers Association, of which all the petitioner companies are members, and which includes manufacturers of more than 90% of the Nation's supply of prescription drugs. They challenged the regulations on the ground that the Commissioner exceeded his authority under the statute by promulgating an order requiring labels, advertisements, and other printed matter relating to prescription drugs to designate the established name of the particular drug involved every time its trade name is used anywhere in such material.

The District Court, on cross motions for summary judgment, granted the declaratory and injunctive relief sought, finding that the statute did not sweep so broadly as to permit the Commissioner's "every time" interpretation. The Court of Appeals for the Third Circuit reversed without reaching the merits of the case. It held first that under the statutory scheme provided by the Federal Food, Drug, and Cosmetic Act pre-enforcement review of these regulations was unauthorized and therefore beyond the jurisdiction of the District Court. Second, the Court of Appeals held that no "actual case or controversy" existed and, for that reason, that no relief under the Administrative Procedure Act or under the Declaratory Judgment Act was in any event available. . . .

I

The first question we consider is whether Congress by the Federal Food, Drug, and Cosmetic Act intended to forbid pre-enforcement review of this sort of regulation promulgated by the Commissioner. The question is phrased in terms of "prohibition" rather than "authorization" because a survey of our cases shows that judicial review of a final agency action by an aggrieved person will not be cut off unless there is persuasive reason to believe that such was the purpose of Congress. Early cases in which this type of judicial review was entertained have been reinforced by the enactment of the Administrative Procedure Act, which embodies the basic presumption of judicial review to one "suffering legal wrong because of agency action, or adversely affected or aggrieved by agency action within the meaning of a relevant statute," so long as no statute precludes such relief or the action is not one committed by law to agency discretion. The Administrative Procedure Act provides specifically not only for review of "agency action made reviewable by statute" but also for review of "final agency action for which there is no other adequate remedy in a court." . . .

Given this standard, we are wholly unpersuaded that the statutory scheme in the food and drug area excludes this type of action. . . .

* * * *

II

A further inquiry must, however, be made. The injunctive and declaratory judgment remedies are discretionary, and courts traditionally have been reluctant to apply them to administrative determinations unless these arise in the context of a controversy "ripe" for judicial resolution. Without undertaking to survey the intricacies of the ripeness doctrine it is fair to say that its basic rationale is to prevent the courts, through avoidance of premature adjudication, from entangling themselves in abstract disagreements over administrative policies, and also to protect the agencies from judicial interference until an administrative decision has been formalized and its effects felt in a concrete way by the challenging parties. The problem is best seen in a twofold aspect, requiring us to evaluate both the fitness of the issues for judicial decision and the hardship to the parties of withholding court consideration.

As to the former factor, we believe the issues presented are appropriate for judicial resolution at this time. First, all parties agree that the issue tendered is a purely legal one: whether the statute was properly construed by the Commissioner to require the established name of the drug to be used *every time* the proprietary name is employed. Both sides moved for summary judgment in the District Court, and no claim is made here that further administrative proceedings are contemplated. . . .

Second, the regulations in issue we find to be "final agency action" within the meaning of § 10 of the Administrative Procedure Act, 5 U.S.C. § 704, as construed in judicial decisions. An "agency action" includes any "rule," defined by the Act as "an agency statement of general or particular applicability and future effect designed to implement, interpret, or prescribe law or policy." The cases dealing with judicial review of administrative actions have interpreted the "finality" element in a pragmatic way. . . .

* * * *

This is also a case in which the impact of the regulations upon the petitioners is sufficiently direct and immediate as to render the issue appropriate for judicial review at this stage. These regulations purport to give an authoritative interpretation of a statutory provision that has a direct effect on the day-to-day business of all prescription drug companies; its promulgation puts petitioners in a dilemma that it was the very purpose of the Declaratory Judgment Act to ameliorate. As the District Court found on the basis of uncontested allegations, "Either they must comply with the every time requirement and incur the costs of changing over their promotional material and labeling or they must follow their present course and risk prosecution." The regulations are clear-cut, and were made effective immediately upon publication; as noted earlier the agency's counsel represented to the District Court that immediate compliance with their terms was expected. If petitioners wish to comply they must change all their labels, advertisements, and promotional materials; they must destroy stocks of printed matter; and they must invest heavily in new printing type and new supplies. The alternative to compliance — continued use of material which they believe in good faith meets the statutory requirements, but which clearly does not meet the regulation of the Commissioner — may be even more costly. That course would risk serious criminal and civil penalties for the unlawful distribution of "misbranded" drugs.

It is relevant at this juncture to recognize that petitioners deal in a sensitive industry, in which public confidence in their drug products is especially important. To require them to challenge these regulations only as a defense to an action brought by the Government might harm them severely and unnecessarily. Where the legal issue presented is fit for judicial resolution, and where a regulation requires an immediate and significant change in the plaintiffs' conduct of their affairs with serious penalties attached to noncompliance, access to the courts under the Administrative Procedure Act and the Declaratory Judgment Act must be permitted, absent a statutory bar or some other unusual circumstance, neither of which appears here.

The Government does not dispute the very real dilemma in which petitioners are placed by the regulation, but contends that "mere financial expense" is not a justification for pre-enforcement judicial review. It is of course true that . . . a possible financial loss is not by itself a sufficient interest to sustain a judicial challenge to governmental action. But there is no question in the present case that petitioners have sufficient standing as plaintiffs: the regulation is directed at them in particular; it requires them to make significant changes in their everyday business practices; if they fail to observe the Commissioner's rule they are quite clearly exposed to the imposition of strong sanctions. . . .

The Government further contends that the threat of criminal sanctions for noncompliance with a judicially untested regulation is unrealistic; the Solicitor General has represented that if court enforcement becomes necessary, "the Department of Justice will proceed only civilly for an injunction . . . or by condemnation." We cannot accept this argument as a sufficient answer to petitioners' petition. This action at its inception was properly brought and this subsequent representation of the Department of Justice should not suffice to defeat it.

Finally, the Government urges that to permit resort to the courts in this type of case may delay or impede effective enforcement of the Act. We fully recognize the important public interest served by assuring prompt and unimpeded administration of the Pure Food, Drug, and Cosmetic Act, but we do not find the Government's argument convincing. First, in this particular case, a pre-enforcement challenge by nearly all prescription drug manufacturers is calculated to speed enforcement. If the Government prevails, a large part of the industry is bound by the decree; if the Government loses, it can more quickly revise its regulation.

The Government contends, however, that if the Court allows this consolidated suit, then nothing will prevent a multiplicity of suits in various jurisdictions challenging other regulations. The short answer to this contention is that the courts are well equipped to deal with such eventualities.

* * * *

Reversed and remanded.

JUSTICE BRENNAN took no part in the consideration or decision of this case.

[Justice Fortas's dissenting opinion, joined by Chief Justice Warren and Justice Clark, and Justice Clark's dissenting opinion, omitted.]

DISCUSSION AND QUESTIONS

Abbott Labs holds that the controversy is ripe for review even though the challenged law has not yet been enforced against the plaintiffs. What if the Court had refused to consider the case? Is the risk of significant criminal and civil penalties for noncompliance with the challenged law sufficient hardship, in your opinion, to warrant a finding of ripeness at this time? In this light, consider Problem 2-5.

PROBLEM 2-5

Is One Person's Hardship Another's Hardship?

In federal court, a cosmetic manufacturer seeks declaratory relief to invalidate a Food and Drug Administration ("FDA") law that provides FDA open access to all manufacturing processes with respect to color additives. If denied access, the FDA can suspend sale certifications. The governing law also provides that the aggrieved party may challenge any suspension through the administrative channels and then seek federal court review of the administrative denial. The cosmetic manufacturer sues prior to FDA enforcement.

Evaluate whether this matter is ripe for federal court review.

The determination of what constitutes sufficient hardship to justify a finding of ripeness may be tricky. You should focus on the choice the plaintiffs may be faced with if they wait to sue. Must they violate a law and risk suffering sanctions? Must they forgo exercising a right and risk criminal exposure or job loss? Must they refrain from a chosen activity or risk losing their jobs?[15] If the federal judiciary denies court access based on failure to satisfy ripeness, ask if the plaintiffs suffer minimal hardship and maintain routes of review to federal resolution or adequate state court review. Consider the next related hurdle — mootness.

4. *Mootness*

The mootness doctrine, like ripeness, hinges on timing. Instead of focusing on whether a case is premature, mootness focuses on whether a justiciable issue has become stale. It arises, for example, when a dispositive law or fact changes while litigation is pending. For example, a case may become factually moot due to the passage of time before the Court's resolution. *Camreta v. Greene*, 563 U.S. ____, 131 S. Ct. 2020 (2011) (finding mootness where a child grew up and moved across the country such that she would never again be subject to

15. *See, e.g., Adler v. Board of Educ.*, 342 U.S. 485 (1952); *Steffel v. Thompson*, 415 U.S. 452 (1974). *But see Int'l Longshoremen's & Warehousemen's Union Local 37 v. Boyd*, 347 U.S. 222 (1954).

Oregon's allegedly unconstitutional, in-school interviewing practices of sexual abuse victims). A case is not moot, however, even if the claim possesses a low probability of success on the merits or is more likely to be ignored than executed should plaintiff succeed. *Chafin v. Chafin*, 133 S. Ct. 1017 (2013) (reversing a mootness ruling in an international child custody fight in which a United Kingdom citizen filed a federal district court action in Alabama seeking the return of her daughter to Scotland per a multilateral treaty). Despite weak prospects on the merits and the remedy, a claim is not moot if plaintiff's injury is adequately "concrete." *Id.*

As you have learned, standing must exist at the initiation of a federal lawsuit and must remain throughout the course of the litigation. *See Turner v. Rogers*, 564 U.S. ____, 131 S. Ct. 2507 (2011) (finding contemnor's challenge "capable of repetition yet evading review" because his twelve-month sentence for repeated failure to pay child support was too short in duration to be fully litigated through the state courts to arrive at the Court prior to its "expiration" and because more than a "reasonable expectation" existed that he would again be "subjected to the same action"). If justiciability wanes, a mootness issue arises. For example, if after the commencement of federal litigation the legislature repeals an underlying substantive law upon which the decision would turn, the federal court should dismiss the case on mootness grounds *unless* an exception to the mootness doctrine applies.

Like standing, a federal court may address mootness at any moment during the litigation. Events possibly triggering mootness include settlement of the lawsuit, death of a criminal defendant, death of a civil plaintiff where law precludes the suit's survival, repeal or expiration of the challenged law, and alteration of dispositive facts such as completion of a time-limited event upon which a challenge wholly hinges. *See* ERWIN CHEMERINSKY, FEDERAL JURISDICTION 131-33 (6th ed. 2012).

The thrust of mootness is that, if an event occurs causing a resolution of the dispute, then the case or controversy disappears. The matter no longer presents a justiciable controversy, and it would be a waste of time for a federal court to expend resources. Does this sound constitutionally or prudentially rooted? According to the Supreme Court, mootness stems from Article III's prohibition on advisory opinions. *See, e.g., Hall v. Beals*, 396 U.S. 45, 48 (1969). *But see Honing v. Doe*, 484 U.S. 305, 330 (1988) (Rehnquist, C.J., concurring) (contending that mootness determinations rely more on prudential than constitutional grounds). Calling for the Court to reconsider the constitutional classification in favor of a prudential lens is Professor Evan T. Lee in *Deconstitutionalizing Justiciability: The Example of Mootness*, 105 HARV. L. REV. 603, 608 (1992).

Under the Court's current construction, if events cause a mootness problem, then the case is beyond the court's judicial power. Accordingly, enforcing the mootness doctrine serves separation-of-powers interests by keeping tight reins on the scope of federal judicial power. The federal judiciary, applying the mootness doctrine, may be able to focus its resources on resolving actual live disputes in which the result truly matters to the instant litigants, rather than expending time and effort conducting unnecessary interpretations. Although mootness may arise late in the litigation process and there may be sunk costs, mootness principles dictate that federal courts dismiss such cases that have morphed into the realm of hypothetical or academic issues. The mootness doctrine thus helps to maintain the proper role of the federal judiciary in our constitutional design.

Yet the Court does not strictly apply the mootness doctrine; rather, several exceptions exist in the Court's jurisprudence. For instance, there are federal cases in which the dispute appears moot because of resolution of the main injury, yet potential "*collateral*" consequences may constitute sufficient injury to enable the litigant's case to survive a mootness challenge. *See, e.g., Carafas v. LaVallee*, 391 U.S. 234, 237-38 (1968) (permitting a habeas corpus petition to remain in federal court, despite the criminal defendant's unconditional release from custody, because of potential collateral injuries from the conviction on defendant's ability to obtain employment, vote, be elected to a union office, and serve on a jury). In a civil lawsuit, examine whether injunctive relief is necessary to redress plaintiff's injury.

Another exception involves cases where a wrong is "*capable of repetition yet evading review.*" This exception arises when the wrong's relatively short duration frustrates plaintiff's ability to challenge the act within the confines of a lawsuit's lifespan. Focus on whether the context of the injury is inherently of limited duration such as an election cycle, a time-sensitive medical procedure, or a finite experience like school. The context makes it unworkable for the plaintiff to sustain a challenge through the course of litigation. If the federal court believes that the wrong is likely to recur, it may maintain jurisdiction despite the evident mootness. Some precedent indicates that the injury must be likely to recur to the particular plaintiff, although the Supreme Court does not always raise the issue to the individual level of specificity. *Compare Murphy v. Hunt*, 455 U.S. 478 (1982) (applying mootness because no possibility of recurrence of arrest and denial of bond to the same defendant), *with Roe v. Wade*, 410 U.S. 113 (1973) (resolving the merits of plaintiff's constitutional challenge to a state law prohibiting abortion, despite plaintiff's pregnancy completion prior to the Court's resolution).

The remaining exception, "*voluntary cessation*," occurs when defendant chooses to cease the wrongful conduct but is free to resume at any time. In other words, defendant commits an alleged wrong and then, before plaintiff has an opportunity to receive federal court resolution, defendant complies with the law. For example, look for defendant, during the pendency of federal litigation, to change its policy or cease violative behavior. Ask whether "defendant is free to return to his old ways." *United States v. W.T. Grant Co.*, 345 U.S. 629, 632 (1953). The Court will not find mootness—that is, defendant's voluntary cessation will not destroy jurisdiction—*unless* defendant satisfies the high burden of showing "no reasonable expectation" of repeating the wrong. *Id.* at 633. Federal courts have broad discretion to determine what circumstances constitute sufficient likelihood of future injury or inherently shortened injury time span. *See, e.g., Friends of the Earth, Inc. v. Laidlaw Envtl. Servs., Inc.*, 528 U.S. 167 (2000) (declining to dismiss where defendant voluntary conformed behavior during the litigation but failed to carry the "formidable burden of showing that it is absolutely clear the allegedly wrongful behavior could not reasonably be expected to recur"). Of the three exceptions, the exception of wrongs capable of repetition yet evading review arises with sufficient frequency and presents significant complexity that it warrants our focused attention.

Examine how the Supreme Court interprets the mootness doctrine and this slippery exception in the following case.

DEFUNIS v. ODEGAARD

416 U.S. 312 (1974)

PER CURIAM.

In 1971 the petitioner Marco DeFunis, Jr., applied for admission as a first-year student at the University of Washington Law School, a state-operated institution. The size of the incoming first-year class was to be limited to 150 persons, and the Law School received some 1,600 applications for these 150 places. DeFunis was eventually notified that he had been denied admission. He thereupon commenced this suit in a Washington trial court, contending that the procedures and criteria employed by the Law School Admissions Committee invidiously discriminated against him on account of his race in violation of the Equal Protection Clause of the Fourteenth Amendment to the United States Constitution.

DeFunis brought the suit on behalf of himself alone, and not as the representative of any class, against the various respondents, who are officers, faculty members, and members of the Board of Regents of the University of Washington. He asked the trial court to issue a mandatory injunction commanding the respondents to admit him as a member of the first-year class entering in September 1971, on the ground that the Law School admissions policy had resulted in the unconstitutional denial of his application for admission. The trial court agreed with his claim and granted the requested relief. DeFunis was, accordingly, admitted to the Law School and began his legal studies there in the fall of 1971. On appeal, the Washington Supreme Court reversed the judgment of the trial court and held that the Law School admissions policy did not violate the Constitution. By this time DeFunis was in his second year at the Law School.

He then petitioned this Court for a writ of certiorari, and Mr. Justice Douglas, as Circuit Justice, stayed the judgment of the Washington Supreme Court pending the "final disposition of the case by this Court." By virtue of this stay, DeFunis has remained in law school, and was in the first term of his third and final year when this Court first considered his certiorari petition in the fall of 1973. Because of our concern that DeFunis' third-year standing in the Law School might have rendered this case moot, we requested the parties to brief the question of mootness before we acted on the petition. In response, both sides contended that the case was not moot. The respondents indicated that, if the decision of the Washington Supreme Court were permitted to stand, the petitioner could complete the term for which he was then enrolled but would have to apply to the faculty for permission to continue in the school before he could register for another term.[16]

We granted the petition for certiorari on November 19, 1973. The case was in due course orally argued on February 26, 1974.

In response to questions raised from the bench during the oral argument, counsel for the petitioner has informed the Court that DeFunis has now registered "for his final quarter in law school." Counsel for the respondents have made clear that the Law School will not in any way seek to abrogate this registration. In light of DeFunis' recent registration for the last quarter of his final law school year, and the Law School's assurance that his registration is fully

16. [Footnote 2 in Court's opinion.] By contrast, in their response to the petition for certiorari, the respondents had stated that DeFunis "will complete his third year [of law school] and be awarded his J.D. degree at the end of the 1973-74 academic year regardless of the outcome of this appeal."

effective, the insistent question again arises whether this case is not moot, and to that question we now turn.

The starting point for analysis is the familiar proposition that "federal courts are without power to decide questions that cannot affect the rights of litigants in the case before them." The inability of the federal judiciary "to review moot cases derives from the requirement of Art. III of the Constitution under which the exercise of judicial power depends upon the existence of a case or controversy." Although as a matter of Washington state law it appears that this case would be saved from mootness by "the great public interest in the continuing issues raised by this appeal," the fact remains that under Art. III "even in cases arising in the state courts, the question of mootness is a federal one which a federal court must resolve before it assumes jurisdiction."

The respondents have represented that, without regard to the ultimate resolution of the issues in this case, DeFunis will remain a student in the Law School for the duration of any term in which he has already enrolled. Since he has now registered for his final term, it is evident that he will be given an opportunity to complete all academic and other requirements for graduation, and, if he does so, will receive his diploma regardless of any decision this Court might reach on the merits of this case. In short, all parties agree that DeFunis is now entitled to complete his legal studies at the University of Washington and to receive his degree from that institution. A determination by this Court of the legal issues tendered by the parties is no longer necessary to compel that result, and could not serve to prevent it. DeFunis did not cast his suit as a class action, and the only remedy he requested was an injunction commanding his admission to the Law School. He was not only accorded that remedy, but he now has also been irrevocably admitted to the final term of the final year of the Law School course. The controversy between the parties has thus clearly ceased to be "definite and concrete" and no longer "touch[es] the legal relations of parties having adverse legal interests."

It matters not that these circumstances partially stem from a policy decision on the part of the respondent Law School authorities. The respondents, through their counsel, the Attorney General of the State, have professionally represented that in no event will the status of DeFunis now be affected by any view this Court might express on the merits of this controversy. And it has been the settled practice of the Court, in contexts no less significant, fully to accept representations such as these as parameters for decision.

There is a line of decisions in this Court standing for the proposition that the "voluntary cessation of allegedly illegal conduct does not deprive the tribunal of power to hear and determine the case, *i.e.*, does not make the case moot." These decisions and the doctrine they reflect would be quite relevant if the question of mootness here had arisen by reason of a unilateral change in the *admissions procedures* of the Law School. For it was the admissions procedures that were the target of this litigation, and a voluntary cessation of the admissions practices complained of could make this case moot only if it could be said with assurance "that 'there is no reasonable expectation that the wrong will be repeated.'" Otherwise, "the defendant is free to return to his old ways," and this fact would be enough to prevent mootness because of the "public interest in having the legality of the practices settled." But mootness in the present case depends not at all upon a "voluntary cessation" of the admissions practices that were the subject of this litigation. It depends, instead, upon the simple fact that DeFunis is now in the final quarter of the final year of his course of study, and the settled and unchallenged policy of the Law School to permit him to complete the term for which he is now enrolled.

It might also be suggested that this case presents a question that is "capable of repetition, yet evading review," and is thus amenable to federal adjudication even though it might otherwise be considered moot. But DeFunis will never again be required to run the gantlet of the Law School's admission process, and so the question is certainly not "capable of repetition" so far as he is concerned. Moreover, just because this particular case did not reach the Court until the eve of the petitioner's graduation from law school, it hardly follows that the issue he raises will in the future evade review. If the admissions procedures of the Law School remain unchanged, there is no reason to suppose that a subsequent case attacking those procedures will not come with relative speed to this Court, now that the Supreme Court of Washington has spoken. This case, therefore, in no way presents the exceptional situation in which the *Southern Pacific Terminal* doctrine might permit a departure from "the usual rule in federal cases . . . that an actual controversy must exist at stages of appellate or certiorari review, and not simply at the date the action is initiated."

Because the petitioner will complete his law school studies at the end of the term for which he has now registered regardless of any decision this Court might reach on the merits of this litigation, we conclude that the Court cannot, consistently with the limitations of Art. III of the Constitution, consider the substantive constitutional issues tendered by the parties. Accordingly, the judgment of the Supreme Court of Washington is vacated, and the cause is remanded for such proceedings as by that court may be deemed appropriate.

It is so ordered.

[Justice Douglas's dissenting opinion omitted.]

JUSTICE BRENNAN, with whom JUSTICE DOUGLAS, JUSTICE WHITE, and JUSTICE MARSHALL concur, dissenting.

I respectfully dissent. Many weeks of the school term remain, and petitioner may not receive his degree despite respondents' assurances that petitioner will be allowed to complete this term's schooling regardless of our decision. Any number of unexpected events — illness, economic necessity, even academic failure — might prevent his graduation at the end of the term. Were that misfortune to befall, and were petitioner required to register for yet another term, the prospect that he would again face the hurdle of the admissions policy is real, not fanciful; for respondents warn that "Mr. DeFunis would have to take some appropriate action to request continued admission for the remainder of his law school education, and *some discretionary action by the University on such request would have to be taken.*" Thus, respondents' assurances have not dissipated the possibility that petitioner might once again have to run the gantlet of the University's allegedly unlawful admissions policy. The Court therefore proceeds on an erroneous premise in resting its mootness holding on a supposed inability to render any judgment that may affect one way or the other petitioner's completion of his law studies. For surely if we were to reverse the Washington Supreme Court, we could insure that, if for some reason petitioner did not graduate this spring, he would be entitled to re-enrollment at a later time on the same basis as others who have not faced the hurdle of the University's allegedly unlawful admissions policy.

In these circumstances, and because the University's position implies no concession that its admissions policy is unlawful, this controversy falls squarely within the Court's long line of decisions holding that the "mere voluntary cessation of allegedly illegal conduct does not moot a case." Since respondents' voluntary representation to this Court is only that they will permit petitioner to complete this term's studies, respondents have not borne the "heavy burden," of demonstrating that there was not even a "mere possibility" that petitioner would once again be subject to the challenged admissions policy. On the contrary, respondents have positioned themselves so as to be "free to return to [their] old ways."

I can thus find no justification for the Court's straining to rid itself of this dispute. While we must be vigilant to require that litigants maintain a personal stake in the outcome of a controversy to assure that "the questions will be framed with the necessary specificity, that the issues will be contested with the necessary adverseness and that the litigation will be pursued with the necessary vigor to assure that the constitutional challenge will be made in a form traditionally thought to be capable of judicial resolution," *Flast v. Cohen,* there is no want of an adversary contest in this case. Indeed, the Court concedes that, if petitioner has lost his stake in this controversy, he did so only when he registered for the spring term. But petitioner took that action only after the case had been fully litigated in the state courts, briefs had been filed in this Court, and oral argument had been heard. The case is thus ripe for decision on a fully developed factual record with sharply defined and fully canvassed legal issues.

Moreover, in endeavoring to dispose of this case as moot, the Court clearly disserves the public interest. The constitutional issues which are avoided today concern vast numbers of people, organizations, and colleges and universities, as evidenced by the filing of twenty-six *amicus curiae* briefs. Few constitutional questions in recent history have stirred as much debate, and they will not disappear. They must inevitably return to the federal courts and ultimately again to this Court. Because avoidance of repetitious litigation serves the public interest, that inevitability counsels against mootness determinations, as here, not compelled by the record. Although the Court should, of course, avoid unnecessary decisions of constitutional questions, we should not transform principles of avoidance of constitutional decisions into devices for side-stepping resolution of difficult cases.

On what appears in this case, I would find that there is an extant controversy and decide the merits of the very important constitutional questions presented.

DISCUSSION AND QUESTIONS

The Supreme Court decides not to reach the merits of DeFunis's constitutional challenge. Is this determination a matter of constitutional mandate? The Court concludes:

> Because the petitioner will complete his law school studies at the end of the term for which he has now registered regardless of any decision this Court might reach on the merits of this litigation, we conclude that the Court cannot, consistently with the limitations of Art. III of the Constitution, consider the substantive constitutional issues tendered by the parties.

Are you convinced? In an omitted footnote immediately after the above quotation, footnote 5 in the original opinion, the Court expounded:

> It is suggested in dissent that "any number of unexpected events—illness, economic necessity, even academic failure—might prevent his graduation at the end of the term." "But such speculative contingencies afford no basis for our passing on the substantive issues [the petitioner] would have us decide," in the absence of "evidence that this is a prospect of 'immediacy and reality.'"

Justice Brennan, along with three other justices, did not view such unexpected events as pure speculation but rather reasoned that DeFunis might again face injury. Should the Court have found that DeFunis met one of the exceptions to mootness—capable of repetition or voluntary cessation?

Does the significance of the asserted underlying right bear on the determination? Justice Brennan's dissent acknowledges "the Court should, of course, avoid unnecessary decisions of constitutional questions," but maintains that the Court "should not transform principles of avoidance of constitutional decisions into devices for side-stepping resolution of difficult cases." Is Justice Brennan's characterization of the majority's reasoning a fair interpretation? Consider whether the Court manipulates the mootness boundaries in order to avoid a thorny substantive issue. Further, is Justice Brennan finessing the mootness boundaries to reach a decision on the merits that he favors? Evaluate, in contrast, whether DeFunis presented an actual controversy that would remain alive through the completion of federal litigation. Should the inherent time-limited nature of his status help or hurt his chances for federal resolution?

Test your knowledge and explore whether the following problem presents a stronger or weaker case of a live justiciable controversy than *DeFunis.*

PROBLEM 2-6

"It Ain't Over 'til It's Over"—But When Is It Over?

The police respond to a phone call complaint regarding the volume of noise from Apartment 12B. Catherine answers the door and upon seeing it was the police, she instinctively walks into the hallway and closes the apartment door behind her. The police believe this raises reasonable suspicion, so they search Catherine's person, find remnants and paraphernalia of methamphetamine, and seize the drug evidence.

In her Kentucky trial court criminal proceeding, Catherine files an unsuccessful pretrial motion to suppress the evidence, pleads guilty, and preserves her right to appeal. She asserts that the state's search and seizure violates her rights under the Fourth Amendment of the United States Constitution. The Kentucky court convicts Catherine of possession of narcotics. Proceeding in the timeliest fashion feasible, she seeks and loses all state appellate review, but the United States Supreme Court grants certiorari to consider her Fourth Amendment challenge. Meanwhile as a result of the state's having denied bail pending appeal, Catherine has already served the entirety of her six-month sentence for the instant conviction.

At oral argument before the Supreme Court, an associate justice, who rarely speaks at argument, asked: "*Why doesn't the Court have an obligation to dismiss this case for lack of jurisdiction?*" Catherine's *pro bono* counsel responded, "If Catherine were arrested in the future, her conviction might carry a higher penalty due to the presence of this wrongful conviction on her record." Accordingly, Catherine's counsel insisted that Catherine's civil rights still remained at issue. The state's lawyer retorted: "Justices, 'if' . . . 'might'—sounds like conjecture, hypotheses, and advice are what the instant appeal seeks; the Court thus must vacate the lower court decision and remand for dismissal of the action as Catherine has already served the entirety of the sentence." How would you resolve the issue of jurisdiction?

EXPLORING DOCTRINE

Mootness — Now You See It; Now You Don't

Although mootness is an Article III command according to the Supreme Court, it has at least three exceptions for cases where (i) collateral injuries exist; (ii) a wrong is capable of repetition yet evading review; and (iii) voluntary cessation of an illegal behavior occurs where the actor is free to resume at any juncture. What policies support these inroads? Does a prudential approach make more sense? Should the Court revisit the necessity of both the mootness doctrine and the prohibition on advisory opinions? Is maintenance of a flexible mootness doctrine sufficient?

5. *Political Question*

With the political question doctrine, we enter a strange terrain in which the federal court deems that a case raises a political question such that dismissal is proper even though the litigant satisfies standing and the claim is otherwise justiciable. As with the abstention doctrines of Chapter 9, the federal court determines that it should refrain from deciding the justiciable controversy because of the inevitable separation-of-powers tension and other judicial administration considerations. The political question doctrine illustrates the tension within the judicial branch between the instinct and wisdom of judicial restraint—thus dismissing political question cases—and the potential abdication of federal judicial obligation—resolving the justiciable claim, protecting the Constitution, and providing a remedy where a wrong exists.

What are political question cases? Of course, it depends. It is a matter of interpretation. Be sure not to equate political question cases with any case that is political. For determining which matters raise a political question, there are apparent judicial guides, yet this arena remains confusing and complex. In *Baker v. Carr*, 369 U.S. 186 (1962), the Supreme Court addressed whether an equal protection challenge to the apportionment of Tennessee state legislative districts raised a nonjusticiable political question. The Supreme Court declined to find the presence of political question but provided six factors—any one of which may call for application of the doctrine:

1. "textually demonstrable constitutional commitment of the issue to a coordinate political department";
2. "lack of judicially discoverable and manageable standards for resolving it";

3. "impossibility of deciding without an initial policy determination of a kind clearly for nonjudicial discretion";
4. "impossibility of a court's undertaking independent resolution without expressing lack of respect due coordinate branches of government";
5. "unusual need for unquestioning adherence to a political decision already made"; and
6. "potentiality of embarrassment from multifarious pronouncements by various departments on one question."

Although federal courts routinely recite these factors, uttering them may do little to assist you in knowing a political question when you see it. According to Professor Wechsler, the political question doctrine only

> defensibly impl[ies] that the courts are called upon to judge whether the Constitution has committed to another agency of government the autonomous determination of the issue raised, a finding that itself requires an interpretation. . . . [T]he only proper judgment that may lead to an abstention from decision is that the Constitution has committed the determination of the issue to another agency of government than the courts.[17]

Yet evidence of constitutional commitment of an issue to a particular branch may be less than clear. Accordingly, reviewing instances in which the Court has found the doctrine applicable and inapplicable may be our best guide.

The doctrinal emphasis returns us to the proper role of federal courts with special regard to boundaries that the Constitution creates by arguably reserving the resolution of the issue in another branch of government. Still it is the federal judiciary's role to interpret whether the Constitution so commits the decision to a coordinate branch. As you explore the doctrine's potential application, consider whether the political question doctrine is prudential or constitutional. This could become critical in the event that there were a real constitutional crisis between the executive and legislative branches. A constitutional basis for the political question doctrine would presumably preclude federal court intervention in the dispute, while a prudential basis would permit the federal courts to get involved under exceptional circumstances. Note the doctrine's grounding in judicial administrative function and separation-of-powers (but *not* federalism) concerns.

Explore the Supreme Court's consideration of the political question doctrine in the following case.

NIXON v. UNITED STATES

506 U.S. 224 (1993)

CHIEF JUSTICE REHNQUIST delivered the opinion of the Court.

Petitioner Walter L. Nixon, Jr., asks this Court to decide whether Senate Rule XI, which allows a committee of Senators to hear evidence against an individual who has been impeached and to report that evidence to the full Senate, violates the Impeachment Trial Clause, Art. I, § 3, cl. 6. That Clause provides that the

17. FALLON ET AL., HART & WECHSLER'S THE FEDERAL COURTS, *supra*, at 232 (quoting WECHSLER, PRINCIPLES, POLITICS AND FUNDAMENTAL LAW 11-14 (1961)) (first bracket added).

"Senate shall have the sole Power to try all Impeachments." But before we reach the merits of such a claim, we must decide whether it is "justiciable," that is, whether it is a claim that may be resolved by the courts. We conclude that it is not.

Nixon, a former Chief Judge of the United States District Court for the Southern District of Mississippi, was convicted by a jury of two counts of making false statements before a federal grand jury and sentenced to prison. The grand jury investigation stemmed from reports that Nixon had accepted a gratuity from a Mississippi businessman in exchange for asking a local district attorney to halt the prosecution of the businessman's son. Because Nixon refused to resign from his office as a United States District Judge, he continued to collect his judicial salary while serving out his prison sentence.

On May 10, 1989, the House of Representatives adopted three articles of impeachment for high crimes and misdemeanors. The first two articles charged Nixon with giving false testimony before the grand jury and the third article charged him with bringing disrepute on the Federal Judiciary.

After the House presented the articles to the Senate, the Senate voted to invoke its own Impeachment Rule XI, under which the presiding officer appoints a committee of Senators to "receive evidence and take testimony."[18] The Senate committee held four days of hearings, during which 10 witnesses, including Nixon, testified. Pursuant to Rule XI, the committee presented the full Senate with a complete transcript of the proceeding and a Report stating the uncontested facts and summarizing the evidence on the contested facts. Nixon and the House impeachment managers submitted extensive final briefs to the full Senate and delivered arguments from the Senate floor during the three hours set aside for oral argument in front of that body. Nixon himself gave a personal appeal, and several Senators posed questions directly to both parties. The Senate voted by more than the constitutionally required two-thirds majority to convict Nixon on the first two articles. The presiding officer then entered judgment removing Nixon from his office as United States District Judge.

Nixon thereafter commenced the present suit, arguing that Senate Rule XI violates the constitutional grant of authority to the Senate to "try" all impeachments because it prohibits the whole Senate from taking part in the evidentiary hearings. Nixon sought a declaratory judgment that his impeachment conviction was void and that his judicial salary and privileges should be reinstated. The District Court held that his claim was nonjusticiable, and the Court of Appeals for the District of Columbia Circuit agreed. We granted certiorari.

A controversy is nonjusticiable — *i.e.*, involves a political question — where there is "a textually demonstrable constitutional commitment of the issue to

18. [Footnote 1 in Court's opinion.] Specifically, Rule XI provides:

> In the trial of any impeachment the Presiding Officer of the Senate, if the Senate so orders, shall appoint a committee of Senators to receive evidence and take testimony. . . .
>
> Unless otherwise ordered by the Senate, the rules of procedure and practice in the Senate when sitting on impeachment trials shall govern the procedure and practice of the committee so appointed. The committee so appointed shall report to the Senate in writing a certified copy of the transcript of the proceedings and testimony had and given before such committee, and such report shall be received by the Senate and the evidence so received and the testimony so taken shall be considered to all intents and purposes, subject to the right of the Senate to determine competency, relevancy, and materiality, as having been received and taken before the Senate, but nothing herein shall prevent the Senate from sending for any witness and hearing his testimony in open Senate, or by order of the Senate having the entire trial in open Senate.

a coordinate political department; or a lack of judicially discoverable and manageable standards for resolving it. . . ." *Baker v. Carr*, 369 U.S. 186, 217 (1962). But the courts must, in the first instance, interpret the text in question and determine whether and to what extent the issue is textually committed. See *Powell v. McCormack*, 395 U.S. 486, 519 (1969). As the discussion that follows makes clear, the concept of a textual commitment to a coordinate political department is not completely separate from the concept of a lack of judicially discoverable and manageable standards for resolving it; the lack of judicially manageable standards may strengthen the conclusion that there is a textually demonstrable commitment to a coordinate branch.

In this case, we must examine Art. I, § 3, cl. 6, to determine the scope of authority conferred upon the Senate by the Framers regarding impeachment. It provides:

> The Senate shall have the sole Power to try all Impeachments. When sitting for that Purpose, they shall be on Oath or Affirmation. When the President of the United States is tried, the Chief Justice shall preside: And no Person shall be convicted without the Concurrence of two thirds of the Members present.

The language and structure of this Clause are revealing. The first sentence is a grant of authority to the Senate, and the word "sole" indicates that this authority is reposed in the Senate and nowhere else. The next two sentences specify requirements to which the Senate proceedings shall conform: The Senate shall be on oath or affirmation, a two-thirds vote is required to convict, and when the President is tried the Chief Justice shall preside.

Petitioner argues that the word "try" in the first sentence imposes by implication an additional requirement on the Senate in that the proceedings must be in the nature of a judicial trial. From there petitioner goes on to argue that this limitation precludes the Senate from delegating to a select committee the task of hearing the testimony of witnesses, as was done pursuant to Senate Rule XI. "'Try' means more than simply 'vote on' or 'review' or 'judge.' In 1787 and today, trying a case means hearing the evidence, not scanning a cold record." Petitioner concludes from this that courts may review whether or not the Senate "tried" him before convicting him.

There are several difficulties with this position which lead us ultimately to reject it. The word "try," both in 1787 and later, has considerably broader meanings than those to which petitioner would limit it. Older dictionaries define try as "to examine" or "to examine as a judge." In more modern usage the term has various meanings. For example, try can mean "to examine or investigate judicially," "to conduct the trial of," or "to put to the test by experiment, investigation, or trial." Petitioner submits that "try," as contained in T. Sheridan, Dictionary of the English Language (1796), means "to examine as a judge; to bring before a judicial tribunal." Based on the variety of definitions, however, we cannot say that the Framers used the word "try" as an implied limitation on the method by which the Senate might proceed in trying impeachments. "As a rule the Constitution speaks in general terms, leaving Congress to deal with subsidiary matters of detail as the public interests and changing conditions may require. . . ."

The conclusion that the use of the word "try" in the first sentence of the Impeachment Trial Clause lacks sufficient precision to afford any judicially manageable standard of review of the Senate's actions is fortified by the existence of the three very specific requirements that the Constitution does impose on the Senate when trying impeachments: The Members must be under oath, a two-thirds vote is required to convict, and the Chief Justice presides when the President is tried. These limitations are quite precise, and their nature suggests that the Framers did not intend to impose additional limitations on the form of the Senate proceedings by the use of the word "try" in the first sentence.

Petitioner devotes only two pages in his brief to negating the significance of the word "sole" in the first sentence of Clause 6. As noted above, that sentence provides that "the Senate shall have the sole Power to try all Impeachments." We think that the word "sole" is of considerable significance. Indeed, the word "sole" appears only one other time in the Constitution — with respect to the House of Representatives' "*sole* Power of Impeachment." Art. I, § 2, cl. 5 (emphasis added). The commonsense meaning of the word "sole" is that the Senate alone shall have authority to determine whether an individual should be acquitted or convicted. The dictionary definition bears this out. "Sole" is defined as "having no companion," "solitary," "being the only one," and "functioning . . . independently and without assistance or interference." If the courts may review the actions of the Senate in order to determine whether that body "tried" an impeached official, it is difficult to see how the Senate would be "functioning . . . independently and without assistance or interference."

Nixon asserts that the word "sole" has no substantive meaning. To support this contention, he argues that the word is nothing more than a mere "cosmetic edit" added by the Committee of Style after the delegates had approved the substance of the Impeachment Trial Clause. . . . Such a result is at odds with the fact that the Convention passed the Committee's version, and with the well-established rule that the plain language of the enacted text is the best indicator of intent.

Petitioner also contends that the word "sole" should not bear on the question of justiciability because Art. II, § 2, cl. 1, of the Constitution grants the President pardon authority "except in Cases of Impeachment." He argues that such a limitation on the President's pardon power would not have been necessary if the Framers thought that the Senate alone had authority to deal with such questions. But the granting of a pardon is in no sense an overturning of a judgment of conviction by some other tribunal; it is "an executive action that mitigates or sets aside *punishment* for a crime." Authority in the Senate to determine procedures for trying an impeached official, unreviewable by the courts, is therefore not at all inconsistent with authority in the President to grant a pardon to the convicted official. The exception from the President's pardon authority of cases of impeachment was a separate determination by the Framers that executive clemency should not be available in such cases.

Petitioner finally argues that even if significance be attributed to the word "sole" in the first sentence of the Clause, the authority granted is to the Senate, and this means that "the Senate — not the courts, not a lay jury, not a Senate Committee — shall try impeachments." It would be possible to read the first sentence of the Clause this way, but it is not a natural reading. Petitioner's interpretation would bring into judicial purview not merely the sort of claim made by petitioner, but other similar claims based on the conclusion that the word "Senate" has imposed by implication limitations on procedures which the Senate might adopt. Such limitations would be inconsistent with the construction of the Clause as a whole, which, as we have noted, sets out three express limitations in separate sentences.

The history and contemporary understanding of the impeachment provisions support our reading of the constitutional language. The parties do not offer evidence of a single word in the history of the Constitutional Convention or in contemporary commentary that even alludes to the possibility of judicial review in the context of the impeachment powers. This silence is quite meaningful in light of the several explicit references to the availability of judicial review as a check on the Legislature's power with respect to bills of attainder, *ex post facto* laws, and statutes. *See* The Federalist No. 78 ("Limitations . . . can be preserved in practice no other way than through the medium of the courts of justice").

The Framers labored over the question of where the impeachment power should lie. Significantly, in at least two considered scenarios the power was placed with the Federal Judiciary. Indeed, James Madison and the Committee of Detail proposed that the Supreme Court should have the power to determine impeachments. Despite these proposals, the Convention ultimately decided that the Senate would have "the sole Power to try all Impeachments." According to Alexander Hamilton, the Senate was the "most fit depositary of this important trust" because its Members are representatives of the people. The Supreme Court was not the proper body because the Framers "doubted whether the members of that tribunal would, at all times, be endowed with so eminent a portion of fortitude as would be called for in the execution of so difficult a task" or whether the Court "would possess the degree of credit and authority" to carry out its judgment if it conflicted with the accusation brought by the Legislature — the people's representative. . . .

There are two additional reasons why the Judiciary, and the Supreme Court in particular, were not chosen to have any role in impeachments. First, the Framers recognized that most likely there would be two sets of proceedings for individuals who commit impeachable offenses — the impeachment trial and a separate criminal trial. In fact, the Constitution explicitly provides for two separate proceedings. *See* Art. I, § 3, cl. 7. The Framers deliberately separated the two forums to avoid raising the specter of bias and to ensure independent judgments[.]

* * * *

Certainly judicial review of the Senate's "trial" would introduce the same risk of bias as would participation in the trial itself.

Second, judicial review would be inconsistent with the Framers' insistence that our system be one of checks and balances. In our constitutional system, impeachment was designed to be the *only* check on the Judicial Branch by the Legislature. On the topic of judicial accountability, Hamilton wrote:

> The precautions for their responsibility are comprised in the article respecting impeachments. They are liable to be impeached for mal-conduct by the house of representatives, and tried by the senate, and if convicted, may be dismissed from office and disqualified for holding any other. *This is the only provision on the point, which is consistent with the necessary independence of the judicial character, and is the only one which we find in our own constitution in respect to our own judges.*

Judicial involvement in impeachment proceedings, even if only for purposes of judicial review, is counterintuitive because it would eviscerate the "important constitutional check" placed on the Judiciary by the Framers. Nixon's argument would place final reviewing authority with respect to impeachments in the hands of the same body that the impeachment process is meant to regulate.

Nevertheless, Nixon argues that judicial review is necessary in order to place a check on the Legislature. Nixon fears that if the Senate is given unreviewable authority to interpret the Impeachment Trial Clause, there is a grave risk that the Senate will usurp judicial power. The Framers anticipated this objection and created two constitutional safeguards to keep the Senate in check. The first safeguard is that the whole of the impeachment power is divided between the two legislative bodies, with the House given the right to accuse and the Senate given the right to judge. This split of authority "avoids the inconvenience of making the same persons both accusers and judges; and guards against the danger of persecution from the prevalency of a factious spirit in either of those branches." The second safeguard is the two-thirds supermajority vote requirement. Hamilton explained that "as the concurrence of two-thirds of the senate will be requisite to a condemnation, the security to innocence, from this additional circumstance, will be as complete as itself can desire."

In addition to the textual commitment argument, we are persuaded that the lack of finality and the difficulty of fashioning relief counsel against justiciability. *See Baker v. Carr.* We agree with the Court of Appeals that opening the door of judicial review to the procedures used by the Senate in trying impeachments would "expose the political life of the country to months, or perhaps years, of chaos." This lack of finality would manifest itself most dramatically if the President were impeached. The legitimacy of any successor, and hence his effectiveness, would be impaired severely, not merely while the judicial process was running its course, but during any retrial that a differently constituted Senate might conduct if its first judgment of conviction were invalidated. Equally uncertain is the question of what relief a court may give other than simply setting aside the judgment of conviction. Could it order the reinstatement of a convicted federal judge, or order Congress to create an additional judgeship if the seat had been filled in the interim?

Petitioner finally contends that a holding of nonjusticiability cannot be reconciled with our opinion in *Powell v. McCormack.* The relevant issue in *Powell* was whether courts could review the House of Representatives' conclusion that Powell was "unqualified" to sit as a Member because he had been accused of misappropriating public funds and abusing the process of the New York courts. We stated that the question of justiciability turned on whether the Constitution committed authority to the House to judge its Members' qualifications, and if so, the extent of that commitment. Article I, § 5, provides that "Each House shall be the Judge of the Elections, Returns and Qualifications of its own Members." In turn, Art. I, § 2, specifies three requirements for membership in the House: The candidate must be at least 25 years of age, a citizen of the United States for no less than seven years, and an inhabitant of the State he is chosen to represent. We held that, in light of the three requirements specified in the Constitution, the word "qualifications" — of which the House was to be the Judge — was of a precise, limited nature. [*S*]*ee also* The Federalist No. 60 ("The qualifications of the persons who may choose or be chosen, as has been remarked upon another occasion, are defined and fixed in the constitution; and are *unalterable by the legislature*").

Our conclusion in *Powell* was based on the fixed meaning of "qualifications" set forth in Art. I, § 2. . . . The decision as to whether a Member satisfied these qualifications *was* placed with the House, but the decision as to what these qualifications consisted of was not.

In the case before us, there is no separate provision of the Constitution that could be defeated by allowing the Senate final authority to determine the meaning of the word "try" in the Impeachment Trial Clause. We agree with Nixon that courts possess power to review either legislative or executive action that transgresses identifiable textual limits. As we have made clear, "whether the action of [either the Legislative or Executive Branch] exceeds whatever authority has been committed, is itself a delicate exercise in constitutional interpretation, and is a responsibility of this Court as ultimate interpreter of the Constitution." *Baker v. Carr.* But we conclude, after exercising that delicate responsibility, that the word "try" in the Impeachment Trial Clause does not provide an identifiable textual limit on the authority which is committed to the Senate.

For the foregoing reasons, the judgment of the Court of Appeals is *Affirmed.*

JUSTICE STEVENS, concurring.

For me, the debate about the strength of the inferences to be drawn from the use of the words "sole" and "try" is far less significant than the central fact that the Framers decided to assign the impeachment power to the Legislative Branch. The disposition of the impeachment of Samuel Chase in 1805 demonstrated that the Senate is fully conscious of the profound importance of that assignment, and nothing in the subsequent history of the Senate's exercise of this extraordinary power suggests otherwise. Respect for a coordinate branch of the Government forecloses any assumption that improbable hypotheticals like those mentioned by Justice White and Justice Souter will ever occur. Accordingly, the wise policy of judicial restraint, coupled with the potential anomalies associated with a contrary view, provide a sufficient justification for my agreement with the views of The Chief Justice.

JUSTICE WHITE, with whom JUSTICE BLACKMUN joins, concurring in the judgment.

Petitioner contends that the method by which the Senate convicted him on two articles of impeachment violates Art. I, § 3, cl. 6, of the Constitution, which mandates that the Senate "try" impeachments. The Court is of the view that the Constitution forbids us even to consider his contention. I find no such prohibition and would therefore reach the merits of the claim. I concur in the judgment because the Senate fulfilled its constitutional obligation to "try" petitioner.

I

It should be said at the outset that, as a practical matter, it will likely make little difference whether the Court's or my view controls this case. This is so because the Senate has very wide discretion in specifying impeachment trial procedures and because it is extremely unlikely that the Senate would abuse its discretion and insist on a procedure that could not be deemed a trial by reasonable judges. Even taking a wholly practical approach, I would prefer not to announce an unreviewable discretion in the Senate to ignore completely the constitutional direction to "try" impeachment cases. When asked at oral argument whether that direction would be satisfied if, after a House vote to impeach, the Senate, without any procedure whatsoever, unanimously found the accused guilty of being "a bad guy," counsel for the United States answered that the Government's theory "leads me to answer that question yes." Especially in light of this advice from the Solicitor General, I would not issue an invitation to the Senate to find an excuse, in the name of other pressing business, to be dismissive of its critical role in the impeachment process.

Practicalities aside, however, since the meaning of a constitutional provision is at issue, my disagreement with the Court should be stated.

II

* * * *

Of course the issue in the political question doctrine is *not* whether the constitutional text commits exclusive responsibility for a particular governmental function to one of the political branches. There are numerous instances of this sort of textual commitment, *e.g.*, Art. I, § 8, and it is not thought that disputes implicating these provisions are non-justiciable. Rather, the issue is whether the Constitution has given one of the political branches final responsibility for interpreting the scope and nature of such a power.

* * * *

The majority finds a clear textual commitment in the Constitution's use of the word "sole" in the phrase "the Senate shall have the sole Power to try all Impeachments." Art. I, § 3, cl. 6. It attributes "considerable significance" to the fact that this term appears in only one other passage in the Constitution. *See* Art. I, § 2, cl. 5 (the House of Representatives "shall have the sole Power of Impeachment"). The Framers' sparing use of "sole" is thought to indicate that its employment in the Impeachment Trial Clause demonstrates a concern to give the Senate exclusive interpretive authority over the Clause.

In disagreeing with the Court, I note that the Solicitor General stated at oral argument that "we don't rest our submission on sole power to try." The Government was well advised in this respect. The significance of the Constitution's use of the term "sole" lies not in the infrequency with which the term appears, but in the fact that it appears exactly twice, in parallel provisions concerning impeachment. That the word "sole" is found only in the House and Senate Impeachment Clauses demonstrates that its purpose is to emphasize the distinct role of each in the impeachment process. As the majority notes, the Framers, following English practice, were very much concerned to separate the prosecutorial from the adjudicative aspects of impeachment. Giving each House "sole" power with respect to its role in impeachments effected this division of labor. While the majority is thus right to interpret the term "sole" to indicate that the Senate ought to "'function independently and without assistance or interference,'" it wrongly identifies the Judiciary, rather than the House, as the source of potential interference with which the Framers were concerned when they employed the term "sole."

* * * *

The majority's review of the historical record thus explains why the power to try impeachments properly resides with the Senate. It does not explain, however, the sweeping statement that the Judiciary was "not chosen to have any role in impeachments." Not a single word in the historical materials cited by the majority addresses judicial review of the Impeachment Trial Clause. And a glance at the arguments surrounding the Impeachment Clauses negates the majority's attempt to infer nonjusticiability from the Framers' arguments in support of the Senate's power to try impeachments.

What the relevant history mainly reveals is deep ambivalence among many of the Framers over the very institution of impeachment, which, by its nature, is not easily reconciled with our system of checks and balances. . . .

* * * *

The historical evidence reveals above all else that the Framers were deeply concerned about placing in any branch the "awful discretion, which a court of impeachments must necessarily have." Viewed against this history, the discord between the majority's position and the basic principles of checks and balances underlying the Constitution's separation of powers is clear. In essence, the majority suggests that the Framers conferred upon Congress a potential tool of legislative dominance yet at the same time rendered Congress' exercise of that power one of the very few areas of legislative authority immune from any judicial review. While the majority rejects petitioner's justiciability argument as espousing a view "inconsistent with the Framers' insistence that our system be one of checks and balances," it is the Court's finding of nonjusticiability that truly upsets the Framers' careful design. In a truly balanced system, impeachments tried by the Senate would serve as a means of controlling the largely unaccountable Judiciary, even as judicial review would ensure that the Senate adhered to a minimal set of procedural standards in conducting impeachment trials.

* * * *

III

The majority's conclusion that "try" is incapable of meaningful judicial construction is not without irony. One might think that if any class of concepts would fall within the definitional abilities of the Judiciary, it would be that class having to do with procedural justice.

* * * *

The fact that Art. III, § 2, cl. 3, specifically exempts impeachment trials from the jury requirement provides some evidence that the Framers were anxious not to have additional specific procedural requirements read into the term "try." Contemporaneous commentary further supports this view. Hamilton, for example, stressed that a trial by so large a body as the Senate (which at the time promised to boast 26 members) necessitated that the proceedings not "be tied down to . . . strict rules, either in the delineation of the offence by the prosecutors, or in the construction of it by the Judges. . . ." The Federalist No. 65. In his extensive analysis of the Impeachment Trial Clause, Justice Story offered a nearly identical analysis. . . .

* * * *

It is also noteworthy that the delegation of factfinding by judicial and quasi-judicial bodies was hardly unknown to the Framers. Jefferson, at least, was aware that the House of Lords sometimes delegated factfinding in impeachment trials to committees and recommended use of the same to the Senate. . . .

In short, textual and historical evidence reveals that the Impeachment Trial Clause was not meant to bind the hands of the Senate beyond establishing a set of minimal procedures. Without identifying the exact contours of these procedures, it is sufficient to say that the Senate's use of a fact-finding committee under Rule XI is entirely compatible with the Constitution's command that the Senate "try all impeachments." Petitioner's challenge to his conviction must therefore fail.

IV

Petitioner has not asked the Court to conduct his impeachment trial; he has asked instead that it determine whether his impeachment was tried by the Senate. The majority refuses to reach this determination out of a laudable desire to respect the authority of the Legislature. Regrettably, this concern is manifested in a manner that does needless violence to the Constitution.[19] The deference that is owed can be found in the Constitution itself, which provides the Senate ample discretion to determine how best to try impeachments.

JUSTICE SOUTER, concurring in the judgment.

I agree with the Court that this case presents a nonjusticiable political question. Because my analysis differs somewhat from the Court's, however, I concur in its judgment by this separate opinion.

As we cautioned in *Baker v. Carr*, "the 'political question' label" tends "to obscure the need for case-by-case inquiry." The need for such close examination is nevertheless clear from our precedents, which demonstrate that the functional nature of the political question doctrine requires analysis of "the precise facts and posture of the particular case," and precludes "resolution by any semantic cataloguing. . . ."

Whatever considerations feature most prominently in a particular case, the political question doctrine is "essentially a function of the separation of powers," existing to restrain courts "from inappropriate interference in the business of the other branches of Government," and deriving in large part from prudential concerns about the respect we owe the political departments. Not all interference is inappropriate or disrespectful, however, and application of the doctrine ultimately turns, as Learned Hand put it, on "how importunately the occasion demands an answer."

This occasion does not demand an answer. The Impeachment Trial Clause commits to the Senate "the sole Power to try all Impeachments," subject to three procedural requirements: the Senate shall be on oath or affirmation; the Chief Justice shall preside when the President is tried; and conviction shall be upon the concurrence of two-thirds of the Members present. It seems fair to conclude that the Clause contemplates that the Senate may determine, within broad

19. [Footnote 4 in Justice White's concurring opinion.] Although our views might well produce identical results in most cases, the same objection may be raised against the prudential version of political question doctrine presented by Justice Souter. According to the prudential view, judicial determination of whether the Senate has conducted an impeachment trial would interfere unacceptably with the Senate's work and should be avoided except where necessitated by the threat of grave harm to the constitutional order. As articulated, this position is missing its premise: No explanation is offered as to why it would show disrespect or cause disruption or embarrassment to review the action of the Senate in this case as opposed to, say, the enactment of legislation under the Commerce Clause. The Constitution requires the courts to determine the validity of statutes passed by Congress when they are challenged, even though such laws are passed with the firm belief that they are constitutional. The exercise of judicial review of this kind, with all of its attendant risk of interference and disrespect, is not conditioned upon a showing in each case that without it the Republic would be at risk. Some account is therefore needed as to why prudence does not counsel against judicial review in the typical case, yet does so in this case.

In any event, the prudential view cannot achieve its stated purpose. The judgment it wishes to avoid—and the attendant disrespect and embarrassment—will inevitably be cast because the courts still will be required to distinguish cases on their merits. Justice Souter states that the Court ought not to entertain petitioner's constitutional claim because "it seems fair to conclude," that the Senate tried him. In other words, on the basis of a preliminary determination that the Senate has acted within the "broad boundaries" of the Impeachment Trial Clause, it is concluded that we must refrain from making that determination. At best, this approach offers only the illusion of deference and respect by substituting impressionistic assessment for constitutional analysis.

boundaries, such subsidiary issues as the procedures for receipt and consideration of evidence necessary to satisfy its duty to "try" impeachments. Other significant considerations confirm a conclusion that this case presents a nonjusticiable political question: the "unusual need for unquestioning adherence to a political decision already made," as well as "the potentiality of embarrassment from multifarious pronouncements by various departments on one question." As the Court observes, judicial review of an impeachment trial would under the best of circumstances entail significant disruption of government.

One can, nevertheless, envision different and unusual circumstances that might justify a more searching review of impeachment proceedings. If the Senate were to act in a manner seriously threatening the integrity of its results, convicting, say, upon a coin toss, or upon a summary determination that an officer of the United States was simply "'a bad guy,'" judicial interference might well be appropriate. In such circumstances, the Senate's action might be so far beyond the scope of its constitutional authority, and the consequent impact on the Republic so great, as to merit a judicial response despite the prudential concerns that would ordinarily counsel silence. "The political question doctrine, a tool for maintenance of governmental order, will not be so applied as to promote only disorder."

DISCUSSION AND QUESTIONS

The *Nixon* Court declined to resolve the challenge to Senate procedures used to impeach federal district court judge Walter Nixon. Are you persuaded that the Court correctly evaluated the political question doctrine? Justice White's concurrence sees "no such prohibition" and accordingly would resolve the merits and find that the Senate met its constitutional requirement to "try" Judge Nixon. Is there an intolerable tension created between the judiciary and the Senate by a review of the merits? To what extent should we consider prior cases in which the Court addressed the merits of a dispute despite undeniable tensions between the branches such as *Marbury v. Madison* and *Bush v. Gore*, 531 U.S. 98 (2000)?[20] Must the Court apply the political question doctrine rigidly? A flexible model is less predictable but allows the Court to examine the particular context and strike an appropriate balance concerning: the proper role of the judiciary within our constitutional framework, respect for other branches of federal government regarding matters specially committed to them, and interest in judicially resolving the controversy.

The Supreme Court has applied the political question doctrine and dismissed cases concerning the following: (i) republican form of government,[21] (ii) power to conduct foreign affairs,[22] (iii) impeachment trial procedures,[23] (iv) political party regulation,[24] (v) state ratification procedures for amending the

20. In dissent, Justice Breyer maintained that the Supreme Court should have refrained from resolving the presidential election dispute because the case demonstrated "the 'strangeness of the issue,' its 'intractability to principled resolution,' its 'sheer momentousness, . . . which tends to unbalance judicial judgment,' and 'the inner vulnerability, the self-doubt of an institution which is electorally irresponsible and has no earth to draw strength from.'" *Bush v. Gore*, 531 U.S. at 157 (Breyer, J., dissenting) (quoting ALEXANDER M. BICKEL, THE LEAST DANGEROUS BRANCH 184 (1962)).

21. *See Texas v. White*, 74 U.S. (7 Wall.) 700 (1869); *Luther v. Borden*, 48 U.S. 1 (1849).

22. *See, e.g., Goldwater v. Carter*, 444 U.S. 996 (1979).

23. *See Nixon v. United States*, 506 U.S. 224 (1993).

24. *See Cousins v. Wigoda*, 419 U.S. 477 (1975).

Constitution,[25] (vi) power to declare cessation of war,[26] and (vii) National Guard training and weaponry.[27] All of these examples thus represent "nonjusticiable" matters in the Court's eyes. What are the consequences of the federal court's staying its hand with respect to such issues?

There are instances in which the Supreme Court has considered the applicability of the political question doctrine but determined that the doctrine did not prevent it from considering the merits. In *Baker v. Carr*, the Court decided it could evaluate a state legislative apportionment challenge. Although Justice Frankfurther urged in dissent that the equal protection challenge to state legislative apportionment was in effect a matter concerning the "republican form of government" matter and thus nonjusticiable, the Court decided not to treat the matter as a political question and reserved the merits for another day.[28] Other instances in which the Court has declined to dismiss the case as raising the political question doctrine include: President Richard Nixon's claim of executive privilege over the Watergate tapes,[29] Indian Tribes' challenge regarding land purportedly conveyed from the Tribes to a state in violation of a treaty,[30] and exclusion of a representative-elect from taking his seat in Congress.[31] As you can see, whether an issue is constitutionally committed to another branch of the federal government requires delicate interpretation.

A recent political question controversy that the Supreme Court resolved in favor of jurisdiction raised the following issue: "Whether the 'political question doctrine' deprives a federal court of jurisdiction to enforce a federal statute that explicitly directs the Secretary of State how to record the birthplace of an American citizen on a Consular Report of Birth Abroad and on a passport." *M.B.Z. v. Clinton*, 132 S. Ct. 1421 (2012). This case raises controversial questions about congressional power to dictate how the Executive branch completes birth certificates for U.S. citizens born abroad—here the citizen was born in Jerusalem, a city that the U.S. government does not recognize as an official part of Israel. The federal statute orders the State Department to show Israel as the birthplace for citizens born in Jerusalem; the State Department officials refused to do so. The D.C. Circuit Court refused to resolve the case on the grounds of the political question doctrine. The Court interestingly requested the lawyers to argue an added substantive question: whether the federal statute unconstitutionally infringes the President's power to recognize foreign sovereigns. When President George W. Bush signed the statute into law in 2002, he issued a signing statement in which he protested the law on exactly such grounds. Should the Court reach the merits? It determined that the Court has the power in an 8-1 opinion by Chief Justice Roberts. The Court remanded the case for the lower court to consider the merits, including whether the 2002 law unconstitutionally infringes on the President's powers. Justice Breyer dissented. The Court has yet to address the effect that a presidential signing statement has on judicial interpretation of federal statutes. Stay tuned.

Before testing your understanding of the political question doctrine, remember that, despite the federal court's decision to dismiss such cases, the plaintiffs in question demonstrated standing and posed otherwise justiciable claims.

25. *See Coleman v. Miller*, 307 U.S. 433 (1939).
26. *See Commercial Trust Co. v. Miller*, 262 U.S. 51 (1923).
27. *See Gilligan v. Morgan*, 413 U.S. 1 (1973).
28. *See Reynolds v. Sims*, 377 U.S. 533 (1964).
29. *See United States v. Nixon*, 418 U.S. 683 (1974).
30. *See County of Oneida v. Oneida Indian Nation*, 470 U.S. 226 (1985).
31. *See Powell v. McCormack*, 395 U.S. 486 (1969).

We provide a basic illustration contrasting the doctrines of standing, ripeness, mootness, and political question in Figure 2-1.

FIGURE 2-1

Standing, Political Question, Ripeness, and Mootness

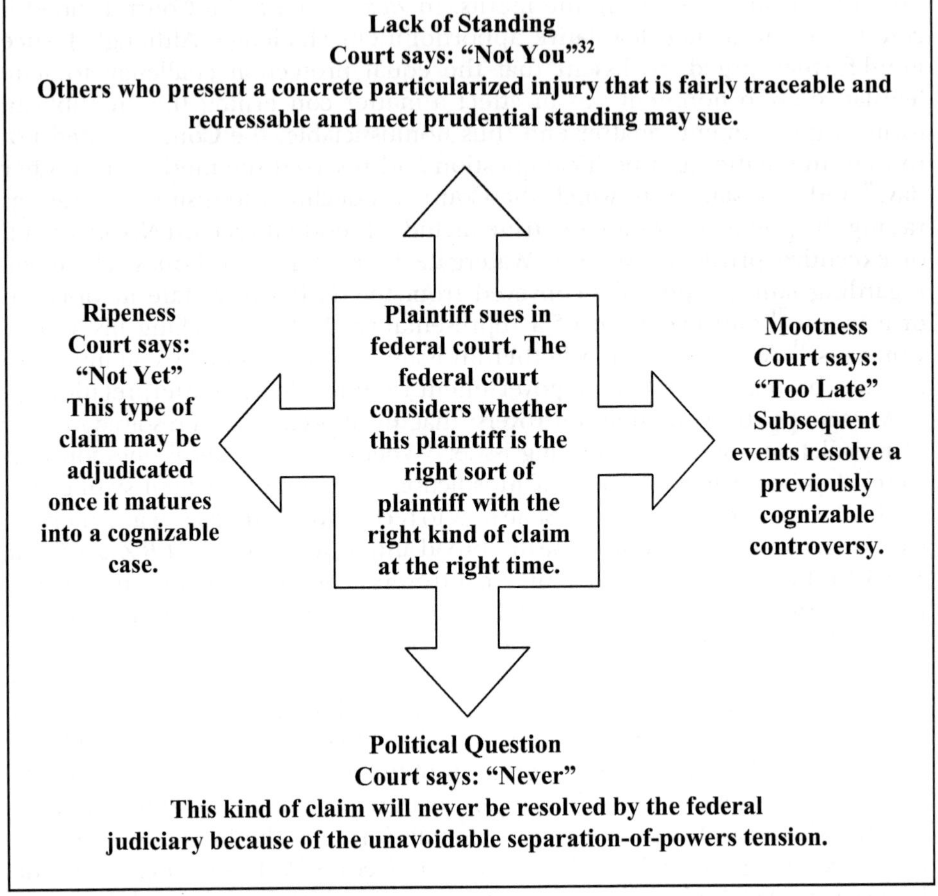

Examine the doctrines of standing, ripeness, mootness, and political question in Problem 2-7.

PROBLEM 2-7

Escalating Branch Tensions—May Each Branch Have Its Say?

A Presidential signing statement is a written or oral pronouncement issued by the President of the United States upon the signing of a bill into law. Throughout history, Presidents have utilized signing statements to provide context to their signatures when approving bills. There is an ongoing

32. The inspiration for this illustration stemmed from Peter M. Shane & Harold H. Bruff, Separation of Powers Law 98 n.1 (3d ed. 2011) ("[A] standing holding only says 'not you,' instead of 'never,' leaving the other branches to wonder whether the Court might someday find a suitable plaintiff if sufficiently tempted to do so.").

separation-of-powers controversy concerning the extensive use of Presidential signing statements, rather than vetoes, to modify the meaning of laws. In July 2006, a task force of the American Bar Association described the use of signing statements to modify the meaning of duly enacted laws as "contrary to the rule of law and our constitutional system of separation of powers." In response, Congress passes a statute, the "Signing Statement Accountability Act," purporting to confer jurisdiction to bring federal court challenges to Presidential signing statements. The statute recognizes two classes of aggrieved parties: Senators and Members of Congress, and persons arguably aggrieved under the statute. Congress is concerned that overuse of signing statements by the Executive might provide the wrong signals to those who carry out the commands of the passed legislation. In other words, if the President signs the bill into law, but notes a serious reservation about the construction of a critical provision, it could create uncertainty and under-enforcement of Congress' will.

After the Signing Statement Accountability Act is enacted, Congress passes legislation creating heightened strictures for warrants to investigate possible illegal immigrants. The President signs the bill but reserves presidential power to disregard certain requirements in the name of national security. Habib Adami, a United States citizen, claims the Executive is violating the federal warrant law. Adami fears the Executive's disregard of warrant requirements will result in the discovery of her live-in mentally and physically unstable immigrant mother who relies on the American health care system. Meanwhile, Senator Luke Valero also files a federal claim seeking declaratory and injunctive relief based upon the President's signing statement attached to the warrant law. Valero, as a Senator who voted in favor of the Signing Statement Accountability Act, wants to see its intent carried out.

Evaluate whether the federal court should decline jurisdiction based on the political question doctrine. Also, review your knowledge by addressing any concerns regarding the prohibition on advisory opinions and the doctrines of standing and ripeness.

D. SOME ADDITIONAL PROBLEMS

The following additional problems provide further opportunity to sharpen your skills regarding the justiciability topics covered in Chapter 2.

PROBLEM 2-8

Enforcing Civil Rights — Standing Broadly or Narrowly Construed: Who Suffers Injury from Discrimination?

Marlowe and Rita are both tenants of a San Francisco apartment complex. In a lawsuit filed in federal district court, they allege that RentCo, owner of the complex, engages in racially discriminatory housing practices in violation of the Civil Rights Act of 1968 (the "Act"). Neither Marlowe, who is black, nor Rita, who is white, were denied housing, but they assert that RentCo discriminates against nonwhites on the basis of race in the rental of apartments in violation of the Act. The alleged discriminatory behavior includes RentCo's making it known that it does not welcome nonwhites, manipulating the waitlist to disfavor nonwhites, delaying nonwhite applications, and using acceptance standards less favorable to nonwhites. Of the 8,200 tenants in the complex, less than 1 percent of the tenants are black. Marlowe and Rita properly exhausted the administrative procedures before seeking redress in federal court.

Marlowe and Rita assert that RentCo's unlawful discrimination has caused them to (1) lose social benefits derived from living in integrated communities; (2) miss professional opportunities and benefits that might have accrued from the integrated association; and (3) suffer embarrassment and economic damage in social and professional undertakings because of stigmatization as residents of a "white ghetto." Section 810 of the Act provides: "an aggrieved person may . . . - commence a civil action in any appropriate United States district court . . . to enforce rights granted or protected by this title." The Act further defines "aggrieved person" as "any person who claims to have been injured by a discriminatory housing practice."

Evaluate whether the federal district court should dismiss because these plaintiffs lack standing. Consider whether Marlowe and Rita possess Article III standing and whether they are within the class of persons entitled to sue under the Act. Also, are there any issues regarding the prohibition on advisory opinions, ripeness, and mootness?

PROBLEM 2-9

How Capable of Repetition Must the Wrong Be to Avoid Mootness?

Nell, a pregnant woman confined in a state prison, seeks an abortion. Nell seeks an injunction in state court; she demands that the prison transport her to an abortion clinic in a bordering state. Case precedent exists regarding the general applicability of the federal constitutional right to prison inmates. The state court judge declines to grant an injunction. After further state appellate court denials, Nell seeks federal court aid given the constitutional right at stake. Before the Supreme Court has the opportunity to resolve the conflict, Nell experiences a miscarriage through natural causes.

Is Nell's case moot? Should the Court keep the case because of the inherent short duration of pregnancies? Must it be likely that this plaintiff will suffer the same injury in the future? How do you balance the federal judicial interest in avoiding advisory opinions, while protecting constitutional rights and maintaining proper interpretation of precedents?

PROBLEM 2-10

Revisiting Problem 2-3 — We Quit; We Promise . . .

Recall David's constitutional challenge and his allegation that he continues to fear the Chicago Police Department will submit him to a life-threatening chokehold again. Before completion of the federal litigation process, the Chicago Board of Police Commissioners issues a six-month moratorium on the use of chokehold for any purpose other than in response to clear imminent deadly force. Based on continuing efforts to analyze and assess alternative police techniques, the Board has extended the moratorium indefinitely.

Evaluate mootness. Be sure to consider these mootness exceptions: (i) capable of repetition yet evading review and (ii) voluntary cessation.

PROBLEM 2-11

Settling One to Moot the Rest?

Plaintiff sues on behalf of herself and similarly situated employees under the Fair Labor Standards Act (FLSA) alleging that her employer unlawfully deducted thirty minutes as unpaid lunch breaks every day despite plaintiff's conducting work during that time. Prior to class certification, employer offered a settlement to compensate plaintiff for her individual claim. Is plaintiff's claim moot? May plaintiff maintain a collective action?

CHAPTER 3

Congressional Control of Federal Jurisdiction and Decisionmaking

This chapter explores the contours of congressional control over the federal judiciary. The following Reference Problem illustrates many of the issues we explore throughout this chapter.

A. A REFERENCE PROBLEM

In the wake of terrorist attacks against the United States, detainees are being held in a U.S. military complex outside the United States (the "Complex"). These individuals are not U.S. citizens but seek access to our court system. Those detainees deemed "enemy combatants" are being held indefinitely without trial. There is a military review tribunal to confirm their status as enemy combatants.

The U.S. Supreme Court has held that these enemy combatants have a statutory right to bring habeas corpus challenges in U.S. federal courts and that the District Court for the District of Columbia should hear such matters. Olem, a detainee, filed a habeas corpus action challenging his detention and arguing that his detention violated the Uniform Code of Military Justice and the Geneva Conventions. The Geneva Conventions provide human rights protections to prisoners of war. For instance, Common Article 3 of the Geneva Conventions requires that one be tried by a "regularly constituted court." The district court granted habeas relief, but the Court of Appeals for the D.C. Circuit reversed. The appellate court declined the government's suggestion of abstention and ruled on the merits. It held that Olem was not entitled to relief. The appellate court determined (i) the Geneva Conventions are not judicially enforceable; (ii) Supreme Court precedent precluded a separation-of-powers challenge to the military commissions' jurisdiction; and (iii) Olem's trial before the commission would violate neither the Uniform Code of Military Justice nor the Armed Forces' regulations implementing the Geneva Conventions.

Thereafter, but before the Supreme Court's ruling in Olem's case, Congress passed, and the President signed, legislation (the "Act"), which provides in pertinent part:

> No court, justice, or judge shall have jurisdiction to consider—
>
> (1) an application for a writ of habeas corpus filed by or on behalf of an alien detained by the Department of Defense at the Complex; or
>
> (2) any other action against the United States or its agents relating to any aspect of detention by the Department of Defense of an alien at the Complex, who—
>
> (A) is currently in military custody; or
>
> (B) has been determined by the United States Court of Appeals for the District of Columbia Circuit in accordance with the procedures set forth elsewhere in the Act to be properly detained as an enemy combatant.

Another provision of the Act grants "exclusive jurisdiction" in the D.C. Circuit Court "to determine the validity of any final decision of a military commission that an alien is properly designated as an enemy combatant." The provision also delimits the scope of the D.C. Court's exclusive jurisdiction to review those final decisions. In particular, the D.C. Circuit Court may only review for consistency with (i) military standards and (ii) the Constitution and federal laws to the extent they apply. The Act generally provides that the "date of enactment of the Act" shall be the "effective date."

During oral argument before the Supreme Court, Olem's attorneys argued that the Act should not apply retroactively to Olem. Further, even if the Act were applicable, they maintained that the legislation is unconstitutional under the Constitution's Suspension Clause, Article I, Section 9, Clause 2. The Suspension Clause provides that habeas corpus "shall not be suspended, unless when in Cases of Rebellion or Invasion the public Safety may require it." How should the Supreme Court resolve this case?

* * * * *

How should one approach Olem's complex challenge to the Act? For now, simply consider the following questions raised (some not so obviously) by the problem:

- Consider the congressional motivations behind the Act. Would you have advised Congress to pass this Act? Does Congress' Act leave any avenue open to federal court review? Is *some* access to federal courts important to the analysis? Is there any floor regarding the substance of any access provided?

- The removal of federal habeas jurisdiction has significant consequences given the limited nature of preexisting habeas jurisdiction and the import of the right at stake. The Suspension Clause is a powerful reminder of the Constitution's vigilant protection of the habeas corpus right. The preexisting limits on habeas jurisdiction are (i) state courts cannot hear federal habeas petitions, and (ii) federal courts do not have common-law habeas jurisdiction. (See Chapter 13.)

- Does Congress possess the power to dictate the jurisdiction of federal courts? What constitutional provisions are relevant? Are there any limits on Congress' power?
- Does the Act strip the Supreme Court of jurisdiction over Olem's habeas corpus case?
- What is the dispositive aspect of the Act that either makes it pass constitutional muster or renders it unconstitutional? Consider what revision you could make to the Act that would alter constitutional analysis.
- Should the Supreme Court endeavor to avoid the constitutional issue if possible? Could the Court avoid the issue altogether on statutory or jurisdictional grounds?
- Does the Act apply retroactively to Olem? Must Congress expressly state that the Act applies retroactively to all pending cases? Does Congress possess the power to authorize retroactive application of the Act?
- Assuming the Act applies to Olem, articulate what the potential separation-of-powers challenges to the Act might be. [Hint: Think about tension between Congress and the Judiciary and tension between the Executive and the Judiciary.] Are there other constitutional challenges worth making?
- What access should alleged enemy combatants have to our American court system? What branch of the U.S. government should have the final say on this issue?
- Would it make a difference to the Court's analysis if under the Act Olem faces criminal prosecution before a military tribunal and a possible sentence of life imprisonment, rather than merely indefinite detention as an enemy combatant?
- Would the exigencies of the national climate after a terrorist attack warrant suspension of habeas corpus review? Can the U.S. government adequately fight terrorism without suspending the writ of habeas corpus? Can a "War on Terror" justify the Act or a suspension? Are there any likely alternatives that could balance the necessity of fighting terrorism with respect for the civil liberties of all individuals, even "enemy combatants?"
- What about the geographic location of the Complex or place of capture might you want to know? Why?

Think through the issues raised by these questions. You may not be able to answer most of these questions now. Keep them in your view as you approach the complex materials that follow, and return to them for review at the conclusion of this chapter. Our hope is that through the course of this chapter you will develop a deeper understanding of this arena and have more tools in your arsenal to appreciate the intricacies of the Reference Problem.

B. CONTEXT AND BACKGROUND

Chapter 2 explored the nature of the judicial function under the Constitution. We focused on the role of courts under our constitutional framework. In particular, we examined the constitutional and prudential requirements that make a case justiciable in our federal courts.

This chapter delves further into the jurisdiction of the federal courts by examining Congress' control over it. You will discover that Congress' attempts to limit the federal judiciary's sphere of influence or dictate its decisionmaking are not always successful. In other words, there are limits to congressional power. This chapter explores those limits—and whether, in some instances, limits should ever be defined.

We will explore two broad categories of congressional control: (1) Congress' control over the jurisdiction of federal courts and (2) Congress' power over the decisionmaking of federal courts. For an exploration of congressional control of state courts and Supreme Court review of state courts, see Chapter 12.

Regarding Congress' jurisdictional authority over federal courts, we will first consider its power over Supreme Court jurisdiction and then its power over the inferior federal courts (i.e., all federal appellate and district courts below the Supreme Court). These two forms of jurisdictional control raise related but distinct concerns.

1. *Constitutional Text*

Jurisdiction of the federal judiciary must be rooted in the Constitution, although you will soon learn that the inquiry hardly ends there. Article III of the Constitution is the source from which all else flows. Section 1 provides in pertinent part:

> The judicial Power of the United States, shall be vested in one supreme Court, and in such inferior Courts as the Congress may from time to time ordain and establish.

This section is known as the "Ordain and Establish" Clause. The key portion of Section 2 of Article III states:

> The judicial Power shall extend to all Cases, in Law and Equity, arising under this Constitution, the Laws of the United States, and Treaties made, or which shall be made, under their Authority; . . . In all [such] Cases . . . , the supreme Court shall have appellate Jurisdiction, both as to Law and Fact, with such Exceptions, and under such Regulations as the Congress shall make.

The first sentence of Section 2 authorizes "arising under" jurisdiction, which we will cover in Chapter 5. The second sentence is known as the "Exceptions" Clause, which is central to our discussion of the Supreme Court's jurisdiction. Before adopting Article III, the Framers debated and struggled with the proper components, powers, and limits of a federal judiciary. Consensus emerged regarding the creation of one national Supreme Court. Article III creates the Supreme Court, although it tells us precious little about that institution. It does vest the Supreme Court with original jurisdiction (i.e., trial jurisdiction) over the matters it lists—none requiring congressional action. The Supreme Court's original jurisdiction is thus self-executory but is not exclusive.[1] Accordingly, with respect to the Supreme Court, we will focus our attention on Congress' exercise of its Article III power to regulate the appellate jurisdiction of the Supreme Court via the Exceptions Clause. As we will see, exactly what this clause empowers Congress to do is a matter of much dispute.

2. *The Framers' Debate*

During the Constitutional Convention, a deadlock about the existence and role of inferior federal courts arose. One contingent of Framers urged the adoption of a constitutional mandate for the creation of lower federal courts. Another contingent pressed a constitutional bar to the lower courts' creation, which they thought unnecessary in light of existing state court tribunals, which would be subject to Supreme Court review. The "Madisonian Compromise" resolved the deadlock by granting Congress the discretion to create lower federal courts, as evidenced by the Ordain and Establish Clause. Congress immediately exercised its discretion in the Judiciary Act of 1789 by creating the lower federal courts. But Congress has never conferred these courts with the full extent of the jurisdictional grant articulated in Article III.

Thus, from the beginning Article III of the Constitution envisioned significant congressional responsibility in creating and controlling the federal judiciary. This power was further affirmed by the Necessary and Proper Clause, U.S. CONST. art. I, § 8, which enables Congress to make any law that is necessary and proper in executing its other enumerated powers, including powers over federal courts.

3. *Interbranch Tension*

The constitutional relationship between Congress and the federal judiciary necessitates some level of interbranch tension. Some level of tension may even be a healthy component of our republican government. We are not strangers to such tension, as evidenced by the debate fueling the compromise adopted in Article III, the strife engulfing the days of *Marbury*, or the acrimony resulting in President Franklin D. Roosevelt's attempts to pack the Supreme Court with Justices friendly to the New Deal. Is there a threshold, however, beyond which rising tension threatens our constitutional equilibrium? When does one branch of government overreach in exercising its ostensible constitutional authority?

Scholars watch with caution as any governmental branch contemplates improvident steps of overreaching. An *overstep* could be a step within a branch's constitutional authority, but nevertheless a step that *should not* be taken. Regardless of any disagreement about the extent of congressional authority over the federal courts, scholars are generally united in their regard for the

1. *See United States v. California*, 297 U.S. 175 (1936) (noting nonexclusive nature of the Supreme Court's original jurisdiction in that Congress has the power to grant such jurisdiction to an inferior federal court); *Wisconsin v. Pelican Ins. Co.*, 127 U.S. 265, 300 (1888) (discussing self-executory nature of Supreme Court original jurisdiction).

wisdom of restraint.[2] In other words, academic commentators have recognized that there is an important difference between the power to take a certain action and the *wisdom* of doing so. Try to keep this distinction in mind as we consider the matters below.

Periodically throughout our history, Congress has considered bills that would strip federal courts of their power to adjudicate controversial issues. Examples include controversial topics like school prayer, abortion, busing, same-sex marriage, and the Pledge of Allegiance. Congress occasionally enacts such limits on jurisdiction, though far less frequently than it considers them. For example, Congress did so in several instances in connection with the "War on Terror" as we discuss below. When confronted with such bans, the Court tends to construe limitations narrowly to avoid addressing the serious constitutional issues that might be implicated if the bans were read as written. In other words, the Court has not definitively ruled on the limits, if any, on congressional control of federal court jurisdiction.

Our goal in this chapter is to work through the various issues that jurisdiction-stripping measures implicate. In the next several paragraphs, we raise a number of issues discussed either in Supreme Court dicta or by legal scholars that help to frame the jurisdiction-stripping debate. Many of these issues may seem foreign to you now. That should not concern you. Rather, try to get a sense of the issues at play in this area and then return to this portion of the chapter after you have studied the materials in the next section.

We begin with a rare occasion in which the Supreme Court offered some guidance on the issue. In *Martin v. Hunter's Lessee,* 14 U.S. 304 (1816), Justice Joseph Story articulated a theory of limited congressional authority over lower federal courts. Justice Story reasoned that because Article III states that the federal "judicial Power *shall* be vested" in the Supreme Court and inferior federal courts, Congress has a duty to vest the full extent of federal judicial power *somewhere* in the federal judiciary. *Id.* at 328-31. In other words, a complete strip of federal jurisdiction would be contrary to the mandate of Article III of the Constitution. *Id.*

4. *Competing Approaches to Congressional Jurisdictional Role*

Unrestrained by a need to have a case or controversy pending before them, legal scholars have contributed a number of analytical frameworks for interpretation of Congress' jurisdictional power under the Constitution. Some scholars have explored and refined Justice Story's approach and articulated various approaches, all of which restrict the ability of Congress to limit federal court jurisdiction in one respect or another.[3] More recently, Professor Akhil Amar

2. *See, e.g.*, Gerald Gunther, *Congressional Power to Curtail Federal Court Jurisdiction: An Opinionated Guide to the Ongoing Debate,* 36 STAN. L. REV. 895, 898 (1984); Henry M. Hart, Jr., *The Power of Congress to Limit the Jurisdiction of Federal Courts: An Exercise in Dialectic,* 66 HARV. L. REV. 1362, 1365 (1953).

3. *See, e.g.*, Lawrence G. Sager, *The Supreme Court 1980 Term–Foreword: Constitutional Limitations on Congress' Authority to Regulate the Jurisdiction of the Federal Courts,* 95 HARV. L. REV. 17, 71 (1981) (advancing the view that some federal forum must be available to decide federal constitutional questions); Robert N. Clinton, *A Mandatory View of Federal Court Jurisdiction: A Guided Quest for the Original Understanding of Article III,* 132 U. PA. L. REV. 741, 749-50 (1984) (contending that Framers intended "shall be vested" to "mandate that Congress allocate to the federal judiciary as a whole each and every type of case or controversy defined as part of the judicial Power" under Article III's Section 2 unless "so trivial that they would pose an unnecessary burden" on federal courts and parties).

provocatively advanced a related rationale for a narrow view of congressional power via a "two-tier" theory of Article III.[4] Professor Amar opines that *some* federal court — the Supreme Court or an inferior federal court — must be available for handling (i) cases arising under federal law, (ii) cases affecting ambassadors, and (iii) admiralty cases. According to Professor Amar, these three categories warrant unique treatment because the word "all" precedes them in Article III, section 2.[5]

Other scholars, however, maintain that Congress has broad power over lower federal court jurisdiction and over Supreme Court appellate jurisdiction.[6] These scholars point to the plain language of Article III and the supporting Supreme Court precedent interpreting the same that we will discuss below.

The debate, however, does not end here. All of the arguments we have discussed thus far have been internal to Article III. That is, they all are founded on the specific language of the portion of the Constitution that creates the federal judiciary. But the scope of congressional power over the federal judiciary implicates myriad sources of constraint that are external to Article III. Among such principles are separation of powers, Due Process, Equal Protection, and the preservation of the essential functions of the Supreme Court in our constitutional scheme.[7]

5. *The Role of Federalism*

There is one final issue to introduce, or more accurately, re-introduce. How does the existence of state courts fit into the mix? If one courthouse door closes as a result of jurisdiction-stripping legislation, does another remain open? In short, does the ability of state courts to adjudicate an issue over which the federal courts no longer have jurisdiction solve all or some of the problems flowing from jurisdiction-stripping efforts? Recall the tenors of the parity debate from

4. *See* Akhil Reed Amar, *Article III and the Judiciary Act of 1978: The Two-Tiered Structure of the Judiciary Act of 1789*, 138 U. PA. L. REV. 1499 (1990) (articulating two-tier position); *see also* Akhil Reed Amar, *A Neo-Federalist View of Article III: Separating the Two Tiers of Federal Jurisdiction*, 65 B.U. L. REV. 205, 231-33 (1985) (building on Justice Story's theory).

5. *Id. Compare* Akhil Reed Amar, *Reports of My Death Are Greatly Exaggerated: A Reply*, 138 U. PA. L. REV. 1651, 1659 (1990) (summarizing the historical support for a two-tier approach to Article III in which "jurisdiction must ('shall') extend to all arising under cases, but not necessarily 'all' cases in other categories . . ."), *with* Daniel Meltzer, *The History and Structure of Article III*, 138 U. PA. L. REV. 1569 (1990) (critiquing Amar's two-tier interpretation); Martin Redish, *Text, Structure, and Common Sense in the Interpretation of Article III*, 138 U. PA. L. REV. 1633 (1990) (rejecting Amar's two-tier approach with its particular emphasis on Article III's "shall" and "all" language and criticizing Amar's textual analysis as "internally inconsistent").

6. *See, e.g.*, Martin H. Redish, *Constitutional Limitations on Congressional Power to Control Federal Jurisdiction: A Reaction to Professor Sager*, 77 NW. U. L. REV. 143, 145 (1982); John C. Harrison, *The Power of Congress to Limit the Jurisdiction of Federal Courts and the Text of Article III*, 64 U. CHI. L. REV. 203 (1997).

7. *See* Hart, *supra* note 2 (warning against sweeping jurisdiction-stripping legislation that "will destroy the essential role of the Supreme Court in the constitutional plan"); *see also* Leonard G. Ratner, *Majoritarian Constraints on Judicial Review: Congressional Control of Supreme Court Jurisdiction*, 27 VILL. L. REV. 929, 935 (1982) (rejecting theories of plenary congressional power as violative of the Supreme Court's core functions to maintain the supremacy and uniformity of federal law); Sager, *supra* note 3, at 89 (arguing that "adoption of any of the bills that are part of the proposed assault on the federal judiciary would set a dangerous and tawdry precedent by sabotaging the integrity of the judicial process"); Leonard G. Ratner, *Congressional Power over the Appellate Jurisdiction of the Supreme Court*, 109 U. PA. L. REV. 157, 201 (1960) (contending that "legislation that precludes Supreme Court review in every case involving a particular subject is an unconstitutional encroachment on the Court's essential functions").

Chapter 1. Can the state courts be trusted to carry such a duty as effectively, or even more effectively, than federal courts? Also, could Congress pass the buck to the state courts on really tough or high-profile legal issues by leaving only the state courts open? Are federal judges simply "better" than state judges? Could state courts be superior in some ways? Regardless of whether one forum is preferable, consider whether state courts are adequate for the resolution of constitutional claims. All of these issues may be raised in the context of jurisdiction-stripping legislation.

As you read the cases and materials that follow, look at each case in its particular context, but also step back and consider how the cases and problems fit into the broader context of our state and federal judicial systems. Throughout this chapter, you will need to remain vigilant and view the issues through broad constitutional and prudential lenses. Examine the text of Article III each time. Think about the Due Process and Equal Protection Clauses. Consider whether any concerns exist regarding the separation of powers, federalism, parity, and the judiciary's essential functions. Also, contemplate the very essence of justice and the American judicial system. Do litigants have any *access* rights to federal courts? Is there a right to a remedy? Is the substantive basis of the claim—for example, the Constitution, federal statute, state claim with complete diversity of parties—dispositive? Given the federal judiciary's birth out of the Madisonian Compromise, what reaction might the Framers have to the issues raised in the cases that follow? Did they envision federal courts, particularly the Supreme Court, to have so much contemporary power?

C. THE LAW AND PROBLEMS

Congress' power over the federal judiciary affects both the jurisdiction and decisionmaking. The characterization of a congressional action as affecting "jurisdiction" or dictating a court's "decision" could determine the ultimate constitutional question. Where jurisdiction ends and substantive decisions begin, however, is often a difficult line to ascertain. As you read the cases below, consider how Congress' control of jurisdiction affects resolution of the underlying merits of the dispute.

1. *Control of Jurisdiction*

Article III provides an impressive start to Congress' assertion of power over the federal judiciary. Both the Ordain and Establish Clause and the Exceptions Clause give power to Congress. But does the text of Article III hold any limitations on that power? Any limits, or implied limits, in the text of Article III are commonly known as "internal" restraints on congressional power. In other words, if one agrees with Justice Story's interpretation of the word "shall" from Article III or Professor Amar's approach to the placement of "all" in Article III, then one has arguments for restraints on congressional power that are internal to Article III. Another example of what Professor Gunther deems an internal limit inherent in Article III is Professor Hart's "essential role" or "core functions" theory, that is, Congress cannot use its "Exceptions" power in a manner that eviscerates the essential functions of the Supreme Court in our constitutional order. Remember, however, that it is possible to read Article III as possessing no significant internal restraints on congressional power. Is Congress' authority over the courts therefore virtually limitless?

You should sense already that there are many other arguments in favor of limitations to Congress' power over the judiciary. Are there other legal boundaries that serve to delimit congressional action in a more mandatory sense? Recall that there are forceful constitutional arguments for restraining Congress, such as the Due Process and Equal Protection Clauses, the Suspension Clause, separation of powers, and access to fundamental federal rights. These constitutional doctrines are generally considered "external" to Article III. For example, a clear external limit stemming from the Due Process and Equal Protection Clauses would prohibit the congressional creation of federal law that denied access to federal courts on the basis of a person's race. What if Congress attempted to strip federal court jurisdiction over particular constitutional rights? The traction of such theories of external constitutional restraints may depend upon whether one believes that state courts are adequate to adjudicate federal constitutional claims. Again, recall discussions of parity from Chapter 1. Recall that some positions of restraint stem from policies favoring the use of caution as a matter of wisdom given the delicate balance of interbranch powers.

As you read the following materials, focus on the text of Congress' legislation. Ask what effect the text has on congressional power over federal courts. For this inquiry, you should think broadly about the legislation's impact on Supreme Court appellate jurisdiction, lower federal court jurisdiction, and state court jurisdiction. Explore each of these arenas individually, while remaining aware of their collective effect. This threshold analysis will dictate your approach as you examine internal, external, and policy-based restraints on congressional power. Consider the following suggested road map for addressing these issues.

REVIEW AND CONSOLIDATION

Assessing Limits on Congressional Power

Threshold Guideposts:

1. What effect does Congress' Act have on the appellate jurisdiction of the Supreme Court?
2. What effect does Congress' Act have on the jurisdiction of the lower federal courts?
3. What effect does Congress' Act have on the jurisdiction of state courts?

Analysis Checklist:

- ✦ Identify which power(s) Congress is utilizing: the Exceptions Clause and/or the Ordain and Establish Clause.
- ✦ Assess whether there are arguments internal to the clause at issue or inherent in Article III generally. Examine how the case law supports or detracts from any textual theory of restraint.

- ✦ Evaluate the applicability and strength of any constitutional arguments that are external to Article III, such as Due Process and Equal Protection. [Hint: Remain cognizant of any valves that remain open to the federal courts.] Consider whether the existence of state court review is sufficient to satisfy constitutional concerns.
- ✦ Consider the relevance of any policy arguments supporting the exercise of congressional restraint.

a. The Supreme Court's Appellate Jurisdiction

Recall that the Exceptions Clause permits Congress to modify the appellate jurisdiction of the Supreme Court. This section explores the breadth and limits of this power.

The following case, *Ex Parte McCardle*, involves a petition for habeas corpus. Habeas corpus constitutes a civil action through which a prisoner seeks relief from unlawful detention. As you analyze *McCardle*, consider what avenues for relief were available to Mr. McCardle before the case, and what, if any, remain after the Supreme Court's decision.

EX PARTE MCCARDLE

74 U.S. (7 Wall.) 506 (1868)

[The Court set forth the text of Article III, sections 1 and 2.]

With these constitutional provisions in existence, Congress, on the 5th February, 1867, by "An act to amend an act to establish the judicial courts of the United States, approved September 24, 1789," provided that the several courts of the United States, and the several justices and judges of such courts, within their respective jurisdiction, in addition to the authority already conferred by law, should have power to grant writs of habeas corpus in all cases where any person may be restrained of his or her liberty in violation of the Constitution, or of any treaty or law of the United States. And that, from the final decision of any judge, justice, or court inferior to the Circuit Court, appeal might be taken to the Circuit Court of the United States for the district in which the cause was heard, and *from the judgment of the said Circuit Court to the Supreme Court of the United States.*

This statute being in force, one McCardle, alleging unlawful restraint by military force, preferred a petition in the court below, for the writ of habeas corpus. The writ was issued, and a return was made by the military commander, admitting the restraint, but denying that it was unlawful.

It appeared that the petitioner was not in the military service of the United States, but was held in custody by military authority for trial before a military commission, upon charges founded upon the publication of articles alleged to be incendiary and libellous, in a newspaper of which he was editor. The custody was alleged to be under the authority of certain acts of Congress.

* * * *

THE CHIEF JUSTICE [CHASE] delivered the opinion of the court.

[During the pendency of the instant appeal, Congress, over presidential veto, passed the Act of March 27, 1868, repealing a jurisdiction-granting provision of the February 5, 1867 Act. The relevant provision of the 1867 Act amended the Judicial Act of 1789 and authorized appeals to the Supreme Court from the decisions of the Circuit Courts in habeas corpus cases. Thus, in an attempt to block review of *McCardle*'s case, Congress revoked, via the 1868 Act, the Court's habeas appellate jurisdiction previously authorized by the 1867 Act.]

The first question necessarily is that of jurisdiction; for, if the act of March, 1868, takes away the jurisdiction defined by the act of February, 1867, it is useless, if not improper, to enter into any discussion of other questions.

[A]ppellate jurisdiction of this court is not derived from acts of Congress. It is, strictly speaking, conferred by the Constitution. But it is conferred "with such exceptions and under such regulations as Congress shall make."

It is unnecessary to consider whether, if Congress had made no exceptions and no regulations, this court might not have exercised general appellate jurisdiction under rules prescribed by itself. For among the earliest acts of the first Congress, at its first session, was the act of September 24th, 1789, to establish the judicial courts of the United States. . . .

The source of that jurisdiction, and the limitations of it by the Constitution and by statute, have been on several occasions subjects of consideration here. In the case of *Durousseau v. The United States*, particularly, the whole matter was carefully examined, and the court held, that while "the appellate powers of this court are not given by the judicial act, but are given by the Constitution," they are, nevertheless, "limited and regulated by that act, and by such other acts as have been passed on the subject." The court said, further, that the judicial act was an exercise of the power given by the Constitution to Congress "of making exceptions to the appellate jurisdiction of the Supreme Court." "They have described affirmatively," said the court, "its jurisdiction, and this affirmative description has been understood to imply a negation of the exercise of such appellate power as is not comprehended within it."

The principle that the affirmation of appellate jurisdiction implies the negation of all such jurisdiction not affirmed having been thus established, it was an almost necessary consequence that acts of Congress, providing for the exercise of jurisdiction, should come to be spoken of as acts granting jurisdiction, and not as acts making exceptions to the constitutional grant of it.

. . . The provision of the act of 1867, affirming the appellate jurisdiction of this court in cases of habeas corpus is expressly repealed. It is hardly possible to imagine a plainer instance of positive exception.

We are not at liberty to inquire into the motives of the legislature. We can only examine into its power under the Constitution; and the power to make exceptions to the appellate jurisdiction of this court is given by express words.

What, then, is the effect of the repealing act upon the case before us? We cannot doubt as to this. Without jurisdiction the court cannot proceed at all in any cause. Jurisdiction is power to declare the law, and when it ceases to exist, the only function remaining to the court is that of announcing the fact and dismissing the cause. . . .

* * * *

[T]he general rule, supported by the best elementary writers, is, that "when an act of the legislature is repealed, it must be considered, except as to transactions past and closed, as if it never existed." . . . [I]t [has been] held that no judgment could be rendered in a suit after the repeal of the act under which it was brought and prosecuted.

It is quite clear, therefore, that this court cannot proceed to pronounce judgment in this case, for it has no longer jurisdiction of the appeal; and judicial duty is not less fitly performed by declining ungranted jurisdiction than in exercising firmly that which the Constitution and the laws confer.

Counsel seem to have supposed, if effect be given to the repealing act in question, that the whole appellate power of the court, in cases of habeas corpus, is denied. But this is an error. The act of 1868 does not except from that jurisdiction any cases but appeals from Circuit Courts under the act of 1867. It does not affect the jurisdiction which was previously exercised.

The appeal of the petitioner in this case must be

DISMISSED FOR WANT OF JURISDICTION.

DISCUSSION AND QUESTIONS

Were you surprised that Congress could pass a bill stripping Supreme Court jurisdiction during the pendency of a case? The *McCardle* Court states emphatically:

> What, then, is the effect of the repealing act upon the case before us? We cannot doubt as to this. Without jurisdiction the court cannot proceed at all in any cause. Jurisdiction is power to declare the law, and when it ceases to exist, the only function remaining to the court is that of announcing the fact and dismissing the cause. . . .

This is forceful language regarding Congress' power to strip jurisdiction. Further, the Court states that it is powerless to "inquire into the motives of the legislature."

McCardle demonstrates that Article III is the source for the Supreme Court's appellate jurisdiction, but that jurisdiction is subject to "such exceptions and under such regulations as Congress shall make." Recall that the *McCardle* Court could not hear the appeal because Congress effectively stripped the Supreme Court of appellate jurisdiction granted by an earlier statute. The petitioner, McCardle, had brought his claim under the 1867 Act, which Congress had repealed with the 1868 Act. Because Congress stripped the Supreme Court of its statutory appellate jurisdiction over petitioner McCardle's case, the Court dismissed the case for want of jurisdiction.

A contrary ruling by the Supreme Court in *McCardle* might have interfered with the process of Reconstruction following the Civil War. During Reconstruction, the Union military took control of the Southern judiciary. Petitioner McCardle was not in the military; he was a civilian newspaper editor being held in custody by the military for printing allegedly libelous material. Petitioner McCardle sought Supreme Court review under the post–Civil War Reconstruction Acts, specifically the 1867 Act. Congress feared how the Supreme Court might rule on the Reconstruction Acts and, accordingly, passed the 1868 Act repealing the Supreme Court's habeas appellate jurisdiction. Is it surprising that, in the wake of the Civil War, a unanimous Supreme Court upheld Congress' jurisdiction-stripping maneuver? To what extent do you think political motivations affected the Supreme Court's ruling? For an in-depth treatment of

McCardle and its historical context, see William W. Van Alstyne, *A Critical Guide to* Ex Parte McCardle, 15 ARIZ. L. REV. 229 (1973). *See also* Daniel L. Meltzer, *The Story of* Ex parte McCardle*: The Power of Congress to Limit the Supreme Court's Appellate Jurisdiction, in* FEDERAL COURTS STORIES 57-86 (Vicki C. Jackson & Judith Resnik eds., 2010) (exploring McCardle's history and lessons to conclude that the scope of congressional power over Supreme Court appellate jurisdiction remains uncertain).

The Supreme Court's validation of Congress' restriction on the Court's appellate jurisdiction in *McCardle* provides support for a plenary view of Congress' power over that appellate jurisdiction. *See Brotherhood of R.R. Trainmen v. Toledo P. & W. R.R.*, 321 U.S. 50, 63-64 (1944) (acknowledging Congress' "plenary control over the jurisdiction of the federal courts").[8] Yet, before we reach this conclusion, consider whether a more limited reading of *McCardle* is plausible.

In the opinion's penultimate paragraph, the Court responds to the counsel's argument that Congress' 1868 Act, if validated by the Court, completely strips the Supreme Court of appellate jurisdiction over habeas corpus matters. The Court responds:

> Counsel seem to have supposed, if effect be given to the repealing act in question, that the whole appellate power of the court, in cases of habeas corpus, is denied. But this is an error. The act of 1868 does not except from that jurisdiction any cases but appeals from Circuit Courts under the act of 1867. It does not affect the jurisdiction which was previously exercised.

At the start of the *McCardle* case, two habeas routes existed. Mr. McCardle chose the first route, proceeding under the 1867 Act. That statute provided federal courts with the authority to consider habeas claims by those held in violation of federal law by state and federal authorities. The second route, via the unrepealed Judiciary Act of 1789, provided the federal courts with habeas jurisdiction for those held in violation of federal law by federal authorities only. Congress' action repealed the 1867 procedural route, leaving only the 1789 device in place. Thus, in a sense, one could say that Mr. McCardle lost because he selected the wrong road to travel.

EXPLORING DOCTRINE

Partial versus Complete Jurisdiction Strips

Why is the distinction between an act that repeals the whole appellate power rather than a portion of appellate power important? Do you think Congress intended to leave unaffected the habeas corpus jurisdiction that the Supreme Court previously exercised? Could Congress have chosen to exercise a broader authority under the Exceptions Clause and eliminated all Supreme Court appellate review of habeas corpus cases? Does *McCardle* suggest limits on Congress' Article III power?

8. *See also* Martin H. Redish, *Congressional Power to Regulate Supreme Court Appellate Jurisdiction Under the Exceptions Clause: An Internal and External Examination*, 27 VILL. L. REV. 900, 913-15 (1982).

Now consider how the Court handles another habeas corpus dispute that came to it shortly after *McCardle.*

EX PARTE YERGER

75 U.S. (8 Wall.) 85 (1868)

THE CHIEF JUSTICE [CHASE] delivered the opinion of the court.

* * * *

The general question of jurisdiction in this case resolves itself necessarily into two . . . questions:

> 1. Has the court jurisdiction, in a case like the present, to inquire into the cause of detention, alleged to be unlawful, and to give relief, if the detention be found to be in fact unlawful, by the writ of habeas corpus, under the Judiciary Act of 1789?
>
> 2. If, under that act, the court possessed this jurisdiction, has it been taken away by the second section of the act of March, 27, 1868, repealing so much of the act of February 5, 1867, as authorizes appeals from Circuit Courts to the Supreme Court?

Neither of these questions is new here. The first has, on several occasions, received very full consideration, and very deliberate judgment.

A cause, so important as that which now invokes the action of this court, seems however to justify a reconsideration. . . .

The great writ of habeas corpus has been for centuries esteemed the best and only sufficient defence of personal freedom.

In England, after a long struggle, it was firmly guaranteed by the famous Habeas Corpus Act of May 27, 1679, "for the better securing of the liberty of the subject," which, as Blackstone says, "is frequently considered as another Magna Charta."

It was brought to America by the colonists, and claimed as among the immemorial rights descended to them from their ancestors.

Naturally, therefore, when the confederated colonies became United States, and the formation of a common government engaged their deliberations in convention, this great writ found prominent sanction in the Constitution. That sanction is in these words:

> The privilege of the writ of habeas corpus shall not be suspended unless when in cases of rebellion or invasion the public safety may require it.

The terms of this provision necessarily imply judicial action. In England, all the higher courts were open to applicants for the writ, and it is hardly supposable that, under the new government, founded on more liberal ideas and principles, any court would be, intentionally, closed to them.

We find, accordingly, that the first Congress under the Constitution, after defining, by various sections of the act of September 24, 1789, the jurisdiction of the District Courts, the Circuit Courts, and the Supreme Court in other cases, proceeded, in the 14th section, to enact, "that all the beforementioned courts of the United States shall have power to issue writs of *scire facias,* habeas corpus, and all other writs, not specially provided by statute, which may be necessary for the exercise of their respective jurisdictions, and agreeable to the principles and usages of law." In the same section, it was further provided "that either of the Justices of the Supreme Court, as well as Judges of the District Courts, shall have power to grant writs of habeas corpus for the purpose of an inquiry into the cause of commitment; provided that writs of habeas corpus shall in no case extend to prisoners in jail, unless they are in custody, under, or by color of the authority of the United States, or are committed for trial before some court of the same, or are necessary to be brought into court to testify."

That this court is one of the courts to which the power to issue writs of habeas corpus is expressly given by the terms of this section has never been questioned. . . .

But the power vested in this court is, in an important particular, unlike that possessed by the English courts. The jurisdiction of this court is conferred by the Constitution, and is appellate; whereas, that of the English courts, though declared and defined by statutes, is derived from the common law, and is original.

The judicial power of the United States extends to all cases in law and equity arising under the Constitution, the laws of the United States, and treaties made under their authority, and to large classes of cases determined by the character of the parties, or the nature of the controversy.

That part of this judicial power vested in this court is defined by the Constitution in these words:

> In all cases affecting ambassadors, other public ministers, and consuls, and those in which a State shall be a party, the Supreme Court shall have original jurisdiction. In all the other cases before mentioned, the Supreme Court shall have appellate jurisdiction, both as to law and fact, with such exceptions, and under such regulations as the Congress shall make.

If the question were a new one, it would, perhaps, deserve inquiry whether Congress might not, under the power to make exceptions from this appellate jurisdiction, extend the original jurisdiction to other cases than those expressly enumerated in the Constitution; and especially, in view of the constitutional guaranty of the writ of habeas corpus, to cases arising upon petition for that writ.

But, in the case of *Marbury v. Madison*, it was determined, upon full consideration, that the power to issue writs of mandamus, given to this court by the 13th section of the Judiciary Act, is, under the Constitution, an appellate jurisdiction, to be exercised only in the revision of judicial decisions. And this judgment has ever since been accepted as fixing the construction of this part of the Constitution.

It was pronounced in 1803. In 1807 the same construction was given to the provision of the 14th section relating to the writ of habeas corpus. . . .

* * * *

The doctrine of the Constitution and of the cases thus far may be summed up in these propositions:

> (1.) The original jurisdiction of this court cannot be extended by Congress to any other cases than those expressly defined by the Constitution.
>
> (2.) The appellate jurisdiction of this court, conferred by the Constitution, extends to all other cases within the judicial power of the United States.
>
> (3.) This appellate jurisdiction is subject to such exceptions, and must be exercised under such regulations as Congress, in the exercise of its discretion, has made or may see fit to make.

(4.) Congress not only has not excepted writs of habeas corpus and *mandamus* from this appellate jurisdiction, but has expressly provided for the exercise of this jurisdiction by means of these writs.

We come, then, to consider the first great question made in the case now before us.

We shall assume, upon the authority of the decisions referred to, what we should hold were the question now for the first time presented to us, that in a proper case this court, under the act of 1789, and under all the subsequent acts, giving jurisdiction in cases of habeas corpus, may, in the exercise of its appellate power, revise the decisions of inferior courts of the United States, and relieve from unlawful imprisonment authorized by them, except in cases within some limitations of the jurisdiction by Congress.

It remains to inquire whether the case before us is a proper one for such interposition. Is it within any such limitation? In other words, can this court inquire into the lawfulness of detention, and relieve from it if found unlawful, when the detention complained of is not by civil authority under a commitment made by an inferior court, but by military officers, for trial before a military tribunal, after an examination into the cause of detention by the inferior court, resulting in an order remanding the prisoner to custody?

* * * *

But it is unnecessary to enter upon this inquiry here. The action which we are asked to revise was that of a tribunal whose decisions are subject to revision by this court in ordinary modes.

We need consider, therefore, only the second branch of the proposition, namely, that the action of the inferior court must have resulted in a commitment for trial in a civil court; and the inference drawn from it, that no relief can be had here, by habeas corpus, from imprisonment under military authority, to which the petitioner may have been remanded by such a court.

This proposition certainly is not supported by authority.

* * * *

We have carefully considered the argument against it, made in this case, and are satisfied that the doctrine heretofore maintained is sound.

The great and leading intent of the Constitution and the law must be kept constantly in view upon the examination of every question of construction.

That intent, in respect to the writ of habeas corpus, is manifest. It is that every citizen may be protected by judicial action from unlawful imprisonment. To this end the act of 1789 provided that every court of the United States should have power to issue the writ. The jurisdiction thus given in law to the Circuit and District Courts is original; that given by the Constitution and the law to this court is appellate. Given in general terms, it must necessarily extend to all cases to which the judicial power of the United States extends, other than those expressly excepted from it.

As limited by the act of 1789, it did not extend to cases of imprisonment after conviction, under sentences of competent tribunals; nor to prisoners in jail, unless in custody under or by color of the authority of the United States, or committed for trial before some court of the United States, or required to be brought into court to testify. But this limitation has been gradually narrowed, and the benefits of the writ have been extended . . . to all cases where any person may be restrained of liberty in violation of the Constitution, or of any treaty or law of the United States.

This brief statement shows how the general spirit and genius of our institutions has tended to the widening and enlarging of the habeas corpus jurisdiction of the courts and judges of the United States; and this tendency, except in one recent instance, has been constant and uniform; and it is in the light of it that we must determine the true meaning of the Constitution and the law in respect to the appellate jurisdiction of this court. We are not at liberty to except from it any cases not plainly excepted by law; and we think it sufficiently appears from what has been said that no exception to this jurisdiction embraces such a case as that now before the court. On the contrary, the case is one of those expressly declared not to be excepted from the general grant of jurisdiction. For it is a case of imprisonment alleged to be unlawful, and to be under color of authority of the United States.

* * * *

We are obliged to hold, therefore, that in all cases where a Circuit Court of the United States has, in the exercise of its original jurisdiction, caused a prisoner to be brought before it, and has, after inquiring into the cause of detention, remanded him to the custody from which he was taken, this court, in the exercise of its appellate jurisdiction, may, by the writ of habeas corpus, aided by the writ of *certiorari*, revise the decision of the Circuit Court, and if it be found unwarranted by law, relieve the prisoner from the unlawful restraint to which he has been remanded.

This conclusion brings us to the inquiry whether the 2d section of the act of March 27th, 1868, takes away or affects the appellate jurisdiction of this court under the Constitution and the acts of Congress prior to 1867.

In *McCardle*'s case, we expressed the opinion that it does not, and we have now re-examined the grounds of that opinion.

The circumstances under which the act of 1868 was passed were peculiar.

On the 5th of February, 1867, Congress passed the act to which reference has already been made, extending the original jurisdiction by habeas corpus of the District and Circuit Courts, and of the several judges of these courts, to all cases of restraint of liberty in violation of the Constitution, treaties, or laws of the United States. This act authorized appeals to this court from judgments of the Circuit Court, but did not repeal any previous act conferring jurisdiction by habeas corpus, unless by implication.

* * * *

The effect of the act was to oust the court of its jurisdiction of the particular case then before it on appeal, and it is not to be doubted that such was the effect intended. Nor will it be questioned that legislation of this character is unusual and hardly to be justified except upon some imperious public exigency.

It was, doubtless, within the constitutional discretion of Congress to determine whether such an exigency existed; but it is not to be presumed that an act, passed under such circumstances, was intended to have any further effect than that plainly apparent from its terms.

It is quite clear that the words of the act reach, not only all appeals pending, but all future appeals to this court under the act of 1867; but they appear to be limited to appeals taken under that act.

The words of the repealing section are, "that so much of the act approved February 5th, 1867, as authorizes an appeal from the judgment of the Circuit

Court to the Supreme Court of the United States, or the exercise of any such jurisdiction by said Supreme Court on appeals which have been, or may be hereafter taken, be, and the same is hereby repealed."

These words are not of doubtful interpretation. They repeal only so much of the act of 1867 as authorized appeals, or the exercise of appellate jurisdiction by this court. They affected only appeals and appellate jurisdiction authorized by that act. They do not purport to touch the appellate jurisdiction conferred by the Constitution, or to except from it any cases not excepted by the act of 1789. They reach no act except the act of 1867.

* * * *

The appeal given by the act of 1867 extended, indeed, to cases within the former acts; and the act, by its grant of additional authority, so enlarged the jurisdiction by habeas corpus that it seems, as was observed in the *McCardle* case, "impossible to widen" it. But this effect does not take from the act its character of an additional grant of jurisdiction, and make it operate as a repeal of jurisdiction theretofore allowed.

Our conclusion is, that none of the acts prior to 1867, authorizing this court to exercise appellate jurisdiction by means of the writ of habeas corpus, were repealed by the act of that year, and that the repealing section of the act of 1868 is limited in terms, and must be limited in effect to the appellate jurisdiction authorized by the act of 1867.

We could come to no other conclusion without holding that the whole appellate jurisdiction of this court, in cases of habeas corpus, conferred by the Constitution, recognized by law, and exercised from the foundation of the government hitherto, has been taken away, without the expression of such intent, and by mere implication, through the operation of the acts of 1867 and 1868.

* * * *

The argument having been confined, by direction of the court, to the question of jurisdiction, this opinion is limited to that question. The jurisdiction of the court to issue the writ prayed for is affirmed.

DISCUSSION AND QUESTIONS

Can *Yerger* be squared with *McCardle*? The Supreme Court rendered both opinions in 1868. Both opinions were unanimous. In one the Court dismissed for want of jurisdiction (*McCardle*), while in the other the Court affirmed jurisdiction (*Yerger*). Does either decision question Congress' power to strip the Court of jurisdiction? Or do the two decisions turn instead on the interpretation of congressional intent?

In *Yerger*, the petitioner sought review under the Judiciary Act of 1789, whereas the petitioner in *McCardle* sought review under the Reconstruction Act of 1867. Why might this be critical? Recall the *Yerger* Court's analysis of the jurisdiction-stripping statute at issue in *McCardle*:

> These words are not of doubtful interpretation. They repeal only so much of the act of 1867 as authorized appeals, or the exercise of appellate jurisdiction by this court. They affected only appeals and appellate jurisdiction authorized by that act.

> They do not purport to touch the appellate jurisdiction conferred by the Constitution, or to except from it any cases not excepted by the act of 1789. They reach no act except the act of 1867.

Does this analysis give any clue concerning whether Congress' power is plenary or limited?

Consider whether there is some value in having uncertainty in separation-of-powers jurisprudence. In other words, keeping both branches in play, one could say, is more consistent with the fundamental constitutional design than assigning "supreme power" to either branch.

Test your understanding of congressional control over Supreme Court jurisdiction after *McCardle* and *Yerger* with Problem 3-1.

PROBLEM 3-1

Dead-End Boulevard or Open Avenue?

Congress' frustration with the volume of successive habeas corpus petitions causes it to pass the Antiterrorism and Effective Death Penalty Act (the "Act"). The Act imposes significant restrictions on state prisoners' second or successive federal habeas corpus petitions, making it more difficult to challenge a conviction. It establishes a "gatekeeping" function requiring that all successive habeas corpus petitions be approved by the United States Court of Appeals under the statutory standard. Congress also prohibits Supreme Court review, either by appeal or writ of certiorari, of the circuit court's gatekeeper decision. Specifically, the statute provides that the appellate court decision "*shall not be appealable and shall not be the subject of a petition for rehearing or for a writ of certiorari.*"

Assume a federal appellate court denies a prisoner's request to file a second habeas petition challenging his death sentence. The prisoner seeks certiorari review of this denial from the Supreme Court.

Assume that, prior to the passage of the Act, there were three potential habeas avenues to the Supreme Court: (1) an appeal from an inferior court's decision on a habeas petition, (2) a petition for writ of certiorari to review an inferior court's decision, and (3) a habeas petition to the Supreme Court as an original matter, that is, in the first instance in the Supreme Court.[9]

Assume the Supreme Court grants certiorari to consider (a) whether the Act unconstitutionally suspended the writ of habeas corpus, and (b) whether the Act unconstitutionally restrains the jurisdiction of the Supreme Court in violation of Article III.

How should the Supreme Court rule on these issues in light of *McCardle* and *Yerger*? Does the Act preclude all avenues of review by the Supreme Court? If not, does the practical availability of some form of review sustain the Act's constitutionality? Does the availability of some form of review provide the Court a means of avoiding the constitutional issue?

9. Granting an original petition for writ of habeas corpus requires exceptional circumstances; the Court has not utilized this avenue since 1925.

Problem 3-1 demonstrates the breadth of *Yerger.* Recall how the *Yerger* Court reasoned that the 1868 Act revoked the Supreme Court's jurisdiction over habeas appeals conferred under the 1867 Act, but that the 1868 repeal did not address habeas jurisdiction authorized by the 1789 Act. How did the *Yerger* Court view the theory that the 1867 Act repealed its habeas jurisdiction by implication?

Is the Court's precedent clear to this point? Consider whether the cases that follow clarify the scope of congressional control.

b. The Inferior Federal Courts

The Supreme Court has declared: "There can be no question of the power of Congress to define and limit the jurisdiction of the inferior courts of the United States." *Lauf v. E.G. Shinner & Co.*, 303 U.S. 323, 330 (1938) (declining to invalidate the Norris-LaGuardia Act, which stripped federal courts of their ability to enjoin labor disputes). Under Article III, Congress has the discretion *to create* lower federal courts. Recall the Ordain and Establish Clause of the Constitution:

> The judicial Power of the United States, shall be vested in one supreme Court, and in such inferior Courts as the Congress may from time to time ordain and establish.

U.S. Const. art. III, § 1. In other words, Congress could have chosen never to establish any federal courts under the Supreme Court. Congress did of course opt to create inferior federal courts at its first session. *See* First Judiciary Act, ch. 20, § 14, 1 Stat. 73 (1789). But Congress took nearly a century before granting lower federal courts a permanent general grant of federal question jurisdiction. And Congress has never vested the full jurisdictional power described in Article III in inferior federal courts. For example, Congress continues to impose an "amount in controversy" limit on diversity-of-citizenship jurisdiction even though no "amount in controversy" requirement is stated in Article III.

Once Congress opted to create lower federal courts, what level of jurisdiction must be conferred on those courts?

Many scholars maintain that Congress' power to create includes the power to destroy.[10] They contend that the "greater power includes the lesser power" in that Congress' power to decide whether to create inferior federal courts necessarily encompasses the "lesser" power to restrict the jurisdiction of lower federal courts.[11] As you will soon learn, the Supreme Court has articulated this rationale

10. *See, e.g.*, Martin H. Redish & Curtis Woods, *Congressional Power to Control the Jurisdiction of Lower Federal Courts: A Critical Review and New Synthesis*, 124 U. Pa. L. Rev. 45, 70 (1975) (endorsing the theory that Congress has unfettered discretion to establish or destroy inferior courts); Gerald Gunther, *Congressional Power to Curtail Federal Court Jurisdiction: An Opinionated Guide to the Ongoing Debate*, 36 Stan. L. Rev. 895, 916 (1984).

11. *See* Paul M. Bator, *Congressional Power over the Jurisdiction of the Federal Courts*, 27 Vill. L. Rev. 1030, 1031 (1982) ("[T]he greater power (not to create such courts at all) must include the lesser (to create them but limit their jurisdiction)."). *But see* Ronald D. Rotunda, *Congressional Power to Restrict the Jurisdiction of the Lower Federal Courts and the Problem of School Busing*, 64 Geo. L.J. 839, 842 (1976) (arguing that the "lesser" power to define jurisdiction is actually greater than the power to create inferior courts).

in a series of cases validating congressional restrictions on the jurisdiction of the inferior federal courts.

EXPLORING DOCTRINE

Unfettered Discretion

What are the potential consequences and dangers in the theory of unfettered congressional discretion? Would Congress' exercise of this discretion pose an increased judicial burden on state courts and fewer avenues for potential federal litigants? Would Congress attempt to restrict the ability of federal judges to hear politically controversial wedge issues? Might a jurisdiction strip benefit the federal courts' docket? Other than the Supreme Court and respect for a true balance of power and cooperation among the coequal branches, what checks Congress in its use of this discretion?

Consider these questions as you review the next set of cases.

SHELDON v. SILL

49 U.S. (8 How.) 441 (1850)

* * * *

JUSTICE GRIER delivered the opinion of the court.

The only question which it will be necessary to notice in this case is, whether the Circuit Court had jurisdiction.

Sill, the complainant below, a citizen of New York, filed his bill in the Circuit Court of the United States for Michigan, against Sheldon, claiming to recover the amount of a bond and mortgage, which had been assigned to him by Hastings, the President of the Bank of Michigan.

Sheldon, in his answer, among other things, pleaded that "the bond and mortgage in controversy, having been originally given by a citizen of Michigan to another citizen of the same state, and the complainant being assignee of them, the Circuit Court had no jurisdiction."

The eleventh section of the Judiciary Act, which defines the jurisdiction of the Circuit Courts, restrains them from taking "cognizance of any suit to recover the contents of any promissory note or other chose in action, in favor of an assignee, unless a suit might have been prosecuted in such court to recover the contents, if no assignment had been made, except in cases of foreign bills of exchange."

The third article of the Constitution declares that "the judicial power of the United States shall be vested in one Supreme Court, and such inferior courts as the Congress may, from time to time, ordain and establish." The second section of the same article enumerates the cases and controversies of which the judicial power shall have cognizance, and, among others, it specifies "controversies between citizens of different states."

It has been alleged, that this restriction of the Judiciary Act, with regard to assignees of choses in action, is in conflict with this provision of the Constitution, and therefore void.

It must be admitted, that if the Constitution had ordained and established the inferior courts, and distributed to them their respective powers, they could not be restricted or divested by Congress. But as it has made no such distribution, one of two consequences must result, — either that each inferior court created by Congress must exercise all the judicial powers not given to the Supreme Court, or that Congress, having the power to establish the courts, must define their respective jurisdictions. The first of these inferences has never been asserted, and could not be defended with any show of reason, and if not, the latter would seem to follow as a necessary consequence. And it would seem to follow, also, that, having a right to prescribe, Congress may withhold from any court of its creation jurisdiction of any of the enumerated controversies. Courts created by statute can have no jurisdiction but such as the statute confers. No one of them can assert a just claim to jurisdiction exclusively conferred on another, or withheld from all.

The Constitution has defined the limits of the judicial power of the United States, but has not prescribed how much of it shall be exercised by the Circuit Court; consequently, the statute which does prescribe the limits of their jurisdiction, cannot be in conflict with the Constitution, unless it confers powers not enumerated therein. Such has been the doctrine held by this court since its first establishment. . . .

In the case of *Turner v. Bank of North America*, it was contended, as in this case, that, as it was a controversy between citizens of different states, the Constitution gave the plaintiff a right to sue in the Circuit Court, notwithstanding he was an assignee within the restriction of the eleventh section of the Judiciary Act. But the court said, — "The political truth is, that the disposal of the judicial power (except in a few specified instances) belongs to Congress; and Congress is not bound to enlarge the jurisdiction of the Federal courts to every subject, in every form which the Constitution might warrant." This decision was made in 1799; since that time, the same doctrine has been frequently asserted by this court. . . .

The only remaining inquiry is, whether the complainant in this case is the assignee of a "chose in action," within the meaning of the statute. The term "chose in action" is one of comprehensive import. It includes the infinite variety of contracts, covenants, and promises, which confer on one party a right to recover a personal chattel or a sum of money from another, by action.

* * * *

The complainant in this case is the purchaser and assignee of a sum of money, a debt, a chose in action, not of a tract of land. He seeks to recover by this action a debt assigned to him. He is therefore the "assignee of a chose in action," within the letter and spirit of the act of Congress under consideration, and cannot support this action in the Circuit Court of the United States, where his assignor could not.

The judgment of the Circuit Court must therefore be reversed, for want of jurisdiction.

DISCUSSION AND QUESTIONS

Review the language of Article III, section 2, which provides that the "judicial Power shall extend to all Cases, in Law and Equity, arising under this Constitution, the Laws of the United States . . . to Controversies . . . between Citizens of different States. . . ." U.S. Const. art. III, § 2. This section enumerates nine categories of cases and controversies over which federal courts may exercise the "judicial Power." Does *Sheldon* suggest any limit on congressional power to either create inferior federal courts or vest them with Article III jurisdiction?

Sheldon upholds Congress' restriction on the diversity jurisdiction of federal courts. The Court's reasoning highlights the breadth of Congress' authority over inferior federal courts. *Sheldon* is oft-cited for the Court's emphatic statement that "Congress may withhold from any court of its creation jurisdiction of any of the enumerated controversies. Courts created by statute can have no jurisdiction but such as the statute confers." According to the Court, Congress' plenary power over the regulation of judicial power is a "political" fact. The Court explicitly declares that Congress has no obligation to provide the full jurisdiction envisioned by Article III.

With *Sheldon* demonstrating the might of Congress' power to withhold jurisdiction from the lower federal courts, does it matter whether state courts are available to hear the sorts of claims that arise when Congress has used its authority to withhold jurisdiction from the lower federal courts? Is access to state courts adequate for the resolution of the claim for satisfaction of the bond? What if the claim at issue in *Sheldon* had been grounded in the Constitution? Professor Hart and others maintain that state courts are competent to interpret the Constitution. Do you agree?

The Supreme Court reaffirmed *Sheldon*'s analysis in a series of cases. In 1922, the Court upheld a restriction in the federal Anti-Injunction Act barring federal courts from issuing injunctions to halt simultaneous state court cases regarding a breach of contract. *Kline v. Burke Constr. Co.*, 260 U.S. 226 (1922). The Court reiterated that Congress, and Congress alone, possesses the power to create jurisdiction of all lower federal courts and that Congress "may give, withhold or restrict such jurisdiction at its discretion provided it be not extended beyond the boundaries fixed by the Constitution." *Id.* at 234. Then, in 1938, the Supreme Court upheld the restriction in a federal statute preventing federal courts from enjoining labor disputes. *Lauf v. E.G. Shinner & Co.*, 303 U.S. 323 (1938). With conviction, the Court announced that congressional authority "to define and limit" lower federal courts was without question. *Id.* at 330.

Shortly thereafter, the Court upheld legislation limiting federal court jurisdiction in actions challenging price-control regulations issued under the Emergency Price Control Act to special three-judge panels deemed "Emergency Courts." *Lockerty v. Phillips*, 319 U.S. 182 (1943). The Court rejected the argument that Congress' scheme of exclusive jurisdiction violated the Constitution. Under the Act, price control regulations issued by federal authorities could only be challenged before the Emergency Courts. The Act stated that "no court, Federal, State, or Territorial, shall have jurisdiction or power to consider the validity of any such regulation." The Court upheld this jurisdictional scheme, concluding that Congress was not obligated to bestow jurisdiction on any given lower federal court. The Court found no reason to "doubt the authority of Congress to require that a plaintiff seeking such equitable relief resort to the Emergency Court." *Id.* at 188. The Court construed Congress' power over the lower federal courts via the Ordain and Establish Clause broadly to encompass "the power of investing them in the exact degrees and character which to Congress may seem proper for the public good." *Id.*

Within a year of *Lockerty,* the Court again reviewed the constitutionality of the exclusive jurisdiction provisions of the Emergency Price Control Act, but this time within the context of a criminal case. In *Yakus v. United States,* criminal defendants prosecuted under the Act argued that its exclusive jurisdiction provisions denied them the opportunity to challenge price-control regulations at their criminal trial. Under the Act, the defendants could be prosecuted for violations of price-control regulations in any federal district court but could challenge the validity of the regulations only in the special Emergency Courts created by the Act. The defendants argued that this limit on federal jurisdiction operated to deny them rights under the Fifth and Sixth Amendments.

Consider whether the Court in *Yakus* may have suggested *some* limit on congressional power to control jurisdiction of inferior federal courts.

YAKUS v. UNITED STATES

321 U.S. 414 (1944)

CHIEF JUSTICE STONE delivered the opinion of the Court.

The questions for our decision are: (1) Whether the Emergency Price Control Act of January 30, 1942, as amended by the Inflation Control Act of October 2, 1942, involves an unconstitutional delegation to the Price Administrator of the legislative power of Congress to control prices; (2) whether § 204(d) of the Act was intended to preclude consideration by a district court of the validity of a maximum price regulation promulgated by the Administrator, as a defense to a criminal prosecution for its violation; (3) whether the exclusive statutory procedure set up by §§ 203 and 204 of the Act for administrative and judicial review of regulations, with the accompanying stay provisions, provide a sufficiently adequate means of determining the validity of a price regulation to meet the demands of due process; and (4) whether, in view of this available method of review, § 204(d) of the Act, if construed to preclude consideration of the validity of the regulation as a defense to a prosecution for violating it, contravenes the Sixth Amendment, or works an unconstitutional legislative interference with the judicial power.

Petitioners in both of these cases were tried and convicted by the District Court for Massachusetts upon several counts of indictments charging violation of §§ 4(a) and 205(b) of the Act by the willful sale of wholesale cuts of beef at prices above the maximum prices prescribed by [the] Revised Maximum Price Regulation No. 169. Petitioners have not availed themselves of the procedure set up by §§ 203 and 204 by which any person subject to a maximum price regulation may test its validity by protest to and hearing before the Administrator, whose determination may be reviewed on complaint to the Emergency Court of Appeals and by this Court on certiorari, see *Lockerty v. Phillips,* 319 U.S. 182. When the indictments were found the 60 days period allowed by the statute for filing protests had expired.

... They specifically raised the question reserved in *Lockerty v. Phillips,* whether the validity of a regulation may be challenged in defense of a prosecution for its violation although it had not been tested by the prescribed administrative procedure and complaint to the Emergency Court of Appeals. The District Court convicted petitioners upon verdicts of guilty. The Circuit Court of Appeals for the First Circuit affirmed, and we granted certiorari.

I.

* * * *

That Congress has constitutional authority to prescribe commodity prices as a war emergency measure, and that the Act was adopted by Congress in the exercise of that power, are not questioned here, and need not now be considered save as they have a bearing on the procedural features of the Act later to be considered which are challenged on constitutional grounds.

* * * *

II.

We consider next the question whether the procedure which Congress has established for determining the validity of the Administrator's regulations is exclusive so as to preclude the defense of invalidity of the Regulation in this criminal prosecution for its violation under §§ 4(a) and 205(b). Section 203(a) sets up a procedure by which "any person subject to any provision of [a] regulation [or] order" may within 60 days after it is issued "file a protest specifically setting forth objections to any such provision and affidavits or other written evidence in support of such objections." He may similarly protest later, on grounds arising after the expiration of the original sixty days. The subsection directs that within a reasonable time and in no event more than thirty days after the filing of a protest or ninety days after the issue of the regulation protested, whichever is later, "the Administrator shall either grant or deny such protest in whole or in part, notice such protest for hearing, or provide an opportunity to present further evidence in connection therewith. In the event that the Administrator denies any such protest in whole or in part, he shall inform the protestant of the grounds upon which such decision is based, and of any economic data and other facts of which the Administrator has taken official notice."

Section 204(c) creates a court to be known as the Emergency Court of Appeals consisting of United States district or circuit judges designated by the Chief Justice of the United States. Section 204(a) authorizes any person aggrieved by the denial or partial denial of his protest to file a complaint with the Emergency Court of Appeals within thirty days after the denial, praying that the regulation, order or price schedule protested be enjoined or set aside in whole or in part. The court may issue such an injunction only if it finds that the regulation, order or price schedule "is not in accordance with law, or is arbitrary or capricious." Subsection (b). It is denied power to issue a temporary restraining order or interlocutory decree. Subsection (c). The effectiveness of any permanent injunction it may issue is postponed for thirty days, and if review by this Court is sought upon writ of certiorari, as authorized by subsection (d), its effectiveness is further postponed until final disposition of the case by this Court by denial of certiorari or decision upon the merits. Subsection (b).

Section 204(d) declares:

> The Emergency Court of Appeals, and the Supreme Court upon review of judgments and orders of the Emergency Court of Appeals, shall have exclusive jurisdiction to determine the validity of any regulation or order issued under section 2, . . . of any price schedule effective in accordance with the provisions of section 206, . . . and of

> any provision of any such regulation, order, or price schedule. Except as provided in this section, no court, Federal, State, or Territorial, shall have jurisdiction or power to consider the validity of any such regulation, order, or price schedule, or to stay, restrain, enjoin, or set aside, in whole or in part, any provision of this Act authorizing the issuance of such regulations or orders, or making effective any such price schedule, or any provision of any such regulation, order, or price schedule, or to restrain or enjoin the enforcement of any such provision.

In *Lockerty v. Phillips*, we held that these provisions conferred on the Emergency Court of Appeals, subject to review by this Court, exclusive equity jurisdiction to restrain enforcement of price regulations of the Administrator and that they withdrew such jurisdiction from all other courts. This was accomplished by the exercise of the constitutional power of Congress to prescribe the jurisdiction of inferior federal courts, and the jurisdiction of all state courts to determine federal questions, and to vest that jurisdiction in a single court, the Emergency Court of Appeals.

The considerations which led us to that conclusion with respect to the equity jurisdiction of the district court, lead to the like conclusion as to its power to consider the validity of a price regulation as a defense to a criminal prosecution for its violation. The provisions of § 204(d), conferring upon the Emergency Court of Appeals and this Court "exclusive jurisdiction to determine the validity of any regulation or order", coupled with the provision that "no court, Federal, State, or Territorial, shall have jurisdiction or power to consider the validity of any such regulation", are broad enough in terms to deprive the district court of power to consider the validity of the Administrator's regulation or order as a defense to a criminal prosecution for its violation.

* * * *

III

We come to the question whether the provisions of the Act, so construed as to deprive petitioners of opportunity to attack the Regulation in a prosecution for its violation, deprive them of the due process of law guaranteed by the Fifth Amendment. At the trial, petitioners offered to prove that the Regulation would compel them to sell beef at such prices as would render it impossible for wholesalers such as they are, no matter how efficient, to conduct their business other than at a loss. . . .

* * * *

The petitioners are not confronted with the choice of abandoning their businesses or subjecting themselves to the penalties of the Act before they have sought and secured a determination of the Regulation's validity. It is true that if the Administrator denies a protest no stay or injunction may become effective before the final decision of the Emergency Court or of this Court if review here is sought. It is also true that the process of reaching a final decision may be time-consuming. But while courts have no power to suspend or ameliorate the operation of a regulation during the pendency of proceedings to determine its validity, we cannot say that the Administrator has no such power or assume that he would not exercise it in an appropriate case.

* * * *

The award of an interlocutory injunction by courts of equity has never been regarded as strictly a matter of right, even though irreparable injury may otherwise result to the plaintiff. Even in suits in which only private interests are involved the award is a matter of sound judicial discretion, in the exercise of which the court balances the conveniences of the parties and possible injuries to them according as they may be affected by the granting or withholding of the injunction. And it will avoid such inconvenience and injury so far as may be, by attaching conditions to the award, such as the requirement of an injunction bond conditioned upon payment of any damage caused by the injunction if the plaintiff's contentions are not sustained.

But where an injunction is asked which will adversely affect a public interest for whose impairment, even temporarily, an injunction bond cannot compensate, the court may in the public interest withhold relief until a final determination of the rights of the parties, though the postponement may be burdensome to the plaintiff. This is but another application of the principle . . . that "Courts of equity may, and frequently do, go much further both to give and withhold relief in furtherance of the public interest than they are accustomed to go when only private interests are involved."

Here, in the exercise of the power to protect the national economy from the disruptive influences of inflation in time of war Congress has seen fit to postpone injunctions restraining the operations of price regulations until their lawfulness could be ascertained by an appropriate and expeditious procedure. In so doing it has done only what a court of equity could have done, in the exercise of its discretion to protect the public interest. What the courts could do Congress can do as the guardian of the public interest of the nation in time of war. The legislative formulation of what would otherwise be a rule of judicial discretion is not a denial of due process or a usurpation of judicial functions.[12]

* * * *

IV

As we have seen Congress, through its power to define the jurisdiction of inferior federal courts and to create such courts for the exercise of the judicial power, could, subject to other constitutional limitations, create the Emergency Court of Appeals, give to it exclusive equity jurisdiction to determine the validity of price regulations prescribed by the Administrator, and foreclose any further or other consideration of the validity of a regulation as a defense to a prosecution for its violation.

Unlike most penal statutes and regulations whose validity can be determined only by running the risk of violation, the present statute provides a mode of testing the validity of a regulation by an independent administrative proceeding. There is no constitutional requirement that that test be made in one tribunal rather than in another, so long as there is an opportunity to be heard and for judicial review which satisfies the demands of due process, as is the case here. This was recognized in *Bradley v. City of Richmond* . . . and has never been

12. [In footnote 8 of this opinion, the Court listed examples of federal legislation restricting federal court power to issue injunctions, including the Norris-La Guardia Act (regulating federal court power to grant injunctions in labor disputes and barring injunctions where "contrary to the public policy" as defined in the Act).]

doubted by this Court. And we are pointed to no principle of law or provision of the Constitution which precludes Congress from making criminal the violation of an administrative regulation, by one who has failed to avail himself of an adequate separate procedure for the adjudication of its validity, or which precludes the practice, in many ways desirable, of splitting the trial for violations of an administrative regulation by committing the determination of the issue of its validity to the agency which created it, and the issue of violation to a court which is given jurisdiction to punish violations. Such a requirement presents no novel constitutional issue.

No procedural principle is more familiar to this Court than that a constitutional right may be forfeited in criminal as well as civil cases by the failure to make timely assertion of the right before a tribunal having jurisdiction to determine it. Courts may for that reason refuse to consider a constitutional objection even though a like objection had previously been sustained in a case in which it was properly taken. . . .

* * * *

We have no occasion to decide whether one charged with criminal violation of a duly promulgated price regulation may defend on the ground that the regulation is unconstitutional on its face. Nor do we consider whether one who is forced to trial and convicted of violation of a regulation, while diligently seeking determination of its validity by the statutory procedure may thus be deprived of the defense that the regulation is invalid. There is no contention that the present regulation is void on its face, petitioners have taken no step to challenge its validity by the procedure which was open to them and it does not appear that they have been deprived of the opportunity to do so. Even though the statute should be deemed to require it, any ruling at the criminal trial which would preclude the accused from showing that he had had no opportunity to establish the invalidity of the regulation by resort to the statutory procedure, would be reviewable on appeal on constitutional grounds. It will be time enough to decide questions not involved in this case when they are brought to us for decision, as they may be, whether they arise in the Emergency Court of Appeals or in the district court upon a criminal trial.

* * * *

Affirmed.

Justice Roberts [dissenting].

I dissent. I find it unnecessary to discuss certain of the questions treated in the opinion of the court. I am of opinion that the Act unconstitutionally delegates legislative power to the Administrator. As I read the opinion of the court it holds the Act valid on the ground that sufficiently precise standards are prescribed to confine the Administrator's regulations and orders within fixed limits, and that judicial review is provided effectively to prohibit his transgression of those limits. I believe that analysis demonstrates the contrary. I proceed, therefore, to examine the statute.

* * * *

Justice Rutledge, dissenting. [Murphy, J., joining]

I agree with the Court's conclusions upon the substantive issues. But I am unable to believe that the trial afforded the petitioners conformed to constitutional requirements. The matter is of such importance as requires a statement of the reasons for dissent.

* * * *

II

* * * *

I have no difficulty with the provision which confers jurisdiction upon the Emergency Court of Appeals to determine the validity of price regulations or, if that had been all, with the mandate which makes its jurisdiction in that respect exclusive. Equally clear is the power of Congress to deprive the other federal courts of jurisdiction to issue stay orders, restraining orders, injunctions or other relief to prevent the operation of price regulations or to set them aside. So much may be rested on Congress' plenary authority to define and control the jurisdiction of the federal courts. Constitution, Article III, Section 2; *Lockerty v. Phillips*, 319 U.S. 182. It may be taken too, for the purposes of this case, that Congress' power to channel enforcement of federal authority through the federal courts sustains the like prohibitions it has placed on the state courts. Without more, the statute's provisions would seem to be unquestionably within the Congressional power.

Congress however was not content to create a single national tribunal, give it exclusive jurisdiction to determine all cases arising under the statute, and deny jurisdiction over them to all other courts. It provided for enforcement by civil and criminal proceedings in the federal district courts and in the state courts throughout the country.

This, too, it could do, though only if adequate proceedings, in the constitutional sense, were authorized. And I agree that the enforcing jurisdiction would not be made inadequate merely by the fact that no stay order or other relief could be had pending the outcome of litigation. Confronted as the nation was with the imminent danger of inflation and therefore the necessity that price controls should become effective at once and continue so without interruption at least until invalidated in particular instances, Congress could require individuals to sustain, in deference to the paramount public interest, whatever harm might ensue during the period of litigation and until each had demonstrated the invalidity of the regulation as it affected himself. Runaway inflation could not have been avoided in any other way. The lid had to go on, go on tight and stay tight. This necessity united with the general presumption of validity which attaches to legislation and Congress' power to control the jurisdiction of the courts to sustain its denial of power to all courts, including the enforcing courts, the Emergency Court and this one, to suspend operation of the regulations pending final determination of validity.

The crux of this case comes, as I see it, in the question whether Congress can confer jurisdiction upon federal and state courts in the enforcement proceedings, more particularly the criminal suit, and at the same time deny them 'jurisdiction or power to consider the validity' of the regulations for which enforcement is thus sought. This question which the Court now says "presents no novel constitutional issue" was expressly and carefully reserved in *Lockerty v. Phillips*. The prohibition is the statute's most novel feature. In combination with others it gives the procedure a culminating summary touch and presents questions different from those arising from the other features.

The prohibition is unqualified. It makes no distinction between regulations invalid on constitutional grounds and others merely departing in some respect from statutory limitations . . .

It is one thing for Congress to withhold jurisdiction. It is entirely another to confer it and direct that it be exercised in a manner inconsistent with constitutional requirements or, what in some instances may be the same thing, without regard to them. Once it is held that Congress can require the courts criminally to enforce unconstitutional laws or statutes, including regulations, or to do so without regard for their validity, the way will have been found to circumvent the supreme law and, what is more, to make the courts parties to doing so. This Congress cannot do. There are limits to the judicial power. Congress may impose others. And in some matters Congress or the President has final say under the Constitution. But whenever the judicial power is called into play, it is responsible directly to the fundamental law and no other authority can intervene to force or authorize the judicial body to disregard it. The problem therefore is not solely one of individual right or due process of law. It is equally one of the separation and independence of the powers of government and of the constitutional integrity of the judicial process, more especially in criminal trials.

* * * *

VII

To sanction conviction of crime in a proceeding which does not accord the accused full protection for his rights under the Fifth and Sixth Amendments, and which entails a substantial legislative incursion on the constitutionally derived judicial power, if indeed this ever could be sustained, would require a showing of the greatest emergency coupled with an inability to accomplish the substantive ends sought in any other way. . . .

[The Court further noted that] the foreclosure of criminal defense should be allowed, if at all, only by a procedure affording its substantial equivalent, in relation to special constitutional issues and in such a manner that the failure to follow it reasonably could be taken as an actual, not a forced waiver. Thus, possibly foreclosure of criminal defense could be sustained, when validity turns on complex economic questions, usually of confiscatory effects of legislation, and proof of complicated facts bearing on them. But, if so, this should be only when the special proceeding is clearly adequate, affording the usual rights to present evidence, cross-examine, and make argument, characteristic of judicial proceedings, so that, if followed, the party would have a substantial equivalent to defense in a criminal trial. . . .

In respect to other questions, such as the drawing of racial or religious lines in orders or by their application, of a character determinable as well by the criminal as by the special tribunal, in my opinion the special constitutional limitations applicable to federal criminal trials, and due enforcement of some substantive requirements as well, require keeping open and available the chance for full and complete defense in the criminal trial itself.

The judgment should be reversed.

DISCUSSION AND QUESTIONS

According to the majority in *Yakus,* the defendants failed to take advantage of the special Emergency Courts in which they might have challenged the validity of price-control regulations under which they were prosecuted. The Court rules, in essence, that the defendants procedurally waived this opportunity. As for the defendants' argument that they were entitled to challenge the price-control regulation in the same court in which they were prosecuted, the Court observed "there is no constitutional requirement that that test be made in one tribunal rather than in another, so long as there is an opportunity to be heard and for judicial review which satisfies the demands of due process, as is the case here."

Justice Rutledge, dissenting, concluded that Congress' jurisdictional scheme violated the Constitution. "It is one thing for Congress to withhold jurisdiction. It is entirely another to confer it and direct that it be exercised in a manner inconsistent with constitutional requirements."

The Supreme Court has reinvigorated debates about the scope of federal court habeas power and limits on congressional authority to regulate habeas jurisdiction (see also Chapters 12 and 13). In *In re Davis*, 130 S. Ct. 1 (2009), the Court, in a one-paragraph opinion, transferred a writ of habeas corpus to a federal district court with instructions to adjudicate the state prisoner's original habeas petition. Justice Stevens, in concurrence, endorsed federal district court power to issue habeas relief and maintained that the Court expressly left open the question whether the Antiterrorism and Effective Death Penalty Act of 1996 (AEDPA) applies to original habeas petitions. *Id.* at 1 (citing *Felker v. Turpin*, 518 U.S. 651, 663 (1996)). He alternatively opined that such a congressional limitation on federal court power to issue a writ of habeas corpus "is arguably unconstitutional to the extent it bars relief for a death row inmate who has established his [actual] innocence." *Id.*

In dissent, Justice Scalia vehemently argued that the federal district court would be powerless to grant any relief as petitioner's claim was a "sure loser" (already fully aired and rejected by the Georgia Supreme Court) and thus barred by AEDPA, which blocks issuance of a writ of habeas corpus regarding "any claim that was adjudicated on the merits in State court proceedings unless adjudication of the claim . . . resulted in a decision that was contrary to, or involved an unreasonable application of, clearly established Federal law, as determined by the Supreme Court of the United States." *Id.* at 2-3 (quoting AEDPA § 2254(d)(1)). Moreover, Justice Scalia reiterated that it is frivolous to maintain that the Constitution requires federal-court screening of all state convictions for constitutional violations. *Id.* at 3. Justice Scalia added, if instead the Court has "new-found doubts regarding the constitutionality of § 2254(d)(1)," the Court should hear the prisoner's application and resolve the issue itself rather than transferring the writ to a federal district court that lacks the power to issue relief— "a fool's errand." *Id.* at 3-4. Who has the better argument—Justice Stevens or Justice Scalia? If limits on congressional authority over the scope of habeas jurisdiction exist, what are the constitutional sources of such limits?

According to the majority and dissenting opinions in *Yakus*, is Congress' power over inferior federal courts' jurisdiction limited by Article III (an "internal" limit) or by some other provision in the Constitution (an "external" limit)? Do these opinions differ about constitutional doctrine, or do they instead differ about how the federal Act restricted defendants' assertion of their criminal defense?

In *Yakus*, the defendants challenged a restriction on federal court jurisdiction that limited their ability to assert a defense to their prosecution. The next case addresses a jurisdictional restriction that limits a civil plaintiff's ability to assert a cause of action offensively.

BATTAGLIA v. GENERAL MOTORS CORP.

169 F.2d 254 (2d Cir. 1948)

CHASE, CIRCUIT JUDGE:

Four separate suits were brought against the appellee in the District Court for the Western District of New York by and in behalf of its employees to recover overtime pay in accordance with the provisions of the Fair Labor Standards Act of 1938, as interpreted by the Supreme Court. . . . While these suits were pending without adjudication, Congress enacted the Portal-to-Portal Act of 1947. The appellee then moved to dismiss each of the complaints, which for present purposes may be treated as identical, on the grounds that no cause of action was alleged and that the court was without jurisdiction by virtue of section 2 of the Portal-to-Portal Act. As the appellants then questioned this statute upon constitutional grounds, notice of that was given the Attorney General and he was allowed to intervene in behalf of the government in support of the validity of the Act. The motions to dismiss were granted. . . . Appeals taken by the plaintiffs from each of those orders were consolidated for hearing.

The complaints alleged a cause of action under section 16(b) of the Fair Labor Standards Act for overtime compensation and an additional equal amount as liquidated damages, together with reasonable attorney's fees, for time upon the employer's premises preliminary to, and after engagement in, the principal activities of the employees. This time was spent by the employees in walking to and from their work stations and walking out of their employers' premises when their principal work was done; in changing their clothes on their employer's premises before and after their main activities; in receiving their orders; in obtaining on such premises their tools and other equipment before, and in disposing of them after, their main activities; in washing and cleansing themselves after their principal work was done; and in lunch and rest periods during which their time was not entirely at their own disposal. It was not alleged that the compensation sought was for activities which were compensable by an express provision of a written or nonwritten contract, or by a custom or practice, in effect at the time of the activities and at the place of employment. Consequently, appellants did not meet the conditions of subdivision (a) of section 2 of the Portal-to-Portal Act on showing the employer's liability under the Fair Labor Standards Act, nor did they comply with the jurisdictional requirements of subdivision (d) of that section of the Act.[13]

. . . We think the dismissal of each cause of action right, for the following reasons.

A few of the district court decisions sustaining section 2 of the Portal-to-Portal Act have done so on the ground that since jurisdiction of federal courts other

13. [Footnote 3 in Court's opinion.] "(a) No employer shall be subject to any liability or punishment under the Fair Labor Standards Act of 1938, as amended, . . . , on account of the failure of such employer to pay an employee minimum wages, or to pay an employee overtime compensation, for or on account of any activity of an employee engaged in prior to May 14, 1947. . . .

* * * *

"(d) No court of the United States, of any State, Territory, or possession of the United States, or of the District of Columbia, shall have jurisdiction of any action or proceeding, whether instituted prior to or after May 14, 1947, to enforce liability or impose punishment for or on account of the failure of the employer to pay minimum wages or overtime compensation under the Fair Labor Standards Act of 1938, as amended, under the Walsh-Healey Act, or under the Bacon-Davis Act, to the extent that such action or proceeding seeks to enforce any liability or impose any punishment with respect to an activity which was not compensable under subsections (a) and (b) of this section."

than the Supreme Court is conferred by Congress, it may at the will of Congress be taken away in whole or in part. Relying upon a statement of the Supreme Court in *Kline v. Burke Construction Co.*, 260 U.S. 226, and on cases like . . . *Ex parte McCardle*, these district court decisions would, in effect, sustain subdivision (d) of section 2 of the Act regardless of whether subdivisions (a) and (b) were valid. We think, however, that the exercise of Congress of its control over jurisdiction is subject to compliance with at least the requirements of the Fifth Amendment. That is to say, while Congress has the undoubted power to give, withhold, and restrict the jurisdiction of courts other than the Supreme Court, it must not so exercise that power as to deprive any person of life, liberty, or property without due process of law or to take private property without just compensation. Thus, regardless of whether subdivision (d) of section 2 had an independent end in itself, if one of its effects would be to deprive the appellants of property without due process or just compensation, it would be invalid. Under this view, subdivision (d) on the one hand and subdivisions (a) and (b) on the other will stand or fall together. We turn then to a consideration of the question whether the appellants have been unconstitutionally deprived of any substantive rights.

It is contended that, while the employees' rights to overtime compensation ultimately flow from the Fair Labor Standards Act, they are also in some sense "contractual" in nature and hence vested. And it is well settled that contracts made by private parties must necessarily be constructed in the light of the applicable law at the time of their execution. These appellants' contracts of employment with the appellee were made before the Fair Labor Standards Act was enacted. Thus it cannot be said that the contracts were 'made,' as the appellants put it, with reference to the provisions of that Act. . . .

* * * *

Thus, there are, we think, three ways in which the employees' rights to compensation for these activities may be viewed: first, as wholly statutory up to the time the Portal-to-Portal Act was enacted; second, as purely statutory up to the time of the Supreme Court decisions and contractual thereafter; and finally, as wholly contractual from the beginning. We . . . think that however appellants' rights are considered, the Portal-to-Portal Act is constitutional.

This seems plain enough, if we take the view that the claims rested purely on statute up to the time the Portal-to-Portal Act was enacted. Clearly, the general rule is that "powers derived wholly from a statute are extinguished by its repeal." The Supreme Court, moreover, has told us that rights granted to employees under the Fair Labor Standards Act have a "private-public character" and has indicated that they are "charged or colored with the public interest." Congress has also found that it "is in the national public interest and for the general welfare, essential to national defense and necessary to aid, protect, and foster commerce" that the Portal-to-Portal Act be enacted. This being true, so long as the claims, if they were purely statutory, had not ripened into final judgment, regardless of whether the activities on which they were based had been performed, they were subject to whatever action Congress might take with respect to them.

If however, the rights were statutory up to the time of the Supreme Court decisions and contractual thereafter, or if they were founded upon contract from the time of the enactment of the Fair Labor Standards Act, the problem is not so simple, for there are a number of cases holding that it is a violation of due process to deprive an individual of previously vested contractual rights.

But the solution to the problem seems quite as clear. The Portal-to-Portal Act, like the Fair Labor Standards Act, was passed as an exercise of the power to regulate commerce from time to time as conditions may require. The Congressional findings, made after investigations which disclosed amply supporting facts, show fully why the enactment of the Portal-to-Portal Act was necessary to avoid great injury to interstate commerce. In the Act Congress saw fit to change the Fair Labor Standards Act, which might be said previously to have made the appellants' contracts of employment include the right to compensation for Portal to Portal activities, by doing away with so much of those contracts in that respect as that statute had added to them. This did not deprive the appellants of any Constitutional right. If the contractual arrangements of these private parties were subject to the Fair Labor Standards Act as it might be interpreted by the courts, or were modified to take into consideration decisions construing that statute, they were also subject to changes made in it by Congress in the exercise of its power to regulate commerce. Very closely in point is *Louisville & Nashville R. Co. v. Mottley*, where a contract to furnish transportation free of charge—valid when made and based upon adequate consideration—was held unenforceable when Congress later, in the exercise of its commerce power, made it unlawful for railroads to provide such transportation. The private contract to furnish free transportation was totally destroyed. The Supreme Court there said: "The agreement between the railroad company and the Mottleys must necessarily be regarded as having been made subject to the possibility that, at some future time, Congress might so exert its whole constitutional power in regulating interstate commerce as to render that agreement unenforceable, or to impair its value. That the exercise of such power may be hampered or restricted to any extent by contracts previously made between individuals or corporations is inconceivable. . . . If that principle be not sound, the result would be individuals and corporations could, by contracts between themselves, in anticipation of legislation, render of no avail the exercise of Congress, to the full extent authorized by the Constitution, of its power to regulate commerce. No power of Congress can be thus restricted." The controlling principle was said . . . to be that: "Not only are existing laws read into contracts in order to fix obligations as between the parties, but the reservation of essential attributes of sovereign power is also read into contracts as postulate of the legal order." And this principle is not limited to cases where the effect of the exercise of Congressional power upon pre-existing contracts is only incidental.

This is not to say, of course, that Congress may exercise its commerce power in a discriminatory or arbitrary manner. We need not go so far. Faced with what it reasonably considered a situation relating to commerce that called for legislative action, Congress, after a thorough investigation, enacted the Portal-to-Portal Act. It cannot be said that, in so doing, Congress acted arbitrarily. It is not even suggested that it acted discriminatorily. Clearly the Act did not violate the Fifth Amendment in so far as it may have withdrawn from private individuals, these appellants, any rights they may said to have had which rested upon private contracts they had made.

Nor is the Portal-to-Portal Act a violation of Article III of the Constitution or an encroachment upon the separate power of the judiciary. True enough, decisions of the Supreme Court played their part in creating the conditions Congress undertook to remedy, as it expressly stated in section 1(a) of the Act. But those decisions were construing a previously enacted statute. The regulatory legislation did not attempt to change these decisions in any way, or to impose upon the courts any rule of decision not in conformity with basic legal concepts, as in *United States v.*

Klein.[14] On the contrary, it left express private contracts and those implied in fact, except to the extent that they may be said to have . . . reference to prior statutory law, untouched and enforceable in the courts as before under the applicable legal principles. It did not require repayment of any money paid in reliance upon the decisions of the Supreme Court. It left valid final judgments for portal-to-portal pay. Since Congress, for the reasons heretofore stated, otherwise had the power to enact the Portal-to-Portal Act, the fact that one of the Act's incidental effects is to prevent the courts from following the *Tennessee Coal Iron & R. Co., Jewell Ridge Coal Corp.*, and *Mt. Clemens Pottery* cases, is of no importance. . . .

Judgments affirmed.

DISCUSSION AND QUESTIONS

After recognizing Congress' authority to restrict the jurisdiction of inferior federal courts, the *Battaglia* court admonished that Congress "must not so exercise that power as to deprive any person of life, liberty, or property without due process of law or to take private property without just compensation." Ultimately, the court avoided rendering Congress' statute unconstitutional by finding that plaintiffs did not possess a sufficient property right to justify due process application. Is this still a significant ruling? Does the Second Circuit's ruling seem consistent with Supreme Court precedent?

To review the material on congressional control over the jurisdiction of inferior federal courts, consider Problem 3-2.

PROBLEM 3-2

A Lethal Dose of Jurisdiction

For years, a number of states have administered lethal injections to execute individuals convicted of capital crimes. Recently, anti–death penalty advocates and criminal defense lawyers have orchestrated a series of legal challenges to lethal injection procedures based on the Eighth Amendment's prohibition against "cruel and unusual punishments." The Supreme Court has issued a splintered ruling on one of these challenges; the Court held the lethal injection at bar to be constitutional. The anti–death penalty challenges persist. Plaintiffs have submitted evidence sufficient to show that certain lethal injection procedures are unconstitutional under the Court's splintered decision.

Assume that, in response to one of these challenges, a federal district court enters a temporary injunction enjoining a state from administering any lethal injections pending further hearings to consider scientific evidence regarding the pain levels incident to such injections.

14. [Footnote 15 in Court's opinion.] It is contended that Congress, by distinguishing more or less between claims arising prior to the enactment of the Act and those arising thereafter, permitting by virtue of section 4 recovery for all activities compensable under the Fair Labor Standards Act and performed after the passage of the Act except those "preliminary to or postliminary to said principal activity or activities," has thus constituted itself "judge and jury" in the "plainest possible violation" of Article III, § 1. We think, however, that such a distinction was a wholly reasonable one to make. One of the primary reasons for the passage of the Portal-to-Portal Act was the fact that, according to the Congressional findings in section 1(a), liabilities for activities performed prior to the Supreme Court decisions were "wholly unexpected" and "retroactive in operation." This of course, was not true as to activities engaged in after the enactment of the Act.

A pro–death penalty majority in Congress, with the support of the administration, is extremely concerned that the lethal injection argument is a Trojan horse designed to erode the state's power to implement capital punishment. To forestall future proceedings in federal court, Congress enacts the "Death Penalty Protection Act," which states:

> No court created by an Act of Congress shall have any jurisdiction, and the Supreme Court shall have no appellate jurisdiction, to hear or decide any question pertaining to the interpretation of the Eighth Amendment of the Constitution or concerning the validity of execution by lethal injection.

Using all of the cases you have encountered thus far, analyze the wisdom and constitutional validity of the Act.

As you might have noticed by this point in the chapter, the limits of congressional power to dictate federal jurisdiction often tend to be tested when there is a significant rift involving separation-of-powers concerns. What would occur if, as illustrated in Problem 3-2, Congress fully flexed its muscle and attempted to strip federal courts of all jurisdiction over a controversial subject matter? Consider the following excerpt from a fictional conversation involving a key member of each of the three branches of government—Senator Roll Call, Attorney General Blanche Mansion, and Justice Life Tenure—during a period of high tension and acrimony:

> SENATOR CALL: Certainly you cannot argue that we lack the power to strip inferior federal courts of jurisdiction. Lower federal courts wouldn't even exist but for the fact that Congress created them. And, we created them under power explicitly given to us from the Constitution. The Framers, in their wisdom, determined that Congress could, at its discretion, "ordain and establish" lower federal courts. Thus, we could have decided to never create lower federal courts at all. It should go without saying that the power to create is the power to destroy. The greater power includes the lesser power. You can't deny that the legislative branch possesses inherent authority to strip jurisdiction of lower federal courts.
>
> ATTORNEY GENERAL MANSION: Isn't the argument even stronger than the implied notion that the greater power includes the lesser power? It's widely accepted that the Constitution is clear that Congress possesses the power to regulate inferior federal courts. It emanates from the Constitutional Convention's Madisonian compromise itself, which included the "agreement that the question whether access to the lower federal courts was necessary to assure the effectiveness of federal law should not be answered as a matter of constitutional principle, but rather, should be left a matter of political and legislative judgment."
>
> JUSTICE TENURE: First, you know that provision was the result of a complex compromise among competing interests of the Framers. The Nationalists, or Federalists, argued to mandate the establishment of lower federal courts in order to ensure enforcement of federal law; while the Localists, or Anti-Federalists, believed that state courts would be adequate to interpret federal law. You are correct that the compromise resulted in Article III leaving the *creation* of lower federal courts to Congress. But, remember, that the driving force behind the Localist stance was that states were competent to conduct an "initial" review bound as they are under the Supremacy Clause and as long as ultimate Supreme Court review remained. Here, Congress is attempting to strip the whole federal forum.

Second, simply because Congress possesses the power to create lower federal courts does not translate into possessing the power to control absolutely. Judicial power is "vested" in the federal courts. Consider the presidential context. Congress may create a Department of Justice that has an Attorney General, but just because Congress created the Attorney General position does not mean that Congress retains all control over the position. Rather, it becomes the President's power to appoint the individual, and Congress cannot dictate who should be selected simply on the basis that Congress created the position. The same is true if you analogize to *INS v. Chadha*. As you will recall, Congress tried to retain budgetary veto authority on the ground that Congress created the Immigration and Naturalization Service, but as you also know the Supreme Court determined that a legislative veto violated the Presentment Clause and impermissibly interfered with the President's veto power. For instance, you can choose to create a child, but you do not retain absolute control over the child. It becomes an independent entity.

SENATOR CALL: I'll buy your child analogy because I think we created Frankenstein. Didn't the Supreme Court already resolve this issue back in the 1800s?

JUSTICE TENURE: I disagree. Congress can create inferior federal courts, but once it has chosen to create them, which it did long ago, those entities take on a constitutional life of their own. Those courts accordingly have all the power and inherent authority that they derive from being a part of a coequal branch of government. The distinction between the power to create and the power to regulate is a central tenet of power sharing within the construct of the separation of powers doctrine.

SENATOR CALL: Congress also has the power to curtail the appellate jurisdiction of the Supreme Court via the Exceptions Clause of the Constitution. There is no limitation on what types of cases that Congress may opt to exclude from the appellate jurisdiction as set forth in the Constitution. Moreover, if the Constitution itself isn't clear enough for you, leading scholars in this arena, such as Professors Van Alstyne, Gunther, and Wechsler, agree that Congress possesses the power as I have described it. All one needs to do is review the testimony from the congressional hearings regarding the Defense of Marriage Act. Preeminent scholars, led by the Majority's witness, Professor Martin Redish, concluded that Congress possesses the power to strip jurisdiction.

JUSTICE TENURE: Again, I can refute the global scope you are asserting with another apt analogy. Similar to the constitutional grant of authority to Congress under the Exceptions Clause, the Constitution also grants Congress the appropriations power. With the appropriations power, Congress again has an express textual grant to handle appropriations; *but* most serious constitutional scholars would agree that even though Congress has a plenary express grant of power to appropriate funds, Congress cannot zero out the budgets for the federal courts because that would be interfering with the core functions of coequal branches and thus would violate separation of powers doctrine. So, while Congress has an express grant of authority to manipulate the Supreme Court's appellate jurisdiction, even this grant comes embedded with limits. The power must be exercised within the permissible sphere of authority and not interfere with the core functions of the Court. The jurisdiction-stripping bills, as passed by the House, do not represent the permissible sphere of authority.

ATTORNEY GENERAL MANSION: You lack any support for your proposition that Congress lacks the power to proceed.

SENATOR CALL: That is because they have no authority for their assertion on this point.

JUSTICE TENURE: To the contrary, I can point to the seminal work of Professor Henry Hart in which he utilized Socratic dialogue to demonstrate that Congress cannot exercise the "exceptions" power without violating the core functions of the Supreme Court. Others have advanced Hart's theory. For example, Professor Leonard Ratner maintains that the essential constitutional functions of the Court are to maintain supremacy and uniformity of federal law. He further asserts that "some avenue must remain open to permit ultimate resolution by the Supreme Court of persistent conflicts between state and federal law or in the interpretation of federal law by lower courts." A former Attorney General for President Ronald Reagan, William French Smith, echoed Ratner's contentions and additionally provided an argument external to Article III in that he insisted that "no one Branch of Government should have the power to eliminate the fundamental constitutional role of either of the other Branches." He knew that the role of the independent judiciary must be protected within the separation of powers scheme. The ultimate failsafe is that Congress cannot strip all avenues to the federal forum without violating due process. According to Professor Akhil Amar, Congress cannot strip jurisdiction from all federal courts because Article III mandates that federal jurisdiction must extend to all "arising under" cases–whether it be via original or appellate jurisdiction. With two inartfully drawn bills, Congress has unconstitutionally left no avenue to a federal forum and thus violated the separation of powers.

ATTORNEY GENERAL MANSION: You appear to be overlooking the trump card in favor of congressional authority — *Ex parte McCardle.* It's Supreme Court precedent no less. You know that *McCardle,* without a doubt, stands for the proposition that Congress possesses the power to limit the Supreme Court's appellate jurisdiction even during the pendency of an appeal. Congress hoped to derail an anticipated adverse ruling from the Supreme Court with its proposed limit on appellate jurisdiction, and the Court upheld Congress' maneuver as a valid exercise of Congress' Article III power under the Exceptions Clause.

SENATOR CALL: According to my Chief Counsel who looked into this issue for me, the Court, in *McCardle,* notably stated: "We are not at liberty to inquire into the motives of the legislature. We can only examine into its power under the Constitution; and the power to make exceptions to the appellate jurisdiction of this court is given by express words."

JUSTICE TENURE: So, your purported conclusive precedent is an 1868 case that is flatly distinguishable from the instant attempts to strip jurisdiction from the entire federal judicial forum? Your read of *McCardle* is inaccurate. The critical ingredient in *McCardle* was that a petitioner could seek a federal forum through a writ of habeas corpus, notwithstanding Congress' appellate jurisdiction-limiting statute. The complete jurisdictional strips that Congress is considering at present would eviscerate the Court's core functions of supremacy and uniformity as envisioned by Justice Joseph Story in *Martin v. Hunter's Lessee,* which upheld the constitutionality of section 25 of the 1789 Judiciary Act against an assault by the highest court in Virginia.

Congress cannot pass an unconstitutional statute and simultaneously strip all federal courts of jurisdiction. Even if the avenue to state courts remains open, individual state courts are beholden to local politics and thus may not uphold the constitutional interest. The essence of *Marbury* would be thwarted. The federal judiciary will not quietly stand by and let this come to pass. We will strike down the strip if necessary.

ATTORNEY GENERAL MANSION: You know good and well that Chief Justice Chase's unanimous opinion in *McCardle* did not rely on the distinction regarding whether an avenue remained open when it upheld Congress' jurisdiction-curbing provision as constitutional.

SENATOR CALL: As for Justice Story, you also know that Supreme Court precedent is weak for your argument because there are "far more numerous statements from the Court suggesting very broad congressional authority" with respect to regulating federal court jurisdiction. These repeated "expressions of deference to congressional delineations of appellate jurisdiction" clearly surpass the ruminations of Justice Story. Even Justice Story himself lobbied for legislation that would be a congressional extension of the Judiciary Act. Isn't it more likely that Justice Story's words represent "exhortations regarding desirable policy [rather] than . . . expressions of constitutional commands"?

JUSTICE TENURE: The bottom line is that the Court has never had to face a situation in which Congress has sought to bar all access to the federal court system over a body of constitutional issues. Assuming *arguendo* that you both are correct, as *Bartlett* [*v. Bowen*, 816 F.2d 695 (D.C. Cir. 1987)] makes clear, to the extent that Article III is inconsistent with the Due Process Clause of the Fifth Amendment, the Fifth Amendment effectively modifies it because of the subsequent adoption of the [Fourteenth] Amendment. For example, if the Court found that denying a right violated the Due Process or Equal Protection Clause, the [Fourteenth] Amendment trumps Article III if the two clauses are inconsistent.

ATTORNEY GENERAL MANSION: The arguments that you now pose are amorphous and without bounds.

JUSTICE TENURE: Well, at any rate, I am not about to concede that Congress has the power. To be honest, I am of two minds about it, but let me be clear that you do not want to make the Supreme Court decide that case. Let me give you a little foreshadowing. If you pass a jurisdiction-stripping bill on a set of constitutional rights for example, then a case *will* reach federal court, and federal courts maintain inherent authority to determine whether jurisdiction is proper. We will find that it is proper and proceed to rule that your bill is unconstitutional as a violation of the separation of powers.

SENATOR CALL: What violation?

JUSTICE TENURE: A violation of the core functions of federal courts, a coequal branch of government. If pressed, we will strike it down as an impermissible encroachment of our core functions. Congress cannot pass an unconstitutional bill and simultaneously strip all federal court jurisdiction. More than violating the essential functions of the third branch, it would violate *Marbury* as the Supreme Court maintains the right "to say what the law is." Accordingly, the jurisdictional strip in the case of an unconstitutional statute is also unconstitutional. The Court certainly retains the authority to so rule.

ATTORNEY GENERAL MANSION: That is a whole lot of bunk.

SENATOR CALL: Last I checked most scholars rejected those arguments.

JUSTICE TENURE: The scholarly verdict is still out, but it is the Court that will have the *last word.*

SENATOR CALL: That's not your Court's precedent. I think you are bluffing.

ATTORNEY GENERAL MANSION: Plus, thanks to *some* of the Executive's predecessors the makeup of the Supreme Court contains a majority of justices who believe that "our federalism" means that states should be respected as able to decide constitutional matters. Based on modern federalist principles, I think the current Supreme Court will uphold Congress' use of power to strip federal court jurisdiction.[15]

15. Caprice L. Roberts, *Jurisdiction Stripping in Three Acts — A Three String Serenade*, 51 VILL. L. REV. 593, 636-46 (2006) (footnotes omitted).

REVIEW AND CONSOLIDATION

The Scope of Judicial Power

Consider at this point how you envision the scope of potential federal court jurisdiction set forth in Article III, section 2. Is that part of the Constitution the end or the beginning of the matters to which the "judicial Power" vested under Article III extends? Professor Chemerinsky has devised a framework for depicting the possible relationship between Article III jurisdiction and Congress.[16] Professor Chemerinsky asks whether the nine categories of jurisdiction stated in Article III, section 2, represent a constitutionally mandated jurisdictional floor, a jurisdictional ceiling, both, or neither. Figure 3-1 offers a graphic summarizing the possibilities identified by Chemerinsky.

FIGURE 3-1

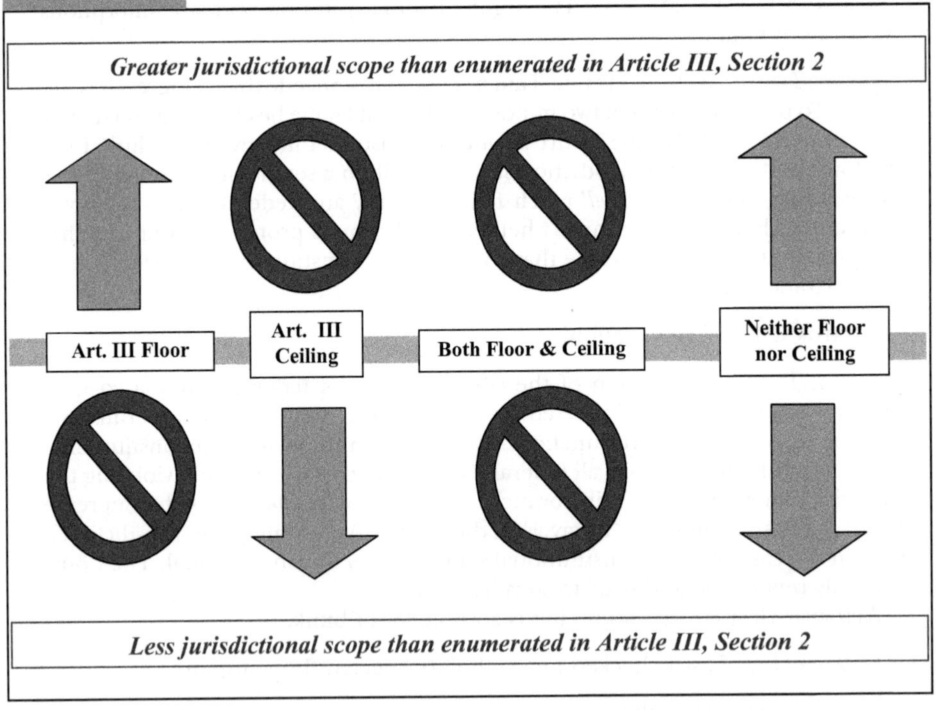

The middle horizontal line in Figure 3-1 represents the nine categories of "cases and controversies" listed in Article III, section 2. Upward pointing arrows illustrate the view that Congress can confer jurisdiction exceeding the express categories of Article III (i.e., Article III is not a ceiling on congressional power). Downward pointing arrows illustrate the view that Congress can confer less jurisdiction than is authorized by Article III (i.e., Article III is not a floor on congressional power). Finally, the slashed circles illustrate the view that

16. Erwin Chemerinsky, Federal Jurisdiction 177-78 (6th ed. 2012).

Congress cannot alter the jurisdictional grants in Article III, either by exceeding those grants or diminishing them.

Now work through some applications of Professor Chemerinsky's framework. Recall the Court's decision in *Sheldon v. Sill, supra,* where the Court held that Congress was not required to vest federal courts with the full diversity of citizenship jurisdiction authorized by Article III. Which constructs in Figure 3-1 might illustrate *Sheldon*'s view of jurisdiction? Which constructs of congressional power are plainly foreclosed by *Sheldon*?

Next consider Justice Joseph Story's view in *Martin v. Hunter's Lessee* that Article III *mandates* that its jurisdictional categories be vested in some federal court. Which of the constructs in Figure 3-1 might illustrate Justice Story's view? Which constructs of congressional power are plainly foreclosed by his view?

The last two constructs are conceptually counterintuitive to some. The third construct, which prevents Congress from either expanding or contracting the judicial powers enumerated in Article III, means that Article III is both a "floor" and a "ceiling." Does any case you have read support this view of Article III jurisdiction? Does Article III itself contain language that might support this view?

The fourth construct represents the view that the nine categories of "cases and controversies" in Article III are neither a floor nor a ceiling. Under this view, Congress can either expand or contract the categories of judicial power stated in Article III. Can you see why this view yields enormous power to Congress? Does this view seem consistent with the constitutional compromise agreed to by the Framers in Article III?

2. *Control of Decisionmaking*

We have explored a wide range of material regarding the roots, contours, and limits of Congress' power to control federal court jurisdiction. We have assumed, correctly, that the power to adjudicate cases arising under Article III is conferred on the judicial branch of government and not on other branches. The fundamental separation of governmental powers in our Constitution prevents Congress from dictating the outcome in Article III cases. Simply put, Congress cannot decide individual cases.

But to what extent does Congress possess the power to *influence* the decisionmaking of Article III courts? In reality, it requires subtle interpretation to determine when statutory maneuvers amount to mandating the result in a particular case — something not allowed — or only establishing the general rules by which federal court adjudication is to proceed. In fact, a spectrum of means exists by which Congress can attempt to influence decisionmaking of the federal judiciary. The key is determining which means are permitted under our constitutional scheme.

As you read the next case, *United States v. Klein,* consider how it relates to the materials you read above in section C.1.a., regarding congressional control over the Supreme Court's appellate jurisdiction. Like *McCardle* and *Yerger,* the *Klein* Court grappled with an effort by Congress to strip federal courts of jurisdiction. But *Klein* also involves an effort by Congress to control judicial decisionmaking. What additional limits on congressional power result from the Court's decision in *Klein*?

UNITED STATES v. KLEIN

80 U.S. 128 (1871)

THE CHIEF JUSTICE [CHASE] delivered the opinion of the court.

[This case involved a series of acts regarding the seizure and forfeiture of property used in support of the rebellion in the Civil War. The Act of March 12, 1863, provided that one could reclaim ownership by proving to the court ownership of the property and offering an oath that he provided no aid or comfort to the rebellion. The President, via the Act of July 17, 1862, possessed the power to pardon rebels fully and restore all property rights. Included among those pardoned in the President's December 8, 1863, proclamation was V.F. Wilson. Following Wilson's death in 1865, the administrator of his estate, Klein, filed a petition setting forth Wilson's ownership of cotton. The Court of Claims decreed $125,300 to Klein as the proceeds of the cotton that the U.S. Treasury possessed.

Prior to Klein's case, the Court considered the case of Padelford, who similarly engaged in the rebellion, deserted his cotton crops, claimed its proceeds, and took the amnesty oath. The Court ruled that the oath cured his participation and secured his right to his property's proceeds. In 1870, soon after the Court's decision in Padelford's case, Congress passed an act declaring: (i) no pardon would be admissible evidence to establish a claimant's right to property; (ii) any pardon previously granted to a person who aided the rebellion would constitute conclusive evidence of giving aid to the rebellion, and (iii) jurisdiction of the court would cease on proof of such a pardon and dismissal of the case would follow. In essence, the act mandated that courts reject (through dismissal for lack of jurisdiction) property claims of persons who had been pardoned by the President. Based on this Act, the U.S. Attorney General moved to dismiss Klein's case pending in the Supreme Court for want of jurisdiction.]

* * * *

It is thus seen that, except to property used in actual hostilities, as mentioned in the first section of the act of March 12th, 1863, no titles were divested in the insurgent States unless in pursuance of a judgment rendered after due legal proceedings. The government recognized to the fullest extent the humane maxims of the modern law of nations, which exempt private property of non-combatant enemies from capture as booty of war. Even the law of confiscation was sparingly applied. The cases were few indeed in which the property of any not engaged in actual hostilities was subjected to seizure and sale.

* * * *

The act directs the officers of the Treasury Department to take into their possession and make sale of all property abandoned by its owners or captured by the national forces, and to pay the proceeds into the national treasury.

That it was not the intention of Congress that the title to these proceeds should be divested absolutely out of the original owners of the property seems clear upon a comparison of different parts of the act.

* * * *

In the case of Padelford we held that the right to the possession of private property was not changed until actual seizure by proper military authority, and that actual seizure by such authority did not divest the title under the provisions of the Abandoned and Captured Property Act. . . .

[The Act] makes the right to the remedy dependent upon proof of loyalty, but implies that there may be proof of ownership without proof of loyalty. The property of the original owner is, in no case, absolutely divested. . . .

It is to be observed, however, that the Abandoned and Captured Property Act was approved on the 12th of March, 1863, and on the 17th of July, 1862, Congress had already passed an act — the same which provided for confiscation — which authorized the President, "at any time hereafter, by proclamation, to extend to persons who may have participated in the existing rebellion, in any State or part thereof, pardon and amnesty, with such exceptions and at such time and on such conditions as he may deem expedient for the public welfare." The act of the 12th of March, 1863, provided for the sale of enemies' property collected under the act, and payment of the proceeds into the treasury, and left them there subject to such action as the President might take under the act of the 17th of July, 1862. What was this action?

The suggestion of pardon by Congress, for such it was, rather than authority, remained unacted on for more than a year. At length, however, on the 8th of December, 1863, the President issued a proclamation, in which he referred to that act, and offered a full pardon, with restoration of all rights of property, except as to slaves and property in which rights of third persons had intervened, to all, with some exceptions, who, having been engaged in the rebellion as actual participants, or as aiders or abettors, would take and keep inviolate a prescribed oath. By this oath the person seeking to avail himself of the offered pardon was required to promise that he would thenceforth support the Constitution of the United States and the union of the States thereunder, and would also abide by and support all acts of Congress and all proclamations of the President in reference to slaves, unless the same should be modified or rendered void by the decision of this court.

In his annual message, transmitted to Congress on the same day, the President said "the Constitution authorizes the Executive to grant or withhold pardon at his own absolute discretion." He asserted his power "to grant it on terms as fully established," and explained the reasons which induced him to require applicants for pardon and restoration of property to take the oath prescribed, in these words: "Laws and proclamations were enacted and put forth for the purpose of aiding in the suppression of the rebellion. To give them their fullest effect there had to be a pledge for their maintenance. In my judgment they have aided, and will further aid, the cause for which they were intended. To now abandon them would not only be to relinquish a lever of power, but would also be a cruel and astounding breach of faith. . . . For these and other reasons it is thought best that support of these measures shall be included in the oath, and it is believed the Executive may lawfully claim it in return for pardon and restoration of forfeited rights, which he has clear constitutional power to withhold altogether or grant upon the terms which he shall deem wisest for the public interest."

* * * *

On the 29th of May, 1865, amnesty and pardon, with the restoration of the rights of property except as to slaves, and that as to which legal proceedings had been instituted under laws of the United States, were again offered to all who had, directly or indirectly, participated in the rebellion, except certain persons included in fourteen classes. All who embraced this offer were required to take and subscribe an oath of like tenor with that required by the first proclamation.

On the 7th of September, 1867, still another proclamation was issued, offering pardon and amnesty, with restoration of property, as before and on the same oath, to all but three excepted classes.

And finally, on the 4th of July, 1868, a full pardon and amnesty was granted, with some exceptions, and on the 25th of December, 1868, without exception, unconditionally and without reservation, to all who had participated in the rebellion, with restoration of rights of property as before. No oath was required.

It is true that the section of the act of Congress which purported to authorize the proclamation of pardon and amnesty by the President was repealed on the 21st of January, 1867; but this was after the close of the war, when the act had ceased to be important as an expression of the legislative disposition to carry into effect the clemency of the Executive, and after the decision of this court that the President's power of pardon "is not subject to legislation"; that "Congress can neither limit the effect of his pardon, nor exclude from its exercise any class of offenders." It is not important, therefore, to refer to this repealing act further than to say that it is impossible to believe, while the repealed provision was in full force, and the faith of the legislature as well as the Executive was engaged to the restoration of the rights of property promised by the latter, that the proceeds of property of persons pardoned, which had been paid into the treasury, were to be withheld from them. The repeal of the section in no respect changes the national obligation, for it does not alter at all the operation of the pardon, or reduce in any degree the obligations of Congress under the Constitution to give full effect to it, if necessary, by legislation.

We conclude, therefore, that the title to the proceeds of the property which came to the possession of the government by capture or abandonment, with the exceptions already noticed, was in no case divested out of the original owner. It was for the government itself to determine whether these proceeds should be restored to the owner or not. The promise of the restoration of all rights of property decides that question affirmatively as to all persons who availed themselves of the proffered pardon. It was competent for the President to annex to his offer of pardon any conditions or qualifications he should see fit; but after those conditions and qualifications had been satisfied, the pardon and its connected promises took full effect. The restoration of the proceeds became the absolute right of the persons pardoned, on application within two years from the close of the war. It was, in fact, promised for an equivalent. "Pardon and restoration of political rights" were "in return" for the oath and its fulfillment. To refuse it would be a breach of faith not less "cruel and astounding" than to abandon the freed people whom the Executive had promised to maintain in their freedom.

What, then, was the effect of the provision of the act of 1870 upon the right of the owner of the cotton in this case? He had done certain acts which this court has adjudged to be acts in aid of the rebellion; but he abandoned the cotton to the agent of the Treasury Department, by whom it has been sold and the proceeds paid into the Treasury of the United States; and he took, and has not violated, the amnesty oath under the President's proclamation. Upon this case the Court of Claims pronounced him entitled to a judgment for the net proceeds in the treasury. This decree was rendered on the 26th of May, 1869; the appeal to this court made on the 3d of June, and was filed here on the 11th of December, 1869.

The judgment of the court in the case of Padelford, which, in its essential features, was the same with this case, was rendered on the 30th of April, 1870. It affirmed the judgment of the Court of Claims in his favor.

Soon afterwards the provision in question was introduced as a proviso to the clause in the general appropriation bill, appropriating a sum of money for the payment of judgments of the Court of Claims, and became a part of the act, with perhaps little consideration in either House of Congress.

This proviso declares in substance that no pardon, acceptance, oath, or other act performed in pursuance, or as a condition of pardon, shall be admissible in evidence in support of any claim against the United States in the Court of Claims, or to establish the right of any claimant to bring suit in that court; nor, if already put in evidence, shall be used or considered on behalf of the claimant, by said court, or by the appellate court on appeal. Proof of loyalty is required to be made according to the provisions of certain statutes, irrespective of the effect of any executive proclamation, pardon, or amnesty, or act of oblivion; and when judgment has been already rendered on other proof of loyalty, the Supreme Court, on appeal, shall have no further jurisdiction of the cause, and shall dismiss the same for want of jurisdiction. It is further provided that whenever any pardon, granted to any suitor in the Court of Claims, for the proceeds of captured and abandoned property, shall recite in substance that the person pardoned took part in the late rebellion, or was guilty of any act of rebellion or disloyalty, and shall have been accepted in writing without express disclaimer and protestation against the fact so recited, such pardon or acceptance shall be taken as conclusive evidence in the Court of Claims, and on appeal, that the claimant did give aid to the rebellion; and on proof of such pardon, or acceptance, which proof may be made summarily on motion or otherwise, the jurisdiction of the court shall cease, and the suit shall be forthwith dismissed.

The substance of this enactment is that an acceptance of a pardon, without disclaimer, shall be conclusive evidence of the acts pardoned, but shall be null and void as evidence of the rights conferred by it, both in the Court of Claims and in this court on appeal.

It was urged in argument that the right to sue the government in the Court of Claims is a matter of favor; but this seems not entirely accurate. It is as much the duty of the government as of individuals to fulfill its obligations. Before the establishment of the Court of Claims claimants could only be heard by Congress. That court was established in 1855 for the triple purpose of relieving Congress, and of protecting the government by regular investigation, and of benefiting the claimants by affording them a certain mode of examining and adjudicating upon their claims. It was required to hear and determine upon claims founded upon any law of Congress, or upon any regulation of an executive department, or upon any contract, express or implied, with the government of the United States. Originally it was a court merely in name, for its power extended only to the preparation of bills to be submitted to Congress.

In 1863 the number of judges was increased from three to five, its jurisdiction was enlarged, and, instead of being required to prepare bills for Congress, it was authorized to render final judgment, subject to appeal to this court and to an estimate by the Secretary of the Treasury of the amount required to pay each claimant. This court being of opinion that the provision for an estimate was inconsistent with the finality essential to judicial decisions, Congress repealed that provision. Since then the Court of Claims has exercised all the functions of a court, and this court has taken full jurisdiction on appeal.

The Court of Claims is thus constituted one of those inferior courts which Congress authorizes, and has jurisdiction of contracts between the government and the citizen, from which appeal regularly lies to this court.

Undoubtedly the legislature has complete control over the organization and existence of that court and may confer or withhold the right of appeal from its decisions. And if this act did nothing more, it would be our duty to give it effect. If it simply denied the right of appeal in a particular class of cases, there could be no doubt that it must be regarded as an exercise of the power of Congress to make "such exceptions from the appellate jurisdiction" as should seem to it expedient.

But the language of the proviso shows plainly that it does not intend to withhold appellate jurisdiction except as a means to an end. Its great and controlling purpose is to deny to pardons granted by the President the effect which this court had adjudged them to have. The proviso declares that pardons shall not be considered by this court on appeal. We had already decided that it was our duty to consider them and give them effect, in cases like the present, as equivalent to proof of loyalty. It provides that whenever it shall appear that any judgment of the Court of Claims shall have been founded on such pardons, without other proof of loyalty, the Supreme Court shall have no further jurisdiction of the case and shall dismiss the same for want of jurisdiction. The proviso further declares that every pardon granted to any suitor in the Court of Claims and reciting that the person pardoned has been guilty of any act of rebellion or disloyalty, shall, if accepted in writing without disclaimer of the fact recited, be taken as conclusive evidence in that court and on appeal, of the act recited; and on proof of pardon or acceptance, summarily made on motion or otherwise, the jurisdiction of the court shall cease and the suit shall be forthwith dismissed.

It is evident from this statement that the denial of jurisdiction to this court, as well as to the Court of Claims, is founded solely on the application of a rule of decision, in causes pending, prescribed by Congress. The court has jurisdiction of the cause to a given point; but when it ascertains that a certain state of things exists, its jurisdiction is to cease and it is required to dismiss the cause for want of jurisdiction.

It seems to us that this is not an exercise of the acknowledged power of Congress to make exceptions and prescribe regulations to the appellate power.

The court is required to ascertain the existence of certain facts and thereupon to declare that its jurisdiction on appeal has ceased, by dismissing the bill. What is this but to prescribe a rule for the decision of a cause in a particular way? In the case before us, the Court of Claims has rendered judgment for the claimant and an appeal has been taken to this court. We are directed to dismiss the appeal, if we find that the judgment must be affirmed, because of a pardon granted to the intestate of the claimants. Can we do so without allowing one party to the controversy to decide it in its own favor? Can we do so without allowing that the legislature may prescribe rules of decision to the Judicial Department of the government in cases pending before it?

We think not; and thus thinking, we do not at all question what was decided in the case of *Pennsylvania v. Wheeling Bridge Company*. In that case, after a decree in this court that the bridge, in the then state of the law, was a nuisance and must be abated as such, Congress passed an act legalizing the structure and making it a post-road; and the court, on a motion for process to enforce the decree, held that the bridge had ceased to be a nuisance by the exercise of the constitutional powers of Congress, and denied the motion. No arbitrary rule of decision was prescribed in that case, but the court was left to apply its ordinary rules to the new circumstances created by the act. In the case before us no new circumstances have been created by legislation. But the court is forbidden to give the effect to evidence which, in its own judgment, such evidence should have, and is directed to give it an effect precisely contrary.

We must think that Congress has inadvertently passed the limit which separates the legislative from the judicial power.

It is of vital importance that these powers be kept distinct. The Constitution provides that the judicial power of the United States shall be vested in one Supreme Court and such inferior courts as the Congress shall from time to time ordain and establish. The same instrument, in the last clause of the same article, provides that in all cases other than those of original jurisdiction, "the Supreme Court shall have appellate jurisdiction both as to law and fact, with such exceptions and under such regulations as the Congress shall make."

Congress has already provided that the Supreme Court shall have jurisdiction of the judgments of the Court of Claims on appeal. Can it prescribe a rule in conformity with which the court must deny to itself the jurisdiction thus conferred, because and only because its decision, in accordance with settled law, must be adverse to the government and favorable to the suitor? This question seems to us to answer itself.

The rule prescribed is also liable to just exception as impairing the effect of a pardon, and thus infringing the constitutional power of the Executive.

It is the intention of the Constitution that each of the great co-ordinate departments of the government—the Legislative, the Executive, and the Judicial—shall be, in its sphere, independent of the others. To the executive alone is intrusted the power of pardon; and it is granted without limit. Pardon includes amnesty. It blots out the offence pardoned and removes all its penal consequences. It may be granted on conditions. In these particular pardons, that no doubt might exist as to their character, restoration of property was expressly pledged, and the pardon was granted on condition that the person who availed himself of it should take and keep a prescribed oath.

Now it is clear that the legislature cannot change the effect of such a pardon any more than the executive can change a law. Yet this is attempted by the provision under consideration. The court is required to receive special pardons as evidence of guilt and to treat them as null and void. It is required to disregard pardons granted by proclamation on condition, though the condition has been fulfilled, and to deny them their legal effect. This certainly impairs the executive authority and directs the court to be instrumental to that end.

We think it unnecessary to enlarge. The simplest statement is the best.

We repeat that it is impossible to believe that this provision was not inserted in the appropriation bill through inadvertence; and that we shall not best fulfill the deliberate will of the legislature by DENYING the motion to dismiss and AFFIRMING the judgment of the Court of Claims; which is
ACCORDINGLY DONE.

Justice Miller (with whom concurred Justice Bradley), dissenting.

I cannot agree to the opinion of the court just delivered in an important matter; and I regret this the more because I do agree to the proposition that the proviso to the act of July 12th, 1870, is unconstitutional, so far as it attempts to prescribe to the judiciary the effect to be given to an act of pardon or amnesty by the President. This power of pardon is confided to the President by the

Constitution, and whatever may be its extent or its limits, the legislative branch of the government cannot impair its force or effect in a judicial proceeding in a constitutional court. But I have not been able to bring my mind to concur in the proposition that, under the act concerning captured and abandoned property, there remains in the former owner, who had given aid and comfort to the rebellion, any interest whatever in the property or its proceeds when it had been sold and paid into the treasury or had been converted to the use of the public under that act. I must construe this act, as all others should be construed, by seeking the intention of its framers, and the intention to restore the proceeds of such property to the loyal citizen, and to transfer it absolutely to the government in the case of those who had given active support to the rebellion, is to me too apparent to be disregarded. In the one case the government is converted into a trustee for the former owner; in the other it appropriates it to its own use as the property of a public enemy captured in war. Can it be inferred from anything found in the statute that Congress intended that this property should ever be restored to the disloyal? I am unable to discern any such intent. But if it did, why was not some provision made by which the title of the government could at some time be made perfect, or that of the owner established? Some judicial proceeding for confiscation would seem to be necessary if there remains in the disloyal owner any right or interest whatever. But there is no such provision, and unless the *act* intended to forfeit absolutely the right of the disloyal owner, the proceeds remain in a condition where the owner cannot maintain a suit for its recovery, and the United States can obtain no perfect title to it.

* * * *

The other case which I refer to is that of *United States v. Padelford.* In that case the opinion makes a labored and successful effort to show that Padelford, the owner of the property, had secured the benefit of the amnesty proclamation *before* the property was seized under the same statute we are now considering. And it bases the right of Padelford to recover its proceeds in the treasury on the fact that *before the capture* his *status* as a loyal citizen had been restored, and with it all his rights of property, although he had previously given aid and comfort to the rebellion. In this view I concurred with all my brethren. And I hold now that as long as the possession or title of property remains in the party, the pardon or the amnesty remits all right in the government to forfeit or confiscate it. But where the property has already been seized and sold, and the proceeds paid into the treasury, and it is clear that the statute contemplates no further proceeding as necessary to divest the right of the former owner, the pardon does not and cannot restore that which has thus completely passed away. And if such was not the view of the court when Padelford's case was under consideration I am at a loss to discover a reason for the extended argument in that case, in the opinion of the court, to show that he had availed himself of the amnesty before the seizure of the property. If the views now advanced are sound, it was wholly immaterial whether Padelford was pardoned before or after the seizure.

DISCUSSION AND QUESTIONS

The exact import of *Klein* eludes scholars and students alike. For helpful elucidation of *Klein* in light of its new import after *Boumediene*— the two occasions in which the Court has struck down explicit congressional limitations on federal court jurisdiction—see Amanda L. Tyler, *The Story of* Klein: *The Scope of Congress' Authority to Shape the Jurisdiction of Federal Courts*, *in* FEDERAL COURTS STORIES 87-113 (2010). *Klein* seems to provide support for both proponents and opponents of jurisdiction striping. Consider the following passage from *Klein*:

> Undoubtedly the legislature has *complete control over the organization and existence* of that court and may confer or withhold the right of appeal from its decisions. And if this act did nothing more, it would be our duty to give it effect. If it simply denied the right of appeal in a particular class of cases, there could be *no doubt* that it must be regarded as an exercise of the power of Congress to make "such exceptions from the appellate jurisdiction" as should seem to it expedient.[17]

Now, consider the next few sentences from the Court's opinion:

> But the language of the proviso shows plainly that it does not intend to withhold appellate jurisdiction except as a means to an end. Its great and controlling purpose is to deny to pardons granted by the President the effect which this court had adjudged them to have.

Given the breadth of the first passage, what limits on Congress' power are added by the second passage? Do other parts of the Court's opinion clarify its notion of the boundaries of congressional power?

Recall that in *Ex Parte McCardle*, the Court stated, "We are not at liberty to inquire into the motives of the legislature" when Congress limits federal jurisdiction. Isn't that what the Court did in *Klein*? Or can these decisions be reconciled by the fact that Congress plainly abrogated presidential pardons in *Klein*, an unconstitutional effect regardless of congressional motive?

The *Klein* Court also expressed concerns about Congress' attempt to dictate the outcome in a case already decided by the lower court and now on review in the Supreme Court. Consider the Court's examination of a related issue in *Plaut v. Spendthrift Farm, Inc.*

PLAUT v. SPENDTHRIFT FARM, INC.

514 U.S. 211 (1995)

JUSTICE SCALIA delivered the opinion of the Court.

The question presented in this case is whether § 27A(b) of the Securities Exchange Act of 1934, to the extent that it requires federal courts to reopen final judgments in private civil actions under § 10(b) of the Act, contravenes the Constitution's separation of powers or the Due Process Clause of the Fifth Amendment.

I

In 1987, petitioners brought a civil action against respondents in the United States District Court for the Eastern District of Kentucky. The complaint alleged that in 1983 and 1984 respondents had committed fraud and deceit in the sale of

17. Emphasis added.

stock in violation of § 10(b) of the Securities Exchange Act of 1934 and Rule 10b-5 of the Securities and Exchange Commission. The case was mired in pretrial proceedings in the District Court until June 20, 1991, when we decided *Lampf, Pleva, Lipkind, Prupis & Petigrow v. Gilbertson*, 501 U.S. 350. *Lampf* held that "[l]itigation instituted pursuant to § 10(b) and Rule 10b-5 . . . must be commenced within one year after the discovery of the facts constituting the violation and within three years after such violation." We applied that holding to the plaintiff-respondents in *Lampf* itself, found their suit untimely, and reinstated a summary judgment previously entered in favor of the defendant-petitioners. On the same day we decided *James B. Beam Distilling Co. v. Georgia*, 501 U.S. 529 (1991), in which a majority of the Court held, albeit in different opinions, that a new rule of federal law that is applied to the parties in the case announcing the rule must be applied as well to all cases pending on direct review. The joint effect of *Lampf* and *Beam* was to mandate application of the 1-year/3-year limitations period to petitioners' suit. The District Court, finding that petitioners' claims were untimely under the *Lampf* rule, dismissed their action with prejudice on August 13, 1991. Petitioners filed no appeal; the judgment accordingly became final 30 days later.

On December 19, 1991, the President signed the Federal Deposit Insurance Corporation Improvement Act of 1991. Section 476 of the Act—a section that had nothing to do with FDIC improvements—became § 27A of the Securities Exchange Act of 1934, and was later codified as 15 U.S.C. § 78aa-1. It provides:

> (a) Effect on pending causes of action
>
> The limitation period for any private civil action implied under section 78j(b) of this title [§ 10(b) of the Securities Exchange Act of 1934] that was commenced on or before June 19, 1991, shall be the limitation period provided by the laws applicable in the jurisdiction, including principles of retroactivity, as such laws existed on June 19, 1991.
>
> (b) Effect on dismissed causes of action
>
> Any private civil action implied under section 78j(b) of this title that was commenced on or before June 19, 1991
>
> (1) which was dismissed as time barred subsequent to June 19, 1991, and
>
> (2) which would have been timely filed under the limitation period provided by the laws applicable in the jurisdiction, including principles of retroactivity, as such laws existed on June 19, 1991,
>
> shall be reinstated on motion by the plaintiff not later than 60 days after December 19, 1991.

On February 11, 1992, petitioners returned to the District Court and filed a motion to reinstate the action previously dismissed with prejudice. The District Court found that the conditions set out in §§ 27A(b)(1) and (2) were met, so that petitioners' motion was required to be granted by the terms of the statute. It nonetheless denied the motion, agreeing with respondents that § 27A(b) is unconstitutional. The United States Court of Appeals for the Sixth Circuit affirmed. We granted certiorari.

II

[In this section of the Court's opinion, respondents argued that the Court could avoid the constitutional issue by interpreting the statute as not requiring federal courts to reopen final judgments. The Court rejected respondents' contentions and concluded that "there is no reasonable construction on which § 27A(b) does not require federal courts to reopen final judgments in suits dismissed with prejudice by virtue of *Lampf*."]

III

Respondents submit that § 27A(b) violates both the separation of powers and the Due Process Clause of the Fifth Amendment. Because the latter submission, if correct, might dictate a similar result in a challenge to state legislation under the Fourteenth Amendment, the former is the narrower ground for adjudication of the constitutional questions in the case, and we therefore consider it first. We conclude that in § 27A(b) Congress has exceeded its authority by requiring the federal courts to exercise "[t]he judicial Power of the United States," U.S. Const., art. III, § 1, in a manner repugnant to the text, structure, and traditions of Article III.

Our decisions to date have identified two types of legislation that require federal courts to exercise the judicial power in a manner that Article III forbids. The first appears in *United States v. Klein*, 13 Wall. 128 (1872), where we refused to give effect to a statute that was said "[to] prescribe rules of decision to the Judicial Department of the government in cases pending before it." Whatever the precise scope of *Klein*, however, later decisions have made clear that its prohibition does not take hold when Congress "amend[s] applicable law." *Robertson v. Seattle Audubon Soc.*, 503 U.S. 429, 441 (1992). Section 27A(b) indisputably does set out substantive legal standards for the Judiciary to apply, and in that sense changes the law (even if solely retroactively). The second type of unconstitutional restriction upon the exercise of judicial power identified by past cases is exemplified by *Hayburn's Case*, 2 Dall. 409 (1792), which stands for the principle that Congress cannot vest review of the decisions of Article III courts in officials of the Executive Branch. Yet under any application of § 27A(b) only courts are involved; no officials of other departments sit in direct review of their decisions. Section 27A(b) therefore offends neither of these previously established prohibitions.

We think, however, that § 27A(b) offends a postulate of Article III just as deeply rooted in our law as those we have mentioned. Article III establishes a "judicial department" with the "province and duty . . . to say what the law is" in particular cases and controversies. *Marbury v. Madison*, 1 Cranch 137, 177 (1803). The record of history shows that the Framers crafted this charter of the judicial department with an expressed understanding that it gives the Federal Judiciary the power, not merely to rule on cases, but to decide them, subject to review only by superior courts in the Article III hierarchy—with an understanding, in short, that "a judgment conclusively resolves the case" because "a 'judicial Power' is one to render dispositive judgments." Easterbrook, *Presidential Review*, 40 Case W. Res. L. Rev. 905, 926 (1990). By retroactively commanding the federal courts to reopen final judgments, Congress has violated this fundamental principle.

A

The Framers of our Constitution lived among the ruins of a system of intermingled legislative and judicial powers, which had been prevalent in the colonies long before the Revolution, and which after the Revolution had produced factional strife and partisan oppression. In the 17th and 18th centuries, colonial assemblies and legislatures functioned as courts of equity of last resort, hearing original actions or providing appellate review of judicial judgments. Often, however, they chose to correct the judicial process through special bills or other enacted legislation. It was common for such legislation not to prescribe a resolution of the dispute, but rather simply to set aside the judgment and order a new trial or appeal. Thus, as described in our discussion of *Hayburn's Case*, such legislation bears not on the problem of interbranch review but on the problem of finality of judicial judgments.

* * * *

[A] sense of a sharp necessity to separate the legislative from the judicial power, prompted by the crescendo of legislative interference with private judgments of the courts, triumphed among the Framers of the new Federal Constitution. The Convention made the critical decision to establish a judicial department independent of the Legislative Branch by providing that "the judicial Power of the United States shall be vested in one supreme Court, and in such inferior Courts as the Congress may from time to time ordain and establish." Before and during the debates on ratification, Madison, Jefferson, and Hamilton each wrote of the factional disorders and disarray that the system of legislative equity had produced in the years before the framing; and each thought that the separation of the legislative from the judicial power in the new Constitution would cure them. Madison's Federalist No. 48, the famous description of the process by which "[t]he legislative department is every where extending the sphere of its activity, and drawing all power into its impetuous vortex," referred to the report of the Pennsylvania Council of Censors to show that in that State "cases belonging to the judiciary department [had been] frequently drawn within legislative cognizance and determination." The Federalist No. 48, pp. 333, 337 (J. Cooke ed. 1961). Madison relied as well on Jefferson's Notes on the State of Virginia, which mentioned, as one example of the dangerous concentration of governmental powers into the hands of the legislature, that "the Legislature . . . in many instances decided rights which should have been left to judiciary controversy."

If the need for separation of legislative from judicial power was plain, the principal effect to be accomplished by that separation was even plainer. As Hamilton wrote in his exegesis of Article III, § 1, in The Federalist No. 81:

> It is not true . . . that the parliament of Great Britain, or the legislatures of the particular states, can rectify the exceptionable decisions of their respective courts, in any other sense than might be done by a future legislature of the United States. The theory neither of the British, nor the state constitutions, authorises the revisal of a judicial sentence, by a legislative act. . . . A legislature without exceeding its province cannot reverse a determination once made, in a particular case; though it may prescribe a new rule for future cases.

The essential balance created by this allocation of authority was a simple one. The Legislature would be possessed of power to "prescrib[e] the rules by which the duties and rights of every citizen are to be regulated," but the power of "[t]he interpretation of the laws" would be "the proper and peculiar province of the courts." The Federalist No. 78. The Judiciary would be, "from the nature of its functions, . . . the [department] least dangerous to the political rights of the constitution," not because its acts were subject to legislative correction, but because the binding effect of its acts was limited to particular cases and controversies. Thus, "though individual oppression may now and then proceed from the courts of justice, the general liberty of the people can never be endangered from that quarter: . . . so long as the judiciary remains truly distinct from both the legislative and executive."

Judicial decisions in the period immediately after ratification of the Constitution confirm the understanding that it forbade interference with the final judgments of courts. In *Calder v. Bull*, 3 Dall. 386 (1798), the Legislature of Connecticut had enacted a statute that set aside the final judgment of a state court in a civil case. Although the issue before this Court was the construction of the Ex Post Facto Clause, Art. I, § 10, Justice Iredell (a leading Federalist who had guided the Constitution to ratification in North Carolina) noted that

> the Legislature of [Connecticut] has been in the uniform, uninterrupted, habit of exercising a general superintending power over its courts of law, by granting new trials. It may, indeed, appear strange to some of us, that in any form, there should exist a power to grant, with respect to suits depending or adjudged, new rights of trial, new privileges of proceeding, not previously recognized and regulated by positive institutions. . . . The power . . . is judicial in its nature; and whenever it is exercised, as in the present instance, it is an exercise of judicial, not of legislative, authority.

The state courts of the era showed a similar understanding of the separation of powers, in decisions that drew little distinction between the federal and state constitutions. To choose one representative example from a multitude: In *Bates v. Kimball*, 2 Chipman 77 (Vt. 1824), . . . The power to annul a final judgment, the court held, was "an assumption of Judicial power," and therefore forbidden.

By the middle of the 19th century, the constitutional equilibrium created by the separation of the legislative power to make general law from the judicial power to apply that law in particular cases was so well understood and accepted that it could survive even *Dred Scott v. Sandford*, 19 How. 393 (1857). In his First Inaugural Address, President Lincoln explained why the political branches could not, and need not, interfere with even that infamous judgment:

> I do not forget the position assumed by some, that constitutional questions are to be decided by the Supreme Court; nor do I deny that such decisions must be binding in any case, upon the parties to a suit, as to the object of that suit. . . . And while it is obviously possible that such decision may be erroneous in any given case, still the evil effect following it, being limited to that particular case, with the chance that it may be over-ruled, and never become a precedent for other cases, can better be borne than could the evils of a different practice.

And the great constitutional scholar Thomas Cooley addressed precisely the question before us in his 1868 treatise: "If the legislature cannot thus indirectly control the action of the courts, by requiring of them a construction of the law according to its own views, it is very plain it cannot do so directly, by setting aside their judgments, compelling them to grant new trials, ordering the discharge of offenders, or directing what particular steps shall be taken in the progress of a judicial inquiry."

B

Section 27A(b) effects a clear violation of the separation-of-powers principle we have just discussed. It is, of course, retroactive legislation, that is, legislation that prescribes what the law was at an earlier time, when the act whose effect is controlled by the legislation occurred — in this case, the filing of the initial Rule 10b-5 action in the District Court. When retroactive legislation requires its own application in a case already finally adjudicated, it does no more and no less than "reverse a determination once made, in a particular case." The Federalist No. 81. Our decisions stemming from Hayburn's Case — although their precise holdings are not strictly applicable here — have uniformly provided fair warning that such an act exceeds the powers of Congress. *See, e.g.*, *Chicago & Southern Air Lines, Inc.*, 333 U.S. at 113 ("Judgments within the powers vested in courts by the Judiciary Article of the Constitution may not lawfully be revised, overturned or refused faith and credit by another Department of Government"); . . . *Hayburn's Case* (opinion of Wilson and Blair, JJ., and Peters, D.J.) ("[R]evision and control" of Article III judgments is "radically inconsistent with the independence of that judicial power which is vested in the courts"); *id.*, at 413 (opinion of Iredell, J., and Sitgreaves, D.J.) ("[N]o decision of any court of the United States can, under any circumstances, . . . be liable to a revision, or even suspension, by the [l]egislature itself, in whom no judicial power of any kind appears to be vested"). Today those clear statements must either be honored, or else proved false.

It is true, as petitioners contend, that Congress can always revise the judgments of Article III courts in one sense: When a new law makes clear that it is retroactive, an appellate court must apply that law in reviewing judgments still on appeal that were rendered before the law was enacted, and must alter the outcome accordingly. Since that is so, petitioners argue, federal courts must apply the "new" law created by § 27A(b) in finally adjudicated cases as well; for the line that separates lower court judgments that are pending on appeal (or may still be appealed), from lower-court judgments that are final, is determined by statute, *see, e.g.*, 28 U.S.C. § 2107(a) (30-day time limit for appeal to federal court of appeals), and so cannot possibly be a constitutional line. But a distinction between judgments from which all appeals have been forgone or completed, and judgments that remain on appeal (or subject to being appealed), is implicit in what Article III creates: not a batch of unconnected courts, but a judicial department composed of "inferior Courts" and "one supreme Court." Within that hierarchy, the decision of an inferior court is not (unless the time for appeal has expired) the final word of the department as a whole. It is the obligation of the last court in the hierarchy that rules on the case to give effect to Congress' latest enactment, even when that has the effect of overturning the judgment of an inferior court, since each court, at every level, must "decide according to existing laws." Having achieved finality, however, a judicial decision becomes the last word of the judicial department with regard to a particular case or controversy, and Congress may not declare by retroactive legislation that the law applicable to that very case was something other than what the courts said it was. Finality of a legal judgment is determined by statute, just as entitlement to a government benefit is a statutory creation; but that no more deprives the former of its constitutional significance for separation-of-powers analysis than it deprives the latter of its significance for due process purposes.

To be sure, § 27A(b) reopens (or directs the reopening of) final judgments in a whole class of cases rather than in a particular suit. We do not see how that makes any difference. The separation-of-powers violation here, if there is any, consists of depriving judicial judgments of the conclusive effect that they had when they were announced, not of acting in a manner—viz., with particular rather than general effect—that is unusual (though, we must note, not impossible) for a legislature. To be sure, a general statute such as this one may reduce the perception that legislative interference with judicial judgments was prompted by individual favoritism; but it is legislative interference with judicial judgments nonetheless. Not favoritism, nor even corruption, but power is the object of the separation-of-powers prohibition. The prohibition is violated when an individual final judgment is legislatively rescinded for even the very best of reasons, such as the legislature's genuine conviction (supported by all the law professors in the land) that the judgment was wrong; and it is violated 40 times over when 40 final judgments are legislatively dissolved.

It is irrelevant as well that the final judgments reopened by § 27A(b) rested on the bar of a statute of limitations. The rules of finality, both statutory and judge made, treat a dismissal on statute-of-limitations grounds the same way they treat a dismissal for failure to state a claim, for failure to prove substantive liability, or for failure to prosecute: as a judgment on the merits. Petitioners suggest, directly or by implication, two reasons why a merits judgment based on this particular ground may be uniquely subject to congressional nullification. First, there is the fact that the length and indeed even the very existence of a statute of limitations upon a federal cause of action is entirely subject to congressional control. But virtually all of the reasons why a final judgment on the merits is rendered on a federal claim are subject to congressional control. Congress can eliminate, for example, a particular element of a cause of action that plaintiffs have found it difficult to establish; or an evidentiary rule that has often excluded essential testimony; or a rule of offsetting wrong (such as contributory negligence) that has often prevented recovery. To distinguish statutes of limitations on the ground that they are mere creatures of Congress is to distinguish them not at all. The second supposedly distinguishing characteristic of a statute of limitations is that it can be extended, without violating the Due Process Clause, after the cause of the action arose and even after the statute itself has expired. But that also does not set statutes of limitations apart. To mention only one other broad category of judgment-producing legal rule: Rules of pleading and proof can similarly be altered after the cause of action arises, and even, if the statute clearly so requires, after they have been applied in a case but before final judgment has been entered. Petitioners' principle would therefore lead to the conclusion that final judgments rendered on the basis of a stringent (or, alternatively, liberal) rule of pleading or proof may be set aside for retrial under a new liberal (or, alternatively, stringent) rule of pleading or proof. This alone provides massive scope for undoing final judgments and would substantially subvert the doctrine of separation of powers.

The central theme of the dissent is a variant on these arguments. The dissent maintains that *Lampf* "announced" a new statute of limitations in an act of "judicial . . . lawmaking" that "changed the law." That statement, even if relevant, would be wrong. The point decided in *Lampf* had never before been addressed by this Court, and was therefore an open question, no matter what the lower courts had held at the time. But the more important point is that *Lampf* as such is irrelevant to this case. The dissent itself perceives that "[w]e would have the same issue to decide had Congress enacted the *Lampf* rule," and that the *Lampf* rule's genesis in judicial lawmaking rather than, shall we say, legislative lawmaking, "should not affect the separation-of-powers analysis." Just so. The issue here is not the validity or even the source of the legal rule that produced the Article III judgments, but rather the immunity from legislative abrogation of those judgments themselves. The separation-of-powers question before us has nothing to do with *Lampf*, and the dissent's attack on *Lampf* has nothing to do with the question before us.

C

Apart from the statute we review today, we know of no instance in which Congress has attempted to set aside the final judgment of an Article III court by retroactive legislation. That prolonged reticence would be amazing if such interference were not understood to be constitutionally proscribed. The closest analogue that the Government has been able to put forward is the statute at issue in *United States v. Sioux Nation*, 448 U.S. 371 (1980). That law required the Court of Claims "'[n]otwithstanding any other provision of law . . . [to] review on the merits, without regard to the defense of res judicata or collateral estoppel,'" a Sioux claim for just compensation from the United States—even though the Court of Claims had previously heard and rejected that very claim. We considered and rejected separation-of-powers objections to the statute based upon *Hayburn's Case* and *United States v. Klein*. The basis for our rejection was a line of precedent that stood, we said, for the proposition that "Congress has the power to waive the res judicata effect of a prior judgment entered in the Government's favor on a claim against the United States." And our holding was as narrow as the precedent on which we had relied: "In sum, . . . Congress' mere waiver of the res judicata effect of a prior judicial decision rejecting the validity of a legal claim against the United States does not violate the doctrine of separation of powers."

* * * *

Finally, petitioners liken § 27A(b) to Federal Rule of Civil Procedure 60(b), which authorizes courts to relieve parties from a final judgment for grounds such as excusable neglect, newly discovered evidence, fraud, or "any other reason justifying relief. . . ." We see little resemblance. Rule 60(b), which authorizes discretionary judicial revision of judgments in the listed situations and in other "'extraordinary circumstances,'" does not impose any legislative mandate to reopen upon the courts, but merely reflects and confirms the courts' own inherent and discretionary power, "firmly established in English practice long before the foundation of our Republic," to set aside a judgment whose enforcement would work inequity. Thus, Rule 60(b), and the tradition that it embodies, would be relevant refutation of a claim that reopening a final judgment is always a denial of property without due process; but they are irrelevant to the claim that legislative instruction to reopen impinges upon the independent constitutional authority of the courts.

* * * *

Finally, we may respond to the suggestion of the concurrence that this case should be decided more narrowly. The concurrence is willing to acknowledge only that "sometimes Congress lacks the power under Article I to reopen an otherwise closed court judgment." In the present context, what it considers critical is that § 27A(b) is "exclusively retroactive" and "appli[es] to a limited number of individuals." If Congress had only "provid[ed] some of the assurances against 'singling out' that ordinary legislative activity normally provides—say, prospectivity and general applicability—we might have a different case."

This seems to us wrong in both fact and law. In point of fact, § 27A(b) does not "single out" any defendant for adverse treatment (or any plaintiff for favorable treatment). Rather, it identifies a class of actions (those filed pre-*Lampf*, timely under applicable state law, but dismissed as time barred post-*Lampf*) which embraces many plaintiffs and defendants, the precise number and identities of whom we even now do not know. The concurrence's contention that the number of covered defendants "is too small *(compared with the number of similar, uncovered firms)* to distinguish meaningfully the law before us from a similar law aimed at a single closed case," (emphasis added), renders the concept of "singling out" meaningless.

More importantly, however, the concurrence's point seems to us wrong in law. To be sure, the class of actions identified by § 27A(b) could have been more expansive (e.g., all actions that were or could have been filed pre-*Lampf*) and the provision could have been written to have prospective as well as retroactive effect (e.g., "all post-*Lampf* dismissed actions, plus all future actions under Rule 10b-5, shall be timely if brought within 30 years of the injury"). But it escapes us how this could in any way cause the statute to be any less an infringement upon the judicial power. The nub of that infringement consists not of the Legislature's acting in a particularized and hence (according to the concurrence) nonlegislative fashion; but rather of the Legislature's nullifying prior, authoritative judicial action. It makes no difference whatever to that separation-of-powers violation that it is in gross rather than particularized (e.g., "we hereby set aside all hitherto entered judicial orders"), or that it is not accompanied by an "almost" violation of the Bill of Attainder Clause, or an "almost" violation of any other constitutional provision.

Ultimately, the concurrence agrees with our judgment only "[b]ecause the law before us embodies risks of the very sort that our Constitution's 'separation of powers' prohibition seeks to avoid." But the doctrine of separation of powers is a structural safeguard rather than a remedy to be applied only when specific harm, or risk of specific harm, can be identified. In its major features (of which the conclusiveness of judicial judgments is assuredly one) it is a prophylactic device, establishing high walls and clear distinctions because low walls and vague distinctions will not be judicially defensible in the heat of interbranch conflict. . . . The delphic alternative suggested by the concurrence (the setting aside of judgments is all right so long as Congress does not "impermissibly tr[y] to apply, as well as make, the law") simply prolongs doubt and multiplies confrontation. Separation of powers, a distinctively American political doctrine, profits from the advice authored by a distinctively American poet: Good fences make good neighbors. . . .

We know of no previous instance in which Congress has enacted retroactive legislation requiring an Article III court to set aside a final judgment, and for good reason. The Constitution's separation of legislative and judicial powers denies it the authority to do so. Section 27A(b) is unconstitutional to the extent that it requires federal courts to reopen final judgments entered before its enactment. The judgment of the Court of Appeals is affirmed.

It is so ordered.

JUSTICE BREYER, concurring in the judgment.

I agree with the majority that § 27A(b) . . . is unconstitutional. In my view, the separation of powers inherent in our Constitution means that at least sometimes Congress lacks the power under Article I to reopen an otherwise closed court judgment. And the statutory provision here at issue, § 27A(b), violates a basic "separation-of-powers" principle — one intended to protect individual liberty. Three features of this law — its exclusively retroactive effect, its application to a limited number of individuals, and its reopening of closed judgments — taken together, show that Congress here impermissibly tried to apply, as well as make, the law. Hence, § 27A(b) falls outside the scope of Article I. But, it is far less clear, and unnecessary for the purposes of this case to decide, that separation of powers "is violated" whenever an "individual final judgment is legislatively rescinded" or that it is "violated 40 times over when 40 final judgments are legislatively dissolved." I therefore write separately.

The majority provides strong historical evidence that Congress lacks the power simply to reopen, and to revise, final judgments in individual cases. The Framers would have hesitated to lodge in the Legislature both that kind of power and the power to enact general laws, as part of their effort to avoid the "despotic government" that accompanies the "accumulation of all powers, legislative, executive, and judiciary, in the same hands." The Federalist No. 47, p. 241 (J. Gideon ed. 1831) (J. Madison); *id.*, No. 48, at 249 (quoting T. Jefferson, Notes on the State of Virginia). For one thing, the authoritative application of a general law to a particular case by an independent judge, rather than by the legislature itself, provides an assurance that even an unfair law at least will be applied evenhandedly according to its terms. *See, e.g.*, 1 Montesquieu, The Spirit of Laws 174 (T. Nugent transl. 1886) (describing one objective of the "separation of powers" as preventing "the same monarch or senate," having "enact[ed] tyrannical laws" from "execut[ing] them in a tyrannical manner"). For another thing, as Justice Powell has pointed out, the Constitution's "separation-of-powers" principles reflect, in part, the Framers' "concern that a legislature should not be able unilaterally to impose a substantial deprivation on one person." The Framers "expressed" this principle, both in "specific provisions, such as the Bill of Attainder Clause," and in the Constitution's "general allocation of power."

Despite these two important "separation-of-powers" concerns, sometimes Congress can enact legislation that focuses upon a small group, or even a single individual. Congress also sometimes passes private legislation. And, sometimes Congress can enact legislation that, as a practical matter, radically changes the effect of an individual, previously entered court decree. Statutes that apply prospectively and (in part because of that prospectivity) to an open-ended class of persons, however, are more than simply an effort to apply, person by person, a previously enacted law, or to single out for oppressive treatment one, or a handful, of particular individuals. Thus, it seems to me, if Congress enacted legislation that reopened an otherwise closed judgment but in a way that mitigated some of the here relevant "separation-of-powers" concerns, by also providing some of the assurances against "singling out" that ordinary legislative activity normally provides — say, prospectivity and general applicability — we might have a different case. Because such legislation, in light of those mitigating circumstances, might well present a different constitutional question, I do not subscribe to the Court's more absolute statement.

* * * *

The upshot is that, viewed in light of the relevant, liberty-protecting objectives of the "separation of powers," this case falls directly within the scope of language in this Court's cases suggesting a restriction on Congress' power to reopen closed court judgments.

At the same time, because the law before us both reopens final judgments and lacks the liberty—protecting assurances that prospectivity and greater generality would have provided, we need not, and we should not, go further—to make of the reopening itself, an absolute, always determinative distinction, a "prophylactic device," or a foundation for the building of a new "high wal[l]" between the branches. Indeed, the unnecessary building of such walls is, in itself, dangerous, because the Constitution blends, as well as separates, powers in its effort to create a government that will work for, as well as protect the liberties of, its citizens. *See* The Federalist No. 48 (J. Madison). That doctrine does not "divide the branches into watertight compartments," nor "establish and divide fields of black and white." And, important separation-of-powers decisions of this Court have sometimes turned, not upon absolute distinctions, but upon degree. As the majority invokes the advice of an American poet, one might consider as well that poet's caution, for he not only notes that "Something there is that doesn't love a wall," but also writes, "Before I built a wall I'd ask to know/ What I was walling in or walling out." R. Frost, *Mending Wall*, The New Oxford Book of American Verse 395-396 (R. Ellmann ed. 1976).

* * * *

Because the law before us embodies risks of the very sort that our Constitution's "separation-of-powers" prohibition seeks to avoid, and because I can find no offsetting legislative safeguards that normally offer assurances that minimize those risks, I agree with the Court's conclusion and I join its judgment.

Justice Stevens, with whom Justice Ginsburg joins, dissenting.

* * * *

Throughout our history, Congress has passed laws that allow courts to reopen final judgments. Such laws characteristically apply to judgments entered before as well as after their enactment. When they apply retroactively, they may raise serious due process questions, but the Court has never invalidated such a law on separation-of-powers grounds until today. Indeed, only last Term we recognized Congress' ample power to enact a law that "in effect 'restored' rights that [a party] reasonably and in good faith thought he possessed before the surprising announcement" of a Supreme Court decision. We conditioned our unambiguous restatement of the proposition that "Congress had the power to enact legislation that had the practical effect of restoring the status quo retroactively" only on Congress' clear expression of its intent to do so.

A large class of investors reasonably and in good faith thought they possessed rights of action before the surprising announcement of the *Lampf* rule on June 20, 1991. When it enacted the 1991 amendment, Congress clearly expressed its intent to restore the rights *Lampf* had denied the aggrieved class. Section 27A comported fully with *Rivers* and with other precedents in which we consistently have recognized Congress' power to enact remedial statutes that set aside classes of final judgments. The only remarkable feature of this enactment is the fact that it remedied a defect in a new judge-made rule rather than in a statute.

The familiar history the Court invokes, involving colonial legislatures' ad hoc decisions of individual cases, "'unfettered by rules,'" provides no support for its holding. On the contrary, history and precedent demonstrate that Congress may enact laws that establish both substantive rules and procedures for reopening final judgments. When it enacted the 1991 amendment to the *Lampf* rule, Congress did not encroach on the judicial power. It decided neither the merits of any 10b-5 claim nor even whether any such claim should proceed to decision on the merits. It did provide that the rule governing the timeliness of 10b-5 actions pending on June 19, 1991, should be the pre-*Lampf* statute of limitations, and it also established a procedure for Article III courts to apply in determining whether any dismissed case should be reinstated. Congress' decision to extend that rule and procedure to 10b-5 actions dismissed during the brief period between this Court's law-changing decision in *Lampf* and Congress' remedial action is not a sufficient reason to hold the statute unconstitutional.

* * * *

III

The lack of precedent for the Court's holding is not, of course, a sufficient reason to reject it. Correct application of separation-of-powers principles, however, confirms that the Court has reached the wrong result. As our most recent major pronouncement on the separation of powers noted, "we have never held that the Constitution requires that the three branches of Government 'operate with absolute independence.'" Rather, our jurisprudence reflects "Madison's flexible approach to separation of powers." In accepting Madison's conception rather than any "hermetic division among the Branches," "we have upheld statutory provisions that to some degree commingle the functions of the Branches, but that pose no danger of either aggrandizement or encroachment." Today's holding does not comport with these ideals.

Section 27A . . . does not decide the merits of any issue in any litigation but merely removes an impediment to judicial decision on the merits. The impediment it removes would have produced inequity because the statute's beneficiaries did not cause the impediment. It requires a party invoking its benefits to file a motion within a specified time and to convince a court that the statute entitles the party to relief. Most important, § 27A(b) specifies both a substantive rule to govern the reopening of a class of judgments — the pre-*Lampf* limitations rule — and a procedure for the courts to apply in determining whether a particular motion to reopen should be granted. These characteristics are quintessentially legislative. They reflect Congress' fealty to the separation of powers and its intention to avoid the sort of ad hoc excesses the Court rightly criticizes in colonial legislative practice. In my judgment, all of these elements distinguish § 27A from "judicial" action and confirm its constitutionality. A sensible analysis would at least consider them in the balance.

Instead, the Court myopically disposes of § 27A(b) by holding that Congress has no power to "requir[e] an Article III court to set aside a final judgment." That holding must mean one of two things. It could mean that Congress may not impose a mandatory duty on a court to set aside a judgment even if the court makes a particular finding, such as a finding of fraud or mistake, that Congress has not made. Such a rule, however, could not be correct. Although Rule 60(b), for example, merely authorizes federal courts to set aside judgments after making appropriate findings, Acts of Congress characteristically set standards that judges are obligated to enforce. Accordingly, Congress surely could add to Rule 60(b) certain instances in which courts must grant relief from final judgments if they make particular findings—for example, a finding that a member of the jury accepted a bribe from the prevailing party. The Court, therefore, must mean to hold that Congress may not unconditionally require an Article III court to set aside a final judgment. That rule is both unwise and beside the point of this case.

A simple hypothetical example will illustrate the practical failings of the Court's new rule. Suppose Congress, instead of endorsing the new limitations rule fashioned by the Court in *Lampf,* had decided to return to the pre-*Lampf* regime (or perhaps to enact a longer uniform statute). Subsection (a) of § 27A would simply have provided that the law in effect prior to June 19, 1991, would govern the timeliness of all 10b-5 actions. In that event, subsection (b) would still have been necessary to remedy the injustice caused by this Court's failure to exempt pending cases from its new rule. In my judgment, the statutory correction of the inequitable flaw in *Lampf* would be appropriate remedial legislation whether or not Congress had endorsed that decision's substantive limitations rule. The Court, unfortunately, appears equally consistent: Even though the class of dismissed 10b-5 plaintiffs in my hypothetical would have been subject to the same substantive rule as all other 10b-5 plaintiffs, the Court's reasoning would still reject subsection (b) as an impermissible exercise of "judicial" power.

The majority's rigid holding unnecessarily hinders the Government from addressing difficult issues that inevitably arise in a complex society. This Court, for example, lacks power to enlarge the time for filing petitions for certiorari in a civil case after 90 days from the entry of final judgment, no matter how strong the equities. If an Act of God, such as a flood or an earthquake, sufficiently disrupted communications in a particular area to preclude filing for several days, the majority's reasoning would appear to bar Congress from addressing the resulting inequity. If Congress passed remedial legislation that retroactively granted movants from the disaster area extra time to file petitions or motions for extensions of time to file, today's holding presumably would compel us to strike down the legislation as an attack on the finality of judgments. Such a ruling, like today's holding, would gravely undermine federal courts' traditional power "to set aside a judgment whose enforcement would work inequity."

Even if the rule the Court announces today were sound, it would not control the case before us. In order to obtain the benefit of § 27A, petitioners had to file a timely motion and persuade the District Court they had timely filed their complaint under pre-*Lampf* law. In the judgment of the District Court, petitioners satisfied those conditions. Congress reasonably could have assumed, indeed must have expected, that some movants under § 27A(b) would fail to do so. The presence of an important condition that the District Court must find a movant to have satisfied before it may reopen a judgment distinguishes § 27A from the unconditional congressional directives the Court appears to forbid.

Moreover, unlike the colonial legislative commands on which the Court bases its holding, § 27A directed action not in "a civil case" but in a large category of civil cases.[18] The Court declares that a legislative direction to reopen a class of 40 cases is 40 times as bad as a direction to reopen a single final judgment because

18. [Footnote 17 in Justice Stevens's dissent.] At the time Congress was considering the bill that became § 27A, a House Subcommittee reported that *Lampf* had resulted in the dismissal of 15 cases, involving thousands of plaintiffs in every State (of whom over 32,000 had been identified) and claims totaling over $692.25 million. In addition, motions to dismiss based on *Lampf* were then pending in 17 cases involving thousands of plaintiffs in every State and claims totaling over $4.578 billion.

"power is the object of the separation-of-powers prohibition." This self-evident observation might be salient if § 27A(b) unconditionally commanded courts to reopen judgments even absent findings that the complaints were timely under pre-*Lampf* law. But Congress did not decide—and could not know how any court would decide—the timeliness issue in any particular case in the affected category. Congress, therefore, had no way to identify which particular plaintiffs would benefit from § 27A. It merely enacted a law that applied a substantive rule to a class of litigants, specified a procedure for invoking the rule, and left particular outcomes to individualized judicial determinations—a classic exercise of legislative power.

"All we seek," affirmed a sponsor of § 27A, "is to give the victims [of securities fraud] a fair day in court." A statute, such as § 27A, that removes an unanticipated and unjust impediment to adjudication of a large class of claims on their merits poses no danger of "aggrandizement or encroachment."[19] This is particularly true for § 27A in light of Congress' historic primacy over statutes of limitations.[20] The statute contains several checks against the danger of congressional overreaching. The Court in *Lampf* undertook a legislative function. Essentially, it supplied a statute of limitations for 10b-5 actions. The Court, however, failed to adopt the transition rules that ordinarily attend alterations shortening the time to sue. Congress, in § 27A, has supplied those rules. The statute reflects the ability of two coequal branches to cooperate in providing for the impartial application of legal rules to particular disputes. The Court's mistrust of such cooperation ill serves the separation of powers.[21]

19. [Footnote 19 in Justice Stevens's dissent.] Today's decision creates a new irony of judicial legislation. A challenge to the constitutionality of § 27A(a) could not turn on the sanctity of final judgments. Section 27A(a) benefits litigants who had filed appeals that *Lampf* rendered frivolous; petitioners and other law-abiding litigants whose claims *Lampf* rendered untimely had acquiesced in the dismissal of their actions. By striking down § 27A(b) on a ground that would leave § 27A(a) intact, the Court indulges litigants who protracted proceedings but shuts the courthouse door to litigants who proceeded with diligence and respect for the *Lampf* judgment.

20. [Footnote 20 in Justice Stevens's dissent.] "Statutes of limitation find their justification in necessity and convenience rather than in logic. They represent expedients, rather than principles. . . . They are by definition arbitrary, and their operation does not discriminate between the just and the unjust claim, or the voidable and unavoidable delay. They have come into the law not through the judicial process but through legislation. They represent a public policy about the privilege to litigate. . . . [T]he history of pleas of limitation shows them to be good only by legislative grace and to be subject to a relatively large degree of legislative control."

21. [Footnote 21 in Justice Stevens's dissent.] Although I agree with Justice Breyer's general approach to the separation-of-powers issue, I believe he gives insufficient weight to two important features of § 27A. First, he fails to recognize that the statute restored a pre-existing rule of law in order to remedy the manifest injustice produced by the Court's retroactive application of *Lampf*. The only "'substantial deprivation'" Congress imposed on defendants was that properly filed lawsuits proceed to decisions on the merits. Second, he understates the class of defendants burdened by § 27A: He finds the statute underinclusive because it provided no remedy for potential plaintiffs who may have failed to file timely actions in reliance on pre-*Lampf* limitations law, but he denies the importance of § 27A(a), which provided a remedy for plaintiffs who appealed dismissals after *Lampf*. The coverage of § 27A is coextensive with the retroactive application of the general rule announced in *Lampf*. If Congress had enacted a statute providing that the *Lampf* rule should apply to all cases filed after the statute's effective date and that the pre-*Lampf* rule should apply to all cases filed before that date, Justice Breyer could not reasonably condemn the statute as special legislation. The only difference between such a statute and § 27A is that § 27A covered all cases pending on the date of *Lampf*—June 20, 1991—rather than on the effective date of the statute—December 19, 1991. In my opinion, § 27A has sufficient generality to avoid the characteristics of a bill of attainder.

IV

The Court has drawn the wrong lesson from the Framers' disapproval of colonial legislatures' appellate review of judicial decisions. The Framers rejected that practice, not out of a mechanistic solicitude for "final judgments," but because they believed the impartial application of rules of law, rather than the will of the majority, must govern the disposition of individual cases and controversies. Any legislative interference in the adjudication of the merits of a particular case carries the risk that political power will supplant evenhanded justice, whether the interference occurs before or after the entry of final judgment. Section 27A(b) neither commands the reinstatement of any particular case nor directs any result on the merits. . . .

"We must remember that the machinery of government would not work if it were not allowed a little play in its joints." The three branches must cooperate in order to govern. We should regard favorably, rather than with suspicious hostility, legislation that enables the judiciary to overcome impediments to the performance of its mission of administering justice impartially, even when, as here, this Court has created the impediment. Rigid rules often make good law, but judgments in areas such as the review of potential conflicts among the three coequal branches of the Federal Government partake of art as well as science. That is why we have so often reiterated the insight of Justice Jackson:

> The actual art of governing under our Constitution does not and cannot conform to judicial definitions of the power of any of its branches based on isolated clauses or even single Articles torn from context. While the Constitution diffuses power the better to secure liberty, it also contemplates that practice will integrate the dispersed powers into a workable government. It enjoins upon its branches separateness but interdependence, autonomy but reciprocity.

We have the authority to hold that Congress has usurped a judicial prerogative, but even if this case were doubtful I would heed Justice Iredell's admonition that "the Court will never resort to that authority, but in a clear and urgent case." An appropriate regard for the interdependence of Congress and the judiciary amply supports the conclusion that § 27A(b) reflects constructive legislative cooperation rather than a usurpation of judicial prerogatives.

Accordingly, I respectfully dissent.

DISCUSSION AND QUESTIONS

As we stated earlier, *Klein* relates to the material on congressional control over Supreme Court appellate jurisdiction as well as control over lower-court decisionmaking. We cover it here for its resonance with *Plaut.* In its simplest form, *Plaut* states loud and clear that one attribute of the judiciary's power is that its final judgments cannot be overruled by a non-court (e.g., Congress). Now consider whether, and how, *Plaut* complements *Klein.*

Opponents of congressional efforts to weaken federal court power embrace *Klein*'s broad language forbidding legislative attempts to "prescribe rules of decision to the Judicial Department of the government in cases pending before it." This language has been used by the modern Court to constrain Congress' authority over federal courts. *See United States v. Sioux Nation*, 448 U.S. 371, 404

(1980) (interpreting *Klein* to invalidate a congressional jurisdictional provision that "prescribed a rule of decision in a case pending before the courts, and did so in a manner that required the courts to decide the controversy in the Government's favor"). One commentator emphasizes, "[i]t was clear to the *Klein* Court that Congress could not manipulate jurisdiction to secure unconstitutional ends."[22]

Yet other scholars question such a broad construction of *Klein*. For example, "courts are obligated to apply law (otherwise valid) as they find it at the time of their decision, including, when a case is on review, new statutes enacted after the judgment below."[23] As the Court commented in *Plaut*, "whatever the precise scope of *Klein* . . . later decisions have made clear that its prohibition does not take hold when Congress 'amend[s] applicable law'" while a case is still pending.

The interpretative limits of *Klein* may appear in the Supreme Court's unanimous ruling in *Robertson v. Seattle Audubon Society*, 503 U.S. 429 (1992). In *Robertson*, the Court reversed the Ninth Circuit's holding that the challenged federal statute was unconstitutional under *Klein*. The statute mandated that the Bureau of Land Management offer certain land for sale and placed restrictions on harvesting from other land. The statute further identified two pending cases alleging unlawful acts by the Bureau and stated that the acts satisfied statutory standards underlying the two cases. The Court found no problem under *Klein*. The Court construed the statute at issue as a valid modification of existing law rather than a mandate that the lower court apply preexisting legal standards in a specific manner.

The Court in *Robertson* appears to view *Klein* as a limit on congressional action that dictates judicial decisionmaking; the limit is not germane when Congress passes a new law governing a pending case. Is the Court's distinction persuasive? The *Robertson* case has not escaped criticism.[24]

Advocates of congressional restraint have reason for hope with the Supreme Court's decision in *Plaut*, at least when litigation has produced a final judgment. The Court in *Plaut* blocked Congress' attempt to undercut the finality of federal court judgments by resuscitating cases dismissed based on the Court's interpretation of the statute of limitations in *Lampf*. The Court held that Congress' action constituted an unconstitutional encroachment on the judiciary's Article III power to render "final" decisions. Drawing upon the spirit of *Marbury v. Madison*, the Court stressed that federal courts hold the authority "not merely to rule on cases, but to decide them."

The *Plaut* Court distinguished *Pennsylvania v. Wheeling & Belmont Bridge Co.*, 59 U.S. (18 How.) 421, 431-32 (1856) (*Wheeling Bridge*), in which the Court reasoned that Congress possessed the power to alter the law providing the foundation for an ongoing injunction. The Court appears to recognize that

22. Sager, *supra* note 3, at 71.

23. FALLON ET AL., HART AND WECHSLER'S THE FEDERAL COURTS, *supra*, at 88 (describing "clear" principle from *United States v. Schooner Peggy*, 5 U.S. (1 Cranch) 103 (1801)). Further, Congress possesses unquestioned power to adopt rules of evidence, standards of review, and so forth. *Id.*

24. *See, e.g.*, Ira Bloom, *Prisons, Prisoners, and Pine Forests: Congress Breaches the Wall Separating Legislative from Judicial Power*, 40 ARIZ. L. REV. 389, 395-98 (1998) (critiquing *Robertson* and the Supreme Court's reluctance to address congressional statutes intended to mandate particular results of a case); Amy D. Ronner, *Judicial Self-Demise: The Test of When Congress Impermissibly Intrudes on Judicial Power after* Robertson v. Seattle Audubon Society *and the Federal Appellate Courts' Rejection of the Separation of Powers Challenges to the New Section of the Securities Exchange Act of 1934*, 35 ARIZ. L. REV. 1037, 1053-54 (1993) (maintaining that *Robertson* and *Klein* are irreconcilable).

Congress can lawfully interfere with existing "judgments" in this context. Unlike monetary damages that operate in a backward-looking manner to remedy past harms, injunctive relief operates into the future by its continuing effect on a defendant's conduct. Accordingly, under *Plaut,* Congress may not undo a final judgment of a federal court, but pursuant to *Wheeling Bridge,* Congress may alter the underlying substantive law with the effect of nullifying a prospective remedy because the law will no longer support ongoing injunctive relief.

It remains unclear, however, what restrains Congress' power to affect the outcome in cases that have not reached finality. *Plaut* obviously did not involve a congressional attempt to strip federal courts of jurisdiction, as was the case in *Klein.* Further, the majority in *Plaut* declined to address the claim that Congress' action violated the Due Process Clause, which might provide an "external" check on Congress' control of the federal judiciary. As Professor Chemerinsky observes, there are limits to the analogy between the two cases.[25]

Test your understanding of the possible boundaries of congressional power over judicial decisionmaking by attempting Problem 3-3.

PROBLEM 3-3

End-of-Life Decisions: A Role for Congress and the Courts?

Reece Baxter lost consciousness for unknown reasons. Her brain was deprived of oxygen, leaving her in what family doctors diagnosed as a persistent vegetative state. Reece's family was left with a difficult set of decisions. Initially, her family agreed to have the hospital provide artificial nutrition and hydration. Over time, consensus among family members waned, and Max Baxter, Reece's husband and legal guardian, requested that a state court consider Reece's wishes regarding whether to be sustained by artificial medical support given her present condition. Reece's parents maintained that Reece's artificial medical support should continue.

After complex and embittered rounds of litigation, every court ruled that under applicable state constitutional and statutory law, Reece was in a persistent vegetative state and would not have wished to continue artificial support under the circumstances. Years of litigation resulted in a state order directing removal of the feeding tube. The tube was removed; but before Reece expired, the state legislature responded by enacting "Reece's Law." This law mandated reinsertion of the feeding tube. More litigation followed. After the state's highest court held Reece's Law unconstitutional in violation of the state constitution's separation-of-powers provision, the hospital removed the feeding tube again.

The struggle continued. At the behest of political affiliates of the right-to-life movement, the President and Congress intervened by passing federal legislation (the "Act") conferring jurisdiction on a particular federal district court encompassing Reece's place of hospitalization "to hear, determine, and render judgment" on any claim brought on behalf of Reece for the violation of any right under the Constitution or federal statutes relating to

25. Chemerinsky, *supra* note 16, at 195-96.

the withdrawal of any artificial medical support. Notably, the Act explicitly purports to

(a) grant "standing" to Reece's parents to bring a claim (expressly repealing the "*Rooker/Feldman*" doctrine that otherwise might prohibit any such claim);

(b) direct the district court not to abstain from deciding any case brought under the Act (which otherwise might be appropriate under Supreme Court abstention doctrine);

(c) alleviate any state exhaustion of remedy requirements (which otherwise might apply under federal statutes); and

(d) instruct the court to conduct "de novo" review of any claimed violation (which otherwise might violate federal law of res judicata).

Reece's parents file suit in the appropriate federal district court pursuant to the Act.

Is Congress' Act subject to challenge under any of the case authority we have studied? Address challenges under both Article III and separation-of-powers doctrine. In assessing challenges to the Act, consider the following questions:

- Does the Act create any substantive law governing the dispute? Why might this matter?
- Does the Act dictate the ultimate outcome of the case?
- Are Congress' motives in passing the Act relevant?
- Which Supreme Court decisions provide strongest support for challenging the Act? For upholding it?

Now consider Problem 3-4, which presents an opportunity to apply *Klein*, *Plaut*, and related jurisprudence to a complex dance among the branches of government.

PROBLEM 3-4

It's Your Move . . . Congress, Judiciary, Executive . . .

The winds in the nation's capital are whipping frostily. Senators are clamoring about the rogue and arbitrary unchecked power of federal courts. Most recently, members of Congress are angry about federal district courts that have issued extensive injunctive relief to correct problems in Veterans' Administration (VA) hospitals.

The suits against VA hospitals are based on a federal law, the Veterans' Administration Reform Act. The Reform Act is designed to ease backlogs in claims and improve patient physical and psychological care. The Reform Act imposes benchmark requirements to ensure that VA hospitals meet the Act's purposes. By and large, VA hospitals have utterly failed to comply with the Reform Act's commands. They have let claims languish; failed to hire psychologists and psychiatrists needed to handle patients with psychological issues; and failed to initiate any new programs since the Act's passage. Veterans feel they are no better off than they were prior to the Reform Act, while VA hospitals claim they are doing the best they can given increased patients and workload.

For years, veterans attempted to obtain governmental or legislative support for their complaints about the VA hospitals' failure to live up to the Reform Act, but bureaucracy and partisan battles created a stalemate. Accordingly, the veterans sought injunctive relief, which some federal courts granted. The injunctions were multi-paragraphed orders instructing the VA hospitals at issue to stop violating the Reform Act and affirmatively to shape up. For example, the injunctions commanded that the VA hospitals (i) process claims for benefits within four weeks; (ii) increase mental health staff to handle posttraumatic stress disorder; and (iii) spend 80 percent of the money appropriated on critical mission functions, that is, on actual services rather than administrative overhead. Some of the courts appointed special masters to conduct on-site monitoring to handle situations before they erupted into contempt proceedings.

Members of Congress are incredibly hostile to such expansive injunctions. In response, Congress passed, and the President signed, a bill (the "Act") that

> (1) requires retroactively that injunctions issued against government healthcare institutions be narrowly tailored to address the court's factual findings;
> (2) allows a motion to terminate prospective relief;
> (3) mandates that any termination motion "shall operate as a stay" beginning on the 30th day after the motion is filed and ending on the date the court enters its final ruling (the "Automatic Stay"); and
> (4) permits the court to delay the Automatic Stay for 60 days, but only upon a showing of "good cause" other than the court's general docket congestion.

Relying on the Act, the government moved to terminate injunctive relief against Fairhaven Veterans Hospital. The injunction at issue had been entered in an action brought by a small group of local veterans against the hospital. In response, the plaintiff-veterans requested that the federal district court enjoin imposition of the Automatic Stay provision. The federal district court granted the veterans' request and enjoined the Automatic Stay provision, which the court found violative of the Due Process Clause and separation-of-powers doctrine. The federal circuit court affirmed.

The case is now pending in the Supreme Court. How should the Court resolve the veterans' challenges to the Act's constitutionality? Here are some avenues for you to explore:

- The veterans raise a federal statutory challenge based on the VA's failure to comport with the Act's requirements. The federal district courts issued the original injunctions against the VA because the veterans established that irreparable injury would result without injunctive relief. In essence, the original injunction ordered the VA to take specific actions in order to achieve compliance with the Act. Do federal courts retain their traditional equitable power to issue injunctions for noncompliance with federal law even if the Act does not explicitly call for injunctive relief? If the Act commanded injunctive relief in the face of a violation of the Act, would a federal court retain power to deny an injunction if plaintiff proved the violation? When does Congress' legislative authority trump court power? If Congress created the federal statutory right, does it retain the power to remove traditionally available remedies because Congress possesses the power to eliminate the right?

- What if precedent supports a federal constitutional right (e.g., a fundamental property right to health care vested pursuant to the Act), and a federal judge determines that injunctions over government entities are necessary in order to cure ongoing violations of the Constitution? Does the federal judge's reliance on federal constitutional law rather than federal statutory law make a plaintiff's claim to injunctive relief stronger? Assuming the federal judge found an ongoing constitutional violation, would Congress have the power to deny the federal court's power to issue an injunction to stop or cure the constitutional violation?
- Does the Act constitute an unconstitutional encroachment on federal court power? Explore any separation-of-powers and federalism issues. Consider the effect of three axes: (i) the federal courts' original injunctions, (ii) the Act's Automatic Stay on the federal courts' injunctions, and (iii) a federal court determination that the Automatic Stay is unconstitutional. Regarding the first axis, for example, the original injunctions are federal judiciary orders telling an executive agency, the VA, how to run its hospitals. The second axis focuses on the Act's Automatic Stay of previously ordered injunctions. The Automatic Stay operates like an injunction of the original injunction — Congress is ordering the end to all orders of the original injunctions authorized by federal courts. The final axis pinpoints the tension that would be created by a federal court using the Constitution to trump Congress' effort to curtail a federal court remedy. Recall also that the purpose of the federal court remedy, the injunction, is to cure the Executive's violation of a federal statutory right that Congress created.
- Compensatory relief compensates *retroactively* for past harm, while injunctive relief operates *prospectively* to stop future harm. Injunctions are considered an "equitable," rather than "legal," remedy. Accordingly, the judge, instead of a jury, orders injunctive relief that operates directly on the defendant, ordering him to take action or cease action. Does Congress possess the power to change the prospective effect of the injunctions previously entered by federal district courts? In your opinion, did Congress (i) dictate the outcome of these cases by telling judges what, when, or how to rule; (ii) reopen a final judgment of the courts; or (iii) alter the underlying substantive law that previously provided the basis for the injunction (e.g., did Congress provide a new legal standard for relief)? [Hint: *Compare Plaut* (holding unconstitutional a federal statute that overturned a Supreme Court decision dismissing certain cases) *with Wheeling Bridge* (upholding a federal statute that validated a bridge that the Supreme Court had previously held an unlawful obstruction).] Then articulate which behavior is constitutionally within Congress' power.
- Under our constitutional system, should Congress, the Executive, or the Supreme Court have the "last word"?

PROBLEM 3-5

Lethal Dose Part II

Review the facts in Problem 3-2. Recall that a federal district court issued an injunction to stop a state from authorizing any legal injections pending further hearings regarding pain levels that may raise "cruel and unusual punishments" under the Eighth Amendment to the Constitution, and then Congress passed the Death Penalty Protection Act to strip federal court jurisdiction over Eighth Amendment claims and lethal injection challenges. Further recall that in *Klein*, the Court distinguished *Wheeling Bridge*, in which the Court applied ordinary rules to new circumstances created by Congress' legislation, from *Klein*, in which Congress did not present new circumstances in its act. In *Klein*, the Court invalidated Congress' attempt to direct how the Court should rule, whereas, in *Wheeling Bridge*, the Court upheld Congress' validation of a bridge that the Court had already held was an invalid nuisance.

What effect would the Death Penalty Protection Act have on the preliminary injunction in place under the supervision of the federal district court? Remember that when the federal district court issued the injunction, it held valid jurisdiction. The issue is whether Congress' jurisdiction-stripping legislation alters a preexisting and ongoing injunctive remedy. Does the substantive basis giving rise to the injunction still exist? Does the district court's power to enforce the injunction still exist? Would your analysis change if, instead of an injunction pending further hearings, the court had ruled that lethal injections violate the Eighth Amendment?

D. SOME ADDITIONAL PROBLEMS

The problems that follow provide additional practice concerning the topics covered in Chapter 3.

PROBLEM 3-6

Inferior-ity Complex

After a series of opinions favoring criminal defendants, the Attorney General and Solicitor General became increasingly vocal about their dissatisfaction with the Supreme Court's criminal justice jurisprudence. Congress held hearings on the Supreme Court's trend of favoring defendants. A few more defendant-friendly Supreme Court opinions followed, and Congress resolved to act. During Congress' deliberations, Senator Phil E. Buster railed against a permissive Supreme Court. He exclaimed, "We can't do business with them anymore." Eventually, a majority emerged supporting Senator Buster's position. Congress passed, and the President signed, the "Safe Jurisdictions Act," which provided: "The Supreme Court shall have no appellate jurisdiction over criminal cases. Appellate jurisdiction over all criminal cases is hereby conferred on the

United States Court of Appeals for the Fourth Circuit, which shall be the final reviewer of all such cases." Proponents of the bill chose the Fourth Circuit because of a reputation for its inhospitable climate for criminal defendants.

For purposes of Problem 3-6, assume that the *grant* of jurisdiction to the Fourth Circuit—a topic that we will cover in Chapter 4–is proper. Instead focus your attention on the strip of Supreme Court jurisdiction over a class of cases rife with constitutional questions. Assuming the Supreme Court retains its original habeas corpus jurisdiction, could the Act pass constitutional muster? What court, if any, would have authority to decide a challenge to the Act? If the Act is valid, would you expect the Supreme Court to breathe life into its original jurisdiction vehicle?

PROBLEM 3-7

The Ready-or-Not Reserve

As part of the global War on Terror, the Defense Department has attempted to maintain troop levels in two theaters of combat operations by calling up "Ready Reserve" components of the military. The Ready Reserve, governed by 10 U.S.C. § 10145, includes certain military personnel who have been released from active duty within the past ten years.

Traditionally, federal courts were loath to allow pre-recall judicial review of Ready Reserve recall orders. Ready Reservists had two exclusive routes to federal court review: (a) as a defense to a criminal prosecution for failure to report for duty or (b) by an action for discharge by means of writ of habeas corpus. However, two years ago an appellate court granted a Ready Reservist pre-recall review for a recall classification she alleged was based on her anti-war activities. In response, Congress passed the following Act:

> No judicial review shall be made of the classification or processing of any Ready Reservist as that term is defined in 10 U.S.C. § 10145 in relation to a recall order except as a defense to a criminal prosecution.

Gary Graystone was honorably discharged from the Marine Corps as a junior officer eight years ago and considers himself a "former Marine." Last year, his wife was killed in a car accident, leaving him the sole breadwinner and sole caretaker for his daughter. When Graystone first heard that components of the Ready Reserve were being called up to active duty, he followed detailed administrative procedures and received a hardship exemption under applicable regulations based on his role as his daughter's sole caregiver. Those regulations also require that he report to the nearest Reserve unit if he moves and keep his "exemption certificate" with him for presentation should his unit be called up.

Since his time on active duty, Graystone has become increasingly disenchanted with the prosecution of the War on Terror. Several months ago, he participated in an anti-war rally to protest the use of the Ready Reserve, at which he and others burned their exemption certificates. Last week, he received a "Notification of Involuntary Recall to Active Duty," and his Reserve Command refused to honor his exemption on the basis of (a) its admitted knowledge of his anti-war activities and (b) his failure to present his exemption certificate. Graystone administratively appealed the decision, and all administrative remedies were exhausted. He has filed suit in federal district court against Reserve Command, alleging he was illegally deprived of his exemption. He argues that, once a person substantively qualifies for an exemption, that person cannot be deprived of it on the basis of unrelated conduct.

Reserve Command moves to dismiss Graystone's suit for lack of jurisdiction. Graystone responds by arguing that the recent Act limiting federal court jurisdiction is unconstitutional. What arguments can Graystone make to support his response? How should the federal court rule on those arguments?

CHAPTER
4

Allocation of Jurisdiction to Non-Article III Tribunals

A. A REFERENCE PROBLEM

In this chapter we principally consider when Congress may allocate Article III jurisdictional powers to non-Article III actors. *See* U.S. Const. art. III, § 2. The Reference Problem below introduces many of the concepts we will explore.

* * * * *

For much of United States history, a person claiming an entitlement to receive a government benefit on account of military service had no recourse to the judicial system if his or her claim was denied. In 1988, that situation changed when Congress created what is today known as the United States Court of Appeals for Veterans Claims (CAVC). Congress stated that it was creating the CAVC "under Article I of the Constitution of the United States." *See* 28 U.S.C. § 7251.

The CAVC is an appellate body comprising nine judges. The judges are appointed by the President with the advice and consent of the Senate. *See* 28

U.S.C. § 7253(b). The judges are usually appointed for terms of fifteen years. *See* 28 U.S.C. § 7253(c). Their salary is set by statute, but there is no statutory provision preventing a reduction in such compensation. Further, Congress provided that the President could remove a CAVC judge "on grounds of misconduct, neglect of duty, or engaging in the practice of law." *See* 28 U.S.C. § 7253(f).

The CAVC has jurisdiction to consider appeals by veterans (or others claiming to be entitled to benefits) denied benefits administered through the United States Department of Veterans Affairs. *See* 28 U.S.C. § 7252(a).[1] The government cannot appeal to the CAVC. *Id.* Decisions of the CAVC may be appealed by any dissatisfied party to the United States Court of Appeals for the Federal Circuit. *See* 28 U.S.C. § 7292. The Federal Circuit is an Article III court that, unlike the other federal courts of appeals, has jurisdiction not based on geography. Instead, the Federal Circuit's appellate jurisdiction is based on specialized subject matter such as taxes and patents, among other things. The Federal Circuit's decisions concerning appeals from the CAVC are subject to review in the Supreme Court of the United States by writ of certiorari. *Id.*

Review of CAVC decisions in the Federal Circuit (and by extension the Supreme Court) is limited. The Federal Circuit has jurisdiction only to review "relevant questions of law, including interpreting constitutional and statutory provisions." *See* 28 U.S.C. § 7292(d)(1). However, unless the appeal presents a constitutional issue, the Federal Circuit is specifically precluded from reviewing "a challenge to a factual determination" or "a challenge to a law or regulation as applied to the facts of a particular case." *See* 28 U.S.C. § 7292(d)(2).

You work for a law firm that represents a veteran who has been denied benefits to which she believes she is entitled. Your firm is preparing the client's appeal of the denial of these benefits to the CAVC. Your boss at the firm is concerned that "something just doesn't feel right about the CAVC." He poses a number of questions for you to consider:

- Can Congress create the CAVC under Article I of the Constitution? He would like you to provide a specific citation to the constitutional authority for the power to create such a body.
- Assuming that Congress has the authority to create such a body under Article I of the Constitution, can it assign the adjudication of your client's claims to a body that is not an Article III court? After all, your client's dispute would seem to be one "arising under . . . the Laws of the United States," a category of claims to which the "judicial Power of the United States" extends under Article III, section 2.
- Assuming that Congress can create the CAVC under Article I and can also assign the adjudication of your client's claim to such a body, is appellate review by an Article III court such as the Federal Circuit required? If it is, is the limited scope of review of the CAVC's decisions sufficient?

* * * * *

In many respects, the questions posed above go to the very heart of the role of federal courts in the American constitutional order. If there is truly something

1. Technically, the final denial of benefits is made by an entity known as the Board of Veterans' Appeals, a body within the Department of Veterans Affairs.

important about the assignment of the "judicial Power" to adjudicators with constitutional tenure and salary protection, then the CAVC Congress created needs to be supported by equally powerful justifications. We consider these issues, and others, in the material that follows.

B. CONTEXT AND BACKGROUND

The starting point for considering the issues discussed in this chapter is Article III of the Constitution. As we have highlighted throughout the text thus far, the Constitution provides that judges serving in the third branch of the federal government "shall hold their Offices during good Behaviour, and shall at stated Times, receive for their Services, a Compensation, which shall not be diminished during their Continuance in Office." *See* U.S. CONST. art. III, § 1. Thus, to be an Article III judge, by constitutional definition, one must have both life tenure and salary protection. Article III then proceeds to catalogue those cases and controversies as to which Article III judges may wield the "judicial Power of the United States." *See* U.S. CONST. art. III, § 2, cl. 1.

The first question we address in this chapter is under what circumstances Congress may constitutionally assign the adjudication of matters listed in Article III, section 2, to which the "judicial Power of the United States" may extend, to adjudicators who do not enjoy the tenure and salary protections of Article III, section 1. This question raises yet again the fundamental issue of what is special about Article III judges in the American constitutional system.

It is tempting to answer this question with a firm, bright line rule that Congress may not under any circumstances assign the adjudication of matters within Article III to a non-Article III actor. One could argue that the Constitution's separation-of-powers principles necessarily lead to the conclusion that a congressional assignment of something coming within the "judicial Power of the United States" to something other than an Article III court undermines the authority of one of the three coordinate branches of government. One might also argue that, apart from Article III's structural role, individual litigants have a personal right to an Article III adjudicator for those matters set forth in Article III, section 2. However, as we will learn, it turns out that the Court has not adopted this strict interpretation of how Article III operates either on a structural or individual rights basis.

From the very early days of the Republic, the Supreme Court has made clear that Congress may, in certain circumstances, assign the adjudication of Article III matters to non-Article III adjudicators. Thus, the Court's effort has been — and our challenge will be — to determine in which cases such an assignment is consistent with the Constitution.

Before previewing what we will learn about this question, it may be useful to consider some examples of non-Article III adjudicators. One type of non-Article III adjudicator that can often be overlooked precisely because it is so obvious is a state court. State court judges are not protected by the tenure and salary guarantees of Article III and, almost universally, do not enjoy those guarantees under state law. Yet no one seriously questions that Congress can assign the adjudication of matters within Article III, section 2, to state courts if it so desires. For example, state courts generally have jurisdiction concurrent with Article III federal courts to adjudicate matters arising under federal law. However, the structural issues we alluded to above concerning the separation of powers do not apply when we consider state courts. These courts are not under the control of Congress and, therefore, we may worry less about the assignment of matters within Article III to them.

Our discussion in this chapter of non-Article III adjudicators will instead focus on *federal* entities to which Congress assigns matters within Article III, section 2. For these entities, the separation-of-powers concern is directly implicated. It is here that we worry about Congress unduly influencing the resolution of controversies because the adjudicator to whom the dispute is assigned lacks the tenure and salary protections designed to foster judicial independence. It is also here that we may be concerned about Congress inappropriately removing from the mix one of the coordinate federal branches.

Generically speaking, there are three types of federal non-Article III adjudicators. First, there are Article I courts (also referred to as legislative courts), such as the United States Tax Court and the United States Court of Appeals for Veterans Claims. *See* U.S. CONST. art. I, § 8, cl. 9 (providing that Congress has the authority to "constitute Tribunals inferior to the Supreme Court"). Like their Article III counterparts, judges serving on Article I courts are generally appointed by the President with the advice and consent of the Senate. However, they lack the Article III salary and tenure protections.

A second entity is what is commonly known as an adjunct to an Article III court. An adjunct is an adjudicator said to be within Article III but who is not an Article III judge. In other words, the adjunct is subject to comprehensive Article III control but does not possess the tenure and salary protections of Article III. Examples of Article III adjuncts are United States Magistrate Judges and United States Bankruptcy Judges.

Finally, the third category of federal non-Article III adjudicators is the administrative agency. As you learn in an Administrative Law course, the modern administrative agency often possesses attributes of legislative, executive, *and* judicial authority. Examples of administrative adjudication abound, including in the areas of immigration, social security benefits, and enforcement of laws concerning marketable securities, to name just a few. While administrative agencies bear similarities to both Article III adjuncts and legislative courts, they are sufficiently distinctive to warrant separate discussion.

Having outlined what is meant by a non-Article III adjudicator, we may return to when Congress may assign Article III matters to such entities. As we will see, the contemporary Court has taken two different approaches to determine when an assignment of an Article III matter to a non-Article III entity is constitutional. At times, the Court has appeared to adopt a categorical approach in which Congress may assign Article III tasks to non-Article III actors only in specifically defined, and potentially narrow, categories. At other times, however, the Court has adopted an ad hoc balancing approach in which the constitutionality of any given assignment of an Article III task to a non-Article III adjudicator is evaluated by balancing the values underlying Article III with Congress' Article I legislative interests. In the materials that follow, we explore each of these approaches. At least until the Court clarifies matters, you will need to understand both of them. This may be especially true today because the Court has quite recently decided several cases that appear to blend these two approaches to the issue that may only serve to muddy the already cloudy waters.

We conclude the chapter by discussing the converse of the issue with which we have been wrestling thus far. Specifically, we consider when Congress may assign a non-Article III task to an Article III court. While matters are not entirely clear in this regard, you will learn that Congress probably cannot assign non-judicial tasks to Article III courts and probably cannot assign the adjudication of judicial matters to Article III courts if those matters do not come within the ambit of Article III, section 2.

As you work through the often difficult material that follows, try to keep the following broad questions in mind, some of which we have considered in other contexts before:

- What is the importance in our constitutional system of having adjudicators who possess Article III tenure and salary protections? Do we lose the benefits associated with these attributes when Congress assigns matters to which the "judicial Power of the United States" extends to non-Article III adjudicators?
- Is the Supreme Court's current doctrine concerning the assignment of Article III matters to non-Article III adjudicators workable? If it is not, how can it be improved?
- Does the Supreme Court's current doctrine concerning assignment of Article III matters to non-Article III adjudicators sufficiently take into account structural concerns involving the separation of powers? What about the individual litigants' interest in fair and impartial adjudicators?

C. THE LAW AND PROBLEMS

1. *Assignment of Judicial Business to Non-Article III Tribunals*

We begin our discussion of the assignment of judicial business to non-Article III tribunals with the Supreme Court's 1982 decision in *Northern Pipeline Construction Co. v. Marathon Pipe Line Co.* This decision is important for two reasons. First, Justice Brennan's plurality opinion sets forth an excellent summary of how doctrine in this area developed during the first nearly two centuries of government under the Constitution. Second, the Brennan plurality opinion describes one approach to the issue, one that is highly categorical. As we will learn, this approach stands in contrast to a more flexible balancing approach the Court used in later cases. And there is at least some reason to believe that the pendulum may be swinging back to this categorical approach — or some version of it.

It is a fair question why we begin, and devote serious attention to, *Northern Pipeline* given its nature (i.e., plurality) and the divergent approach taken in more recent decisions. We believe such attention is important for at least two independent reasons. First, it is difficult to assess the Court's later balancing methodology without understanding the categorical approach Justice Brennan advocates. One can appreciate that approach best by actually reading *Northern Pipeline.* Second, as we will learn, while the Court has used an ad hoc balancing approach in more recent cases, there has also been some indication that the categorical approach at the heart of Justice Brennan's *Northern Pipeline* plurality may still play some role.

We will return to many of these introductory points after you have had an opportunity to read *Northern Pipeline* and the other cases the Court has decided in this area.

NORTHERN PIPELINE CONSTRUCTION CO. v. MARATHON PIPE LINE CO.

458 U.S. 50 (1982)

JUSTICE BRENNAN announced the judgment of the Court and delivered an opinion, in which JUSTICE MARSHALL, JUSTICE BLACKMUN, and JUSTICE STEVENS joined.

The question presented is whether the assignment by Congress to bankruptcy judges of the jurisdiction granted in 28 U. S. C. § 1471 by § 241(a) of the Bankruptcy Act of 1978 violates Art. III of the Constitution.

I

A

In 1978, after almost 10 years of study and investigation, Congress enacted a comprehensive revision of the bankruptcy laws. The Bankruptcy Act of 1978 (Act) made significant changes in both the substantive and procedural law of bankruptcy. It is the changes in the latter that are at issue in this case.

Before the Act, federal district courts served as bankruptcy courts and employed a "referee" system. Bankruptcy proceedings were generally conducted before referees, except in those instances in which the district court elected to withdraw a case from a referee. The referee's final order was appealable to the district court. The bankruptcy courts were vested with "summary jurisdiction" — that is, with jurisdiction over controversies involving property in the actual or constructive possession of the court. And, with consent, the bankruptcy court also had jurisdiction over some "plenary" matters — such as disputes involving property in the possession of a third person.

The Act eliminates the referee system and establishes "in each judicial district, as an adjunct to the district court for such district, a bankruptcy court which shall be a court of record known as the United States Bankruptcy Court for the district." The judges of these courts are appointed to office for 14-year terms by the President, with the advice and consent of the Senate. They are subject to removal by the "judicial council of the circuit" on account of "incompetency, misconduct, neglect of duty or physical or mental disability." In addition, the salaries of the bankruptcy judges are set by statute and are subject to adjustment under the Federal Salary Act.

The jurisdiction of the bankruptcy courts created by the Act is much broader than that exercised under the former referee system. Eliminating the distinction between "summary" and "plenary" jurisdiction, the Act grants the new courts jurisdiction over all "civil proceedings arising under title 11 [the Bankruptcy title] or arising in or *related to* cases under title 11." 28 U.S.C. § 1471(b) (emphasis added).[2] This jurisdictional grant empowers bankruptcy courts to entertain a

2. [Footnote 3 in Justice Brennan's opinion.] Although the Act initially vests this jurisdiction in district courts, 28 U.S.C. § 1471(a), it subsequently provides that "[the] bankruptcy court for the district in which a case under title 11 is commenced shall exercise *all* of the jurisdiction conferred

wide variety of cases involving claims that may affect the property of the estate once a petition has been filed under Title 11. Included within the bankruptcy courts' jurisdiction are suits to recover accounts, controversies involving exempt property, actions to avoid transfers and payments as preferences or fraudulent conveyances, and causes of action owned by the debtor at the time of the petition for bankruptcy. The bankruptcy courts can hear claims based on state law as well as those based on federal law.

The judges of the bankruptcy courts are vested with all of the "powers of a court of equity, law, and admiralty," except that they "may not enjoin another court or punish a criminal contempt not committed in the presence of the judge of the court or warranting a punishment of imprisonment." In addition to this broad grant of power, Congress has allowed bankruptcy judges the power to hold jury trials; to issue declaratory judgments; to issue writs of habeas corpus under certain circumstances; to issue all writs necessary in aid of the bankruptcy court's expanded jurisdiction; and to issue any order, process or judgment that is necessary or appropriate to carry out the provisions of Title 11.

The Act also establishes a special procedure for appeals from orders of bankruptcy courts. The circuit council is empowered to direct the chief judge of the circuit to designate panels of three bankruptcy judges to hear appeals. These panels have jurisdiction of all appeals from final judgments, orders, and decrees of bankruptcy courts, and, with leave of the panel, of interlocutory appeals. If no such appeals panel is designated, the district court is empowered to exercise appellate jurisdiction. The court of appeals is given jurisdiction over appeals from the appellate panels or from the district court. If the parties agree, a direct appeal to the court of appeals may be taken from a final judgment of a bankruptcy court.[3]

* * * *

B

This case arises out of proceedings initiated in the United States Bankruptcy Court for the District of Minnesota after appellant Northern Pipeline Construction Co. (Northern) filed a petition for reorganization in January 1980. In March 1980 Northern, pursuant to the Act, filed in that court a suit against appellee Marathon Pipe Line Co. (Marathon). Appellant sought damages for alleged breaches of contract and warranty, as well as for alleged misrepresentation, coercion, and duress. Marathon sought dismissal of the suit, on the ground that the Act unconstitutionally conferred Art. III judicial power upon judges who lacked life tenure and protection against salary diminution. The United States intervened to defend the validity of the statute.

The Bankruptcy Judge denied the motion to dismiss. But on appeal the District Court entered an order granting the motion, on the ground that "the delegation of authority in 28 U. S. C. § 1471 to the Bankruptcy Judges to try cases which are otherwise relegated under the Constitution to Article III judges" was unconstitutional. Both the United States and Northern filed notices of appeal in this Court.

---

by this section on the district courts," § 1471 (c) (emphasis added). Thus the ultimate repository of the Act's broad jurisdictional grant is the bankruptcy courts.

3. [Footnote 5 in Justice Brennan's opinion.] Although no particular standard of review is specified in the Act, the parties in the present cases seem to agree that the appropriate one is the clearly-erroneous standard. . . .

II

A

Basic to the constitutional structure established by the Framers was their recognition that "[the] accumulation of all powers, legislative, executive, and judiciary, in the same hands, whether of one, a few, or many, and whether hereditary, self-appointed, or elective, may justly be pronounced the very definition of tyranny." The Federalist No. 47 (J. Madison). To ensure against such tyranny, the Framers provided that the Federal Government would consist of three distinct Branches, each to exercise one of the governmental powers recognized by the Framers as inherently distinct. "The Framers regarded the checks and balances that they had built into the tripartite Federal Government as a self-executing safeguard against the encroachment or aggrandizement of one branch at the expense of the other."

The Federal Judiciary was therefore designed by the Framers to stand independent of the Executive and Legislature — to maintain the checks and balances of the constitutional structure, and also to guarantee that the process of adjudication itself remained impartial. Hamilton explained the importance of an independent Judiciary:

"Periodical appointments, however regulated, or by whomsoever made, would, in some way or other, be fatal to [the courts'] necessary independence. If the power of making them was committed either to the Executive or legislature, there would be danger of an improper complaisance to the branch which possessed it; if to both, there would be an unwillingness to hazard the displeasure of either; if to the people, or to persons chosen by them for the special purpose, there would be too great a disposition to consult popularity, to justify a reliance that nothing would be consulted but the Constitution and the laws." The Federalist No. 78.

The Court has only recently reaffirmed the significance of this feature of the Framers' design: "A Judiciary free from control by the Executive and Legislature is essential if there is a right to have claims decided by judges who are free from potential domination by other branches of government."

As an inseparable element of the constitutional system of checks and balances, and as a guarantee of judicial impartiality, Art. III both defines the power and protects the independence of the Judicial Branch. It provides that "The judicial Power of the United States, shall be vested in one supreme Court, and in such inferior Courts as the Congress may from time to time ordain and establish." Art. III, § 1. The inexorable command of this provision is clear and definite: The judicial power of the United States must be exercised by courts having the attributes prescribed in Art. III. Those attributes are also clearly set forth:

"The Judges, both of the supreme and inferior Courts, shall hold their Offices during good Behaviour, and shall, at stated Times, receive for their Services, a Compensation, which shall not be diminished during their Continuance in Office." Art. III, § 1.

The "good Behaviour" Clause guarantees that Art. III judges shall enjoy life tenure, subject only to removal by impeachment. The Compensation Clause guarantees Art. III judges a fixed and irreducible compensation for their services. Both of these provisions were incorporated into the Constitution to ensure the independence of the Judiciary from the control of the Executive and

Legislative Branches of government.[4] As we have only recently emphasized, "[the] Compensation Clause has its roots in the longstanding Anglo-American tradition of an independent Judiciary," while the principle of life tenure can be traced back at least as far as the Act of Settlement in 1701. To be sure, both principles were eroded during the late colonial period, but that departure did not escape notice and indignant rejection by the Revolutionary generation. Indeed, the guarantees eventually included in Art. III were clearly foreshadowed in the Declaration of Independence, "which, among the injuries and usurpations recited against the King of Great Britain, declared that he had 'made judges dependent on his will alone, for the tenure of their offices, and the amount and payment of their salaries.'" The Framers thus recognized:

"Next to permanency in office, nothing can contribute more to the independence of the judges than a fixed provision for their support. . . . In the general course of human nature, *a power over a man's subsistence amounts to a power over his will.*" The Federalist No. 79 (A. Hamilton) (emphasis in original).

In sum, our Constitution unambiguously enunciates a fundamental principle — that the "judicial Power of the United States" must be reposed in an independent Judiciary. It commands that the independence of the Judiciary be jealously guarded, and it provides clear institutional protections for that independence.

B

It is undisputed that the bankruptcy judges whose offices were created by the Bankruptcy Act of 1978 do not enjoy the protections constitutionally afforded to Art. III judges. The bankruptcy judges do not serve for life subject to their continued "good Behaviour." Rather, they are appointed for 14-year terms, and can be removed by the judicial council of the circuit in which they serve on grounds of "incompetency, misconduct, neglect of duty, or physical or mental disability." Second, the salaries of the bankruptcy judges are not immune from diminution by Congress. In short, there is no doubt that the bankruptcy judges created by the Act are not Art. III judges.

That Congress chose to vest such broad jurisdiction in non-Art. III bankruptcy courts, after giving substantial consideration to the constitutionality of the Act, is of course reason to respect the congressional conclusion. But at the same time, "[deciding] whether a matter has in any measure been committed by the Constitution to another branch of government, or whether the action of that branch exceeds whatever authority has been committed, is itself a delicate exercise in constitutional interpretation, and is a responsibility of this Court as ultimate interpreter of the Constitution."

With these principles in mind, we turn to the question presented for decision: whether the Bankruptcy Act of 1978 violates the command of Art. III that the judicial power of the United States must be vested in courts whose judges enjoy the protections and safeguards specified in that Article.

4. [Footnote 10 in Justice Brennan's opinion.] These provisions serve other institutional values as well. The independence from political forces that they guarantee helps to promote public confidence in judicial determinations. See The Federalist No. 78 (A. Hamilton). The security that they provide to members of the Judicial Branch helps to attract well-qualified persons to the federal bench. The guarantee of life tenure insulates the individual judge from improper influences not only by other branches but by colleagues as well, and thus promotes judicial individualism.

Appellants suggest two grounds for upholding the Act's conferral of broad adjudicative powers upon judges unprotected by Art. III. First, it is urged that "pursuant to its enumerated Article I powers, Congress may establish legislative courts that have jurisdiction to decide cases to which the Article III judicial power of the United States extends." Referring to our precedents upholding the validity of "legislative courts," appellants suggest that "the plenary grants of power in Article I permit Congress to establish non-Article III tribunals in 'specialized areas having particularized needs and warranting distinctive treatment,'" such as the area of bankruptcy law. Second, appellants contend that even if the Constitution does require that this bankruptcy-related action be adjudicated in an Art. III court, the Act in fact satisfies that requirement. "Bankruptcy jurisdiction was vested in the district court" of the judicial district in which the bankruptcy court is located, "and the exercise of that jurisdiction by the adjunct bankruptcy court was made subject to appeal as of right to an Article III court." Analogizing the role of the bankruptcy court to that of a special master, appellants urge us to conclude that this "adjunct" system established by Congress satisfies the requirements of Art. III. We consider these arguments in turn.

III

Congress did not constitute the bankruptcy courts as legislative courts. Appellants contend, however, that the bankruptcy courts could have been so constituted, and that as a result the "adjunct" system in fact chosen by Congress does not impermissibly encroach upon the judicial power. In advancing this argument, appellants rely upon cases in which we have identified certain matters that "congress may or may not bring within the cognizance of [Art. III courts], as it may deem proper." *Murray's Lessee v. Hoboken Land & Improvement Co.*, 18 How. 272, 284 (1856).[5] But when properly understood, these precedents represent no broad departure from the constitutional command that the judicial power of the United States must be vested in Art. III courts.[6] Rather, they reduce to three narrow situations not subject to that command, each recognizing a circumstance in which the grant of power to the Legislative and Executive Branches was historically and constitutionally so exceptional that the congressional assertion of a power to create legislative courts was consistent with, rather than threatening to, the constitutional mandate of separation of powers. These precedents simply acknowledge that the literal command of Art. III, assigning the judicial power of the United States to courts insulated from Legislative or Executive interference,

5. [Footnote 14 in Justice Brennan's opinion.] At one time, this Court suggested a rigid distinction between those subjects that could be considered only in Art. III courts and those that could be considered only in legislative courts. But this suggested dichotomy has not withstood analysis. Our more recent cases clearly recognize that legislative courts may be granted jurisdiction over some cases and controversies to which the Art. III judicial power might also be extended.

6. [Footnote 15 in Justice Brennan's opinion.] Justice White's dissent finds particular significance in the fact that Congress could have assigned all bankruptcy matters to the state courts. But, of course, virtually all matters that might be heard in Art. III courts could also be left by Congress to state courts. This fact is simply irrelevant to the question before us. Congress has no control over state-court judges; accordingly the principle of separation of powers is not threatened by leaving the adjudication of federal disputes to such judges. The Framers chose to leave to Congress the precise role to be played by the lower federal courts in the administration of justice. But the Framers did not leave it to Congress to define the character of those courts—they were to be independent of the political branches and presided over by judges with guaranteed salary and life tenure.

must be interpreted in light of the historical context in which the Constitution was written, and of the structural imperatives of the Constitution as a whole.

Appellants first rely upon a series of cases in which this Court has upheld the creation by Congress of non-Art. III "territorial courts." This exception from the general prescription of Art. III dates from the earliest days of the Republic, when it was perceived that the Framers intended that as to certain geographical areas, in which no State operated as sovereign, Congress was to exercise the general powers of government. . . .

The Court followed the same reasoning when it reviewed Congress' creation of non-Art. III courts in the District of Columbia. It noted that there was in the District "no division of powers between the general and state governments. Congress has the entire control over the district for every purpose of government; and it is reasonable to suppose, that in organizing a judicial department here, all judicial power necessary for the purposes of government would be vested in the courts of justice."

Appellants next advert to a second class of cases — those in which this Court has sustained the exercise by Congress and the Executive of the power to establish and administer courts-martial. The situation in these cases strongly resembles the situation with respect to territorial courts: It too involves a constitutional grant of power that has been historically understood as giving the political Branches of Government extraordinary control over the precise subject matter at issue. Article I, § 8, cls. 13, 14, confer upon Congress the power "[to] provide and maintain a Navy," and "[to] make Rules for the Government and Regulation of the land and naval Forces." The Fifth Amendment, which requires a presentment or indictment of a grand jury before a person may be held to answer for a capital or otherwise infamous crime, contains an express exception for "cases arising in the land or naval forces." And Art. II, § 2, cl. 1, provides that "The President shall be Commander in Chief of the Army and Navy of the United States, and of the Militia of the several States, when called into the actual Service of the United States." Noting these constitutional directives, the Court in *Dynes v. Hoover*, 20 How. 65 (1857), explained:

"These provisions show that Congress has the power to provide for the trial and punishment of military and naval offences in the manner then and now practiced by civilized nations; and that the power to do so is given without any connection between it and the 3d article of the Constitution defining the judicial power of the United States; indeed, that the two powers are entirely independent of each other."[7]

Finally, appellants rely on a third group of cases, in which this Court has upheld the constitutionality of legislative courts and administrative agencies created by Congress to adjudicate cases involving "public rights."[8] The "public rights" doctrine was first set forth in *Murray's Lessee v. Hoboken Land & Improvement Co.*, 18 How, 272 (1856):

"[We] do not consider congress can either withdraw from judicial cognizance any matter which, from its nature, is the subject of a suit at the common law, or in equity, or admiralty; nor, on the other hand, can it bring under the judicial

7. [Footnote 17 in Justice Brennan's opinion.] But this Court has been alert to ensure that Congress does not exceed the constitutional bounds and bring within the jurisdiction of the military courts matters beyond that jurisdiction, and properly within the realm of "judicial power."

8. [Footnote 18 in Justice Brennan's opinion.] Congress' power to create legislative courts to adjudicate public rights carries with it the lesser power to create administrative agencies for the same purpose, and to provide for review of those agency decisions in Art. III courts.

power a matter which, from its nature, is not a subject for judicial determination. At the same time there are matters, *involving public rights,* which may be presented in such form that the judicial power is capable of acting on them, and which are susceptible of judicial determination, but which congress may or may not bring within the cognizance of the courts of the United States, as it may deem proper." (emphasis added).

This doctrine may be explained in part by reference to the traditional principle of sovereign immunity, which recognizes that the Government may attach conditions to its consent to be sued. But the public-rights doctrine also draws upon the principle of separation of powers, and a historical understanding that certain prerogatives were reserved to the political Branches of Government. The doctrine extends only to matters arising "between the Government and persons subject to its authority in connection with the performance of the constitutional functions of the executive or legislative departments," *Crowell v. Benson,* 285 U.S. 22, 50 (1932), and only to matters that historically could have been determined exclusively by those departments. The understanding of these cases is that the Framers expected that Congress would be free to commit such matters completely to nonjudicial executive determination, and that as a result there can be no constitutional objection to Congress' employing the less drastic expedient of committing their determination to a legislative court or an administrative agency.

The public-rights doctrine is grounded in a historically recognized distinction between matters that could be conclusively determined by the Executive and Legislative Branches and matters that are "inherently . . . judicial." For example, the Court in *Murray's Lessee* looked to the law of England and the States at the time the Constitution was adopted, in order to determine whether the issue presented was customarily cognizable in the courts. Concluding that the matter had not traditionally been one for judicial determination, the Court perceived no bar to Congress' establishment of summary procedures, outside of Art. III courts, to collect a debt due to the Government from one of its customs agents. . . .[9]

The distinction between public rights and private rights has not been definitively explained in our precedents.[10] Nor is it necessary to do so in the present cases, for it suffices to observe that a matter of public rights must at a minimum arise "between the government and others."[11] In contrast, "the liability of one individual to another under the law as defined" is a matter of private rights.

9. [Footnote 20 in Justice Brennan's opinion.] Doubtless it could be argued that the need for independent judicial determination is greatest in cases arising between the Government and an individual. But the rationale for the public-rights line of cases lies not in political theory, but rather in Congress' and this Court's understanding of what power was reserved to the Judiciary by the Constitution as a matter of historical fact.

10. [Footnote 22 in Justice Brennan's opinion.] *Crowell v. Benson* attempted to catalog some of the matters that fall within the public-rights doctrine: "Familiar illustrations of administrative agencies created for the determination of such matters are found in connection with the exercise of the congressional power as to interstate and foreign commerce, taxation, immigration, the public lands, public health, the facilities of the post office, pensions and payments to veterans."

11. [Footnote 23 in Justice Brennan's opinion.] Congress cannot "withdraw from [Art. III] judicial cognizance *any* matter which, *from its nature,* is the subject of a suit at the common law, or in equity, or admiralty." *Murray's Lessee v. Hoboken Land & Improvement Co.* It is thus clear that the presence of the United States as a proper party to the proceeding is a necessary but not sufficient means of distinguishing "private rights" from "public rights." And it is also clear that even with respect to matters that arguably fall within the scope of the "public rights" doctrine, the presumption is in favor of Art. III courts. Moreover, when Congress assigns these matters to administrative agencies, or to legislative courts, it has generally provided, and we have suggested that it may be required to provide, for Art. III judicial review.

Our precedents clearly establish that *only* controversies in the former category may be removed from Art. III courts and delegated to legislative courts or administrative agencies for their determination.[12] Private-rights disputes, on the other hand, lie at the core of the historically recognized judicial power.

In sum, this Court has identified three situations in which Art. III does not bar the creation of legislative courts. In each of these situations, the Court has recognized certain exceptional powers bestowed upon Congress by the Constitution or by historical consensus. Only in the face of such an exceptional grant of power has the Court declined to hold the authority of Congress subject to the general prescriptions of Art. III.[13]

We discern no such exceptional grant of power applicable in the cases before us. The courts created by the Bankruptcy Act of 1978 do not lie exclusively outside the States of the Federal Union, like those in the District of Columbia and the Territories. Nor do the bankruptcy courts bear any resemblance to courts-martial, which are founded upon the Constitution's grant of plenary authority over the Nation's military forces to the Legislative and Executive Branches. Finally, the substantive legal rights at issue in the present action cannot be deemed "public rights." Appellants argue that a discharge in bankruptcy is indeed a "public right," similar to such congressionally created benefits as "radio station licenses, pilot licenses, or certificates for common carriers" granted by administrative agencies. But the restructuring of debtor-creditor relations, which is at the core of the federal bankruptcy power, must be distinguished from the adjudication of state-created private rights, such as the right to recover contract damages that is at issue in this case. The former may well be a "public right," but the latter obviously is not. Appellant Northern's right to recover contract damages to augment its estate is "one of private right, that is, of the liability of one individual to another under the law as defined." *Crowell v. Benson.*

Recognizing that the present cases may not fall within the scope of any of our prior cases permitting the establishment of legislative courts, appellants argue that we should recognize an additional situation beyond the command of Art. III, sufficiently broad to sustain the Act. Appellants contend that Congress' constitutional authority to establish "uniform Laws on the subject of Bankruptcies throughout the United States," Art. I, § 8, cl. 4, carries with it an inherent power to establish legislative courts capable of adjudicating "bankruptcy-related controversies". . . .

12. [Footnote 24 in Justice Brennan's opinion.] Of course, the public-rights doctrine does not extend to any criminal matters, although the Government is a proper party.

13. [Footnote 25 in Justice Brennan's opinion.] The "unifying principle" that Justice White's dissent finds lacking in all of these cases is to be found in the exceptional constitutional grants of power to Congress with respect to certain matters. Although the dissent is correct that these grants are not explicit in the language of the Constitution, they are nonetheless firmly established in our historical understanding of the constitutional structure. When these three exceptional grants are properly constrained, they do not threaten the Framers' vision of an independent Federal Judiciary. What clearly remains subject to Art. III are all private adjudications in federal courts within the States — matters from their nature subject to "a suit at common law or in equity or admiralty" — and all criminal matters, with the narrow exception of military crimes. There is no doubt that when the Framers assigned the "judicial Power" to an independent Art. III Branch, these matters lay at what they perceived to be the protected core of that power.

Although the dissent recognizes that the Framers had something important in mind when they assigned the judicial power of the United States to Art. III courts, it concludes that our cases and subsequent practice have eroded this conception. Unable to find a satisfactory theme in our precedents for analyzing these cases, the dissent rejects all of them, as well as the historical understanding upon which they were based, in favor of an ad hoc balancing approach in which Congress can essentially determine for itself whether Art. III courts are required. But even the dissent recognizes that the notion that Congress rather than the Constitution should determine whether there is a need for independent federal courts cannot be what the Framers had in mind.

Appellants' contention, in essence, is that pursuant to any of its Art. I powers, Congress may create courts free of Art. III's requirements whenever it finds that course expedient. This contention has been rejected in previous cases. Although the cases relied upon by appellants demonstrate that independent courts are not required for *all* federal adjudications, those cases also make it clear that where Art. III does apply, all of the legislative powers specified in Art. I and elsewhere are subject to it.

The flaw in appellants' analysis is that it provides no limiting principle. It thus threatens to supplant completely our system of adjudication in independent Art. III tribunals and replace it with a system of "specialized" legislative courts. True, appellants argue that under their analysis Congress could create legislative courts pursuant only to some "specific" Art. I power, and "only when there is a particularized need for distinctive treatment." They therefore assert that their analysis would not permit Congress to replace the independent Art. III Judiciary through a "wholesale assignment of federal judicial business to legislative courts." But these "limitations" are wholly illusory. For example, Art. I, § 8, empowers Congress to enact laws, *inter alia*, regulating interstate commerce and punishing certain crimes. Art. I, § 8, cls. 3, 6. On appellants' reasoning Congress could provide for the adjudication of these and "related" matters by judges and courts within Congress' exclusive control. The potential for encroachment upon powers reserved to the Judicial Branch through the device of "specialized" legislative courts is dramatically evidenced in the jurisdiction granted to the courts created by the Act before us. The broad range of questions that can be brought into a bankruptcy court because they are "related to cases under title 11" is the clearest proof that even when Congress acts through a "specialized" court, and pursuant to only one of its many Art. I powers, appellants' analysis fails to provide any real protection against the erosion of Art. III jurisdiction by the unilateral action of the political Branches. In short, to accept appellants' reasoning, would require that we replace the principles delineated in our precedents, rooted in history and the Constitution, with a rule of broad legislative discretion that could effectively eviscerate the constitutional guarantee of an independent Judicial Branch of the Federal Government.[14]

* * * *

In sum, Art. III bars Congress from establishing legislative courts to exercise jurisdiction over all matters related to those arising under the bankruptcy laws. The establishment of such courts does not fall within any of the historically

14. [Footnote 28 in Justice Brennan's opinion.] Justice White's suggested "limitations" on Congress' power to create Art. I courts are even more transparent. Justice White's dissent suggests that Art. III "should be read as expressing one value that must be balanced against competing constitutional values and legislative responsibilities," and that the Court retains the final word on how the balance is to be struck. The dissent would find the Art. III "value" accommodated where appellate review by Art. III courts is provided and where the Art. I courts are "designed to deal with issues likely to be of little interest to the political branches." But the dissent's view that appellate review is sufficient to satisfy either the command or the purpose of Art. III is incorrect. And the suggestion that we should consider whether the Art. I courts are designed to deal with issues likely to be of interest to the political Branches would undermine the validity of the adjudications performed by most of the administrative agencies, on which validity the dissent so heavily relies.

In applying its ad hoc balancing approach to the facts of this case, the dissent rests on the justification that these courts differ from standard Art. III courts because of their "extreme specialization." As noted above, "extreme specialization" is hardly an accurate description of bankruptcy courts designed to adjudicate the entire range of federal and state controversies. Moreover, the special nature of bankruptcy adjudications is in no sense incompatible with performance of such functions in a tribunal afforded the protection of Art. III. . . .

recognized situations in which the general principle of independent adjudication commanded by Art. III does not apply. Nor can we discern any persuasive reason, in logic, history, or the Constitution, why the bankruptcy courts here established lie beyond the reach of Art. III.

IV

Appellants advance a second argument for upholding the constitutionality of the Act: that "viewed within the entire judicial framework set up by Congress," the bankruptcy court is merely an "adjunct" to the district court, and that the delegation of certain adjudicative functions to the bankruptcy court is accordingly consistent with the principle that the judicial power of the United States must be vested in Art. III courts. As support for their argument, appellants rely principally upon *Crowell v. Benson*, 285 U.S. 22 (1932), and *United States v. Raddatz*, 447 U.S. 667 (1980), cases in which we approved the use of administrative agencies and magistrates as adjuncts to Art. III courts. The question to which we turn, therefore, is whether the Act has retained "the essential attributes of the judicial power," *Crowell v. Benson*, in Art. III tribunals.[15]

The essential premise underlying appellants' argument is that even where the Constitution denies Congress the power to establish legislative courts, Congress possesses the authority to assign certain factfinding functions to adjunct tribunals. It is, of course, true that while the power to adjudicate "private rights" must be vested in an Art. III court: "this Court has accepted factfinding by an administrative agency, . . . as an adjunct to the Art. III court, analogizing the agency to a jury or a special master and permitting it in admiralty cases to perform the function of the special master. *Crowell v. Benson.*

The use of administrative agencies as adjuncts was first upheld in *Crowell v. Benson.* The congressional scheme challenged in *Crowell* empowered an administrative agency, the United States Employees' Compensation Commission, to make initial factual determinations pursuant to a federal statute requiring employers to compensate their employees for work-related injuries occurring upon the navigable waters of the United States. The Court began its analysis by noting that the federal statute administered by the Compensation Commission provided for compensation of injured employees "irrespective of fault," and that the statute also prescribed a fixed and mandatory schedule of compensation. The agency was thus left with the limited role of determining "questions of fact as to the circumstances, nature, extent and consequences of the injuries sustained by the employee for which compensation is to be made." The agency did not possess the power to enforce any of its compensation orders: On the contrary, every compensation order was appealable to the appropriate federal district court, which had the sole power to enforce it or set it aside, depending upon whether the court determined it to be "in accordance with law" and supported by evidence in the record. The Court found that in view of these limitations upon the Compensation

15. [Footnote 29 in Justice Brennan's opinion.] Justice White's dissent fails to distinguish between Congress' power to create adjuncts to Art. III courts, and Congress' power to create Art. I courts in limited circumstances. Congress' power to create adjuncts and assign them limited adjudicatory functions is in no sense an "exception" to Art. III. Rather, such an assignment is consistent with Art. III, so long as "the essential attributes of the judicial power" are retained in the Art. III court, *Crowell v. Benson*, and so long as Congress' adjustment of the traditional manner of adjudication can be sufficiently linked to its legislative power to define substantive rights.

Commission's functions and powers, its determinations were "closely analogous to findings of the amount of damages that are made, according to familiar practice, by commissioners or assessors." Observing that "there is no requirement that, in order to maintain the essential attributes of the judicial power, all determinations of fact in constitutional courts shall be made by judges," the Court held that Art. III imposed no bar to the scheme enacted by Congress.

Crowell involved the adjudication of congressionally created rights. But this Court has sustained the use of adjunct factfinders even in the adjudication of constitutional rights—so long as those adjuncts were subject to sufficient control by an Art. III district court. In *United States v. Raddatz*, the Court upheld the 1978 Federal Magistrates Act, which permitted district court judges to refer certain pretrial motions, including suppression motions based on alleged violations of constitutional rights, to a magistrate for initial determination. The Court observed that the magistrate's proposed findings and recommendations were subject to *de novo* review by the district court, which was free to rehear the evidence or to call for additional evidence. Moreover, it was noted that the magistrate considered motions only upon reference from the district court, and that the magistrates were appointed, and subject to removal, by the district court. In short, the ultimate decisionmaking authority respecting all pretrial motions clearly remained with the district court. Under these circumstances, the Court held that the Act did not violate the constraints of Art. III.

Together these cases establish two principles that aid us in determining the extent to which Congress may constitutionally vest traditionally judicial functions in non-Art. III officers. First, it is clear that when Congress creates a substantive federal right, it possesses substantial discretion to prescribe the manner in which that right may be adjudicated—including the assignment to an adjunct of some functions historically performed by judges.[16] Thus *Crowell* recognized that Art. III does not require "all determinations of fact [to] be made by judges" with respect to congressionally created rights, some factual determinations may be made by a specialized factfinding tribunal designed by Congress, without constitutional bar. Second, the functions of the adjunct must be limited in such a way that "the essential attributes" of judicial power are retained in the Art. III court. Thus in upholding the adjunct scheme challenged in *Crowell*, the Court emphasized that "the reservation of full authority to the court to deal with matters of law provides for the appropriate exercise of the judicial function in this class of cases." And in refusing to invalidate the Magistrates Act at issue in *Raddatz*, the Court stressed that under the congressional scheme "'[the] authority—and the responsibility—to make an informed, final determination . . . remains with the judge'"; the statute's delegation of power was therefore permissible, since "the ultimate decision is made by the district court."

These two principles assist us in evaluating the "adjunct" scheme presented in these cases. Appellants assume that Congress' power to create "adjuncts" to consider all cases related to those arising under Title 11 is as great as it was in the circumstances of *Crowell*. But while *Crowell* certainly endorsed the

16. [Footnote 32 in Justice Brennan's opinion.] Contrary to Justice White's suggestion, we do not concede that "Congress may provide for initial adjudications by Art. I courts or administrative judges of all rights and duties arising under otherwise valid federal laws." Rather we simply reaffirm the holding of *Crowell*—that Congress may assign to non-Art. III bodies some adjudicatory functions. *Crowell* itself spoke of "specialized" functions. These cases do not require us to specify further any limitations that may exist with respect to Congress' power to create adjuncts to assist in the adjudication of federal statutory rights.

proposition that Congress possesses broad discretion to assign factfinding functions to an adjunct created to aid in the adjudication of congressionally created statutory rights, *Crowell* does not support the further proposition necessary to appellants' argument—that Congress possesses the same degree of discretion in assigning traditionally judicial power to adjuncts engaged in the adjudication of rights *not* created by Congress. Indeed, the validity of this proposition was expressly denied in *Crowell*, when the Court rejected "the untenable assumption that the constitutional courts may be deprived in all cases of the determination of facts upon evidence even though a *constitutional* right may be involved"[17] and stated that "the essential independence of the exercise of the judicial power of the United States in the enforcement of *constitutional* rights requires that the Federal court should determine . . . an issue [of agency jurisdiction] upon its own record and the facts elicited before it." (emphasis added).[18]

Appellants' proposition was also implicitly rejected in *Raddatz*. Congress' assignment of adjunct functions under the Federal Magistrates Act was substantially narrower than under the statute challenged in *Crowell*. Yet the Court's scrutiny of the adjunct scheme in *Raddatz*—which played a role in the adjudication of *constitutional* rights—was far stricter than it had been in *Crowell*. Critical to the Court's decision to uphold the Magistrates Act was the fact that the ultimate decision was made by the district court.

Although *Crowell* and *Raddatz* do not explicitly distinguish between rights created by Congress and other rights, such a distinction underlies in part *Crowell*'s and *Raddatz*' recognition of a critical difference between rights created by federal statute and rights recognized by the Constitution. Moreover, such a distinction seems to us to be necessary in light of the delicate accommodations required by the principle of separation of powers reflected in Art. III. The constitutional system of checks and balances is designed to guard against "encroachment or aggrandizement" by Congress at the expense of the other branches of government. But when Congress creates a statutory right, it clearly has the discretion, in defining that right, to create presumptions, or assign burdens of proof, or prescribe remedies; it may also provide that persons seeking to vindicate that right must do so before particularized tribunals created to perform the specialized adjudicative tasks related to that right.[19] Such provisions do, in a sense, affect the exercise of judicial power, but they are also incidental to

17. [Footnote 33 in Justice Brennan's opinion.] The Court in *Crowell* found that the requirement of *de novo* review as to certain facts was not "simply the question of due process in relation to notice and hearing," but was "rather a question of the appropriate maintenance of the Federal judicial power." The dissent agreed that some factual findings cannot be made by adjuncts, on the ground that "under certain circumstances, the constitutional requirement of due process is a requirement of [Art. III] judicial process." (Brandeis, J., dissenting).

18. [Footnote 34 in Justice Brennan's opinion.] *Crowell*'s precise holding, with respect to the review of "jurisdictional" and "constitutional" facts that arise within ordinary administrative proceedings, has been undermined by later cases. But the general principle of *Crowell*—distinguishing between congressionally created rights and constitutionally recognized rights—remains valid. . . .

19. [Footnote 35 in Justice Brennan's opinion.] Drawing the line between permissible extensions of legislative power and impermissible incursions into judicial power is a delicate undertaking, for the powers of the Judicial and Legislative Branches are often overlapping. As Justice Frankfurter noted in a similar context: "To be sure the content of the three authorities of government is not to be derived from an abstract analysis. The areas are partly interacting, not wholly disjointed." *Youngstown Sheet & Tube Co. v. Sawyer* (concurring opinion). The interaction between the Legislative and Judicial Branches is at its height where courts are adjudicating rights wholly of Congress' creation. Thus where Congress creates a substantive right, pursuant to one of its broad powers to make laws, Congress may have something to say about the proper manner of adjudicating that right.

Congress' power to define the right that it has created. No comparable justification exists, however, when the right being adjudicated is not of congressional creation. In such a situation, substantial inroads into functions that have traditionally been performed by the Judiciary cannot be characterized merely as incidental extensions of Congress' power to define rights that it has created. Rather, such inroads suggest unwarranted encroachments upon the judicial power of the United States, which our Constitution reserves for Art. III courts.

We hold that the Bankruptcy Act of 1978 carries the possibility of such an unwarranted encroachment. Many of the rights subject to adjudication by the Act's bankruptcy courts, like the rights implicated in *Raddatz*, are not of Congress' creation. Indeed, the cases before us, which center upon appellant Northern's claim for damages for breach of contract and misrepresentation, involve a right created by *state* law, a right independent of and antecedent to the reorganization petition that conferred jurisdiction upon the Bankruptcy Court.[20] Accordingly, Congress' authority to control the manner in which that right is adjudicated, through assignment of historically judicial functions to a non-Art. III "adjunct," plainly must be deemed at a minimum. Yet it is equally plain that Congress has vested the "adjunct" bankruptcy judges with powers over Northern's state-created right that far exceed the powers that it has vested in administrative agencies that adjudicate only rights of Congress' own creation.

Unlike the administrative scheme that we reviewed in *Crowell*, the Act vests all "essential attributes" of the judicial power of the United States in the "adjunct" bankruptcy court. First, the agency in *Crowell* made only specialized, narrowly confined factual determinations regarding a particularized area of law. In contrast, the subject-matter jurisdiction of the bankruptcy courts encompasses not only traditional matters of bankruptcy, but also "all civil proceedings arising under title 11 or arising in or *related to* cases under title 11." 28 U. S. C. § 1471(b) (emphasis added). Second, while the agency in *Crowell* engaged in statutorily channeled factfinding functions, the bankruptcy courts exercise "*all* of the jurisdiction" conferred by the Act on the district courts, § 1471(c) (emphasis added). Third, the agency in *Crowell* possessed only a limited power to issue compensation orders pursuant to specialized procedures, and its orders could be enforced only by order of the district court. By contrast, the bankruptcy courts exercise all ordinary powers of district courts, including the power to preside over jury trials, the power to issue declaratory judgments, the power to issue writs of habeas corpus, and the power to issue any order, process, or judgment appropriate for the enforcement of the provisions of Title 11. Fourth, while orders issued by the agency in *Crowell* were to be set aside if "not supported by the evidence," the judgments of the bankruptcy courts are apparently subject to review only under the more deferential "clearly erroneous" standard. Finally, the agency in *Crowell* was required by law to seek enforcement of its compensation orders in the district court. In contrast, the bankruptcy courts issue final judgments, which are binding and enforceable even in the absence of an appeal. In short, the "adjunct" bankruptcy courts created by the Act exercise jurisdiction behind the facade of a grant to the district courts, and

20. [Footnote 36 in Justice Brennan's opinion.] Of course, bankruptcy adjudications themselves, as well as the manner in which the rights of debtors and creditors are adjusted, are matters of federal law. Appellant Northern's state-law contract claim is now in federal court because of its relationship to Northern's reorganization petition. But Congress has not purported to prescribe a rule of decision for the resolution of Northern's contractual claims.

are exercising powers far greater than those lodged in the adjuncts approved in either *Crowell* or *Raddatz*.[21]

We conclude that 28 U.S.C. § 1471, as added by § 241(a) of the Bankruptcy Act of 1978, has impermissibly removed most, if not all, of "the essential attributes of the judicial power" from the Art. III district court, and has vested those attributes in a non-Art. III adjunct. Such a grant of jurisdiction cannot be sustained as an exercise of Congress' power to create adjuncts to Art. III courts.

V

[In Part V, the plurality determined that its decision was to be applied prospectively. In addition, the Court stayed its order for a period of time to allow Congress "an opportunity to reconstitute the bankruptcy courts or adopt other valid means of adjudication, without impairing the interim administration of the bankruptcy laws."]

It is so ordered.

JUSTICE REHNQUIST, with whom JUSTICE O'CONNOR joins, concurring in the judgment.

Were I to agree with the plurality that the question presented by these cases is "whether the assignment by Congress to bankruptcy judges of the jurisdiction granted in 28 U.S.C. § 1471 by § 241(a) of the Bankruptcy Act of 1978 violates Art. III of the Constitution," I would with considerable reluctance embark on the duty of deciding this broad question. But appellee Marathon Pipe Line Co. has not been subjected to the full range of authority granted Bankruptcy Courts by § 1471. It was named as a defendant in a suit brought by appellant Northern Pipeline Construction Co. in a United States Bankruptcy Court. The suit sought damages for, *inter alia*, breaches of contract and warranty. Marathon moved to dismiss the action on the grounds that the Bankruptcy Act of 1978, which authorized the suit, violated Art. III of the Constitution insofar as it established

21. [Footnote 39 in Justice Brennan's opinion.] Appellants suggest that *Crowell* and *Raddatz* stand for the proposition that Art. III is satisfied so long as some degree of appellate review is provided. But that suggestion is directly contrary to the text of our Constitution: "The Judges, *both* of the supreme and inferior Courts, shall hold their Offices during good Behaviour, and shall . . . - receive [undiminished] Compensation." Art. III, § 1 (emphasis added). Our precedents make it clear that the constitutional requirements for the exercise of the judicial power must be met at all stages of adjudication, and not only on appeal, where the court is restricted to considerations of law, as well as the nature of the case as it has been shaped at the trial level. The Court responded to a similar suggestion in *Crowell* by stating that to accept such a regime "would be to sap the judicial power as it exists under the Federal Constitution, and to establish a government of bureaucratic character alien to our system, wherever fundamental rights depend, as not infrequently they do depend, upon the facts, and finality as to facts becomes in effect finality in law."

Justice White's dissent views the function of the Third Branch as interpreting the Constitution in order to keep the other two Branches in check, and would accordingly find the purpose, if not the language, of Art. III satisfied where there is an appeal to an Art. III court. But in the Framers' view, Art. III courts would do a great deal more than, in an abstract way, announce guidelines for the other two Branches. While "expounding" the Constitution was surely one vital function of the Art. III courts in the Framers' view, the tasks of those courts, for which independence was an important safeguard, included the mundane as well as the glamorous, matters of common law and statute as well as constitutional law, issues of fact as well as issues of law. As Hamilton noted, "it is not with a view to infractions of the Constitution only, that the independence of the judges may be an essential safeguard against the effects of occasional ill humors in the society." The Federalist No. 78. In order to promote the independence and improve the quality of federal judicial decisionmaking in all of these areas, the Framers created a system of independent federal courts. See The Federalist Nos. 78-82.

bankruptcy judges whose tenure and salary protection do not conform to the requirements of Art. III.

With the cases in this posture, Marathon has simply been named defendant in a lawsuit about a contract, a lawsuit initiated by appellant Northern after having previously filed a petition for reorganization under the Bankruptcy Act. Marathon may object to proceeding further with this lawsuit on the grounds that if it is to be resolved by an agency of the United States, it may be resolved only by an agency which exercises "[the] judicial power of the United States" described by Art. III of the Constitution. But resolution of any objections it may make on this ground to the exercise of a different authority conferred on bankruptcy courts by the 1978 Act should await the exercise of such authority.

* * * *

Particularly in an area of constitutional law such as that of "Art. III Courts," with its frequently arcane distinctions and confusing precedents, rigorous adherence to the principle that this Court should decide no more of a constitutional question than is absolutely necessary accords with both our decided cases and with sound judicial policy.

From the record before us, the lawsuit in which Marathon was named defendant seeks damages for breach of contract, misrepresentation, and other counts which are the stuff of the traditional actions at common law tried by the courts at Westminster in 1789. There is apparently no federal rule of decision provided for any of the issues in the lawsuit; the claims of Northern arise entirely under state law. No method of adjudication is hinted, other than the traditional common-law mode of judge and jury. The lawsuit is before the Bankruptcy Court only because the plaintiff has previously filed a petition for reorganization in that court.

The cases dealing with the authority of Congress to create courts other than by use of its power under Art. III do not admit of easy synthesis. . . . I need not decide whether these cases in fact support a general proposition and three tidy exceptions, as the plurality believes, or whether instead they are but landmarks on a judicial "darkling plain" where ignorant armies have clashed by night, as Justice White apparently believes them to be. None of the cases has gone so far as to sanction the type of adjudication to which Marathon will be subjected against its will under the provisions of the 1978 Act. To whatever extent different powers granted under that Act might be sustained under the "public rights" doctrine of *Murray's Lessee v. Hoboken Land & Improvement Co.*, and succeeding cases, I am satisfied that the adjudication of Northern's lawsuit cannot be so sustained.

I am likewise of the opinion that the extent of review by Art. III courts provided on appeal from a decision of the bankruptcy court in a case such as Northern's does not save the grant of authority to the latter under the rule espoused in *Crowell v. Benson.* All matters of fact and law in whatever domains of the law to which the parties' dispute may lead are to be resolved by the bankruptcy court in the first instance, with only traditional appellate review by Art. III courts apparently contemplated. Acting in this manner the bankruptcy court is not an "adjunct" of either the district court or the court of appeals.

I would, therefore, hold so much of the Bankruptcy Act of 1978 as enables a Bankruptcy Court to entertain and decide Northern's lawsuit over Marathon's objection to be violative of Art. III of the United States Constitution. Because I agree with the plurality that this grant of authority is not readily severable from the remaining grant of authority to bankruptcy courts under § 1471 I concur in the judgment. I also agree with the discussion in Part V of the plurality opinion respecting retroactivity and the staying of the judgment of this Court.

[The dissenting opinion of Chief Justice Burger is omitted.]

JUSTICE WHITE, with whom THE CHIEF JUSTICE and JUSTICE POWELL join, dissenting.

* * * *

Any reader could easily take this provision to mean that although Congress was free to establish such lower courts as it saw fit, any court that it did establish would be an "inferior" court exercising "judicial Power of the United States" and so must be manned by judges possessing both life tenure and a guaranteed minimal income. This would be an eminently sensible reading and one that, as the plurality shows, is well founded in both the documentary sources and the political doctrine of separation of powers that stands behind much of our constitutional structure.

If this simple reading were correct and we were free to disregard 150 years of history, these would be easy cases and the plurality opinion could end with its observation that "[it] is undisputed that the bankruptcy judges whose offices were created by the Bankruptcy Act of 1978 do not enjoy the protections constitutionally afforded to Art. III judges." The fact that the plurality must go on to deal with what has been characterized as one of the most confusing and controversial areas of constitutional law itself indicates the gross oversimplification implicit in the plurality's claim that "our Constitution unambiguously enunciates a fundamental principle—that the 'judicial Power of the United States' must be reposed in an independent Judiciary [and] provides clear institutional protections for that independence." While this is fine rhetoric, analytically it serves only to put a distracting and superficial gloss on a difficult question.

That question is what limits Art. III places on Congress' ability to create adjudicative institutions designed to carry out federal policy established pursuant to the substantive authority given Congress elsewhere in the Constitution. Whether fortunate or unfortunate, at this point in the history of constitutional law that question can no longer be answered by looking only to the constitutional text. This Court's cases construing that text must also be considered. In its attempt to pigeonhole these cases, the plurality does violence to their meaning and creates an artificial structure that itself lacks coherence.

I

There are, I believe, two separate grounds for today's decision. First, non-Art. III judges, regardless of whether they are labeled "adjuncts" to Art. III courts or "Art. I judges," may consider only controversies arising out of federal law. Because the immediate controversy in these cases—Northern Pipeline's claim against Marathon—arises out of state law, it may only be adjudicated, within the federal system, by an Art. III court. Second, regardless of the source of law that governs the controversy, Congress is prohibited by Art. III from establishing Art. I courts, with three narrow exceptions. Adjudication of bankruptcy proceedings does not fall within any of these exceptions. I shall deal with the first of these contentions in this section.

The plurality concedes that Congress may provide for initial adjudications by Art. I courts or administrative judges of all rights and duties arising under otherwise valid federal laws. There is no apparent reason why this principle should not extend to matters arising in federal bankruptcy proceedings. The plurality attempts to escape the reach of prior decisions by contending that the bankrupt's claim against Marathon arose under state law. Non-Article III judges, in its view, cannot be vested with authority to adjudicate such issues. It then proceeds to strike down 28 U.S.C. § 1471 on this ground. For several reasons, the Court's judgment is unsupportable.

First, clearly this ground alone cannot support the Court's invalidation of § 1471 on its face. The plurality concedes that in adjudications and discharges in bankruptcy, "the restructuring of debtor-creditor relations, which is at the core of the federal bankruptcy power," and "the manner in which the rights of debtors and creditors are adjusted," are matters of federal law. Under the plurality's own interpretation of the cases, therefore, these matters could be heard and decided by Art. I judges. But because the bankruptcy judge is also given authority to hear a case like that of appellant Northern against Marathon, which the Court says is founded on state law, the Court holds that the section must be stricken down on its face. This is a grossly unwarranted emasculation of the scheme Congress has adopted. Even if the Court is correct that such a state-law claim cannot be heard by a bankruptcy judge, there is no basis for doing more than declaring the section unconstitutional as applied to the claim against Marathon, leaving the section otherwise intact. In that event, cases such as these would have to be heard by Art. III judges or by state courts — unless the defendant consents to suit before the bankruptcy judge — just as they were before the 1978 Act was adopted. But this would remove from the jurisdiction of the bankruptcy judge only a tiny fraction of the cases he is now empowered to adjudicate and would not otherwise limit his jurisdiction.

Second, the distinction between claims based on state law and those based on federal law disregards the real character of bankruptcy proceedings. The routine in ordinary bankruptcy cases now, as it was before 1978, is to stay actions against the bankrupt, collect the bankrupt's assets, require creditors to file claims or be forever barred, allow or disallow claims that are filed, adjudicate preferences and fraudulent transfers, and make pro rata distributions to creditors, who will be barred by the discharge from taking further actions against the bankrupt. The crucial point to be made is that in the ordinary bankruptcy proceeding the great bulk of creditor claims are claims that have accrued under state law prior to bankruptcy — claims for goods sold, wages, rent, utilities, and the like. "[The] word debt as used by the Act is not confined to its technical common law meaning but . . . extends to liabilities arising out of breach of contract . . . to torts . . . and to taxes owing to the United States or state or local governments." Every such claim must be filed and its validity is subject to adjudication by the bankruptcy court. The existence and validity of such claims recurringly depend on state law. Hence, the bankruptcy judge is constantly enmeshed in state-law issues.

The new aspect of the Bankruptcy Act of 1978, in this regard, therefore, is not the extension of federal jurisdiction to state-law claims, but its extension to particular kinds of state-law claims, such as contract cases against third parties or disputes involving property in the possession of a third person. Prior to 1978, a claim of a bankrupt against a third party, such as the claim against Marathon in this case, was not within the jurisdiction of the bankruptcy judge. The old limits were based, of course, on the restrictions implicit within the concept of *in rem* jurisdiction; the new extension is based on the concept of *in personam* jurisdiction. "The bankruptcy court is given in personam jurisdiction as well as in rem jurisdiction to handle everything that arises in a bankruptcy case." The difference between the new and old Acts, therefore, is not to be found in a distinction between state-law and federal-law matters; rather, it is in a distinction between *in rem* and *in personam* jurisdiction. The majority at no place explains why this distinction should have constitutional implications.

Third, all that can be left of the majority's argument in this regard is that state-law claims adjudicated within the federal system must be heard in the first instance by Art. III judges. I shall argue below that any such attempt to distinguish Art. I from Art. III courts by the character of the controversies they may adjudicate fundamentally misunderstands the historical and constitutional significance of Art. I courts. Initially, however, the majority's proposal seems to turn the separation-of-powers doctrine, upon which the majority relies, on its head: Since state-law claims would ordinarily not be heard by Art. III judges — *i.e.*, they would be heard by state judges — one would think that there is little danger of a diminution of, or intrusion upon, the power of Art. III courts, when such claims are assigned to a non-Art. III court. The plurality misses this obvious point because it concentrates on explaining how it is that federally created rights can ever be adjudicated in Art. I courts — a far more difficult problem under the separation-of-powers doctrine. The plurality fumbles when it assumes that the rationale it develops to deal with the latter problem must also govern the former problem. In fact, the two are simply unrelated and the majority never really explains the separation-of-powers problem that would be created by assigning state-law questions to legislative courts or to adjuncts of Art. III courts.

* * * *

In theory and fact, therefore, I can find no basis for that part of the majority's argument that rests on the state-law character of the claim involved here. Even if, prior to 1978, the referee could not generally participate in cases aimed at collecting the assets of a bankrupt estate, he nevertheless repeatedly adjudicated issues controlled by state law. There is very little reason to strike down § 1471 on its face on the ground that it extends, in a comparatively minimal way, the referees' authority to deal with state-law questions. To do so is to lose all sense of proportion.

II

The plurality unpersuasively attempts to bolster its case for facial invalidity by asserting that the bankruptcy courts are now "exercising powers far greater than those lodged in the adjuncts approved in either *Crowell* or *Raddatz*." In support of this proposition it makes five arguments in addition to the "state-law" issue. Preliminarily, I see no basis for according standing to Marathon to raise any of these additional points. The state-law objection applies to the Marathon case. Only that objection should now be adjudicated.[22]

I also believe that the major premise of the plurality's argument is wholly unsupported: There is no explanation of why *Crowell v. Benson* and

22. [Footnote 6 in Justice White's dissent.] On this point I am in agreement with the Justices concurring in the judgment.

United States v. Raddatz define the outer limits of constitutional authority. Much more relevant to today's decision are, first, the practice in bankruptcy prior to 1978, which neither the majority nor any authoritative case has questioned, and, second, the practice of today's administrative agencies. Considered from this perspective, all of the plurality's arguments are unsupportable abstractions, divorced from the realities of modern practice.

The first three arguments offered by the plurality focus on the narrowly defined task and authority of the agency considered in *Crowell*: The agency made only "specialized, narrowly confined factual determinations" and could issue only a narrow class of orders. Regardless of whether this was true of the Compensation Board at issue in *Crowell*, it certainly was not true of the old bankruptcy courts, nor does it even vaguely resemble current administrative practice. As I have already said, general references to bankruptcy judges, which was the usual practice prior to 1978, permitted bankruptcy judges to perform almost all of the functions of a bankruptcy court. . . .

* * * *

The plurality's fourth argument fails to point to any difference between the new and old Bankruptcy Acts. While the administrative orders in *Crowell* may have been set aside by a court if "not supported by the evidence," under both the new and old Acts at issue here, orders of the bankruptcy judge are reviewed under the "clearly erroneous standard." Indeed, judicial review of the orders of bankruptcy judges is more stringent than that of many modern administrative agencies. Generally courts are not free to set aside the findings of administrative agencies, if supported by substantial evidence. But more importantly, courts are also admonished to give substantial deference to the agency's interpretation of the statute it is enforcing. No such deference is required with respect to decisions on the law made by bankruptcy judges.

Finally, the plurality suggests that, unlike the agency considered in *Crowell*, the orders of a post-1978 bankruptcy judge are final and binding even though not appealed. To attribute any constitutional significance to this, unless the plurality intends to throw into question a large body of administrative law, is strange. More directly, this simply does not represent any change in bankruptcy practice. It was hornbook law prior to 1978 that the authorized judgments and orders of referees, including turnover orders were final and binding and res judicata unless appealed and overturned. . . .

Even if there are specific powers now vested in bankruptcy judges that should be performed by Art. III judges, the great bulk of their functions are unexceptionable and should be left intact. Whatever is invalid should be declared to be such; the rest of the 1978 Act should be left alone. I can account for the majority's inexplicably heavy hand in this case only by assuming that the Court has once again lost its conceptual bearings when confronted with the difficult problem of the nature and role of Art. I courts. To that question I now turn.

III

A

The plurality contends that the precedents upholding Art. I courts can be reduced to three categories. First, there are territorial courts, which need not satisfy Art. III constraints because "the Framers intended that as to certain geographical areas . . . Congress was to exercise the general powers of government." Second, there are courts-martial, which are exempt from Art. III limits because of a constitutional grant of power that has been "historically understood as giving the political Branches of Government extraordinary control over the precise subject matter at issue." Finally, there are those legislative courts and administrative agencies that adjudicate cases involving public rights — controversies between the Government and private parties — which are not covered by Art. III because the controversy could have been resolved by the executive alone without judicial review. Despite the plurality's attempt to cabin the domain of Art. I courts, it is quite unrealistic to consider these to be only three "narrow" limitations on or exceptions to the reach of Art. III. In fact, the plurality itself breaks the mold in its discussion of "adjuncts" in Part IV, when it announces that "when Congress creates a substantive federal right, it possesses substantial discretion to prescribe the manner in which that right may be adjudicated." Adjudications of federal rights may, according to the plurality, be committed to administrative agencies, as long as provision is made for judicial review.

The first principle introduced by the plurality is geographical: Art. I courts presumably are not permitted within the States. The problem, of course, is that both of the other exceptions recognize that Art. I courts can indeed operate within the States. The second category relies upon a new principle: Art. I courts are permissible in areas in which the Constitution grants Congress "extraordinary control over the precise subject matter." Preliminarily, I do not know how we are to distinguish those areas in which Congress' control is "extraordinary" from those in which it is not. Congress' power over the Armed Forces is established in Art. I, §8, cls. 13, 14. There is nothing in those Clauses that creates congressional authority different in kind from the authority granted to legislate with respect to bankruptcy. But more importantly, in its third category, and in its treatment of "adjuncts," the plurality itself recognizes that Congress can create Art. I courts in virtually all the areas in which Congress is authorized to act, regardless of the quality of the constitutional grant of authority. At the same time, territorial courts or the courts of the District of Columbia, which are Art. I courts, adjudicate private, just as much as public or federal, rights.

Instead of telling us what it is Art. I courts can and cannot do, the plurality presents us with a list of Art. I courts. When we try to distinguish those courts from their Art. III counterparts, we find — apart from the obvious lack of Art. III judges — a series of nondistinctions. By the plurality's own admission, Art. I courts can operate throughout the country, they can adjudicate both private and public rights, and they can adjudicate matters arising from congressional actions in those areas in which congressional control is "extraordinary." I cannot distinguish this last category from the general "arising under" jurisdiction of Art. III courts.

The plurality opinion has the appearance of limiting Art. I courts only because it fails to add together the sum of its parts. Rather than limiting each other, the principles relied upon complement each other; together they cover virtually the whole domain of possible areas of adjudication. Without a unifying principle, the plurality's argument reduces to the proposition that because bankruptcy courts are not sufficiently like any of these three exceptions, they may not be either Art. I courts or adjuncts to Art. III courts. But we need to know why bankruptcy courts cannot qualify as Art. I courts in their own right.

B

The plurality opinion is not the first unsuccessful attempt to articulate a principled ground by which to distinguish Art. I from Art. III courts. The concept of a legislative, or Art. I, court was introduced by an opinion authored by Chief Justice Marshall [in *American Insurance Co. v. Canter* decided in 1828)]. Not only did he create the concept, but at the same time he started the theoretical controversy that has ever since surrounded the concept. . . .

The proposition was simple enough: Constitutional courts exercise the judicial power described in Art. III of the Constitution; legislative courts do not and cannot.

There were only two problems with this proposition. First, *Canter* itself involved a case in admiralty jurisdiction, which is specifically included within the "judicial power of the United States" delineated in Art. III. How, then, could the territorial court not be exercising Art. III judicial power? Second, and no less troubling, if the territorial courts could not exercise Art. III power, how could their decisions be subject to appellate review in Art. III courts, including this one, that can exercise only Art. III "judicial" power? Yet from early on this Court has exercised such appellate jurisdiction. The attempt to understand the seemingly unexplainable was bound to generate "confusion and controversy." This analytic framework, however—the search for a principled distinction—has continued to burden the Court.

The first major elaboration on the *Canter* principle was in *Murray's Lessee v. Hoboken Land & Improvement Co.* The plaintiff in that case argued that a proceeding against a customs collector for the collection of moneys claimed to be due to the United States was an exercise of "judicial power" and therefore had to be carried out by Art. III judges. The Court accepted this premise: "It must be admitted that, if the auditing of this account, and the ascertainment of its balance, and the issuing of this process, was an exercise of the judicial power of the United States, the proceeding was void; for the officers who performed these acts could exercise no part of that judicial power." Having accepted this premise, the Court went on to delineate those matters which could be determined only by an Art. III court, *i.e.*, those matters that fall within the nondelegable "judicial power" of the United States. The Court's response to this was twofold. First, it suggested that there are certain matters which are inherently "judicial": "[We] do not consider congress can either withdraw from judicial cognizance any matter which, from its nature, is the subject of a suit at the common law, or in equity, or admiralty." Second, it suggested that there is another class of issues that, depending upon the form in which Congress structures the decisionmaking process, may or may not fall within "the cognizance of the courts of the United States." This latter category consisted of the so-called "public rights." Apparently, the idea was that Congress was free to structure the adjudication of "public rights" without regard to Art. III.

Having accepted the plaintiff's premise, it is hard to see how the Court could have taken too seriously its first contention. The Court presented no examples of such issues that are judicial "by nature" and simply failed to acknowledge that Art. I courts already sanctioned by the Court—*e.g.*, territorial courts—were deciding such issues all the time. The second point, however, contains implicitly a critical insight; one that if openly acknowledged would have undermined the entire structure. That insight follows from the Court's earlier recognition that the term "judicial act" is broad enough to encompass all administrative action involving inquiry into facts and the application of law to those facts.

If administrative action can be characterized as "judicial" in nature, then obviously the Court's subsequent attempt to distinguish administrative from judicial action on the basis of the manner in which Congress structures the decision cannot succeed. There need be no Art. III court involvement in any adjudication of a "public right," which the majority now interprets as any civil matter arising between the Federal Government and a citizen. In that area, whether an issue is to be decided by an Art. III court depends, finally, on congressional intent.

Although *Murray's Lessee* implicitly undermined Chief Justice Marshall's suggestion that there is a difference in kind between the work of Art. I and that of Art. III courts, it did not contend that the Court must always defer to congressional desire in this regard. The Court considered the plaintiff's contention that removal of the issue from an Art. III court must be justified by "necessity." Although not entirely clear, the Court seems to have accepted this proposition: "[It] seems to us that the just inference from the entire law is, that there was such a necessity for the warrant."[23]

The Court in *Murray's Lessee* was precisely right: Whether an issue can be decided by a non-Art. III court does not depend upon the judicial or nonjudicial character of the issue, but on the will of Congress and the reasons Congress offers for not using an Art. III court. This insight, however, was completely disavowed in the next major case to consider the distinction between Art. I and Art. III courts, *Ex parte Bakelite Corp.*, 279 U.S. 438 (1929), in which the Court concluded that the Court of Customs Appeals was a legislative court. The Court there directly embraced the principle also articulated in *Murray's Lessee* that Art. I courts may not consider any matter "which inherently or necessarily requires judicial determination," but only such matters as are "susceptible of legislative or executive determination." It then went on effectively to bury the critical insight of *Murray's Lessee*, labeling as "fallacious" any argument that "assumes that whether a court is of one class or the other depends on the intention of Congress, whereas the true test lies in the power under which the court was created and in the jurisdiction conferred."

The distinction between public and private rights as the principle delineating the proper domains of legislative and constitutional courts respectively received its death blow, I had believed, in *Crowell v. Benson*, 285 U.S. 22 (1932). In that case, the Court approved an administrative scheme for the determination, in the first instance, of maritime employee compensation claims. Although acknowledging the framework set out in *Murray's Lessee* and *Ex parte Bakelite Corp.*, the Court specifically distinguished the case before it: "The present case does not fall within the categories just described but is one of private right, that is, of the liability of one individual to another under the law as defined." Nevertheless, the Court approved of the use of an Art. I adjudication mechanism on the new theory that "there is no requirement that, in order to maintain the essential attributes of the judicial power, all determinations of fact in constitutional courts shall be made by judges." Article I courts could deal not only with public rights, but also, to an extent, with private rights. The Court now established a distinction between questions of fact and law: "[The] reservation of full

23. [Footnote 9 in Justice White's dissent.] By stating that "of this necessity congress alone is the judge," the Court added some serious ambiguity to the standard it applied. Because this statement ends the Court's analysis of the merits of the claim, it does not seem to mean that the Court will simply defer to congressional judgment. Rather, it appears to mean that the Court will review the legislative record to determine whether there appeared to Congress to be compelling reasons for not establishing an Art. III court.

authority to the court to deal with matters of law provides for the appropriate exercise of the judicial function in this class of cases."[24]

[Justice White then went on to canvass other decisions, ultimately concluding that the Court had not established clear rules in this area even after "[o]ne hundred and fifty years of constitutional history."]

IV

The complicated and contradictory history of the issue before us leads me to conclude that . . . [t]here is no difference in principle between the work that Congress may assign to an Art. I court and that which the Constitution assigns to Art. III courts. Unless we want to overrule a large number of our precedents upholding a variety of Art. I courts — not to speak of those Art. I courts that go by the contemporary name of "administrative agencies" — this conclusion is inevitable. It is too late to go back that far; too late to return to the simplicity of the principle pronounced in Art. III and defended so vigorously and persuasively by Hamilton in The Federalist Nos. 78-82.

To say that the Court has failed to articulate a principle by which we can test the constitutionality of a putative Art. I court, or that there is no such abstract principle, is not to say that this Court must always defer to the legislative decision to create Art. I, rather than Art. III, courts. Article III is not to be read out of the Constitution; rather, it should be read as expressing one value that must be balanced against competing constitutional values and legislative responsibilities. This Court retains the final word on how that balance is to be struck.

Despite the principled, although largely mistaken, rhetoric expanded by the Court in this area over the years, such a balancing approach stands behind many of the decisions upholding Art. I courts. [Justice White then reviewed decisions that he read to embody the balancing approach in this area of law.]

I do not suggest that the Court should simply look to the strength of the legislative interest and ask itself if that interest is more compelling than the values furthered by Art. III. The inquiry should, rather, focus equally on those Art. III values and ask whether and to what extent the legislative scheme accommodates them or, conversely, substantially undermines them. The burden on Art. III values should then be measured against the values Congress hopes to serve through the use of Art. I courts.

To be more concrete: *Crowell* suggests that the presence of appellate review by an Art. III court will go a long way toward insuring a proper separation of powers. Appellate review of the decisions of legislative courts, like appellate review of state-court decisions, provides a firm check on the ability of the political institutions of government to ignore or transgress constitutional limits on their own authority. Obviously, therefore, a scheme of Art. I courts that provides for appellate review by Art. III courts should be substantially less controversial than a legislative attempt entirely to avoid judicial review in a constitutional court.

24. [Footnote 12 in Justice White's dissent.] *Crowell* also suggests that certain facts — constitutional or jurisdictional — must also be subject to *de novo* review in an Art. III court. I agree with the plurality that this aspect of *Crowell* has been "undermined by later cases." As a matter of historical interest, however, I would contend that *Crowell's* holding with respect to these "facts" turned more on the questions of law that were inseparably tied to them, than on some notion of the inadequacy of a non-Art. III factfinder.

Similarly, as long as the proposed Art. I courts are designed to deal with issues likely to be of little interest to the political branches, there is less reason to fear that such courts represent a dangerous accumulation of power in one of the political branches of government. Chief Justice Vinson suggested as much when he stated that the Court should guard against any congressional attempt "to transfer jurisdiction . . . for the purpose of emasculating" constitutional courts. *National Insurance Co. v. Tidewater Co.*

V

I believe that the new bankruptcy courts established by the Bankruptcy Act of 1978 satisfy this standard.

First, ample provision is made for appellate review by Art. III courts. Appeals may in some circumstances be brought directly to the district courts. Decisions of the district courts are further appealable to the court of appeals. In other circumstances, appeals go first to a panel of bankruptcy judges and then to the court of appeals. In still other circumstances—when the parties agree—appeals may go directly to the court of appeals. In sum, there is in every instance a right of appeal to at least one Art. III court. Had Congress decided to assign all bankruptcy matters to the state courts, a power it clearly possesses, no greater review in an Art. III court would exist. Although I do not suggest that this analogy means that Congress may establish an Art. I court wherever it could have chosen to rely upon the state courts, it does suggest that the critical function of judicial review is being met in a manner that the Constitution suggests is sufficient.

Second, no one seriously argues that the Bankruptcy Act of 1978 represents an attempt by the political branches of government to aggrandize themselves at the expense of the third branch or an attempt to undermine the authority of constitutional courts in general. Indeed, the congressional perception of a lack of judicial interest in bankruptcy matters was one of the factors that led to the establishment of the bankruptcy courts: Congress feared that this lack of interest would lead to a failure by federal district courts to deal with bankruptcy matters in an expeditious manner. Bankruptcy matters are, for the most part, private adjudications of little political significance. Although some bankruptcies may indeed present politically controversial circumstances or issues, Congress has far more direct ways to involve itself in such matters than through some sort of subtle, or not so subtle, influence on bankruptcy judges. Furthermore, were such circumstances to arise, the Due Process Clause might very well require that the matter be considered by an Art. III judge: Bankruptcy proceedings remain, after all, subject to all of the strictures of that constitutional provision.

* * * *

The real question is not whether Congress was justified in establishing a specialized bankruptcy court, but rather whether it was justified in failing to create a specialized, Art. III bankruptcy court. My own view is that the very fact of extreme specialization may be enough, and certainly has been enough in the past, to justify the creation of a legislative court. Congress may legitimately consider the effect on the federal judiciary of the addition of several hundred specialized judges: We are, on the whole, a body of generalists. The addition of several hundred specialists may substantially change, whether for good or bad, the character of the federal bench. Moreover, Congress may have desired to maintain some flexibility in its possible future responses to the general problem of bankruptcy. There is no question that the existence of several hundred bankruptcy judges with life tenure would have severely limited Congress' future options. Furthermore, the number of bankruptcies may fluctuate, producing a substantially reduced need for bankruptcy judges. Congress may have thought that, in that event, a bankruptcy specialist should not as a general matter serve as a judge in the countless nonspecialized cases that come before the federal district courts. It would then face the prospect of large numbers of idle federal judges. Finally, Congress may have believed that the change from bankruptcy referees to Art. I judges was far less dramatic, and so less disruptive of the existing bankruptcy and constitutional court systems, than would be a change to Art. III judges.

For all of these reasons, I would defer to the congressional judgment. Accordingly, I dissent.

Discussion and Questions

There is much to consider in *Northern Pipeline.* The decision allows us to get a sense of the shape of the forest as well as get a fairly good look at the trees at least as of 1982. Despite the lack of a majority opinion in the case, there are important elements of doctrinal agreement among the justices. All three of the opinions excerpted above agree that there are serious constitutional issues implicated by the assignment of Article III judicial business to non-Article III tribunals. At the same time, however, all three opinions also recognize that it is not *per se* unconstitutional for Congress to make such assignments. The critical difference, which we will explore in this discussion, is how one determines when a given assignment is consistent with the Constitution.

Before we consider that issue, think about the broader constitutional values that are implicated in this complicated area of the law. Justice Brennan's plurality opinion (as well as the concurring and dissenting opinions) discuss two distinct but interrelated constitutional concerns. The first concern is *structural,* involving the separation of powers and the concomitant preservation of an independent judiciary. The Court is concerned that Congress does not eviscerate the Framers' constitutional design by assigning "too much" Article III business to actors who do not enjoy the Article III tenure and salary protections. Those features of the Judicial Branch are thought to be central to the maintenance of an institution that can stand up to Congress and the Executive. Thus, the assignment of Article III business to state courts — also non-Article III institutions — does not raise this concern because state courts are not subject to the potential congressional or executive pressures that federal adjudicators without Article III tenure might be. *See* footnote 15 in Justice Brennan's opinion (footnote 6 in this chapter).

The second concern is focused on an *individual* right "that the process of adjudication itself remain[s] impartial." As we will see in the cases following *Northern Pipeline,* the scope of this individual right is far from certain. In any event, these two concerns are fused in Justice Brennan's statement about the functions of Article III: "As an inseparable element of the constitutional system of checks and balances, and as a guarantee of impartiality, Art. III both defines the power and protects the independence of the Judicial Branch." Thus, no matter which approach one follows to judge the constitutionality of the assignment of Article III business to non-Article III tribunals, the importance of separation of powers, as well as the individual right to a fair adjudication, will be a part of the equation. You should remain alert to these values as you consider the balance of this chapter.

EXPLORING DOCTRINE

Is There a Missing Constitutional Value?

As discussed, the Court has identified separation of powers and the individual right to a fair adjudication as the values that animate its jurisprudence in this area. Is there another value that the Court should consider? Specifically, what about federalism? After all, the specific issue at play in *Northern Pipeline* concerned the adjudication by a non-Article III tribunal of a *state law* claim. As a part of the "plan of the Convention" the States certainly agreed that particular state law matters could be heard in federal courts under Article III. A prime example is reflected in diversity jurisdiction. But did the states agree that such claims—or even broader ones perhaps (i.e., between non-diverse parties)—could be heard in federal adjudicative bodies other than those created under Article III? At the very least, shouldn't the Court consider this value? What arguments can you make on both sides of this question?

Justice Brennan and Justice White may agree about the underlying values at stake in an abstract way. However, they articulate two quite different means to evaluate whether these values have been honored in a given case. It is worth spending a moment to understand the fundamental differences in these approaches.[25]

Justice Brennan's approach seeks to preserve the relevant constitutional values by adopting a formalistic, rule-based means to evaluate the assignment of Article III business to non-Article III tribunals. He begins with a rule—or at least a very strong presumption—that Article III business belongs in Article III courts. He then identifies a series of relatively narrow exceptions to that rule, intimating at least that those exceptions provide the universe of situations in which Congress may assign Article III judicial business to non-Article III tribunals. We will consider in a moment Justice Brennan's exceptions. For now, the point is that his opinion is based on a broad, generally applicable rule with narrow, pre-defined exceptions.

Justice White eschews a categorical approach. Instead, Justice White advocates a case-by-case balancing approach that is far more flexible than the plurality's position. Justice White argues in dissent that "Article III is not to be read out of the Constitution; rather it should be read as expressing one value that must be balanced against competing constitutional values and legislative responsibilities." He continues:

> I do not suggest that the Court should simply look to the strength of the legislative interest and ask itself if that interest is more compelling than the values furthered

25. Justice Rehnquist's concurring opinion does not take a position on the correct approach more generally.

> by Article III. The inquiry should, rather, focus equally on those Article III values and ask whether and to what extent the legislative scheme accommodates them or, conversely, substantially undermines them. The burden on Article III values should then be measured against the values Congress hopes to serve through the use of [non-Article III tribunals].

We quote at length from Justice White's dissent because, as we will explore below, the Court *may* have moved away from Justice Brennan's categorical approach and toward the views Justice White espoused. And interestingly, if the Court did move away from the categorical approach, it may be in the midst of a shift back toward it. In any event, we will leave consideration of this possibility for later.

Having considered the broader issues concerning (1) constitutional values and (2) methodologies for evaluating the assignment of judicial business to non-Article III adjudicators, we now turn to the details. Justice Brennan does a good job of outlining the development of the law in this area through 1982. In particular, one can draw from his opinion the broad landscape of non-Article III adjudicators to which Congress may, in certain cases, assign Article III business. We have depicted this landscape, and included examples of these bodies, in Figure 4-1.

FIGURE 4-1

Assignment of Judicial Business to Non-Article III Adjudicators: The Landscape

Legislative or Article I Courts	Administrative Agencies	Article III Adjuncts
• Territorial Courts • Military Courts • Courts to adjudicate "public rights" disputes, such as ○ United States Tax Court ○ United States Court of Appeals for Veterans Claims ○ United States Court of Federal Claims	Examples of administrative adjudication abound, including • Securities and Exchange Commission • Social Security Administration • Federal Communications Commission	• Magistrate Judges • Post-1984 Bankruptcy Courts

We consider each of these three types of non-Article III adjudicators below.

a. Legislative or Article I Courts

The first category of non-Article III adjudicators is referred to as legislative or Article I courts. Congress creates these tribunals as courts but staffs them with judges who do not possess the tenure and salary protections provided in Article III. There was a time when the Supreme Court held the view that Congress could not assign Article III business to Article I tribunals. However, as Justice Brennan noted in *Northern Pipeline*, the modern view is "that legislative courts may be granted jurisdiction over some controversies to which the Art. III judicial power might also be extended." The key, of course, is determining which "controversies" may be assigned to a legislative court.

Recall that Justice Brennan's view was categorical as to the use of non-Article III adjudicators. Such bodies could be used only in certain specific situations. In his opinion, Justice Brennan identifies the three exceptions he gleaned from the Court's precedents justifying the use of an Article I tribunal: (1) territorial courts; (2) military courts; and (3) courts to adjudicate disputes concerning "public rights." According to Justice Brennan, these three exceptions to Article III jurisdiction were justified by the Constitution's assignment of "exceptional" control of these matters to the other branches of the federal government.

We consider each of these bodies in turn, although our principal focus is on those tribunals concerning public rights disputes.

i. *Territorial Courts*

Justice Brennan's first category concerns Congress's power to establish Article I tribunals for territories the United States possesses as well as other areas not within the control of any state, such as the District of Columbia. This category has a long pedigree having been recognized by the Court in an opinion by Chief Justice Marshall in 1828. *See American Ins. Co. v. Cantor*, 26 U.S. 511 (1828) (upholding the constitutionality of territorial courts in Florida). It remains viable as a basis for decision in the modern era as well. *See, e.g., Palmore v. United States*, 411 U.S. 389 (1972) (upholding the constitutionality of courts in Washington, D.C., to adjudicate criminal cases). The rationale for allowing Article I tribunals with respect to the territories and areas such as the District of Columbia is that the Constitution provides Congress with sweeping powers to regulate these geographic regions. *See* U.S. CONST. art. IV, § 3, cl. 2 ("The Congress shall have Power to dispose of and make all needful Rules and Regulations respecting the Territory or other Property belonging to the United States . . ."); U.S. CONST. art. I, § 8, cl. 17 (Congress shall have Power . . . To exercise exclusive Legislation in all Cases whatsoever, over such District . . . as may . . . become the Seat of Government of the United States . . .").

This category clearly did not provide a basis under Justice Brennan's categorical approach for Congress's power to create the bankruptcy courts at issue in *Northern Pipeline.*

ii. *Military Courts*

The second exception Justice Brennan identifies concerned military courts. This category, too, has a long history. The first Congress authorized the use of military courts. The Supreme Court affirmed the constitutionality of such entities to try members of the armed forces more than 150 years ago. *See Dynes v. Hoover*, 61 U.S. 65 (1858). Today, the highest court with jurisdiction over members of the military is the United States Court of Appeals for the Armed Forces, a court whose members—all civilian—are appointed to 15-year terms by the President with the Senate's advice and consent.

The military court exception to Article III is based on the Court's conclusion that the Constitution assigns the political branches of the federal government exceptional powers over the armed forces. *See, e.g.,* U.S. CONST. art. I, § 8, cl. 11

("Congress shall have Power . . . To declare War . . ."); U.S. CONST. art. I § 8, cl. 12 (Congress shall have Power . . . To raise and support armies . . ."); U.S. CONST. art. I, § 8, cl. 13 ("Congress shall have Power . . . To provide and maintain a Navy."); U.S. CONST. art. II, § 2, cl. 1 ("The President shall be Commander in Chief of the Army and Navy of the United States . . ."). The military court exception also was not relevant to the bankruptcy courts at issue in *Northern Pipeline.*

Traditionally, the most prominent military court was a court-martial concerning members of the Armed Services. But the power also extends to the use of military commissions that have been much in the news of late. We consider issues related to the military commissions constituted after the September 11 terrorist attacks elsewhere in the book in the context of (1) the ability of Congress to control the jurisdiction of the federal courts, see Chapter 3; and (2) habeas corpus, see Chapter 13.

iii. Courts to Adjudicate Disputes Concerning "Public Rights"

The third categorical exception is the most important and the most complex. Justice Brennan states that Congress had the power to assign to Article I courts disputes concerning what the Court has termed "public rights." What precisely is a public right? The Court does not say. Indeed, Justice Brennan forthrightly recognizes that "[t]he distinction between public rights and private rights has not been definitively explained in our precedents." He does, however, give some definitional clues:

- "The doctrine extends only to matters arising between the Government and persons subject to its authority in connection with the performance of the constitutional functions of the executive or legislative departments." (Citation and internal quotation marks omitted.)
- "A matter of public rights must at a minimum arise between the government and others. In contrast, the liability of one individual to another under the law as defined is a matter of private rights." (Citation and internal quotation marks omitted.) As we will see, the Court later qualified this statement in important respects.
- "*Crowell v. Benson* attempted to catalog some of the matters that fall within the public-rights doctrine: 'Familiar illustrations of administrative agencies created for the determination of such matters are found in connection with the exercise of the congressional power as to interstate and foreign commerce, taxation, immigration, the public lands, public health, the facilities of the post office, pensions and payments to veterans.'"
- "Congress cannot 'withdraw from [Art. III] judicial cognizance *any* matter which, *from its nature,* is the subject of a suit at the common law, or in equity, or admiralty.' *Murray's Lessee v. Hoboken Land & Improvement Co.* It is thus clear that the presence of the United States as a proper party to the proceeding is a necessary but not sufficient means of distinguishing 'private rights' from 'public rights.' And it is also clear that even with respect to matters that arguably fall within the scope of the 'public rights' doctrine, the presumption is in favor of Art. III courts."
- "Of course, the public-rights doctrine does not extend to any criminal matters, although the Government is a proper party."

As we discuss near the end of this section, the Court returned to the public/private rights distinction several times after *Northern Pipeline.* We leave it to the reader to decide whether it did a better job of defining the difference between what is a "private right" and what qualifies as a "public right." However, one can get at least a glimpse of what public rights might be from *Northern Pipeline.* They seem to be non-criminal matters in which the government is a party and the dispute concerns matters that are not the stuff of traditional common law (or equitable) adjudication. Approaching matters from the converse perspective, the Court has referred to private right adjudications as "inherently judicial," although that may not be very helpful either.

The public/private rights distinction does not mean that the Article III courts are out of the business of adjudicating public rights. First, Congress is not required to assign such disputes to non-Article III tribunals. These disputes would necessarily "arise under" federal law and, therefore, could be assigned for resolution to federal courts under Article III, section 2. Second, the Court has noted "that when Congress assigns these matters to administrative agencies, or to legislative courts, it has generally provided, and we have suggested that it may be required to provide, for Art. III judicial review." However, the Court has not explained why such appellate review is required. In some measure, it seems inconsistent with the rationales articulated for the doctrine in the first instance.

Before exploring why the matter at issue in *Northern Pipeline* was not a public right, consider the rationale for the public/private rights distinction in the first place. The Court has indicated that there are two fundamental reasons supporting the public rights doctrine. First, Justice Brennan refers to the concept of sovereign immunity by which the government may only be sued with its consent. It follows, according to the Court, that the government may condition that consent to be sued on adjudication contesting receipt of the public right in an Article I tribunal. Second, and seemingly more important for the Court, Justice Brennan noted that public rights involved the constitutional allocation of power to one of the political branches of government. In other words, the Constitution granted power to take a certain action and, when taking that action, the political branches should be given significant authority to dictate the scope of the "right" conferred. Are you persuaded by these justifications for the public/private rights distinction?

EXPLORING DOCTRINE

The "Public Rights" Irony

There is a certain irony with respect to the public rights doctrine. Under the doctrine, Congress may more easily assign the adjudication of a dispute concerning a right it creates—a public right—to a body whose members do not enjoy the salary and compensation protections afforded Article III judges than it can assign disputes concerning private rights between private litigants. But isn't it the case that we should be *more* concerned with pressure on adjudicators in the public rights context than in an entirely private dispute? Justice Brennan recognizes this possibility but rejects it on historical grounds. *See* footnote 20 in Justice Brennan's opinion (footnote 9 in this chapter). Do you accept Justice Brennan's position? If not, does this irony cast broader doubts on the public/private rights distinction in the context of Article III?

Having considered the bases for the public/private rights distinction, it is possible to practice applying the distinction by evaluating the Court's invalidation of the provisions of the Bankruptcy Act of 1978 at issue in *Northern Pipeline.* Recall what was actually at issue in the case. The portion of the statute with which the Court dealt concerned the power bestowed on the bankruptcy court to adjudicate state-law counterclaims. The issue did not concern the jurisdiction of the bankruptcy court over the "restructuring of debtor-creditor relations"—in other words, the core of bankruptcy. Justice Brennan indicated that such restructuring "may well be a 'public right.'" Both Justice Rehnquist in his concurrence and Justice White in his dissent appear to agree that such restructuring would be a public right. Is it in your view?

Turning to the precise issue in the case concerning state-law counterclaims, one can first see Justice Brennan's categorical approach at work. The only possible category into which the state-law counterclaim jurisdiction could fit would be the public rights group. He concludes that the state-law counterclaim was not a public right because it was a garden-variety common-law claim (i.e., breach of contract) between two private parties. The government was absent. Congress did not create the right. Thus, Congress could not assign that "private right" for adjudication before an Article I court. Justice Rehnquist agrees with this assessment in his concurrence but declines to make broader pronouncements concerning the generic categories of controversies that Congress could assign to Article I tribunals.

How does Justice White view the situation? Here, we can see Justice White apply his balancing approach. He considers the Article I goals Congress could have sought to advance—for example, efficiency in the bankruptcy process, the preservation of an elite Article III judiciary, and the retention of flexibility in future bankruptcy matters. Against these goals, he balances Article III values; in particular, he considers whether Congress sought to undermine those values. In this regard, he concludes that the adjudication of state-law counterclaims in bankruptcy actions would "likely be of little interest to the political branches" and, therefore, "there is less reason to fear that such courts [i.e., the bankruptcy courts] represent a dangerous accumulation of powers in one of the political branches of government." And, finally, in a sort of backstop argument, Justice White comments that Article III appellate review provided under the Act "will go a long way toward insuring a proper separation of powers."

Which approach do you find most persuasive? You may wish to consider which approach best preserves Article III values as well as which approach is easiest to apply?

You can test your understanding of the Court's approaches to Article I courts (at least as of *Northern Pipeline*) with Problem 4-1.

PROBLEM 4-1

Bankruptcy Revisited

Assume that you are the legal counsel to a United States Senator. The Supreme Court has just decided *Northern Pipeline.* The Senator for whom you work would like to introduce a bill that reconstitutes the bankruptcy court as an Article I tribunal in a manner that would be constitutional. She has asked for your advice about how to go about doing so. Prepare a memorandum to your boss explaining how the bankruptcy court could be reconstituted to satisfy the constitutional objections of the plurality as well as the concurring justices. If you do not believe it is possible to do so (1) explain why and (2) suggest other options that could be pursued. [Note: You may wish to re-consider your answer to this problem after you have had the opportunity to consider the Court's most recent opinions in this area, all of which deal with bankruptcy.]

b. Article III Adjuncts

After concluding that the courts established under the Bankruptcy Act of 1978 could not qualify as valid Article I tribunals, Justice Brennan then considers a second possibility. Could these tribunals qualify as an adjunct to an Article III court? The plurality concluded that they could not. In this section, we consider why that is so and also explore the more general concept of the use of adjuncts.

When the Court refers to an adjunct to an Article III court it means an adjudicator who does not possess the tenure and salary protection of an Article III judge but who is located within the structure of Article III. As you might imagine, all things being equal, the separation-of-powers concerns that underlie much of the Court's work concerning Article I tribunals are reduced when considering an adjunct to an Article III court. When such an adjunct is properly constituted, one need not be concerned—or at least not be as concerned—with the political branches' undermining the independence of the judicial branch.

Justice Brennan draws "two principles" from the Court's precedents that were central to evaluating whether assignment of matters to an adjunct to an Article III court was proper. The first principle harkens back to the public/private rights distinction discussed above: "When Congress creates a substantive federal right, it possesses substantial discretion to prescribe the manner in which that right may be adjudicated—including the assignment to an adjunct of some functions historically performed by judges."

The second principle is broader in that it concerns both congressionally created rights as well as rights derived from the Constitution or common law. Justice Brennan concludes that "the functions of the adjunct must be limited in such a way that 'the essential attributes' of judicial power are retained in the Art. III court."

Justice Brennan concludes that the bankruptcy courts established under the 1978 Act could not qualify as adjuncts under these two principles. First, the right at issue was a state-law created right and, therefore, Congress had less latitude to assign its adjudication to an adjunct. Second, Justice Brennan concludes that the Act did not leave "the essential attributes of the judicial power" in an Article III court. Some of the provisions he cited were (1) the bankruptcy court's power to enforce its own orders; (2) the relatively limited standard of review applied on appeal to an Article III court (i.e., the orders were to be set aside only if "clearly erroneous"); (3) the broad assignment of "all the jurisdiction" of the Article III court to the bankruptcy tribunal, and (4) the jurisdiction of the bankruptcy courts to hear "all civil proceedings . . . arising in or related to" a bankruptcy petition.

The classic example of an appropriate adjunct to an Article III court is the office of United States Magistrate Judge. Magistrate judges are appointed by the district judges in the various United States District Courts.[26] They serve for eight-year terms and may be removed by the district court for various cause-based reasons. Compensation of magistrate judges may not be reduced while in office under statute.

Congress has assigned a number of Article III judicial functions to magistrate judges. As of 2013, there were approximately 550 full-time United States Magistrate Judges and 40 part-time magistrate judges. Section 636 of Title 28 of the United States Code describes in full the duties of magistrate judges. Some of those duties include

- In criminal matters, the magistrate judge initially sets bail and otherwise conducts initial appearances. Bail issues may be appealed to the district court which conducts a *de novo* determination of the matter.
- The magistrate judge may try misdemeanor criminal matters.
- In civil matters, the magistrate judge may be assigned non-dispositive matters subject to limited review in the district court.
- In civil matters, the district judge may refer to the magistrate judge dispositive matters with respect to which the magistrate judge will make a report and recommendation to the district judge. The parties may object to such report and recommendation and the district judge will consider the matter *de novo.*
- The parties in a civil case may consent to have a case assigned to a magistrate judge for all purposes, including trial. Any appeal from such a case would be to the appropriate circuit court of appeals.

Magistrate judges conduct a great deal of judicial business in the federal courts and, thus, are collectively an essential part of the contemporary federal court structure. In the period from October 2012 through September 2013 United States Magistrate Judges ruled on an aggregate of 1,179,358 matters.[27] The following table illustrates some of the more common activities of these important judicial actors:

Type of Proceeding	*Number of Actions*
Class A Misdemeanor Adjudications	8,385
Petty Offenses Adjudications	114,771
Felony Preliminary Proceedings Conducted	377,176
Non-Dispositive Civil Pretrial Matters Adjudicated	229,276
Reports and Recommendations Concerning Dispositive Civil Matters Issued	21,990
Civil Matters Assigned to Magistrate Judges on Consent of Parties	15,804

The Supreme Court has rendered a number of decisions over the past two decades concerning magistrate judges. Several of these decisions were statutory, concluding that Congress had not, in fact, authorized certain tasks to be

26. The relevant statutory provisions concerning United States Magistrate Judges can be found at 28 U.S.C. §§ 631-639.

27. The statics are available in a report prepared by the Administrative Office of the United States Courts. *See* 2012 Judicial Business of the United States Courts, *available at* http://www.uscourts.gov/Statistics/JudicialBusiness/2013/tables/S17Sep13.pdf.

assigned to magistrate judges.[28] When confronted with the question whether the statutory assignment of a task to a magistrate judge was constitutional, the Court has consistently upheld the statutory grant of authority.[29]

Another example of an adjunct to an Article III court is the current bankruptcy court. Under the current statute, the relevant court of appeals appoints bankruptcy judges to terms of 14 years. These judges are said to be officers of the appropriate district courts. The district court may—but need not—refer all bankruptcy matters to the applicable bankruptcy court. We will consider the bankruptcy court in more detail later in this chapter because the Supreme Court's most recent cases in this area have focused on what Congress did to address the *Northern Pipeline* decision.

c. Administrative Agencies

One of the hallmarks of modern American government is the administrative agency. It would be rare to spend a week reading the newspapers during which you would not see something about such a federal agency. Just consider the last time you read about the Environmental Protection Agency, the Federal Elections Commission, the Consumer Product Safety Commission, the Federal Communications Commission, or the Federal Aviation Administration. And these are only a few of the examples we could have listed.

You should be under no illusion concerning the ubiquity of administrative adjudication in modern American law. For example, in 1999 (the last year for which a comparative date is available) there were 834 life-tenured Article III judges. That number was dwarfed, however, by the approximately 1,400 administrative law judges adjudicating claims in the federal system.[30] Thus, statistically speaking, one was far more likely to encounter federal adjudication with an administrative agency than with an Article III judge.

As you may have gathered from Justice Brennan's opinion in *Northern Pipeline*, in terms of their adjudicative functions, administrative agencies seem a bit like both a legislative court and an adjunct to an Article III court. Indeed, at various points the Supreme Court has analogized administrative agencies to both of these other institutions. Therefore, many of the constitutional issues concerning the use of non-Article III adjudicators discussed in the context of those bodies are applicable to administrative agencies.

However, as mentioned above, administrative agencies are different from these other bodies in some important respects. For example, one prominent Federal Courts resource has indicated that there are three significant differences between administrative agencies and many legislative courts:[31]

(1) Judgments rendered in administrative agencies are generally enforceable only upon an order of an Article III court;

28. *See, e.g.*, *Gomez v. United States*, 490 U.S. 858 (1989); *Wing v. Wedding*, 418 U.S. 461 (1974).

29. *See, e.g.*, *Gonzales v. United States*, 128 S. Ct. 1765 (2008); *Roell v. Withrow*, 538 U.S. 580 (2003); *Peretz v. United States*, 501 U.S. 923 (1991); *McCarthy v. Bronson*, 500 U.S. 136 (1991); *United States v. Raddatz*, 447 U.S. 667 (1980).

30. *See* Judith Resnik, *"Uncle Sam Modernizes His Justice": Inventing the Federal District Courts of the Twentieth Century for the District of Columbia and the Nation*, 90 Geo. L.J. 607, 621 (2002).

31. *See* Richard H. Fallon, Jr., et al., Hart and Wechsler's The Federal Courts and the Federal System 342 (6th ed. 2009).

(2) Administrative agencies have formal and informal policymaking functions in addition to adjudicative responsibilities; and
(3) There are "traditional justifications" in which legislative courts are considered as Article I exceptions to Article III while administrative agencies are considered as part of the Article II executive function in many respects. In other words, the historical development of each institution sets boundaries for the future.

Whether one accepts these distinctions, they have resulted in administrative agencies' being treated differently than other non-Article III adjudicators in a number of respects. For example, a court will defer to an agency's interpretation of an ambiguous federal statute when that interpretation is reasonable and Congress has intended the agency to fill statutory gaps. *See, e.g., Chevron U.S.A., Inc. v. Natural Res. Def. Council, Inc.*, 467 U.S. 837 (1984). You will have the opportunity to explore more fully the operation of administrative agencies in Administrative Law. For present purposes, we simply want you to be aware that these institutions raise issues concerning the Article III judicial power that are similar to those addressed in the context of legislative courts and Article III adjuncts. But you should also know that the administrative agency remains a controversial part of the American constitutional order. A prime example is the following passage written by Justice Kennedy several years ago: "The dynamics of the three branches of Government are well understood as a general matter. But the role and position of the agency, and the exact locus of its powers, present questions that are delicate, subtle, and complex. The Federal Government could not perform its duties in a responsible and effective way without administrative agencies. Yet the amorphous character of the administrative agency in the constitutional system escapes simple explanation." *FCC v. Fox Television Stations, Inc.*, 556 U.S. 502, 536 (2009) (Kennedy, J., concurring).

* * * * *

We have just considered the state of the law largely as matters stood when the Court decided *Northern Pipeline* in 1982. In that discussion, we noted some post-1982 developments in several areas. But much of the Court's work after *Northern Pipeline* focused on the third of Justice Brennan's legislative court categories—those involving the adjudication of public rights disputes. We now consider these post-1982 developments.

In 1985, the Court decided *Thomas v. Union Carbide Agricultural Products Co.*, 473 U.S. 568 (1985). That decision moved decidedly away from the categorical approach of Justice Brennan's plurality opinion in *Northern Pipeline* and channeled Justice White's more functional balancing methodology.

Thomas concerned a complicated statutory regime under the Federal Insecticide, Fungicide and Rodenticide Act (FIFRA), 7 U.S.C. §§ 136 *et seq.* Under that statute, participants in FIFRA's chemical registration process were required under certain circumstances to provide data to other participants on commercially reasonable terms. The Act provided that if the participants could not agree on a price, they would be required to address their dispute in binding arbitration with only limited judicial review.

A participant in the mandatory arbitration program challenged the procedure as a violation of the assignment of Article III tasks to non-Article III adjudicators. Justice Sandra Day O'Connor, writing for the Court, rejected that challenge. While Justice Brennan agreed in a concurring opinion, the prime importance of *Thomas* and Justice O'Connor's majority opinion is the reasoning.

Justice O'Connor first reaffirmed the fundamental principle that Congress may in certain circumstances assign jurisdiction over Article III matters to non-Article III adjudicators. The major change came in how the Court appeared to evaluate when such an assignment is constitutional. Recall that Justice Brennan's plurality opinion in *Northern Pipeline* employed a categorical approach to this question. Justice O'Connor dealt with this approach in two ways. As an initial matter, she limited *Northern Pipeline* to its precise facts. In this regard, she described the issue in that case as follows: "The Court's holding [in *Northern Pipeline*] established only that Congress may not vest in a non-Article III court the power to adjudicate, render final judgment, and issue binding orders in a traditional contract action arising under state law, without consent of the litigants, and subject only to ordinary appellate review."

Having thus limited *Northern Pipeline*, Justice O'Connor next cast serious doubt on the plurality's categorical approach to the issue. She stated that "practical attention to substance rather than doctrinaire reliance on formal categories should inform application of Article III." Justice O'Connor continued to evaluate the public/private rights issue implicated in *Thomas* in a manner far more consistent with the balancing approach advocated in Justice White's *Northern Pipeline* dissent. Key to this analysis, Justice O'Connor wrote that "the public rights doctrine reflects simply a pragmatic understanding that when Congress selects a quasi-judicial method of resolving matters that 'could be exclusively determined by the Executive and Legislative branches,' the danger of encroaching on the judicial power is reduced."

Applying this "practical" approach, Justice O'Connor concluded that Congress was within its rights to craft the compensation dispute resolution system at issue in FIFRA. She first considered the right at issue more akin to a traditional public right. She also indicated that the complex nature of the congressional regulatory scheme underlying FIFRA cuts in favor of allowing Congress latitude in assigning adjudication of compensation disputes in the manner it did. She specifically noted that there was meaningful appellate review in an Article III court.[32] Based on these factors, Justice O'Connor concluded that "we do not think the system [under FIFRA] threatens the independent role of the Judiciary in our constitutional scheme."

Justice Brennan concurred in the judgment. He reaffirmed the categorical approach of the *Northern Pipeline* plurality. He was able to concur in this case because he expanded in some measure his view of a public right. In this regard, Justice Brennan wrote: "Although a compensation dispute under FIFRA ultimately involves a determination of the duty owed one private party by another, at its heart the dispute involves the exercise of authority by a Federal Government arbitrator in the course of administration of FIFRA's comprehensive regulatory scheme." This fact was enough to make the right "public" and, therefore, Congress's assignment of its adjudication to a non-Article III actor fits within one of the exceptions recognized in the *Northern Pipeline* plurality.

Thomas was not the Court's last word for long. In 1986, the Court decided *Commodity Futures Trading Commission v. Schor*, in which it again considered the public/private rights distinction as it related to legislative courts. Excerpts of

32. Again, it is worth considering why such appellate review would be required at all given the other arguments the Court advances in support of its decision.

that decision appear below. Note the continued reliance in *Schor* on a consideration that was mentioned several times in *Thomas*—the importance (or at least relevance) of the parties' consent when adjudicative functions are assigned to non-Article III entities. As we will see later in this chapter, consent continued to be a vexing issue in this area of law.

COMMODITY FUTURES TRADING COMMISSION v. SCHOR

478 U.S. 833 (1986)

JUSTICE O'CONNOR delivered the opinion of the Court.

The question presented is whether the Commodity Exchange Act (CEA or Act) empowers the Commodity Futures Trading Commission (CFTC or Commission) to entertain state law counterclaims in reparation proceedings and, if so, whether that grant of authority violates Article III of the Constitution.

I

The CEA broadly prohibits fraudulent and manipulative conduct in connection with commodity futures transactions. In 1974, Congress "overhauled" the Act in order to institute a more "comprehensive regulatory structure to oversee the volatile and esoteric futures trading complex." Congress also determined that the broad regulatory powers of the CEA were most appropriately vested in an agency which would be relatively immune from the "political winds that sweep Washington." It therefore created an independent agency, the CFTC, and entrusted to it sweeping authority to implement the CEA.

Among the duties assigned to the CFTC was the administration of a reparations procedure through which disgruntled customers of professional commodity brokers could seek redress for the brokers' violations of the Act or CFTC regulations. Thus, § 14 of the CEA provides that any person injured by such violations may apply to the Commission for an order directing the offender to pay reparations to the complainant and may enforce that order in federal district court. Congress intended this administrative procedure to be an "inexpensive and expeditious" alternative to existing fora available to aggrieved customers, namely, the courts and arbitration.

In conformance with the congressional goal of promoting efficient dispute resolution, the CFTC promulgated a regulation in 1976 which allows it to adjudicate counterclaims "[arising] out of the transaction or occurrence or series of transactions or occurrences set forth in the complaint." This permissive counterclaim rule leaves the respondent in a reparations proceeding free to seek relief against the reparations complainant in other fora.

The instant dispute arose in February 1980, when respondents Schor and Mortgage Services of America, Inc., invoked the CFTC's reparations jurisdiction by filing complaints against petitioner ContiCommodity Services, Inc. (Conti), a commodity futures broker, and Richard L. Sandor, a Conti employee. Schor had an account with Conti which contained a debit balance because Schor's net futures trading losses and expenses, such as commissions, exceeded the funds deposited in the account. Schor alleged that this debit balance was the result of Conti's numerous violations of the CEA.

Before receiving notice that Schor had commenced the reparations proceeding, Conti had filed a diversity action in Federal District Court to recover the debit balance. Schor counterclaimed in this action, reiterating his charges that the debit balance was due to Conti's violations of the CEA. Schor also moved on two separate occasions to dismiss or stay the District Court action, arguing that the continuation of the federal action would be a waste of judicial resources and an undue burden on the litigants in view of the fact that "[the] reparations proceedings . . . will fully . . . resolve and adjudicate all the rights of the parties to this action with respect to the transactions which are the subject matter of this action."

Although the District Court declined to stay or dismiss the suit, Conti voluntarily dismissed the federal court action and presented its debit balance claim by way of a counterclaim in the CFTC reparations proceeding. Conti denied violating the CEA and instead insisted that the debit balance resulted from Schor's trading, and was therefore a simple debt owed by Schor.

After discovery, briefing, and a hearing, the Administrative Law Judge (ALJ) in Schor's reparations proceeding ruled in Conti's favor on both Schor's claims and Conti's counterclaims. After this ruling, Schor for the first time challenged the CFTC's statutory authority to adjudicate Conti's counterclaim. The ALJ rejected Schor's challenge, stating himself "bound by agency regulations and published agency policies." The Commission declined to review the decision and allowed it to become final at which point Schor filed a petition for review with the Court of Appeals for the District of Columbia Circuit. Prior to oral argument, the Court of Appeals, *sua sponte*, raised the question whether CFTC could constitutionally adjudicate Conti's counterclaims in light of *Northern Pipeline Construction Co.* v. *Marathon Pipe Line Co.* in which this Court held that "Congress may not vest in a non-Article III court the power to adjudicate, render final judgment, and issue binding orders in a traditional contract action arising under state law, without consent of the litigants, and subject only to ordinary appellate review." *Thomas v. Union Carbide Agricultural Products Co.*

After briefing and argument, the Court of Appeals upheld the CFTC's decision on Schor's claim in most respects, but ordered the dismissal of Conti's counterclaims on the ground that "the CFTC lacks authority (subject matter competence) to adjudicate" common law counterclaims. . . .

* * * *

II

[In this portion of the opinion, the Court considered whether the Act authorized the CFTC to entertain state law counterclaims. In concluded:

"In view of the abundant evidence that Congress both contemplated and authorized the CFTC's assertion of jurisdiction over Conti's common law counterclaim, we conclude that the Court of Appeals' analysis is untenable. The canon of construction that requires courts to avoid unnecessary constitutional adjudication did not empower the Court of Appeals to manufacture a restriction on the CFTC's jurisdiction that was nowhere contemplated by Congress and to reject plain evidence of congressional intent because that intent was not specifically embodied in a statutory mandate. We therefore are squarely faced with the question whether the CFTC's assumption of jurisdiction over common law counterclaims violates Article III of the Constitution."]

III

Article III, § 1, directs that the "judicial Power of the United States shall be vested in one supreme Court and in such inferior Courts as the Congress may from time to time ordain and establish," and provides that these federal courts shall be staffed by judges who hold office during good behavior, and whose compensation shall not be diminished during tenure in office. Schor claims that these provisions prohibit Congress from authorizing the initial adjudication of common law counterclaims by the CFTC, an administrative agency whose adjudicatory officers do not enjoy the tenure and salary protections embodied in Article III.

Although our precedents in this area do not admit of easy synthesis, they do establish that the resolution of claims such as Schor's cannot turn on conclusory reference to the language of Article III. Rather, the constitutionality of a given congressional delegation of adjudicative functions to a non-Article III body must be assessed by reference to the purposes underlying the requirements of Article III. This inquiry, in turn, is guided by the principle that "practical attention to substance rather than doctrinaire reliance on formal categories should inform application of Article III."

A

Article III, § 1, serves both to protect "the role of the independent judiciary within the constitutional scheme of tripartite government" and to safeguard litigants' "right to have claims decided before judges who are free from potential domination by other branches of government." Although our cases have provided us with little occasion to discuss the nature or significance of this latter safeguard, our prior discussions of Article III, § 1's guarantee of an independent and impartial adjudication by the federal judiciary of matters within the judicial power of the United States intimated that this guarantee serves to protect primarily personal, rather than structural, interests.

Our precedents also demonstrate, however, that Article III does not confer on litigants an absolute right to the plenary consideration of every nature of claim by an Article III court. Moreover, as a personal right, Article III's guarantee of an impartial and independent federal adjudication is subject to waiver, just as are other personal constitutional rights that dictate the procedures by which civil and criminal matters must be tried. Indeed, the relevance of concepts of waiver to Article III challenges is demonstrated by our decision in *Northern Pipeline*, in which the absence of consent to an initial adjudication before a non-Article III tribunal was relied on as a significant factor in determining that Article III forbade such adjudication.

In the instant cases, Schor indisputably waived any right he may have possessed to the full trial of Conti's counterclaim before an Article III court. Schor expressly demanded that Conti proceed on its counterclaim in the reparations proceeding rather than before the District Court and was content to have the entire dispute settled in the forum he had selected until the ALJ ruled against him on all counts; it was only after the ALJ rendered a decision to which he objected that Schor raised any challenge to the CFTC's consideration of Conti's counterclaim.

Even were there no evidence of an express waiver here, Schor's election to forgo his right to proceed in state or federal court on his claim and his decision to seek relief instead in a CFTC reparations proceeding constituted an effective waiver. . . .

B

As noted above, our precedents establish that Article III, § 1, not only preserves to litigants their interest in an impartial and independent federal adjudication of claims within the judicial power of the United States, but also serves as "an inseparable element of the constitutional system of checks and balances." Article III, § 1, safeguards the role of the Judicial Branch in our tripartite system by barring congressional attempts "to transfer jurisdiction [to non-Article III tribunals] for the purpose of emasculating" constitutional courts and thereby preventing "the encroachment or aggrandizement of one branch at the expense of the other." To the extent that this structural principle is implicated in a given case, the parties cannot by consent cure the constitutional difficulty for the same reason that the parties by consent cannot confer on federal courts subject-matter jurisdiction beyond the limitations imposed by Article III, § 2. When these Article III limitations are at issue, notions of consent and waiver cannot be dispositive because the limitations serve institutional interests that the parties cannot be expected to protect.

In determining the extent to which a given congressional decision to authorize the adjudication of Article III business in a non-Article III tribunal impermissibly threatens the institutional integrity of the Judicial Branch, the Court has declined to adopt formalistic and unbending rules. Although such rules might lend a greater degree of coherence to this area of the law, they might also unduly constrict Congress' ability to take needed and innovative action pursuant to its Article I powers. Thus, in reviewing Article III challenges, we have weighed a number of factors, none of which has been deemed determinative, with an eye to the practical effect that the congressional action will have on the constitutionally assigned role of the federal judiciary. Among the factors upon which we have focused are the extent to which the "essential attributes of judicial power" are reserved to Article III courts, and, conversely, the extent to which the non-Article III forum exercises the range of jurisdiction and powers normally vested only in Article III courts, the origins and importance of the right to be adjudicated, and the concerns that drove Congress to depart from the requirements of Article III . . .

An examination of the relative allocation of powers between the CFTC and Article III courts in light of the considerations given prominence in our precedents demonstrates that the congressional scheme does not impermissibly intrude on the province of the judiciary. The CFTC's adjudicatory powers depart from the traditional agency model in just one respect: the CFTC's jurisdiction over common law counterclaims. While wholesale importation of concepts of pendent or ancillary jurisdiction into the agency context may create greater constitutional difficulties, we decline to endorse an absolute prohibition on such jurisdiction out of fear of where some hypothetical "slippery slope" may deposit us. . . .

In the instant cases, we are likewise persuaded that there is little practical reason to find that this single deviation from the agency model is fatal to the congressional scheme. Aside from its authorization of counterclaim jurisdiction, the CEA leaves far more of the "essential attributes of judicial power" to

Article III courts than did that portion of the Bankruptcy Act found unconstitutional in *Northern Pipeline.* The CEA scheme in fact hews closely to the agency model approved by the Court in *Crowell v. Benson.*

The CFTC, like the agency in *Crowell,* deals only with a "particularized area of law," whereas the jurisdiction of the bankruptcy courts found unconstitutional in *Northern Pipeline* extended to broadly "all civil proceedings arising under title 11 or arising in or *related to* cases under title 11." 28 U.S.C. § 1471(b) (quoted in *Northern Pipeline*) (emphasis added). CFTC orders, like those of the agency in *Crowell,* but unlike those of the bankruptcy courts under the 1978 Act, are enforceable only by order of the district court. CFTC orders are also reviewed under the same "weight of the evidence" standard sustained in *Crowell,* rather than the more deferential standard found lacking in *Northern Pipeline.* The legal rulings of the CFTC, like the legal determinations of the agency in *Crowell,* are subject to *de novo* review. Finally, the CFTC, unlike the bankruptcy courts under the 1978 Act, does not exercise "all ordinary powers of district courts," and thus may not, for instance, preside over jury trials or issue writs of habeas corpus.

Of course, the nature of the claim has significance in our Article III analysis quite apart from the method prescribed for its adjudication. The counterclaim asserted in this litigation is a "private" right for which state law provides the rule of decision. It is therefore a claim of the kind assumed to be at the "core" of matters normally reserved to Article III courts. Yet this conclusion does not end our inquiry; just as this Court has rejected any attempt to make determinative for Article III purposes the distinction between public rights and private rights, *Thomas,* there is no reason inherent in separation of powers principles to accord the state law character of a claim talismanic power in Article III inquiries.

We have explained that "the public rights doctrine reflects simply a pragmatic understanding that when Congress selects a quasi-judicial method of resolving matters that 'could be conclusively determined by the Executive and Legislative Branches,' the danger of encroaching on the judicial powers" is less than when private rights, which are normally within the purview of the judiciary, are relegated as an initial matter to administrative adjudication. *Thomas* (quoting *Northern Pipeline*). Similarly, the state law character of a claim is significant for purposes of determining the effect that an initial adjudication of those claims by a non-Article III tribunal will have on the separation of powers for the simple reason that private, common law rights were historically the types of matters subject to resolution by Article III courts. The risk that Congress may improperly have encroached on the federal judiciary is obviously magnified when Congress "[withdraws] from judicial cognizance any matter which, from its nature, is the subject of a suit at the common law, or in equity, or admiralty" and which therefore has traditionally been tried in Article III courts, and allocates the decision of those matters to a non-Article III forum of its own creation. *Murray's Lessee v. Hoboken Land & Improvement Co.* Accordingly, where private, common law rights are at stake, our examination of the congressional attempt to control the manner in which those rights are adjudicated has been searching. *See, e.g., Northern Pipeline.* In this litigation, however, "[looking] beyond form to the substance of what" Congress has done, we are persuaded that the congressional authorization of limited CFTC jurisdiction over a narrow class of common law claims as an incident to the CFTC's primary, and unchallenged, adjudicative function does not create a substantial threat to the separation of powers. *Thomas.*

It is clear that Congress has not attempted to "withdraw from judicial cognizance" the determination of Conti's right to the sum represented by the debit balance in Schor's account. Congress gave the CFTC the authority to adjudicate such matters, but the decision to invoke this forum is left entirely to the parties and the power of the federal judiciary to take jurisdiction of these matters is unaffected. In such circumstances, separation of powers concerns are diminished, for it seems self-evident that just as Congress may encourage parties to settle a dispute out of court or resort to arbitration without impermissible incursions on the separation of powers, Congress may make available a quasi-judicial mechanism through which willing parties may, at their option, elect to resolve their differences. This is not to say, of course, that if Congress created a phalanx of non-Article III tribunals equipped to handle the entire business of the Article III courts without any Article III supervision or control and without evidence of valid and specific legislative necessities, the fact that the parties had the election to proceed in their forum of choice would necessarily save the scheme from constitutional attack. But this case obviously bears no resemblance to such a scenario, given the degree of judicial control saved to the federal courts as well as the congressional purpose behind the jurisdictional delegation, the demonstrated need for the delegation, and the limited nature of the delegation.

When Congress authorized the CFTC to adjudicate counterclaims, its primary focus was on making effective a specific and limited federal regulatory scheme, not on allocating jurisdiction among federal tribunals. Congress intended to create an inexpensive and expeditious alternative forum through which customers could enforce the provisions of the CEA against professional brokers. Its decision to endow the CFTC with jurisdiction over such reparations claims is readily understandable given the perception that the CFTC was relatively immune from political pressures and the obvious expertise that the Commission possesses in applying the CEA and its own regulations. This reparations scheme itself is of unquestioned constitutional validity. It was only to ensure the effectiveness of this scheme that Congress authorized the CFTC to assert jurisdiction over common law counterclaims. Indeed, as was explained above, absent the CFTC's exercise of that authority, the purposes of the reparations procedure would have been confounded.

It also bears emphasis that the CFTC's assertion of counterclaim jurisdiction is limited to that which is necessary to make the reparations procedure workable. The CFTC adjudication of common law counterclaims is incidental to, and completely dependent upon, adjudication of reparations claims created by federal law, and in actual fact is limited to claims arising out of the same transaction or occurrence as the reparations claim.

In such circumstances, the magnitude of any intrusion on the Judicial Branch can only be termed *de minimis.* Conversely, were we to hold that the Legislative Branch may not permit such limited cognizance of common law counterclaims at the election of the parties, it is clear that we would "defeat the obvious purpose of the legislation to furnish a prompt, continuous, expert and inexpensive method for dealing with a class of questions of fact which are peculiarly suited to examination and determination by an administrative agency specially assigned to that task." *Crowell v. Benson.* We do not think Article III compels this degree of prophylaxis.

* * * *

[B]right-line rules cannot effectively be employed to yield broad principles applicable in all Article III inquiries. Rather, due regard must be given in each case to the unique aspects of the congressional plan at issue and its practical consequences in light of the larger concerns that underlie Article III. We conclude that the limited jurisdiction that the CFTC asserts over state law claims as a necessary incident to the adjudication of federal claims willingly submitted by the parties for initial agency adjudication does not contravene separation of powers principles or Article III.

C

Schor asserts that Article III, § 1, constrains Congress for reasons of federalism, as well as for reasons of separation of powers. He argues that the state law character of Conti's counterclaim transforms the central question in this litigation from whether Congress has trespassed upon the judicial powers of the Federal Government into whether Congress has invaded the prerogatives of state governments.

At the outset, we note that our prior precedents in this area have dealt only with separation of powers concerns, and have not intimated that principles of federalism impose limits on Congress' ability to delegate adjudicative functions to non-Article III tribunals. This absence of discussion regarding federalism is particularly telling in *Northern Pipeline,* where the Court based its analysis solely on the separation of powers principles inherent in Article III despite the fact that the claim sought to be adjudicated in the bankruptcy court was created by state law.

Even assuming that principles of federalism are relevant to Article III analysis, however, we are unpersuaded that those principles require the invalidation of the CFTC's counterclaim jurisdiction. The sole fact that Conti's counterclaim is resolved by a *federal* rather than a *state* tribunal could not be said to unduly impair state interests, for it is established that a federal court could, without constitutional hazard, decide a counterclaim such as the one asserted here under its ancillary jurisdiction, even if an independent jurisdictional basis for it were lacking. Given that the federal courts can and do exercise ancillary jurisdiction over counterclaims such as the one at issue here, the question becomes whether the fact that a federal agency rather than a federal Article III court initially hears the state law claim gives rise to a cognizably greater impairment of principles of federalism.

Schor argues that those Framers opposed to diversity jurisdiction in the federal courts acquiesced in its inclusion in Article III only because they were assured that the federal judiciary would be protected by the tenure and salary provisions of Article III. He concludes, in essence, that to protect this constitutional compact, Article III should be read to absolutely preclude any adjudication of state law claims by federal decisionmakers that do not enjoy the Article III salary and tenure protections. We are unpersuaded by Schor's novel theory, which suffers from a number of flaws, the most important of which is that Schor identifies no historical support for the critical link he posits between the provisions of Article III that protect the independence of the federal judiciary and those provisions that define the extent of the judiciary's jurisdiction over state law claims.

The judgment of the Court of Appeals for the District of Columbia Circuit is reversed, and the case is remanded for further proceedings consistent with this opinion.

It is so ordered.

JUSTICE BRENNAN, with whom JUSTICE MARSHALL joins, dissenting.

Article III, § 1, of the Constitution provides that "[the] judicial Power of the United States, shall be vested in one supreme Court, and in such inferior Courts as the Congress may from time to time ordain and establish." It further specifies that the federal judicial power must be exercised by judges who "shall hold their Offices during good Behaviour, and [who] shall, at stated Times, receive for their Services a Compensation, which shall not be diminished during their Continuance in Office."

On its face, Article III, § 1, seems to prohibit the vesting of *any* judicial functions in either the Legislative or the Executive Branch. The Court has, however, recognized three narrow exceptions to the otherwise absolute mandate of Article III: territorial courts; courts-martial; and courts that adjudicate certain disputes concerning public rights. Unlike the Court, I would limit the judicial authority of non-Article III federal tribunals to these few, long-established exceptions and would countenance no further erosion of Article III's mandate.

I

The Framers knew that "[the] accumulation of all powers, Legislative, Executive, and Judiciary, in the same hands, whether of one, a few, or many, and whether hereditary, self-appointed, or elective, may justly be pronounced the very definition of tyranny." The Federalist No. 46 (J. Madison). In order to prevent such tyranny, the Framers devised a governmental structure composed of three distinct branches — "a vigorous Legislative Branch," "a separate and wholly independent Executive Branch," and "a Judicial Branch equally independent." The separation of powers and the checks and balances that the Framers built into our tripartite form of government were intended to operate as a "self-executing safeguard against the encroachment or aggrandizement of one branch at the expense of the other." "'The fundamental necessity of maintaining each of the three general departments of government entirely free from the control or coercive influence, direct or indirect, of either of the others, has often been stressed and is hardly open to serious question.'" The federal judicial power, then, must be exercised by judges who are independent of the Executive and the Legislature in order to maintain the checks and balances that are crucial to our constitutional structure.

The Framers also understood that a principal benefit of the separation of the judicial power from the legislative and executive powers would be the protection of individual litigants from decisionmakers susceptible to majoritarian pressures. Article III's salary and tenure provisions promote impartial adjudication by placing the judicial power of the United States "in a body of judges insulated from majoritarian pressures and thus able to enforce [federal law] without fear of reprisal or public rebuke." As Alexander Hamilton observed, "[that] inflexible and uniform adherence to the rights of the Constitution, and of individuals, which we perceive to be indispensable in the Courts of justice can certainly not be expected from Judges who hold their offices by a temporary commission." The Federalist No. 78. This is so because "[if] the power of making [periodic appointments] was committed either to the Executive or Legislature, there would be danger of an improper complaisance to the branch which possessed it; if to both, there would be an unwillingness to hazard the displeasure of either; if to the People, or to persons chosen by them for the special purpose, there would be too great a disposition to consult popularity, to justify a reliance that nothing would be consulted but the Constitution and the laws." "Next to permanency in office," Hamilton added, "nothing can contribute more to the independence of the Judges than a fixed provision for their support" because *"a power over a man's subsistence amounts to a power over his will."* (emphasis in original).

These important functions of Article III are too central to our constitutional scheme to risk their incremental erosion. The exceptions we have recognized for territorial courts, courts-martial, and administrative courts were each based on "certain exceptional powers bestowed upon Congress by the Constitution or by historical consensus." Here, however, there is no equally forceful reason to extend further these exceptions to situations that are distinguishable from existing precedents. The Court, however, engages in just such an extension. By sanctioning the adjudication of state-law counterclaims by a federal administrative agency, the Court far exceeds the analytic framework of our precedents.

More than a century ago, we recognized that Congress may not "withdraw from [Article III] judicial cognizance any matter *which, from its nature, is the subject of a suit at the common law,* or in equity, or admiralty." *Murray's Lessee* (emphasis added [by Court]). More recently, in *Northern Pipeline* the view of a majority of the Court that the breach-of-contract and misrepresentation claims at issue in that case lay "at the core of the historically recognized judicial power" and were "the stuff of the traditional actions at common law tried by the courts at Westminster in 1789," contributed significantly to the Court's conclusion that the bankruptcy courts could not constitutionally adjudicate Northern Pipeline's common-law claims. In the instant litigation, the Court lightly discards both history and our precedents. The Court attempts to support the substantial alteration it works today in our Article III jurisprudence by pointing, *inter alia,* to legislative convenience; to the fact that Congress does not altogether eliminate federal-court jurisdiction over ancillary state-law counterclaims; and to Schor's "consent" to CFTC adjudication of ContiCommodity's counterclaims. In my view, the Court's effort fails.

II

The Court states that in reviewing Article III challenges, one of several factors we have taken into account is "the concerns that drove Congress to depart from the requirements of Article III." The Court identifies the desire of Congress "to create an inexpensive and expeditious alternative forum through which customers could enforce the provisions of the CEA against professional brokers" as the motivating congressional concern here. The Court further states that "[it] was only to ensure the effectiveness of this scheme that Congress authorized the CFTC to assert jurisdiction over common-law counterclaims[;] . . . absent the CFTC's exercise of that authority, the purposes of the reparations procedure would have been confounded." Were we to hold that the CFTC's authority to decide common-law counterclaims offends Article III, the Court declares, "it is clear that we would 'defeat the obvious purpose of the legislation.'" Article III, the Court concludes, does not "[compel] this degree of prophylaxis."

I disagree—Article III's prophylactic protections were intended to prevent just this sort of abdication to claims of legislative convenience. The Court requires that the legislative interest in convenience and efficiency be weighed against the competing interest in judicial independence. In doing so, the Court pits an interest the benefits of which are immediate, concrete, and easily understood against one, the benefits of which are almost entirely prophylactic, and thus often seem remote and not worth the cost in any single case. Thus, while this balancing creates the illusion of objectivity and ineluctability, in fact the result was foreordained, because the balance is weighted against judicial independence. The danger of the Court's balancing approach is, of course, that as individual cases accumulate in which the Court finds that the short-term benefits of efficiency outweigh the long-term benefits of judicial independence, the protections of Article III will be eviscerated.

Perhaps the resolution of reparations claims such as respondents' may be accomplished more conveniently under the Court's decision than under my approach, but the Framers foreswore this sort of convenience in order to preserve freedom. As we [recently] explained: "The choices we discern as having been made in the Constitutional Convention impose burdens on governmental processes that often seem clumsy, inefficient, even unworkable, but those hard choices were consciously made by men who had lived under a form of government that permitted arbitrary governmental acts to go unchecked. . . . With all the obvious flaws of delay [and] untidiness . . . , we have not yet found a better way to preserve freedom than by making the exercise of power subject to the carefully crafted restraints spelled out in the Constitution."

* * * *

III

According to the Court, the intrusion into the province of the Federal Judiciary caused by the CFTC's authority to adjudicate state-law counterclaims is insignificant, both because the CFTC *shares* in, rather than displaces, federal district court jurisdiction over these claims and because only a very narrow class of state-law issues are involved. The "sharing" justification fails under the reasoning used by the Court to support the CFTC's authority. If the administrative reparations proceeding is so much more convenient and efficient than litigation in federal district court that abrogation of Article III's commands is warranted, it seems to me that complainants would rarely, if ever, choose to go to district court in the first instance. Thus, any "sharing" of jurisdiction is more illusory than real.

More importantly, the Court, in emphasizing that *this litigation* will permit solely a narrow class of state-law claims to be decided by a non-Article III court, ignores the fact that it establishes a broad principle. The decision today may authorize the administrative adjudication only of state-law claims that stem from the same transaction or set of facts that allow the customer of a professional commodity broker to initiate reparations proceedings before the CFTC, but the *reasoning* of this decision strongly suggests that, given "legislative necessity" and party consent, any federal agency may decide state-law issues that are ancillary to federal issues within the agency's jurisdiction. Thus, while in this litigation "the magnitude of any intrusion on the Judicial Branch" may conceivably be characterized as *"de minimis,"* the potential impact of the Court's decision on federal-court jurisdiction is substantial. The Court dismisses warnings about the dangers of its approach, asserting simply that it does not fear the slippery slope, and that this litigation does not involve the creation by Congress of a "phalanx of non-Article III tribunals equipped to handle the entire business of the Article III courts." A healthy respect for the precipice on which we stand is warranted, however, for this reason: Congress can seriously impair Article III's structural and individual protections without assigning away "the *entire* business of the Article III courts." It can do so by *diluting* the judicial power of the federal courts. And, contrary to the Court's intimations, dilution of judicial power operates to impair the protections of Article III regardless of whether Congress acted with the "good intention" of providing a more efficient dispute resolution system or with the "bad intention" of strengthening the Legislative Branch at the expense of the Judiciary.

IV

The Court's reliance on Schor's "consent" to a non-Article III tribunal is also misplaced. The Court erroneously suggests that there is a clear division between the separation of powers and the impartial adjudication functions of Article III. The Court identifies Article III's structural, or separation-of-powers, function as preservation of the Judiciary's domain from encroachment by another branch. The Court identifies the impartial adjudication function as the protection afforded by Article III to individual litigants against judges who may be dominated by other branches of government.

In my view, the structural and individual interests served by Article III are inseparable. The potential exists for individual litigants to be deprived of impartial decisionmakers only where federal officials who exercise judicial power are susceptible to congressional and executive pressure. That is, individual litigants may be harmed by the assignment of judicial power to non-Article III federal tribunals only where the Legislative or Executive Branches have encroached upon judicial authority and have thus threatened the separation of powers. The Court correctly recognizes that to the extent that Article III's structural concerns are implicated by a grant of judicial power to a non-Article III tribunal, "the parties cannot by consent cure the constitutional difficulty for the same reason that the parties by consent cannot confer on federal courts subject-matter jurisdiction beyond the limitations imposed by Article III, § 2." Because the individual and structural interests served by Article III are coextensive, I do not believe that a litigant may ever waive his right to an Article III tribunal where one is constitutionally required. In other words, consent is irrelevant to Article III analysis.

V

Our Constitution unambiguously enunciates a fundamental principle — that the "judicial Power of the United States" be reposed in an independent Judiciary. It is our obligation zealously to guard that independence so that our tripartite system of government remains strong and that individuals continue to be protected against decisionmakers subject to majoritarian pressures. Unfortunately, today the Court forsakes that obligation for expediency. I dissent.

Discussion and Questions

Justice O'Connor appears to continue the movement away from the categorical approach of the *Northern Pipeline* plurality. She evaluates the assignment of adjudicative responsibilities of certain state-law counterclaims to a non-Article III adjudicator by doing precisely what Justice White advocated in his *Northern Pipeline* dissent: balancing Article III values against the Article I needs of Congress.

The Court concludes that the balance in this case tips in favor of Congress's decision to assign to the CFTC authority to adjudicate the state-law counterclaims at issue. Factors that the Court considered important in this regard included

- what the Court perceived as the relatively narrow scope of the allocation of Article III jurisdiction to the non-Article III adjudicator;
- the need for enforcement of the ultimate order by an Article III court;
- a standard of review in an Article III court (e.g., based on the "weight of the evidence") that was said to be more searching than the one at issue in *Northern Pipeline*;
- the ability of the Article III court to review legal issues *de novo*; and
- the fact that the CFTC was not granted "all" the jurisdiction of an Article III court as was the bankruptcy court at issue in *Northern Pipeline*.

The Court in *Schor* rejects the notion that, because the right at issue was a "private" one under any definition, this rendered the allocation at issue unconstitutional. The Court agrees that, when the right is private, the Court's review should be "searching." However, Justice O'Connor treats the matter as simply an element of a broader balancing approach.

Justice Brennan's spirited dissent rejects the majority's position. He once again asserts his categorical approach. He also expands on why he believes that approach is superior. He argues that a categorical approach was effectively the only way to preserve Article III values in the long term. He worries that a case-by-case approach will allow Article III to be sapped of its strength over time because any incremental withdrawal of Article III jurisdiction will seem inconsequential, yet over the long haul such withdrawals can make the judiciary far less powerful as a constitutional actor. The majority rejects this argument, reasoning that the Court will be vigilant to ensure that Congress does not do piecemeal what it cannot do all at once. Which view is more persuasive to you?

Justice O'Connor also articulates in one of the most straightforward ways we have seen that the issues underlying the Court's concerns are based on two distinct constitutional values: (1) the importance of an independent judiciary as reflected in Article III and (2) an individual's interest in having claims adjudicated "before judges who are free from potential domination by other branches of government." Justice Brennan agrees that both values are implicated but argues that they are not, in fact, separate. Rather, for Justice Brennan they are part of single, unified constitutional command.

Justice O'Connor also puts a fair amount of weight on Schor's consent to have the state-law counterclaim adjudicated outside Article III. She suggests that this consent or waiver cured the individual rights concern. It did not, she opines, resolve the structural issues concerning an independent judiciary. However, it is difficult to read the majority opinion without the consent/waiver gloss's having at least some impact—even if below the surface—on the structural concerns. For Justice Brennan, Schor's consent and/or waiver made no difference because the individual rights concern could not be separated from the structural constitutional concerns.

Finally, it is worth mentioning that Justice O'Connor discusses the role—or more appropriately the lack of role—that federalism plays as a constitutional value in this area. We asked you to consider this question earlier in this chapter. Have your views changed based on Justice O'Connor's explicit rejection of federalism as a value to consider as part of the constitutional equation?

Test your knowledge of the material thus far with Problem 4-2.

PROBLEM 4-2

An Expansion of the Jurisdiction of the Court of Appeals for Veterans Claims

Return for a moment to the Court of Appeals for Veterans Claims discussed in the Reference Problem at the beginning of this chapter. Recall that the CAVC's jurisdiction is currently limited to appeals from decisions of the Department of Veterans Affairs denying benefits to veterans (or others claiming to be entitled to benefits administered by that department).

Assume that Congress decided to expand the CAVC's jurisdiction. Specifically, assume that Congress enacted a statute that made it a violation of federal law to discriminate against a veteran in the provision of rental housing. The statute prohibited landlords who receive any federal funding for their properties from (1) refusing to rent to a veteran because of status as a veteran or (2) evicting a person on that basis. Congress was concerned that anti-war sentiment based on the ongoing conflicts in Iraq and Afghanistan might provoke some landlords to refuse to rent to veterans.

Assume further that Congress provided that a veteran who believed that he or she was subject to discrimination based on veteran status in rental housing had a private right of action against a landlord. Congress directed that claims for violating the statute had to be brought in the CAVC. Congress further specifically provided that such veteran could join with his or her claim of rental discrimination "any other matter relating to or arising out of the rental relationship." Appeals from the CAVC's decision would lie in the Federal Circuit under the same terms outlined in the Reference Problem.

Jennifer Rambo, a citizen of California, is a veteran who had served in the United States Marine Corps. She lived in a rental apartment unit in San Diego, California. Rambo had served in Iraq. Her landlord, John Dove, also a citizen of California, vehemently opposed the presence of the United States in Iraq. Dove made his anger about the war, and Rambo's participation in it, plain whenever he saw her. One day when Rambo complained about some repairs that had not been made in her apartment, Dove said that she was a disruptive tenant and began eviction proceedings. Dove received federal funding under several programs in connection with his ownership of the building in which Rambo lived.

Rambo files suit against Dove in the CAVC. She asserts two claims. The first one is under the federal statute concerning rental discrimination. The second one is based on California law. Specifically, she claims that Dove has breached the obligation to maintain her apartment in a habitable condition. She seeks an injunction prohibiting her eviction as a violation of the federal statute and money damages for the violation of California law.

Rambo prevails in the CAVC. The CAVC concludes as a matter of fact that Dove had discriminated against Rambo because of her status as a veteran. It further finds that Dove had failed to maintain Rambo's apartment in a habitable condition. The court enters the injunction Rambo requested and awards her compensatory damages on the habitability claim.

Dove appeals the CAVC's judgment to the Federal Circuit. Among his arguments on appeal is that Congress exceeded its powers under the Constitution by assigning the adjudication of both of Rambo's claims to the CAVC. You are a law clerk to a Federal Circuit judge. She has asked you to prepare a memorandum discussing how Dove's claims should be evaluated under relevant law. She has also asked you to suggest an outcome. Prepare a memorandum for your judge.

If one were to stop at *Schor*, it would seem that Justice White's balancing approach from *Northern Pipeline* would have carried the day. The difficulty is that three years after *Schor* the Court decided *Granfinanciera, S.A. v. Nordberg*, 492 U.S. 33 (1989), a case that made matters far less clear than *Schor* might have suggested.

Granfinanciera returns us once again to the bankruptcy courts, now reconstituted as purported adjuncts to Article III courts after the Court's *Northern Pipeline* decision. The issue in the case did *not* concern the constitutionality of that reorganization, at least not directly. The bankruptcy trustee had asserted a claim against the creditor based on an allegedly "fraudulent" transfer of money under the Bankruptcy Code. The trustee argued the transfer was void and the money at issue should be returned to the bankrupt's estate. The Court considered whether the trustee's claim required a jury trial under the Seventh Amendment even though the creditor had not asserted a claim against the estate.[33]

Granfinanciera is relevant to our discussion not so much because of the precise issue it considered (although that issue is most certainly both important and interesting) but rather for the Court's approach to that question. After determining that a claim for fraudulent transfer was a legal claim that would entitle a party to a jury in an Article III court, Justice Brennan, writing for the Court, turned to whether Congress could avoid the Seventh Amendment by assigning adjudication of the claim to a non-Article III adjudicator. The Court held that the answer to this question should be determined by applying the Court's precedents concerning the assignment of the adjudicatory function to a non-Article III tribunal in the first instance. The Court thus brought into play *Northern Pipeline, Thomas*, and *Schor*.

One can quibble with the Court's approach, but there still is no uncertainty added to the constitutional mix. The problem is that the Court did not apply the

33. The Seventh Amendment provides: "In Suits at common law, where the value in controversy shall exceed twenty dollars, the right of trial by jury shall be preserved, and no fact tried to a jury, shall be otherwise re-examined in any Court of the United States, than according to the rules of the common law."

balancing approach that seemed to carry the day in *Thomas* and *Schor*. Rather, Justice Brennan returned to the categorical approach he articulated for the *Northern Pipeline* plurality. He stated that a jury trial was required in this situation because the matter was a "private right." It was not a claim between the government and a private party and it was not so closely tied to a comprehensive federal regulatory scheme (as in *Thomas*) that it had the hallmarks of a public right.[34]

The Court remanded the case, leaving two questions unanswered. First, did the statute authorizing the bankruptcy courts provide for the conduct of jury trials? Congress later mooted this question by specifically providing the bankruptcy courts with authority to conduct jury trials. *See* Bankruptcy Reform Act of 1994, 108 Stat. 4106. The second question is more vexing: assuming that there was statutory authorization, is such authority consistent with both the Seventh Amendment and Article III?

The Court has not returned to the Seventh Amendment question. It has, however, continued to address the constitutional ability of the bankruptcy courts to adjudicate certain matters and, along the way, shed more light—although not necessarily more clarity—on the ability of Congress to assign Article III tasks to non-Article III adjudicators. We begin with perhaps the most comprehensive decision in this area in the last quarter-century.

STERN v. MARSHALL

131 S. Ct. 2594 (2011)

CHIEF JUSTICE ROBERTS delivered the opinion of the Court.

... This is the second time we have had occasion to weigh in on this long-running dispute between Vickie Lynn Marshall and E. Pierce Marshall over the fortune of J. Howard Marshall II, a man believed to have been one of the richest people in Texas. The Marshalls' litigation has worked its way through state and federal courts in Louisiana, Texas, and California, and two of those courts—a Texas state probate court and the Bankruptcy Court for the Central District of California—have reached contrary decisions on its merits. The Court of Appeals below held that the Texas state decision controlled, after concluding that the Bankruptcy Court lacked the authority to enter final judgment on a counterclaim that Vickie brought against Pierce in her bankruptcy proceeding.[35] To determine whether the Court of Appeals was correct in that regard, we must resolve two issues: (1) whether the Bankruptcy Court had the statutory authority under 28 U.S.C. § 157(b) to issue a final judgment on Vickie's counterclaim; and (2) if so, whether conferring that authority on the Bankruptcy Court is constitutional.

Although the history of this litigation is complicated, its resolution ultimately turns on very basic principles. Article III, § 1, of the Constitution commands that "[t]he judicial Power of the United States, shall be vested in one supreme Court, and in such inferior Courts as the Congress may from time to time ordain and establish." That Article further provides that the judges of those courts shall

34. Perhaps significantly, Justice Scalia concurred and argued that a public rights dispute *must* involve the government as a litigant.

35. [Footnote 1 in Court's opinion.] Because both Vickie and Pierce passed away during this litigation, the parties in this case are Vickie's estate and Pierce's estate. We continue to refer to them as "Vickie" and "Pierce."

hold their offices during good behavior, without diminution of salary. Those requirements of Article III were not honored here. The Bankruptcy Court in this case exercised the judicial power of the United States by entering final judgment on a common law tort claim, even though the judges of such courts enjoy neither tenure during good behavior nor salary protection. We conclude that, although the Bankruptcy Court had the statutory authority to enter judgment on Vickie's counterclaim, it lacked the constitutional authority to do so.

I

Of current relevance are two claims Vickie filed in an attempt to secure half of J. Howard's fortune. Known to the public as Anna Nicole Smith, Vickie was J. Howard's third wife and married him about a year before his death. Although J. Howard bestowed on Vickie many monetary and other gifts during their courtship and marriage, he did not include her in his will. Before J. Howard passed away, Vickie filed suit in Texas state probate court, asserting that Pierce—J. Howard's younger son—fraudulently induced J. Howard to sign a living trust that did not include her, even though J. Howard meant to give her half his property. Pierce denied any fraudulent activity and defended the validity of J. Howard's trust and, eventually, his will.

After J. Howard's death, Vickie filed a petition for bankruptcy in the Central District of California. Pierce filed a complaint in that bankruptcy proceeding, contending that Vickie had defamed him by inducing her lawyers to tell members of the press that he had engaged in fraud to gain control of his father's assets. The complaint sought a declaration that Pierce's defamation claim was not dischargeable in the bankruptcy proceedings. Pierce subsequently filed a proof of claim for the defamation action, meaning that he sought to recover damages for it from Vickie's bankruptcy estate. Vickie responded to Pierce's initial complaint by asserting truth as a defense to the alleged defamation and by filing a counterclaim for tortious interference with the gift she expected from J. Howard. As she had in state court, Vickie alleged that Pierce had wrongfully prevented J. Howard from taking the legal steps necessary to provide her with half his property.

On November 5, 1999, the Bankruptcy Court issued an order granting Vickie summary judgment on Pierce's claim for defamation. On September 27, 2000, after a bench trial, the Bankruptcy Court issued a judgment on Vickie's counterclaim in her favor. The court later awarded Vickie over $400 million in compensatory damages and $25 million in punitive damages.

In post-trial proceedings, Pierce argued that the Bankruptcy Court lacked [statutory] jurisdiction over Vickie's counterclaim. . . . The Bankruptcy Court in this case concluded that [it] . . . had the "power to enter judgment" [under the Bankruptcy Act]. . . .

The District Court disagreed. . . . The District Court accordingly concluded that . . . it was required to treat the Bankruptcy Court's judgment as "proposed[,] rather than final," and engage in an "independent review" of the record. Although the Texas state court had by that time conducted a jury trial on the merits of the parties' dispute and entered a judgment in Pierce's favor, the District Court declined to give that judgment preclusive effect and went on to decide the matter itself. Like the Bankruptcy Court, the District Court found that Pierce had tortiously interfered with Vickie's expectancy of a gift from J. Howard. The District Court awarded Vickie compensatory and punitive damages, each in the amount of $44,292,767.33.

The Court of Appeals reversed the District Court on a different ground, and we — in the first visit of the case to this Court — reversed the Court of Appeals on that issue. On remand from this Court, the Court of Appeals held that § 157 [of the Bankruptcy Act] mandated "a two-step approach" under which a bankruptcy judge may issue a final judgment in a proceeding only if the matter both "meets Congress' definition of a core proceeding *and* arises under or arises in title 11," the Bankruptcy Code. The court also reasoned that allowing a bankruptcy judge to enter final judgments on all counterclaims raised in bankruptcy proceedings "would certainly run afoul" of this Court's decision in *Northern Pipeline.* With those concerns in mind, the court concluded that Vickie's counterclaim did not meet that test. That holding made "the Texas probate court's judgment . . . the earliest final judgment entered on matters relevant to this proceeding," and therefore the Court of Appeals concluded that the District Court should have "afford[ed] preclusive effect" to the Texas "court's determination of relevant legal and factual issues."

We again granted certiorari.

II

[In this section of the opinion, the Court concluded that the Bankruptcy Code provided statutory authorization for the bankruptcy court to enter a final judgment on the state-law counterclaim.]

III

Although we conclude that § 157(b)(2)(C) permits the Bankruptcy Court to enter final judgment on Vickie's counterclaim, Article III of the Constitution does not.

A

Article III, § 1, of the Constitution mandates that "[t]he judicial Power of the United States, shall be vested in one supreme Court, and in such inferior Courts as the Congress may from time to time ordain and establish." The same section provides that the judges of those constitutional courts "shall hold their Offices during good Behaviour" and "receive for their Services[ ] a Compensation[ ] [that] shall not be diminished" during their tenure.

As its text and our precedent confirm, Article III is "an inseparable element of the constitutional system of checks and balances" that "both defines the power and protects the independence of the Judicial Branch." *Northern Pipeline.* Under "the basic concept of separation of powers . . . that flow[s] from the scheme of a tripartite government" adopted in the Constitution, "the 'judicial Power of the United States' . . . can no more be shared" with another branch than "the Chief Executive, for example, can share with the Judiciary the veto power, or the Congress share with the Judiciary the power to override a Presidential veto."

In establishing the system of divided power in the Constitution, the Framers considered it essential that "the judiciary remain[ ] truly distinct from both the legislature and the executive." The Federalist No. 78. As Hamilton put it, quoting Montesquieu, "'there is no liberty if the power of judging be not separated from the legislative and executive powers.'" *Ibid.*

We have recognized that the three branches are not hermetically sealed from one another, but it remains true that Article III imposes some basic limitations that the other branches may not transgress. Those limitations serve two related purposes. "Separation-of-powers principles are intended, in part, to protect each branch of government from incursion by the others. Yet the dynamic between and among the branches is not the only object of the Constitution's concern. The structural principles secured by the separation of powers protect the individual as well."

Article III protects liberty not only through its role in implementing the separation of powers, but also by specifying the defining characteristics of Article III judges. . . . By appointing judges to serve without term limits, and restricting the ability of the other branches to remove judges or diminish their salaries, the Framers sought to ensure that each judicial decision would be rendered, not with an eye toward currying favor with Congress or the Executive, but rather with the "[c]lear heads . . . and honest hearts" deemed "essential to good judges."

Article III could neither serve its purpose in the system of checks and balances nor preserve the integrity of judicial decisionmaking if the other branches of the Federal Government could confer the Government's "judicial Power" on entities outside Article III. That is why we have long recognized that, in general, Congress may not "withdraw from judicial cognizance any matter which, from its nature, is the subject of a suit at the common law, or in equity, or admiralty." *Murray's Lessee.* When a suit is made of "the stuff of the traditional actions at common law tried by the courts at Westminster in 1789," *Northern Pipeline* (Rehnquist, J., concurring in judgment), and is brought within the bounds of federal jurisdiction, the responsibility for deciding that suit rests with Article III judges in Article III courts. . . .

B

This is not the first time we have faced an Article III challenge to a bankruptcy court's resolution of a debtor's suit. In *Northern Pipeline,* we considered whether bankruptcy judges serving under the Bankruptcy Act of 1978 — appointed by the President and confirmed by the Senate, but lacking the tenure and salary guarantees of Article III — could "constitutionally be vested with jurisdiction to decide [a] state-law contract claim" against an entity that was not otherwise part of the bankruptcy proceedings. . . . The Court concluded that assignment of such state law claims for resolution by those judges "violates Art. III of the Constitution." . . .

The plurality in *Northern Pipeline* recognized that there was a category of cases involving "public rights" that Congress could constitutionally assign to "legislative" courts for resolution. That opinion concluded that this "public rights" exception extended "only to matters arising between" individuals and the Government "in connection with the performance of the constitutional functions of the executive or legislative departments . . . that historically could have been determined exclusively by those" branches. A full majority of the Court, while not agreeing on the scope of the exception, concluded that the doctrine did not encompass adjudication of the state law claim at issue in that case. . . .

A full majority of Justices in *Northern Pipeline* also rejected the debtor's argument that the bankruptcy court's exercise of jurisdiction was constitutional because the bankruptcy judge was acting merely as an adjunct of the district court or court of appeals. . . .

After our decision in *Northern Pipeline,* Congress revised the statutes governing bankruptcy jurisdiction and bankruptcy judges. In the 1984 Act, Congress . . . permitted the newly constituted bankruptcy courts to enter final judgments only in "core" proceedings.

With respect to such "core" matters, however, the bankruptcy courts under the 1984 Act exercise the same powers they wielded under the Bankruptcy Act of 1978. . . . As in *Northern Pipeline,* for example, the newly constituted bankruptcy courts are charged . . . with resolving "[a]ll matters of fact and law in whatever domains of the law to which" a counterclaim may lead. . . . As in *Northern Pipeline,* the new courts in core proceedings "issue final judgments, which are binding and enforceable even in the absence of an appeal." And, as in *Northern Pipeline,* the district courts review the judgments of the bankruptcy courts in core proceedings only under the usual limited appellate standards. That requires marked deference to, among other things, the bankruptcy judges' findings of fact.

C

Vickie and the dissent argue that the Bankruptcy Court's entry of final judgment on her state common law counterclaim was constitutional, despite the similarities between the bankruptcy courts under the 1978 Act and those exercising core jurisdiction under the 1984 Act. We disagree. It is clear that the Bankruptcy Court in this case exercised the "judicial Power of the United States" in purporting to resolve and enter final judgment on a state common law claim, just as the court did in *Northern Pipeline.* No "public right" exception excuses the failure to comply with Article III in doing so, any more than in *Northern Pipeline.* Vickie argues that this case is different because the defendant is a creditor in the bankruptcy. But the debtors' claims in the cases on which she relies were themselves federal claims under bankruptcy law, which would be completely resolved in the bankruptcy process of allowing or disallowing claims. Here Vickie's claim is a state law action independent of the federal bankruptcy law and not necessarily resolvable by a ruling on the creditor's proof of claim in bankruptcy. *Northern Pipeline* and our subsequent decision in *Granfinanciera* rejected the application of the "public rights" exception in such cases.

Nor can the bankruptcy courts under the 1984 Act be dismissed as mere adjuncts of Article III courts, any more than could the bankruptcy courts under the 1978 Act. The judicial powers the courts exercise in cases such as this remain the same, and a court exercising such broad powers is no mere adjunct of anyone.

1

Vickie's counterclaim cannot be deemed a matter of "public right" that can be decided outside the Judicial Branch. As explained above, in *Northern Pipeline* we rejected the argument that the public rights doctrine permitted a bankruptcy court to adjudicate a state law suit brought by a debtor against a company that had not filed a claim against the estate. Although our discussion of the public rights exception since that time has not been entirely consistent, and the exception has been the subject of some debate, this case does not fall within any of the various formulations of the concept that appear in this Court's opinions.

We first recognized the category of public rights in *Murray's Lessee.* That case involved the Treasury Department's sale of property belonging to a customs collector who had failed to transfer payments to the Federal Government that he had collected on its behalf. The plaintiff, who claimed title to the same land through a different transfer, objected that the Treasury Department's calculation of the deficiency and sale of the property was void, because it was a judicial act that could not be assigned to the Executive under Article III.

"To avoid misconstruction upon so grave a subject," the Court laid out the principles guiding its analysis. It confirmed that Congress cannot "withdraw from judicial cognizance any matter which, from its nature, is the subject of a suit at the common law, or in equity, or admiralty." The Court also recognized that "[a]t the same time there are matters, involving public rights, which may be presented in such form that the judicial power is capable of acting on them, and which are susceptible of judicial determination, but which congress may or may not bring within the cognizance of the courts of the United States, as it may deem proper."

As an example of such matters, the Court referred to cases [in which] "it depends upon the will of congress whether a remedy in the courts shall be allowed at all," so Congress could limit the extent to which a judicial forum was available. The challenge in *Murray's Lessee* to the Treasury Department's sale of the collector's land likewise fell within the "public rights" category of cases, because it could only be brought if the Federal Government chose to allow it by waiving sovereign immunity. The point of *Murray's Lessee* was simply that Congress may set the terms of adjudicating a suit when the suit could not otherwise proceed at all.

Subsequent decisions from this Court contrasted cases within the reach of the public rights exception — those arising "between the Government and persons subject to its authority in connection with the performance of the constitutional functions of the executive or legislative departments" — and those that were instead matters "of private right, that is, of the liability of one individual to another under the law as defined."[36] *Crowell v. Benson*. . . .

Shortly after *Northern Pipeline*, the Court rejected the limitation of the public rights exception to actions involving the Government as a party. The Court has continued, however, to limit the exception to cases in which the claim at issue derives from a federal regulatory scheme, or in which resolution of the claim by an expert government agency is deemed essential to a limited regulatory objective within the agency's authority. In other words, it is still the case that what makes a right "public" rather than private is that the right is integrally related to particular federal government action. . . .

Our decision in *Thomas v. Union Carbide Agricultural Products Co.*, for example, involved a data-sharing arrangement between companies under a federal statute providing that disputes about compensation between the companies would be

36. [Footnote 6 in Court's opinion.] Although the Court in *Crowell* went on to decide that the facts of the private dispute before it could be determined by a non-Article III tribunal in the first instance, subject to judicial review, the Court did so only after observing that the administrative adjudicator had only limited authority to make specialized, narrowly confined factual determinations regarding a particularized area of law and to issue orders that could be enforced only by action of the District Court. In other words, the agency in *Crowell* functioned as a true "adjunct" of the District Court. That is not the case here. See *infra*, at 34-36.

Although the dissent suggests that we understate the import of *Crowell* in this regard, the dissent itself recognizes — repeatedly — that *Crowell* by its terms addresses the determination of *facts* outside Article III. . . . *Crowell* may well have additional significance in the context of expert administrative agencies that oversee particular substantive federal regimes, but we have no occasion to and do not address those issues today. . . .

decided by binding arbitration. This Court held that the scheme did not violate Article III, explaining that "[a]ny right to compensation . . . results from [the statute] and does not depend on or replace a right to such compensation under state law."

Commodity Futures Trading Commission v. Schor concerned a statutory scheme that created a procedure for customers injured by a broker's violation of the federal commodities law to seek reparations from the broker before the Commodity Futures Trading Commission. A customer filed such a claim to recover a debit balance in his account, while the broker filed a lawsuit in Federal District Court to recover the same amount as lawfully due from the customer. The broker later submitted its claim to the CFTC, but after that agency ruled against the customer, the customer argued that agency jurisdiction over the broker's counterclaim violated Article III. This Court disagreed, but only after observing that (1) the claim and the counterclaim concerned a "single dispute" — the same account balance; (2) the CFTC's assertion of authority involved only "a narrow class of common law claims" in a "'particularized area of law'"; (3) the area of law in question was governed by "a specific and limited federal regulatory scheme" as to which the agency had "obvious expertise"; (4) the parties had freely elected to resolve their differences before the CFTC; and (5) CFTC orders were "enforceable only by order of the district court." Most significantly, given that the customer's reparations claim before the agency and the broker's counterclaim were competing claims to the same amount, the Court repeatedly emphasized that it was "necessary" to allow the agency to exercise jurisdiction over the broker's claim, or else "the reparations procedure would have been confounded."

The most recent case in which we considered application of the public rights exception — and the only case in which we have considered that doctrine in the bankruptcy context since *Northern Pipeline* — is *Granfinanciera*. . . . In *Granfinanciera* we rejected a bankruptcy trustee's argument that a fraudulent conveyance action filed on behalf of a bankruptcy estate against a noncreditor in a bankruptcy proceeding fell within the "public rights" exception. We explained that, "[i]f a statutory right is not closely intertwined with a federal regulatory program Congress has power to enact, and if that right neither belongs to nor exists against the Federal Government, then it must be adjudicated by an Article III court." We reasoned that fraudulent conveyance suits were "quintessentially suits at common law that more nearly resemble state law contract claims brought by a bankrupt corporation to augment the bankruptcy estate than they do creditors' hierarchically ordered claims to a pro rata share of the bankruptcy res." As a consequence, we concluded that fraudulent conveyance actions were "more accurately characterized as a private rather than a public right as we have used those terms in our Article III decisions."

Vickie's counterclaim — like the fraudulent conveyance claim at issue in *Granfinanciera* — does not fall within any of the varied formulations of the public rights exception in this Court's cases. It is not a matter that can be pursued only by grace of the other branches, as in *Murray's Lessee*, or one that "historically could have been determined exclusively by" those branches, *Northern Pipeline*. The claim is instead one under state common law between two private parties. It does not "depend[ ] on the will of congress," *Murray's Lessee*; Congress has nothing to do with it.

In addition, Vickie's claimed right to relief does not flow from a federal statutory scheme, as in *Thomas*. It is not "completely dependent upon" adjudication of a claim created by federal law, as in *Schor*. And in contrast to the objecting party in *Schor*, Pierce did not truly consent to resolution of Vickie's claim in the bankruptcy court proceedings. He had nowhere else to go if he wished to recover from Vickie's estate.

Furthermore, the asserted authority to decide Vickie's claim is not limited to a "particularized area of the law," as in *Crowell, Thomas*, and *Schor*. We deal here not with an agency but with a court, with substantive jurisdiction reaching any area of the *corpus juris*. This is not a situation in which Congress devised an "expert and inexpensive method for dealing with a class of questions of fact which are particularly suited to examination and determination by an administrative agency specially assigned to that task." The "experts" in the federal system at resolving common law counterclaims such as Vickie's are the Article III courts, and it is with those courts that her claim must stay.

The dissent reads our cases differently, and in particular contends that more recent cases view *Northern Pipeline* as "'establish[ing] only that Congress may not vest in a non-Article III court the power to adjudicate, render final judgment, and issue binding orders in a traditional contract action arising under state law, without consent of the litigants, and subject only to ordinary appellate review.'" Just so: Substitute "tort" for "contract," and that statement directly covers this case.

We recognize that there may be instances in which the distinction between public and private rights — at least as framed by some of our recent cases — fails to provide concrete guidance as to whether, for example, a particular agency can adjudicate legal issues under a substantive regulatory scheme. Given the extent to which this case is so markedly distinct from the agency cases discussing the public rights exception in the context of such a regime, however, we do not in this opinion express any view on how the doctrine might apply in that different context.

What is plain here is that this case involves the most prototypical exercise of judicial power: the entry of a final, binding judgment *by a court* with broad substantive jurisdiction, on a common law cause of action, when the action neither derives from nor depends upon any agency regulatory regime. If such an exercise of judicial power may nonetheless be taken from the Article III Judiciary simply by deeming it part of some amorphous "public right," then Article III would be transformed from the guardian of individual liberty and separation of powers we have long recognized into mere wishful thinking.

2

Vickie and the dissent next attempt to distinguish *Northern Pipeline* and *Granfinanciera* on the ground that Pierce, unlike the defendants in those cases, had filed a proof of claim in the bankruptcy proceedings. Given Pierce's participation in those proceedings, Vickie argues, the Bankruptcy Court had the authority to adjudicate her counterclaim under [other of the Court's] decisions. . . .

We do not agree. . . . Pierce's claim for defamation in no way affects the nature of Vickie's counterclaim for tortious interference as one at common law that simply attempts to augment the bankruptcy estate — the very type of claim that we held in *Northern Pipeline* and *Granfinanciera* must be decided by an Article III court.

* * * *

. . . In light of all the foregoing, we . . . see no reason to treat Vickie's counterclaim any differently from the fraudulent conveyance action in *Granfinanciera*. *Granfinanciera*'s distinction between actions that seek "to augment the bankruptcy estate" and those that seek "a pro rata share of the bankruptcy res," reaffirms that Congress may not bypass Article III simply because a proceeding may have *some* bearing on a bankruptcy case; the question is whether the action at issue stems from the bankruptcy itself or would necessarily be resolved in the claims allowance process. Vickie has failed to demonstrate that her counterclaim falls within one of the "limited circumstances" covered by the public rights exception, particularly given our conclusion that, "even with respect to matters that arguably fall within the scope of the 'public rights' doctrine, the presumption is in favor of Art. III courts." *Northern Pipeline* (plurality opinion).

3

Vickie additionally argues that the Bankruptcy Court's final judgment was constitutional because bankruptcy courts under the 1984 Act are properly deemed "adjuncts" of the district courts. We rejected a similar argument in *Northern Pipeline,* and our reasoning there holds true today.

To begin, as explained above, it is still the bankruptcy court itself that exercises the essential attributes of judicial power over a matter such as Vickie's counterclaim. The new bankruptcy courts, like the old, do not "ma[k]e only specialized, narrowly confined factual determinations regarding a particularized area of law" or engage in "statutorily channeled factfinding functions." *Northern Pipeline.* Instead, bankruptcy courts under the 1984 Act resolve "[a]ll matters of fact and law in whatever domains of the law to which" the parties' counterclaims might lead. *Id.*

In addition, whereas the adjunct agency in *Crowell v. Benson* "possessed only a limited power to issue compensation orders . . . [that] could be enforced only by order of the district court," a bankruptcy court resolving a counterclaim under [the Code] has the power to enter "appropriate orders and judgments"—including final judgments—subject to review only if a party chooses to appeal. It is thus no less the case here than it was in *Northern Pipeline* that "[t]he authority—and the responsibility—to make an informed, final determination . . . remains with" the bankruptcy judge, not the district court. Given that authority, a bankruptcy court can no more be deemed a mere "adjunct" of the district court than a district court can be deemed such an "adjunct" of the court of appeals. We certainly cannot accept the dissent's notion that judges who have the power to enter final, binding orders are the "functional[ ]" equivalent of "law clerks[ ] and the Judiciary's administrative officials." And even were we wrong in this regard, that would only confirm that such judges should not be in the business of entering final judgments in the first place.

* * * *

D

Finally, Vickie and her *amici* predict as a practical matter that restrictions on a bankruptcy court's ability to hear and finally resolve compulsory counterclaims will create significant delays and impose additional costs on the bankruptcy process. It goes without saying that "the fact that a given law or procedure is efficient, convenient, and useful in facilitating functions of government, standing alone, will not save it if it is contrary to the Constitution."

In addition, we are not convinced that the practical consequences of such limitations on the authority of bankruptcy courts to enter final judgments are as significant as Vickie and the dissent suggest. . . . [T]he framework Congress adopted in the 1984 Act already contemplates that certain state law matters in bankruptcy cases will be resolved by judges other than those of the bankruptcy courts. . . .

As described above, the current bankruptcy system also requires the district court to review *de novo* and enter final judgment on any matters that are "related to" the bankruptcy proceedings, and permits the district court to withdraw from the bankruptcy court any referred case, proceeding, or part thereof. . . . We do not think the removal of counterclaims such as Vickie's from core bankruptcy jurisdiction meaningfully changes the division of labor in the current statute; we agree with the United States that the question presented here is a "narrow" one.

If our decision today does not change all that much, then why the fuss? Is there really a threat to the separation of powers where Congress has conferred the judicial power outside Article III only over certain counterclaims in bankruptcy? The short but emphatic answer is yes. A statute may no more lawfully chip away at the authority of the Judicial Branch than it may eliminate it entirely. "Slight encroachments create new boundaries from which legions of power can seek new territory to capture." Although "[i]t may be that it is the obnoxious thing in its mildest and least repulsive form," we cannot overlook the intrusion: "illegitimate and unconstitutional practices get their first footing in that way, namely, by silent approaches and slight deviations from legal modes of procedure." We cannot compromise the integrity of the system of separated powers and the role of the Judiciary in that system, even with respect to challenges that may seem innocuous at first blush. . . .

Article III of the Constitution provides that the judicial power of the United States may be vested only in courts whose judges enjoy the protections set forth in that Article. We conclude today that Congress, in one isolated respect, exceeded that limitation in the Bankruptcy Act of 1984. The Bankruptcy Court below lacked the constitutional authority to enter a final judgment on a state law counterclaim that is not resolved in the process of ruling on a creditor's proof of claim. Accordingly, the judgment of the Court of Appeals is affirmed.

It is so ordered.

JUSTICE SCALIA, concurring.

I agree with the Court's interpretation of our Article III precedents, and I accordingly join its opinion. I adhere to my view, however, that — our contrary precedents notwithstanding — "a matter of public rights . . . must at a minimum arise between the government and others."

The sheer surfeit of factors that the Court was required to consider in this case should arouse the suspicion that something is seriously amiss with our jurisprudence in this area. I count at least seven different reasons given in the Court's opinion for concluding that an Article III judge was required to adjudicate this lawsuit: that it was one "under state common law" which was "not a matter that can be pursued only by grace of the other branches," that it was "not 'completely dependent upon' adjudication of a claim created by federal law," that "Pierce did not truly consent to resolution of Vickie's claim in the bankruptcy court proceedings," that "the asserted authority to decide Vickie's claim is not limited to a 'particularized area of the law,'" that "there was never any reason to believe that the process of adjudicating Pierce's proof of claim would necessarily resolve Vickie's counterclaim," that the trustee was not "asserting a right of recovery created by federal bankruptcy law," and that the Bankruptcy Judge "ha[d] the power to enter 'appropriate orders and judgments'—including final judgments—subject to review only if a party chooses to appeal."

Apart from their sheer numerosity, the more fundamental flaw in the many tests suggested by our jurisprudence is that they have nothing to do with the text or tradition of Article III. For example, Article III gives no indication that state-law claims have preferential entitlement to an Article III judge; nor does it make pertinent the extent to which the area of the law is "particularized." The multifactors relied upon today seem to have entered our jurisprudence almost randomly.

Leaving aside certain adjudications by federal administrative agencies, which are governed (for better or worse) by our landmark decision in *Corwell v. Benson*, in my view an Article III judge is required in *all* federal adjudications, unless there is a firmly established historical practice to the contrary. For that reason—and not because of some intuitive balancing of benefits and harms—I agree that Article III judges are not required in the context of territorial courts, courts-martial, or true "public rights" cases. . . . Vickie points to no historical practice that authorizes a non-Article III judge to adjudicate a counterclaim of the sort at issue here.

JUSTICE BREYER, with whom JUSTICE GINSBURG, JUSTICE SOTOMAYOR, and JUSTICE KAGAN join, dissenting.

* * * *

. . . The question before us is whether the Bankruptcy Court possessed jurisdiction to adjudicate Vickie Marshall's counterclaim. I agree with the Court that the bankruptcy statute authorizes the bankruptcy court to adjudicate the counterclaim. But I do not agree with the majority about the statute's constitutionality. I believe the statute is consistent with the Constitution's delegation of the "judicial Power of the United States" to the Judicial Branch of Government. Art. III, § 1. Consequently, it is constitutional.

I

My disagreement with the majority's conclusion stems in part from my disagreement about the way in which it interprets, or at least emphasizes, certain precedents. In my view, the majority overstates the current relevance of statements this Court made in an 1856 case, *Murray's Lessee*, and it overstates the importance of an analysis that did not command a Court majority in *Northern Pipeline*, and that was subsequently disavowed. At the same time, I fear the Court understates the importance of a watershed opinion widely thought to demonstrate the constitutional basis for the current authority of administrative agencies to adjudicate private disputes, namely, *Crowell v. Benson*. And it fails to follow the analysis that this Court more recently has held applicable to the evaluation of claims of a kind before us here, namely, claims that a congressional delegation of adjudicatory authority violates separation-of-powers principles derived from Article III. See *Thomas v. Union Carbide Agricultural Products Co., Commodity Futures Trading Comm'n v. Schor*,. . . .

I shall describe these cases in some detail in order to explain why I believe we should put less weight than does the majority upon the statement in *Murray's Lessee* and the analysis followed by the *Northern Pipeline* plurality and instead should apply the approach this Court has applied in *Crowell, Thomas*, and *Schor*.

A

In *Murray's Lessee*, the Court held that the Constitution permitted an executive official, through summary, nonjudicial proceedings, to attach the assets of a customs collector whose account was deficient. . . . In the course of its opinion, the Court wrote:

> "[W]e do not consider congress can either withdraw from judicial cognizance any matter which, from its nature, is the subject of a suit at the common law, or in equity, or admiralty; nor, on the other hand, can it bring under the judicial power a matter which, from its nature, is not a subject for judicial determination. At the same time there are matters, involving public rights, which may be presented in such form that the judicial power is capable of acting on them, and which are susceptible of judicial determination, but which congress may or may not bring within the cognizance of the courts of the United States, as it may deem proper."

The majority reads the first part of the statement's first sentence as authoritatively defining the boundaries of Article III. I would read the statement in a less absolute way. For one thing, the statement is in effect dictum. For another, it is the remainder of the statement, announcing a distinction between "public rights" and "private rights," that has had the more lasting impact. Later Courts have seized on that distinction when *upholding* non-Article III adjudication, not when striking it down. The one exception is *Northern Pipeline*, where a plurality, not a majority, read the statement roughly in the way the Court does today.

B

At the same time, I believe the majority places insufficient weight on *Crowell*, a seminal case that clarified the scope of the dictum in *Murray's Lessee*. In that case, the Court considered whether Congress could grant to an Article I administrative agency the power to adjudicate an employee's workers' compensation claim against his employer. The Court assumed that an Article III court would review the agency's decision *de novo* in respect to questions of law but it would conduct a less searching review (looking to see only if the agency's award was "supported by evidence in the record") in respect to questions of fact. The Court pointed out that the case involved a dispute between private persons (a matter of "private rights") and . . . it upheld Congress' delegation of primary factfinding authority to the agency. . . .

Crowell has been hailed as "the greatest of the cases validating administrative adjudication." Yet, in a footnote, the majority distinguishes *Crowell* as a case in which the Court upheld the delegation of adjudicatory authority to an administrative agency simply because the agency's power to make the "specialized, narrowly confined factual determinations" at issue arising in a "particularized area of law," made the agency a "true 'adjunct' of the District Court." Were *Crowell's* holding as narrow as the majority suggests, one could question the validity of Congress' delegation of authority to adjudicate disputes among private parties to other agencies . . . thereby resurrecting important legal questions previously thought to have been decided.

C

The majority, in my view, overemphasizes the precedential effect of the plurality opinion in *Northern Pipeline*. . . . Four Members of the Court wrote that Congress could grant adjudicatory authority to a non-Article III judge only where (1) the judge sits on a "territorial cour[t]" (2) the judge conducts a "courts-martial," or (3) the case involves a "public right," namely, a "matter" that "at a minimum arise[s] 'between the government and others.'" Two other Members of the Court, without accepting these limitations, agreed with the result because the case involved a breach of contract claim brought by the bankruptcy trustee on behalf of the bankruptcy estate against a third party who was not part of the bankruptcy proceeding, and none of the Court's preceding cases (which, the two Members wrote, "do not admit of easy synthesis") had "gone so far as to sanction th[is] type of adjudication."

Three years later, the Court held that *Northern Pipeline*

> "establishes only that Congress may not vest in a non-Article III court the power to adjudicate, render final judgment, and issue binding orders in a traditional contract action arising under state law, without consent of the litigants, and subject only to ordinary appellate review." *Thomas.*

D

Rather than leaning so heavily on the approach taken by the plurality in *Northern Pipeline,* I would look to this Court's more recent Article III cases *Thomas* and *Schor*—cases that commanded a clear majority. In both cases the Court took a more pragmatic approach to the constitutional question. It sought to determine whether, in the particular instance, the challenged delegation of adjudicatory authority posed a genuine and serious threat that one branch of Government sought to aggrandize its own constitutionally delegated authority by encroaching upon a field of authority that the Constitution assigns exclusively to another branch.

1

In *Thomas,* the statute in question required pesticide manufacturers to submit to binding arbitration claims for compensation owed for the use by one manufacturer of the data of another to support its federal pesticide registration. After describing *Northern Pipeline*'s holding . . . the Court stated that "*practical attention to substance* rather than doctrinaire reliance on formal categories should inform application of Article III." It indicated that Article III's requirements could not be "determined" by "the identity of the parties alone," or by the "private rights"/"public rights" distinction. And it upheld the arbitration provision of the statute.

The Court pointed out that the right in question was created by a federal statute, it "represent[s] a pragmatic solution to the difficult problem of spreading [certain] costs," and the statute "does not preclude review of the arbitration proceeding by an Article III court." The Court concluded:

> "Given the nature of the right at issue and the concerns motivating the Legislature, we do not think this system threatens the independent role of the Judiciary in our constitutional scheme."

2

. . . The question at issue in *Schor* involved a delegation of authority to an agency to adjudicate a counterclaim. A customer brought before the Commodity Futures Trading Commission (CFTC) a claim for reparations against his commodity futures broker. The customer noted that his brokerage account showed that he owed the broker money, but he said that the broker's unlawful actions had produced that debit balance, and he sought damages. The broker brought a counterclaim seeking the money that the account showed the customer owed. This Court had to decide whether agency adjudication of such a counterclaim is consistent with Article III.

In doing so, the Court expressly "declined to adopt formalistic and unbending rules." Rather, it "weighed a number of factors, none of which has been deemed determinative, with an eye to the practical effect that the congressional action will have on the constitutionally assigned role of the federal judiciary." Those relevant factors include (1) "the origins and importance of the right to be adjudicated"; (2) "the extent to which the non-Article III forum exercises the range of jurisdiction and powers normally vested only in Article III courts"; (3) the extent to which the delegation nonetheless reserves judicial power for exercise by Article III courts; (4) the presence or "absence of consent to an initial adjudication before a non-Article III tribunal"; and (5) "the concerns that drove Congress to depart from" adjudication in an Article III court.

* * * *

Applying this analysis, the Court upheld the agency's authority to adjudicate the counterclaim. The Court conceded that the adjudication might be of a kind traditionally decided by a court and that the rights at issue were "private," not "public." But, the Court said, the CFTC deals only with a "'particularized area of law'"; the decision to invoke the CFTC forum is "left entirely to the parties"; Article III courts can review the agency's findings of fact under "the same 'weight of the evidence' standard sustained in *Crowell*" and review its "legal determinations . . . *de novo*"; and the agency's "counterclaim jurisdiction" was necessary to make "workable" a "reparations procedure," which constitutes an important part of a congressionally enacted "regulatory scheme." The Court concluded that for these and other reasons "the magnitude of any intrusion on the Judicial Branch can only be termed *de minimis.*"

II

A

This case law, as applied in *Thomas* and *Schor*, requires us to determine . . . through an examination of [the five] relevant factors [from *Schor*] whether that delegation constitutes a significant encroachment by the Legislative or Executive Branches of Government upon the realm of authority that Article III reserves for exercise by the Judicial Branch of Government. . . . The presence of "private rights" does not automatically determine the outcome of the question but requires a more "searching" examination of the relevant factors.

Insofar as the majority would apply more formal standards, it simply disregards recent, controlling precedent. . . .

B

Applying *Schor's* approach here, I conclude that the delegation of adjudicatory authority before us is constitutional. A grant of authority to a bankruptcy court to adjudicate compulsory counterclaims does not violate any constitutional separation-of-powers principle related to Article III.

First, I concede that *the nature of the claim to be adjudicated* argues against my conclusion. Vickie Marshall's counterclaim—a kind of tort suit—resembles "a suit at the common law." *Murray's Lessee.* Although not determinative of the question, a delegation of authority to a non-Article III judge to adjudicate a claim of that kind poses a heightened risk of encroachment on the Federal Judiciary. . . .

At the same time the significance of this factor is mitigated here by the fact that bankruptcy courts often decide claims that similarly resemble various common-law actions. . . .

Of course, in this instance the state-law question is embedded in a debtor's counterclaim, not a creditor's claim. But the counterclaim is "compulsory." It "arises out of the transaction or occurrence that is the subject matter of the opposing party's claim." Fed. Rule Civ. Proc. 13(a); Fed. Rule Bkrtcy. Proc. 7013. Thus, resolution of the counterclaim will often turn on facts identical to, or at least related to, those at issue in a creditor's claim that is undisputedly proper for the bankruptcy court to decide.

Second, *the nature of the non-Article III tribunal* argues in favor of constitutionality. That is because the tribunal is made up of judges who enjoy considerable protection from improper political influence. Unlike the 1978 Act . . . current law provides that the federal courts of appeals appoint federal bankruptcy judges. Bankruptcy judges are removable by the circuit judicial counsel . . . and only for cause. Their salaries are pegged to those of federal district court judges, and the cost of their courthouses and other work-related expenses are paid by the Judiciary,. . . . [F]unctionally, bankruptcy judges can be compared to magistrate judges, law clerks, and the Judiciary's administrative officials, whose lack of Article III tenure and compensation protections do not endanger the independence of the Judicial Branch.

Third, *the control exercised by Article III judges over bankruptcy proceedings* argues in favor of constitutionality. Article III judges control and supervise the bankruptcy court's determinations—at least to the same degree that Article III judges supervised the agency's determinations in *Crowell,* if not more so. Any party may appeal those determinations to the federal district court, where the federal judge will review all determinations of fact for clear error and will review all determinations of law *de novo.* . . .

Moreover, in one important respect Article III judges maintain greater control over the bankruptcy court proceedings at issue here. . . . The District Court here may "withdraw, in whole or in part, any case or proceeding referred [to the Bankruptcy Court] . . . on its own motion or on timely motion of any party, for cause shown." . . .

Fourth, the fact that *the parties have consented* to Bankruptcy Court jurisdiction argues in favor of constitutionality, and strongly so. Pierce Marshall . . . appeared voluntarily in Bankruptcy Court as one of Vickie Marshall's creditors. . . . He need not have filed a claim . . . he could have litigated it in a state or federal court after distribution. Thus, Pierce Marshall likely had "an alternative forum to the bankruptcy court in which to pursue [his] clai[m]." *Granfinanciera.*

* * * *

. . . The majority argues that Pierce Marshall "did not truly consent" to bankruptcy jurisdiction, but filing a proof of claim was sufficient in . . . *Granfinanciera,* and there is no relevant distinction between the claims filed in those cases and the claim filed here.

Fifth, *the nature and importance of the legislative purpose served* by the grant of adjudicatory authority to bankruptcy tribunals argues strongly in favor of constitutionality. . . . Article I, § 8, of the Constitution explicitly grants Congress the "Power To . . . establish . . . uniform Laws on the subject of Bankruptcies throughout the United States." . . .

* * * *

The consequent importance to the total bankruptcy scheme of permitting the trustee in bankruptcy to assert counterclaims against claimants, *and resolving those counterclaims in a bankruptcy court,* is reflected in the fact that Congress included "counterclaims by the estate against persons filing claims against the estate" on its list of "[c]ore proceedings." And it explains the difference, reflected in this Court's opinions, between a claimant's and a nonclaimant's constitutional right to a jury trial. . . .

Consequently a bankruptcy court's determination of such matters has more than "some bearing on a bankruptcy case." It plays a critical role in Congress' constitutionally based effort to create an efficient, effective federal bankruptcy system. At the least, that is what Congress concluded. We owe deference to that determination, which shows the absence of any legislative or executive motive, intent, purpose, or desire to encroach upon areas that Article III reserves to judges to whom it grants tenure and compensation protections.

Considering these factors together, I conclude that, as in *Schor,* "the magnitude of any intrusion on the Judicial Branch can only be termed *de minimis.*" I would similarly find the statute before us constitutional.

III

The majority predicts that as a "practical matter" today's decision "does not change all that much." But I doubt that is so. Consider a typical case: A tenant files for bankruptcy. The landlord files a claim for unpaid rent. The tenant asserts a counterclaim for damages suffered by the landlord's (1) failing to fulfill his obligations as lessor, and (2) improperly recovering possession of the premises by misrepresenting the facts in housing court. . . . This state-law counterclaim does not "ste[m] from the bankruptcy itself," it would not "necessarily be resolved in the claims allowance process," and it would require the debtor to prove damages suffered by the lessor's failures, the extent to which the landlord's representations to the housing court were untrue, and damages suffered by improper recovery of possession of the premises. Thus, under the majority's holding, the federal district judge, not the bankruptcy judge, would have to hear and resolve the counterclaim.

Why is that a problem? Because these types of disputes arise in bankruptcy court with some frequency. Because the volume of bankruptcy cases is staggering, involving almost 1.6 million filings last year, compared to a federal district court docket of around 280,000 civil cases and 78,000 criminal cases. . . . Because . . . compulsory counterclaims involve the same factual disputes as the claims that may be finally adjudicated by the bankruptcy courts. Because under these circumstances, a constitutionally required game of jurisdictional ping-pong between courts would lead to inefficiency, increased cost, delay, and needless additional suffering among those faced with bankruptcy.

For these reasons, with respect, I dissent.

Discussion and Questions

Stern is a truly significant case in this area. The Court appears to adopt a more categorical approach to these issues than was suggested in *Thomas* and *Schor*. Yet Chief Justice Roberts cites both of those decisions in his opinion. How is that possible? We suppose the true answer is that we do not know, at least not yet.

Notice also that the Court continues to be coy concerning the import of a party's consent to adjudication before a non-Article III adjudicator. Should consent matter given the values at stake? Why or why not?

The Supreme Court has continued its interest in this area of the law in the aftermath of *Stern*. In *Executive Benefits Insurance Agency v. Arkinson*, 134 S. Ct. 2165 (2014), the Court considered how a bankruptcy court (and by extension a federal district court) should proceed when confronted with a *Stern* claim. In other words, when there is a claim before a bankruptcy judge that Congress has described as one over which the bankruptcy court could statutorily enter final judgment, but that claim is also one that the Court has held in *Stern* cannot be constitutionally finally adjudicated in a non-Article III tribunal, what can be done?

In *Arkinson*, the Court determined that when confronted with this situation "the proper course is [for the bankruptcy court] to issue proposed findings of fact and conclusions of law. The district court will then review the claims *de novo* and enter judgment. This approach accords with the bankruptcy statute and does not implicate the constitutional defect identified by *Stern*." *Id.* at 2170. The interesting thing about *Stern* and *Arkinson* in combination is that they make a dramatic constitutional statement about separation of power—*Stern*—but make the practical import of the constitutional holding negligible—*Arkinson.*

And it appears that the Court is not done in this area. It granted certiorari in *Wellness International Net-Work Ltd. v. Sharif* to be heard in the October 2014 Term after this text will have gone to print. As relevant to the present discussion, the Court will decide an issue left open in both *Stern* and *Arkinson*: whether the consent of the parties may cure a *Stern* defect. In the case under review, the United States Court of Appeals for the Seventh Circuit stated: "We hold that a constitutional objection based on *Stern* is not waivable because it implicates separation-of-powers principles." *Wellness Int'l Net-Work, Ltd. v. Sharif*, 727 F.3d 751, 755 (7th Cir. 2013).

PROBLEM 4-3

Are Magistrate Judges Next?

Smith and Jones entered into a contract. Thereafter, Smith claimed that Jones breached the agreement, and Smith filed a lawsuit in a federal district court. Jurisdiction was based on diversity of citizenship. Pursuant to a standing order of the district court, when the case was filed the Clerk of Court sent the parties a form inquiring whether they would both agree to have the matter assigned to a United States Magistrate Judge for all purposes including entry of a final judgment. Both Smith and Jones executed the form and returned it to the Clerk. The case was thereafter randomly assigned to a United States Magistrate Judge for all purposes.

After discovery, Jones filed a motion for summary judgment under Federal Rule of Civil Procedure 56. The Magistrate Judge granted the motion and entered final judgment in favor of Jones. Smith filed a timely appeal.

On appeal, one of Smith's arguments is that *Stern* (and *Arkinson*) suggest that the Supreme Court's prior decisions affirming the constitutionality of the authority magistrate judges wield have been undermined. Moreover, Smith argues that the defect in the assignment of this case to a magistrate judge cannot be cured by his consent.

You are a clerk to a judge on the court of appeals considering the case. What will you tell your judge about Smith's arguments? Why?

Where do matters stand on this issue today? The true answer is that we really do not know. It is difficult to reconcile *Northern Pipeline, Thomas, Schor, Granfinanciera, Stern,* and *Arkinson.* We have attempted to do so in Figure 4-2 below, which is based in some measure on a synthesis articulated in RICHARD H. FALLON, JR., ET AL., HART AND WECHSLER'S THE FEDERAL COURTS AND THE FEDERAL SYSTEM 401 (5th ed. 2003), an earlier edition of a major text in the Federal Courts arena.

FIGURE 4-2

Non-Article III Adjudicators A Checklist (of Sorts)

STEP ONE

Is the assignment of the adjudication constitutional under Article III?

A. Does the assignment come within one of the following "exceptions" to Article III:

1. Territorial Courts
2. Military Courts
3. Disputes concerning public rights

OR

B. Does a balancing of Article I and Article III values justify the assignment?

STEP TWO

Even if the assignment is permissible under Article III, are there individual rights issues that render the assignment unconstitutional? Such issues could include:

A. Due Process;
B. Equal Protection;
C. The Habeas Corpus Suspension Clause; or
D. The Seventh Amendment.

A FINAL THOUGHT ABOUT THE FUTURE

Up until this point, we have largely been assuming that Congress has assigned a matter otherwise falling within the categories to which the Constitution provides that the "judicial Power" might extend to some *domestic* body other than an Article III court. That body might be a tribunal established under Article I, an administrative agency, or an Article III adjunct. However, the common feature is that all of these bodies are themselves part of the American constitutional system.

There is another possibility (in addition to a state court). What if Congress were to assign an Article III matter to a supra-national entity? Imagine, for example, that the United States entered into a multilateral treaty by which it agreed that disputes by citizens of signatory nations concerning the validity of patents would be resolved by an entity to be formed called the World Court for Patent Disputes. Judgments of this court would be enforceable in the domestic courts of signatory nations. If a United States citizen challenged the assignment of the adjudication of such disputes to the World Court for Patent Disputes, how should that argument be resolved? Should one use the same rubric utilized in the Article I court context? Or is it more appropriate to evaluate such assignments to supra-national bodies in the same way one would evaluate the assignment of adjudicator tasks to state courts? The answer really is that we do not know because the issue has received scant attention thus far. It seems likely, however, that it is on the horizon.[37]

You can test your understanding of the material we have covered thus far by considering Problem 4-4:

PROBLEM 4-4

Is NAFTA Nifty Under Article III

Generally, United States trade law prohibits the "dumping" of foreign goods in the United States as well as the sale of foreign goods here that are subject to a "countervailing subsidy" in the importing nation.[38] When complaints concerning these issues are lodged with the United States Department of Commerce, an administrative agency called the International Trade Commission (ITC) must investigate. If the ITC concludes that the complaint has merit, countervailing duties or other equalizing measures are taken to address the violation of the relevant trade laws.

Review of ITC decisions is available in the United States Court of International Trade, an Article III court. Appeals from this court may be taken to the United States Court of Appeals for the Federal Circuit and, thereafter, by writ of certiorari to the Supreme Court.

In 1992, the United States, Mexico, and Canada entered into the North American Free Trade Agreement (NAFTA). NAFTA essentially creates a free trade zone among these three nations. Congress approved NAFTA and enacted the North American Free Trade Implementation Act, 107 Stat. 2057 (the "Act"), to bring into force certain aspects of the Agreement. For present purposes, you should know that Chapter 19 of NAFTA as implemented by the Act alters the means by which decisions of the ITC are reviewed. Specifically, these provisions allow an "interested party" (usually the foreign business found to have imported goods in violation of United States trade law) to request that review of the ITC determination be had by a NAFTA binational panel, referred to as a BNP.

The BNPs are made up of private individuals selected from a preexisting list of panel members maintained for service on these tribunals. The BNPs are required to review the ITC's decision under the same United States domestic law standards as would United States courts. Decisions of the BNPs are final and

37. Depicted visually, the issue we raise here would be akin to adding a fourth box to Figure 4-1, *supra*, that would include relevant supra-national adjudicatory bodies.

38. Dumping refers to the sale of imported goods at below-market prices. A countervailing subsidy concerns a situation in which a foreign nation provides certain types of economic subsidies to its businesses without similar benefits' being made available to non-domestic businesses.

binding on all parties subject only to very limited review to a superior BNP within the NAFTA structure. Appeals to domestic courts are expressly prohibited.

Is the assignment of these matters under United States trade law to a BNP constituted under Chapter 19 of NAFTA and the Act constitutional? Do the doctrines we have discussed thus far answer the question or do we need additional theories to address the issue? Even if the assignment of these matters to a BNP is constitutional, is there nevertheless a problem because there is no Article III appellate review?

2. *Assignment of Non-Article III Matters to Article III Courts*

To this point, we have been considering when Congress may appropriately bestow jurisdiction over a matter set forth in Article III, section 2, to a non-Article III adjudicator. This part briefly considers the converse issue: Is it appropriate for Congress to empower an Article III court to undertake tasks outside the jurisdictional grants of Article III, section 2? You may likely guess given what you have learned thus far in this course that the state of the law in this area is not entirely clear. It is not, however, as murky as many other areas of law we study in the Federal Courts course.

The question we address in this section itself breaks down into two distinct situations. First, when, if ever, may Congress constitutionally assign to Article III courts tasks that are non-judicial in nature? Second, when, if ever, may Congress assign to Article III courts the adjudication of cases (i.e., judicial tasks) that do not come within the scope of the jurisdictional grants in Article III, section 2? We consider each of these situations in turn.

a. Assignment of Non-Judicial Tasks to Article III Courts

There are strong constitutional reasons why Congress has, at most, extremely limited authority to assign non-judicial tasks to Article III courts. As we learned in Chapter 2, there are several constitutional doctrines designed to ensure that Article III courts decide only live disputes between or among litigants with actual stakes in the matter at hand. It is for this reason that the Court has interpreted Article III to require a "case" or "controversy" as the key to the federal courthouse door.

If the federal courts were able to act outside a concrete case or controversy, it would potentially raise serious and fundamental constitutional issues. First, the placement of such power in the Article III branch of the federal government would arguably expand the power of that branch well beyond that envisioned by the vesting of the "judicial Power of the United States." *See* U.S. CONST. art. III, § 1. Without a case or controversy, one could say that the Article III adjudicator is no longer acting as a court; instead it is acting as a legislature or executive entity in form if not substance. While the Constitution may tolerate and even embrace the counter-majoritarian nature of the Article III courts in cases and controversies, there would at the very least be serious arguments concerning the anti-democratic effects of allowing this governmental entity to exercise power without the "case or controversy" constraint.

A second reason for not allowing Article III courts to perform non-judicial tasks is that doing so raises the risk of conflicts between and among the branches. When Congress assigns a non-judicial task to an Article III court, it is far more tempting for it to attach conditions or requirements that could set the branches on a collision course with one another than when Congress merely assigns the adjudication of a case to the court. Take for example the situation in *Hayburn's Case,* 2 U.S. 408 (1792). Congress had enacted legislation directing federal judges to set the amount of pensions to be paid to veterans of the Revolutionary War. However, these decisions were subject to revision by the Secretary of War, an executive branch official. The Court essentially held that Article III judges could not perform this task because the decisions made were not final. We have discussed the general importance of finality elsewhere.[39] Our point here is that the assignment of this at least arguably non-judicial task led to a conflict among the branches that likely would have been avoided if the assigned task had been truly judicial in nature.

It would be useful if there were a hard-and-fast rule that Congress may not assign non-judicial functions to Article III courts. And this *probably* is the rule. The difficulty comes with two decisions rendered in the 1980s that create at least some arguable ambiguity in the area. In *Morrison v. Olson,* 487 U.S. 654 (1988), the Court upheld a statute authorizing a panel of Article III judges to make certain decisions concerning the appointment and conduct of independent counsel.[40] Second, in *Mistretta v. United States,* 488 U.S. 361 (1989), the Court upheld the constitutionality of including Article III judges on the United States Sentencing Commission, an entity Congress created to, among other things, establish uniform guidelines for federal criminal sentencing.

It is possible to read *Morrison* and *Mistretta* as moving away from a prohibition against the assignment of non-judicial tasks to Article III judges. On the other hand, it is also possible to fit these decisions within the rule in that they each dealt with matters very closely connected to adjudication even if not precisely in the context of a specific case. At a minimum, they cast some question over the likely rule. As unsatisfying as it may be, this is the state of the law.

b. Assignment of the Adjudication of Cases to Article III Courts Outside the Scope of the Jurisdictional Grants in Article III, Section 2

The concerns that underlie the likely rule discussed above concerning non-judicial tasks do not have weight if Congress assigns to Article III courts the adjudication of actual cases or controversies outside the ambit of Article III, section 2. One need not be concerned that a court is not acting as a court when deciding an actual case; after all, that is what courts do. Nor are the concerns about inter-branch tensions likely to be heightened in this context. Nevertheless, the Court has indicated—albeit not with a single voice—that Congress likely does not have the authority to assign such matters for adjudication by an Article III court.

39. See, e.g., Chapter 3.

40. By "independent counsel" we refer to individuals appointed to investigate potential crimes or other misdeeds by high-ranking government officials. Perhaps the most famous contemporary example of an independent counsel is Kenneth Starr, who investigated President Clinton in connection with, among other things, the Monica Lewinsky scandal.

The starting point for discussion is the confusing set of opinions in *National Mutual Insurance Co. v. Tidewater Transfer Co.*, 337 U.S. 582 (1949). The issue in that case concerned the constitutionality of a federal statute providing that a citizen of the District of Columbia was to be considered a citizen of a "state" for purposes of diversity jurisdiction in federal court. A corporate citizen of Virginia sued a corporate citizen of the District of Columbia in federal court. The district court dismissed the suit on the ground that Congress could not authorize such a suit under Article III because the District was not a state. The Court of Appeals affirmed the dismissal.

The Supreme Court reversed, but the Court was unable to marshal a majority opinion. Justice Jackson announced the judgment of the Court and wrote for himself as well as Justices Black and Burton. Jackson concluded that the District was not a state for Article III purposes but that this did not mean that Congress lacked power to extend federal court jurisdiction over the case at hand. He argued that so long as the extension of federal court jurisdiction was "necessary and proper," *see* U.S. Const. art. I, § 8, cl. 18, to utilize an Article I power, Congress had the power to make the assignment. In *Tidewater*, Jackson concluded that Congress was utilizing its power to make laws and regulations concerning the District of Columbia, *see* U.S. Const. art. I, § 8, cl. 17, and, therefore, the assignment of suits involving District citizens in diversity situations was appropriate.

All six other justices strongly rejected Jackson's position.[41] They all agreed that Congress could not constitutionally extend federal jurisdiction to cases or controversies outside the scope of Article III, section 2. According to these justices, Article III, section 2, sets the absolute limit of the potential jurisdiction of federal courts. To go beyond these limits would unconstitutionally expand the power of the federal courts at the expense of the states, thus raising an issue of federalism. Justice Frankfurter also argued in his dissent that allowing Congress to assign cases outside the scope of Article III, section 2, to federal courts would be a dangerous precedent in terms of separation of powers. Using what we would think of as a slippery-slope argument, Frankfurter argued that, if Congress could assign such matters for adjudication in Article III courts, what would prevent Congress from directing federal courts to issue advisory opinions? If Congress could take that action, it could undermine one of the fundamental distinctions separating the judiciary from other governmental actors.

Where are we left after *Tidewater*? The Court itself has not directly returned to the issue since. One can say with certainty that a majority of the Court has never embraced the power of Congress to assign non-Article III cases to Article III courts. On the other hand, no single opinion of the Court has squarely rejected the point either. There are strong reasons based on both federalism and separation of powers to believe that, if push came to shove, the Court would not approve of the assignment of these cases to Article III courts. Yet there is enough uncertainty here to warrant caution in approaching the issue. We leave the point

41. The Court ultimately reversed the lower court ruling because two of these six justices (Justice Rutledge and Justice Murphy) believed that an earlier decision holding that the word "state" in Article III did not include the District should be overruled. Therefore, they concluded that the case at issue did come within the scope of Article III, section 2. They thus concurred only in the judgment and not Justice Jackson's reasoning. Indeed, Justice Rutledge began his dissent by stating, "I strongly dissent from the reasons assigned to support [the judgment] in the opinion of Mr. Justice Jackson." *National Mut. Ins. Co.*, 337 U.S. at 604 (Rutledge, J., dissenting).

for now. However, we will return to it in another form in Chapter 5 concerning "arising under" jurisdiction when we consider the theory of protective jurisdiction.

D. SOME ADDITIONAL PROBLEMS

The problems that follow provide additional practice concerning the topics covered in this chapter:

PROBLEM 4-5

An Article I (or Article IV) Infection?

In 2003, the Supreme Court decided *Nguyen v. United States*, 539 U.S. 69 (2003). Nguyen had been convicted of violating certain federal drug laws. He appealed his conviction to the United States Court of Appeals for the Ninth Circuit. His appeal was heard by a panel of three judges. All three judges voted to affirm the conviction.

The issue in the case concerned the nature of the panel that heard the appeal. Two of the three panel members were Circuit Judges on the Ninth Circuit. In other words, they were Article III judges. The third panel member was not. Instead, he was the Chief Judge of the District Court for the Northern Mariana Islands. That court is a territorial court that Congress established under Article IV of the Constitution, and its judges do not enjoy the tenure and salary protections afforded Article III judges. The territorial judge had been appointed to the panel pursuant to a statute that allowed the Chief Judge of the relevant circuit to appoint "one or more district judges within the circuit [to sit on a circuit court panel] whenever the business of the court so requires." *See* 28 U.S.C. § 292(a). Nguyen argued that the territorial court judge did not qualify under this statute and, therefore, that the panel that affirmed his conviction was unlawfully constituted.

The Court agreed with Nguyen. It held (in a 5-4 decision) that the relevant statute did not authorize the appointment of a territorial judge to sit on a circuit court panel. The majority made reference to a possible constitutional issue in footnote 9 of the opinion:

> [Nguyen] contend[s] that the participation of an Article IV judge on the panel violated structural constitutional guarantees embodied in Article III and in the Appointments Clause, Art. II, § 2, cl. 2, of the Constitution. We find it unnecessary to discuss the constitutional questions because the statutory violation is clear.

Assume that in response to *Nguyen* Congress amended the relevant statute to provide that the Chief Judge of the relevant circuit could appoint "one or more district judges or judges of territorial courts within the circuit [to sit on a circuit court panel] whenever the business of that court so requires." Bill Smith was convicted of a federal drug offense and appealed his conviction to the Ninth Circuit Court of Appeals. The panel hearing his appeal consisted of two Ninth Circuit Judges and one district judge from the District Court for

Guam, a territorial court Congress created under Article IV of the Constitution.

Smith's conviction was unanimously affirmed by the Ninth Circuit panel. He has appealed the conviction to the Supreme Court. You are a clerk to one of the justices. One of Smith's arguments is that the presence of an Article IV judge on the Ninth Circuit panel is unconstitutional and in violation of Article III. Your justice believes that the statute clearly authorizes the appointment of the territorial judge in this situation. She has asked your opinion as to how to address the constitutional issue. How would you advise her?

PROBLEM 4-6

An Environmental Court

Congress has enacted a complex and comprehensive web of statutes dealing with environmental matters. Such statutes include, but by no means are limited to, the Clean Water Act, the Clean Air Act, the Water Quality Act, the National Environmental Policy Act, and the Endangered Species Act. Some would say that the effectiveness of some of these statutes has been limited by federal court decisions making it difficult for individual citizens to establish standing to litigate cases.[42]

Assume that Congress has decided to address the perceived enforcement problem of these environmental statutes. It is considering establishing under its Article I powers the United States Court for Environmental Protection (the "Environmental Court").[43] The judges of the Environmental Court will be appointed by the President to ten-year non-renewable terms. The Senate will have to provide its advice and consent to the President's nominations. The judges of the Environmental Court will not have salary protection. The judges can be removed from office by the President or the Administrator of the Environmental Protection Agency for "mental or physical disability or for neglect of duty."

The Environmental Court will have jurisdiction to adjudicate the following matters:

- claims by individuals that entities regulated under a listed set of federal laws (or agency regulations promulgated thereunder) are in violation of those laws, including the ones set forth above; and
- claims by individuals or regulated entities that agency regulations promulgated under the list of federal statutes are unlawful.

The Environmental Court's jurisdiction over these matters is exclusive of all other courts. Appeals from the Environmental Court's decisions will lie in the

42. *See, e.g., Lujan v. Defenders of Wildlife*, 504 U.S. 555 (1992); *Sierra Club v. Morton*, 405 U.S. 727 (1972). We have discussed these cases in Chapter 2.

43. The idea for this problem comes generally from a student law review note. *See* Timothy C. Hodits, Note: *The Fatal Flaw of Standing: A Proposal for an Article I Tribunal for Environmental Claims*, 84 WASH. U. L. REV. 1907 (2006).

United States Court of Appeals for the District of Columbia Circuit. The proposed statute provides that the D.C. Circuit will review questions of law *de novo* and may reverse a factual determination of the Environmental Court only if clearly erroneous. A party dissatisfied with a ruling of the D.C. Circuit can seek a writ of certiorari in the United States Supreme Court.

You are a lawyer working for a United States Senator. She has asked you for your opinion concerning the constitutionality of the proposed Environmental Court. Please prepare a memorandum for your boss addressing the possible constitutional issues implicated in the proposal. Also, make a recommendation concerning both how the constitutional issue is likely to be resolved and the wisdom of creating the Environmental Court.

CHAPTER 5

"Arising Under" Jurisdiction

A. A REFERENCE PROBLEM

In this chapter we consider when a case "arises under" federal law for purposes of subject matter jurisdiction. The Reference Problem below introduces many of the concepts we will explore.

* * * * *

Gary Flyer was a Minnesota citizen whose passion was recreational aviation. After years of saving, he bought his own airplane, a Cirrus SR-22 single engine aircraft. The Cirrus SR-22 was designed, manufactured, and sold by Cirrus Design Company ("Cirrus"), a business incorporated under Minnesota law. Shortly after purchasing the plane, Gary was killed when the plane crashed as he attempted to land at a local airport in poor weather conditions.

Flyer's Estate ("Flyer") has sued Cirrus in a Minnesota state court. Flyer claims that Cirrus failed to properly instruct the deceased about how to land the plane in adverse weather. Flyer alleges that the deceased was not licensed under federal law to operate the plane in adverse weather (referred to in the field as "IMC" conditions). Flyer further alleges that Cirrus knew the deceased was not licensed to fly in IMC conditions and undertook to instruct the deceased in use of the plane's automatic pilot instruments to land in those conditions. According to Flyer, Cirrus's instruction was negligent.

The complaint is limited to state-law negligence claims. There is no federal law expressly granting Flyer a right to seek damages.

Cirrus removes Flyer's case to the United States District Court for the District of Minnesota. Cirrus claims that removal is proper because Flyer's case "arises under" federal law. Specifically, Cirrus asserts that the Federal Aviation Act (FAA) and related federal aviation regulations (FARs) raise important federal issues insofar as

- The FAA and FARs provide an implied federal *defense* to Flyer's claims because flight instruction and pilot licensing are exclusively the responsibility of federally licensed flight instructors, and Cirrus never attempted to provide such flight instruction.
- Even if the FAA and FARs do not provide a defense, Flyer's negligence claims must be *construed in light of* the federal pilot licensing law referenced in Flyer's complaint.
- Finally, aviation has been so federalized that the *only law applicable* to air traffic safety is federal law. In other words, Flyer's claims — no matter how they look on their face — are necessarily federal ones.

Flyer believes it advantageous to litigate the case in state court. Accordingly, Flyer files a timely motion to remand. How will a United States District Judge likely decide the motion to remand?

* * * * *

As you think about your response, consider the following questions raised (some not so obviously) by the problem:

- How does one determine whether a plaintiff's claim arises under federal law? Must federal law explicitly grant plaintiff the right to sue for some remedy like damages? Or is it sufficient that federal law imposes some duty on the defendant and that state law provides the remedy? Alternatively, does a plaintiff's claim arise under federal law when the court will be called on to interpret or apply federal law? Are there ever circumstances where *any* claim asserted by a plaintiff must necessarily "arise under" federal law?
- If the defendant has a federal defense to liability, does it matter whether the plaintiff's claim arises under federal law? Is the argument for arising under jurisdiction strengthened if the defendant asserts that federal law totally displaces state law?
- Assuming that arising under jurisdiction exists based on any one of the grounds mentioned above, what federal policies are promoted by conferral of jurisdiction?
- Assuming that arising under jurisdiction exists based on any one of the grounds mentioned above, what might that say about the relative competence of the Minnesota state courts to adjudicate the case?

You will probably not be able to answer most of these questions now. You should be able to do so at the conclusion of this chapter.

B. CONTEXT AND BACKGROUND

In Chapter 3 we learned the importance of congressional control of federal court jurisdiction. We principally focused on the *limits* of Congress' power to restrict the courts' jurisdiction.

This chapter also concerns the jurisdiction of the federal courts, but the focus is different. Here, we address the *breadth* of Congress' power to grant jurisdiction rather than limits on that power. Our specific focus is the first of the jurisdictional grants in Article III, section 2, conferring federal court jurisdiction over "all Cases, in Law and Equity, arising under this Constitution, the Laws of the United States and Treaties made, or which shall be made, under their Authority." This jurisdictional grant is referred to as "arising under" or "federal question" jurisdiction. In this chapter we address the original (or trial) jurisdiction of the federal district courts under the arising under provision; in Chapter 12 we consider both the original and appellate jurisdiction of the Supreme Court of the United States.

As we discussed in Chapter 1, Article III of the Constitution enumerates the cases or controversies to which the judicial power of the United States potentially extends. The Supreme Court has consistently held that Congress' power to confer federal court jurisdiction is limited by the grants set forth in Article III. Further, litigants cannot consent to a federal court's exercise of jurisdiction not included within Article III (and an appropriate statutory grant). We begin by considering the breadth of the constitutional language authorizing arising under jurisdiction.

The second principal issue we consider is whether Congress has, in fact, granted jurisdiction within that constitutionally permissible range. This question focuses not on the Constitution but rather on statutes. Today, general federal question jurisdiction is authorized by 28 U.S.C. § 1331. Section 1331 provides that federal district courts "shall have original jurisdiction of all civil actions arising under the Constitution, laws, or treaties of the United States." This language is nearly identical to the language used in the Constitution.

In federal court practice, the conclusion that a case comes within statutory "arising under" jurisdiction usually entails that it satisfies the Constitution's grant of such jurisdiction, at least when one considers the plaintiff's claims. But the statutory and constitutional questions remain analytically distinct. The Court has consistently held that Congress did *not* intend the general statutory grant to extend to the constitutional limits.

Why did the Framers include federal question jurisdiction in the Constitution, and why did Congress deem it important to enact a statute granting some form of that jurisdiction to the federal courts? The most common rationales for authorizing arising under jurisdiction focus on (1) enhancing the uniformity of federal law; (2) ensuring the supremacy of federal law; (3) providing for tribunals that in some sense specialize in federal law; and (4) validating federal authority more generally. Another less commonly invoked rationale is the efficacy of providing a federal *forum* for one reason or another. In other words, there might be something about the federal courts as an institution — such as the procedural rules by which lawsuits are resolved — that provides support for enacting a jurisdictional statute. Each of these justifications can be criticized and debated. However, at the heart of all of them one finds echoes of the "parity debate" we discussed in Chapter 1. Are federal courts somehow necessary to vindicate federal rights? Are they in some measure "better" than state courts for interpreting and enforcing federal law? Are the state courts systematically biased against federal rights?

Whatever the theoretical importance of arising under jurisdiction, many students are surprised to learn that, with the exception of a very brief period from 1801-1802, there was no general federal question jurisdiction as one finds in today's § 1331 until 1875. During that period, cases arising under federal law had to be tried in state court unless there was a specific grant of statutory jurisdiction (such as that concerning copyright[1]). There are many potential reasons for this lack of federal question jurisdiction. There were far fewer federal statutory rights at the time. In addition, the Bill of Rights was not yet applicable to the states. But the practical reality was that the state courts were the principal adjudicators of what federal rights existed. Does the failure of early Congresses to enact a general federal question statute tell us anything about the parity debate as it existed at the time?

This state of affairs changed in 1875 when Congress enacted the precursor of today's § 1331. That statute (which at the time also required that there be a minimum amount in controversy[2]) did not eliminate state courts' power to adjudicate federal questions. State courts enjoy a "presumption of concurrent jurisdiction that lies at the core of our federal system" unless Congress expressly states otherwise. *Yellow Freight System, Inc. v. Donnelly*, 494 U.S. 820, 826 (1990). The concept of concurrency means that the plaintiff usually has a choice whether to pursue a case arising under federal law in federal or state court. However, Congress has given a defendant the option of trumping a plaintiff's choice of forum by removing the case to federal court in those situations in which the plaintiff could have filed a case arising under federal law in federal court but declined to do so. *See* 28 U.S.C. § 1441.

It may have taken nearly a century for Congress to confer general federal question jurisdiction, but cases arising under federal law are now a staple of the federal courts' civil dockets. According to the Administrative Office of the United States Courts, in fiscal year 2013, there were 284,604 cases filed originally in federal court. Of those originally filed cases, 145,007 (51 percent) were federal question cases. *See* 2013 Judicial Business of the United States Courts, *available at* http://www.uscourts.gov/judbususc/judbus.html. In other words, federal question jurisdiction has great practical significance for the day-to-day functioning of the federal judicial system.

1. Even today with a general federal question statutory grant on the books, there remain numerous specific grants of federal question jurisdiction as well. Many of these grants are duplicative of the general provision, while several contain important differences, such as making federal jurisdiction exclusive. Our focus will generally be on § 1331's provision for general federal question jurisdiction.

2. Congress eliminated the amount-in-controversy requirement for federal question cases in 1980.

C. THE LAW AND PROBLEMS

1. *The Constitutional Scope of "Arising Under" Jurisdiction*

a. The Basic Rule

The Constitution provides that the judicial power of the United States extends to "all Cases, in Law and Equity, arising under this Constitution, the Laws of the United States and Treaties made, or which shall be made, under their Authority." U.S. CONST. art. III, § 2. As with many of the bedrock principles of American constitutional law, enunciation of arising under jurisdiction begins with the great Chief Justice John Marshall.

OSBORN v. BANK OF THE UNITED STATES

22 U.S. (9 Wheat.) 738 (1824)

MR. CHIEF JUSTICE MARSHALL delivered the opinion of the Court. . . .

[*Osborn* is one of several cases decided in the first part of the nineteenth century concerning the federal government's establishment of a national bank. Perhaps the most famous of these cases is *McCulloch v. Maryland,* in which the Supreme Court (again in an opinion by Chief Justice Marshall) confirmed the authority of Congress to establish the Bank and held that the states were precluded from taxing it. 17 U.S. (4 Wheat.) 316 (1819). But the Court's decision in *McCulloch* did not quell dissension concerning the Bank.

The State of Ohio had taxed the Bank and then placed a levy on the Bank's property. The State eventually seized some of the Bank's property—namely, deposits. Ohio did so even though a federal court had issued an injunction against such action. Thereafter, the Bank sued Osborn, the Ohio State Auditor, and others in federal court, seeking the return of the confiscated funds.]

* * * *

The appellants contest the jurisdiction of the Court on two grounds:

1st. That the act of Congress [Editors' note: The Court is referring to the act establishing the Bank of the United States.] has not given it.

2d. That, under the constitution, Congress cannot give it.

1. The first part of the objection depends entirely on the language of the act. The words are, that the Bank shall be "made able and capable in law," "to sue and be sued, plead and be impleaded, answer and be answered, defend and be defended, in all State Courts having competent jurisdiction, and in any Circuit Court of the United States."

These words seem to the Court to admit of but one interpretation. They cannot be made plainer by explanation. They give, expressly, the right "to sue and be sued," "in every Circuit Court of the United States," and it would be difficult to substitute other terms which would be more direct and appropriate for the purpose. . . .

* * * *

2. We will now consider the constitutionality of the clause in the act of incorporation, which authorizes the Bank to sue in the federal Courts.

In support of this clause, it is said, that the legislative, executive, and judicial powers, of every well constructed government, are co-extensive with each other; that is, they are potentially co-extensive. The executive department may constitutionally execute every law which the Legislature may constitutionally make, and the judicial department may receive from the Legislature the power of construing every such law. All governments which are not extremely defective in their organization, must possess, within themselves, the means of expounding, as well as enforcing, their own laws. If we examine the constitution of the United States, we find that its framers kept this great political principle in view. The 2d article vests the whole executive power in the President; and the 3d article declares, "that the judicial power shall extend to all cases in law and equity arising under this constitution, the laws of the United States, and treaties made, or which shall be made, under their authority."

This clause enables the judicial department to receive jurisdiction to the full extent of the constitution, laws, and treaties of the United States, when any question respecting them shall assume such a form that the judicial power is capable of acting on it. That power is capable of acting only when the subject is submitted to it by a party who asserts his rights in the form prescribed by law. It then becomes a case, and the constitution declares, that the judicial power shall extend to all cases arising under the constitution, laws, and treaties of the United States.

The suit of *The Bank of the United States v. Osborn and others,* is a case, and the question is, whether it arises under a law of the United States?

The appellants contend, that it does not, because several questions may arise in it, which depend on the general principles of the law, not on any act of Congress.

* * * *

We ask, then, if it can be sufficient to exclude this jurisdiction, that the case involves questions depending on general principles? A cause may depend on several questions of fact and law. Some of these may depend on the construction of a law of the United States; others on principles unconnected with that law. If it be a sufficient foundation for jurisdiction, that the title or right set up by the party, may be defeated by one construction of the constitution or law of the United States, and sustained by the opposite construction, provided the facts necessary to support the action be made out, then all the other questions must be decided as incidental to this, which gives that jurisdiction. Those other questions cannot arrest the proceedings. Under this construction, the judicial power of the Union extends effectively and beneficially to that most important class of cases, which depend on the character of the cause. On the opposite construction, the judicial power never can be extended to a whole case, as expressed by the constitution, but to those parts of cases only which present the particular question involving the construction of the constitution or the law. We say it never can be extended to the whole case, because, if the circumstance that other points are involved in it, shall disable Congress from authorizing the Courts of the Union to take jurisdiction of the original cause, it equally disables Congress from authorizing those Courts to take jurisdiction of the whole cause, on an appeal, and thus will be restricted to a single question in that cause; and words obviously intended to secure to those who claim rights under the constitution, laws, or treaties of the United States, a trial in the federal Courts, will be restricted to the insecure remedy of an appeal upon an insulated point, after it has received that shape which may be given to it by another tribunal, into which he is forced against his will.

We think, then, that when a question to which the judicial power of the Union is extended by the constitution, forms an ingredient of the original cause, it is in the power of Congress to give the Circuit Courts jurisdiction of that cause, although other questions of fact or of law may be involved in it.

The case of the Bank is, we think, a very strong case of this description. The charter of incorporation not only creates it, but gives it every faculty which it possesses. The power to acquire rights of any description, to transact business of any description, to make contracts of any description, to sue on those contracts, is given and measured by its charter, and that charter is a law of the United States. This being can acquire no right, make no contract, bring no suit, which is not authorized by a law of the United States. It is not only itself the mere creature of a law, but all its actions and all its rights are dependant on the same law. Can a being, thus constituted, have a case which does not arise literally, as well as substantially, under the law?

Take the case of a contract, which is put as the strongest against the Bank.

When a Bank sues, the first question which presents itself, and which lies at the foundation of the cause, is, has this legal entity a right to sue? Has it a right to come, not into this Court particularly, but into any Court? This depends on a law of the United States. The next question is, has this being a right to make this particular contract? If this question be decided in the negative, the cause is determined against the plaintiff; and this question, too, depends entirely on a law of the United States. These are important questions, and they exist in every possible case. The right to sue, if decided once, is decided for ever; but the power of Congress was exercised antecedently to the first decision on that right, and if it was constitutional then, it cannot cease to be so, because the particular question is decided. It may be revived at the will of the party, and most probably would be renewed, were the tribunal to be changed. But the question respecting the right to make a particular contract, or to acquire a particular property, or to sue on account of a particular injury, belongs to every particular case, and may be renewed in every case. The question forms an original ingredient in every cause. Whether it be in fact relied on or not, in the defence, it is still a part of the cause, and may be relied on. The right of the plaintiff to sue, cannot depend on the defence which the defendant may choose to set up. His right to sue is anterior to that defence, and must depend on the state of things when the action is brought. The questions which the case involves, then, must determine its character, whether those questions be made in the cause or not.

The appellants say, that the case arises on the contract; but the validity of the contract depends on a law of the United States, and the plaintiff is compelled, in every case, to show its validity. The case arises emphatically under the law. The act of Congress is its foundation. The contract could never have been made, but under the authority of that act. The act itself is the first ingredient in the case, is its origin, is that from which every other part arises. That other questions may also arise, as the execution of the contract, or its performance, cannot change the case, or give it any other origin than the charter of incorporation. The action still originates in, and is sustained by, that charter.

* * * *

Upon the best consideration we have been able to bestow on this subject, we are of opinion, that the clause in the act of incorporation, enabling the Bank to sue in the Courts of the United States, is consistent with the constitution, and to be obeyed in all Courts.

* * * *

[In the omitted portion of Chief Justice Marshall's opinion, the Court dealt with the merits of the action.]

We think, then, that there is no error in the decree of the Circuit Court for the district of Ohio, so far as it directs restitution of the specific sum of 98,000 dollars, which was taken out of the Bank unlawfully, and was in the possession of the defendant, Samuel Sullivan, when the injunction was awarded, in September, 1820, to restrain him from paying it away, or in any manner using it; and so far as it directs the payment of the remaining sum of 2000 dollars, by the defendants, Ralph Osborne and John L. Harper; but that the same is erroneous, so far as respects the interest on the coin, part of the said 98,000 dollars, it being the opinion of this Court, that, while the parties were restrained by the authority of the Circuit Court from using it, they ought not to be charged with interest. The decree of the Circuit Court for the district of Ohio is affirmed, as to the said sums of 98,000 dollars, and 2000 dollars; and reversed, as to the residue.

MR. JUSTICE JOHNSON [dissenting].

The argument in this cause presents three questions: 1. Has Congress granted to the Bank of the United States, an unlimited right of suing in the Courts of the United States? 2. Could Congress constitutionally grant such a right? and 3. Has the power of the Court been legally and constitutionally exercised in this suit?

* * * *

[The initial portion of Justice Johnson's opinion largely focuses on contesting the Court's holding that the statute authorizing the Second Bank of the United States bestowed arising under jurisdiction.]

In the present instances, I cannot persuade myself that the constitution sanctions the vesting of the right of action in this Bank, in cases in which the privilege is exclusively personal or in any case, merely on the ground that a question might *possibly* be raised in it, involving the constitution, or constitutionality of a law, of the United States.

* * * *

I will dwell no longer on a point, which is in fact secondary and subordinate; for if Congress can vest this jurisdiction, and the people will it, the act may be amended, and the jurisdiction vested. I next proceed to consider, more distinctly, the constitutional question, on the right to vest the jurisdiction to the extent here contended for.

And here I must observe, that I altogether misunderstood the counsel, who argued the cause for the plaintiff in error, if any of them contended against the jurisdiction, on the ground that the cause involved questions depending on general principles. No one can question, that the Court which has jurisdiction of the principal question, must exercise jurisdiction over every question. Neither did I understand them as denying, that if Congress could confer on the Circuit Courts appellate, they could confer original jurisdiction. The argument went to deny the right to assume jurisdiction on a mere hypothesis. It was one of description, identity, definition; they contended, that until a question involving the construction or administration of the laws of the United States did actually arise, the *casus federis* [Editors' note: A federal cause of action.] was not presented, on which the constitution authorized the government to take to itself the jurisdiction of the cause. That until such a question actually arose, until such a case was actually presented . . . , but the cause depended upon general principles, exclusively cognizable in the State Courts; that neither the letter nor the spirit of the constitution sanctioned the assumption of jurisdiction on the part of the United States at any previous stage.

* * * *

I have never understood any one to question the right of Congress to vest original jurisdiction in its inferior Courts, in cases coming properly within the description of "cases arising under the laws of the United States"; but surely it must first be ascertained, in some proper mode, that the cases are such as the constitution describes. By possibility, a constitutional question may be raised in any conceivable suit that may be instituted; but that would be a very insufficient ground for assuming universal jurisdiction; and yet, that a question has been made, as that, for instance, on the Bank charter, and may again be made, seems still worse, as a ground for extending jurisdiction. For, the folly of raising it again in every suit instituted by the Bank, is too great, to suppose it possible. Yet this supposition, and this alone, would seem to justify vesting the Bank with an unlimited right to sue in the federal Courts. Indeed, I cannot perceive how, with ordinary correctness, a question can be said to be involved in a cause, which only may possibly be made, but which, in fact, is the very last question that there is any probability will be made; or rather, how that can any longer be denominated a question, which has been put out of existence by a solemn decision. The constitution presumes, that the decisions of the supreme tribunal will be acquiesced in; and after disposing of the few questions which the constitution refers to it, all the minor questions belong properly to the State jurisdictions, and never were intended to be taken away in mass.

Efforts have been made to fix the precise sense of the constitution, when it vests jurisdiction in the general government, in "cases arising under the laws of the United States." To me, the question appears susceptible of a very simple solution; that all depends upon the identity of the case supposed; according to which idea, a case may be such in its very existence, or it may become such in its progress. An action may "live, move, and have its being," in a law of the United States; such is that given for the violation of a patent-right, and four or five different actions given by this act of incorporation; particularly that against the President and Directors for over-issuing; in all of which cases the plaintiff must count upon the law itself as the ground of his action. And of the other description, would have been an action of trespass, in this case, had remedy been sought for an actual levy of the tax imposed. Such was the case of the former Bank against *Deveaux*, and many others that have occurred in this Court, in which the suit, in its form, was such as occur in ordinary cases, but in which the pleadings or evidence raised the question on the law or constitution of the United States. In this class of cases, the occurrence of a question makes the case, and transfers it, as provided for under the twenty-fifth section of the Judiciary Act, to the jurisdiction of the United States. And this appears to me to present the only sound and practical construction of the constitution on this subject; for no other cases does it regard as necessary to place under the control of the general government. It is only when the case exhibits one or the other of these characteristics, that it is acted upon by the constitution. Where no question is raised, there can be no contrariety of construction; and what else had the constitution to guard against? As to cases of the first description, *ex necessitate rei* [Editors' note: From the necessity of the thing.], the Courts of the United States must be susceptible of original jurisdiction; and as to all other cases, I should hold them, also, susceptible of original jurisdiction, if it were practicable, in the nature of things, to make out the definition of the case, so as to bring it under the constitution judicially, upon an original suit. But until the plaintiff can control the defendant in his pleadings, I see no practical mode of determining when the case does occur, otherwise than by permitting the cause to advance until the case for which the constitution provides shall actually arise. If it never occurs, there can be nothing to complain of; and such are the provisions of the twenty-fifth section. The cause might be transferred to the Circuit Court before an adjudication takes place; but I can perceive no earlier stage at which it can possibly be predicated of such a case, that it is one within the constitution; nor any possible necessity for transferring it then, or until the Court has acted upon it to the prejudice of the claims of the United States. It is not, therefore, because Congress may not vest an *original* jurisdiction, where they can constitutionally vest in the Circuit Courts *appellate* jurisdiction, that I object to this general grant of the right to sue; but, because that the peculiar nature of this jurisdiction is such, as to render it impossible to exercise it in a strictly original form, and because the principle of a possible occurrence of a question as a ground of jurisdiction, is transcending the bounds of the constitution, and placing it on a ground which will admit of an *enormous accession*, if not an *unlimited assumption*, of jurisdiction.

* * * *

Upon the whole, I feel compelled to dissent from the Court, on the point of jurisdiction; and this renders it unnecessary for me to express my sentiments on the residue of the points in the cause.

DISCUSSION AND QUESTIONS

The Court clearly articulates the requirement that, for there to be subject matter jurisdiction in the lower federal courts, a statute must grant such jurisdiction *and* that statutory grant must comport with the Constitution. The Court interpreted a statute authorizing the Bank to "sue or be sued . . . in all State Courts having competent jurisdiction, and in any Circuit Court of the United States" as a congressional grant of federal question jurisdiction. Chief Justice Marshall then turned to the constitutional question for which perhaps *Osborn* is most famous.

Taken at its fullest, the scope of constitutional federal question jurisdiction in *Osborn* is about as broad as one could imagine such a grant could be. Although there are portions of the opinion using a narrower articulation,[3] *Osborn* has come to be associated with this description of arising under jurisdiction:

3. The potentially narrower version of *Osborn*'s holding is captured in the following statement: "[I]t is a sufficient foundation for jurisdiction, that the title or right set up by the party, may be defeated by one construction of the Constitution or laws of the United States and sustained by the opposite construction." *Osborn*, 22 U.S. at 822.

> We think, then, that when a question to which the judicial power of the Union is extended by the constitution, *forms an ingredient of the original cause*, it is in the power of Congress to give the Circuit Courts jurisdiction of that cause, although other questions of fact or of law may be involved in it.

Osborn, 22 U.S. at 823 (emphasis added).

As Justice Johnson argues in his dissent, the Court's requirement of a mere federal "ingredient" to justify jurisdiction permits Congress to endow the federal courts with jurisdiction over a huge variety of matters. To take one simple and oft-cited example, much land in the western portion of the United States can trace its roots to federal land grants. Could Congress constitutionally extend jurisdiction to any dispute in the West dealing with property having its origin in a federal land grant? Justice Johnson would almost certainly find this statutory grant unconstitutional. Yet, if the majority is taken seriously, jurisdiction would be appropriate. Take time to think about this issue to explore the fundamental divide between Chief Justice Marshall and Justice Johnson, two giants of the early Supreme Court.

The scope of jurisdiction under *Osborn* is even more expansive when one considers the Court's intimation that the federal ingredient need not actually be at issue in a lawsuit in order to support arising under jurisdiction. Rather, it is sufficient if there is a *possibility* that the federal ingredient could be raised. Thus, in *Osborn* itself the federal ingredient was the federal law creating the Bank and, according to Chief Justice Marshall, it was always possible in any case in which the Bank was a party that someone could challenge that federal law (even if the issue had been raised and resolved in other cases). In *Osborn*, this possibility supported constitutional jurisdiction even though it appeared certain that Ohio was not going to contest congressional authority to create the Bank or the Bank's ability to bring a lawsuit under federal law.

Finally, *Osborn* makes clear that the scope of federal jurisdiction, once it attaches, extends to the entire "case," not merely a federal issue. Even Justice Johnson appears to agree with this point. *See Osborn*, 22 U.S. at 884-85. This principle is critical to the modern concept of supplemental jurisdiction that we consider in Chapter 7.

One might be tempted to rationalize *Osborn* based on the Court's strong interest in addressing the significant federal issue concerning the national Bank's immunity from state taxation. After all, that was the issue at the heart of the landmark Supreme Court decision in *McCulloch v. Maryland*, 17 U.S. (4 Wheat.) 316 (1819). However, on the same day as *Osborn*, the Court decided another case concerning the Bank that did not raise the immunity issue. The case was also held to be within the jurisdiction of the federal courts on the same basis articulated in *Osborn*. *See Bank of the United States v. Planters' Bank of Ga.*, 22 U.S. (9 Wheat.) 904 (1824).

Try your hand at applying *Osborn* by considering Problem 5-1.

PROBLEM 5-1

Tainted Blood and Federal Courts

Jane Smith is a citizen of New Hampshire. She received a blood transfusion during surgery and, as a result, contracted AIDS. The blood Smith received was contaminated with the HIV virus. She sued a number of parties in New Hampshire state court, asserting negligence in connection with the blood transfusion.

One of the parties Smith sued was the American National Red Cross (the "Red Cross"). The Red Cross was founded in 1881 as part of an international effort to address wartime suffering. Over the years, its mission has expanded to include a number of charitable and public service activities. One such activity is to provide certain services in connection with the civilian blood supply. Smith alleged that the Red Cross was negligent under New Hampshire law in providing the tainted blood at issue.

The Red Cross is a federally chartered corporation. Its current charter provides that the Red Cross may "sue and be sued in courts of law and equity, State or Federal, within the jurisdiction of the United States."

The Red Cross timely removed Ms. Smith's suit to the United States District Court for the District of New Hampshire. You should assume that the only claimed basis for removal is that Ms. Smith's suit arises under federal law. Ms. Smith has filed a timely motion to remand to state court. She argues that the federal court lacks constitutional authority to hear the removed case. You are a United States District Judge in the District of New Hampshire. How do you rule on the motion to remand and why?

As Problem 5-1 demonstrates, it is truly difficult to overstate the sweep of *Osborn*'s jurisdictional holding. While *Osborn*'s holding has been the subject of some criticism, the modern Court has declined invitations to reconsider it although intimating that it might read *Osborn* more narrowly someday. As the Court opined in *Verlinden B.V. v. Central Bank of Nigeria*:

> *Osborn* . . . reflects a broad conception of arising under jurisdiction, according to which Congress may confer on the federal courts jurisdiction over any case or controversy that might call for the application of federal law. The breadth of that conclusion has been questioned. It has been observed that, taken at its broadest, *Osborn* might be read as permitting assertion of original federal jurisdiction on the remote possibility of presentation of a federal question. We need not now resolve that issue or decide the precise boundaries of Article III jurisdiction, however, since the present case does not involve a mere speculative possibility that a federal question may arise at some point in the proceeding. . . .

461 U.S. 480, 492-93 (1983) (internal quotation marks and citations omitted).

EXPLORING DOCTRINE

What Should the Court Consider in Defining the Scope of "Arising Under" Jurisdiction?

Assume that *Osborn* is correct. That is, the Constitution allows Congress to bestow arising under jurisdiction on the federal courts in any case in which a federal ingredient is conceivably present. Does this suggest anything concerning the Framers' trust in state courts?

Now consider the modern Court's reluctance to embrace the full potential of *Osborn.* Does this reluctance reflect changing beliefs about the trustworthiness of state courts? Or might the Court be concerned about contemporary institutional factors, for example, the modern proliferation of federal law and its potential impact on the federal courts' workload? Are such institutional factors relevant when the constitutional question concerns the *Framers'* intent?

b. Where Is the Constitutional Frontier?

In the previous section, we saw that the Constitution allows Congress to extend jurisdiction whenever there is a federal "ingredient" in a case, apparently regardless of whether the federal issue will actually arise. A common feature in all the cases in which a federal ingredient is found is the existence of some federal law, even if in the deep background. In *Osborn,* the federal ingredient was a statute creating the Second Bank of the United States. In *American National Red Cross v. S.G.,* 505 U.S. 247 (1992) (the case on which Problem 5-1 is based), it was a statute incorporating the Red Cross.

But does Article III allow Congress to extend federal question jurisdiction to situations in which there is no federal statute, treaty, or constitutional provision providing a possible rule of decision in a case? Some legal scholars have argued for "protective jurisdiction," permitting federal courts to exercise jurisdiction over cases involving important federal interests where Congress has not yet chosen to legislate specific rules of decision. The Supreme Court has not fully resolved the constitutionality of protective jurisdiction. The next case contains excerpts from the most influential discussion of protective jurisdiction by a member of the Court, dissenting Justice Frankfurter.

TEXTILE WORKERS UNION OF AMERICA v. LINCOLN MILLS OF ALABAMA

353 U.S. 448 (1957)

[This case involved a dispute concerning a collective bargaining agreement between a union and an employer. A part of that agreement required the parties to submit certain disputes to arbitration. The employer refused to do so. The union then commenced suit in a federal court.

The union based subject matter jurisdiction on section 301(a) of the Labor Management Relations Act of 1947, providing that

> [s]uits for violation of contracts between an employer and a labor organization representing employees in an industry affecting commerce as defined in this chapter, or between any such labor organizations, may be brought in any district court of the United States having jurisdiction of the parties, without respect to the amount in controversy or without regard to the citizenship of the parties.

Justice Douglas, writing for the majority, concluded that jurisdiction was proper because section 301(a) did more than simply confer subject matter jurisdiction. Justice Douglas held that this statute directed the federal courts to craft "federal common law" concerning labor-management agreements. As we discuss in Chapter 11, cases can arise under federal common law just as they arise under federal statutes. Justice Douglas explained:

> There is no constitutional difficulty. Article III, § 2, extends the judicial power to cases "arising under . . . the Laws of the United States. . . ." The power of Congress to regulate these labor-management controversies under the Commerce Clause is plain. A case or controversy arising under § 301(a) is, therefore, one within the purview of judicial power defined in Article III.

353 U.S. at 457 (citations omitted). The Court then reversed the lower court's holding that the union's suit must be dismissed for lack of subject matter jurisdiction.

Other members of the Court disagreed with Justice Douglas's ruling that federal common law provided the law governing the labor dispute. Justice Burton found that arising under jurisdiction was proper but based his opinion on the conclusion that "some" federal law might be involved in the case even though state law primarily governed the parties' "substantive" rights. Justice Frankfurter, in contrast, concluded that no federal law governed the suit. As a consequence, Justice Frankfurter had to address the constitutional limits of "protective jurisdiction." What follows are excerpts from the opinions of Justices Burton and Frankfurter.]

MR. JUSTICE BURTON, whom MR. JUSTICE HARLAN joins, concurring in the result.

This suit was brought in a United States District Court under § 301 of the Labor Management Relations Act of 1947 seeking specific enforcement of the arbitration provisions of a collective-bargaining contract. The District Court had jurisdiction over the action since it involved an obligation running to a union — a union controversy — and not uniquely personal rights of employees sought to be enforced by a union. Having jurisdiction over the suit, the court was not powerless to fashion an appropriate federal remedy. The power to decree specific performance of a collectively bargained agreement to arbitrate finds its source in § 301 itself, and in a Federal District Court's inherent equitable powers, nurtured by a congressional policy to encourage and enforce labor arbitration in industries affecting commerce.

I do not subscribe to the conclusion of the Court that the substantive law to be applied in a suit under § 301 is federal law. At the same time, I agree with [a Court of Appeals holding] that some federal rights may necessarily be involved in a § 301 case, and hence that the constitutionality of § 301 can be upheld as a congressional grant to Federal District Courts of what has been called "protective jurisdiction."

MR. JUSTICE FRANKFURTER, dissenting.

[The first portion of Justice Frankfurter's dissent focused primarily on Justice Douglas's conclusion that section 301(a) authorized the federal courts to craft a body of federal common law to govern labor-management relations. Justice Frankfurter disagreed with that conclusion.]

The second ground of my dissent from the Court's action is more fundamental. Since I do not agree with the Court's conclusion that federal substantive law is to govern in actions under § 301, I am forced to consider the serious constitutional question that was [avoided in an earlier case], the constitutionality of a grant of jurisdiction to federal courts over contracts that came into being entirely by virtue of state substantive law, a jurisdiction not based on diversity of citizenship, yet one in which a federal court would, as in diversity cases, act in effect merely as another court of the State in which it sits. The scope of allowable federal judicial power that this grant must satisfy is constitutionally described as "Cases, in Law and Equity, arising under this Constitution, the Laws of the United States, and Treaties made, or which shall be made, under their Authority." Art. III, § 2. While interpretive decisions are legion under general statutory grants of jurisdiction strikingly similar to this constitutional wording, it is generally recognized that the full constitutional power has not been exhausted by these statutes. . . .

Almost without exception, decisions under the general statutory grants have tested jurisdiction in terms of the presence, as an integral part of plaintiff's cause of action, of an issue calling for interpretation or application of federal law. Although it has sometimes been suggested that the "cause of action" must derive from federal law, it has been found sufficient that some aspect of federal law is essential to plaintiff's success. The litigation-provoking problem has been the degree to which federal law must be in the forefront of the case and not collateral, peripheral or remote. [Editors' note: We return to this point, pertaining more to statutory federal question jurisdiction, in the next part of this chapter.]

In a few exceptional cases, arising under special jurisdictional grants, the criteria by which the prominence of the federal question is measured against constitutional requirements have been found satisfied under circumstances suggesting a variant theory of the nature of these requirements. The first, and the leading case in the field, is *Osborn.* There, Chief Justice Marshall sustained federal jurisdiction in a situation — hypothetical in the case before him but presented by the companion case of *Bank of the United States v. Planters' Bank of Georgia* involving suit by a federally incorporated bank upon a contract. Despite the assumption that the cause of action and the interpretation of the contract would be governed by state law, the case was found to "arise under the laws of the United States" because the propriety and scope of a federally granted authority to enter into contracts and to litigate might well be challenged. This reasoning was subsequently applied to sustain jurisdiction in actions against federally chartered railroad corporations. *Pacific Railroad Removal* Cases. The traditional interpretation of this series of cases is that federal jurisdiction under the "arising" clause of the Constitution, though limited to cases involving potential federal questions, has such flexibility that Congress may confer it whenever there exists in the background some federal proposition that might be challenged, despite the remoteness of the likelihood of actual presentation of such a federal question.

* * * *

With this background, many theories have been proposed to sustain the constitutional validity of § 301. In [a lower court opinion it was] suggested, among other possibilities, that § 301 might be read as containing a direction that controversies affecting interstate commerce should be governed by federal law incorporating state law by reference, and that such controversies would then arise under a valid federal law as required by Article III. Whatever may be said of the assumption regarding the validity of federal jurisdiction under an affirmative declaration by Congress that state law should be applied as federal law by federal courts to contract disputes affecting commerce, we cannot argumentatively legislate for Congress when Congress has failed to legislate. To do so disrespects legislative responsibility and disregards judicial limitations.

Another theory, relying on *Osborn* . . . , has been proposed. . . . [At this point, Justice Frankfurter cited a number of authorities, including an influential law review article by Professor Herbert Wechsler.] Called "protective jurisdiction," the suggestion is that in any case for which Congress has the constitutional power to prescribe federal rules of decision and thus confer "true" federal question jurisdiction, it may, without so doing, enact a jurisdictional statute, which will provide a federal forum for the application of state statute and decisional law. Analysis of the "protective jurisdiction" theory might also be attempted in terms of the language of Article III — construing "laws" to include jurisdictional statutes where Congress could have legislated substantively in a field. This is but another way of saying that because Congress could have legislated substantively and thereby could give rise to litigation under a statute of the United States, it can provide a federal forum for state-created rights although it chose not to adopt state law as federal law or to originate federal rights.

Surely the truly technical restrictions of Article III are not met or respected by a beguiling phrase that the greater power here must necessarily include the lesser. In the compromise of federal and state interests leading to distribution of jealously guarded judicial power in a federal system, it is obvious that very different considerations apply to cases involving questions of federal law and those turning solely on state law. It may be that the ambiguity of the phrase "arising under the laws of the United States" leaves room for more than traditional theory could accommodate. But, under the theory of "protective jurisdiction," the "arising under" jurisdiction of the federal courts would be vastly extended. For example, every contract or tort arising out of a contract affecting commerce might be a potential cause of action in the federal courts, even though only state law was involved in the decision of the case. At least in *Osborn* . . . , a substantive federal law was present somewhere in the background. But this theory rests on the supposition that Congress could enact substantive federal law to govern the particular case. It was not held in those cases, nor is it clear, that federal law could be held to govern . . . all suits of a Bank of the United States.

"Protective jurisdiction," once the label is discarded, cannot be justified under any view of the allowable scope to be given to Article III. "Protective jurisdiction" is a misused label for the statute we are here considering. That rubric is properly descriptive of safeguarding some of the indisputable, staple business of the federal courts. It is a radiation of an existing jurisdiction. "Protective jurisdiction" cannot generate an independent source for adjudication outside of the Article III sanctions and what Congress has defined. The theory must have as its sole justification a belief in the inadequacy of state tribunals in determining state law. The Constitution reflects such a belief in the specific situation within which the Diversity Clause was confined. The intention to remedy such supposed defects was exhausted in this provision of Article III. That this "protective" theory was not adopted by Chief Justice Marshall at a time when conditions might have presented more substantial justification strongly suggests its lack of constitutional merit. Moreover, Congress in its consideration of § 301 nowhere suggested dissatisfaction with the ability of state courts to administer state law properly. Its concern was to provide access to the federal courts for easier enforcement of state-created rights.

Another theory also relies on *Osborn* . . . as an implicit recognition of the propriety of the exercise of some sort of "protective jurisdiction" by the federal courts.

[At this point, Justice Frankfurter cited another influential law review article on the topic, this one by Professor Paul Mishkin.] Professor Mishkin tends to view the assertion of such a jurisdiction, in the absence of any exercise of substantive powers, as irreconcilable with the "arising" clause since the case would then arise only under the jurisdictional statute itself, and he is reluctant to find a constitutional basis for the grant of power outside Article III. Professor Mishkin also notes that the only purpose of such a statute would be to insure impartiality to some litigant, an objection inconsistent with Article III's recognition of "protective jurisdiction" only in the specified situation of diverse citizenship. But where Congress has "an articulated and active federal policy regulating a field, the 'arising under' clause of Article III apparently permits the conferring of jurisdiction on the national courts of all cases in the area—including those substantively governed by state law." In such cases, the protection being offered is not to the suitor, as in diversity cases, but to the "congressional legislative program." Thus he supports § 301: "even though the rules governing collective bargaining agreements continue to be state-fashioned, nonetheless the mode of their application and enforcement may play a very substantial part in the labor-management relations of interstate industry and commerce—an area in which the national government has labored long and hard."

Insofar as state law governs the case, Professor Mishkin's theory is quite similar to that advanced by Professors Hart and Wechsler and followed by the Court of Appeals for the First Circuit: The substantive power of Congress, although not exercised to govern the particular "case," gives "arising under" jurisdiction to the federal courts despite governing state law. The second "protective jurisdiction" theory has the dubious advantage of limiting incursions on state judicial power to situations in which the State's feelings may have been tempered by early substantive federal invasions.

Professor Mishkin's theory of "protective jurisdiction" may find more constitutional justification if there is not merely an "articulated and active" congressional policy regulating the labor field but also federal rights existing in the interstices of actions under § 301. [Justice Frankfurter then went on to reject that this was the case.]

* * * *

If there is in the phrase "arising under the laws of the United States" leeway for expansion of our concepts of jurisdiction, the history of Article III suggests that the area is not great and that it will require the presence of some substantial federal interest, one of greater weight and dignity than questionable doubt concerning the effectiveness of state procedure. . . .

In the wise distribution of governmental powers, this Court cannot do what a President sometimes does in returning a bill to Congress. We cannot return this provision to Congress and respectfully request that body to face the responsibility placed upon it by the Constitution to define the jurisdiction of the lower courts with some particularity and not to leave these courts at large. Confronted as I am, I regretfully have no choice. For all the reasons elaborated in this dissent, even reading into § 301 the limited federal rights consistent with the purposes of that section, I am impelled to the view that it is unconstitutional in cases such as the present ones where it provides the sole basis for exercise of jurisdiction by the federal courts.

[A lengthy appendix to Justice Frankfurter's dissent is omitted.]

DISCUSSION AND QUESTIONS

Justice Douglas was able to avoid discussing "protective jurisdiction" by construing section 301 of the Labor Management Relations Act of 1947 to authorize federal court creation of federal common law. As a result, the jurisdictional question was simple: the case clearly arose under federal law.

The Supreme Court has consistently taken the approach Justice Douglas used in *Lincoln Mills* when confronted with the possibility that Congress sought to utilize some type of protective jurisdiction. For example, in *Verlinden B.V. v. Central Bank of Nigeria*, 461 U.S. 480 (1983), the issue concerned jurisdiction under the Foreign Sovereign Immunities Act (FSIA). Among other things, that statute purported to confer arising under jurisdiction in all non-jury cases filed against a foreign state. In *Verlinden*, a foreign national sued a foreign state under the FSIA on a breach of contract claim. The Court of Appeals held that the FSIA exceeded the jurisdictional limitations of Article III.

The Supreme Court unanimously reversed. The Court determined that the FSIA did more than merely grant jurisdiction. According to the Court, it also created substantive federal law governing the scope of foreign states' sovereign immunity from suit. Thus, *Verlinden* presented an easy case for arising under jurisdiction, much as *Lincoln Mills* presented an easy case for Justice Douglas. As the Court put it:

> In view of our conclusion that proper actions by foreign plaintiffs under the Foreign Sovereign Immunities Act are within Article III arising under jurisdiction, we need not consider petitioner's alternative argument that the Act is constitutional as an aspect of so-called "protective jurisdiction."

Verlinden, 461 U.S. at 491 n.17 (citation omitted).

Similarly, in *Mesa v. California*, 489 U.S. 121 (1989), the Court refused to recognize some form of protective jurisdiction when interpreting 28 U.S.C. § 1442(1), a statutory provision authorizing federal agents to remove to federal court cases filed against them in state court. The Court interpreted the statute such that removal was permitted only when the defendant asserts some substantive federal defense to the state court action. Although the Court did not repudiate the theory of protective jurisdiction *per se*, it emphasized that Congress cannot base arising under jurisdiction on statutes that "do nothing more than grant jurisdiction over a particular class of cases." 489 U.S. at 136 (quoting *Verlinden, B.V. v. Central Bank of Nig.*, 461 U.S. 480, 491 (1983)). The Court found no "federal interests" requiring protective jurisdiction when a federal agent fails to assert a federal defense to the state court action and where there is no allegation of "state court hostility or interference." *Id.* at 137. According to the Court, the defense's theory of protective removal jurisdiction raised a "serious" constitutional question that it was able to avoid by interpreting the statute to require a federal defense as a basis for removal. *Id.* at 136.

The Court's most extensive discussion of protective jurisdiction remains that of Justice Frankfurter in his *Lincoln Mills* dissent. Some form of the concept was implicated several years earlier in *National Mutual Insurance Co. of District of Columbia v. Tidewater Transfer Co.*, 337 U.S. 582 (1949), a case we first discussed in Chapter 4. This case concerned Congress' decision to provide for federal court diversity jurisdiction in actions between citizens of a state and citizens of the District of Columbia. The Court upheld the statute against constitutional attack. *Tidewater's* meaning is obscured by the lack of a majority opinion and shifting coalitions among the justices. However, in some language of Justice Jackson announcing the judgment of the Court and most notably in Justice Frankfurter's dissent, one can see the beginnings of the dispute more fully aired in *Lincoln Mills.*

Keep in mind that Justice Frankfurter in *Lincoln Mills* articulates two versions of the theory, both of which he rejects. The first type of protective jurisdiction is most often associated with Professor Herbert Wechsler. Professor Wechsler's basic thesis has been described as "the greater power includes the lesser one." In his own words, federal question jurisdiction may constitutionally extend to

> all cases in which Congress has authority to make the rule to govern disposition of the controversy but is content instead to let the states provide the rule so long as jurisdiction to enforce it has been vested in a federal court. Where, for example, Congress by the commerce power can declare as federal law that contracts of a given kind are valid and enforceable, it must be free to take the lesser step of drawing suits upon such contracts to the district courts without displacement of the states as sources of the operative, substantive law. A grant of jurisdiction is, in short, one mode by which Congress may assert its regulatory powers.

Herbert Wechsler, *Federal Jurisdiction and the Revision of the Judicial Code,* 13 Law & Contemp. Probs. 217, 224-25 (1948).

Justice Frankfurter's second articulation of protective jurisdiction is associated with Professor Paul Mishkin. That view requires more than congressional power to act in an area standing alone. Professor Mishkin would require that Congress actually exercise its power in an area before protective jurisdiction is constitutionally permissible. As he explains it, "where there is an articulated and active federal policy regulating a field, the 'arising under' clause of Article III apparently permits the conferring of jurisdiction on the national courts of all cases in the area — including those substantively governed by state law." Paul J. Mishkin, *The Federal "Question" in the District Courts,* 53 Colum. L. Rev. 157, 192 (1953).

Justice Burton insists in his concurrence in *Lincoln Mills* that "protective jurisdiction" supports federal question jurisdiction in the case, but he is not specific concerning what he understands that term to mean. Would it matter whether Justice Burton was referring to protective jurisdiction as articulated by Professor Wechsler or Professor Mishkin?

To review your understanding of constitutional arising under jurisdiction, consider the following problem based on an event that is, sadly, etched in our collective memories.

PROBLEM 5-2

Federal Jurisdiction and September 11, 2001

Most of us who were alive and old enough at the time to have been able to watch television remember exactly where we were on September 11, 2001. That event will likely have lasting ramifications in many areas of American life — and law — for years to come. It could also have an impact on federal jurisdiction. This problem explores that issue.

In the wake of the terrorist attacks, Congress passed and President Bush signed into law the Air Transportation Safety and System Stabilization Act (ATSSSA). A part of this statute created the September 11th Victim Compensation Fund (the "Fund"). The Fund provided compensation to individuals injured in the attacks or their relatives so long as they agreed not to file civil lawsuits against anyone other than the terrorists or their sponsors.[4]

Section 408 of the ATSSSA created as an alternative to Fund participation a "federal cause of action for damages arising out of the hijacking and subsequent crashes [of the aircraft involved]." Such action was "the exclusive remedy for damages arising out of the hijacking and subsequent crashes of such flights." Moreover, the action could only be filed in the United States District Court for the Southern District of New York. This action is the only legal remedy for victims who opted out of the Fund.

The ATSSSA contained two other provisions relevant to our inquiry. First, it capped the damages that certain defendants (such as airlines and New York City) faced in any civil action related to the attacks.[5] Second, the Act stated that "[t]he substantive law for decision in any such suit [under the ATSSSA] shall be derived from the law, including choice of law principles, of the State in which the crash occurred unless such law is inconsistent with or preempted by Federal law."

Does the arising under provision of Article III support subject matter jurisdiction in a case filed in federal court under the ATSSSA? Does the Act's constitutionality require resort to the doctrine of "protective jurisdiction"? Explore all possible arguments in support of jurisdiction.

EXPLORING DOCTRINE

Protective Jurisdiction and the Constitution

As should be evident to you now, protective jurisdiction (whatever that term means) raises a host of constitutional issues. One strand of argument is that protective jurisdiction is inconsistent with fundamental principles of separation of powers. Another strand is that protective jurisdiction is inconsistent with federalism.

Is any notion of protective jurisdiction consistent with either separation-of-powers principles or federalism? Does your answer depend on whether one considers the views of either Professor Wechsler or Professor Mishkin?

4. *See* 49 U.S.C. § 40101. The Fund eventually distributed more than $7 billion to eligible claimants. The Special Master appointed to manage the Fund determined that nearly every eligible family elected to participate in the Fund.

5. Liability was capped at the amount of available liability insurance.

REVIEW AND CONSOLIDATION

The Constitutional Scope of "Arising Under" Jurisdiction

- Congress must affirmatively exercise its power to bestow jurisdiction under Article III. Therefore, one must both identify a statute granting arising under jurisdiction and ensure that the jurisdiction granted comports with the Constitution.
- The scope of arising under jurisdiction in Article III is broad. Under *Osborn* there need only be a federal "ingredient" in the case, and that federal ingredient need not be in dispute.
- The theory of "protective jurisdiction" pushes the outer limit of the Constitution's arising under jurisdiction. Protective jurisdiction, if it exists, must be tied either to an "articulated and active" federal policy or more broadly to the protection of identified federal interests. Recognition of protective jurisdiction would enhance congressional power as well as that of the federal courts. To date, the Supreme Court has declined to either endorse or reject protective jurisdiction.

2. *The Statutory Scope of "Arising Under" Jurisdiction*

We have seen that arising under jurisdiction encompassed by Article III is quite broad. But Article III is not self-executing. An act of Congress is required to implement arising under jurisdiction. We now consider congressional implementation of its power.

There are many examples of Congress' exercise of the power to confer federal question jurisdiction. For example, Congress has specifically granted federal question jurisdiction for actions arising under the patent, copyright, and trademark laws (28 U.S.C. § 1338), actions arising under federal statutes relating to the postal service (28 U.S.C. § 1339), and actions on bonds executed under federal law (28 U.S.C. § 1352). We could continue this list for some time. Some of these jurisdictional grants go beyond providing a basis for federal court jurisdiction by also making that jurisdiction exclusive.[6]

The specific grants of arising under jurisdiction may occasionally be significant. As mentioned, a specific grant of jurisdiction may make federal court the only option, or it may expand a defendant's ability to remove a case to federal court more liberally than would otherwise be possible. By and large, however, these more specific jurisdictional grants are artifacts of a period in which there needed to be a certain amount in controversy under the general federal question statute. Now that this requirement has been removed from the general jurisdictional statute, specific jurisdictional statutes are often superfluous.

Our focus will be on the general federal question jurisdictional provision, 28 U.S.C. § 1331. This section provides: "The district courts shall have original jurisdiction of all civil actions arising under the Constitution, laws, or treaties of

6. *See, e.g.*, 28 U.S.C. § 1338(a) (providing for exclusive federal jurisdiction for, among other things, copyright and patent cases).

the United States."[7] As mentioned earlier, despite the similarity between the language of the Constitution and § 1331, the Court has consistently interpreted the statute to provide a narrower scope of jurisdiction than Article III. In federal court practice, interpretation of § 1331 is usually far more practically important than interpretation of Article III.

a. Where (and How) to Look: The Well-Pleaded Complaint Rule

The starting point for considering the Supreme Court's interpretation of § 1331 is the famous case concerning Erasmus and Annie Mottley and their epic battle with the Louisville and Nashville Railroad. The Mottleys' story began when they were injured on one of defendant's trains and sued for negligence. The parties entered into a settlement agreement that released the Railroad from liability in exchange for lifetime passes valid for free transportation. Everything went well for the Mottleys until 1907 when the Railroad, for reasons explained below, refused to honor their free passes any longer. The Mottleys sued in federal court, seeking specific performance of the Railroad's promise to honor the free passes.

LOUISVILLE & NASHVILLE RAILROAD CO. v. MOTTLEY

211 U.S. 149 (1908)

MR. JUSTICE MOODY . . . delivered the opinion of the court.

Two questions of law were raised . . . by appeal, and have been argued before us. They are, first, whether that part of the act of Congress of June 29, 1906, which forbids the giving of free passes or the collection of any different compensation for transportation of passengers than that specified in the tariff filed, makes it unlawful to perform a contract for transportation of persons, who in good faith, before the passage of the act, had accepted such contract in satisfaction of a valid cause of action against the railroad; and, second, whether the statute, if it should be construed to render such a contract unlawful, is in violation of the Fifth Amendment of the Constitution of the United States. We do not deem it necessary, however, to consider either of these questions, because, in our opinion, the court below was without jurisdiction of the cause. Neither party has questioned that jurisdiction, but it is the duty of this court to see to it that the jurisdiction of the Circuit Court, which is defined and limited by statute, is not exceeded. This duty we have frequently performed of our own motion.

There was no diversity of citizenship and it is not and cannot be suggested that there was any ground of jurisdiction, except that the case was a "suit . . . arising under the Constitution and laws of the United States." [The Court cited the then-current version of today's 28 U.S.C. § 1331.] It is the settled interpretation of these words, as used in this statute, conferring jurisdiction, that a suit arises under the Constitution and laws of the United States only when the plaintiff's statement of his own cause of action shows that it is based upon those laws or that Constitution. It is not enough that the plaintiff alleges some anticipated defense

7. Arising under jurisdiction pursuant to § 1331 is concurrent with that of the state courts.

to his cause of action and asserts that the defense is invalidated by some provision of the Constitution of the United States. Although such allegations show that very likely, in the course of the litigation, a question under the Constitution would arise, they do not show that the suit, that is, the plaintiff's original cause of action, arises under the Constitution. In *Tennessee v. Union & Planters' Bank*, the plaintiff, the State of Tennessee, brought suit in the Circuit Court of the United States to recover from the defendant certain taxes alleged to be due under the laws of the State. The plaintiff alleged that the defendant claimed an immunity from the taxation by virtue of its charter, and that therefore the tax was void, because in violation of the provision of the Constitution of the United States, which forbids any State from passing a law impairing the obligation of contracts. The cause was held to be beyond the jurisdiction of the Circuit Court, the court saying, "a suggestion of one party, that the other will or may set up a claim under the Constitution or laws of the United States, does not make the suit one arising under that Constitution or those laws." Again, in *Boston & Montana Consolidated Copper & Silver Mining Company v. Montana Ore Purchasing Company*, the plaintiff brought suit in the Circuit Court of the United States for the conversion of copper ore and for an injunction against its continuance. The plaintiff then alleged, for the purpose of showing jurisdiction, in substance, that the defendant would set up in defense certain laws of the United States. The cause was held to be beyond the jurisdiction of the Circuit Court, the court saying,

> "It would be wholly unnecessary and improper in order to prove complainant's cause of action to go into any matters of defence which the defendants might possibly set up and then attempt to reply to such defence, and thus, if possible, to show that a Federal question might or probably would arise in the course of the trial of the case. To allege such defence and then make an answer to it before the defendant has the opportunity to itself plead or prove its own defence is inconsistent with any known rule of pleading so far as we are aware, and is improper.
>
> "The rule is a reasonable and just one that the complainant in the first instance shall be confined to a statement of its cause of action, leaving to the defendant to set up in his answer what his defence is and, if anything more than a denial of complainant's cause of action, imposing upon the defendant the burden of proving such defence.
>
> "Conforming itself to that rule the complainant would not, in the assertion or proof of its cause of action, bring up a single Federal question. The presentation of its cause of action would not show that it was one arising under the Constitution or laws of the United States.
>
> "The only way in which it might be claimed that a Federal question was presented would be in the complainant's statement of what the defence of defendants would be and complainant's answer to such defence. . . ."

* * * *

It is ordered that the judgment be reversed and the case remitted to the Circuit Court with instructions to dismiss the suit for want of jurisdiction.[8]

8. After this decision the Mottleys refiled their suit in Kentucky state court. The state courts ruled in favor of the Mottleys, ultimately ordering that the Railroad specifically perform under the terms of the settlement agreement. The Supreme Court once again heard the case on appeal from the Court of Appeals of Kentucky. The Court reversed the state court judgment and held the federal statute made enforcement of the contract's terms unlawful and that the statute was constitutional. *See Louisville & Nashville R.R. Co. v. Mottley*, 219 U.S. 467 (1911).

DISCUSSION AND QUESTIONS

Mottley is a first-year Civil Procedure staple, so you will likely have read the opinion before. In *Mottley* the Court sets forth the so-called well-pleaded complaint rule that helps define arising under jurisdiction under § 1331.

At its heart, the well-pleaded complaint rule concerns both *where* and *how* to determine whether a given lawsuit falls within statutory arising under jurisdiction. As to where, Justice Moody makes clear we must examine the *plaintiff's complaint.* This has several important consequences. First, one determines whether a suit arises under federal law at the beginning of a lawsuit upon filing of the complaint. Second, the plaintiff has considerable power when drafting the complaint to control jurisdiction, assuming the plaintiff has an option of alleging a federal claim. Finally, the defendant's response to the complaint is irrelevant. Even if a federal defense is asserted in response to the plaintiff's non-federal claim, there is no federal question jurisdiction. Similarly, the well-pleaded complaint rule renders irrelevant the assertion of a federal counterclaim in the defendant's responsive pleading. *See Holmes Grps., Inc. v. Vorando Air Circulation Sys., Inc.*, 535 U.S. 826 (2002) (construing the phrase arising under in 28 U.S.C. § 1338 to exclude jurisdiction based on the assertion of a federal patent counterclaim).[9]

The *Mottley* Court also provides some information as to how one looks at the plaintiff's complaint. It is not enough that the plaintiff refers to federal law in the complaint. After all, the Mottleys raised issues in their complaint about both a federal statute and the United States Constitution. Rather, one looks at the complaint to determine whether the plaintiff relies on federal law to establish its claim—hence the requirement that there be a *well-pleaded* complaint. A plaintiff cannot plead itself into federal court under § 1331 by anticipating a federal issue that should be properly alleged in the defendant's well-pleaded answer. The federal issue in the complaint must be one that is a part of the *plaintiff's* case.[10] In other words, the rule asks one to consider what the plaintiff would have to prove in order to win on the merits, assuming the defendant raised no defenses.

The combined impact of the rule's components is that the scope of jurisdiction under § 1331 is but a subset of the federal question jurisdiction Congress could potentially confer under the constitutional standard stated in *Osborne.* One can visualize this relationship as displayed in Figure 5-1.

9. Congress has overruled the statutory holding in *Holmes Group*, which specifically concerned the specific jurisdictional grant in 28 U.S.C. § 1338 dealing with patents. In the 2012 America Invents Act, Congress expanded such jurisdiction to include counterclaims. *See* Pub. L. No. 112-29, codified in scattered sections of Title 28 of the United States Code. This development reflects both the Court's strong commitment to the well-pleaded complaint principle and also Congress' ability to alter that statutory rule.

10. We consider the well-pleaded complaint rule in the context of declaratory judgment actions below. See section C.2.c.

FIGURE 5-1

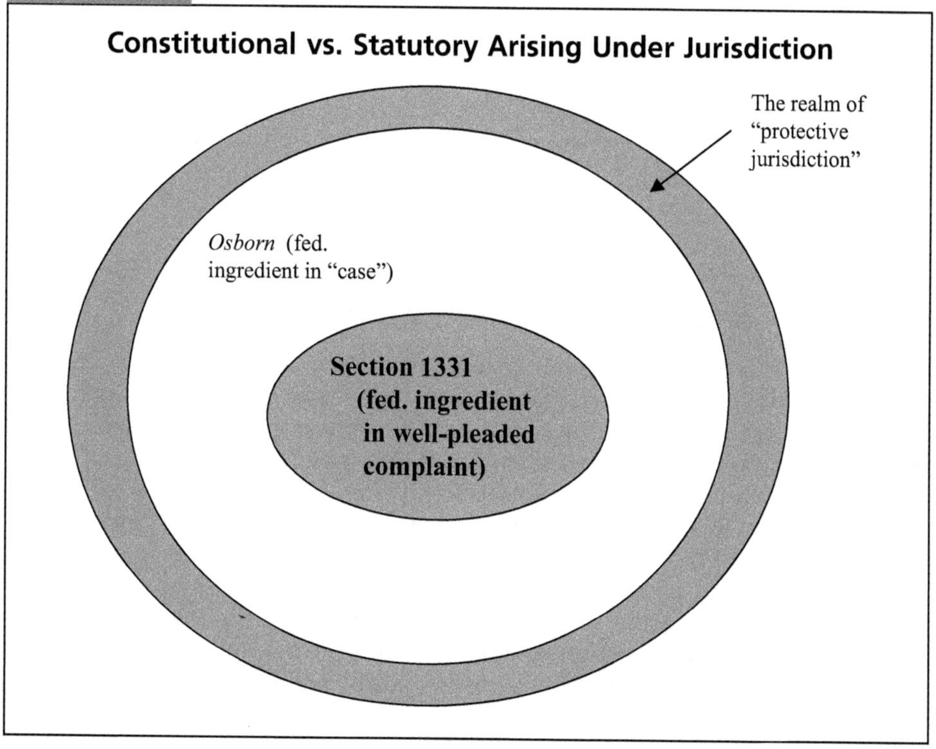

The well-pleaded complaint rule applies most obviously when a plaintiff files its case in federal court. It also applies, however, when a plaintiff has filed a lawsuit in state court and a defendant wishes to remove that suit to federal court. Under 28 U.S.C. § 1441, a defendant's ability to remove a civil action is generally tied to whether the plaintiff could have filed in federal court in the first place.[11] Thus, one still must consider the plaintiff's complaint—and only that document—to judge whether removal is appropriate.[12]

The well-pleaded complaint rule has come under criticism over the years because of its rigidity. Its effect is to exclude from the federal courts certain cases in which there will unquestionably be an important federal issue at play as a result of a federal defense or a federal counterclaim. These cases will be resolved by state courts with only the slim possibility of federal review through the Supreme Court in connection with a writ of certiorari. If one mistrusts state courts when resolving federal issues, such a state of affairs is unsettling. But despite scholarly criticism, the Supreme Court has shown no inclination to

11. The Court has held that, while the plaintiff is the master of the case filed, it may not thwart a defendant's ability to remove a case by "artful pleading." In other words, a plaintiff cannot omit material that would support federal jurisdiction in order to avoid removal. Of course, balancing the "master of the complaint" and "artful pleading" doctrines can prove difficult in certain cases. We do not explore details of this area of federal question jurisdiction.

12. In certain limited circumstances, Congress has made removal available based on a federal defense. *See, e.g.*, 28 U.S.C. § 1442 (allowing removal of an action in state court against a federal "agency" or "officer" based on a federal defense); 28 U.S.C. § 1443 (providing removal in certain actions implicating civil rights). Congress has also precluded removal in certain cases when it would otherwise be appropriate. *See, e.g.*, 28 U.S.C. § 1445 (listing several actions that are not removable, such as actions under workers' compensation laws and certain actions against railroads).

change its interpretation of § 1331.[13] In addition, Congress has shown no willingness to amend the statute. Some of this unwillingness to alter the rule may stem from the courts' institutional self-preservation. Imagine the flood of cases that could swamp the federal courts if the full *Osborn* scope of arising under jurisdiction were grafted onto § 1331.

Test your understanding of the well-pleaded complaint rule as it stands today by considering Problem 5-3.

PROBLEM 5-3

Native American Tribes, States, and Taxes

The Chickasaw Nation of Native Americans (the "Nation") owns and operates a facility in Oklahoma at which it conducts bingo games and sells cigarettes. Under Oklahoma statutes, the Nation is required to pay excise taxes on its sales of cigarettes and proceeds from the bingo games. For a period of years, the Nation failed to pay the required excise taxes.

The State of Oklahoma filed suit in an Oklahoma state court against the Nation, seeking to collect the unpaid excise taxes. The Nation removed the case to federal court, arguing that arising under jurisdiction was proper because the Nation is immune from suit under federal law. You should assume that the Nation is correct that it possesses such immunity from suit and you should ignore any claim the state may have under the Eleventh Amendment, a topic we consider in Chapter 8.

The state has moved to remand the case to state court based on a lack of federal question jurisdiction. How should the district court judge rule? Would it make a difference if the state pled in its complaint the reasons why the Nation may not be immune under federal law? What if Oklahoma law provides that, when suing an entity having a colorable claim of immunity, a plaintiff must plead why immunity does not apply?

REVIEW AND CONSOLIDATION

The Well-Pleaded Complaint Rule

- Under § 1331, one looks to the plaintiff's well-pleaded *complaint,* and the complaint alone, to determine whether the case arises under federal law. One does not consider a defendant's anticipated or actual defenses or counterclaims.
- The key is the plaintiff's *well-pleaded* complaint. The plaintiff is not allowed to circumvent the rule by including in the complaint allegations about an anticipated federal defense or counterclaim.

13. This is the case even though the Court has described the rule as being based more on "history than logic." *See Franchise Tax Bd. of Cal. v. Construction Laborers Vacation Trust for S. Cal.,* 463 U.S. 1, 4 (1983). The Supreme Court continues to adhere to the well-pleaded complaint rule in terms of excluding both answers as well as counterclaims that may be based on federal law. *See Vaden v. Discover Bank,* 556 U.S. 49, 59-62 (2009).

One considers only what the plaintiff must plead in order to prevail under substantive law.

✦ The same well-pleaded complaint rule governs a defendant's removal of a case to federal court. Removal is proper only if the well-pleaded complaint filed by the plaintiff in state court would have arisen under federal law if filed in federal court in the first instance.

b. What to Look For?

The well-pleaded complaint rule is clearly significant. However, the rule is really only the beginning of the analysis. The next question is: what does one look for in the well-pleaded complaint when deciding whether it arises under federal law? We now address that question.

We consider three issues in turn. First, we discuss the rule that captures the great majority of complaints arising under federal law—namely, complaints where federal law creates the plaintiff's cause of action. Second, we consider the very limited situations in which the plaintiff's cause of action is created by state law but there is embedded in the plaintiff's state-law cause of action a federal issue of such importance that the case qualifies as one arising under federal law. Finally, we conclude by considering the special, although narrow, situation in which federal law has so completely occupied a field that even something that looks like a state cause of action is, in reality, one that arises under federal law. This doctrine is referred to as "complete preemption."

i. The "Cause of Action" Rule

The overwhelming majority of cases that fall within the scope of § 1331's grant of jurisdiction are captured by the rule Justice Oliver Wendell Holmes laid down in the following case.

AMERICAN WELL WORKS CO. v. LAYNE & BOWLER CO.

241 U.S. 257 (1916)

MR. JUSTICE HOLMES delivered the opinion of the Court:

[Plaintiff commenced an action for libel and slander in state court. Plaintiff's complaint alleged that defendant was falsely defaming its pump by representing that it violated defendant's own patented pump. In the opinion excerpted below, Justice Holmes examines whether plaintiff's complaint arises under federal patent law and was properly removed to federal court.]

Of course the question depends upon the plaintiff's declaration. That may be summed up in a few words. The plaintiff alleges that it owns, manufactures, and sells a certain pump, has or has applied for a patent for it, and that the pump is known as the best in the market. It then alleges that the defendants have falsely and maliciously libeled and slandered the plaintiff's title to the pump by stating that the pump and certain parts thereof are infringements upon the defendant's pump and certain parts thereof, and that without probable cause they have brought suits against some parties who are using the plaintiff's pump, and that they are threatening suits against all who use it. The allegation of the defendants' libel or slander is repeated in slightly varying form, but it all comes to statements to various people that the plaintiff was infringing the defendants' patent, and that the defendant would sue both seller and buyer if the plaintiff's pump was used. Actual damage to the plaintiff in its business is alleged to the extent of $50,000, and punitive damages to the same amount are asked.

It is evident that the claim for damages is based upon conduct; or, more specifically, language, tending to persuade the public to withdraw its custom from the plaintiff, and having that effect to its damage. Such conduct, having such effect, is equally actionable whether it produces the result by persuasion, by threats, or by falsehood and it is enough to allege and prove the conduct and effect, leaving the defendant to justify if he can. If the conduct complained of is persuasion, it may be justified by the fact that the defendant is a competitor, or by good faith and reasonable grounds. If it is a statement of fact, it may be justified, absolutely or with qualifications, by proof that the statement is true. But all such justifications are defenses, and raise issues that are no part of the plaintiff's case. In the present instance it is part of the plaintiff's case that it had a business to be damaged; whether built up by patents or without them does not matter. It is no part of it to prove anything concerning the defendants' patent, or that the plaintiff did not infringe the same — still less to prove anything concerning any patent of its own. The material statement complained of is that the plaintiff infringes, — which may be true notwithstanding the plaintiff's patent. That is merely a piece of evidence. Furthermore, the damage alleged presumably is rather the consequence of the threat to sue than of the statement that the plaintiff's pump infringed the defendants' rights.

A suit for damages to business caused by a threat to sue under the patent law is not itself a suit under the patent law. And the same is true when the damage is caused by a statement of fact, that the defendant has a patent which is infringed. What makes the defendants' act a wrong is its manifest tendency to injure the plaintiff's business; and the wrong is the same whatever the means by which it is accomplished. But whether it is a wrong or not depends upon the law of the state where the act is done, not upon the patent law, and therefore the suit arises under the law of the state. A suit arises under the law that creates the cause of action. The fact that the justification may involve the validity and infringement of a patent is no more material to the question under what law the suit is brought than it would be in an action of contract. If the state adopted for civil proceedings the saying of the old criminal law: the greater the truth, the greater the libel, the validity of the patent would not come in question at all. In Massachusetts the truth would not be a defense if the statement was made from disinterested malevolence. The state is master of the whole matter, and if it saw fit to do away with actions of this type altogether, no one, we imagine, would suppose that they still could be maintained under the patent laws of the United States. Judgment reversed.

MR. JUSTICE MCKENNA dissents, being of opinion that the case involves a direct and substantial controversy under the patent laws.

DISCUSSION AND QUESTIONS

American Well Works reaffirms the well-pleaded complaint rule. Justice Holmes leaves no doubt that whether the plaintiff's case arises under federal law depends on the complaint. But Justice Holmes also gives us important instruction about what to look for when determining whether the complaint arises under federal law.

What American Well Works means. *American Well Works* stands for the proposition that "[a] suit arises under the law that creates the cause of action." 241 U.S. at 260. In *American Well Works*, Massachusetts law had created the right to sue for slander of title. The fact that the alleged slander concerned federal patents did not mean that federal law created the cause of action. The federal patents were merely evidence relevant to a state-created cause of action.

A prime advantage of the "cause of action" rule is that it is clear. One asks what creates the plaintiff's right to sue. If the right to sue for a cause of action is created by federal law, the case arises under federal law. If not, the case is not within the statutory grant. Of course, a potential disadvantage of the rule is its rigidity. By focusing on one issue — what law creates the cause of action — federal courts are denied jurisdiction even though plaintiff's well-pleaded complaint discloses that a federal issue is important to proving her state cause of action.

Whatever the merits are in a debate about the rule, it remains a fixture. The Supreme Court reaffirmed the vitality of the "cause of action" rule in its 2011 Term. In *Mims v. Arrow Financial Services, LLC*, the Court addressed a provision of a federal statute dealing with abuses telemarketing practices: the Telephone Consumer Protection Act of 1991, 47 U.S.C § 227. 132 S. Ct. 740 (2012). Of present importance, this statute created a private right of action for consumers and also provided that such actions could be brought in state court. The question was whether the provision for state court jurisdiction meant that a case correspondingly could not be brought in federal court. The Supreme Court ruled unanimously that federal courts possessed subject matter jurisdiction under § 1331. 132 S. Ct. at 745. The Court first underscored the centrality of the "cause of action" rule from *American Well Works. Id.* at 748. Then the Court made clear that absent congressional direction to the contrary, the mere provision of jurisdiction to state courts to adjudicate claims arising under a federal statute does not divest federal courts of general federal question jurisdiction under § 1331. Such jurisdiction is presumed to be concurrent. *Id.* at 753.

Over time, the Supreme Court has come to view the *American Well Works* test as "more useful for describing the vast majority of cases that come within the district courts' original jurisdiction than it is for describing which cases are beyond district court jurisdiction." *Franchise Tax Bd. of Cal. v. Construction Laborers Vacation Trust for S. Cal.*, 463 U.S. 1, 9 (1983). In other words, the "cause of action" test does not describe the *only* circumstances in which a case can be said to arise under federal law. We will turn in the next subpart to those situations in which a claim may arise under federal law even though the plaintiff's right to sue is created by state law. For now, we explore the *American Well Works* test in greater detail.

How does one determine whether a cause of action is created by federal law? How does one determine whether a cause of action is, in fact, created by federal law such that *American Well Works* supports jurisdiction? In an overwhelming number of situations the answer is clear: a federal statute will expressly provide that a person may bring a lawsuit. We have already seen an example of such a statute in this chapter. See *supra* Problem 5-2 (discussing the ATSSA that creates a "federal cause of action" for certain claims arising out of the September 11 terrorist attacks).

However, such express statutory causes of action do not exhaust the situations in which a plaintiff's right to sue is created by federal law. First, rights of action may be implied by the Constitution, federal statutes, and treaties. To the extent that any of these sources of federal law are interpreted to provide a private right of action, the *American Well Works* formulation would support arising under jurisdiction. Second, a cause of action may arise under federal common law as well as under a federal statute. *See, e.g., Illinois v. City of Milwaukee,* 406 U.S. 91, 100 (1972). We discuss both implied causes of action and federal common law more generally in Chapter 11.

Exceptions to the rule. Of course, what would a rule be without exceptions? There are two such exceptions we briefly highlight.[14] First, 16 years before *American Well Works* the Supreme Court decided *Shoshone Mining Co. v. Rutter,* 177 U.S. 505 (1900). *Shoshone Mining* concerned competing claims for exclusive grants to certain mining rights. The plaintiff filed its suit under the provisions of a federal statute. However, that statute directed that the rights of competing parties were to be determined by "local customs or rules of miners in the several mining districts, so far as the same are applicable and not inconsistent with the laws of the United States." Under the formulation that was to come in *American Well Works,* the case would be one that arose under federal law because the right to sue flowed from a federal statute. The Court in *Shoshone Mining* held, however, that federal jurisdiction was improper because the suit "to determine the right of possession [for mining] may not involve any question as to the construction or effect of the Constitution or laws of the United States, but may present simply a question of fact [concerning local matters], or a determination of the meaning and effect of certain local rules and customs . . . or the effect of state statutes. . . ." 177 U.S. at 509.

One might be tempted to say that, whatever *Shoshone Mining* meant when it was decided, it was seriously undercut if not effectively overruled by the Court's later decision in *American Well Works.* However, the Supreme Court has consistently stated that *Shoshone Mining* remains good law. *See, e.g., Grable & Sons Metal Prods., Inc. v. Darue Eng'g & Mfg.,* 545 U.S. 308, 317 n.5 (2005) (describing *Shoshone* as "an extremely rare exception" to the "cause of action" rule); *Merrell Dow Pharms., Inc. v. Thompson,* 478 U.S. 804, 814 n. 12 (1986) (citing *Shoshone* with approval).

What, then, is one to make of *Shoshone Mining*? One way to reconcile the case with general doctrine is to use the classic dodge of limiting it to its facts. It would thus be restricted to federal mining claims. Another tack to reconcile *Shoshone Mining* with modern doctrine is to argue that the "federal interest" in that case was insufficient to justify exercise of federal question jurisdiction. As we discuss in the next section, this approach has some support in jurisdictional precedent. But no attempt to reconcile *Shoshone Mining* with modern jurisdictional doctrine is fully satisfying.

The second exception to the "cause of action" rule recognizes that the federal cause of action alleged in the complaint may be "frivolous" or so "insubstantial" that the federal courts lacks jurisdiction. *See Bell v. Hood,* 327 U.S. 678 (1946). When the federal cause of action is insubstantial, a court may have authority to

14. As we discuss later, it is also possible that one could classify the "complete preemption" doctrine as an exception to the *American Well Works* rule. Indeed, at times the Supreme Court has done so. *See Aetna Health Inc. v. Davila,* 542 U.S. 200, 208 (2004). See section C.2.b.iii.

either dismiss for lack of jurisdiction or dismiss for "failure to state a claim" under Federal Rule of Civil Procedure 12(b)(6).[15] The difficulty is that the Court has not been consistent as to which approach is appropriate. As then-Justice Rehnquist once wrote, "to me the decision in *Bell* is one of the most cryptic in the recent history of this Court's jurisprudence." *Yazoo Country Indus. Dev. Corp. v. Suthoff,* 454 U.S. 1157 (1982) (dissenting from denial of certiorari). Despite or perhaps because of the doctrinal confusion, jurisdictional dismissals based on an insubstantial or frivolous claim are quite rare. They are, however, possible and qualify the "cause of action" approach announced in *American Well Works.*

REVIEW AND CONSOLIDATION

American Well Works "Cause of Action" Rule

- In the great majority of cases, a suit arises under federal law for purposes of § 1331 if federal law creates the plaintiff's right to sue. That right can be an express or implied right of action under the Constitution, a federal statute, or a treaty. It can also be based on federal common law.
- The "cause of action" rule is one of inclusion, not exclusion. It describes well what comes within arising under jurisdiction but does not necessarily exclude other causes of action from federal court jurisdiction.
- There *may* be the rare exception to the "cause of action" rule when federal law provides the right to sue but the case does not arise under federal law for purposes of § 1331.
- The plaintiff may plead a federal cause of action that is so frivolous or insubstantial that it is dismissed for lack of jurisdiction.

ii. The State-Created Cause of Action That "Arises Under" Federal Law

As described in the previous subpart, the "cause of action" rule outlined by Justice Holmes in *American Well Works* describes the great majority of situations in which a case arises under federal law for purposes of § 1331. Federal jurisdiction exists when federal law confers a right and judicial remedy on the plaintiff. But

15. The distinction might be important when the plaintiff has alleged both federal and state claims. If the sole federal claim is dismissed for failure to state a claim, the court might still exercise supplemental jurisdiction over state claims. *See* 28 U.S.C. § 1367(c) (recognizing court's authority to dismiss or retain supplemental state claims when "claims over which it has original jurisdiction" have been dismissed). If the federal claim is dismissed for want of jurisdiction, the remaining state claims must be dismissed because there is no basis for exercising supplemental jurisdiction. The distinction could also have important consequences for a plaintiff's ability to refile a claim in state court. A dismissal for lack of subject matter jurisdiction would usually not have any claim- or issue-preclusive effect in a state court. A dismissal for failure to state a federal claim, however, could preclude such a claim from being tried anywhere else even if it is repled as a "state" claim.

the Court has consistently disavowed any bright-line rule limiting jurisdiction to this situation. In the words of Justice Cardozo:

> This Court has had occasion to point out how futile is the attempt to define "cause of action" without reference to context. To define broadly and in the abstract "a case arising under the Constitution or laws of the United States" has hazards of a kindred order. What is needed is something of that common-sense accommodation of judgment to kaleidoscopic situations which characterizes the law in its treatment of problems of causation.

Gully v. First Nat'l Bank of Meridian, 299 U.S. 109, 118 (1936). As we consider evolving concepts of arising under jurisdiction, ask yourself whether modern doctrine has become more predictable than Justice Cardozo's comments suggest.

The Law Before Grable and Gunn. Current doctrine concerning when a state-created cause of action arises under federal law is principally framed by *Grable* and *Gunn,* the two principal opinions excerpted below. In order to understand these opinions, it helps to explore prior precedent interpreting § 1331 and its predecessors.

In 1921, the Court decided *Smith v. Kansas City Title & Trust Co.,* 255 U.S. 180 (1921). The plaintiff Smith was a shareholder in the defendant corporation, which was organized under Missouri law. He filed suit in a federal court in Missouri, seeking to enjoin the defendant from investing in certain "farm loan bonds" issued pursuant to a federal statute, the Federal Farm Loan Act. Smith claimed that investment in the bonds violated Missouri law. Specifically, he asserted that corporate directors would violate their fiduciary duty under Missouri law if they invested in bonds not issued pursuant to a valid law. He alleged that Congress lacked the constitutional authority to authorize issuance of bonds under the Federal Farm Loan Act. Therefore, Smith reasoned, the defendant corporation should be enjoined from investing in the bonds because they were not lawfully issued.

The defendant corporation removed the case to federal court, claiming Smith's complaint arose under federal law. If *American Well Works* provided an exclusive test for arising under jurisdiction, Smith had an easy argument to defeat jurisdiction: Smith's right to sue arose under Missouri law, not federal law.

The Supreme Court concluded, however, that Smith's case arose under federal law for purposes of § 1331. In sustaining jurisdiction, the Court held:

> The general rule is that, where it appears from the [plaintiff's complaint] that the right to relief depends upon the construction or application of the Constitution or laws of the United States, and that such federal claim is not merely colorable, and rests upon a reasonable foundation, the District Court has jurisdiction [under § 1331].

255 U.S. at 199. Applying its test, the Court concluded jurisdiction was proper based on the following reasoning:

> In the instant case the averments of the bill show that the directors were proceeding to make the investments in view of the act authorizing the bonds about to be purchased, maintaining that the act authorizing them was constitutional and the

> bonds valid and desirable investments. The objecting shareholder avers in the bill that the securities were issued under an unconstitutional law, and hence of no validity. It is therefore apparent that the controversy concerns the constitutional validity of an act of Congress which is directly drawn in question. The decision depends upon the determination of this issue.

Id. at 201. Justice Holmes strenuously dissented, insisting that his opinion in *American Well Works* defined the full scope of statutory arising under jurisdiction.

Smith thus expands the *American Well Works* definition of when a case arises under federal law. *Smith* does *not* call into question the well-pleaded complaint rule, as there still must be some allegations pertaining to federal law in plaintiff's well-pleaded complaint. In *Smith* those allegations concerned the unconstitutionality of federal bonds, which, according to state law, prevented the corporation from investing in them. Notice that if Smith's complaint had not alluded to federal law and, instead, the defendant had asserted federal law as a defense to Smith's claim, the situation would have been the same as in *Mottley*. There would have been no federal jurisdiction.

A second important precursor to modern doctrine is the Court's decision in *Moore v. Chesapeake & Ohio Railway Co.*, 291 U.S. 205 (1934). Moore was an employee of the defendant railroad injured at work. Moore sued his employer in federal court, basing his suit on Kentucky's Employer Liability Act. This Act precluded defenses of contributory negligence or assumption of risk if an employee's injury resulted from the employer's violation of any state or federal statute enacted for the safety of employees. Moore alleged that his injury resulted from his employer's violation of the Federal Safety Appliance Act.

The Court held in *Moore* that the case did not arise under federal law for statutory purposes. The Court might have relied on *Mottley*'s well-pleaded complaint rule and concluded that Moore's complaint alleged federal law merely in anticipation of the defendant's assertion of contributory negligence. Instead, the Court treated the case as if Moore had alleged a federal ingredient as part of his state cause of action, as occurred in *Smith v. Kansas City Title & Trust Co.*

But the Court seemingly departed from *Smith* in rejecting arising under jurisdiction. The Court stressed first that the plaintiff's cause of action was created by Kentucky law. The Court then gave this rationale for rejecting arising under jurisdiction:

> The Federal Safety Appliance Act prescribed duties, and injured employees are entitled to recover for injuries sustained through the breach of these duties. Questions arising in actions in state courts to recover for injuries sustained by employees in intrastate commerce and relating to the scope or construction of the Federal Safety Appliance Acts are, of course, federal questions which may appropriately be reviewed in this Court. But it does not follow that a suit brought under the state statute which defines liability to employees who are injured while engaged in intrastate commerce, and brings within the purview of the statute a breach of the duty imposed by the federal statute should be regarded as a suit arising under the laws of the United States and cognizable in the federal court in the absence of diversity of citizenship. The Federal Safety Appliances Act, while prescribing absolute duties, and thus creating correlative rights in favor of injured employees, did not attempt to lay down rules governing actions in enforcing these rights. . . .

Moore, 291 U.S. at 214-15.

PROBLEM 5-4

Reconciling Smith *and* Moore

How is one to reconcile the holdings of *Smith* and *Moore*? It has been argued that the holdings cannot be reconciled. Before despairing of a reconciliation, try to develop a theory of arising under jurisdiction that accommodates these holdings within the framework of the well-pleaded complaint rule. Recall that *Smith* involved an underlying question of whether the defendant corporation should be enjoined from investing in federally authorized bonds. *Moore*, on the other hand, involved a question of whether the defendant railroad should be precluded from asserting a defense of contributory negligence to a state cause of action because it violated federal safety statutes. Does this distinction suggest a basis for reconciling the two cases and developing a consistent theory of arising under jurisdiction? Are there other distinctions between *Moore* and *Smith* that might explain their different results?

We are now ready to consider how the modern-day Court views state-created causes of action that include a federal ingredient. We begin with the Court's decision in *Merrell Dow Pharmaceuticals, Inc. v. Thompson*, 478 U.S. 804 (1986). *Merrell Dow* concerned a claim by plaintiffs alleging that the drug Bendectin was defective, leading to injuries sustained by children born of mothers who had taken the drug. Plaintiffs brought claims only under state law. However, in support of those state-law claims, they alleged that the defendant's purported violation of a federal statute, the Food, Drug, and Cosmetic Act, constituted a rebuttable presumption of negligence as a matter of state law. Plaintiffs filed their suit in state court. The defendant removed to federal court, claiming that the case was one that arose under federal law.

We can pause a moment to review. The case did not arise under federal law in the *American Well Works* sense. All agreed that the plaintiffs' right to sue was derived from state law because all of their claims were based on either state common law or state statutes as the basis for providing the right to sue. Thus, federal jurisdiction was proper only if the embedded reference to federal law in the plaintiffs' state law action provided a basis for removal. The Court held that it did not. Importantly, however, it also reaffirmed that there were situations in which a federal issue embedded in a state-law cause of action could provide the basis for jurisdiction under § 1331. But to do so the federal ingredient needed to be sufficiently substantial.

To better understand the Court's decision in *Merrell Dow* and set the stage for the cases that follow it, it helps to distinguish between express and implied causes of action. Most federal statutes relied on by plaintiffs provide them express rights and remedies. For example, Title VII provides employees the right to be free of discrimination in employment and also provides aggrieved employees an equitable or monetary remedy. Such express causes of action, which bundle rights and remedies, unquestionably satisfy federal question jurisdiction as defined in *American Well Works*.

However, many federal statutes regulating conduct fail to expressly create private causes of action. One example of such a statute was the Food, Drug, and Cosmetic Act at issue in *Merrell Dow*. Such statutes regulate certain conduct, such as drug labeling, but any rights or remedies for private enforcement must be inferred by the courts — that is, the courts must recognize an "implied" cause of action. Although one could argue that Congress' failure to expressly provide a cause of action under a statute denies plaintiffs any federal relief, the Supreme Court has long held that statutory silence does not necessarily foreclose private suits. Provided there is strong indication that Congress wanted persons to have the right to sue for violations of a statute, the Court is willing to recognize an implied cause of action.

We explore implied causes of action more fully in Chapter 11. Such implied rights are controversial. For present purposes, understanding private causes of action is important to understanding *Merrell Dow.* Do not get confused. The issue in the case was not directly whether the Food, Drug, and Cosmetic Act provided either an express or an implied cause of action. That would have been the question had one of the plaintiffs' claims been asserted under that statute itself. Rather, the question was what impact, if any, the express/implied cause of action had on whether the reference to the federal statute in a state cause of action provided the basis for federal jurisdiction *over that state-law created cause of action.*

First, there was no question that the federal statute embedded in the plaintiffs' complaint did not expressly create a federal cause of action. Second, the Court assumed that there was no implied cause of action under the statute either. Apparently based largely on these two conclusions, the Court stated that there was no arising under jurisdiction over plaintiffs' defective drug claims. Stated succinctly, the federal ingredient was insufficiently substantial.

While the bottom-line result was clear, the actual impact of the absence of an express or implied federal cause of action with respect to the embedded federal ingredient on that result was not. In other words, the question of how one is to separate a substantial federal issue from one that is not remained obscure. As Justice Brennan pointed out in his dissent, the concept of substantiality is susceptible of a wide range of meanings. After *Merrell Dow* the lower federal courts developed a number of approaches to resolving this question. Debate often centered on the existence of a private right of action, whether express or implied. Some courts required that there be an express or implied right of action under federal law in order to sustain jurisdiction. Others held that it was possible to have a substantial federal issue under *Smith, Moore,* and *Merrell Dow* even in the absence of a federal cause of action. The Supreme Court resolved this disagreement in the next two opinions and also provided the most recent, extensive statements concerning when a state-created cause of action arises under federal law.

GRABLE & SONS METAL PRODUCTS, INC. v. DARUE ENGINEERING & MANUFACTURING

545 U.S. 308 (2005)

JUSTICE SOUTER delivered the opinion of the Court.

The question is whether want of a federal cause of action to try claims of title to land obtained at a federal tax sale precludes removal to federal court of a state action with non-diverse parties raising a disputed issue of federal title law. We answer no, and hold that the national interest in providing a federal forum for federal tax litigation is sufficiently substantial to support the exercise of federal question jurisdiction over the disputed issue on removal, which would not distort any division of labor between the state and federal courts, provided or assumed by Congress.

I

In 1994, the Internal Revenue Service seized Michigan real property belonging to petitioner Grable & Sons Metal Products, Inc., to satisfy Grable's federal tax delinquency. [Certain portions of the Internal Revenue Code] required the IRS to give notice of the seizure, and there is no dispute that Grable received actual notice by certified mail before the IRS sold the property to respondent Darue Engineering & Manufacturing. Although Grable also received notice of the sale itself, it did not exercise its statutory right to redeem the property within 180 days of the sale and after that period had passed, the Government gave Darue a quitclaim deed.

Five years later, Grable brought a quiet title action in state court, claiming that Darue's record title was invalid because the IRS had failed to notify Grable of its seizure of the property in the exact manner required by [the Internal Revenue Code], which provides that written notice must be "given by the Secretary to the owner of the property [or] left at his usual place of abode or business." Grable said that the statute required personal service, not service by certified mail.

Darue removed the case to Federal District Court as presenting a federal question, because the claim of title depended on the interpretation of the notice statute in the federal tax law. The District Court declined to remand the case at Grable's behest after finding that the "claim does pose a significant question of federal law," and ruling that Grable's lack of a federal right of action to enforce its claim against Darue did not bar the exercise of federal jurisdiction. On the merits, the court granted summary judgment to Darue, holding that although [the relevant portion of the Internal Revenue Code] by its terms required personal service, substantial compliance with the statute was enough.

The Court of Appeals for the Sixth Circuit affirmed. On the jurisdictional question, the panel thought it sufficed that the title claim raised an issue of federal law that had to be resolved, and implicated a substantial federal interest (in construing federal tax law). The court went on to affirm the District Court's judgment on the merits. We granted certiorari on the jurisdictional question alone to resolve a split within the Courts of Appeals on whether [*Merrell Dow*] always requires a federal cause of action as a condition for exercising federal-question jurisdiction. We now affirm.

II

Darue was entitled to remove the quiet title action if Grable could have brought it in federal district court originally [28 U.S.C. § 1441(b)] as a civil action "arising under the Constitution, laws, or treaties of the United States," [28 U.S.C. § 1331]. This provision for federal-question jurisdiction is invoked by and large by plaintiffs pleading a cause of action created by federal law. . . . There is, however, another longstanding, if less frequently encountered, variety of federal "arising under" jurisdiction, this Court having recognized for nearly 100 years that in certain cases federal question jurisdiction will lie over state-law claims that implicate significant federal issues. The doctrine captures the commonsense notion that a federal court ought to be able to hear claims recognized under state law that nonetheless turn on substantial questions of federal law, and thus justify resort to the experience, solicitude, and hope of uniformity that a federal forum offers on federal issues. . . .

The classic example is [*Smith*], a suit by a shareholder claiming that the defendant corporation could not lawfully buy certain bonds of the National Government because their issuance was unconstitutional. Although Missouri law provided the cause of action, the Court recognized federal-question jurisdiction because the principal issue in the case was the federal constitutionality of the bond issue. *Smith* thus held, in a somewhat generous statement of the scope of the doctrine, that a state-law claim could give rise to federal-question jurisdiction so long as it "appears from the [complaint] that the right to relief depends upon the construction or application of [federal law]."

The *Smith* statement has been subject to some trimming to fit earlier and later cases recognizing the vitality of the basic doctrine, but shying away from the expansive view that mere need to apply federal law in a state-law claim will suffice to open the "arising under" door. As early as 1912, this Court had confined federal-question jurisdiction over state-law claims to those that "really and substantially involv[e] a dispute or controversy respecting the validity, construction or effect of [federal] law." This limitation was the ancestor of Justice Cardozo's later explanation that a request to exercise federal-question jurisdiction over a state action calls for a "common-sense accommodation of judgment to [the] kaleidoscopic situations" that present a federal issue, in "a selective process which picks the substantial causes out of the web and lays the other ones aside." [*Gully*]. It has in fact become a constant refrain in such cases that federal jurisdiction demands not only a contested federal issue, but a substantial one, indicating a serious federal interest in claiming the advantages thought to be inherent in a federal forum.

But even when the state action discloses a contested and substantial federal question, the exercise of federal jurisdiction is subject to a possible veto. For the federal issue will ultimately qualify for a federal forum only if federal jurisdiction is consistent with congressional judgment about the sound division of labor between state and federal courts governing the application of § 1331. Thus, *Franchise Tax Bd.* explained that the appropriateness of a federal forum to hear an embedded issue could be evaluated only after considering the "welter of issues regarding the interrelation of federal and state authority and the proper management of the federal judicial system." Because arising-under jurisdiction to hear a state-law claim always raises the possibility of upsetting the state-federal line drawn (or at least assumed) by Congress, the presence of a disputed federal issue and the ostensible importance of a federal forum are never necessarily dispositive; there must always be an assessment of any disruptive portent in exercising federal jurisdiction.

These considerations have kept us from stating a "single, precise, all-embracing" test for jurisdiction over federal issues embedded in state-law claims between nondiverse parties. We have not kept them out simply because they appeared in state raiment [Editors' note: Clothing.], as Justice Holmes would have done, see [*Smith*], but neither have we treated "federal issue" as a password opening federal courts to any state action embracing a point of federal law. Instead, the question is, does a state-law claim necessarily raise a stated federal issue, actually disputed and substantial, which a federal forum may entertain without disturbing any congressionally approved balance of federal and state judicial responsibilities.

III

A

This case warrants federal jurisdiction. Grable's state complaint must specify "the facts establishing the superiority of [its] claim," Mich. Ct. Rule 3.411(B)(2)(c), and Grable has premised its superior title claim on a failure by the IRS to give it adequate notice, as defined by federal law. Whether Grable was given notice within the meaning of the federal statute is thus an essential element of its quiet title claim, and the meaning of the federal statute is actually in dispute; it appears to be the only legal or factual issue contested in the case. The meaning of the federal tax provision is an important issue of federal law that sensibly belongs in a federal court. The Government has a strong interest in the "prompt and certain collection of delinquent taxes," and the ability of the IRS to satisfy its claims from the property of delinquents requires clear terms of notice to allow buyers like Darue to satisfy themselves that the Service has touched the bases necessary for good title. The Government thus has a direct interest in the availability of a federal forum to vindicate its own administrative action, and buyers (as well as tax delinquents) may find it valuable to come before judges used to federal tax matters. Finally, because it will be the rare state title case that raises a contested matter of federal law, federal jurisdiction to resolve genuine disagreement over federal tax title provisions will portend only a microscopic effect on the federal-state division of labor.

This conclusion puts us in venerable company, quiet title actions having been the subject of some of the earliest exercises of federal-question jurisdiction over state-law claims. . . . [16] Consistent with those cases, the recognition of federal jurisdiction is in order here.

B

[*Merrell Dow*], on which Grable rests its position, is not to the contrary. [*Merrell Dow*] considered a state tort claim resting in part on the allegation that the defendant drug company had violated a federal misbranding prohibition, and was thus presumptively negligent under Ohio law. The Court assumed that federal law would have to be applied to resolve the claim, but after closely examining the strength of the federal interest at stake and the implications of opening the federal forum, held federal jurisdiction unavailable. Congress had not provided a private federal cause of action for violation of the federal branding requirement, and the Court found "it would . . . flout, or at least undermine, congressional intent to conclude that federal courts might nevertheless exercise federal-question jurisdiction and provide remedies for violations of that federal statute solely because the violation . . . is said to be a . . . 'proximate cause' under state law."

Because federal law provides for no quiet title action that could be brought against Darue, Grable argues that there can be no federal jurisdiction here,

16. [Footnote 3 in Court's opinion.] The quiet title cases also show the limiting effect of the requirement that the federal issue in a state-law claim must actually be in dispute to justify federal-question jurisdiction. In [one early case], this Court found that there was no federal question jurisdiction to hear a plaintiff's quiet title claim in part because the federal statutes on which title depended were not subject to "any controversy respecting their validity, construction, or effect." As the Court put it, the requirement of an actual dispute about federal law was "especially" important in "suit[s] involving rights to land acquired under a law of the United States," because otherwise "every suit to establish title to land in the central and western states would so arise [under federal law], as all titles in those States are traceable back to those laws."

stressing some broad language in *Merrell Dow* (including the passage just quoted) that on its face supports Grable's position. But an opinion is to be read as a whole, and *Merrell Dow* cannot be read whole as overturning decades of precedent, as it would have done by effectively adopting the Holmes dissent in *Smith,* and converting a federal cause of action from a sufficient condition for federal-question jurisdiction[17] into a necessary one.

In the first place, *Merrell Dow* disclaimed the adoption of any bright-line rule, as when the Court reiterated that "in exploring the outer reaches of § 1331, determinations about federal jurisdiction require sensitive judgments about congressional intent, judicial power, and the federal system." The opinion included a lengthy footnote explaining that questions of jurisdiction over state-law claims require "careful judgments" about the "nature of the federal interest at stake." And as a final indication that it did not mean to make a federal right of action mandatory, it expressly approved the exercise of jurisdiction sustained in *Smith* despite the want of any federal cause of action available to *Smith's* shareholder plaintiff. *Merrell Dow* then, did not toss out, but specifically retained the contextual enquiry that had been *Smith's* hallmark for over 60 years. At the end of *Merrell Dow* Justice Holmes was still dissenting.

Accordingly, *Merrell Dow* should be read in its entirety as treating the absence of a federal private right of action as evidence relevant to, but not dispositive of, the "sensitive judgments about congressional intent" that § 1331 requires. The absence of any federal cause of action affected *Merrell Dow's* result two ways. The Court saw the fact as worth some consideration in the assessment of substantiality. But its primary importance emerged when the Court treated the combination of no federal cause of action and no preemption of state remedies for misbranding as an important clue to Congress' conception of the scope of jurisdiction to be exercised under § 1331. The Court saw the missing cause of action not as a missing federal door key, always required, but as a missing welcome mat, required in the circumstances, when exercising federal jurisdiction over a state misbranding action would have attracted a horde of original filings and removal cases raising other state claims with embedded federal issues. For if the federal labeling standard without a federal cause of action could get a state claim into federal court, so could any other federal standard without a federal cause of action. And that would have meant a tremendous number of cases.

One only needed to consider the treatment of federal violations generally in garden variety state tort law. "The violation of federal statutes and regulations is commonly given negligence per se effect in state tort proceedings." Restatement (Third) of Torts (proposed final draft) § 14, Comment *a.* A general rule of exercising federal jurisdiction over state claims resting on federal mislabeling and other statutory violations would thus have heralded a potentially enormous shift of traditionally state cases into federal courts. Expressing concern over the "increased volume of federal litigation," and noting the importance of adhering to "legislative intent," *Merrell Dow* thought it improbable that the Congress, having made no provision for a federal cause of action, would have meant to welcome any state-law tort case implicating federal law "solely because the violation of the federal statute is said to [create] a rebuttable presumption [of negligence] . . . under state law." In this situation, no welcome

17. [Footnote 5 in Court's opinion.] For an extremely rare exception to the sufficiency of a federal right of action, *see* [*Shoshone Mining*].

mat meant keep out. *Merrell Dow*'s analysis thus fits within the framework of examining the importance of having a federal forum for the issue, and the consistency of such a forum with Congress' intended division of labor between state and federal courts.

As already indicated, however, a comparable analysis yields a different jurisdictional conclusion in this case. Although Congress also indicated ambivalence in this case by providing no private right of action to Grable, it is the rare state quiet title action that involves contested issues of federal law. Consequently, jurisdiction over actions like Grable's would not materially affect, or threaten to affect, the normal currents of litigation. Given the absence of threatening structural consequences and the clear interest the Government, its buyers, and its delinquents have in the availability of a federal forum, there is no good reason to shirk from federal jurisdiction over the dispositive and contested federal issue at the heart of the state-law title claim.[18]

IV

The judgment of the Court of Appeals, upholding federal jurisdiction over Grable's quiet title action, is affirmed.

It is so ordered.

Justice Thomas concurring.

The Court faithfully applies our precedents interpreting 28 U.S.C. § 1331 to authorize federal-court jurisdiction over some cases in which state law creates the cause of action but requires determination of an issue of federal law, *e.g.*, [*Smith; Merrell Dow*]. In this case, no one has asked us to overrule those precedents and adopt the rule Justice Holmes set forth in [*American Well Works*], limiting § 1331 jurisdiction to cases in which federal law creates the cause of action pleaded on the face of the plaintiff's complaint. In an appropriate case, and perhaps with the benefit of better evidence as to the original meaning of § 1331's text, I would be willing to consider that course.[19]

Jurisdictional rules should be clear. Whatever the virtues of the *Smith* standard, it is anything but clear . . .

Whatever the vices of the *American Well Works* rule, it is clear. Moreover, it accounts for the "'vast majority'" of cases that come within § 1331 under our

18. [Footnote 7 in Court's opinion.] At oral argument, Grable's counsel espoused the position that after *Merrell Dow*, federal-question jurisdiction over state-law claims absent a federal right of action, could be recognized only where a constitutional issue was at stake. There is, however, no reason in text or otherwise to draw such a rough line. As *Merrell Dow* itself suggested, constitutional questions may be the more likely ones to reach the level of substantiality that can justify federal jurisdiction. But a flat ban on statutory questions would mechanically exclude significant questions of federal law like the one this case presents.

19. [Footnote * in Justice Thomas's concurrence.] This Court has long construed the scope of the statutory grant of federal-question jurisdiction more narrowly than the scope of the constitutional grant of such jurisdiction. I assume for present purposes that this distinction is proper—that is, that the language of 28 U.S.C. § 1331, "[t]he district courts shall have original jurisdiction of all *civil actions arising under* the Constitution, laws, or treaties of the United States" (emphasis added), is narrower than the language of Art. III, § 2, cl. 1 of the Constitution, "[t]he judicial Power shall extend to all *Cases*, in Law and Equity, *arising under* this Constitution, the Laws of the United States, and Treaties made, or which shall be made, under their Authority . . ." (emphases added by Justice Thomas).

current case law,—further indication that trying to sort out which cases fall within the smaller *Smith* category may not be worth the effort it entails. Accordingly, I would be willing in appropriate circumstances to reconsider our interpretation of § 1331.

GUNN v. MINTON

133 S. Ct. 1059 (2013)

CHIEF JUSTICE ROBERTS delivered the opinion of the Court.

Federal courts have exclusive jurisdiction over cases "arising under any Act of Congress relating to patents." 28 U.S.C. § 1338(a). The question presented is whether a state law claim alleging legal malpractice in the handling of a patent case must be brought in federal court.

I

In the early 1990s, respondent Vernon Minton developed a computer program and telecommunications network designed to facilitate securities trading. In March 1995, he leased the system—known as the Texas Computer Exchange Network, or TEXCEN—to R.M. Stark & Co., a securities brokerage. A little over a year later, he applied for a patent for an interactive securities trading system that was based substantially on TEXCEN. The U.S. Patent and Trademark Office issued the patent in January 2000.

Patent in hand, Minton filed a patent infringement suit in Federal District Court against the National Association of Securities Dealers, Inc. (NASD) and the NASDAQ Stock Market, Inc. He was represented by Jerry Gunn and the other petitioners. NASD and NASDAQ moved for summary judgment on the ground that Minton's patent was invalid under the "on sale" bar. That provision specifies that an inventor is not entitled to a patent if "the invention was . . . on sale in [the United States], more than one year prior to the date of the application," and Minton had leased TEXCEN to Stark more than one year prior to filing his patent application. Rejecting Minton's argument that there were differences between TEXCEN and the patented system that precluded application of the on-sale bar, the District Court granted the summary judgment motion and declared Minton's patent invalid.

Minton then filed a motion for reconsideration in the District Court, arguing for the first time that the lease agreement with Stark was part of ongoing testing of TEXCEN and therefore fell within the "experimental use" exception to the on-sale bar. The District Court denied the motion.

Minton appealed to the U.S. Court of Appeals for the Federal Circuit. That court affirmed, concluding that the District Court had appropriately held Minton's experimental-use argument waived.

Minton, convinced that his attorneys' failure to raise the experimental-use argument earlier had cost him the lawsuit and led to invalidation of his patent, brought this malpractice action in Texas state court. His former lawyers defended on the ground that the lease to Stark was not, in fact, for an experimental use, and that therefore Minton's patent infringement claims would have failed even if the experimental-use argument had been timely raised. The trial court agreed, holding that Minton had put forward "less than a scintilla of proof" that the lease had been for an experimental purpose. It accordingly granted summary judgment to Gunn and the other lawyer defendants.

On appeal, Minton raised a new argument: Because his legal malpractice claim was based on an alleged error in a patent case, it "aris[es] under" federal patent law for purposes of 28 U.S.C. § 1338(a). And because, under § 1338(a), "[n]o State court shall have jurisdiction over any claim for relief arising under any Act of Congress relating to patents," the Texas court—where Minton had originally brought his malpractice claim—lacked subject matter jurisdiction to decide the case. Accordingly, Minton argued, the trial court's order should be vacated and the case dismissed, leaving Minton free to start over in the Federal District Court.

A divided panel of the Court of Appeals of Texas rejected Minton's argument. Applying the test we articulated in *Grable* . . . it held that the federal interests implicated by Minton's state law claim were not sufficiently substantial to trigger § 1338 "arising under" jurisdiction. It also held that finding exclusive federal jurisdiction over state legal malpractice actions would, contrary to *Grable*'s commands, disturb the balance of federal and state judicial responsibilities. Proceeding to the merits of Minton's malpractice claim, the Court of Appeals affirmed the trial court's determination that Minton had failed to establish experimental use and that arguments on that ground therefore would not have saved his infringement suit.

The Supreme Court of Texas reversed. . . . The Court concluded that Minton's claim involved "a substantial federal issue" within the meaning of *Grable* "because the success of Minton's malpractice claim is reliant upon the viability of the experimental use exception as a defense to the on-sale bar." Adjudication of Minton's claim in federal court was consistent with the appropriate balance between federal and state judicial responsibilities, it held, because "the federal government and patent litigants have an interest in the uniform application of patent law by courts well-versed in that subject matter."

* * * *

II

"Federal courts are courts of limited jurisdiction," possessing "only that power authorized by Constitution and statute." There is no dispute that the Constitution permits Congress to extend federal court jurisdiction to a case such as this one, see *Osborn*; the question is whether Congress has done so.

As relevant here, Congress has authorized the federal district courts to exercise original jurisdiction in "all civil actions arising under the Constitution, laws, or treaties of the United States," 28 U.S.C. § 1331, and, more particularly, over "any civil action arising under any Act of Congress relating to patents," § 1338(a). Adhering to the demands of "[l]inguistic consistency," we have interpreted the phrase "arising under" in both sections identically, applying our § 1331 and § 1338(a) precedents interchangeably. For cases falling within the patent-specific arising under jurisdiction of § 1338(a), however, Congress has not only provided for federal jurisdiction but also eliminated state jurisdiction, decreeing that "[n]o State court shall have jurisdiction over any claim for relief arising under any Act of Congress relating to patents." To determine whether jurisdiction was proper in the Texas courts, therefore, we must determine whether it would have been proper in a federal district court—whether, that is, the case "aris[es] under any Act of Congress relating to patents."

For statutory purposes, a case can "aris[e] under" federal law in two ways. Most directly, a case arises under federal law when federal law creates the cause of action asserted. *See American Well Works Co.* As a rule of inclusion, this "creation" test admits of only extremely rare exceptions, see, *e.g., Shoshone Mining Co.*, and accounts for the vast bulk of suits that arise under federal law, *see Franchise Tax Bd. of Cal.* . . .

But even where a claim finds its origins in state rather than federal law—as Minton's legal malpractice claim indisputably does—we have identified a "special and small category" of cases in which arising under jurisdiction still lies. In outlining the contours of this slim category, we do not paint on a blank canvas. Unfortunately, the canvas looks like one that Jackson Pollock got to first.

In an effort to bring some order to this unruly doctrine several Terms ago, we condensed our prior cases into the following inquiry: Does the "state-law claim necessarily raise a stated federal issue, actually disputed and substantial, which a federal forum may entertain without disturbing any congressionally approved balance of federal and state judicial responsibilities"? *Grable.* That is, federal jurisdiction over a state law claim will lie if a federal issue is: (1) necessarily raised, (2) actually disputed, (3) substantial, and (4) capable of resolution in federal court without disrupting the federal-state balance approved by Congress. Where all four of these requirements are met, we held, jurisdiction is proper because there is a "serious federal interest in claiming the advantages thought to be inherent in a federal forum," which can be vindicated without disrupting Congress' intended division of labor between state and federal courts.

III

Applying *Grable*'s inquiry here, it is clear that Minton's legal malpractice claim does not arise under federal patent law. Indeed, for the reasons we discuss, we are comfortable concluding that state legal malpractice claims based on underlying patent matters will rarely, if ever, arise under federal patent law for purposes of § 1338(a). Although such cases may necessarily raise disputed questions of patent law, those cases are by their nature unlikely to have the sort of significance for the federal system necessary to establish jurisdiction.

A

To begin, we acknowledge that resolution of a federal patent question is "necessary" to Minton's case. Under Texas law, a plaintiff alleging legal malpractice must establish four elements: (1) that the defendant attorney owed the plaintiff a duty; (2) that the attorney breached that duty; (3) that the breach was the proximate cause of the plaintiff's injury; and (4) that damages occurred. In cases like this one, in which the attorney's alleged error came in failing to make a particular argument, the causation element requires a "case within a case" analysis of whether, had the argument been made, the outcome of the earlier litigation would have been different. To prevail on his legal malpractice claim, therefore, Minton must show that he would have prevailed in his federal patent infringement case if only petitioners had timely made an experimental-use argument on his behalf. That will necessarily require application of patent law to the facts of Minton's case.

B

The federal issue is also "actually disputed" here — indeed, on the merits, it is the central point of dispute. Minton argues that the experimental-use exception properly applied to his lease to Stark, saving his patent from the on-sale bar; petitioners argue that it did not. This is just the sort of "'dispute . . . respecting the . . . effect of [federal] law'" that *Grable* envisioned.

C

Minton's argument founders on *Grable*'s next requirement, however, for the federal issue in this case is not substantial in the relevant sense. In reaching the opposite conclusion, the Supreme Court of Texas focused on the importance of the issue to the plaintiff's case and to the parties before it. As our past cases show, however, it is not enough that the federal issue be significant to the particular parties in the immediate suit; that will *always* be true when the state claim "necessarily raise[s]" a disputed federal issue, as *Grable* separately requires. The substantiality inquiry under *Grable* looks instead to the importance of the issue to the federal system as a whole.

In *Grable* itself, for example, the Internal Revenue Service had seized property from the plaintiff and sold it to satisfy the plaintiff's federal tax delinquency. Five years later, the plaintiff filed a state law quiet title action against the third party that had purchased the property, alleging that the IRS had failed to comply with certain federally imposed notice requirements, so that the seizure and sale were invalid. In holding that the case arose under federal law, we primarily focused not on the interests of the litigants themselves, but rather on the broader significance of the notice question for the Federal Government. We emphasized the Government's "strong interest" in being able to recover delinquent taxes through seizure and sale of property, which in turn "require[d] clear terms of notice to allow buyers . . . to satisfy themselves that the Service has touched the bases necessary for good title." The Government's "direct interest in the availability of a federal forum to vindicate its own administrative action" made the question "an important issue of federal law that sensibly belong[ed] in a federal court."

A second illustration of the sort of substantiality we require comes from *Smith*, which *Grable* described as "[t]he classic example" of a state claim arising under federal law. In *Smith*, the plaintiff argued that the defendant bank could not purchase certain bonds issued by the Federal Government because the Government had acted unconstitutionally in issuing them. We held that the case arose under federal law, because the "decision depends upon the determination" of "the constitutional validity of an act of Congress which is directly drawn in question." Again, the relevant point was not the importance of the question to the parties alone but rather the importance more generally of a determination that the Government "securities were issued under an unconstitutional law, and hence of no validity."

Here, the federal issue carries no such significance. Because of the backward-looking nature of a legal malpractice claim, the question is posed in a merely hypothetical sense: *If* Minton's lawyers had raised a timely experimental-use argument, would the result in the patent infringement proceeding have been different? No matter how the state courts resolve that hypothetical "case within a case," it will not change the real-world result of the prior federal patent litigation. Minton's patent will remain invalid.

Nor will allowing state courts to resolve these cases undermine "the development of a uniform body of [patent] law." Congress ensured such uniformity by vesting exclusive jurisdiction over actual patent cases in the federal district courts and exclusive appellate jurisdiction in the Federal Circuit. In resolving the non-hypothetical patent questions those cases present, the federal courts are of course not bound by state court case-within-a-case patent rulings. In any event, the state court case-within-a-case inquiry asks what would have happened in the prior federal proceeding if a particular argument had been made. In answering that question, state courts can be expected to hew closely to the pertinent federal precedents. It is those precedents, after all, that would have applied had the argument been made.

As for more novel questions of patent law that may arise for the first time in a state court "case within a case," they will at some point be decided by a federal court in the context of an actual patent case, with review in the Federal Circuit. If the question arises frequently, it will soon be resolved within the federal system, laying to rest any contrary state court precedent; if it does not arise frequently, it is unlikely to implicate substantial federal interests. The present case is "poles apart from *Grable*," in which a state court's resolution of the federal question "would be controlling in numerous other cases."

* * * *

Nor can we accept the suggestion that the federal courts' greater familiarity with patent law means that legal malpractice cases like this one belong in federal court. It is true that a similar interest was among those we considered in *Grable*. But the possibility that a state court will incorrectly resolve a state claim is not, by itself, enough to trigger the federal courts' exclusive patent jurisdiction, even if the potential error finds its root in a misunderstanding of patent law.

There is no doubt that resolution of a patent issue in the context of a state legal malpractice action can be vitally important to the particular parties in that case. But something more, demonstrating that the question is significant to the federal system as a whole, is needed. That is missing here.

D

It follows from the foregoing that *Grable*'s fourth requirement is also not met. That requirement is concerned with the appropriate "balance of federal and state judicial responsibilities." We have already explained the absence of a substantial federal issue within the meaning of *Grable*. The States, on the other hand, have "a special responsibility for maintaining standards among members of the licensed professions." Their "interest . . . in regulating lawyers is especially great since lawyers are essential to the primary governmental function of administering justice, and have historically been officers of the courts." We have no reason to suppose that Congress — in establishing exclusive federal jurisdiction over patent cases — meant to bar from state courts state legal malpractice claims simply because they require resolution of a hypothetical patent issue.

* * * *

As we recognized a century ago, "[t]he Federal courts have exclusive jurisdiction of all cases arising under the patent laws, but not of all questions in which a patent may be the subject-matter of the controversy." In this case, although the state courts must answer a question of patent law to resolve Minton's legal malpractice claim, their answer will have no broader effects. It will not stand as binding precedent for any future patent claim; it will not even affect the validity of Minton's patent. Accordingly, there is no "serious federal interest in claiming the advantages thought to be inherent in a federal forum," *Grable.* Section 1338(a) does not deprive the state courts of subject matter jurisdiction.

The judgment of the Supreme Court of Texas is reversed, and the case is remanded for further proceedings not inconsistent with this opinion.

It is so ordered.

FURTHER DISCUSSION

While it may be difficult to predict the cases that will ultimately fall within the *Grable/ Gunn* formulation, it is clear that it represents a "slim category" of federal jurisdiction. *Empire HealthChoice Assurance, Inc. v. McVeigh,* 547 U.S. 677, 701 (2006). In any event, Justice Souter provides a four-part test at the end of Section II of his opinion in *Grable* as a guide for determining whether a state-created cause of action arises under federal law for purposes of § 1331. Chief Justice Roberts reemphasizes that test in *Gunn* at the end of Section II of that opinion. We summarize that test in the checklist below:

REVIEW AND CONSOLIDATION

When Do State-Created Causes of Action Create "Arising Under" Jurisdiction? The Grable/Gunn Test

- ✦ Does the state-law claim on the face of the well-pleaded complaint include a federal issue necessary to that claim? Or, stated somewhat differently, is the federal issue "necessarily raised" in plaintiff's claim?
- ✦ Is the federal issue "actually disputed"?
- ✦ Is the federal issue "substantial"?
- ✦ Can the federal courts "entertain [the federal issue] without disturbing any congressionally approved balance of federal-state judicial responsibilities"?

Practice using the checklist and gauge your understanding of *Grable* and *Gunn* by considering Problems 5-5 and 5-6.[20]

20. For some additional practice, revisit Problem 5-3 above. Would arising under jurisdiction be appropriate there under the *Grable/Gunn* analysis? You can also consider this issue by exploring the matters raised in Problem 5-10 in section D below.

PROBLEM 5-5

Tax Advice Gone Bad: Is it a Federal Case?

Debbie Investor ("Investor"), a Florida citizen, recently received a modest inheritance from a long-lost aunt. Investor decided she needed financial help. She turned to Ben & Noah Investing Services, Inc. ("B&N"), a Florida corporation.

B&N convinced Investor to use an investment strategy the firm had developed in which she would invest in foreign currency options (the "Strategy"). The Strategy was designed to produce substantial profits or (more likely) generate losses to be used to offset Investor's other income. Investor took B&N's advice, invested using the Strategy, and reported the losses generated on her federal income tax forms. The Internal Revenue Service (IRS) later assessed penalties and interest against Investor on the basis that the losses generated by the Strategy could not be used to offset other income. The IRS has concluded that the Strategy itself is unlawful.

Investor has filed a lawsuit in Florida state court against B&N, seeking to recover the penalties and interest assessed by the IRS. Among other things, Investor asserts that B&N breached its contract with her, breached its fiduciary duties to her, and committed professional malpractice. All of Investor's claims are based on state law. The central portion of Investor's complaint alleges that B&N breached its duties to her (and otherwise violated state law) by failing to

- disclose that if she claimed losses generated by the Strategy, the IRS might contend she was liable for penalties and interest under federal tax law;
- advise her that the design of the Strategy made no economic or investment sense and, as such, losses generated by the Strategy might not be proper ones for deductions; and
- advise her about the existence and implications of certain IRS notices that indicated the Strategy was unlawful.

B&N removes Investor's suit to the appropriate federal court. The sole basis for removal is that Investor's suit arises under federal law as provided by 28 U.S.C. § 1331. You are the federal judge to whom the case has been assigned. How do you rule on Investor's motion to remand the case to Florida state court? What is the basis for your ruling? If there is any additional information you need to make your decision, identify such information and explain its relevance to your decision.

PROBLEM 5-6

Lobsters and Federal Jurisdiction

In 1942, Congress consented to a compact (or agreement) among several states called the Atlantic Marine Fisheries Compact (the Compact). The Compact provides means by which states would provide joint regulatory oversight of fishing through the development of interstate fishery management plans. While participation in such plans by states entering into the Compact was originally voluntary, in 1993 Congress made participation mandatory.

Along with making participation in management plans compulsory, Congress also designated a federal body, the Atlantic States Marine Fisheries Commission (the Commission), as the body that would prepare and adopt interstate fishery management plans. Such plans were generally species specific, and one plan focused on the American lobster.

Once the Commission adopts a plan, each affected state is required to implement it. Such implementation would generally entail the adoption of state statutes or regulations.

Stocks of American lobsters (the types of lobsters one associates with New England) have been declining for some time. Concerned about overfishing in connection with this decline, the Commission began to take action. One such action was known as "Addendum VII." Addendum VII addressed a specific area in the Atlantic Ocean off the coasts of Massachusetts and Rhode Island. As relevant, Addendum VII required states to allocate lobster traps to people based on a person's documented lobster catch during 2001-2003.

In 2012, the Rhode Island Department of Environmental Management (the DEM) adopted Regulation X for the purpose of "bring[ing] the State of Rhode Island into compliance with Addendum VII." Under Regulation X, in order to obtain the license required under Rhode Island law, a person would need to show that the person (1) held a state (or federal) license to catch lobsters in the relevant section of the Atlantic off Rhode Island at some point in the period 2001-2003; and (2) had documented lobster catches in that period in the relevant area.

Tommy is a commercial lobsterman living in Rhode Island. He did not have a license in the relevant period. He very much wants to engage in the lobster industry in the area off the Rhode Island coast but cannot under Regulation X. He filed a lawsuit against the DEM in Rhode Island state court, claiming that the adoption of Regulation X violated the Rhode Island Constitution and a number of Rhode Island statutes. The central point of Tommy's claim is that Regulation X adopts a "retroactive control date." In other words, it bases eligibility for a license on events that have occurred in the past. Specifically, Tommy's complaint cites R.I. Gen. Laws § 1-2-3, which states that "retroactive control dates are prohibited and shall not be used or implemented, unless expressly required by federal law, regulation or court decision."

The DEM has removed Tommy's suit, claiming that it is one that "arises under" federal law under 28 U.S.C. § 1331. Tommy has filed a timely motion to remand his lawsuit. Tommy asserts that his claims all arise under Rhode Island law and, therefore, federal jurisdiction is lacking.

You are a United States District Judge in the District of Rhode Island. How do you rule on Tommy's motion to remand? Make sure to explain your decision.

EXPLORING DOCTRINE

What Is the Correct Spin on Grable? *Version 5-C*

Is federal jurisdiction in a case such as *Grable* a power grab by the Court in that it is taking authority away from Congress? Or is it instead the Court's implicit recognition of the adequacy of state courts? These quite differing interpretations of *Grable* (and one would infer *Smith* as well) are increasingly debated among scholars. Why might the decision be interpreted as a "power grab" raising issues of separation of powers? Why might the decision be interpreted as the Court's show of respect toward state courts?

iii. The Special Case of "Complete Preemption"

Assume that a former smoker brings a products-liability suit in state court against a tobacco company. The plaintiff claims that the defendant misled the public about the dangers of cigarettes. The plaintiff's claim is based entirely on state-law principles and makes no reference to federal law. Based on what we have studied thus far, you should be able to determine that the defendant cannot remove to federal court. The well-pleaded complaint neither alleges a federal cause of action nor raises a federal issue satisfying the *Grable/Gunn* test.

But what if the relevant federal statute concerning cigarette labeling provides that the tobacco company's compliance with the federally mandated warnings is a complete defense to state-law failure-to-warn allegations? You should also recognize that this federal defense is irrelevant to removal. Under the well-pleaded complaint rule, a federal defense does not create arising under jurisdiction, whether referred to in plaintiff's complaint or in defendant's answer.

Now assume we have a different suit. This one is brought by a plaintiff against a bank. The plaintiff's claim is that the bank charged interest rates that were usurious and, therefore, unlawful under state law. Once again, the plaintiff makes no reference to federal law in the complaint. The defendant-bank removes the case to federal court on the basis that it arises under federal law. Its notice of removal recites that the interest it charged was lawful under the federal National Bank Act, and that this Act provides bank customers' exclusive rights and remedies concerning the loans at issue (i.e., all state regulation of the loans is preempted). Is this case removable?

It would appear the case against the bank is no different from the one against the tobacco company. Jurisdiction seems lacking in both cases because federal law enters the case only through defensive pleadings. However, the Supreme Court has held that in limited circumstances a federal statute may "preempt" state law so completely that a claim based on state law actually becomes one arising under federal law.[21] This doctrine is known, not surprisingly, as

21. It is for this reason that the complete preemption doctrine can be considered either an exception to or an application of the well-pleaded complaint rule. To the extent that one goes beyond the complaint to evaluate the jurisdictional issue, it is easy to see the doctrine as an exception. However, if one accepts that in the narrow band of situations covered by "complete preemption" a state claim is *really* a federal one, then the Court is only applying the rule laid down in *Mottley* because what the plaintiff has pled, even if it looks like a state claim, is actually a federal one.

"complete preemption." We generally explore the concept of complete preemption in the balance of this subpart.

As you learned in your basic Constitutional Law course, preemption has its roots in the Supremacy Clause of the Constitution. Under that Clause, validly enacted federal law trumps any inconsistent state law.[22] In the great run of cases, federal preemption of state law is merely a defense, albeit an incredibly powerful one. Thus, a preemption defense usually does not justify removal under *Mottley*'s well-pleaded complaint. *See Caterpillar Inc. v. Williams*, 482 U.S. 386 (1987). However, "if Congress intended [the federal statute at issue] to provide the exclusive cause of action" in the relevant area, the plaintiff's state-law claim is said to actually be a federal one. *See, e.g., Beneficial National Bank v. Anderson*, 539 U.S. 1, 9 (2003). Accordingly, removal of such claims is appropriate because "[w]hen the federal statute completely pre-empts the state-law cause of action, a claim which comes within the scope of that cause of action, even if pleaded in terms of state law, is in reality based on federal law." *Id.* at 8.

The rule seems relatively easy to state in the abstract. Unfortunately, distinguishing those situations in which a federal law is *so* preemptive that it converts a state law claim into a federal one (e.g., the bank example) from those in which the preemptive federal law is merely a defense (e.g., the cigarette example) is notoriously difficult.

To date, the Supreme Court has identified only three federal statutory provisions that "completely preempt" state law for jurisdictional purposes: section 502 of the Employee Retirement Income Security Act (ERISA), *see Metropolitan Life Ins. Co. v. Taylor*, 481 U.S. 58 (1987); section 301of the Labor Management Relations Act of 1947 (the provision of law at issue in *Lincoln Mills, supra*), *see Avco Corp. v. Machinists*, 390 U.S. 557 (1968); and sections 85 and 86 of the National Bank Act, discussed in *Beneficial National Bank*. In each of these cases, the Court stressed two related features of the statutes at issue. First, the Court concluded that Congress intended to exercise its powers to the fullest and totally eliminate state regulation in the area. This is what the Court appears to mean when it states that a federal statute provides the "exclusive cause of action." Second, the statutes at issue were construed to provide a remedial framework supplanting remedies otherwise provided by state law. When these two features are present—and the plaintiff in fact pleads a state-law claim within the preemptive scope of the federal statute—the only claim that can lawfully be pressed is one that arises under federal law.

We will return to the complete preemption doctrine in the final part of this chapter when we consider *Franchise Tax Board of California v. Construction Laborers Vacation Trust for Southern California*, 463 U.S. 1 (1983). For now, test your understanding of the basic workings of the complete preemption doctrine (and review some of the other statutory arising under jurisprudence) by considering Problem 5-7.

22. Preemption can also extend beyond this situation of so-called "conflict preemption." For example, preemption can include situations where Congress intends to preempt an entire area ("field preemption") regardless of whether there is specific conflict between federal and state law.

PROBLEM 5-7

Southern Discomfort

Bob Brown ("Brown") bought an airline ticket on Southern Airlines ("Southern"). Both Brown and Southern are citizens of Texas. In addition to his fare, Brown also paid a September 11th Security Fee mandated by the federal government (the "Fee"). Brown's ticket was non-refundable. Under its terms, the ticket had to be used within one year of purchase or Brown would forfeit the fare. Brown did not use the ticket within one year of purchase, and Southern canceled the ticket according to its terms. Brown sought return of the Fee, claiming that Southern did not have to pay the Fee to the government until Brown traveled. Because Brown did not travel, Southern would never pay the Fee to the government. Finally, Brown asserted that his contract with Southern referred only to forfeiting the fare, not any associated fees.

Brown files a lawsuit in Texas state court against Southern, claiming breach of contract and unjust enrichment, both state-law theories of recovery. Southern removes the case to federal court, claiming it arose under federal law based on the doctrine of complete preemption. Southern emphasizes several provisions of the Aviation and Transportation Security Act (ATSA). These provisions state that (1) airlines are required to collect the Fee and pay it to the government within a specified period of time after a person's flight; (2) the Secretary of Transportation "may refund any fee paid by mistake or any amount paid in excess" of the amount properly to be collected; and (3) compliance with the schedule of fees and the procedures for their assessment as set forth in the ATSA shall be a defense to any claims of unlawful conduct in connection with the collection or retention of such fees by airlines.

Brown moves to remand the case to state court. You are the district judge assigned to the case. How do you rule on Brown's motion? If there is any additional information you would like in order to make your decision, identify it and explain why it is important to your decision.

We have considered the Court's varying interpretations of § 1331 and arising under jurisdiction. Figure 5-2 depicts the three principal forms such jurisdiction can take.

FIGURE 5-2

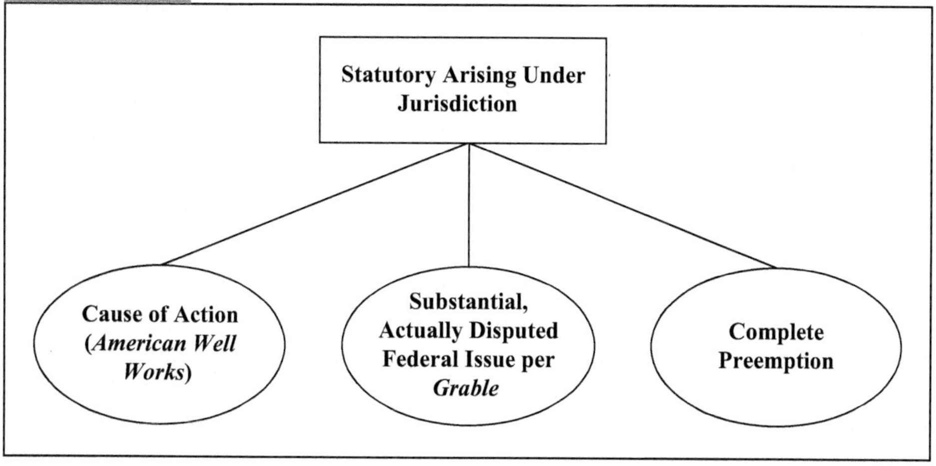

c. Where (and How) to Look Redux: Declaratory Judgments

You should now be comfortable with the well-pleaded complaint rule and understand what to look for in the complaint when assessing whether statutory federal question jurisdiction is present. The last topic we address concerns arising under jurisdiction in the context of declaratory judgments.

In order to understand the jurisdictional implications of seeking a declaratory judgment, you first must understand the basics of that remedy. Most remedies are "coercive" in that they compel a defendant to take some action. For example, a plaintiff may obtain an award of damages compelling the defendant to pay or risk attachment of its property. Or a plaintiff may obtain an injunction compelling the defendant to take (or refrain from taking) certain action. If a defendant acts contrary to the injunction, contempt sanctions are possible.

A declaratory judgment operates differently than coercive remedies such as damages or injunctions. A declaratory judgment resolves a currently disputed issue between adversarial parties. It does so, however, without compelling either party to take any action. For example, if a state threatened to enforce a new tax against a railroad that the railroad believed was unconstitutional, the railroad could seek a judgment declaring the tax invalid. All states and the federal government have in place some form of declaratory judgment statute.

You might be wondering why anyone would seek a declaratory judgment instead of a coercive remedy. There are several reasons, strategic as well as substantive, you may discuss if you take a Remedies course. One reason important for jurisdictional purposes is that a declaratory judgment allows a potential defendant to become a plaintiff. For example, assume that Company X manufactures widgets. Company Y holds a patent on a process to manufacture widgets. Company Y informs Company X that it believes Company X is infringing Company Y's patent. What is Company X to do if it believes that it is not infringing the patent but Company Y has not yet filed a suit for patent infringement? If Company X keeps manufacturing the widgets using the allegedly infringing process, it could be liable for significant damages. The declaratory judgment procedure allows Company X—which would be the defendant in a coercive patent infringement suit—to become the plaintiff in a declaratory judgment action. As plaintiff in this action, Company X seeks a declaration resolving the current dispute concerning whether its manufacturing process violates Company Y's patent.

The potential reversal of plaintiff and defendant roles in declaratory actions complicates the jurisdictional issue. The question arises, how does the reversal of party roles affect application of the well-pleaded complaint rule?

An early, important decision on this question is *Skelly Oil Co. v. Phillips Petroleum Co.*, 339 U.S. 667 (1950). Skelly and Phillips had a contract concerning the sale of natural gas. Under the terms of the contract, Skelly Oil could terminate the deal after December 1, 1946, *unless* the Federal Power Commission issued a certain certificate to a third-party pipeline business. On November 30, 1946, the Commission issued a "conditional certificate" to the pipeline business but did not make that action public until December 2, 1946.

Skelly notified Phillips that it was terminating the contract because no certificate had been issued by December 1. Phillips responded by seeking a declaration in federal court that the certificate the Commission issued was valid under federal law and, therefore, Skelly could not terminate the contract.

The Supreme Court held in *Skelly Oil* that Phillips's suit did not arise under federal law. The Court reasoned that the federal Declaratory Judgment Act was not intended to increase federal court jurisdiction. In other words, the Act created a cause of action but did not expand the federal courts' arising under jurisdiction. To determine whether a declaratory judgment suit arose under federal law, the Court focused on the "coercive" action that *might* have been brought in lieu of the declaratory action. In *Skelly Oil*, the coercive suit would be one for breach of contract by Phillips in which the federal issue concerning the Commission certificate would arise, if at all, only as a defense.[23] Because this hypothetical coercive suit did not arise under federal law, a preemptive declaratory suit did not either.

The next case is the Court's most prominent modern consideration of federal question jurisdiction in declaratory judgment suits. It is also a review of removal jurisdiction and the complete preemption doctrine.

FRANCHISE TAX BOARD OF THE STATE OF CALIFORNIA v. CONSTRUCTION LABORERS VACATION TRUST FOR SOUTHERN CALIFORNIA

463 U.S. 1 (1983)

JUSTICE BRENNAN delivered the opinion of the Court.

The principal question in dispute between the parties is whether the Employment Retirement Income Security Act of 1974 (ERISA) permits state tax authorities to collect unpaid state income taxes by levying on funds held in trust for the taxpayers under an ERISA-covered vacation benefit plan. The issue is an important one, which affects thousands of federally regulated trusts and all nonfederal tax collection systems, and it must eventually receive a definitive, uniform resolution. Nevertheless, for reasons involving perhaps more history than logic, we hold that the lower federal courts had no jurisdiction to decide the question in the case before us, and we vacate the judgment and remand the case with instructions to remand it to the state court from which it was removed.

I

None of the relevant facts is in dispute. Appellee Construction Laborers Vacation Trust for Southern California (CLVT) is a trust established by an agreement between four associations of employers active in the construction industry in Southern California and the Southern California District Council of Laborers, an arm of the District Council and affiliated locals of the Laborers' International Union of North America. The purpose of the agreement and trust was to establish a mechanism for administering the provisions of a collective bargaining agreement that grants construction workers a yearly paid vacation. The trust agreement expressly proscribes any assignment, pledge, or encumbrance of funds held in trust by CLVT. The plan that CLVT administers is unquestionably an "employee welfare benefit plan" within the meaning of § 3

23. According to the parties' contract, the Commission's failure to issue a valid certificate provided a defense to contract enforcement in the nature of a "condition subsequent" whose occurrence excused performance.

of ERISA, and CLVT and its individual trustees are thereby subject to extensive regulation under titles I and III of ERISA.

Appellant Franchise Tax Board is a California agency charged with enforcement of that State's personal income tax law. California law authorizes appellant to require any person in possession of "credits or other personal property belonging to a taxpayer" "to withhold . . . the amount of any tax, interest, or penalties due from the taxpayer . . . and to transmit the amount withheld to the Franchise Tax Board." Any person who, upon notice by the Franchise Tax Board, fails to comply with its request to withhold and to transmit funds becomes personally liable for the amounts identified in the notice.

In June 1980, the Franchise Tax Board filed a complaint in state court against CLVT and its trustees. Under the heading "First Cause of Action," appellant alleged that CLVT had failed to comply with three levies issued under [California tax law] concluding with the allegation that it had been "damaged in a sum . . . not to exceed $380.56 plus interest from June 1, 1980." Under the heading "Second Cause of Action," appellant incorporated its previous allegations and added:

> "There was at the time of the levies alleged above and continues to be an actual controversy between the parties concerning their respective legal rights and duties. The Board [appellant] contends that defendants [CLVT] are obligated and required by law to pay over to the Board all amounts held . . . in favor of the Board's delinquent taxpayers. On the other hand, defendants contend that section 514 of ERISA preempts state law and that the trustees lack the power to honor the levies made upon them by the State of California. ". . . [D]efendants will continue to refuse to honor the Board's levies in this regard. Accordingly, a declaration by this court of the parties' respective rights is required to fully and finally resolve this controversy."

In a prayer for relief, appellant requested damages for defendants' failure to honor the levies and a declaration that defendants are "legally obligated to honor all future levies by the Board."

CLVT removed the case to the United States District Court for the Central District of California, and the court denied the Franchise Tax Board's motion for remand to the state court. On the merits, the District Court ruled that ERISA did not preempt the State's power to levy on funds held in trust by CLVT. CLVT appealed, and the Court of Appeals reversed. . . . We now hold that this case was not within the removal jurisdiction conferred by 28 U.S.C. § 1441, and therefore we do not reach the merits of the preemption question.

II

The jurisdictional structure at issue in this case has remained basically unchanged for the past century. With exceptions not relevant here, "any civil action brought in a State court of which the district courts of the United States have original jurisdiction, may be removed by the defendant or the defendants, to the district court of the United States for the district and division embracing the place where such action is pending." 28 U.S.C. § 1441. If it appears before final judgment that a case was not properly removed, because it was not within the original jurisdiction of the United States district courts, the district court must remand it to the state court from which it was removed. For this case — as for many cases where there is no diversity of citizenship between the parties — the propriety of removal turns on whether the case falls within the original "federal question" jurisdiction of the United States district courts: "The district courts shall have jurisdiction of all civil actions arising under the Constitution, laws, or treaties of the United States." 28 U.S.C. § 1331.

Since the first version of § 1331 was enacted, the statutory phrase "arising under the Constitution, laws, or treaties of the United States" has resisted all attempts to frame a single, precise definition for determining which cases fall within, and which cases fall outside, the original jurisdiction of the district courts. Especially when considered in light of § 1441's removal jurisdiction, the phrase "arising under" masks a welter of issues regarding the interrelation of federal and state authority and the proper management of the federal judicial system.

The most familiar definition of the statutory "arising under" limitation is Justice Holmes' statement, "A suit arises under the law that creates the cause of action." [*American Well Works*]. However, it is well settled that Justice Holmes' test is more useful for describing the vast majority of cases that come within the district courts' original jurisdiction than it is for describing which cases are beyond district court jurisdiction. We have often held that a case "arose under" federal law where the vindication of a right under state law necessarily turned on some construction of federal law, see, *e.g.*, [*Smith*], and even the most ardent proponent of the Holmes test has admitted that it has been rejected as an exclusionary principle. . . .

One powerful doctrine has emerged, however — the "well-pleaded complaint" rule — which as a practical matter severely limits the number of cases in which state law "creates the cause of action" that may be initiated in or removed to federal district court, thereby avoiding more-or-less automatically a number of potentially serious federal-state conflicts. . . .

Thus, a federal court does not have original jurisdiction over a case in which the complaint presents a state-law cause of action, but also asserts that federal law deprives the defendant of a defense he may raise, [*Mottley*], or that a federal defense the defendant may raise is not sufficient to defeat the claim. "Although such allegations show that very likely, in the course of the litigation, a question under the Constitution would arise, they do not show that the suit, that is, the plaintiff's original cause of action, arises under the Constitution." [*Mottley*] For better or worse, under the present statutory scheme as it has existed since 1887, a defendant may not remove a case to federal court unless the *plaintiff's* complaint establishes that the case "arises under" federal law. . . .[24]

For many cases in which federal law becomes relevant only insofar as it sets bounds for the operation of state authority, the well-pleaded complaint rule makes sense as a quick rule of thumb. . . .

The rule, however, may produce awkward results, especially in cases in which neither the obligation created by state law nor the defendant's factual failure to

24. [Footnote 9 in Court's opinion.] The well-pleaded complaint rule applies to the original jurisdiction of the district courts as well as to their removal jurisdiction. It is possible to conceive of a rational jurisdictional system in which the answer as well as the complaint would be consulted before a determination was made whether the case "arose under" federal law, or in which original and removal jurisdiction were not coextensive. Indeed, until the 1887 amendments to the 1875 Act [establishing federal question jurisdiction], the well-pleaded complaint rule was not applied in full force to cases removed from state court; the defendant's petition for removal could furnish the necessary guarantee that the case necessarily presented a substantial question of federal law. Commentators have repeatedly proposed some mechanism be established to permit removal of cases in which a federal defense may be dispositive. But those proposals have not been adopted.

comply are in dispute, and both parties admit that the only question for decision is raised by a federal preemption defense. Nevertheless, it has been correctly understood to apply in such situations. As we said in *Gully*, "By unimpeachable authority, a suit brought upon a state statute does not arise under an act of Congress or the Constitution of the United States because prohibited thereby."[25]

III

Simply to state these principles is not to apply them to the case at hand. Appellants' complaint sets forth two "causes of action," one of which expressly refers to ERISA; if either comes within the original jurisdiction of the federal courts, removal was proper as to the whole case. Although appellant's complaint does not specifically assert any particular statutory entitlement for the relief it seeks, the language of the complaint suggests (and the parties do not dispute) that appellant's "first cause of action" states a claim under [California's revenue law], and its "second cause of action" states a claim under California's Declaratory Judgment Act. As an initial proposition, then, the "law that creates the cause of action" is state law, and original federal jurisdiction is unavailable unless it appears that some substantial, disputed question of federal law is a necessary element of one of the well-pleaded state claims, or that one or the other claim is "really" one of federal law.

A

Even though state law creates appellant's causes of action, its case might still "arise under" the laws of the United States if a well-pleaded complaint established that its right to relief under state law requires resolution of a substantial question of federal law in dispute between the parties. For appellant's first cause of action — to enforce its levy, under [California law] — a straightforward application of the well-pleaded complaint rule precludes original federal court jurisdiction. California law establishes a set of conditions, without reference to federal law, under which a tax levy may be enforced; federal law becomes relevant only by way of a defense to an obligation created entirely by state law, and then only if appellant has made out a valid claim for relief under state law. The well-pleaded complaint rule was framed to deal with precisely such a situation. . . . [S]ince 1887 it has been settled law that a case may not be removed to federal court on the basis of a federal defense, including the defense of preemption, even if the defense is anticipated in the plaintiff's complaint, and even if both parties admit that the defense is the only question truly at issue in the case.

Appellant's declaratory judgment action poses a more difficult problem. Whereas the question of federal preemption is relevant to appellant's first cause of action only as a potential defense, it is a necessary element of the declaratory judgment claim. Under [California law], a party with an interest in property may bring an action for a declaration of another party's legal rights

25. [Footnote 12 in Court's opinion.] Note, however, that a claim of federal preemption does not always arise as a defense to a coercive action. And, of course, the absence of original jurisdiction does not mean that there is no federal forum in which a preemption defense may be heard. If the state courts reject a claim of federal preemption, that decision may ultimately be reviewed on appeal by this Court.

and duties with respect to that property upon showing that there is an "actual controversy relating to the respective rights and duties" of the parties. The only questions in dispute between the parties in this case concern the rights and duties of CLVT and its trustees under ERISA. Not only does appellant's request for a declaratory judgment under California law clearly encompass questions governed by ERISA, but appellant's complaint identifies no other questions as a subject of controversy between the parties. Such questions must be raised in a well-pleaded complaint for a declaratory judgment. Therefore, it is clear on the face of its well-pleaded complaint that appellant may not obtain the relief it seeks in its second cause of action ("[t]hat the court declare defendants legally obligated to honor all future levies by the Board upon [CLVT],") without a construction of ERISA and/or an adjudication of its preemptive effect and constitutionality—all questions of federal law.

Appellant argues that original federal court jurisdiction over such a complaint is foreclosed by our decision in *Skelly Oil*]. As we shall see, however, *Skelly Oil* is not directly controlling. [The Court then provided the factual background of *Skelly Oil.*]

* * * *

. . . *Skelly Oil* has come to stand for the proposition that "if, but for the availability of the declaratory judgment procedure, the federal claim would arise only as a defense to a state created action, jurisdiction is lacking."

1. As an initial matter, we must decide whether the doctrine of *Skelly Oil* limits original federal court jurisdiction under § 1331—and by extension removal jurisdiction under § 1441—when a question of federal law appears on the face of a well-pleaded complaint for a state law declaratory judgment. . . . Our interpretation of the federal Declaratory Judgment Act in *Skelly Oil* does not apply of its own force to *state* declaratory judgment statutes, many of which antedate the federal statute.

Yet while *Skelly Oil* itself is limited to the federal Declaratory Judgment Act, fidelity to its spirit leads us to extend it to state declaratory judgment actions as well. If federal district courts could take jurisdiction, either originally or by removal, of state declaratory judgment claims raising questions of federal law, without regard to the doctrine of *Skelly Oil*, the federal Declaratory Judgment Act—with the limitations *Skelly Oil* read into it—would become a dead letter. For any case in which a state declaratory judgment action was available, litigants could get into federal court for a declaratory judgment despite our interpretation of [the federal DJ Act] simply by pleading an adequate state claim for a declaration of federal law. Having interpreted the [federal DJ Act] to include certain limitations on the jurisdiction of federal district courts to entertain declaratory judgment suits, we should be extremely hesitant to interpret [§§ 1331 and 1441] in a way that renders the limitations in the later statute nugatory. Therefore, we hold that under the jurisdictional statutes as they now stand[26] federal courts do not have original jurisdiction, nor do they acquire jurisdiction on removal, when a federal question is presented by a complaint for

26. [Footnote 17 in Court's opinion.] It is not beyond the power of Congress to confer a right to a declaratory judgment on a case or controversy arising under federal law—within the meaning of the Constitution or of § 1331—without regard to *Skelly Oil's* particular application of the well-pleaded complaint rule. . . . Nevertheless, Congress has declined to make such a change. At this point, any adjustment in the system that has evolved under the *Skelly Oil* rule must come from Congress.

a state declaratory judgment, but *Skelly Oil* would bar jurisdiction if the plaintiff had sought a federal declaratory judgment.

2. The question, then, is whether a federal district court could take jurisdiction of appellant's declaratory judgment claim had it been brought under [the federal DJ Act].[27] The application of *Skelly Oil* to such a suit is somewhat unclear. Federal courts have regularly taken original jurisdiction over declaratory judgment suits in which, if the declaratory judgment defendant brought a coercive action to enforce its rights, that suit would necessarily present a federal question.[28] Section 502(a)(3) of ERISA specifically grants trustees of ERISA-covered plans like CLVT a cause of action for injunctive relief when their rights and duties under ERISA are at issue, and that action is exclusively governed by federal law. If CLVT could have sought an injunction under ERISA against application to it of state regulations that require acts inconsistent with ERISA, does a declaratory judgment suit by the State "arise under" federal law?

We think not. We have always interpreted [28 U.S.C. § 1331] with an eye to practicality and necessity. "What is needed is something of that common-sense accommodation of judgment to kaleidoscopic situations which characterizes the law in its treatment of causation . . . a selective process which picks the substantial causes out of the web and lays the other ones aside." [*Gully*] There are good reasons why the federal courts should not entertain suits by the States to declare the validity of their regulations despite possibly conflicting federal law. States are not significantly prejudiced by an inability to come to federal court for a declaratory judgment in advance of a possible injunctive suit by a person subject to federal regulation. They have a variety of means by which they can enforce their own laws in their own courts, and they do not suffer if the preemption questions such enforcement may raise are tested there.[29] The express grant of federal jurisdiction in ERISA is limited to suits brought by certain parties as to whom Congress presumably determined that a right to enter federal court was necessary to further the statute's purposes. It did not go so far as to provide that any suit *against* such parties must also be brought in federal court when they themselves did not choose to sue. The situation presented by a State's suit for a declaration of the validity of state law is sufficiently removed from the spirit of necessity and careful limitation of district court jurisdiction that informed our statutory interpretation in *Skelly Oil* and *Gully* to convince us that, until Congress informs us otherwise, such a suit is not within the original jurisdiction of the United States district courts. Accordingly, the same suit brought originally in state court is not removable either.

27. [Footnote 18 in Court's opinion.] It may seem odd that, for purposes of determining whether removal was proper, we analyze a claim bought under state law, in state court, by a party who has continuously objected to district court jurisdiction over its case, as if that party had been trying to get original federal court jurisdiction all along. That irony, however, is a more-or-less constant feature of the removal statute, under which a case is removable if a federal district court could have taken jurisdiction had the same complaint been filed.

28. [Footnote 19 in Court's opinion.] For instance, federal courts have consistently adjudicated suits by alleged patent infringers to declare a patent invalid, on the theory that an infringement suit by the declaratory judgment defendant would raise a federal question over which the federal courts have exclusive jurisdiction. . . .

29. [Footnote 22 in Court's opinion.] Indeed, as [the Board's] strategy in this case shows, they may often be willing to go to great lengths to avoid federal-court resolution of a preemption question. Realistically, there is little prospect that States will flood the federal courts with declaratory judgment actions; most questions will arise, as in this case, because a State has sought a declaration in state court and the defendant has removed the case to federal court. Accordingly, it is perhaps appropriate to note that considerations of comity make us reluctant to snatch cases which a State has brought from the courts of that State, unless some clear rule demands it.

B

CLVT also argues that [the Board's] "causes of action" are, in substance, federal claims. Although we have often repeated that "the party who brings the suit is master to decide what law he will rely upon," it is an independent corollary of the well-pleaded complaint rule that a plaintiff may not defeat removal by omitting to plead necessary federal questions in a complaint.

CLVT's best argument stems from our decision in *Avco Corp. v. Aero Lodge No. 735*. In that case, the petitioner filed suit in state court alleging simply that it had a valid contract with the respondent, a union, under which the respondent had agreed to submit all grievances to binding arbitration and not to cause or sanction any "work stoppages, strikes, or slowdowns." The petitioner further alleged that the respondent and its officials had violated the agreement by participating in the sanctioning work stoppages, and it sought temporary and permanent injunctions against further breaches. It was clear that, had petitioner invoked it, there would have been a federal cause of action under § 301 of the Labor Management Relations Act of 1947 (LMRA) and that, even in state court, any action to enforce an agreement within the scope of § 301 would be controlled by federal law. . . .

[The Court held] that the petitioner's action "arose under" § 301, and thus could be removed to federal court, although the petitioner had undoubtedly pleaded an adequate claim for relief under the state law of contracts and had sought a remedy available *only* under state law. The necessary ground of decision was that the preemptive force of § 301 is so powerful as to displace entirely any state cause of action "for violation of contracts between an employer and a labor organization." Any such suit is purely a creature of federal law, notwithstanding the fact that state law would provide a cause of action in the absence of § 301. *Avco* stands for the proposition that if a federal cause of action completely preempts a state cause of action any complaint that comes within the scope of the federal cause of action necessarily "arises under" federal law.

CLVT argues by analogy that ERISA, like § 301, was meant to create a body of federal common law, and that "any state court action which would require the interpretation or application of ERISA to a plan document 'arises under' the laws of the United States." ERISA contains provisions creating a series of express causes of action in favor of participants, beneficiaries, and fiduciaries of ERISA-covered plans, as well as the Secretary of Labor. § 502(a). It may be that, as with § 301 as interpreted in *Avco*, any state action coming within the scope of § 502(a) of ERISA would be removable to federal district court, even if an otherwise adequate state cause of action were pleaded without reference to federal law. It does not follow, however, that either of appellant's claims in this case comes within the scope of one of ERISA's causes of action.

The phrasing of § 502(a) is instructive. Section 502(a) specifies which persons — participants, beneficiaries, fiduciaries, or the Secretary of Labor — may bring actions for particular kinds of relief. It neither creates nor expressly denies any cause of action in favor of state governments, to enforce tax levies or for any other purpose. It does not purport to reach every question relating to plans covered by ERISA.[30]

30. [Footnote 28 in Court's opinion.] In contrast, § 301(a) of the LMRA applies to all "[s]uits for violation of contracts between an employer and a labor organization representing employees in an industry affecting commerce . . . or between any such labor organization." We have not taken a restrictive view of *who* may sue under § 301 for violations of such contracts. But even under § 301 we have never intimated that any action merely relating to a contract within the coverage of § 301 arises exclusively under that section. For instance, a state battery suit growing out of a violent strike would not arise under § 301 simply because the strike may have been a violation of an employer-union contract.

Furthermore, § 514(b)(2)(A) of ERISA makes clear that Congress did not intend to preempt entirely every state cause of action relating to such plans. With important, but express limitations, it states that "nothing in this subchapter shall be construed to relieve any person from any law of any State which regulates insurance, banking, or securities."

Against this background, it is clear that a suit by state tax authorities under a statute like [the California law at issue] does not "arise under" ERISA. Unlike the contract rights at issue in *Avco*, the State's right to enforce its tax levies is not of central concern to the federal statute. For that reason, . . . on the face of a well-pleaded complaint there are many reasons completely unrelated to the provisions and purposes of ERISA why the State may or may not be entitled to the relief it seeks.[31] Furthermore, ERISA does not provide an alternative cause of action in favor of the State to enforce its rights, while § 301 expressly supplied the plaintiff in *Avco* with a federal cause of action to replace its preempted state contract claim. Therefore, even though the Court of Appeals may well be correct that ERISA precludes enforcement of the State's levy in the circumstances of this case, an action to enforce the levy is not itself preempted by ERISA.

Once again, [the Board's] declaratory judgment cause of action presents a somewhat more difficult issue. The question on which a declaration is sought—that of the CLVT trustees' "power to honor the levies made upon them by the State of California"—is undoubtedly a matter of concern under ERISA. It involves the meaning and enforceability of provisions in CLVT's trust agreement forbidding the trustees to assign or otherwise to alienate funds held in trust, and thus comes within the class of questions for which Congress intended that federal courts create federal common law.[32] Under § 502(a)(3)(B) of ERISA, a participant, beneficiary, or fiduciary of a plan covered by ERISA may bring a declaratory judgment action in federal court to determine whether the plan's trustees may comply with a state levy on funds held in trust. Nevertheless, CLVT's argument that [the Board's] second cause of action arises under ERISA fails for the second reason given above. ERISA carefully enumerates the parties entitled to seek relief under § 502; it does not provide anyone other than participants, beneficiaries, or fiduciaries with an express cause of action for a declaratory judgment on the issues in this case. A suit for similar relief by some other party does not "arise under" that provision.

IV

Our concern in this case is consistent application of a system of statutes conferring original federal court jurisdiction, as they have been interpreted by this Court over many years. Under our interpretations, Congress has given the lower

31. [Footnote 29 in Court's opinion.] In theory (looking only at the complaint), it may turn out that the levy was improper under state law, or that in fact the defendant had complied with the levy. . . .

32. [Footnote 30 in Court's opinion.] Of course, in suggesting that the trustees' power to comply with a state tax levy is—as a subset of the trustees' general duties with respect to CLVT—a matter of concern under ERISA, we express no opinion as to whether ERISA forbids the trustees to comply with the levies in this case or otherwise preempts the State's power to levy on funds held in trust. The same is true of our holding that ERISA does not preempt the State's causes of action entirely. Merely to hold that ERISA does not have the same effect on appellant's suit in this case that § 301 of the LMRA had on the petitioner's contract suit in *Avco* is not to prejudge the merits of CLVT's preemption claim.

federal courts jurisdiction to hear, originally or by removal from a state court, only those cases in which a well-pleaded complaint establishes either that federal law creates the cause of action or that the plaintiff's right to relief necessarily depends on resolution of a substantial question of federal law. We hold that a suit by state tax authorities both to enforce its levies against funds held in trust pursuant to an ERISA-covered employee benefit plan, and to declare the validity of the levies notwithstanding ERISA, is neither a creature of ERISA itself nor a suit of which the federal courts will take jurisdiction because it turns on a question of federal law. Accordingly, we vacate the judgment of the Court of Appeals and remand so that this case may be remanded to the Superior Court of the State of California for the County of Los Angeles.

DISCUSSION AND QUESTIONS

Franchise Tax Board is a difficult opinion. One needs to take things one step at a time. First, an important holding of the case is that the same rules established in *Skelly Oil* for considering federal declaratory judgment actions apply to state declaratory judgment actions removed to federal court.

There were two claims at issue in *Franchise Tax Board*. The Court considers each one separately, as should you. The first claim is one provided for by California's substantive tax laws. The claim has nothing to do with a declaratory judgment. The right to sue is created by state law and the well-pleaded complaint does not contain an embedded federal ingredient. Under the rules we have discussed above, that claim does not arise under federal law. While the Trust could conceivably argue that ERISA preempts state law, that issue would be a defense.[33] Thus, federal jurisdiction existed, if at all, based on the Board's second claim.

The Board's second claim sought a declaratory judgment that ERISA *did not* preempt California law, allowing the Board to collect the taxes from the Trust. The Court first makes clear that the face of the declaratory judgment complaint is still important in the analysis. That document must still set forth a federal issue. Here, the condition was clearly satisfied by the central place of ERISA in the declaration sought.

Next, the Court set about determining whether a coercive suit *by either party* would arise under federal law. There had been dispute after *Skelly Oil* whether it was appropriate to consider a coercive suit by the declaratory defendant or only the declaratory plaintiff. Justice Brennan appears to adopt the broader reading of *Skelly Oil* in which a coercive suit by either party is properly considered. Some justices have since questioned this broader reading, but this aspect of *Franchise Tax Board* has not been repudiated by the Court. *See Textron Lycoming Reciprocating Engine Div., Avco Corp. v. UAW*, 523 U.S. 653, 659 (1998). Accordingly, the second step in the analysis is to consider whether a coercive suit by either party would arise under federal law, under the "cause of action" rule announced in *American Well Works*, the *Grable/ Gunn* test, or the complete preemption doctrine.

The Court next considered whether a coercive suit by either the Board or the Trust would arise under federal law. This is where matters become cloudy.

33. Nor would the claim arise under federal law through the complete preemption doctrine. The Court concluded that the Board was not within the class of persons for whom ERISA provided a right of action. *See* Section III.B of the Court's opinion. Thus, while ERISA might provide the Trust with a defense, it did not transform the Board's state-law claim for collection of taxes into one under federal law.

The Court concluded that a coercive suit by the Board against the Trust would not arise under federal law. That part of the analysis is straightforward; after all, count I of the complaint sought coercive relief solely under state law,

What about a coercive suit by the Trust against the Board? Near the end of section III.A, the Court suggests that such a suit likely would arise under federal law: "Section 502(a)(3) of ERISA specifically grants trustees of ERISA-covered plans like CLVT a cause of action for injunctive relief when their rights and duties under ERISA are at issue, and that action is exclusively governed by federal law." 463 U.S. at 19-20. If a coercive suit by one of the parties would arise under federal law, why then does the Court conclude there is no jurisdiction?

This question leads us to the third—and most controversial—aspect of arising under jurisdiction in the declaratory judgment context. The Court concluded there was no jurisdiction through the use of an ad hoc exception in which "practicality and necessity" trump what would otherwise be a finding of jurisdiction under § 1331. The primary factor the Court cited as a jurisdictional trump card was its conclusion that a *state* does not need federal court protection to enforce its laws. That rationale is odd since the *Trust*, not the state, sought a federal forum (recall the case was removed).

The test the Court crafts for determining jurisdiction over declaratory judgment claims is relatively easy to state. We do so in a flow chart in Figure 5-3, a graphic representation that is consistent with the Court's most recent comments in this area. *See Medtronic, Inc. v. Mirowski Family Ventures, LLC,* 134 S. Ct. 843, 848-49 (2014). The difficulty is how to determine in any given case whether "practicality and necessity" trump an otherwise valid claim of jurisdiction under § 1331. In many ways, this analysis is akin to deciding whether a federal issue embedded in a state-created cause of action is "substantial" under *Grable* and *Gunn.* Perhaps the best one can do is understand the test and be creative within the confines of precedent in applying it.

Test your understanding of jurisdiction over declaratory judgment actions—as well as the other doctrines concerning statutory federal question jurisdiction—with Problem 5-8.

PROBLEM 5-8

Labor Unrest

Union and Employer are parties to a collective bargaining agreement subject to section 301 of the Labor Management Relations Act of 1947. That statutory provision (the same one that was at issue in *Lincoln Mills, supra*) governs the interpretation and enforcement of all collective bargaining agreements entered into between unions and employers. The specific rules governing these agreements are crafted as a matter of federal common law. A provision of the parties' agreement is that the Union will not institute a strike against the Employer for any reason during the term of the agreement. The Union has recently learned that the Employer is planning to subcontract certain work that is currently being done by Union members. The agreement does not prevent such subcontracting. However, the Union contends that the Employer intentionally misled it concerning the subcontracting issue during the negotiations that led to the adoption of the current collective bargaining agreement.

The Union would like to be able to credibly threaten to strike if the Employer continues to subcontract jobs to non-union members. It is concerned, however,

FIGURE 5-3

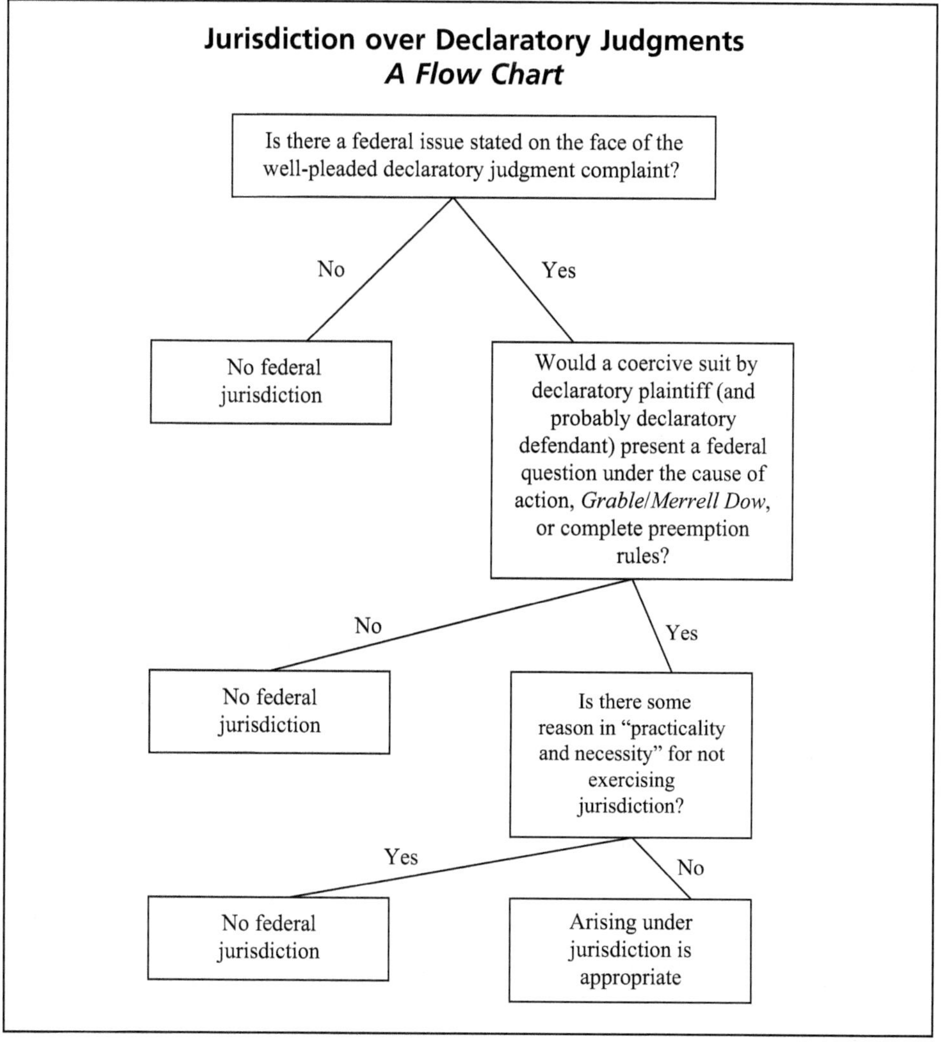

that the no-strike clause in the collective bargaining agreement will render such action a breach of contract. Accordingly, the Union files a lawsuit against the Employer in state court under the state declaratory judgment act. The Union seeks a declaration that the existing collective bargaining agreement is voidable at the option of the Union based on the alleged misrepresentations of the Employer. The Union does not allege that either the Employer or the Union has ever violated the express terms of the collective bargaining agreement.

The Employer removes the case to federal court on the basis that the Union's lawsuit arises under federal law within the meaning of 28 U.S.C. § 1331. The Union has moved to remand the case to state court. You are the federal judge to whom the case has been assigned. How do you rule on the motion to remand? What is the basis of your ruling?

FIGURE 5-4

An Ultimate Checklist

Having now evaluated the Constitution and congressional statutes, how should one approach a "federal question" problem? We suggest a broad, three-step approach.

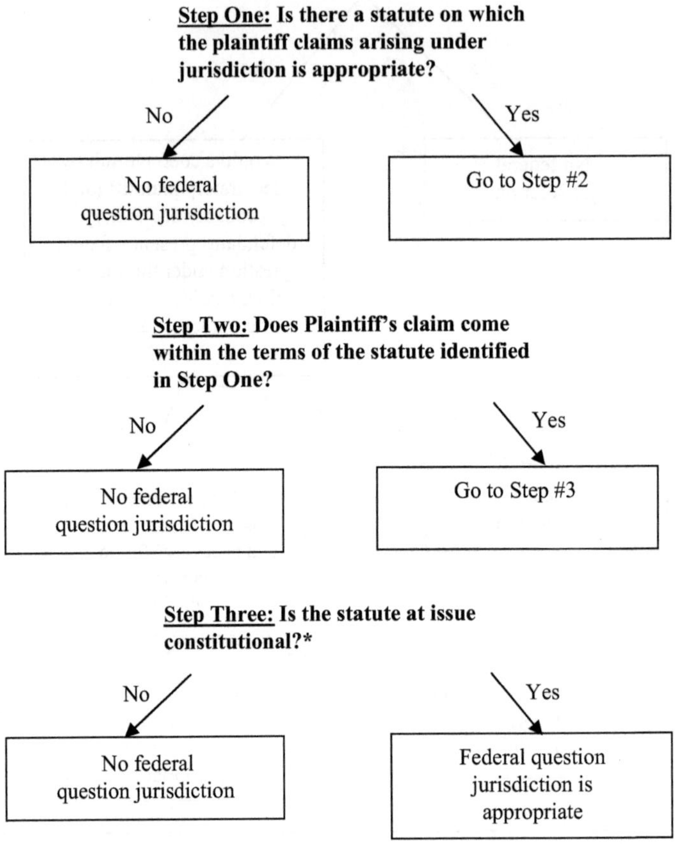

***If the statute is § 1331, one need not engage in this step because § 1331 is by definition narrower in scope than the constitution grant of federal question jurisdiction.**

D. SOME ADDITIONAL PROBLEMS

The problems that follow provide additional practice concerning the topics covered in Chapter 5.

PROBLEM 5-9

Medical Malpractice and Federal Courts

You are a lawyer working as a staff counsel for a Committee of the United States Senate. You have been asked to provide advice concerning a bill that a senator wishes to introduce. The bill is premised on a congressional finding that medical malpractice lawsuits in the aggregate have a significant impact on interstate commerce. Based on this conclusion, the proposed bill would allow any claim by a person alleging medical malpractice to be filed in or removed to federal district court regardless of the citizenship of the parties or the amount in controversy.

Is it possible to uphold this jurisdictional grant without resort to the concept of protective jurisdiction? If the proposed bill is based on protective jurisdiction, does it matter whether one accepts either Professor Mishkin's or Professor Wechsler's theory of the constitutional basis for protective jurisdiction? See section C.1.c. Please prepare a memorandum for the Committee addressing these issues.

PROBLEM 5-10

A Nursing Home Death

Mildred Rose ("Rose"), a citizen of Georgia, was a resident in the Grace Retirement and Nursing Home ("Grace") in Athens, Georgia. Grace is a corporation organized under Georgia law. Georgia law provides residents of facilities such as the one operated by Grace with certain rights. One of those rights, the violation of which will support an award of damages or other appropriate relief, is compliance with all regulations promulgated under the federal Medicare and Medicaid Acts. One of those regulations provides that a covered facility must ensure that "a resident who enters the facility without pressure sores does not develop such sores unless such development is unavoidable based on an individual's specific medical condition."

Rose entered Grace with no pressure sores. She did not suffer from any medical condition that would cause such sores. However, Rose developed pressure sores and died on account of the infection resulting from them. Rose's children have sued Grace in Georgia state court for violation of the Georgia statute. They allege that Grace is liable under the statute because of Grace's violation of the federal regulation. They do not assert any claims under the regulation itself, which does not convey a private right of action.

Grace removes the case to federal court, claiming that it arises under federal law under the terms of 28 U.S.C. § 1331. Rose's children move to remand the case to state court. You are the federal judge to whom the case has been assigned. How do you rule on the remand motion? What is the basis for your ruling?

PROBLEM 5-11

A Blue Cross/Blue Shield Conundrum

The Federal Employees Health Benefits Act of 1959 (FEHBA) establishes a comprehensive program of health insurance for federal employees. FEHBA authorizes a federal agency, the Office of Personnel Management (the "Agency"), to contract with private health insurers to offer federal employees various health care plans. The largest provider of such plans is Blue Cross/ Blue Shield ("Blue Cross").

Under the terms of the Blue Cross contract with the Agency, the federal government pays 75 percent of the premiums and the employee pays the balance. All premiums are deposited in a Treasury Fund out of which payments are made to plan beneficiaries. The federal government pays Blue Cross based on a flat rate specified in the contract between the Agency and Blue Cross.

FEHBA does not itself deal with reimbursement by the beneficiary of any benefits paid by the plan should the beneficiary recover damages in a tort action. However, the statement of benefits (a contract) Blue Cross provides to plan beneficiaries provides as follows in relevant part:

> If another person or entity . . . causes you to suffer an injury or illness, and if we [Blue Cross] pay benefits for that injury or illness, you agree to the following:
>
> All recoveries you obtain (whether by lawsuit, settlement, or otherwise), no matter how described or designated, must be used to reimburse us [Blue Cross] in full for benefits we paid. Our share of any recovery extends only to the amount of benefits we have paid or will pay to you or, if applicable, to your heirs, administrators, successors, or assignees.

Further relating to the reimbursement issue, the Agency–Blue Cross contract provides that Blue Cross must make a "reasonable effort to seek recovery of amounts . . . it is entitled to recover in cases . . . brought to its attention."

There are two other provisions of FEHBA that may be relevant. First, one section of the statute provides as follows:

> The provisions of any contract under this chapter which relate to the nature or extent of coverage or benefits (including payments with respect to benefits) shall supersede and preempt any State or local law, or any regulation issued thereunder, which relates to health insurance or plans.

The other potentially relevant provision is that the federal district courts are vested with "original jurisdiction, concurrent with the United States Court of Federal Claims, of a civil action or claim against the United States founded on [FEHBA]."

In June 2007, Tony Stone ("Stone") was severely injured in an accident in his home state of New York. Stone is a federal employee covered under a health plan administered by Blue Cross under the Agency–Blue Cross contract under FEHBA. Stone eventually died as a result of the injuries he sustained in the accident. Under the health plan, Blue Cross paid $150,000 in benefits on Stone's behalf.

Stone's estate brought a state-law claim against the person whose negligence injured Stone. That state court action was ultimately settled for $3,000,000. Having been notified of the settlement, Blue Cross demanded reimbursement of the $150,000 it had paid. Stone's estate contested the demand and refused to pay.

You are a lawyer retained by Blue Cross. Blue Cross would like to file a lawsuit against Stone's estate to recover the $150,000 as provided in the Statement of Benefits. It would like to file the suit in a federal court. There is no diversity of citizenship between Blue Cross and Stone's estate. Please prepare a memorandum to Blue Cross advising it of all possible jurisdictional grounds for filing suit in federal court. Be as comprehensive and creative as possible. Be sure to provide an assessment of the likely success of the various jurisdictional theories you advance.

CHAPTER
6

Diversity Jurisdiction

A. A REFERENCE PROBLEM

On February 20, 2003, a deadly fire destroyed a nightclub in West Warwick, Rhode Island, known to its patrons as "The Station." The fire was caused by the negligent pyrotechnics of performing band members, all of whom were from California. The fire left 100 people dead and more than 200 injured. Only seventy-seven people were reported to have escaped the building without physical harm.[1]

1. The facts in the opening paragraph are taken directly from the court's opinion in *Passa v. Derderian*, 308 F. Supp. 2d 43 (D.R.I. 2004). Other facts in the Reference Problem are fictionalized.

One of those who escaped unharmed was Alex Seay. Seay had just exited the building to go to his car when the fire broke out. His only personal loss was damage to his car caused by an emergency vehicle. Seay was later contacted by a Rhode Island lawyer representing many victims of the fire and their family members. When asked, Seay declined to join as plaintiff in a suit the lawyer had filed in Rhode Island state court.

Seay did permit a lawyer friend, who primarily does probate work, to file a small claim on his behalf in a Rhode Island state court. The suit seeks to recover for damage to Seay's car, much of which his auto insurer has refused to cover. Seay has sued the owners of the nightclub, both of whom are citizens of Rhode Island like Seay. Seay's lawyer initially believed the defendants would settle once served with a complaint.

To Seay's surprise, the defendant nightclub owners have now removed his small suit to federal court. Seay's lawyer is at a loss to explain why his suit has ended up in federal court. As she explains to Seay, "I don't get it. We haven't sued under federal law. Everybody is a Rhode Islander. I'm not even admitted to practice in the federal district court. I think the nightclub's lawyer made a mistake. I'll contact him."

What Seay's lawyer learned from defense counsel surprised her. It seems the nightclub owners (acting on the directions of their insurer) are removing all suits filed against them to federal court. More than a dozen removed suits against the nightclub owners and the California band members who started the fire are now pending in federal court. Even though Rhode Islanders make up almost half the victims, and Rhode Island law will likely govern all fire-related claims, defense counsel claims a new "diversity-of-citizenship" statute gives the federal court jurisdiction over all these claims.

Seay's lawyer looks up the federal statute, 28 U.S.C. § 1369(a), to verify that defense counsel has read it correctly. It appears counsel has. Section 1369(a) states in pertinent part that subject matter jurisdiction exists if there is at least one state citizen whose interests are "adverse" to those of a citizen of another state. Seay's lawyer wonders to herself: "What happened to the complete diversity rule I learned about in law school? Why would Congress give Rhode Island defendants the right to remove a case from their own state's court? And I thought the current amount in controversy was $75,000? This just doesn't make sense."

* * * *

As we discover in this chapter, the musty topic of diversity jurisdiction has been re-invigorated in recent years. Since 2002, Congress has twice conferred new forms of diversity jurisdiction that are unprecedented in the federal courts' history. One form is the basis for federal jurisdiction in the Reference Problem. Congress' action has given new and controversial life to diversity jurisdiction at a time when many thought prejudice against out-of-state citizens — the ill supposedly targeted by diversity jurisdiction — was confined to collegiate sports rivalries.

In recent years there has also been increased scrutiny of the Framers' intent in authorizing diversity jurisdiction. Hardly anyone who has examined constitutional history believes that the Framers had some generalized fear that Virginians could not be trusted to adjudicate disputes between their fellow citizens and New Yorkers. But what exactly the Framers did fear, and how federal jurisdiction was to placate those fears, is still disputed. For several critics, Congress has now exceeded its constitutional power to authorize federal court jurisdiction over "Controversies . . . between Citizens of different States." According to these critics, unless diversity jurisdiction is constrained by its historical purposes Congress will have acquired a vast new power to subvert the sovereignty of state courts.

Among the issues we will explore in this chapter are:

- Why did the constitutional Framers single out disputes between diverse citizens as meriting a special grant of federal jurisdictional power? What apprehensions about state courts motivated the Framers, and what was supposed to change when diversity actions were transferred to federal court?
- Does conventional diversity jurisdiction currently serve the purposes envisioned by the constitutional Framers? Especially in the case of those business entities who most often invoke diversity jurisdiction, does current diversity law make good sense?
- Are there meaningful limits on Congress' power to confer diversity jurisdiction? What are those limits? Have they been transgressed by Congress in the past decade?
- Does recent diversity legislation knock down one of the long-standing props of federalism, the belief that state courts can be trusted to exercise their powers with restraint and due regard for the national interest?

As you can see from the issues highlighted above, in this chapter we take a different approach to diversity of citizenship than the one you likely took in Civil Procedure. Instead of revisiting topics like how citizenship is defined or how the amount in controversy is calculated under federal statutes, we focus on the larger implications of the diversity power for Congress, federal and state courts, and the regulation of America's legal and economic affairs.

B. CONTEXT AND BACKGROUND

1. *Why Diversity Jurisdiction?*[2]

In Chapter Five we examined the federal courts' authority to adjudicate cases arising under federal law. We can intuitively grasp many of the reasons the Framers, and eventually Congress, conferred arising under jurisdiction on federal courts. Federally appointed judges are presumably more hospitable to the enforcement of the laws of the sovereign that empowers them to act. And as federal judges specialize in the enforcement of federal law, presumably this specialization will lead to greater expertise in interpreting federal law.

But why diversity jurisdiction? On first examination, the answer seems apparent. The Framers believed that federal courts would provide a less biased forum than state courts when non-citizens litigate against local citizens. The need for an impartial federal forum seems to be reaffirmed by other Article III grants of jurisdiction, like that conferred over controversies "between two or more states" and controversies "between a State and citizens of another State." In fact, the

2. The term "diversity jurisdiction" is widely used to designate two related forms of jurisdiction. The most important form today, emphasized in this chapter, is diversity jurisdiction based on the different state citizenship of American nationals. *See* 28 U.S.C. § 1332(a)(1). The second form is referred to as "alienage" jurisdiction, which exists when a state citizen litigates against a citizen of a foreign state. *See* 28 U.S.C. § 1332(a)(2).

role of federal courts as impartial tribunals seemed especially important to the Framers. When many of them convened as members of the first Congress, they used their Article III power mainly to confer diversity and alienage jurisdiction on federal courts; arising under jurisdiction was entrusted to state courts. Without the authorization of diversity jurisdiction, it has been said, "the circuit courts created by the First Judiciary Act would have had very little to do."[3]

Today diversity jurisdiction generates an important part of the federal courts' business. Roughly one-third of private civil cases docketed in federal court are based on diversity jurisdiction.[4] Although one can discern a steady trend toward the contraction of diversity jurisdiction in conventional litigation in the late twentieth century (for example, increasingly higher amount-in-controversy requirements), more recently Congress has significantly expanded jurisdiction by giving federal courts power over many class actions. *See* 28 U.S.C. §§ 1332, 1453 (the "Class Action Fairness Act of 2005"). This may suggest that Congress still finds need for impartial tribunals to avoid "home state" bias against non-citizens.

But there is reason to question appearances. According to several federal courts scholars, the historical record belies the conventional explanation that diversity jurisdiction was intended to provide a class of litigants, out-of-state citizens, an impartial forum. The *real* reason the Framers created diversity jurisdiction, it is argued, is quite different. According to one view, diversity jurisdiction was created to protect a distinct group of litigants — creditors and commercial interests — from the pro-debtor bias of state judges and state legislatures. According to yet another view, diversity jurisdiction was motivated by the Framers' interest in creating a new federal judiciary with power to develop a new form of "common law" conducive to the nation's emerging commerce. More recently, one scholar has argued an interpretation of diversity jurisdiction that suggests the Framers' motives were less than admirable. According to this interpretation, the Framers were motivated by a much larger concern in creating diversity jurisdiction — a fear that state court juries would exercise unrestrained "democratic" control over legal disputes. Under this view, the Framers' call for diversity jurisdiction to avoid bias against non-citizens was a pretext. What the Framers actually sought was the authority to rein in populist state court juries and the corresponding power to manipulate federal juries to carry out the political agenda of the dominant Federalist party.

These discrepant interpretations highlight how, more than two-hundred years after diversity jurisdiction was authorized, there is until no consensus about the Framers' intent. Were the Framers apprehensive about state legislatures, state judges, or state court juries? What perceived biases, in particular, prompted the creation of diversity jurisdiction? And how was diversity jurisdiction to eliminate these biases?

In thinking about bias against out-of-staters, it helps to conceive of how bias might manifest itself in state courts. One form of bias is biased *law*. For example, state legislatures might enact laws that single out non-citizens for less favorable treatment under the law. Alternatively, state courts might promulgate common-law or procedural rules that disfavor non-citizens. A more subtle form of biased law might take the form of legal rules that appear to apply even-handedly to citizen and non-citizen alike, yet which disfavor a class of litigants in which non-citizens predominate. For example, a debt-ridden agrarian state might enact

3. Henry Friendly, Federal Jurisdiction: A General View 141 (1973).
4. *See http://www.uscourts.gov/uscourts/Statistics/JudicialBusiness/2013/appendices/C08Sep13.pdf.*

laws unfavorable to creditors and commercial interests knowing they will be used largely against non-citizens.

To the extent that apprehensions about biased state law motivated the Framers, the transfer of power to federal courts through diversity jurisdiction would have to result in a change in the applicable law. As we learn, some scholars view diversity jurisdiction as a mechanism for displacing state law, although they disagree about how this displacement was to be achieved.

Another form of bias is *adjudicatory* bias. The most obvious form of such bias is juror bias. Another form of adjudicatory bias is that of the state court judge. Even when state court judges are applying seemingly-neutral legal rules, the discretion inherent in much adjudication often provides opportunity to tip the scales toward locals. To the extent that apprehensions about adjudicatory bias motivated the Framers, they would have anticipated that transfer of jurisdictional power to federal court would resulted in more impartial decisionmakers. Diversity jurisdiction clearly substitutes federal judges for state judges, but how does it affect the composition of the jury? After all, state and federal juries are drawn from the same general population of state citizens.

If we can identify the Framers' purpose(s) in creating diversity jurisdiction, we can better assess the legitimacy of Congress' recent, controversial uses of diversity jurisdiction in special settings. We can also better assess whether more conventional diversity jurisdiction continues to justify its substantial demand on the federal courts.

2. *Plan of Coverage*

We begin by considering the principal theories of the Framers' intent in authorizing diversity jurisdiction. We first consider the "orthodox" interpretation of the Framers' intent, that they sought to provide non-citizens an impartial forum for the adjudication of their disputes with local citizens. This orthodox interpretation is routinely relied on by the Court and Congress but is frequently questioned by commentators, who discern no evidence of non-citizen bias during the Framers' era. We consider whether such evidence has perhaps been overlooked.

We next consider the theory that the Framers intended to affect the application of state law by authorizing diversity jurisdiction. One version of this theory argues that the Framers hoped federal judges would be less parochial in their application of choice-of-law theory, moderating the tendency of state courts to apply local law to transactions with stronger connections to other jurisdictions. Another version of this theory argues that the Framers authorized diversity jurisdiction for the express purpose of having federal courts independently develop common law rules to replace state court rules. We ask whether this theory overlooks the potential importance of federal courts as a check on the application of unconstitutional state law.

We then consider a more recent interpretation of the Framers' intent, which argues that they created diversity jurisdiction to shift control of juries from state to federal officials — particularly, Federalist officials. We examine the important contribution this theory makes to our understanding of the eighteenth-century jury, particularly the jury's role in lawmaking. We consider how a better understanding of the eighteenth-century jury discloses another reason for conferring diversity jurisdiction on the federal courts. As with all theories of the

Framers' intent, however, we ask whether undue focus on one justification for diversity jurisdiction interferes with our appreciation of what may have been a mixture of motives.

Having reviewed the principal theories of diversity jurisdiction, we consider the evolution in the law of corporate diversity. Corporate diversity is important in its own right because of the prevalence of corporate players in diversity litigation. But the debate over the proper bounds of corporate diversity also provides opportunity to consider the larger debate over the continued justification for devoting more than a third of the federal courts' business to diversity litigation.

We then consider Congress' most recent implementations of diversity jurisdiction in the Multiparty, Multiforum Trial Jurisdiction Act of 2002 and the Class Action Fairness Act of 2005. These statutes authorize unprecedented mechanisms for invoking diversity jurisdiction to achieve far more ambitious ends than Congress has previously sought to attain. We ask whether Congress has exploited the theory of "minimal diversity" to expand federal control over litigation previously entrusted to state courts. We also ask whether Congress has unmasked its belief that, at least in the context of class actions, it has lost confidence in state courts.

Finally, we consider whether there are workable limits on Congress' power to confer diversity jurisdiction, particularly its power to confer "minimal diversity" jurisdiction. If there are such limits, have they been exceeded by Congress in recent diversity legislation? As we discover, the search for limits on Congress' diversity power takes us back to an examination of the Framers' intent in authorizing diversity jurisdiction. Eighteenth-century constitutional history has never been more important.

C. THE LAW AND PROBLEMS

1. *The Framers' Intent(s)*

Diversity jurisdiction has been the subject of dispute and attempted reform throughout its history. For many, reform must be premised on a sound understanding of the Framers' intent in authorizing diversity jurisdiction. Consider these comments of one of the twentieth century's most esteemed federal judges:

> When we know why the federal courts were given this jurisdiction and how they handled it in their early years, we shall have taken one small step toward understanding the problem today.[5]

These words were written almost a century ago by the late Judge Henry Friendly, in response to then-pending reform efforts. Since Judge Friendly wrote, there have been many attempts to take the "one small step" toward understanding the Framers' intent. Despite many elaborations of the Framers' intent, however, at least some critics argue that the more pressing task facing constitutional

5. Henry Friendly, *The Historic Basis of Diversity Jurisdiction*, 41 HARV. L. REV. 483, 483 (1928).

historians it to rid the literature of "misconceptions" that Judge Friendly and others have introduced.[6] We will examine this critique in later discussion.

Judge Friendly's observation emphasizes the need to consider two distinct aspects of historical diversity jurisdiction: (1) why the Framers authorized it, and (2) how it was implemented by early federal courts. These two aspects of the inquiry are related. The first Congress to confer diversity jurisdiction was dominated by Federalist proponents of the Constitution's jurisdictional provisions. Further, the Framers were largely lawyers and presumably had some appreciation for how the transfer of cases from state to federal court would affect diversity disputes.[7]

While commentators and courts have long expressed opinions about the Framers' purposes in authorizing diversity jurisdiction (the "why"), fewer have opined about how federal courts would achieve those purposes. Did the Framers believe that federal courts would interpret and apply the same law (state law) differently than state courts? Or did the Framers believe federal courts would apply a different law altogether? Who were the state court players (*e.g.*, judges, juries) the Framers sought to circumvent by allocating diversity suits to federal court? Further, what political, social, and economic conditions in eighteenth-century America might have been the immediate motivation for authorizing diversity jurisdiction?

In the following discussion, we highlight three (or so) interpretations of the Framers' intent, ranging from the "orthodox" interpretation that emerged soon after diversity jurisdiction was authorized to a more recent, unflattering interpretation that views diversity jurisdiction as a manipulative political ploy by the Federalists who dominated the constitutional convention. After surveying these interpretations, we discuss whether any is fully convincing. We also consider whether the differing interpretations might be synthesized into a more plausible, if less monolithic, portrayal of the Framers' intent.

At times we will distinguish "alienage" jurisdiction from the broader category of "diversity" jurisdiction of which alienage is a part. As discussed below, alienage jurisdiction was debated and approved together with jurisdiction over disputes between diverse American citizens. Yet while alienage jurisdiction is often assimilated into discussion of domestic diversity jurisdiction, at times it will be important to distinguish the two.[8]

a. Diversity to Protect Non-citizen Litigants: The "Orthodox" Interpretation

The Framers' intent in authorizing diversity jurisdiction seems apparent, at least if one takes at face value public comments of leading Federalists who supported diversity jurisdiction. James Madison, for example, expressed apprehensions that local citizens might harbor "strong prejudice" against

6. *See, e.g.*, Robert L. Jones, *Finishing a Friendly Argument: The Jury and the Historical Origins of Diversity Jurisdiction*, 82 N.Y.U. L. Rev. 997, 1091 (2007).

7. *See* Forrest McDonald, Novus Ordo Seclorum: The Intellectual Origins of the Constitution 220 (1985) (observing that 34 of the 55 delegates to the Constitutional Convention were lawyers).

8. As Professor Kevin R. Johnson has demonstrated, alienage jurisdiction historically served purposes similar to but distinct from those served by citizen-versus-citizen jurisdiction. Kevin R. Johnson, *Why Alienage Jurisdiction? Historical Foundations and Modern Justifications for Federal Jurisdiction Over Disputes Involving Noncitizens*, 21 Yale J. Int'l L. 1 (1996).

non-citizens "who might have claims against them."[9] Alexander Hamilton similarly spoke of the wisdom of providing "impartial" tribunals in disputes between citizens of different states.[10] This view of the Framers' intent was echoed in early Supreme Court decisions. As Chief Justice Marshall observed in *Bank of the United States v. Deveaux*, 9 U.S. (5 Cranch) 61, 87 (1809):

> The judicial department was introduced into the American constitution under impressions, and with views, which are too apparent not to be perceived by all. However true the fact may be, that the tribunals of the states will administer justice as impartially as those of the nation, to parties of every description, it is not less true that the constitution itself either entertains apprehensions on this subject, or views with such indulgence the possible fears and apprehensions of suitors, that it has established national tribunals for the decisions of controversies between aliens and a citizen, or between citizens of different states.

Two centuries later, Justice Frankfurter echoed Chief Justice Marshall's view that feared bias against non-citizens underlies the creation of diversity jurisdiction:

> It was believed that, consciously or otherwise, the courts of a state may favor their own citizens. Bias against outsiders may become embedded in a judgment of a state court and yet not be sufficiently apparent to be made the basis of a federal claim.

Lumbermen's Mut. Cas. Co. v. Elbert, 348 U.S. 48, 54 (1954).

The view that diversity jurisdiction addresses *adjudicatory* bias against non-citizens is often mentioned in current debates about the continued need for diversity jurisdiction. *See, e.g.*, Graham C. Lilly, Making Sense of Nonsense: Reforming Supplemental Jurisdiction, 74 IND. L.J. 181, 190 (1998) ("The principal argument for diversity jurisdiction is the protection of out-of-state litigants from local prejudice."). And as we will see, Congress continues to rely on this rationale as the basis for extending diversity jurisdiction to more controversial contexts.

But the orthodox interpretation has been challenged. The most influential critique is that of Judge Friendly. Judge Friendly observes, "Madison does not point out any specific examples of prejudice, does not allege that any exist; Marshall even gives the innuendo that none do exist."[11] Judge Friendly reached the tentative conclusion based on his review of reported cases that there was no evidence of "undue prejudice" against non-citizens in state court in the years preceding the creation of diversity jurisdiction.[12] Other, contemporary theorists of diversity jurisdiction agree with Judge Friendly that there is no "direct support" for the prejudice rationale, and like Judge Friendly question the sincerity of the Federalists' defense of diversity jurisdiction.[13]

9. 10 DOCUMENTARY HISTORY OF THE RATIFICATION 1414 (John P. Kaminski & Gaspare J. Saladino eds., 1993)

10. THE FEDERALIST No. 80.

11. *See* Friendly, *supra* note 5, at 493.

12. *Id.* at 493-94.

13. *See* Jones, *supra* note 6, at 1008-09 ("We must resist the temptation to interpret the historical struggle solely through the lens of those who emerged victorious."). *See also* 1 JULIUS GOEBEL, JR., HISTORY OF THE SUPREME COURT OF THE UNITED STATES, ANTECEDENTS AND BEGINNINGS TO 1801 at xx ("The so-called diversity jurisdiction conferred upon the federal [judiciary] had been contrived among other reasons to provide a forum where British creditors could pursue their claims without impediment as covenanted in the treaty of peace").

b. Diversity to Restrain or Prevent the Application of State Law

Judge Friendly offered an alternative interpretation of the Framers' intent that appears to have gained ascendance among many federal courts' scholars. According to Judge Friendly, the Framers' primary motivation in creating diversity jurisdiction was not a "vague" fear that state courts would harbor general prejudice against non-citizens. Instead, the Framers had a well-supported fear that state courts would be inhospitable to *creditors* in post-Revolutionary War America. According to Judge Friendly, the Framers believed that state courts would primarily implement their anti-creditor "bias" through *legislative* means.

Judge Friendly focused on the post-war proliferation of state laws intended to ameliorate the widespread indebtedness of Americans. Following the war, the states owed overwhelming debt to private creditors as well as to soldiers who had served in the Continental army and state militias.[14] Common citizens, most of them farmers, shared in the states' plight because many of them were debtors themselves. In addition, they were expected to fund the repayment of state debt through increased taxes. Adding to debtors' antipathies toward creditors was the fact that many creditors were British citizens whose compatriots had ravaged the countryside and economy of America.[15]

Many states responded to this debt crisis by enacting laws to relieve financial pressures on agrarian communities.[16] For example, some state laws relieved debtors of interest incurred during the war or permitted protracted repayment of debt through installments. One especially controversial form of debt relief was to authorize state issuance of "paper money." State-issued paper money could be used to finance public debt (in lieu of taxes), to help farmers refinance private debt, and to provide a means of debt repayment with inflated paper money instead of scarce hard currency. The issuance of paper money enjoyed substantial support in agrarian communities and was staunchly opposed by most creditors, including those in the nation's urban commercial centers.

The post-war experience with repayment of debt in state court weighed on the minds of diversity proponents, who were largely aligned with creditor interests. According to Judge Friendly's highly-influential thesis:[17]

> [T]he Federalists seem to have cherished a vague feeling that these new [federal] courts would have none of paper money. . . . [W]e may say that the desire to protect creditors against legislation favorable to debtors was a principal reason for the grant of diversity jurisdiction, and that as a reason it was by no means without validity. . . . There was a vague feeling that the new courts would be strong courts, creditors' courts, business men's courts.[18]

Judge Friendly's insight into the role of creditor relief in prompting the creation of diversity jurisdiction seems, in retrospect, obvious and compelling.

14. One of the best introductions to the debt crisis confronted after the Revolutionary War is found in Wythe Holt, *"To Establish Justice": Politics, the Judiciary Act of 1789, and the Invention of the Federal Courts*, 1989 DUKE L.J. 1421.

15. For example, among those creditors filing collection suits in Virginia circuit court during the period from 1790-97, 74 percent were citizens of Great Britain. *See* Jones, *supra* note 6, at 1015 n.71.

16. *See generally* Holt, *supra* note 14.

17. Judge Friendly's interpretation is often relied on to support the claim that bias against non-citizens may not have been of substantial concern to the Framers. *See, e.g.*, RUSSELL R. WHEELER & CYNTHIA HARRISON, CREATING THE FEDERAL COURT SYSTEM 6 (Federal Judicial Ctr. 1994).

18. *See* Friendly, *supra* note 5, at 495, 496-97, 498.

As one author has observed, "the push . . . for a strong central government that resulted in the Constitutional Convention came in large part from creditor interests."[19] As observed by another, "the problem of debts and the paper money, tender, and other laws lay heavy over the whole proceedings of the Convention."[20] Not surprisingly, "the supporters of the Constitution in ratifying conventions and in the public press . . . repeatedly referred to biased state laws" when promoting their avowedly pro-creditor agenda.[21] That diversity jurisdiction might be envisioned as one means of promoting inter-state and international credit arrangements now seems uncontroversial. But Judge Friendly's insight appeared to break new ground when he published his views in 1928.

The pro-creditor interpretation of diversity jurisdiction has several important implications. First, Judge Friendly's thesis attributes to the Framers the intent to promote the new nation's *economic* interests by improving the credit market.[22] Diversity jurisdiction is thus seen as a companion piece to other constitutional measures that helped promote creditor interests, including the Constitution's requirement that states restrict debt repayment to "gold and silver Coin" (art. I, sec. 10); that states honor public debts incurred under the Articles of Confederation (art. VI); that states give "full faith and credit" to the judgments of sister states (art. IV); and that states not enact laws "impairing the Obligation of Contracts" (art. I, sec. 10). Second, Judge Friendly's pro-creditor interpretation downplays the orthodox rationale that the Framers harbored a generic, apolitical concern about state court prejudice against non-citizen litigants. After all, the pro-debtor laws of concern to the Framers were presumably applied by state courts against all creditors, local or foreign. It was the very enforcement of such laws, more than their selective enforcement, which concerned the proponents of diversity jurisdiction.

Another important contribution of Judge Friendly was his attempt to explain *how* the pro-creditor policies of diversity jurisdiction would be implemented in the new federal courts. After all, why should the adjudication of creditor disputes in federal court make a difference? Other than constitutional protections like those mentioned above, there were no new federal laws governing creditors' rights. Consequently, would not federal judges in diversity cases apply the same state laws as state judges?

Judge Friendly's analysis largely turned on his understanding of how *choice-of-law* rules would be applied by the new federal courts. A dispute involving a debtor-creditor relationship between parties from different states or nations would usually require courts to apply choice-of-law principles to determine which jurisdiction's laws governed. Federalist John Marshall indicated as much when, upon being asked at a ratifying convention whose law would apply in diversity suits, he answered that these suits "would be governed by the laws of the state where the contract was made."[23] Although Marshall's

19. Patrick Borchers, The Origins of Diversity Jurisdiction, the Rise of Legal Positivism, and a Brave New World for Erie and Klaxon, 72 TEX. L. REV. 79, 89 (1993).

20. Holt, *supra* note 14, at 1461.

21. *See* Borchers, *supra* note 19, at 95.

22. *See* Larry Kramer, *Diversity Jurisdiction*, 1990 B.Y.U.L. REV. 98 (arguing that one of "the most important concerns in establishing federal courts" was "to foster a secure environment for interstate commerce.")

23. 3 THE DEBATES IN THE SEVERAL STATE CONVENTIONS ON THE ADOPTION OF THE FEDERAL CONSTITUTION 556-57 (Jonathan Elliot ed., 2d ed. 1836) (John Marshall, Speech to the Va. Convention (June 20, 1788).

response may have oversimplified the choice-of-law question, it affirms an understanding that diversity suits would be governed by emerging choice-of-law principles derived from international law.[24] In other words, suits between diverse parties would not *necessarily* be governed by the commercial law of the state where suit was filed.[25] Based on notions of interstate and international "comity," a court–whether state or federal—might forebear from applying its own law and instead apply the law of another jurisdiction (*e.g.*, the law of the place where a contract was made).[26]

But this still does not give a satisfactory explanation for shifting diverse commercial disputes from state court to federal court. As Judge Friendly observed, "in either court the same rules of conflict of laws should be applied and the same decision given."[27] Judge Friendly concluded, however, that federal courts would be less prone than state courts to *interpret and apply* emerging choice-of-law theory in preference of local state law favoring debtors.[28] In support of his suspicions, Judge Friendly quoted the remarks of an early Justice expressing misgivings about the propensity of state courts to manipulate "metaphysical" choice-of-law theory: "I had no doubt [diversity jurisdiction] was introduced . . . into the Constitution, to prevent, among other evils, the assertion of a power [by state court] over the rights of the citizens of other States, upon the metaphysical ideas of the British Courts on the subject of the jurisdiction over contracts." *Ogden v. Saunders*, 12 Wheat. 213, 365 (1827).

Professor Patrick Borchers has argued an alternative version of Judge Friendly's theory that choice of law motivated the Framers in creating diversity jurisdiction. According to Professor Borchers, Congress fully anticipated that federal diversity courts would *independently* develop "general" common law rules to govern interstate and international commercial transactions. In other words, diversity courts would not be limiting to choosing among different states' laws; they could develop their own.[29] Although Professor Borchers is swimming against the tide of opinion since *Erie Railroad v. Tompkins*[30]—where the Court repudiated any federal court power to independently develop general common law—his *historical* observation about what eighteenth-century lawyers and courts likely understood remains sound: "American lawyers near the time the federal courts were created also believed in general law, applicable to transstate and transnational cases."[31] Based on the legal community's view of "general" law in the eighteenth century, federal diversity courts would not be bound to follow state law or state court precedent, including state law that favored debtors to the detriment of the nation's future economic development. Professor Borchers continues, "From the beginning, federal courts in diversity cases applied . . . general law in general matters," which encompassed "commercial law . . . and conflict of laws."[32]

24. *See generally* Eugene F. Scoles et al., Conflict of Laws 18-19 (4th ed. 2004).
25. As is currently the case, federal trial court jurisdiction was organized along state jurisdictional boundaries.
26. Perhaps the most influential choice-of-law scholar in early America was the Netherlander, Ulrich Huber, who developed the principle of comity. *See Scoles, supra* note 24, at 14-15.
27. *See* Friendly, *supra* note 5, at 495.
28. *Id.* at 496.
29. *See* Borchers, *supra* note 19, at 109-10, 111-15. This is a modern interpretation of the federal courts' law-making authority, since courts at that time conceived of "general" common law as having an existence independent of the judges who "discerned" that law.
30. 304 U.S. 64 (1938).
31. *See* Borchers, *supra* note 19, at 111.
32. *Id.* at 112-13.

Consequently, Professor Borchers concludes that the Framers foresaw the new federal courts would develop and apply legal rules different from those that might be applied in state court. According to Professor Borchers, "diversity jurisdiction would be a weapon against . . . prejudice *only* if it allowed federal courts to apply different substantive rules in diversity cases."[33] Professor Borchers thus agrees with Judge Friendly in part–the Framers anticipated that the law applied in diversity suits might differ from that which state courts applied. But Professor Borchers does not place much stock in Judge Friendly's suggestion that possible divergence in state and federal court interpretations of the *same* choice-of-law rules would alone have motivated the Framers to confer diversity jurisdiction. The power of diversity courts to develop an independent body of law to govern commerce gave the Framers much stronger incentive to create diversity jurisdiction.

In sum, under both Judge Friendly's and Professor Borchers' interpretation of diversity jurisdiction, the Framers viewed diversity as a check on the states' legislative power. As we will see later, recent legislation indicates that Congress until believes diversity jurisdiction can serve such a role.

c. Diversity to Restrain the Jury: New Insights

The orthodox interpretation of diversity allegedly fails for want of evidence that state courts demonstrated *adjudicatory* prejudice toward non-citizens. The pro-creditor interpretation shifts focuses away from prejudice against non-citizens, and emphasizes that diversity jurisdiction was created to curtail *legislative* bias against creditors.

Recently, Professor Robert Jones has proffered a new theory of the Framers' intent, which calls for a revised understanding of how eighteenth-century juries functioned. Professor Jones' analysis builds on Judge Friendly's pro-creditor rationale. But Professor Jones argues that Judge Friendly and other legal scholars have missed the point. Diversity jurisdiction, he argues, was not motivated by the desire to harness state judges' propensity to apply local law. Instead, diversity jurisdiction targeted the real eighteenth-century lawgiver—the *jury*.

Professor Jones argues that contemporary lawyers and scholars have an "anachronistic" understanding of the early jury's power. Unlike the modern jury, the eighteenth-century jury (1) had the power to engage in factfinding virtually unencumbered by modern jury-control devices like the directed verdict;[34] and (2) had the ultimate power to *interpret and create law.*[35] Professor Jones observes:

> By virtue of their extensive prerogatives, eighteenth-century American juries did more than simply apply established legal norms to the cases that came before them. Instead, they played a substantial role throughout this period in shaping and creating the substantive law of their jurisdictions.[36]

33. Borchers, *supra* note 19, at 94 (emphasis added).
34. *See* Jones, *supra* note 6, at 1033 ("[A]lmost no American jurisdiction at the time allowed the bench to set aside a jury verdict.").
35. *Id.* at 1025-37.
36. *Id.* at 1036.

The point is not original with Professor Jones,[37] but he may be the first to directly incorporate it into a revised interpretation of diversity jurisdiction.

If state court juries were in fact "creating" substantive commercial law, as well as finding facts without judicial oversight, the pro-creditor Framers had more to fear from state court juries than state court judges. "American juries' decisions on matters of private litigation, when aggregated, were the functional equivalent of legislation."[38] For this reason, Professor Jones contends that Judge Friendly's focus on the role of state court judges in promoting pro-debtor law is "fundamentally flawed."[39]

According to Professor Jones, the inability of creditors to reliably recover debts in state court offered the Framers "a tangible example of the injustice and shortsightedness of the majoritarian hegemony of state court juries."[40] The Framers responded in part by excluding a right to trial by jury in federal civil trials. Although they were later overruled when Anti-Federalists secured ratification of the Seventh Amendment, even that amendment fails to affirm the jury's law-making role.[41]

But the Federalists co-opted the role of the jury in federal trials. When they reconvened as members of the first Congress that met in 1789, they (1) enacted legislation that had the ultimate effect of permitting U.S. marshals (virtually all of whom were Federalists during the presidencies of Washington and Adams) to handpick federal jurors; (2) eliminated historical "vicinage" requirements that mandated the selection of jurors from relevant local communities distributed throughout the state; and (3) located federal courts in the nation's commercial centers, where the jury pool would be populated by elites sharing the characteristics and attitudes of the Federalists themselves.[42] Professor Jones argues:

> The creation of the lower federal courts effectively circumvented state court juries because it bestowed federal officials with the power to dictate the composition of federal juries. Throughout the eighteenth century, it was not an uncommon practice for those who controlled the courts to manipulate the composition of juries. At the time of the Constitutional Convention, the majority of states provided local sheriffs with virtually unlimited discretion to impanel juries of their own choosing. The Framers knew that simply adopting the prevailing contemporary state practice would provide federal marshals—the analogues of state sheriffs—with a plenary power to dictate the compositions of federal juries. Similarly, the Framers would have known that it would be a simple task for those administering the federal courts to dictate the geography of the federal jury pools and, in so doing, to pervasively control the political, economic, and social composition of the federal juries.[43]

By this point, Professor Jones has made a compelling case that the creation of diversity jurisdiction cannot be understood without appreciating the much

37. *See, e.g.*, William E. Nelson, *The Eighteenth-Century Background of John Marshall's Jurisprudence*, 76 MICH. L. REV. 893, 916 (1978) ("It . . . seems safe to conclude that juries in most, if not all, eighteenth-century American jurisdictions normally had the power to determine law as well as fact in both civil and criminal cases.").

38. *See* Jones, *supra* note 6, at 1039 (expressing the "logic" of Madison's view).

39. *Id.* at 1017.

40. *Id.* at 1040.

41. The Seventh Amendment provides that "no *fact* tried by a jury shall be otherwise re-examined in any Court of the United States, than according to the rules of common law."

42. *See* Jones, *supra* note 6, at 1054-90. The possibility that new U.S. marshals might manipulate jury composition was earlier noted by Holt, *supra* note 14, at 1458.

43. Jones, *supra* note 6, at 1004.

greater role served by eighteenth-century jury–especially its "lawmaking" role — and the opportunity the Federalists had to control or reduce this role by moving cases from state to federal court. One is convinced that the prospect of jury control influenced at least some of the Framers, many of whom were wise in the ways of how courts really function. Diversity jurisdiction took a significant amount of commercial litigation out of the hands of "ungovernable" state court jurors, who had virtually unlimited power to find facts and "create" law favorable to their fellow debtors.

But Professor Jones' argument does not end here. Not only was jury control an important, previously overlooked factor influencing the creation of diversity jurisdiction, it was the "single most important driving force."[44] The overwhelming importance of the Framers' power to manipulate[45] juries through diversity jurisdiction leads Professor Jones to a far more ambitious contention. He argues that legal scholars have too narrowly focused on the credit crisis of immediate concern to the Framers. The Framers set their sights beyond any "single socio-economic issue" like that of "simply ensuring that creditors would be able to collect their debts."[46]

> The perceived superiority of federal juries to state juries in the Framers' eyes . . . was not limited to the ways in which they favored creditors or even commercial litigants in general. By virtue of their belief that federal juries would be drawn from "the better sort" of society, the Framers had faith that the federal courts would provide a superior alternative to state courts — not just with respect to one issue and not just with respect to events that might transpire during their own lifetimes. Instead, the Framers had reason to believe that, because of the juries that decided their cases, *the lower federal courts would be a superior forum for every type of litigation that could arise under diversity jurisdiction, not just during their own lives but for the life of the nation.*[47]

In short, diversity jurisdiction was a very large Trojan horse. Through diversity jurisdiction, the Federalists-Framers intended to secure a jury-authored body of law that would advance the interests of elites for the remainder of the nation's life.

DISCUSSION

A reformed orthodoxy? The work of scholars like Friendly and Borchers compels modification of the orthodox view that diversity jurisdiction derives from a *generic* concern with state court bias against non-citizens. Article III history cannot be divorced from the compelling problems of debtor-creditor relations that confronted the new nation. As Professor Holt has commented, "The pressure to facilitate debt recovery in forums not subject to local debtor pressures played a significant, perhaps controlling, part in the introduction of the[] heads of federal court jurisdiction."[48] But if debtor-creditor relations present the essential context for understanding diversity jurisdiction, does this lead to the conclusion of Judge Friendly and others that state court bias against non-citizens

44. *Id.* at 1005.
45. *Id.* at 1094.
46. *Id.* at 1086.
47. *Id.* at 1025 (emphasis added).
48. Holt, *supra* note 14, at 1464.

was at best a "vague" concern unsupported by historical experience, and at worst a pretext?

Judge Friendly's assessment of the historical record was, by his own admission, based on reported appellate decisions that comprise only an "infinitesimal fragment of the total amount of litigation."[49] Nonetheless Judge Friendly ventured a decisive and still influential opinion.[50] More recent research by legal historian Wythe Holt, however, indicates that Judge Friendly was likely mistaken. Professor Holt draws upon his own research, as well as that of other historians, to show the Framers had substantial reason to fear that state court judges *and* juries might be biased against non-citizens. He reviews trials in state admiralty courts involving contests over "prizes of war" and discovers bias against both non-citizens and the judgments of other state courts.[51] Based on his review of trial court records in the Framers' era, Professor Holt concludes, "These examples demonstrate why local bias against nonlocal citizens, both American and foreign, was obvious to many in the prize litigation emanating from the Revolution."[52]

Professor Holt also draws an important connection between the record of bias in admiralty cases and the members of the Constitutional Convention. Of the Convention's 55 members, 20 had either practiced before admiralty courts or served as judges in those courts; only 1 of these 20 opposed the Constitution.[53] As Professor Holt concludes, these members "presumably understood the problems of localism that the national experience with admiralty had presented during the Confederation."[54]

Professor Holt has also searched for evidence of state court bias in debt enforcement proceedings in the sparse archives of state trial courts. He identifies evidence of prejudice against British creditors by state court judges, as well as evidence of jury bias against non-citizens. One particularly important trial involves a local creditor's suit against a *non-resident debtor* in North Carolina state court. The debtor was Robert Morris, a signer of the Declaration of Independence, a delegate to the Constitutional Convention, and a member of the first Senate.[55] In a case of "blatant bias by local juries against a famous out-of-state person of wealth," the jury awarded a local creditor three times the amount of damages he had demanded from Morris in his complaint.[56] Presumably Morris retained strong memories of his experience in the courts of North Carolina when he finally had the opportunity to address bias against non-citizens at the Constitutional Convention.

Does Professor Holt's review of the "sparse" state court archives rehabilitate the theory that non-citizen bias was a legitimate concern of the Framers? If court records are indeed sparse, can historians ever make a truly convincing case concerning the Framers' views on non-citizen bias? Are we ultimately required to reach some judgment about the sincerity of the Framers' argued defense of diversity jurisdiction, which focuses on non-citizen bias? In addition, might

49. Friendly, *supra* note 5, at 493.
50. "We have seen . . . that there was little cause to fear that the state tribunals would be hostile to litigants from other states." *Id.* at 497.
51. *See* Holt, *supra* note 14, at 1427-30.
52. *Id.* at 1429.
53. *Id.*
54. *Id.* at 1430.
55. *See id.* at 1456-57.
56. *See id.* at 1457.

concerns with state court prejudice against creditors *and* non-citizens have conjoined in the Framers' press for diversity jurisdiction?

Notice that diversity jurisdiction is not the only constitutional provision addressing the problem of discrimination against non-citizens. Article IV, section 1, requires that states give "full faith and credit" to the judgments of sister states. One of the historical problems prompting adoption of this provision was the refusal of state courts to enforce judgments obtained in sister state courts. The party seeking to enforce such a judgment was often a non-citizen.[57] Section 2 of Article IV also reflects a concern with discrimination against non-citizens by providing that "the citizens of each state shall be entitled to all Privileges and Immunities of Citizens in the several states."[58] Do these provisions add legitimacy to the Framers' claim that diversity jurisdiction was needed to combat bias against non-citizens?

Shifting lawmaking power to the federal judiciary. Professor Borchers and Professor Jones present quite different theories of how the Framers intended diversity jurisdiction to combat "legislative" prejudice. According to Professor Borchers, "diversity jurisdiction would be a weapon against . . . prejudice *only* if it allowed federal courts to apply different substantive rules in diversity cases."[59] Professor Jones argues, in contrast, that traditional accounts of diversity jurisdiction mistakenly focus on state judges and ignore the more critical role played by juries.[60]

To assess Professor Borchers's theory one must avoid the "anachronistic" conclusion that diversity courts are required to apply state law under the *Erie* doctrine.[61] We explore the *Erie* doctrine in Chapter 11, but for the time being recall that *Erie* overturned *Swift v. Tyson*, 16 U.S. (Pet.) 1 (1842), and a century-old practice of applying "federal" common law in diversity suits. Professor Borchers argues that *Swift* confirmed a practice prevailing since the creation of the federal court system—diversity courts applied "general law" (or, in modern understanding, made federal common law) in commercial disputes.[62] Professor Borchers emphasizes that lawyers in the eighteenth century (among them many of the Framers) would have appreciated that a body of general law principles governed "transstate and transnational cases," and that these principles were neither "state law" nor "federal law." Consequently, the Framers anticipated that the new federal courts would adjudicate diversity disputes based on non-parochial principles of general commercial law. In fact, Professor Borchers argues the first Congress may well have dictated that diversity courts apply this general law in the Judiciary Act of 1789.[63]

Professor Borchers's interpretation is of more than historical interest. He advocates that modern diversity courts *reinstitute* the practice of developing

57. *See* Michael S. Finch, *Giving Full Faith and Credit to Punitive Damages Awards: Will Florida Rule the Nation?*, 86 MINN. L. REV. 497, 512-13 (2002).

58. Another, unsavory, example of apprehended bias against non-citizens is the Fugitive Slave Clause, found in section 2 of Article IV. This clause required that a state return slaves or indentured servants lawfully bound under the laws of another state to the person claiming the right to the escaped person's "service or labour."

59. *See* Borchers, *supra* note 19, at 94.

60. *See* Jones, *supra* note 6, at 1019-21.

61. *See* Borchers, *supra* note 19, at 110-11.

62. *See id.* at 110-15.

63. *Id.* at 98-111. This is the Rules of Decision Act, currently codified at 28 U.S.C. § 1652, which directs courts to apply the "laws of the several states" when appropriate. The reference to "laws of the several states," it is argued, may have been understood to refer to general law.

choice-of-law rules to govern disputes involving multiple jurisdictions.[64] As we discuss later, such a practice would complement Congress' recent efforts to use diversity jurisdiction to rein in the perceived excesses of state courts in applying state law to multistate disputes.

One cannot minimize the intense focus on pro-debtor state law that preceded authorization of diversity jurisdiction. After the war, virtually every state enacted some form of legislation restricting debt recovery.[65] Although the United States was required by a 1783 peace treaty with Great Britain to eliminate "legal impediments" to the recovery of debt owed to foreign creditors, few states complied by repealing unfavorable laws, and some even enacted new laws.[66]

But does the existence of objectionable state law lead to the conclusion that the new federal courts could "only" fight prejudice against non-citizens by developing a *new* "general" law of commercial relations? Or has Professor Borchers overlooked an alternative means of circumventing objectionable state law—by a federal court's refusal to enforce state law under the Supremacy Clause? Article VI mandates the supremacy of federal law, including federal treaties, and it also validates debts entered into before the adoption of the Constitution. Could federal diversity courts cure part of the credit problem by invoking the Contract Clause or the 1783 Treaty and refusing to enforce state laws that abrogate the claims of non-citizens.[67] Does Congress' failure to authorize arising under jurisdiction in the early years of the nation in any way undermine the authority of federal diversity courts to refuse enforcement of unconstitutional state laws? Does the power of federal courts to refuse enforcement of objectionable state laws provide an alternative explanation for the creation of diversity jurisdiction, or simply an additional reason?

Shifting lawmaking power to federal juries. Professor Jones does not attach great importance to the role of federal diversity judges in developing or applying law. He views juries as the primary "lawgivers" targeted by the Framers. He contends "it was the juries—not the judges—that decided cases and chose the substantive law in the courts of eighteenth-century America."[68] That is why the Framers authorized diversity jurisdiction and the first Congress established methods to strictly control the composition of juries: "[I]t was the very prospect of such control that most motivated the Framers to establish diversity jurisdiction and the lower federal courts when they met in Philadelphia."[69]

If we are persuaded by Professor Jones's interpretation of the Framers' intent, what are its implications? Does it imply that modern diversity jurisdiction serves *no* continuing purpose, at least none envisioned by the Framers? After all, modern procedural systems in both state and federal court (1) clearly allocate the task of interpreting or "making" law to someone other than the jury; and

64. *See* Borchers, *supra* note 19, at 123-31.

65. *See* Wythe Holt, *The Origins of Alienage Jurisdiction*, 14 OKLA. CITY U. L. REV. 547, 560-61 (1996).

66. *See id.* Eventually the United States would assume responsibility for debts whose collection was prevented by state "legal impediments" through the Jay Treaty. *See* Henry Paul Monaghan, *Article III and Supranational Judicial Review*, 107 COLUM. L. REV. 833, 852-53 (2007).

67. Article I, section 10, invalidates state laws "impairing the Obligation of Contracts," and it also invalidates state laws authorizing "paper money" as repayment of debts.

68. Jones, *supra* note 6, at 1021.

69. *Id.* at 1095.

(2) the jury's power to determine the facts in civil cases is now specifically curtailed by rules permitting trial and appellate courts to reverse aberrant verdicts.[70]

Has Professor Jones minimized both the historical importance of state legislatures in making pro-debtor laws, and the historical power of federal judges to decline enforcement of those laws? Professor Jones ably argues that juries usually had the *de facto* power to disregard the bench's view of the "law" and in essence create their own law to govern a dispute. But does it follow that juries routinely exercised that power or even needed to? After all, if state laws often favored debtors — the principal complaint addressed by the peace treaty with Great Britain — how often was jury "lawmaking" critical to verdicts favoring debtors? Jury lawmaking might sometimes be critical, as might the jury's almost unlimited power to find facts. But was the jury's power to make law to govern a specific case the driving force behind creation of diversity jurisdiction? How would one go about investigating this thesis?

Consider also the numerous contexts in which state "law" of the legislative variety emerged as important during the Framers' era. The Treaty of 1783 required the United States to eliminate "legal impediments" to enforcement of foreign debt. In ratification debates, one of the principal grounds on which Anti-Federalists opposed diversity jurisdiction was their "genuine fear that diversity courts would not defer to state law."[71] The Judiciary Act of 1789 mandated that diversity courts apply the "law of the several states." Do these references suggest that state "law" was envisioned as something distinct from jurors' subjective views of the right result? Or were the speakers making circumspect references to the role of state juries?

Although Professor Jones has made a valuable contribution to our understanding of the eighteenth-century jury and how its role might have influenced the creation of federal courts, has he oversold his thesis? Consider the following:

- The Framers clearly mandated that federal law (including the explicit constitutional protections of contractual debt, and the nation's express treaty obligations to eliminate legal impediments to foreign debt) was to be "supreme." Is it plausible to assume the Framers thought federal juries had power to override the Constitution and, consequently, the nation's jurisprudential future turned on control of the jury?
- The Framers succeeded in *excluding* a right to jury trial in civil cases from the original Constitution. That right was introduced by a later constitutional amendment at the behest of Anti-Federalists. Why would the driving force in creating diversity jurisdiction have been the control of civil juries not required by the Constitution and not wanted by Federalist Framers?[72]
- If the Federalists sought to use diversity jurisdiction to seize lawmaking power from state juries and vest it in controlled federal juries, why did they immediately enact legislation (a) giving state courts exclusive jurisdiction

70. *See, e.g.*, Fed. R. Civ. P. 50, 59.

71. Borchers, *supra* note 19, at 97.

72. The Federalists' antipathy to civil juries continued throughout the eighteenth century. In one instance, a prominent Federalist justice in Massachusetts succeeded in having the state legislature enact a law to limit the jury's power to interpret law. *See* Stephan Landsman, *The Civil Jury in America: Scenes from an Unappreciated History*, 44 HASTINGS L.J. 579, 602 (1993).

over cases arising under federal law; (b) giving state courts concurrent jurisdiction over diversity cases; and (c) denying federal courts jurisdiction over suits between diverse citizens when neither resided in the state where suit was filed?[73]

- The Framers allegedly created their manipulative scheme of diversity jurisdiction to guide the federal courts "for the life of the nation." But their scheme would succeed only so long as they maintained control of the federal government, giving them power to appoint the federal marshals who selected jurors. Especially in light of the fact that the Federalists permanently lost majority power with the election of Thomas Jefferson in 1801, does it seem realistic to conclude they devised a constitutional plan "for the life of the nation" that depended on their maintenance of political power?

We return to the question of the Framers' intent later, when we consider how various interpretations of that intent (1) influence the continuing debate over whether general diversity jurisdiction should be retained, and (2) influence the debate over whether Congress has exceeded its constitutional power in enacting recent diversity legislation. As challenging as it may be to infer the intent of intensely political figures from the eighteenth century, the attempt cannot be avoided.

EXPLORING DOCTRINE

A New Synthesis of Diversity Jurisdiction?

Consider the differing views of the Framers' intent in authorizing diversity jurisdiction that we have discussed. Can you articulate an interpretation of that intent that synthesizes the varying views, at least those you find plausible? Does your synthesis provide guidance as to the breadth of Congress' constitutional power to confer diversity jurisdiction in the twenty-first century?

The concept of the "Framers' intent" is a legal construct to guide the implementation of diversity jurisdiction by Congress and the courts. There is ultimately no single "Framers' intent" since the Framers—even the dominant Federalists—were of different minds on diversity. But consider whether the following hypothetical letter from a Framer, who shares the prejudices of his era yet believes he is ultimately acting in the country's best interests, is plausible.[74]

73. Section 11 of the Judiciary Act of 1789 granted diversity jurisdiction only when "the suit is between a citizen of the State where the suit is brought, and a citizen of another State." It also established an amount-in-controversy requirement of $500.

74. Some of the phrasings are directly borrowed, without attribution, from the writings of prominent Federalists.

July 14, 1787

Dear Patrick,

Thank you for the opportunity to share my thoughts on the proposal to create federal courts with power to resolve disputes among diverse citizens. As I have said before, there is urgency to this proposal. Great Britain continues to press us on the fulfillment of treaty promises to rid state-created obstacles to the enforcement of their citizens' claims. Though I share with you some distaste for the assembly of Tories, loyalists, and war-time speculators who stand to profit from debt recovery, the nation's prospects are dire if we do not act to provide creditors meaningful protection. Is it not necessary, if we mean to restore public and private credit, that foreigners and Americans alike have a just and impartial tribunal to which they may resort? And is it not imaginable that, failing to satisfy our treaty obligations, the British will go forth from their outposts in our western territories and precipitate renewed hostilities? Could our nation survive another war when it has proven itself incapable of satisfying the obligations assumed to finance the last one?

The most immediate need is to rescue commerce interests from the creditor hells our state courts have become. In some localities, creditors' counsel risks physical assault if they attempt to present their clients' claims in state court. And when not deterred by force, creditors confront a judiciary unwilling or afraid to administer justice. Legitimate claims are either rejected or enforced with such delay that creditors despair of recovery within their lifespan. State legislators, intimidated by the debtor mob, or members of the mob themselves, erect legal barriers to just and speedy recovery. Members of the bench, many who have never laid eyes on a lawbook, discover legal rules unknown to the law of nations. Local debtors take turns serving as jurors in the disputes of their fellow debtors, and inevitably discover facts or rules of "conscience" that put an end to the creditor's case.

As long as commercial interests must pursue defaulting debtors into local state courts — often a practical necessity when debtors withdraw their persons and property into the security of home borders[75] — the problem is insoluble. As our own professional experience with admiralty courts in the late war makes apparent, inter-state jealousy is endemic to state courts. Mister Morris poignantly testifies to the hostility faced when one of our citizens enters the courts of another state.

Much of our current situation can be ameliorated by the creation of an independent federal judiciary. We have the opportunity to create a bench unbeholden to state or local interests that will administer the law with impartiality. If the protections of our new Constitution are to mean anything, they must be implemented by judges owing no allegiance to the states. In time, our new courts will ensure that the nation's commerce is governed by the same general principles recognized by competent jurists in other civilized nations.

75. Recall that traditional jurisdictional doctrine emphasized a state's power of persons or property found within the state's territorial borders. Long-arm jurisdiction was unknown.

We can also hope to defeat the introduction into federal courts of that pernicious instrument of majority oppression, the jury. Failing that—and the opposition is already agitating for some constitutional endorsement of juries—we can trust to the same mechanisms that have enabled state court officials to fashion juries to serve local interests. With careful selection of suitable men of education and character, drawn from the nation's commercial centers where the new courts will be located, we need not fear the reign of debtors now found in state court.

This I say to you in confidence. The same factions that presently dominate our state courts will appear at ratification conventions, especially in the New England states. For the time being, it is important that we secure approval of a new constitution and leave to later its implementation. We may need to blindfold the mare if she is to be led to safety.

Your most humble & obedient servant etc., James

d. A Note on Alienage Jurisdiction

One of the oddities of federal jurisdiction is that the Framers' historical priorities have been reversed over time. "Arising under" jurisdiction, which predominates in private civil litigation in federal court, was not generally conferred by Congress until 1875. As discussed above, diversity jurisdiction involving American citizens was a very important basis for jurisdiction during the federal courts' first century of operation. Nonetheless, it has been said that "historically the single most important grant of national court jurisdiction embodied in the [Judiciary Act of 1789] was the grant over alienage cases,"[76] even though this form of jurisdiction is a relatively minor part of the federal courts' business today.

We have seen how the interests of creditors were of paramount concern to the Framers. A "staggering" amount of debt was owed to British and Scottish merchants, and alien creditors were the target of the most extreme hostilities expressed in state court—not surprising, given the lingering enmities between the former combatants.[77] Yet the most disfavored creditor class was also the most important to the nation's future. Four of the five plans for federal jurisdiction included a provision for alienage jurisdiction, while only one addressed jurisdiction over disputes between American citizens.[78] There appears to have been little disagreement at the Constitutional Convention about the need to provide a national forum for disputes between aliens and American citizens so as to promote the nation's future prosperity, peace, and status in the international community.

The importance of alienage jurisdiction to the Framers introduces an additional note of uncertainty when attempting to ascertain their intent. Post-war experience with foreign creditors may have colored the debate about citizen-versus-citizen diversity, and perhaps was decisive in securing the creation of

76. *See* Holt, *supra* note 14, at 548.

77. *See id.* at 556. *See also* Friendly, *supra* note 5, at 484 n.6 ("Several states had failed to give foreigners proper protection under the treaties concluded with England at the end of the Revolution. . . . Local animosity was so great that only national tribunals could compel the enforcement of a national treaty.").

78. *See* Kevin R. Johnson, *supra* note 8, at 10.

diversity jurisdiction.[79] Today, when citizen-versus-citizen diversity is such a prominent part of the federal courts' workload and Congress has begun employing diversity in unprecedented ways, it is tempting to discover portentous meaning in the Framers' decisions when, in fact, they may have been thinking of other things.

2. *Implementation of Conventional Diversity Jurisdiction*

Almost all students explore the technical elements of conventional diversity jurisdiction in Civil Procedure. The subject can be exceedingly complex, which is one reason contemporary opponents argue that federal judges could better spend their time on other matters.[80]

Further exploration of the intricacies of diversity we leave to other courses. In this brief section, we summarize some of the rudiments of diversity jurisdiction you became acquainted with in Civil Procedure. This summary provides useful background for the issues we more fully explore in later discussion.

Diversity jurisdiction in conventional litigation is largely prescribed by 28 U.S.C. §§ 1332(a)-(c) and 1441(a), (b). Most rules of diversity are found in the statutes, but some have been developed by the courts ostensibly implementing Congress' inferred intent. Among the important rules of diversity applied in routine litigation[81] are these:

- All plaintiffs must be of diverse citizenship from all defendants, that is, the "complete diversity" requirement. Assuming the amount-in-controversy requirement is satisfied, plaintiffs may file suit in federal court even if that court is located within the plaintiffs' home state.
- When plaintiffs file suit in state court, defendants may remove to federal court as long as complete diversity is satisfied.
- Provided that one plaintiff satisfies the amount-in-controversy requirement, a federal court may hear the claims of other plaintiffs seeking less than the required amount if their claims are part of the same "case or controversy" as the plaintiff who satisfies the amount-in-controversy requirement.[82]
- The citizenship of each party is usually determined at the time the complaint is first filed; in the case of suits removed to federal court, citizenship must also be proper (e.g., complete diversity must exist) at the time of removal.

79. One advocate in the Supreme Court remarked that "[t]he jurisdiction given to the federal courts in cases between citizens of different states, was, at the time of the adoption of the constitution, supposed to be of very little importance to the people. . . ." *Hepburn v. Ellzey*, 6 U.S. (2 Cranch) 445, 450 (1805). Judge Friendly commented on the "astounding . . . apathy of the defense" of diversity jurisdiction at the Constitutional Convention. Friendly, *supra* note 5, at 487.

80. *See* Thomas D. Rowe, Jr., *Abolishing Diversity Jurisdiction: Positive Side Effects and Potential for Future Reforms*, 92 HARV. L. REV. 963 (1979).

81. This excludes, for example, class actions and interpleader actions, which we discuss separately.

82. *See Exxon Mobil Corp. v. Allapattah Servs., Inc.*, 545 U.S. 546 (2005). The Court's decision, construing 28 U.S.C. § 1367, overturns long-standing precedent requiring each plaintiff to satisfy the amount requirement independently.

- A party's citizenship is based on definitions usually provided by Congress, but occasionally developed by the courts. Among important definitions of citizenship are these:
  - the state citizenship of a natural person is derived from both (a) her physical residence in a state and (b) her intent to make that residence home;
  - the citizenship of a foreign national is based on her legal status as an alien under foreign law;
  - foreign nationals admitted to the United States for permanent residence are treated as citizens of the state where they are domiciled;
  - the citizenship of persons who represent the interests of others is sometimes that of the representative (e.g., many fiduciaries, and traditionally the representative of a class in a class action); in other situations, the citizenship of the person represented is determinative (e.g., legal representatives of estates, infants, and incompetents);
  - the citizenship of corporations (especially domestic corporations) is both (a) the state of incorporation and (b) the state of the corporation's principal place of business; and,
  - the citizenship of partnerships and other non-incorporated entities is usually that of all its partners or members.
- With some exceptions, courts exercising diversity jurisdiction must usually apply the law, including the common law, of the state encompassing the federal district where suit has been filed if that law is either "substantive" or "outcome determinative."

Changes to diversity and alienage jurisdiction were enacted in 2011 through the "Federal Court Jurisdiction and Venue Clarification Act of 2011." While the jurisdictional guidelines cited in the text remain accurate, the 2011 Act clarifies a few aspects of jurisdiction concerning foreign litigants. Among the changes are these: (1) diversity jurisdiction is further restricted in suits between state citizens and foreign nationals admitted for permanent residence and domiciled in the "same" state (amending 28 U.S.C. § 1332(a)(2)); and (2) the test for corporate citizenship extends to corporations that are incorporated in or have their principal place of business in a foreign nation (amending 28 U.S.C. § 1332(c)(1), (2)). The 2011 Act makes important changes governing the removal of cases to federal court, which are discussed in Chapter 7.

Many features of modern diversity jurisdiction were unknown to early American courts. For example, corporations lacked any status as state "citizens," an issue we return to shortly. Similarly, modern procedural devices like the class action and interpleader were unknown, as were the jurisdictional complexities they generate.

Yet several basic features of modern diversity jurisdiction can be traced back to the first Judiciary Act. In particular, the first Judiciary Act (1) permitted suit to be filed in federal court by a diverse plaintiff even if that plaintiff was a citizen of the state encompassing the federal court; (2) denied removal of a diverse action if a defendant was a citizen of the state where suit was filed; (3) required that the plaintiff satisfy an "amount in controversy" requirement; and (4) gave state courts concurrent jurisdiction over diversity actions.[83] Even the venerable "complete diversity" rule was part of the first Judiciary Act, at least according to the Court.

83. *See* Holt, *supra* note 14, at 1485-90.

Do these features of original statutory diversity permit inferences about the Framers' intent, especially given the significant number of Framers who were members of the first Congress? To the extent some of these features persist in modern practice, do they have continued justification? We can tentatively explore these questions in the context of the historical problem that most concerned the Framers, a creditor's suit brought against a diverse debtor. Recall that two of the competing interpretations of the Framers' intent argue that (1) diversity jurisdiction was intended to prevent state court bias against non-citizens ("non-citizen bias"); or alternatively, (2) diversity was intended to prevent state court bias against creditors generally ("creditor bias"). Consider how the law of diversity plays out in the following scenarios.

PROBLEM 6-1

Attempting to Reconcile Diversity Rules and Diversity Policy

The geographic setting for the following disputes is Virginia, a state we assume has demonstrated antipathy toward creditors. One litigant is Vinnie, from New York, and the other is Fauntleroy of Virginia. Assume all claims satisfy relevant amount-in-controversy requirements.

(a) Vinnie files suit in a Virginia federal court seeking to recover a debt from Fauntleroy. Diversity jurisdiction is proper under both the 1789 Act and current § 1332.
(b) Vinnie files suit in a Virginia state court seeking to recover a debt from Fauntleroy. Fauntleroy cannot remove the suit to federal court under either the 1789 Act or current § 1441.
(c) Fauntleroy files suit in a Virginia federal court seeking to recover a debt from Vinnie. Diversity jurisdiction is proper under both the 1789 Act and current § 1332.
(d) Fauntleroy files suit in a Virginia state court seeking to recover a debt from Vinnie. Vinnie is permitted to remove the suit to federal court under either the 1789 Act or current § 1441.

Now consider these questions:

(1) Based on the "non-citizen bias" interpretation of the Framers' intent, can you fully explain the outcomes reached by applying jurisdictional statutes?
(2) Based on the "creditor bias" interpretation of the Framers' intent, can you fully explain the outcomes reached by applying jurisdictional statutes?
(3) Relying on *both* interpretations, can you fully explain the jurisdictional outcomes?
(4) The scenarios described above seem to always result in the creditor's gaining access to a federal court if he wants it. Does this shed any light on the Framers' intent?
(5) If Congress currently avows that non-citizen bias is an essential element of diversity protection, do any of the jurisdictional outcomes *not* make sense?

3. *Evolution in Diversity Doctrine*

Diversity jurisdiction dominated the federal courts' business for almost a century, reaching its greatest expanse in 1875. An 1875 act of Congress eliminated the long-standing jurisdictional requirement that jurisdiction over a suit between diverse parties existed only if it was filed in a state where one of the parties was a citizen. The act also authorized removal by a defendant who was a citizen of the state where suit was filed.[84] At the same time as diversity jurisdiction was expanded, general arising under jurisdiction was conferred on federal courts for the first time. After 1875, federal courts were "deluged with new business" and Congress (aided by the Court)[85] soon commenced its seemingly endless task of reforming diversity jurisdiction.[86]

One significant decision by the first Congress was to refrain from conferring the full diversity jurisdiction authorized by Article III. As illustrated in Problem 6-1, some of the limits on diversity jurisdiction appear to reflect Congress' belief that the threat of non-citizen bias was minimal or nonexistent. Other statutory limits on diversity jurisdiction reflected concerns with the federal courts' administration of diversity jurisdiction. For example, Congress likely imposed an "amount in controversy" requirement of $500 to spare poor and "middling" debtors the expense of litigating in more distant federal courts.[87]

The history of diversity reform (both in Congress and in the Court) reveals a variety of concerns, some implicating the Framers' vision but many more addressing pragmatic issues in the implementation of diversity jurisdiction. These concerns include

- revising jurisdictional law to reflect the perceived realities of *bias* against certain types of litigants like business entities;
- reducing the burden of diversity jurisdiction on the federal judiciary by limiting its use to "*important*" litigation, like suits involving a specified amount in controversy;
- reducing litigants' use of *manipulative strategies* to create or destroy diversity jurisdiction (i.e., forum shopping);
- reducing the federal courts' *workload*;
- developing methods that permit federal courts to *defer* to state courts when interpreting uncertain state law or when litigation threatens important state interests; and
- more generally, promoting the perceived *federalism* policy of letting state courts adjudicate most disputes arising solely under state law.

As recently as 1990, one federal courts scholar could confidently state that concerns like these have led inexorably to the contraction of diversity jurisdiction: "[W]hile other facets of federal jurisdiction have steadily expanded over the last

84. *See, e.g.,* James William Moore & Donald T. Weckstein, *Diversity Jurisdiction: Past, Present, and Future,* 43 TEX. L. REV. 1, 5-8 (1964). Congress eventually restored the restriction on a local defendant's right of removal.

85. *See* James M. Underwood, *The Late, Great Diversity Jurisdiction,* 57 CASE W. RES. L. REV. 179, 189-96 (2006) (discussing Court restrictions on diversity jurisdiction, like that requiring each plaintiff to independently satisfy the amount-in-controversy requirement).

86. *See* Moore & Weckstein, *supra* note 84, at 8.

87. *See, e.g.,* Holt, *supra* note 14, at 1519; Moore & Weckstein, *supra* note 84, at 4. Professors Moore and Weckstein mention that the costs of defending appeals to the Supreme Court were of special concern to the opponents of diversity jurisdiction.

century, diversity has been consistently restricted."[88] As we will soon see, this opinion aptly describes the evolution of conventional diversity jurisdiction, but it no longer reflects Congress' rediscovery of diversity's potential to address contemporary problems of complex, multistate litigation.

a. Corporations and Diversity

The Framers' immediate purpose in authorizing diversity jurisdiction seems to have been the rehabilitation of the nation's failed credit markets and the reinvigoration of the nation's commerce. Throughout the nineteenth century and well into the twentieth century, diversity jurisdiction played an important role in facilitating the development of interstate commerce.[89] The commercial thrust of diversity jurisdiction is reflected in modern diversity practice as well, where corporations are the principal private litigants, often in business disputes with other corporations.[90] It is not surprising that corporations are major players in diversity litigation, since their use of interstate commerce (not to mention cyberspace) frequently leads them to transact business with the citizens of other states and nations. The evolving role of corporations in diversity history well illustrates the struggle of Congress and the courts to adapt diversity jurisdiction to changing conditions.

In the first year diversity jurisdiction was implemented, there were fewer than three dozen private corporations.[91] When corporations first appeared in federal court, jurisdiction over their disputes was apparently unobjectionable.[92] But in *Bank of the United States v. Deveaux*, 9 U.S. (5 Cranch) 61 (1809), Chief Justice Marshall concluded that a corporation was a mere "legal entity" lacking independent status as a citizen under diversity legislation. It was the corporation's members who counted for diversity purposes. Combined with the Court's prior ruling in *Strawbridge v. Curtiss*, 3 Cranch 267 (1806), requiring "complete diversity" between plaintiffs and defendants, *Deveaux* substantially reduced the availability of diversity jurisdiction in suits involving corporate litigants.

Some 30 years later, in *Louisville, Cincinnati & Charleston Railroad v. Letson*, 43 U.S. (2 How.) 497 (1844), the Court receded from *Deveaux* and indicated that a corporation could acquire the citizenship of the state that chartered it. In a subsequent decision, the Court reconciled earlier precedent by returning to the view that a corporation's citizenship *was* that of its shareholders, but conclusively presuming that its shareholders were citizens of the state of incorporation.[93] Through a series of legal fictions, the Court had given corporations a state of citizenship.

88. *See* Kramer, *supra* note 22, at 102.

89. *See generally* David Marcus, Erie, *The Class Action Fairness Act, and Some Federalism Implications of Diversity Jurisdiction*, 48 WM. & MARY L. REV. 1247 (2007).

90. *See* Walter H. Beckman III, *The View from the Chair*, 25 BRIEF 2 (Summer 1996) ("[I]n federal court, businesses are their own worst enemy. It appears that businesses sue each other as often as they are sued. Between 1985 and 1991 business disagreements made up nearly half of all federal litigation, with suits over contracts outpacing any other single category.). *See also* Adrienne J. Marsh, *Diversity Jurisdiction: Scapegoat of Overcrowded Federal Courts*, 48 BROOK. L. REV. 197, 209 n.60 (1982) (reporting estimates that more than 75 percent of diversity suits involve corporate parties).

91. *See* Charles Warren, *Corporations and Diversity of Citizenship*, 19 VA. L. REV. 661, 662-63 (1933) (identifying 30 private corporations in 1790).

92. *See* Moore & Weckstein, *supra* note 84, at 7.

93. *See Marshall v. Baltimore & Ohio R. Co.*, 16 How. 314 (1844).

At the time, the extension of diversity jurisdiction to corporations was not thought a victory for corporations. As Charles Warren has remarked:

> [T]he doctrine that a corporation could be treated as a citizen and hence as suable in Federal Courts was established against the opposition and protest of the corporation. It was not a doctrine which the Supreme Court promoted for the benefit of the corporation, but rather to benefit the citizen suing the corporation by enabling him to keep out of the Courts of the State which chartered the corporation. The possible prejudice in State Courts, against which the diversity of citizenship jurisdiction of the Federal Courts was serving as a protection, was the apprehended prejudice in favor of the State corporation and against the individual plaintiff; it was not an apprehended prejudice against a corporation and in favor of the individual.[94]

In other words, state courts were then perceived as biased in *favor* of local commercial interests, a reversal of prejudices perceived during the Framers' era. But in time corporations would come to prefer a federal forum, especially in suits brought against railroads by injured employees, allegedly because the additional cost and delay incurred in federal court led to more favorable settlements.[95] Perceived abuses of diversity jurisdiction by corporations led to several unsuccessful attempts in Congress to deny corporations the power to invoke diversity jurisdiction.[96]

A corporation's ability to control its citizenship through the act of incorporating in a particular state gave it potential power to manipulate the substantive law applicable to its legal disputes. As discussed earlier, federal diversity courts began applying "general" common law shortly after they commenced business in 1789. In many cases, the common law developed by federal courts was more advantageous to corporations than was local state law. Although some scholars argue the Framers anticipated that diversity courts would develop common law favorable to business interests,[97] the blatant manipulation of diversity jurisdiction in *Black & White Taxicab & Transfer Co. v. Brown & Yellow Taxicab & Transfer Co.*, 276 U.S. 518 (1928), likely exceeded the Framers' expectations. In *Black & White Taxicab*, a former corporate citizen of Kentucky dodged Kentucky state law preventing monopolies in taxicab service by re-incorporating in Tennessee. By re-incorporating in Tennessee, the company was permitted to invoke diversity jurisdiction and secure application of federal common law, which permitted the exclusive service contract the company had with a Kentucky railroad station. *Black & White Taxicab*, you may recall from your study of *Erie*, illustrated the evils of "general federal common law" and forum shopping that eventually led the Court to reject such common lawmaking power.

Despite congressional proposals to repeal corporate use of diversity jurisdiction in the early twentieth century, change did not come until 1958. In 1958, Congress enacted what may be its greatest set of reforms of diversity jurisdiction, including a redefinition of corporation citizenship. A corporation's citizenship now includes both the state of incorporation *and* the principal place of business. *See* 28 U.S.C. § 1332(c). Locally based corporations can no longer transform

94. *See* Warren, *supra* note 91, at 670.

95. *See* David W. Jackson, Note, *Federal Court Diversity Jurisdiction and the Corporation*, 8 Tulsa L.J. 120, 122-23 (1972).

96. *See id.* at 123-24.

97. See section C.1.b earlier in this chapter.

themselves into non-citizens by the simple act of incorporation, and they stand on equal footing with other locally based corporations organized under local state law. Congress' redefinition of corporate citizenship worked a "substantial curtailment" of diversity jurisdiction.[98] To the extent that the Framers were concerned with both bias against non-citizens and bias against commercial interests, the new definition of citizenship emphasized the first purpose. In addition, Congress' action reflected what seems to have become the principal goal in modern diversity reform — reducing the workload of the federal courts.

In *Hertz Corp. v. Friend*, 130 S. Ct. 1181 (2010), the Supreme Court resolved an issue that has troubled lower federal courts for decades — how does one determine a corporation's "principal place of business" when the corporation carries on appreciable business in several states? Lower courts have used a variety of multi-factor tests, some of which focus on a corporation's "nerve center," some of which focus on the location of principal business activities (e.g., sales or manufacturing), and some of which combine these and even other factors. *Id.* at 1191.

In *Hertz Corp.*, the Court endorsed the "nerve center" test:

> We conclude that "principal place of business" is best read as referring to the place where a corporation's officers direct, control, and coordinate the corporation's activities. It is the place that Courts of Appeals have called the corporation's "nerve center." And in practice it should normally be the place where the corporation maintains its headquarters — provided that the headquarters is the actual center of direction, control, and coordination, i.e., the "nerve center," and not simply an office where the corporation holds its board meetings (for example, attended by directors and officers who have traveled there for the occasion).

Id. at 1192. The Court adopted this test largely to promote "administrative simplicity" for courts applying the diversity statutes and to make jurisdictional assessments more "predictable." *Id.* at 1193-94.

The Court conceded that its test might not achieve the "general purpose" of diversity jurisdiction, namely, to avoid prejudice against non-resident litigants. But the Court thought this quest "doomed to failure" anyway. The Court commented:

> After all, the relevant purposive concern — prejudice against an out-of-state party — will often depend upon factors that courts cannot easily measure, for example, a corporation's image, its history, and its advertising, while the factors that courts can more easily measure, for example, its office or plant location, its sales, its employment, or the nature of the goods or services it supplies, will sometimes bear no more than a distant relation to the likelihood of prejudice.

Id. at 1192.

Note that the Court's definition of "principal place of business" will apply to corporations incorporated in or having their principal place of business in a foreign nation in light of the treatment of such corporations prescribed by the Federal Court Jurisdiction and Venue Clarification Act of 2011. *See* 28 U.S.C. § 1332(c)(1), (2).

98. *See* Moore & Weckstein, *supra* note 84, at 12.

b. The Continuing Debate over the Value of Conventional Diversity Jurisdiction

Congress' revision of corporate "citizenship" in 1958 did not please all. Some critics argued Congress did not go far enough in restricting diversity jurisdiction in corporate disputes, while a few argued it went too far. The debate over corporate diversity in many ways condenses the larger debate over the continuing value of conventional diversity jurisdiction. Let's consider some of the disputants' main arguments.

According to Professors Moore and Weckstein, strong supporters of the "principal place of business" standard, the standard is "analogous to the residence of a natural person. Treating a corporation as a citizen of such state also bears a rational relationship to the facts of business life as well as to the local prejudice basis of diversity jurisdiction."[99] At the same time, Professors Moore and Weckstein argue against broader definitions of corporate citizenship that might reduce or eliminate the availability of diversity jurisdiction to corporate litigants. While "fear of local prejudice" may no longer be the primary reason corporations prefer a federal forum, it remains one reason.

More important, Professors Moore and Weckstein contend that corporate diversity jurisdiction need not stand or fall based on proof of non-citizen bias. They emphasize as well the Framers' belief that diversity jurisdiction was wedded to the nation's commercial prospects:

> [A]nother of the traditional justifications for diversity applies with particular force to the invocation of the jurisdiction by corporate litigants. Several commentators have contended that diversity jurisdiction was primarily intended to assuage the apprehensions of commercial suitors and investors, and the jurisdiction has been credited with exercising a great influence in fostering interstate commerce and investment, sustaining the public credit and sanctity of contracts, and welding the states into a single nation. It is even more true today than it was in the early days of the Republic that corporations frequently serve as the source of, as well as the medium for, investment, and incorporated enterprises are more often than not parties to important commercial transactions. These corporations feel they have need to use and frequently do use the federal courts when litigation becomes necessary. Fear of local prejudice may no longer be the primary reason for corporations to seek federal jurisdiction but other reasons are not lacking.[100]

Professors Moore and Weckstein emphasize several features of contemporary federal courts that might make them more appealing forums for corporate litigants. First, federal judges are appointed and tenured for life. Unlike state judges (both in 1789 and today in most states), federal judges need not stand for reelection or rely on the support of local constituencies (like lawyers who appear before them). Further, federal court procedure is thought to be superior to that in some state courts, and corporate litigants have less reason to fear that disputes will be resolved according to "the sporting theory of justice."[101] Note that this view can be construed to support diversity jurisdiction even when there is no fear of local bias against a corporation. This view, for example, supports the current

99. *See* James W. Moore & Donald T. Weckstein, *Corporations and Diversity of Citizenship: A Supreme Court Fiction Revisited*, 77 Harv. L. Rev. 1426, 1446 (1964).
100. *See id.* at 1448-49.
101. *See id.* at 1449.

statutory scheme permitting *local* plaintiffs to invoke diversity jurisdiction despite the fact they are suing in their home state.

Critics of corporate diversity jurisdiction attack it on several grounds. First, some argue that the definition of corporate citizenship needs to be broader (and hence the situations supporting diversity narrower) if it is to have any practical relationship to actual prejudice against corporations. Alternative approaches to the current statutory scheme include (1) denying diversity jurisdiction to a corporation that has a "permanent local" business establishment in a state in any suit related to activities of that local establishment;[102] (2) treating a corporation as a citizen of any state where it is either licensed to do business or does business;[103] or (3) treating a corporation as a citizen of any state where it conducts business.[104] Second, critics question the existence of prejudice against non-citizens today ("lawyers' fears, not the reality of bias"[105]), especially in suits involving corporations.

Critics also dispute the contention that federal courts and federal judges are somehow "superior" to their state counterparts, and in any event argue that this provides no reason to give non-citizens a federal forum. As Professor Kramer asserts, "If state courts are inadequate, improve them."[106] What is more, federal juries like state juries are drawn from the same state citizenry,[107] and neither state nor federal juries enjoy the broad factfinding and law-interpreting power of the eighteenth-century jury. Finally, since *Erie Railroad v. Tompkins*, federal judges have lost the power to develop common law that might promote development of the nation's commerce.

Research sheds some light on what factors — fear of prejudice, preference for a superior procedural system — motivate the choice of forum by corporate litigants. The researchers' conclusions are admittedly tentative and may represent only the views of those lawyer populations studied. But many of the findings are supported by multiple studies, and in any event they provide the best available evidence of what motivates corporate litigants (and likely other forms of litigants) to select a federal forum. Relevant research findings include the following:[108]

- Diversity jurisdiction is most often invoked by *local* plaintiffs suing non-citizen corporations.[109]
- A substantial majority of federal practitioners believe the *citizenship* of a party is an important reason for choosing a federal forum, while a substantial fraction also believe that the *corporate status* of a party is an important factor.[110]

102. *See* Moore & Weckstein, *supra* note 84, at 24 (discussing an American Law Institute proposal).

103. *See id.* at 14.

104. *See* Charles W. Joiner, *Corporations as Citizens of Every State Where They Do Business: A Needed Change in Diversity Jurisdiction*, 70 JUDICATURE 291 (1987).

105. *See* Kramer, *supra* note 22, at 119.

106. *See id.* at 118. Professor Kramer acknowledges, nonetheless, that non-citizens lack the political opportunity to reform the court systems of other states.

107. Of course, federal juries are drawn from the local federal district and division, whose boundaries may differ from those of the local state court.

108. These findings, incorporating the author's own research as well as that of others, are found in Victor E. Flango, *Litigant Choice Between State and Federal Courts*, 46 S.C. L. REV. 961 (1995).

109. *See id.* at 971 (reporting that, in fiscal year 1993, 16,473 diversity plaintiffs were local citizens from a total of 30,399 diversity suits filed.)

110. *See id.* at 967-68 (reporting that 71 percent of federal practitioners found the citizenship of a litigant to be an important factor in forum selection, while 41 percent found the litigant's corporate status to be an important factor).

- Most practitioners indicate that "*institutional*" factors like the quality of judges, court procedures, and general familiarity with the court system are important factors in selecting a federal or state forum.[111]

All sides of the diversity debate can find some support in these findings. The predominance of local plaintiffs in diversity suits suggests that, if non-citizen bias is the principal purpose of diversity jurisdiction—and many argue it is the sole remaining purpose—much diversity litigation is unjustified. Similarly, federal practitioners' emphasis on the role of institutional factors in selecting a federal forum (e.g., the quality of the federal judiciary) also undermines the historical rationale for providing diverse litigants a federal forum. At the same time, advocates of diversity jurisdiction can point out that a clear majority of federal practitioners think a party's citizenship is an important influence on forum selection. In addition, these practitioners believe that corporate status influences forum selection, arguably supporting the pro-commerce rationale for diversity jurisdiction.[112]

While the value of retaining conventional diversity jurisdiction remains highly contentious, there is little disagreement about the tangible costs of implementing diversity in federal court. As mentioned earlier, diversity jurisdiction is the basis for one-third of the federal courts' private-party caseload, and its demand on the courts' adjudicatory work may be even greater. Federal judges may spend a disproportionate amount of time trying diversity cases (relative to the number pending),[113] and may also spend a disproportionate amount of time resolving pretrial disputes—like those presented in determining a corporation's citizenship under current standards.[114] Critics argue that the burdens imposed on federal courts, and the encroachment on the state courts' adjudicatory authority, are unjustified by what is ultimately the insistence of trial lawyers that they be permitted to "forum shop."

PROBLEM 6-2

Reforming Diversity for Business Entities

Corporations are not the only type of commercial litigants to pose problems for the exercise of diversity jurisdiction. The courts have struggled with the appropriate test of citizenship for other business entities like partnerships and unincorporated associations. Currently, most such entities are treated as conglomerates of individuals, and the citizenship of each individual "counts" in diversity analysis. *See, e.g., Carden v. Arkoma Assocs.*, 494 U.S. 185 (1990) (the citizenship of all partners must be considered in determining that of the partnership). While this may appear to reduce the availability of diversity jurisdiction

111. *See id.* 972-73 (reporting that 79 percent of federal practitioners believed that the competence and quality of the judiciary were important in forum selection).

112. At the same time, when federal courts are perceived to be inhospitable to business, the corporate defendant will be at a disadvantage insofar as a diverse plaintiff can file suit in federal court and deprive the defendant of a more hospitable state court.

113. *See* Dolores K. Sloviter, *A Federal Judge Views Diversity Jurisdiction Through the Lens of Federalism*, 78 VA. L. REV. 1671, 1674 (1992) (estimating that "about one of every two federal civil trials" is based on diversity jurisdiction).

114. *See* Kramer, *supra* note 22, at 100. *See also* Federal Courts Study Comm., Report to the Federal Courts Study Committee of the Subcommittee on the Role of the Federal Courts and Their Relation to the States 422-24 (Working Papers and Subcommittee Reports, Vol. 1, July 1, 1990); John Kozyris, *Corporate Wars and Choice of Law*, 1989 DUKE L.J. 1, 53 (commenting on the "incredible difficulties" courts have faced in applying the "principal place of business" test for corporate citizenship).

in suits involving such entities, it can lead to anomalous results. For example, a partnership may carry on business exclusively in one state and yet, when sued by local state citizens, remove to federal court based on diversity jurisdiction because all its partners are citizens of states other than the one where the partnership carries on its business.[115]

Might there be a better, uniform method for assessing the citizenship of all entities, including corporations and partnerships? Assess the merits of a proposed amendment to diversity statutes that would treat all business entities as citizens of *every* state where they have conducted "continual" business activity for at least one year. Assume that this amendment defines business activity in a state to include (1) maintenance of a local business office, (2) employment of three or more state citizens, or (3) regular advertising, sales, or service activities in the state.

Discuss whether such an amendment to diversity statutes would better effectuate the historical goals of diversity jurisdiction while reducing unnecessary litigation in federal court. Also consider whether such an amendment could be implemented by federal courts without presenting the complex factual inquiries presented by the "principal place of business" standard.

Toward the close of the twentieth century, diversity jurisdiction had few defenders other than the lawyers who regularly used it. In 1988, Congress authorized an elite panel of judges, legal scholars, and practitioners to conduct the "most comprehensive examination of the federal court system in the last half century."[116] The panel recommended that most diversity jurisdiction be abolished:

> We believe that diversity jurisdiction should be virtually eliminated for two simple reasons: On the one hand, no other class of cases has a weaker claim on federal judicial resources. On the other hand, no other step will do anywhere nearly as much to reduce federal case load pressures and contain the growth of the federal judiciary. Given all the demands on the federal courts, there is little reason to use them for contract disputes or automobile accident suits simply because the parties live across state boundaries—especially when litigants who do not live in different states must bring otherwise identical suits in state courts.[117]

While diversity jurisdiction has not been abolished, Congress continues to restrict its availability in conventional litigation. For example, Congress has (1) increased the amount-in-controversy requirement to $75,000; (2) required that foreign nationals admitted to the United States as "permanent residents" be treated as state citizens; and (3) disregarded the citizenship of the chosen representatives of estates, infants, and incompetents in assessing diversity of citizenship. *See* 28 U.S.C. § 1332(a)(4), (c)(2).

One of the strongest objections to diversity jurisdiction to gain prominence in recent decades is the impact of such jurisdiction on the state courts. According to one federal jurist, Judge Sloviter of the Third Circuit, diversity results "in the inevitable erosion of the state courts' sovereign right and duty to develop state

115. One of the authors was involved in such a suit. In a dispute between two stores in a local shopping center, the defendant removed the suit to federal court because the partnership that owned the defendant-store consisted of partners who were citizens of other states. The partnership's sole business activity consisted of the local store.

116. 101st Cong. Report of the Federal Courts Study Comm. at 3.

117. *Id.* at 39.

law as they deem appropriate."[118] Judge Sloviter reviews a variety of untoward consequences resulting from federal diversity courts' interpretations of state law. Under the *Erie* doctrine, federal courts must often "predict" how state law would be interpreted by a state's highest court—an interpretive opportunity denied state courts because of diversity jurisdiction. Federal diversity courts often find no clear guidance in reported state court decisions. Federal courts must venture tentative opinions on a variety of important state-law issues and, according to Judge Sloviter, they often "guess wrong."[119] Bad guesses "inevitably skew the decisions of persons and businesses who rely on them and inequitably affect the losing federal litigant who cannot appeal the decision to the state supreme court."[120] State sovereignty is compromised as issues of important state legal policy are decided by federal courts, with authoritative state court interpretations deferred until later litigation. While federal courts often have the power to certify state-law issues to a state's supreme court, inherent limits of certification make it at best an "incomplete solution to the problem."[121]

We will soon examine yet other federalism concerns raised by recent developments in diversity jurisdiction. Before we do, reflect on the federalism implications of conventional diversity jurisdiction for the development of state law.

EXPLORING DOCTRINE

Diversity and Federalism

Judge Sloviter asserts that "little or no attention" has been given to the impact of diversity jurisdiction on federalism concerns. Could one argue that these concerns merit the little attention they have received? How would you respond to the following observations?:

- *Erie* has eliminated the most serious encroachment on state sovereignty, the power of federal courts to develop general common law.
- Our constitutional court scheme does not impose a rigid separation of legislative and judicial authority, giving each sovereign's courts exclusive power to adjudicate cases arising under its own laws. State courts exercise concurrent jurisdiction over cases arising under federal law, and much federal law interpretation is made by state courts.
- While federal diversity courts may make inaccurate predictions about the meaning of state law, state courts similarly err in predicting how the federal courts will ultimately interpret federal law. Further, state court misinterpretations of federal law are reviewable only by the Supreme Court, which seldom exercises its oversight power. What "federalism" concerns result from the exercise of diversity jurisdiction that do not similarly result from state courts' exercise of concurrent jurisdiction in cases arising under federal law?

118. *See* Sloviter, *supra* note 114, at 1671 (1992). Professor Kramer agrees with many of Judge Sloviter's criticisms. *See* Kramer, *supra* note 22, at 103-04.

119. *See* Sloviter, *supra* note 112, at 1679.

120. *Id.* at 1681.

121. *See id.* at 1686. Judge Sloviter points out that some states authorize certification only by federal appellate courts, not trial courts.

4. *Diversity Jurisdiction Receives New and Controversial Life*

Many critics concede that diversity jurisdiction retains an important role in discrete, limited settings. For example, diversity jurisdiction over suits involving foreign nationals is supported because "it is important in the relations of this country with other nations that any possible appearance of injustice or tenable ground for resentment be avoided."[122] The perceived needs of international relations and the modest impact of alienage jurisdiction on the federal courts' workload have even led some commentators to support abrogation of the "complete diversity" requirement and substitution of a "minimal diversity" standard in alienage jurisdiction.[123]

Critics of conventional diversity jurisdiction have also recognized a role for a specialized jurisdictional power in complex litigation with interstate and international dimensions. In 1986, Professors Rowe and Sibley argued that a new "multiparty, multiforum" version of diversity jurisdiction might well replace the conventional diversity power exercised by federal courts.[124] The main focus of their proposal, as well as those of others, has relatively little to do with prejudice against non-citizens. Rather, diverse citizenship provided a constitutional platform for addressing the "problem of scattered litigation,"[125] and the "unavailability of any single state court forum in which to consolidate scattered, related litigation."[126] The problem of scattered litigation has arisen often in past decades when consumers file products-liability actions.

The problem of scattered litigation was largely unknown to the Framers. It arose in the twentieth century as the result of many factors. First, interstate commerce eclipsed local economies. Regional and nationwide markets for products and services emerged, and large corporations extended their activities into these markets. Second, "long-arm" jurisdiction broadened the power of state courts to adjudicate disputes affecting their citizens without regard to whether defendants were somehow "present" in the state. Third, state common law evolved to create new legal rights not dependent on concepts of "privity" (e.g., products-liability law) at the same time states enacted legislation for the protection of consumers. Fourth, procedural innovations like the class action enabled plaintiffs to champion the legal rights of many, increasing the potential recovery by class representatives and their lawyers while accentuating the risks to corporate defendants. Finally, the Court announced relatively relaxed limitations on the power of state courts to apply local law to events or defendants beyond their state borders.[127]

Despite its potential implications for interstate commerce, in the past scattered litigation was not amenable to solution by the federal courts. Congress has never invoked its interstate commerce power to enact legislation that might broadly federalize tort and commercial disputes and provide the basis for arising

122. American Law Inst., Study of the Division of Jurisdiction Between State and Federal Courts 108 (1969).

123. *See, e.g.*, Kramer, *supra* note 22, at 122.

124. *See* Thomas D. Rowe, Jr., & Kenneth D. Sibley, Beyond Diversity: Federal Multiparty, Multiforum Jurisdiction, 135 U. PA. L. REV. 7, 47 (1986).

125. *Id.* at 20.

126. *Id.* at 9.

127. *See Allstate Ins. Co. v. Hague*, 449 U.S. 302 (1981) (permitting application of a state's substantive law to transactions having minimal contacts with the state); *Sunoil Co. v. Wortman*, 486 U.S. 717 (1988) (permitting application of a state's "procedural" law, e.g., statutes of limitation, based on the law's traditional characterization regardless of the existence of factual contacts with the underlying dispute).

under jurisdiction. And faithful to its understanding of congressional intent, the Court has historically interpreted diversity jurisdiction to require "complete diversity" between all plaintiffs and all defendants, and until recently has required that each plaintiff class member independently satisfy amount-in-controversy requirements.[128] Consumer class actions thus had to be litigated in state court. Further, in one of the jurisdictional oddities of class actions, class citizenship was based on the *representatives'* citizenship rather than that of the class members themselves.[129] Consequently, plaintiffs enjoyed the power to select class representatives to create or destroy complete diversity, even though such forum shopping is prohibited in many other contexts.[130]

The litigation world of the late-twentieth century thus created the potential for "mischief," both intended and unintended. Such mischief included the following:

- A single state court might lack the ability to resolve all legal claims arising from a discrete accident, the use of a single product, or discrete misconduct by a defendant. As a consequence, litigation was often dispersed throughout state and federal courts, leading to the possibility of multiple, inconsistent outcomes.
- A plaintiff might forum shop and select a state court with known propensities to favor particular litigants, thereby securing the biased forum for an entire class of litigants.
- A state court might liberally construe choice-of-law principles to maximize the application of local law to events or parties outside the state, giving it power to effectively regulate the conduct of interstate businesses or to force defendants to enter into costly settlements.

As early as 1969, Congress considered legislation to transfer class actions to federal court where they might be resolved in some coordinated, efficient manner.[131] At the time, Congress explored the possibility of vesting federal courts with "protective jurisdiction," a controversial form of arising under jurisdiction we considered in Chapter 5. Legislative proposals failed, however, in part because of the organized opposition of business groups.[132]

a. Multiparty, Multiforum Trial Jurisdiction Act

In 2002, efforts to address scattered litigation through the intervention of federal courts resulted in a minor victory. Congress enacted the Multiparty,

128. *See Zahn v. International Paper Co.*, 414 U.S. 291 (1973).
129. *See Snyder v. Harris*, 394 U.S. 332 (1969).
130. For example, 28 U.S.C. § 1359 bars "collusive" joinder to gain access to federal court but not to frustrate access. The Court has also protected a defendant's right of removal when the plaintiff attempts to join a non-diverse defendant against whom the plaintiff has no bona fide claim. *See Wecker v. National Enameling & Stamping Co.*, 204 U.S. 176 (1907). Further, courts must "look beyond the pleadings" to verify that a party's designation as "plaintiff" or "defendant" reflects the party's actual interests in a suit. *See City of Dawson v. Columbia Ave. Sav. Fund*, 197 U.S. 178 (1905). In addition, statutory rules for determining citizenship have mitigated a party's power to select litigation representatives in other contexts (e.g., estate litigation) so as to either create or destroy diversity. *See, e.g.*, 28 U.S.C. § 1332(c)(2).
131. *See* James E. Pfander, *Protective Jurisdiction, Aggregate Litigation, and the Limits of Article III*, 95 Cal. L. Rev. 1423, 1446 (2007).
132. *See id.*

Multiforum Trial Jurisdiction Act (MMTJA)[133] to "achieve judicial and litigant economy, as well as fairness to litigants, by preventing repetitive litigation and inconsistent outcomes resulting from multiple federal and state proceedings arising out of the same transactions or events."[134] The MMTJA targets the ills associated with scattered litigation, but in a very limited setting—when a "single accident" has resulted in substantial death.[135] The MMTJA does not purport to remedy bias against non-citizens.

The Act anticipates that most suits arising from a mass disaster will eventually end up in federal court, either by original filing or removal from state court. Once in federal court, multiple actions can be consolidated for discovery and trial. To assist the placement of suits in federal court, the MMTJA expands federal court power by authorizing "minimal diversity" jurisdiction. The Act provides:

> The district courts shall have original jurisdiction of any civil action involving minimal diversity between adverse parties that arises from a single accident, where at least 75 natural persons have died in the accident at a discrete location, if—
>
> (1) a defendant resides in a State and a substantial part of the accident took place in another State or other location, regardless of whether that defendant is also a resident of the State where a substantial part of the accident took place;
> (2) any two defendants reside in different States, regardless of whether such defendants are also residents of the same State or States; or
> (3) substantial parts of the accident took place in different States.

28 U.S.C. § 1369(a). The Act specifies that "minimal diversity" exists if there are "adverse parties" consisting of at least one citizen of a state, and a citizen of either another state or a foreign nation.

The Act also reflects Congress' concern with federalism values by directing that federal courts abstain from exercising jurisdiction over what have been called "local controversies." Abstention is required when

> (1) the substantial majority of all plaintiffs are citizens of a single State of which the primary defendants are also citizens; and
> (2) the claims asserted will be governed primarily by the laws of that State.

28 U.S.C. § 1369(b).

Although the practical impact of the MMTJA is limited, it inaugurates several important changes in diversity jurisdiction with broader implications. These are found primarily in the Act's removal provisions, which amend the general removal provisions of § 1441. First, any defendant may remove to federal court, and the concurrence of other defendants is no longer required. Second, the fact that the defendant initiating removal is also a citizen of the state where suit has been filed does not preclude removal. Third, and most significant, a defendant may remove *any* state court action that "arises from the same accident" as an action satisfying the jurisdictional requirements of § 1369[136] *regardless*

133. 28 U.S.C. § 1369.

134. C. Douglas Floyd, *The* Limits of Minimal Diversity, 55 HASTINGS L.J. 613, 614 (2004).

135. The reference to an "accident" in the MMTJA has been construed to exclude litigation resulting from Hurricane Katrina. *See, e.g.*, Flint v. Louisiana Farm Bureau Mut. Ins. Co., 2006 WL 2375593 (E.D. La. 2006).

136. The Act also permits a non-diverse party to intervene in pending federal litigation.

of whether the removed action satisfies federal jurisdictional requirements. *See* 28 U.S.C. § 1441(e). In other words, a state court action arising from the same accident as another action satisfying jurisdictional requirements can be removed even if all the parties are citizens of the same state. The "minimal diversity" required is that between two adverse parties involved in the *same accident.*

There is much to say for federal intervention after public disasters. Congress was properly credited for its intervention in the wake of 9/11,[137] and President Bush's administration was sorely criticized for its delayed intervention following Hurricane Katrina. Nonetheless, the MMTJA announces unprecedented jurisdictional rules in a context where non-citizen bias is not a concern.

Fortunately the MMTJA's jurisdictional provisions have been seldom used. One exceptional use occurred in the aftermath of the highly publicized nightclub fire at "The Station" in West Warwick, Rhode Island. The tragic circumstances of the fire are described in the federal district court's opinion in *Passa v. Derderian*, 308 F. Supp. 2d 43 (D.R.I. 2004), and illustrate how the MMTJA can be used to federalize litigation following such mass disasters.

> On February 20, 2003, a deadly fire destroyed a nightclub located in West Warwick, Rhode Island, known to its patrons as "The Station." The fire started during the first minutes of a performance by the rock band Great White, while the club itself was crowded with spectators, staff, and performers. When defendants, Jack Russell, Mark Kendall, David Filice, and Eric Powers, members of the band "Great White" (hereafter referred to as "Band Members") took the stage that night, they and their tour manager, Daniel Bichele, ignited pyrotechnic devices as a part of their performance. These "pyrotechnics," also described as stage fireworks, or sparklers, caused flaming sparks to explode behind the stage area. According to witnesses, the sparks from these fireworks ignited foam insulation material previously installed in the club's ceiling and walls for soundproofing purposes. Once started, the fire quickly spread throughout The Station, creating a fiery inferno in its wake. In less than three minutes, the entire establishment was ablaze, and a reported 412 people inside the building that night were scrambling to escape the conflagration. According to this Court's best estimates, this tragic fire left 100 individuals dead and more than 200 injured. Only seventy-seven people are reported to have escaped the building without physical harm, yet, even for these lucky few who escaped bodily injury, the disaster continues to haunt their memories and affect their lives.
>
> In the wake of this tragedy, numerous lawsuits have been filed throughout southern New England in both state and federal courts. At present, this Court is concerned with five of these cases, two originally filed here in the United States District Court for the District of Rhode Island. . . . Three of these cases are civil actions filed by fire victims, their estates, and surviving family members alleging a variety of different state law tort claims against a host of different named Defendants. These named Defendants include the surviving Band Members, their management company, and their record label; nightclub owners, a corporation, a real estate company; insulation manufacturers; pyrotechnic manufacturer; event sponsors such as Anheuser-Busch Companies, Inc.; and representatives of government agencies establishing fire code regulations and enforcing compliance, and the State itself.

Id. at 46-47.

137. *See* Air Transportation Safety and System Stabilization Act, Pub. L. No. 107-42, 115 Stat. 230 (2001) (creating a federal cause of action for injuries suffered in plane crashes occurring on 9/11). We discussed this statute earlier. See Chapter 5.

The court in *Passa* readily found minimal diversity between at least two adverse parties (many plaintiffs were citizens of Rhode Island, and the band members who started the fire were Californians). The court then had to determine whether the "local controversy" exception required it to abstain, an issue that turned on whether a "substantial majority" of the plaintiffs and the "primary defendants" were citizens of the same state. The court eventually concluded it was not required to abstain because (1) fewer than 50 percent of those injured or killed in the accident were citizens of Rhode Island, and (2) the "primary defendants" directly liable for starting the fire included the band members and their manager, all from California. The court also declined to exercise its discretion to abstain based on "federalism and comity" concerns, even though it recognized that a Rhode Island state court had already invested considerable time and effort towards the proper management of cases arising from the Station nightclub fire, and the case had a "large impact" in the state. *See id.* at 64.

DISCUSSION AND QUESTIONS

Article III extends federal judicial power to "Controversies . . . between Citizens of different states." Does this language literally require complete diversity, or can it be construed as well to authorize minimal diversity? In other words, does a literal approach to the construction of Article III dictate any particular form of citizenship diversity? Note that in *Strawbridge v. Curtiss,* 3 Cranch 267 (1806), Chief Justice Marshall construed the federal diversity statute to require complete diversity and did not purport to construe Article III.

Even if you conclude that Article III does not literally require complete diversity, must it be construed so as to promote *some* purpose intended by the Framers? Based on our prior discussion of the Framers' intent in authorizing diversity jurisdiction, can you identify any original purpose promoted by the MMTJA? Do you agree with one critic's comment that the Act is unrelated to diversity's historical purposes because it "is not aimed at preventing local bias against out-of-state litigants or even at promoting 'nationalization' by assuring a competent and neutral federal forum for multistate business enterprises conducting business away from home"?[138]

On one prior occasion the Court has considered the constitutionality of minimal diversity. In *State Farm Fire & Casualty Co. v. Tashire,* 386 U.S. 523 (1967), the Court affirmed the constitutionality of Congress' authorization of minimal diversity in the federal interpleader statute, 28 U.S.C. § 1335. That statute uses language similar to language used in the MMTJA when it permits federal courts to exercise jurisdiction if there is diversity between "two or more adverse claimants" to property in the possession of an interpleader plaintiff. The Court in *Tashire* apparently thought the question of Congress' constitutional power so uncontroversial that it was content to simply cite lower court and academic authorities endorsing minimal diversity. *Id.* at 531 n.7.

In some respects, statutory interpleader discussed in *Tashire* is analogous to the consolidation mechanisms made possible by the MMTJA. Both statutory schemes provide the solution to a problem of complex litigation not amenable to resolution in state court. For example, statutory interpleader authorizes

138. *See* Floyd, *supra* note 133, at 628.

nationwide service of process and the exercise of personal jurisdiction not available in state court.[139] And like the MMTJA, statutory interpleader helps protect a party (the stakeholder) from the threat of multiple, inconsistent judgments. *See id.* at 534. Finally, both statutory schemes require the application of state substantive law, including state choice-of-law rules, and so do not displace state legislative authority.[140]

But there is one significant difference between the MMTJA and statutory interpleader. Whereas statutory interpleader confers diversity jurisdiction over a discrete dispute centered on a "stake" over which the federal court has jurisdiction, the MMTJA lacks such a unifying factual nucleus. MMTJA plaintiffs may share the commonality of a "single accident," but they assert independent tort claims whose success is not directly affected by the outcome in other plaintiffs' suits. As we discuss later, the reduced factual commonality in consolidated suits under the MMTJA calls into question Congress' ready reliance on *Tashire* to endorse the constitutionality of the MMTJA.

b. Class Action Fairness Act of 2005

The MMTJA should have relatively few applications given its requirement of a "single accident" with catastrophic consequences. The same cannot be said of Congress' most recent authorization of minimal diversity jurisdiction in the Class Action Fairness Act of 2005 (CAFA). *See* 28 U.S.C. §§ 1332, 1453. To appreciate the implications of CAFA, it helps to understand aspects of the modern class action that led to the enactment of this legislation.

One of the most important procedural innovations of the federal courts, later adopted by state courts, is the class action. *See* Fed. R. Civ. P. 23. No procedural innovation has invoked greater controversy, especially the type of class authorized by Rule 23(b)(3). The (b)(3) class action permits the joinder of numerous plaintiffs[141] even though their claims do not arise from a "common transaction or occurrence" (as is required for conventional plaintiff joinder under Rule 20.) The (b)(3) class action generally requires (1) "questions of law or fact" common to the class that predominate over questions affecting individual class members, and (2) a finding that the class device is superior to other methods for fairly and efficiently resolving members' disputes.

The plaintiffs' class representatives in (b)(3) are initially self-chosen (usually by class lawyers), and they may seek to represent a class as broad or narrow as the trial court thinks appropriate. For example, class representatives in a products-liability case may seek to represent a statewide, regional, or nationwide class of plaintiffs. When a trial court certifies such a class, settlement is often precipitated as the defendant comes to appreciate the economic risks of litigation. The terms of a settlement must be approved by the court, which exercises considerable discretion in deciding what is fair to the plaintiff class, their lawyers, and the defendant.

In class actions to enforce state-law claims, federal and state courts often labor under the same restrictions. Federal courts' personal jurisdictional power over

139. For example, Federal Rule of Civil Procedure 4(k)(1) authorizes nationwide service of process in statutory interpleader actions.

140. *See Griffin v. McCoach*, 313 U.S. 498 (1941).

141. We focus solely on the plaintiffs' use of the (b)(3) action, although defendant classes are also permitted under the Rule.

defendants is largely coextensive with that of the local state court.[142] In addition, federal courts must apply the same choice-of-law rules as local state courts, subject to the same constitutional restrictions.[143] But unlike state courts, which have "general" subject matter jurisdiction, federal courts enforcing solely state-law claims are limited by the requirements of diversity jurisdiction. As mentioned earlier, federal courts often lacked diversity jurisdiction over consumer class actions in the past because of the "complete diversity" requirement and the requirement that each class member satisfy the amount-in-controversy requirement. In 2005, a divided Court concluded that federal courts can now assert "supplemental jurisdiction" over class members' claims falling below the amount-in-controversy requirement provided at least one named plaintiff member satisfies this requirement.[144] But this change in diversity law still requires that at least one plaintiff satisfy the amount-in-controversy requirement (currently $75,000), a requirement not likely satisfied in many consumer class actions.

Consequently, state courts have provided the exclusive forum for most (b)(3)-type class actions in recent decades. And toward the end of the twentieth century, Congress became convinced that several state courts were abusing their power to adjudicate class actions. Business groups that had opposed expanded federal jurisdiction over class actions circa 1969 now had a change of heart. Professor Richard Marcus has summarized the perceived abuses resulting in the enactment of CAFA:

> Although defendants began in the 1980s to employ the class action to resolve large numbers of mass claims with some frequency, the use of the device in consumer-type situations drew growing criticism. This criticism focused particularly on state-court class actions that asserted claims on behalf of nationwide classes, or classes made up of claimants from many states. In part, this was a result of the likely application of the law of the forum state to transactions happening elsewhere, where one could argue that those engaged in transactions in other states had no meaningful way to foresee that their conduct would be measured by the standards of the state in which the suit was filed.
>
> But a greater concern was that plaintiff lawyers would carefully file such nationwide class actions in a state court in a county that was highly favorable to class action plaintiffs. These localities became known as "plaintiffs' paradise." On occasion it seemed that there was a close relationship between the elected state-court judges in these localities and members of the plaintiffs' bar, who were major contributors to these judges' campaigns. Because it was often possible to file such a class action wherever any member of the class resided, these cases came to offer what was known as "universal venue," giving plaintiff lawyers easy access to plaintiffs' paradise jurisdictions.
>
> The favored solution to this problem, from the defense perspective, was to have the cases heard by federal courts. At first blush, this may seem odd. The Federal Rules, after all, were the source of the expansion of class action practice . . . . And the relaxed pleading and broad discovery features of American litigation were also derived from the Federal Rules' breakthrough reforms. But federal judges are not only part of the nationwide federal judicial system, they are appointed for life and do not stand for election. Beyond that, there may have been some feeling that federal judges — most of them appointed

142. *See* Fed. R. Civ. P. 4(e), (h).
143. *See Klaxon Co. v. Stentor Elec. Mfg. Co.*, 313 U.S. 487 (1941).
144. *See Exxon Mobil Corp. v. Allapattah Servs., Inc.*, 545 U.S. 546 (2005).

> by Republican presidents—would be more sympathetic to defendants' concerns than some state-court judges. And the federal rules concerning what evidence could be used in court—particularly expert evidence—may have been viewed as more favorable by defendants. As a consequence, plaintiff lawyers had attempted to configure their suits to prevent them from being removed to federal court, often by making sure there was a local defendant who would defeat diversity of citizenship, which was required for cases based on state law to be in federal court.
>
> At the same time, it is important to note that the possibility of aggressive state-court measures in class actions contained the possibility of disrupting the operation of the federal-court systems. There were certainly examples of federal class action proceedings that had seemingly been undermined by conflicting rulings by state-court judges in competing class actions. Sometimes, after a federal judge decided that class certification should not be allowed, a state-court judge would permit a class action in virtually identical circumstances. Similarly, on occasion a state-court judge would approve a proposed class-action settlement that a federal judge had earlier found inadequate or unfair.[145]

The legislative history to CAFA regales the reader with examples of abuse and outrage, although opponents argue this history is skewed. Among the problems identified by Congress were several thought to implicate federalism concerns: (1) plaintiff-friendly state courts authorizing relief on behalf of nonresidents based on dubious interpretations of their home states' laws ("Why should a state court judge elected by the several thousand residents of a small county in Alabama tell New York or California the meaning of their laws?"), S. Rep. No. 109-14, at 61; (2) state courts employing dubious choice-of-law analysis to dictate the application of local law to other states ("Why should an Alabama state court tell 20 million people in all 50 states what kind of airbags they can have in their cars?"), *id.* at 24; and (3) state courts chosen because of the known propensity of local juries to award large verdicts, resulting in coerced settlements by interstate businesses, *see generally* S. Rep. No. 109-14; H.R. Rep. No. 107-370.

Congress also expressed concern with state courts "sometimes acting in ways that demonstrate bias against out-of-State defendants," including "interstate enterprises." S. Rep. No. 109-14, at 12. "Interstate class actions which often involve millions of parties from numerous states present the precise concerns that diversity jurisdiction was designed to prevent: frequently in such cases there appears to be state court provincialism against out-of-state defendants or a judicial failure to recognize the interests of other states in the litigation." *Id.* at 6. These and other abuses, Congress indicated, undermine "our Federal system and the intent of the framers of the Constitution in creating diversity jurisdiction." *Id.*

Reform of state court class actions was approved with "uncharacteristically strong bipartisan support."[146] Congress' solution was to modify conventional diversity rules that apply to class actions, specifically the "complete diversity"

145. Richard L. Marcus, *Modes of Procedural Reform*, 31 Hastings Int'l & Comp. L. Rev. 157, 180-81 (2008).

146. *See* Underwood, *supra* note 84, at 212 (noting that three-fourths of the Senate voted for CAFA).

and "amount in controversy" requirements thought to be easily manipulated by class lawyers. *See id.* at 11-12. Section 1332(d) now provides:

> The district courts shall have original jurisdiction of any civil action in which the matter in controversy exceeds the sum or value of $5,000,000, exclusive of interest and costs, and is a class action in which—
>
> (A) any member of a class of plaintiffs is a citizen of a State different from any defendant;
> (B) any member of a class of plaintiffs is a foreign state or a citizen or subject of a foreign state and any defendant is a citizen of a State; or
> (C) any member of a class of plaintiffs is a citizen of a State and any defendant is a foreign state or a citizen or subject of a foreign state.

CAFA thus authorizes federal diversity jurisdiction in class actions when (a) there is minimal diversity between *some* member of the plaintiff class and one defendant, and (b) the aggregate value of class members' claims exceeds $5 million. CAFA also eliminates the statutory restriction preventing removal of diversity cases when one defendant is a citizen of the state where a suit is filed. *See* 28 U.S.C. § 1453(b). This is intended to prevent "artful pleading" by plaintiffs to defeat the right of removal. *See* S. Rep. No. 109-14, at 11. Commentators agree that CAFA will "shift[] a wide range of consumer class actions to federal court."[147]

Like the MMTJA, CAFA contains "local controversy" exceptions that either permit or require a federal court to decline jurisdiction. *See* 28 U.S.C. § 1332(d)(3), (4). Excerpted below are the rococo criteria of § 1332(d)(4), mandating abstention:

> A district court shall decline to exercise jurisdiction . . .
> (A)(i) over a class action in which—
> (I) greater than two-thirds of the members of all proposed plaintiff classes in the aggregate are citizens of the State in which the action was originally filed;
> (II) at least 1 defendant is a defendant—
> (aa) from whom significant relief is sought by members of the plaintiff class;
> (bb) whose alleged conduct forms a significant basis for the claims asserted by the proposed plaintiff class; and
> (cc) who is a citizen of the State in which the action was originally filed; and
> (III) principal injuries resulting from the alleged conduct or any related conduct of each defendant were incurred in the State in which the action was originally filed; *and*
> (ii) during the 3-year period preceding the filing of that class action, no other class action has been filed asserting the same or similar factual allegations against any of the defendants on behalf of the same or other persons; *or*
> (B) two-thirds or more of the members of all proposed plaintiff classes in the aggregate, and the primary defendants, are citizens of the State in which the action was originally filed.

The greatest impact of CAFA will likely result from its provisions for *removal* of class actions filed by plaintiffs in state court. Not only does CAFA expand

147. James E. Pfander, *Protective Jurisdiction, Aggregate Litigation, and the Limits of Article III*, 95 Cal. L. Rev. 1423, 1444 (2007).

diversity jurisdiction to make more class actions removable, it eliminates several important restrictions on removal that apply in other contexts.[148] First, a defendant's right to removal does not expire one year after a state court suit is filed. *See* 28 U.S.C. § 1453(b). Second, the minimal diversity requirement of CAFA permits removal even if one or more defendants are citizens of the state where suit is originally filed. *See id.* Third, CAFA eliminates any requirement that all defendants consent to removal. *See id.* CAFA's unique removal provisions were intended by Congress to prevent state court plaintiffs from "gaming" the judicial system. *See* S. Rep. No. 109-14, at 4.

In *Standard Fire Insurance Co. v. Knowles*, 133 S. Ct. 1345 (2013), the Court held that a class action plaintiff could not avoid removal under CAFA by stipulating that the class would not seek more than $5 million in damages. Until the class was certified and the plaintiff had authority to make stipulations binding the class, the plaintiff could not limit the class's recovery and so defeat removal.

In *Mississippi ex rel. Hood v. AU Optronics Corp.*, 134 S. Ct. 736 (2014), the Court held that CAFA's requirement that at least "100 persons" join as class plaintiffs is not satisfied when a state sues as sole plaintiff and seeks restitution based on injuries suffered by its citizens. *See* 28 U.S.C. Ï 1332(d)(11)(B)(i). The Court concluded that Congress used the term *persons* selectively to refer to joined plaintiffs, and the 100-person requirement was not satisfied based on the underlying interests of unnamed persons on whose behalf the state was acting.

Before we explore the constitutional implications of CAFA, let's examine how CAFA may operate to federalize future class actions.

PROBLEM 6-3

Flicks

GreatFlicks, Inc., is a nationwide franchisor whose franchisees operate film rental stores in all 50 states. GreatFlicks is incorporated in Delaware and has its principal place of business in California.

GreatFlicks is currently defending against class actions filed in several state and federal courts. The plaintiff class in each of these suits alleges that GreatFlicks's ambiguous "late return" policy on film rentals has allowed it to defraud customers of tens of millions of dollars.

One class action has been filed in Kansas City, Kansas, on behalf of all citizens of Kansas who have been defrauded by GreatFlicks during the past five years. The complaint requests compensatory and punitive damages "not to exceed $5 million." Named defendants include GreatFlicks, as well as several dozen franchisees who operate GreatFlicks stores in Kansas. Approximately 95 percent of these franchisees are citizens of Kansas; the remainder are citizens of surrounding states. The complaint alleges legal claims under the common law of Kansas.

GreatFlicks has removed the Kansas class action to federal court, based on CAFA. In response, the plaintiffs' representatives have moved to remand to state court based on the contention that the federal court lacks jurisdiction.

148. See Chapter 7 (discussing removal requirements applicable to most civil actions).

(1) Based on these facts, how should the federal court rule?
(2) How would the jurisdictional issue be resolved by diversity law that applied prior to the enactment of CAFA?

Congressional debate preceding enactment of CAFA elicited numerous comments about the historical purposes of diversity jurisdiction and whether the statute promotes any of those purposes. Consider how both supporters and opponents of the Act interpret the Framers' intent in the committee report excerpted below. We begin with the proponents' interpretation:

> [T]he whole purpose of diversity jurisdiction is to . . . allow[] state-law based claims to be removed from local courts to federal courts, so as to ensure that all parties can litigate on a level playing field and thereby protect interstate commerce interests. Article III of the Constitution ensures that there will be a fair, uniform, and efficient forum (a federal court) for adjudicating interstate commercial disputes, so as to nurture interstate commerce. Some scholars have persuasively argued that diversity jurisdiction, of all the powers exercised under the Constitution, has had the greatest influence in melding the United States into a single nation, by fostering interstate commerce, communication and the uninterrupted flow of capital for investment into various parts of the Union, and sustaining the public credit and the sanctity of private contracts.
>
> [CAFA] promotes these important constitutional norms. The statutory "gatekeeper" for federal diversity jurisdiction—28 U.S.C. § 1332—generally allows federal courts to hear cases that are large (that is, cases with large "amounts in controversy") and that have interstate implications (that is, cases involving citizens from multiple jurisdictions). These requirements were intended to ensure that diversity jurisdiction is preserved for those cases with significant interstate and economic impacts. Class actions would normally satisfy these requirements because they usually involve big dollar amounts and parties from multiple jurisdictions. Yet, because section 1332 was enacted prior to the existence of the modern-day class action, it does not take into account the unique circumstances presented by class actions. Consequently, section 1332, as presently drafted, tends to exclude the overwhelming majority of class actions from federal courts, while inviting into federal courts much smaller single-plaintiff cases having few (if any) interstate ramifications. Such a result is inconsistent with the federal judiciary's proper jurisdictional role. [CAFA] would correct this technical problem and thereby promote the underlying goals of diversity jurisdiction. As former Clinton Administration Acting Solicitor General Walter Dellinger has testified in congressional hearings, if Congress were to now re-write the federal diversity jurisdiction statute, interstate class actions undoubtedly would be one of the first categories of cases to be included within the scope of the statute. This makes plain sense insofar as class action lawsuits typically involve more people, more money, and more interstate commerce issues than any other type of case. [CAFA] will simply fix the technical problem in section 1332 and judicial interpretation of the diversity requirements that keep most class actions in state court.

S. Rep. No. 109-14, at 53-54.

Dissenting members of Congress criticized what they thought might be an unconstitutional usurpation of state court authority to adjudicate class actions based on state law. They also offered the following comments in response to the argument that CAFA helped reduce the "bias" some non-citizens encountered in state court:

Arguments that the bill is nonetheless justified because state courts are "biased" against out of state defendants in class action suits also lacks foundation. First, the Supreme Court has already made clear that state courts are constitutionally required to provide due process and other fairness protections to the parties in class action cases.

Secondly, it is important to note that as fears of local court prejudice have subsided and concerns about diverting Federal courts from their core responsibilities increased, the policy trend in recent years has been towards limiting Federal diversity jurisdiction. For example, less than 6 years ago Congress enacted the Federal Courts Improvement Act of 1996, which increased the amount in controversy requirement needed to remove a diversity case to Federal court from $50,000 to $75,000. This statutory change was based on the Judicial Conference's determination that fear of local prejudice by state courts was no longer relevant and that it was important to keep the Federal judiciary's efforts focused on Federal issues. In this same regard, the American Law Institute has found "there is no longer the kind of prejudice against citizens of other states that motivated the creation of diversity jurisdiction," and the most recent Federal Courts Study Committee report on the subject concluded that local bias "is no longer a major threat to litigation fairness" particularly when compared to other types of prejudice that litigants may face, such as on account of religion, race or economic status. Indeed, in 1978, the House twice passed legislation that would have abolished general diversity jurisdiction.

Thirdly, as the legislation is currently written, it assumes a defendant will be automatically subject to prejudice in any state where the corporation is not formally incorporated (typically Delaware) or maintains its principal place of business. In so doing, it can be said the bill ignores the fact that many large businesses have a substantial commercial presence in more than one state, through factories, business facilities or employees. For example, if General Motors or Ford were to be sued by a class of plaintiffs in Ohio, where they have numerous factories and tens of thousands of employees, it does not seem reasonable to expect the defendants to face any great risk of bias. Similarly, if the Disney Corporation, one of Florida's largest employers, were to face a class action brought by a class of plaintiffs in a Florida court, it would make little sense to involve the Federal courts [out] of concern of local prejudice. Yet under [CAFA], both of these hypothetical cases would be subject to removal to Federal court.

It is for these reasons that the State courts believe that the enactment of the legislation goes against the underlying judicial principles of our system of government. Specifically, the Conference of Chief Justices said in a letter opposing a predecessor version of the bill, "So drastic a distortion and disruption of judicial federalism is not justified, absent clear evidence of the inability of the state judicial systems to process and decide class action cases in a fair and impartial manner and in timely fashion."

H.R. Rep. No. 107-370, at 127-28.

DISCUSSION AND QUESTIONS

CAFA is properly viewed as an "historic expansion of diversity jurisdiction"[149] that will "federalize consumer class actions."[150] Based on the excerpts from

149. *See* Underwood, *supra* note 84, at 215.

150. *See* Pfander, *supra* note 146, at 1444. An important exception to this generalization, however, is the situation where a large majority of class members are local citizens targeting conduct of a local defendant, which would likely be governed by local state law. Nonetheless, CAFA can be accurately interpreted as the federalization of substantial class actions (i.e., those seeking more than $5 million) having any appreciable interstate component.

legislative history quoted above, which theory of the Framers' intent has Congress embraced to support CAFA? To the extent that non-citizen bias is offered as a justification for CAFA, does bias truly seem to be a prominent concern when you consider (a) the abuses of the class action emphasized by proponents, and (b) the jurisdictional provisions of CAFA?

In earlier discussion we identified several mechanisms through which state courts allegedly worked their mischief in the eighteenth century. These include (a) enforcement of state laws adverse to commercial interests; (b) application of local state law to transactions significantly related to other jurisdictions; and (c) adjudication by state judges and juries that was prejudiced against either non-citizens or commercial interests generally. To what extent does CAFA suggest that some of these mechanisms are at work in the twenty-first century? Does contemporary experience with class actions in state court revive concerns akin to those shared by the Framers?

What does the enactment of CAFA imply for the "parity" debate we have discussed in previous chapters? As opponents of CAFA pointed out in the legislative history excerpted above, state court justices view the new law as a "drastic . . . distortion and disruption of judicial federalism," calling into question the ability of state courts to resolve class actions "in a fair and impartial manner and in timely fashion." One academic critic of CAFA has observed, "Since the mid-1990s, federal courts have demonstrated a systematic impatience with the aggressive use of Rule 23 in multistate cases with state law causes of action. . . . CAFA supporters' confidence in federalization rests in large measure on a perception of this . . . hostility."[151] Regardless of whether the federal judges' disposition toward class actions can be accurately characterized as "hostility," CAFA does seem to anticipate that class action abuse will be lessened by simply replacing state judges with federal judges. If state courts (at least some prominent ones) cannot be trusted to fairly resolve disputes arising under *state* law, should they be trusted to fairly apply federal law? Has the enactment of CAFA uncovered continuing beliefs—dismissed until recently by those who believe diversity jurisdiction is antiquated—that state judges are not fungible with federal judges?

Does CAFA raise second thoughts about what abstractions like "federalism" mean in a concrete political setting? Professor Pfander points out that Congress previously considered expanding federal court jurisdiction to transfer consumer class actions to federal court in 1969. At that time, proponents of expanded federal jurisdiction thought consumer classes might *benefit* by using the more liberal joinder procedures under federal class action rules. Proposals to expand federal jurisdiction over class actions were opposed by business interests.[152] Is it too cynical to conclude that federalism is a protean concept invoked by those who like the results coming out of state court, and ignored by those who do not?

5. *In Search of Limits to Diversity Jurisdiction*

The proponents of CAFA identified many abuses of the class action mechanism occurring in at least some state courts. For example, some state courts were inducing interstate businesses to enter into costly settlements to avoid even

151. *See* Marcus, *supra* note 144, at 1281.
152. *See* Pfander, *supra* note 146, at 1446.

more costly jury verdicts. Some state courts seemed eager to press the proper bounds of their regulatory authority by either applying local law to conduct having stronger connections with other states, or by misinterpreting other states' laws to promote local legal policy. Congress likely had the power to prevent such abuses through direct legislation. For example, under its interstate commerce power Congress likely has the authority to enact legislation preempting or limiting state laws that adversely affect national businesses. Similarly, Congress could exercise its power to implement the Full Faith and Credit Clause by establishing national choice-of-law rules to govern interstate commerce.[153]

Instead, Congress has used diversity jurisdiction to achieve substantive legal change, based on its confidence that federal judges will adjudicate class actions differently than state judges would. The use of diversity jurisdiction to achieve substantive change is not unprecedented. As we have learned, the Framers likely authorized diversity jurisdiction in part to alter the outcomes in creditor litigation. But are there no limits to the uses to which Congress can put diversity jurisdiction? Has Congress an unlimited power to redefine the citizenship of litigants, institute minimal diversity requirements, and confer diversity jurisdiction without regard to whether there is plausible threat of non-citizen bias?

The enactment of CAFA has prompted some legal scholars to argue limits to Congress' power to confer diversity jurisdiction.[154] Perhaps the leading advocate of a more restricted view of Congress' power is Professor James Pfander. According to Professor Pfander, a principled basis for limiting Congress' power is found in the language of Article III authorizing jurisdiction over "*controversies*" between citizens of different states. Inherent in the concept of a controversy, he argues, is the notion of a "head-to-head dispute involving two opposing parties from different states."[155] Each plaintiff in the typical (b)(3) "common question" class action, for example, is involved in a separate "controversy" with the class defendant. The fact that each plaintiff may be complaining about her use of the same product does not mean that all plaintiffs are part of a single "controversy." According to Professor Pfander, Article III generally imposes a "requirement of jurisdictional self-sufficiency" for each head-to-head dispute between a plaintiff and a defendant. This interpretation of Article III casts doubt on the constitutionality of the minimal diversity approach used in CAFA, and even in the MMTJA.

Professor Pfander recognizes that he is contending against Congress and perhaps the Court, both of which seem to accept the constitutionality of minimal diversity. But he maintains that Court precedent has been over-interpreted. The Court's approval of minimal diversity in *State Farm Fire & Casualty Co. v. Tashire*, 386 U.S. 523 (1967), occurred in the special context of interpleader. *Tashire* affirms minimal diversity because it is *necessary* in an interpleader dispute if the diverse parties are to resolve the controversy between them fully and fairly.[156] Professor Pfander similarly distinguishes

153. *See* Scoles & Hay, *supra* note 24, at 2 ("the United States Constitution provides the power to federalize the law of interstate conflicts").

154. *See, e.g., id.*; Floyd, *supra* note 133. In 1990, Professor Richard Epstein cautioned that the consolidation of non-diverse actions in federal court might exceed Congress' authority under Article III, although he did not have occasion to develop his theory of constitutional limits. *See* Richard A. Epstein, *The Consolidation of Complex Litigation: A Critical Evaluation of the ALI Proposal*, 10 J.L. & Com. 1 (1990).

155. Pfander, *supra* note 146, at 1449.

156. *See id.* at 1453-54.

other Court precedent,[157] leading him to conclude that "the Court's relaxation of the strict version of the complete diversity rule does not imply the absence of all limits; its leading cases allow the removal of separate claims or the assertion of ancillary jurisdiction over the claims of parties needed for a just adjudication."[158]

Professor Pfander concludes that non-diverse adversaries should be permitted to tag along in the controversies of diverse adversaries only when "necessary for the just adjudication" of the diverse parties' dispute. CAFA, he argues, lacks such a justification. Congress may pursue other tacks for transferring class actions to federal court—including enacting federal law under which non-diverse controversies can "arise"—but it should not be permitted to employ the concept of minimal diversity to federalize disputes arising under state law. CAFA thus provides a future opportunity for the Court to announce limits to Congress' power under the diversity clause.[159]

Professor C. Douglas Floyd agrees with Professor Pfander that the Constitution's requirement of a "controversy" between diverse parties precludes facile use of minimal diversity.[160] Professor Floyd argues that, even when there is minimal diversity in a class action, Congress bears the burden of providing constitutional justification for legislation. To begin with, Professor Floyd rejects the contention that the Framers were familiar with an analogue to the modern (b)(3) class action, and thus rejects a "historic" justification for minimal diversity in statutes like CAFA.[161] This leads Professor Floyd to consider whether Congress might have authority under the Necessary and Proper Clause to confer minimal diversity jurisdiction.

Professor Floyd acknowledges that *McCulloch v. Maryland*, 17 U.S. (4 Wheat.) 316 (1819), broadly interprets Congress' "necessary and proper" power, an interpretation that would sustain the MMTJA and CAFA if they "arguably relate" to "ends" promoted by the constitutional diversity power.[162] But he argues that the Court has more recently shown a renewed interest in federalism concerns, and that the Court's new temperament requires a "moderately demanding necessary and proper review."[163] According to Professor Floyd, both the MMTJA and significant parts of the CAFA do not survive such a review.

Professor Floyd scrutinizes the stated purposes of the MMTJA and CAFA. For the most part, he concludes that the only legitimate purposes of these statutes pertain to the protection of non-citizens litigating in state court. This leads him to question jurisdictional provisions that confer diversity jurisdiction where there is no apparent threat of non-citizen bias. For example, he criticizes removal provisions in the MMTJA and CAFA, which permit removal by a defendant-citizen of the state court where an action is pending.[164] He also questions the right of non-diverse litigants to remove under MMTJA simply

157. *See id.* at 1454-58. For example, the Court approved ancillary jurisdiction over claims asserted by non-diverse *defending* parties in *Owen Equipment & Erection Co. v. Kroger*, 437 U.S. 365 (1978), based in part on notions of fairness to parties who had not chosen to be in federal court.

158. Pfander, *supra* note 146, at 1458.

159. *See id.* at 1465-68.

160. *See* Floyd, *supra* note 133, at 636.

161. *See id.* at 637-42. Professor Floyd published before enactment of CAFA and so his comments pertain to drafts of the Act.

162. *See id.* at 644.

163. *See id.* at 650.

164. *See id.* at 661-62, 674-75.

because their dispute arises from the same "single accident" as another dispute between diverse parties.[165]

Professor Floyd's conclusion that the prevention of non-citizen bias is the *central* purpose of diversity jurisdiction leads him to conclude that many important goals underlying the MMTJA and CAFA are simply "impermissible." For example, he criticizes CAFA's attempt to promote "interstate commercial intercourse": "The fact that litigation may involve large numbers of parties, or a large sum of money, or have 'interstate commerce ramifications' does not, standing alone, bring it within the rationale of the diversity jurisdiction."[166] He concludes that the MMTJA is founded on impermissible purposes insofar as its primary goal is to provide for more efficient litigation of multiparty claims arising from a single accident: "Diversity claims arising from one accident . . . may be entirely and successfully litigated in federal court without the joinder of non-diverse claims. . . . The contention that it would be more rational and efficient if they all were resolved in one forum has no apparent connection to the purposes of the diversity jurisdiction."[167]

Professor Floyd also believes CAFA cannot be defended based on the argument that state courts have "inappropriately applied their own procedural and substantive law to cases involving litigants from other states."[168] This rationale is said to be "both tenuous and unconnected to the purpose of the Diversity Clause." Professional Floyd argues that the Due Process Clause places an ultimate constraint on state courts that improperly extend local law to non-local events, and in any event federal courts are required under *Erie* "to make the same choice" as state courts.

In summary, Professor Floyd contends that minimal diversity jurisdiction is permissible only if it serves the interests of the non-citizens who are the "intended beneficiaries of the Diversity Clause."[169] To the extent that the MMTJA and CAFA are "baldly . . . predicated on the need to achieve judicial and litigant economy and consistent outcomes between federal and state litigation arising from the same events or transactions, the proposals on their face seek to achieve ends that are unrelated to the purposes of the Diversity Clause."[170]

DISCUSSION AND QUESTIONS

The argument that "Controversies . . . between Citizens of different States" literally confers jurisdiction over head-to-head disputes between diverse citizens—and not much more—is indirectly supported by Court precedent construing "arising under" jurisdiction. As we learn in Chapter 7, the Court has limited the power of federal courts to adjudicate state claims in federal question disputes to those state claims sharing a "common nucleus of operative fact" with federal claims. This limit on "supplemental" jurisdiction derives from the Court's interpretation of the boundaries of a constitutional case or controversy within the meaning of Article III. One can argue that minimal diversity exceeds

165. *See id.* at 675.
166. *See id.* at 656.
167. *See id.* at 673.
168. *See id.* at 657.
169. *See id.* at 693.
170. *See id.* at 694.

the constitutional boundaries of a "controversy" when it permits a federal court to litigate disputes between non-diverse parties that do not arise from a "common nucleus of operative fact" shared by diverse litigants. According to Professor Floyd, the MMTJA and CAFA extend minimal diversity jurisdiction beyond constitutional limits; in fact, Congress appears to have assumed that one diverse dispute satisfies Article III and has shown no regard for whether the non-diverse disputes are factually related to diverse disputes.[171] Keep this issue in mind as you explore supplemental jurisdiction in Chapter 7.

One of the challenges faced by opponents of a broad-ranging minimal diversity power is Court precedent. The requirement of complete diversity was announced as a statutory limit on jurisdiction in *Strawbridge v. Curtiss*, and Justice Marshall eventually expressed regrets about having given such a limiting interpretation.[172] The Court has repeatedly permitted the exercise of minimal diversity, *Tashire* being the most prominent example, and it recently reaffirmed that "the complete diversity requirement is not mandated by the Constitution." *Exxon Mobil Corp. v. Allapattah Servs., Inc.*, 545 U.S. 546, 553 (2005).[173] Although Professor Pfander does a skillful job restricting Court precedent to its facts, one wonders whether the Court is willing to announce and develop new restrictions on Congress' jurisdictional power. As Professor Pfander candidly acknowledges, "it may be too late to establish a workable limit on Congressional use of minimal diversity."[174]

Consider whether workable limits on the use of minimal diversity can be derived from an examination of the historical purposes of diversity jurisdiction, which is Professor Floyd's approach. Earlier we examined different theories of the Framers' intent in authorizing diversity jurisdiction. We saw that some Framers may have been influenced by

- fears that state courts (judges or juries) would show adjudicatory bias toward non-citizens;
- fears that state courts would show adjudicatory bias toward commercial interests;
- fears that state courts would apply state law inconsistent with the Constitution and federal treaties;
- fears that state courts would apply state law to non-local business transactions through indulgent interpretation of choice-of-law theory; and
- fears that state courts (again including judges or juries) would develop legal rules damaging to the nation's developing economy.

First, even though these concerns may have *motivated* some of the Framers, should they all be considered in defining the *purposes* of constitutional diversity jurisdiction? Professor Floyd finds that the prevention of non-citizen bias is the measuring stick for the legitimacy of minimal diversity. In *Allapattah, supra*, 545 U.S. at 553-54, the Court recently stated that "a principal reason" for conferring

171. *See id.* at 678-81.

172. *See Louisville, Cincinnati & Charleston R.R. v. Letson*, 43 U.S. (2 How.) 497, 555 (1844) ("By no one was the correctness of them more questioned than by the late chief justice who gave them. It is within the knowledge of several of us, that he repeatedly expressed regret that those decisions had been made, adding, whenever the subject was mentioned, that if the point of jurisdiction was an original one, the conclusion would be different").

173. Professor Floyd wrote before the Court announced its opinion in *Allapattah*.

174. *See* Pfander, *supra* note 146, at 1470.

diversity jurisdiction is "to provide a federal forum for important disputes where state courts might favor, or be perceived as favoring, home-state litigants." Are you convinced that the constitutionality of minimal diversity should turn on its specific impact on non-citizen litigants? Does the fact that the Framers authorized this form of jurisdiction based explicitly on diverse citizenship mean that factors like "interstate commerce" have relevance *only* when related to the interests of diverse parties? After all, the Framers did not confer jurisdiction over "disputes affecting interstate commerce" or "disputes involving creditor-debtor relations." If Congress must support diversity legislation based on some credible concern with the prevention of non-citizen bias, does the MMTJA survive scrutiny? If you think this interpretation of Congress' power is too restrictive, can you think of a less restrictive interpretation that imposes some workable limits? Or can Congress use the adventitious presence of two diverse disputants to justify any conferral of diversity jurisdiction?

Or has Professor Floyd too narrowly defined the historical purposes of diversity jurisdiction? Consider, for example, his conclusion that Congress had no legitimate basis for regulating the choice-of-law decisions of state courts through CAFA. Judge Friendly, we have seen, believed that the fear of errant choice-of-law decisions by state courts may have been a primary concern of the Framers. Professor Borchers believes that the Framers specifically *intended* to displace state law, including state choice-of-law theory, when it authorized diversity jurisdiction. While it may be true that, after *Erie* and *Klaxon*, federal diversity courts must follow state choice-of-law directives, does it follow that they must "make the same choice" as state courts, as Professor Floyd argues? Is it possible that, given the great amount of discretion involved in deciding when and how to apply state law to interstate events, Congress might properly conclude that some state courts exercise their discretion more often to benefit local citizens, consumers, or even the local plaintiffs' bar? Professor Floyd contends that state courts are already subject to constitutional constraints when they make choice-of-law decisions. But did not the Framers authorize diversity jurisdiction in part to prevent the continued enforcement of unconstitutional state laws? Stated differently, even though state courts cannot apply state law in an unconstitutional manner, can Congress confer diversity jurisdiction to aid the enforcement of constitutional restrictions?

To the extent that Congress justified the MMTJA and CAFA because of the "interstate commerce ramifications" of multi-jurisdictional litigation, was Congress' purpose "impermissible" under the diversity clause? Admittedly, these new federal laws operate in circumstances that often have no colorable relationship to a non-citizen's plight. But does the Constitution require such a relationship? Is the "hook" of two diverse claimants sufficient to support any exercise of congressional power that alleviates problems in state court affecting the national economy?[175] To the extent we understand the Framers' intent(s) in authorizing diversity jurisdiction, do you believe they would have objected to statutes like the MMTJA or CAFA?

Yet another perspective on diversity of citizenship has been offered by Professors Charles Cooper and Howard Nelson, Jr. They argue that a complete-diversity requirement was never intended by the First Congress and "very well may be a requirement that Congress lacked constitutional authority to impose in

175. Professor Floyd has written about Congress' misuse of the "interstate commerce" rationale to expand diversity jurisdiction. *See* C. Douglas Floyd, *The Inadequacy of the Interstate Commerce Justification for the Class Action Fairness Act of 2005*, 55 EMORY L.J. 487 (2006).

any event."[176] If they are correct, arguably it does not matter whether statutes requiring less than complete diversity serve any specific goal such as the promotion of national commerce.

D. SOME ADDITIONAL PROBLEMS

PROBLEM 6-4

Punishment Enough

In response to state court rulings authorizing substantial punitive damages against several large national businesses, Congress enacts new diversity legislation. Congress recites the need for "efficient, coordinated litigation to avoid the threat of duplicative, excess awards of punitive damages that might adversely affect interstate commerce." The new statute creates a limited *removal* jurisdiction for defendants sued in state court. In any suit where the plaintiff(s) seek more than $250,000 in total damages and make some demand for punitive damages, the defendant may remove to federal court if it is diverse from at least *one* of the plaintiffs. After at least one such suit has been removed to federal court, the statute authorizes removal of any *other* state court action seeking punitive damages from that same business, provided the claims in that action arise from the same conduct, transaction, or series of conduct or transactions that are the basis for a previously removed action. Removal of subsequent suits is permitted regardless of the litigants' citizenship. Upon removal of punitive damages suits that have the required factual relationship, the statute authorizes consolidation of these suits in one federal district.

(1) Discuss whether the statute raises constitutional concerns based on any of the theories of constitutional diversity jurisdiction we have examined.
(2) Reflect back on our study of arising under jurisdiction in Chapter 5. As an alternative to the diversity statute described above, could Congress exercise its Commerce Clause power by enacting criteria to govern the award of punitive damages against businesses engaged in interstate commerce, and then confer removal jurisdiction over state court suits seeking punitive damages based on arising under jurisdiction?

PROBLEM 6-5

Saving Ronald

Assume that, at some point in the near future, a few plaintiffs begin succeeding in their efforts to reform American fast-food cuisine through litigation. In particular, lower courts in two states have upheld new applications of negligence

176. Charles J. Cooper & Howard C. Nelson, Jr., *Complete Diversity and the Closing of the Federal Courts,* 37 Harv. J.L. & Pub. Pol'y 295, 326 (2014).

law to permit persons with various health problems to sue fast-food restaurants that promote consumption of large quantities of fat-saturated foods. Already, McDonald's has been forced to reach costly settlements to avoid the threat of devastating jury verdicts.

In response to court decisions in these path-breaking states, Congress is considering amendments to diversity law. Proponents of the amendments argue that "controversial rulings in several state courts now threaten to give single states the power to dictate the eating habits of the consumers in other states. While state supreme courts have the authority to correct such errant precedent, and in time likely will, delays in state court appeals permit bad precedent to fester and work its harmful effects on the nation's food industry." Consequently, new diversity rules are proposed to govern commercial dining and take-out establishments that operate under a franchise relationship with large national franchisors (e.g., McDonald's, Burger King, Subway). The new diversity statute provides that the citizenship of national franchisors and local franchisees will be that of the *state of their incorporation.* This is intended to make most franchisors and franchisees diverse from plaintiffs in problem states, based on the assumption that businesses will incorporate (or re-incorporate) in "safe" states not likely to authorize controversial applications of negligence law. The new statute also authorizes minimal diversity jurisdiction to prevent plaintiffs from joining parties whose presence will defeat federal jurisdiction. Note that the statute omits any amount-in-controversy requirement, and it applies to conventional lawsuits involving small numbers of plaintiffs (i.e., it is not a class action reform proposal). As a constraint on the new legislation, Congress specifically restricts its citizenship rules to disputes attempting to link plaintiffs' adverse medical conditions to the nutritional content of foods.

Discuss whether the proposed statute raises constitutional concerns based on any of the theories of constitutional diversity jurisdiction we have examined.

CHAPTER 7

Augmenting Federal Courts' Power Through the Exercise of Supplemental and Removal Jurisdiction

A. A REFERENCE PROBLEM

In this chapter we address two forms of jurisdiction that augment the federal trial courts' power to adjudicate controversies—supplemental jurisdiction and removal jurisdiction. The Reference Problem below introduces some of the issues that arise when these forms of jurisdiction are exercised.

* * * *

Larry Gottfried has a small law practice specializing in the representation of consumers. Recently he filed suit in federal court on behalf of two clients, Janice Primmer and Darryl Wheeler. The plaintiffs' suit arises from these facts:

Primmer and Wheeler graduated from Illinois School of Cosmetology a few years ago. To help them meet school expenses, each independently obtained private loans from Student Friendly Loans, Inc. ("SFL"). Primmer borrowed $75,000 from SFL, while Wheeler borrowed a more modest $25,000.

When Primmer and Wheeler contracted for their loans, SFL's agent, Liz Gilley, emphasized that "we appreciate that cosmetology students often need a little time after graduation to secure permanent employment, and so we routinely defer any repayment obligation until you're established in the profession and earning a salary sufficient to make loan repayment manageable. You needn't worry about that." After graduating, the Primmer and Wheeler were unable to find full-time employment in the field of cosmetology and, instead, accepted low-paying jobs in retail sales. Yet shortly after graduating from cosmetology school, Primmer and Wheeler received invoices from SFL requesting the first payments on their loans. When they contacted Liz Gilley, she pointed out that the loan agreements they signed specifically state that repayment must commence within three months of graduation and contain no payment-deferral option. "You must have misunderstood me when you originally applied for your loans," Gilley told them.

Primmer and Wheeler argued vigorously with Gilley. When they threatened to sue SFL, Gilley told them, "You'll either make payment immediately or we'll spread the word through the cosmetology community that you're a couple of deadbeats. Then you'll see how hard jobs are to come by. We've done it before and we'll do it again."

Primmer and Wheeler contacted attorney Gottfried to seek legal assistance in their disputes with SFL. Gottfried soon spoke with SFL's vice president, who denied that SFL ever represented that the plaintiffs could defer student loans beyond the repayment deadline found in the loan agreements. The VP also stated that neither Liz Gilley nor anyone one else ever made the threats alleged by the plaintiffs. The VP demanded that Primmer and Wheeler immediately begin repaying the loans and threatened to take legal action if they did not. That's when Gottfried filed a federal suit against SFL and its agent, Liz Gilley.

The plaintiffs' complaint alleges three causes of action[1] on behalf of each plaintiff: (1) a claim under 15 U.S.C. §§1692 *et seq.*, the Fair Debt Collection Practices Act ("FDCPA"); (2) a claim under the Illinois counterpart to the FDCPA (the "Illinois Act"); and (3) a claim under state common law for fraud. Gilley is named as defendant solely to the fraud claim, as neither the FDCPA nor the Illinois Act authorizes a cause of action against Gilley individually. You may assume that the alleged threats to harm the plaintiffs' professional careers are actionable under the FDCPA and the Illinois Act, and that the alleged misrepresentations about deferment of loan repayments constitute actionable fraud under state common law.

In response to the suit, the defendants (represented by the same law firm) take these actions:

1. Although the federal statute is real, we have fabricated elements of both federal and state law. If you have independent knowledge of federal or state law, please ignore it in answering the Reference Problem.

(a) defendant SFL moves to dismiss Primmer's *federal claim* because it was filed one week after the applicable statute of limitations expired;
(b) defendants SFL and Gilley move to dismiss the *state fraud claims* for lack of federal subject matter jurisdiction; and,
(c) defendant SFL also files an answer in which it asserts a counterclaim under state law to recover monies owed by the plaintiffs under their loan agreement.

In light of the defendants' responses to the complaint, consider the following questions:

(1) If SFL succeeds in having Primmer's federal claim dismissed as untimely, must the federal court dismiss the remaining state claims she alleges?
(2) Regardless of what rulings the court makes on other pending defense motions, does the court have subject matter jurisdiction over the state claims?
(3) Regardless of what rulings the court makes on other pending defense motions, does the court have jurisdiction over SFL's counterclaim for breach of contract?
(4) If the plaintiffs had originally filed their complaint in *state* court, would the defendants have been permitted to remove the suit to federal court?

* * * *

The Reference Problem illustrates issues that can arise when federal and state claims are presented in a single lawsuit. Among the issues we consider in this chapter are:

- When are claims based on state law part of the same "case or controversy" as claims based on federal law?
- What are the justifications for permitting a federal court to entertain claims based on state law? How much discretion does a federal court have in exercising its supplemental jurisdiction over state-law claims?
    - When can a state court defendant remove a case to federal court, despite the plaintiff's preference for a state court forum? And what options are available to defendants when a plaintiff employs procedural strategies for the purpose of defeating removal?

B. CONTEXT AND BACKGROUND

1. *Augmenting the Jurisdiction of Federal Trial Courts*

By now you have come to appreciate how seriously federal courts take the question of their subject matter jurisdiction. Any doubts about that jurisdiction can overshadow trial and appellate proceedings because of the possibility that the litigants' efforts will come to nothing.[2]

2. *See, e.g,* Fed. R. Civ. P. 12(h)(3) (permitting a party to object to subject matter jurisdiction at any time); *Mitchell v. Maurer,* 293 U.S. 237, 244 (1934) (an appellate court has an independent duty to verify that both trial and appellate proceedings satisfy jurisdictional requirements).

Despite the potential consequences of jurisdictional error, litigants often have strong incentive to invoke federal jurisdiction and resolve in one proceeding as many aspects of the dispute as possible. Modern Rules of procedure encourage litigants to do what good sense dictates—include as many claims and parties as necessary to achieve a client's litigation goals. Modern Rules encourage the assertion of all viable claims one has against an adversary, *see, e.g.*, Fed. R. Civ. P. 13, 18; and the joining of all parties against whom relief is needed or desired. *See, e.g.*, Fed. R. Civ. P. 14, 19, 20. Sometimes the assertion of multiple claims is not only encouraged but is required. Under what is loosely referred to as "res judicata" doctrine, a litigant can forfeit the opportunity to litigate a claim or an issue if it is not raised in a pending proceeding.

A plaintiff wishing to assert all available federal and state claims can usually achieve this goal by simply filing suit in state court. Almost all state courts have adopted liberal joinder rules similar to those followed by federal courts. Further, state courts are courts of "general jurisdiction" and usually have power to adjudicate all issues raised by a controversy whether based on federal or state law. Consequently, state courts usually provide a forum for the comprehensive resolution of a dispute involving multiple claims or multiple parties.[3]

But even when a state court has comprehensive jurisdictional power to adjudicate all aspects of a dispute, litigants may prefer a federal forum. If federal courts lacked the power to adjudicate all claims arising from a dispute, including those that, standing alone, fall outside the courts' jurisdictional power, plaintiffs might be discouraged from using the federal forum. And defendants compelled to defend themselves in federal court could suffer significant disadvantages if they were not permitted to assert their own claims arising from the dispute—for example, counterclaims, crossclaims, and third-party claims—that lack independent jurisdictional foundation. For reasons such as these,[4] Congress has conferred "supplemental jurisdiction" on the federal courts. In this chapter we begin with an analysis of supplemental jurisdiction and its legitimacy under Article III's case-or-controversy requirement.

Federal statutes authorizing removal jurisdiction augment the federal courts' power in a different way. Removal jurisdiction promotes *defendants'* access to federal court by permitting them to remove based on the nature of the case that *plaintiffs* have constructed. Even though a plaintiff is content to litigate in state court a case that might have been filed in federal court, a defendant usually can override the plaintiff's choice of forum. Somewhat anomalously, a defendant's right of removal is not based on its own interest in securing a federal forum for federal defenses and counterclaims it has asserted. As you learned in Civil Procedure, a defendant's right of removal focuses on the same item considered in determining the plaintiff's right to file suit in federal court—the well-pleaded complaint.[5]

3. There are exceptions. Sometimes state courts lack the power to adjudicate all aspects of a controversy. For example, a federal court may have exclusive jurisdiction over particular federal claims, or exclusive control over property that is the focus of a dispute. In such circumstances, a federal court may provide the only possible forum for fully adjudicating all aspects of a controversy.

4. *See generally* Robert G. Bone, *Revisiting the Policy Case for Supplemental Jurisdiction*, 74 Ind. L.J. 139 (1998).

5. See Louisville & Nashville Railroad Co. v. Mottley, 219 U.S. 467 (1911).

Yet plaintiffs — "masters" of the lawsuit — can at times structure their suits so as to improperly deny defendants the right of removal. So as we learn later in this chapter, Congress and the courts have devised several strategies to restrain plaintiffs' use of improper or "fraudulent" procedural tactics to frustrate defendants' right of removal.

2. *Plan of Coverage*

a. Supplemental Jurisdiction

No doubt you have examined supplemental jurisdiction in Civil Procedure. In this chapter we review some of the principal uses of supplemental jurisdiction in routine federal practice. We then consider the Constitution's case-or-controversy requirement and how that requirement affects the use of supplemental jurisdiction. In so doing, we examine the contemporary dialogue between Congress and the Court about the permissible scope of supplemental jurisdiction.

As we learn, Congress has seemingly endorsed a more limited interpretation of the case-or-controversy requirement than that suggested by earlier Court precedent and advocated by some commentators. According to critics of the Court's current interpretation, it unjustifiably deprives federal courts of jurisdictional power they might usefully employ. While the current interpretation of what constitutes a constitutional case accommodates many of the joinder devices promulgated by the Court in federal procedural rules, it does not accommodate all. To expand our understanding of what constitutes a constitutional case, we examine the current dispute among federal courts concerning how supplemental jurisdiction should apply to one important joinder device, the counterclaim.

We also examine the important element of discretion built into both supplemental jurisdiction doctrine and federal procedural rules. Some of this discretion is guided by Congress' federalism concerns, as when federal courts are permitted to decline adjudicating state-law issues that are novel or complex or to decline adjudicating disputes that largely turn on claims arising state law. At other times, courts exercise discretion to promote federal-law policies without explicit direction from Congress. To explore this controversial exercise of discretion, we again focus on the counterclaim.

b. Removal Jurisdiction[6]

Our brief study of removal addresses defendants' right to remove cases where a plaintiff (1) joins claims based on both federal and state law or (2) uses procedural strategies for the purpose of frustrating defendants' right of removal. We begin by discussing the statute most widely used in private civil litigation, 28 U.S.C. § 1441, and how it extends the exercise of removal jurisdiction to otherwise non-removable claims that are part of the case or controversy that underlies removable claims. We then consider recent statutory

6. In 2013, more than 284,000 civil cases were filed in federal district courts. *See* http://www.uscourts.gov/uscourts/Statistics/JudicialBusiness/2013/appendices/C08Sep13.pdf. About 32,000 or 11 percent of these were removed from state court.

amendments that protect defendants' right of removal when plaintiffs join removable with non-removable claims that don't arise from the same case or controversy. Finally, we consider statutory and judicially developed responses to plaintiffs who attempt to defeat defendants' right of removal by improperly using procedural rules governing joinder of claims and removal of cases.

C. THE LAW AND PROBLEMS

1. *Supplemental Jurisdiction*

In prior chapters we considered the various forms of original jurisdictional power authorized by Article III of the Constitution and focused specifically on two forms, federal question and diversity of citizenship jurisdiction. See Chapters 5 and 6. The doctrine of supplemental jurisdiction applies generally to all forms of original jurisdiction exercised by the district courts, *see* 28 U.S.C. § 1367(a), but the Supreme Court has emphasized that its more expansive interpretations of supplemental jurisdiction apply when courts exercise federal question jurisdiction. *See Exxon Mobil Corp. v. Allapattah Servs. Inc.*, 545 U.S. 546, 553 (2005). In part for this reason, and in part to facilitate a more manageable discussion of what can be a highly technical subject, we emphasize the role that supplemental jurisdiction plays when courts exercise federal question jurisdiction. At the same time, we indicate from time to time where Congress has enacted special restrictions on the extension of supplemental jurisdiction to suits based on diversity of citizenship.

a. The Constitutional Foundation of Supplemental Jurisdiction

The Constitution extends federal judicial power to "all Cases" arising under federal law. U.S. CONST. art. III, § 2. In Chapter 2, we considered how the case-or-controversy language has been interpreted to require, among other things, that parties demonstrate they have a "ripe" dispute and "standing" to litigate that dispute. As the Court recently emphasized in *DaimlerChrysler Corp. v. Cuno,* 547 U.S. 332 (2006), these case-or-controversy requirements must be satisfied even when a party invokes a court's supplemental jurisdiction power.

The doctrine of supplemental jurisdiction presents a distinct issue under the case-or-controversy requirement. Supplemental jurisdiction assumes the parties have presented a sufficiently developed dispute that they have standing to litigate, that is, there is some form of case. The question raised by supplemental jurisdiction is a different one: does the "case" encompass claims that, standing alone, would not fall within one of the original forms of jurisdiction authorized by the Constitution? *See United Mine Workers of Am. v. Gibbs,* 383 U.S. 715, 725 n.12 (1966). In a suit based on federal question jurisdiction, the question is whether claims based on state law can be viewed as part of the same "case."

In *Osborn v. Bank of the United States,* 22 U.S. (9 Wheat) 738 (1824), Chief Justice Marshall suggested that the breadth of a constitutional case is quite broad. *Osborn,* which we discussed more fully in Chapter 4 when studying federal question jurisdiction, indicated that a case arises under federal law when a non-federal cause of action contains an "ingredient" of federal law. Chief Justice Marshall's famous description of "arising under" power states:

> [W]hen a question to which the judicial power of the Union is extended by the constitution, forms an ingredient of the original cause, *it is in the power of Congress to give the Circuit Courts jurisdiction of that cause,* although other questions of fact or of law may be involved in it.

Id. at 823 (emphasis added).

Chief Justice Marshall observes several times that a court has jurisdiction over a "case" involving an ingredient of federal law. But notice that Chief Justice Marshall's famous statement of federal jurisdiction quoted above addresses when a "cause" arises under federal law. Is there a distinction between a case and a cause of action? Can a case involve two causes and, if so, does constitutional jurisdiction extend to both causes?

In later cases, the Court seemed to focus on Chief Justice Marshall's use of the term "cause," and to distinguish such causes from the case itself. For example, in *Hurns v. Oursler,* 289 U.S. 238, 243 (1933), the Court emphasized that a federal court does not have power to adjudicate nonfederal causes of action simply because they are asserted in the same complaint as federal causes. As the Court observed, "the Rule does not go so far as to permit a federal court to assume jurisdiction of a *separate and distinct* nonfederal cause of action because it is joined in the same complaint with a federal cause of action." *Id.* at 245-46 (emphasis added). Although the Court quoted without objection the holding in *Osborn,* it plainly rejected an interpretation of *Osborn* that would permit a federal court to adjudicate *any* claim asserted in a suit simply because a "federal ingredient" is part of one claim.

Professor Richard A. Matasar has made a highly plausible argument that Osborn authorizes federal jurisdiction over all claims in a suit containing a single federal "cause," provided the additional claims are properly joined under conventional Rules of civil procedure. *See* Richard A. Matasar, *Rediscovering "One Constitutional Case": Procedural Rules and the Rejection of the* Gibbs *Test for Supplemental Jurisdiction,* 71 CAL. L. REV. 1399, 1477-90 (1983). In theory this could greatly expand the current scope of supplemental jurisdiction, since Congress has extended that jurisdiction to any "claims" that "form part of the same case or controversy" as claims coming within the federal courts' original jurisdiction.[7]

The modern Court, in *United Mine Workers of America v. Gibbs,* has reaffirmed that the question of supplemental jurisdiction is cause-specific, or more precisely, claim-specific.[8] Excerpted below is the Court's current articulation of the constitutional scope of supplemental jurisdiction. In *Gibbs,* a former mine superintendent (Gibbs), sued United Mine Workers because it had allegedly threatened him, prevented the opening of the mine Gibbs was to supervise, and prevented Gibbs from performing under a contract he had with mine owners.

7. This is solely in theory because Congress enacted § 1367 in light of the Court's decision in *Gibbs,* which defines the case or controversy requirement more narrowly than does Professor Matasar.

8. Again we emphasize that our focus is the use of supplemental jurisdiction where at least one claim arises under federal law. The analysis in cases based on diversity of citizenship differs because the focus shifts to the parties' citizenship and the amount in controversy, not the nature of the claim (which are by definition claims not arising under federal law).

These actions, Gibbs alleged, violated federal labor law as well as state common law (tortious interference with a contract). In *Gibbs*, the Court was asked to determine whether a federal trial court could exercise supplemental jurisdiction over Gibbs' state law claim. Note that the doctrine of supplemental jurisdiction was then referred to in its different forms as "pendent" jurisdiction (the form addressed in *Gibbs*) and "ancillary" jurisdiction.[9]

As you read *Gibbs*, try to distinguish constitutional requirements for the exercise of supplemental jurisdiction, and non-constitutional discretionary factors a court may consider when deciding whether to decline to exercise its supplemental jurisdictional power. This distinction will be important when we consider Congress' express authorization of this jurisdictional power in § 1367, which appears to implement the Court's ruling in *Gibbs*.

UNITED MINE WORKERS OF AMERICA v. GIBBS

383 U.S. 715 (1966)

MR. JUSTICE BRENNAN delivered the opinion of the Court.

* * * *

The Court held in Hurn v. Oursler, 289 U.S. 238 (1933) that state law claims are appropriate for federal court determination if they form a separate but parallel ground for relief also sought in a substantial claim based on federal law. The Court distinguished permissible from non-permissible exercises of federal judicial power over state law claims by contrasting a case where two distinct grounds in support of a single cause of action are alleged, one only of which presents a federal question, and a case where two separate and distinct causes of action are alleged, one only of which is federal in character. In the former, where the federal question averred is not plainly wanting in substance, the federal court, even though the federal ground be not established, may nevertheless retain and dispose of the case upon the nonfederal ground; in the latter it may not do so upon the nonfederal cause of action. . . . *Hurn* was decided in 1933, before the unification of law and equity by the Federal Rules of Civil Procedure. At the time, the meaning of "cause of action" was a subject of serious dispute; the phrase might "mean one thing for one purpose and something different for another."

* * * *

With the adoption of the Federal Rules of Civil Procedure and the unified form of action, Fed. Rule Civ. Proc. 2, much of the controversy over "cause of action" abated. The phrase [that] remained as the keystone of the *Hurn* test, however, . . . has been the source of considerable confusion. Under the Rules, the impulse is toward entertaining the broadest possible scope of action consistent with fairness to the parties; joinder of claims, parties and remedies is strongly encouraged. Yet because the *Hurn* question involves issues of jurisdiction as well as convenience, there has been some tendency to limit its application to cases in which the state and federal claims are, as in *Hurn*, "little more than

9. One way of distinguishing pendent and ancillary jurisdiction is offered by Professor Chemerinsky: "Pendent jurisdiction can be thought of as claims contained in the *plaintiff's complaint* for which there are not independent bases for federal court jurisdiction. In contrast, ancillary jurisdiction can be understood as claims that are asserted *after the filing of the original complaint* that do not independently meet the requirements for federal court jurisdiction. ERWIN CHEMERINSKY, FEDERAL JURISDICTION 358 (Aspen 6th ed. 2012) (emphasis in original).

the equivalent of different epithets to characterize the same group of circumstances."

This limited approach is unnecessarily grudging. Pendent jurisdiction, in the sense of judicial power, exists whenever there is a claim "arising under [the] Constitution, the Laws of the United States, and Treaties made, or which shall be made, under their Authority . . . ," U.S.Const., Art. III, § 2, and the relationship between that claim and the state claim permits the conclusion that the entire action before the court comprises but one constitutional "case." The federal claim must have substance sufficient to confer subject matter jurisdiction on the court. The state and federal claims must derive from a common nucleus of operative fact. But if, considered without regard to their federal or state character, a plaintiff's claims are such that he would ordinarily be expected to try them all in one judicial proceeding, then, assuming substantiality of the federal issues, there is power in federal courts to hear the whole.

That power need not be exercised in every case in which it is found to exist. It has consistently been recognized that pendent jurisdiction is a doctrine of discretion, not of plaintiff's right. Its justification lies in considerations of judicial economy, convenience and fairness to litigants; if these are not present a federal court should hesitate to exercise jurisdiction over state claims, even though bound to apply state law to them [under Erie R. Co. v. Tompkins]. Needless decisions of state law should be avoided both as a matter of comity and to promote justice between the parties, by procuring for them a surer-footed reading of applicable law. Certainly, if the federal claims are dismissed before trial, even though not insubstantial in a jurisdictional sense, the state claims should be dismissed as well. Similarly, if it appears that the state issues substantially predominate, whether in terms of proof, of the scope of the issues raised, or of the comprehensiveness of the remedy sought, the state claims may be dismissed without prejudice and left for resolution to state tribunals. There may, on the other hand, be situations in which the state claim is so closely tied to questions of federal policy that the argument for exercise of pendent jurisdiction is particularly strong. In the present case, for example, the allowable scope of the state claim implicates the federal doctrine of pre-emption; while this interrelationship does not create statutory federal question jurisdiction, citing Louisville & N.R. Co. v. Mottley, its existence is relevant to the exercise of discretion. Finally, there may be reasons independent of jurisdictional considerations, such as the likelihood of jury confusion in treating divergent legal theories of relief, that would justify separating state and federal claims for trial, Fed. Rule Civ. Proc. 42(b). If so, jurisdiction should ordinarily be refused.

The question of power will ordinarily be resolved on the pleadings. But the issue whether pendent jurisdiction has been properly assumed is one which remains open throughout the litigation. Pretrial procedures or even the trial itself may reveal a substantial hegemony of state law claims, or likelihood of jury confusion, which could not have been anticipated at the pleading stage. Although it will of course be appropriate to take account in this circumstance of the already completed course of the litigation, dismissal of the state claim might even then be merited. For example, it may appear that the plaintiff was well aware of the nature of his proofs and the relative importance of his claims; recognition of a federal court's wide latitude to decide ancillary questions of state law does not imply that it must tolerate a litigant's effort to impose upon it what is in effect only a state law case. Once it appears that a state claim constitutes the real body of a case, to which the federal claim is only an appendage, the state claim may fairly be dismissed.

* * * *

[Justice Harlan's concurring opinion, agreeing with the majority's discussion of supplemental jurisdiction, is omitted.]

DISCUSSION AND QUESTIONS

The constitutional power to exercise supplemental jurisdiction. The Court in *Gibbs* announces two criteria (or three, depending on how they are categorized), for deciding whether federal and state law claims form a single constitutional "case" authorizing federal court jurisdiction. First, the federal claim must have "substance sufficient to confer subject matter jurisdiction on the court." The requirement that a federal claim have "substance" is not a demanding one. The case relied on by *Gibbs* explains the concept of an unsubstantial federal claim: "the federal question averred may be plainly unsubstantial either because obviously without merit, or because its unsoundness so clearly results from the previous decisions of this court as to foreclose the subject and leave no room for the inference that the questions sought to be raised can be the subject of controversy." *Levering & Garrigues Co. v. Morrin,* 289 U.S. 103, 105 (1933). Note that substance exists when the allegations of a complaint suggest the possibility of a meritorious federal claim, regardless of whether there is evidentiary support for the claim. As the Court more recently observed in *Hagans v. Levine,* an alleged federal claim is substantial unless "prior decisions inescapably render the claims frivolous." 415 U.S. 528, 538 (1974). This means that a facially adequate federal claim will not be rendered unsubstantial when it is later shown that no evidence supports the claim.

Gibbs's second requirement is usually the decisive one: "The state and federal claims must derive from a common nucleus of operative fact," such that a plaintiff "would ordinarily be expected to try them all in one judicial proceeding." This requirement clearly departs from a more expansive definition of a case or controversy like that suggested by Chief Justice Marshall in *Osborn. See Finley v. United States,* 490 U.S. 545, 549 (1989) (*Gibbs* "common nucleus of operative fact" test defines when federal and state claims compromise a single "constitutional case").

Contrast *Osborn*'s constitutional ruling that a claim arises under federal law if federal law is an ingredient of a claim, and *Gibbs'* constitutional ruling that a state law claim must be factually related to a federal law claim to constitute a single case. Are these rulings inconsistent or difficult to reconcile? Or do they address distinct constitutional concerns requiring different resolutions? If *Gibbs* had ruled that a constitutional case encompasses all claims alleged in a complaint where there is some federal law ingredient, what impact would that have had on the workload of federal courts? Note that, while some federal rules limit the joinder of claims and parties to factually related allegations, *see, e.g.,* Fed. R. Civ. P. 13(a), 14(a), 20, other rules omit any requirement that additional claims be related. *See, e.g.,* Fed. R. Civ. P. 18(a), 13(b). Does the potential breadth of an *Osborne*-like definition of a constitutional case raise concerns that either (a) federal courts would be unduly burdened by a surfeit of state law claims or (b) federal courts would usurp jurisdictional power properly allocated to state courts? Does the fact that federal courts have discretion to exercise supplemental jurisdiction under *Gibbs,* discussed below, make these concerns less troublesome?

PROBLEM 7-1

A Statutory Simplification of Supplemental Jurisdiction

Assume that, in 2015, Congress is asked by the Federal Judicial Center to simplify what has become a confusing body of judicial interpretation of supplemental jurisdiction. The Center suggests a statutory amendment whose central provision is the following:

> In all cases filed in the federal district courts to which the United States is not a party where original jurisdiction is based on the presence of a claim arising under the laws of the United States, the courts shall have supplemental jurisdiction over any nonfederal claims properly asserted by the parties under the Federal Rules of Civil Procedure.

The Center opines that Congress has authority to enact the proposed amendment under its power to confer original jurisdiction on the federal courts as well as its "Necessary and Proper" clause power to make the exercise of federal jurisdiction more efficient.

The proposed amendment expressly precludes use of its newly-authorized supplemental jurisdiction in cases involving large numbers of plaintiffs or defendants or in cases seeking class relief. The statute also grants federal courts broad discretion to dismiss nonfederal claims when the assertion of jurisdiction over them would make adjudication less manageable or would undermine "important state interests."

Discuss any problems, practical or legal, you find with the proposed legislation. Also consider what factors, if any, commend Congress' enactment of the proposal.

Judicial discretion in exercising supplemental jurisdiction. The Court recognizes that the exercise of supplemental jurisdiction is discretionary, not obligatory as is usually the case when a court is asked to adjudicate claims arising under federal law. This discretion should be exercised to promote "judicial economy, convenience and fairness to litigants," and a court has power to revisit its decision as the case progresses. In *Gibbs,* the Court identifies several factors bearing on a district court's exercise of discretion, all of which were later affirmed when Congress enacted § 1367.

First, the Court comments that "needless decisions of state law should be avoided . . . by procuring for them a surer-footed reading of applicable law." The Court alludes to the desirability of permitting state courts the opportunity to interpret state law whose meaning is unclear. As we learn in Chapter 10, such deference to the paramount role of state courts in interpreting state law has led to the development of one form of abstention doctrine, whereby federal courts sometimes stay proceedings to permit the parties to request an authoritative interpretation of state law from a state court. As an alternative to such abstention, federal district courts often have the authority to certify state law questions to a state's supreme court. When these strategies are available to a federal district court, they may be employed in lieu of dismissing supplemental claims.

The Court also states in *Gibbs* that, if all federal claims are "dismissed before trial," supplemental state claims should be dismissed as well. This situation differs from that where federal claims alleged in a complaint are insubstantial or frivolous on their face. When such insubstantial federal claims are the foundation for federal jurisdiction, a federal court lacks constitutional power to adjudicate the case. But where federal claims are facially sound but are dismissed before trial (e.g., by motion for summary judgment), the Court adjures federal courts to dismiss the remaining state claims.

The Court also remarks that, when state issues "substantially predominate" in a federal suit, they may be dismissed by the federal court. Similarly, when state issues present the "likelihood of jury confusion," a federal court should consider dismissing state claims. Note that the appropriate response to this situation, like the response to claims based on unclear state law, is to dispose of the *state* claim. Federal courts are normally required to adjudicate federal claims properly within their mandatory jurisdiction.

b. The Emerging Importance of Congressional Intent

Gibbs addressed a federal court's power to adjudicate a plaintiff's parallel state claim arising out of the same factual occurrence as a federal claim. Yet the Court recognized long before *Gibbs* that supplemental jurisdiction may also be available to persons other than the plaintiff. For example, in *Freeman v. Howe,* 65 U.S. (24 How.) 450 (1860), the Court permitted persons to intervene in a pending federal court action to assert their interests in property seized by federal officials even though they asserted no independent basis for jurisdiction. Such "ancillary" jurisdiction was again affirmed in *Dewey v. West Fairmont Gas Coal Co.,* 123 U.S. 329 (1887), where a third-party defendant was joined in a diversity-of-citizenship action even though the third party shared citizenship with the plaintiff. And in *Moore v. New York Cotton Exchange,* 270 U.S. 593 (1926), the Court permitted a federal court defendant to assert a state-law counterclaim against the plaintiff that arose from the same facts as the plaintiff's federal claim.

In the years following *Gibbs,* the Court indicated that its decision was not a broad endorsement of supplemental jurisdiction over any and all claims sharing a "common nucleus of operative fact" with claims coming within the federal courts' original jurisdiction. To limit the potential scope of *Gibbs,* the Court introduced a consideration not addressed in *Gibbs* itself. The Court began asking whether *Congress* had endorsed the use of supplemental jurisdiction when it enacted the jurisdiction statute on which the federal part of a particular suit was founded. The situation that first prompted the Court's new attention to congressional intent was the exercise of pendent party jurisdiction, where additional parties who could not independently satisfy jurisdictional requirements are joined in a federal suit.

For example, in *Aldinger v. Howard,* 427 U.S. 1 (1976), the Court considered whether a jurisdictional statute, 28 U.S.C. § 343, permitted a plaintiff to join as a pendent party defendant to a civil rights action a county that was sued solely under state law. The Court rejected supplemental jurisdiction over the county, even though the plaintiff's claim against the county arose from the same nucleus of facts as the plaintiff's claim against the defendants sued under federal law (42 U.S.C. §983). Because Congress has excluded counties from the coverage of §1983,[10] the Court concluded that Congress had impliedly preempted use of supplemental jurisdiction to join the county as a pendent party. 427 U.S. at 17.

In *Zahn v. International Paper Co.*, 414 U.S. 291 (1973), the Court refused to let a plaintiff join in a diversity class action when his claim was worth less than the amount-in-controversy requirement then in force under 28 U.S.C. §1332. The Court concluded that such use of supplemental jurisdiction was inconsistent with Congress' intent to limit diversity actions to controversies involving greater stakes, even though the pendent party's dispute was part of the same constitutional case as the claims of plaintiff class members who satisfied the amount-in-controversy requirement.

In yet another case, the Court refused to extend supplemental jurisdiction in a suit founded on diversity of citizenship. The Court concluded that the plaintiff in a diversity action could not assert a claim against a non-diverse party who had been impleaded as a third-party defendant. *See Owen Equipment & Erection Co. v. Kroger*, 437 U.S. 365 (1978). The Court emphasized that *Gibbs*'s common-nucleus standard "does not end the inquiry into whether a federal court has power to hear the nonfederal claims along with the federal ones. Beyond this constitutional minimum, there must be an examination of the posture in which the nonfederal claim is asserted and of the specific statute that confers jurisdiction over the federal claim." *Id.* at 373. As in *Zahn*, the Court in *Kroger* concluded that permitting the plaintiff to assert a claim against the non-diverse third-party defendant would violate congressional limits contained in the relevant jurisdictional statute, 28 U.S.C. §1332.

The Court's final curtailment of supplemental jurisdiction before Congress intervened came in *Finley v. United States*, 490 U.S. 545 (1989). *Finley*, even better than prior decisions, captures the ongoing debate within the Court concerning Congress' voice in the development of supplemental jurisdiction. Although the Court's specific ruling in *Finley* was ultimately reversed by Congress, its discussion of the relative roles of Congress and the Court in elaborating the scope of subject matter jurisdiction remains relevant.

FINLEY v. UNITED STATES

490 U.S. 545 (1989)

JUSTICE SCALIA delivered the opinion of the Court.

On the night of November 11, 1983, a twin-engine plane carrying petitioner's husband and two of her children struck electric transmission lines during its approach to a San Diego, California, airfield. No one survived the resulting crash. Petitioner brought a tort action in state court, claiming that San Diego Gas and Electric Company had negligently positioned and inadequately illuminated the transmission lines, and that the city of San Diego's negligent maintenance of the airport's runway lights had rendered them inoperative the night of the crash. When she later discovered that the Federal Aviation Administration (FAA) was in fact the party responsible for the runway lights, petitioner filed the present action against the United States in the United States District Court for

10. In Chapter 9 we study how this interpretation of §1983 was ultimately overruled by the Court.

the Southern District of California. The complaint based jurisdiction upon the Federal Tort Claims Act (FTCA), 28 U.S.C. § 1346(b), alleging negligence in the FAA's operation and maintenance of the runway lights and performance of air traffic control functions. Almost a year later, she moved to amend the federal complaint to include claims against the original state-court defendants, as to which no independent basis for federal jurisdiction existed. The District Court granted petitioner's motion and asserted "pendent" jurisdiction under [*Gibbs*], finding it "clear" that "judicial economy and efficiency" favored trying the actions together, and concluding that they arose "from a common nucleus of operative facts." The District Court certified an interlocutory appeal to the Court of Appeals for the Ninth Circuit. . . . That court summarily reversed. . . . We granted certiorari to resolve a split among the Circuits on whether the FTCA permits an assertion of pendent jurisdiction over additional parties.

The FTCA provides that "the district courts . . . shall have exclusive jurisdiction of civil actions on claims against the United States" for certain torts of federal employees acting within the scope of their employment. 28 U.S.C. § 1346(b). Petitioner seeks to append her claims against the city and the utility to her FTCA action against the United States, even though this would require the District Court to extend its authority to additional parties for whom an independent jurisdictional base—such as diversity of citizenship, 28 U.S.C. § 1332(a)(1)—is lacking.

In 1807 Chief Justice Marshall wrote for the Court that "courts which are created by written law, and whose jurisdiction is defined by written law, cannot transcend that jurisdiction. It is unnecessary to state the reasoning on which this opinion is founded, because it has been repeatedly given by this court; and with the decisions heretofore rendered on this point, no member of the bench has, even for an instant, been dissatisfied." It remains rudimentary law that "[a]s regards all courts of the United States inferior to this tribunal, two things are necessary to create jurisdiction, whether original or appellate. The Constitution must have given to the court the capacity to take it, and an act of Congress must have supplied it. . . . To the extent that such action is not taken, the power lies dormant."

Despite this principle, in a line of cases by now no less well established we have held, without specific examination of jurisdictional statutes, that federal courts have "pendent" claim jurisdiction—that is, jurisdiction over nonfederal claims between parties litigating other matters properly before the court—to the full extent permitted by the Constitution. Gibbs, which has come to stand for the principle in question, held that "[p]endent jurisdiction, in the sense of judicial power, exists whenever there is a claim 'arising under [the] Constitution, the Laws of the United States, and Treaties made, or which shall be made, under their Authority . . . ,' U.S. Const., Art. III, § 2, and the relationship between that claim and the state claim permits the conclusion that the entire action before the court comprises but one constitutional 'case.'" The requisite relationship exists, Gibbs said, when the federal and nonfederal claims "derive from a common nucleus of operative fact" and are such that a plaintiff "would ordinarily be expected to try them in one judicial proceeding." Petitioner contends that the same criterion applies here, leading to the result that her state-law claims against San Diego Gas and Electric Company and the city of San Diego may be heard in conjunction with her FTCA action against the United States.

Analytically, petitioner's case is fundamentally different from Gibbs in that it brings into question what has become known as pendent-party jurisdiction, that is, jurisdiction over parties not named in any claim that is independently cognizable by the federal court. We may assume, without deciding, that the constitutional criterion for pendent-party jurisdiction is analogous to the constitutional criterion for pendent-claim jurisdiction, and that petitioner's state-law claims pass that test. Our cases show, however, that with respect to the addition of parties, as opposed to the addition of only claims, we will not assume that the full constitutional power has been congressionally authorized, and will not read jurisdictional statutes broadly. [The Court then discusses its prior decisions in *Zahn, Aldinger,* and *Kroger,* where it limited application of supplemental jurisdiction.]

* * * *

The most significant element of "posture" or of "context in the present case (as in Zahn, Aldinger, and Kroger) is precisely that the added claims involve added parties over whom no independent basis of jurisdiction exists. While in a narrow class of cases a federal court may assert authority over such a claim "ancillary" to jurisdiction otherwise properly vested—for example, when an additional party has a claim upon contested assets within the court's exclusive control, or when necessary to give effect to the court's judgment—we have never reached such a result solely on the basis that the Gibbs test has been met. And little more basis than that can be relied upon by petitioner here. As in Kroger, the relationship between petitioner's added claims and the original complaint is one of "mere factual similarity," which is of no consequence since "neither the convenience of the litigants nor considerations of judicial economy can suffice to justify extension of the doctrine of ancillary jurisdiction." . . . It is true that here, unlike in Kroger, the party seeking to bring the added claims had little choice but to be in federal rather than state court, since the FTCA permits the Federal Government to be sued only there. But that alone is not enough, since we have held that suits against the United States under the Tucker Act (which can of course be brought only in federal court) cannot include private defendants.

The second factor invoked by Kroger, the text of the jurisdictional statute at issue, likewise fails to establish petitioner's case. The FTCA, § 1346(b), confers jurisdiction over "civil actions on claims against the United States." It does not say "civil actions on claims that include requested relief against the United States," nor "civil actions in which there is a claim against the United States"—formulations one might expect if the presence of a claim against the United States constituted merely a minimum jurisdictional requirement, rather than a definition of the permissible scope of FTCA actions. Just as the statutory provision "between . . . citizens of different States" has been held to mean citizens of different States and no one else, see Kroger, so also here we conclude that "against the United States" means against the United States and no one else.[11] "Due regard for the rightful independence of state governments . . . requires that [federal courts] scrupulously confine their own jurisdiction to the

11. [Footnote 5 in Court's opinion.] Justice Stevens would distinguish (and *Zahn v. International Paper Co.*) from the present case on the ground that, where Congress "has unequivocally indicated its intent that the federal right be litigated in a federal forum, there is reason to believe that Congress did not intend that the substance of the federal right be diminished by the increased costs in efficiency and convenience of litigation in two forums." It seems to us, however, that one could say precisely the same thing about the diversity jurisdiction involved in *Kroger* and *Zahn*: When Congress has unequivocally indicated its intent that a plaintiff have a right to bring a diversity action in federal court, there is reason to believe that Congress did not intend that the substance of that right be diminished, etc. We simply do not agree with the inference, in either context.

precise limits which the statute has defined." The statute here defines jurisdiction in a manner that does not reach defendants other than the United States.

Petitioner contends, however, that an affirmative grant of pendent-party jurisdiction is suggested by changes made to the jurisdictional grant of the FTCA as part of the comprehensive 1948 revision of the Judicial Code. In its earlier form, the FTCA had conferred upon district courts "exclusive jurisdiction to hear, determine, and render judgment on any claim against the United States" for specified torts. In the 1948 revision, this provision was changed to "exclusive jurisdiction of civil actions on claims against the United States." Petitioner argues that this broadened the scope of the statute, permitting the assertion of jurisdiction over any "civil action," so long as that action includes a claim against the United States. We disagree.

Under established canons of statutory construction, "it will not be inferred that Congress, in revising and consolidating the laws, intended to change their effect unless such intention is clearly expressed." Concerning the 1948 recodification of the Judicial Code in particular, we have stated that "no changes in law or policy are to be presumed from changes of language in the revision unless an intent to make such changes is clearly expressed." We have found no suggestion, much less a clear expression, that the minor rewording at issue here imported a substantive change. The change from "claim against the United States" to "civil actions on claims against the United States" would be a strange way to express the substantive revision asserted by petitioner — but a perfectly understandable way to achieve another objective. The 1948 recodification came relatively soon after the adoption of the Federal Rules of Civil Procedure, which provide that "[t]here shall be one form of action to be known as 'civil action.'" Fed. Rule Civ. Proc. 2. Consistent with this new terminology, the 1948 revision inserted the expression "civil action" throughout the provisions governing district-court jurisdiction.

Reliance upon the 1948 recodification also ignores the fact that the concept of pendent-party jurisdiction was not considered remotely viable until Gibbs liberalized the concept of pendent-claim jurisdiction — nearly 20 years later. Indeed, in 1948 even a relatively limited substantive expansion of pendent-claim jurisdiction with respect to unfair competition actions provoked considerable discussion, and was described by the chief reviser as one of a dozen "major changes of law" effected by his handiwork That change, in the already accepted realm of pendent-claim jurisdiction, was accomplished by wording that could not be mistaken, referring to "any civil action asserting a claim of unfair competition when joined with a substantial and related claim under the copyright, patent, or trademark laws." It is inconceivable that the much more radical change of adopting pendent-party jurisdiction would have been effected by the minor and obscure change of wording at issue here — especially when that revision is more naturally understood as stylistic.

Because the FTCA permits the Government to be sued only in federal court, our holding that parties to related claims cannot necessarily be sued there means that the efficiency and convenience of a consolidated action will sometimes have to be forgone in favor of separate actions in state and federal courts. We acknowledged this potential consideration in Aldinger, but now conclude that the present statute permits no other result.

As we noted at the outset, our cases do not display an entirely consistent approach with respect to the necessity that jurisdiction be explicitly conferred. The *Gibbs* line of cases was a departure from prior practice, and a departure that we have no intent to limit or impair. But *Aldinger* indicated that the *Gibbs* approach would not be extended to the pendent-party field, and we decide today to retain that line. Whatever we say regarding the scope of jurisdiction conferred by a particular statute can of course be changed by Congress. What is of paramount importance is that Congress be able to legislate against a background of clear interpretive Rules, so that it may know the effect of the language it adopts. All our cases — *Zahn*, Aldinger, and *Kroger* — have held that a grant of jurisdiction over claims involving particular parties does not itself confer jurisdiction over additional claims by or against different parties. Our decision today reaffirms that interpretive Rule; the opposite would sow confusion.

For the foregoing reasons, the judgment of the Court of Appeals is Affirmed.

JUSTICE BLACKMUN, dissenting.

If Aldinger v. Howard required us to ask whether the Federal Tort Claims Act embraced "an affirmative grant of pendent-party jurisdiction," I would agree with the majority that no such specific grant of jurisdiction is present. But, in my view, that is not the appropriate question under Aldinger. I read the Court's opinion in that case, rather, as requiring us to consider whether Congress has demonstrated an intent to exempt "the party as to whom jurisdiction pendent to the principal claim" is asserted from being haled into federal court. And, as those of us in dissent in *Aldinger* observed, the *Aldinger* test would be rendered meaningless if the required intent could be found in the failure of the relevant jurisdictional statute to mention the type of party in question, "because all instances of asserted pendent-party jurisdiction will by definition involve a party as to whom Congress has impliedly 'addressed itself' by not expressly conferring subject-matter jurisdiction on the federal courts."

In Aldinger, the Court found the requisite intent to exclude municipalities from the relevant jurisdictional statute, because (the Court then thought) municipalities had been affirmatively excluded by Congress from the scope of 42 U.S.C. § 1983. In such a case, the Court barred the use of the pendent-party doctrine, for otherwise the doctrine would permit an end run around an express congressional limitation of federal power.

In the present case, I find no such substantive limitation. Nor, in my view, is there any other expression of congressional intent to exclude private defendants from federal tort claims litigation.

* * * *

In a case not controlled by any express intent to limit the scope of a constitutional "case," *Aldinger* suggests that the appropriateness of pendent-party jurisdiction might turn on the "alignmen[t] of parties and claims," and that one significant factor is whether "the grant of jurisdiction to [the] federal court is exclusive," as is the situation here. Where, as here, Congress' preference for a federal forum for a certain category of claims makes the federal forum the only possible one in which the constitutional case may be heard as a whole, the sensible result is to permit the exercise of pendent-party jurisdiction. *Aldinger* imposes no obstacle to that result, and I would not reach out to create one. I therefore dissent.

JUSTICE STEVENS, with whom JUSTICE BRENNAN and JUSTICE MARSHALL join, dissenting.

The case before us today is one in which the United States is a party. Given the plain language of Article III, there is not even an arguable basis for questioning the federal court's constitutional power to decide it. Moreover, by enacting the Federal Tort Claims Act (FTCA) in 1946, Congress unquestionably authorized the District Court to accept jurisdiction of "civil actions on claims against the United States." Thus, it is perfectly clear that the District Court has both constitutional and statutory power to decide this case.

It is also undisputed that this power will not be defeated by the joinder of two private defendants. Rule 14(a) of the Federal Rules of Civil Procedure expressly authorizes the defendant to implead joint tortfeasors, and this Rule is applicable to FTCA cases. Moreover, if the claim against nonfederal defendants had been properly brought in a federal court, those defendants could require the United States to defend their claim for contribution in that action. The dispute between all the parties derives from a common nucleus of operative fact. There is accordingly ample basis for regarding this entire three-cornered controversy as a single "case" and for allowing petitioner to assert additional claims against the nonfederal defendants as she is authorized to do by Rule 20(a) of the Federal Rules.

Prior to the adoption of the Federal Rules of Civil Procedure in 1938, the federal courts routinely decided state-law claims in cases in which they had subject-matter jurisdiction, and granted relief against nondiverse parties on state claims as to which there was no independent basis for federal jurisdiction. Although the contours of the federal cause of action — or "case" — were then more narrowly defined than they are today, the doctrine of "pendent" or "ancillary" jurisdiction had long been firmly established. The relevant change that was effectuated by the adoption of the Rules in 1938 was, in essence, a statutory broadening of the dimensions of the cases that federal courts may entertain.

* * * *

I would thus hold that the grant of jurisdiction to hear "civil actions on claims against the United States" authorizes the federal courts to hear state-law claims against a pendent party. As many other judges have recognized, the fact that such claims are within the exclusive federal jurisdiction, together with the absence of any evidence of congressional disapproval of the exercise of pendent-party jurisdiction in FTCA cases, provides a fully sufficient justification for applying the holding in *Gibbs* to this case.

* * * *

The Court treats the absence of an affirmative grant of jurisdiction by Congress as though it constituted the kind of implicit rejection of pendent jurisdiction that we found in *Aldinger v. Howard.* Its opinion laboriously demonstrates that the FTCA "defines jurisdiction in a manner that does not reach defendants other than the United States," and that the language of the statute cannot be construed as "adopting pendent-party jurisdiction." That, of course, is always the predicate for the question whether a federal court may rely on the doctrine of ancillary or pendent jurisdiction to fill a gap in the relevant jurisdictional statute. If the Court's demonstration were controlling, *Gibbs*, Hurn, and Moore, as well as a good many other cases, were incorrectly decided.[12]

In Aldinger, we adopted a Rule of construction that assumed the existence of pendent jurisdiction unless "Congress in the statutes conferring jurisdiction has . . . expressly or by implication negated its existence." We rejected the

12. [Footnote 26 in Justice Stevens's dissent.] The Court is mistaken in asserting that this approach is somehow inconsistent with the principle that a court does not have subject-matter jurisdiction over an action unless an Act of Congress has supplied it. The District Court clearly had jurisdiction over this case, and the only question is the scope of its authority to consider specific claims.

assertion of pendent-party jurisdiction there because it arose "not in the context of congressional silence or tacit encouragement, but in quite the opposite context." Congress' exclusion of municipal corporations from the definition of persons under § 1983, we concluded, evinced an intent to preclude the exercise of federal-court jurisdiction over them. If congressional silence were sufficient to defeat pendent jurisdiction, the careful reasoning in our *Aldinger* opinion was wholly unnecessary, for obviously the civil rights statutes do not affirmatively authorize the joinder of any state-law claims.

A similar approach, focusing on a legislative intent to bar a party from federal court, guided our analysis in Zahn v. International Paper Co., and *Owen Equipment & Erection Co. v. Kroger.* In Zahn, we surveyed the "firmly rooted" law that "multiple plaintiffs with separate and distinct claims must each satisfy the jurisdictional-amount requirement for suit in federal courts," and refused to adopt a Rule that would allow putative plaintiffs who could not meet the jurisdictional amount to assert claims pendent to jurisdictionally sufficient claims. We noted that adoption of such a Rule "would undermine the purpose and intent of Congress in providing that plaintiffs in diversity cases must present claims in excess of the specified jurisdictional amount" and would depart from "the historic construction of the jurisdictional statutes, left undisturbed by Congress over these many years." In Kroger, the Rule at issue was the requirement that a plaintiff invoking diversity jurisdiction plead complete diversity. After noting the historical evidence demonstrating "a congressional mandate that diversity jurisdiction is not to be available when any plaintiff is a citizen of the same State as any defendant," we held that that jurisdictional requirement could not be circumvented through the exercise of pendent jurisdiction.

The Court today adopts a sharply different approach. Without even so much as acknowledging our statement in *Aldinger* that before a federal court may exercise pendent-party jurisdiction it must satisfy itself that Congress "has not expressly or by implication negated its existence," it now instructs that "a grant of jurisdiction over claims involving particular parties does not itself confer jurisdiction over additional claims by or against different parties." This Rule, the Court asserts, is necessary to provide Congress "a background of clear interpretative Rules" and to avoid sowing confusion. But as a method of statutory interpretation, the Court's approach is neither clear nor faithful to our judicial obligation to discern congressional intent. While with respect to the joinder of additional defendants on pendent state claims, the Court's mandate is now clear, its approach offers little guidance with respect to the many other claims that a court must address in the course of deciding a constitutional case. Because the Court provides no reason why the joinder of pendent defendants over whom there is no other basis of federal jurisdiction should differ from the joinder of pendent claims and other pendent parties, I fear that its approach will confuse more than it clarifies.

How much more clear to assume — especially when the courts have long so held — that with respect to all of these situations Congress intended the Federal Rules to govern unless Congress has indicated otherwise.

The Court's focus on diversity cases may explain why it also loses sight of the purpose behind the principle of pendent jurisdiction. The doctrine of pendent jurisdiction rests in part on a recognition that forcing a federal plaintiff to litigate his or her case in both federal and state courts impairs the ability of the federal court to grant full relief, and "imparts a fundamental bias against utilization of the federal forum owing to the deterrent effect imposed by the needless requirement of duplicate litigation if the federal forum is chosen." "The courts, by recognizing pendent jurisdiction, are effectuating Congress' decision to provide the plaintiff with a federal forum for litigating a jurisdictionally sufficient claim." This is especially the case when, by virtue of the grant of exclusive federal jurisdiction, "only in a federal court may all of the claims be tried together." In such circumstances, in which Congress has unequivocally indicated its intent that the federal right be litigated in a federal forum, there is reason to believe that Congress did not intend that the substance of the federal right be diminished by the increased costs in efficiency and convenience of litigation in two forums. No such special federal interest is present when federal jurisdiction is invoked on the basis of the diverse citizenship of the parties and the state-law claims may be litigated in a state forum. To be sure "[w]hatever we say regarding the scope of jurisdiction conferred by a particular statute can . . . be changed by Congress," but that does not relieve us of our responsibility to be faithful to the congressional design. The Court is quite incorrect to presume that because Congress did not sanction the exercise of pendent-party jurisdiction in the diversity context, it has not permitted its exercise with respect to claims within the exclusive federal jurisdiction.

* * * *

DISCUSSION AND QUESTIONS

Dueling interpretive principles. Justice Scalia begins his analysis by asserting the "rudimentary" proposition that a constitutional grant of federal court jurisdiction remains "dormant" until Congress implements that grant through legislation. As we learned in Chapter 5, the proposition is unassailable. Justice Scalia then notes it is also "well established" in Court precedent that supplemental jurisdiction exists over factually related *claims*, even though this precedent fails to address the issue of congressional authorization. Justice Scalia is unwilling to challenge Court precedent, apparently in deference to the principle of stare decisis.

Justice Scalia is willing to assume that the constitutional case-or-controversy standard announced in *Gibbs* applies equally to the joinder of additional parties as well as claims. But he is unwilling to extend *Gibbs* to pendent parties without congressional authorization. He rejects the contention that judicial efficiency and litigant economy alone justify extending *Gibbs*, even if this means plaintiffs like Finley must split their tort litigation between federal and state courts. (Do you understand why separate suits are the result of the Court's ruling in *Finley*?) Justice Scalia requires proof that Congress expressly or impliedly authorized pendent-party jurisdiction in suits under the FTCA, and he finds no such proof. A change in the FTCA's jurisdictional language from the authorization of "claims" to the authorization of "civil actions on claims" is not sufficient. To the contrary, the fact that Congress revised this jurisdictional language in 1948 undermines the plaintiffs' contention, since *Gibbs* was decided almost 20 years later and the doctrine of pendent-party jurisdiction was in a nascent stage.

Is Justice Scalia's analysis persuasive? Did not *Gibbs* overlook the question of congressional authorization of supplemental jurisdiction? At the same time, does the majority show proper respect for the constitutional role of Congress in requiring statutory support for novel applications of supplemental jurisdiction? By requiring congressional authorization of pendent-party jurisdiction while excusing *Gibbs*'s failure to require such authorization for pendent claims, did Justice Scalia speak "out of both sides of his mouth"?[13]

Justice Blackmun, dissenting, observes that a party asserting supplemental jurisdiction will inevitably fail the Court's new requirement of congressional authorization, since evidence that Congress authorized supplemental jurisdiction would effectively moot a party's need to rely on the judicially developed doctrine. Do you agree? In any event, does Justice Blackmun justify his interpretive presumption that, absent indication that Congress would oppose the use of supplemental jurisdiction, such use is proper? Can this presumption be squared with the long-standing requirement that Congress must authorize exercise of federal court jurisdiction? Was the Court's *de facto* use of this presumption in prior cases (e.g., *Aldinger, Zahn,* and *Kroger*) a sufficient justification for extending that presumption to the exercise of pendent-party jurisdiction? Consider that the Court has permitted exercise of ancillary jurisdiction throughout the twentieth century, apparently without congressional authorization. Does this further support Justice Blackmun's presumption?

Justice Stevens's dissenting opinion sharply criticizes the majority on every point. First, he finds that "by enacting the Federal Tort Claims Act (FTCA) in 1946, Congress unquestionably authorized the United States District Court to accept jurisdiction of "civil actions on claims against the United States." Based on this language, Justice Stevens finds it "perfectly clear" that Congress authorized jurisdiction beyond the mere assertion of claims against the United States itself. In a related, but somewhat different argument, Justice Stevens also challenges Justice Scalia's view that the long-standing principle requiring congressional authorization of jurisdiction necessitates authorization of supplemental jurisdiction in particular. According to Justice Stevens, the constitutional requirement of congressional authorization is satisfied by the grant of jurisdiction contained in the FTCA—supplemental jurisdiction properly derives from that grant and does not require its own specific authorization.

Which justice's view of the required congressional authorization do you find most persuasive? Is it simply a question of how specific statutory authorization must be? Has one justice trivialized the constitutional requirement of congressional authorization? Which one?

Justice Stevens also emphasizes that jurisdiction under the FTCA is exclusive, and the majority's ruling results in duplicative litigation in federal and state court. He is willing to attribute a more practical, sensible intent to Congress permitting consolidated litigation in federal court. Do you agree with Justice Stevens's pragmatism, or has he invoked policy arguments to justify usurpation of congressional control over federal jurisdiction?

c. Congress Responds to the Court

In *Finley*, Justice Scalia invited Congress to express its intent about the federal courts' power to exercise supplemental jurisdiction. In 1990 Congress swiftly responded by enacting 28 U.S.C. § 1367. Subsection (a) of this statute provides:

13. Richard D. Freer, *Compounding Confusion and Hampering Diversity: Life After* Finley *and the Supplemental Jurisdiction Act,* 40 Emory L.J. 445, 466 (1991).

> Except as provided in subsections (b) and (c) or as expressly provided otherwise by Federal statute, in any civil action of which the district courts have original jurisdiction, the district courts shall have supplemental jurisdiction over all other claims that are so related to claims in the action within such original jurisdiction that they form part of the same case or controversy under Article III of the United States Constitution. Such supplemental jurisdiction shall include claims that involve the joinder or intervention of additional parties.

Section 1367(a) accomplishes several things:

- it authorizes the exercise of supplemental jurisdiction "in *any* civil action of which the district courts have original jurisdiction";
- it authorizes such jurisdiction when supplemental claims are part of "the same case or controversy" within the meaning of the Constitution, a likely reference to the *Gibbs* standard of constitutionality;[14] and
- it extends supplemental jurisdiction to the joinder or intervention of "additional parties," indicating that the former doctrine of "pendent party" jurisdiction is no less permissible than pendent claim or ancillary jurisdiction.

At the same time, § 1367(b) signals Congress' rejection of many uses of supplemental jurisdiction that would undermine the traditional requirements for diversity of citizenship. When a federal court's jurisdiction is based solely on 28 U.S.C. § 1332, plaintiffs cannot assert claims against persons "made parties" under Federal Rule 14 (impleader), Rule 19 (necessary parties), Rule 20 (joinder of defendants), or Rule 24 (intervention) if complete diversity would be destroyed. Nor can a court assert supplemental jurisdiction over plaintiffs joined under Rule 19 or seeking to intervene under Rule 24 if complete diversity would be destroyed.

Section 1367(b)'s restrictions on supplement jurisdiction in diversity cases are inartfully drafted, as members of the Court have remarked. Without delving into the varied applications of § 1367(b), we point out one significant Court interpretation that actually *expands* the traditional scope of diversity jurisdiction. In *Exxon Mobil Corp. v. Allapatah Services, Inc.*, 545 U.S. 546 (2005), a 5-4 Court concluded that supplemental jurisdiction modifies the traditional rule that usually requires *each* plaintiff to satisfy the amount-in-controversy requirement of the diversity statute. As the Court held in *Allapatah Services*, "where the other elements of jurisdiction are present and at least one named plaintiff in the action satisfies the amount-in-controversy requirement, § 1367 does authorize supplemental jurisdiction over the claims of other plaintiffs in the same Article III case or controversy, even if those claims are for less than the jurisdictional amount specified in the statute setting forth the requirements for diversity jurisdiction." *Id.* at 549. The Court's ruling overturns its prior decision in *Zahn v. International Paper Co.*, 414 U.S. 291 (1973). The Court also indicated that § 1367(b)'s relaxation of the amount-in-controversy requirement applies to both the joinder of plaintiffs under Rule 20 and class actions under Rule 23.

Section 1367(c) reaffirms much of the Court's opinion in *Gibbs* recognizing lower court discretion to dismiss supplemental claims in appropriate

14. *See City of Chicago v. International Coll. of Surgeons*, 522 U.S. 156, 172-73 (1997).

circumstances.[15] Thus, a court may decline to exercise jurisdiction over supplemental claims when "(1) the claim raises a novel or complex issue of State law, (2) the claim substantially predominates over the claim or claims over which the district court has original jurisdiction, (3) the district court has dismissed all claims over which it has original jurisdiction, or (4) in exceptional circumstances, there are other compelling reasons for declining jurisdiction." Beyond the listing of these factors, Congress gave courts little assistance in determining whether to exercise discretion to dismiss supplemental claims. Questions yet to be finally resolved include, if one of the enumerated factors is present, must a federal court dismiss supplemental claims? And may a court go beyond the enumerated statutory factors and incorporate other, so-called *Gibbs* factors, which include "considerations of judicial economy, convenience and fairness to litigants"? *See generally* CHARLES ALLEN WRIGHT, ARTHUR R. MILLER, & EDWARD H. COOPER, 6 FEDERAL PRACTICE AND PROCEDURE § 3523.1 (2014).

In *Carlsbad Technology Inc. v. HIF Bio, Inc.*, 556 U.S. 635 (2009), the Supreme Court held that, when a district court declines to exercise jurisdiction over supplemental state claims otherwise within its power under § 1367, that decision may be appealed. The prohibition found in 28 U.S.C. § 1447(d) — precluding the appeal of remand orders based on the federal court's lack of subject matter jurisdiction — is not applicable when a district court exercises its discretionary power to remand state claims under § 1367(c). But because the district court's decision to remand is discretionary, the appeal may be limited to the issue whether the court "abused" its discretion. *Id.* at 644 (Breyer, J., concurring).

d. Integrating Supplemental Jurisdiction and Federal Procedural Rules

We have seen how *Gibbs* and § 1367 affirm a constitutional definition of a case or controversy that requires sufficient factual relationship between the federal and state components of a lawsuit. In affirming this definition of a constitutional case, the Court implicitly rejected Chief Justice Marshall's more expansive definition in *Osborn v. Bank of the United States,* which arguably would empower federal courts to entertain all claims properly joined under the federal rules provided the required federal "ingredient" was present.[16]

Since 1938, the Federal Rules of Civil Procedure have provided an independent framework for determining what claims may be asserted in a federal court suit. These Rules, as you learned in Civil Procedure, dictate what claims and parties may be asserted in a "civil action" filed in federal court. But as you also learned in Civil Procedure, the Federal Rules do not "extend or limit" federal subject matter jurisdiction. Fed. R. Civ. P. 82. Consequently, the joinder of claims and parties in a federal civil action requires consideration of two factors: (1) does a federal rule permit joinder, and (2) does the joined claim or party satisfy jurisdictional requirements?

To help us explore the implementation of federal joinder rules in the context of supplemental jurisdiction, we again focus on the very common situation in federal court litigation where the complaint alleges at least one claim arising

15. *See id.* at 173.
16. See Chapter 5.

under federal law and a party attempts to join a nonfederal claim.[17] This is the historical context for most of the Court's decisions addressing the scope of a constitutional case and, as mentioned earlier, has the virtue of rendering a challenging body of jurisdictional law more manageable for our specific purposes.[18]

You will recall from Chapter 5 that the great majority of claims arising under federal law are based on a federal statute giving the plaintiff both a right and a remedy. As alleged in a federal complaint, this combined right-remedy takes the form of a claim or count. You will also recall that neither the defendant's defenses nor her counterclaims matter when determining whether the plaintiff's well-pleaded complaint arises under federal law. But the question we now address is not whether the plaintiff's federal claim arises under federal law—that is a given in the scenarios described below—but whether other claims, both plaintiffs' and defendants', are part of the same constitutional case as the federal claim. In addressing the jurisdictional question, analysis must be *claim specific.* Each claim must be assessed as an independent "unit" of litigation in determining the proper scope of supplemental jurisdiction when a federal claim is present.

i. The Plaintiff's Perspective[19]

Joinder of claims. After a federal plaintiff alleges a federal claim against the defendant, she is permitted to join any other claim she "has" against her opponent. Rule 18(a) requires no factual relatedness between the added claim and the foundational federal claim. But since procedural rules cannot enhance a court's jurisdiction, additional claims must also be supported by a jurisdictional statute. If the added claim itself arises under federal law, the jurisdictional requirement is satisfied (i.e., jurisdiction can be based on 28 U.S.C. § 1331). But if the claim arises solely under state law, supplemental jurisdiction under § 1367 is needed. Such supplemental jurisdiction, as *Gibbs* tells us, requires that a non-federal claim have a sufficient factual relationship to a federal claim (it must arise from a "common nucleus of operative fact"). For example, if the plaintiff asserts a federal constitutional claim against a police officer for excessive force, she can assert a state-law claim against that same officer for assault and battery. Given the factual relationship between the two claims, they constitute one constitutional case. Such "parallel" claims are very common in litigation given the overlapping regulatory powers of federal and state government.

17. Court statistics for 2012-2013 indicate that arising under jurisdiction is the basis for about 62 percent of private civil suits filed in federal court. http://www.uscourts.gov/uscourts/Statistics/JudicialBusiness/2013/appendices/C02Sep13.pdf.

18. We thus avoid addressing many of the complex issues that arise when supplemental jurisdiction is asserted in a case based solely on diversity-of-citizenship jurisdiction. As previously noted, § 1367(b) signals Congress' intent that diversity cases be subject to special limitations that do not apply when jurisdiction is based on other forms of original jurisdiction.

19. In discussing whether a party can join claims or parties, it helps to "construct" a suit from the bottom up, with the "bottom" being a single federal claim against a single defendant. In actual practice, of course, the construction is usually done simultaneously in the drafting of a single pleading (the complaint or the answer) containing all of a party's claims. So, our step-by-step construction of the federal suit does not imply that a litigant is literally joining additional claims through a series of procedural actions.

Joinder of parties. Rule 20 governs the joinder of additional parties, whether additional plaintiffs or defendants. Unlike Rule 18, Rule 20 requires a factual relationship when new parties are joined. In the case of additional plaintiffs, the second plaintiff must assert a claim that arises "out of the same transaction, occurrence or series of transactions or occurrences" as *some* claim asserted by the first plaintiff. In addition, the claim by the second plaintiff must present "a question of law or fact" common to both plaintiffs. The same analysis applies when a plaintiff seeks to add a second defendant. That is, the plaintiff must show that she is asserting a claim against the second defendant factually related to her claim against the first defendant as the relationship is defined by Rule 20.

If the claim asserted by a second plaintiff, or the claim asserted against a second defendant, arises under federal law, then supplemental jurisdiction is unnecessary. But similar to the joinder of nonfederal claims under Rule 18, the joinder of a party whose dispute is based on state law must rely on supplemental jurisdiction. This means that the claim asserted by the second plaintiff, or the claim asserted against the second defendant, must arise from a "common nucleus of operative fact" as a *federal* claim asserted against another party.[20] For example, if the first plaintiff asserts a federal statutory claim against her employer for sexual harassment, she would be permitted to join as second defendant a job supervisor who has been sued because behavior factually related to the harassment constitutes a battery under state law. But she would not be permitted to join as second defendant a co-employee who owed her money (a contract claim under state law), because the claim would satisfy neither Rule 20 nor supplemental jurisdiction. Stated in another way, the claim against her co-employee is not part of the same constitutional case as the federal claim against her employer for sexual harassment.

Because Rule 20 has its own requirement of factual relatedness, it might seem that the proper joinder of an additional plaintiff or defendant rather automatically indicates that supplemental jurisdiction exists. In fact, one court has observed that, not only is the test for supplemental jurisdiction "similar to the transaction and common question requirements of Rule 20," "the jurisdictional sweep may be *broader* than the Rule." *Travelers Ins. Co. v. Intraco, Inc.* 163 F.R.D. 554, 557 (S.D. Iowa 1995) (emphasis added).[21] But one caveat is in order. Rule 20 requires a factual relationship only between (1) a claim asserted by or against the joined party and (2) "a" claim asserted by or against an existing party. It is possible, for example, that Rule 20 can be satisfied if the original plaintiff asserts a state claim against a second defendant that is factually related to a *state* claim already asserted against the first defendant (rather than being related to a federal claim asserted against the first defendant). Consequently, even though the factual relationship required by Rule 20 may be more demanding than that required by supplemental jurisdiction, it is still important to verify that there is a sufficient factual relationship with an existing *federal* claim. This is another manifestation of the principle that jurisdiction is claim-specific.

Cumulative use of joinder rules. Once an additional plaintiff or defendant is joined in a suit, Rule 18's liberal authorization of the joinder of claims is

20. Note that § 1367(b) specifically forbids a plaintiff from using supplemental jurisdiction to join a second defendant in a *diversity of citizenship* suit.

21. *See also Fidelity Nat'l Title Co. v. U.S. Small Bus. Admin.*, 2014 WL 1883939 (E.D. Cal. May 12, 2014) (noting that some federal circuits conclude that certain permissive counterclaims can be considered under a court's supplemental jurisdiction power).

available to any party seeking relief. For example, the plaintiff may assert *all* claims she has against a second defendant properly joined in the suit, in addition to the factually related claim that supported joinder of the defendant under Rule 20. It also means that a second plaintiff can assert any claims he has against the defendant, besides the claim that supports the second plaintiff's joinder under Rule 20. As always, each claim asserted must have jurisdictional support.

In practice, the joint operation of joinder rules and supplemental jurisdiction often become intuitive to counsel. But since that day has not yet arrived for most students, we will work through a few sample problems.

PROBLEM 7-2

Trouble on the Job

Khadija Mustafa was an accomplished translator who worked for a company, Far Horizons, that facilitates international business between American companies and companies in the Middle East. Khadija, an expatriate from Iran, is a practicing Shiite Muslim, as are a few other employees of Far Horizons.

A few years ago, Khadija began working for a new job supervisor, Abd al-Rahman. Al-Rahman is a native of Saudi Arabia and a Sunni Muslim. At the beginning of their working relationship, Khadija and al-Rahman worked well together. Since both were single, they even socialized together on occasion. But later their relationship deteriorated, and Khadija was terminated by Far Horizons.

Khadija has filed a federal suit against Far Horizons, al-Rahman, and Corporate Benefits, Inc. (CBI). In her complaint she alleges these claims:

1. a federal claim for religious discrimination against Far Horizons, based on allegations the company terminated her at the behest of al-Rahman, who in turn was motivated by antipathy toward Khadija's religious affiliation;
2. a state claim for religious discrimination against Far Horizons, based on state law that provides protections similar to those found in federal law;
3. a state claim against al-Rahman for tortious interference with a business relationship, based on allegations al-Rahman maliciously induced Far Horizons to terminate her;
4. another state claim against al-Rahman for assault and battery, based on allegations he improperly touched Khadija when they were socializing several months before her termination (this incident was apparently the catalyst for deteriorating relations between the two);
5. a state claim against Far Horizons for breach of contract, based on allegations it failed to pay her accrued vacation pay when she was terminated; and,
6. a state claim against CBI for violation of its fiduciary duty as custodian of her employer's benefits plan, based on allegations CBI improperly advised Far Horizons it should not pay Khadija her accrued vacation pay.[22]

From the outset of the suit, Khadija's lawyer has been aware that state law prohibiting religious discrimination arguably does not apply to small

22. Ignore the fact that federal law might govern CBI's legal duties.

employers like Far Horizons. She hopes this important issue will be resolved in Khadija's suit.

Discuss all plausible strategies the defendants might use to have some or all of Khadija's claims dismissed.

---

ii. The Defendant's Perspective

Counterclaims. Federal joinder rules take a very even-handed approach to litigants, whether they are formally styled plaintiffs or defendants. A defendant, for example, is not frozen into the defensive role but shares the plaintiff's procedural option of seeking relief through the assertion of claims and joinder of parties. Such a defendant also shares the plaintiff's obligation to show that each of his claims is supported by a jurisdictional statute. *See* Fed. R. Civ. P. 8(a) (requiring that a party allege the jurisdictional basis for all forms of claims).

The most common claim asserted by a defendant is the counterclaim. As you learned in Civil Procedure, Rule 13 recognizes both "compulsory" and "permissive" counterclaims. A compulsory counterclaim under Rule 13(a) must be asserted (with some exceptions) or else the defendant will be prevented from asserting the underlying claim in a later suit. There is no obligation to assert a permissive counterclaim under Rule 13(b), so the defendant's decision to assert such a counterclaim is determined largely by litigation strategy and efficiency—and, in federal court, jurisdiction.

The compulsory counterclaim Rule, like Rule 20 authorizing joinder of parties, requires an element of factual relatedness between claims. Specifically, a compulsory counterclaim "arises out of the transaction or occurrence that is the subject matter of the opposing party's claim." Fed. R. Civ. P. 13(a). Rule 13(a)'s language referring to factual commonality seems highly similar to the *Gibbs* standard for supplemental jurisdiction, which requires a "common nucleus of operative fact." Leading commentators on federal practice conclude that "supplemental jurisdiction permits courts to hear compulsory counterclaims, under Rule 13(a), but permissive counterclaims, under Rule 13(b), require independent jurisdictional grounds." CHARLES ALAN WRIGHT & MARY KAY KANE, 20 FEDERAL PRACTICE & PROCEDURE DESKBOOK § 10 (2013). This view is often taught to students in Civil Procedure.

But some federal courts disagree that all permissive counterclaims necessarily fail to satisfy supplemental jurisdiction. According to some courts, a permissive counterclaim—which by definition does not arise from the same transaction or occurrence as an opponent's claim—may nonetheless be part of the same case or controversy as an opponent's claim. Shortly we will consider a line of decisions that take this position and scrutinize whether a permissive counterclaim can arise out of a common nucleus of operative fact even though it does not arise out of the same "transaction or occurrence" as the opponent's claim. Before we do, we will complete our overview of some of the more important joinder devices that might qualify for supplemental jurisdiction.

Crossclaims. Rule 13(g) authorizes crossclaims between co-plaintiffs or co-defendants "if the claim arises out of the transaction or occurrence that is the subject matter of the original action or of a counterclaim." As with compulsory counterclaims, the factual relationship required by Rule 13(g) leads most commentators to conclude that crossclaims almost inevitably satisfy supplemental jurisdiction requirements. *See* Wright & Kay, *supra.*

Third-party claims. Rule 14 permits a "defending party" to add an additional party as a "third-party defendant" when the third party "is or may be liable to it for all or part of the claim against" the defending party. This is the joinder device known as "impleader." By its nature, an impleader action joins a third-party defendant to defray liability that might result from a claim already alleged in a pending federal suit. And any such alleged claim must itself have a jurisdictional foundation. Consequently, third-party claims derivative of claims pending in a federal suit should qualify for supplemental jurisdiction.[23]

Permissive joinder of additional claims. Many of the counter-offensive devices like compulsory counterclaims, crossclaims, and third-party claims require a factual relationship with existing claims. For that reason, supplemental jurisdiction will usually permit a federal court to hear those counter-offensive claims (assuming they do not satisfy some other jurisdictional basis like arising under jurisdiction). Why? Because the existing claims to which the new claims are related must themselves have a jurisdictional foundation.[24] Thus, the constitutional case can branch out through the joinder of factually related state-law claims.

However, a party asserting a counterclaim, a crossclaim, or a third-party claim shares with the plaintiff the right to join *any* other claims the pleader has against an adversary. *See* Fed. R. Civ. P. 18(a). Rule 18 thus invites defending parties to join further claims that might not satisfy requirements for supplemental jurisdiction. Consequently, defending parties attempting to join additional claims under Rule 18 must, like the plaintiff, verify that the additional claims have jurisdictional support.

Other forms of party joinder available to defending parties.[25] As mentioned, federal joinder Rules are evenhanded. Consequently, just as a plaintiff may add co-plaintiffs or additional defendants under Rule 20, so may defending parties who assert counterclaims or crossclaims. *See* Fed. R. Civ. P. 13(h). When they do, the same analysis of joinder Rules and jurisdiction previously discussed would apply.[26]

The best way to reaffirm your understanding of these sometimes abstract joinder devices is to apply them in a discrete fact setting. Consider Problem 7-3.

23. *See, e.g., Olan Mills Inc., v. Hy-Vee Food Stores, Inc.*, 731 F. Supp. 1416, 1420-21 (N.D. Iowa 1990). Once a third-party defendant is joined, Rule 14 authorizes the assertion of a variety of claims among the new assembly of parties. Those claims, too, require a jurisdictional foundation like supplemental jurisdiction. Notice that § 1367(b) specifically denies supplemental jurisdiction over a *plaintiff*'s claims against the third-party defendant when original jurisdiction is based on diversity of citizenship.

24. Recall that our discussion addresses supplemental jurisdiction where the foundational claim is a federal claim. Cases based on diversity of citizenship require a different analysis.

25. Still other potential uses of supplemental jurisdiction include Rule 22 interpleader, Rule 23 class actions, and Rule 24 intervention. We defer treatment of these challenging joinder devices to other courses like Complex Litigation.

26. Rule 13(h) also gives counterclaimants and crossclaimants the same right as plaintiffs to use Rule 19 to compel the joinder of necessary or indispensable parties. When such parties are added in federal question cases, supplemental jurisdiction is available. However, § 1367(b) prohibits a plaintiff's use of supplemental jurisdiction to join Rule 19 parties.

PROBLEM 7-3

Far Horizon's Counter-Offensive

Recall that, in Problem 7-2, Khadija has sued her employer, Far Horizons, for religious discrimination and its failure to pay accrued vacation earnings.

Several months after the suit was filed, Far Horizons moved to amend its answer to include a new counterclaim. It alleges that Khadija and three other ex-employees "converted" office supplies by taking them home after work. The allegedly converted office supplies include pens, paper, printer ink cartridges etc. In addition to seeking permission to add this counterclaim against Khadija, Far Horizons also seeks permission to join the other ex-employees as defendants to the counterclaim for conversion.

Discuss any grounds on which Khadija might object to Far Horizon's motion to amend.

e. Counterclaims and Supplemental Jurisdiction — a Constitutional Borderland?

Now that we have surveyed many of the more common joinder devices where supplemental jurisdiction may prove important, we return to the question posed earlier. Can a permissive counterclaim, which by definition does not arise from the same transaction or occurrence as the plaintiff's claim, nonetheless be part of the same constitutional case as the plaintiff's claim? Or is conventional wisdom, namely, that Rule 13's division of compulsory and permissive counterclaims corresponds to a division between claims falling within, or without, a federal court's supplemental jurisdiction, correct?

As you read *Sparrow v. Mazda American Credit*, consider the court's explanation of how § 1367 expands federal jurisdiction to include some forms of permissive counterclaims. In addition, consider the court's analysis of another important issue presented when courts implement supplemental jurisdiction — what "exceptional circumstances" permit a court to dismiss state claims despite the existence of supplemental jurisdiction?

SPARROW v. MAZDA AMERICAN CREDIT

385 F. Supp. 2d 1063 (E.D. Cal. 2005)

* * * *

This case arises out of Plaintiff's allegation that Defendant violated state and federal law by engaging in abusive practices in its attempts to collect a debt from Plaintiff. Cal. Civ.Code §§ 1788 et seq. (Rosenthal Fair Debt Collection Practices Act ("RFDCPA")); 15 U.S.C. §§ 1692, et seq. (Fair Debt Collection Practices Act ("FDCPA")). Plaintiff filed the original complaint in the Superior Court of the State of California. . . . [Defendant then removed to federal court and filed counterclaims for breach of contract and to recover the underlying debt owed by Plaintiff.] Plaintiff argues that Defendant's counterclaims are not compulsory and that therefore, this court does not have supplemental jurisdiction over them. Defendant filed opposition to Plaintiff's motion, arguing that its counterclaims are compulsory and that supplemental jurisdiction exists.

III. Legal Standard

"It is a fundamental precept that federal courts are courts of limited jurisdiction." Federal courts have original jurisdiction over all civil actions "arising under the Constitution, laws, or treatises of the United States" and in all civil actions where complete diversity of citizenship exists and the amount in controversy exceeds $75,000. 28 U.S.C. §§ 1331, 1332. Here, while original jurisdiction exists over Plaintiff's claims under the FDCPA, which was created by federal law, original jurisdiction does not exist over Defendant's state-law counterclaims. Diversity jurisdiction cannot provide an independent jurisdictional basis for Defendant's counterclaims because the amount Defendant is claiming is not over $75,000, as 28 U.S.C. § 1332 requires. The only basis for jurisdiction over Defendant's counterclaims is the supplemental jurisdiction statute, 28 U.S.C. § 1367.

Plaintiff moves to dismiss Defendant's state law counterclaims for lack of subject matter jurisdiction on the basis that supplemental jurisdiction over those claims is improper. Plaintiff moves under Rule 12(b)(1) of the Federal Rules of Civil Procedure, which allows a party to move to dismiss a claim or counterclaim for lack of subject matter jurisdiction. Once a party challenges subject matter jurisdiction, the non-moving party bears the burden to establish that subject matter jurisdiction exists. The supplemental jurisdiction statute, 28 U.S.C. § 1367, grants federal courts supplemental jurisdiction over claims over which no original jurisdiction exists. Section 1367(a) grants supplemental jurisdiction over state law counterclaims "that are so related to claims in the action within such original jurisdiction that they form part of the same case or controversy under Article III of the United States Constitution." Section 1367 applies to state law claims brought by a plaintiff as well as to counterclaims brought by a defendant.

Rule 13 of the Federal Rules of Civil Procedure defines two types of counterclaims: compulsory and permissive. "Compulsory" counterclaims are claims that "arise[ ] out of the transaction or occurrence that is the subject matter of the opposing party's claim." Fed. R. Civ. P. 13(a). The Ninth Circuit applies a "logical relationship test" to determine whether a counterclaim is compulsory. Under this test, the court "analyze[s] whether the essential facts of the various claims are so logically connected that considerations of judicial economy and fairness dictate that all the issues be resolved in one lawsuit." If a defendant fails to bring a compulsory counterclaim, he is barred from asserting that claim in a future proceeding. Fed. R. Civ. P. 13(a). The traditional Rule is that federal courts have supplemental jurisdiction over compulsory counterclaims, since a plaintiff would otherwise lose his opportunity to be heard on that claim.

All counterclaims that are not compulsory are "permissive." Permissive counterclaims are claims that do "not aris[e] out of the transaction or occurrence that is the subject matter of the opposing party's claim." Fed. R. Civ. P. 13(b). Before 1990, when Congress enacted the supplemental jurisdiction statute, the Rule was clear that federal courts did not have jurisdiction over permissive counterclaims absent an independent basis for federal subject matter jurisdiction. After Congress enacted 28 U.S.C. § 1367, however, at least two circuits (the

Seventh and the Second) have held that a federal court may exercise supplemental jurisdiction over certain permissive counterclaims. Channell, 89 F.3d at 384; Rothman v. Emory Univ., 123 F.3d 446, 454 (7th Cir.1997); Jones, 358 F.3d at 212-13. These courts have altogether abandoned the analysis for determining whether supplemental jurisdiction exists based on whether a counterclaim is compulsory or permissive. *See, e.g.*, Adams St. Joint Venture, 231 F. Supp. 2d at 761-62; Jones, 358 F.3d at 212-13. These courts reason that the issue whether supplemental jurisdiction exists over counterclaims is determined by the language of § 1367 alone. In other words, whether supplemental jurisdiction exists over a counterclaim depends on whether the state counterclaim and the federal claim are "so related . . . that they form part of the same case or controversy under Article III of the United States Constitution."

The language of § 1367 derives from the test for supplemental jurisdiction as stated in Mine Workers v. Gibbs, in which the Supreme Court held that federal courts have supplemental jurisdiction over a state law claim where the state claim and the federal claim "derive from a common nucleus of operative fact," such that "the relationship between [the federal] claim and the state claim permits the conclusion that the entire action before the court comprises but one constitutional 'case.'" By definition, compulsory counterclaims "form part of the same [Article III] case or controversy" as the federal claims since compulsory counterclaims "arise out of the same transaction or occurrence" as the primary claims. The § 1367 test for supplemental jurisdiction is broader than the test for compulsory counterclaims, so counterclaims that are compulsory under the "same transaction or occurrence" test automatically pass the § 1367 "same Article III case or controversy" test.

The difficulty with the traditional Rule arises when the § 1367 supplemental jurisdiction analysis is applied to permissive counterclaims. The § 1367 same case or controversy test is clearly broader than the "same transaction or occurrence" test for compulsory counterclaims, but the § 1367 test also appears to be broader than the test for permissive counterclaims. The test for permissive counterclaims is that the state law claim does not arise out of the same transaction or occurrence as the federal claim. However, just because a state law claim does not arise out of the same transaction or occurrence as the federal law claim does not mean that the state law claim does not arise out of facts that bear some relationship to the facts from which the federal claim arises so that the state claim and the federal claim are considered part of the same constitutional "case."

The Ninth Circuit does not appear to have explicitly addressed the issue whether the compulsory/permissive counterclaim analysis should be abandoned altogether. The Ninth Circuit did cite the Seventh Circuit's *Channell* decision with approval in CE Distrib., LLC v. New Sensor Corp., 380 F.3d 1107, 1114 (9th Cir. 2004). The issue in *CE Distrib.*, however, involved a question of pendent personal jurisdiction, and did not address supplemental subject matter jurisdiction.

IV. Analysis[27]

Whether supplemental jurisdiction can be exercised over Defendant's counterclaims under § 1367 is a question of law. In this case, if Defendant's

27. The court inadvertently labeled both the "legal standard" and "analysis" sections as section "III."

counterclaims are compulsory, supplemental jurisdiction exists and the inquiry ends. If, however, Defendant's counterclaims are permissive, the question is whether supplemental jurisdiction exists over those claims under § 1367(a). If yes, the next question is whether the court should exercise its discretion to decline to assert supplemental jurisdiction over those claims.

A. WHETHER DEFENDANT'S COUNTERCLAIMS ARE COMPULSORY

The first question is whether Defendant's counterclaims for the debt underlying Plaintiff's unfair collection practices claims are compulsory. Several courts have considered the question whether a claim for the underlying debt in an action originally brought by the plaintiff under the FDCPA is a compulsory counterclaim under Rule 13(a). Plaintiff cites two published cases holding that counterclaims for the underlying debt are not compulsory. Leatherwood v. Universal Bus. Serv. Co., 115 F.R.D. 48 (W.D.N.Y. 1987); Hart v. Clayton-Parker and Assoc., Inc., 869 F. Supp. 774 (D. Ariz. 1994). Another district court in the Ninth Circuit has held the same. Taylor v. Bryant, Inc., 275 F. Supp. 2d 1305 (D. Nev. 2003). These courts reason that breach of contract counterclaims for the underlying debt are not "logically connected" to the unfair-collection-practices claim, despite that they both relate to the same debt. While the debt does provide some factual connection between the claims, because they arise out of the debt, the legal issues and evidence relating to the claims are considered sufficiently distinct so as not to meet the logical-relationship test.

This reasoning may, on the surface, seem contrary to the logical-relationship test for compulsory counterclaims. Nevertheless, this reasoning has its source in three overlapping inquiries and policy concerns identified in Leatherwood. First, the Leatherwood court noted that the issues raised by the FDCPA claim and the counterclaim for the debt are distinct:

> The [FDCPA claim] relates to the application of the FDCPA and focuses on a narrow realm of facts concerning the use of abusive, deceptive and/or unfair debt collection practices by the defendants. On the other hand, [the defendant's] counterclaim encompasses a private duty under state law and requires a broad proof of facts establishing the existence and performance of a contract, the validity of the contract's provisions, a breach of the contract by the plaintiff and monetary damages resulting from the breach. The claim and counterclaim are, of course, "offshoots" of the same basic transaction, but they do not represent the same basic controversy between the parties.

115 F.R.D. at 49.

Second, the court noted that the evidence needed to support each claim differs. The plaintiff needs to produce evidence of the allegedly abusive collection practices, including evidence regarding the specific actions of the defendant, such as phone calls and letters, on certain dates and times; whereas the defendant needs to produce evidence of the existence of a valid contract and breach.

Third, the *Leatherwood* court noted that the claims are not related on a "transactional" level:

> [T]he FDCPA claim involves the enforcement of federal policy and federal statutory law concerning a debt collector's conduct in collecting a debt. This claim does

> not concern any obligations created by the underlying debt. In contrast, the counterclaim alleges that the plaintiff has defaulted on a private contract governed by state law.

Two district courts in the Ninth Circuit (District of Arizona and District of Nevada) cited Leatherwood with approval and have applied similar reasoning in almost identical fact situations.

Defendant argues that its counterclaims are compulsory under the Ninth Circuit's logical-relationship test. However, Defendant cites no published cases holding that a claim for the underlying debt in a FDCPA action was held to be compulsory. The facts in this case are almost identical to the facts in three other district court cases holding that a counterclaim for the underlying debt in an unfair debt collection action is not compulsory. Defendant provides no argument as to the relationship and/or overlap between the evidence about the counterclaims to collect the debt (including evidence "regarding the origination of [Plaintiff's] debt and payments that she made to reduce the debt") and evidence of Defendant's allegedly abusive actions in collecting the debt. Whether a plaintiff in an unfair debt collection practices action actually has outstanding debt is irrelevant to the merits of that claim. Defendant's claims are not compulsory and supplemental jurisdiction does not exist on that basis.

B. WHETHER SUPPLEMENTAL JURISDICTION EXISTS OVER DEFENDANT'S COUNTERCLAIMS

The analysis of the district courts in *Hart* and *Taylor* determined that the claim for the underlying debt was a permissive counterclaim and that supplemental jurisdiction therefore did not exist. Despite that each case was decided after 1990 (when § 1367 took effect), each court held that supplemental jurisdiction could not be exercised on the basis that the claims were permissive. The court in *Hart* did not discuss § 1367. The *Taylor* court did discuss § 1367, and cited to authority holding that § 1367 maintained the compulsory/permissive distinction:

> Defendant maintains that under section 1367(a), the court may exercise jurisdiction over the counterclaim regardless of whether federal subject matter jurisdictional requirements are independently met. Defendant's argument, however, overlooks the fact that even under section 1367(a), courts must still distinguish between compulsory and permissive counterclaims: federal courts have supplemental jurisdiction over compulsory counterclaims, but permissive counterclaims require their own jurisdictional basis.

Taylor was decided in 1994, before the Seventh and Second Circuits addressed this issue and held the opposite, in 1996 and 2004, respectively. Based upon the language of § 1367 and the holdings of the Seventh and Second Circuits in *Channell* and *Jones*, the analysis no longer ends with the compulsive/permissive counterclaim distinction. Because Defendant's counterclaims are not compulsory, the next question is whether supplemental jurisdiction over the counterclaims nevertheless exists under 28 U.S.C. § 1367(a). The inquiry, referred to as the "case or controversy" test, as discussed above, is whether the counterclaim is "so related to claims in the action within such original jurisdiction that they form part of the same case or controversy under Article III of the United States Constitution."

The next question is whether the court should nevertheless decline to exercise jurisdiction under § 1367(c), which provides that a district court may decline to exercise supplemental jurisdiction in one of four situations:

> The district courts may decline to exercise supplemental jurisdiction over a claim under subsection (a) if—
>
> (1) the claim raises a novel or complex issue of State law,
> (2) the claim substantially predominates over the claim or claims over which the district court has original jurisdiction,
> (3) the district court has dismissed all claims over which it has original jurisdiction, or
> (4) in exceptional circumstances, there are other compelling reasons for declining jurisdiction.

The applicable subsection here is § 1367(c)(4). Even if supplemental jurisdiction exists over Defendant's counterclaims, a court may decline to exercise that jurisdiction where compelling reasons exist. In a case such as this one, strong policy reasons favor declining to exercise jurisdiction. As the court states in *Leatherwood,* allowing a debt collector to bring an action for the underlying debt in a case brought under the FDCPA may deter litigants from pursuing their rights under that statute:

> To allow a debt collector defendant to seek to collect the debt in the federal action to enforce the FDCPA might well have a chilling effect on persons who otherwise might and should bring suits such as this. Moreover, it would involve this Court in questions of no federal significance. Given the remedial nature of the FDCPA "and the broad public policy which it serves, federal courts should be loath to become immersed in the debt collection suits of . . . the target of the very legislation under which" a FDCPA plaintiff states a cause of action.

A major purpose of the FDCPA is to protect individuals from unfair debt collection practices regardless of whether the individual actually owes a debt. Strong policy reasons exist to prevent the chilling effect of trying FDCPA claims in the same case as state law claims for collection of the underlying debt. This policy satisfies the exceptional circumstances requirement to support an order declining to exercise supplemental jurisdiction over Defendant's state law claims to enforce the debt.

V. Conclusion

For all the foregoing reasons, Plaintiff's motion to dismiss Defendant's counterclaims is GRANTED. Defendant's counterclaims are DISMISSED WITHOUT PREJUDICE. SO ORDERED.

DISCUSSION AND QUESTIONS

The court in *Sparrow* addresses two related issues concerning counterclaims: (1) when is a counterclaim compulsory; and (2) do some permissive counterclaims qualify for supplemental jurisdiction? Since the enactment of § 1367, the second issue has arisen most often in one setting. In that setting, plaintiffs attempt to recover damages for violations of federal law generally regulating (a) the terms of lending agreements (the Truth in Lending Act, 15 U.S.C. §§1667-1667e), and (b) the manner in which debts can be collected (the FDCPA relied on in *Sparrow*).[28] *See, e.g., Channell v. Citicorp Nat'l Servs., Inc.*, 89 F.3d 379 (7th Cir. 1996). When defendants respond with counterclaims seeking to recover (or set off) the underlying debt, plaintiffs object that these state-law claims have no jurisdictional support because they are permissive counterclaims. Alternatively, plaintiffs ask the court to exercise its discretion under § 1367(c) to dismiss the state-law claims.

We begin by considering the strategic implications of the defendant's assertion of a counterclaim to collect the debt. The plaintiff often would prefer to litigate the federal claim without responding to a counterclaim for the debt. If the counterclaim is entertained by the court, the plaintiff has in a manner of speaking initiated a debt collection proceeding against himself. Further, the presence of the counterclaim broadens the evidence heard by the jury to include the debt's history and the plaintiff's payment history, which may place the plaintiff in a bad light. If the counterclaim is not added, the plaintiff may be permitted to stipulate to the existence of the underlying debt and prevent the introduction of possibly adverse evidence concerning the debt's history. And, of course, the plaintiff prefers not to have his judgment reduced by the defendant's recovery under a counterclaim.

The defendant, in contrast, would obviously prefer to have the court consider all aspects of the debt's history and collection and would also like the suit to result in a final accounting of all monies owed by the parties. In addition, if the defendant fails to assert a counterclaim for debt collection, and a court later finds the counterclaim was compulsory, the defendant may have forfeited the right to collect the debt.

Same case, different transaction. The use of the phrase "same transaction or occurrence" in federal joinder rules shares a history with the development of supplemental jurisdiction doctrine. For example, in *Moore v. New York Cotton Exchange*, 270 U.S. 593 (1926), the Court upheld what was then called "ancillary" jurisdiction over a counterclaim. The Court, interpreting a rule of equity permitting the assertion of counterclaims arising from a common "transaction," observed that the word "[t]ransaction" is a word of flexible meaning. It may comprehend a series of many occurrences, depending not so much upon the immediateness of their connection as upon their logical relationship."[29] *Id.* at 610.

The phrase "transaction or occurrence" in federal joinder rules derives from the term "transaction" interpreted in *Moore. See* Douglas D. McFarland, *In Search of the Transaction or Occurrence: Counterclaims*, 40 CREIGHTON L. REV. 699, 703-04 (2007). As Professor McFarland has observed, "the primary point of all the joinder Rules — including the counterclaim — is whenever feasible to settle all controversies between the litigants in one suit." *Id.* at 702. Like the *Gibbs*

28. The issue also arises when consumers finance purchases by agreeing to make payments automatically through electronic transfers from their bank accounts. *See, e.g., Miller v. Interstate Auto Grp., Inc.*, 2014 WL 4437675 (W.D. Wis. Sept. 9, 2014) (alleging that a sales contract for the purchase of an auto contains terms that violated the Electronic Fund Transfer Act.).

29. Notice that Rule 13(a) uses the phrase "transaction or occurrence" while Rule 20 governing party joinder uses the phrase "transaction, occurrence, or series of transactions or occurrences." *Moore* suggests that the Rule 13(a) terminology encompasses the terminology in Rule 20.

test for determining the scope of a constitutional case, federal joinder rules emphasize a fact-intensive inquiry. But a seemingly pragmatic, case-specific standard has transmuted into a variety of tests, most of them unsatisfactory. *See, e.g.*, CHARLES ALLEN WRIGHT, ARTHUR R. MILLER, & EDWARD H. COOPER, 6 FEDERAL PRACTICE AND PROCEDURE § 1425 (2014).

The court in *Sparrow* seems to combine elements of several different tests courts have developed to define a "common transaction or occurrence." The court mentions three reasons why the defendant's debt claim presents a separate transaction/occurrence from the plaintiff's debt collection claim. First, the plaintiff's federal claim focuses on a "narrow realm of facts" whereas the defendant's state claim "requires a broad proof of facts." The two claims are "offshoots" of the same "basic transaction" but are not the "same basic controversy." Second, the evidence needed to support each claim differs. Third, the claims "are not related on a transactional level" because one concerns debt-collection conduct while the other concerns the underlying debt.

Does the court in *Sparrow* provide three reasons for concluding the defendant's counterclaim is not compulsory, or is there but one reason stated in different ways? Is the court's interpretation of common transaction/occurrence consistent with the Supreme Court's interpretation of the term "common transaction" in *Moore v. New York Cotton Exchange, supra*? In *Moore*, the plaintiff, an odd-lot cotton exchange, sued the defendant under federal law, alleging that it had created a monopoly over wire information used to report commodity prices and bids. The defendant counterclaimed, seeking to enjoin the plaintiff from using some of this wire information that the plaintiff had allegedly stolen from it. The Court found that the defendant's refusal to share wire information with the plaintiff was common to the claim and counterclaim, and affirmed that the lower court had ancillary jurisdiction over the counterclaim. Under the court's analysis in *Sparrow*, could one argue that the claim and counterclaim in *Moore* did not involve the same "basic controversy" because different facts underlay the plaintiff's proof that the defendant had a monopoly over wire information and the defendant's proof that the plaintiff was stealing some of that wire information? After all, proof of the plaintiff's alleged theft differed from proof that the defendant exercised a monopoly over wire information. Can *Moore* and *Sparrow* be reconciled?

Does the court's interpretation of the common transaction/occurrence standard disregard the intent of federal joinder rules, which admonish courts "to settle all controversies between the litigants in one suit" whenever feasible? *See* McFarland, *supra*, at 702. Is there any doubt that the parties' larger controversy cannot be finally resolved unless there is both a resolution of the debt and debt collection disputes? Recall that in *Gibbs* the Court explained that "if, considered without regard to their federal or state character, a plaintiff's claims are such that he would ordinarily be expected to try them all in one judicial proceeding, then, assuming substantiality of the federal issues, there is power in federal courts to hear the whole." Does this constitutional standard address the same concern as the standard for joinder used in federal rules? Measured by this standard, would one normally expect the debtor and creditor in *Sparrow* to resolve their dispute in one lawsuit?

An appreciable number of courts agree with the court's conclusion in *Sparrow* and find that a creditor's debt arises from a different transaction/occurrence than the plaintiff's claim for improper lending or debt-collection practices. *See, e.g.*, *Whigham v. Beneficial Fin. Co. of Fayetteville, Inc.*, 599 F.2d 1322 (4th Cir. 1979); *Martin v. Law Offices of John F. Edwards*, 262 F.R.D. 534 (S.D. Cal. 2009); *Cabrera v. Courtesy Auto, Inc.*, 192 F. Supp. 2d 1012 (D. Neb. 2002). But other courts reach a different conclusion. *See, e.g., Plant v. Blazer Fin. Servs., Inc.*, 598 F.2d 1357 (5th Cir. 1979); *Mims v. Dixie Fin. Corp.*, 426 F. Supp. 627 (N.D. Ga. 1976).

Expanding supplemental jurisdiction to encompass permissive counterclaims. Because of the *Sparrow* court's limited interpretation of the compulsory counterclaim standard, it is required to consider the defendant's alternative argument that some permissive counterclaims qualify for supplemental jurisdiction. The court relies on the seminal case recognizing that supplemental jurisdiction may encompass some permissive counterclaims, the Seventh Circuit's decision in *Channell v. Citicorp National Services, Inc.*, 89 F.3d 379 (7th Cir. 1996). In *Channell*, the court explained why, prior to the enactment of § 1367, the scope of compulsory counterclaims was more limited:

> Now the jurisdictional distinction between permissive and compulsory counterclaims was developed before Congress enacted 28 U.S.C. § 1367 to codify, and to an extent extend, the supplemental jurisdiction (formerly known as the pendent jurisdiction). Section 1367(a) says that district courts have supplemental jurisdiction "over all other claims that are so related to claims in the action within [the] original jurisdiction that they form part of the same case or controversy under Article III of the United States Constitution."
>
> The distinction between permissive and compulsory counterclaims served an important function when every assertion of pendent jurisdiction was of doubtful propriety, because not supported by statute, but in which the law of preclusion required compulsory counterclaims to be presented or lost. (That's why they are called compulsory. No one has to make a "compulsory" counterclaim, but it is lost if not presented.) Refusal to entertain a compulsory counterclaim might lead to its forfeiture. Refusal to entertain a permissive counterclaim did not create such a risk—while hearing the counterclaim could exceed the powers granted to a court of limited jurisdiction. Now that Congress has codified the supplemental jurisdiction in § 1367(a), courts should use the language of the statute to define the extent of their powers.

Id. at 385.

The court in *Channell* suggests that the traditional rule, limiting supplemental jurisdiction to compulsory counterclaims, reflected both doubts about the constitutionality of supplemental jurisdiction and solicitude for the interests of *defendants*—who risked losing compulsory counterclaims if they were not adjudicated by the court under its supplemental jurisdictional power. In one important respect, the court appears mistaken. Forfeiture of a counterclaim would not occur if a court found it lacked jurisdiction to hear the counterclaim; Rule 13(a) cannot conceivably be construed to penalize a defendant for failing to assert a claim the court cannot hear.

Channell concludes that Congress intended to authorize supplemental jurisdiction that extends beyond the scope of a common transaction/occurrence encompassed by Rule 13(a).[30] Rather than expand Rule 13(a) to encompass the

30. Some have argued that § 1367 announces a broader constitutional standard for supplemental jurisdiction than recognized in *Gibbs. See, e.g.*, Graham Beck, *Supplemental Jurisdiction Over Permissive Counterclaims in Light of* Exxon v. Allapattah, 41 U.S.F. L. Rev. 45, 47 (2006). But this view is not supported. First, in § 1367(a) Congress extended supplemental jurisdiction to the limits of the case-or-controversy standard. Because that standard had been authoritatively interpreted by the Court in *Gibbs*, and because Congress did not purport to offer a differing interpretation, *Gibbs* remains good law. Second, the Court's recent interpretations of § 1367 do not suggest that Congress has expanded the constitutional standard announced in *Gibbs. See generally Exxon Mobil Corp. v. Allapattah Servs. Inc.*, 545 U.S. 546, 553 (2005).

full scope of the *Gibbs* standard,[31] the court fills in the slack by extending supplemental jurisdiction to some counterclaims under Rule 13(b). Which tack seems better? Could the court in *Channel* (and the court in *Sparrow*) have avoided introducing yet another note of uncertainty to supplemental jurisdiction doctrine by simply adopting a more flexible standard for compulsory counterclaims? Could one justify a broader interpretation of the compulsory counterclaim Rule by arguing that Congress knew of the historical congruity of compulsory counterclaims and supplemental jurisdiction and intended to perpetuate it in § 1367? Professor Martin Redish has argued that, when the issue is a court's supplemental jurisdictional power, Rule 13(a)'s transaction/occurrence requirement should be interpreted more broadly than it has been in other contexts. *See* Martin H. Redish, *Reassessing the Allocation of Judicial Business Between State and Federal Courts: Federal Jurisdiction and "The Martian Chronicles,"* 78 VA. L. REV. 1769 (1992).

While there is much to commend Professor Redish's approach, it would have been at odds with the *Sparrow* court's goal of eliminating debtor counterclaims under the FDCPA. Perhaps this is the key to understanding the court's narrow construction of transaction/occurrence.

If the court had ruled that debt counterclaims were compulsory, but eliminated them from the debtor's suit by invoking its discretionary power to dismiss under § 1367(c), consider the consequences for future consumer suits. Such a ruling would have likely encouraged creditors to file debt counterclaims, not at all what the court wanted. Creditors would have seemingly been *required* to assert debt counterclaims, since compulsory counterclaims are forfeited when omitted. The fact that creditors could have anticipated that courts might exercise their *discretion* to dismiss debt counterclaims would not mitigate their obligation to assert "compulsory" counterclaims. Consequently, the court's ruling in *Sparrow,* that debt counterclaims are permissive, promoted its goal of reducing the assertion of such counterclaims in consumer suits.

The approach adopted by *Channell* and *Sparrow* has been followed by only a minority of federal circuits. Other circuits currently hew to the traditional approach limiting supplemental jurisdiction to compulsory counterclaims. *See* M. Evan Lacke, *The New Breed of Permissive Counterclaim: Supplemental Jurisdiction After 28 U.S.C. § 1367,* 56 S.C. L. REV. 607, 619 (2005). And some courts finding debt counterclaims to be permissive reject the conclusion that such counterclaims nonetheless qualify for supplemental jurisdiction. *See, e.g., Cabrera v. Courtesy Auto, Inc.,* 192 F. Supp. 2d 1012, 1021 (D. Neb. 2002) ("If CMAC's counterclaim for a deficiency judgment on the Pontiac loan does not arise out of the same transaction or occurrence as Cabrera's claim regarding CMAC's alleged failure to disclose federally-required information when making the loan, it is difficult to conclude that Cabrera's additional state-law claims for breach of contract, conversion, etc., involve the same case or controversy as her claim arising under federal law. In other words, I seriously question whether the court has supplemental jurisdiction over some or all of Cabrera's state-law claims.")

A court's discretion to dismiss permissive state claims. After going to the effort of extending supplemental jurisdiction to some permissive counterclaims, the

31. Indirect support for the court's approach can be found in the fact that a congressional subcommittee's proposal to use the common transaction/occurrence language in § 1367 was not ultimately followed by Congress. *See* Michael D. Conway,.

court in *Sparrow* nonetheless dismisses the permissive counterclaim of the defendant. The court finds "exceptional circumstances" under § 1367(c) justifying dismissal of the defendant's claim for unpaid debt. The court observes that "a major purpose of the FDCPA is to protect individuals from unfair debt collection practices regardless of whether the individual actually owes a debt. Strong policy reasons exist to prevent the chilling effect of trying FDCPA claims in the same case as state law claims for collection of the underlying debt." A few other courts have employed the same reasoning when exercising their discretion to dismiss debt counterclaims in FDCPA cases. *See, e.g.*, *Robles v. Ally Bank*, 2013 WL 28773 (S.D. Cal. Jan. 2, 2013); *Avery v. First Resolution Mgmt. Corp.*, 2007 WL 1560653 (D. Or. 2007).

Are you persuaded by the *Sparrow* court's justification for dismissing the debt counterclaim? Does your assessment of this justification turn on whether you imagine the plaintiff as a beleaguered debtor exploited by unscrupulous creditors or debt collectors (an experience some of you may share)? If you find the policy argument persuasive, is it preferable for a court to effect policy by (a) ruling that a debt counterclaim is simply not covered by supplemental jurisdiction or (b) declining to exercise supplemental jurisdiction?

In *Bakewell v. Federal Financial Group, Inc.*, 2006 WL 739807 (N.D. Ga. 2006), the district court agreed with *Sparrow* and found that a defendant's debt counterclaim was permissive yet within its supplemental jurisdiction. But the court declined to dismiss the counterclaim, expressly disagreeing with the court's rationale in *Sparrow*:

> While some courts have exercised their discretion and declined to assert supplemental jurisdiction over claims for underlying debt in FDCPA cases citing public policy reasons, this court declines to follow this course of action. The court finds that there are also public policy reasons for allowing both claims under one suit. First, it is inherently more efficient to deal with both matters in one consolidated action. Second, to bar Defendant's counterclaim would be to favor one litigant's claim over another, a practice courts should not engage in.

Id. at *4.

Notice that the court in *Bakewell* finds procedural policy paramount to the alleged substantive policy underlying FDCPA claims. The court concludes it is both more efficient and fairer to resolve a creditor's counterclaim in the debtor's suit. Do you agree with the court's reasoning? Does *Bakewell* seem more consistent with the even-handed approach to joinder endorsed by the federal rules? Does a court's consideration of the *substantive* policy underlying a federal plaintiff's claims seem consistent with the tenor of other grounds enumerated in § 1367(c), which specifically address procedural policy?

Professor McFarland, criticizing some courts' willingness to deny jurisdiction over creditors' counterclaims in Truth-In-Lending-Act cases, challenges the view that dismissal of debt counterclaims promotes congressional intent:

> Congress did not provide for exclusive federal jurisdiction and enforcement. Congress provided concurrent jurisdiction with the states. A plaintiff who sues in state court is without question subject to the debt counterclaim in every state—even those that provide only for permissive counterclaims. Congress obviously did not believe its enforcement scheme would be undermined in state court enforcement actions. So why would Congress have believed its enforcement scheme would be

> undermined in federal courts by allowing a debt counterclaim? Even more anomalous would be a TILA case brought in state court and removed to federal court. The result that follows is that upon removal, and not before, the federal enforcement scheme is undermined by allowing the debt counterclaim.

Douglas D. McFarland, *In Search of the Transaction or Occurrence: Counterclaims,* 40 Creighton L. Rev. 699, 727 (2007).

Notice that the "anomalous" scenario described by Professor McFarland is the same one presented in *Sparrow.* The plaintiff-debtor in *Sparrow* originally filed suit in state court, after which the case was removed to federal court by the defendant. Does the procedural history of *Sparrow* undermine the court's assertion that a creditor's assertion of a debt counterclaim will deter debtors from bringing suits under the FDCPA?

In *Channell,* Judge Easterbrook offered a law-and-economics perspective on the wisdom of denying creditors the opportunity to recover on their loans when they are sued for violations of federal law:

> Lessors extend credit (this is what long-term auto leases effectively are) only when the returns equal or exceed what they can earn by investing money elsewhere. Debts that must be written off, and legal expenses of collection, are part of the cost of credit and ultimately are paid by lessees. Legal Rules that increase collections and reduce expenses may require these lessees to pay more, but the cost of leases will fall for consumers as a group—for in competition any reduction in costs flows to consumers. Consideration of consumers' interests therefore favors adjudicating rather than dismissing Citicorp's counterclaim.

89 F.3d at 386.

Are you persuaded by Judge Easterbrook's argument?

PROBLEM 7-4

The College Strikes Back

Professor Wade Hannity was a highly controversial faculty member at Red River College, a community college in New Mexico. Over the ten years he taught at the college, he antagonized some students and many alumni. Last year, in a course Professor Hannity teaches in "Military Adventurism in U.S. Foreign Policy," he offered a particularly acerbic critique of persons who serve in the military, and some of his comments were construed to disparage minorities serving in the military.

The college administration, in response to student and alumni complaints, began reviewing transcripts of Professor Hannity's classroom comments. While doing so, they learned from an anonymous source that the professor may have falsified his credentials when he originally applied for a faculty position. Further investigation indicated that Professor Hannity likely misrepresented his own status as a military veteran. Professor Hannity was immediately suspended from his teaching position, with full pay, until formal proceedings were conducted to consider the both his representations of veteran status and his alleged criticisms of minorities serving in the military.

Professor Hannity quickly sued the college in federal court. He alleged his suspension and the pending proceedings violated (1) his First Amendment rights (the college was "retaliating" against him for expressing his opinions), and (2) procedural due process. Professor Hannity seeks full reinstatement to his teaching position and an injunction preventing the college from continuing with the pending proceedings.

In its answer to the professor's complaint, the college asserts counterclaims seeking a declaratory judgment that Professor Hannity committed fraud and breach of contract by misrepresenting his status as a veteran. The counterclaims are based on state law.

Professor Hannity has now moved to dismiss the college's counterclaims. He argues that the claims have no jurisdictional basis and that, in any event, the federal court should exercise its discretion to dismiss the counterclaims because they threaten to "chill" exercise of his constitutional rights.

How should the court rule?

f. The Consequences of Dismissal Under Section 1367(c)

What happens after a plaintiff's supplemental state claim is dismissed under § 1367(c)? Presumably the plaintiff's remaining federal claim(s) continue to be adjudicated by the federal court. But the plaintiff may decide that it is preferable to litigate the entire dispute in state court. Because state courts usually share concurrent power with federal courts to adjudicate federal claims, plaintiffs can often litigate all federal and state claims in a single state court proceeding.[32] In such circumstances, the plaintiff may consider voluntarily dismissing the case under Rule 41(a) and refiling in state court.

According to Rule 41(a), a plaintiff's power to voluntarily dismiss a federal suit after supplemental claims are dismissed is limited. If the defendant has previously served an answer to the complaint or a motion for summary judgment, a plaintiff may voluntarily dismiss only if opposing parties consent. Otherwise, a plaintiff must obtain court permission to dismiss. One factor a federal court must consider when asked to dismiss is whether the court will continue to have jurisdiction over any remaining *counterclaims*. Supplemental jurisdiction confers such jurisdiction over counterclaims provided they satisfy the *Gibbs* test. As we learned earlier, a court has the power to adjudicate factually related state claims—including counterclaims—even after federal claims are dismissed.

But a federal court is not required to adjudicate supplemental counterclaims once the plaintiff dismisses his own claims. One of the discretionary factors in § 1367(c) permits a federal court to dismiss supplemental state-law claims if claims coming within the court's "original jurisdiction" have been dismissed. Consequently, a federal court may grant the plaintiff's requested order for dismissal and also exercise its jurisdiction to dismiss state-law counterclaims as well. *See, e.g., Piedra v. Mentor Graphics Corp.*, 979 F. Supp. 2d 1297, 1299 (D. Or. 1997). In such circumstances, the plaintiff will attain his objective of resolving the dispute in a single lawsuit.

32. This assumes any remaining federal law claim does not come within the exclusive jurisdiction of the federal courts.

A *defendant* whose state counterclaims are dismissed by a federal court has few options but to assert those counterclaims in a new state court action. Federal courts have no authority under § 1367(c) to dismiss the plaintiff's pending federal claims.

When supplemental state claims are dismissed, § 1367(d) provides an important protection for the party who must now file a separate suit in state court. State statutes of limitation are "tolled" while the federal action is pending and for an additional 30 days after state claims are dismissed. Since most jurisdictions measure the timeliness of a suit based on the day it is filed, *see, e.g.*, Fed. R. Civ. P. 3, the party whose state claims are dismissed must act expeditiously in filing a state court action.

Section 1367(d) is another means through which Congress encourages parties to use a federal court forum to adjudicate all related claims. A litigant can at least attempt to assert supplemental claims in federal court without fearing that, while the federal action is pending, the limitations period on those supplemental claims will expire. Without § 1367(d), a litigant might be compelled to file a separate state court action while the federal action is proceeding so as to preserve supplemental claims if they are ultimately dismissed by the federal court.

The constitutionality of § 1367(d)'s tolling provision has been challenged twice in the Court. In *Kimel v. Florida Board of Regents*, 528 U.S. 62 (2000), the Court concluded that § 1367(d) does not apply when a plaintiff's action against the *state* has been dismissed by a federal court. The Court's interpretation of § 1367(d) permitted it to avoid the "serious" constitutional question whether Congress can control the terms and conditions governing suits against a state in its own courts. In Chapter 8, we examine the constitutional issues of sovereign immunity referred to in *Kimel*.

The Court refused to extend *Kimel* to the situation where a federal court dismisses supplemental claims against a local government entity. In *Jinks v. Richland County*, 538 U.S. 456 (2003), the Court held that suits against local government do not raise the sovereign immunity issues raised when the state itself is a defendant. In Chapter 9 we examine one of the rationales underlying the *Jinks* decision when we consider how local government is generally denied the immunity from federal actions enjoyed by the state.

2. *Removal Jurisdiction*

We have now examined the three statutory bases for federal court jurisdiction relied on most frequently in private civil litigation. These include two statutes conferring "original" jurisdiction — 28 U.S.C. § 1331 (arising under jurisdiction) and § 1332 (diversity jurisdiction) — and one statute augmenting that jurisdiction when non-federal claims are part of the same constitutional case. 28 U.S.C. § 1367.

Jurisdictional statutes addressing removal of a case from state to federal court complement original federal jurisdiction in one of three ways. First, removal statutes most commonly give the federal courts a derivative power to entertain suits that could have been originally filed in federal court.[33] This derivative removal jurisdiction is the type most frequently invoked by defendants.

33. These categories of removal jurisdiction are discussed in depth in Scott Dodson, *In Search of Removal Jurisdiction*, 102 Nw. U. L. Rev. 55, 61-66 (2008).

REVIEW AND CONSOLIDATION

Supplemental Jurisdiction Under Section 1367

- Supplemental jurisdiction permits the joinder of claims outside the federal courts' original jurisdiction when they arise from the same "case or controversy" as claims within the courts' original jurisdiction.
- Supplemental jurisdiction encompasses the joinder of additional parties.
- Congress and the Court have endorsed a definition of a constitutional "case or controversy" that emphasizes the factual relatedness of federal and non-federal claims, even though earlier Court precedent suggests a more expansive view.
- Supplemental jurisdiction is specifically limited in cases founded solely on diversity-of-citizenship jurisdiction. These limitations apply to plaintiffs, or would-be plaintiffs, who seek to assert claims against defendants joined under specified federal rules.
- In cases based on federal question jurisdiction, courts usually have supplemental jurisdiction over compulsory counterclaims, crossclaims, and third-party claims, as well as parties joined under Rule 20. Other claims must be assessed to determine whether they arise from a "common nucleus of operative fact" underlying federal claims.
- Federal courts have the discretion to dismiss supplemental claims for reasons specified in § 1367 as well as other compelling reasons yet to be enunciated by the courts.

Second, removal statutes occasionally give federal courts the power to entertain suits that could not have been filed there originally. One example of such removal power is found in 28 U.S.C. § 1442, which permits a federal officer sued or prosecuted in state court to remove the action to federal court if the officer relies on a federal defense.[34]

Third, removal statutes sometimes *restrict* the removal of cases that could have been originally filed in federal court by the plaintiff. For example, in Chapter 6 we discussed 28 U.S.C. § 1441(b), which prevents a defendant from removing a diversity action that might have been filed in federal court by the plaintiff if any defendant resides in the state where the suit has been filed.[35]

A defendant's power to remove a case from state to federal court can serve the goals that federal jurisdiction is intended to promote. These include permitting federal courts to adjudicate federal claims based on their presumably greater

34. *See Mesa v. California*, 489 U.S. 121, 137 (1989) (holding that § 1442 "overcomes" the well-pleaded complaint rule).

35. See Chapter 6. Professor Dodson offers other examples of where Congress has restricted the removal of cases otherwise within the federal courts' original jurisdiction. *See* Dodson, *supra* note 33, at 63-66. As Professor Dodson explains, whether these restrictions on removal are deemed "jurisdictional" or "procedural" in nature can have a significant impact on the outcome of litigation. *See id.* at 77.

expertise in interpreting federal law and their greater solicitude for enforcement of federal law; and averting prejudice that non-citizens might experience if forced to litigate in the home state court of their adversaries. But defendants often choose a federal forum for litigation advantage rather than to fulfill the purposes for which federal jurisdiction was conferred. *See* Kevin M. Clermont & Theodore Eisenberg, *"Do Case Outcomes Really Reveal Anything About the Legal System? Win Rates and Removal Jurisdiction," 83 CORNELL L. REV. 581 (1998).* For example, Professor Clermont and Professor Eisenberg's research found that defendants' success rate escalated in cases removed to federal court. This removal effect, they concluded, might reflect in part the "incompetence" of plaintiffs' attorneys who fail to structure litigation so as to prevent its removal to less hospitable federal courts. *Id.* at 582. Their conclusion assumes, of course, that competent attorneys can structure litigation to prevent its removal to federal court.

In the following discussion, we address how litigation can be structured to both create and defeat federal court jurisdiction. We consider whether plaintiffs are "masters of their cases" to the extent that they can control whether the suit is litigated in state or federal court. And we consider whether defendants can override plaintiffs' choice of a state forum when plaintiffs have used procedural rules to frustrate their removal.

Congress and the courts have experimented with numerous solutions to the problems of jurisdiction manipulation. We examine several recent solutions, including (1) statutory changes affecting the removal of cases in which federal and state claims are joined and (2) statutory changes and court-created doctrines affecting the removal of suits based on diversity of citizenship. To place this discussion in context, we begin by reviewing some common features of removal jurisdiction that you likely studied in Civil Procedure.

a. Removal Under 28 U.S.C. § 1441(a)

In most private litigation, the plaintiff has much to say about whether a dispute that could be transformed into a federal case actually is. The plaintiff's "well-pleaded complaint" determines whether the suit alleges a claim arising under federal law. Likewise, a plaintiff can usually select the configuration of plaintiffs and defendants whose joinder will determine whether diversity jurisdiction exists.[36] And even when the plaintiff has the choice of invoking a federal court's jurisdiction, the existence of "concurrent" state court jurisdiction usually means the plaintiff can initiate suit in state court.

The most commonly used federal removal statute, 28 U.S.C. § 1441, restores jurisdictional choice to the defendant.[37] If the plaintiff could have filed the complaint in federal court but chose not to, the defendant can often supersede the plaintiff's choice and remove the suit to federal court. As stated in § 1441(a), a defendant may remove to the appropriate federal district court "any civil

36. Most decisions regarding the joinder of plaintiffs and defendants are governed by Federal Rule of Civil Procedure 20, which permits but does not require that all potential plaintiffs and defendants be joined. And most state court rules generally authorizing joinder are similar to Rule 20.

37. Recall from Chapter 5 that a defendant cannot usually create federal jurisdiction by interjecting federal defenses or federal claims.

action brought in a State court of which the district courts of the United States have original jurisdiction."

You have studied removal under § 1441 in Civil Procedure, where you learned some of its constituent provisions. These include the following:

- a civil suit that could have been filed originally in federal court usually can be removed to federal court by the defendant(s);[38]
- the right to removal mentioned above is restricted when the basis for original jurisdiction is solely diversity of citizenship; in such diversity cases, removal is prohibited if one of the defendants is a citizen of the state where the action was originally filed;[39]
- usually all properly joined defendants must consent to removal;[40]
- a defendant's right of removal usually must be exercised expeditiously, within 30 days after receiving a copy of the initial pleading showing that a case is removable;[41] and
- the federal court to which a case has been removed[42] must remand the case back to state court if it lacks jurisdiction over the case, or if some procedural error in the removal process is timely raised.[43]

The symmetry of original jurisdiction and removal jurisdiction in most cases permits litigants to reliably determine whether removal is proper. The question of removal jurisdiction under § 1441(a) usually presents the same question presented when a court determines its original jurisdiction.

This symmetry also extends to the doctrine of supplemental jurisdiction, which we discussed earlier in the chapter. As the Court observed in *City of Chicago v. International College of Surgeons*, 522 U.S. 156, 165 (1997), when a federal district court has original jurisdiction over federal claims, it can "exercise supplemental jurisdiction over the accompanying state law claims so long as those claims . . . form part of the same case or controversy."[44] Thus, a plaintiff who asserts claims under federal law can't defeat removal by joining factually related state-law claims that, standing alone, could not be adjudicated in federal court.[45]

But what of the situation where the plaintiff alleges federal claims and joins state claims that aren't factually related and thus not within a federal court's supplemental jurisdiction? For example, Federal Rule of Civil Procedure 18 and similar state rules permit a party asserting a claim to join additional claims

38. 28 U.S.C. § 1441(a). Plaintiffs lack authority to remove cases they have filed in state court. *See Shamrock Oil & Gas Corp. v. Sheets*, 313 U.S. 100 (1941).
39. 28 U.S.C. § 1441(b).
40. 28 U.S.C. §§ 1446(b)(2)(A), 1441(c)(2).
41. 28 U.S.C. § 1446(b).
42. Section 1441(a) states that a case is removed to "the district court of the United States for the district and division embracing the place where such action is pending." But § 1441(e)(6) preserves the authority of that district court to "transfer or dismiss an action on the ground of inconvenient forum."
43. 28 U.S.C. § 1447(c). These restrictions on removal are further explored in Dodson, *supra* note 33.
44. Similarly, the restrictions on supplemental jurisdiction contained in § 1367(b) also govern in removed cases.
45. Plaintiffs can avoid removal by alleging only the state claims, assuming they are willing to forgo the possible benefits of including related federal claims. The principal exception to this tack occurs in very limited situations where federal law completely preempts state-law regulation of a subject. In those situations, plaintiffs' legal claims necessarily arise under federal law. See Chapter 6.

regardless of whether they are factually related.[46] Does the presence of non-removable claims defeat removal of the case? If not, is the entire case removed to federal court or only parts of it? And which parts of the case can be adjudicated by a federal court after removal?

b. Removal Under 28 U.S.C. § 1441(c)

For more than a century, Congress has tinkered with removal jurisdiction to address the situation where a case filed in state court contains a mixture of claims or parties, some within the federal courts' jurisdictional power and others without.[47] Much of that tinkering is found in 28 U.S.C. § 1441(c).

Section 1441(c), as revised in 2011, now provides in relevant part:

> If a civil action includes . . . a claim arising under the Constitution, laws, or treaties of the United States . . . and a claim not within the original or supplemental jurisdiction of the district court or a claim that has been made nonremovable by statute, the entire action may be removed if the action would be removable without the inclusion of the [nonremovable] claim. . . .[48]

Once such a civil action is removed to federal court, the court severs any non-removable claim and remands it to state court:

> Upon removal of an action . . . the district court shall sever from the action all [nonremovable] claims . . . and shall remand the severed claims to the State court from which the action was removed.

To further protect a defendant's right of removal under § 1441(c), the statute modifies the normal requirement that all defendants join in the removal petition. Instead, only those defendants against whom is asserted a claim arising under federal law need consent to removal.[49] And if the plaintiff defers pleading a federal claim until later in the state court action, § 1446(b) permits the defendant to remove the case within 30 days of learning the case has become removable.

Prior to 2011, § 1441(c) authorized the removal of cases where the plaintiff joined removable claims with "separate and independent" nonremovable claims. Courts sometimes struggled in determining what was a "separate and independent" claim. They also had to confront the issue whether their exercise of removal jurisdiction under § 1441(c) might lead them to adjudicate claims exceeding their constitutional power. Section 1441(c) gave federal courts

46. Although Rule 20 governing joinder of parties requires that there be factual commonality among the joined parties (i.e., joinder is permitted when claims asserted by co-plaintiffs or claims asserted against co-defendants arise from "the same transaction, occurrence, or series of transactions or occurrences"), that commonality is required only between *some* claim ("any right to relief"). Thus, a plaintiff can join an additional defendant to a state-law claim that has been properly asserted under Rule 18 even though the claim against that new defendant is unrelated to any federal claim asserted by the plaintiff.

47. Charles Allen Wright, Arthur R. Miller, & Edward H. Cooper, 14C Federal Practice and Procedure § 3722 (2014).

48. By its terms, § 1441(c) only applies to suits involving claims arising under federal law that include claims not within a federal court's original or supplemental jurisdiction. Thus it doesn't apply to pure diversity actions involving no federal claim.

49. *See* 28 U.S.C. § 1441(c)(2).

discretion to "determine all issues . . . or, . . . remand all matters in which State law predominates." In other words, federal courts had discretion to adjudicate "separate and independent" claims that came within neither their original nor their supplemental jurisdiction. And this seemed to imply that Congress had extended the courts' jurisdiction to state claims that did not arise from *Gibbs*'s "common nucleus of operative fact" and thus were not part of the same constitutional case as the federal claim. While adjudicating separate and independent claims might promote a defendant's access to federal court by permitting the defendant to remove federal and state claims for adjudication in one proceeding, some commentators concluded that this power exceeded Congress' constitutional authority to confer jurisdiction on the federal courts.[50]

Another possible implication of the earlier version of § 1441(c) was that *any* case filed in state court that joined federal and state claims was removable. As Professors Wright, Miller, and Cooper surmised:

> [I]f the federal and the nonfederal claims are separate and independent, the entire case will be removable under Section 1441(c); if the two claims are not separate and independent, the case will be removable under Section 1441(b) with the nonfederal claim being brought along under the supplemental jurisdiction of the federal courts provided for in Section 1367.[51]

Several courts seemed to agree with this interpretation of the earlier version of § 1441(c).[52]

Effective in 2012,[53] § 1441(c) has eliminated several of the constitutional and statutory issues posed by the prior statute. The revised statute operates in conjunction with § 1367 so that

- A federal court's power to adjudicate a removed case combining federal and state claims is equivalent to its original jurisdictional power — that is, the court must adjudicate federal claims[54] and has the power under § 1367 to adjudicate supplemental state claims.[55]
- A federal court must remand state claims that lack jurisdictional foundation under § 1367 (or some other federal statute), and it retains discretion to remand state claims that otherwise qualify for supplemental jurisdiction provided one of the remand criteria in § 1367(c) is satisfied.

Thus, a state court defendant's right to remove federal claims can't be thwarted by the plaintiff's joining of state claims. At the same time, federal courts can't exercise their removal jurisdiction to entertain claims that are not part of the same constitutional case as the federal claims. Either the entire case can be removed to and heard by the federal court based on its exercise of original and

50. *See, e.g.*, Lewin, *The Federal Courts' Hospitable Back Door — Removal of "Separate and Independent" Non-Federal Causes of Action*, 66 Harv. L. Rev. 423 (1953).

51. Charles Allen Wright, Arthur R. Miller, & Edward H. Cooper, 14C Federal Practice and Procedure § 3722 (2014).

52. *See, e.g., Salei v. Boardwalk Regency Corp.*, 913 F. Supp. 993 (E.D. Mich. 1996).

53. Section 1441(c) was revised in the Federal Court Jurisdiction and Venue Clarification Act of 2011, Pub. L. No. 112-63, 125 Stat. 758, and took effect in 2012.

54. Some courts interpreted the prior version of § 1441(c) to permit remand of any claims in the removed case, including federal claims. *See, e.g., Moore v. DeBiase*, 766 F. Supp. 1311, 1315-22 (D.N.J. 1991).

55. As mentioned, § 1441(c) addresses state claims that come within neither "the original [n]or supplemental jurisdiction of the district court."

supplemental jurisdiction, or the entire case is removed and the nonremovable claims are remanded to state court.

c. Regulating the Removal of Diversity Actions

In Chapter 6 we examined the persistence of diversity jurisdiction despite doubts about whether prejudice against out-of-state citizens justifies the burden this form of jurisdiction imposes on the federal courts' docket. We also considered how litigants often invoke diversity jurisdiction for litigation advantage rather than to avoid state court prejudice against non-citizens.[56]

Federal statutes are less solicitous of diversity jurisdiction than federal-question jurisdiction. For example, the amount-in-controversy requirement, the complete-diversity requirement, and the one-year limit on removing diversity cases found in § 1446(c)(1)[57] prevent federal courts from exercising the breadth of diversity jurisdiction permitted by the Constitution. Likewise, § 1359 of the Judicial Code prevents a federal court from exercising jurisdiction when a party has been "improperly or collusively joined to invoke the jurisdiction of such court," thus prohibiting improper joinder of parties for the purpose of creating diversity jurisdiction

But § 1359 does not address improper joinder of parties to *defeat* a defendant's right of removal. Nonetheless, both Congress and the courts have recognized limits on the ability of plaintiffs to manipulate procedural rules so as to defeat removal of diversity suits. We briefly address some of the principal limitations.

Improper joinder of parties to defeat diversity jurisdiction. A state court plaintiff has several options for defeating removal of a suit that might otherwise be removable based on diversity jurisdiction. For example, a plaintiff can join a defendant sharing the plaintiff's state of citizenship and so defeat removal based on the complete-diversity requirement. Or a plaintiff can join as defendant someone who is a citizen of the state where suit has been filed and take advantage of § 1441(b)'s prohibition of the removal of such suits.[58] In most cases, plaintiffs have the right to choose which defendants to sue even when their choice is made to defeat removal.

But in some cases, courts conclude that a plaintiff's selection of parties exceeds the bounds of fair play. One judicially developed response to unfair use of party joinder is the doctrine of "fraudulent joinder."[59] Fraudulent joinder occurs either when there is no possibility that a state court plaintiff can state a cause of action against a non-diverse defendant, or when the plaintiff has committed outright fraud in selecting the defendants.[60] The first form of

56. *See E. Farish Percy, Making a Federal Case of It: Removing Civil Cases to Federal Court Based on Fraudulent Joinder*, 91 Iowa L. Rev. 189, 206 & n.110 (2005), (describing a "variety of factors that may influence plaintiffs' general preference to litigate in state court," including local attorneys' comfort with home-state court systems, the increased chances of summary judgment in federal courts, the cost of federal pretrial activities, and the relative liberality of state rules governing permissive joinder).

57. *See* 28 U.S.C. § 1446(c) (preventing removal of a diversity case more than one year after an action is commenced).

58. These tactics to defeat removal are discussed in Paul Rosenthal, *Improper Joinder: Confronting Plaintiffs' Attempts to Destroy Federal Subject Matter Jurisdiction*, 59 Am. U. L. Rev. 49 (2009).

59. The dimensions of the problem are explored in E. Farish Percy, *Making a Federal Case of It: Removing Civil Cases to Federal Court Based on Fraudulent Joinder*, 91 Iowa L. Rev. 189, 240 (2005).

60. *Gottlieb v. Westin Hotel Co.*, 990 F.3d 323, 327 (7th Cir. 2003).

fraudulent joinder, where the plaintiff's claim against the diversity-destroying defendant is meritless, is the more common form. An illustration of this form of fraudulent joinder is found in pharmaceutical litigation. A plaintiff suing a pharmaceutical manufacturer for product liability sometimes names as co-defendant a local pharmaceutical representative sharing the plaintiff's citizenship.[61] The manufacturer removes the suit based on complete diversity between it and the plaintiff and asks the court to disregard the diversity-destroying defendant. If the manufacturer can meet its heavy burden of showing the plaintiff has no plausible claim against the pharmaceutical representative, a federal court will dismiss this co-defendant and deny the plaintiff's motion to remand for lack of diversity jurisdiction.[62]

Yet another form of fraudulent joinder—"procedural misjoinder"—has emerged in some circuits[63] to address the situation where a plaintiff joins a diversity-defeating defendant against whom the plaintiff may have a viable claim yet where joinder of that defendant is procedurally flawed.[64] Such flawed-party joinder occurs when a plaintiff joins a defendant based on claims that arise from factually unrelated incidents. Federal Rule of Civil Procedure 20, and similar state rules, limit the joinder of co-defendants to situations where some "right to relief" asserted against co-defendants arises "out of the same transaction, occurrence, or series of transactions or occurrences." The doctrine of fraudulent procedural joinder can be invoked when a court concludes that claims against co-defendants arise from separate transactions or occurrences and that the plaintiff's misuse of joinder rules is intended to defeat removal jurisdiction. In recognizing this form of fraudulent joinder, one circuit court has remarked, "Misjoinder may be just as fraudulent as the joinder of a resident defendant against whom a plaintiff has no possibility of a cause of action."[65] In cases of procedural misjoinder, courts usually sever the misjoined claim against the non-diverse defendant[66] and remand that part of the case to state court.

Another variation on fraudulent misjoinder is an adaptation of 28 U.S.C. § 1359, which prohibits improper or "collusive" joinder of a party intended to *create* diversity jurisdiction. Although § 1359 does not apply to the misuse of joinder to defeat diversity jurisdiction, several courts have concluded that guidelines developed under § 1359 can be used when plaintiffs collude to defeat the removal of diversity disputes.[67] One important guideline addresses a party's assignment of its claim against a defendant, or a share of its claim, when the assignment is intended to create a plaintiff who shares the citizenship of the defendant, thus violating the complete-diversity rule. Courts construing § 1359 have developed criteria to identify "collusive" assignments, and these criteria are sometimes used when the assignment of a claim permits a plaintiff to defeat removal. For example, in *Grassi v. Ciba-Geigy, Ltd.*, 894 F. 2d 181 (5th Cir. 1990), the Fifth Circuit upheld removal of a case when the plaintiff had assigned

61. *See, e.g., Legg v. Wyeth*, 428 F.3d 1317 (11th Cir. 2005); *In re Diet Drugs Prods. Liab. Litig.*, 220 F. Supp. 2d 414 (E.D. Pa. 2002).

62. *See, e.g., Florence v. Crescent Res., LLC*, 484 F.3d 1293, 1297 (11th Cir. 2007).

63. The leading case recognizing the principle of fraudulent joinder is *Tapscott v. MS Dealer Service Corp.*, 77 F.3d 1353 (11th Cir. 2000).

64. *See, e.g.*, Jason Harmon, *Procedural Misjoinder: The Quest for a Uniform Standard*, 62 KAN. L. REV. 1439 (2014).

65. *Tapscott v. MS Dealer Serv. Corp.*, 77 F.3d 1353, 1360 (11th Cir. 2000).

66. Federal Rule of Civil Procedure 21 authorizes the severing of misjoined claims or parties.

67. *See generally* CHARLES ALLEN WRIGHT, ARTHUR R. MILLER, & EDWARD H. COOPER, 6 FEDERAL PRACTICE AND PROCEDURE § 3641 (2014).

a 2 percent interest in its claim to a co-plaintiff for the purpose of defeating diversity jurisdiction.

Post-filing changes in parties that might defeat diversity jurisdiction. In most cases, the requirements for diversity jurisdiction must be satisfied both at the time the case is filed in state court and at the time it is removed.[68] And since parties may be added or dropped after a case is filed in state court or after it is removed to federal court, these changes can create or destroy diversity jurisdiction after filing. Congress has addressed the possibility that post-filing party changes might be used to defeat a defendant's right of removal through two revisions of removal statutes.

First, Congress has modified a restriction on removing diversity cases found in § 1446(c), which requires that such cases be removed no later than "1 year after commencement of the action" in state court.[69] This one-year limit does not apply if "the district court finds that the plaintiff has acted in bad faith to prevent a defendant from removing the action."[70] Such a rule complements the court-made doctrine of fraudulent joinder discussed earlier insofar as it prevents strategic delay of party joinder even when joinder is otherwise proper.[71] Such a strategic delay may constitute "bad faith" and so suspend operation of the one-year limit on removing diversity cases.[72]

Another provision in federal joinder statutes, § 1447(e), addresses the situation where a plaintiff seeks to join diversity-destroying defendants after a case has been properly removed to federal court. According to § 1447(e), a federal court asked to permit joinder of a diversity-destroying defendant "may deny joinder, or permit joinder and remand the action to State court." One would expect courts to deny joinder when they suspect that a plaintiff's primary motive in seeking joinder is to defeat jurisdiction.

Removal and the amount-in-controversy requirement. Diversity cases are removable to federal court only when the amount in controversy exceeds $75,000. But in many states, plaintiffs are not permitted to allege the amount of damages sought or, if they do, are not limited to the amount demanded in the original complaint.[73] This presents the question, how does a defendant seeking to remove a suit between diverse parties satisfy the amount-in-controversy requirement when the well-pleaded complaint fails to allege damages exceeding $75,000?

68. *Pullman Co. v. Jenkins*, 305 U.S. 534 (1939). Exceptions to this generalization are discussed in Richard D. Freer, Civil Procedure 243-44 (3d ed. 2012).

69. 28 U.S.C. § 1446(c)(1).

70. *Id.*

71. Section 1446(b)(2)(c) addresses another possible obstacle to removal, the general requirements that (a) defendants timely move for removal within 30 days of service of the pleading showing a right of removal exists, and (b) all defendants consent to removal. If a new defendant is added, and that defendant has the right to remove the case based on diversity of citizenship, the fact that other defendants failed to timely exercise the right of removal does not prevent the new defendant from seeking the consent of the earlier-named defendants to removal of the suit.

72. For example, the plaintiff might sue a non-diverse defendant and, a year later, dismiss that defendant and join as a new defendant a diverse party. Or the plaintiff might sue co-defendants, one of whom destroys complete diversity, and later dismiss the non-diverse defendant. Because many state courts don't employ case management and scheduling rules like Federal Rule of Civil Procedure 16, it's quite possible that a plaintiff can amend the pleading to change parties more than a year after suit is filed.

73. *See* Richard D. Freer, Civil Procedure 244-45 (3d ed. 2012)

In 2011, Congress addressed this question by amending § 1446(c)(2). Thus, when the plaintiff's complaint can't allege the specific amount of damages sought because of state procedural rules, or the plaintiff can recover damages in excess of what is alleged, diverse defendants can remove to federal court by alleging in their *notice of removal* that the amount in controversy actually exceeds $75,000. If the plaintiff disputes this claim, the federal court must determine based on "the preponderance of the evidence" whether the defendants' claim is true. Further, this section includes an anti-fraud provision. If the defendants attempt to remove a diversity dispute after the one-year limit on removal has expired, and the federal court "finds that the plaintiff deliberately failed to disclose the amount in controversy to prevent removal," the plaintiff's nondisclosure constitutes "bad faith" and the one-year limit does not apply.[74]

PROBLEM 7-5

The Limits of Removal Jurisdiction

Lance and Bert formerly worked as firemen for small communities in northern Kentucky. Lance was employed by the town of Billings, Kentucky, while Bert was employed by the neighboring town of Everton.[75] Each of the men eventually left their jobs because of harassment they suffered based on their known sexual orientation. Lance continues to live in Billings, Kentucky, but Bert moved across the border to Illinois after leaving his job in Everton.

Lance recently sued the town of Billings and alleged that it discriminated against him based on his sexual orientation in violation of state law. Assume that Kentucky law authorizes a cause of action for victims of sexual-orientation discrimination in employment. Successful plaintiffs can recover economic damages and noneconomic damages for pain and suffering, humiliation, emotional distress, and the like. Punitive damages are not recoverable.

Shortly after Lance filed suit against the town of Billings, Bert contacted Lance's lawyer. Eventually counsel recommended that Bert join Lance as co-plaintiff and add the town of Everton as co-defendant. Based on this advice, Lance's lawyer filed an amended complaint that included Bert as co-plaintiff and the town of Everton as co-defendant. In the amended complaint, each of the two plaintiffs alleges a claim for employment discrimination under state law. The amended complaint also alleges that Lance is currently a citizen of Kentucky and Bert is currently a citizen of Illinois.

Each plaintiff demands economic and noneconomic damages. The complaint does not allege the amount of damages the plaintiffs seek—state procedural law does not require an allegation specifying the amount of damages sought. But in the "Civil Filing Form" that plaintiffs must file along with a complaint, each plaintiff alleges economic damages (lost wages and benefit) of about $50,000 along with noneconomic damages "in an amount to be determined by the jury."

74. *See* 28 U.S.C. § 1446(c)(1), (c)(3)(B). A plaintiff can stipulate that she will not seek more than $75,000 and defeat removal. *See, e.g., Standard Fire Insurance Co. v. Knowles*, 133 S. Ct. 1345 (2013) (stating that a plaintiff class representative could defeat removal by stipulating to recovery of less than the amount-in-controversy requirement of the Class Action Fairness Act but only after she had authority to make binding stipulations for the class), But after removal, a plaintiff can't force remand by making such a stipulation. *See* Richard D. Freer, Civil Procedure 245 (3d ed. 2012).

75. Both the towns and the laws mentioned in this hypothetical are fictional.

The plaintiffs' lawyer filed the amended complaint "as a matter of right" and did not need court permission. But in the "notice of filing" accompanying the amended complaint, Lance's lawyer stated that "this amended complaint is submitted in accordance with Kentucky Rule of Civil Procedure 20." Both plaintiffs assert claims under Kentucky's Employment Discrimination Act based on discriminatory job action of the adjoining towns of Billings and Everton, Kentucky. The plaintiffs allege that the discriminatory job action arises from a practice and culture of hostility toward persons of their sexual orientation prevailing in Billings, Everton, and other communities in this part of the state." Rule 20, you may assume, is identical to Federal Rule of Civil Procedure 20.

The town of Everton has now filed a notice of removal that removes the entire case to the federal court presiding in this part of Kentucky. Everton alleges that removal is proper because it is a citizen of Kentucky, plaintiff Bert is a citizen of Illinois, and plaintiff Bert alleges a controversy in which damages may exceed $75,000. Everton also alleges that the citizenship of plaintiff Lance should be ignored because his claim has been improperly and collusively joined to that of plaintiff Bert.

1. What arguments can the plaintiffs assert if they seek to have all, or part, of the removed case remanded to state court? Are they likely to prevail in seeking remand?
2. Assume that, in the amended complaint filed in state court, Bert had included a second claim that Everton violated his rights under federal law by failing to compensate him for overtime work he performed when he was employed by the town. How would Bert's assertion of this federal claim alter the federal court's analysis of its removal jurisdiction?

d. Other Removal Statutes

As mentioned at the outset of our discussion of removal, several other subject- or defendant-specific statutes authorize removal. By omitting discussion of these statutes, we do not minimize their importance. Some of these statutes may be covered in other courses you take, such as courses in civil rights and securities regulation. We offer brief comment on two of these statutes, both of which authorize removal based on the nature of the defenses asserted by a defendant.

First, 28 U.S.C. § 1442 permits federal officers, federal agencies, and the United States itself to remove certain civil or criminal cases filed in state court when these parties assert a federal law *defense. See Mesa v. California*, 489 U.S. 121 (1989). In *Mesa*, the Court reaffirmed that the well-pleaded complaint rule (which ignores a defendant's federal defenses) is not derived from the Constitution and can be abrogated by Congress. But the Court expressed "grave constitutional concerns" about whether Congress could confer removal power on federal officials who asserted no defense based on federal law. *Id.* at 137.

Second, 28 U.S.C. § 1443 permits defendants to remove cases to federal court when they are denied the protection of laws providing for "equal civil rights," or when a defendant is acting under the authority of such laws. In Chapter 9 we consider the unique role played by the federal courts in the enforcement of constitutional rights, including the enforcement of federal rights threatened by pending state court action. Section 1443 was enacted in the aftermath of the Civil War, and authorizes removal of both civil and criminal actions.

Removal under § 1443 need not detain us long because it has been so narrowly construed that it has little practical use. According to the Court, unless a defendant is affected by a *specific* state law denying him "equal rights," removal is unavailable under the first part of the act. *See, e.g., Georgia v. Rachel*, 384 U.S. 780 (1966). With the demise of state and local laws authorizing de jure discrimination, this part of the statute has little utility.

The second part of § 1443, authorizing removal by defendants acting "under the authority" of civil rights laws, also has little if any practical value today. According to the Court in *City of Greenwood v. Peacock*, 384 U.S. 808 (1966), this form of statutory removal is available solely to governmental officials. As a consequence, this removal provision is largely redundant of removal statutes like § 1442 (referred to above).[76]

REVIEW AND CONSOLIDATION

Removal in Conventional Civil Litigation

- A defendant may usually remove a civil action filed in state court if the plaintiff could have originally filed the action in federal court. The principal exception occurs in diversity-of-citizenship cases where some properly named defendant is a citizen of the state where suit has been filed.
- Removal jurisdiction extends to cases alleging federal claims together with state claims that satisfy the requirements for supplemental jurisdiction.
- A defendant against whom is asserted a claim arising under federal law can remove a case despite the joinder of other claims or parties not within a federal court's supplemental jurisdiction. But those claims lacking a jurisdictional basis must be remanded to state court.
- When a state court plaintiff improperly uses rules of joinder to defeat a defendant's right of removal, federal statutes or judicial doctrine may permit removal and a federal court can adjudicate those parts of the case within its jurisdiction.
- Specialized federal statutes both authorize, and limit, removal in certain settings.

76. *See generally* Martin H. Redish, *Revitalizing Civil Rights Removal Jurisdiction*, 64 MINN. L. REV. 523 (1980).

D. SOME ADDITIONAL PROBLEMS

PROBLEM 7-6

To sell a car

Two plaintiffs, Toody and Muldoon (neighbors), have joined in a state court suit in Missouri against Dependable Cars, Inc. (DCI). Each plaintiff purchased a used auto from DCI last year in separate transactions. Both financed their purchases through DCI's credit program (i.e., there is no independent financing company). The two purchasers have joined as plaintiffs because each challenges the terms of the loan documents. According to the plaintiffs' complaint, DCI charged the plaintiffs a fee of $45 for "license, title, registration, and inspection" even though the state's actual charge for these items is only $20. What is more, the $45 fee was added to the loan balance, thus requiring the plaintiffs to pay interest on the fee. The complaint alleges that DCI's "fee scheme" violates the federal Truth in Lending Act, as well as Missouri's "Fair Lending Practices Act" (a fictionalized statute).

Each plaintiff is also unhappy with the auto he purchased. Toody alleges that DCI failed to disclose his auto had been previously damaged in a flood, causing rust to develop in the auto's chassis (a condition recently discovered by Toody). Muldoon alleges that his auto was also damaged in a prior accident, and that the "original paint" representation made by DCI was false. The new paint job is beginning to fail.

In response to the suit, DCI denies all charges. In addition, it asserts counterclaims against Toody and Muldoon to recover monies owed under their lending agreements. It also asserts a counterclaim against Toody for defamation, based on Toody's recent appearance on a television show, "Looking out for you!" where Toody said that "DCI is a bunch of crooks. They will lie, steal, or do anything else to sell a car."

DCI has now filed a timely notice removing the plaintiffs' suit to federal court. Please discuss all responses available to the plaintiffs to have all, or part, of the suit remanded to state court.

PROBLEM 7-7

I Wrote That Script!

As you learned in Chapter 5, the Supreme Court has held that some subjects are "completely preempted" by federal law, with the consequence that claims appearing to be based on state law actually "arise under" federal law. As the Court observed in *Beneficial National Bank v. Anderson*, 539 U.S. 1, 8 (2003), "When the federal statute completely pre-empts the state-law cause of action, a claim which comes within the scope of that cause of action, even if pleaded in terms of state law, is in reality based on federal law."

Assume that Milton has sued Big Lion Studios (Studios) for the wrongful use of television scripts written by Milton. One script, "Never Trust a Gambler," was actually copyrighted by Milton before Studios used it in a TV show. A second script, "Strange Bedfellows," was never copyrighted. The complaint, filed in California state court, alleges (1) a federal copyright violation claim against Studios for its unauthorized use of "Never Trust a Gambler"; (2) a state common-law conversion claim for Studios' use of "Strange Bedfellows."

Studios' lawyer conducts appropriate research and concludes (a) Milton's copyright infringement claim is unsupported because Milton failed to timely register his copyright as required by federal law; and (b) Milton's conversion claim is tantamount to a claim under federal copyright law and so is completely preempted.

Discuss Studios' strategic options for responding to Milton's suit, including the option of removing the suit to federal court.

PROBLEM 7-8

In Pursuit of the Bad-Faith Insurance Company

Mildred was injured in a car accident when an uninsured motorist ran a red light. When the insurance company from whom she purchased uninsured motorist coverage refused to pay her full policy limits of $25,000, she sued her insurer in state court for breach of contract. Mildred is a citizen of Texas, while her insurer is a corporate citizen of Oklahoma.

Eighteen months after filing her suit against the defendant insurer, Mildred moved to amend her complaint to add a claim under state law for "bad-faith representation." The state court granted Mildred's motion to amend. If Mildred succeeds in proving bad faith, she can recover all her accident damages from the insurer, which will not be limited by the policy limits of $25,000. In compliance with state procedural law, Mildred has not pleaded the amount of damages she seeks in her complaint.

Defendant insurer filed a notice of removal in the local federal court within 30 days of being served with Mildred's amended complaint. The notice alleged that Mildred's case is removable based on diversity jurisdiction. If Mildred files a motion to remand the case to state court because the insurer failed to "timely remove" the action, will she succeed?

CHAPTER 8

The Eleventh Amendment and State Sovereign Immunity

A. A REFERENCE PROBLEM

In this chapter we consider the Eleventh Amendment to the United States Constitution and the broader concept of state sovereign immunity from suit in federal courts that it is said to reflect. The Reference Problem below introduces many of the concepts we will explore.

* * * * *

Jane Jett ("Jett") was a promising high school soccer player who lived in Davenport, Iowa. She was highly recruited by several colleges based on her athletic ability. One of these institutions was the University of Iowa (the

"University"). The University was created by the Iowa State Constitution, which provides that the University's funds and lands "shall be under the control and management of the General Assembly of this State." Approximately 20 percent of the University's funds come through state appropriations. The balance of its funds come from other sources, including tuition and federal government grants. Iowa state law considers the University to be a state agency.

Jett was contacted in her junior year of high school by the University's athletic director, Tom Field ("Field"). Field actively recruited Jett, keeping in touch almost weekly with Jett and her parents. Field ultimately convinced Jett that Iowa was the school to attend. No small part of Jett's decision was based on the University's offer of a full athletic scholarship should she attend and play soccer.

Unfortunately, in addition to possessing great athletic talent, Jett also had a serious learning disability. Despite having an above-average IQ score, she was diagnosed early in her elementary school years as having difficulty in organizing and processing information. As a result, Jett needed extra time to take tests, required assistance in studying and organizing materials, and performed better in very small classes. In order to accommodate her learning disability, a majority of Jett's classes in high school were in a special education setting, and she was allowed to take standardized tests such as the SAT in an untimed format.

The University is a member of the National Collegiate Athletic Association (NCAA), the primary governing body for intercollegiate athletics in the United States. One function the NCAA serves is determining whether incoming college freshman are academically eligible to play college sports. Through its membership in the organization, the University agreed to abide by the NCAA's eligibility determinations. The NCAA makes its eligibility determinations by considering, among other things, a high school student's transcript to determine that the courses taken were at least at a "regular academic instruction level." The NCAA also considers the student's SAT score in its eligibility determinations.

The NCAA determined that Jett was a "non-qualifying" student for athletic eligibility purposes. A student designated as "non-qualifying" cannot be a member of a collegiate sports team and cannot informally associate with such a team by, among other things, attending team meetings or workouts. Part of the NCAA's reasoning, which it disclosed to the University, was based on its determination that (1) Jett's SAT score could not be relied upon because it was based on an untimed test and (2) many of Jett's high school special education courses were not taught at a "regular academic instruction level." When the University received the NCAA's designation of Jett as "non-qualifying," it ceased its recruiting efforts. Field informed Jett and her parents that he could no longer offer Jett a scholarship to attend the University.

Jett has filed a lawsuit in the United States District Court for the Southern District of Iowa against, among others, the University and Field in his position as the University's athletic director. The jurisdictional basis asserted in the complaint is that Jett's cause of action arises under federal law. *See* 28 U.S.C. § 1331. The gist of Jett's lawsuit is that the University and Field as its agent discriminated against her because of her disability. Specifically, Jett asserts claims under two federal statutes: the Rehabilitation Act of 1973 and Title II of the Americans with Disabilities Act of 1990 (ADA). For remedies, Jett seeks monetary damages (which are provided for under both statutes) from the University and an injunction against both the University and Field as its athletic director prohibiting them from future action respecting Jett in violation of either statute.

Section 504 of the Rehabilitation Act prohibits discrimination on the basis of disability in federally funded programs or activities. It provides: "No otherwise qualified individual with a disability in the United States . . . shall, solely by reason of her or his disability, be excluded from the participation in, be denied the benefits of, or be subjected to discrimination under any program or activity receiving Federal financial assistance. . . ." The statute makes clear that a "program or activity" includes "the entity of [a] State or local government that distributes" the federal assistance. Finally, the statute includes the following provision: "A state shall not be immune under the Eleventh Amendment of the Constitution of the United States from suit in Federal court for a violation of section 504 of the Rehabilitation Act of 1973. . . ." The relevant portions of the Rehabilitation Act were enacted pursuant to Congress'so-called Spending Power. *See* U.S. CONST. art. I, § 8, cl. 1 ("The Congress shall have Power [t]o . . . provide for the common Defence and general Welfare of the United States. . . ."). The University received federal funds in connection with its athletic programs.

Title II of the ADA prohibits any public entity from discriminating against qualified persons with disabilities in the provision or operation of public services, programs, or activities. The term "public entitles" specifically includes state and local governments as well as their instrumentalities. Finally, the statute provides that a "State shall not be immune under the Eleventh Amendment to the Constitution of the United States from an action in [a] Federal or State court of competent jurisdiction."

The ADA was enacted pursuant to Congress' power to "regulate Commerce . . . among the several States . . .", *see* U.S. CONST. art. I, § 8, cl. 3, and under section 5 of the Fourteenth Amendment, *see* U.S. CONST. amend. XIV, § 5 ("The Congress shall have power to enforce, by appropriate legislation, the provisions of this article."). Congress enacted the ADA after several years of investigation concerning discrimination in American society against persons with disabilities. As part of that work, congressional committees collected examples of such discrimination by public educational institutions.

Both the University and Field have moved to dismiss Jett's complaint in its entirety on the ground that they are immune from suit in federal court with respect to all her claims (and for all the remedies sought) by virtue of the Eleventh Amendment to the United States Constitution and the principles of state sovereign immunity it reflects. You are the United States District Judge to whom the case has been assigned. How do you rule on the motion? Why? If you need additional information, what would you like to know and why would that information be relevant to your inquiry?

* * * *

As you think about your response, consider the following questions this Reference Problem raises:

- Look at the text of the Eleventh Amendment. Based on its language, does the Amendment support any claim for immunity in this case? Even if the Amendment or some other constitutional principle could support a state immunity defense, should the *University* get the benefit of that defense?
- As a policy matter, what arguments could be used to support immunity from suit in federal court for states? What arguments cut against recognizing such immunity?

- Assuming that either one or both of the federal statutes Jett sues under allow her to proceed in federal court despite a broad state immunity from suit, how could such a result be justified? Are there other policy or constitutional issues at play here concerning, for example, deference to congressional judgments?
- Assuming that the University would be entitled to immunity from suit on all of Jett's claims, is there any basis for allowing her request for an injunction to proceed against Field? Assuming that the law is such that the claim would be allowed to proceed, why might the law have developed in this way?

You will almost certainly not be able to answer most of these questions now. You should be able to do so at the conclusion of this chapter.

B. CONTEXT AND BACKGROUND

The Eleventh Amendment reads in full as follows:

> The Judicial power of the United States shall not be construed to extend to any suit in law or equity, commenced or prosecuted against one of the United States by Citizens of another State, or by Citizens or Subjects of any Foreign State.

These 43 words have spawned hundreds of Supreme Court decisions over the past 200 years and voluminous commentary by some of the most distinguished scholars in the federal courts world. Yet there is still deep disagreement about what this Amendment means. At least as far as accepted doctrine goes, as with the proverbial iceberg, there is much more to the Eleventh Amendment than one might guess by looking at its surface alone. This chapter explores what lies in these often murky depths.

As we will see, the Eleventh Amendment and the immunity from suit it both reflects and confers on the states of the Union raise many of the issues that are central in a Federal Courts class. What is the proper role of the federal courts in ensuring the supremacy of federal law? What is the proper role of federal courts in policing the interaction between the "People" and the states? Are state courts up to the task of doing either of these things? What is the proper role of Congress in policing the boundaries of federalism? And, finally for now, what is the proper role of the federal courts in judging Congress's actions concerning the balance of authority between federal and state governments? In short, this chapter is replete with fundamental questions going to the heart of American constitutional federalism and separation of powers.

One of the most significant initial challenges in studying the Eleventh Amendment is that, as retired Justice John Paul Stevens has written, there are in important respects "two Eleventh Amendments." *See Pennsylvania v. Union Gas Co.*, 491 U.S. 1, 23 (1990) (Stevens, J., concurring). What Justice Stevens meant is that there is, first, the meaning of the Eleventh Amendment itself on the ability of states to be sued in a federal court. But there is also according to the Court a broader immunity from suit that is a part of our federal system of government. Exploring that broader immunity is challenging because there is no precise constitutional text to study. The Court treats immunity, like the air we breathe, as all around us even if we cannot see it. In this chapter, you will see that both we — as well as the Court — refer to the states' immunity from suit at times as "Eleventh Amendment immunity" and at other junctures as some form of "state sovereign immunity." You should treat these phrases as interchangeable unless the context requires otherwise.

To understand this area of the law, a student must first have some grasp of the basic notion of sovereign immunity itself. Historically, sovereign immunity was captured in the phrase "the King can do no wrong." This concept, evoking images of monarchs from ages past, never truly meant that the ruler was infallible. Rather, the immunity from suit was a recognition that as the sovereign the monarch could not be called to account in his or her court without royal consent. The "right" to avoid suit was thus said to be bound up with the status as sovereign.

Of course, we have no monarch in America. Nevertheless, the basic notion of sovereign immunity traversed the Atlantic Ocean and was recognized as a part of American law when the colonies gained their independence. That is, the newly independent states were said to be immune from suits in their courts unless they consented to such a suit.

But saying that the states possessed some form of immunity from suit in their own courts does not necessarily tell us what immunity from suit these sovereigns had with respect to courts established under the Constitution. The basic reason for this uncertainty is that the states technically could not have had immunity in federal courts before the Constitution was ratified because there were no federal courts before the Constitution created the Supreme Court and Congress ordained and established the inferior federal courts in the famous Judiciary Act of 1789. The uncertainty is compounded because the text of the Constitution says nothing expressly about state immunity from suit in federal courts. What does that silence mean? As we will see, a bare majority of the Supreme Court has consistently taken the position that this silence actually reflects the universal recognition of sovereign immunity. In other words, because it was so accepted, the Court has said that nothing needed to be expressed about it in the document.

We begin the next section by considering this fundamental issue concerning the existence of sovereign immunity from suit in the original Constitution and what the Eleventh Amendment's ratification in response to a controversial Supreme Court decision not recognizing such immunity should be interpreted to mean. As we will learn, by the end of the 1800s, the Supreme Court had held that the Eleventh Amendment reflected a much broader immunity that existed at the time the Constitution was ratified and that survived ratification intact.

We then turn from our initial exploration of the nature and scope of sovereign immunity to consider three ways in which it is possible to avoid or get around it. First, a state may consent to suit in federal court or otherwise waive its immunity. Second, it is possible for a plaintiff to avoid sovereign immunity by suing a state official in her official capacity and requesting prospective injunctive relief to stop an ongoing violation of federal law. We will see that this doctrine, most commonly referred to in shorthand form as *Ex parte Young* relief, is the Court's attempt to balance the federalism values that sovereign immunity reflects with the importance of the supremacy of federal law. Third, and finally, it is possible for Congress to abrogate — or void — a state's immunity from suit provided that it acts pursuant to a power that permits it to do so. The key is that the Court has interpreted the Constitution to limit Congress's ability in that regard in several important respects.

The final section of the chapter turns to several decisions the Court rendered around the turn of the twenty-first century. As we will explore, these decisions both expand the scope of state sovereign immunity and, somewhat inconsistently, introduce uncertainty about the basic immunity states enjoy from suit in federal court. In many respects, you will see that the doctrine today is as unsettled as it has been at many other points in American constitutional history.

C. THE LAW AND PROBLEMS

1. *The Foundations and Scope of Constitutional State Sovereign Immunity*

a. The Historical Backstory to Modern Doctrine

As with so much else in this course, a good beginning to the questions we will explore is Article III of the Constitution. As originally ratified, Article III extended the "judicial Power of the United States" to, among other matters, "Controversies . . . between a State and Citizens of another State." U.S. CONST. art. III, § 2, cl. 1. Relying on that provision, the executor of the estate of a citizen of South Carolina sued the State of Georgia in federal court, claiming that Georgia had breached a contract to pay for supplies provided in connection with the American Revolutionary War.[1] Georgia refused to appear to defend the case, arguing that as a sovereign state it was immune from suit without its consent.

In a 4-1 decision the Supreme Court rejected Georgia's immunity-based argument. *Chisholm v. Georgia*, 2 U.S. (2 Dall.) 419 (1793). *Chisholm*'s underlying rationale is not as easy to determine as one might think. One reason is that, at the time of the case, the Court announced its decisions *seriatim*. Each justice gave his own reasons for ruling as he did. There was no "opinion of the Court," a concept that would not be introduced until John Marshall became Chief Justice.

Chisholm is discussed in many of the cases we have excerpted in this chapter. As you will see, exactly what *Chisholm* did, whether the decision was correct, and the import of what happened in response to it are all highly contested. In some respects, it may be more important what the Court has said about *Chisholm* than what *Chisholm* actually said itself. For present purposes, however, it is sufficient to understand only a few central points from this important constitutional decision. First, a central basis on which the Court ruled was the plain language of Article III that certainly appeared to address the situation the Court faced. Indeed, two of the justices seemed to rely essentially exclusively on this rationale for their positions.[2] Second, the other justices in the majority, while also relying on the language of Article III, more thoroughly discussed the concept of a state's

1. The case was actually filed in the Supreme Court pursuant to a provision of the Judiciary Act of 1789 giving the Supreme Court original jurisdiction in such cases. *See* 1 Stat. 73, § 13.

2. *See Chisholm*, 2 U.S. at 450-53 (opinion of Blair, J.); *id.* at 466-69 (opinion of Cushing, J.).

sovereignty in the new federal system.[3] However, there cannot be said to have been any "rule" of a majority of the *Chisholm* Court concerning how, precisely, the sovereignty of the several states from the pre-constitutional period applied with respect to lawsuits in the new federal courts. Third, Justice Iredell, the lone dissenter, also discussed the general importance of sovereign immunity to the states in the pre-constitutional period, but he ultimately based his dissent on an absence of specific legislation authorizing the suit.[4] As we will see, precisely what Justice Iredell's dissent means has been an important point of dispute in the modern Eleventh Amendment cases. Fourth, all five justices on the *Chisholm* Court had been deeply involved in the drafting and/or ratification of the then-newly operative Constitution. They were all Framers and/or ratifiers of the document.

As the Supreme Court interpreted it in our first principal case below, *Chisholm* was said to have "created . . . a shock of surprise throughout the country." *Hans v. Louisiana*, 134 U.S. 1, 11 (1890). While this description is certainly somewhat hyperbolic, it is the case that Congress moved swiftly after *Chisholm* to amend the Constitution to, at a minimum, reverse the Supreme Court's interpretation of Article III in that case. What would become the Eleventh Amendment was introduced in Congress within days of the decision. The Eleventh Amendment certainly prohibits a suit such as the one the Court faced in *Chisholm*. The question is what else — if anything — does the Amendment do? Our journey to answer that question — or at least see how the Supreme Court has answered it — begins with *Hans v. Louisiana* in 1890.

HANS v. LOUISIANA

134 U.S. 1 (1890)

MR. JUSTICE BRADLEY . . . delivered the opinion of the [C]ourt.

[Mr. Hans claimed that he held valid bonds issued by the State of Louisiana on which certain payments were due. Nevertheless, Hans asserted, the State refused to pay on the bonds, relying on an amendment to the Louisiana Constitution that purported to "remit" such outstanding state-issued instruments. Hans argued that this remittance violated the Contracts Clause of the United States Constitution. *See* U.S. CONST. art. I, § 10, cl. 1. Hans filed suit against the State of Louisiana in federal court. The state objected to the federal court's jurisdiction, claiming that it could not be sued in federal court without its consent. The lower court dismissed the suit based on the state's argument. Hans appealed to the Supreme Court of the United States.]

The question is presented, whether a State can be sued in a Circuit Court of the United States by one of its own citizens upon a suggestion that the case is one that arises under the Constitution or laws of the United States.

The ground taken is, that under the Constitution, as well as under the act of Congress passed to carry it into effect, a case is within the jurisdiction of the federal courts, without regard to the character of the parties, if it arises under the

3. *See id.* at 453-66 (opinion of Wilson, J.); *id.* at 470-79 (opinion of Jay, C.J.).

4. Specifically, Justice Iredell argued that there was no statute expressly conferring federal jurisdiction over breach of contract actions against the states. In the absence of such specific congressional authorization, Iredell argued that Article III's general language was insufficient to justify jurisdiction against an unconsenting state given the importance of sovereign immunity in the young federal system. *See, e.g., Chisholm*, 2 U.S. at 434-35 (Iredell, J., dissenting).

Constitution or laws of the United States, or, which is the same thing, if it necessarily involves a question under said Constitution or laws. The language relied on is that clause of the 3d article of the Constitution, which declares that "the judicial power of the United States shall extend to all cases in law and equity arising under this Constitution, the laws of the United States, and treaties made, or which shall be made, under their authority"; and the corresponding clause of [the then-current version of 28 U.S.C. § 1331 conferring arising under jurisdiction on the lower federal courts]. It is said that these jurisdictional clauses make no exception arising from the character of the parties, and, therefore, that a State can claim no exemption from suit, if the case is really one arising under the Constitution, laws or treaties of the United States. It is conceded that where the jurisdiction depends alone upon the character of the parties, a controversy between a State and its own citizens is not embraced within it; but it is contended that though jurisdiction does not exist on that ground, it nevertheless does exist if the case itself is one which necessarily involves a federal question; and with regard to ordinary parties this is undoubtedly true. The question now to be decided is, whether it is true where one of the parties is a State, and is sued as a defendant by one of its own citizens.

That a State cannot be sued by a citizen of another State, or of a foreign state, on the mere ground that the case is one arising under the Constitution or laws of the United States, is clearly established by the decisions of this court in several recent cases. Those were cases arising under the Constitution of the United States, upon laws complained of as impairing the obligation of contracts, one of which was the constitutional amendment of Louisiana complained of in the present case. Relief was sought against state officers who professed to act in obedience to those laws. This court held that the suits were virtually against the States themselves and were consequently violative of the Eleventh Amendment of the Constitution, and could not be maintained. It was not denied that they presented cases arising under the Constitution; but, notwithstanding that, they were held to be prohibited by the amendment referred to.

In the present case the plaintiff in error [Hans] contends that he, being a citizen of Louisiana, is not embarrassed by the obstacle of the Eleventh Amendment, inasmuch as that amendment only prohibits suits against a State which are brought by the citizens of another State, or by citizens or subjects of a foreign State. It is true, the amendment does so read: and if there were no other reason or ground for abating his suit, it might be maintainable; and then we should have this anomalous result, that in cases arising under the Constitution or laws of the United States, a State may be sued in the federal courts by its own citizens, though it cannot be sued for a like cause of action by the citizens of other States, or of a foreign state; and may be thus sued in the federal courts, although not allowing itself to be sued in its own courts. If this is the necessary consequence of the language of the Constitution and the law, the result is no less startling and unexpected than was the original decision of this court, that under the language of the Constitution and of the judiciary act of 1789, a State was liable to be sued by a citizen of another State, or of a foreign country. That decision was made in the case of *Chisholm v. Georgia* and created such a shock of surprise throughout the country that, at the first meeting of Congress thereafter, the Eleventh Amendment to the Constitution was almost unanimously proposed, and was in due course adopted by the legislatures of the States. This amendment, expressing the will of the ultimate sovereignty of the whole country, superior to all legislatures and all courts, actually reversed the decision of the Supreme Court.

It did not in terms prohibit suits by individuals against the States, but declared that the Constitution should not be construed to import any power to authorize the bringing of such suits. The language of the amendment is that "the judicial power of the United States shall not be construed to extend to any suit in law or equity, commenced or prosecuted against one of the United States by citizens of another State or by citizens or subjects of any foreign state." The Supreme Court had construed the judicial power as extending to such a suit, and its decision was thus overruled. . . .

This view of the force and meaning of the amendment is important. It shows that, on this question of the suability of the States by individuals, the highest authority of this country was in accord rather with the minority than with the majority of the court in the decision of the case of *Chisholm v. Georgia*; and this fact lends additional interest to the able opinion of Mr. Justice Iredell on that occasion. The other justices were more swayed by a close observance of the letter of the Constitution, without regard to former experience and usage; and because the letter said that the judicial power shall extend to controversies "between a State and citizens of another State;" and "between a State and foreign states, citizens or subjects," they felt constrained to see in this language a power to enable the individual citizens of one State, or of a foreign state, to sue another State of the Union in the federal courts. Justice Iredell, on the contrary, contended that it was not the intention to create new and unheard of remedies, by subjecting sovereign States to actions at the suit of individuals, (which he conclusively showed was never done before,) but only, by proper legislation, to invest the federal courts with jurisdiction to hear and determine controversies and cases, between the parties designated, that were properly susceptible of litigation in courts.

Looking back from our present standpoint at the decision in *Chisholm v. Georgia*, we do not greatly wonder at the effect which it had upon the country. Any such power as that of authorizing the federal judiciary to entertain suits by individuals against the States, had been expressly disclaimed, and even resented, by the great defenders of the Constitution whilst it was on its trial before the American people. As some of their utterances are directly pertinent to the question now under consideration, we deem it proper to quote them.

The eighty-first number of the Federalist, written by Hamilton, has the following profound remarks:

> It has been suggested that an assignment of the public securities of one State to the citizens of another, would enable them to prosecute that State in the federal courts for the amount of those securities; a suggestion which the following considerations prove to be without foundation:
>
> It is inherent in the nature of sovereignty not to be amenable to the suit of an individual without its consent. This is the general sense and the general practice of mankind; and the exemption, as one of the attributes of sovereignty, is now enjoyed by the government of every State in the Union. Unless, therefore, there is a surrender of this immunity in the plan of the convention, it will remain with the States, and the danger intimated must be merely ideal. The circumstances which are necessary to produce an alienation of state sovereignty were discussed in considering the article of taxation, and need not be repeated here. A recurrence to the principles there established will satisfy us, that there is no color to pretend that the state governments would, by the adoption of that plan, be divested of the privilege of paying their own debts in their own way, free from every constraint but that which flows from the obligations of good

> faith. The contracts between a nation and individuals are only binding on the conscience of the sovereign, and have no pretension to a compulsive force. They confer no right of action independent of the sovereign will. To what purpose would it be to authorize suits against States for the debts they owe? How could recoveries be enforced? It is evident that it could not be done without waging war against the contracting State; and to ascribe to the federal courts by mere implication, and in destruction of a pre-existing right of the state governments, a power which would involve such a consequence, would be altogether forced and unwarrantable.

The obnoxious clause to which Hamilton's argument was directed, and which was the ground of the objections which he so forcibly met, was that which declared that "the judicial power shall extend to all . . . controversies between a State and citizens of another State, . . . and between a State and foreign states, citizens or subjects." It was argued by the opponents of the Constitution that this clause would authorize jurisdiction to be given to the federal courts to entertain suits against a State brought by the citizens of another State, or of a foreign state. Adhering to the mere letter, it might be so; and so, in fact, the Supreme Court held in *Chisholm v. Georgia*; but looking at the subject as Hamilton did, and as Mr. Justice Iredell did, in the light of history and experience and the established order of things, the views of the latter were clearly right,—as the people of the United States in their sovereign capacity subsequently decided.

But Hamilton was not alone in protesting against the construction put upon the Constitution by its opponents. In the Virginia convention the same objections were raised by George Mason and Patrick Henry, and were met by Madison and Marshall as follows. Madison said: "Its jurisdiction [the federal jurisdiction] in controversies between a State and citizens of another State is much objected to, and perhaps without reason. It is not in the power of individuals to call any State into court. The only operation it can have is that, if a State should wish to bring a suit against a citizen, it must be brought before the federal court. This will give satisfaction to individuals, as it will prevent citizens on whom a State may have a claim being dissatisfied with the state courts. . . . It appears to me that this [clause] can have no operation but this—to give a citizen a right to be heard in the federal courts; and if a State should condescend to be a party, this court may take cognizance of it." Marshall, in answer to the same objection, said: "With respect to disputes between a State and the citizens of another State, its jurisdiction has been decried with unusual vehemence. I hope that no gentleman will think that a State will be called at the bar of the federal court. . . . It is not rational to suppose that the sovereign power should be dragged before a court. The intent is to enable States to recover claims of individuals residing in other States. . . . But, say they, there will be partiality in it if a State cannot be defendant—if an individual cannot proceed to obtain judgment against a State, though he may be sued by a State. It is necessary to be so, and cannot be avoided. I see a difficulty in making a State defendant which does not prevent its being plaintiff."

It seems to us that these views of those great advocates and defenders of the Constitution were most sensible and just; and they apply equally to the present case as to that then under discussion. The letter is appealed to now, as it was then, as a ground for sustaining a suit brought by an individual against a State. The reason against it is as strong in this case as it was in that. It is an attempt to strain the Constitution and the law to a construction never imagined or dreamed of. Can we suppose that, when the Eleventh Amendment was adopted, it was understood to be left open for citizens of a State to sue their own state in the federal courts, whilst the idea of suits by citizens of other states, or of foreign states, was indignantly repelled? Suppose that Congress, when proposing the Eleventh Amendment, had appended to it a proviso that nothing therein contained should prevent a State from being sued by its own citizens in cases arising under the Constitution or laws of the United States: can we imagine that it would have been adopted by the States? The supposition that it would is almost an absurdity on its face.

* * * *

The suability of a State without its consent was a thing unknown to the law. This has been so often laid down and acknowledged by courts and jurists that it is hardly necessary to be formally asserted. It was fully shown by an exhaustive examination of the old law by Mr. Justice Iredell in his opinion in *Chisholm v. Georgia*; and it has been conceded in every case since, where the question has, in any way been presented, even in the cases which have gone farthest in sustaining suits against the officers or agents of States. *Osborn v. Bank of United States*. . . . In all these cases the effort was to show, and the court held, that the suits were not against the State or the United States, but against the individuals; conceding that if they had been against either the State or the United States, they could not be maintained.

* * * *

Undoubtedly a State may be sued by its own consent. . . . Chief Justice Taney . . . said: "It is an established principle of jurisprudence in all civilized nations that the sovereign cannot be sued in its own courts, or in any other, without its consent and permission; but it may, if it thinks proper, waive this privilege and permit itself to be made a defendant in a suit by individuals, or by another State. And as this permission is altogether voluntary on the part of the sovereignty, it follows that it may prescribe the terms and conditions on which it consents to be sued, and the manner in which the suit shall be conducted, and may withdraw its consent whenever it may suppose that justice to the public requires it. . . ."

* * * *

But besides the presumption that no anomalous and unheard-of proceedings or suits were intended to be raised up by the Constitution—anomalous and unheard of when the Constitution was adopted—an additional reason why the jurisdiction claimed for the Circuit Court does not exist, is the language of the act of Congress by which its jurisdiction is conferred. The words are these: "The circuit courts of the United States shall have original cognizance, concurrent with the courts of the several States, of all suits of a civil nature at common law or in equity, . . . arising under the Constitution or laws of the United States, or treaties," etc.—"Concurrent with the courts of the several States." Does not this qualification show that Congress, in legislating to carry the Constitution into effect, did not intend to invest its courts with any new and strange jurisdictions? The state courts have no power to entertain suits by individuals against a State without its consent. Then how does the Circuit Court, having only concurrent jurisdiction, acquire any such power? It is true that the same qualification existed in the judiciary act of 1789, which was before the court in *Chisholm v. Georgia*, and the majority of the court did not think that it was sufficient to limit the jurisdiction of the Circuit Court. Justice Iredell thought differently. In view of the manner in which that decision was received by the country, the adoption of the Eleventh Amendment, the light of history and the reason of the thing, we think we are at liberty to prefer Justice Iredell's views in this regard.

Some reliance is placed by the plaintiff upon the observations of Chief Justice Marshall, in *Cohens v. Virginia.* The Chief Justice was there considering the power of review exercisable by this court over the judgments of a state court, wherein it might be necessary to make the State itself a defendant in error. He showed that this power was absolutely necessary in order to enable the judiciary of the United States to take cognizance of all cases arising under the Constitution and laws of the United States. He also showed that making a State a defendant in error was entirely different from suing a State in an original action in prosecution of a demand against it, and was not within the meaning of the Eleventh Amendment; that the prosecution of a writ of error against a State was not the prosecution of a suit in the sense of that amendment, which had reference to the prosecution, by suit, of claims against a State. "Where," said the Chief Justice, "a State obtains a judgment against an individual, and the court rendering such judgment overrules a defence set up under the Constitution or laws of the United States, the transfer of this record into the Supreme Court for the sole purpose of inquiring whether the judgment violates the Constitution of the United States, can, with no propriety, we think, be denominated a suit commenced or prosecuted against the State whose judgment is so far reexamined. Nothing is demanded from the State. No claim against it of any description is asserted or prosecuted. The party is not to be restored to the possession of any thing. . . . The universally received opinion is that no suit can be commenced or prosecuted against the United States; that the judiciary act does not authorize such suits. Yet writs of error, accompanied with citations, have uniformly issued for the removal of judgments in favor of the United States into a superior court. . . .

After thus showing by incontestable argument that a writ of error to a judgment recovered by a State, in which the State is necessarily the defendant in error, is not a suit commenced or prosecuted against a State in the sense of the amendment, he added, that if the court were mistaken in this, its error did not affect that case, because the writ of error therein was not prosecuted by "a citizen of another State" or "of any foreign state," and so was not affected by the amendment; but was governed by the general grant of judicial power, as extending "to all cases arising under the Constitution or laws of the United States, without respect to parties."

It must be conceded that the last observation of the Chief Justice does favor the argument of the plaintiff. But the observation was unnecessary to the decision, and in that sense extra judicial, and though made by one who seldom used words without due reflection, ought not to outweigh the important considerations referred to which lead to a different conclusion. With regard to the question then before the court, it may be observed, that writs of error to judgments in favor of the crown, or of the State, had been known to the law from time immemorial; and had never been considered as exceptions to the rule, that an action does not lie against the sovereign.

To avoid misapprehension it may be proper to add that, although the obligations of a State rest for their performance upon its honor and good faith, and cannot be made the subjects of judicial cognizance unless the State consents to be sued, or comes itself into court; yet where property or rights are enjoyed under a grant or contract made by a State, they cannot wantonly be invaded. Whilst the State cannot be compelled by suit to perform its contracts, any attempt on its part to violate property or rights acquired under its contracts, may be judicially resisted; and any law impairing the obligation of contracts under which such property or rights are held is void and powerless to affect their enjoyment.

It is not necessary that we should enter upon an examination of the reason or expediency of the rule which exempts a sovereign State from prosecution in a court of justice at the suit of individuals. This is fully discussed by writers on public law. It is enough for us to declare its existence. The legislative department of a State represents its polity and its will; and is called upon by the highest demands of natural and political law to preserve justice and judgment, and to hold inviolate the public obligations. Any departure from this rule, except for reasons most cogent, (of which the legislature, and not the courts, is the judge,) never fails in the end to incur the odium of the world, and to bring lasting injury upon the State itself. But to deprive the legislature of the power of judging what the honor and safety of the State may require, even at the expense of a temporary failure to discharge the public debts, would be attended with greater evils than such failure can cause.

The judgment of the Circuit Court is affirmed.

MR. JUSTICE HARLAN, concurring.

I concur with the court in holding that a suit directly against a State by one of its own citizens is not one to which the judicial power of the United States extends, unless the State itself consents to be sued. Upon this ground alone I assent to the judgment. But I cannot give my assent to many things said in the opinion. The comments made upon the decision in *Chisholm v. Georgia* do not meet my approval. They are not necessary to the determination of the present case. Besides, I am of opinion that the decision in that case was based upon a sound interpretation of the Constitution as that instrument then was.

DISCUSSION

Hans is a centerpiece of modern state sovereign immunity doctrine. To understand what the case itself did (and did not) decide, it is important to proceed deliberately. First, be clear about the jurisdictional basis on which Mr. Hans claimed to be entitled to proceed in federal court. He argued that state action violated the Constitution. In other words, he asserted arising under jurisdiction. Compare this situation with what the Court faced in *Chisholm.* There, jurisdiction was based on party status. There was no substantive federal issue at play. Thus, the *Hans* Court's decision to recognize state sovereign immunity from suit in federal court implicates the essential role of the federal judiciary in enforcing federal law in a way *Chisholm* did not need to consider.

Second, correctly or not, *Hans* reflects a theme we will see displayed even more prominently in modern Court decisions: the divorce of state sovereign immunity principles from specific constitutional text. As the *Hans* Court itself recognized, a literal reading of the Eleventh Amendment would not have prohibited Hans's suit against Louisiana because Mr. Hans was not "a Citizen[] of another State, or . . . [a] Citizen[] or subject[] of any Foreign State." *See* U.S. Const. amend. XI. *Hans* rejected the notion that the full scope of state sovereign immunity from suit in federal court is reflected in the Eleventh Amendment. Rather, the Court treated the Amendment's provisions as merely one reflection of some broader immunity the states possessed. It is for this reason that describing the topic of this chapter solely as "Eleventh Amendment immunity" is misleading. The immunity the states enjoy is far broader.

Third, notice Justice Bradley's reliance on the debates concerning ratification of the Constitution as support for the Court's assertion that *Chisholm* was wrongly decided. We will see a more in-depth consideration of the ratification debates below in Justice Souter's dissent in *Seminole Tribe.* See section C.2.c. For now, note the considerable irony in this line of reasoning to attack *Chisholm* given the prominence the members of the *Chisholm* majority played during the founding period. Consider this temporal issue as you evaluate the modern Court's reliance on *Hans*'s historical conclusions.

Fourth, one sees in *Hans* the seeds of several modern theories about the meaning of the Eleventh Amendment and the scope of state sovereign immunity from suit in federal court. It will be helpful to keep these theories in mind as you study this chapter. We outline them below:

Option #1: The Literal Interpretation

A quite obvious interpretation of the meaning of the Eleventh Amendment begins and ends with the constitutional text. Thus, all one needs to know to operate under this option is the citizenship of a plaintiff suing a state in federal court. If the plaintiff is a citizen of another state or a foreign country, the suit is barred no matter what the specific jurisdictional basis. A literal interpretation of the Eleventh Amendment would not relieve all concerns about arising under jurisdiction because a federal question claim asserted by a citizen of another state would still be barred. This option rejects any notion that there is some background principle of state sovereign immunity; the full extent of such immunity is reflected on the face of the Amendment. Moreover, it assumes that *Chisholm* was correctly decided. The *Hans* Court expressly rejected this option in part because of what it perceived as the incongruity of allowing Hans's claim to proceed in federal court when an identical claim by a citizen of Mississippi (or any state other than Louisiana) would be barred. No member of the modern Court has advocated for a literal interpretation of the Eleventh Amendment.

Option #2: The Diversity Interpretation

A second interpretation of the Eleventh Amendment is not literal but does focus on constitutional text. Like the literal interpretation, the diversity view maintains that the Eleventh Amendment defines the full scope of state sovereign immunity from suit in federal court. Therefore, this approach too rejects a background principle of immunity and acknowledges that *Chisholm* was correctly decided. The diversity view differs from the literal interpretation in that it would restrict state sovereign immunity only to those cases in which federal court jurisdiction is based *solely* on party-based status. If jurisdiction were based on another Article III head of jurisdiction, most importantly perhaps a question arising under federal law, the Eleventh Amendment immunity would not apply.

Proponents of the diversity interpretation support their view in part by comparing the language of the Amendment with that of Article III. Article III sets forth nine heads of jurisdiction. Two of these jurisdictional bases concerned states and citizens of other sovereigns (i.e., other states and foreign nations). Those supporting the diversity view point out that the Eleventh Amendment acts as an erasure of only those two Article III bases of jurisdiction based on party status. They highlight that it leaves the rest of Article III intact. Thus, because there is no background principle of sovereign immunity and other bases of jurisdiction have not been erased from the constitutional text, it remains appropriate for the federal courts to hear cases based on grounds such as federal questions and admiralty even for an unconsenting state.

This interpretation of the Eleventh Amendment is more solicitous of the role of federal courts in interpreting and enforcing federal law than is either the literal view or the view taken in *Hans*. Unlike the literal interpretation, the diversity interpretation was not expressly rejected in *Hans*, but the decision is inconsistent with it. Also unlike the literal interpretation, the diversity view has had strong proponents on the modern Court. Indeed, there has often been a solid minority of three or four justices who have advocated this interpretation of the Amendment. The most recent articulation of this interpretative philosophy is Justice Souter's important dissenting opinion in *Seminole Tribe*. See section C.2.c.

Option #3: Background State Sovereign Immunity

The third interpretative option is the one *Hans* adopts. We will see later what the modern Court *says Hans* meant. For now, consider only the opinion itself. First, there is no doubt that *Hans* considers state sovereign immunity from suit to be broader than the Eleventh Amendment. The Amendment is important because it corrected what this view considers to have been an erroneous decision in *Chisholm*, thus restoring the preexisting immunity the states enjoyed. Under this option as opposed to the previous two, there existed some constitutionally recognized state sovereign immunity from suit in federal court before the Eleventh Amendment was ratified. In the words of Justice Bradley, before *Chisholm* "[t]he suability of a State without its consent was a thing unknown to the law." *Hans*, 134 U.S. at 16.

Before considering the *nature* of the background immunity *Hans* recognized, consider two points that the Court did not discuss. First, under the Court's view, the Eleventh Amendment needed only to reverse the *Chisholm* Court's error because, after doing so, the supposed preexisting immunity would be restored. If that is so, how significant is it that the Eleventh Amendment by its plain terms unquestionably does *more* than reverse *Chisholm*? The Amendment mentions suits against states by citizens of other states, which describes the factual scenario in *Chisholm*. However, it also discusses suits brought by citizens or subjects of foreign nations, something indisputably not at issue in *Chisholm*.

Second, the *Hans* Court does not discuss alternative versions of what would become the Eleventh Amendment that Congress did not adopt. One of these competing versions was introduced by Representative Theodore Sedgwick of Massachusetts. It provided:

> [N]o state shall be liable to be made a party defendant, in any of the judicial courts, established, or which shall be established under the authority of the United States, at the suit of any person or persons, whether a citizen or citizens, or a foreigner or foreigners, or of any body politic or corporate, whether within or without the United States.[5]

Does the failure of Congress to adopt this proposal, which would have barred on its face all federal court jurisdiction over unconsenting states, weaken *Hans*?

Whatever its merits (a question we will reconsider at several later parts of this chapter as we discuss the debates in this area on the modern Court), *Hans*'s view of state sovereign immunity is incredibly broad. In a nutshell, states have immunity from suit in federal court that is independent of the Eleventh Amendment and that covers all bases of federal court jurisdiction in Article III, including, perhaps most notably, arising under jurisdiction.[6] But *Hans* leaves unanswered the nature of that immunity. Is it one that is a common-law background principle that may be altered through congressional legislation as are other common-law doctrines? Or is state sovereign immunity itself a feature of the original Constitution and is, therefore, not subject to alteration by Congress at least under the powers originally vested in that body under the Constitution ratified in 1789? *Hans* did not address this point because either view would have led to the same result in the case because there was no federal statute advanced that purported to authorize *Hans*'s suit. Thus, this third interpretative option in reality has two subparts that one could label the "common-law immunity" view and the "constitutional immunity" view. The modern Court has adopted its interpretation of the scope of immunity (the constitutional view), but we defer discussion of this issue until later in the chapter. See section C.2.c.

We summarize the various interpretative approaches to the Eleventh Amendment in Figure 8-1.

As we will see, the modern Court has returned to debate the meaning of the Eleventh Amendment and what *Hans* said about state sovereign immunity. Understanding this debate is dependent on being comfortable with the competing interpretative approaches we have discussed above. Problem 8-1 allows one to apply these various interpretive approaches.

5. *See Seminole Tribe of Fla. v. Florida*, 517 U.S. 44, 111 (1996) (Souter, J., dissenting) (quoting *Gazette of the United States* 303 (Feb. 20, 1793)).

6. Technically, of course, *Hans* dealt only with arising under jurisdiction. However, as we outline later in this subsection, the Court has extended *Hans*'s reasoning to cover the full range of jurisdictional bases on which citizens of the United States and foreign states could sue an unconsenting state in federal court.

FIGURE 8-1

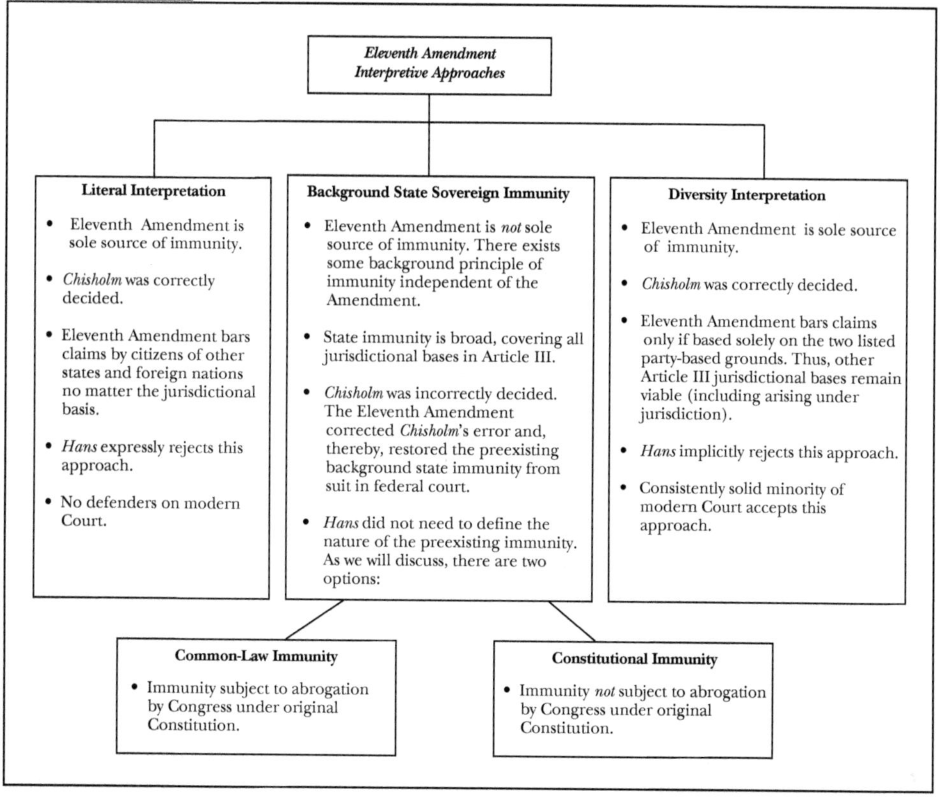

PROBLEM 8-1

Applying Competing Eleventh Amendment Theories

Scenario #1. Paula is a citizen of the State of Delaware. She has filed a lawsuit in a federal court against the State of Pennsylvania, claiming that Pennsylvania breached a contract to hire her as an architect for the new state capitol. Would Pennsylvania succeed on a defense of state immunity from suit in federal court under any of the three interpretative approaches outlined above? Why?

Scenario #2. Paula is a citizen of the State of Delaware. She has filed a lawsuit in a federal court against the State of Pennsylvania, claiming that Pennsylvania has violated the Privileges and Immunities Clause of Article IV of the Constitution prohibiting certain types of discrimination against non-citizens. Assume that Paula has sued directly under the Constitution and not relied on any federal statute. Would Pennsylvania succeed on a defense of state immunity from suit in federal court under any of the three interpretative approaches outlined above? Why?

Scenario #3. Paula is a citizen of the State of Delaware. She has filed a lawsuit against the State of Delaware in a federal court, claiming that Delaware has violated the Second Amendment's prohibition against infringing on the right of citizens to bear arms. Assume that Paula sued directly under the Constitution and has not relied on any federal statute. Would Delaware succeed on a defense of state immunity from suit in federal court under any of the three interpretative approaches outlined above? Why?

Scenario #4. Paula is a citizen of the State of Delaware. She has filed a lawsuit against the State of Delaware in a federal court, claiming that Delaware has violated a federal statute purporting to limit a state's ability to take land by eminent domain. Assume that Congress enacted this statute solely under its Article I power to regulate "Commerce . . . among the several States." *See* U.S. CONST. art. I, § 8, cl. 3. Paula has sued only under this federal statute, which states expressly that any citizen shall have the right to sue a state in federal court for the violation of the statute. Would Delaware succeed on a defense of state immunity from suit in federal court under any of the three interpretative approaches outlined above? Why?

We know that *Hans* recognized a broad background immunity from suit in federal court. In the next subsection we discuss what entities are entitled to assert that immunity. Before doing so, however, we briefly outline several additional decisions marking the boundaries of the immunity *Hans* recognized. To begin with, the Court made clear after *Hans* that state sovereign immunity from suit extended to all jurisdictional bases set forth in Article III, including not only arising under jurisdiction, which was at issue in *Hans*, but also to admiralty[7] as well as actions commenced by foreign nations.[8]

The Court also held that states do *not* enjoy sovereign immunity from suit in federal courts in several areas despite *Hans*'s sweeping language. Four of the most important examples are

1. Suits brought by the United States;[9]
2. Suits brought by other states;[10]
3. Some suits of an *in rem* nature (e.g., to allocate property rights) when the state does not have physical possession of the property at issue;[11] and
4. Actions in the Supreme Court based on its appellate jurisdiction when the underlying action has been litigated in the state courts.[12]

Yet another introductory point concerns the status of state sovereign immunity from suit as a defense. It is clear that sovereign immunity is more than merely a defense to liability. It is an entitlement not to be sued at all. An important implication of this characterization is that a decision denying sovereign immunity is immediately appealable.[13] But the Court has struggled with the

7. *See, e.g., Ex parte New York*, 256 U.S. 490, 497-98 (1921).

8. *See, e.g., Principality of Monaco v. Mississippi*, 292 U.S. 313, 320-31 (1934).

9. *See, e.g., United States v. Mississippi*, 380 U.S. 128, 140-41 (1965).

10. *See, e.g., Kansas v. Colorado*, 533 U.S. 1, 7-9 (2001). However, a state may not consistent with sovereign immunity sue another state as merely a proxy for the interests of private citizens. The state-plaintiff must have its own direct interest. *See id.* at 8. In addition, the Court has held that suits by Indian Tribes against unconsenting states *do* trigger state sovereign immunity from suit in federal court. *See, e.g., Blatchford v. Native Vill. of Noatak*, 501 U.S. 775, 779-82 (1991).

11. *See, e.g, Tennessee Student Assistance Corp. v. Hood*, 541 U.S. 440 (2004) (certain actions in bankruptcy are *in rem* and do not raise sovereign immunity concerns); *California v. Deep Sea Research, Inc.*, 523 U.S. 491 (1998) (*in rem* actions in admiralty do not raise state sovereign immunity concerns when the property is not in the possession of the state).

12. *See, e.g., McKesson Corp. v. Div. of Alcoholic Beverages & Tobacco, Dep't of Bus. Regulation of Fla.*, 496 U.S. 18, 26-31 (1990) ("[T]he Eleventh Amendment does not constrain the appellate jurisdiction of the Supreme Court over cases arising from State courts."); *Cohens v. Virginia*, 19 U.S. (6 Wheat.) 264, 412 (1821) (same). Note that the *Hans* Court discussed Chief Justice Marshall's opinion in *Cohens* and, in some measure, worked to avoid dicta in that decision at odds with the broad immunity *Hans* recognized.

13. *See, e.g., Puerto Rico Aqueduct & Sewer Auth. v. Metcalf & Eddy, Inc.*, 506 U.S. 139 (1993) (holding that denial of sovereign immunity claim is immediately appealable under the collateral order doctrine).

more fundamental question of whether state sovereign immunity is jurisdictional in the same sense as other Article III limitations. As we have seen when discussing subject matter jurisdiction in other parts of the course, characterizing something as "jurisdictional" has consequences such as the inability of the parties to consent to jurisdiction in such a case, the inability of Congress to direct the federal courts to consider such cases, the requirement that a federal court raise the matter on its own, and a prohibition on waiving the jurisdictional defense by inadvertence.

The Court seems to have decided that state sovereign immunity is quasi-jurisdictional. First, as we will see below, the Court allows a state to affirmatively consent to jurisdiction despite a valid affirmative defense and to waive the defense through, among other things, litigation conduct. See section C.2.a. Second, in limited circumstances Congress may abrogate state immunity, thus allowing unconsenting states to be sued in federal court. See section C.2.c. Third, the Court has stated that "we have never held that [a defense based on state sovereign immunity] is jurisdictional in the sense that it must be raised and decided by this Court on its own motion." *See Patsy v. Board of Regents*, 457 U.S. 496, 516 n.19 (1982). Yet the Court has stated that "the Eleventh Amendment defense sufficiently partakes of the nature of a jurisdictional bar" that a state may raise it for the first time on appeal. *See Edelman v. Jordan*, 415 U.S. 651, 677-78 (1974), excerpted below, see section C.2.b.

We conclude this section with the following question that will recur throughout the chapter:

EXPLORING DOCTRINE

What Values Are Served by State Sovereign Immunity?

A central question concerning the interpretation of the Eleventh Amendment is what values are served by the doctrine of state sovereign immunity. While one can draw something about this question from *Hans*, the Court was not particularly explicit about underlying values. We will see that the modern Court has more consciously considered this question. In particular, the Court has articulated two primary values immunity serves, although their relative importance has changed over time: (1) protection of the state treasury and (2) recognition of the state's "dignity" as a sovereign.

We will consider this issue further below. For now, do these values justify the broad immunity *Hans* recognized? Are they both legitimate? Are there other values that state sovereign immunity might serve?

b. What Entities Are Entitled to Sovereign Immunity from Suit in Federal Court?

In the previous subsection we explored the broad scope of state sovereign immunity from suit in federal court. In this subsection we briefly consider what entities in addition to the states themselves are entitled to assert that immunity, and what entities are not. As a preliminary matter, it is important to note that the Court has held that sovereign immunity is not merely a functional doctrine. That is, a state is able to assert its immunity even if it is indemnified by another party and, therefore, would not have to pay any judgment that might be rendered in a given case. *See, e.g., Regents of the Univ. of Cal. v. Doe*, 519 U.S. 425 (1997). Thus, if a state is named in a suit to which sovereign immunity applies, that state may assert its immunity from suit in federal court even if it would not in reality be forced to pay a judgment.

In addition to the states themselves, there are two other actors that obtain the benefits of the immunity the Eleventh Amendment reflects. First, a state official may assert the state's immunity from suit in federal court when the relief the plaintiff requests would require the payment of money from the state. *See, e.g., Ford Motor Co. v. Dep't of Treasury of Ind.*, 323 U.S. 459 (1945). We consider this aspect of the law below in connection with our discussion of the *Ex parte Young* doctrine. See section C.2.b.

Second, "arms of the state" may assert the state's sovereign immunity from suit in federal court. *See, e.g., Hess v. Port Auth. Trans-Hudson Corp.*, 513 U.S. 30 (1994). The rule is easy to state in the abstract. However, application is a more challenging matter because the law as to which entities are entitled to such immunity is inconsistent at best.[14] While we will not explore this area of sovereign immunity in this text, it suffices to say that the analysis for determining whether a given entity is an arm of the state is highly contextual. The Court has looked to several factors, such as the extent of state control over the entity, whether officials of the entity are state appointees, and how state law characterizes the entity. But the most important factor seems to be whether a monetary judgment rendered against the entity in question would be required to be paid by the state.

Equally important as what entities may assert immunity is what entities may not do so. The Court has long held that counties and local governments are not entitled to immunity from suit in federal court even though these entities ultimately derive their authority from the state itself. *See, e.g., Northern Ins. Co. of N.Y. v. Chatham Cnty.*, 547 U.S. 189 (2006); *Lincoln Cnty. v. Luning*, 133 U.S. 529, 530 (1890). This limitation on state sovereign immunity is practically quite significant. If localities were entitled to immunity from suit in federal court, much of the law you will learn about when you study § 1983 civil rights litigation would never have been written. See Chapter 9. The only crack in this long-established doctrine is that a county official administering a state program such that the relief the plaintiff requests would run against the state is entitled to assert the same immunity as would a state or a state official. *See, e.g., Pennhurst State Sch. & Hosp. v. Halderman*, 465 U.S. 89, 124 n.34 (1984).

2. *Ways to Avoid State Sovereign Immunity from Suit in Federal Court*

The previous section considered the historical scope and foundation of the states' sovereign immunity from suit in federal court. Assuming that immunity is applicable based on the defendant sued and the causes of action asserted, a plaintiff will need to consider whether there are means to avoid or get around immunity. This section considers the three principal means to do so.

The first method focuses on actions of the state itself. The Court has made clear that a state may waive its immunity and thereby consent to a suit in federal court. The second way around the Eleventh Amendment concerns the plaintiff's choice in structuring the lawsuit. In this regard, the plaintiff can avoid immunity

14. A distinct question is whether a state may assert Eleventh Amendment immunity when it is used by such an "arm of the state" in an original proceeding in the Supreme Court. A majority of the Supreme Court declined to answer that question. *See Alabama v. North Carolina*, 130 S. Ct. 2295, 2314-16 (2010). Chief Justice Roberts, joined by Justice Thomas, would have held that a state may assert immunity from suit in such a situation. *Id.* at 2317-19 (Roberts, C.J., concurring in part and dissenting in part).

by suing an individual state officer—rather than the state itself—for certain types of relief. Finally, Congress can avoid state sovereign immunity in certain cases by "abrogating" the immunity clearly enough in a federal statute, provided that Congress has the power to do so under a given constitutional grant of authority. We consider each of these ways to avoid state sovereign immunity from suit in federal court in turn.

a. The State: Waiver of Immunity and Consent to Suit

Although inconsistent with the notion that state sovereign immunity from suit in federal court is jurisdictional in nature, the Supreme Court has "long recognized that a State's sovereign immunity is 'a personal privilege which it may waive at its pleasure.'" *College Sav. Bank v. Florida Prepaid Postsecondary Educ. Expense Bd.*, 527 U.S. 666, 675 (1999) (quoting *Clark v. Barnard*, 108 U.S. 436, 447 (1883)). Such waiver of immunity and consequent consent to suit can take place either before litigation has been filed or after suit has been commenced. We provide a brief description of the current state of the law of waiver in both these contexts.

i. Pre-litigation Waiver and Consent to Suit

In the pre-litigation context, the "test for determining whether a State has waived its immunity from federal court jurisdiction is a stringent one." *Atascadero State Hosp. v. Scanlon*, 473 U.S. 234, 241 (1985). For example, it is not enough if a state has consented to suit in its own courts on a given cause of action.[15] Nor is it sufficient to establish waiver if the arm of the state at issue was created with language that it was capable of suing and being sued[16] or that it could be sued in "any court of competent jurisdiction."[17] "Thus, in order for a state statute or constitutional provision to constitute a waiver of Eleventh Amendment immunity, it must specify the State's intention to subject itself to suit in *federal* court." *Id.* at 241 (emphasis in original).

The Court briefly experimented with the doctrine of "constructive waiver," by which a state was held to consent to suit in federal court when it voluntarily engaged in activities that were the subject of federal regulation. Thus, the Court held that employees of a state-owned railroad could sue the state in federal court under the Federal Employers' Liability Act (FELA) because the state had impliedly agreed to be subject to such suits by engaging in the activity FELA regulated. *See Parden v. Terminal Ry. of Ala. Docks Dep't*, 377 U.S. 184 (1964). This constructive waiver doctrine never fit comfortably in the Court's sovereign immunity jurisprudence. After being undermined to varying degrees in other decisions, the Court fully overruled *Parden* in 1999. *See College Sav. Bank*, 527 U.S. at 676-87. Today, a state will not be deemed to have constructively waived its immunity merely by participating in an activity subject to federal regulation.

Matters can be quite different when a state elects to accept federal funds and receipt of those funds is conditioned on the waiver of the state's immunity from suit in federal court with respect to the program at issue. "Mere receipt of

15. *See, e.g., Smith v. Reeves*, 178 U.S. 436, 441-45 (1900).
16. *See, e.g., Florida Dep't of Health & Rehab. Servs. v. Florida Nursing Home Ass'n*, 450 U.S. 147, 149-50 (1981).
17. *See, e.g., Kennecott Copper Corp. v. State Tax Comm'n*, 327 U.S. 573, 577-79 (1946).

federal funds" is not sufficient to establish waiver in this context. *Atascadero State Hosp.*, 473 U.S. at 246. Rather, the federal statute at issue must "manifest[] a clear intent to condition participation in the programs funded under the [statute] on a State's waiver of its constitutional immunity" in order for the receipt of federal funds to constitute consent to suit. *Id.* at 247. In this context, the state has a free choice to accept federal funds and waive its immunity or decline the funds and retain that protection from suit. So long as Congress validly acts pursuant to its power under the Spending Clause and the choice is clear to the state, waiver in this context is constitutionally permissible.

In 2011, the Supreme Court reaffirmed that in order for a state to waive its immunity from suit in federal court based on the acceptance of federal funds, the agreement to waive immunity must be clear and unambiguous. In *Sossamon v. Texas*, 131 S. Ct. 1651 (2011), the Court considered whether a state's acceptance of funds concerning prisons amounted to a waiver of sovereign immunity pursuant to the terms of the Religious Land Use and Institutionalized Persons Act of 2000 (RLUIPA). RLUIPA provided in relevant part that when a state's actions infringed on a prisoner's religious freedom, the state would need to show that it had a compelling interest for its actions and that what was done was the least restrictive means by which to serve that interest. *See* 42 U.S.C. § 2000cc-1(a). A person claiming a violation of RLUIPA could bring a private cause of action to enforce the statute. The statute also provided that by accepting federal prison funds, the state agreed to waive sovereign immunity concerning the award of "appropriate relief." 42 U.S.C. § 2000cc-2(a). The Court held that the phrase "appropriate relief" was insufficiently clear to be certain that the state knew it was consenting to the award of monetary relief. *Sossamon*, 131 S. Ct. at 1658-62. Accordingly, the Court determined that Texas retained its immunity from a suit for monetary relief in federal court under the statute. *Id.* at 1663.

ii. Waiver at or After Commencement of Suit

A state can also waive its immunity from suit in federal court in the context of an action commenced in that forum. Most directly, a state waives its immunity if it invokes the jurisdiction of the federal court by voluntarily commencing a lawsuit or makes a clear declaration after being sued that it intends to submit to federal court jurisdiction. *See College Sav. Bank*, 527 U.S. at 675-76.

What about a state's removal to federal court of a lawsuit filed against it in state court? In 2002, the Court stated, "The question before us is whether the State's act of removing a lawsuit from state court to federal court waives its immunity. We hold that it does." *Lapides v. Board of Regents*, 535 U.S. 613, 616 (2002). Despite the breadth of this statement, the Court later in its opinion made clear that its holding was actually more limited. The Court stated that it was deciding whether removal constituted waiver of immunity only in "the context of state-law claims, in respect to which the State has explicitly waived immunity from state-court proceedings." Thus, the full import of removal with respect to waiver of sovereign immunity is not entirely clear.

b. The Plaintiff: Suits Against State Officials

The second means by which one can avoid the operation of sovereign immunity concerns the entities sued and the claims asserted. This method for getting around immunity is largely in the hands of the plaintiff. Of course, the plaintiff can avoid state sovereign immunity most easily (and obviously) by suing only entities not entitled to such immunity or with respect to claims not covered by immunity. However, in most cases, a plaintiff will not have the luxury to pick and choose among such claims and parties and still obtain the relief she seeks.

This section of the chapter considers the means by which a plaintiff can sue an individual state official and obtain relief that he would not otherwise be able to obtain against the state itself. As we will see, this ability is an incredibly important counterpart to the broad immunity the *Hans* Court recognized. We begin by considering the doctrine's origin and basic scope. We then turn to certain limitations on it.

i. The Origins: Ex parte Young

Less than two decades after announcing in *Hans v. Louisiana* that the Eleventh Amendment was only a reflection of a much broader state sovereign immunity from suit in federal court, the Court decided *Ex parte Young*, one of the Court's most important constitutional decisions. As you read the opinion below, consider how it is possible for *Hans* and *Young* to coexist. Also, consider what constitutional values are at issue in *Young* in relation to those reflected in *Hans*.

EX PARTE YOUNG

209 U.S. 123 (1908)

MR. JUSTICE PECKHAM . . . delivered the opinion of the Court.

[Minnesota enacted certain statutes setting maximum rates railroads could charge for passenger and freight routes. Shareholders of various railroads brought suit in a federal court to enjoin enforcement of these statutes on the ground that they violated the Fourteenth Amendment. The defendant was Edward T. Young, who as Attorney General of Minnesota was charged with enforcing the laws in question.

The trial court entered a temporary restraining order prohibiting Young from enforcing the challenged statutes. Despite that order, Young brought enforcement proceedings against certain railroads. Thereafter, the trial court held Young in contempt and ordered him jailed. The trial court rejected Young's argument that it was without jurisdiction in the case on account of the Eleventh Amendment.

Young then filed a petition for a writ of habeas corpus directly in the Supreme Court of the United States. This opinion denied the writ.]

* * * *

[The Court addressed in some detail whether there was arising under jurisdiction in the case as framed. At the end of this analysis, the Court stated:] We conclude that the Circuit Court had jurisdiction in the case before it, because it involved the decision of Federal questions arising under the Constitution of the United States.

* * * *

[The Court then considered the merits of the railroads' claims and concluded:] We hold, therefore, that the provisions of the acts relating to the enforcement of the rates, either for freight or passengers, by imposing such enormous fines and possible imprisonment as a result of an unsuccessful effort to test the validity of the laws themselves, are unconstitutional on their face, without regard to the question of the insufficiency of those rates. We also hold that the Circuit Court had jurisdiction . . . to inquire whether the rates permitted by these acts or orders were too low and therefore confiscatory, and if so held, that the court then had jurisdiction to permanently enjoin the railroad company from putting them in force, and that it also had power, while the inquiry was pending, to grant a temporary injunction to the same effect.

* * * *

We have, therefore, upon this record the case of an unconstitutional act of the state legislature and an intention by the Attorney General of the State to endeavor to enforce its provisions, to the injury of the company, in compelling it, at great expense, to defend legal proceedings of a complicated and unusual character, and involving questions of vast importance to all employees and officers of the company, as well as to the company itself. The question that arises is whether there is a remedy that the parties interested may resort to, by going into a Federal court of equity, in a case involving a violation of the Federal Constitution, and obtaining a judicial investigation of the problem, and pending its solution obtain freedom from suits, civil or criminal, by a temporary injunction, and if the question be finally decided favorably to the contention of the company, a permanent injunction restraining all such actions or proceedings.

This inquiry necessitates an examination of the most material and important objection made to the jurisdiction of the Circuit Court, the objection being that the suit is, in effect, one against the State of Minnesota, and that the injunction issued against the Attorney General illegally prohibits state action, either criminal or civil, to enforce obedience to the statutes of the State. This objection is to be considered with reference to the Eleventh and Fourteenth Amendments to the Federal Constitution. The Eleventh Amendment prohibits the commencement or prosecution of any suit against one of the United States by citizens of another State or citizens or subjects of any foreign State. The Fourteenth Amendment provides that no State shall deprive any person of life, liberty or property without due process of law, nor shall it deny to any person within its jurisdiction the equal protection of the laws.

The case before the Circuit Court proceeded upon the theory that the orders and acts heretofore mentioned would, if enforced, violate rights of the complainants protected by the latter Amendment. We think that whatever the rights of complainants may be, they are largely founded upon that Amendment, but a decision of this case does not require an examination or decision of the question whether its adoption in any way altered or limited the effect of the earlier Amendment. We may assume that each exists in full force, and that we must give to the Eleventh Amendment all the effect it naturally would have, without cutting it down or rendering its meaning any more narrow than the language, fairly interpreted, would warrant. It applies to a suit brought against a State by one of its own citizens as well as to a suit brought by a citizen of another State. *Hans v. Louisiana.* It was adopted after the decision of this court in *Chisholm v. Georgia* where it was held that a State might be sued by a citizen of another State. Since that time there have been many cases decided in this court involving the Eleventh Amendment, among them being *Osborn v. United States Bank,* which held that the Amendment applied only to those suits in which the State was a party on the record. . . . [The Court then discussed (and in some cases distinguished) numerous cases decided between *Osborn* and *Young*.]

* * * *

The various authorities we have referred to furnish ample justification for the assertion that individuals, who, as officers of the State, are clothed with some duty in regard to the enforcement of the laws of the State, and who threaten and are about to commence proceedings, either of a civil or criminal nature, to enforce against parties affected an unconstitutional act, violating the Federal Constitution, may be enjoined by a Federal court of equity from such action.

* * * *

In making an officer of the State a party defendant in a suit to enjoin the enforcement of an act alleged to be unconstitutional it is plain that such officer must have some connection with the enforcement of the act, or else it is merely making him a party as a representative of the State, and thereby attempting to make the State a party.

* * * *

The answer to all [Young's objections] is the same as made in every case where an official claims to be acting under the authority of the State. The act to be enforced is alleged to be unconstitutional, and if it be so, the use of the name of the State to enforce an unconstitutional act to the injury of complainants is a proceeding without the authority of and one which does not affect the State in its sovereign or governmental capacity. It is simply an illegal act upon the part of a state official in attempting by the use of the name of the State to enforce a legislative enactment which is void because unconstitutional. If the act which the state Attorney General seeks to enforce be a violation of the Federal Constitution, the officer in proceeding under such enactment comes into conflict with the superior authority of that Constitution, and he is in that case stripped of his official or representative character and is subjected in his person to the consequences of his individual conduct. The State has no power to impart to him any immunity from responsibility to the supreme authority of the United States. It would be an injury to complainant to harass it with a multiplicity of suits or litigation generally in an endeavor to enforce penalties under an unconstitutional enactment, and to prevent it ought to be within the jurisdiction of a court of equity. If the question of unconstitutionality with reference, at least, to the Federal Constitution be first raised in a Federal court that court, as we think is shown by the authorities cited hereafter, has the right to decide it to the exclusion of all other courts.

* * * *

It is further objected (and the objection really forms part of the contention that the State cannot be sued) that a court of equity has no jurisdiction to enjoin criminal proceedings, by indictment or otherwise, under the state law. This, as a general rule, is true. But there are exceptions. When such indictment or proceeding is brought to enforce an alleged unconstitutional statute, which is the subject matter of inquiry in a suit already pending in a Federal court, the latter court having first obtained jurisdiction over the subject matter, has the right, in both civil and criminal cases, to hold and maintain such jurisdiction, to the exclusion of all other courts, until its duty is fully performed. But the Federal court cannot, of course, interfere in a case where the proceedings were already pending in a state court.

* * * *

It is proper to add that the right to enjoin an individual, even though a state official, from commencing suits under circumstances already stated, does not include the power to restrain a court from acting in any case brought before it, either of a civil or criminal nature, nor does it include power to prevent any investigation or action by a grand jury. The latter body is part of the machinery of a criminal court, and an injunction against a state court would be a violation of the whole scheme of our Government. If an injunction against an individual is disobeyed, and he commences proceedings before a grand jury or in a court, such disobedience is personal only, and the court or jury can proceed without incurring any penalty on that account.

The difference between the power to enjoin an individual from doing certain things, and the power to enjoin courts from proceeding in their own way to exercise jurisdiction is plain, and no power to do the latter exists because of a power to do the former.

It is further objected that there is a plain and adequate remedy at law open to the complainants and that a court of equity, therefore, has no jurisdiction in such case. It has been suggested that the proper way to test the constitutionality of the act is to disobey it, at least once, after which the company might obey the act pending subsequent proceedings to test its validity. But in the event of a single violation the prosecutor might not avail himself of the opportunity to make the test, as obedience to the law was thereafter continued, and he might think it unnecessary to start an inquiry. If, however, he should do so while the company was thereafter obeying the law, several years might elapse before there was a final determination of the question, and if it should be determined that the law was invalid the property of the company would have been taken during that time without due process of law, and there would be no possibility of its recovery.

Another obstacle to making the test on the part of the company might be to find an agent or employee who would disobey the law, with a possible fine and imprisonment staring him in the face if the act should be held valid. Take the passenger rate act, for instance: A sale of a single ticket above the price mentioned in that act might subject the ticket agent to a charge of felony, and upon conviction to a fine of five thousand dollars and imprisonment for five years. It is true the company might pay the fine, but the imprisonment the agent would have to suffer personally. It would not be wonderful if, under such circumstances, there would not be a crowd of agents offering to disobey the law. The wonder would be that a single agent should be found ready to take the risk.

* * * *

To await proceedings against the company in a state court grounded upon a disobedience of the act, and then, if necessary, obtain a review in this court by writ of error to the highest state court, would place the company in peril of large loss and its agents in great risk of fines and imprisonment if it should be finally determined that the act was valid. This risk the company ought not to be required to take. . . .

All the objections to a remedy at law as being plainly inadequate are obviated by a suit in equity, making all who are directly interested parties to the suit, and enjoining the enforcement of the act until the decision of the court upon the legal question.

* * * *

Finally it is objected that the necessary result of upholding this suit in the Circuit Court will be to draw to the lower Federal courts a great flood of litigation of this character, where one Federal judge would have it in his power to enjoin proceedings by state officials to enforce the legislative acts of the State, either by criminal or civil actions. To this it may be answered, in the first place, that no injunction ought to be granted unless in a case reasonably free from doubt. We think such rule is, and will be, followed by all the judges of the Federal courts.

And, again, it must be remembered that jurisdiction of this general character has, in fact, been exercised by Federal courts from the time of *Osborn v. United States Bank* up to the present; the only difference in regard to the case of *Osborn* and the case in hand being that in this case the injury complained of is the threatened commencement of suits, civil or criminal, to enforce the act, instead of, as in the *Osborn* case, an actual and direct trespass upon or interference with tangible property. A bill filed to prevent the commencement of suits to enforce an unconstitutional act, under the circumstances already mentioned, is no new invention, as we have already seen. The difference between an actual and direct interference with tangible property and the enjoining of state officers from enforcing an unconstitutional act, is not of a radical nature, and does not extend, in truth, the jurisdiction of the courts over the subject matter. In the case of the interference with property the person enjoined is assuming to act in his capacity as an official of the State, and justification for his interference is claimed by reason of his position as a state official. Such official cannot so justify when acting under an unconstitutional enactment of the legislature. So, where the state official, instead of directly interfering with tangible property, is about to commence suits, which have for their object the enforcement of an act which violates the Federal Constitution, to the great and irreparable injury of the complainants, he is seeking the same justification from the authority of the State as in other cases. The sovereignty of the State is, in reality, no more involved in one case than in the other. The State cannot in either case impart to the official immunity from responsibility to the supreme authority of the United States.

This supreme authority, which arises from the specific provisions of the Constitution itself, is nowhere more fully illustrated than in the series of decisions under the Federal habeas corpus statute in some of which cases persons in the custody of state officers for alleged crimes against the State have been taken from that custody and discharged by a Federal court or judge, because the imprisonment was adjudged to be in violation of the Federal Constitution. The right to so discharge has not been doubted by this court, and it has never been supposed there was any suit against the State by reason of serving the writ upon one of the officers of the State in whose custody the person was found. In some of the cases the writ has been refused as matter of discretion, but in others it has been granted, while the power has been fully recognized in all.

It is somewhat difficult to appreciate the distinction which, while admitting that the taking of such a person from the custody of the State by virtue of service of the writ on the state officer in whose custody he is found, is not a suit against the State, and yet service of a writ on the Attorney General to prevent his enforcing an unconstitutional enactment of a state legislature is a suit against the State.

There is nothing in the case before us that ought properly to breed hostility to the customary operation of Federal courts of justice in cases of this character.

The rule to show cause is discharged and the petition for writs of habeas corpus and certiorari is dismissed.

So ordered.

MR. JUSTICE HARLAN, dissenting.

[Justice Harlan began with a lengthy description of the facts and the procedural history of the case.]

Let it be observed that the suit . . . was, as to the defendant Young, one against him *as, and only because he was,* Attorney General of Minnesota. No relief was sought against him individually but only in his capacity *as* Attorney General. And the manifest, indeed the avowed and admitted, object of seeking such relief was *to tie the hands* of the *State* so that it could not in any manner or by any mode of proceeding, *in its own courts,* test the validity of the statutes and orders in question. It would therefore seem clear that within the true meaning of the Eleventh Amendment the suit brought in the Federal court was one, in legal effect, against the State — as much so as if the State had been formally named on the record as a party — and therefore it was a suit to which, under the Amendment, so far as the State or its Attorney General was concerned, the judicial power of the United States did not and could not extend. If this proposition be sound it will follow — indeed, it is conceded that if, so far as relief is sought against the Attorney General of Minnesota, this be a suit against the State — then the order of the Federal court enjoining that officer from taking any action, suit, step or proceeding to compel the railway company to obey the Minnesota statute was beyond the jurisdiction of that court and wholly void; in which case, that officer was at liberty to proceed in the discharge of his official duties as defined by the laws of the State, and the order adjudging him to be in contempt for bringing the mandamus proceeding in the state court was a nullity.

The fact that the Federal Circuit Court had, prior to the institution of the mandamus suit in the state court, preliminarily (but not finally) held the statutes of Minnesota and the orders of its Railroad and Warehouse Commission in question to be in violation of the Constitution of the United States, was no reason why that court should have laid violent hands upon the Attorney General of Minnesota and by its orders have deprived the State of the services of its constitutional law officer in its own courts. Yet that is what was done by the Federal Circuit Court; for, the intangible thing, called a State, however extensive its powers, can never appear or be represented or known in any court in a litigated case, except by and through its officers. When, therefore, the Federal court forbade the defendant Young, as Attorney General of Minnesota, from taking any action, suit, step or proceeding whatever looking to the enforcement of the statutes in question, it said in effect to the State of Minnesota: "It is true that the powers not delegated to the United States by the Constitution, nor prohibited by it to the States, are reserved to the States respectively or to its people, and it is true that under the Constitution the judicial power of the United States does not extend to any suit brought against a State by a citizen of another State or by a citizen or subject of a foreign State, yet the Federal court adjudges that you, the State, although a sovereign for many important governmental purposes, shall not appear in your own courts, by your law officer, with the view of enforcing, or even for determining the validity of the state enactments which the Federal court has, upon a preliminary hearing, declared to be in violation of the Constitution of the United States."

This principle, if firmly established, would work a radical change in our governmental system. It would inaugurate a new era in the American judicial system and in the relations of the National and state governments. It would enable the subordinate Federal courts to supervise and control the official action of the States as if they were "dependencies" or provinces. It would place the States of the Union in a condition of inferiority never dreamed of when the Constitution was adopted or when the Eleventh Amendment was made a part of the Supreme Law of the Land. I cannot suppose that the great men who framed the Constitution ever thought the time would come when a subordinate Federal court, having no power to compel a State, in its corporate capacity, to appear before it as a litigant, would yet assume to deprive a State of the right to be represented in its own courts by its regular law officer. That is what the court below did, as to Minnesota, when it adjudged that the appearance of the defendant Young *in the state court,* as the Attorney General of Minnesota, representing his State as its chief law officer, was a contempt of the authority of the Federal court, punishable by fine and imprisonment. Too little consequence has been attached to the fact that the courts of the States are under an obligation equally strong with that resting upon the courts of the Union to respect and enforce the provisions of the Federal Constitution as the Supreme Law of the Land, and to guard rights secured or guaranteed by that instrument. We must assume — a decent respect for the States requires us to assume — that the state courts will enforce every right secured by the Constitution. If they fail to do so, the party complaining has a clear remedy for the protection of his rights; for, he can come by writ of error, in an orderly, judicial way, from the highest court of the State to this tribunal for redress in respect of every right granted or secured by that instrument and denied by the state court. The state courts, it should be remembered, have jurisdiction concurrent with the courts of the United States of all suits of a civil nature, at common law or equity . . . arising under the Constitution or laws of the United States. . . . Upon the state courts, equally with the courts of the Union, rests the obligation to guard, enforce, and protect every right granted or secured by the Constitution of the United States and the laws made in pursuance thereof, whenever those rights are involved in any suit or proceeding before them; for the judges of the state courts are required to take an oath to support that Constitution, and they are bound by it, and the laws of the United States made in pursuance thereof, and all treaties made under their authority, as the supreme law of the land, 'anything in the Constitution or laws of any State to the contrary notwithstanding.' If they fail therein, and withhold or deny rights, privileges, or immunities secured by the Constitution and laws of the United States, the party aggrieved may bring the case from the highest court of the State in which the question could be decided to this court for final and conclusive determination." So that an order of the Federal court preventing the State from having the services of its Attorney General in one of its own courts, except at the risk of his being fined and arrested, cannot be justified upon the ground that the question of constitutional law, involved in the enforcement of the statutes in question, was beyond the competency of a state court to consider and determine, primarily, as between the parties before it in a suit brought by the State itself.

* * * *

. . . The essential and only question now before us or that need be decided is whether an order by the Federal court which prevents the State from being represented in its own courts, by its chief law officer, upon an issue involving the constitutional validity of certain state enactments, does not make a suit against the State within the meaning of the Eleventh Amendment. If it be a suit of that kind, then, it is conceded, the Circuit Court was without jurisdiction to fine and imprison the petitioner and he must be discharged, whatever our views may be as to the validity of those state enactments. This must necessarily be so unless the Amendment has less force and a more restricted meaning now than it had at the time of its adoption, and unless a suit against the Attorney General of a State, in his official capacity, is not one against a State under the Eleventh Amendment when its determination depends upon a question of constitutional power or right under the Fourteenth Amendment. In that view I cannot concur. In my opinion the Eleventh Amendment has not been modified in the slightest degree as to its scope or meaning by the Fourteenth Amendment, and a suit which, in its essence, is one against the State remains one of that character and is forbidden even when brought to strike down a state statute alleged to be in violation of that clause of the Fourteenth Amendment forbidding the deprivation by a State of life, liberty or property without due process of law. If a suit be commenced in a state court, and involves a right secured by the Federal Constitution, the way is open under our incomparable judicial system to protect that right, first, by the judgment of the state court, and ultimately by the judgment of this court, upon writ of error. But such right cannot be protected by means of a suit which, at the outset, is, directly or in legal effect, one against the State whose action is alleged to be illegal. That mode of redress is absolutely forbidden by the Eleventh Amendment and cannot be made legal by mere construction, or by any consideration of the consequences that may follow from the operation of the statute. Parties cannot, in any case, obtain redress by a suit *against the State.* Such has been the uniform ruling in this court, and it is most unfortunate that it is now declared to be competent for a Federal Circuit Court, by exerting its authority over the chief law officer of the State, without the consent of the State, to exclude the State, in its sovereign capacity, from its own courts when seeking to have the ruling of those courts as to its powers under its own statutes. Surely, the right of a State to invoke the jurisdiction of its own courts is not less than the right of individuals to invoke the jurisdiction of a Federal court. The preservation of the dignity and sovereignty of the States, within the limits of their constitutional powers, is of the last importance, and vital to the preservation of our system of government. The courts should not permit themselves to be driven by the hardships, real or supposed, of particular cases to accomplish results, even if they be just results, in a mode forbidden by the fundamental law. The country should never be allowed to think that the Constitution can, in any case, be evaded or amended by mere judicial interpretation, or that its behests may be nullified by an ingenious construction of its provisions.

* * * *

... [T]o forbid the Attorney General of a State (under the penalty of being punished as for contempt) from representing his State in suits of a particular kind, in its own courts, is to forbid the State itself from appearing and being heard in such suits. Neither the words nor the policy of the Eleventh Amendment will, under our former decisions, justify any order of a Federal court the necessary effect of which will be to exclude a State from its own courts. Such an order attended by such results cannot, I submit, be sustained consistently with the powers which the States, according to the uniform declarations of this court, possess under the Constitution. I am justified, by what this court has heretofore declared, in now saying that the men who framed the Constitution and who caused the adoption of the Eleventh Amendment would have been amazed by the suggestion that a State of the Union can be prevented by an order of a subordinate Federal court from being represented by its Attorney General in a suit brought by it in one of its own courts; and that such an order would be inconsistent with the dignity of the States as involved in their constitutional immunity from the judicial process of the Federal courts (except in the limited cases in which they may constitutionally be made parties in this court) and would be attended by most pernicious results.

I dissent from the opinion and judgment.

DISCUSSION AND QUESTIONS

Ex parte Young holds that a plaintiff may sue a state official in his or her official capacity without running afoul of the Eleventh Amendment even when the plaintiff could not sue the state itself because of its sovereign immunity. To begin with, how is that possible? The Court's answer is that when state officials act unlawfully, they are stripped of their state authority and, therefore, state immunity from suit is no longer applicable.

Do not be deceived. The theory on which *Ex parte Young* is based is most certainly a fiction. As a practical matter it must be a fiction because if the state official was no longer truly a state official, the plaintiff would often not be entitled to the relief it sought. For example, if Attorney General Young really was stripped of his state authority, an order directing that he not enforce the statute at issue would be meaningless. If he had no state authority, he could not enforce the statute in any event.

Ex parte Young must also be a fiction on constitutional grounds. As you all learned in your first-year Constitutional Law course, in order for there to be a constitutional violation, there must be state action. If Attorney General Young had really been stripped of his state authority, he could not have engaged in state action sufficient to violate the terms of the Fourteenth Amendment. Thus, under *Ex parte Young* it is possible — indeed, it is necessary — that an official sued in his official capacity qualifies as a state actor for purposes of the Fourteenth Amendment but not for purposes of the Eleventh Amendment.

But to say that *Ex parte Young* is a fiction is not to say that the case was wrongly decided. In fact, there is wide agreement that *Ex parte Young* is necessary to ensure that federal law remains supreme. If it were not for *Ex parte Young* and its fiction, the immunity *Hans* recognized based on the important values of federalism would greatly limit the ability of federal courts to be involved in the interpretation of federal law, something that many believe is itself an important attribute of federalism. There are, therefore, in the *Ex parte Young* doctrine strong undercurrents of the parity debate we have seen so often in our study of Federal Courts.

The Court recently reaffirmed the important place the *Ex parte Young* doctrine plays in the constitutional structure in *Virginia Office for Protection & Advocacy v. Stewart*, 131 S. Ct. 1632 (2011). The case concerned a claim by a state agency that another state actor was violating federal rights the state agency was authorized to protect as a matter of *federal* law. The state agency sought an injunction against a state official for prospective compliance with federal law. The Court rejected Virginia's challenge that *Ex parte Young* did not apply. Along the way, the Court noted that the doctrine had coexisted for nearly the entire period after *Hans* and that it played an important role in ensuring that federal rights were enforced while balancing the need to preserve state sovereignty principles reflected in the Eleventh Amendment.

In the next subsection, we consider four important limitations the Court has put on the *Ex parte Young* doctrine over the past century-plus. Despite these limitations, however, the Court has made clear that the core of *Ex parte Young* remains intact and is a vital part of overall state sovereignty jurisprudence. As the Court stated relatively recently: "[T]he *Young* doctrine has been accepted as necessary to permit the federal courts to vindicate federal rights and hold state officials responsible to the supreme authority of the United States." *Pennhurst State Sch. & Hosp. v. Halderman*, 465 U.S. 89, 105 (1984) (citations and internal quotation marks omitted).

In 1997, Justice Kennedy, joined by Chief Justice Rehnquist, argued that the Court should significantly alter the way in which it employed *Ex parte Young. See Idaho v. Coeur d'Alene Tribe of Idaho*, 521 U.S. 261, 271-80 (1997) (opinion of Kennedy, J.). Justice Kennedy argued that *Young* was not actually a rule into which a plaintiff could necessarily plead. Instead, he argued that the doctrine required "a careful balancing and accommodation of state interests when determining whether the *Young* exception applies in a given case." *Id.* at 278. Consideration in this case-by-case balancing would be given to factors such as whether a state forum was available for the plaintiff to pursue and whether there were undefined "other factors" that suggested a federal court should not apply the *Young* fiction. Seven members of the Court rejected Justice Kennedy's suggestion to redefine the doctrine and reaffirmed its place in American law. But Justice Kennedy's critique of the doctrine remains fodder for future development by another Court.

EXPLORING DOCTRINE

Young*: A Necessary Fiction or an Evisceration of State Sovereignty?*

A solid majority of the Court rejected Justice Kennedy's argument that *Ex parte Young* should be considered a case-by-case balancing exercise. Nevertheless, the Court did balance competing values when it adopted the doctrine, and it has reaffirmed the doctrine over the years. On the one hand are the values of federalism at the core of *Hans*. On the other hand are the values associated with the protection of individual rights and the supremacy of federal law.

Assuming that *Young* was correctly decided in 1908, does its balancing of these important competing values hold true today? If the balance is not true across the board, was Justice Kennedy correct to argue for a more nuanced case-by-case approach?

ii. Limitations on the Ex parte Young *Doctrine*

In this section, we consider various limitations the Court has crafted on the *Ex parte Young* doctrine. There are four main limitations on the doctrine: limitations based on (1) the remedies the plaintiff seeks; (2) the source of the legal violation alleged; (3) whether the matter at issue is the equivalent of a quiet title action (or perhaps some other "special sovereignty interest"); and (4) whether Congress intended to preclude resort to *Ex parte Young* in connection with a federal statutory right. We consider each in turn.

Limitation #1: Remedy Sought

We begin with *Edelman v. Jordan*, in which the Court limits *Ex parte Young* based on the types of remedies sought.

EDELMAN v. JORDAN

415 U.S. 651 (1974)

MR. JUSTICE REHNQUIST delivered the opinion of the Court.

Respondent John Jordan filed a complaint in the United States District Court for the Northern District of Illinois, individually and as a representative of a class, seeking declaratory and injunctive relief against two former directors of the Illinois Department of Public Aid, the director of the Cook County Department of Public Aid, and the comptroller of Cook County. Respondent alleged that these state officials were administering the federal-state programs of Aid to the Aged, Blind, or Disabled (AABD) in a manner inconsistent with various federal regulations and with the Fourteenth Amendment to the Constitution.

[The federal AABD program required that states make eligibility determinations within either 30 or 45 days of an application, depending on the various bases asserted for the receipt of benefits.] Respondent's complaint charged that the Illinois defendants, operating under [various state] regulations, were improperly authorizing grants to commence only with the month in which an application was approved and not including prior eligibility months for which an applicant was entitled to aid under federal law. The complaint also alleged that the Illinois defendants were not processing the applications within the applicable time requirements of the federal regulations; specifically, respondent alleged that his own application for disability benefits was not acted on by the Illinois Department of Public Aid for almost four months. Such actions of the Illinois officials were alleged to violate federal law and deny the equal protection of the laws. Respondent's prayer requested declaratory and injunctive relief, and specifically requested "a permanent injunction enjoining the defendants to award to the entire class of plaintiffs all AABD benefits wrongfully withheld."

[The district court ruled against the state officials. It entered a permanent injunction requiring future compliance with the federal AABD regulations.] The District Court . . . also ordered the state officials to "release and remit AABD benefits wrongfully withheld to all applicants for AABD in the State of Illinois who applied between July 1, 1968 [the date of the federal regulations] and April 16, 197[1] [the date of the preliminary injunction issued by the District Court] and were determined eligible. . . ."

[The United States Court of Appeals for the Seventh Circuit affirmed the district court's judgments. The Supreme Court granted a petition for a writ of certiorari.] Because we believe the Court of Appeals erred in its disposition of the Eleventh Amendment claim [the state officials made], we reverse that portion of the Court of Appeals decision which affirmed the District Court's order that retroactive benefits be paid by the Illinois state officials.

The historical basis of the Eleventh Amendment has been oft stated, and it represents one of the more dramatic examples of this Court's effort to derive meaning from the document given to the Nation by the Framers nearly 200 years ago. . . .

The issue [of the susceptibility of a State to suit in federal court] was squarely presented to the Court in a suit brought at the August 1792 Term by two citizens of South Carolina, executors of a British creditor, against the State of Georgia. After a year's postponement for preparation on the part of the State of Georgia, the Court, after argument, rendered in February 1793, its shortlived decision in *Chisholm v. Georgia.* The decision in that case, that a State was liable to suit by a citizen of another State or of a foreign country, literally shocked the Nation. Sentiment for passage of a constitutional amendment to override the decision rapidly gained momentum, and five years after *Chisholm* the Eleventh Amendment was officially announced by President John Adams. . . .

While the Amendment by its terms does not bar suits against a State by its own citizens, this Court has consistently held that an unconsenting State is immune from suits brought in federal courts by her own citizens as well as by citizens of another State. *Hans v. Louisiana.* It is also well established that even though a State is not named a party to the action, the suit may nonetheless be barred by the Eleventh Amendment. In *Ford Motor Co.* v. *Department of Treasury* [in 1945] the Court said: "When the action is in essence one for the recovery of money from the state, the state is the real, substantial party in interest and is entitled to invoke its sovereign immunity from suit even though individual officials are nominal defendants."

Thus the rule has evolved that a suit by private parties seeking to impose a liability which must be paid from public funds in the state treasury is barred by the Eleventh Amendment.

The Court of Appeals in this case, while recognizing that the *Hans* line of cases permitted the State to raise the Eleventh Amendment as a defense to suit by its own citizens, nevertheless concluded that the Amendment did not bar the award of retroactive payments of the statutory benefits found to have been wrongfully withheld. The Court of Appeals held that the above-cited cases, when read in light of this Court's landmark decision in *Ex parte Young* do not preclude the grant of such a monetary award in the nature of equitable restitution.

Petitioner concedes that *Ex parte Young* is no bar to that part of the District Court's judgment that prospectively enjoined petitioner's predecessors from failing to process applications within the time limits established by the federal regulations. Petitioner argues, however, that *Ex parte Young* does not extend so far as to permit a suit which seeks the award of an accrued monetary liability which must be met from the general revenues of a State, absent consent or waiver by the State of its Eleventh Amendment immunity, and that therefore the award of retroactive benefits by the District Court was improper.

Ex parte Young was a watershed case in which this Court held that the Eleventh Amendment did not bar an action in the federal courts seeking to enjoin the Attorney General of Minnesota from enforcing a statute claimed to violate the Fourteenth Amendment of the United States Constitution. This holding has permitted the Civil War Amendments to the Constitution to serve as a sword, rather than merely as a shield, for those whom they were designed to protect. But the relief awarded in *Ex parte Young* was prospective only; the Attorney General of Minnesota was enjoined to conform his future conduct of that office to the requirement of the Fourteenth Amendment. Such relief is analogous to that awarded by the District Court in the prospective portion of its order under review in this case.

But the retroactive portion of the District Court's order here, which requires the payment of a very substantial amount of money which that court held should have been paid, but was not, stands on quite a different footing. These funds will obviously not be paid out of the pocket of petitioner Edelman.

... The funds to satisfy the award in this case must inevitably come from the general revenues of the State of Illinois, and thus the award resembles far more closely the monetary award against the State itself, *Ford Motor Co.* v. *Department of Treasury*, than it does the prospective injunctive relief awarded in *Ex parte Young*.

The Court of Appeals, in upholding the award in this case, held that it was permissible because it was in the form of "equitable restitution" instead of damages, and therefore capable of being tailored in such a way as to minimize disruptions of the state program of categorical assistance. But we must judge the award actually made in this case, and not one which might have been differently tailored in a different case, and we must judge it in the context of the important constitutional principle embodied in the Eleventh Amendment.[18]

We do not read *Ex parte Young* or subsequent holdings of this Court to indicate that any form of relief may be awarded against a state officer, no matter how closely it may in practice resemble a money judgment payable out of the state treasury, so long as the relief may be labeled "equitable" in nature. The Court's opinion in *Ex parte Young* hewed to no such line.

As in most areas of the law, the difference between the type of relief barred by the Eleventh Amendment and that permitted under *Ex parte Young* will not in many instances be that between day and night. The injunction issued in *Ex parte Young* was not totally without effect on the State's revenues, since the state law which the Attorney General was enjoined from enforcing provided substantial monetary penalties against railroads which did not conform to its provisions. Later cases from this Court have authorized equitable relief which has probably had greater impact on state treasuries than did that awarded in *Ex parte Young*. ... But the fiscal consequences to state treasuries in these cases were the necessary result of compliance with decrees which by their terms were prospective in nature. State officials, in order to shape their official conduct to the mandate of the Court's decrees, would more likely have to spend money from the state treasury than if they had been left free to pursue their previous course of conduct. Such an ancillary effect on the state treasury is a permissible and often an inevitable consequence of the principle announced in *Ex parte Young*.

But that portion of the District Court's decree which petitioner challenges on Eleventh Amendment grounds goes much further than any of the cases cited. It requires payment of state funds, not as a necessary consequence of compliance in the future with a substantive federal-question determination, but as a form of compensation to those whose applications were processed on the slower time

18. [Footnote 11 in Court's opinion.] It may be true, as stated by our Brother Douglas in dissent, that "most welfare decisions by federal courts have a financial impact on the States." But we cannot agree that such a financial impact is the same where a federal court applies *Ex parte Young* to grant prospective declaratory and injunctive relief, as opposed to an order of retroactive payments as was made in the instant case. It is not necessarily true that "whether the decree is prospective only or requires payments for the weeks or months wrongfully skipped over by the state officials, the nature of the impact on the state treasury is precisely the same." This argument neglects the fact that where the State has a definable allocation to be used in the payment of public aid benefits, and pursues a certain course of action such as the processing of applications within certain time periods as did Illinois here, the subsequent ordering by a federal court of retroactive payments to correct delays in such processing will invariably mean there is less money available for payments for the continuing obligations of the public aid system.

schedule at a time when petitioner was under no court-imposed obligation to conform to a different standard. While the Court of Appeals described this retroactive award of monetary relief as a form of "equitable restitution," it is in practical effect indistinguishable in many aspects from an award of damages against the State. It will to a virtual certainty be paid from state funds, and not from the pockets of the individual state officials who were the defendants in the action. It is measured in terms of a monetary loss resulting from a past breach of a legal duty on the part of the defendant state officials.

[The Court went on to hold that Illinois had neither waived its immunity from suit in federal court nor consented to such suit by agreeing to participate in the AABD program.]

* * * *

For the foregoing reasons we decide that the Court of Appeals was wrong in holding that the Eleventh Amendment did not constitute a bar to that portion of the District Court decree which ordered retroactive payment of benefits found to have been wrongfully withheld. The judgment of the Court of Appeals is therefore reversed and the cause remanded for further proceedings consistent with this opinion.

So ordered.

[A dissenting opinion by Justice Douglas is omitted.]

MR. JUSTICE BRENNAN, dissenting.

This suit is brought by Illinois citizens against Illinois officials. In that circumstance, Illinois may not invoke the Eleventh Amendment, since that Amendment bars only federal court suits against States by citizens of other States. Rather, the question is whether Illinois may avail itself of the nonconstitutional but ancient doctrine of sovereign immunity as a bar to respondent's claim for retroactive AABD payments. In my view Illinois may not assert sovereign immunity . . . : the States surrendered that immunity in Hamilton's words, "in the plan of the Convention," that formed the Union, at least insofar as the States granted Congress specifically enumerated powers. Congressional authority to enact the Social Security Act, of which AABD is a part, is to be found in Art. I, § 8, cl. 1, one of the enumerated powers granted Congress by the States in the Constitution. I remain of the opinion that "because of its surrender, no immunity exists that can be the subject of a congressional declaration or a voluntary waiver," and thus have no occasion to inquire whether or not Congress authorized an action for AABD retroactive benefits, or whether or not Illinois voluntarily waived the immunity by its continued participation in the program against the background of precedents which sustained judgments ordering retroactive payments.

I would affirm the judgment of the Court of Appeals.

[A dissenting opinion by Justice Marshall joined by Justice Blackmun, arguing that the state had waived its immunity, is omitted.]

DISCUSSION

Edelman establishes the first limitation on the *Ex parte Young* doctrine. The Court's limitation is easy to state although perhaps not so easy to apply. A federal court may use the *Ex parte Young* fiction only to award prospective injunctive relief or declaratory relief that is itself concerned with the prospective enforcement of federal rights. A federal court may not use *Young* to award money damages against a state official in her official capacity,[19] injunctive or other equitable relief that as in *Edelman* was the functional equivalent of damages, or declaratory relief with no ongoing violation of federal law.

The Court made clear in a later case that *Edelman*'s limitation on *Young* was part of the delicate (but categorical) balancing of interests at work in the area of state sovereign immunity. As the Court explained:

> Both prospective and retrospective relief implicate Eleventh Amendment concerns, but the availability of prospective relief of the sort awarded in *Ex Parte Young* gives life to the Supremacy Clause. Remedies designed to end a continuing violation of federal law are necessary to vindicate the federal interest in assuring the supremacy of that law. But compensatory or deterrence interests are insufficient to overcome the dictates of the Eleventh Amendment.

Green v. Mansour, 474 U.S. 64, 68 (1985) (citations omitted).

The line drawing required by *Edelman* has not always been easy for the Court nor has it necessarily led to predictable results. We provide the following brief descriptions of some of the Court's decisions applying *Edelman*'s prospective/ retrospective distinction:

- *Milliken v. Bradley*, 433 U.S. 267 (1977). This case concerned the long-running school desegregation litigation in Detroit, Michigan. The district court had found certain state defendants had acted unconstitutionally and, as a result, were partially responsible for the segregated state of the schools in Detroit. The district court ordered the state defendants to pay for certain programs to eliminate the vestiges of racial segregation. The state defendants challenged the district court's order as being the equivalent of damages and thus inappropriate under *Edelman*. The Supreme Court rejected the state defendants' contention. The Court reasoned that the order was prospective in nature because it sought to eliminate the future effects of past unlawful conduct. Moreover, the Court rejected the notion that the high cost of such future relief was itself a reason to preclude resort to *Ex parte Young*.
- *Hutto v. Finney*, 437 U.S. 678 (1978). *Hutto* was another institutional reform case, this one dealing with truly deplorable conditions in the Arkansas prison system. The litigation had many facets, and the district court ultimately concluded that the state officials sued had, in bad faith, failed to cure the constitutional violation found. As a result, the district court ordered that the state pay the plaintiffs' attorney's fees. The Supreme Court rejected an Eleventh Amendment challenge to the fee award. The Court held that the award of fees was "ancillary" to the main order in the case concerning prospective injunctive relief. As such, the award was not barred by the Eleventh Amendment under the principles of *Young* and *Edelman*.
- *Quern v. Jordan*, 440 U.S. 332 (1979). This case was a continuation of the *Edelman* litigation itself. On remand after the Supreme Court's decision,

19. A plaintiff is free to sue a state official in her individual capacity in an attempt to obtain monetary relief from that individual personally. We will consider this issue when we discuss litigation under 42 U.S.C. § 1983. See Chapter 9.

the district judge eventually ordered the defendant government officials to send a notice to the members of the plaintiff-class informing the class of (1) the court's finding concerning the violation of the federal regulations at issue and (2) the availability of state administrative proceedings by which the plaintiffs could seek recovery for the wrongfully withheld benefits. The Supreme Court upheld the district court's order directing such notice over an Eleventh Amendment objection. The Court reasoned that there was prospective relief at issue and the notice, even though dealing with the past, would not necessarily require the state to pay any money from its treasury. The Court stated that if any money were to be paid, it would be as a result of independent state action and not a federal court order. It was not enough that the federal court action under *Young* was merely part of a causal chain that could lead to the payment of money concerning past acts.

- *Green v. Mansour*, 474 U.S. 64 (1985). *Green* was a class action challenging state officials' implementation of the federal Aid to Families with Dependent Children (AFDC) program. The state officials were not in compliance with the relevant federal law. During the litigation, Congress amended the statutes at issue such that the state officials' conduct now conformed to federal law. As a result, there was no ongoing violation of federal law for which the federal court could issue prospective injunctive relief under *Young*. The district court thereafter refused to issue notice relief similar to that approved in *Quern* on the ground that such relief under these facts was barred by the Eleventh Amendment. The Supreme Court affirmed, agreeing that notice relief in this case was barred. The Court reasoned as follows: "[A] request for a limited notice order will escape the Eleventh Amendment bar if the notice is ancillary to the grant of some other appropriate relief that can be 'noticed.' Because there is no continuing violation of federal law to enjoin in this case, an injunction is not available. Therefore, notice cannot be justified as a mere case-management device that is ancillary to a judgment awarding valid prospective relief." *Id.* at 71.

Limitation #2: Source of Legal Violation

The second limitation on *Ex parte Young* relief concerns the source of the law the state official is alleged to have violated. Recall that when justifying its decision, the *Young* Court opined that when a state official acted in violation of law, he was stripped of his state character and, therefore, was not entitled to assert the state's immunity from suit in federal court. The Court also stated that *Young* was necessary in order to support the supremacy of federal law. So long as the law alleged to have been violated is federal, both of these statements lead to the availability of relief under *Young*. The question is what if the alleged violation concerns a *state* law. In that case only the authority-stripping rationale would support relief. The supremacy concern would not be present.

In *Pennhurst State School & Hospital v. Halderman*, 465 U.S. 89 (1984), the Court held that relief under *Ex parte Young* was available only with respect to an alleged violation of federal law. The Court reasoned that *Young* was based on a need to balance the competing interests of federalism and the supremacy of federal law. It continued:

> This need to reconcile competing interests is wholly absent, however, when a plaintiff alleges that a state official has violated *state* law. In such a case the entire basis for the doctrine of *Young* and *Edelman* disappears. A federal court's grant of relief against state officials on the basis of state law, whether prospective or retroactive, does not vindicate the supreme authority of federal law. On the contrary, it is difficult to think of a greater intrusion on state sovereignty than when a federal court instructs state officials on how to conform their conduct to state law. Such a result conflicts directly with the principles of federalism that underlie the Eleventh Amendment. We conclude that *Young* and *Edelman* are inapplicable in a suit against state officials on the basis of state law.

Pennhurst, 465 U.S. at 106 (emphasis in original).

The Court went on to hold that it was impermissible to base jurisdiction on what today would be called supplemental jurisdiction under 28 U.S.C. § 1367. Thus, even if a plaintiff sought relief with respect to federal law, a federal court would be without jurisdiction to order prospective relief concerning state-law violations.

Limitation #3: Claims That Are the Equivalent of Quiet Title Actions and (Perhaps) Those Implicating "Other Special Sovereignty Interests"

The third limitation on *Young* is in one respect quite narrow. However, planted within that narrow exception is a potentially much broader restriction on the doctrine. The Coeur d'Alene Tribe of Native Americans sued the State of Idaho in federal court, claiming that the Tribe held title to certain submerged lands in Lake Coeur d'Alene in Idaho. The Tribe's claim to ownership of these submerged lands was based on federal law. For our purposes, the Tribe sought an injunction (and related declaratory relief) prohibiting certain state officials sued in their official capacity from exercising any regulatory control over the lands in which the Tribe claimed an ownership interest. *See Idaho v. Coeur d'Alene Tribe of Idaho,* 521 U.S. 261 (1997).

The state officials sought dismissal based on Idaho's sovereign immunity from suit in federal court. The Court recognized that a straightforward application of *Young, Edelman,* and *Pennhurst* would require it to reject the state officials' immunity argument. The Tribe alleged an ongoing violation of federal law and sought prospective injunctive relief with respect to that federal violation. Nevertheless, the Court held that under the particular facts of this case, *Ex parte Young* relief was not appropriate.[20]

The Court reasoned that the Tribe's requested relief was equivalent to a request to quiet title to land. The Court stated that the "relief the Tribe seeks is close to the functional equivalent of quiet title in that substantially all benefits to ownership and control would shift from the State to the Tribe. . . . To pass this off as a judgment causing little or no offense to Idaho's sovereign authority and its standing in the Union would be to ignore the realities of the relief the Tribe demands." *Coeur d'Alene,* 521 U.S. at 282.

20. This is the case in which Justice Kennedy argued for a case-by-case balancing approach in connection with *Ex parte Young.* A majority of the Court rejected that argument. The discussion in this section concerns the more categorical restriction on *Young* the Court adopted.

In a narrow sense, relief that would otherwise be allowed under *Young* and its progeny that is the equivalent of an action to quiet title in real property is barred because of its strong impact on a state's sovereign authority. In dissent, Justice Souter argued that there was no meaningful distinction between the relief the Tribe sought and the relief the railroad sought against Attorney General Young. In both cases, Justice Souter argued, the plaintiff sought an order prohibiting a state from enforcing its laws. Who has the better of that argument? Is ownership in land truly so different that one should reach opposite results in *Young* and *Coeur d'Alene*?

Whatever one concludes about Justice Souter's arguments, there is also a potentially broader implication of the decision. In introducing its reasoning rejecting relief under *Young*, the Court summarized that "the Tribe's suit is the functional equivalent of a quiet title action *which implicates special sovereignty interests*." *Id.* at 281 (emphasis added). Some commentators have argued that the Court's language suggests that being "the functional equivalent of a quiet title action" is merely one example of something that "implicates a special sovereignty interest." Seen in this light, the *Coeur d'Alene* holding is narrow but contains an embedded suggestion that could lead to a far broader limitation on *Young*.

In *Virginia Office for Protection & Advocacy v. Stewart*, 131 S. Ct. 1632 (2011), the Court declined Virginia's invitation to expand the "special sovereignty interest" language to include a situation in which a state is sued in federal court under *Ex parte Young* by an independent state agency. As described above, this case concerned a claim by an independent state agency that other state officials were acting in violation of a federal law. The state agency was authorized by state law to enforce the federal mandate. Virginia claimed that such enforcement, even if allowed by *Ex parte Young* standing alone, would violate the state's "special sovereignty interests." In an opinion by Justice Scalia, the Court rejected the argument largely on the basis that it was the state itself that had set up the agency to enforce the federal mandate. Thus, there could be no violation of the state's "special sovereignty interests." *Id.* at 1640-41.

Thus, we are left with a narrow limitation on the cases the Court has decided in this area. Yet the tools are there with which to build on the Court's narrow position.

Limitation #4: Congressional Displacement

The final limitation on relief under *Ex parte Young* concerns Congress. The Court held that "where Congress has prescribed a detailed remedial scheme for the enforcement against a State of a statutorily created right, a court should hesitate before casting aside those limitations and permitting an action against a state officer based upon *Ex parte Young*." *Seminole Tribe of Fla. v. Florida*, 517 U.S. 44, 74 (1996).[21] Thus, unlike the other limitations on the doctrine we have discussed, this final one is in the hands of Congress to control.

In *Seminole Tribe*, an Indian Tribe sued the Governor of Florida in federal court claiming that the Governor was violating the Indian Gaming Regulatory Act (the "Act"). The Act concerned Indian Tribes' ability to engage in certain types of

21. We return to *Seminole Tribe* in the next section when we consider congressional abrogation of a state's sovereign immunity from suit in federal court.

gambling activities on Tribal lands, some of which required the approval of the state within which such Tribal lands were located. The Act contained intricate procedures by which a Tribe could attempt to compel a state to negotiate with it if the state had refused to do so. When Florida refused to negotiate, the Tribe filed suit in federal court under the Act.

As we will learn in the next section of the chapter, the Court first held that Congress did not have the constitutional authority to abrogate the states' immunity from suit under the so-called Indian Commerce Clause, the basis it articulated for enacting the statute. The Tribe, however, argued that it could prevail even if Congress could not remove state immunity because *Ex parte Young* allowed it to obtain an injunction compelling the Governor to bargain under the Act. In short, the Tribe sought prospective injunctive relief with respect to an ongoing violation of federal law. The Court rejected the argument because, somewhat ironically given the fact that it had held that Congress could not abrogate state sovereign immunity, the detailed nature of the remedial scheme in the Act indicated that Congress had meant to displace relief under *Ex parte Young*.

How broad is the *Seminole Tribe* exception to *Young*? First, you should be clear that it is capable of application by its own terms only with respect to violations of federal *statutory* law. Second, in its most recent statement on the matter the Court has indicated that it will not read that exception broadly as it relates to such statutes. It is not enough that Congress has enacted a comprehensive statutory scheme. Rather, Congress must intend to replace the *Young* remedy with another, more limited remedy. *See Verizon Md., Inc. v. Public Serv. Comm'n of Md.*, 535 U.S. 635, 647-48 (2002) (rejecting a challenge to using *Ex parte Young* to enforce the provisions of the Telecommunications Act of 1996 because, while detailed, the regulatory scheme Congress crafted "places no restriction on the relief a court can award").

We have seen in this section that *Ex parte Young* and its progeny allow a federal court to order a state official sued in his or her official capacity (or an official of some other entity entitled to Eleventh Amendment immunity) to comply with federal law prospectively. We have also seen that there are several exceptions to the basic *Ex parte Young* doctrine. Figures 8-2 and 8-3 summarize this important aspect of state sovereign immunity law:

FIGURE 8-2

Ex parte Young: What Can Plaintiffs Get?

Relief Allowed	Relief Not Allowed
• Prospective injunctive relief, or appropriate declaratory relief, with respect to an ongoing violation of federal law. • Relief ancillary to such prospective injunctive or declaratory relief, including in appropriate cases reasonable attorney's fees.	• Money damages, or its equivalent, to compensate for a past wrong when suing the state official in his or her official capacity. • Injunctive or declaratory relief if there is no ongoing violation of federal law.

Once one determines that *Ex parte Young* allows the relief sought, then one should ensure that none of the other exceptions to the doctrine would bar relief. Figure 8-3 illustrates how one might go about evaluating those exceptions.

FIGURE 8-3

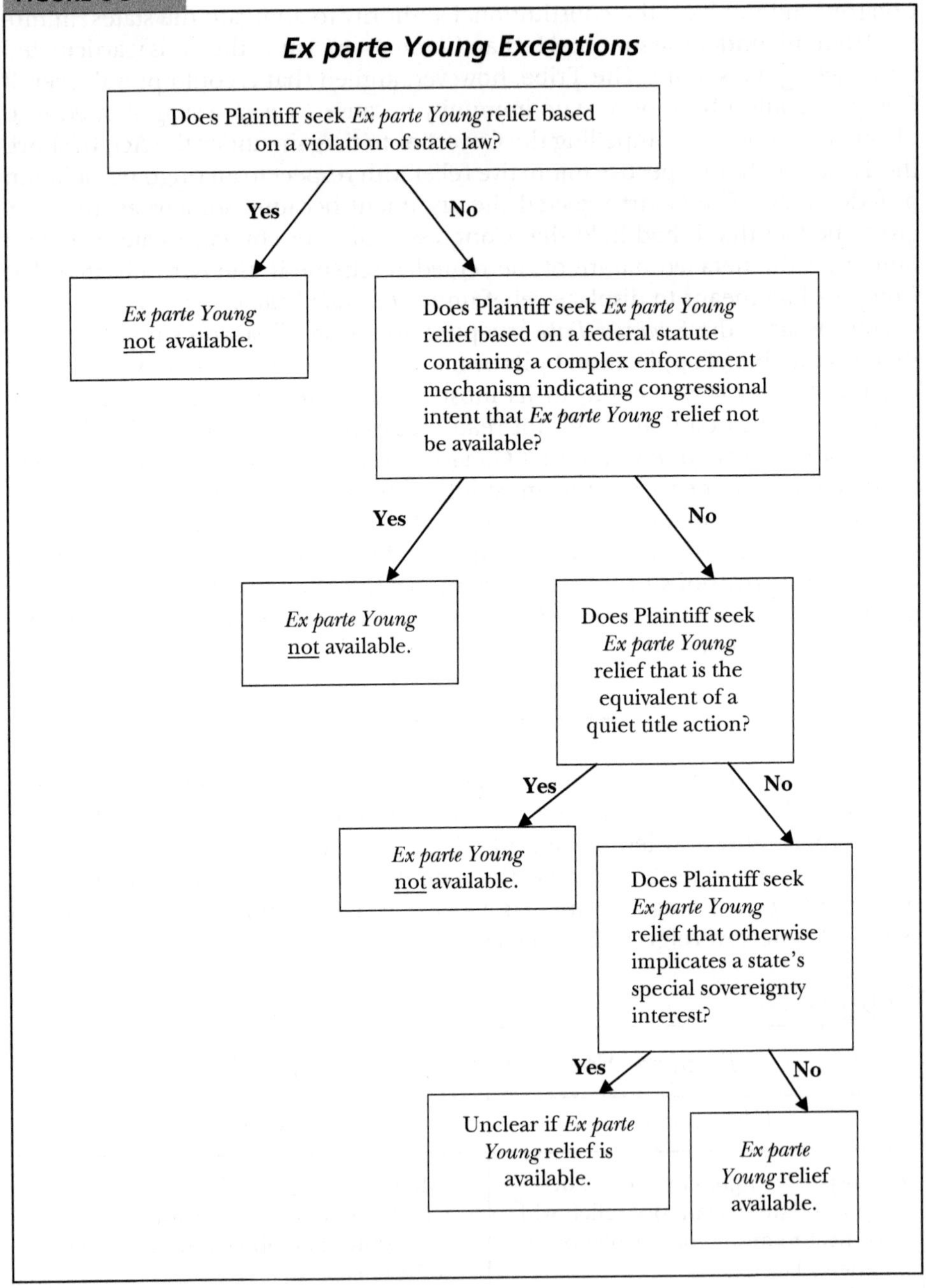

Problem 8-2 below allows you to work through some of the issues we have discussed in this section concerning *Ex parte Young* and its progeny.

PROBLEM 8-2

The Quadriplegic, the Wheelchair, and the Stingy State

Richard Costa ("Costa") is a quadriplegic as a result of multiple sclerosis. He has lived in a skilled nursing facility in Connecticut for the past 14 years. He requires 24-hour-a-day care and assistance in his daily living activities. He cannot move his legs or his right arm. He has limited mobility in his left hand, which allows him to operate a mechanical wheelchair. He currently uses a 15-year-old power wheelchair that he brought to the nursing home on his admission.

Due to his deteriorating condition, Costa's doctors concluded that he required a new mechanical wheelchair. The applicable Connecticut state regulations require that a vendor of durable medical devices such as a mechanical wheelchair must look to a nursing facility for payment first unless there is a prior authorization from the State Department of Social Services (the "Department") for direct payment from that entity. The funds the Department disburses for such purchases come from the federal Medicaid program. Given the substantial cost involved, the nursing facility refused to order Costa's new wheelchair without such prior authorization.

Costa sought pre-authorization from the Department for the mechanical wheelchair. The Department approved pre-payment for a non-power-driven wheelchair only. The Department's policy was that mechanical wheelchairs are not medically necessary for patients in 24-hour-per-day skilled nursing facilities.

Costa has filed suit in the United States District Court for the District of Connecticut against the Secretary of the Department in his official capacity, asserting that the Department's position (1) is inconsistent with relevant Department policies, and (2) to the extent consistent with those policies, is in violation of the relevant federal Medicaid statutes and regulations. Costa sought (1) a declaration that the Department's action was inconsistent with state law; (2) a declaration that to the extent the Department's action was consistent with state law, it was in violation of federal law; (3) an injunction ordering the Department to pre-approve the wheelchair request in its entirety and advance the funds for its immediate purchase; and (4) damages for emotional pain and suffering that he has been caused as a result of the Department's unlawful action.

The Secretary has moved to dismiss Costa's complaint in its entirety based on Connecticut's state sovereign immunity from suit in federal court. How should the District Judge rule on the Secretary's motion? Is there anything you would want to know about the relevant federal Medicaid statutes and regulations concerning the immunity issue? What would you want to know and why would you want to know it?

c. The Congress: Abrogation of Immunity

The third way in which it is possible to avoid state sovereign immunity from suit in federal court is if Congress has abrogated the immunity. This approach strongly implicates not only federalism values that underlie much debate in this area, but also principles of separation of powers. The fundamental question here is whether, assuming that *Hans* was correct that there exists some broad principle of state sovereign immunity beyond that recognized in the text of the Eleventh Amendment, Congress can remove or abrogate that immunity. Recall that *Hans* itself did not need to address that question because there was no relevant statute on which Hans relied to proceed against the State of Louisiana. We begin our consideration of congressional abrogation with *Fitzpatrick v. Bitzer.*

FITZPATRICK v. BITZER

427 U.S. 445 (1976)

MR. JUSTICE REHNQUIST delivered the opinion of the Court.

In the 1972 Amendments to Title VII of the Civil Rights Act of 1964, Congress, acting under § 5 of the Fourteenth Amendment, authorized federal courts to award money damages in favor of a private individual against a state government found to have subjected that person to employment discrimination on the basis of "race, color, religion, sex, or national origin." The principal question presented by these cases is whether, as against the shield of sovereign immunity afforded the State by the Eleventh Amendment Congress has the power to authorize federal courts to enter such an award against the State as a means of enforcing the substantive guarantees of the Fourteenth Amendment. The Court of Appeals for the Second Circuit held that the effect of our decision in *Edelman* was to foreclose Congress' power. We granted certiorari to resolve this important constitutional question. We reverse.

I

Petitioners . . . sued in the United States District Court for the District of Connecticut on behalf of all present and retired male employees of the State of Connecticut. Their amended complaint asserted, *inter alia,* that certain provisions in the State's statutory retirement benefit plan discriminated against them because of their sex, and therefore contravened Title VII. Title VII, which originally did not include state and local governments, had in the interim been amended to bring the States within its purview.

The District Court held that the Connecticut State Employees Retirement Act violated Title VII's prohibition against sex-based employment discrimination. It entered prospective injunctive relief in petitioners' favor against respondent state officials. Petitioners also sought an award of retroactive retirement benefits as compensation for losses caused by the State's discrimination. . . . But the District Court held that [such recovery] would constitute recovery of money damages from the State's treasury, and [was] therefore precluded by the Eleventh Amendment and by this Court's decision in *Edelman v. Jordan.*

On petitioners' appeal, the Court of Appeals . . . agreed with the District Court that the action, "insofar as it seeks damages, is in essence against the state and as such is subject to the Eleventh Amendment." The Court of Appeals also found that under the 1972 Amendments to Title VII, "Congress intended to authorize a private suit for backpay by state employees against the state." Notwithstanding this statutory authority, the Court of Appeals affirmed the District Court and held that under *Edelman* a "private federal action for retroactive damages" is not a "constitutionally permissible method of enforcing

Fourteenth Amendment rights." . . . The petition filed here by the state employees . . . contends that Congress does possess the constitutional power under § 5 of the Fourteenth Amendment to authorize their Title VII damages action against the State. . . .

II

In *Edelman* this Court held that monetary relief awarded by the District Court to welfare plaintiffs, by reason of wrongful denial of benefits which had occurred previous to the entry of the District Court's determination of their wrongfulness, violated the Eleventh Amendment. Such an award was found to be indistinguishable from a monetary award against the State itself which had been prohibited in [an earlier decision]. It was therefore controlled by that case rather than by *Ex parte Young*, which permitted suits against state officials to obtain prospective relief against violations of the Fourteenth Amendment.

Edelman went on to hold that the plaintiffs in that case could not avail themselves of the doctrine of waiver expounded in cases such as *Parden v. Terminal R. Co.*, because the necessary predicate for that doctrine was congressional intent to abrogate the immunity conferred by the Eleventh Amendment. We concluded that none of the statutes relied upon by plaintiffs in *Edelman* contained any authorization by Congress to join a State as defendant. . . .

All parties in the instant litigation agree with the Court of Appeals that the suit for retroactive benefits by the petitioners is in fact indistinguishable from that sought to be maintained in *Edelman*, since what is sought here is a damages award payable to a private party from the state treasury.

Our analysis begins where *Edelman* ended, for in this Title VII case the "threshold fact of congressional authorization," to sue the State as employer is clearly present. This is, of course, the prerequisite found present in *Parden*. . . . The congressional authorization involved in *Parden* was based on the power of Congress under the Commerce Clause; here, however, the Eleventh Amendment defense is asserted in the context of legislation passed pursuant to Congress' authority under § 5 of the Fourteenth Amendment.

As ratified by the States after the Civil War, that Amendment quite clearly contemplates limitations on their authority. [The Court then quoted sections 1 and 5 of the Fourteenth Amendment.]

The substantive provisions are by express terms directed at the States. Impressed upon them by those provisions are duties with respect to their treatment of private individuals. Standing behind the imperatives is Congress' power to "enforce" them "by appropriate legislation."

The impact of the Fourteenth Amendment upon the relationship between the Federal Government and the States, and the reach of congressional power under § 5, were examined at length by this Court in *Ex parte Virginia*. A state judge had been arrested and indicted under a federal criminal statute prohibiting the exclusion on the basis of race of any citizen from service as a juror in a state court. The judge claimed that the statute was beyond Congress' power to enact under either the Thirteenth or the Fourteenth Amendment. The Court first observed that these Amendments "were intended to be, what they really are, limitations of the power of the States and enlargements of the power of Congress." . . .

Ex parte Virginia's early recognition of this shift in the federal-state balance has been carried forward by more recent decisions of this Court.

There can be no doubt that this line of cases has sanctioned intrusions by Congress, acting under the Civil War Amendments, into the judicial, executive, and legislative spheres of autonomy previously reserved to the States. The legislation considered in each case was grounded on the expansion of Congress' powers—with the corresponding diminution of state sovereignty—found to be intended by the Framers and made part of the Constitution upon the States' ratification of those Amendments, a phenomenon aptly described as a "carv[ing] out" in *Ex parte Virginia.*

It is true that none of these previous cases presented the question of the relationship between the Eleventh Amendment and the enforcement power granted to Congress under § 5 of the Fourteenth Amendment. But we think that the Eleventh Amendment, and the principle of state sovereignty which it embodies, see *Hans v. Louisiana,* are necessarily limited by the enforcement provisions of § 5 of the Fourteenth Amendment. In that section Congress is expressly granted authority to enforce "by appropriate legislation" the substantive provisions of the Fourteenth Amendment, which themselves embody significant limitations on state authority. When Congress acts pursuant to § 5, not only is it exercising legislative authority that is plenary within the terms of the constitutional grant, it is exercising that authority under one section of a constitutional Amendment whose other sections by their own terms embody limitations on state authority. We think that Congress may, in determining what is "appropriate legislation" for the purpose of enforcing the provisions of the Fourteenth Amendment, provide for private suits against States or state officials which are constitutionally impermissible in other contexts.[22]

* * * *

The judgment . . . is *Reversed.*

Mr. Justice Brennan, concurring in the judgment.

. . . In my view Connecticut may not assert sovereign immunity [because] . . . [t]he States surrendered that immunity, in Hamilton's words, "in the plan of the Convention" that formed the Union, at least insofar as the States granted Congress specifically enumerated powers. Congressional authority to enact the provisions of Title VII at issue in this case is found in the Commerce Clause, Art. I, § 8, cl. 3, and in § 5 of the Fourteenth Amendment, two of the enumerated powers granted Congress in the Constitution. I remain of the opinion that "because of its surrender, no immunity exists that can be the subject of a congressional declaration or a voluntary waiver."

I therefore concur in the judgment of the Court.

[An opinion of Justice Stevens concurring in the judgment is omitted.]

DISCUSSION

Fitzpatrick is a critical case in late twentieth-century Eleventh Amendment jurisprudence. It is important, therefore, to consider carefully what it does

22. [Footnote 11 in Court's opinion.] Apart from their claim that the Eleventh Amendment bars enforcement of the remedy established by Title VII in this case, respondent state officials do not contend that the substantive provisions of Title VII as applied here are not a proper exercise of congressional authority under § 5 of the Fourteenth Amendment.

and does not hold. The Court starts from the position that state sovereign immunity applies in the case absent some appropriate congressional action. In other words, *Fitzpatrick* fully accepts the broad immunity *Hans* recognized. The Court's focus is on whether Congress has successfully altered that broad immunity. Note that Justice Brennan in his concurrence approaches matters quite differently. For him, there is no immunity in the first place because *Hans* was incorrectly decided.

Having recognized that sovereign immunity would ordinarily bar the suit, the Court turns to congressional abrogation. The Court's first consideration is whether Congress intended to abrogate state sovereign immunity when it enacted Title VII. This question is a statutory one. In later cases, the Court has made clear that because of the importance of state sovereign immunity in the federal system, Congress must be extraordinarily clear about its intent to alter the federal-state balance. "Congress may abrogate the States' constitutionally secured immunity from suit in federal court only by making its intention unmistakably clear in the language of the statute." *Atascadero State Hosp. v. Scanlon*, 473 U.S. 234, 242 (1985). And the Court later held, "Legislative history generally will be irrelevant to a judicial inquiry into whether Congress intended to abrogate the Eleventh Amendment." *Dellmuth v. Muth*, 491 U.S. 223, 230 (1989).

The clear statement rule can be a significant hurdle to overcome and has been employed with important consequences. Perhaps the most significant example of its impact concerns 42 U.S.C. § 1983. The Court held that this important civil rights statute, about which you will learn later in the course, see Chapter 9, was insufficiently clear in terms of Congress's intent to abrogate the states' immunity from suit. *See Quern v. Jordan*, 440 U.S. 332 (1979).[23] In other words, the clear statement rule itself should not be discounted in the abrogation calculus.

In any event, the *Fitzpatrick* Court held that Congress's *intention* to abrogate immunity was clear. It then needed to address whether Congress had the *power* to do so. As is implicit at least in *Fitzpatrick* and made explicit in later cases, the first step in determining whether Congress has the power to act is to identify the specific constitutional provision on which Congress bases its abrogation. The relevant provision in *Fitzpatrick* was section 5 of the Fourteenth Amendment. The Court held that when acting within the scope of section 5, Congress may abrogate the states' immunity. Note, however, that *Fitzpatrick* does *not* address the *scope* of Congress' power under section 5 itself because the state officials did not raise that issue on appeal. *See* note 11 in the Court's opinion, note 22 in this chapter.

Justice Rehnquist also explained for the Court why action taken within the scope of Congress' section 5 powers could affect the Eleventh Amendment and "the principle of state sovereignty which it embodies." The key was that the Fourteenth Amendment, one of the Civil War Amendments, was meant to change the balance of power between the states and the federal government. Thus, Congress was acting pursuant to a constitutional provision the Court recognized as both taking something way from the states while simultaneously giving something to the federal Congress. The very nature of sovereignty in the United States had been altered.

23. The Court later held that actions under § 1983 in state courts were also not allowed because the word "person" in the statute did not include states. *See Will v. Michigan Dep't of State Police*, 491 U.S. 58 (1989).

Notice, however, that *Fitzpatrick* did not address whether Congress had the authority to abrogate state sovereign immunity from suit in federal court if it acted pursuant to any of the powers enumerated in Article I, section 8, of the original Constitution. The Court turned to that question several years later in *Pennsylvania v. Union Gas. Co.*, 491 U.S. 1 (1989). Without a single opinion commanding a majority, the Court concluded in *Union Gas* that at least when acting pursuant to Congress' Article I power to "regulate Commerce . . . among the several States," *see* U.S. CONST. art. I, § 8, cl. 3, Congress could validly abrogate state sovereign immunity.

The difficulty with *Union Gas* is that it was an incredibly fractured decision. A plurality opinion by Justice Brennan that garnered only four votes articulated a view that the broad immunity *Hans* recognized was not itself constitutional. Rather, it was akin to a background common-law principle that Congress could alter by acting pursuant to one of its enumerated powers. The idea was that the states had entered into the federal union with their immunity intact (thus preserving *Hans*'s vitality) but had implicitly agreed that Congress could change that state of affairs if acting pursuant to an enumerated power. Justice White concurred in the plurality's conclusion but, rather unhelpfully, stated that "I do not agree with much of [Justice Brennan's reasoning]." *Union Gas Co.*, 491 U.S. at 57. Four other justices dissented.

The result of *Union Gas* was that the Court provided an answer to the question concerning whether Congress could validly abrogate the states' sovereign immunity when it acted under its Article I powers, but it was unable to agree on why that was the case. Such instability in the rationale for such an important constitutional decision marked *Union Gas* as a decision likely to be reconsidered. It was in the next principal case, *Seminole Tribe v. Florida.* The detailed opinions in this case, in particular Justice Souter's dissent, not only consider congressional abrogation but also review much of the fundamental doctrine concerning the scope of state sovereign immunity from suit in federal court itself. In our view, it is important to read a significant portion of the opinions in *Seminole Tribe*, unquestionably a key decision in this area of law.

SEMINOLE TRIBE OF FLORIDA v. FLORIDA

517 U.S. 44 (1996)

CHIEF JUSTICE REHNQUIST delivered the opinion of the Court.

The Indian Gaming Regulatory Act provides that an Indian tribe may conduct certain gaming activities only in conformance with a valid compact between the tribe and the State in which the gaming activities are located. The Act, passed by Congress under the Indian Commerce Clause, U.S. Const., Art. I, § 8, cl. 3, imposes upon the States a duty to negotiate in good faith with an Indian tribe toward the formation of a compact and authorizes a tribe to bring suit in federal court against a State in order to compel performance of that duty. We hold that notwithstanding Congress' clear intent to abrogate the States' sovereign immunity, the Indian Commerce Clause does not grant Congress that power, and therefore [the Act] cannot grant jurisdiction over a State that does not consent to be sued. We further hold that the doctrine of *Ex parte Young* may not be used to enforce [the Act] against a state official.

I

Congress passed the [Act] in 1988 in order to provide a statutory basis for the operation and regulation of gaming by Indian tribes. The Act divides gaming on Indian lands into three classes—I, II, and III—and provides a different regulatory scheme for each class. Class III gaming—the type with which we are here concerned—is defined as "all forms of gaming that are not class I gaming or class II gaming," and includes such things as slot machines, casino games, banking card games, dog racing, and lotteries. It is the most heavily regulated of the three classes. The Act provides that class III gaming is lawful only where it is: (1) authorized by an ordinance or resolution that (a) is adopted by the governing body of the Indian tribe, (b) satisfies certain statutorily prescribed requirements, and (c) is approved by the National Indian Gaming Commission; (2) located in a State that permits such gaming for any purpose by any person, organization, or entity; and (3) "conducted in conformance with a Tribal-State compact entered into by the Indian tribe and the State under paragraph (3) that is in effect."

The "paragraph (3)" to which the last prerequisite [quoted above] . . . describes the permissible scope of a Tribal-State compact, and provides that the compact is effective "only when notice of approval by the Secretary [of the Interior] of such compact has been published by the Secretary in the Federal Register." More significant for our purposes, however, is that [the Act] describes the process by which a State and an Indian tribe begin negotiations toward a Tribal-State compact. [The Court then described the Act's requirements in this regard. For present purposes, the key provisions concerned a State's refusal to enter into negotiations with a Tribe concerning class III gambling. In such case, the Act provided that a federal district court had jurisdiction to order the State to enter into such negotiations. If no agreement is reached after the court-ordered process, there followed mediation and, eventually, a determination of the issue by the Secretary of the Interior of the terms of a compact concerning class III gambling.]

In September 1991, the Seminole Tribe of Florida, petitioner, sued the State of Florida and its Governor, Lawton Chiles, respondents. Invoking jurisdiction under [the Act], as well as 28 U.S.C. §§ 1331 and 1362 [providing federal district courts original jurisdiction in cases brought by Indian tribes asserting a claim that "arises under the Constitution, laws, or treaties of the United States"], petitioner alleged that respondents had "refused to enter into any negotiation for inclusion of [certain gaming activities] in a tribal-state compact," thereby violating the "requirement of good faith negotiation" contained in [the Act]. Respondents moved to dismiss the complaint, arguing that the suit violated the State's sovereign immunity from suit in federal court. The District Court denied respondents' motion and respondents took an interlocutory appeal of that decision. [The United States Court of Appeals for the Eleventh Circuit reversed.]

* * * *

Petitioner sought our review of the Eleventh Circuit's decision and we granted certiorari in order to consider two questions: (1) Does the Eleventh Amendment prevent Congress from authorizing suits by Indian tribes against States for prospective injunctive relief to enforce legislation enacted pursuant to the Indian Commerce Clause?; and (2) Does the doctrine of *Ex parte Young* permit suits against a State's Governor for prospective injunctive relief to enforce the good-faith bargaining requirement of the Act? We answer the first question in the affirmative, the second in the negative, and we therefore affirm the Eleventh Circuit's dismissal of petitioner's suit.

* * * *

Although the text of the [Eleventh] Amendment would appear to restrict only the Article III diversity jurisdiction of the federal courts, "we have understood the Eleventh Amendment to stand not so much for what it says, but for the presupposition . . . which it confirms." That presupposition, first observed over a century ago in *Hans v. Louisiana* has two parts: first, that each State is a sovereign entity in our federal system; and second, that "'it is inherent in the nature of sovereignty not to be amenable to the suit of an individual without its consent.'" For over a century we have reaffirmed that federal jurisdiction over suits against unconsenting States "was not contemplated by the Constitution when establishing the judicial power of the United States." *Hans.*

Here, petitioner has sued the State of Florida and it is undisputed that Florida has not consented to the suit. Petitioner nevertheless contends that its suit is not barred by state sovereign immunity. First, it argues that Congress through the Act abrogated the States' sovereign immunity. Alternatively, petitioner maintains that its suit against the Governor may go forward under *Ex parte Young.* We consider each of those arguments in turn.

II

Petitioner argues that Congress through the Act abrogated the States' immunity from suit. In order to determine whether Congress has abrogated the States' sovereign immunity, we ask two questions: first, whether Congress has "unequivocally expressed its intent to abrogate the immunity"; and second, whether Congress has acted "pursuant to a valid exercise of power."

A

[In this part of its opinion, the Court concluded that "Congress intended through the Act to abrogate the States' sovereign immunity from suit."]

B

Having concluded that Congress clearly intended to abrogate the States' sovereign immunity . . . , we turn now to consider whether the Act was passed "pursuant to a valid exercise of power." Before we address that question here, however, we think it necessary first to define the scope of our inquiry.

Petitioner suggests that one consideration weighing in favor of finding the power to abrogate here is that the Act authorizes only prospective injunctive relief rather than retroactive monetary relief. But we have often made it clear that the relief sought by a plaintiff suing a State is irrelevant to the question whether the suit is barred by the Eleventh Amendment. We think it follows *a fortiori* from this proposition that the type of relief sought is irrelevant to whether Congress has power to abrogate States' immunity. The Eleventh Amendment does not exist solely in order to "preven[t] federal-court judgments that must be paid out of a State's treasury"; it also serves to avoid "the indignity of subjecting a State to the coercive process of judicial tribunals at the instance of private parties."

Similarly, petitioner argues that the abrogation power is validly exercised here because the Act grants the States a power that they would not otherwise have, viz., some measure of authority over gaming on Indian lands. It is true enough that the Act extends to the States a power withheld from them by the Constitution. Nevertheless, we do not see how that consideration is relevant to the question whether Congress may abrogate state sovereign immunity. The Eleventh Amendment immunity may not be lifted by Congress unilaterally deciding that it will be replaced by grant of some other authority.

Thus our inquiry into whether Congress has the power to abrogate unilaterally the States' immunity from suit is narrowly focused on one question: Was the Act in question passed pursuant to a constitutional provision granting Congress the power to abrogate? See, *e. g., Fitzpatrick v. Bitzer.* Previously, in conducting that inquiry, we have found authority to abrogate under only two provisions of the Constitution. In *Fitzpatrick,* we recognized that the Fourteenth Amendment, by expanding federal power at the expense of state autonomy, had fundamentally altered the balance of state and federal power struck by the Constitution. We noted that § 1 of the Fourteenth Amendment contained prohibitions expressly directed at the States and that § 5 of the Amendment expressly provided that "The Congress shall have power to enforce, by appropriate legislation, the provisions of this article." We held that through the Fourteenth Amendment, federal power extended to intrude upon the province of the Eleventh Amendment and therefore that § 5 of the Fourteenth Amendment allowed Congress to abrogate the immunity from suit guaranteed by that Amendment.

In only one other case has congressional abrogation of the States' Eleventh Amendment immunity been upheld. In *Pennsylvania v. Union Gas Co.*, a plurality of the Court found that the Interstate Commerce Clause, Art. I, § 8, cl. 3, granted Congress the power to abrogate state sovereign immunity, stating that the power to regulate interstate commerce would be "incomplete without the authority to render States liable in damages." Justice White added the fifth vote necessary to the result in that case, but wrote separately in order to express that he "[did] not agree with much of [the plurality's] reasoning."

In arguing that Congress through the Act abrogated the States' sovereign immunity, petitioner does not challenge the Eleventh Circuit's conclusion that the Act was passed pursuant to neither the Fourteenth Amendment nor the Interstate Commerce Clause. Instead, accepting the lower court's conclusion that the Act was passed pursuant to Congress' power under the Indian Commerce Clause, petitioner now asks us to consider whether that Clause grants Congress the power to abrogate the States' sovereign immunity. [The Court then considered whether there was a meaningful distinction for sovereign immunity purposes between the Indian Commerce Clause and the Interstate Commerce Clause. The Court ultimately concluded that "the plurality opinion in *Union Gas* allows no principled distinction in favor of the States to be drawn between [the two clauses."]

* * * *

Respondents argue, however, that we need not conclude that the Indian Commerce Clause grants the power to abrogate the States' sovereign immunity. Instead, they contend that if we find the rationale of the *Union Gas* plurality to extend to the Indian Commerce Clause, then "*Union Gas* should be reconsidered and overruled." Generally, the principle of *stare decisis,* and the interests that it serves, viz., "the evenhanded, predictable, and consistent development of legal principles, . . . reliance on judicial decisions, and . . . the actual and perceived integrity of the judicial process," counsel strongly against reconsideration of our precedent. Nevertheless, we always have treated *stare decisis* as a "principle of policy" and not as an "inexorable command," "When governing decisions are unworkable or are badly reasoned, 'this Court has never felt constrained to follow precedent.'" Our willingness to reconsider our earlier decisions has been "particularly true in constitutional cases, because in such cases 'correction through legislative action is practically impossible.'"

The Court in *Union Gas* reached a result without an expressed rationale agreed upon by a majority of the Court. We have already seen that Justice Brennan's opinion received the support of only three other Justices. Of the other five, Justice White, who provided the fifth vote for the result, wrote separately in order to indicate his disagreement with the plurality's rationale and four Justices joined together in a dissent that rejected the plurality's rationale. Since it was issued, *Union Gas* has created confusion among the lower courts that have sought to understand and apply the deeply fractured decision.

The plurality's rationale also deviated sharply from our established federalism jurisprudence and essentially eviscerated our decision in *Hans*. It was well established in 1989 when *Union Gas* was decided that the Eleventh Amendment stood for the constitutional principle that state sovereign immunity limited the federal courts' jurisdiction under Article III. The text of the Amendment itself is clear enough on this point: "The Judicial power of the United States shall not be construed to extend to any suit. . . ." And our decisions since *Hans* had been equally clear that the Eleventh Amendment reflects "the fundamental principle of sovereign immunity [that] limits the grant of judicial authority in Art. III." As the dissent in *Union Gas* recognized, the plurality's conclusion — that Congress could under Article I expand the scope of the federal courts' jurisdiction under Article III — "contradicted our unvarying approach to Article III as setting forth the *exclusive* catalog of permissible federal-court jurisdiction."

Never before the decision in *Union Gas* had we suggested that the bounds of Article III could be expanded by Congress operating pursuant to any constitutional provision other than the Fourteenth Amendment. Indeed, it had seemed fundamental that Congress could not expand the jurisdiction of the federal courts beyond the bounds of Article III. *Marbury v. Madison*. . . .

The plurality's extended reliance upon our decision in *Fitzpatrick v. Bitzer*, that Congress could under the Fourteenth Amendment abrogate the States' sovereign immunity was also, we believe, misplaced. *Fitzpatrick* was based upon a rationale wholly inapplicable to the Interstate Commerce Clause, viz., that the Fourteenth Amendment, adopted well after the adoption of the Eleventh Amendment and the ratification of the Constitution, operated to alter the pre-existing balance between state and federal power achieved by Article III and the Eleventh Amendment. As the dissent in *Union Gas* made clear, *Fitzpatrick* cannot be read to justify "limitation of the principle embodied in the Eleventh Amendment through appeal to antecedent provisions of the Constitution."

In the five years since it was decided, *Union Gas* has proved to be a solitary departure from established law. Reconsidering the decision in *Union Gas*, we conclude that none of the policies underlying *stare decisis* require our continuing adherence to its holding. The decision has, since its issuance, been of questionable precedential value, largely because a majority of the Court expressly disagreed with the rationale of the plurality. The case involved the interpretation of the Constitution and therefore may be altered only by constitutional amendment or revision by this Court. Finally, both the result in *Union Gas* and the plurality's rationale depart from our established understanding of the Eleventh Amendment and undermine the accepted function of Article III. We feel bound to conclude that *Union Gas* was wrongly decided and that it should be, and now is, overruled.

The dissent makes no effort to defend the decision in *Union Gas*, but nonetheless would find congressional power to abrogate in this case. Contending that our decision is a novel extension of the Eleventh Amendment, the dissent chides us for "attending" to dicta. We adhere in this case, however, not to mere *obiter dicta*, but rather to the well-established rationale upon which the Court based the results of its earlier decisions. When an opinion issues for the Court, it is not only the result but also those portions of the opinion necessary to that result by which we are bound. For over a century, we have grounded our decisions in the oft-repeated understanding of state sovereign immunity as an essential part of the Eleventh Amendment. . . . It is true that we have not had occasion previously to apply established Eleventh Amendment principles to the question whether Congress has the power to abrogate state sovereign immunity (save in *Union Gas*). But consideration of that question must proceed with fidelity to this century-old doctrine.

The dissent, to the contrary, disregards our case law in favor of a theory cobbled together from law review articles and its own version of historical events. The dissent cites not a single decision since *Hans* (other than *Union Gas*) that supports its view of state sovereign immunity, instead relying upon the now-discredited decision in *Chisholm v. Georgia*. Its undocumented and highly speculative extralegal explanation of the decision in *Hans* is a disservice to the Court's traditional method of adjudication.

The dissent mischaracterizes the *Hans* opinion. That decision found its roots not solely in the common law of England, but in the much more fundamental "'jurisprudence in all civilized nations.'" The dissent's proposition that the common law of England, where adopted by the States, was open to change by the Legislature is wholly unexceptionable and largely beside the point: that common law provided the substantive rules of law rather than jurisdiction. It also is noteworthy that the principle of state sovereign immunity stands distinct from other principles of the common law in that only the former prompted a specific constitutional amendment.

Hans—with a much closer vantage point than the dissent—recognized that the decision in *Chisholm* was contrary to the well-understood meaning of the Constitution. The dissent's conclusion that the decision in *Chisholm* was "reasonable," certainly would have struck the Framers of the Eleventh Amendment as quite odd: That decision created "such a shock of surprise that the Eleventh Amendment was at once proposed and adopted." The dissent's lengthy analysis of the text of the Eleventh Amendment is directed at a straw man—we long have recognized that blind reliance upon the text of the Eleventh Amendment is "'to strain the Constitution and the law to a construction never imagined or dreamed of.'" The text dealt in terms only with the problem presented by the decision in *Chisholm*; in light of the fact that the federal courts did not have federal-question jurisdiction at the time the Amendment was passed (and would not have it until 1875), it seems unlikely that much thought was given to the prospect of federal-question jurisdiction over the States.

That same consideration causes the dissent's criticism of the views of Marshall, Madison, and Hamilton to ring hollow. The dissent cites statements made by those three influential Framers, the most natural reading of which would preclude all federal jurisdiction over an unconsenting State. Struggling against this reading, however, the dissent finds significant the absence of any contention that sovereign immunity would affect the new federal-question jurisdiction. But the lack of any statute vesting general federal-question jurisdiction in the federal courts until much later makes the dissent's demand for greater specificity about a then-dormant jurisdiction overly exacting.[24]

In putting forward a new theory of state sovereign immunity, the dissent develops its own vision of the political system created by the Framers, concluding with the statement that "the Framers. principal objectives in rejecting English theories of unitary sovereignty . . . would have been impeded if a new concept of sovereign immunity had taken its place in federal-question cases, and would have been substantially thwarted if that new immunity had been held untouchable by any congressional effort to abrogate it."[25] This sweeping statement ignores the fact that the Nation survived for nearly two centuries without the question of the existence of such power ever being presented to this Court. And Congress itself waited nearly a century before even conferring federal-question jurisdiction on the lower federal courts.

In overruling *Union Gas* today, we reconfirm that the background principle of state sovereign immunity embodied in the Eleventh Amendment is not so ephemeral as to dissipate when the subject of the suit is an area, like the regulation of Indian commerce, that is under the exclusive control of the Federal Government. Even when the Constitution vests in Congress complete law-making authority over a particular area, the Eleventh Amendment prevents congressional authorization of suits by private parties against unconsenting States. The Eleventh Amendment restricts the judicial power under Article III, and Article I cannot be used to circumvent the constitutional limitations placed upon federal jurisdiction. Petitioner's suit against the State of Florida must be dismissed for a lack of jurisdiction.

III

[In this part of its opinion, the Court considered whether *Ex parte Young* provided jurisdiction over the Tribe's claims against Florida Governor Chiles, in which it sought prospective injunctive relief. As we discussed in the previous section of this chapter, the Court held that it did not based on congressional intent when adopting the Act.]

24. [Footnote 13 in Court's opinion.] Although the absence of any discussion dealing with federal-question jurisdiction is therefore unremarkable, what is notably lacking in the Framers' statements is any mention of Congress' power to abrogate the States' immunity. The absence of any discussion of that power is particularly striking in light of the fact that the Framers virtually always were very specific about the exception to state sovereign immunity arising from a State's consent to suit. . . .

25. [Footnote 14 in Court's opinion.] This argument wholly disregards other methods of ensuring the States' compliance with federal law: The Federal Government can bring suit in federal court against a State; an individual can bring suit against a state officer in order to ensure that the officer's conduct is in compliance with federal law, *see, e. g., Ex parte Young*; and this Court is empowered to review a question of federal law arising from a state-court decision where a State has consented to suit, *see, e. g., Cohens v. Virginia.*

IV

The Eleventh Amendment prohibits Congress from making the State of Florida capable of being sued in federal court. The narrow exception to the Eleventh Amendment provided by the *Ex parte Young* doctrine cannot be used to enforce [the Act] because Congress enacted a remedial scheme specifically designed for the enforcement of that right. The Eleventh Circuit's dismissal of petitioner's suit is hereby affirmed.

It is so ordered.

JUSTICE STEVENS, dissenting.

This case is about power—the power of the Congress of the United States to create a private federal cause of action against a State, or its Governor, for the violation of a federal right. In *Chisholm v. Georgia*, the entire Court—including Justice Iredell whose dissent provided the blueprint for the Eleventh Amendment—assumed that Congress had such power. In *Hans v. Louisiana*—a case the Court purports to follow today—the Court again assumed that Congress had such power. In *Fitzpatrick v. Bitzer* and *Pennsylvania v. Union Gas Co.* the Court squarely held that Congress has such power. In a series of cases . . . the Court formulated a special "clear statement rule" to determine whether specific Acts of Congress contained an effective exercise of that power. Nevertheless, in a sharp break with the past, today the Court holds that with the narrow and illogical exception of statutes enacted pursuant to the Enforcement Clause of the Fourteenth Amendment, Congress has no such power.

The importance of the majority's decision to overrule the Court's holding in *Pennsylvania v. Union Gas Co.* cannot be overstated. The majority's opinion does not simply preclude Congress from establishing the rather curious statutory scheme under which Indian tribes may seek the aid of a federal court to secure a State's good-faith negotiations over gaming regulations. Rather, it prevents Congress from providing a federal forum for a broad range of actions against States, from those sounding in copyright and patent law, to those concerning bankruptcy, environmental law, and the regulation of our vast national economy.

There may be room for debate over whether, in light of the Eleventh Amendment, Congress has the power to ensure that such a cause of action may be enforced in federal court by a citizen of another State or a foreign citizen. There can be no serious debate, however, over whether Congress has the power to ensure that such a cause of action may be brought by a citizen of the State being sued. Congress' authority in that regard is clear.

As Justice Souter has convincingly demonstrated, the Court's contrary conclusion is profoundly misguided. Despite the thoroughness of his analysis, supported by sound reason, history, precedent, and strikingly uniform scholarly commentary, the shocking character of the majority's affront to a coequal branch of our Government merits additional comment.

[The remainder of Justice Stevens's dissent is omitted.]

* * * *

JUSTICE SOUTER, with whom JUSTICE GINSBURG and JUSTICE BREYER join, dissenting.

In holding the State of Florida immune to suit under the Indian Gaming Regulatory Act, the Court today holds for the first time since the founding of the Republic that Congress has no authority to subject a State to the jurisdiction of a federal court at the behest of an individual asserting a federal right. Although the Court invokes the Eleventh Amendment as authority for this proposition, the only sense in which that amendment might be claimed as pertinent here was tolerantly phrased by Justice Stevens in his concurring opinion in *Pennsylvania v. Union Gas Co.* There, he explained how it has come about that we have two Eleventh Amendments, the one ratified in 1795, the other (so-called) invented by the Court nearly a century later in *Hans v. Louisiana.* Justice Stevens saw in that second Eleventh Amendment no bar to the exercise of congressional authority under the Commerce Clause in providing for suits on a federal question by individuals against a State, and I can only say that after my own canvass of the matter I believe he was entirely correct in that view, for reasons given below. His position, of course, was also the holding in *Union Gas,* which the Court now overrules and repudiates.

The fault I find with the majority today is not in its decision to reexamine *Union Gas,* for the Court in that case produced no majority for a single rationale supporting congressional authority. Instead, I part company from the Court because I am convinced that its decision is fundamentally mistaken, and for that reason I respectfully dissent.

I

It is useful to separate three questions: (1) whether the States enjoyed sovereign immunity if sued in their own courts in the period prior to ratification of the National Constitution; (2) if so, whether after ratification the States were entitled to claim some such immunity when sued in a federal court exercising jurisdiction either because the suit was between a State and a nonstate litigant who was not its citizen, or because the issue in the case raised a federal question; and (3) whether any state sovereign immunity recognized in federal court may be abrogated by Congress.

The answer to the first question is not clear, although some of the Framers assumed that States did enjoy immunity in their own courts. The second question was not debated at the time of ratification, except as to citizen-state diversity jurisdiction; there was no unanimity, but in due course the Court in *Chisholm v. Georgia* answered that a state defendant enjoyed no such immunity. As to federal-question jurisdiction, state sovereign immunity seems not to have been debated prior to ratification, the silence probably showing a general understanding at the time that the States would have no immunity in such cases.

The adoption of the Eleventh Amendment soon changed the result in *Chisholm,* not by mentioning sovereign immunity, but by eliminating citizen-state diversity jurisdiction over cases with state defendants. I will explain why the Eleventh Amendment did not affect federal-question jurisdiction, a notion that needs to be understood for the light it casts on the soundness of *Hans*'s holding that States did enjoy sovereign immunity in federal-question suits. The *Hans* Court erroneously assumed that a State could plead sovereign immunity against a noncitizen suing under federal-question jurisdiction, and for that reason held that a State must enjoy the same protection in a suit by one of its citizens. The error of *Hans*'s reasoning is underscored by its clear inconsistency with the Founders' hostility to the implicit reception of common-law doctrine as federal law, and with the Founders' conception of sovereign power as divided between the States and the National Government for the sake of very practical objectives.

The Court's answer today to the third question is likewise at odds with the Founders' view that common law, when it was received into the new American legal system, was always subject to legislative amendment. In ignoring the reasons for this pervasive understanding at the time of the ratification, and in holding that a nontextual common-law rule limits a clear grant of congressional power under Article I, the Court follows a course that has brought it to grief before in our history, and promises to do so again.

* * * *

A

The doctrine of sovereign immunity comprises two distinct rules, which are not always separately recognized. The one rule holds that the King or the Crown, as the font of law, is not bound by the law's provisions; the other provides that the King or Crown, as the font of justice, is not subject to suit in its own courts. The one rule limits the reach of substantive law; the other, the jurisdiction of the courts. We are concerned here only with the latter rule, which took its common-law form in the high Middle Ages. "At least as early as the thirteenth century, during the reign of Henry III (1216-1272), it was recognized that the king could not be sued in his own courts."

The significance of this doctrine in the nascent American law is less clear, however, than its early development and steady endurance in England might suggest. While some colonial governments may have enjoyed some such immunity the scope (and even the existence) of this governmental immunity in pre-Revolutionary America remains disputed.

Whatever the scope of sovereign immunity might have been in the Colonies, however, or during the period of Confederation, the proposal to establish a National Government under the Constitution drafted in 1787 presented a prospect unknown to the common law prior to the American experience: the States would become parts of a system in which sovereignty over even domestic matters would be divided or parcelled out between the States and the Nation, the latter to be invested with its own judicial power and the right to prevail against the States whenever their respective substantive laws might be in conflict. With this prospect in mind, the 1787 Constitution might have addressed state sovereign immunity by eliminating whatever sovereign immunity the States previously had, as to any matter subject to federal law or jurisdiction; by recognizing an analogue to the old immunity in the new context of federal jurisdiction, but subject to abrogation as to any matter within that jurisdiction; or by enshrining a doctrine of inviolable state sovereign immunity in the text, thereby giving it constitutional protection in the new federal jurisdiction.

The 1787 draft in fact said nothing on the subject, and it was this very silence that occasioned some, though apparently not widespread, dispute among the Framers and others over whether ratification of the Constitution would preclude a State sued in federal court from asserting sovereign immunity as it could have done on any matter of nonfederal law litigated in its own courts. As it has come down to us, the discussion gave no attention to congressional power under the proposed Article I but focused entirely on the limits of the judicial power provided in Article III. And although the jurisdictional bases together constituting the judicial power of the national courts under § 2 of Article III included questions arising under federal law and cases between States and individuals who are not citizens, it was only upon the latter citizen-state diversity provisions that preratification questions about state immunity from suit or liability centered.

Later in my discussion I will canvass the details of the debate among the Framers and other leaders of the time; for now it is enough to say that there was no consensus on the issue. There was, on the contrary, a clear disagreement, which was left to fester during the ratification period, to be resolved only thereafter. One other point, however, was also clear: the debate addressed only the question whether ratification of the Constitution would, in diversity cases and without more, abrogate the state sovereign immunity or allow it to have some application. We have no record that anyone argued for the third option mentioned above, that the Constitution would affirmatively guarantee state sovereign immunity against any congressional action to the contrary. Nor would there have been any apparent justification for any such argument, since no clause in the proposed (and ratified) Constitution even so much as suggested such a position. It may have been reasonable to contend (as we will see that Madison, Marshall, and Hamilton did) that Article III would not alter States' pre-existing common-law immunity despite its unqualified grant of jurisdiction over diversity suits against States. But then, as now, there was no textual support for contending that Article III or any other provision would "constitutionalize" state sovereign immunity, and no one uttered any such contention.

B

The argument among the Framers and their friends about sovereign immunity in federal citizen-state diversity cases, in any event, was short lived and ended when this Court, in *Chisholm v. Georgia* chose between the constitutional alternatives of abrogation and recognition of the immunity enjoyed at common law. The 4-to-1 majority adopted the reasonable (although not compelled) interpretation that the first of the two Citizen-State Diversity Clauses abrogated for purposes of federal jurisdiction any immunity the States might have enjoyed in their own courts, and Georgia was accordingly held subject to the judicial power in a common-law assumpsit action by a South Carolina citizen suing to collect a debt.[26] The case also settled, by implication, any question there could possibly have been about recognizing state sovereign immunity in actions depending on the federal question (or "arising under") head of jurisdiction as well. The constitutional text on federal-question jurisdiction, after all, was just as devoid of immunity language as it was on citizen-state diversity, and at the time of *Chisholm* any influence that general common-law immunity might have had as an interpretive force in construing constitutional language would presumably

26. [Footnote 5 in Justice Souter's dissent.] This lengthy discussion of the history of the Constitution's ratification, the Court's opinion in *Chisholm v. Georgia* and the adoption of the Eleventh Amendment is necessary to explain why, in my view, the contentions in some of our earlier opinions that *Chisholm* created a great "shock of surprise" misread the history. See *Principality of Monaco v. Mississippi.* The Court's response to this historical analysis is simply to recite yet again *Monaco*'s erroneous assertion that *Chisholm* created "such a shock of surprise that the Eleventh Amendment was at once proposed and adopted." This response is, with respect, no response at all. *Monaco*'s *ipse dixit* that *Chisholm* created a "shock of surprise" does not make it so. This Court's opinions frequently make assertions of historical fact, but those assertions are not authoritative as to history in the same way that our interpretations of laws are authoritative as to them. . . . Moreover, in this case, there is ample evidence contradicting the "shock of surprise" thesis. Contrary to *Monaco*'s suggestion, the Eleventh Amendment was not "at once proposed and adopted." Congress was in session when *Chisholm* was decided, and a constitutional amendment in response was proposed two days later, but Congress never acted on it, and in fact it was not until two years after *Chisholm* was handed down that an Amendment was ratified.

have been no greater when addressing the federal-question language of Article III than its Diversity Clauses.

Although Justice Iredell's dissent in *Chisholm* seems at times to reserve judgment on what I have called the third question, whether Congress could authorize suits against the States, his argument is largely devoted to stating the position taken by several federalists that state sovereign immunity was cognizable under the Citizen-State Diversity Clauses, not that state immunity was somehow invisibly codified as an independent constitutional defense. . . . Justice Iredell's dissent focused on the construction of the Judiciary Act of 1789, not Article III. This would have been an odd focus, had he believed that Congress lacked the constitutional authority to impose liability. Instead, on Justice Iredell's view, States sued in diversity retained the common-law sovereignty "where no special act of Legislation controuls it, to be in force in each State, as it existed in England, (unaltered by any statute) at the time of the first settlement of the country." While in at least some circumstances States might be held liable to "the authority of the United States," any such liability would depend upon "laws passed under the Constitution and in conformity to it." Finding no congressional action abrogating Georgia's common-law immunity, Justice Iredell concluded that the State should not be liable to suit.[27]

C

The Eleventh Amendment, of course, repudiated *Chisholm* and clearly divested federal courts of some jurisdiction as to cases against state parties. . . . There are two plausible readings of [the Amendment's] text. Under the first, it simply repeals the Citizen-State Diversity Clauses of Article III for all cases in which the State appears as a defendant. Under the second, it strips the federal courts of jurisdiction in any case in which a state defendant is sued by a citizen not its own, even if jurisdiction might otherwise rest on the existence of a federal question in the suit. Neither reading of the Amendment, of course, furnishes authority for the Court's view in today's case, but we need to choose between the competing readings for the light that will be shed on the *Hans* doctrine and the legitimacy of inflating that doctrine to the point of constitutional immutability as the Court has chosen to do.

The history and structure of the Eleventh Amendment convincingly show that it reaches only to suits subject to federal jurisdiction exclusively under the Citizen-State Diversity Clauses. In precisely tracking the language in Article III providing for citizen-state diversity jurisdiction, the text of the Amendment does, after all, suggest to common sense that only the Diversity Clauses are being addressed. If the Framers had meant the Amendment to bar federal-question suits as well, they could not only have made their intentions clearer very easily, but could simply have adopted the first post-*Chisholm* proposal, introduced in the House of Representatives by Theodore Sedgwick of Massachusetts

27. [Footnote 7 in Justice Souter's dissent.] Of course, even if Justice Iredell had concluded that state sovereign immunity was not subject to abrogation, it would be inappropriate to assume (as it appears the Court does today, and *Hans* did as well) that the Eleventh Amendment (regardless of what it says) "constitutionalized" Justice Iredell's dissent, or that it simply adopted the opposite of the holding in *Chisholm*. It is as odd to read the Eleventh Amendment's rejection of *Chisholm* (which held that States may be sued in diversity) to say that States may not be sued on a federal question as it would be to read the Twenty-Sixth Amendment's rejection of *Oregon v. Mitchell* (which held that Congress could not require States to extend the suffrage to 18-year-olds) to permit Congress to require States to extend the suffrage to 12-year-olds.

on instructions from the Legislature of that Commonwealth. Its provisions would have had exactly that expansive effect:

> No state shall be liable to be made a party defendant, in any of the judicial courts, established, or which shall be established under the authority of the United States, at the suit of any person or persons, whether a citizen or citizens, or a foreigner or foreigners, or of any body politic or corporate, whether within or without the United States.

With its references to suits by citizens as well as noncitizens, the Sedgwick amendment would necessarily have been applied beyond the Diversity Clauses, and for a reason that would have been wholly obvious to the people of the time. Sedgwick sought such a broad amendment because many of the States, including his own, owed debts subject to collection under the Treaty of Paris. Suits to collect such debts would "arise under" that Treaty and thus be subject to federal-question jurisdiction under Article III. . . .

Congress took no action on Sedgwick's proposal, however, and the Amendment as ultimately adopted two years later could hardly have been meant to limit federal-question jurisdiction, or it would never have left the States open to federal-question suits by their own citizens. To be sure, the majority of state creditors were not citizens, but nothing in the Treaty would have prevented foreign creditors from selling their debt instruments (thereby assigning their claims) to citizens of the debtor State. If the Framers of the Eleventh Amendment had meant it to immunize States from federal-question suits like those that might be brought to enforce the Treaty of Paris, they would surely have drafted the Amendment differently.

* * * *

In sum, reading the Eleventh Amendment solely as a limit on citizen-state diversity jurisdiction has the virtue of coherence with this Court's practice, with the views of John Marshall, with the history of the Amendment's drafting, and with its allusive language. Today's majority does not appear to disagree, at least insofar as the constitutional text is concerned; the Court concedes, after all, that "the text of the Amendment would appear to restrict only the Article III diversity jurisdiction of the federal courts."

Thus, regardless of which of the two plausible readings one adopts, the further point to note here is that there is no possible argument that the Eleventh Amendment, by its terms, deprives federal courts of jurisdiction over all citizen law-suits against the States. Not even the Court advances that proposition, and there would be no textual basis for doing so. Because the plaintiffs in today's case are citizens of the State that they are suing, the Eleventh Amendment simply does not apply to them. We must therefore look elsewhere for the source of that immunity by which the Court says their suit is barred from a federal court.[28]

28. [Footnote 13 in Justice Souter's dissent.] The majority chides me that the "lengthy analysis of the text of the Eleventh Amendment is directed at a straw man." But plain text is the Man of Steel in a confrontation with "background principle[s]" and "'postulates which limit and control." An argument rooted in the text of a constitutional provision may not be guaranteed of carrying the day, but insubstantiality is not its failing. This is particularly true in construing the jurisdictional provisions of Art. III, which speak with a clarity not to be found in some of the more open-textured provisions of the Constitution. That the Court thinks otherwise is an indication of just how far it has strayed beyond the boundaries of traditional constitutional analysis.

II

The obvious place to look elsewhere, of course, is *Hans v. Louisiana*, and *Hans* was indeed a leap in the direction of today's holding, even though it does not take the Court all the way. The parties in *Hans* raised, and the Court in that case answered, only what I have called the second question, that is, whether the Constitution, without more, permits a State to plead sovereign immunity to bar the exercise of federal-question jurisdiction. Although the Court invoked a principle of sovereign immunity to cure what it took to be the Eleventh Amendment's anomaly of barring only those state suits brought by noncitizen plaintiffs, the *Hans* Court had no occasion to consider whether Congress could abrogate that background immunity by statute. Indeed (except in the special circumstance of Congress's power to enforce the Civil War Amendments), this question never came before our Court until *Union Gas*, and any intimations of an answer in prior cases were mere dicta. In *Union Gas* the Court held that the immunity recognized in *Hans* had no constitutional status and was subject to congressional abrogation. Today the Court overrules *Union Gas* and holds just the opposite. In deciding how to choose between these two positions, the place to begin is with *Hans*'s holding that a principle of sovereign immunity derived from the common law insulates a State from federal-question jurisdiction at the suit of its own citizen. A critical examination of that case will show that it was wrongly decided, as virtually every recent commentator has concluded. It follows that the Court's further step today of constitutionalizing *Hans*'s rule against abrogation by Congress compounds and immensely magnifies the century-old mistake of *Hans* itself and takes its place with other historic examples of textually untethered elevations of judicially derived rules to the status of inviolable constitutional law.

A

* * * *

Hans . . . addressed the issue implicated (though not directly raised) in the preratification debate about the Citizen-State Diversity Clauses and implicitly settled by *Chisholm:* whether state sovereign immunity was cognizable by federal courts on the exercise of federal-question jurisdiction. According to *Hans*, and contrary to *Chisholm*, it was. But that is all that *Hans* held. Because no federal legislation purporting to pierce state immunity was at issue, it cannot fairly be said that *Hans* held state sovereign immunity to have attained some constitutional status immunizing it from abrogation.

Taking *Hans* only as far as its holding, its vulnerability is apparent. The Court rested its opinion on avoiding the supposed anomaly of recognizing jurisdiction to entertain a citizen's federal question suit, but not one brought by a noncitizen. There was, however, no such anomaly at all. As already explained, federal-question cases are not touched by the Eleventh Amendment, which leaves a State open to federal-question suits by citizens and noncitizens alike. If Hans had been from Massachusetts the Eleventh Amendment would not have barred his action against Louisiana.

Although there was thus no anomaly to be cured by *Hans*, the case certainly created its own anomaly in leaving federal courts entirely without jurisdiction to enforce paramount federal law at the behest of a citizen against a State that broke it. It destroyed the congruence of the judicial power under Article III with the substantive guarantees of the Constitution, and with the provisions of statutes passed by Congress in the exercise of its power under Article I: when a State injured an individual in violation of federal law no federal forum could provide direct relief. . . .

How such a result could have been threatened on the basis of a principle not so much as mentioned in the Constitution is difficult to understand. But history provides the explanation. [Justice Souter then discussed a historical theory suggesting that the *Hans* Court was concerned that its orders would not be enforced with respect to the relatively newly empowered Southern states.] Given the likelihood that a judgment against the State could not be enforced, it is not wholly surprising that the *Hans* Court found a way to avoid the certainty of the State's contempt.

So it is that history explains, but does not honor, *Hans*. The ultimate demerit of the case centers, however, not on its politics but on the legal errors on which it rested.[29] Before considering those errors, it is necessary to address the Court's contention that subsequent cases have read into *Hans* what was not there to begin with, that is, a background principle of sovereign immunity that is constitutional in stature and therefore unalterable by Congress.

B

The majority does not dispute the point that *Hans v. Louisiana* had no occasion to decide whether Congress could abrogate a State's immunity from federal-question suits. The Court insists, however, that the negative answer to that question that it finds in *Hans* and subsequent opinions is not "mere *obiter dicta,* but rather . . . the well-established rationale upon which the Court based the results of its earlier decisions." The exact rationale to which the majority refers, unfortunately, is not easy to discern. The Court's opinion says, immediately after its discussion of *stare decisis,* that "for over a century, we have grounded our decisions in the oft-repeated understanding of state sovereign immunity as an essential part of the Eleventh Amendment." This cannot be the "rationale," though, because this Court has repeatedly acknowledged that the Eleventh Amendment standing alone cannot bar a federal-question suit against a State brought by a state citizen. [Justice Souter then went on to explore the Court's statements after *Hans* concerning the nature of state sovereign immunity.]

* * * *

III

Three critical errors in *Hans* weigh against constitutionalizing its holding as the majority does today. The first we have already seen: the *Hans* Court misread the Eleventh Amendment. It also misunderstood the conditions under which common-law doctrines were received or rejected at the time of the founding, and it fundamentally mistook the very nature of sovereignty in the young Republic that was supposed to entail a State's immunity to federal-question jurisdiction

29. [Footnote 17 in Justice Souter's dissent.] Today's majority condemns my attention to *Hans*'s historical circumstances as "a disservice to the Court's traditional method of adjudication." The point, however, is not that historical circumstance may undermine an otherwise defensible decision; on the contrary, it is just because *Hans* is so utterly indefensible on the merits of its legal analysis that one is forced to look elsewhere in order to understand how the Court could have gone so far wrong. . . .

in a federal court. While I would not, as a matter of *stare decisis*, overrule *Hans* today, an understanding of its failings on these points will show how the Court today simply compounds already serious error in taking *Hans* the further step of investing its rule with constitutional inviolability against the considered judgment of Congress to abrogate it.

A

There is and could be no dispute that the doctrine of sovereign immunity that *Hans* purported to apply had its origins in the "familiar doctrine of the common law" . . . "derived from the laws and practices of our English ancestors."[30] Although statutes came to affect its importance in the succeeding centuries, the doctrine was never reduced to codification, and Americans took their understanding of immunity doctrine from Blackstone. Here, as in the mother country, it remained a common-law rule.

* * * *

1

[In this section, Justice Souter canvassed American colonial experience and concluded that English common law was not uniformly adopted.]

* * * *

2

While the States had limited their reception of English common law to principles appropriate to American conditions, the 1787 draft Constitution contained no provision for adopting the common law at all. This omission stood in sharp contrast to the state constitutions then extant, virtually all of which contained explicit provisions dealing with common-law reception. Since the experience in the States set the stage for thinking at the national level, this failure to address the notion of common-law reception could not have been inadvertent. Instead, the Framers chose to recognize only particular common-law concepts, such as the writ of habeas corpus, U.S. Const., Art. I, § 9, cl. 2, and the distinction between law and equity, U.S. Const., Amdt. VII, by specific reference in the constitutional text. This approach reflected widespread agreement that ratification would not itself entail a general reception of the common law of England.

* * * *

B

Given the refusal to entertain any wholesale reception of common law, given the failure of the new Constitution to make any provision for adoption of common law as such, and given the protests already quoted that no general reception had occurred, the *Hans* Court and the Court today cannot reasonably

30. [Footnote 27 in Justice Souter's dissent.] The Court seeks to disparage the common-law roots of the doctrine, and the consequences of those roots which I outline by asserting that *Hans* "found its roots not solely in the common law of England, but in the much more fundamental '"jurisprudence in all civilized nations."'" (quoting *Hans*). The *Hans* Court, however, relied explicitly on the ground that a suit against the State by its own citizen was "not known . . . at the common law" and was not among the departures from the common law recognized by the Constitution. Moreover, *Hans* explicitly adopted the reasoning of Justice Iredell's dissent in *Chisholm*, and that opinion could hardly have been clearer in relying exclusively on the common law.

argue that something like the old immunity doctrine somehow slipped in as a tacit but enforceable background principle. The evidence is even more specific, however, that there was no pervasive understanding that sovereign immunity had limited federal-question jurisdiction.

1

As I have already noted briefly, the Framers and their contemporaries did not agree about the place of common-law state sovereign immunity even as to federal jurisdiction resting on the Citizen-State Diversity Clauses. Edmund Randolph argued in favor of ratification on the ground that the immunity would not be recognized, leaving the States subject to jurisdiction. Patrick Henry opposed ratification on the basis of exactly the same reading. On the other hand, James Madison, John Marshall, and Alexander Hamilton all appear to have believed that the common-law immunity from suit would survive the ratification of Article III, so as to be at a State's disposal when jurisdiction would depend on diversity. This would have left the States free to enjoy a traditional immunity as defendants without barring the exercise of judicial power over them if they chose to enter the federal courts as diversity plaintiffs or to waive their immunity as diversity defendants. As Hamilton stated in The Federalist No. 81,

> "It is inherent in the nature of sovereignty, not to be amenable to the suit of an individual *without its consent.* This is the general sense and the general practice of mankind; and the exemption, as one of the attributes of sovereignty, is now enjoyed by the government of every state in the Union. Unless therefore, there is a surrender of this immunity in the plan of the convention, it will remain with the states, and the danger intimated must be merely ideal."

The majority sees in these statements, and chiefly in Hamilton's discussion of sovereign immunity in The Federalist No. 81, an unequivocal mandate "which would preclude all federal jurisdiction over an unconsenting State." But there is no such mandate to be found.

As I have already said, the immediate context of Hamilton's discussion in Federalist No. 81 has nothing to do with federal-question cases. It addresses a suggestion "that an assignment of the public securities of one state to the citizens of another, would enable them to prosecute that state in the federal courts for the amount of those securities." Hamilton is plainly talking about a suit subject to a federal court's jurisdiction under the Citizen-State Diversity Clauses of Article III.

* * * *

The most that can be inferred from this is, as noted above, that in diversity cases applying state contract law the immunity that a State would have enjoyed in its own courts is carried into the federal court. When, therefore, the *Hans* Court relied in part upon Hamilton's statement, its reliance was misplaced; Hamilton was addressing diversity jurisdiction, whereas *Hans* involved federal-question jurisdiction under the Contracts Clause. No general theory of federal-question immunity can be inferred from Hamilton's discussion of immunity in contract suits. . . .

* * * *

2

[The Court has held] that "the States entered the federal system with their sovereignty intact," but we surely did not mean that they entered that system with the sovereignty they would have claimed if each State had assumed independent existence in the community of nations, for even the Articles of Confederation allowed for less than that. While there is no need here to calculate exactly how close the American States came to sovereignty in the classic sense prior to ratification of the Constitution, it is clear that the act of ratification affected their sovereignty in a way different from any previous political event in America or anywhere else. For the adoption of the Constitution made them members of a novel federal system that sought to balance the States' exercise of some sovereign prerogatives delegated from their own people with the principle of a limited but centralizing federal supremacy.

As a matter of political theory, this federal arrangement of dual delegated sovereign powers truly was a more revolutionary turn than the late war had been. Before the new federal scheme appeared, 18th-century political theorists had assumed that "there must reside somewhere in every political unit a single, undivided, final power, higher in legal authority than any other power, subject to no law, a law unto itself." The American development of divided sovereign powers, which "shattered . . . the categories of government that had dominated Western thinking for centuries," was made possible only by a recognition that the ultimate sovereignty rests in the people themselves. The people possessing this plenary bundle of specific powers were free to parcel them out to different governments and different branches of the same government as they saw fit. As James Wilson emphasized, the location of ultimate sovereignty in the People meant that "they can distribute one portion of power to the more contracted circle called State governments; they can also furnish another proportion to the government of the United States."

* * * *

Given this metamorphosis of the idea of sovereignty in the years leading up to 1789, the question whether the old immunity doctrine might have been received as something suitable for the new world of federal-question jurisdiction is a crucial one. The answer is that sovereign immunity as it would have been known to the Framers before ratification thereafter became inapplicable as a matter of logic in a federal suit raising a federal question. The old doctrine, after all, barred the involuntary subjection of a sovereign to the system of justice and law of which it was itself the font, since to do otherwise would have struck the common-law mind from the Middle Ages onward as both impractical and absurd. But the ratification demonstrated that state governments were subject to a superior regime of law in a judicial system established, not by the State, but by the people through a specific delegation of their sovereign power to a National Government that was paramount within its delegated sphere. When individuals sued States to enforce federal rights, the Government that corresponded to the "sovereign" in the traditional common-law sense was not the State but the National Government, and any state immunity from the jurisdiction of the Nation's courts would have required a grant from the true sovereign, the people, in their Constitution, or from the Congress that the Constitution had empowered. . . .

* * * *

Given the Framers' general concern with curbing abuses by state governments, it would be amazing if the scheme of delegated powers embodied in the Constitution had left the National Government powerless to render the States judicially accountable for violations of federal rights. And of course the Framers did not understand the scheme to leave the Government powerless. In The Federalist No. 80, Hamilton observed that "no man of sense will believe that such prohibitions [running against the States] would be scrupulously regarded, without some effectual power in the government to restrain or correct the infractions of them," and that "an authority in the federal courts, to over-rule such as might be in manifest contravention of the articles of union" was the Convention's preferred remedy. By speaking in the plural of an authority in the federal "courts," Hamilton made it clear that he envisioned more than this Court's exercise of appellate jurisdiction to review federal questions decided by state courts. Nor is it plausible that he was thinking merely of suits brought against States by the National Government itself, which The Federalist's authors did not describe in the paternalistic terms that would pass without an eyebrow raised today. Hamilton's power of the Government to restrain violations of citizens' rights was a power to be exercised by the federal courts at the citizens' behest.

This sketch of the logic and objectives of the new federal order is confirmed by what we have previously seen of the preratification debate on state sovereign immunity, which in turn becomes entirely intelligible both in what it addressed and what it ignored. It is understandable that reasonable minds differed on the applicability of the immunity doctrine in suits that made it to federal court only under the original Diversity Clauses, for their features were not wholly novel. While they were, of course, in the courts of the new and, for some purposes, paramount National Government, the law that they implicated was largely the old common law (and in any case was not federal law). It was not foolish, therefore, to ask whether the old law brought the old defenses with it. But it is equally understandable that questions seem not to have been raised about state sovereign immunity in federal-question cases. The very idea of a federal question depended on the rejection of the simple concept of sovereignty from which the immunity doctrine had developed; under the English common law, the question of immunity in a system of layered sovereignty simply could not have arisen. The Framers' principal objectives in rejecting English theories of unitary sovereignty, moreover, would have been impeded if a new concept of sovereign immunity had taken its place in federal-question cases, and would have been substantially thwarted if that new immunity had been held to be untouchable by any congressional effort to abrogate it.

Today's majority discounts this concern. Without citing a single source to the contrary, the Court dismisses the historical evidence regarding the Framers' vision of the relationship between national and state sovereignty, and reassures us that "the Nation survived for nearly two centuries without the question of the existence of [the abrogation] power ever being presented to this Court." But we are concerned here not with the survival of the Nation but the opportunity of its citizens to enforce federal rights in a way that Congress provides. The absence of any general federal-question statute for nearly a century following ratification of Article III (with a brief exception in 1800) hardly counts against the importance of that jurisdiction either in the Framers' conception or in current reality; likewise, the fact that Congress has not often seen fit to use its power of abrogation (outside the Fourteenth Amendment context, at least) does not compel a conclusion that the power is not important to the federal scheme. In the end, is it plausible to contend that the plan of the convention was meant to leave the National Government without any way to render individuals capable of enforcing their federal rights directly against an intransigent State?

C

The considerations expressed so far, based on text, *Chisholm*, caution in common-law reception, and sovereignty theory, have pointed both to the mistakes inherent in *Hans* and, even more strongly, to the error of today's holding. Although for reasons of *stare decisis* I would not today disturb the century-old precedent, I surely would not extend its error by placing the common-law immunity it mistakenly recognized beyond the power of Congress to abrogate. In doing just that, however, today's decision declaring state sovereign immunity itself immune from abrogation in federal-question cases is open to a further set of objections peculiar to itself. For today's decision stands condemned alike by the Framers' abhorrence of any notion that such common-law rules as might be received into the new legal systems would be beyond the legislative power to alter or repeal, and by its resonance with this Court's previous essays in constitutionalizing common-law rules at the expense of legislative authority.

1

[In this section, Justice Souter explored the traditional rule that common-law doctrines (which for his purposes here included sovereign immunity) could be altered by statute.]

2

History confirms the wisdom of Madison's abhorrence of constitutionalizing common-law rules to place them beyond the reach of congressional amendment. The Framers feared judicial power over substantive policy and the ossification of law that would result from transforming common law into constitutional law, and their fears have been borne out every time the Court has ignored Madison's counsel on subjects that we generally group under economic and social policy. It is, in fact, remarkable that as we near the end of this century the Court should choose to open a new constitutional chapter in confining legislative judgments on these matters by resort to textually unwarranted common-law rules, for it was just this practice in the century's early decades that brought this Court to the nadir of competence that we identify with *Lochner v. New York*.

It was the defining characteristic of the *Lochner* era, and its characteristic vice, that the Court treated the common-law background (in those days, common-law property rights and contractual autonomy) as paramount, while regarding congressional legislation to abrogate the common law on these economic matters as constitutionally suspect. And yet the superseding lesson that seemed clear after *West Coast Hotel Co. v. Parrish* [in 1937] that action within the legislative power is not subject to greater scrutiny merely because it trenches upon the case law's ordering of economic and social relationships, seems to have been lost on the Court.

The majority today, indeed, seems to be going *Lochner* one better. When the Court has previously constrained the express Article I powers by resort to common-law or background principles, it has done so at least in an ostensible effort to give content to some other written provision of the Constitution, like the Due Process Clause, the very object of which is to limit the exercise of governmental power. Some textual argument, at least, could be made that the Court was doing no more than defining one provision that happened to be at odds with another. Today, however, the Court is not struggling to fulfill a responsibility to reconcile two arguably conflicting and Delphic constitutional provisions, nor is it struggling with any Delphic text at all. For even the Court concedes that the Constitution's grant to Congress of plenary power over relations with Indian tribes at the expense of any state claim to the contrary is unmistakably clear, and this case does not even arguably implicate a textual trump to the grant of federal-question jurisdiction.

* * * *

IV

[In Part IV of his dissent, Justice Souter rejected the Court's conclusions that *Ex parte Young* did not apply in the circumstances of this case. We have discussed this issue earlier in this chapter in section C.2.b.ii.]

V

Absent the application of *Ex parte Young*, I would, of course, follow *Union Gas* in recognizing congressional power under Article I to abrogate *Hans* immunity. Since the reasons for this position, as explained in Parts II-III tend to unsettle *Hans* as well as support *Union Gas*, I should add a word about my reasons for continuing to accept *Hans*'s holding as a matter of *stare decisis*.

The *Hans* doctrine was erroneous, but it has not previously proven to be unworkable or to conflict with later doctrine or to suffer from the effects of facts developed since its decision (apart from those indicating its original errors). I would therefore treat *Hans* as it has always been treated in fact until today, as a doctrine of federal common law. For, as so understood, it has formed one of the strands of the federal relationship for over a century now, and the stability of that relationship is itself a value that *stare decisis* aims to respect.

In being ready to hold that the relationship may still be altered, not by the Court but by Congress, I would tread the course laid out elsewhere in our cases. The Court has repeatedly stated its assumption that insofar as the relative positions of States and Nation may be affected consistently with the Tenth Amendment they would not be modified without deliberately expressed intent. The plain statement rule, which "assures that the legislature has in fact faced, and intended to bring into issue, the critical matters involved in the judicial decision," is particularly appropriate in light of our primary reliance on "the effectiveness of the federal political process in preserving the States' interests." Hence, we have required such a plain statement when Congress pre-empts the historic powers of the States imposes a condition on the grant of federal moneys or seeks to regulate a State's ability to determine the qualifications of its own officials.

When judging legislation passed under unmistakable Article I powers, no further restriction could be required. Nor does the Court explain why more could be demanded. In the past, we have assumed that a plain statement requirement is sufficient to protect the States from undue federal encroachments upon their traditional immunity from suit. It is hard to contend that this rule has set the bar too low, for (except in *Union Gas*) we have never found the requirement to be met outside the context of laws passed under § 5 of the Fourteenth Amendment. The exception I would recognize today proves the rule, moreover, because the federal abrogation of state immunity comes as part of a regulatory scheme which is itself designed to invest the States with regulatory powers that Congress need not extend to them. This fact suggests to me that the political safeguards of federalism are working, that a plain-statement rule is an adequate check on congressional over-reaching, and that today's abandonment of that approach is wholly unwarranted.

There is an even more fundamental "clear statement" principle, however, that the Court abandons today. John Marshall recognized it over a century and a half ago in the very context of state sovereign immunity in federal-question cases:

> "The jurisdiction of the court, then, being extended by the letter of the constitution to all cases arising under it, or under the laws of the United States, it follows that those who would withdraw any case of this description from that jurisdiction, must sustain the exemption they claim on the spirit and true meaning of the constitution, which spirit and true meaning must be so apparent as to overrule the words which its framers have employed." *Cohens v. Virginia.*

Because neither text, precedent, nor history supports the majority's abdication of our responsibility to exercise the jurisdiction entrusted to us in Article III, I would reverse the judgment of the Court of Appeals.

DISCUSSION AND QUESTIONS

There is a great deal that one can glean from *Seminole Tribe.* In the following discussion, we highlight some significant points from the decision, raise questions that the decision implicates, and explore the growth of congressional abrogation doctrine since 1996.

In terms of black-letter doctrine, the *Seminole Tribe* majority overrules *Union Gas* and concludes that Congress does not have the power to abrogate state sovereign immunity when acting under its Article I, section 8, power to "regulate Commerce." The Court in dicta in *Seminole Tribe*[31] and similar dicta in later decisions[32] appeared to take the position that Congress could never abrogate state sovereign immunity when acting pursuant to its Article I powers. There have actually been only two holdings concerning specific Article I powers in which the Court concluded that abrogation was inappropriate: the power to regulate commerce under Article I, section 8, clause 3, *Seminole Tribe,* and the so-called "patent power" under Article I, section 8, clause 8,[33]

31. *See Seminole Tribe,* 517 U.S. at 72-73 ("The Eleventh Amendment restricts the judicial power under Article III, and Article I cannot be used to circumvent the constitutional limitations placed upon federal jurisdiction.").

32. *See, e.g., Board of Trs. v. Garrett,* 531 U.S. 356, 364 (2001) ("Congress may not, of course, base its abrogation of the States' Eleventh Amendment immunity upon powers enumerated in Article I."); *Florida Prepaid Postsecondary Educ. Expense Bd. v. College Sav. Bank,* 527 U.S. 627, 636 (1999) ("*Seminole Tribe* makes clear that Congress may not abrogate state sovereign immunity pursuant to its Article I powers.").

33. *See* U.S. Const. art. I, § 8, cl 8 ("Congress shall have power . . . [t]o promote the Progress of the Science and useful arts, by securing for limited Times to Authors and Inventors the exclusive Right to their respective Writings and Discoveries.").

see Florida Prepaid Postsecondary Educ. Expense Bd. v. College Sav. Bank, 527 U.S. 627 (1999).

As we will see in the next section, while the Court's broad dicta concerning Article I and abrogation remains in place, it is at least somewhat deceptive in that the Court has relatively recently held that, with respect to at least one Article I power (bankruptcy), no immunity exists in the first place. See section C.3. For now, however, we can take the Court at its word that abrogation of immunity under Article I powers is not constitutionally permissible.

At the same time it overruled *Union Gas*, however, the *Seminole Tribe* Court also reaffirmed the holding of *Fitzpatrick v. Bitzer* that Congress does have the power to abrogate state sovereign immunity when acting pursuant to its power under section 5 of the Fourteenth Amendment. Understanding why the Court reaches this conclusion is important. The first step in the Chief Justice's analysis concerns the nature of the broad immunity *Hans* recognized. As we highlighted earlier, *Hans* recognized that the states retained at the time of the Constitution's ratification a sovereign immunity from suit that was broad enough to immunize them from suit in the newly created federal courts. However, *Hans* had no occasion to consider the nature of that immunity. Was it a background common-law principle that could be altered by legislation, or was it a constitutional principle that coexisted with the more explicitly articulated principles set forth in the Constitution? *Seminole Tribe* adopts the constitutional immunity position.

The rest of the decision's logic essentially follows from the basic timeline set forth in Figure 8-4:

FIGURE 8-4

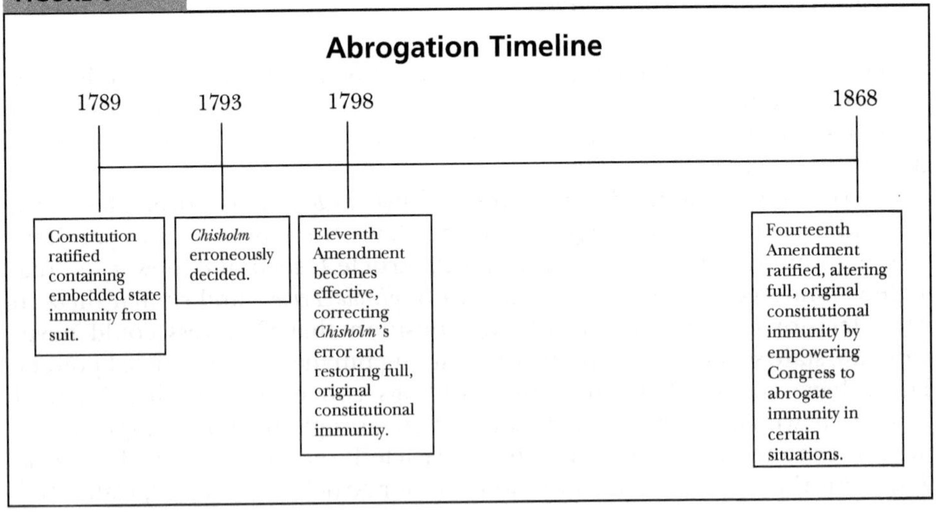

Notice that there are at least two ways in which Justice Souter attacks the majority's reasoning in his dissent. The first focuses on the Court's assessment of what happened in 1789 when the Constitution became effective. In other words, Justice Souter reignites the debate about whether *Hans* was correctly decided in the first place. This debate fundamentally concerns federalism. What did Article I's enumeration of powers really bestow on Congress with respect to the states? The discussion in *Seminole Tribe* leaves no doubt that after more than two and a quarter centuries, this issue is still subject to uncertainty.

Justice Souter argues at length that *Hans* was incorrectly decided and that there is no background principle of immunity. He explains why he concludes that the better interpretation of the Eleventh Amendment is the diversity view earlier advanced by Justice Brennan. Nevertheless, Justice Souter does not advocate that *Hans* be overruled given the importance of *stare decisis.* Instead, he accepts *Hans*'s recognition that there is some background principle of immunity. His disagreement with the majority on this score is whether that immunity is of a common law or constitutional nature. He sees it as one of common law and thus alterable by legislation as other common-law rules generally are.

Of course, this debate, too, concerns federalism. But it also has a strong separation-of-powers flavor. The Court's decision that immunity is constitutional restricts Congress' power. Instead of resting the decision with Congress about keeping the states' immunity from suit in place, as would be the case with a broad common-law immunity, the decision was made by the Court in constitutionalizing the immunity. Thus, we see in Justice Souter's multifaceted dissent that there are several decision-points in the Court's immunity jurisprudence at which one can take different paths, depending on federalism and separation-of-powers principles.

EXPLORING DOCTRINE

Who Should Be the "Guardians of Federalism"?

A part of the debate evident in *Seminole Tribe* concerns which of the many entities in the American constitutional structure should be the guardians of federalism. The majority in *Seminole Tribe* embraces the Article III judiciary's role as guardian. The *Seminole Tribe* dissenters at least implicitly consider the "political" branches of the federal government to be more appropriate to serve in that role.

Given the current constitutional structure, prevailing partisan political realities, and the practical difficulties with Article V amendments, which side of the debate has the better side of the argument?

After *Seminole Tribe,* then, Congress does not appear to have constitutional authority to abrogate state sovereign immunity from suit in federal court when acting pursuant to its Article I powers, but it may do so when acting under section 5 of the Fourteenth Amendment. Therefore, it is important to identify the constitutional basis on which Congress purports to act in passing any given piece of legislation. If Congress acts under the Fourteenth Amendment, one must ensure that the statute at issue satisfies the clear statement rule. Assuming that it does, what happens next?

Unfortunately, the answer to that question is difficult on two scores. First, it involves questions that go beyond the scope of traditional Federal Courts courses and, instead, are more aptly described as raising issues more generally applicable in constitutional law. Second, the Court's decisions in this area have hardly been a model of clarity. Nevertheless, because of the importance of section 5 abrogation in the context of state sovereign immunity, we describe below the general development of the law in this area.

Fitzpatrick recognized that section 5 provides a basis on which Congress may abrogate state sovereign immunity. The Court has made clear that section 5 is a grant of power to Congress but that it also contains a limitation on the power granted. Congress may enact only "appropriate legislation," and that legislation must be "to enforce" the terms of the Fourteenth Amendment. Thus, in order to validly abrogate state sovereign immunity from suit in federal court under section 5, Congress'action must comport with these self-contained limitations on its power.

In a number of decisions beginning with *City of Boerne v. Flores*, 521 U.S. 507 (1997), the Court has created a checklist of sorts by which to assess Congress'actions under section 5. First, one must "identify with some precision the scope of the constitutional right at issue." *Board of Trs. v. Garrett*, 531 U.S. 356, 365 (2001). Next, the Court has insisted that Congress assemble sufficient evidence of the state violations of the constitutional right at issue. *See, e.g., id.* at 368. Without a sufficient body of evidence indicating a pattern of constitutional violation, the Court has held that Congress would not be acting in the required remedial capacity of "enforcing" the Fourteenth Amendment's guarantees. *Id.*

How much evidence of constitutional violations is required? This has been a challenging issue for the Court to decide, and its opinions have not necessarily been consistent. However, what does appear fairly clear now is that the quantum of evidence required to sustain legislation under section 5 is related to the nature of the constitutional right at issue. If the constitutional right at issue is one for which a court would apply heightened scrutiny if a private citizen challenged government conduct, it is "easier for Congress to show a pattern of state constitutional violations" sufficient to act under section 5. *See Nevada Dep't of Human Res. v. Hibbs*, 538 U.S. 721, 736 (2003). So, for example, it would be easier for Congress to amass sufficient evidence to act under section 5 with respect to racial discrimination, for which strict scrutiny is required, than it would with respect to discrimination based on age, which is judged only for rationality.

Assuming that Congress amassed sufficient evidence of state constitutional violations, the Court's next step is to assess whether the remedy Congress enacted under its section 5 powers is an appropriate response to the problem. Congress is *not* limited only to correcting a violation of the Fourteenth Amendment itself. Rather, Congress can permissibly prohibit conduct going beyond that which the Constitution prohibits as a prophylactic means of preventing actual constitutional violations. *See, e.g., Kimel v. Florida Bd. of Regents*, 528 U.S. 62, 81 (2000). The difficulty is determining what Congress may and may not do in this regard.

To answer this question, the Court has held that the remedy Congress enacts must be "congruent and proportional to the targeted violation." *Garrett*, 531 U.S. at 374. The congruence and proportionality test has been notoriously difficult to apply and even at times difficult for the Court to explain. In a nutshell, a remedy is "congruent" if it matches a violation qualitatively. It is "proportionate" if it matches the size of the problem; in other words, a remedy may not be overkill.

Applying these principles, the Court has concluded that Congress did not have the authority to abrogate state sovereign immunity from suit in federal court with respect to the following statutes: (1) Title I of the Americans with

Disabilities Act of 1990, which prohibits discrimination against persons with disabilities in connection with employment;[34] (2) the Trademark Remedy Clarification Act;[35] (3) the Patent and Plant Variety Protection Remedy Clarification Act;[36] and (4) the Age Discrimination in Employment Act of 1967.[37]

On the other hand, in addition to its decision in *Fitzpatrick v. Bitzer*, upholding abrogation with respect to Title VII of the Civil Rights Act of 1964, the Court has upheld congressional abrogation of state sovereign immunity from suit in federal court under section 5 with respect to the following statutes and/or claims: (1) the Family and Medical Leave Act;[38] (2) Title II of the ADA (concerning discrimination in the provision of "public services, program and activities") with respect to a claim based on access to courts;[39] and (3) Title II of the ADA with respect to a claim by a handicapped prisoner concerning state conduct that actually violated the Eighth Amendment's prohibition against "cruel and unusual punishment."[40] As these last two decisions make clear, the abrogation decision under section 5 must be made on a claim-by-claim basis instead of on a statute-by-statute basis.

An excellent recent illustration of the difficulty in this area is the Court's 2012 decision in *Coleman v. Court of Appeals of Maryland*, 132 S. Ct. 1327 (2012). At issue in *Coleman* was a claim by an employee of a Maryland state court that he was terminated in violation of the Family and Medical Leave Act (FMLA). *Id.* at 1332. The legal issue presented was whether Congress had validly abrogated the state's immunity from suit under section 5 of the Fourteenth Amendment when it enacted the FMLA. *Id.* at 1333. The Court held 5-4 that Congress's attempt to abrogate immunity was inappropriate.

There are several points that one can take from *Coleman*. First, the decision underscores the point we have made above about how difficult this area of the law is. Second, the decision reiterates that the abrogation question is one that cannot be made on a statute-by-statute basis. Instead, one must proceed at a more detailed level. In the *Coleman* context, this point is made clear because the Court had already ruled that in certain provisions of the FMLA, Congress had validly abrogated state sovereign immunity from suit. *See Nevada Dep't of Human Res. v. Hibbs*, 538 U.S. 721 (2003). *Coleman* found that abrogation was inappropriate under different provisions in the FMLA.

The final point from *Coleman* concerns the fundamental reason for the difference between the result in that case and the one the Court reached several years earlier in *Hibbs*. The Court explained that the provisions at issue in *Hibbs* dealt with sex-based discrimination. On the other hand, the Court explained that the statutory provision at issue in *Coleman* did not seek to address that issue. *See, e.g., Coleman*, 132 S. Ct. at 1333-37. Thus, this aspect of the decision underscores the greater ability of Congress to use its section 5 powers to address issues in which the Court would apply a higher level of constitutional scrutiny when assessing state action. As you recognize well by now, there are many challenging

34. *See Board of Trs. v. Garrett*, 531 U.S. 536 (2001).
35. *See College Sav. Bank v. Florida Prepaid Postsecondary Educ. Expense Bd.*, 527 U.S. 666 (1999).
36. *See Florida Prepaid Postsecondary Educ. Expense Bd. v. College Sav. Bank*, 527 U.S. 627 (1999).
37. *See Kimel v. Florida Bd. of Regents*, 528 U.S. 62 (2000).
38. *See Nevada Dep't of Human Res. v. Hibbs*, 538 U.S. 721 (2003).
39. *See Tennessee v. Lane*, 541 U.S. 509 (2004).
40. *See United States v. Georgia*, 546 U.S. 151 (2006).

issues associated with congressional abrogation of state sovereign immunity from suit in federal court. These issues run the gamut from the highly theoretical ones concerning who should be the guardians of federalism to the far more mundane (although no less important) question of whether Congress's intent to abrogate immunity is sufficiently clear. We have attempted in Figure 8-5 to summarize the steps to consider in terms of abrogation. This chart should assist you both in practically applying the doctrine and in situating the important theoretical debates in the larger constitutional structure.

FIGURE 8-5

Congressional Abrogation of State Sovereign Immunity a Flow Chart

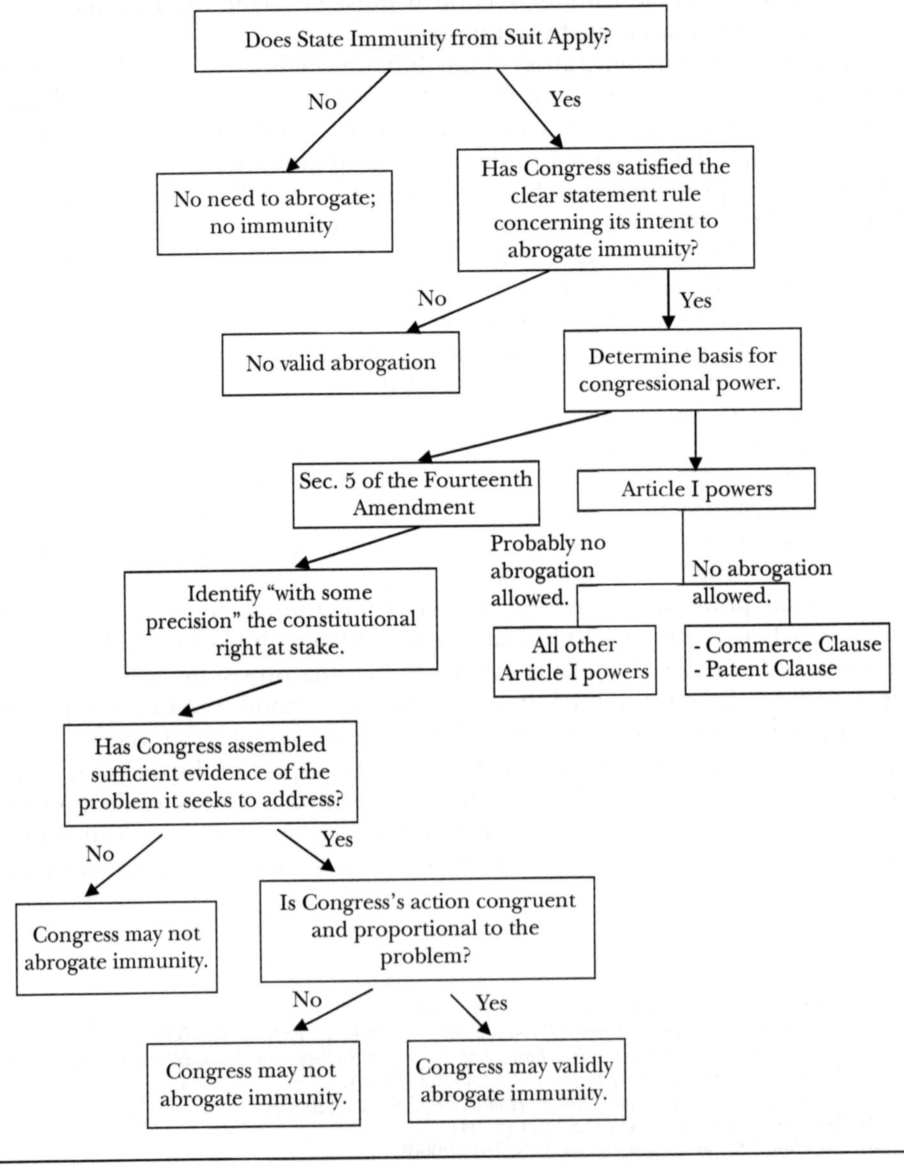

Try your hand working through abrogation with Problem 8-3 below:

PROBLEM 8-3

The Over-Taxed Railroad

Monopoly Railroad, Inc. ("Monopoly") operates an interstate network of railroads in 23 states, including New York. Monopoly owns physical assets in all of the states in which it operates and has taxable property in 28 of New York's 62 counties.

The scheme by which New York taxes Monopoly's property is complex. The Executive Department of Taxation of New York State (the "Department") is charged by state statute with administering all real property taxation in the state. New York State law provides interstate railroads with a form of tax exemption through a so-called "railroad ceiling." A railroad ceiling is the maximum value on which a county or other taxing district may levy real property taxes on a railroad's real property. Railroad property is exempt from taxation by such counties or other taxing districts to the extent its value exceeds the applicable railroad ceiling. The Department is responsible for establishing all railroad ceilings in the state.

There is one other statute of which you need to be aware. In 1976, Congress passed pursuant to its power to regulate interstate commerce and its authority to enforce the terms of the Fourteenth Amendment the Railroad Revitalization and Regulatory Reform Act (the "4-R Act"). The 4-R Act prohibits a state or any subdivision of a state from assessing railroad property at a higher percentage of the property's true market value than the percentage applied to other commercial or industrial property. It also provides that the 4-R Act may be enforced in "an appropriate state court or in an appropriate district court of the United States."

The 4-R Act was passed after 15 years of off-and-on congressional consideration. One of the principal goals of the 4-R Act was to combat what Congress concluded was a discriminatory over-taxing of interstate railroads. Congress held a number of hearings at which committees took evidence of examples of states and localities taxing the property of interstate railroads at percentages far greater than other commercial and industrial property. Congress concluded that such railroads were, as non-residents, easy targets for discriminatory treatment. In fact, a House of Representatives Report prepared in conjunction with the legislative debate concerning the 4-R Act stated that "interstate railroads are over-taxed by at least $50 million each year."

Monopoly believes that the method the Department uses to determine railroad ceilings violates the restrictions of the 4-R Act in certain respects. It has filed suit in the United States District Court for the Southern District of New York against the Department, seeking a declaration that the method for calculating the railroad ceiling is unlawful under the 4-R Act and an injunction against continuing to use that method in the future. The Department has moved to dismiss Monopoly's complaint under the Eleventh Amendment.

How would a court go about evaluating whether the Department's motion should be granted? Assuming the motion were granted, is there anything Monopoly might do in another lawsuit to obtain the relief it seeks in this one?

We summarize our discussion of the ways to avoid a state's sovereign immunity in Figure 8-6.

FIGURE 8-6

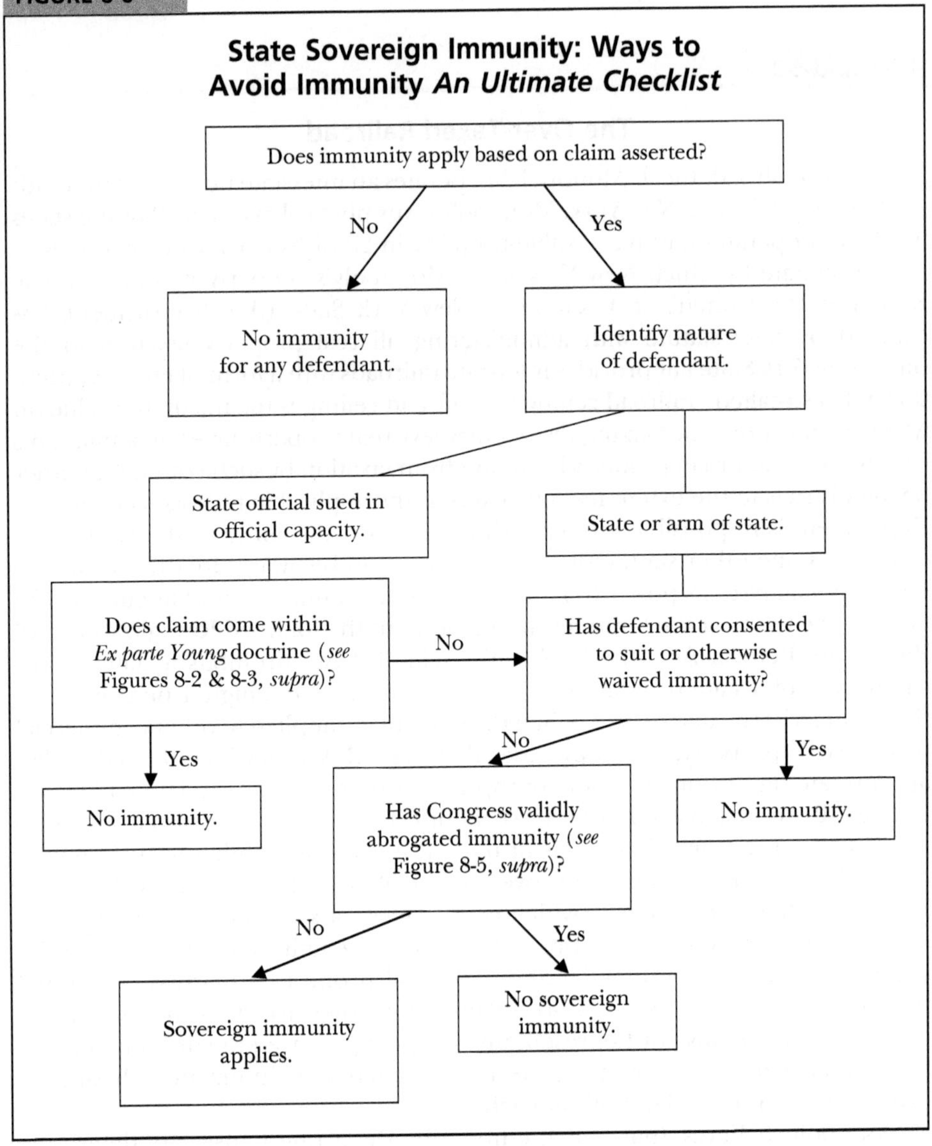

3. *A Return to the Scope of Constitutional State Sovereign Immunity: Expansion and Some Surprising Retrenchment at the Dawn of the Twenty-first Century*

The Court's debates concerning the meaning of the Eleventh Amendment and the deeper state sovereign immunity from suit have not ended. Indeed, the Court has rendered several important decisions concerning the fundamental nature of that immunity as the twenty-first century dawned. In this concluding section, we consider these important developments.

An initial challenge for anyone studying this area of the law is that the Court's decisions have not been consistent even in the basic direction in which they point. Some of them have considerably broadened the nature of the states' immunity, while others have pointed, at least tentatively, to a restriction on that immunity. The one thing that can be said with certainty is that the Court is still wrestling with the nature and scope of the immunity the Eleventh Amendment reflects.

ALDEN v. MAINE: ***Forum to Substantive Immunity.*** As we have seen, the *Hans* Court adopted a broad view of state sovereign immunity, holding that the Eleventh Amendment merely reflected a broader immunity coexisting with the Constitution. As a result, over the years the Court employed the doctrine of sovereign immunity to limit the reach of the "judicial power" beyond what was set forth on the face of the Amendment. But all of these decisions were forum-based. That is, a state was immune from suit *in a federal court.*

In 1999, the Supreme Court altered the nature of state sovereign immunity in an important and unexpected respect with its decision in *Alden v. Maine,* 527 U.S. 706 (1999). *Alden* was a suit by state probation officers filed in the Maine state courts claiming that they were entitled to overtime wages under the federal Fair Labor Standards Act (FLSA). Congress enacted the FLSA under its power to regulate commerce among the several states. It provided for concurrent jurisdiction in state and federal courts.

As you should be aware at this point in the chapter, *Seminole Tribe* would have prevented Congress from using its power over interstate commerce to authorize suits under the FLSA in federal court. Significantly, however, the Supreme Court held in *Alden* that the lawsuit also could not proceed in state court because of the sovereign immunity the states enjoyed at the time the Constitution was ratified. In the Court's words: "We hold that the powers delegated to Congress under Article I of the United States Constitution do not include the power to subject nonconsenting States to private suits for damages in state courts." *Id.* at 712. *Alden* expanded the nature of sovereign immunity from a forum-based immunity to one that was far more substantive. It was not simply that the Article III courts could not hear a claim; now the Article I legislative branch was substantively precluded from exercising its enumerated powers to allow for suits in a state forum.

While the Court took the position that *Alden* was a natural extension of longstanding precedent, for many it was a surprising expansion of the nature of the sovereign immunity the states enjoyed. It now encompassed Article I as well as Article III in a way even more serious than the abrogation decision at issue in *Seminole Tribe.* As we will see below, the Court later expanded sovereign immunity to include the Article II executive branch. We turn to that development next.

FEDERAL MARITIME COMMISSION v. SOUTH CAROLINA STATE PORTS AUTHORITY: ***Movement from Article III To Article II Immunity.*** South Carolina Maritime Services, Inc. ("Maritime Services") owned a cruise ship that it used in one respect or another to bring people into international waters so that they could gamble. The South Carolina State Ports Authority (the "Ports Authority") refused the cruise ship permission to dock in Charleston, South Carolina. Maritime Services believed that the Ports Authority's refusal was unlawful discrimination under the federal Shipping Act. Accordingly, Maritime Services filed a complaint with a federal administrative agency, the Federal Maritime Commission (the "FMC").

When the FMC receives a complaint it employs an administrative adjudicative procedure in which an Administrative Law Judge (ALJ) determines whether the complaint has merit. If the ALJ determines that the complaint has merit, the FMC can enter a wide range of orders. Any such order may be enforced by an action in a federal district court brought by the FMC or the Attorney General.

The Ports Authority moved to dismiss the proceeding before the ALJ on the ground that a state's sovereign immunity from suit precluded a proceeding that resembled litigation even if such a proceeding itself was not before an Article III federal court. The Supreme Court ultimately agreed with this argument. In an opinion by Justice Thomas, the Court held that subjecting an unconsenting state to proceedings of an adjudicative nature before a federal administrative agency was "contrary to [the Framers'] constitutional design" and, therefore, the states enjoyed a constitutional immunity from such proceedings. *Fed. Maritime Comm'n v. South Carolina Ports Auth.*, 535 U.S. 743, 769 (2002).

The decision is no doubt important for its expansion of state sovereign immunity from the Article III judiciary to the Article II federal administrative agency context. On a more theoretical level, the decision is also significant for its rhetoric concerning the purpose of state immunity in the constitutional design:

> While state sovereign immunity serves the important function of shielding state treasuries and thus preserving the States' ability to govern in accordance with the will of their citizens," the doctrine's central purpose is to accord the States the respect owed them as joint sovereigns.

Id. at 765 (citations and internal quotation marks omitted).

The Court's decision seemed to reflect the ever increasing scope of state sovereign immunity from suit in the federal system. Quite surprisingly, the Court thereafter took a different turn.

CENTRAL VIRGINIA COMMUNITY COLLEGE v. KATZ: *Back to the "Plan of the Convention."* The final development we highlight came as a surprise to many Court watchers. It has the potential to upset much of the fundamental law in this area, although it remains uncertain at this point how aggressively courts will explore the potential power of the decision. In *Central Virginia Community College v. Katz* the Court returned to the fundamental question of what the states "gave up" when they entered into the federal union in 1789.

CENTRAL VIRGINIA COMMUNITY COLLEGE v. KATZ

546 U.S. 356 (2006)

JUSTICE STEVENS delivered the opinion of the Court.

Article I, § 8, cl. 4, of the Constitution provides that Congress shall have the power to establish "uniform Laws on the subject of Bankruptcies throughout the United States." In *Tennessee Student Assistance Corporation v. Hood*, we granted certiorari to determine whether this Clause gives Congress the authority to abrogate States' immunity from private suits. Without reaching that question, we upheld the application of the Bankruptcy Code to proceedings initiated by a debtor against a state agency to determine the dischargeability of a student loan debt. In this case we consider whether a proceeding initiated by a bankruptcy trustee to set aside preferential transfers by the debtor to state agencies is barred by sovereign immunity. Relying in part on our reasoning in *Hood*, we reject the sovereign immunity defense advanced by the state agencies.

I

Petitioners are Virginia institutions of higher education that are considered "arms of the State" entitled to sovereign immunity. Wallace's Bookstores, Inc., did business with petitioners before it filed a petition for relief under chapter 11 of the Bankruptcy Code in the United States Bankruptcy Court for the Eastern District of Kentucky. Respondent, Bernard Katz, is the court-appointed liquidating supervisor of the bankrupt estate. He has commenced proceedings in the Bankruptcy Court . . . to avoid and recover alleged preferential transfers to each of the petitioners made by the debtor when it was insolvent. Petitioners' motions to dismiss those proceedings on the basis of sovereign immunity were denied by the Bankruptcy Court.

The denial was affirmed by the District Court and the Court of Appeals for the Sixth Circuit on the authority of the Sixth Circuit's prior determination that Congress has abrogated the States' sovereign immunity in bankruptcy proceedings. We granted certiorari to consider the question left open by our opinion in *Hood*: whether Congress' attempt to abrogate state sovereign immunity in 11 U.S.C. § 106(a)[41] is valid. As we shall explain, however, we are persuaded that the enactment of that provision was not necessary to authorize the Bankruptcy Court's jurisdiction over these preference avoidance proceedings.

Bankruptcy jurisdiction, at its core, is *in rem*. As we noted in *Hood*, it does not implicate States' sovereignty to nearly the same degree as other kinds of jurisdiction. That was as true in the 18th century as it is today. Then, as now, the jurisdiction of courts adjudicating rights in the bankrupt estate included the power to issue compulsory orders to facilitate the administration and distribution of the res.

It is appropriate to presume that the Framers of the Constitution were familiar with the contemporary legal context when they adopted the Bankruptcy Clause — a provision which, as we explain in Part IV, *infra*, reflects the States' acquiescence in a grant of congressional power to subordinate to the pressing goal of harmonizing bankruptcy law sovereign immunity defenses that might have been asserted in bankruptcy proceedings. The history of the Bankruptcy Clause, the reasons it was inserted in the Constitution, and the legislation both proposed and enacted under its auspices immediately following ratification of the Constitution demonstrate that it was intended not just as a grant of legislative authority to Congress, but also to authorize limited subordination

41. [Footnote 2 in Court's opinion.] Section 106(a), as amended in 1994, provides in part as follows: "Notwithstanding an assertion of sovereign immunity, sovereign immunity is abrogated as to a governmental unit . . . with respect to [specified Bankruptcy Code provisions]." . . . The term "governmental unit" is defined to include a "State," a "municipality," and a "department, agency, or instrumentality of . . . a State." § 101(27). The above-quoted version of § 106(a) is the product of revisions made in the wake of some of our precedents. The Bankruptcy Reform Act of 1978 contained a provision indicating only that "governmental units," defined to include States, were deemed to have "waived sovereign immunity" with respect to certain proceedings in bankruptcy and to be bound by a court's determinations under certain provisions of the Act "notwithstanding any assertion of sovereign immunity." This Court[ ] held that Congress had failed to make sufficiently clear in the predecessor to § 106(a) its intent either to "abrogate" state sovereign immunity or to waive the Federal Government's immunity. [This holding] prompted Congress in 1994 to enact the text of § 106(a) now in force.

of state sovereign immunity in the bankruptcy arena. Foremost on the minds of those who adopted the Clause were the intractable problems, not to mention the injustice, created by one State's imprisoning of debtors who had been discharged (from prison and of their debts) in and by another State. As discussed below, to remedy this problem, the very first Congresses considered, and the Sixth Congress enacted, bankruptcy legislation authorizing federal courts to, among other things, issue writs of habeas corpus directed at state officials ordering the release of debtors from state prisons.

We acknowledge that statements in both the majority and the dissenting opinions in *Seminole Tribe of Fla. v. Florida* reflected an assumption that the holding in that case would apply to the Bankruptcy Clause. Careful study and reflection have convinced us, however, that that assumption was erroneous. . . .

II

Critical features of every bankruptcy proceeding are the exercise of exclusive jurisdiction over all of the debtor's property, the equitable distribution of that property among the debtor's creditors, and the ultimate discharge that gives the debtor a "fresh start" by releasing him, her, or it from further liability for old debts. "Under our longstanding precedent, States, whether or not they choose to participate in the proceeding, are bound by a bankruptcy court's discharge order no less than other creditors." *Hood.* Petitioners here, like the state agencies that were parties in *Hood,* have conceded as much.

The history of discharges in bankruptcy proceedings demonstrates that the state agencies' concessions, and *Hood*'s holding, are correct. The term "discharge" historically had a dual meaning; it referred to both release of debts and release of the debtor from prison. Indeed, the earliest English statutes governing bankruptcy and insolvency authorized discharges of persons, not debts. . . .

Well into the 18th century, imprisonment for debt was still ubiquitous in England and the American Colonies. . . .

Common as imprisonment itself was, the American Colonies, and later the several States, had wildly divergent schemes for discharging debtors and their debts. At least four jurisdictions offered relief through private Acts of their legislatures. Those Acts released debtors from prison upon surrender of their property, and many coupled the release from prison with a discharge of debts. Other jurisdictions enacted general laws providing for release from prison and, in a few places, discharge of debt. Others still granted release from prison, but only in exchange for indentured servitude. Some jurisdictions provided no relief at all for the debtor.

The difficulties posed by this patchwork of insolvency and bankruptcy laws were peculiar to the American experience. In England, where there was only one sovereign, a single discharge could protect the debtor from his jailer and his creditors. As two cases — one litigated before the Constitutional Convention in Philadelphia and one litigated after it — demonstrate, however, the uncoordinated actions of multiple sovereigns, each laying claim to the debtor's body and effects according to different rules, rendered impossible so neat a solution on this side of the Atlantic.

In the first case, *James v. Allen,* a Pennsylvania creditor [sought] recovery from a debtor who had been released from prison in New Jersey. Shortly after his release, the debtor traveled to Pennsylvania, where he was arrested for nonpayment of the Pennsylvania debt. In seeking release from the Pennsylvania prison, he argued that his debt had been discharged by the New Jersey court. [The creditor] responded that the order granting relief under New Jersey's insolvency laws "only discharged the person of the debtor from arrest within the State of New Jersey." The [Pennsylvania state] court agreed: Whatever effect the order might have had in New Jersey, the court said, it "goes no further than to discharge [the debtor] from his imprisonment in the Gaol of Essex County in the State of New Jersey; which, if the fullest obedience were paid to it, could not authorize a subsequent discharge from imprisonment in another Gaol, in another State." The court further observed that "insolvent laws subsist in every State in the Union, and are probably all different from each other. . . . Even the Bankrupt Laws of England, while we were the subjects of that country, were never supposed to extend here, so as to exempt the persons of the Bankrupts from being arrested."

[T]he second case, *Millar v. Hall*, which was decided the year after the Philadelphia Convention, [concerns] a debtor named Hall, [who] had been "discharged under an insolvent law of the state of Maryland, which is in the nature of a general bankruptcy law. Prior to his discharge, Hall had incurred a debt to a Pennsylvanian named Millar. Hall neglected to mention that debt in his schedule of creditors presented to the Maryland court, or to personally notify Millar of the looming discharge. Following the Maryland court's order, Hall traveled to Pennsylvania and was promptly arrested for the unpaid debt to Millar.

Responding to Millar's . . . argument that the holding of *James* controlled, [Hall] urged adoption of a rule that "the discharge of the Defendant in one state ought to be sufficient to discharge [a debtor] in every state." Absent such a rule, [Hall] continued, "perpetual imprisonment must be the lot of every man who fails; and all hope of retrieving his losses by honest and industrious pursuits, will be cut off from the unfortunate bankrupt." The [Pennsylvania state] court accepted this argument. Allowing a creditor to execute "upon [a debtor's] person out of the state in which he has been discharged," the court explained, "would be giving a superiority to some creditors, and affording them a double satisfaction — to wit, a proportionable dividend of his property there, and the imprisonment of his person here." Indeed, the debtor having already been obliged to surrender all of his effects, "to permit the taking [of] his person here, would be to attempt to compel him to perform an impossibility, that is, to pay a debt after he has been deprived of every means of payment, — an attempt which would, at least, amount to perpetual imprisonment, unless the benevolence of his friends should interfere to discharge [his] account."

These two cases illustrate the backdrop against which the Bankruptcy Clause was adopted. In both *James* and *Millar*, the debtors argued that the earlier discharge should be given preclusive effect pursuant to the Full Faith and Credit Clause of the Articles of Confederation. That possibility was the subject of discussion at the Constitutional Convention when a proposal to encompass legislative Acts, and insolvency laws in particular, within the coverage of the Full Faith and Credit Clause of the Constitution was committed to the Committee of Detail[42] together with a proposal "'to establish uniform laws upon the

42. [Footnote 8 in Court's opinion.] The Committee of Detail was created by the Convention on July 25, 1787, to prepare a draft text of the Constitution based on delegates' proposals.

subject of bankruptcies, and respecting the damages arising on the protest of foreign bills of exchange.'" A few days after this proposal was taken under advisement, the Committee of Detail reported that it had recommended adding the power "'to establish uniform laws upon the subject of bankruptcies'" to the Naturalization Clause of what later became Article I.

The Convention adopted the Committee's recommendation with very little debate two days later. Roger Sherman of Connecticut alone voted against it, apparently because he was concerned that it would authorize Congress to impose upon American citizens the ultimate penalty for debt then in effect in England: death. The absence of extensive debate over the text of the Bankruptcy Clause or its insertion indicates that there was general agreement on the importance of authorizing a uniform federal response to the problems presented in cases like *James* and *Millar.*[43]

III

Bankruptcy jurisdiction, as understood today and at the time of the framing, is principally *in rem* jurisdiction. In bankruptcy, "the court's jurisdiction is premised on the debtor and his estate, and not on the creditors." *Hood.* As such, its exercise does not, in the usual case, interfere with state sovereignty even when States' interests are affected.

The text of Article I, § 8, cl. 4, of the Constitution, however, provides that Congress shall have the power to establish "uniform Laws on the subject of Bankruptcies throughout the United States." Although the interest in avoiding unjust imprisonment for debt and making federal discharges in bankruptcy enforceable in every State was a primary motivation for the adoption of that provision, its coverage encompasses the entire "subject of Bankruptcies." The power granted to Congress by that Clause is a unitary concept rather than an amalgam of discrete segments.

The Framers would have understood that laws "on the subject of Bankruptcies" included laws providing, in certain limited respects, for more than simple adjudications of rights in the res. The first bankruptcy statute, for example, gave bankruptcy commissioners appointed by the district court the power, *inter alia,* to imprison recalcitrant third parties in possession of the estate's assets. More generally, courts adjudicating disputes concerning bankrupts' estates historically have had the power to issue ancillary orders enforcing their *in rem* adjudications

Our decision in *Hood* illustrates the point. As the dissenters [including Justice Thomas] in that case pointed out, it was at least arguable that the particular procedure that the debtor pursued to establish dischargeability of her student loan could have been characterized as a suit against the State rather than a purely *in rem* proceeding. But because the proceeding was merely ancillary to the Bankruptcy Court's exercise of its *in rem* jurisdiction, we held that it did not implicate

43. [Footnote 9 in Court's opinion.] Of course, the Bankruptcy Clause, located as it is in Article I, is "'intimately connected'" not just with the Full Faith and Credit Clause, which appears in Article IV of the Constitution, but also with the Commerce Clause. That does not mean, however, that the state sovereign immunity implications of the Bankruptcy Clause necessarily mirror those of the Commerce Clause. Indeed, the Bankruptcy Clause's unique history, combined with the singular nature of bankruptcy courts' jurisdiction, discussed *infra,* have persuaded us that the ratification of the Bankruptcy Clause does represent a surrender by the States of their sovereign immunity in certain federal proceedings. That conclusion is implicit in our holding in *Tennessee Student Assistance Corporation v. Hood.*

state sovereign immunity. The point is also illustrated by Congress' early grant to federal courts of the power to issue *in personam* writs of habeas corpus directing States to release debtors from state prisons, discussed in Part IV, *infra.*

The interplay between *in rem* adjudications and orders ancillary thereto is evident in the case before us. Respondent first seeks a determination under 11 U.S.C. § 547 that the various transfers made by the debtor to petitioners qualify as voidable preferences. The § 547 determination, standing alone, operates as a mere declaration of avoidance. That declaration may be all that the trustee wants; for example, if the State has a claim against the bankrupt estate, the avoidance determination operates to bar that claim until the preference is turned over. See § 502(d). In some cases, though, the trustee, in order to marshal the entirety of the debtor's estate, will need to recover the subject of the transfer pursuant to § 550(a). A court order mandating turnover of the property, although ancillary to and in furtherance of the court's *in rem* jurisdiction, might itself involve *in personam* process.

As we explain in Part IV, *infra,* it is not necessary to decide whether actions to recover preferential transfers pursuant to § 550(a) are themselves properly characterized as *in rem.* Whatever the appropriate appellation, those who crafted the Bankruptcy Clause would have understood it to give Congress the power to authorize courts to avoid preferential transfers and to recover the transferred property. Petitioners do not dispute that that authority has been a core aspect of the administration of bankrupt estates since at least the 18th century. And it, like the authority to issue writs of habeas corpus releasing debtors from state prisons, see Part IV, *infra,* operates free and clear of the State's claim of sovereign immunity.

IV

Insofar as orders ancillary to the bankruptcy courts' *in rem* jurisdiction, like orders directing turnover of preferential transfers, implicate States' sovereign immunity from suit, the States agreed in the plan of the Convention not to assert that immunity. So much is evidenced not only by the history of the Bankruptcy Clause, which shows that the Framers' primary goal was to prevent competing sovereigns' interference with the debtor's discharge, see Part II, *supra,* but also by legislation considered and enacted in the immediate wake of the Constitution's ratification.

Congress considered proposed legislation establishing uniform federal bankruptcy laws in the first and each succeeding Congress until 1800, when the first Bankruptcy Act was passed. The Bankruptcy Act of 1800 was in many respects a copy of the English bankruptcy statute then in force. It was, like the English law, chiefly a measure designed to benefit creditors. Like the English statute, its principal provisions permitted bankruptcy commissioners, on appointment by a federal district court, to arrest the debtor; to "cause the doors of the dwelling-house of [the] bankrupt to be broken,"; to seize and collect the debtor's assets; to examine the debtor and any individuals who might have possession of the debtor's property; and to issue a "certificate of discharge" once the estate had been distributed.

The American legislation differed slightly from the English, however. That difference reflects both the uniqueness of a system involving multiple sovereigns and the concerns that lay at the core of the Bankruptcy Clause itself. The English statute gave a judge sitting on a court where the debtor had obtained his discharge the power to order a sheriff, "Bailiff or Officer, Gaoler or Keeper of any Prison" to release the "Bankrupt out of Custody" if he were arrested subsequent to the discharge. The American version of this provision was worded differently; it specifically granted federal courts the authority to issue writs of habeas corpus effective to release debtors from state prisons.

This grant of habeas power is remarkable not least because it would be another 67 years, after ratification of the Fourteenth Amendment, before the writ would be made generally available to state prisoners.[44] Moreover, the provision of the 1800 Act granting that power was considered and adopted during a period when state sovereign immunity could hardly have been more prominent among the Nation's concerns. *Chisholm v. Georgia*, the case that had so "shocked" the country in its lack of regard for state sovereign immunity, *Principality of Monaco v. Mississippi*, was decided in 1793. The ensuing five years that culminated in adoption of the Eleventh Amendment were rife with discussion of States' sovereignty and their amenability to suit. Yet there appears to be no record of any objection to the bankruptcy legislation or its grant of habeas power to federal courts based on an infringement of sovereign immunity.

This history strongly supports the view that the Bankruptcy Clause of Article I, the source of Congress' authority to effect this intrusion upon state sovereignty, simply did not contravene the norms this Court has understood the Eleventh Amendment to exemplify. Petitioners, ignoring this history, contend that nothing in the *words* of the Bankruptcy Clause evinces an intent on the part of the Framers to alter the "background principle" of state sovereign immunity. Specifically, they deny that the word "uniform" in the Clause implies anything about pre-existing immunities or Congress' power to interfere with those immunities. Whatever the merits of petitioners' argument,[45] it misses the point; text aside, the Framers, in adopting the Bankruptcy Clause, plainly intended to give Congress the power to redress the rampant injustice resulting from States' refusal to respect one another's discharge orders. As demonstrated by the First Congress' immediate consideration and the Sixth Congress' enactment of a provision granting federal courts the authority to release debtors from state prisons, the power to enact bankruptcy legislation was understood to carry with it the power to subordinate state sovereignty, albeit within a limited sphere.

44. [Footnote 11 in Court's opinion.] The Judiciary Act of 1789 authorized issuance of the writ, but only to release those held in *federal* custody. Also, in the interim between 1800 and 1867, Congress authorized limited issuance of the writ in response to two crises it viewed as sufficiently pressing to warrant a federal response: The South Carolina nullification controversy of 1828-1833 and the imprisonment of a foreign national by New York State a few years later [in 1842]. The 1833 statute made the writ available to U.S. citizens imprisoned by States for actions authorized by federal law, while the 1842 statute gave federal judges the power to release foreign nationals imprisoned for actions authorized by foreign governments.

45. [Footnote 13 in Court's opinion.] Petitioners make much of precedents suggesting that the word "uniform" represents a limitation, rather than an expansion, of Congress' legislative power in the bankruptcy sphere. . . . Based on these authorities, petitioners argue that the word "uniform" in the Bankruptcy Clause cannot be interpreted to confer upon Congress any greater authority to impinge upon state sovereign immunity than is conferred, for example, by the Commerce Clause.

Petitioners' logic is not persuasive. Although our analysis does not rest on the peculiar text of the Bankruptcy Clause as compared to other Clauses of Article I, we observe that, if anything, the mandate to enact "uniform" laws supports the historical evidence showing that the States agreed not to assert their sovereign immunity in proceedings brought pursuant to "Laws on the subject of Bankruptcies." That Congress is constrained to enact laws that are uniform in application, whether geographically or otherwise, does not imply that it *lacks power* to enact bankruptcy legislation that is uniform in a more robust sense. As our holding today demonstrates, Congress has the power to enact bankruptcy laws the purpose and effect of which are to ensure uniformity in treatment of state and private creditors.

The ineluctable conclusion, then, is that States agreed in the plan of the Convention not to assert any sovereign immunity defense they might have had in proceedings brought pursuant to "Laws on the subject of Bankruptcies."[46] The scope of this consent was limited; the jurisdiction exercised in bankruptcy proceedings was chiefly *in rem*—a narrow jurisdiction that does not implicate state sovereignty to nearly the same degree as other kinds of jurisdiction. But while the principal focus of the bankruptcy proceedings is and was always the res, some exercises of bankruptcy courts' powers—issuance of writs of habeas corpus included—unquestionably involved more than mere adjudication of rights in a res. In ratifying the Bankruptcy Clause, the States acquiesced in a subordination of whatever sovereign immunity they might otherwise have asserted in proceedings necessary to effectuate the *in rem* jurisdiction of the bankruptcy courts.[47]

V

Neither our decision in *Hood*, which held that States could not assert sovereign immunity as a defense in adversary proceedings brought to adjudicate the dischargeability of student loans, nor the cases upon which it relied, rested on any statement Congress had made on the subject of state sovereign immunity. Nor does our decision today. The relevant question is not whether Congress has "abrogated" States' immunity in proceedings to recover preferential transfers. See 11 U.S.C. § 106(a). The question, rather, is whether Congress' determination that States should be amenable to such proceedings is within the scope of its power to enact "Laws on the subject of Bankruptcies." We think it beyond peradventure that it is.

Congress may, at its option, either treat States in the same way as other creditors insofar as concerns "Laws on the subject of Bankruptcies" or exempt them from operation of such laws. Its power to do so arises from the Bankruptcy Clause itself; the relevant "abrogation" is the one effected in the plan of the Convention, not by statute.

The judgment of the Court of Appeals for the Sixth Circuit is affirmed.

It is so ordered.

JUSTICE THOMAS, with whom THE CHIEF JUSTICE, JUSTICE SCALIA, and JUSTICE KENNEDY join, dissenting.

Under our Constitution, the States are not subject to suit by private parties for monetary relief absent their consent or a valid congressional abrogation, and it is "settled doctrine" that nothing in Article I of the Constitution establishes those preconditions. Yet the majority today casts aside these long-established

46. [Footnote 14 in Court's opinion.] One might object that the writ of habeas corpus was no infringement on state sovereignty, and would not have been understood as such, because that writ, being in the nature of an injunction against a state official, does not commence or constitute a suit against the State. See *Ex parte Young*. While that objection would be supported by precedent today, it would not have been apparent to the Framers. The *Ex parte Young* doctrine was not finally settled until over a century after the Framing and the enactment of the first bankruptcy statute. Indeed, we have recently characterized the doctrine as an expedient "fiction" necessary to ensure the supremacy of federal law.

47. [Footnote 15 in Court's opinion.] We do not mean to suggest that every law labeled a "bankruptcy" law could, consistent with the Bankruptcy Clause, properly impinge upon state sovereign immunity.

principles to hold that the States are subject to suit by a rather unlikely class of individuals—bankruptcy trustees seeking recovery of preferential transfers for a bankrupt debtor's estate. This conclusion cannot be justified by the text, structure, or history of our Constitution. In addition, today's ruling is . . . impossible to square with this Court's settled state sovereign immunity jurisprudence.

The majority maintains that the States' consent to suit can be ascertained from the history of the Bankruptcy Clause. But history confirms that the adoption of the Constitution merely established federal power to legislate in the area of bankruptcy law, and did not manifest an additional intention to waive the States' sovereign immunity against suit. Accordingly, I respectfully dissent.

I

The majority does not appear to question the established framework for examining the question of state sovereign immunity under our Constitution. The Framers understood, and this Court reiterated [quoting Hamilton in Federalist No. 81] over a century ago in *Hans v. Louisiana* that

> It is inherent in the nature of sovereignty not to be amenable to the suit of an individual without its consent. This is the general sense and the general practice of mankind; and the exemption, as one of the attributes of sovereignty, is now enjoyed by the government of every state in the Union. *Unless, therefore, there is a surrender of this immunity in the plan of the convention, it will remain with the states. . . .*

These principles were further reinforced early in our Nation's history, when the people swiftly rejected this Court's decision in *Chisholm v. Georgia*, by ratifying the Eleventh Amendment less than two years later. Thus, "for over a century [since *Hans*] we have reaffirmed that federal jurisdiction over suits against unconsenting States 'was not contemplated by the Constitution when establishing the judicial power of the United States.'" *Seminole Tribe.*

The majority finds a surrender of the States' immunity from suit in Article I of the Constitution, which authorizes Congress "to establish . . . uniform Laws on the subject of Bankruptcies throughout the United States." §8, cl. 4. But nothing in the text of the Bankruptcy Clause suggests an abrogation or limitation of the States' sovereign immunity. Indeed, as this Court has noted on numerous occasions, "the Eleventh Amendment restricts the judicial power under Article III, and Article I cannot be used to circumvent the constitutional limitations placed upon federal jurisdiction." *Seminole Tribe.* "It is settled doctrine that neither substantive federal law nor attempted congressional abrogation under Article I bars a State from raising a constitutional defense of sovereign immunity in federal court." *Alden.* And we have specifically applied this "settled doctrine" to bar abrogation of state sovereign immunity under various clauses within §8 of Article I. *See, e.g., Seminole Tribe* (the Interstate and Indian *Commerce Clauses*); *Florida Prepaid Postsecondary Ed. Expense Bd. v. College Savings Bank* (the Patents Clause).

It is difficult to discern an intention to abrogate state sovereign immunity through the Bankruptcy Clause when no such intention has been found in any of the other clauses in Article I. Indeed, our cases are replete with acknowledgments that there is nothing special about the Bankruptcy Clause in this regard. *See Seminole Tribe.*

* * * *

[In short], today's decision makes clear that *no action* of Congress is needed because the Bankruptcy Clause itself manifests the consent of the States to be sued.

II

The majority supports its break from precedent by relying on historical evidence that purportedly reveals the Framers' intent to eliminate state sovereign immunity in bankruptcy proceedings. The Framers undoubtedly wanted to give Congress the authority to enact a national law of bankruptcy, as the text of the Bankruptcy Clause confirms. But the majority goes further, contending that the Framers found it intolerable that bankruptcy laws could vary from State to State, and demanded the enactment of a single, uniform national body of bankruptcy law. The majority then concludes that, to achieve a uniform national bankruptcy law, the Framers must have intended to waive the States' sovereign immunity against suit. Both claims are unwarranted.

A

In contending that the States waived their immunity from suit by adopting the Bankruptcy Clause, the majority conflates two distinct attributes of sovereignty: the authority of a sovereign to enact legislation regulating its own citizens, and sovereign immunity against suit by private citizens.[48] Nothing in the history of the Bankruptcy Clause suggests that, by including that clause in Article I, the founding generation intended to waive the latter aspect of sovereignty. These two attributes of sovereignty often do not run together—and for purposes of enacting a uniform law of bankruptcy, they need not run together.

For example, Article I also empowers Congress to regulate interstate commerce and to protect copyrights and patents. These provisions, no less than the Bankruptcy Clause, were motivated by the Framers' desire for nationally uniform legislation. Thus, we have recognized that "the need for uniformity in the construction of patent law is undoubtedly important." *Florida Prepaid.* Nonetheless, we have refused, in addressing patent law, to give the need for uniformity the weight the majority today assigns it in the context of bankruptcy, instead recognizing that this need "is a factor which belongs to the Article I patent-power calculus, rather than to any determination of whether a state plea of sovereign immunity deprives a patentee of property without due process of law.".

Nor is the abrogation of state sovereign immunity from suit necessary to the enactment of nationally uniform bankruptcy laws. The sovereign immunity of the States against suit does not undermine the objective of a uniform national law of bankruptcy, any more than does any differential treatment between different categories of creditors.

B

The majority also greatly exaggerates the depth of the Framers' fervor to enact a national bankruptcy regime. The idea of authorizing Congress to enact a nationally uniform bankruptcy law did not arise until late in the Constitutional

48. [Footnote 2 in Justice Thomas's dissent.] Immunity against suit is just "one of the attributes of sovereignty, . . . enjoyed by the government of every state in the Union." The Federalist No. 81. The sovereign power to legislate is a distinct attribute of sovereignty; it is discussed, for example, in a completely separate portion of the Federalist than immunity from suit. *See, e.g., id.,* No. 32.

Convention, which began in earnest on May 25, 1787. The Convention charged the Committee of Detail with putting forth a comprehensive draft Constitution, which it did on August 6. Yet the Convention did not consider the language that eventually became the Bankruptcy Clause until September 1, and it adopted the provision with little debate two days later. Under the majority's analysis, which emphasizes the Framers' zeal to enact a national law of bankruptcy, this timing is difficult to explain.

The majority's premise fares even worse in explaining the postratification period. The majority correctly notes that the practice of the early Congresses can provide valuable insight into the Framers' understanding of the Constitution. But early practice undermines, rather than supports, the majority's theory. "For over a century after the Constitution, . . . the Bankruptcy Clause [authority] remained largely unexercised by Congress. . . . Thus, states were free to act in bankruptcy matters for all but 16 of the first 109 years after the Constitution was ratified." And when Congress did act, it did so only in response to a major financial disaster, and it repealed the legislation in each instance shortly thereafter.[49] It was not until 1898, well over a century after the adoption of the Bankruptcy Clause, that Congress adopted the first permanent national bankruptcy law.

The historical record thus refutes, rather than supports, the majority's premise that the Framers placed paramount importance on the enactment of a nationally uniform bankruptcy law. In reality, for most of the first century of our Nation's history, the country survived without such a law, relying instead on the laws of the several States.

Moreover, the majority identifies *no* historical evidence suggesting that the Framers or the early legislatures, even if they were anxious to establish a national bankruptcy law, contemplated that the States would subject themselves to private suit as creditors under that law. In fact, the historical record establishes that the Framers' held the opposite view. To the Framers, it was a particularly grave offense to a State's sovereignty to be hauled into court by a private citizen and forced to make payments on debts. Alexander Hamilton, the author of Federalist No. 81, followed his general discussion of state sovereign immunity by emphasizing that the Constitution would be especially solicitous of state sovereignty within the specific context of payment of state debts:

> There is no color to pretend that the state governments would, by the adoption of that plan, be divested of the privilege of paying their own debts in their own way, free from every constraint but that which flows from the obligations of good faith. The contracts between a nation and individuals are only binding on the conscience of the sovereign, and have no pretension to a compulsive force. They confer no right of action independent of the sovereign will. To what purpose would it be to authorize suits against States for the debts they owe? How could recoveries be enforced? It is evident that it could not be done without waging war against the

49. [Footnote 3 in Justice Thomas's dissent.] For over a dozen years after the ratification of the Constitution, Congress failed to adopt a single bankruptcy law. It was not until April 4, 1800, that the Sixth Congress finally adopted our Nation's first bankruptcy law, and even that law left an ample role for state law, (By contrast, the very first Congress enacted, *inter alia,* patent and copyright legislation.)

Moreover, that first Act was short-lived; Congress repealed it just three years later. And over a decade later, this Court confirmed what Congress' inattention had already communicated — that the Bankruptcy Clause does not vest exclusive power in Congress, but instead leaves an ample role for the States. It was not until 1841 that Congress would enact another bankruptcy law, only to repeal it less than two years later. The economic upheaval of the Civil War caused Congress to pass another bankruptcy law in 1867, but that too was repealed after just over a decade.

contracting State; and to ascribe to the federal courts by mere implication, and in destruction of a pre-existing right of the state governments, a power which would involve such a consequence, would be altogether forced and unwarrantable.

C

The majority attempts to bolster its historical argument by making three additional observations about the bankruptcy power: (1) Congress' early provision of habeas corpus relief in bankruptcy to forbid the imprisonment of a debtor by one State, in violation of a discharge order issued by the courts of another State; (2) the inability of debtors, first in the American Colonies and then under the Articles of Confederation, to enforce in one state court a discharge order issued by another state court; and (3) the historical understanding that bankruptcy jurisdiction is principally *in rem.* The implication is that, if these specific observations about bankruptcy are correct, then States must necessarily be subject to suit in transfer recovery proceedings, if not also in other bankruptcy settings. But none of these observations comes close to demonstrating that, under the Bankruptcy Clause, the States may be sued by private parties for monetary relief.[50]

1

The availability of habeas relief in bankruptcy between 1800 and 1803 does not support respondent's effort to obtain monetary relief in bankruptcy against state agencies today.[51] The habeas writ was well established by the time of the Framing, and consistent with then-prevailing notions of sovereignty. In *Ex parte Young,* this Court held that a petition for the writ is a suit against a state official, not a suit against a State, and thus does not offend the Eleventh Amendment. . . .

This Court has reaffirmed *Young* repeatedly—including in *Seminole Tribe.* Although the majority observes that *Young* was not issued "until over a century after the Framing and the enactment of the first bankruptcy statute," this observation does nothing to reconcile the majority's analysis with *Young,* as the majority does not purport to question the historical underpinnings of *Young*'s holding. The availability of federal habeas relief to debtors in state prisons thus has no bearing whatsoever on whether the Bankruptcy Clause authorizes suits against the States for money damages.[52]

50. [Footnote 4 in Justice Thomas's dissent.] To be sure, the majority opinion adds, in a footnote, that "we do not mean to suggest that every law labeled a 'bankruptcy' law could, consistent with the Bankruptcy Clause, properly impinge upon state sovereign immunity." But the majority offers no explanation of this statement; certainly it offers no principled basis on which to draw distinctions in future cases.

51. [Footnote 5 in Justice Thomas's dissent.] This is particularly so given the absence of any known application of that law (let alone any test of its validity) during that time. . . .

52. [Footnote 6 in Justice Thomas's dissent.] The majority also contends that the provision for habeas relief in the 1800 bankruptcy law is "remarkable not least because it would be another 67 years, after ratification of the Fourteenth Amendment, before the writ would be made generally available to state prisoners." The implication is that the Bankruptcy Clause shares a similar pedigree with the Fourteenth Amendment, which (unlike Article I of the Constitution) authorizes Congress to abrogate state sovereign immunity against suit. *See, e.g., Fitzpatrick v. Bitzer.* But as the majority recognizes Congress *did* enact other habeas provisions prior to the Fourteenth Amendment. The Fourteenth Amendment bears no relevance to this discussion in any event, because as I have explained above, habeas relief simply does not offend the Framers' view of state sovereign immunity.

2

The majority's second observation — that the Framers were concerned that, under the Articles of Confederation, debtors were unable to obtain discharge orders issued by the court of one State that would be binding in the court of another State, — implicates nothing more than the application of full faith and credit, as is apparent from the majority opinion itself. Accordingly, it has nothing to do with state sovereign immunity from suit.

To support its observation, the majority describes at length two Pennsylvania court rulings issued under the Articles of Confederation. *See James v. Allen*; *Millar v. Hall.* But as the majority's explanation makes clear, the problem demonstrated by these cases is the need for recognition of sister-state judgments by state courts, not disregard for state sovereign immunity against suit in federal courts. Both *James* and *Millar* involved litigation between a private debtor and a private creditor. In both cases, the creditor filed suit in a Pennsylvania court to enforce a debt. And in both cases, the debtor sought but failed to obtain recognition of a judgment of discharge that had previously been entered by a court of another State.

Accordingly, it is unsurprising that, when the issue of bankruptcy arose at the Constitutional Convention, it was also within the context of full faith and credit. As the majority correctly points out, the Framers "plainly intended to give Congress the power to redress the rampant injustice resulting from States' refusal to respect one another's discharge orders." But redress of that "rampant injustice" turned entirely on binding state courts to respect the discharge orders of their sister States under the Full Faith and Credit Clause, not on the authorization of private suits against the States.

3

Finally, the majority observes that the bankruptcy power is principally exercised through *in rem* jurisdiction. The fact that certain aspects of the bankruptcy power may be characterized as *in rem*, however, does not determine whether or not the States enjoy sovereign immunity against such *in rem* suits. And it certainly does not answer the question presented in this case: whether the Bankruptcy Clause subjects the States to transfer recovery proceedings — proceedings the majority describes as "ancillary to and in furtherance of the court's *in rem* jurisdiction," though not necessarily themselves *in rem.*

Two years ago, this Court held that a State is bound by a bankruptcy court's discharge order, notwithstanding the State's invocation of sovereign immunity, because such actions arise out of *in rem* jurisdiction. *See Tennessee Student Assistance Corporation v. Hood.* In doing so, however, the Court explicitly distinguished recovery of preferential transfers, noting that the debt discharge proceedings there were "unlike an adversary proceeding by the bankruptcy trustee seeking to recover property in the hands of the State on the grounds that the transfer was a voidable preference."

[Justice Thomas then went on to critique and reject the Majority's analysis concerning the *in rem* nature of an action to recover a preferential transfer.]

It would be one thing if the majority simply wanted to overrule *Seminole Tribe* altogether. That would be wrong, but at least the terms of our disagreement would be transparent. The majority's action today, by contrast, is difficult to comprehend. Nothing in the text, structure, or history of the Constitution indicates that the Bankruptcy Clause, in contrast to all of the other provisions of Article I, manifests the States' consent to be sued by private citizens.

I respectfully dissent.

DISCUSSION AND QUESTIONS

Katz is a surprising twist in the state sovereign immunity journey. Be clear about its focus. Technically speaking, *Katz* does *not* concern Congress' power to abrogate the states' sovereign immunity. In other words, it is not held out as part of the line of cases such as *Fitzpatrick, Seminole Tribe,* and the other decisions discussed in section C.2.c of this chapter. Rather, taken literally, *Katz* is about the nature and scope of the states' immunity in the first instance. Thus, it is more akin to *Hans, Alden,* and *South Carolina Ports Authority.*

Katz returns to the fundamental question with which the Court has been concerned at least since *Hans*: What immunity did the states have when the Constitution entered into force? After *Hans,* it seemed that the Court's position was that there was a universal type of background immunity from suit in federal court in place. After *Seminole Tribe* it seemed clear that this immunity was itself constitutional in nature. And after *Alden* and *South Carolina* it appeared that the immunity the states enjoyed extended beyond the forum of a federal court and included state courts and federal administrative bodies.

With *Katz* the Court has to some degree thrown these basic postulates into question. Under *Katz* one must go back to the founding and ask, apparently on a power-by-power basis, whether or not the states gave up their immunity from suit in the "plan of the convention." This makes *Katz* a *potentially* powerful force to upset the settled scope of immunity. It has in some measure moved the immunity debate away from congressional abrogation — on which much of the law in the last almost three decades has focused — and back to the existence of immunity in the first instance. Under *Katz,* Congress need not have power to abrogate immunity because there might be no immunity in the first place.

But *Katz* is only *potentially* powerful. First, it technically only deals with the enumerated power to "establish . . . uniform Laws on the subject of Bankruptcies. . . ." U.S. Const. art. I, § 8, cl. 4. And even as to that power, the Court indicates that *Katz* does not hold that all laws enacted pursuant to the Bankruptcy Clause necessarily avoid sovereign immunity concerns. *See Katz,* 546 U.S. at 378 n.15 ("We do not mean to suggest that every law labeled a 'bankruptcy' law could, consistent with the Bankruptcy Clause, properly impinge upon state sovereign immunity."). Thus, on a doctrinal level it is not clear how much authority under the Bankruptcy Clause or which other Article I powers, if any, could be implicated by *Katz*'s reasoning.

A second limiting factor is more practical. *Katz* was a 5-4 decision. It was one of the last decisions announced while Justice Sandra Day O'Connor served on the Court. She was in the majority. Her replacement, Justice Samuel Alito, might not share Justice O'Connor's views (and even now we know little about his fundamental views in this area) and, if that is the case, *Katz* might have a very limited impact on sovereign immunity doctrine. In the end, and as we have said about other matters discussed in this chapter, only time will tell the full import of this potentially significant decision.

D. SOME ADDITIONAL PROBLEMS

The problems that follow provide additional practice concerning the topics covered in Chapter 8.

PROBLEM 8-4

The Overturned Gasoline Truck and State Sovereign Immunity

Assume that the Department of Defense ("DoD") believed that the addition of a certain chemical ("Chemical X") to gasoline would allow its vehicles to run more productively. Therefore, the DoD ordered its gasoline producers to include Chemical X in gasoline delivered to the DoD. The DoD's gasoline producer for its California installations was Gas Corp., Inc., a corporation organized under California law with its principal place of business in California. Gas Corp. complied with the DoD's directive and included Chemical X in the gasoline it delivered to the DoD in California.

A Gas Corp. truck on its way to deliver fuel to the Navy base in San Diego had an accident in California and spilled fuel that contaminated a state-owned piece of property. California believes that the damage to the property was greater than it otherwise would have been because of Gas Corp.'s failure to include in the gasoline formulation another chemical to counteract certain negative effects of Chemical X. Accordingly, the State of California filed a lawsuit in California state court against Gas Corp. This lawsuit was based on basic state-law negligence principles and sought monetary damages for damage to the state property.

Gas Corp. removed the lawsuit to the United States District Court for the Southern District of California based on 28 U.S.C. § 1442(a)(1), which allows for removal of a civil action brought against "any person acting under" an officer of the United States. Gas Corp. claims it added Chemical X to its gasoline as a result of the direction of a federal officer, the Secretary of Defense, acting pursuant to the appropriate congressional statute, and that removal is therefore appropriate. You should assume that such removal is, in fact, appropriate.[53]

(1) The State of California has filed a motion to remand its lawsuit against Gas Corp., claiming that the doctrine of state sovereign immunity bars the suit. How should the judge rule on the state's motion to remand? Why?

(2) Assume the judge denied the motion to remand and allowed the case to proceed in federal court. Now assume that Gas Corp. has filed a counterclaim against the State pursuant to Federal Rule of Civil Procedure 13(a), requiring that a party "state as a counterclaim any claim which . . . [Gas Corp.] has against any opposing party, if it arise out of the transaction or occurrence that is the subject matter of the opposing party's claim. . . ." Specifically, Gas Corp. wishes to assert a counterclaim against California, claiming that when cleaning up the spill at the property in question, California seized and later destroyed certain of the company's property. Gas Corp. seeks monetary damages for these actions. Despite the hypothetical ruling of the court rejecting the remand motion, California has moved to dismiss the counterclaim based on principles of state sovereign immunity. How should the judge rule on the state's motion to dismiss? Why?

---

53. There is a strong argument that such a case would be removable. *See Watson v. Philip Morris Cos.*, 127 S. Ct. 2301 (2007) (rejecting removal by a cigarette company claiming that the highly regulated nature of the industry provided a basis for removal under § 1442 but contrasting the situation where a company produced a given product at the specific direction of the federal government).

PROBLEM 8-5

The Double-Crossing State

Adam Jones ("Jones") lives in Texas and is the father of a child eligible for certain services provided under Medicaid. These services are designed to catch physical, mental, and emotional problems in children as early as possible. They are often called "Early Intervention" services. Medicaid itself is a program under which the federal government provides funding for certain medical services such as Early Intervention.

In 2003, Jones filed a lawsuit pursuant to 42 U.S.C. § 1983 against the Commissioner of the Texas state agency charged with administering the Early Intervention services. The Commissioner was represented in this litigation by the office of the Texas Attorney General. On behalf of himself and a class of similarly situated Texans, Jones alleged that the Texas Early Intervention program did not comply with certain federal requirements. The district court certified the requested class pursuant to Federal Rule of Civil Procedure 23.

After certification, the parties entered into extensive settlement negotiations. They ultimately reached an agreement that was memorialized in a consent decree. A consent decree is an order of a court that embodies a settlement agreement reached by parties to the litigation. It has certain advantages to a purely private settlement because a breach of a consent decree is also subject to contempt sanctions.

The consent decree on which the parties agreed and that the district judge entered as an order went beyond the specific terms of federal law. The Commissioner agreed not only to comply with federal law but also to do certain things not required by federal law. For example, the Commissioner agreed to establish and maintain a toll-free telephone number for parents of eligible children to seek assistance in obtaining Early Intervention benefits.

By 2005, and despite the terms of the decree, the Commissioner had still not complied with many of the terms of the decree that went beyond the federal Medicaid requirements. For example, he had not established the toll-free telephone number. After numerous attempts to get the Commissioner to perform his obligations under the decree, Jones filed a motion to enforce the consent decree with the federal court.

The Commissioner has appeared and offered only a single defense. He claims that the federal court lacks jurisdiction over him pursuant to the Eleventh Amendment and principles of state sovereign immunity. You should assume that it is undisputed that the State of Texas is now in compliance with the applicable federal Medicaid regulations concerning Early Intervention services. The only noncompliance is with respect to those portions of the consent decree that the Commissioner agreed to that go beyond federal law.

You are a clerk for a United States District Court Judge handling the case. He has asked you for advice concerning how he should rule on the Commissioner's arguments concerning sovereign immunity. Make sure to consider the various arguments that can be marshaled in support of your conclusion. The judge has also asked you whether there would be any Eleventh Amendment problem if he were to hold the Commissioner in contempt and award monetary sanctions against him payable to Jones as compensation for the costs of having to seek enforcement of the decree.

PROBLEM 8-6

The Evicted War Veteran

The Armed Forces have been stretched thin as a result of the conflicts in Iraq and Afghanistan as well as other obligations around the world. Recognizing this problem, assume that Congress decided that it needed to take steps to make service in the military more attractive. One step it took was enacting the Prevention of Discrimination in Rental Housing Against War on Terror Veterans Act (the "Act"), which the President signed into law.[54] The Act makes it unlawful to discriminate against veterans who served in either Iraq or Afghanistan in the period after September 11, 2001 (a group referred to as "covered veterans") in the provision of rental housing.

Under the Act, if a veteran establishes that (1) he or she served in Iraq or Afghanistan in the relevant time, and (2) was not rented an available rental housing unit or was evicted or threatened with eviction from a rental housing unit, he or she will have made out a prima facie case of liability under the Act. At that point, the defendant has the burden of establishing that there was a lawful reason for the failure to rent (or the eviction or threat of eviction) that was unrelated to the covered veteran status of the plaintiff. A defendant held liable under the Act could be subject to an order not to continue its discrimination against covered veterans and could be liable for damages awarded to compensate the plaintiff for economic and noneconomic (i.e., pain and suffering, humiliation, etc.) damages.

Congress indicated in the preamble to the Act that it believed it had the authority to enact the statute under four separate provisions of the Constitution: (1) the Interstate Commerce Clause (U.S. CONST. art. I, § 8, cl. 3, in conjunction with the Necessary and Proper Clause, U.S. CONST. art. I, § 8, cl. 18); (2) the War Power Clause (U.S. CONST. art. I, § 8, cl. 11, also in conjunction with the Necessary and Proper Clause); (3) the powers to raise and support an army and a navy (U.S. CONST. art. I, § 8, cl. 12 and cl. 13, yet again in conjunction with the Necessary and Proper Clause); and (4) the enforcement clause of the Fourteenth Amendment (U.S. CONST. amend. XIV, § 5).

The legislation was enacted in a relatively short period of time. It seems to have been prompted most directly by two stories that appeared in newspapers on opposite ends of the country. In Maine, the City of Bangor had refused to rent an apartment in a city-owned building to a U.S. Army veteran who served in Iraq. There appeared to be some indication that the City Council was expressing its hostility to the conflict in Iraq in refusing to rent the apartment at issue. Second, a private landlord in Seattle also refused to rent to a U.S. Army veteran expressly for anti-war reasons. Beyond these two incidents, most of the legislative history contains only second-hand anecdotes of stories about discrimination in housing with respect to veterans.

What is certainly clear from the debates concerning the Act is that many members of Congress were quite concerned with the need to ensure a well-functioning armed forces. There was much talk, for example, of the need to be prepared to "fight the war." There was also some pushback on this point by those who pointed out that Congress had not, in fact, declared war against

54. For your information, there are various federal statutes dealing with discrimination on the basis of service in the military. However, the Act discussed in this question is fictional.

anyone, including Iraq and Afghanistan. Rather, the Congress had passed a law—the Authorization for the Use of Military Force—that authorized the President to take certain military action. Nevertheless, all seemed to agree that regardless of the status of the conflicts in Iraq or Afghanistan as a technical "war," steps certainly needed to be taken to ensure that enrollment in the military would be sufficient to carry out the military's various duties. It seemed that providing various types of legal protections—like those in the Act—was at the very least a step in the right direction.

The final provision of the Act that is relevant for present purposes is the following: "A State is subject to suit for a violation of the Act in a United States District Court. Congress expressly abrogates any immunity from suit that any State of the Union might otherwise possess."

Hans Tribe ("Tribe") is a veteran of service in the United States Army in Iraq. He served in Iraq from January 2005 through June 2006, at which time he was honorably discharged from the Army. Tribe is a "covered veteran" under the Act. He returned to the United States and moved back into his apartment in Tallahassee, Florida. The apartment building in which Tribe rented was owned by the State of Florida. Thomas Trainer ("Trainer") was the Florida Secretary of State. One of his responsibilities in that position was managing the rental properties the state owned, including the one in which Tribe rented his apartment.

Tribe's time in Iraq fundamentally changed him. He returned a fervent pacifist. He took every opportunity to express his distaste for the fighting in Iraq, including by holding gatherings in his apartment at all times of the day and night. Tribe's anti-war sentiments as well as his gatherings did not sit well with many of his neighbors, who complained about both the content of his demonstrations as well as their disruptive nature. In response to his neighbors' complaints, the State of Florida refused to renew Tribe's lease, claiming that he was disruptive.

Tribe consulted a local lawyer who was an expert in laws concerning veterans' benefits. That lawyer decided to file a lawsuit under the Act. His theory was that Florida had failed to renew Tribe's lease because of Tribe's covered veteran status. At the very least, the lawyer believed that Tribe could make out a prima facie case under the Act.

Tribe sued the following two parties in the United States District Court for the Northern District of Florida: the State of Florida and Secretary Trainer, whom Tribe sued in his role as Secretary of State and, therefore, ultimate authority over Florida's state-owned rental operations. Tribe first sought damages against both defendants under the Act for the emotional distress he has suffered as a result of the eviction. Second, Tribe sought an injunction against Secretary Trainer, precluding him from acting in violation of the Act in the future by discriminating against Tribe in housing on account of his veteran status. Both defendants have moved to dismiss Tribe's action on the ground that all the relief he seeks is barred by the doctrine of state sovereign immunity.

You are a law clerk to the United States District Court Judge to whom Tribe's case has been assigned. The judge has asked you to prepare a memorandum advising her as to how she should rule on the motion of each defendant concerning state sovereign immunity. The judge understands that you may not have all the substantive constitutional law knowledge to make a full and complete assessment. However, she would like you to explain the process by which you would decide the various issues. You should make sure to address the issue with respect to both defendants and with respect to the various types of relief sought.

CHAPTER 9

The Special Case of Section 1983

"Every person who, under color of any statute, ordinance, regulation, custom, or usage, of any State . . . subjects . . . any citizen of the United States or other person within the jurisdiction thereof to the deprivation of any rights, privileges, or immunities secured by the Constitution and laws, shall be liable to the party injured in an action at law, suit in equity, or other proper proceeding for redress. . . ." 42 U.S.C. § 1983.

A. A REFERENCE PROBLEM

Section 1983 is one of the more important statutes in the U.S. Code. It serves as the foundation of most suits seeking to enforce constitutional rights against state and local government officials. In this chapter we consider a variety of issues that arise when interpreting § 1983. The Reference Problem below introduces many of those issues.

* * * *

A few years ago the Montana Legislature authorized municipalities to enact youth curfew ordinances. The legislature acted in response to testimony about the growing problems of juvenile drug use and crime in Montana cities and towns. Because there is wide variation in the size and character of Montana municipalities, the legislature declined to draft a curfew statute of statewide application.

The City of Bozeman, Montana, recently enacted a youth curfew ordinance. Four of the five city commissioners voted for the ordinance, and the only opposition came from a commissioner who believed the ordinance was an "unconstitutional" solution to a "non-existent" problem. The ordinance stated, among other things: (1) all persons under the age of 17 were subject to the ordinance; (2) any person violating the ordinance was subject to a civil penalty including a fine and community service; and (3) parents who "knowingly" permitted children in their lawful custody to violate the ordinance were subject to criminal misdemeanor charges. The ordinance prohibited persons under 17 from being in any "public place" during specified nighttime hours. Exceptions were recognized for persons (a) accompanied by a parent or lawful custodian, (b) traveling to or from a place of employment, or (c) generally in "emergency" situations.

Jake Gruden was recently arrested for violating the Bozeman ordinance. After working at the local Burger King one Saturday evening, Jake was waiting for an older employee to finish work and drive Jake home. The employee's car was parked across the street in a public parking lot next to a city park. While waiting for his ride home, Jake sat on a park bench. Jake observed several teenagers playing around noisily on the park's playground equipment. Jake did not join the group. When the police later arrived, several of the teenagers began taunting them. Soon all the youths in the park were arrested, including Jake. Jake tried to explain to the two arresting officers that he was simply waiting for a ride home from work and was not associated with the group of rowdy teenagers. The officers asked Jake if he was under 17 years old. When he admitted he was 16, he was arrested with the other teenagers. Jake was taken to the city's police station.

Jake was placed in a jail cell with five other youths. Several of the youths were plainly intoxicated. One passed out while in the cell, while another regurgitated on the floor. After waiting about an hour in the cell, Jake was allowed to call his parents at home. Unfortunately, the phone line was busy when Jake called so he had to leave a message on their voicemail. Jake then returned to the cell to await his parents' receipt of his message and arrival at the jail. Within 15 minutes of returning to the cell, Jake began feeling confused, tired, and terribly thirsty. He asked a jail guard, Sylvester, to let him go to the bathroom. Sylvester took Jake to the bathroom, and as they were returning Jake stumbled and fell. Sylvester helped Jake up and took him back to his cell. Throughout this episode, Jake was wearing an arm bracelet stating he was a diabetic.

Jake's parents arrived within the hour. When they were taken to his cell, they found him passed out. Sylvester told the parents, "He was awake when I left him." Jake's father immediately asked Sylvester to call an ambulance: "Didn't Jake tell you he's diabetic? I think he may be in some sort of coma." Sylvester immediately called 911 and an ambulance soon arrived. Jake was taken to a local hospital, where he remained for several days receiving treatment for diabetic ketoacidosis.

The city's prosecutor eventually dropped all charges against Jake, but only after Jake's parents incurred substantial legal costs. Jake and his parents remain unhappy about his arrest. They have retained local counsel, who is willing to file a suit (1) seeking damages resulting from Jake's arrest, and (2) seeking declaratory or injunctive relief prohibiting continued enforcement of the Bozeman ordinance. Counsel considers naming as defendants to the suit (a) the City of Bozeman, (b) the city commissioners who enacted the ordinance, (c) the officers who arrested Jake, and (d) the prosecutor who belatedly dismissed charges against Jake. Counsel also considers expanding the suit to seek declaratory and injunctive relief invalidating the state statute that authorized enactment of the ordinance.

Jake's counsel has considered asserting various constitutional claims. These include (1) a claim the curfew ordinance violates the Equal Protection Clause, and (2) a claim Jake was denied due process at the jail when his jailers were indifferent to his medical condition. Further, the Montana Constitution seems to provide parallel protections to Jake, essentially duplicating the rights provided Jake under the U.S. Constitution.

As you will discover in this chapter, Jake's counsel must address a variety of questions in determining what claims and defendants to include in the suit. Even if Jake has suffered a violation of his *substantive* constitutional rights, counsel must negotiate through a complex array of remedial issues. Important issues include the following:

- Which individuals can be sued for damages? City commissioners? City police officers? The city prosecutor?
- What defenses can the individual defendants assert, apart from arguing that their actions did not violate the Constitution?
- Can the City of Bozeman be sued for damages based on its enactment of an unconstitutional ordinance? Can it be sued for injunctive or declaratory relief to prevent future enforcement of its ordinance?
- Can the State of Montana be sued for injunctive or declaratory relief to prevent future enforcement of the state statute authorizing curfew ordinances?
- If Jake asserts any of the claims mentioned above, what forms of monetary relief can he seek? In particular, can he recover (a) compensatory damages, (b) punitive damages, or (c) attorney's fees?
- Do the answers to the questions stated above depend on whether suit is filed in federal or state court?

Unless you have previously studied § 1983 in another course, you probably have little idea how to answer these remedial questions. You should be able to see, however, that these questions have immense importance for Jake's case. Even if Jake has solid claims under the substantive provisions of the Constitution, resolution of these remedial issues will dictate who is sued, what relief is sought, and even whether the suit is worth the investment of time and money.

B. CONTEXT AND BACKGROUND

The rights guaranteed by the U.S. Constitution include those found in the Bill of Rights, such as the freedoms of speech and religion, as well as other rights protected by the Fourteenth Amendment's Equal Protection and Due Process Clauses.

The Constitution is largely silent about what remedies are available to a person whose rights have been violated. One uncommon exception is a person's entitlement to "just compensation" when private property has been taken for public use without adequate compensation. *See* U.S. CONST. amend. V. But otherwise, the Constitution fails to expressly authorize suits in law or equity to enforce the rights it confers.

Beginning with post–Civil War amendments, the Constitution's drafters became more explicit about Congress' power to enact enforcing legislation. *See, e.g.*, U.S. CONST. amends. XIII, XIV, XV, XVIII, XIX, XXIV, & XXVI. This chapter addresses the most important exercise of that power to date, 42 U.S.C. § 1983. Today, almost all constitutional litigation against state and local government officials relies on § 1983. As we will see, § 1983 is also available to sue these officials to enforce numerous statutory rights.

Section 1983 has not always been a popular remedy. Enacted in 1871 to respond to the scourge of the Ku Klux Klan, § 1983 was seldom used during the first 90 years of its existence. *See* Comment, *The Civil Rights Act: Emergence of an Adequate Federal Civil Remedy?* 26 IND. L.J. 361 (1951). As recently as 1966, the federal courts reported only 218 cases founded on § 1983. National Ctr. for State Courts, 4 *Caseload Highlights: Examining the Work of State Courts* no. 2 (1998).

Today, suits based on § 1983 constitute an appreciable fraction of the federal courts' civil docket. A substantial portion of these suits are filed by prisoners, often litigating *pro se*.[1] In 1995, the phenomenon of prisoner suits prompted Congress to do what it rarely does — enact specific restrictions on the use of the section 1983 remedy. *See* Prison Litigation Reform Act, 42 U.S.C. § 1997e (and related legislation).

The sharp increase in § 1983 suits during the past half-century has been attributed to numerous factors. One important factor is the Supreme Court's interpretation of § 1983 to expand its remedial scope. We will examine several of the Court's more important decisions, including the seminal decision in *Monroe v. Pape*, 365 U.S. 167 (1961). A second factor contributing to the proliferation of § 1983 filings is Congress' authorization, in 1976, of attorney's fees for parties who prevail in civil rights actions. *See* 42 U.S.C. § 1988. We will examine a few of the more important Court decisions construing § 1988 and the impact they have on § 1983 litigation.

A third factor contributing to the increase in § 1983 suits is the federal courts' elaboration and expansion of substantive constitutional rights. Prior to the 1970s, for example, there was no recognized constitutional right of access to an abortion, nor was there a well-formed body of jurisprudence governing gender discrimination. The expanding scope of constitutional rights has naturally led to increased filings under § 1983. Finally, the increase in § 1983 litigation is likely a consequence of the overall increase in case filings in federal and state court in recent decades, the so-called "litigation explosion."

1. *Recurring Themes and New Themes*

Section 1983 expands on several themes encountered in other chapters of this book. For example, we revisit the question of parity. Can state courts be trusted

1. *See* Statistics for 2012-2013 indicate that prisoners file about one-third of civil cases classified as "civil rights." http://www.uscourts.gov/uscourts/Statistics/JudicialBusiness/2013/appendices/C02Sep13.pdf.

to enforce federal rights? Or does § 1983, and its companion jurisdictional statute, 28 U.S.C. § 1343(3), reflect fundamental misgivings about the solicitude of state courts for federal law? Further, when state courts are asked to adjudicate claims under § 1983, must they surrender their traditional power over "remedial" and procedural issues and defer to federal remedial law such as § 1983?

A related theme is the obligation, if any, of federal courts to defer to pending state court litigation related to § 1983 claims. To what extent does the Anti-Injunction Act[2] or judicially crafted abstention doctrines require that federal courts stay proceedings that might interfere with the state courts? And when state court proceedings result in a final judgment, to what extent are federal courts precluded from relitigating issues resolved by the state court? We examine these questions in the next chapter after completing our introduction to § 1983.

Our study of § 1983 also raises new and distinctive themes. As we will see, the Supreme Court's interpretation of § 1983 often turns on its resolution of very important policy questions. Among the important policy questions are these:

- Should there always be *some* remedy for the violation of constitutional rights? Is the notion of unredressible constitutional violations unacceptable in our scheme of government?
- Should the costs of remedying constitutional violations be borne *individually* by public servants like police officers or public school teachers? Will such costs deter individuals from entering into public service, or deter them from carrying out their duties? Has the Court successfully devised liability standards that accommodate (1) the public interest in having government employees zealously perform their duties, and (2) the public interest in having these employees comply with constitutional strictures?
- When should a *government entity* (i.e., taxpayers) bear the costs of its employees' constitutional violations? Should government be vicariously liable for its employees' violations based on the tort concept of respondeat superior? Or should liability be limited to the transgressions of higher-up policymakers directly accountable to the public?
- Is government obligated to *educate* its employees in the current requirements of constitutional doctrine? Do employees have the obligation to educate themselves? Is it realistic to hold government officials responsible for knowledge of the law when the courts themselves disagree about what the law means?

Resolving these policy questions would tax the institutional competence of a twenty-first-century Congress. But Congress has been unwilling to address the questions. While the Supreme Court is ostensibly interpreting § 1983 to further the intent of a nineteenth-century Congress, it is often difficult to read the Court's decisions as mere interpretations of Congress' intent. Both government and the Constitution have changed dramatically since 1871. Not even the most prescient member of Congress could have anticipated in 1871 the issues courts would confront in later centuries.

As we will observe in our study of the Court's decisions, the justices draw on many interpretive aids when construing § 1983. These include (1) literal meanings of the statute's language, (2) legislative history, (3) related statutory and

2. 28 U.S.C. § 2283.

constitutional provisions, and (4) precedent. But you may find after studying the Court's decisions that little of its interpretation is mandated by these aids. Instead, the Court often appears driven by policy considerations, whether express or implicit.

2. *Plan of Coverage*

The study of § 1983 merits a course unto itself. Our goals in this chapter are to acquaint you with several of the important rudiments of § 1983 and to relate § 1983 to other topics covered in the text. Any student committed to a thorough understanding of § 1983 or constitutional litigation should enroll in a course dedicated to that study.

We begin by examining the liability of individual government officials under § 1983. At the outset we consider when an official acts "under color of" state law, a prerequisite to liability. We then consider some of the more important forms of qualified and absolute immunity enjoyed by officials.

Qualified or good faith immunity, we will see, is enjoyed by most officials. Qualified immunity is one of the most litigated issues in § 1983 suits. In many cases, it is also the most important protection for government officials sued for damages. Qualified immunity provides officials an expeditious way of bringing suits against them to a halt, sometimes before discovery is even commenced. As we will see, the current standard for determining qualified immunity stresses whether a "reasonable" official would know he or she is violating federal law when acting. Plaintiffs may find this standard very difficult to satisfy when the precise contours of constitutional law, and the application of law to specific situations, are not clear. If plaintiffs do satisfy this standard, on the other hand, the defendant is often subject to costly monetary sanctions, including compensatory damages, punitive damages, and attorney's fees.

Certain officials performing important government functions enjoy an absolute immunity from liability. Prominent examples include local legislators, judges, and prosecutors. Absolute immunity protects these officials in different ways. Some are immune only from damages suits, while others are immune from any form of relief. As we will see, both absolute and qualified immunity are important to resolving issues raised in the Reference Problem.

We next consider the liability of government entities for violations of federal law. While government entities enjoy no qualified immunity, their exposure to liability is limited in another way. These entities are liable only if wrongdoing by their agents rises to the level of a government "policy" or custom. There is no vicarious liability for the misconduct of a government's agents simply because they are acting under color of state law. We explore evolving standards for determining what constitutes government policy, and the impact this has on the viability of suits under § 1983. We also consider the wisdom of the current distribution of liability among government employees and government entities, and what this distribution says about accountability for constitutional violations.

We then consider what federal rights are enforceable under § 1983. Almost all of what we consider to be constitutional "rights," we will see, can be enforced through § 1983. But special problems arise when interpreting the Due Process Clause, which has generated a complex variety of protections in § 1983 litigation. We consider the distinction between "substantive" and "procedural" due process, and the role of state law in applying these protections. Finally, we briefly consider the enforcement of federal statutory rights under § 1983, and the Court's devices for limiting such enforcement.

Our final topic is attorney's fees in § 1983 suits. We consider several principles that govern the recovery of attorney's fees and their strategic impact. As we will see, fees are recoverable by "prevailing" plaintiffs but seldom by prevailing defendants. At the same time, the concept of a prevailing party has been severely circumscribed by recent Court decisions. We will see how the law of attorney's fees can shape constitutional litigation, including parties' decisions about whether to sue (or defend) and whether to settle.

At the conclusion of this chapter, you will appreciate the basic questions constitutional lawyers must ask when assessing whether claims based on § 1983 are viable. You will also be familiar with many of the most important defenses available to government and its agents sued under § 1983. From time to time, you will have the opportunity to affirm your understanding as we return to issues raised in the Reference Problem.

C. THE LAW AND PROBLEMS

1. *When Do Violators of Federal Law Act "Under Color of" State Law?*

Section 1983 provides a remedy for violations of federal law by persons acting "under color of" state law, including both positive law (e.g., statutes) and "custom or usage."[3] In this respect, § 1983 lacks the comprehensive coverage of two other civil rights statutes enacted in the aftermath of the Civil War. For example, 42 U.S.C. § 1981 grants all persons, regardless of color, the right to, among other things, "make and enforce contracts." Because § 1981 does not require that violators act under color of state law, the Supreme Court has construed § 1981 to reach discrimination by private actors. *See Runyon v. McCrary*, 427 U.S. 160 (1976). A companion statute, 42 U.S.C. § 1982, prohibits certain forms of racial discrimination in property transactions and likewise omits any requirement that violators act under color of state law. This statute has also been applied to reach discrimination by private actors. *See Jones v. Alfred H. Mayer Co.*, 392 U.S. 409 (1968).

Before the Court rendered its 1961 decision in *Monroe v. Pape*, it was unclear whether the unauthorized misconduct of rogue government employees occurred "under color of" state law. On one hand, there was apparently a "long-standing assumption" that § 1983 "reached only misconduct either officially authorized or so widely tolerated as to amount to 'custom or usage.'" PETER LOW, JOHN JEFFRIES, & CURTIS A. BRADLEY, FEDERAL COURTS AND THE LAW OF FEDERAL-STATE RELATIONS 917 (7th ed. 2013). For example, government employees implementing state-mandated segregation in public education acted under color of state law, whereas the employee discriminating without government's endorsement did not. On the other hand, the under-color-of-law requirement was found

3. The concept of "state" law also includes local government law. Local government powers historically derive from delegated state powers, and so the drafters of § 1983 considered local law to be a form of state law.

satisfied when applying post-bellum, federal criminal statutes even though government employees engaged in *unauthorized* misconduct. *See United States v. Classic,* 313 U.S. 299 (1941); *Screws v. United States,* 325 U.S. 91 (1945).

In *Monroe v. Pape,* the Court squarely addressed the issue whether § 1983 applies to constitutional violations by government actors unauthorized by state law. The Court's decision had obvious, widespread consequences for the enforcement of constitutional rights. State and local governments do not routinely authorize unconstitutional conduct, with some notable exceptions like the *de jure* racial segregation then existing in many states. To the contrary, state law often prohibits conduct similar to that prohibited by the Constitution.

In *Monroe,* the Court was asked to hold that law enforcement officers acted under color of state law when they violated the Fourth Amendment without authorization of state or local law. In fact, state law even appeared to provide the plaintiffs a tort remedy against the officers involved. Did § 1983 provide the plaintiffs an additional remedy?

MONROE v. PAPE

365 U.S. 167 (1961)

MR. JUSTICE DOUGLAS delivered the opinion of the Court.

This case presents important questions concerning the construction of . . . 42 U.S.C. section 1983. . . .

The complaint alleges that 13 Chicago police officers broke into petitioners' home in the early morning, routed them from bed, made them stand naked in the living room, and ransacked every room, emptying drawers and ripping mattress covers. It further alleges that Mr. Monroe was then taken to the police station and detained on "open" charges for 10 hours, while he was interrogated about a two-day-old murder, that he was not taken before a magistrate, though one was accessible, that he was not permitted to call his family or attorney, that he was subsequently released without criminal charges being preferred against him. It is alleged that the officers had no search warrant and no arrest warrant and that they acted "under color of the statutes, ordinances, regulations, customs and usages" of Illinois and of the City of Chicago. . . .

The City of Chicago moved to dismiss the complaint on the ground that it is not liable under the Civil Rights Acts nor for acts committed in performance of its government functions. All defendants moved to dismiss, alleging that the complaint alleged no cause of action under those Acts or under the Federal Constitution. The District Court dismissed the complaint. The Court of Appeals affirmed. . . .

Petitioners claim that the invasion of their home and the subsequent search without a warrant and the arrest and detention of Mr. Monroe without a warrant and without arraignment constituted a deprivation of their "rights, privileges, or immunities secured by the Constitution" within the meaning of section 1983. . . .

Section 1983 came onto the books as section 1 of the Ku Klux Act of April 20, 1871. It was one of the means whereby Congress exercised the power vested in it by section 5 of the Fourteenth Amendment to enforce the provisions of that Amendment. . . .

* * * *

Its purpose is plain from the title of the legislation, "An Act to enforce the Provisions of the Fourteenth Amendment to the Constitution of the United States, and for other Purposes." Allegation of facts constituting a deprivation under color of state authority of a right guaranteed by the Fourteenth Amendment satisfies to that extent the requirement of section 1983. So far petitioners are on solid ground. For the guarantee against unreasonable searches and seizures contained in the Fourth Amendment has been made applicable to the States by reason of the Due Process Clause of the Fourteenth Amendment.

There can be no doubt at least since *Ex parte Virginia* that Congress has the power to enforce provisions of the Fourteenth Amendment against those who carry a badge of authority of a State and represent it in some capacity, whether they act in accordance with their authority or misuse it. The question with which we now deal is the narrower one of whether Congress, in enacting section 1983, meant to give a remedy to parties deprived of constitutional rights, privileges and immunities by an official's abuse of his position. We conclude that it did so intend.

It is argued that "under color of" enumerated state authority excludes acts of an official or policeman who can show no authority under state law, state custom, or state usage to do what he did. In this case it is said that these policemen, in breaking into petitioners' apartment, violated the Constitution and laws of Illinois. It is pointed out that under Illinois law a simple remedy is offered for that violation and that, so far as it appears, the courts of Illinois are available to give petitioners that full redress which the common law affords for violence done to a person; and it is earnestly argued that no "statute, ordinance, regulation, custom or usage" of Illinois bars that redress.

* * * *

The legislation — in particular the section with which we are now concerned — had several purposes. There are threads of many thoughts running through the debates. One who reads them in their entirety sees that the present section had three main aims.

First, it might, of course, override certain kinds of state laws. Mr. Sloss of Alabama, in opposition, spoke of that object and emphasized that it was irrelevant because there were no such laws:

> The first section of this bill prohibits any invidious legislation by States against the rights or privileges of citizens of the United States. The object of this section is not very clear, as it is not pretended by its advocates on this floor that any State has passed any laws endangering the rights or privileges of the colored people.

Second, it provided a remedy where state law was inadequate. That aspect of the legislation was summed up as follows by Senator Sherman of Ohio: ". . . it is said the reason is that any offense may be committed upon a negro by a white man, and a negro cannot testify in any case against a white man, so that the only way by which any conviction can be had in Kentucky in those cases is in the United States courts, because the United States courts enforce the United States laws by which negroes may testify."

But the purposes were much broader. The third aim was to provide a federal remedy where the state remedy, though adequate in theory, was not available in practice. The opposition to the measure complained that "It overrides the reserved powers of the States," just as they argued that the second section of the bill "absorb[ed] the entire jurisdiction of the State over their local and domestic affairs."

This Act of April 20, 1871, sometimes called "the third force bill," was passed by a Congress that had the Klan "particularly in mind." The debates are replete with references to the lawless conditions existing in the South in 1871. There was available to the Congress during these debates a report, nearly 600 pages in length, dealing with the activities of the Klan and the inability of the state governments to cope with it. This report was drawn on by many of the speakers. It was not the unavailability of state remedies but the failure of certain States to enforce the laws with an equal hand that furnished the powerful momentum behind this "force bill."

* * * *

While one main scourge of the evil—perhaps the leading one—was the Ku Klux Klan, the remedy created was not a remedy against it or its members but against those who representing a State in some capacity were unable or unwilling to enforce a state law.

* * * *

There was, it was said, no quarrel with the state laws on the books. It was their lack of enforcement that was the nub of the difficulty.

* * * *

The debates were long and extensive. It is abundantly clear that one reason the legislation was passed was to afford a federal right in federal courts because, by reason of prejudice, passion, neglect, intolerance or otherwise, state laws might not be enforced and the claims of citizens to the enjoyment of rights, privileges, and immunities guaranteed by the Fourteenth Amendment might be denied by the state agencies.

* * * *

Although the legislation was enacted because of the conditions that existed in the South at that time, it is cast in general language and is as applicable to Illinois as it is to the States whose names were mentioned over and again in the debates. It is no answer that the State has a law which if enforced would give relief. The federal remedy is supplementary to the state remedy, and the latter need not be first sought and refused before the federal one is invoked. Hence the fact that Illinois by its constitution and laws outlaws unreasonable searches and seizures is no barrier to the present suit in the federal court.

* * * *

MR. JUSTICE HARLAN, whom MR. JUSTICE STEWART joins, concurring.

* * * *

The dissent considers that the "under color of" provision of section 1983 distinguishes between unconstitutional actions taken without state authority, which only the State should remedy, and unconstitutional actions authorized by the State, which the Federal Act was to reach. If so, then the controlling difference for the enacting legislature must have been either that the state remedy was more adequate for unauthorized actions than for authorized ones or that there was, in some sense, greater harm from unconstitutional actions authorized by the full panoply of state power and approval than from unconstitutional actions not so authorized or acquiesced in by the State. I find less than compelling the evidence that either distinction was important to that Congress.

If the state remedy was considered adequate when the official's unconstitutional act was unauthorized, why should it not be thought equally adequate when the unconstitutional act was authorized? For if one thing is very clear in the legislative history, it is that the Congress of 1871 was well aware that no action requiring state judicial enforcement could be taken in violation of the Fourteenth Amendment without that enforcement being declared void by this Court on direct review from the state courts. And presumably it must also have been understood that there would be Supreme Court review of the denial of a state damage remedy against an official on grounds of state authorization of the unconstitutional action. It therefore seems to me that the same state remedies would, with ultimate aid of Supreme Court review, furnish identical relief in the two situations. . . .

Since the suggested narrow construction of section 1983 presupposes that state measures were adequate to remedy unauthorized deprivations of constitutional rights and since the identical state relief could be obtained for state-authorized acts with the aid of Supreme Court review, this narrow construction would reduce the statute to having merely a jurisdictional function, shifting the load of federal supervision from the Supreme Court to the lower courts and providing a federal tribunal for fact findings in cases involving authorized action. Such a function could be justified on various grounds. It could, for example, be argued that the state courts would be less willing to find a constitutional violation in cases involving "authorized action" and that therefore the victim of such action would bear a greater burden in that he would more likely have to carry his case to this Court, and once here, might be bound by unfavorable state court findings. But the legislative debates do not disclose congressional concern about the burdens of litigation placed upon the victims of "authorized" constitutional violations contrasted to the victims of unauthorized violations. Neither did Congress indicate an interest in relieving the burden placed on this Court in reviewing such cases.

The statute becomes more than a jurisdictional provision only if one attributes to the enacting legislature the view that a deprivation of a constitutional right is significantly different from and more serious than a violation of a state right and therefore deserves a different remedy even though the same act may constitute both a state tort and the deprivation of a constitutional right. This view, by no means unrealistic as a common-sense matter, is, I believe, more consistent with the flavor of the legislative history than is a view that the primary purpose of the statute was to grant a lower court forum for fact findings.[4]

* * * *

4. [Footnote 5 in Justice Harlan's concurring opinion.] There will be many cases in which the relief provided by the state to the victim of a use of state power which the state either did not or could not constitutionally authorize will be far less than what Congress may have thought would be fair reimbursement for deprivation of a constitutional right. I will venture only a few examples. There may be no damage remedy for the loss of voting rights or for the harm from psychological coercion leading to a confession. And what is the dollar value of the right to go to unsegregated schools? Even the remedy for such an unauthorized search and seizure as Monroe was allegedly subjected to may be only the nominal amount of damages to physical property allowable in an action for trespass to land. It would indeed be the purest coincidence if the state remedies for violations of common-law rights by private citizens were fully appropriate to redress those injuries which only a state official can cause and against which the Constitution provides protection.

MR. JUSTICE FRANKFURTER, dissenting [in relevant part].

* * * *

If the question whether due process forbids this kind of police invasion were before us in isolation, the answer would be quick. If, for example, petitioners had sought damages in the state courts of Illinois and if those courts had refused redress on the ground that the official character of the respondents clothed them with civil immunity . . . we would have no hesitation in saying that were a State affirmatively to sanction such police incursion into privacy it would run counter to the guaranty of the Fourteenth Amendment. If that issue is not reached in this case it is not because the conduct which the record here presents can be condoned. But by bringing their action in a Federal District Court petitioners cannot rest on the Fourteenth Amendment *simpliciter.* They invoke the protection of a specific statute by which Congress restricted federal judicial enforcement of its guarantees to particular enumerated circumstances. They must show not only that their constitutional rights have been infringed, but that they have been infringed, "under color of [state] statute, ordinance, regulation, custom, or usage," as that phrase is used in the relevant congressional enactment.

* * * *

This case squarely presents the question whether the intrusion of a city policeman for which that policeman can show no such authority at state law as could be successfully interposed in defense to a state-law action against him, is nonetheless to be regarded as "under color" of state authority within the meaning of Section 1983. Respondents, in breaking into the Monroe apartment, violated the laws of the State of Illinois. Illinois law appears to offer a civil remedy for unlawful searches; petitioners do not claim that none is available. Rather they assert that they have been deprived of due process of law and of equal protection of the laws under color of state law, although from all that appears the courts of Illinois are available to give them the fullest redress which the common law affords for the violence done them, nor does any "statute, ordinance, regulation, custom, or usage" of the State of Illinois bar that redress. . . .

* * * *

[A]ll the evidence converges to the conclusion that Congress by section 1983 created a civil liability enforceable in the federal courts only in instances of injury for which redress was barred in the state courts because some "statute, ordinance, regulation, custom, or usage" sanctioned the grievance complained of. This purpose, manifested even by the so-called "Radical" Reconstruction Congress in 1871, accords with the presuppositions of our federal system. The jurisdiction which Article III of the Constitution conferred on the national judiciary reflected the assumption that the state courts, not the federal courts, would remain the primary guardians of that fundamental security of person and property which the long evolution of the common law had secured to one individual as against other individuals. The Fourteenth Amendment did not alter this basic aspect of our federalism.

* * * *

But, of course, in the present case petitioners argue that the wrongs done them were committed not by individuals but by the police as state officials. There are two senses in which this might be true. It might be true if petitioners alleged that the redress which state courts offer them against the respondents is different than that which those courts would offer against other individuals, guilty of the same conduct, who were not the police. This is not alleged. It might also be true merely because the respondents are the police — because they are clothed with an appearance of official authority which is in itself a factor of significance in dealings between individuals. Certainly the night-time intrusion of the man with a star and a police revolver is a different phenomenon than the night-time intrusion of a burglar. The aura of power which a show of authority carries with it has been created by state government. For this reason the national legislature, exercising its power to implement the Fourteenth Amendment, might well attribute responsibility for the intrusion to the State and legislate to protect against such intrusion. The pretense of authority alone might seem to Congress sufficient basis for creating an exception to the ordinary rule that it is to the state tribunals that individuals within a State must look for redress against other individuals within that State. The same pretense of authority might suffice to sustain congressional legislation creating the exception. But until Congress has declared its purpose to shift the ordinary distribution of judicial power for the determination of causes between co-citizens of a State, this Court should not make the shift. Congress has not in section 1983 manifested that intention.

The unwisdom of extending federal criminal jurisdiction into areas of conduct conventionally punished by state penal law is perhaps more obvious than that of extending federal civil jurisdiction into the traditional realm of state tort law. But the latter, too, presents its problems of policy appropriately left to Congress. Suppose that a state legislature or the highest court of a State should determine that within its territorial limits no damages should be recovered in tort for pain and suffering, or for mental anguish, or that no punitive damages should be recoverable. Since the federal courts went out of the business of making "general law," Erie R. Co. v. Tompkins, 304 U.S. 64 (1938), questions of local policy have admittedly been the exclusive province of state lawmakers. Should the civil liability for police conduct which can claim no authority under local law, which is actionable as common-law assault or trespass in the local courts, comport different rules? Should an unlawful intrusion by a policeman in Chicago entail different consequences than an unlawful intrusion by a hoodlum? These are matters of policy in its strictly legislative sense, not for determination by this Court. And if it be, as it is, a matter for congressional choice, the legislative evidence is overwhelming that section 1983 is not expressive of that choice. Indeed, its precise limitation to acts "under color" of state statute, ordinance or other authority appears on its face designed to leave all questions of the nature and extent of liability of individuals to the laws of the several States except when a State seeks to shield those individuals under the special barrier of state authority. To extend Civil Rights Act liability beyond that point is to interfere in areas of state policymaking where Congress has not determined to interfere.

* * * *

In concluding that police intrusion in violation of state law is not a wrong remediable under section 1983, the pressures which urge an opposite result are duly felt. The difficulties which confront private citizens who seek to vindicate in traditional common-law actions their state-created rights against lawless invasion of their privacy by local policemen are obvious, and obvious is the need for more effective modes of redress. The answer to these urgings must be regard for our federal system which presupposes a wide range of regional autonomy in the kinds of protection local residents receive. If various common—law concepts make it possible for a policeman—but no more possible for a policeman than for any individual hoodlum intruder—to escape without liability when he has vandalized a home, that is an evil. But, surely, its remedy devolves, in the first instance, on the States. Of course, if the States afford less protection against the police, as police, than against the hoodlum—if under authority of state "statute, ordinance, regulation, custom, or usage" the police are specially shielded—section 1983 provides a remedy which dismissal of petitioners' complaint in the present case does not impair. Otherwise, the protection of the people from local delinquencies and shortcomings depends, as in general it must, upon the active consciences of state executives, legislators and judges. Federal intervention, which must at best be limited to securing those minimal guarantees afforded by the evolving concepts of due process and equal protection, may in the long run do the individual a disservice by deflecting responsibility from the state lawmakers, who hold the power of providing a far more comprehensive scope of protection. Local society, also, may well be the loser, by relaxing its sense of responsibility and, indeed, perhaps resenting what may appear to it to be outside interference where local authority is ample and more appropriate to supply needed remedies. . . .

DISCUSSION AND QUESTIONS

The relevance, and irrelevance, of state law after Monroe. The Court identified "three main aims" of § 1983. First, it overturned state laws authorizing racial discrimination. Second, it provided a remedy for unlawful conduct "where state law was inadequate." Third, it provided a remedy for unlawful conduct where "the state remedy, though adequate in theory, was not available in practice." Only the second and third aims were conceivably served by applying § 1983 to the misconduct challenged in *Monroe.*

Did the Court discuss whether the remedy provided by Illinois law was "inadequate" or "not available in practice?" Notice that, in addressing state remedies, Justice Douglas wrote, "The federal remedy is supplementary to the state remedy, and the latter need not be first sought or refused before the federal one is invoked." Does this comment suggest that the inadequacy of state law is not really the issue? If so, has the Court been true to the expressed intent of Congress in 1871?

At the same time, can you imagine what difficulties would arise if § 1983 plaintiffs first had to litigate in state court and, having failed to secure an adequate remedy, then had to file a second action in federal court? Would such a process tend to deter plaintiffs from bringing suit? Would it potentially lead to unseemly conflicts between the state and federal judiciary? In a later chapter, we examine how the Court's concern about such conflicts has led the Court to develop a limitation on the § 1983 remedy known as *Younger* abstention. See Chapter 10.

Justice Harlan's concurring opinion takes greater care exploring the adequacy of state-law remedies. For one thing, he points out that the deprivation of a constitutional right "is significantly different from and more serious than a violation of a state right. . . ." Further, Justice Harlan took care to note that state courts, as well as federal ones, are bound to enforce the Constitution. He observes there is "substantial overlap between the protections granted by state constitutional provisions and those granted by the 14th amendment." But Justice Harlan is concerned that the remedies afforded by state law are inadequate insofar as they may *under-compensate.* He observes, "There will be many cases in which the relief provided by the state to the victim of the use of state power . . . - will be far less than what Congress may have thought would be a fair reimbursement for deprivation of a constitutional right." According to Justice Harlan, remedies afforded by state common law are not devised to redress the specific injuries resulting from unconstitutional conduct: "It would indeed by the purest coincidence if the state remedies for violation of common-law rights by private citizens were fully appropriate to redress those injuries which only a state official can cause and against which the Constitution provides protection."

Monroe thus views § 1983 as a remedial alternative to the assertion of claims under state law. One practical consequence of this view is that § 1983 plaintiffs usually assert state-law claims in their complaints. At times, these state-law claims do little if anything to enhance the plaintiff's recovery. For example, state law often places caps on the damages recoverable from government defendants and precludes recovery of attorney's fees. But at other times state law may truly supplement the remedies available under § 1983. For example, state law may impose vicarious liability on a government entity for the wrongdoing of its employees. This may provide plaintiffs a defendant who can actually satisfy a substantial judgment. As we will see, there is no such vicarious liability under § 1983.

A § 1983 plaintiff may normally join state and federal claims regardless of whether suit is filed in state or federal court. The Court has held that state courts are obligated to entertain claims under § 1983 even when the defendant enjoys sovereign immunity from state-law claims. *See Howlett v. Rose,* 496 U.S. 356 (1990). At the same time, federal courts have the power to hear state-law claims related to federal ones as part of their supplemental jurisdiction. *See* 28 U.S.C. § 1367.[5]

Wearing the "badge" of government authority. In *Monroe,* the Court observed that the Fourteenth Amendment can be enforced against those who carry "a badge of authority of a state and represent it in some capacity," even when they misuse their authority. The question arises, when does a government official take off the badge of authority and become a private actor? This question arises in different contexts. It may arise, for example, when an off-duty police officer uses his authority to facilitate wrongful conduct like sexual battery. *See, e.g., Roe v. Humke,* 128 F.3d 1213 (8th Cir. 1997). Or it may arise when a state-university professor sexually harasses a student. *See, e.g., Hayut v. State Univ. of N.Y.,* 352 F.3d 733 (2d Cir. 2003).

Courts considering whether a government official is wearing the badge of authority when engaged in wrongdoing consider many factors, including whether the official was on or off duty, whether the official actually professed to be exercising government authority, and whether the official had responsibilities that extended to off-duty settings. *See generally* David W. Lee, 2005 Handbook of Section 1983 Litigation 40-44 (Aspen 2005).

5. One important exception arises when a plaintiff sues state government based on state law and the state has not surrendered its sovereign immunity from suit in federal court. For example, a — § 1983 plaintiff may have federal claims against state officials, and state claims against the state itself. In such a situation, the § 1983 plaintiff cannot assert supplemental jurisdiction over the state in a federal court action. *See, e.g., Pennhurst State Sch. & Hosp. v. Halderman,* 465 U.S. 89 (1984). The plaintiff may, however, be able to join both defendants in state court.

At the same time, a purely private individual not employed by government can be subject to suit under § 1983. If a private individual or entity engages in state action—thus implicating constitutional protections—it will also have acted "under color of" state law. *See Lugar v. Edmondson Oil Co.,* 457 U.S. 922 (1982). For example, in *Lugar* an oil company was found to have engaged in state action and acted under color of state law when it used state pre-judgment attachment procedures to seize the plaintiff's property unlawfully. You probably have examined this facet of the state action doctrine in Constitutional Law.

A private party may also conspire with state actors and be subject to suit under § 1983. *See, e.g., Williams v. Seniff,* 342 F.3d 774 (7th Cir. 2003). Such a conspiracy requires both an agreement between the alleged conspirators and concerted action. *Id.* Conspiracies under § 1983 should be distinguished from conspiracies under a related statute, 42 U.S.C. § 1985. Actionable conspiracies under § 1985 are confined to those intended to deprive a person of "equal protection" and similar rights. *See, e.g., Griffin v. Breckenridge,* 403 U.S. 88 (1971).

Individual and government liability under Monroe. The Court's decision in *Monroe v. Pape* is often cited as the catalyst for the ensuing proliferation of suits under § 1983. *Monroe* authorizes suits against government officials *individually* when they have violated federal law. It is irrelevant whether their conduct was authorized or unauthorized by state law.

But what of the City of Chicago, for whom the officers were working at the time they broke into Mr. Monroe's home? Was the city also liable for the officers' misconduct? The Court said "no." The Court concluded with little hesitation that local government entities are not "persons" subject to suit under § 1983. According to the Court's opinion, the reconstruction Congress specifically addressed and rejected the imposition of liability on local government. We will return to the issue of government's liability later in this chapter and observe how the Court later overrules *Monroe* on this point.

For the time being, focus on the implications of *Monroe*'s holding that individual officials are subject to suit under § 1983. None of us is likely troubled by the Court's imposition of liability on the specific defendants in *Monroe*—after all, these law enforcement officers broke into a home, ransacked every room, and then arrested the homeowner and subjected him to interrogation without providing him access to a lawyer. Their actions appeared to violate their own state's law, and even dissenting Justice Frankfurter would appear to support a § 1983 remedy under those circumstances. But *Monroe* also recognizes liability for government officials whose actions were *authorized* by state or local law. Consider possible implications of *Monroe* in a situation like that presented by the Reference Problem.

PROBLEM 9-1

An Appropriate Liability Standard for Government Officials

We will soon consider the Court's development of liability standards for government officials. Before your perspective on liability is shaped by the Court's, consider what standard seems intuitively sound in the context of the Reference Problem.

Assume that, when the Bozeman police arrested Jake Gruden, they believed they were enforcing a valid ordinance against an apparent lawbreaker (Jake was out past the curfew and did not appear to be traveling home from work). But assume that a trial court later concludes that (1) the ordinance was unconstitutional, and, in any event, (2) the totality of evidence indicates Jake satisfied the ordinance's exception for youth traveling to or from work. Does it seem just to impose liability on the police officers, who thought they were enforcing a valid ordinance against a lawbreaker? Should their good-faith belief they were lawfully doing their duty immunize them from liability? Should they be entitled to rely on a city ordinance presumably passed by elected officials having greater legal expertise than the officers? If the officers are required to defend themselves in a civil suit, and possibly pay a costly judgment and Jake's legal fees, how will that affect the hiring and retention of police officers in Bozeman?

On the other hand, if the officers are exonerated because they acted unlawfully but in good faith, where does that leave Jake (especially if the city itself is not subject to suit)? And what message will that send to the city commission, and to the police department, about the importance of enacting and enforcing laws consistently with the Constitution?

Questions like those posed in Problem 9-1 led to the Court's decades-long struggle to define liability standards in the wake of *Monroe v. Pape*. We now consider the evolution of the qualified-immunity doctrine, which has come to be the most important—and most litigated—issue in suits against government officials.

2. *Under What Circumstances Are Individuals Sued Under Section 1983 Immune from Damages?*

Section 1983 says nothing about a defendant's immunity from damages for good-faith actions. A ruthlessly literal interpretation of the statute might conclude there is no immunity. But § 1983 does not stand alone. A related statute, 42 U.S.C. § 1988, empowers courts to apply state "common law" when § 1983 is "deficient."[6] Although § 1988 raises significant interpretive questions in its own right, the statute lends support to the notion that courts should consider common-law principles when applying § 1983. Not surprisingly, the Court's recognition of immunity under § 1983 has at times been greatly influenced by its view of the "immunity historically accorded the relevant official at common law." *Imbler v. Pachtman*, 424 U.S. 409, 421 (1976). At the same time, the Court's evolving standard of qualified immunity reflects its resolution of difficult policy issues as much, if not more, than its investigation of common-law history. *See Harlow v. Fitzgerald*, 457 U.S. 800, 813 n.20 (1980) ("The relevant judicial inquiries . . . encompass considerations of public policy, the importance of which should be confirmed either by reference to the common law or, more likely, our constitutional heritage and structure."); *Anderson v. Creighton*, 483 U.S. 635, 645 n.5 (1987) ("[W]e have never suggested that the precise contours of official immunity can and should be slavishly derived from the often arcane rules of the common law."). One aspect of immunity is clear: The scope of immunities

6. Section 1988 provides in relevant part that "the common law, as modified and changed by the constitution and statutes of the State wherein the court having jurisdiction of such civil or criminal cause is held, so far as same is not inconsistent with the Constitution and the law of the United States, shall be extended to and govern the said courts" when federal law is otherwise "not adapted to the object, or [is] deficient in the provisions necessary to furnish suitable remedies. . . ."

presents an issue of federal law and, while the Court may consider state-law immunities in its quest to enunciate immunities under § 1983, state law does not apply of its own force. *See Haywood v. Drown*, 129 S. Ct. 2108, 2115 n.5 (2009) (affirming that state-law immunities for government officials are preempted when claims are asserted under § 1983).

In *Wood v. Strickland*, 420 U.S. 308 (1975), the Court announced a standard of qualified, or good-faith immunity, comprising two prongs. One prong consisted of a subjective test: an official "must be acting sincerely and with a belief he is doing right." But the Court declined to immunize the official (in *Wood*, a school board member) who acts with subjective good faith and yet undertakes action that is clearly foreclosed by existing constitutional precedent. Consequently, the Court recognized a second prong to qualified immunity: an official must conform his behavior to "basic, unquestioned constitutional rights." In a nutshell, the Court decided that an official will not be immune from a damages action under § 1983 if he "knew or reasonably should have known that the action he took . . . would violate the constitutional rights of [the plaintiff] or if he took the action with the malicious intention to cause a deprivation of constitutional rights or other injury. . . ."

The two-pronged test for qualified immunity in *Wood* meant that a plaintiff could recover damages by proving either that the defendant acted with ill will or ignored established constitutional law. Well-intentioned but plainly unlawful conduct was actionable. And even if governing principles of constitutional law were not established at the time the defendant acted, or their application to the facts of the defendant's conduct was unclear, the defendant might still be liable if he acted with subjective bad faith.

Dissenting in *Wood*, Justices Powell and Rehnquist were deeply troubled by the new, objective prong of qualified immunity. They pointed out that defendants like the school board members in *Wood* served without compensation, lacked ready access to legal counsel, and "possess[ed] no unique competency in divining the law." As for the "settled, indisputable" constitutional law that defendant-officials had to know, its meaning was unlikely to be "self-evident to constitutional law scholars — much less the average school board member. . . ."

Seven years later, Justice Powell commanded a majority that revised the defense of qualified immunity announced in *Wood*. But rather than abandon the objective prong of qualified immunity so objectionable to him in *Wood*, Justice Powell embraced that prong as the sole standard for assessing immunity.

HARLOW v. FITZGERALD[7]

457 U.S. 800 (1982)

[Fitzgerald was discharged from the Air Force, allegedly as the result of a conspiracy against him by former President Nixon and his senior executive aides. After extensive discovery, these aides moved for summary judgment on the ground they were absolutely immune from suit for activities conducted in

7. *Harlow* addresses immunity for federal officials, who usually are not subject to suit under § 1983 because they do not act "under color of" state law. However, the court has applied its developing concept of qualified immunity equally to federal defendants sued under the judicially developed analogue to a § 1983 claim. *See Bivens v. Six Unknown Named Agents of the Fed. Bureau of Narcotics* 403 U.S. 388 (1971).

their capacity as aides to the President. The district court denied their motion, a ruling affirmed by the circuit court. On review, the Supreme Court agreed that the aides were not entitled to absolute immunity but held that they could assert a defense of qualified immunity. In the excerpted opinion that follows, the Court explains its revised standard of qualified immunity.]

MR. JUSTICE POWELL delivered the opinion of the Court.

Even if they cannot establish that their official functions require absolute immunity, petitioners assert that public policy at least mandates an application of the qualified immunity standard that would permit the defeat of insubstantial claims without resort to trial. We agree.

* * * *

The resolution of immunity questions inherently requires a balance between the evils inevitable in any available alternative. In situations of abuse of office, an action for damages may offer the only realistic avenue for vindication of constitutional guarantees. It is this recognition that has required the denial of absolute immunity to most public officers. At the same time, however, it cannot be disputed seriously that claims frequently run against the innocent as well as the guilty—at a cost not only to the defendant officials, but to society as a whole. These social costs include the expenses of litigation, the diversion of official energy from pressing public issues, and the deterrence of able citizens from acceptance of public office. Finally, there is the danger that fear of being sued will "dampen the ardor of all but the most resolute, or the most irresponsible [public officials], in the unflinching discharge of their duties."

In identifying qualified immunity as the best attainable accommodation of competing values, we relied on the assumption that this standard would permit "[i]nsubstantial lawsuits [to] be quickly terminated." Yet petitioners advance persuasive arguments that the dismissal of insubstantial lawsuits without trial—a factor presupposed in the balance of competing interests struck by our prior cases—requires an adjustment of the "good faith" standard established by our decisions.

Qualified or "good faith" immunity is an affirmative defense that must be pleaded by a defendant official. Decisions of this Court have established that the "good faith" defense has both an "objective" and a "subjective" aspect. The objective element involves a presumptive knowledge of and respect for "basic, unquestioned constitutional rights." The subjective component refers to "permissible intentions." *Ibid.* Characteristically the Court has defined these elements by identifying the circumstances in which qualified immunity would *not* be available. Referring both to the objective and subjective elements, we have held that qualified immunity would be defeated if an official "*knew or reasonably should have known* that the action he took within his sphere of official responsibility would violate the constitutional rights of the [plaintiff], *or* if he took the action *with the malicious intention* to cause a deprivation of constitutional rights or other injury. . . ."

The subjective element of the good-faith defense frequently has proved incompatible with our admonition in *Butz* that insubstantial claims should not proceed to trial. Rule 56 of the Federal Rules of Civil Procedure provides that disputed questions of fact ordinarily may not be decided on motions for summary judgment. And an official's subjective good faith has been considered to be a question of fact that some courts have regarded as inherently requiring resolution by a jury.

In the context of *Butz*' attempted balancing of competing values, it now is clear that substantial costs attend the litigation of the subjective good faith of government officials. Not only are there the general costs of subjecting officials to the risks of trial—distraction of officials from their government duties, inhibition of discretionary action, and deterrence of able people from public service. There are special costs to "subjective" inquiries of this kind. Immunity generally is available only to officials performing discretionary functions. In contrast with the thought processes accompanying "ministerial" tasks, the judgments surrounding discretionary action almost inevitably are influenced by the decision-maker's experiences, values, and emotions. These variables explain in part why questions of subjective intent so rarely can be decided by summary judgment. Yet they also frame a background in which there often is no clear end to the relevant evidence. Judicial inquiry into subjective motivation therefore may entail broad-ranging discovery and the deposing of numerous persons, including an official's professional colleagues. Inquiries of this kind can be peculiarly disruptive of effective government.

* * * *

Consistently with the balance at which we aimed in *Butz*, we conclude today that bare allegations of malice should not suffice to subject government officials either to the costs of trial or to the burdens of broad-reaching discovery. We therefore hold that government officials performing discretionary functions generally are shielded from liability for civil damages insofar as their conduct does not violate clearly established statutory or constitutional rights of which a reasonable person would have known.

Reliance on the objective reasonableness of an official's conduct, as measured by reference to clearly established law, should avoid excessive disruption of government and permit the resolution of many insubstantial claims on summary judgment. On summary judgment, the judge appropriately may determine, not only the currently applicable law, but whether that law was clearly established at the time an action occurred. If the law at that time was not clearly established, an official could not reasonably be expected to anticipate subsequent legal developments, nor could he fairly be said to "know" that the law forbade conduct not previously identified as unlawful. Until this threshold immunity question is resolved, discovery should not be allowed. If the law was clearly established, the immunity defense ordinarily should fail, since a reasonably competent public official should know the law governing his conduct. Nevertheless, if the official pleading the defense claims extraordinary circumstances and can prove that he neither knew nor should have known of the relevant legal standard, the defense should be sustained. But again, the defense would turn primarily on objective factors.

By defining the limits of qualified immunity essentially in objective terms, we provide no license to lawless conduct. The public interest in deterrence of unlawful conduct and in compensation of victims remains protected by a test that focuses on the objective legal reasonableness of an official's acts. Where an official could be expected to know that certain conduct would violate statutory or constitutional rights, he should be made to hesitate; and a person who suffers injury caused by such conduct may have a cause of action. But where an official's duties legitimately require action in which clearly established rights are not implicated, the public interest may be better served by action taken "with independence and without fear of consequences."

* * * *

JUSTICE BRENNAN, with whom JUSTICE MARSHALL, and JUSTICE BLACKMUN join, concurring.

I agree with the substantive standard announced by the Court today, imposing liability when a public-official defendant "knew or should have known" of the constitutionally violative effect of his actions. This standard would not allow the official who *actually knows* that he was violating the law to escape liability for his actions, even if he could not "reasonably have been expected" to know what he actually did know. Thus the clever and unusually well-informed violator of constitutional rights will not evade just punishment for his crimes. I also agree that this standard applies "across the board," to all "government officials performing discretionary functions." I write separately only to note that given this standard, it seems inescapable to me that some measure of discovery may sometimes be required to determine exactly what a public-official defendant did "know" at the time of his actions. In this respect the issue before us is very similar to that addressed in Herbert v. Lando, 441 U.S. 153 (1979), in which the Court observed that "[t]o erect an impenetrable barrier to the plaintiff's use of such evidence on his side of the case is a matter of some substance, particularly when defendants themselves are prone to assert their goo[d f]aith. . . ." Of course, as the Court has already noted, summary judgment will be readily available to public-official defendants whenever the state of the law was so ambiguous at the time of the alleged violation that it could not have been "known" then, and thus liability could not ensue. In my view, summary judgment will also be readily available whenever the plaintiff cannot prove, as a threshold matter, that a violation of his constitutional rights actually occurred. I see no reason why discovery of defendants' "knowledge" should not be deferred by the trial judge pending decision of any motion of defendants for summary judgment on grounds such as these.

[Brennan, White, Marshall, and Blackmun together are credited as authoring the brief statement.]

DISCUSSION AND QUESTIONS

The need for qualified immunity. All members of the Court agreed that some form of qualified immunity was needed for officials performing discretionary functions. Officials performing "ministerial" functions, on the other hand, receive no qualified immunity. Such ministerial functions are usually defined as acts that an official must perform without exercising discretion. For example, in *Groton v. California,* 251 F.3d 844 (9th Cir. 2001), the court found that qualified immunity was not available to officials who refused to provide application papers to a real estate appraiser as mandated by state law. Challenges to ministerial functions are not common in § 1983 litigation.

Consider the competing concerns that underlie the decision whether to recognize some form of qualified immunity. Possible justifications for granting immunity include

- the unfairness of imposing liability on public servants, many of whom receive moderate compensation;
- the unfairness of imposing liability on public servants, like police officers, who must often act in situations where legal parameters are unclear;

- the potential deterrence of lawful, zealous performance of important government activities ("overdeterrence"); and
- the diversion of public monies to litigation expenses, and the diversion of public officials' time and attention to defending a suit.

Possible justifications for denying immunity include

- compensation for the plaintiff's injuries, especially when the government entity employing an official is not responsible for damages;
- vindication of the plaintiff's rights; and
- deterrence of future misconduct.

You can doubtlessly elaborate on these rationales. There is abundant legal commentary on the pros and cons of qualified immunity. *Compare* David Rudovsky, *Running in Place: The Paradox of Expanded Rights and Restricted Remedies,* 25 U. ILL. L. REV. 1199, 1217-26 (2005) (questioning whether current immunity doctrine adequately deters misconduct), *with* John C. Jeffries, *In Praise of the Eleventh Amendment and Section 1983,* 84 VA. L. REV. 49, 73-78 (1998) (arguing that current doctrine avoids undesirable overdeterrence of official behavior).

Some rationales involve largely normative questions. Should persons whose constitutional rights have been violated *always* be compensated for their losses regardless of the external costs to government or the public? Should public officials be held to the same standard of reasonable care to which private citizens are held (e.g., under negligence law)? Does a higher threshold for public official liability send the wrong message about the value society places on constitutional rights?

Some of the rationales, by comparison, ultimately rest on empirical assumptions. Will imposition of liability on offending government employees deter future misconduct? Or will liability result in overdeterrence of legitimate government activity? Will the time and costs diverted to defending a suit have appreciable impact on the operation of government? Further, how often do individual officials actually pay litigation costs and resulting judgments? It has been suggested that government entities or their insurers bear most of the costs of litigation, often based on statutes authorizing indemnification of officials. *See, e.g.,* Martin A. Schwartz, *Should Juries Be Informed that Municipality Will Indemnify Officer's § 1983 Liability for Constitutional Wrongdoing?,* 86 IOWA L. REV. 1209, 1216-19 (2001); Alexandra White Dunahoe, *Revisiting the Cost-Benefit Calculus of the Misbehaving Prosecutor: Deterrence Economics and Transitory Prosecutors,* 61 N.Y.U. ANN. SURVEY AM. LAW 45, 63 (2005) (asserting that indemnification of officials in suits under § 1983 is "near[ly] universal").

Your view of the wisdom of individual immunity might also be influenced by an understanding of *government* liability for constitutional wrongs. We will address government liability in the next section of the chapter. As we will see, government entities can usually avoid liability for the discretionary acts of their employees, particularly "street-level" employees like the patrolling police officer. This means that, for an appreciable number of § 1983 plaintiffs, recovery from the individual official is the only federal remedy they have.

Qualified immunity and private actors. The Court has occasionally considered whether private actors acting under color of state law enjoy qualified immunity. The Court's disparate rulings make it difficult to offer reliable generalizations. At times, the Court has declined to extend the qualified-immunity defense to

EXPLORING DOCTRINE

Assessing the Costs and Benefits of Qualified Immunity

One important factual issue underlying qualified immunity is the relative degree of deterrence (of misconduct) and overdeterrence (of zealous public service) resulting from official liability. Assume you serve as legislative assistant to a member of Congress who would like to actually measure the phenomena of deterrence and overdeterrence. Can you imagine some form of study at the local government level that might provide useful clues about these phenomena? How would you measure deterrence? Overdeterrence? Can they be reliably measured? In light of your attempts to imagine how these phenomena might be studied, do you have confidence that courts and commentators arguing the effects of qualified immunity actually know what these effects really are?

some private actors.[8] But more recently, in *Filarsky v. Delia*, 132 S. Ct. 1657 (2012), the Court extended the qualified-immunity defense to a private attorney retained to help in the investigation of a firefighter. Based on both common-law and policy considerations, the Court held that private attorneys retained to carry out the "public's business" should be permitted to assert a defense of qualified immunity. In so ruling, the Court distinguished prior decisions denying immunity to (1) private individuals using state replevin law for purely private purposes and (2) guards working for a privately run prison facility. *Id.* at 1667. The Court concluded in *Filarsky* that a private attorney retained by local government to aid in a governmental investigation should enjoy an immunity defense given the attorney's supervision by government officials and absence of a private, profit motive.

The Court emphasized that qualified immunity helps avoid "unwarranted timidity in performance of public duties, ensuring that talented candidates are not deterred from public service, and preventing the harmful distractions from carrying out the work of government that can often accompany damages suits." *Id.* at 1665. In contrast, prior decisions denying immunity to private actors often involved defendants "using the mechanisms of government to achieve their own ends," as when private attorneys use state replevin statutes to obtain relief for their clients. *Id.* at 1667.

Qualified immunity and the evolution of constitutional law. In *Marbury v. Madison*, Chief Justice Marshall famously observed, "It is emphatically the province and duty of the judicial department to say what the law is. Those who apply the rule to particular cases, must of necessity expound and interpret that rule." 5 U.S. (7 Cranch) 137, 177 (1813). But does the qualified-immunity standard compromise this duty? Consider the situation where a court concludes that the

8. *See, e.g.*, *Wyatt v. Cole*, 504 U.S. 158 (1992) (denying immunity to a private attorney using the state's replevin statutes); *Richardson v. McKnight*, 521 U.S. 399 (1997) (denying immunity to private prison guards charged with violating prisoners' constitutional rights).

right asserted by the plaintiff is not "clearly established" by existing precedent. The court might dispose of the plaintiff's claim based on qualified immunity and never clarify the meaning of the underlying constitutional right. This could compromise the duty announced in *Marbury*, retard the development of constitutional law, and so fail to give guidance about how officials should act if they confront a similar situation in the future.

Until 2009, the court tried to minimize these consequences by instructing trial courts to first address the constitutional question when ruling on qualified immunity. In *Saucier v. Katz*, 533 U.S. 194, 201 (2001), the Court advised trial courts to follow this procedure:

> A court required to rule upon the qualified immunity issue must consider . . . this threshold question: Taken in the light most favorable to the party asserting the injury, do the facts alleged show the officer's conduct violated a constitutional right? This must be the initial inquiry. In the course of determining whether a constitutional right was violated on the premises alleged, a court might find it necessary to set forth principles which will become the basis for a holding that a right is clearly established. This is the process for the law's elaboration from case to case, and it is one reason for our insisting upon turning to the existence or non-existence of a constitutional right as the first inquiry. The law might be deprived of this explanation were a court simply to skip ahead to the question whether the law clearly established that the officer's conduct was unlawful in the circumstances of the case.

But in *Pearson v. Callahan*, 555 U.S. 223 (2009), the Court held that the procedures outlined in *Saucier* were no longer mandatory. Instead, trial courts may exercise discretion in deciding whether to follow the *Saucier* procedure. *Pearson* thus restores the court's option of first deciding whether the meaning of constitutional law was clearly established when the official acted; if this meaning was not clearly established, the court need not decide whether a constitutional right was violated.[9]

In *Pearson*, the Court mentioned several factors supporting its modification of *Saucier*. These include (1) avoiding unnecessary interpretations of the Constitution; (2) reducing the court's and the parties' investment of resources in a suit; and (3) avoiding "soft" rulings on constitutional issues where the court knows that the actual outcome of the suit will be determined by qualified immunity. The Court also rejected arguments that its new discretionary approach might retard the development of constitutional law. The Court noted that the meaning of the Constitution will still be elaborated in criminal cases, in § 1983 cases against government (which enjoys no qualified immunity), and in § 1983 suits seeking injunctive relief. Further, trial courts still have discretion to address the constitutional issue under *Saucier* and contribute to the development of constitutional precedent.

It remains to be seen whether the discretion trial courts enjoy under *Pearson* will often be exercised to avoid ruling on constitutional issues, and what factors will influence the court's exercise of that discretion. What factors *should* a trial court consider when exercising its discretion under *Pearson*?

9. In other contexts, federal courts lack even the discretion to decide an unsettled issue of federal law. For example, when federal courts review state court proceedings to determine whether to issue a writ of habeas corpus, they may act only if the state court decision "involve[s] an unreasonable application[ ] of clearly established Federal law." 28 U.S.C. § 2254(d)(1).

Applying Harlow's standard of qualified immunity. *Harlow* holds that officials engaged in discretionary activities are immune from damages unless their conduct violates "clearly established statutory or constitutional rights of which a reasonable person would have known." The Court has emphasized that the issue of qualified immunity is a legal issue to be resolved by the court, not the fact-finder. *See Hunter v. Bryant*, 502 U.S. 224, 229 (1991). Can you see why qualified immunity is decided as a matter of law?

Determining whether a legal right is clearly established can be simple or enormously complicated. For example, it is now clear that a police officer may not use deadly force to stop a non-violent, fleeing felon. *See Tennessee v. Garner*, 471 U.S. 1 (1985). But consider one of the central legal questions presented by the Reference Problem concerning youth curfews: Was the Bozeman ordinance implementing curfews clearly unconstitutional at the time the police officers enforced it against Jake Gruden? To assist you in working through this application of the qualified-immunity issue, consider the additional, hypothetical facts provided below.

PROBLEM 9-2

The Constitutionality of Youth Curfews

Jake Gruden's attorney would like to assert a damages claim against the officers who arrested Jake, based on the contention that the ordinance they enforced violated the Constitution. He appreciates that this claim will fly only if he can show the ordinance was "clearly unconstitutional." If he cannot show this, the claim will be dismissed and the officers might even seek sanctions against Jake and his lawyer under Federal Rule of Civil Procedure 11 for filing a claim unsupported by law.

Jake's lawyer knows that the constitutionality of the ordinance was an issue at the city commission meeting where the ordinance was passed. The commission heard from one local civil rights activist that "this ordinance will be struck down in federal court. You are exposing the city to a lawsuit and damages." But the commission also heard from the city attorney, who opined that "I think the cases involving ordinances support what we're doing here."

Assume that there are three reported curfew decisions [In truth, there are many more, but we will ignore them and work with the three cases fabricated for use with this problem.] The first case is *Ramos v. Elmira*, a 2009 decision of the United States Court of Appeals for the Second Circuit. *Ramos* holds (1) that youth curfews raise concerns under the Equal Protection Clause because they restrict youths' freedom of movement; (2) that such curfews are subject to "intermediate scrutiny," meaning the curfews must "substantially" promote "important" government objectives; and (3) that a curfew ordinance that fails to permit responsible parents to authorize their children's presence on public property does not satisfy intermediate scrutiny. (Jake's parents, by the way, approved of his employment at the local Burger King and gave him permission to ride home after work with the older employee.)

The second case is *Hutchins v. Oldtown*, a 2005 decision of the United States Court of Appeals for the District of Columbia Circuit. *Hutchins* held that the "rational basis" test applies to youth curfews, and that test is readily satisfied by a town's interest in banning unsupervised youth from public places during nighttime hours. *Hutchins* was decided by a three-judge panel, and one judge dissented, arguing curfews should be subject to "strict scrutiny."

The third decision is *Hodkins v. Longwood*, a 2013 decision of the United States District Court for the Central District of California. *Hodkins* struck down a town curfew based on the same reasoning used by the court in *Ramos*.

There is no relevant decision from the United States District Court for the District of Montana or from the Ninth Circuit, which encompasses the District of Montana.

Finally, there is one unpublished decision rendered by a Montana state trial judge in 2005. That judge enjoined enforcement of a youth curfew adopted by a town in eastern Montana (Bozeman is in western Montana). The trial judge determined that the state statute authorizing youth curfews in Montana (the one relied on by the City of Bozeman) violates the Montana Constitution.

Should Jake's attorney assert a § 1983 claim for damages against the officers? Or will the claim be dismissed based on qualified immunity?

You likely found, in considering Problem 9-2, that subsidiary questions arose concerning how one determines whether the law is clearly established. For example, which courts' decisions do we look at in determining whether law is established? How on point must precedent be? You may also have wondered whether an official like a police officer can be found liable for violating clearly established law when persons with formal legal training (e.g., the city's attorney) find the law unclear. Let's consider these and similar questions raised by the Reference Problem.

"Following the law." The police officers who arrested Jake arguably had good reason to believe the curfew ordinance was valid, or at least not clearly invalid. After all, the town's legislative body enacted the ordinance, apparently with the support of legal counsel. Can't officers reasonably assume enacted law is valid? Or must they second-guess other officials with greater legal expertise?

Courts appear willing to consider the fact that an official has relied on the presumed validity of a law in determining qualified immunity, but such reliance is not conclusive. The defense of "just following the law" may constitute an "extraordinary circumstance" that, under *Harlow*, exonerates an official, even when the law is clearly invalid. *See Harlow*, 457 U.S. at 819 ("If the official pleading the defense claims extraordinary circumstances and can prove that he neither knew nor should have known of the relevant legal standard, the defense should be sustained."). *See* Karen M. Blum, *Qualified Immunity, Discretionary Function, Extraordinary Circumstances, and Other Nuances*, 27 TOURO L. REV. 57, 69 (2007). But following the law does not automatically exonerate the official. Similarly, reliance on the advice of legal counsel can greatly assist an official asserting qualified immunity, but it is not a determinative factor. *See id.* at 67-68. This was brought home by the Court's decision in *Groh v. Ramirez*, 540 U.S. 551 (2004), where the Court denied immunity to an officer who executed a search warrant signed by a magistrate. Because the officer prepared a warrant that "plainly" failed to satisfy constitutional requirements (apparently due to the officer's oversight), he could not rely on the magistrate's approval of the warrant. *Id.* at 563-64.

What legal precedent determines whether law is clearly established? One of the challenges faced by first-year law students is determining what "the law" is. This challenge requires that students distinguish facts of similar cases, distinguish holdings from dicta, and know the hierarchy of courts in establishing binding precedent. A similar challenge is faced by the non-lawyer official who must be aware of clearly established law.

The rulings of the Supreme Court, as well as those of the federal circuit in which the challenged conduct occurred, are sufficient to establish the applicable federal law. But beyond that generalization, it is unclear which courts' precedent an official must know and follow.[10] For example, the Eleventh Circuit has concluded that law is clearly established within that circuit only by decisions of the Supreme Court, the Eleventh Circuit itself, or "the highest court of the pertinent state." *See Marsh v. Butler Cnty.*, 268 F.3d 1014, 1032 n.10 (11th Cir. 2001). The Sixth Circuit, on the other hand, does not require legal precedent directly binding in that circuit. *See Durham v. Nu'Man*, 97 F.3d 862, 866 (6th Cir. 1996). The Supreme Court has not committed itself on this issue, although the Court has suggested that a "consensus of persuasive authority" might clearly establish precedent. *See Wilson v. Layne*, 526 U.S. 603, 617 (1999).

Recall that hypothetical precedent in Problem 9-1 includes two conflicting circuit court decisions, neither of which is binding on federal courts in Montana. The only other federal precedent assessing the validity of curfews comes from a district court in California. Can Jake argue that this precedent constitutes a "consensus of persuasive authority"? There is, of course, the unpublished decision by a state trial court in Montana. But that decision construes Montana state law. The Court has indicated that it is *federal* law that must be clearly established. *See Davis v. Scherer*, 468 U.S. 183 (1984).

The difficulties that can arise when determining whether precedent is clearly established were brought home in *Hope v. Pelzer*, 536 U.S. 730 (2002). In *Hope*, a majority of the Court concluded the unconstitutionality of the officials' conduct was clearly established despite the fact that three dissenting justices found existing precedent "ambiguous."

How specific must legal precedent be? The legal issue we considered in Problem 9-1 can be stated fairly precisely: Does a curfew ordinance prohibiting a minor's presence on public property despite parental consent violate the Constitution? Jake's lawyer would need to identify legal precedent that speaks to that well-defined issue, or at least precedent that is highly analogous, when researching whether the police officers violated a "clearly established" right.

But recall that Jake seeks to assert several claims in his suit. The law underlying *each* legal claim in Jake's suit must be clearly established or that claim is subject to dismissal. In other words, immunity analysis is claim-specific. A defendant may be sued for damages respecting some violations of rights while enjoying immunity for other violations.

Several important constitutional rights are clearly established and easily summarized in a legal proposition, but their application is highly dependent on the facts. Consider, for example, the Fourth Amendment's prohibition of warrantless searches unless an officer can show both "probable cause" and "exigent circumstances." Any competent officer must be aware of this legal rule at his

10. *See generally*, Martin A. Schwartz, Section 1983 Litigation Claims and Defenses § 9A.09 (2014).

peril. But awareness of established Fourth Amendment law does not necessarily entail that it will be clear to an officer that he lacks "probable cause" or "exigent circumstances" at the time he conducts a warrantless search. *See generally* John E. Taylor, *Using Suppression Hearing Testimony to Prove Good Faith Under* United States v. Leon, 54 U. KAN. L. REV. 155 (2005). The question arises: How does qualified immunity apply when the application of a clear legal standard is highly *fact specific?*

The Court's answer to that question came in its 1987 decision in *Anderson v. Creighton,* excerpted below. *Anderson* discusses the qualified-immunity defense pertaining to federal officials sued in *Bivens* actions. We will consider *Bivens* actions later in the chapter, but for now simply be aware that the qualified-immunity standard applicable to such actions is the same as that applicable to claims under § 1983. In addition to elaborating on qualified immunity, *Anderson* also affirms important procedural law governing the trial court's determination of qualified immunity. Consider how *Anderson* affects the burden of a plaintiff who seeks to overcome the qualified-immunity defense.

ANDERSON v. CREIGHTON

483 U.S. 536 (1987)

JUSTICE SCALIA delivered the opinion of the Court.

The question presented is whether a federal law enforcement officer who participates in a search that violates the Fourth Amendment may be held personally liable for money damages if a reasonable officer could have believed that the search comported with the Fourth Amendment.

I

Petitioner Russell Anderson is an agent of the Federal Bureau of Investigation. On November 11, 1983, Anderson and other state and federal law enforcement officers conducted a warrantless search of the home of respondents, the Creighton family. The search was conducted because Anderson believed that Vadaain Dixon, a man suspected of a bank robbery committed earlier that day, might be found there. He was not.

The Creightons later filed suit against Anderson in a Minnesota state court, asserting among other things a claim for money damages under the Fourth Amendment. After removing the suit to Federal District Court, Anderson filed a motion to dismiss or for summary judgment, arguing that the *Bivens* claim was barred by Anderson's qualified immunity from civil damages liability. *See* Harlow v. Fitzgerald, 457 U.S. 800 (1982). Before any discovery took place, the District Court granted summary judgment on the ground that the search was lawful, holding that the undisputed facts revealed that Anderson had had probable cause to search the Creighton's home and that his failure to obtain a warrant was justified by the presence of exigent circumstances.

The Creightons appealed to the Court of Appeals for the Eighth Circuit, which reversed. The Court of Appeals held that the issue of the lawfulness of the search could not properly be decided on summary judgment, because unresolved factual disputes made it impossible to determine as a matter of law that the warrantless search had been supported by probable cause and exigent circumstances. The Court of Appeals also held that Anderson was not entitled to summary judgment on qualified immunity grounds, since the right Anderson was alleged to have violated — the right of persons to be protected from warrantless searches of their home unless the searching officers have probable cause and there are exigent circumstances — was clearly established.

* * * *

II

When government officials abuse their offices, "action[s] for damages may offer the only realistic avenue for vindication of constitutional guarantees." On the other hand, permitting damages suits against government officials can entail substantial social costs, including the risk that fear of personal monetary liability and harassing litigation will unduly inhibit officials in the discharge of their duties. Our cases have accommodated these conflicting concerns by generally providing government officials performing discretionary functions with a qualified immunity, shielding them from civil damages liability as long as their actions could reasonably have been thought consistent with the rights they are alleged to have violated. Somewhat more concretely, whether an official protected by qualified immunity may be held personally liable for an allegedly unlawful official action generally turns on the " objective legal reasonableness" of the action assessed in light of the legal rules that were "clearly established" at the time it was taken.

The operation of this standard, however, depends substantially upon the level of generality at which the relevant "legal rule" is to be identified. For example, the right to due process of law is quite clearly established by the Due Process Clause, and thus there is a sense in which any action that violates that Clause (no matter how unclear it may be that the particular action is a violation) violates a clearly established right. Much the same could be said of any other constitutional or statutory violation. But if the test of "clearly established law" were to be applied at this level of generality, it would bear no relationship to the "objective legal reasonableness" that is the touchstone of *Harlow*. Plaintiffs would be able to convert the rule of qualified immunity that our cases plainly establish into a rule of virtually unqualified liability simply by alleging violation of extremely abstract rights. *Harlow* would be transformed from a guarantee of immunity into a rule of pleading. Such an approach, in sum, would destroy "the balance that our cases strike between the interests in vindication of citizens' constitutional rights and in public officials' effective performance of their duties," by making it impossible for officials "reasonably [to] anticipate when their conduct may give rise to liability for damages." It should not be surprising, therefore, that our cases establish that the right the official is alleged to have violated must have been "clearly established" in a more particularized, and hence more relevant, sense: The contours of the right must be sufficiently clear that a reasonable official would understand that what he is doing violates that right. This is not to say that an official action is protected by qualified immunity unless the very action in question has previously been held unlawful, but it is to say that in the light of pre-existing law the unlawfulness must be apparent.[11]

Anderson contends that the Court of Appeals misapplied these principles. We agree. The Court of Appeals' brief discussion of qualified immunity consisted of little more than an assertion that a general right Anderson was alleged to have violated — the right to be free from warrantless searches of one's home unless the searching officers have probable cause and there are exigent circumstances — was clearly established. The Court of Appeals specifically refused to consider the argument that it was *not* clearly established that the circumstances with which Anderson was confronted did not constitute probable cause and exigent circumstances. The previous discussion should make clear that this refusal was erroneous. It simply does not follow immediately from the conclusion that it was firmly established that warrantless searches not supported by probable cause and exigent circumstances violate the Fourth Amendment that Anderson's search was objectively legally unreasonable. We have recognized that it is inevitable that law enforcement officials will in some cases reasonably but mistakenly conclude that probable cause is present, and we have indicated that in such cases those officials — like other officials who act in ways they reasonably believe to be lawful — should not be held personally liable. The same is true of their conclusions regarding exigent circumstances.

It follows from what we have said that the determination whether it was objectively legally reasonable to conclude that a given search was supported by probable cause or exigent circumstances will often require examination of the information possessed by the searching officials. But contrary to the Creightons' assertion, this does not reintroduce into qualified immunity analysis the inquiry into officials' subjective intent that *Harlow* sought to minimize. The relevant question in this case, for example, is the objective (albeit fact-specific) question whether a reasonable officer could have believed Anderson's warrantless search to be lawful, in light of clearly established law and the information the searching officers possessed. Anderson's subjective beliefs about the search are irrelevant.

The principles of qualified immunity that we reaffirm today require that Anderson be permitted to argue that he is entitled to summary judgment on the ground that, in light of the clearly established principles governing warrantless searches, he could, as a matter of law, reasonably have believed that the search of the Creightons' home was lawful.

* * * *

The general rule of qualified immunity is intended to provide government officials with the ability "reasonably [to] anticipate when their conduct may give rise to liability for damages." Where that rule is applicable, officials can know

11. [Footnote 5 in Court's opinion.] The dissent, which seemingly would adopt this approach, seeks to avoid the unqualified liability that would follow by advancing the suggestion that officials generally (though not law enforcement officials and officials accused of violating the Fourth Amendment) be permitted to raise a defense of reasonable good faith, which apparently could be asserted and proved only at trial. But even when so modified (and even for the fortunate officials to whom the modification applies) the approach would totally abandon the concern — which was the driving force behind *Harlow*'s substantial reformulation of qualified-immunity principles — that "insubstantial claims" against government officials be resolved prior to discovery and on summary judgment if possible. A passably clever plaintiff would always be able to identify an abstract clearly established right that the defendant could be alleged to have violated, and the good-faith defense envisioned by the dissent would be available only at trial.

that they will not be held personally liable as long as their actions are reasonable in light of current American law. That security would be utterly defeated if officials were unable to determine whether they were protected by the rule without entangling themselves in the vagaries of the English and American common law. We are unwilling to Balkanize the rule of qualified immunity by carving exceptions at the level of detail the Creightons propose. We therefore decline to make an exception to the general rule of qualified immunity for cases involving allegedly unlawful warrantless searches of innocent third parties' homes in search of fugitives.[12]

JUSTICE STEVENS, with whom JUSTICE BRENNAN and JUSTICE MARSHALL join, dissenting.

This case is beguiling in its apparent simplicity. The Court accordingly represents its task as the clarification of the settled principles of qualified immunity that apply in damages suits brought against federal officials. Its opinion, however, announces a new rule of law that protects federal agents who make forcible nighttime entries into the homes of innocent citizens without probable cause, without a warrant, and without any valid emergency justification for their warrantless search. The Court stunningly restricts the constitutional accountability of the police by creating a false dichotomy between police entitlement to summary judgment on immunity grounds and damages liability for every police misstep, by responding to this dichotomy with an uncritical application of the precedents of qualified immunity that we have developed for a quite different group of high public office holders, and by displaying remarkably little fidelity to the countervailing principles of individual liberty and privacy that infuse the Fourth Amendment.

* * * *

The effect of the Court's (literally unwarranted) extension of qualified immunity, I fear, is that it allows federal agents to ignore the limitations of the probable-cause and warrant requirements with impunity. The Court does so in the name of avoiding interference with legitimate law enforcement activities even though the probable-cause requirement, which limits the police's exercise of coercive authority, is itself a form of immunity that frees them to exercise that power without fear of strict liability.

The warrant requirement safeguards this bedrock principle of the Fourth Amendment, while the immunity bestowed on a police officer who acts with probable cause permits him to do his job free of constant fear of monetary liability. The Court rests its doctrinally flawed opinion upon a double standard

12. [Footnote 6 in Court's opinion.] Noting that no discovery has yet taken place, the Creightons renew their argument that, whatever the appropriate qualified immunity standard, some discovery would be required before Anderson's summary judgment motion could be granted. We think the matter somewhat more complicated. One of the purposes of the *Harlow* qualified immunity standard is to protect public officials from the "broad-ranging discovery" that can be "peculiarly disruptive of effective government." For this reason, we have emphasized that qualified immunity questions should be resolved at the earliest possible stage of a litigation. Thus, on remand, it should first be determined whether the actions the Creightons allege Anderson to have taken are actions that a reasonable officer could have believed lawful. If they are, then Anderson is entitled to dismissal prior to discovery. If they are not, and if the actions Anderson claims he took are different from those the Creightons allege (and are actions that a reasonable officer could have believed lawful), then discovery may be necessary before Anderson's motion for summary judgment on qualified immunity grounds can be resolved. Of course, any such discovery should be tailored specifically to the question of Anderson's qualified immunity.

of reasonableness which unjustifiably and unnecessarily upsets the delicate balance between respect for individual privacy and protection of the public servants who enforce our laws.

* * * *

DISCUSSION AND QUESTIONS

Reconsidering what constitutes clearly established law. Anderson refines qualified immunity by requiring that a plaintiff show (1) that a constitutional right is clearly established, and (2) that the individual defendant should have known "what he is doing violates that right." Consequently, qualified immunity often becomes a very particularized inquiry into legal precedent. Again, the task is similar to that faced by first-year law students attempting to analogize to or distinguish legal precedent.

Looking at this standard of qualified immunity from the *defendant's* perspective, do you think it fair or sensible to require that non-lawyer officials develop the ability to interpret case law and draw conclusions about its application? Has the Court forgotten the concern expressed by Justice Powell in *Wood v. Strickland,* that government employees should not be expected to make themselves into "constitutional law scholars"? Of course, *Anderson* might send a message to government entities that they must educate their employees—presumably with instruction by legal counsel—about how constitutional law applies to their conduct. But if this is one of the messages, should officials be liable for constitutional wrongs when government itself has failed to fulfill its educational responsibility? Later, we will see how the Court has addressed government's responsibility by recognizing liability for failure to train. See *infra* pp.____. This form of government liability, however, complements rather than substitutes for individual liability.

Looking at qualified immunity from the *plaintiff's* perspective, do you think *Anderson* too easily exonerates individual defendants? As Justice Stevens's dissent emphasizes, defendants already enjoy substantial protection under the "reasonableness" standard that governs searches under the Fourth Amendment. The majority's interpretation of qualified immunity makes it doubly difficult for the victim of constitutional wrongdoing to recover. Not only must the victim prove the officer's search was unreasonable given the circumstances, the victim must show that this unreasonableness was clear under existing legal precedent. Has the Court diminished the protections afforded by the Fourth Amendment and erred on the side of government?

Whether *Anderson*'s refined standard of qualified immunity sets too high a hurdle for plaintiffs depends in part on how fastidious courts are in demanding analogous precedent. The Court has emphasized that a plaintiff need not show that "the very action in question has previously been held unlawful." *Wilson v. Layne,* 526 U.S. 603, 615 (1999). As the Court has commented, "a general constitutional rule already identified in the decisional law may apply with obvious clarity to the specific conduct in question" even when no court has previously applied the rule to similar facts." *See United States v. Lanier,* 520 U.S. 259 (1997). But such "obvious clarity" may be limited to more egregious examples of misconduct. *Lanier,* for example, involved a state court judge who allegedly committed sexual assault on court employees. And a more recent

Court decision denying qualified immunity to prison guards involved handcuffing a prisoner to a hitching post for seven hours without regular water or bathroom breaks. *See Hope v. Pelzer*, 536 U.S. 730 (2002).

Numerous constitutional rights are defined in broad terms whose application turns on highly specific facts. Many arise during encounters with law enforcement, both before and after incarceration. In addition to the Fourth Amendment right against unreasonable searches and seizures at issue in *Anderson*, are (1) the right not to be subjected to "excessive force" by police officers; (2) the right not to be subjected to "cruel or unusual punishment" by prison officials; (3) the right not to be subjected to violence by fellow inmates; and (4) the right to receive attention to basic sanitary and medical needs while incarcerated. *See generally* DAVID W. LEE, HANDBOOK OF SECTION 1983 LITIGATION ch 2 (2013 ed.).

Still other situational rights arise in settings not involving law enforcement. Examples include (1) regulation of the speech of public employees, *see Pickering v. Board of Educ.*, 391 U.S. 563 (1968); (2) regulation of the speech of public school students, *see Tinker v. Des Moines Indep. Sch. Dist.*, 393 U.S. 503 (1969); and (3) decisions regarding academic performance and discipline by public universities, *see Regents of Univ. of Mich. v. Ewing*, 474 U.S. 214 (1985).

Recent Court decisions illustrate the challenges faced by plaintiffs seeking to find precedent sufficiently analogous to clearly establish governing law:

- In *Safford Unified School District No. 1 v. Redding*, 557 U.S. 364 (2009), the Court held that a school official's search of a student's underwear to detect prescription-strength ibuprofen and naproxen violated her Fourth Amendment rights, but also held that precedent failed to clearly establish that this particular search was "unreasonable."
- In *Stanton v. Sims*, 134 S. Ct. 3 (2013), the Court granted immunity to a police officer who entered the plaintiff's home, without a warrant, in hot pursuit of a person suspected of having committed a jailable misdemeanor offense. The Court noted that "federal and state courts nationwide are sharply divided on the question whether an officer with probable cause to arrest a suspect for a misdemeanor may enter a home without a warrant while in hot pursuit of that suspect." *Id.* at 5. The Court also relied on (1) lower state court decisions that had affirmed the lawfulness of the officer's entry and (2) federal district court decisions in California finding that the unlawfulness of the entry was not clearly established.
- In *Wood v. Moss*, 134 S. Ct. 2056 (2014), a unanimous Supreme Court granted qualified immunity to two Secret Service officials who allegedly interfered with the activity of persons protesting President George W. Bush based on antipathy toward the protestors' viewpoint. Not surprisingly, the Court found no precedent establishing that Secret Service agents must supervise persons in the vicinity of the President in a way that ensures that all are treated equally regardless of their differing viewpoints.
- In *Lane v. Franks*, 134 S. Ct. 2369 (2014), the Court held that "the First Amendment protects a public employee from retaliation when he provides truthful sworn testimony, compelled by subpoena, outside the scope of his ordinary job responsibilities. *Id.* at 2378. But the Court granted qualified immunity to the public employer because neither controlling circuit court precedent nor Court precedent established that retaliation under such circumstances violated the First Amendment. *Id.* at 2381-83.

- Finally, in *Plumhoff v. Rickard,* 134 S. Ct. 2012 (2014), the Court held that police officers engaged in a high-speed chase who fired 15 shots at the fleeing suspect's car were entitled to qualified immunity. At the time the officers acted (July 2004), earlier Court precedent did not "clearly establish[] that it was unconstitutional to shoot a fleeing driver to protect those whom his flight might endanger." *Id.* at 2023. And the plaintiffs could neither distinguish that earlier precedent nor point to "a controlling case or a robust consensus of cases" that had altered precedent in the interim. *Id.* at 2024.

In Problem 9-3, below, we examine how qualified immunity might apply to one of Jake Gruden's claims against his jail keepers. Before we do, let's examine more fully the procedures through which immunity issues are resolved.

Pleading and proving qualified immunity. The qualified immunity enjoyed by individual defendants has been described as immunity from "suit," not merely immunity from damages. Qualified immunity is intended to spare officials the cost and distraction of the litigation process itself. *Anderson* admonishes trial courts to make immunity decisions as soon as possible during litigation, prior to discovery if possible, otherwise on motion for summary judgment after limited discovery "tailored specifically to the question . . . of qualified immunity."

Qualified immunity is an affirmative defense that officials must plead. *Gomez v. Toledo,* 446 U.S. 635 (1980). But the plaintiff's complaint remains highly relevant to assessing qualified immunity in many cases. According to *Anderson,* a defendant may ask that the court dismiss a claim if, based on the facts and legal rights alleged by the plaintiff in her complaint, a violation of federal law is not clearly established. The motion to dismiss by definition assumes that the facts alleged by the plaintiff are true. *See* Fed. R. Civ. P. 12(b)(6). Federal circuit courts have repeatedly asserted that it is the *plaintiff's* obligation to allege the existence of a clearly established federal right. *See generally* Lee, *supra,* §7.03[B][2].

If the plaintiff has alleged a clearly established violation of federal law, the defendant official can then challenge the truth of the complaint's factual allegations through a motion for summary judgment. When using summary judgment to resolve the qualified-immunity issue, the defendant attempts to show that "indisputable" facts demonstrate that the legal violation alleged by the plaintiff was not clearly established at the time the defendant acted. A defendant's summary judgment motion may, or may not, require discovery. According to *Crawford-El v. Britton,* 523 U.S. 574 (1998), the trial court should tailor discovery to exploration of the qualified-immunity defense. The immunity issue presents a question of law that "ordinarily should be decided by the court long before trial." *Hunter v. Bryant,* 502 U.S. 224, 228 (1991).

The Court has recently emphasized that a trial court's ruling on a qualified-immunity defense does not alter application of the summary judgment standard found in Federal Rule of Civil Procedure 56. In *Tolan v. Cotton,* 134 S. Ct. 1861 (2014), the Court emphasized that a ruling on summary judgment requires that all inferences be drawn in favor of the nonmovant-plaintiff "even when a court decides only the clearly-established prong" of the qualified-immunity standard. *Id.* at 1866. In *Tolan,* the Court reversed a summary judgment based on the trial court's improper weighing of the evidence and its failure to construe evidence most favorably to the nonmovant-plaintiff. *See also Ortiz v. Jordan,* 131 S. Ct. 884

(2011) (holding that interlocutory appellate review is not available when a trial court denies qualified immunity before trial based solely on the existence of underlying factual issues).

If the trial court rejects a qualified-immunity defense as a matter of law, the defendant has the option of filing an interlocutory appeal in federal circuit court. In *Ashcroft v. Iqbal*, 129 S. Ct. 1937 (2009), the Court authorized interlocutory appeal of a district court's decision denying the defendant's motion to dismiss a complaint for failure to state a claim. The district court denied the defendant's motion to dismiss based on its conclusion that the complaint sufficiently alleged a "clearly established" violation of federal law. The Court reasoned that such a non-final order comes within the "collateral order" doctrine permitting interlocutory review because it turns on an "issue of law." *Id.* at 1945-46. Although *Ashcroft* concerns the immunity of federal officials, its holding applies equally to suits against state officials under § 1983.

At times, a defendant may be permitted to file *two* interlocutory appeals concerning qualified immunity—one after losing a motion to dismiss for failure to state a claim and, if the case continues, another after losing a motion for summary judgment. *See Behrens v. Pelletier*, 516 U.S. 299 (1996). But if the immunity defense is denied based on the existence of unresolved factual issues central to the defense, interlocutory review will not be permitted. *See id.* at 312-13.

PROBLEM 9-3

Qualified Immunity and Fact-Intensive Claims

Consider again the Reference Problem, this time focusing on Jake Gruden's treatment while in jail. Recall that Jake believes his constitutional rights were violated when jail guards failed to notice he was experiencing a diabetic reaction. Also recall that Jake was wearing an arm bracelet stating he was a diabetic. As a consequence of the guards' failure, Jake suffered diabetic ketoacidosis, requiring hospitalization.

You may assume that it is clearly established that a person in custody has the right not to have serious medical needs ignored through the "deliberate indifference" of his custodians. The claim has both objective and subjective aspects. First, a plaintiff must present evidence showing that his condition posed "a substantial risk of serious harm." *See, e.g., Estelle v. Gamble*, 429 U.S. 97 (1976) (discussing the deliberate-indifference standard applicable to inmates under the Eighth Amendment).

Second, a claim of deliberate indifference requires that the defendant "knew of and disregarded a substantial risk of serious harm to [the plaintiff's] health and safety." *Id.* That is, the plaintiff must show that the defendant was "aware of facts from which the inference could be drawn that a substantial risk of serious harm exist[ed] and must actually draw the inference." *See Farmer v. Brennan*, 511 U.S. 825, 837 (1994). The Ninth Circuit, which embraces Montana, has held that a defendant's subjective awareness can be proved by circumstantial evidence, that is, a jury can infer subjective awareness. *See Lemire v. California Dep't of Corr. & Rehab.*, 726 F.3d 1062, 1078 (9th Cir. 2013).

Attorneys for the parties have researched the cases addressing deliberate indifference. The most analogous case anyone can find comes from the Sixth Circuit. In *Garretson v. City of Madison Heights*, 407 F.3d 789 (6th Cir. 2005), the court rejected a qualified-immunity defense when the jail guards were informed that the plaintiff was insulin dependent and yet permitted her to suffer symptoms of insulin deprivation, including diabetic ketoacidosis. At the same time, jail officials who were not informed of her insulin dependence were granted immunity. *Id.* at 797.

Assume that, during an internal police investigation open to the public, guard Sylvester testified that he "can't recall exactly whether he noticed the diabetes bracelet." As he recalled, Jake seemed to be acting "a little drunk like some of the other kids arrested with him." The guard's supervisor, Shenk, testified that he was "unaware of the young man's diabetic condition," although he did notice at one point that Jake appeared a little confused and "shaky." Both guards have been sued.

Discuss whether one or both guards have a viable defense of qualified immunity based on the information presented. How would the defense best be asserted? If you need additional information to answer the question, indicate what information you would want.

REVIEW AND CONSOLIDATION

Asserting the Defense of Qualified Immunity

The qualified-immunity defense affords individual defendants numerous opportunities to challenge claims for monetary relief. They include

- Challenging the sufficiency of the complaint for failure to allege the *violation* of a federal right
- Challenging the sufficiency of the complaint for failure to allege the violation of a *clearly established* right
- Seeking to limit discovery to inquiries directly relevant to the existence of qualified immunity
- Seeking summary judgment by arguing that undisputed facts fail to show either that the conduct violated a federal right, or that the violation was clearly established.
- Seeking interlocutory review of any decision denying the qualified immunity defense
- Requesting specific jury findings on those facts relevant to the qualified immunity defense, and seeking judgment as a matter of law if those findings fail to show the violation of a clearly established federal right

Concluding notes on qualified immunity. Problem 9-3 illustrates one important variation on the qualified-immunity defense. It is often said that qualified immunity poses an objective legal question concerning whether "a reasonable official" could have believed his conduct lawful. In many cases, qualified immunity insulates a particular defendant from discovery concerning his actual motives and beliefs. As the Court has commented, "evidence concerning the defendant's subjective intent is simply irrelevant to the . . . defense." *Crawford-El v. Britton*, 523 U.S. 574, 588 (1998).

But as demonstrated in Problem 9-3, the *nature* of the constitutional violation may necessitate inquiry into a defendant's subjective thinking at the time he acted. The deliberate-indifference standard, for example, requires inquiry into the facts known by the defendant and the inferences he drew from those facts. The qualified-immunity issue cannot be resolved by a purely objective inquiry into what a reasonable official might have thought.

Still other constitutional rights may require investigation into the defendant's subjective beliefs and motive. For example, claims of intentional discrimination or retaliation hinge on the defendant's motive. *See, e.g., Scott v. Churchill*, 377 F.3d 565 (6th Cir. 2004) (alleged retaliatory action of prison guard in response to prisoner's exercise of First Amendment rights). Even when constitutional claims based on knowledge and motive are asserted, however, courts often scrutinize the claims more closely when qualified immunity is raised. Consequently, courts may demand more specific allegations of wrongful motive in the plaintiff's complaint, and they may insist that the plaintiff produce specific evidence of motive in order to survive summary judgment. *See, e.g., id.* at 572 (summary judgment denied where plaintiff produced specific evidence of retaliatory motive); *Hicks v. City of Watonga*, 942 F.2d 737, 742 (10th Cir. 1991) (conclusory allegations were insufficient to withstand a motion for summary judgment).

Finally, the qualified-immunity doctrine insulates individual defendants from *damages* claims. Courts have rejected the argument that qualified immunity is a valid defense to claims for injunctive relief. *See, e.g., Kikumura v. Hurley*, 242 F.3d. 950, 962-63 (10th Cir. 2001); *Williams v. Klien*, 2014 WL 716982, at *3 (D. Colo. Feb. 24, 2014). In explaining why government officials do not need qualified immunity to insulate them from suits for injunctive relief, one court has observed, "[W]hile government officials might experience frustration and annoyance, it is unlikely that the possibility of injunctions will deter officials from the decisive exercise of their duties. Similarly, we doubt that anyone would avoid public service because he or she might be subject to an injunction affecting the exercise of the authority of a public office." *American Fire, Theft, & Collision Managers, Inc. v. Gillespie*, 932 F.2d 816, 818 (9th Cir. 1991).

The qualified-immunity defense often poses a substantial hurdle to plaintiffs seeking to recover damages from government officials. As the Court observed in *Malley v. Briggs*, qualified immunity protects "all but the plainly incompetent or those who knowingly violate the law." 475 U.S. 335, 341 (1986). Plaintiffs who sue officials who are neither "incompetent" nor willful violators of federal law must obtain relief from the government entity itself if they are to obtain relief at all. We will soon consider the viability of damages actions against government entities. Before we do, we consider a form of immunity available to certain government officials that is even more preemptory of litigation—absolute immunity.

3. *Under What Circumstances Are Individuals Sued Under Section 1983 Absolutely Immune from Suit?*

Qualified immunity extends broadly to most discretionary activities of government officials. Immunity does not turn on the type of activity performed by the official; rather, it turns on whether the official should have known the activity violated established federal law.

Absolute immunity does not hinge on the state of federal law or the official's constructive knowledge of that law. Instead, it carves out a sphere of activity where the official can, more or less, act without regard for whether she is violating the law. Obviously such immunity cannot be extended broadly to government officials in a representative democracy without risk to the rule of law. Consequently, the Court has observed that the "presumption is that qualified immunity rather than absolute immunity is sufficient to protect government officials in the exercise of their duties." *Burns v. Reed,* 500 U.S. 478, 486-87 (1991). Yet the common law has long recognized that certain government functions require absolute immunity from liability if government officials are to fulfill their obligations adequately. It is this common-law tradition that has shaped the Supreme Court's fashioning of absolute immunity from suit under § 1983.

In this section we briefly address three government functions where absolute immunity has greatest impact on claims under § 1983. These functions are (1) the legislative function; (2) the judicial function; and (3) the prosecutorial function.

The legislative function. The broadest form of absolute immunity is extended to persons performing legislative functions. Legislators are immune from *both* damages and equitable relief. Immunity from equitable relief, we will see, is highly uncommon.

The Constitution grants absolute immunity to members of Congress in its "Speech or Debate Clause." *See* U.S. Const. art. I, § 6. The Court has extended similar protection to members of state legislatures. *See, e.g., Tenney v. Brandhove,* 341 U.S. 367 (1951). This immunity means that legislators performing "legislative" tasks are immune from suit for those activities.

In 1998, the Supreme Court had the opportunity to explain whether legislative immunity was also available to local government legislators. The Court's unanimous decision in *Bogan v. Scott-Harris* affirms that legislative immunity extends to local government and elaborates on the rationale for that immunity.

BOGAN v. SCOTT-HARRIS

523 U.S. 44 (1998)

[Respondent Scott-Harris was administrator of the Department of Health and Human Services for the City of Fall River, Massachusetts. Scott-Harris filed a complaint against a department employee, alleging she had made racial and ethnic slurs against her colleagues. The accused employee then used her political connections to mitigate punishment by the town council. Her punishment was further reduced by Mayor Bogan. While the employee's complaint was pending, Mayor Bogan proposed a city budget eliminating Scott-Harris's department. The budget was approved by the town council by a 6-2 vote, including the vote of one city council member, Roderick, who was apparently connected to the disciplined employee. Scott-Harris subsequently sued the city, Mayor Bogan, council member Roderick, and other city officials under § 1983. She alleged that her department was eliminated because of the defendants' racial prejudice and in retaliation for the disciplinary action she initiated against the employee. A jury ultimately awarded Scott-Harris damages against the city, Bogan, and Roderick based on its finding they acted in retaliation for her assertion of

First Amendment rights. The Court of Appeals affirmed the verdict against Bogan and Roderick, although the court recognized that officials engaged in "legislative" activities enjoy absolute immunity. The court held that the officials were engaged in "administrative," not legislative activities, when they retaliated against Scott-Harris because they "relied on facts relating to a particular individual [respondent] in the decisionmaking calculus."]

JUSTICE THOMAS delivered the opinion of the Court.

It is well established that federal, state, and regional legislators are entitled to absolute immunity from civil liability for their legislative activities. In this case, petitioners argue that they, as local officials performing legislative functions, are entitled to the same protection. They further argue that their acts of introducing, voting for, and signing an ordinance eliminating the government office held by respondent constituted legislative activities. We agree on both counts and therefore reverse the judgment below.

* * * *

The principle that legislators are absolutely immune from liability for their legislative activities has long been recognized in Anglo-American law. This privilege "has taproots in the Parliamentary struggles of the Sixteenth and Seventeenth Centuries" and was "taken as a matter of course by those who severed the Colonies from the Crown and founded our Nation." The Federal Constitution, the Constitutions of many of the newly independent States, and the common law thus protected legislators from liability for their legislative activities.

Recognizing this venerable tradition, we have held that state and regional legislators are entitled to absolute immunity from liability under § 1983 for their legislative activities. We explained that legislators were entitled to absolute immunity from suit at common law and that Congress did not intend the general language of § 1983 to "impinge on a tradition so well grounded in history and reason." Because the common law accorded local legislators the same absolute immunity it accorded legislators at other levels of government, and because the rationales for such immunity are fully applicable to local legislators, we now hold that local legislators are likewise absolutely immune from suit under § 1983 for their legislative activities.

* * * *

Absolute immunity for local legislators under § 1983 finds support not only in history, but also in reason. The rationales for according absolute immunity to federal, state, and regional legislators apply with equal force to local legislators. Regardless of the level of government, the exercise of legislative discretion should not be inhibited by judicial interference or distorted by the fear of personal liability. Furthermore, the time and energy required to defend against a lawsuit are of particular concern at the local level, where the part-time citizen-legislator remains commonplace. And the threat of liability may significantly deter service in local government, where prestige and pecuniary rewards may pale in comparison to the threat of civil liability.

Moreover, certain deterrents to legislative abuse may be greater at the local level than at other levels of government. Municipalities themselves can be held liable for constitutional violations, whereas States and the Federal Government are often protected by sovereign immunity. And, of course, the ultimate check on legislative abuse—the electoral process—applies with equal force at the local level, where legislators are often more closely responsible to the electorate.

Absolute legislative immunity attaches to all actions taken "in the sphere of legitimate legislative activity." The Court of Appeals held that petitioners' conduct in this case was not legislative because their actions were specifically targeted at respondent. Relying on the jury's finding that respondent's constitutionally protected speech was a substantial or motivating factor behind petitioners' conduct, the court concluded that petitioners necessarily "relied on facts relating to a particular individual" and "devised an ordinance that targeted [respondent] and treated her differently from other managers employed by the City." Although the Court of Appeals did not suggest that intent or motive can overcome an immunity defense for activities that are, in fact, legislative, the court erroneously relied on petitioners' subjective intent in resolving the logically prior question of whether their acts were legislative.

Whether an act is legislative turns on the nature of the act, rather than on the motive or intent of the official performing it. The privilege of absolute immunity "would be of little value if [legislators] could be subjected to the cost and inconvenience and distractions of a trial upon a conclusion of the pleader, or to the hazard of a judgment against them based upon a jury's speculation as to motives."

This leaves us with the question whether, stripped of all considerations of intent and motive, petitioners' actions were legislative. We have little trouble concluding that they were. Most evidently, petitioner Roderick's acts of voting for an ordinance were, in form, quintessentially legislative. Petitioner Bogan's introduction of a budget and signing into law an ordinance also were formally legislative, even though he was an executive official. We have recognized that officials outside the legislative branch are entitled to legislative immunity when they perform legislative functions; Bogan's actions were legislative because they were integral steps in the legislative process.

Respondent, however, asks us to look beyond petitioners' formal actions to consider whether the ordinance was legislative in *substance.* We need not determine whether the formally legislative character of petitioners' actions is alone sufficient to entitle petitioners to legislative immunity, because here the ordinance, in substance, bore all the hallmarks of traditional legislation. The ordinance reflected a discretionary, policymaking decision implicating the budgetary priorities of the city and the services the city provides to its constituents. Moreover, it involved the termination of a position, which, unlike the hiring or firing of a particular employee, may have prospective implications that reach well beyond the particular occupant of the office. And the city council, in eliminating DHHS, certainly governed "in a field where legislators traditionally have power to act." Thus, petitioners' activities were undoubtedly legislative.

For the foregoing reasons, the judgment of the Court of Appeals is reversed.

DISCUSSION

Legislative immunity and the functional approach. The Court's decision in *Bogan* confirms that local government officials can assert absolute legislative immunity. Note that the city's mayor, an office traditionally classified as "executive" not "legislative," enjoys legislative immunity for *acts* deemed part of the legislative process. In *Bogan,* the mayor's legislative acts were the submission of a budget for consideration by the city council and his signing of the enacted budget. This aspect of *Bogan* emphasizes that it is an official's function, not the classification of her office, that determines whether absolute immunity applies.

The Court indicated various factors suggesting that the challenged government acts were legislative. First, the Court observed that the defendants' actions "bore all the hallmarks of traditional legislation." Second, the Court observed that the defendants' acts had "prospective implications that reach well beyond the particular occupant of the office." In other words, what appeared to be the *de facto* firing of the plaintiff—more of an administrative decision—acquired legislative coloring because it was implemented through adoption of the city's budget and had implications beyond the plaintiff. *Compare Davis v. Passman*, 442 U.S. 228 (1979) (Congressman's personal preference for male legislative aids was an actionable administrative decision); *Canary v. Osborn*, 211 F.3d 324 (6th Cir. 2000) (ad hoc personnel decisions are not immune).

Legislative immunity has been granted to a variety of government officials not conventionally thought of as legislators, including members of local zoning boards, local school boards, and county commissions engaged in legislative activity. *See, e.g., Acierno v. Cloutier*, 40 F.3d 597 (3d Cir. 1994). And in *Supreme Court of Virginia v. Consumers Union of the United States, Inc*, 446 U.S. 719 (1980), members of a state supreme court enjoyed absolute immunity relating to their promulgation of rules regulating members of the state's bar.

The question arises: given legislative immunity from both equitable and injunctive relief, are there viable alternatives for challenging an unconstitutional law? As you might guess, there are. In most cases, a plaintiff seeking to challenge an unconstitutional law sues a government official charged with *enforcing* the law or, in appropriate circumstances, the government *entity itself.* For example, suit might be brought against a state's attorney general to enjoin enforcement of a state law. We address such *Ex parte Young* actions in Chapter 8. In addition, legislative immunity does not extend to *government entities*—only to individual officials performing legislative activities on their behalf. As we will see later in this chapter, local government entities can be sued to enjoin unconstitutional local policy (including formal laws) and may even be subject to suit for damages arising from the enforcement of such policy.

The judicial function. The Supreme Court has repeatedly affirmed that "judges defending against § 1983 actions enjoy absolute immunity from damages liability for acts performed in their judicial capacities." *Dennis v. Sparks*, 449 U.S. 24, 27 (1980). The rule of absolute judicial immunity focuses on the action, or function, carried out by judicial personnel, not on their job status. This has two implications. First, judicial immunity usually extends to persons performing a judicial or quasi-judicial function even though they occupy jobs normally classified as "executive" or "administrative." For example, the Supreme Court has extended judicial immunity to federal hearing examiners, parole board members, administrative law judges, and others engaged in the adjudicative process. *See, e.g., Butz v. Economou*, 438 U.S. 478 (1978).[13] Second, even a judge may take action not encompassed by the judicial function and would not

13. Some of you may be interested to know that judicial immunity has been extended to law clerks assisting judges. *See, e.g., Moore v. Brewster*, 96 F.3d 1240, 1244 (9th Cir. 1996); *Oliva v. Heller*, 839 F.2d 37, 39-40 (2d Cir. 1988).

be absolutely immune for such action. For example, a judge's employment decisions are non-immune administrative acts. *See Forrester v. White*, 484 U.S. 219 (1988). And occasionally what appear to be judicial acts may trigger no immunity because a judge acts in the "clear absence of all jurisdiction." *See, e.g., Zarcone v. Perry*, 572 F.2d 52 (2d Cir. 1978) (judge who had courthouse vendor handcuffed for selling "putrid" coffee had no immunity from damages). Notice, however, that a judge does not lose immunity simply because she has acted in violation of "clearly established" law. Even judicial action plainly foreclosed by legal precedent enjoys immunity provided the judge has arguable "jurisdiction" to act.

Judicial immunity differs from legislative immunity in one important respect. In 1984, the Supreme Court held that "absolute" judicial immunity does not grant immunity from prospective *injunctive* relief. *See Pulliam v. Allen*, 466 U.S. 522 (1984). Although the Court observed that injunctive relief against a judge will rarely be justified, it is not barred by absolute immunity:

> For the most part, injunctive relief against a judge raises concerns different from those addressed by the protection of judges from damages awards. The limitations already imposed by the requirements for obtaining equitable relief against any defendant—a showing of an inadequate remedy at law and of a serious risk of irreparable harm—severely curtail the risk that judges will be harassed and their independence compromised by the threat of having to defend themselves against suits by disgruntled litigants. Similar limitations serve to prevent harassment of judges through use of the writ of mandamus. Because mandamus has "the unfortunate consequence of making the judge a litigant, obliged to obtain personal counsel or to leave his defense to one of the litigants before him," the Court has stressed that it should be "reserved for really extraordinary causes." Occasionally, however, there are "really extraordinary causes" and, in such cases, there has been no suggestion that judicial immunity prevents the supervising court from issuing the writ.

Id. at 537-38.[14]

The extraordinary injunctive relief theoretically permitted by *Pulliam* has now been curtailed by Congress. In 1998, § 1983 was amended to preclude injunctive relief against a judge unless declaratory relief is either unavailable or an order of such relief has been violated. *See* 42 U.S.C. § 1983 ("in any action brought against a judicial officer for an act or omission taken in such officer's judicial capacity, injunctive relief shall not be granted unless a declaratory decree was violated or declaratory relief was unavailable"). Further, attorney's fees or costs can be awarded against judicial officers only if the challenged action "was clearly in excess of such officer's jurisdiction." *See* 42 U.S.C. § 1988(b).

The prosecutorial function. Prosecutors engaged in prosecutorial functions enjoy absolute immunity from damages under § 1983. *See Imbler v. Pachtman*, 424 U.S. 409 (1976). The Court has addressed the scope of this immunity on several occasions, and one of its more important decisions is *Buckley v. Fitzsimmons*, 509 U.S. 259 (1993). In *Buckley*, a unanimous Court emphasized that absolute prosecutorial immunity pertains to acts "intimately associated with

14. The Court cited as an example of an "extraordinary cause[]" the situation where civil rights plaintiffs obtained a writ of mandamus to order desegregation of Louisiana's school system after their case had been pending for 11 years. *Id.* at 522 n.19.

the judicial phase of the criminal process." Other acts by a prosecutor enjoy only qualified immunity. Consider how the Court analyses the specific prosecutorial acts in *Buckley*.

BUCKLEY v. FITZSIMMONS

509 U.S. 259 (1993)

JUSTICE STEVENS delivered the opinion of the Court.

In an action brought under 42 U.S.C. § 1983, petitioner seeks damages from respondent prosecutors for allegedly fabricating evidence during the preliminary investigation of a crime and making false statements at a press conference announcing the return of an indictment. The questions presented are whether respondents are absolutely immune from liability on either or both of these claims.

* * * *

[W]e have recognized two kinds of immunities under § 1983. Most public officials are entitled only to qualified immunity. Under this form of immunity, government officials are not subject to damages liability for the performance of their discretionary functions when "their conduct does not violate clearly established statutory or constitutional rights of which a reasonable person would have known." In most cases, qualified immunity is sufficient to "protect officials who are required to exercise their discretion and the related public interest in encouraging the vigorous exercise of official authority."

* * * *

In *Imbler v. Pachtman*, we held that a state prosecutor had absolute immunity for the initiation and pursuit of a criminal prosecution, including presentation of the state's case at trial. Noting that our earlier cases had been "predicated upon a considered inquiry into the immunity historically accorded the relevant official at common law and the interests behind it," we focused on the functions of the prosecutor that had most often invited common-law tort actions. We concluded that the common-law rule of immunity for prosecutors was "well settled" and that "the same considerations of public policy that underlie the common-law rule likewise countenance absolute immunity under § 1983." Those considerations supported a rule of absolute immunity for conduct of prosecutors that was "intimately associated with the judicial phase of the criminal process." In concluding that "in initiating a prosecution and in presenting the State's case, the prosecutor is immune from a civil suit for damages under § 1983," we did not attempt to describe the line between a prosecutor's acts in preparing for those functions, some of which would be absolutely immune, and his acts of investigation or "administration," which would not.

We applied the *Imbler* analysis two Terms ago in Burns v. Reed, 500 U.S. 478 (1991). There the § 1983 suit challenged two acts by a prosecutor: (1) giving legal advice to the police on the propriety of hypnotizing a suspect and on whether probable cause existed to arrest that suspect, and (2) participating in a probable-cause hearing. We held that only the latter was entitled to absolute immunity. Immunity for that action under § 1983 accorded with the common-law absolute immunity of prosecutors and other attorneys for eliciting false or defamatory testimony from witnesses or for making false or defamatory statements during, and related to, judicial proceedings. Under that analysis, appearing before a judge and presenting evidence in support of a motion for a search warrant involved the prosecutor's "'role as advocate for the State.'" Because issuance of a search warrant is a judicial act, appearance at the probable-cause hearing was "'intimately associated with the judicial phase of the criminal process.'"

We further decided, however, that prosecutors are not entitled to absolute immunity for their actions in giving legal advice to the police. We were unable to identify any historical or common-law support for absolute immunity in the performance of this function. We also noted that any threat to the judicial process from "the harassment and intimidation associated with litigation" based on advice to the police was insufficient to overcome the "[a]bsen[ce] [of] a tradition of immunity comparable to the common-law immunity from malicious prosecution, which formed the basis for the decision in Imbler." And though we noted that several checks other than civil litigation prevent prosecutorial abuses in advising the police, "one of the most important checks, the judicial process," will not be effective in all cases, especially when in the end the suspect is not prosecuted. In sum, we held that providing legal advice to the police was not a function "closely associated with the judicial process."

* * * *

The question, then, is whether the prosecutors have carried their burden of establishing that they were functioning as "advocates" when they were endeavoring to determine whether the bootprint at the scene of the crime had been made by petitioner's foot.[15] A careful examination of the allegations concerning the conduct of the prosecutors during the period before they convened a special grand jury to investigate the crime provides the answer. The prosecutors do not contend that they had probable cause to arrest petitioner or to initiate judicial proceedings during that period. Their mission at that time was entirely investigative in character. A prosecutor neither is, nor should consider himself to be, an advocate before he has probable cause to have anyone arrested.

It was well after the alleged fabrication of false evidence concerning the bootprint that a special grand jury was empaneled. And when it finally was convened, its immediate purpose was to conduct a more thorough investigation of the crime — not to return an indictment against a suspect whom there was already probable cause to arrest. Buckley was not arrested, in fact, until 10 months after the grand jury had been convened and had finally indicted him. Under these circumstances, the prosecutors' conduct occurred well before they could properly claim to be acting as advocates. Respondents have not cited any authority that supports an argument that a prosecutor's fabrication of false evidence during the preliminary investigation of an unsolved crime was immune from liability at common law, either in 1871 or at any date before the enactment of § 1983. It therefore remains protected only by qualified immunity.

After Burns [v. Reed, 500 U.S. 478 (1991) (conferring only qualified immunity to prosecutors giving legal advice to police)], it would be anomalous, to say

15. In attempting to determine whether a bootprint left at the victim's home matched a pair of boots provided by the suspect, the prosecutors obtained a positive identification from an anthropologist "allegedly well known for her willingness to fabricate unreliable expert testimony." This identification occurred during the early stages of investigation before the prosecutors convened a special grand jury — which eventually returned an indictment against the suspect more than eight months after it convened.

the least, to grant prosecutors only qualified immunity when offering legal advice to police about an unarrested suspect, but then to endow them with absolute immunity when conducting investigative work themselves in order to decide whether a suspect may be arrested. That the prosecutors later called a grand jury to consider the evidence this work produced does not retroactively transform that work from the administrative into the prosecutorial. A prosecutor may not shield his investigative work with the aegis of absolute immunity merely because, after a suspect is eventually arrested, indicted, and tried, that work may be retrospectively described as "preparation" for a possible trial; every prosecutor might then shield himself from liability for any constitutional wrong against innocent citizens by ensuring that they go to trial. When the functions of prosecutors and detectives are the same, as they were here, the immunity that protects them is also the same.

* * * *

[Respondents also argue that their press-conference comments are clothed with absolute prosecutorial immunity.] Comments to the media have no functional tie to the judicial process just because they are made by a prosecutor. At the press conference, Fitzsimmons did not act in "'his role as advocate for the State.'" The conduct of a press conference does not involve the initiation of a prosecution, the presentation of the state's case in court, or actions preparatory for these functions. Statements to the press may be an integral part of a prosecutor's job and they may serve a vital public function. But in these respects a prosecutor is in no different position than other executive officials who deal with the press, and, qualified immunity is the norm for them.

* * * *

DISCUSSION

Buckley distinguishes between the acts of "initiating a prosecution and . . . presenting the State's case," which enjoy absolute immunity, and acts of "investigation" or "administration," which enjoy only qualified immunity. The dividing line between investigation and prosecution may not always be clear, and one often leads to the other. *Buckley* provides guidance concerning when this divide is crossed by emphasizing the point at which a prosecutor has probable cause to initiate an arrest.

But even this distinction may not always be adequate to identify acts enjoying absolute immunity. In *Kalina v. Fletcher*, 522 U.S. 118 (1997), the Court considered whether a prosecutor's preparation of "charging" documents, including an arrest warrant, enjoyed absolute immunity. The Court found that this preparation was part of the "advocate's function," but with one important exception. When the prosecutor offered sworn testimony about facts underlying the warrant, she abandoned the prosecutorial role and took on the role of a "complaining witness." *Id.* at 131. While the Court was unanimous in denying absolute immunity to the prosecutor-as-complaining-witness, Justice Scalia commented on the peculiar twists of the Court's immunity doctrine. *Id.* at 135. In a prior decision, the Court had held that a police officer giving perjured testimony *at trial* enjoyed absolute immunity from suit under §1983. *See Briscoe v. LaHue*, 460 U.S. 325 (1983). In *Rehberg v. Paulk*, 132 S. Ct. 1497 (2012), the Court extended its ruling in *Briscoe* and held that

FIGURE 9-1

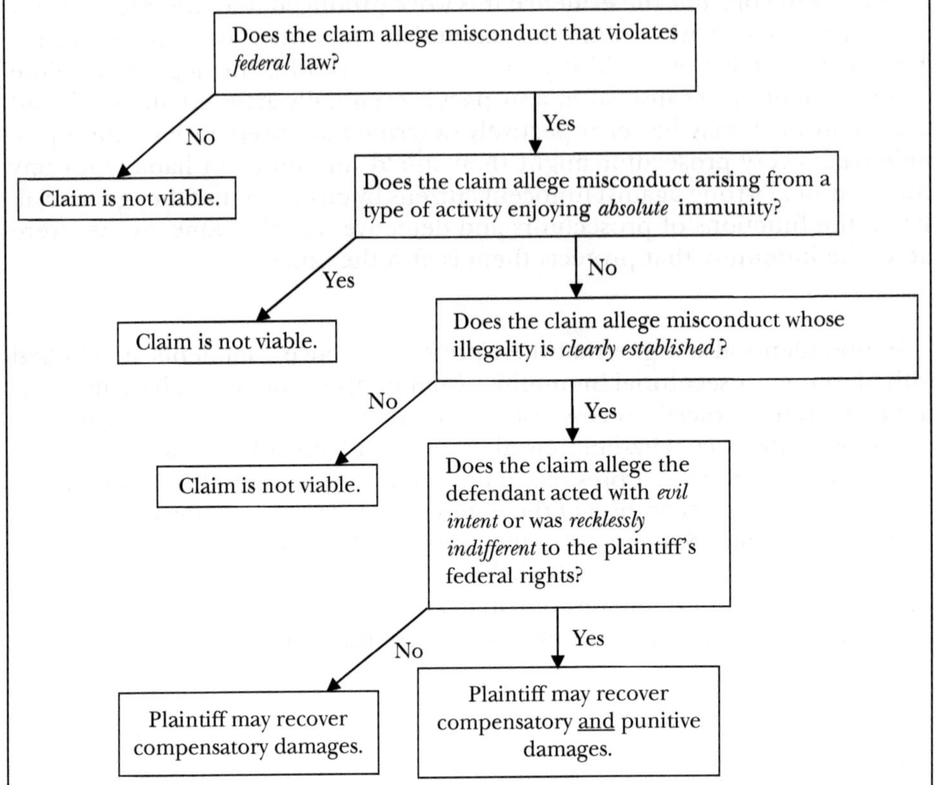

Questions to Consider When Assessing Whether an *Individual* Official Is Potentially Liable for *Damages*

prosecutors and an investigative officer enjoyed absolute immunity when testifying before a grand jury despite allegations that the defendants fabricated evidence.

In *Van de Kamp v. Goldstein*, 555 U.S. 335 (2009), the Court affirmed that supervisory prosecutors sued for failing to adequately train and supervise lower-level prosecutors enjoy absolute immunity. The Court rejected plaintiffs' argument that the supervisory prosecutors were engaged in non-immune "administrative" activities. According to the Court, the supervisory prosecutors were engaged in activity intimately related to the prosecutorial function when they trained and supervised others in their constitutional duty to disclose impeachment evidence to criminal defendants.

Absolute immunity for prosecutorial activities, like that for judicial activities, applies to § 1983 actions seeking monetary relief. But prosecutors are granted no statutory immunity from injunctive actions and are often named as defendants in § 1983 actions seeking to enjoin unconstitutional conduct.

* * * *

Now that we have considered both qualified immunity and a few important forms of absolute immunity, see how these immunities might apply to the following variations on the Reference Problem.

FIGURE 9-2

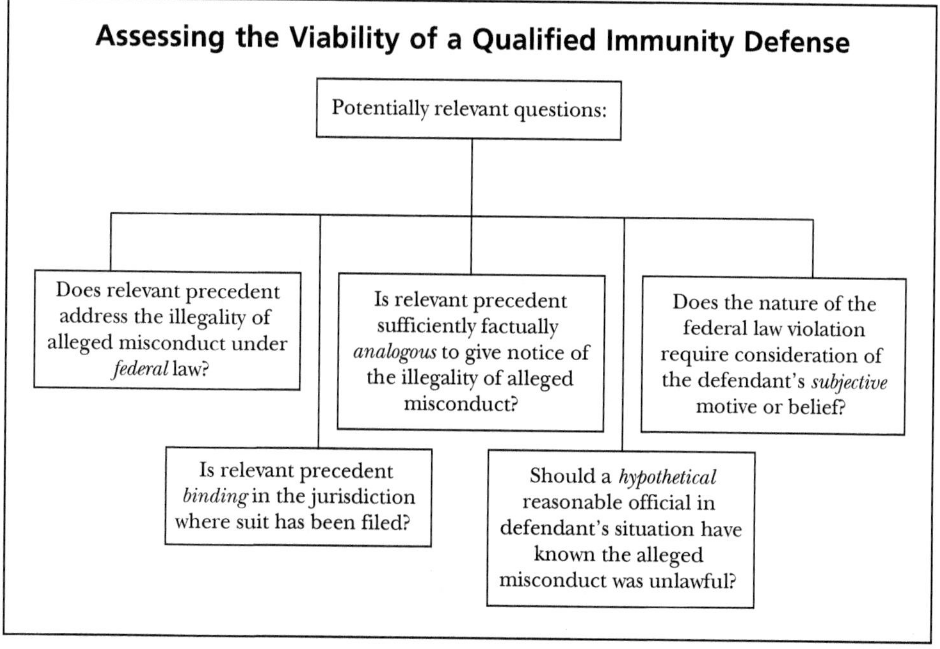

PROBLEM 9-4

Who's Immune from What?

Assume that the curfew ordinance that is the subject of the Reference Problem has led others to consider legal action. In particular, the local chapter of the ACLU has agreed to represent several youths who are affected by the ordinance. While all youths, and their parents, stand opposed to the ordinance, their fact situations vary.

One youth, Simon, has encountered Bozeman police on two occasions while skateboarding in a public park. These encounters occurred at dusk before the hour at which the curfew went into effect. On both occasions, the police threatened to arrest Simon unless he went home. Simon complied but under protest.

Another youth, Brad, was less cooperative when he encountered the police. Brad argued forcefully with the police that the ordinance was unconstitutional and refused to go home as directed. As a result, Brad was arrested even though the curfew hour had not technically arrived. The city's prosecutor has been informed by Brad's ACLU lawyer that the police lacked probable cause to arrest Brad. The prosecutor seems to be aware that the police acted prematurely, but he has still not dropped charges. The prosecutor has asked Brad to sign a "release" agreeing not to bring claims against the police department based on his arrest.

The ACLU lawyer representing Simon and Brad has also learned that the city prosecutor advised city police that the curfew ordinance was constitutional shortly before the boys' encounters with the police.

The lawyer for Simon and Brad is researching all plausible claims for both monetary and injunctive (or declaratory) relief. She would like to obtain an injunction forbidding the police (or city) from enforcing the ordinance. She would also like to have charges against Brad dismissed and recover damages for his improper arrest and prosecution.

At this preliminary stage of research, the youths' lawyer is considering suit against the following persons: (1) members of the town council who enacted the ordinance; (2) the city attorney who advised the town council that the proposed ordinance was constitutional; (3) the city prosecutor; and (4) the city police officers who have been charged with enforcing the ordinance (apparently the same two officers have done the enforcement).

Discuss what immunity defenses will be asserted if the ACLU lawyer sues the individual defendants listed above. Make sure you address both absolute and qualified immunities, as they pertain to all forms of relief sought. You may assume that the boys have "standing" and otherwise satisfy any requirements for obtaining equitable relief.

A final note on remedies available against government officials. When officials are sued individually, their monetary exposure can be substantial, at least in theory. Officials are liable for compensatory damages, including both economic and noneconomic damages (e.g., emotional distress). But juries are not permitted to award damages based on their assessment of the value or importance of a constitutional right. *See Memphis Cmty. Sch. Dist. v. Stachura*, 477 U.S. 299 (1986). Individual officials are also liable for punitive damages if they intentionally violate a plaintiff's constitutional rights or act with "reckless or callous indifference" to those rights. *See Smith v. Wade*, 461 U.S. 51 (1983); *see also* Caprice L. Roberts, *Ratios, (Ir)rationality and Civil Rights Punitive Awards*, 39 AKRON L. REV. 1019, 1026-27 (2006) (noting that most jurisdictions require an award of compensatory damages as a prerequisite of punitive damages). This standard appears to turn on the subjective state of mind of the defendant. *See Kolstad v. American Dental Ass'n*, 527 U.S. 526, 536 (1999).

When a plaintiff prevails in a suit against an official, the plaintiff is entitled to attorney's fees under 42 U.S.C. § 1988. Later in this chapter we will consider some of the more important issues that arise in determining whether fees should be awarded. For present purposes, suffice it to say that attorney's fees can often be a significant exposure to officials sued under § 1983.

4. *Under What Circumstances Are Government Entities Liable for Damages Under Section 1983?*

We have seen how qualified immunity and absolute immunity preclude damages suits against many government officials accused of wrongdoing. In such cases, the only remedy remaining against these officials will be one authorized by state law. Recall that, in *Monroe v. Pape*, the Court rejected the argument that a government entity is a "person" within the meaning of § 1983. The Court rejected entity liability despite the plaintiffs' contention that "municipal liability will not only afford plaintiffs responsible defendants but cause those defendants to eradicate abuses that exist at the police level."

Monroe's rejection of government liability resulted from the Court's interpretation of legislative history. The Court emphasized that Congress had rejected

REVIEW AND CONSOLIDATION

Limits on Section 1983 Remedies Against Individual Defendants

CLAIMS FOR EQUITABLE RELIEF:

- ✦ A defendant enjoys *absolute* immunity from equitable relief challenging activity that is part of the *legislative* function.
- ✦ A defendant enjoys *limited* statutory protections from injunctive relief challenging activity that is part of the *judicial* function.

CLAIMS FOR DAMAGES:

- ✦ A defendant enjoys *absolute* immunity from damages claims for activity that is part of the *legislative, judicial,* or *prosecutorial function.*
- ✦ Otherwise, a defendant enjoys *qualified* immunity from damages claims for *discretionary* activity.

an amendment to § 1983, the "Sherman amendment," that would have made local government liable for certain acts of violence committed by private citizens. This amendment was rejected, the Court observed, because Congress doubted its constitutional power to impose duties on local governments charged with implementing state law. *Id.* at 190. Given Congress' fundamental doubts about constitutional power to impose such duties, the Court inferred that Congress could not have intended that § 1983 create local government liability.

Seventeen years later, in *Monell v. Department of Social Services*, 436 U.S. 658 (1978), the Court reversed itself. The Court concluded that local government entities were "persons" subject to suit under § 1983. Although the Court based this reversal on its revised history of § 1983, the Court was also aware of the incongruity between its holding in *Monroe* and contemporaneous developments in the law. In particular, federal courts had often issued remedial orders directed to local school boards in desegregation suits. As long as *Monroe*'s limited interpretation of § 1983 persisted, courts needed to devise some means of imposing obligations on government entities. One option was to use the *Ex parte Young* device of suing local government officials in their "official" capacities, thereby effectively obtaining relief against the entity the officials represented. We considered the *Ex parte Young* actions in greater depth in Chapter 8. As you will observe in reading *Monell*, this device was used by the plaintiffs in an attempt to obtain some form of monetary relief from the local government entity, even though the device was traditionally restricted to suits seeking declaratory or injunctive relief.

According to one commentator, *Monroe*'s interpretation of the word *person* presented "a very serious danger" to desegregation suits against school boards. *See* William D. Murphy, *Reinterpreting "Person" in Section 1983: The Hidden Influence of* Brown v. Board of Education, 9 Black L.J. 97 (1985). If the Court did not revise its interpretation of "person," it might be compelled to consider whether a cause of action should be inferred *directly* under the Fourteenth Amendment, as the Court had done recently in so-called "*Bivens*" suits against federal officials. By reversing its decision in *Monroe*, these issues were avoided.

MONELL v. DEPARTMENT OF SOCIAL SERVICES

436 U.S. 658 (1978)

MR. JUSTICE BRENNAN delivered the opinion of the Court.

Petitioners, a class of female employees of the Department of Social Services and of the Board of Education of the city of New York, commenced this action under 42 U.S.C. § 1983 in July 1971. The gravamen of the complaint was that the Board and the Department had as a matter of official policy compelled pregnant employees to take unpaid leaves of absence before such leaves were required for medical reasons. The suit sought injunctive relief and backpay for periods of unlawful forced leave. Named as defendants in the action were the Department and its Commissioner, the Board and its Chancellor, and the city of New York and its Mayor. In each case, the individual defendants were sued solely in their official capacities.

* * * *

Although, after plenary consideration, we have decided the merits of over a score of cases brought under § 1983 in which the principal defendant was a school board—and, indeed, in some of which § 1983 and its jurisdictional counterpart, 28 U.S.C. § 1343, provided the only basis for jurisdiction—we indicated last Term that the question presented here was open and would be decided "another day." That other day has come and we now overrule *Monroe v. Pape*, insofar as it holds that local governments are wholly immune from suit under § 1983.

I

In *Monroe v. Pape*, we held that "Congress did not undertake to bring municipal corporations within the ambit of [§ 1983]." The basis for this conclusion was an inference drawn from Congress' rejection of the "Sherman amendment" to the bill which became the Civil Rights Act of 1871, the precursor of § 1983. The Amendment would have held a municipal corporation liable for damage done to the person or property of its inhabitants by *private* persons "riotously and tumultuously assembled." Although the Sherman amendment did not seek to amend § 1 of the Act, which is now § 1983, and although the nature of the obligation created by that amendment was vastly different from that created by § 1, the Court nonetheless concluded in *Monroe* that Congress must have meant to exclude municipal corporations from the coverage of § 1 because "'the House [in voting against the Sherman amendment] had solemnly decided that in their judgment Congress had no constitutional power to impose any *obligation* upon county and town organizations, the mere instrumentality for the administration of state law.'" This statement, we thought, showed that Congress doubted its "constitutional power . . . to impose *civil liability* on municipalities," and that such doubt would have extended to any type of civil liability.

A fresh analysis of the debate on the Civil Rights Act of 1871, and particularly of the case law which each side mustered in its support, shows, however, that *Monroe* incorrectly equated the "obligation" of which Representative Poland spoke with "civil liability."

* * * *

House opponents of the Sherman amendment—whose views are particularly important since only the House voted down the amendment—did not dispute that the Fourteenth Amendment created a federal right to protection, but they argued that the local units of government upon which the amendment fastened liability were not obligated to keep the peace at state law and further that the Federal Government could not constitutionally require local governments to create police forces, whether this requirement was levied directly, or indirectly by imposing damages for breach of the peace on municipalities. The most complete statement of this position is that of Representative Blair:

> The proposition known as the Sherman amendment . . . is entirely new. It is altogether without a precedent in this country. . . . That amendment claims the power in the General Government to go into the States of this Union and lay such obligations as it may please upon the municipalities, which are the creations of the States alone. . . .
>
> [H]ere it is proposed, not to carry into effect an obligation which rests upon the municipality, but to create that obligation, and that is the provision I am unable to assent to. [T]here are certain rights and duties that belong to the States, . . . there are certain powers that inhere in the State governments. They create these municipalities, they say what their powers shall be and what their obligations shall be. If the Government of the United States can step in and add to those obligations, may it not utterly destroy the municipality? If it can say that it shall be liable for damages occurring from a riot, . . . where [will] its power . . . stop and what obligations . . . might [it] not lay upon a municipality[?]. . . .
>
> Now, only the other day, the Supreme Court . . . decided [in Collector v. Day, 11 Wall. 113, 20 L.Ed. 122 (1871)] that there is no power in the Government of the United States, under its authority to tax, to tax the salary of a State officer. Why? Simply because the power to tax involves the power to destroy, and it was not the intent to give the Government of the United States power to destroy the government of the States in any respect. It was held also in the case of Prigg v. Pennsylvania, 16 Pet. 539, 10 L.Ed. 1060 (1842) that it is not within the power of the Congress of the United States to lay duties upon a State officer; that we cannot command a State officer to do any duty whatever, as such; and I ask . . . the difference between that and commanding a municipality, which is equally the creature of the State, to perform a duty.

Any attempt to impute a unitary constitutional theory to opponents of the Sherman amendment is, of course, fraught with difficulties, not the least of which is that most Members of Congress did not speak to the issue of the constitutionality of the amendment. Nonetheless, two considerations lead us to conclude that opponents of the Sherman amendment found it unconstitutional substantially because of the reasons stated by Representative Blair: First, Blair's analysis is precisely that of Poland, whose views were quoted as authoritative in *Monroe*, and that analysis was shared in large part by all House opponents who addressed the constitutionality of the Sherman amendment. Second, Blair's exegesis of the reigning constitutional theory of his day, as we shall explain, was clearly supported by precedent—albeit precedent that has not survived—

and no other constitutional formula was advanced by participants in the House debates. *Collector v. Day,* cited by Blair, was the clearest and, at the time of the debates, the most recent pronouncement of a doctrine of coordinate sovereignty that, as Blair stated, placed limits on even the enumerated powers of the National Government in favor of protecting state prerogatives. There, the Court held that the United States could not tax the income of Day, a Massachusetts state judge, because the independence of the States within their legitimate spheres would be imperiled if the instrumentalities through which States executed their powers were "subject to the control of another and distinct government." Although the Court in *Day* apparently rested this holding in part on the proposition that the taxing "power acknowledges no limits but the will of the legislative body imposing the tax," the Court had in other cases limited other national powers in order to avoid interference with the States.

In *Prigg v. Pennsylvania,* for example, Mr. Justice Story, in addition to confirming a broad national power to legislate under the Fugitive Slave Clause, held that Congress could not "insist that states . . . provide means to carry into effect the duties of the national government." And Mr. Justice McLean agreed that, "[a]s a general principle," it was true "that Congress had no power to impose duties on state officers, as provided in the [Act of Feb. 12, 1793]." Nonetheless he wondered whether Congress might not impose "positive" duties on state officers where a clause of the Constitution, like the Fugitive Slave Clause, seemed to require affirmative government assistance, rather than restraint of government, to secure federal rights.

Had Mr. Justice McLean been correct in his suggestion that, where the Constitution envisioned affirmative government assistance, the States or their officers or instrumentalities could be required to provide it, there would have been little doubt that Congress could have insisted that municipalities afford by "positive" action the protection owed individuals under § 1 of the Fourteenth Amendment whether or not municipalities were obligated by state law to keep the peace. However, any such argument, largely foreclosed by *Prigg,* was made impossible by the Court's holding in *Kentucky v. Dennison.* There, the Court was asked to require Dennison, the Governor of Ohio, to hand over Lago, a fugitive from justice wanted in Kentucky, as required by § 1 of the Act of Feb. 12, 1793, which implemented Art. IV, § 2, cl. 2, of the Constitution. Mr. Chief Justice Taney, writing for a unanimous Court, refused to enforce that section of the Act:

> [W]e think it clear, that the Federal Government, under the Constitution, has no power to impose on a State officer, as such, any duty whatever, and compel him to perform it; for if it possessed this power, it might overload the officer with duties which would fill up all his time, and disable him from performing his obligations to the State, and might impose on him duties of a character incompatible with the rank and dignity to which he was elevated by the State.

The rationale of *Dennison*—that the Nation could not impose duties on state officers since that might impede States in their legitimate activities—is obviously identical to that which animated the decision in *Collector v. Day.* And, as Blair indicated, municipalities as instrumentalities through which States executed their policies could be equally disabled from carrying out state policies if they were also obligated to carry out federally imposed duties. Although no one cited *Dennison* by name, the principle for which it stands was well known to Members of Congress, many of whom discussed *Day* as well as a series of State

Supreme Court cases in the mid-1860's which had invalidated a federal tax on the process of state courts on the ground that the tax threatened the independence of a vital state function. Thus, there was ample support for Blair's view that the Sherman amendment, by putting municipalities to the Hobson's choice of keeping the peace or paying civil damages, attempted to impose obligations on municipalities by indirection that could not be imposed directly, thereby threatening to "destroy the government of the States."

If municipal liability under § 1 of the Civil Rights Act of 1871 created a similar Hobson's choice, we might conclude, as *Monroe* did, that Congress could not have intended municipalities to be among the " persons" to which that section applied. But this is not the case.

First, opponents expressly distinguished between imposing an obligation to keep the peace and merely imposing civil liability for damages on a municipality that was obligated by state law to keep the peace, but which had not in violation of the Fourteenth Amendment. Representative Poland, for example, reasoning from Contract Clause precedents, indicated that Congress could constitutionally confer jurisdiction on the federal courts to entertain suits seeking to hold municipalities liable for using their authorized powers in violation of the Constitution—which is as far as § 1 of the Civil Rights Act went:

> I presume . . . that where a State had imposed a duty [to keep the peace] upon [a] municipality . . . an action would be allowed to be maintained against them in the courts of the United States under the ordinary restrictions as to jurisdiction. But the enforcing a liability [sic], existing by their own contract, or by a State law, in the courts, is a very widely different thing from devolving a new duty or liability upon them by the national Government, which has no power either to create or destroy them, and no power or control over them whatever.

* * * *

Second, the doctrine of dual sovereignty apparently put no limit on the power of federal courts to enforce the Constitution against municipalities that violated it. Under the theory of dual sovereignty set out in *Prigg*, this is quite understandable. So long as federal courts were vindicating the Federal Constitution, they were providing the "positive" government action required to protect federal constitutional rights and no question was raised of enlisting the States in "positive" action. The limits of the principles announced in *Dennison* and *Day* are not so well defined in logic, but are clear as a matter of history. It must be remembered that the same Court which rendered *Day* also vigorously enforced the Contract Clause against municipalities—an enforcement effort which included various forms of "positive" relief, such as ordering that taxes be levied and collected to discharge federal-court judgments, once a constitutional infraction was found. Thus, federal judicial enforcement of the Constitution's express limits on state power, since it was done so frequently, must, notwithstanding anything said in *Dennison* or *Day*, have been permissible, at least so long as the interpretation of the Constitution was left in the hands of the judiciary. Since § 1 of the Civil Rights Act simply conferred jurisdiction on the federal courts to enforce § 1 of the Fourteenth Amendment—a situation precisely analogous to the grant of diversity jurisdiction under which the Contract Clause was enforced against municipalities—is no reason to suppose that opponents of the Sherman amendment would have found any constitutional barrier to § 1 suits against municipalities.

Finally, the very votes of those Members of Congress, who opposed the Sherman amendment but who had voted for § 1, confirm that the liability imposed by § 1 was something very different from that imposed by the amendment. Section 1 without question could be used to obtain a damages judgment against state or municipal *officials* who violated federal constitutional rights while acting under color of law. However, for *Prigg-Dennison-Day* purposes, as Blair and others recognized, there was no distinction of constitutional magnitude between officers and agents — including corporate agents — of the State: Both were state instrumentalities and the State could be impeded no matter over which sort of instrumentality the Federal Government sought to assert its power. *Dennison* and *Day*, after all, were not suits against municipalities but against *officers*, and Blair was quite conscious that he was extending these cases by applying them to municipal corporations. Nonetheless, Senator Thurman, who gave the most exhaustive critique of § 1 — *inter alia*, complaining that it would be applied to state officers — and who opposed both § 1 and the Sherman amendment, the latter on *Prigg* grounds, agreed unequivocally that § 1 was constitutional. Those who voted for § 1 must similarly have believed in its constitutionality despite *Prigg*, *Dennison*, and *Day*.

From the foregoing discussion, it is readily apparent that nothing said in debate on the Sherman amendment would have prevented holding a municipality liable under § 1 of the Civil Rights Act for its own violations of the Fourteenth Amendment. The question remains, however, whether the general language describing those to be liable under § 1 — "any person" — covers more than natural persons. An examination of the debate on § 1 and application of appropriate rules of construction show unequivocally that § 1 was intended to cover legal as well as natural persons.

* * * *

In both Houses, statements of the supporters of § 1 corroborated that Congress, in enacting § 1, intended to give a broad remedy for violations of federally protected civil rights. Moreover, since municipalities through their official acts could, equally with natural persons, create the harms intended to be remedied by § 1, and, further, since Congress intended § 1 to be broadly construed, there is no reason to suppose that municipal corporations would have been excluded from the sweep of § 1. One need not rely on this inference alone, however, for the debates show that Members of Congress understood "persons" to include municipal corporations.

* * * *

Representative Bingham, for example, in discussing § 1 of the bill, explained that he had drafted § 1 of the Fourteenth Amendment with the case of *Barron v. Mayor of Baltimore* especially in mind. "In [that] case the *city* had taken private property for public use, without COMPENSATION . . . , AND THERE WAS NO REDRESS FOR THE wrong. . . ." Bingham's further remarks clearly indicate his view that such takings by cities, as had occurred in *Barron*, would be redressable under § 1 of the bill. More generally, and as Bingham's remarks confirm, § 1 of the bill would logically be the vehicle by which Congress provided redress for takings, since that section provided the only civil remedy for Fourteenth Amendment violations and that Amendment unequivocally prohibited uncompensated takings. Given this purpose, it beggars reason to suppose that Congress would have exempted municipalities from suit, insisting instead that compensation for a taking come from an officer in his individual capacity rather than from the government unit that had the benefit of the property taken.

In addition, by 1871, it was well understood that corporations should be treated as natural persons for virtually all purposes of constitutional and statutory analysis. . . .

That the "usual" meaning of the word "person" would extend to municipal corporations is also evidenced by an Act of Congress which had been passed only months before the Civil Rights Act was passed. This Act provided that "in all acts hereafter passed . . . the word 'person' may extend and be applied to bodies politic and corporate . . . unless the context shows that such words were intended to be used in a more limited sense."

Municipal corporations in 1871 were included within the phrase "bodies politic and corporate" and, accordingly, the "plain meaning" of § 1 is that local government bodies were to be included within the ambit of the persons who could be sued under § 1 of the Civil Rights Act. . . .

* * * *

Our analysis of the legislative history of the Civil Rights Act of 1871 compels the conclusion that Congress *did* intend municipalities and other local government units to be included among those persons to whom § 1983 applies. Local governing bodies, therefore, can be sued directly under § 1983 for monetary, declaratory, or injunctive relief where, as here, the action that is alleged to be unconstitutional implements or executes a policy statement, ordinance, regulation, or decision officially adopted and promulgated by that body's officers. Moreover, although the touchstone of the § 1983 action against a government body is an allegation that official policy is responsible for a deprivation of rights protected by the Constitution, local governments, like every other § 1983 "person," by the very terms of the statute, may be sued for constitutional deprivations visited pursuant to government "custom" even though such a custom has not received formal approval through the body's official decisionmaking channels. As Mr. Justice Harlan, writing for the Court, said in *Adickes v. S. H. Kress & Co.*: "Congress included customs and usages [in § 1983] because of the persistent and widespread discriminatory practices of state officials. . . . Although not authorized by written law, such practices of state officials could well be so permanent and well settled as to constitute a 'custom or usage' with the force of law."

On the other hand, the language of § 1983, read against the background of the same legislative history, compels the conclusion that Congress did not intend municipalities to be held liable unless action pursuant to official municipal policy of some nature caused a constitutional tort. In particular, we conclude that a municipality cannot be held liable *solely* because it employs a tortfeasor—or, in other words, a municipality cannot be held liable under § 1983 on a *respondeat superior* theory.

We begin with the language of § 1983 as originally passed:

> *[A]ny person who,* under color of any law, statute, ordinance, regulation, custom, or usage of any State, *shall subject, or cause to be subjected,* any person . . . to the deprivation of any rights, privileges, or immunities secured by the Constitution of the United States, shall, any such law, statute, ordinance, regulation, custom, or usage of the State to the contrary notwithstanding, be liable to the party injured in any action at law, suit in equity, or other proper proceeding for redress. . . .

The italicized language plainly imposes liability on a government that, under color of some official policy, "causes" an employee to violate another's constitutional rights. At the same time, that language cannot be easily read to impose liability vicariously on governing bodies solely on the basis of the existence of an employer-employee relationship with a tortfeasor. Indeed, the fact that Congress did specifically provide that A's tort became B's liability if B "caused" A to subject another to a tort suggests that Congress did not intend § 1983 liability to attach where such causation was absent.

The primary constitutional justification for the Sherman amendment was that it was a necessary and proper remedy for the failure of localities to protect citizens as the Privileges or Immunities Clause of the Fourteenth Amendment required. And according to Sherman, Shellabarger, and Edmunds, the amendment came into play only when a locality was at fault or had knowingly neglected its duty to provide protection. But other proponents of the amendment apparently viewed it as a form of vicarious liability for the unlawful acts of the citizens of the locality. And whether intended or not, the amendment as drafted did impose a species of vicarious liability on municipalities since it could be construed to impose liability even if a municipality did not know of an impending or ensuing riot or did not have the wherewithal to do anything about it. Indeed, the amendment held a municipality liable even if it had done everything in its power to curb the riot. While the first conference substitute was rejected principally on constitutional grounds, it is plain from the text of the second conference substitute — which limited liability to those who, having the power to intervene against Ku Klux Klan violence, "neglect[ed] or refuse[d] so to do," and which was enacted as § 6 of the 1871 Act and is now codified as 42 U.S.C. § 1986 — that Congress also rejected those elements of vicarious liability contained in the first conference substitute even while accepting the basic principle that the inhabitants of a community were bound to provide protection against the Ku Klux Klan. Strictly speaking, of course, the fact that Congress refused to impose vicarious liability for the wrongs of a few private citizens does not conclusively establish that it would similarly have refused to impose vicarious liability for the torts of a municipality's employees. Nonetheless, when Congress' rejection of the only form of vicarious liability presented to it is combined with the absence of any language in § 1983 which can easily be construed to create *respondeat superior* liability, the inference that Congress did not intend to impose such liability is quite strong.

Equally important, creation of a federal law of *respondeat superior* would have raised all the constitutional problems associated with the obligation to keep the peace, an obligation Congress chose not to impose because it thought imposition of such an obligation unconstitutional. To this day, there is disagreement about the basis for imposing liability on an employer for the torts of an employee when the sole nexus between the employer and the tort is the fact of the employer-employee relationship. Nonetheless, two justifications tend to stand out. First is the common-sense notion that no matter how blameless an employer appears to be in an individual case, accidents might nonetheless be reduced if employers had to bear the cost of accidents. Second is the argument that the cost of accidents should be spread to the community as a whole on an insurance theory.

The first justification is of the same sort that was offered for statutes like the Sherman amendment: "The obligation to make compensation for injury resulting from riot is, by arbitrary enactment of statutes, affirmatory law, and the reason of passing the statute is to secure a more perfect police regulation." This justification was obviously insufficient to sustain the amendment against perceived constitutional difficulties and there is no reason to suppose that a more general liability imposed for a similar reason would have been thought less constitutionally objectionable. The second justification was similarly put forward as a justification for the Sherman amendment: "we do not look upon [the Sherman amendment] as a punishment. . . . It is a mutual insurance." Again, this justification was insufficient to sustain the amendment.

We conclude, therefore, that a local government may not be sued under § 1983 for an injury inflicted solely by its employees or agents. Instead, it is when execution of a government's policy or custom, whether made by its lawmakers or by those whose edicts or acts may fairly be said to represent official policy, inflicts the injury that the government as an entity is responsible under § 1983. Since this case unquestionably involves official policy as the moving force of the constitutional violation found by the District Court, we must reverse the judgment below. In so doing, we have no occasion to address, and do not address, what the full contours of municipal liability under § 1983 may be. We have attempted only to sketch so much of the § 1983 cause of action against a local government as is apparent from the history of the 1871 Act and our prior cases, and we expressly leave further development of this action to another day.

Although we have stated that *stare decisis* has more force in statutory analysis than in constitutional adjudication because, in the former situation, Congress can correct our mistakes through legislation, we have never applied *stare decisis* mechanically to prohibit overruling our earlier decisions determining the meaning of statutes. Nor is this a case where we should "place on the shoulders of Congress the burden of the Court's own error."

First, *Monroe v. Pape*, insofar as it completely immunizes municipalities from suit under § 1983, was a departure from prior practice. Thus, while we have reaffirmed *Monroe* without further examination on three occasions, it can scarcely be said that *Monroe* is so consistent with the warp and woof of civil rights law as to be beyond question.

Second, the principle of blanket immunity established in *Monroe* cannot be cabined short of school boards. Yet such an extension would itself be inconsistent with recent expressions of congressional intent. In the wake of our decisions, Congress not only has shown no hostility to federal-court decisions against school boards, but it has indeed rejected efforts to strip the federal courts of jurisdiction over school boards. Moreover, recognizing that school boards are often defendants in school desegregation suits, which have almost without exception been § 1983 suits, Congress has twice passed legislation authorizing grants to school boards to assist them in complying with federal-court decrees. . . .

Finally, even under the most stringent test for the propriety of overruling a statutory decision proposed by Mr. Justice Harlan in *Monroe*— "that it appear beyond doubt from the legislative history of the 1871 statute that [*Monroe*] misapprehended the meaning of the [section]" — the overruling of *Monroe* insofar as it holds that local governments are not "persons" who may be defendants in § 1983 suits is clearly proper. It is simply beyond doubt that, under the 1871 Congress' view of the law, were § 1983 liability unconstitutional as to local governments, it would have been equally unconstitutional as to state officers. Yet everyone — proponents and opponents alike — knew § 1983 would be applied to state officers and nonetheless stated that § 1983 was constitutional. And, moreover, there can be no doubt that § 1 of the Civil Rights Act was intended to provide a remedy, to be broadly construed, against all forms of official violation of federally protected rights. Therefore, absent a clear statement in the legislative history supporting the conclusion that § 1 was not to apply to the official acts of a municipal corporation—which simply is not present—there is no justification for excluding municipalities from the "persons" covered by § 1.

For reasons stated above, therefore, we hold that *stare decisis* does not bar our overruling of *Monroe* insofar as it is inconsistent with . . . this opinion.

Since the question whether local government bodies should be afforded some form of official immunity was not presented as a question to be decided on this petition and was not briefed by the parties or addressed by the courts below, we express no views on the scope of any municipal immunity beyond holding that municipal bodies sued under § 1983 cannot be entitled to an absolute immunity, lest our decision that such bodies are subject to suit under § 1983 "be drained of meaning."

[Justice Powell's concurrence is omitted.]

MR. JUSTICE REHNQUIST, with whom THE CHIEF JUSTICE [BURGER] joins, dissenting.

Seventeen years ago, in *Monroe v. Pape*, this Court held that the 42d Congress did not intend to subject a municipal corporation to liability as a "person" within the meaning of 42 U.S.C. § 1983. Since then, the Congress has remained silent, but this Court has reaffirmed that holding on at least three separate occasions. Today, the Court abandons this long and consistent line of precedents, offering in justification only an elaborate canvass of the same legislative history which was before the Court in 1961. Because I cannot agree that this Court is "free to disregard these precedents," which have been "considered maturely and recently" by this Court, I am compelled to dissent.

* * * *

The decision in *Monroe v. Pape* was the fountainhead of the torrent of civil rights litigation of the last 17 years. Using § 1983 as a vehicle, the courts have articulated new and previously unforeseeable interpretations of the Fourteenth Amendment. At the same time, the doctrine of municipal immunity enunciated in *Monroe* has protected municipalities and their limited treasuries from the consequences of their officials' failure to predict the course of this Court's constitutional jurisprudence. None of the Members of this Court can foresee the practical consequences of today's removal of that protection. Only the Congress, which has the benefit of the advice of every segment of this diverse Nation, is equipped to consider the results of such a drastic change in the law. It seems all but inevitable that it will find it necessary to do so after today's decision.

DISCUSSION AND QUESTIONS

The plaintiffs in *Monell* filed suit to challenge a mandatory pregnancy leave policy three years *before* the Supreme Court announced such a policy was unconstitutional. *Cleveland Bd. of Educ. v. LaFleur*, 414 U.S. 632 (1974). They sought to both enjoin continuation of the policy and recover backpay, but chose not to sue individually the officials who adopted the policy or who enforced it. Based on your current understanding of qualified and absolute immunity, what immunities might these defendants have asserted had they been sued?

The Court declines to answer the question whether local government enjoys qualified immunity from monetary relief. It does, however, deny local government any form of absolute immunity. What form of absolute immunity might the city have asserted in connection with its adoption of a mandatory pregnancy leave policy? In light of *Monell*, which defendants, individual or entity, should a plaintiff sue when a municipality adopts an unconstitutional policy?

Monell concludes that local government entities are persons under § 1983. Among other things, the Court observed that "municipal corporations" were encompassed by congressional legislation defining the word *person* to include "bodies politic and corporate." According to the Court, the "plain meaning" of Congress was that local government bodies were subject to suit under § 1983.

But what of *state* government? The primary significance of whether a state is a § 1983 person arises when a plaintiff seeks to sue the state for damages. The current Supreme Court interprets the Eleventh Amendment to preclude federal court suits seeking damages from the state unless Congress has "clearly" stated its intent to abrogate state immunity. *See, e.g., Atascadero State Hosp. v. Scanlon*, 473 U.S. 234 (1985). One year after *Monell*, the Court concluded that § 1983 did not "clearly" override state sovereign immunity in federal court suits. *Quern v. Jordan*, 440 U.S. 332 (1979).

Quern did not resolve the question whether a § 1983 plaintiff might assert a § 1983 damages claim in *state* court. That question turned on whether the state was a person within the meaning of § 1983. This question was resolved a decade later in *Will v. Michigan Department of State Police*, 491 U.S. 58 (1989), when the Court concluded a state was not a § 1983 person. In *Will*, the Court considered both the history of state sovereign immunity as well as evidence that the phrase "bodies politic and corporate" used in nineteenth-century legislation was not intended to include state government.

Consequently, a state official sued individually is a person under § 1983, while the government he or she represents is not. Further, the state's sovereign immunity does not extend to its officials sued in their individual capacities. *See Hafer v. Melo*, 502 U.S. 21 (1991). Individual state officials are generally subject to the same liabilities, and enjoy similar immunities, as local government officials.

The meaning of "policy." *Monell* squarely rejects respondeat superior liability for local government. However, local government can be sued for "monetary, declaratory, or injunctive relief where the action that is alleged to be unconstitutional implements or executes a policy statement, ordinance, regulation, or decision officially adopted and promulgated by that body's officers." According to the Court, two criteria must be satisfied to impose liability on government: (1) there must be an "official policy," which includes unwritten "custom or usage," and (2) that policy must "cause" the violation of a plaintiff's federal rights.[16]

The official "policy" challenged in *Monell* was obvious, as was the fact that this policy "caused" the plaintiffs to lose their employment while pregnant. Actions taken to carry out such legislative-type policies present an easy case for municipal liability under *Monell*. But *Monell* leaves unresolved what other forms of government action rise to the level of policy. Does policy include

16. The Court held in *Los Angeles County v. Humphries*, 131 S. Ct. 447 (2010), that a municipal policy must also be identified before local government can be ordered to give prospective (e.g., injunctive or declaratory) relief under § 1983. In the absence of a municipal policy, the plaintiff is unable to obtain relief under § 1983 and so can't recover attorney's fees under § 1988. When there is no municipal policy to challenge in an injunctive action under § 1983, the plaintiff may still be able to bring an *Ex parte Young* action (discussed in Chapter 8). But the plaintiff may be denied attorney's fees if there is no counterpart to § 1988 authorizing them.

- misconduct that has occurred on several occasions without being remedied by responsible government officials;
- misconduct that could have been prevented by responsible government officials if only they had better trained municipal employees;
- misconduct ordered on an ad hoc basis by a government official with final say in the matter; or
- misconduct by a lower-level employee that officials with the final say decline to remedy?

The Court considered these variations on policy as it elaborated on government liability in decisions following *Monell.* We now consider those decisions.

Municipal liability for formal policymaking. While municipal liability for formal policies like those in *Monell* is often an easy case, sometimes it is not. Lower-level officials in a municipality, or individual offices of the municipality, sometimes make policy to govern their own limited operations. For example, a branch office manager might announce a new office rule forbidding the wearing of religious paraphernalia at work. Is this type of policymaking sufficient to create municipal liability? Is policymaking authority diffused throughout all levels of management within a government entity?

The Court has been unwilling to extend policymaking authority throughout municipal management simply because lower-level managers exercise some discretion in performing their job function. Instead, the Court has indicated that *state law* usually dictates who can make policy that implicates local government. As the plurality wrote in *City of St. Louis v. Praprotnick,* "we can be confident that state law (which may include valid local ordinances and regulations) will always direct a court to some official or body that has the responsibility for making law or setting policy in any given area of a local government's business." 485 U.S. 112, 125 (1988). At the same time, the Court conceded that state law will not always "speak with perfect clarity." *Id.*

Sometimes local officials are called upon to implement decisions of state policymakers, raising the issue whether local government should be liable for policy not of its own making. Lower federal courts have responded to this issue differently. One approach requires that courts examine how much discretion local officials have in choosing to enforce state (or sometimes federal) policy. *Compare Bethesda Lutheran Homes & Servs., Inc. v. Leean,* 154 F.3d 716 (7th Cir. 1998) (finding no municipal liability when municipal officials are "acting under compulsion of state or federal law"), *with Cooper v. Dillon,* 403 F.3d 1208 (11th Cir. 2005) (local police chief's "deliberate decision to enforce [state] statute" renders municipality liable).

Custom or usage. Custom or usage is sometimes referred to as "bottom-up policymaking." Custom or usage refers to an unlawful practice sufficiently widespread and persistent to have acquired the force of a municipal policy. One clue to whether unlawful practice has become a custom is government's response to the practice. For example, if government fails to take disciplinary action in response to unlawful behavior, it risks tacitly endorsing that behavior as policy. *See, e.g., Brown v. City of Margate,* 842 F. Supp. 515, 518 (S.D. Fla. 1993) ("[A] smaller number of incidents where the investigation and resulting disciplinary actions were inadequate may be more indicative of a pattern than a larger number of incidents where the department fully and satisfactorily addressed the matter and responded appropriately."). Consequently, government can best avoid "bottom-up policymaking" by monitoring suspected unlawful behavior and responding to it. *See, e.g., Griffin v. City of Opa-Locka*, 261 F.3d 1295 (11th Cir. 2001) (where mayor and city commissioners knew of former city manager's sexual harassment in the workplace and neither investigated the misconduct nor instituted a sexual harassment policy, "custom" existed despite injured parties' failure to file formal complaints with EEOC).

Ad hoc policymaking. When the local government adopted its mandatory leave policy at issue in *Monell*, it announced a rule that was to be followed in the future when teachers became pregnant. But what if the decision had come about under different circumstances? For example, what if the school superintendent had simply been asked by a local school principal whether it was permissible to order a pregnant teacher at the principal's school to take a leave of absence? Would the school superintendent have made policy by responding to the ad hoc request of the principal? Or could it be said that the superintendent's decision was merely the solution to a discrete problem falling short of policymaking?

The Court addressed an analogous question in *Pembaur v. City of Cincinnati*, 475 U.S. 469 (1986). In *Pembaur*, a county prosecutor was asked to give advice to law enforcement officers who had arrived at Pembaur's medical clinic to serve arrest warrants on two clinic employees. The officers had no warrant authorizing them to enter Pembaur's clinic and so Pembaur refused the officers entry. The officers then called their supervisor for advice, who in turn referred them to the county prosecutor. The prosecutor told the officers to "go in and get" the employees by forcible entry if necessary.

Pembaur sued a variety of defendants, including the city and county and the law enforcement officers involved, and sought $20 million in compensatory and punitive damages. Pembaur alleged that the defendants violated his Fourth and Fourteenth Amendment rights because the officers lacked either a warrant or exigent circumstances to search his clinic for the sought-after employees. Pembaur did not sue the county prosecutor because his counsel thought the prosecutor enjoyed absolute immunity while giving advice to the officers. Having studied absolute immunity, do you think counsel's opinion about absolute immunity is supported by current immunity doctrine?

One day after Pembaur filed his suit, and nearly four years after the incident at Pembaur's clinic, the Supreme Court held that it was unconstitutional for officers to search premises when they lacked either a warrant or exceptional circumstances. *See Steagald v. United States*, 451 U.S. 204 (1981). As you can now appreciate, the individual officers had a viable claim of qualified immunity based on the contention that Pembaur's constitutional right was not "clearly established" at the time they acted. The government defendants lacked such immunity, however, because the Supreme Court had previously held that government entities enjoy *no* qualified immunity from damages actions. *See Owen v. City of Independence*, 445 U.S. 622 (1980). In *Owen*, the Court discounted the threat that government liability might deter vigorous execution of government functions, which had been one of its rationales for granting immunity to individuals.

Consequently, government liability in *Pembaur* hinged on whether the officers' unlawful entry resulted from some form of municipal policy.

PEMBAUR v. CITY OF CINCINNATI

475 U.S. 469 (1986)

[JUSTICE BRENNAN announced the judgment of the Court and delivered the opinion of the Court, except as to Part II-B.]

II

A

Our analysis must begin with the proposition that "Congress did not intend municipalities to be held liable unless action pursuant to official municipal policy of some nature caused a constitutional tort."

Monell is a case about responsibility. In the first part of the opinion, we held that local government units could be made liable under § 1983 for deprivations of federal rights, overruling a contrary holding in *Monroe v. Pape.* In the second part of the opinion, we recognized a limitation on this liability and concluded that a municipality cannot be made liable by application of the doctrine of *respondeat superior.* In part, this conclusion rested upon the language of § 1983, which imposes liability only on a person who "subjects, or causes to be subjected," any individual to a deprivation of federal rights; we noted that this language "cannot easily be read to impose liability vicariously on government bodies solely on the basis of the existence of an employer-employee relationship with a tortfeasor." Primarily, however, our conclusion rested upon the legislative history, which disclosed that, while Congress never questioned its power to impose civil liability on municipalities for their *own* illegal acts, Congress did doubt its constitutional power to impose such liability in order to oblige municipalities to control the conduct of *others.* We found that, because of these doubts, Congress chose not to create such obligations in § 1983. Recognizing that this would be the effect of a federal law of *respondeat superior,* we concluded that § 1983 could not be interpreted to incorporate doctrines of vicarious liability.

* * * *

With this understanding, it is plain that municipal liability may be imposed for a single decision by municipal policymakers under appropriate circumstances. No one has ever doubted, for instance, that a municipality may be liable under § 1983 for a single decision by its properly constituted legislative body— whether or not that body had taken similar action in the past or intended to do so in the future—because even a single decision by such a body unquestionably constitutes an act of official government policy. But the power to establish policy is no more the exclusive province of the legislature at the local level than at the state or national level. *Monell's* language makes clear that it expressly envisioned other officials "whose acts or edicts may fairly be said to represent official policy," and whose decisions therefore may give rise to municipal liability under § 1983.

Indeed, any other conclusion would be inconsistent with the principles underlying § 1983. To be sure, "official policy" often refers to formal rules or understandings—often but not always committed to writing—that are intended to, and do, establish fixed plans of action to be followed under similar circumstances consistently and over time. That was the case in *Monell* itself, which involved a written rule requiring pregnant employees to take unpaid leaves of absence before such leaves were medically necessary. However . . . a government frequently chooses a course of action tailored to a particular situation and not intended to control decisions in later situations. If the decision to adopt that particular course of action is properly made by that government's authorized decisionmakers, it surely represents an act of official government "policy" as that term is commonly understood. More importantly, where action is directed by those who establish government policy, the municipality is equally responsible whether that action is to be taken only once or to be taken repeatedly. To deny compensation to the victim would therefore be contrary to the fundamental purpose of § 1983.

B

Having said this much, we hasten to emphasize that not every decision by municipal officers automatically subjects the municipality to § 1983 liability. Municipal liability attaches only where the decisionmaker possesses final authority to establish municipal policy with respect to the action ordered. The fact that a particular official — even a policymaking official — has discretion in the exercise of particular functions does not, without more, give rise to municipal liability based on an exercise of that discretion. The official must also be responsible for establishing final government policy respecting such activity before the municipality can be held liable. Authority to make municipal policy may be granted directly by a legislative enactment or may be delegated by an official who possesses such authority, and of course, whether an official had final policymaking authority is a question of state law. However, like other government entities, municipalities often spread policymaking authority among various officers and official bodies. As a result, particular officers may have authority to establish binding county policy respecting particular matters and to adjust that policy for the county in changing circumstances. We hold that municipal liability under § 1983 attaches where — and only where — a deliberate choice to follow a course of action is made from among various alternatives by the official or officials responsible for establishing final policy with respect to the subject matter in question.

C

Applying this standard to the case before us, we have little difficulty concluding that the Court of Appeals erred in dismissing petitioner's claim against the county. The Deputy Sheriffs who attempted to serve the capiases at petitioner's clinic found themselves in a difficult situation. Unsure of the proper course of action to follow, they sought instructions from their supervisors. The instructions they received were to follow the orders of the County Prosecutor. The Prosecutor made a considered decision based on his understanding of the law and commanded the officers forcibly to enter petitioner's clinic. That decision directly caused the violation of petitioner's Fourth Amendment rights.

Respondent argues that the County Prosecutor lacked authority to establish municipal policy respecting law enforcement practices because only the County Sheriff may establish policy respecting such practices. Respondent suggests that the County Prosecutor was merely rendering "legal advice" when he ordered the Deputy Sheriffs to "go in and get" the witnesses. Consequently, the argument concludes, the action of the individual Deputy Sheriffs in following this advice and forcibly entering petitioner's clinic was not pursuant to a properly established municipal policy.

We might be inclined to agree with respondent if we thought that the Prosecutor had only rendered "legal advice." However, the Court of Appeals concluded, based upon its examination of Ohio law, that both the County Sheriff and the County Prosecutor could establish county policy under appropriate circumstances, a conclusion that we do not question here. [Ohio law] provides that county officers may "require . . . instructions from [the County Prosecutor] in matters connected with their official duties." Pursuant to standard office procedure, the Sheriff's Office referred this matter to the Prosecutor and then followed his instructions. The Sheriff testified that his Department followed this practice under appropriate circumstances and that it was "the proper thing to do" in this case. We decline to accept respondent's invitation to overlook this delegation of authority by disingenuously labeling the Prosecutor's clear command mere "legal advice." In ordering the Deputy Sheriffs to enter petitioner's clinic the County Prosecutor was acting as the final decisionmaker for the county, and the county may therefore be held liable under § 1983.

The decision of the Court of Appeals is reversed, and the case is remanded for further proceedings consistent with this opinion.

JUSTICE WHITE, concurring.

The forcible entry made in this case was not then illegal under federal, state, or local law. The city of Cincinnati frankly conceded that forcible entry of third-party property to effect otherwise valid arrests was standard operating procedure. There is no reason to believe that respondent county would abjure using lawful means to execute the capiases issued in this case or had limited the authority of its officers to use force in executing capiases. Further, the county officials who had the authority to approve or disapprove such entries opted for the forceful entry, a choice that was later held to be inconsistent with the Fourth Amendment. Vesting discretion in its officers to use force and its use in this case sufficiently manifested county policy to warrant reversal of the judgment below.

This does not mean that every act of municipal officers with final authority to effect or authorize arrests and searches represents the policy of the municipality. It would be different if Steagald v. United States had been decided when the events at issue here occurred, if the State Constitution or statutes had forbidden forceful entries without a warrant, or if there had been a municipal ordinance to this effect. Local law enforcement officers are expected to obey the law and ordinarily swear to do so when they take office. Where the controlling law places limits on their authority, they cannot be said to have the authority to make contrary policy. Had the Sheriff or Prosecutor in this case failed to follow an existing warrant requirement, it would be absurd to say that he was nevertheless executing county policy in authorizing the forceful entry in this case and even stranger to say that the county would be liable if the Sheriff had secured a warrant and it turned out that he and the Magistrate had mistakenly thought there was probable cause for the warrant. If deliberate or mistaken acts like this, admittedly contrary to local law, expose the county to liability, it must be on the basis of *respondeat superior* and not because the officers' acts represent local policy.

Such results would not conform to *Monell* and the cases following it. I do not understand the Court to hold otherwise in stating that municipal liability attaches where "a deliberate choice to follow a course of action is made from among various alternatives by the official or officials responsible for establishing final policy with respect to the subject matter in question." A sheriff, for example, is not the final policymaker with respect to the probable-cause requirement for a valid arrest. He has no alternative but to act in accordance with the established standard; and his deliberate or mistaken departure from the controlling law of arrest would not represent municipal policy.

In this case, however, the Sheriff and the Prosecutor chose a course that was not forbidden by any applicable law, a choice that they then had the authority to make. This was county policy, and it was no less so at the time because a later decision of this Court declared unwarranted forceful entry into third-party premises to be violation of the Fourth Amendment. Hence, I join the Court's opinion and judgment.

[The concurring opinion of Justice Stevens is omitted.]

JUSTICE O'CONNOR, concurring in part and concurring in the judgment.

For the reasons stated by Justice White, I agree that the municipal officers here were acting as policymakers within the meaning of *Monell.* As the city of Cincinnati freely conceded, forcible entry of third-party property to effect an arrest was standard operating procedure in May 1977. Given that this procedure was consistent with federal, state, and local law at the time the case arose, it seems fair to infer that respondent county's policy was no different. Moreover, under state law as definitively construed by the Court of Appeals, the county officials who opted for the forcible entry "had the authority to approve or disapprove such entries." Given this combination of circumstances, I agree with Justice White that the decision to break down the door "sufficiently manifested county policy to warrant reversal of the judgment below." Because, however, I believe that the reasoning of the majority goes beyond that necessary to decide the case, and because I fear that the standard the majority articulates may be misread to expose municipalities to liability beyond that envisioned by the Court in *Monell*, I join only Parts I and II-A of the Court's opinion and the judgment.

JUSTICE POWELL, with whom THE CHIEF JUSTICE [BURGER] and JUSTICE REHNQUIST join, dissenting.

The Court today holds Hamilton County liable for the forcible entry in May 1977 by Deputy Sheriffs into petitioner's office. The entry and subsequent search were pursuant to capiases for third parties — petitioner's employees — who had failed to answer a summons to appear as witnesses before a grand jury investigating petitioner. When petitioner refused to allow the Sheriffs to enter, one of them, at the request of his supervisor, called the office of the County Prosecutor for instructions. The Assistant County Prosecutor received the call, and apparently was in doubt as to what advice to give. He referred the question to the County Prosecutor, who advised the Deputy Sheriffs to "go in and get them [the witnesses]" pursuant to the capiases.

This five-word response to a single question over the phone is now found by this Court to have created an official county policy for which Hamilton County is liable under § 1983. This holding is wrong for at least two reasons. First, the Prosecutor's response and the Deputies' subsequent actions did not violate any constitutional right that existed at the time of the forcible entry. Second, no official county policy could have been created solely by an off-hand telephone response from a busy County Prosecutor.

* * * *

[P]etitioner has failed to demonstrate the existence of an official policy for which Hamilton County can be liable. The action said to have created policy here was nothing more than a brief response to a single question over the telephone. The Deputy Sheriffs sought instructions concerning a situation that had never occurred before, at least in the memory of the participants. That in itself, and the fact that the Assistant Prosecutor had to obtain advice from the County Prosecutor, strongly indicate that no prior policy had been formed. Petitioner therefore argues that the County Prosecutor's reaction *in this case* formed county policy. The sparse facts supporting petitioner's theory—adopted by the Court today—do not satisfy the requirement in *Monell*, that local government liability under § 1983 be imposed only when the injury is caused by government policy.

Under *Monell*, local government units may be liable only when "the action that is alleged to be unconstitutional implements or executes a policy statement, ordinance, regulation, or decision officially adopted and promulgated by that body's officers." This case presents the opportunity to define further what was meant in *Monell* by "official policy." Proper resolution of the case calls for identification of the applicable principles for determining when policy is created. The Court today does not do this, but instead focuses almost exclusively on the status of the decisionmaker. Its reasoning is circular: it contends that policy is what policymakers make, and policymakers are those who have authority to make policy.

The Court variously notes that if a decision "is properly made by that government's authorized decisionmakers, it surely represents an act of official government 'policy' as that term is commonly understood," and that "where action is directed by those who establish government policy, the municipality is equally responsible. . . ." Thus, the Court's test for determining the existence of policy focuses only on whether a decision was made "by the official or officials responsible for establishing final policy with respect to the subject matter in question."

In my view, the question whether official policy—in any normal sense of the term—has been made in a particular case is not answered by explaining who has final authority to make policy. The question here is not "*could* the County Prosecutor make policy?" but rather, "*did* he make policy?" By focusing on the authority granted to the official under state law, the Court's test fails to answer the key federal question presented. The Court instead turns the question into one of state law. Under a test that focuses on the authority of the decisionmaker, the Court has only to look to state law for the resolution of this case. Here the Court of Appeals found that "both the County Sheriff and the County Prosecutor [had authority under Ohio law to] establish county policy under appropriate circumstances." Apparently that recitation of authority is all that is needed under the Court's test because no discussion is offered to demonstrate that the Sheriff or the Prosecutor actually used that authority to establish official county policy in this case.

Moreover, the Court's reasoning is inconsistent with *Monell*. Today's decision finds that policy is established because a policymaking official made a decision on the telephone that was within the scope of his authority. The Court ignores the fact that no business organization or government unit makes binding policy decisions so cavalierly. The Court provides no mechanism for distinguishing those acts or decisions that cannot fairly be construed to create official policy from the normal process of establishing an official policy that would be followed by a responsible public entity. Thus, the Court has adopted in part what it rejected in *Monell*: local government units are now subject to *respondeat superior* liability, at least with respect to a certain category of employees, *i.e.*, those with final authority to make policy. The Court's reliance on the status of the employee carries the concept of policy far beyond what was envisioned in *Monell*.

In my view, proper resolution of the question whether official policy has been formed should focus on two factors: (i) the nature of the decision reached or the action taken, and (ii) the process by which the decision was reached or the action was taken. Focusing on the nature of the decision distinguishes between policies and mere ad hoc decisions. Such a focus also reflects the fact that most policies embody a rule of general applicability. That is the tenor of the Court's statement in *Monell* that local government units are liable under § 1983 when the action that is alleged to be unconstitutional "implements or executes a policy statement, ordinance, regulation, or decision officially adopted and promulgated by that body's officers." The clear implication is that policy is created when a rule is formed that applies to all similar situations — a "governing principle [or] plan." Webster's New Twentieth Century Dictionary 1392 (2d ed. 1979). When a rule of general applicability has been approved, the government has taken a position for which it can be held responsible.

Another factor indicating that policy has been formed is the process by which the decision at issue was reached. Formal procedures that involve, for example, voting by elected officials, prepared reports, extended deliberation, or official records indicate that the resulting decisions taken "may fairly be said to represent official policy." Owen v. City of Independence, 445 U.S. 622 (1980), provides an example. The City Council met in a regularly scheduled meeting. One member of the Council made a motion to release to the press certain reports that cast an employee in a bad light. After deliberation, the Council passed the motion with no dissents and one abstention. Although this official action did not establish a rule of general applicability, it is clear that policy was formed because of the process by which the decision was reached.

Applying these factors to the instant case demonstrates that no official policy was formulated. Certainly, no rule of general applicability was adopted. The Court correctly notes that the Sheriff "testified that the Department had no written policy respecting the serving of capiases on the property of third persons and that the proper response in any given situation would depend upon the circumstances." Nor could he recall a specific instance in which entrance had been denied and forcibly gained. The Court's result today rests on the implicit conclusion that the Prosecutor's response — "go in and get them" — altered the prior case-by-case approach of the Department and formed a new rule to apply in all similar cases. Nothing about the Prosecutor's response to the inquiry over the phone, nor the circumstances surrounding the response, indicates that such a rule of general applicability was formed.

Similarly, nothing about the way the decision was reached indicates that official policy was formed. The prosecutor, without time for thoughtful consideration or consultation, simply gave an off-the-cuff answer to a single question. There was no *process* at all. The Court's holding undercuts the basic rationale of *Monell*, and unfairly increases the risk of liability on the level of government least able to bear it. I dissent.

DISCUSSION AND QUESTIONS

Governmental liability for policymaking. A majority of the Court agreed that municipal policy is made when "a deliberate choice to follow a course of action is made from among various alternatives by the official or officials responsible for establishing final policy with respect to the subject matter in question." Given the Court's conclusion that the county prosecutor had final policymaking authority for police search procedures, was there any way the prosecutor could have *avoided* making policy when advising the police? Is policy always made when an official with legal authority to make policy renders a decision? In other words, is the plaintiff's task in proving government liability reduced to (1) establishing under state or local law which person(s) has policymaking authority, and (2) identifying a decision by that person that led to the violation of federal law?

Justices White and O'Connor seem to agree that the unlawful search policy was "standard operating procedure" of the municipality. But they indicate they would not have found the county prosecutor's decision to be government policy had that decision conflicted with state or local law. This analysis makes sense insofar as contrary state or local law constitutes government policy, and effectively "repeals" the authority of local officials to modify that policy. Could a government entity take advantage of this limit on official policymaking by adopting a law mandating that all officials generally "comply with federal law" or stating that "any decision or action" inconsistent with federal law is null and void"?

The Court plainly rejects the contention that policymaking authority is "the limited province of the legislature at the local level." That is, policy can be made by officials other than those constituting the legislative branch of local government. Recall that *individual* officials engaged in the legislative function enjoy absolute immunity from suit. Could one argue that officials engaged in policymaking are the functional equivalent of legislators immune from suit? If so, then the county prosecutor who was found to have made policy in *Pembaur* would enjoy absolute legislative immunity. While this argument is plausible, it runs afoul of the Court's more narrowly tailored explanation of legislative immunity in cases like *Bogan v. Scott-Harris*, 523 U.S. 44 (1998). *Bogan* limited legislative immunity to persons performing acts intimately connected to the legislative, not policymaking, function. The county prosecutor's act of advising law enforcement officers bore none of the "hallmarks of traditional legislation" protected by the Court in the immunity cases. Consequently, § 1983 interpretation requires that we distinguish the legislative function enjoying absolute immunity from "policymaking" activity, which may (*Monell*) or may not (*Pembaur*) result from exercise of legislative power.

Justice Powell's dissenting opinion seems to have something akin to legislation in mind in rejecting the contention that the county prosecutor in *Pembaur* engaged in policymaking. According to Justice Powell, criteria for assessing whether policy is being made include (1) did officials use "established procedures" to make policy, (2) did officials disseminate the policy to their constituent audience, and (3) did officials intend to develop a rule of "general applicability?" Justice Powell believes the Court has confused the authority to make policy with the actual making of policy: "The Court provides no mechanism for distinguishing those acts or decisions that cannot fairly be construed to create official policy from the normal process of establishing an official policy that would be followed by a responsible public entity."

Was Justice Powell correct when he concluded the Court had re-instituted a form of respondeat superior liability for all persons having the power to make policy for government? Consider again how someone like the county prosecutor in *Pembaur* can make a situational decision without risking government liability. What would be the consequences of adopting Justice Powell's narrower definition of policymaking? Would that definition be fairer to blameless taxpayers who must ultimately satisfy liability judgments? On the other hand, does Justice Powell's view shift the costs of unlawful conduct to the blameless plaintiff? And would Justice Powell's view encourage policymakers to eschew "established procedures" for making policy so as to minimize government liability?

Delegating final authority to make policy. In *Pembaur*, the Court relies in part on the fact that the county sheriff's office had delegated to the county prosecutor the final authority to make law enforcement policy. But this "delegation" was consistent with state statutes. Under Ohio law, the county prosecutor shared statutory authority with the county sheriff's office. Consequently, *Pembaur* presented a case of one final policymaker deferring to another final policymaker.

Another form of delegation is probably more common in local government—delegation of decisionmaking authority to a subordinate who has no express legal authority to make final policy. Does such delegation render the subordinate a "final policymaker" whose misconduct implicates local government?

The Court addressed this issue in *City of St. Louis v. Praprotnick*, 485 U.S. 112 (1988). In *Praprotnick*, a former city official alleged that his transfer and eventual termination were in retaliation for his exercise of First Amendment rights, and that the explanation for these job actions was pretextual (a violation of due process). He sued various officials and the City of St. Louis. The supervisors who allegedly took wrongful action against Praprotnick lacked legal authority to make final policy on personnel matters. Yet the court of appeals believed they might nonetheless be "final" policymakers if their decisions were not subject to *de novo* review by the legally designated final authority. This final authority, the city's Civil Service Commission, had declined on technical grounds to review the merits of the action taken against Praprotnick by his supervisors. The court of appeals concluded that the supervisors' actions constituted *de facto* final policy and affirmed a jury verdict against the city.

The Supreme Court reversed. It rejected the court of appeals' position that the supervisors had *de facto* authority to make final policy because the legal policymaker's review had been "highly circumscribed." Justice O'Connor, writing for only four justices, articulated the limited circumstances where subordinates can be found to have exercised delegated final authority.

CITY OF ST. LOUIS v. PRAPROTNICK

485 U.S. 112 (1988)

Justice O'Connor announced the judgment of the Court and delivered an opinion in which The Chief Justice, Justice White, and Justice Scalia joined.

This case calls upon us to define the proper legal standard for determining when isolated decisions by municipal officials or employees may expose the municipality itself to liability under 42 U.S.C. § 1983.

* * * *

In the years since *Monell* was decided, the Court has considered several cases involving isolated acts by government officials and employees. We have assumed that an unconstitutional government policy could be inferred from a single decision taken by the highest officials responsible for setting policy in that area of the government's business. . . .

Two Terms ago, in *Pembaur,* we undertook to define more precisely when a decision on a single occasion may be enough to establish an unconstitutional municipal policy. Although the Court was unable to settle on a general formulation, Justice BRENNAN's opinion articulated several guiding principles. First, a majority of the Court agreed that municipalities may be held liable under § 1983 only for acts for which the municipality itself is actually responsible, "that is, acts which the municipality has officially sanctioned or ordered." Second, only those municipal officials who have "final policymaking authority" may by their actions subject the government to § 1983 liability (plurality opinion). Third, whether a particular official has "final policymaking authority" is a question of *state law* (plurality opinion). Fourth, the challenged action must have been taken pursuant to a policy adopted by the official or officials responsible under state law for making policy in *that area* of the city's business.

* * * *

We begin by reiterating that the identification of policymaking officials is a question of state law. "Authority to make municipal policy may be granted directly by a legislative enactment or may be delegated by an official who possesses such authority, and of course, whether an official had final policymaking authority is a question of state law." Thus the identification of policymaking officials is not a question of federal law, and it is not a question of fact in the usual sense. The States have extremely wide latitude in determining the form that local government takes, and local preferences have led to a profusion of distinct forms. Among the many kinds of municipal corporations, political subdivisions, and special districts of all sorts, one may expect to find a rich variety of ways in which the power of government is distributed among a host of different officials and official bodies. Without attempting to canvass the numberless factual scenarios that may come to light in litigation, we can be confident that state law (which may include valid local ordinances and regulations) will always direct a court to some official or body that has the responsibility for making law or setting policy in any given area of a local government's business. . . .

In the case before us . . . it appears that the Mayor and Aldermen are authorized to adopt such ordinances relating to personnel administration as are compatible with the City Charter. . . . The Civil Service Commission, for its part, is required to "prescribe . . . rules for the administration and enforcement of the provisions of this article, and of any ordinance adopted in pursuance thereof, and not inconsistent therewith." Assuming that applicable law does not make the decisions of the Commission reviewable by the Mayor and Aldermen, or vice versa, one would have to conclude that policy decisions made either by the Mayor and Aldermen or by the Commission would be attributable to the city itself. In any event, however, a federal court would not be justified in assuming that municipal policymaking authority lies somewhere other than where the applicable law purports to put it.

As the plurality in *Pembaur* recognized, special difficulties can arise when it is contended that a municipal policymaker has delegated his policymaking authority to another official. If the mere exercise of discretion by an employee could give rise to a constitutional violation, the result would be indistinguishable from *respondeat superior* liability. If, however, a city's lawful policymakers could insulate the government from liability simply by delegating their policymaking authority to others, § 1983 could not serve its intended purpose. It may not be possible to draw an elegant line that will resolve this conundrum, but certain principles should provide useful guidance.

First, whatever analysis is used to identify municipal policymakers, egregious attempts by local governments to insulate themselves from liability for unconstitutional policies are precluded by a separate doctrine. Relying on the language of § 1983, the Court has long recognized that a plaintiff may be able to prove the existence of a widespread practice that, although not authorized by written law or express municipal policy, is "so permanent and well settled as to constitute a 'custom or usage' with the force of law." That principle, which has not been affected by *Monell* or subsequent cases, ensures that most deliberate municipal evasions of the Constitution will be sharply limited.

Second, as the *Pembaur* plurality recognized, the authority to make municipal policy is necessarily the authority to make *final* policy. When an official's discretionary decisions are constrained by policies not of that official's making, those policies, rather than the subordinate's departures from them, are the act of the municipality. Similarly, when a subordinate's decision is subject to review by the municipality's authorized policymakers, they have retained the authority to measure the official's conduct for conformance with *their* policies. If the authorized policymakers approve a subordinate's decision and the basis for it, their ratification would be chargeable to the municipality because their decision is final.

* * * *

The city cannot be held liable under § 1983 unless respondent proved the existence of an unconstitutional municipal policy. Respondent does not contend that anyone in city government ever promulgated, or even articulated, such a policy. Nor did he attempt to prove that such retaliation was ever directed against anyone other than himself. Respondent contends that the record can be read to establish that his supervisors were angered by his 1980 appeal to the Civil Service Commission; that new supervisors in a new administration chose, for reasons passed on through some informal means, to retaliate against respondent two years later by transferring him to another agency; and that this transfer was part of a scheme that led, another year and a half later, to his layoff. Even if one assumes that all this was true, it says nothing about the actions of those whom the law established as the makers of municipal policy in matters of personnel administration. The Mayor and Aldermen enacted no ordinance designed to retaliate against respondent or against similarly situated employees. On the contrary, the city established an independent Civil Service Commission and empowered it to review and correct improper personnel actions. Respondent does not deny that his repeated appeals from adverse personnel decisions repeatedly brought him at least partial relief, and the Civil Service Commission never so much as hinted that retaliatory transfers or layoffs were permissible. Respondent points to no evidence indicating that the Commission delegated to anyone its final authority to interpret and enforce [local law]. . . .

A majority of the Court of Appeals panel determined that the Civil Service Commission's review of individual employment actions gave too much deference to the decisions of [subordinates]. Simply going along with discretionary decisions made by one's subordinates, however, is not a delegation to them of the authority to make policy. It is equally consistent with a presumption that the subordinates are faithfully attempting to comply with the policies that are supposed to guide them. It would be a different matter if a particular decision by a subordinate was cast in the form of a policy statement and expressly approved by the supervising policymaker. It would also be a different matter if a series of decisions by a subordinate official manifested a "custom or usage" of which the supervisor must have been aware. In both those cases, the supervisor could realistically be deemed to have adopted a policy that happened to have been formulated or initiated by a lower-ranking official. But the mere failure to investigate the basis of a subordinate's discretionary decisions does not amount to a delegation of policymaking authority, especially where (as here) the wrongfulness of the subordinate's decision arises from a retaliatory motive or other unstated rationale. In such circumstances, the purposes of § 1983 would not be served by treating a subordinate employee's decision as if it were a reflection of municipal policy. . . .

JUSTICE BRENNAN, with whom JUSTICE MARSHALL and JUSTICE BLACKMUN join, concurring in the judgment.

[Justice Brennan's concurring opinion disagrees with the plurality's position that municipal liability is avoided except when those with final decisionmaking authority approve a subordinate's decision and the basis for it. Justice Brennan would permit juries to determine whether *de facto* final authority lies with subordinates.]

Attempting to place a gloss on *Pembaur*'s finality requirement, the plurality suggests that whenever the decisions of an official are subject to some form of review — however limited — that official's decisions are nonfinal. Under the plurality's theory, therefore, even where an official wields policymaking authority with respect to a challenged decision, the city would not be liable for that official's policy decision unless *reviewing* officials affirmatively approved both the "decision and the basis for it." Reviewing officials, however, may as a matter of practice never invoke their plenary oversight authority, or their review powers may be highly circumscribed. Under such circumstances, the subordinate's decision is in effect the final municipal pronouncement on the subject. Certainly a § 1983 plaintiff is entitled to place such considerations before the jury, for the law is concerned not with the niceties of legislative draftsmanship but with the realities of municipal decisionmaking, and any assessment of a municipality's actual power structure is necessarily a factual and practical one.

[Justice Stevens's dissenting opinion is omitted.]

DISCUSSION AND QUESTIONS

Note the difference between the policy found in *Pembaur* and that argued in *Praprotnick*. In *Pembaur*, the plaintiff showed that local government had endorsed a policy permitting police searches without a warrant or exigent circumstances. In *Praprotnick*, the plaintiff attempted to show that the City of St. Louis had a policy endorsing retaliation against outspoken employees. One suspects that few municipalities — certainly not a major city like St. Louis — would endorse an official policy of retaliation, and this presented a challenge to the plaintiff in *Praprotnick.*

According to *Pembaur* the single decision of a final policymaker can create municipal policy, and consequently the ill-intentioned decision of a policymaker to retaliate might implicate government. Praprotnick's burden was somewhat eased by the view of policy adopted in *Pembaur,* but he still had to link retaliatory motive to a final policymaker. He attempted to do this by arguing that his supervisors were *de facto* final policymakers because their decisions were not effectively reviewed by the *de jure* policymakers. In other words, Praprotnick argued, the *de jure* policymakers had delegated their authority to the supervisors, and these supervisors decided to implement a policy of retaliation. (Observe that, according to Justice Powell's view of policy stated in *Pembaur,* a municipality would rarely endorse a policy of retaliation since this would require that it consciously adopt that policy through a deliberative process and disseminate its unsavory policy to constituents.)

The plurality in *Praprotnick* was unwilling to recognize delegation of policymaking authority inconsistent with state or local law. Once the *legal* issue of policymaking authority is determined by a court, the plaintiff must show that this policymaking authority "caused" the injury to the plaintiff.

In defense of this limited view of policymaking liability, can it be said that the plurality properly defers to local government to choose *who* will speak for it? In other words, given *Pembaur's* holding that a policymaker's ad hoc decisions may give rise to municipal liability, *Praprotnick* recognizes a municipality's right to select who will wield this power. And these designated policymakers may not delegate their authority in a manner contrary to local law.

But this view of non-delegable policymaking authority can lead to mischief and evasion. In situations like that of Mr. Praprotnick, the final policymakers (the civil service commission) would obviously have known that supervisors were accused of retaliation. And it is extremely unlikely that even ill-intentioned or indifferent policymakers would use Praprotnick's appeal as the occasion to officially endorse a policy of retaliation. However, such policymakers could permit unlawful conduct to occur through subordinates by simply (1) affirming the subordinates' decision while offering a lawful but pretextual rationale for affirmance, or (2) affirming without stating any rationale.

Do you agree with this reading of *Praprotnick?*

The plurality is aware that its view of delegated policymaking authority might suborn misconduct. Its response is to point out at least a partial solution to the problem — if a "series of decisions" shows that policymakers are tolerating misconduct by subordinates, a municipality may be liable for the "custom" it has tolerated.

But such a custom may be difficult to prove. Assume that a particular supervisor has made a series of employment decisions that suggest he is prejudiced against female employees. An affected employee sues the municipality and argues that its civil service commission has permitted the conduct to go on by not granting employees relief when appeals were filed with the commission. How does the plaintiff-employee prove the commission has acquiesced in the supervisor's misconduct? The *Praprotnick* plurality observes that "[s]imply going along with discretionary decisions made by one's subordinates, however, is not a delegation to them of the authority to make policy. It is equally consistent with a presumption that the subordinates are faithfully attempting to comply with the policies that are supposed to guide them." And later the plurality observes,

"[T]he mere failure to investigate the basis of a subordinate's discretionary decisions does not amount to a delegation of policymaking authority."

Consequently, the plurality's working assumption — that policymakers often defer to subordinates for legitimate reasons — undercuts the plaintiff's argument that policymakers were condoning a "custom" of discrimination. Without strong evidence policymakers are turning a blind eye to the obvious, the plaintiff's custom argument may be difficult to prove.

The plurality commented that "[i]f the authorized policymakers approve a subordinate's decision *and the basis for it*, their ratification would be chargeable to the municipality because their decision is final." How likely is it that policymakers will affirm an unlawful "basis" for a subordinate's action? If you were legal adviser to a civil service commission entertaining appeals from employees claiming they were victims of intentional misconduct by their supervisors, what advice would you give the commission so as to reduce the municipality's legal exposure?

Of course, employees who have been harmed by intentional, unlawful conduct will have a remedy under § 1983 against the *individual* wrongdoer. Further, the defense of qualified immunity will not be available to an individual defendant accused of intentional misconduct based on an improper motive. At the same time, the plaintiff will not be assured of actually recovering damages awarded against individual defendants. Employee indemnification programs as well as insurance coverage may exclude intentional misconduct.

Failure to train. We have seen that government liability for damages under § 1983 is limited to situations where government has caused the wrongdoing through its policies or customs. A plaintiff's best tack for asserting government liability is usually to identify either a formal policy or an express decision by a final policymaker. In both instances, policy derives from the deliberate choice of those who make policy for government.

To this point in our study of government liability, we have examined cases where policymakers made deliberate choices leading to *action.* In *Monell*, the city ordered its pregnant teachers to take unpaid leave; in *Pembaur*, the county prosecutor directed law enforcement to forcibly enter the plaintiff's clinic; and in *Praprotnick*, the civil service commission affirmed (in some sense) the job action against Praprotnick. None of these cases addressed whether a municipality might be liable because it deliberately chooses *not to act.*

In *City of Canton v. Harris*, 489 U.S. 378 (1989), the Court considered whether a municipality might be liable for failing to train its employees. Harris had been arrested by Canton police officers and taken to the police station. She twice slumped unconsciously to the floor of the station, but attending officers summoned no medical aid (she apparently suffered from mental illness). Eventually she was taken by her family to a hospital after being released from jail. She subsequently sued the City of Canton, alleging the city had failed to provide its police adequate training in the detection and treatment of arrestees' medical problems. A jury awarded Harris damages against the city, and the court of appeals affirmed that municipal liability arises when the municipality acts recklessly, intentionally, or with gross negligence in failing to train its officers. Notice that municipal liability was not premised on a finding that the city had adopted an unconstitutional policy (as in *Monell* and *Praprotnick*). The city had a policy requiring that jailers take unconscious persons to a local hospital.

CITY OF CANTON v. HARRIS

489 U.S. 378 (1989)

JUSTICE WHITE delivered the opinion of the Court.

In this case, we are asked to determine if a municipality can ever be liable under 42 U.S.C. § 1983 for constitutional violations resulting from its failure to train municipal employees. We hold that, under certain circumstances, such liability is permitted by the statute.

* * * *

[O]ur first inquiry in any case alleging municipal liability under § 1983 is the question whether there is a direct causal link between a municipal policy or custom and the alleged constitutional deprivation. The inquiry is a difficult one; one that has left this Court deeply divided in a series of cases that have followed *Monell*; one that is the principal focus of our decision again today.

Based on the difficulty that this Court has had defining the contours of municipal liability in these circumstances, petitioner urges us to adopt the rule that a municipality can be found liable under § 1983 only where "the policy in question [is] itself unconstitutional." Whether such a rule is a valid construction of § 1983 is a question the Court has left unresolved. Under such an approach, the outcome here would be rather clear: we would have to reverse and remand the case with instructions that judgment be entered for petitioner. There can be little doubt that on its face the city's policy regarding medical treatment for detainees is constitutional. The policy states that the city jailer "shall . . . have [a person needing medical care] taken to a hospital for medical treatment, with permission of his supervisor. . . ." It is difficult to see what constitutional guarantees are violated by such a policy.

Nor, without more, would a city automatically be liable under § 1983 if one of its employees happened to apply the policy in an unconstitutional manner, for liability would then rest on *respondeat superior*. The claim in this case, however, is that if a concededly valid policy is unconstitutionally applied by a municipal employee, the city is liable if the employee has not been adequately trained and the constitutional wrong has been caused by that failure to train. For reasons explained below, we conclude, as have all the Courts of Appeals that have addressed this issue, that there are limited circumstances in which an allegation of a "failure to train" can be the basis for liability under § 1983. Thus, we reject petitioner's contention that only unconstitutional policies are actionable under the statute.

Though we agree with the court below that a city can be liable under § 1983 for inadequate training of its employees, we cannot agree that the District Court's jury instructions on this issue were proper, for we conclude that the Court of Appeals provided an overly broad rule for when a municipality can be held liable under the "failure to train" theory. Unlike the question whether a municipality's failure to train employees can ever be a basis for § 1983 liability—on which the Courts of Appeals have all agreed—there is substantial division among the lower courts as to what *degree of fault* must be evidenced by the municipality's inaction before liability will be permitted. We hold today that the inadequacy of police training may serve as the basis for § 1983 liability only where the failure to train amounts to deliberate indifference to the rights of persons with whom the police come into contact. This rule is most consistent with our admonition in *Monell* that a municipality can be liable under § 1983 only where its policies are the "moving force [behind] the constitutional violation." Only where a municipality's failure to train its employees in a relevant respect evidences a "deliberate indifference" to the rights of its inhabitants can such a shortcoming be properly thought of as a city "policy or custom" that is actionable under § 1983. As Justice Brennan's opinion in Pembaur put it: "[M]unicipal liability under § 1983 attaches where—and only where—a deliberate choice to follow a course of action is made from among various alternatives" by city policymakers. Only where a failure to train reflects a "deliberate" or "conscious" choice by a municipality—a "policy" as defined by our prior cases—can a city be liable for such a failure under § 1983.

Monell's rule that a city is not liable under § 1983 unless a municipal policy causes a constitutional deprivation will not be satisfied by merely alleging that the existing training program for a class of employees, such as police officers, represents a policy for which the city is responsible. That much may be true. The issue in a case like this one, however, is whether that training program is adequate; and if it is not, the question becomes whether such inadequate training can justifiably be said to represent "city policy." It may seem contrary to common sense to assert that a municipality will actually have a policy of not taking reasonable steps to train its employees. But it may happen that in light of the duties assigned to specific officers or employees the need for more or different training is so obvious, and the inadequacy so likely to result in the violation of constitutional rights, that the policymakers of the city can reasonably be said to have been deliberately indifferent to the need.[17] In that event, the failure to provide proper training may fairly be said to represent a policy for which the city is responsible, and for which the city may be held liable if it actually causes injury.

In resolving the issue of a city's liability, the focus must be on adequacy of the training program in relation to the tasks the particular officers must perform. That a particular officer may be unsatisfactorily trained will not alone suffice to fasten liability on the city, for the officer's shortcomings may have resulted from factors other than a faulty training program. It may be, for example, that an otherwise sound program has occasionally been negligently administered. Neither will it suffice to prove that an injury or accident could have been avoided if an officer had had better or more training, sufficient to equip him to avoid the particular injury-causing conduct. Such a claim could be made about almost any encounter resulting in injury, yet not condemn the adequacy of the program to enable officers to respond properly to the usual and recurring situations with which they must deal. And plainly, adequately trained officers occasionally make mistakes; the fact that they do says little about the training program or the legal basis for holding the city liable.

Moreover, for liability to attach in this circumstance the identified deficiency in a city's training program must be closely related to the ultimate injury. Thus in the case at hand, respondent must still prove that the deficiency in training

17. [Footnote 10 in Court's opinion.] For example, city policymakers know to a moral certainty that their police officers will be required to arrest fleeing felons. The city has armed its officers with firearms, in part to allow them to accomplish this task. Thus, the need to train officers in the constitutional limitations on the use of deadly force, see Tennessee v. Garner, 471 U.S. 1 (1985), can be said to be "so obvious," that failure to do so could properly be characterized as "deliberate indifference" to constitutional rights. It could also be that the police, in exercising their discretion, so often violate constitutional rights that the need for further training must have been plainly obvious to the city policymakers, who, nevertheless, are "deliberately indifferent" to the need.

actually caused the police officers' indifference to her medical needs. Would the injury have been avoided had the employee been trained under a program that was not deficient in the identified respect? Predicting how a hypothetically well-trained officer would have acted under the circumstances may not be an easy task for the factfinder, particularly since matters of judgment may be involved, and since officers who are well trained are not free from error and perhaps might react very much like the untrained officer in similar circumstances. But judge and jury, doing their respective jobs, will be adequate to the task.

To adopt lesser standards of fault and causation would open municipalities to unprecedented liability under § 1983. In virtually every instance where a person has had his or her constitutional rights violated by a city employee, a § 1983 plaintiff will be able to point to something the city "could have done" to prevent the unfortunate incident. Thus, permitting cases against cities for their "failure to train" employees to go forward under § 1983 on a lesser standard of fault would result in *de facto respondeat superior* liability on municipalities — a result we rejected in *Monell.* It would also engage the federal courts in an endless exercise of second-guessing municipal employee-training programs. This is an exercise we believe the federal courts are ill suited to undertake, as well as one that would implicate serious questions of federalism.

Consequently, while claims such as respondent's — alleging that the city's failure to provide training to municipal employees resulted in the constitutional deprivation she suffered — are cognizable under § 1983, they can only yield liability against a municipality where that city's failure to train reflects deliberate indifference to the constitutional rights of its inhabitants.

* * * *

[Justice Brennan's concurring opinion is omitted.[18]]

DISCUSSION

Given the Court's rigorous standards for proving an affirmative municipal policy, plaintiffs often consider alleging municipal liability based on a failure to train. But the Court's opinion in *Harris* establishes an equally high standard for failure-to-train cases — a plaintiff must prove the municipality was "deliberately indifferent" to training needs. Mere negligence in training employees, or in seeing the need for training, is not enough.

In *Connick v. Thompson,* 131 S. Ct. 1350 (2011), the Court reviewed a failure-to-train claim alleging that a district attorney's office failed to train its employees concerning their obligation under *Brady v. Maryland,* 373 U.S. 83 (1963), to disclose exculpatory evidence (DNA evidence) to the accused. Although the DA agreed that the *Brady* rule had been violated, he argued that "he could not have been deliberately indifferent to an obvious need for more or different *Brady* training because there was no evidence that he was aware of a pattern of similar *Brady* violations." 131 S. Ct. at 1357. The Eleventh Circuit rejected the DA's argument, affirmed the jury's finding of municipal liability, and ruled that "attorneys, often fresh out of law school, would undoubtedly be required to confront *Brady* issues while at the DA's Office, that erroneous decisions regarding *Brady* evidence would result in serious constitutional violations, that

18. Justice Kennedy did not participate in the decision.

resolution of *Brady* issues was often unclear, and that training in *Brady* would have been helpful." *Id.* at 1358.

The Supreme Court reversed, holding that the type of single-incident liability referred to in *Harris* was not supported. The Court distinguished the obvious need to train police officers in the use of deadly force (*Tennessee v. Garner*) from the need to train prosecutors who have received formal legal education: "Attorneys are trained in the law and equipped with the tools to interpret and apply legal principles, understand constitutional limits, and exercise legal judgment." *Id.* at 1361. The Court concluded:

> In light of this regime of legal training and professional responsibility, recurring constitutional violations are not the "obvious consequence" of failing to provide prosecutors with formal in-house training about how to obey the law. Prosecutors are not only equipped but are also ethically bound to know what *Brady* entails and to perform legal research when they are uncertain. A district attorney is entitled to rely on prosecutors' professional training and ethical obligations in the absence of specific reason, such as a pattern of violations, to believe that those tools are insufficient to prevent future constitutional violations in "the usual and recurring situations with which [the prosecutors] must deal." A licensed attorney making legal judgments, in his capacity as a prosecutor, about *Brady* material simply does not present the same "highly predictable" constitutional danger as *Canton*'s untrained officer.

Id. at 1363.

Four justices argued in dissent that "the evidence demonstrated that misperception and disregard of *Brady*'s disclosure requirements were pervasive" in the DA's office. Such deliberate indifference, the dissent insisted, supported the jury's finding of a municipal policy. *Id.* at 1370.

By the way, the prosecutor in Orleans Parish, Louisiana, was Harry Connick (senior).

Circuit courts have struggled in defining deliberate indifference. *See* Harold S. Lewis, Jr. & Elizabeth J. Norman, Civil Rights Law and Practice 214-16 (2d ed. 2004). Perhaps an important clue to the Court's intended meaning is its observation in *Harris*, "it may happen that in light of the duties assigned to specific officers or employees the need for more or different training is so obvious, and the inadequacy so likely to result in the violation of constitutional rights, that the policymakers of the city can reasonably be said to have been deliberately indifferent to the need." The Court elaborated on this comment in footnote 10 (reproduced earlier), where it provided two examples of deliberate indifference. First, the Court observed that some risks of constitutional violation are so "obvious," that failure to train for these risks is actionable. In support, the Court cited its decision in *Tennessee v. Garner*, which bans the use of deadly force to apprehend a non-violent, fleeing felon. The Court suggests that municipalities should institute training to advise employees of fundamental constitutional rules pertinent to their work. One can imagine several, fundamental rules with which particular employees should be familiar, including the right of arrested persons to receive *Miranda* warnings, or the right of public employees to receive some form of notice and a hearing before being terminated. If employees can be held liable for the failure to follow "clearly established" law, it is only fair that employers share liability when they ignore the need to educate employees about that law.

But as we have seen, much constitutional law is not clear, especially as it applies in particular factual settings. The Court in *Harris* offers another clue relevant to constitutional obligations that are not susceptible to bright-line instruction. A public employer may learn from *experience* that its employees regularly encounter problems in reconciling their official duties with constitutional imperatives. ("It could also be that the police, in exercising their discretion, so often violate constitutional rights that the need for further training must have been plainly obvious.") So, for example, a police department may discover that its officers are repeatedly misusing restraint techniques and are in need of better training. At the same time, the Court emphasizes that training cannot be expected to substitute for an employee's judgment, nor can it fully prevent acts of employee negligence.

In *Praprotnick* the Court stressed that the question whether a government actor making an affirmative decision is a "final policymaker" is a legal question for the court. But the deliberate-indifference brand of policymaking may more frequently present a jury question. Recognizing the added role of juries in resolving some failure-to-train claims, the Court in *Harris* expressed its confidence that "judge and jury, doing their respective jobs, will be adequate to the task" of assessing these claims. At the same time, Justices O'Connor, Scalia, and Kennedy disagreed that the particular plaintiff's failure-to-train claim, based on a single incident of inadequate medical attention, merited a jury trial.

The Court in *Harris* cautioned that the causation requirement in failure-to-train cases should be carefully scrutinized. The Court required that the municipality's deliberate indifference and failure to train be "closely related to the ultimate injury." In *Board of County Commissioners of Bryan County, Oklahoma v. Brown*, 520 U.S. 397 (1997), the Court applied the deliberate-indifference standard in a case where the county was sued because of a sheriff's failure to adequately *screen* a new police hire. The plaintiff, who had been subjected to excessive force at the hands of the new hire, alleged the county sheriff was deliberately indifferent to the new hire's prior record of driving violations and misdemeanors involving physical force. Because the sheriff was the legal policymaker for his office, his deliberate indifference in hiring was alleged as the basis for imputing liability to the county.

The Court concluded the county was not liable for the single, poor hiring decision of the county sheriff. Although the Court recognized that a "single decision" by a policymaker may result in government liability, the Court emphasized that "rigorous standards of culpability and causation" must govern such a decision. The Court elaborated on its decision in *Harris* and indicated that deliberate indifference will most often be found when a plaintiff proves "programmatic" deficits in a municipality's training:

> We concluded in *Canton* that an "inadequate training" claim could be the basis for § 1983 liability in "limited circumstances." We spoke, however, of a deficient training "program," necessarily intended to apply over time to multiple employees. Existence of a "program" makes proof of fault and causation at least possible in an inadequate training case. If a program does not prevent constitutional violations, municipal decisionmakers may eventually be put on notice that a new program is called for. Their continued adherence to an approach that they know or should know has failed to prevent tortious conduct by employees may establish the conscious disregard for the consequences of their action—the "deliberate

> indifference"—necessary to trigger municipal liability. In addition, the existence of a pattern of tortious conduct by inadequately trained employees may tend to show that the lack of proper training, rather than a one-time negligent administration of the program or factors peculiar to the officer involved in a particular incident, is the "moving force" behind the plaintiff's injury.

520 U.S. at 407-08.

The Court then addressed the special difficulties of showing that deliberate indifference to a job applicant's past record caused the plaintiff to suffer an infliction of excessive force:

> We assume that a jury could properly find in this case that Sheriff Moore's assessment of Burns' background was inadequate. Sheriff Moore's own testimony indicated that he did not inquire into the underlying conduct or the disposition of any of the misdemeanor charges reflected on Burns' record before hiring him. But this showing of an instance of inadequate screening is not enough to establish "deliberate indifference." In layman's terms, inadequate screening of an applicant's record may reflect "indifference" to the applicant's background. For purposes of a legal inquiry into municipal liability under § 1983, however, that is not the *relevant* "indifference." A plaintiff must demonstrate that a municipal decision reflects deliberate indifference to the risk that a violation of a particular constitutional or statutory right will follow the decision. Only where adequate scrutiny of an applicant's background would lead a reasonable policymaker to conclude that the plainly obvious consequence of the decision to hire the applicant would be the deprivation of a third party's federally protected right can the official's failure to adequately scrutinize the applicant's background constitute "deliberate indifference."
>
> * * * *
>
> Even assuming without deciding that proof of a single instance of inadequate screening could ever trigger municipal liability, the evidence in this case was insufficient to support a finding that, in hiring Burns, Sheriff Moore disregarded a known or obvious risk of injury. To test the link between Sheriff Moore's hiring decision and respondent's injury, we must ask whether a full review of Burns' record reveals that Sheriff Moore should have concluded that Burns' use of excessive force would be a plainly obvious consequence of the hiring decision. On this point, respondent's showing was inadequate.

Id. at 411-13.

Brown imposes an exceedingly difficult burden of proof when a plaintiff seeks to show that a single instance of deliberate indifference caused his constitutional injury. A plaintiff must show that the specific constitutional violation was a "plainly obvious consequence" of the policymaker's indifference. In *Brown*, the new employee's record did not make it obvious he would use unconstitutional excessive force against a citizen.

How might a plaintiff meet this difficult burden? For example, if the new employee had previously been disciplined for use of excessive force in a prior job, does that make it plainly obvious he will use excessive force again? Allegations of excessive force are made fairly often by persons arrested. Do these allegations mean that police departments risk municipal liability if they hire an officer with a charge of excessive force on his record? If a department retains such an officer after a charge has been made? Or does the "plainly obvious" standard mean the police department can make a considered judgment that such an officer has been falsely charged, or perhaps learned his lesson, and avoid municipal liability?

Remedies against local government. As mentioned, local government enjoys no qualified immunity. Even if federal law is not clearly established, government is liable for violations resulting from its policies. Government does enjoy one advantage not enjoyed by individual defendants, however—it cannot be found liable for punitive damages. *See City of Newport v. Fact Concerts, Inc.*, 453 U.S. 247, 271 (1981). In *Fact Concerts*, the Court reasoned among things that (1) assessing punitive damages against an entity would punish taxpayers rather than the wrongdoer, and (2) deterrence of misconduct is sufficiently insured by requiring government to pay compensatory damages.

In suits against local government, one often finds that plaintiffs join both individual officials and the entity itself. You can now appreciate how differing liability standards, and perhaps differing remedies, apply to individuals and the entity. At the outset of litigation, plaintiffs may not be sure exactly how the liability case against individuals and the entity will develop during discovery. Naming both officials and the entity employing them preserves the plaintiffs' options.

One also finds in suits against local government that plaintiffs often name individual officials in both their individual and official capacities. The question arises: what does the plaintiff add by suing a local official in his "official" capacity?

The answer is usually "nothing." The allegation of official capacity against individuals employed by local government is usually unnecessary and often confusing. Such official-capacity allegations are largely a hangover from earlier days of § 1983 jurisprudence. Recall that, until the Court's decision in *Monell*, local government entities were not persons suable under § 1983. To circumvent this limitation in injunctive suits against local government (e.g., desegregation actions against local school boards), plaintiffs named individual officials in their official capacity. As we explored in Chapter 8, the official-capacity suit has long been a tool to enjoin unconstitutional action by state government when government itself is not subject to suit.

After *Monell* held that local governments were persons within the meaning of § 1983, official-capacity suits against local government officials essentially became obsolete. *See Hafer v. Melo*, 502 U.S. 21, 25 (1991). Plaintiffs can now simply name the local government as a defendant and pray for appropriate relief. Plaintiffs rarely add anything of value by suing individuals in their official capacities. To the contrary, use of official-capacity suits against local government officials has potential to mislead the plaintiff into making errors. For example, a government entity is entitled to notice that suit has been filed against it, *see Brandon v. Holt*, 469 U.S. 464, 472-72 (1985), and plaintiffs' counsel could overlook this requirement and assume that service of the official named in his official capacity is perfectly adequate to give notice to an entity. Equally troublesome, plaintiffs' counsel lacking familiarity with § 1983 may be confused about which liability standards apply in official-capacity suits.

On rare occasions, however, allegations of official-capacity liability against local-government officials may have justification. If, for example, in a suit seeking injunctive relief a plaintiff is unsure whether a government entity is truly "local" or instead part of the "state" (and not subject to suit under § 1983), he might name a key government official in his "official capacity" and so preserve the right to obtain equitable relief if the entity is ultimately deemed to be part of state government. Sometimes the status of a government entity is truly in doubt. *See, e.g., McMillian v. Monroe Cnty., Ala.*, 520 U.S. 781 (1997) (finding a county sheriff's office was part of state government). But this situation is uncommon, and plaintiffs can usually distinguish with confidence those entities that are local government subject to suit under *Monell.*

Now that we have canvassed the principal bases for imposing liability on local-government entities, try to apply your understanding to the following problem:

PROBLEM 9-5

Identifying Municipal Policy

Return to the Reference Problem involving curfew enforcement in Bozeman, Montana. Assume that after attempting to enforce the curfew ordinance, the City Commission was flooded with complaints by parents who thought it unfair that they could not make decisions about their children. The county attorney examined state law and concluded the city was free to tailor its curfew ordinance to grant parents the authority to "exempt" their children from curfew requirements. The Commission responded by granting this authority to parents, subject to the requirement that youths claiming parental permission provide "reasonable verification" of such permission.

Assume that, shortly after the curfew ordinance was amended, Bozeman police encountered a group of youths hanging out after hours at a public baseball field. Since it was well past the starting curfew time, the police arrested the youths. At least two of the arrested youths protested that they had parental permission to be out. When the police asked for verification, these two youths offered the arresting officers their cell phones and gave the officers their parents' home phone numbers. The officers refused to make calls to the parents and told these youths, "next time have some written permission with you. We can't be responsible for calling your parents when we find you out late."

The two youths later brought suit against the City of Bozeman (one sub-unit of which is the police department), alleging their arrests violated both the U.S. and Montana Constitutions. You may assume that there is legal precedent providing some support for their claim that they had a constitutional right to be on public property with parental consent.

The complaint filed by the youths alleged their wrongful arrest resulted from two city "policies." They allege as policy (1) the amended Bozeman ordinance, and (2) policymaking decisions of the Bozeman police department. In response to the city's motion to dismiss their complaint, the plaintiffs argue that the chief of police and his department have final policymaking authority over the enforcement of local ordinances and the training of city police officers. They further argue that, after the curfew ordinance was amended, the police chief issued a written directive to city officers advising them that "under the new curfew ordinance, any youth claiming parental permission to be on public property must provide 'reasonable verification' of permission, which includes signed, written permission of his or her parents." Finally, they argue that the police department "failed to train" its officers in proper implementation of the amended ordinance.

Discuss whether the plaintiffs appear to have a viable claim against the City of Bozeman. If you need further information to offer an opinion, identify what information you would need.

FIGURE 9-3

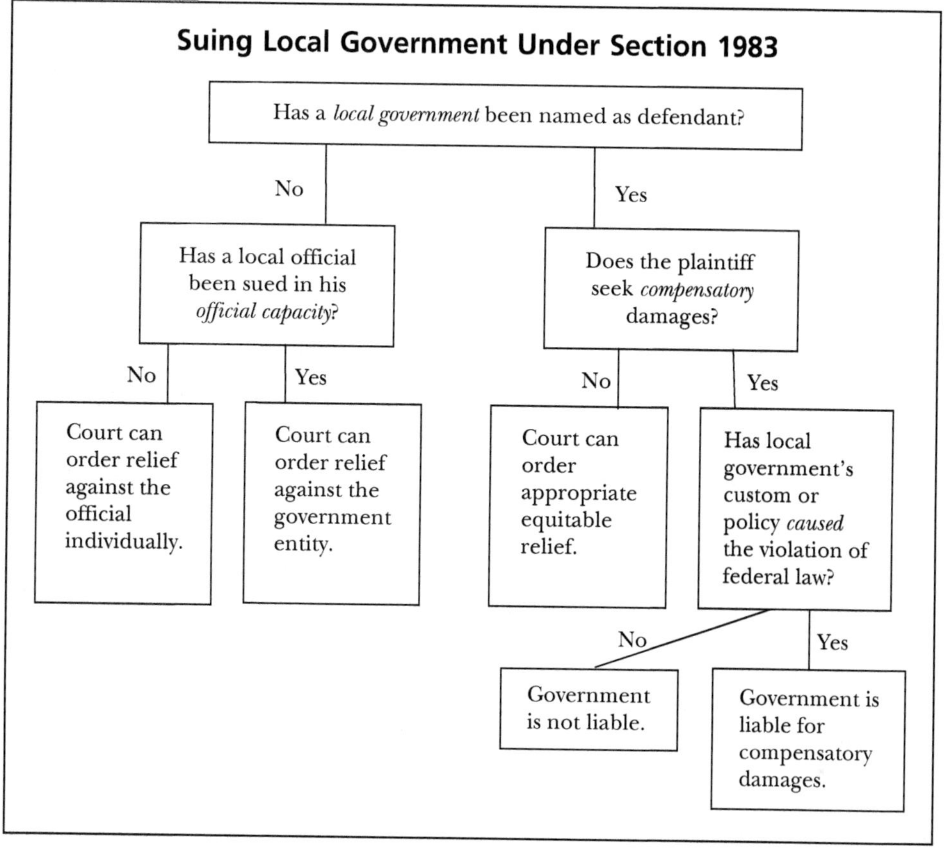

5. *Which Constitutional Rights Are Enforceable Under Section 1983?*

Section 1983 provides a remedy for the deprivation of "rights . . . secured by the Constitution and laws" of the United States. Although § 1983 was enacted to remedy the particular forms of unconstitutional conduct occurring in the aftermath of the Civil War, the remedy has not been limited to these forms. For example, it has not been limited to enforcement of "equal rights," a limitation found in the jurisdictional statute associated with § 1983. *See* 42 U.S.C. § 1343(a)(3).

For the most part, one can readily determine whether a constitutional provision extends "rights" to a plaintiff. The Bill of Rights is a principal source of rights enforceable under the Constitution, as we discuss below. Sometimes, however, the Constitution may be construed to restrict state action without simultaneously conferring "rights" on injured parties enforceable under § 1983. For example, the Supremacy Clause does not directly create rights enforceable under § 1983. *See Golden State Transit Corp. v. City of Los Angeles*, 493 U.S. 103 (1989).[19]

19. A related but distinct issue is whether plaintiffs may challenge state law on the ground that it conflicts with federal law and so is preempted by the Supremacy Clause. In *Douglas v. Independent Living Center of Southern California*, 132 S. Ct. 1204 (2012), five justices voted to remand a suit

FIGURE 9-4

Forms of Local Government Policy Making That Support an Award of Compensatory Damages

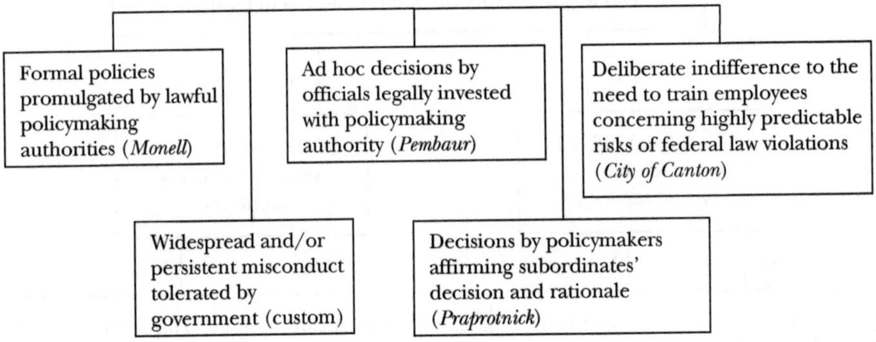

Similarly, the Court has held that *Miranda* violations do not give rise to a right enforceable under § 1983. According to *Chavez v. Martinez*, 538 U.S. 760, 772 (2003), the failure to warn a criminal suspect of the "right" to remain silent and the "right" to speak with a lawyer constitutes a violation of a "prophylactic" rule developed by the Court to foster the purposes of the Fifth Amendment. But the Fifth Amendment itself creates no "right" to remain silent or to have access to counsel.

Consequently, local or state law may be preempted by federal law without simultaneously conferring a right on affected parties to sue for damages under § 1983. In such a case, affected parties must consider whether the *specific* federal law preempting state law is the source of enforceable rights.

Due process. If § 1983 is the most important remedial law in constitutional litigation, the Due Process Clause of the Fourteenth Amendment is the most important source of substantive rights. Due process is the springboard for many, if not most, constitutional claims asserted under § 1983. And the Court's elaboration of the Due Process Clause has often figured prominently in § 1983 litigation.

The Court's due process jurisprudence can at times appear confusing and impossible to describe. But many useful generalizations can be derived from the due process literature, provided we always bear in mind that they are generalizations and not invariable rules.

To begin with, it helps to recall some of the key interpretations of § 1983 that provide background to an understanding of due process. These include (1) random, unauthorized action by government agents is usually "state action"; (2) random, unauthorized action by government agents usually occurs "under

brought to enforce provisions of the federal Medicaid statutes. The plaintiffs asserted a right under the Supremacy Clause to challenge state law said to conflict with the federal statutes. The majority saw no need to "address whether the Ninth Circuit properly recognized a Supremacy Clause action to enforce this federal statute before the agency took final action." *Id.* at 1211. The four dissenting justices argued that recognition of the plaintiffs' right to sue under the Supremacy Clause would permit an "end-round" around § 1983 jurisprudence, where the Court has usually required that plaintiffs identify a specific "right" under federal law. *Id.* at 1213.

color of" state law (recall *Monroe v. Pape*); (3) plaintiffs are generally not required to exhaust state-law remedies before filing suit under § 1983; and (4) the existence of state-law remedies does not usually preempt use of the § 1983 remedy.

The Fourteenth Amendment's Due Process Clause, in turn, provides that the state (including local government) may not "deprive any person of life, liberty, or property, without due process of law. . . ." The forms of "liberty" and "property" protected by due process are extensive. "Liberty" includes not only freedom from physical restraint but also freedom from physical or psychic injury. And "property" includes not only real and personal property but also things like driver's licenses and, in some circumstances, one's interest in continued employment (in appropriate contexts).

Some of the more challenging questions presented historically to the Court concern what constitutes a "deprivation" of life, liberty, or property, as well as what "process" is due a person threatened with a deprivation. For example, one could argue that a common motor vehicle accident results in a denial of due process when the negligent driver is employed by government. After all, a person is arguably deprived of her property (a vehicle) and her liberty (physical injury) when a sanitation department employee negligently operates a truck, causing a vehicular collision. Further, the injured person is obviously not given a notice and a hearing (due process) before the deprivation occurs.

In theory, then, the breadth of § 1983 and the potential breadth of due process combine to create a comprehensive tort-type remedy against government actors. But as we will see, the Court has interpreted due process more narrowly to avoid such a result.

Substantive due process. The concept of due process seems literally to provide *procedural* protections. That is, the state is not prevented from depriving one of life, liberty, or property; rather, before doing so it must provide adequate process. Nonetheless, the Court has interpreted due process to provide both procedural *and* substantive protections. *See, e.g., Daniels v. Williams,* 474 U.S. 327, 331 (1990) (due process guarantees more than "fair process" and bars "certain government actions regardless of the fairness of the procedures used to implement them"). The "substantive" form of due process is critical to modern constitutional law because it provides the mechanism through which constitutional protections like those provided by the First Amendment, the Fourth Amendment, and the Eighth Amendment have been "selectively incorporated" and applied against state action. *See, e.g., Gitlow v. New York,* 268 U.S. 652 (1925) (incorporation of free speech rights); *Wolf v. Colorado,* 338 U.S. 25 (1949) (incorporation of right to be free from unreasonable searches and seizures). The principal means for enforcing these incorporated due process rights in civil suits has been § 1983. If you reflect on the Court decisions we have studied in this chapter, you will find that the large majority involve the use of § 1983 to enforce rights incorporated through the Due Process Clause. These interpretations of § 1983 have greatly expanded the significance of earlier incorporation decisions by providing aggrieved persons a civil remedy not found in the constitutional provision itself.

The other form of substantive due process recognized by the Court is sometimes referred to as "due process *simpliciter.*" *See* Mark R. Brown, *De-Federalizing Common Law Torts: Empathy for* Parratt, Hudson, *and* Daniels, 28 B.C. L. Rev. 813 (1987). This form of substantive due process protects against "arbitrary or conscience shocking" behavior. *See County of Sacramento v. Lewis,* 523 U.S. 833, 847 (1998). This shocks-the-conscience standard was first employed by the Court in *Rochin v. California,* 342 U.S. 165 (1952), where it found unconstitutional the forced pumping of a criminal suspect's stomach to obtain illegal narcotics.

The Court has emphasized that violations of due process *simpliciter* are not easily found. First, when a legal claim is otherwise encompassed within another constitutional provision — like one of the incorporated provisions of the Bill of Rights — due process *simpliciter* does not provide an alternative approach. *See County of Sacramento, supra,* 523 U.S. at 842. For example, if a plaintiff asserting a right alleges he was injured by a police officer's use of excessive force while effecting an arrest, he must satisfy the Fourth Amendment standard governing excessive force and may not attempt to prove an alternative claim of due process *simpliciter* based on the same misconduct. *See Graham v. Connor,* 490 U.S. 386 (1989) (excessive force claims must be assessed based on "the specific constitutional standard that governs that right"). As Justice Souter commented in *Graham,* this approach is "underscored by pragmatic concerns about subjecting government actors to two (potentially inconsistent) standards for the same conduct and needlessly imposing on trial courts the unenviable burden of reconciling well-established jurisprudence under [specific constitutional protections] with the ill-defined contours of some novel due process right."

Second, due process *simpliciter* lies at the "end of the tort spectrum of culpability" where government conduct is "unjustifiable by any government interest." *Id.* at 848-49. In *County of Sacramento,* for example, the Court rejected a due process claim when police engaged in a risky high-speed chase, resulting in the death of a man. The Court held that "high-speed chases with no intent to harm suspects physically or to worsen their legal plight do not give rise to liability under the Fourteenth Amendment redressible by an action under § 1983." *Id.* at 854. Likewise, in *District Attorney's Office for the Third Judicial District v. Osborne,* 557 U.S. 52 (2009), the Court rejected the argument that a prisoner has a substantive due process right to obtain post-conviction access to a state's evidence so he can subject it to DNA testing. The Court reiterated that, "[a]s a general matter, the Court has always been reluctant to expand the concept of substantive due process because guideposts for responsible decisionmaking in this unchartered [sic] area are scarce and open-ended." *Id.* at 72 (internal citation omitted).

Procedural due process. Substantive due process as described above confers rights that cannot be abrogated by the state no matter what procedures the state provides. State procedures leading to the deprivation are simply irrelevant. In addition to substantive guarantees, however, the Due Process Clause also "encompasses . . . a guarantee of fair procedure." *See Zinermon v. Burch,* 494 U.S. 113, 125 (1990). As the Court observed in *Zinermon,* "In procedural due process claims, the deprivation by state action of a constitutionally protected interest in 'life, liberty, or property' is not in itself unconstitutional; what is unconstitutional is the deprivation of such an interest *without due process of law.*" *Id.* Consequently, in procedural due process cases, a plaintiff challenges the constitutionality of state procedures leading to a deprivation of life, liberty, or property, not the deprivation per se.

Procedural due process doctrine makes a distinction between deprivations resulting from (1) established state procedures, and (2) random behavior of officials not authorized by state law. The latter form of procedural due process challenges has caused the greatest confusion in recent decades.

When a plaintiff challenges the sufficiency of established state procedures, the Court applies the test of *Mathews v. Eldridge*, 424 U.S. 319 (1976). The *Mathews* test requires consideration of three factors:

> First, the private interest that will be affected by the official action; second, the risk of an erroneous deprivation of such interest through the procedures used, and the probable value, if any, of additional or substitute procedural safeguards; and [third], the Government's interest, including the function involved and the fiscal and administrative burdens that the additional or substitute procedural requirement would entail.

Id. at 335.

Core requirements of procedural due process include (1) notice of the proposed deprivation and (2) an opportunity to be heard. The Court has indicated that notice and the opportunity to be heard should usually be provided *before* the deprivation occurs. However, in certain circumstances where a pre-deprivation hearing is not practiced, due process can be satisfied, for example, by providing an expeditious hearing after the deprivation or by providing some form of common-law remedy to correct an erroneous deprivation. *See Zinermon, supra,* 494 U.S. at 128.

As an example of post-deprivation process that satisfies constitutional requirements, consider *Mackey v. Montrym*, 443 U.S. 1 (1979). In *Mackey*, the plaintiff's driver's license was automatically suspended because, when stopped by an officer having reasonable suspicion he was driving under the influence of alcohol, the plaintiff refused to take a breathalyzer test. After the plaintiff's license was suspended, state law provided him the right to demand an immediate hearing to test the lawfulness of the suspension. Applying the test in *Mathews v. Eldridge*, the Court upheld state law. The Court concluded that the risk of an erroneous suspension of a driver's license (a recognized form of "property") was not sufficiently substantial to require a pre-deprivation hearing, and found the state had a strong interest in deterring drunk driving by immediately suspending the driver's license.

At other times, however, the Court has rejected the constitutionality of post-deprivation process. For example, in *Goss v. Lopez*, 419 U.S. 565 (1975), the Court held that *some* form of hearing (even an informal hearing) was required before a student can be suspended from public school.

Suppose prison guards negligently lose a prisoner's property. Arguably the prisoner has been "deprived" of his property without due process. The same could be said if, instead of losing the prisoner's property, guards negligently caused him injury (which is considered to be a loss of "liberty"). If these occurrences violate procedural due process, § 1983 provides a remedy.

But these arguments presuppose a few things. First, they presuppose that a negligent loss of property or liberty is a deprivation. Second, they presuppose that post-deprivation state-law remedies that might be available to the prisoner against his guards or the state do not provide him sufficient "due process."

Over a relatively short five-year period the Supreme Court addressed and rejected these arguments. But during that period, the Court's reason for rejecting these arguments — and its ultimate interpretation of procedural due process — changed dramatically.

In *Parratt v. Taylor*, 451 U.S. 527 (1981), the Court held that negligent loss of a prisoner's property was in fact a "deprivation." The Court rejected the contention that either the Due Process Clause or § 1983 required that governmental deprivations be intentional. But the Court still rejected the prisoner's claim. It concluded that the prisoner had been afforded sufficient "due process" to redress his deprivation. The Court distinguished more conventional claims of procedural due process, where plaintiffs challenge "established state procedure." When established state procedures are challenged, the state can usually anticipate the risk of a deprivation and provide some meaningful form of process to prevent wrongful deprivations. But the negligent loss of the prisoner's property in *Parratt* was the result of "unauthorized" conduct by prison guards. It was "not only impracticable, but impossible, to provide a meaningful hearing before the deprivation." *Id.* at 541.

Because pre-deprivation process was not feasible when deprivations occur through negligence, the Court considered whether the state provided the prisoner an adequate form of post-deprivation process. The Court found that state law satisfied due process by providing the prisoner the right to assert a tort claim against the state and recover the value of his lost property. This was adequate process even though the prisoner could not recover punitive damages or attorney's fees, as he could have under § 1983. To require more of due process than this would be to transform the constitutional right into a "font of tort law." *Id.* at 544.

Justice Powell, concurring in *Parratt,* argued that "deprivation" includes only intentional deprivations. Under his view, the issue of whether the state provided adequate post-deprivation process was irrelevant.

After *Parratt,* the Court had several occasions to consider how due process applies to random, unauthorized deprivations of property and liberty. In *Hudson v. Palmer,* 468 U.S. 517 (1984), the Court extended its *Parratt* analysis to the *intentional* destruction of a prisoner's property. As in *Parratt,* the Court found that state procedures provided adequate post-deprivation process by granting the prisoner the right to sue the offending guard based on tort law. The Court also rejected the contention that pre-deprivation process was practicable before the intentional deprivation occurred since the guards were aware of the pending deprivation before effecting it. According to the Court, "the controlling inquiry is whether *the state* is in a position to provide predeprivation process." *Id.* at 534 (emphasis added).

Notice that *Parratt-Hudson* altered § 1983 precedent in one significant way. Under *Monroe v. Pape,* a § 1983 claim is viable regardless of whether state law provides an alternative remedy to the plaintiff. *Parratt-Hudson* affirms, however, that procedural due process claims based on random, unauthorized deprivations turn on the availability of an alternative state-law remedy. The relevance of state law results *not* from an interpretation of § 1983, but from interpretation of the underlying due process *right* enforced through a § 1983 action.

Perhaps the most challenging question left unresolved by *Parratt-Hudson* was what forms of state-law remedies were adequate to provide post-deprivation due process. *Hudson* affirmed that state law did not have to provide one of the more vital components of a § 1983 remedy, attorney's fees. But what if state tort law provided defendants a complete defense to liability, like sovereign immunity? This issue was presented to the Court in *Daniels v. Williams,* 474 U.S. 327 (1986), but became moot when the Court concluded that negligent deprivations of property are not constitutional "deprivations" at all. In other words, Justice Powell's position in *Parratt* had become the new majority view. In a companion case, *Davidson v. Cannon,* 474 U.S. 344 (1986), the Court took the logical step of extending its revised interpretation of deprivations to unauthorized inflictions of injury resulting from negligence. After *Daniels* and *Davidson*, the random, unauthorized negligence committed by government employees was not encompassed by procedural due process.

Daniels and *Davidson* do not address random, unauthorized misconduct that is intended by the perpetrator. Such intentional action would still be cognizable under procedural due process because intentional deprivations of liberty or property are constitutional deprivations. However, *Daniels* and *Davidson* leave several questions unanswered. First, are random, unauthorized deprivations actionable when the wrongdoer has acted with gross negligence or recklessness, that is, something between negligent and intentional conduct? *Daniels* expressly avoids answering this question. 474 U.S. at 334 n.3. Second, when intentional deprivations occur through random, unauthorized conduct, what form of state-law remedy provides due process? In *Daniels*, state sovereign immunity appeared to provide the state a full defense to liability. Somewhat surprisingly, Justice Stevens concurred in *Daniels* based on his opinion that sovereign immunity did not render the state-law remedy constitutionally inadequate. He commented, "[T]he mere fact that a State elects to provide some of its agents with a sovereign immunity defense in certain cases does not justify the conclusion that its remedial system is constitutionally inadequate." *Id.* at 342. According to Justice Stevens, a state prisoner was no worse off than other state citizens whose claims might be barred by sovereign immunity.

In sum, after *Daniels* and *Davidson*, the Court seemed to have reached consensus on several important doctrinal issues. First, procedural due process challenges to "established state procedure" were to be resolved by applying the multi-factor test in *Mathews v. Eldridge.* Second procedural due process challenges to "random, unauthorized" conduct required that the plaintiff show (1) that his loss resulted from intentional misconduct, or perhaps something close like recklessness or deliberate indifference; and (2) that alternative state-law remedies were constitutionally inadequate.

This was the setting for the Court's decision in *Zinermon v. Burch. Zinermon* offers an overview of both § 1983 principles and procedural due process. After reading *Zinermon*, consider whether the apparent doctrinal clarity of *Daniels* and *Davidson* has been compromised.

ZINERMON v. BURCH

494 U.S. 113 (1990)

JUSTICE BLACKMUN delivered the opinion of the Court.

Respondent Darrell Burch brought this suit under 42 U.S.C. § 1983 against the 11 petitioners, who are physicians, administrators, and staff members at Florida State Hospital (FSH) in Chattahoochee, and others. Respondent alleges that petitioners deprived him of his liberty, without due process of law, by admitting him to FSH as a "voluntary" mental patient when he was incompetent to give informed consent to his admission. Burch contends that in his case petitioners should have afforded him procedural safeguards required by the Constitution before involuntary commitment of a mentally ill person, and that petitioners' failure to do so violated his due process rights. . . . Petitioners argue that Burch's complaint failed to state a claim under § 1983 because, in their view, it alleged only a random, unauthorized violation of the Florida statutes governing admission of mental patients. . . .

* * * *

Florida's statutory provisions for "voluntary" admission are part of a comprehensive statutory scheme under which a person may be admitted to a mental hospital in several different ways.

First, Florida provides for short-term emergency admission. If there is reason to believe that a person is mentally ill and likely "to injure himself or others" or is in "need of care or treatment and lacks sufficient capacity to make a responsible application on his own behalf," he may immediately be detained for up to 48 hours. A mental health professional, a law enforcement officer, or a judge may effect an emergency admission. After 48 hours, the patient is to be released unless he "voluntarily gives express and informed consent to evaluation or treatment," or a proceeding for court-ordered evaluation or involuntary placement is initiated.

Second, under a court order a person may be detained at a mental health facility for up to five days for evaluation, if he is likely "to injure himself or others" or if he is in "need of care or treatment which, if not provided, may result in neglect or refusal to care for himself and . . . such neglect or refusal poses a real and present threat of substantial harm to his well-being." Anyone may petition for a court-ordered evaluation of a person alleged to meet these criteria. After five days, the patient is to be released unless he gives "express and informed consent" to admission and treatment, or unless involuntary placement proceedings are initiated.

Third, a person may be detained as an involuntary patient, if he meets the same criteria as for evaluation, and if the facility administrator and two mental health professionals recommend involuntary placement. Before involuntary placement, the patient has a right to notice, a judicial hearing, appointed counsel, access to medical records and personnel, and an independent expert examination. If the court determines that the patient meets the criteria for involuntary placement, it then decides whether the patient is competent to consent to treatment. If not, the court appoints a guardian advocate to make treatment decisions. After six months, the facility must either release the patient, or seek a court order for continued placement by stating the reasons therefor, summarizing the patient's treatment to that point, and submitting a plan for future treatment.

Finally, a person may be admitted as a voluntary patient. Mental hospitals may admit for treatment any adult "making application by express and informed consent" if he is "found to show evidence of mental illness and to be suitable for treatment." "Express and informed consent" is defined as "consent voluntarily given in writing after sufficient explanation and disclosure . . . to enable the person . . . to make a knowing and willful decision without any element of force, fraud, deceit, duress, or other form of constraint or coercion." A voluntary patient may request discharge at any time. If he does, the facility administrator must either release him within three days or initiate the involuntary placement process. At the time of his admission and each six months thereafter, a voluntary patient and his legal guardian or representatives must be notified in writing of the right to apply for a discharge.

Burch, in apparent compliance with [Florida statutes], was admitted by signing forms applying for voluntary admission. He alleges, however, that petitioners violated this statute in admitting him as a voluntary patient, because they knew or should have known that he was incapable of making an informed decision as to his admission. He claims that he was entitled to receive the procedural safeguards provided by Florida's involuntary placement procedure, and that petitioners violated his due process rights by failing to initiate this procedure. The question presented is whether these allegations suffice to state a claim under § 1983, in light of *Parratt* and *Hudson*.

To understand the background against which this question arises, we return to the interpretation of § 1983 articulated in Monroe v. Pape. In *Monroe*, this Court rejected the view that § 1983 applies only to violations of constitutional rights that are authorized by state law, and does not reach abuses of state authority that are forbidden by the State's statutes or Constitution or are torts under the State's common law. It explained that § 1983 was intended not only to "override" discriminatory or otherwise unconstitutional state laws, and to provide a remedy for violations of civil rights "where state law was inadequate," but also to provide a federal remedy "where the state remedy, though adequate in theory, was not available in practice." The Court said: "It is no answer that the State has a law which if enforced would give relief. The federal remedy is supplementary to the state remedy, and the latter need not be first sought and refused before the federal one is invoked."

Thus, overlapping state remedies are generally irrelevant to the question of the existence of a cause of action under § 1983. A plaintiff, for example, may bring a § 1983 action for an unlawful search and seizure despite the fact that the search and seizure violated the State's Constitution or statutes, and despite the fact that there are common-law remedies for trespass and conversion. As was noted in *Monroe*, in many cases there is "no quarrel with the state laws on the books"; instead, the problem is the way those laws are or are not implemented by state officials.

This general rule applies in a straightforward way to two of the three kinds of § 1983 claims that may be brought against the State under the Due Process Clause of the Fourteenth Amendment. First, the Clause incorporates many of the specific protections defined in the Bill of Rights. A plaintiff may bring suit under § 1983 for state officials' violation of his rights to, *e.g.*, freedom of speech or freedom from unreasonable searches and seizures. Second, the Due Process Clause contains a substantive component that bars certain arbitrary, wrongful government actions "regardless of the fairness of the procedures used to implement them." As to these two types of claims, the constitutional violation actionable under § 1983 is complete when the wrongful action is taken. A plaintiff, under *Monroe v. Pape*, may invoke § 1983 regardless of any state-tort remedy that might be available to compensate him for the deprivation of these rights.

The Due Process Clause also encompasses a third type of protection, a guarantee of fair procedure. A § 1983 action may be brought for a violation of procedural due process, but here the existence of state remedies *is* relevant in a special sense. In procedural due process claims, the deprivation by state action of a constitutionally protected interest in "life, liberty, or property" is not in itself unconstitutional; what is unconstitutional is the deprivation of such an interest *without due process of law*. The constitutional violation actionable under § 1983 is not complete when the deprivation occurs; it is not complete unless and until the State fails to provide due process. Therefore, to determine whether a constitutional violation has occurred, it is necessary to ask what process the State provided, and whether it was constitutionally adequate. This inquiry would examine the procedural safeguards built into the statutory or administrative procedure of effecting the deprivation, and any remedies for erroneous deprivations provided by statute or tort law.

In this case, Burch does not claim that his confinement at FSH violated any of the specific guarantees of the Bill of Rights. Burch's complaint could be read to include a substantive due process claim, but that issue was not raised in the petition for certiorari, and we express no view on whether the facts Burch alleges could give rise to such a claim. The claim at issue falls within the third, or procedural, category of § 1983 claims based on the Due Process Clause.

Due process, as this Court often has said, is a flexible concept that varies with the particular situation. To determine what procedural protections the Constitution requires in a particular case, we weigh several factors: "First, the private interest that will be affected by the official action; second, the risk of an erroneous deprivation of such interest through the procedures used, and the probable value, if any, of additional or substitute procedural safeguards; and finally, the Government's interest, including the function involved and the fiscal and administrative burdens that the additional or substitute procedural requirement would entail." *Mathews v. Eldridge.*

Applying this test, the Court usually has held that the Constitution requires some kind of a hearing *before* the State deprives a person of liberty or property. . . . In some circumstances, however, the Court has held that a statutory provision for a postdeprivation hearing, or a common-law tort remedy for erroneous deprivation, satisfies due process.

This is where the *Parratt* rule comes into play. *Parratt* and *Hudson* represent a special case of the general *Mathews v. Eldridge* analysis, in which postdeprivation tort remedies are all the process that is due, simply because they are the only remedies the State could be expected to provide.

Petitioners argue that the dismissal under Rule 12(b)(6) was proper because, as in *Parratt* and *Hudson,* the State could not possibly have provided predeprivation process to prevent the kind of "random, unauthorized" wrongful deprivation of liberty Burch alleges, so the postdeprivation remedies provided by Florida's statutory and common law necessarily are all the process Burch was due. . . .

* * * *

[The Court indicated that Burch agreed he had remedies under Florida law for his unlawful confinement. The Court also decided that the rule in *Parratt* could apply to deprivations of "liberty" as well as property.]

To determine whether, as petitioners contend, the *Parratt* rule necessarily precludes § 1983 liability in this case, we must ask whether predeprivation procedural safeguards could address the risk of deprivations of the kind Burch alleges. To do this, we examine the risk involved. The risk is that some persons who come into Florida's mental health facilities will apparently be willing to sign forms authorizing admission and treatment, but will be incompetent to give the "express and informed consent" required for voluntary placement. Indeed, the very nature of mental illness makes it foreseeable that a person needing mental health care will be unable to understand any proffered "explanation and disclosure of the subject matter" of the forms that person is asked to sign, and will be unable "to make a knowing and willful decision" whether to consent to admission. A person who is willing to sign forms but is incapable of making an informed decision is, by the same token, unlikely to benefit from the voluntary patient's statutory right to request discharge. Such a person thus is in danger of being confined indefinitely without benefit of the procedural safeguards of the involuntary placement process, a process specifically designed to protect persons incapable of looking after their own interests. . . .

We now consider whether predeprivation safeguards would have any value in guarding against the kind of deprivation Burch allegedly suffered. Petitioners urge that here, as in *Parratt* and *Hudson,* such procedures could have no value at all, because the State cannot prevent its officials from making random and unauthorized errors in the admission process. We disagree.

The Florida statutes, of course, do not allow incompetent persons to be admitted as "voluntary" patients. But the statutes do not direct any member of the facility staff to determine whether a person is competent to give consent, nor to initiate the involuntary placement procedure for every incompetent patient. A patient who is willing to sign forms but incapable of informed consent certainly cannot be relied on to protest his "voluntary" admission and demand that the involuntary placement procedure be followed. The staff are the *only* persons in a position to take notice of any misuse of the voluntary admission process and to ensure that the proper procedure is followed.

Florida chose to delegate to petitioners a broad power to admit patients to FSH, *i.e.*, to effect what, in the absence of informed consent, is a substantial deprivation of liberty. Because petitioners had state authority to deprive persons of liberty, the Constitution imposed on them the State's concomitant duty to see that no deprivation occur without adequate procedural protections.

It may be permissible constitutionally for a State to have a statutory scheme like Florida's, which gives state officials broad power and little guidance in admitting mental patients. But when those officials fail to provide constitutionally required procedural safeguards to a person whom they deprive of liberty, the state officials cannot then escape liability by invoking *Parratt* and *Hudson.* It is immaterial whether the due process violation Burch alleges is best described as arising from petitioners' failure to comply with state procedures for admitting involuntary patients, or from the absence of a requirement that petitioners determine whether a patient is competent to consent to voluntary admission. Burch's suit is neither an action challenging the facial adequacy of a State's statutory procedures, nor an action based only on state officials' random and unauthorized violation of state laws. Burch is not simply attempting to blame the State for misconduct by its employees. He seeks to hold state officials accountable for their abuse of their broadly delegated, uncircumscribed power to effect the deprivation at issue.

This case, therefore, is not controlled by *Parratt* and *Hudson,* for three basic reasons:

First, petitioners cannot claim that the deprivation of Burch's liberty was unpredictable. Under Florida's statutory scheme, only a person competent to give informed consent may be admitted as a voluntary patient. There is, however, no specified way of determining, before a patient is asked to sign admission forms, whether he is competent. It is hardly unforeseeable that a person requesting treatment for mental illness might be incapable of informed consent, and that state officials with the power to admit patients might take their apparent willingness to be admitted at face value and not initiate involuntary placement procedures. Any erroneous deprivation will occur, if at all, at a specific, predictable point in the admission process—when a patient is given admission forms to sign.

* * * *

Second, we cannot say that predeprivation process was impossible here. Florida already has an established procedure for involuntary placement. The problem is only to ensure that this procedure is afforded to all patients who cannot be admitted voluntarily, both those who are unwilling and those who are unable to give consent.

* * * *

Here . . . there is nothing absurd in suggesting that, had the State limited and guided petitioners' power to admit patients, the deprivation might have been averted. Burch's complaint alleges that petitioners "knew or should have known" that he was incompetent, and nonetheless admitted him as a voluntary patient in "willful, wanton, and reckless disregard" of his constitutional rights. Understood in context, the allegation means only that petitioners disregarded their duty to ensure that the proper procedures were followed, not that they, like the prison guard in *Hudson,* were bent upon effecting the substantive deprivation and would have done so despite any and all predeprivation safeguards. Moreover, it would indeed be strange to allow state officials to escape § 1983 liability for failing to provide constitutionally required procedural protections by assuming that those procedures would be futile because the same state officials would find a way to subvert them.

Third, petitioners cannot characterize their conduct as "unauthorized" in the sense the term is used in *Parratt* and *Hudson.* The State delegated to them the power and authority to effect the very deprivation complained of here, Burch's confinement in a mental hospital, and also delegated to them the concomitant duty to initiate the procedural safeguards set up by state law to guard against unlawful confinement. In *Parratt* and *Hudson,* the state employees had no similar broad authority to deprive prisoners of their personal property, and no similar duty to initiate (for persons unable to protect their own interests) the procedural safeguards required before deprivations occur. The deprivation here is "unauthorized" only in the sense that it was not an act sanctioned by state law, but, instead, was a "depriv[ation] of constitutional rights . . . by an official's abuse of his position."

We conclude that petitioners cannot escape § 1983 liability by characterizing their conduct as a "random, unauthorized" violation of Florida law which the State was not in a position to predict or avert, so that all the process Burch could possibly be due is a postdeprivation damages remedy. Burch, according to the allegations of his complaint, was deprived of a substantial liberty interest without either valid consent or an involuntary placement hearing, by the very state officials charged with the power to deprive mental patients of their liberty and the duty to implement procedural safeguards. Such a deprivation is foreseeable, due to the nature of mental illness, and will occur, if at all, at a predictable point in the admission process. Unlike *Parratt* and *Hudson,* this case does not represent the special instance of the *Mathews* due process analysis where postdeprivation process is all that is due because no predeprivation safeguards would be of use in preventing the kind of deprivation alleged.

We express no view on the ultimate merits of Burch's claim; we hold only that his complaint was sufficient to state a claim under § 1983 for violation of his procedural due process rights.

JUSTICE O'CONNOR, with whom THE CHIEF JUSTICE [REHNQUIST], JUSTICE SCALIA, and JUSTICE KENNEDY join, dissenting.

Application of *Parratt* and *Hudson* indicates that respondent has failed to state a claim allowing recovery under 42 U.S.C. § 1983. Petitioners' actions were unauthorized: they are alleged to have wrongly and without license departed from established state practices. Florida officials in a position to establish safeguards commanded that the voluntary admission process be employed only for consenting patients and that the involuntary hearing procedures be used to admit unconsenting patients. Yet it is alleged that petitioners "with willful, wanton and reckless disregard of and indifference to" Burch's rights contravened both commands. As in *Parratt*, the deprivation "occurred as a result of the unauthorized failure of agents of the State to follow established state procedure." The wanton or reckless nature of the failure indicates it to be random. The State could not foresee the particular contravention and was hardly "in a position to provide for predeprivation process," to ensure that officials bent upon subverting the State's requirements would in fact follow those procedures. For this wrongful deprivation resulting from an unauthorized departure from established state practice, Florida provides adequate postdeprivation remedies, as two courts below concluded, and which the Court and respondent do not dispute. *Parratt* and *Hudson* thus should govern this case and indicate that respondent has failed to allege a violation of the Fourteenth Amendment.

The allegedly wanton nature of the subversion of the state procedures underscores why the State cannot in any relevant sense anticipate and meaningfully guard against the random and unauthorized actions alleged in this case. The Court suggests that the State could foresee "that a person requesting treatment for mental illness might be incapable of informed consent." While foreseeability of that routine difficulty in evaluating prospective patients is relevant in considering the general adequacy of Florida's voluntary admission procedures, *Parratt* and *Hudson* address whether the State can foresee and thus be required to forestall the deliberate or reckless departure from established state practice. Florida may be able to predict that over time some state actors will subvert its clearly implicated requirements. Indeed, that is one reason that the State must implement an adequate remedial scheme. But Florida "cannot predict precisely when the loss will occur," and the Due Process Clause does not require the State to do more than establish appropriate remedies for any wrongful departure from its prescribed practices.

* * * *

A claim of negligence will not support a procedural due process claim. Respondent, if not the Court, avoids these pitfalls. According to Burch, petitioners "knew" him to be incompetent or were presented with such clear evidence of his incompetence that they should be charged with such knowledge. Petitioners also knew that Florida law required them to provide an incompetent prospective patient with elaborate procedural safeguards. Far from alleging inadvertent or negligent disregard of duty, respondent alleges that petitioners "acted with willful, wanton and reckless disregard of and indifference" to his rights by treating him without providing the hearing that Florida requires. That is, petitioners did not bumble or commit "errors" by taking Burch's "apparent willingness to be admitted at face value." Rather, they deliberately or recklessly subverted his rights and contravened state requirements.

The unauthorized and wrongful character of the departure from established state practice makes additional procedures an "impracticable" means of preventing the deprivation. "The underlying rationale of *Parratt* is that when deprivations of property are effected through random and unauthorized conduct of a state employee, predeprivation procedures are simply 'impracticable' since the state cannot know when such deprivations will occur." The Court suggests that additional safeguards surrounding the voluntary admission process would have quite possibly reduced the risk of deprivation. This reasoning conflates the value of procedures for preventing error in the repeated and usual case (evaluated according to the test set forth in *Mathews v. Eldridge*) with the value of additional predeprivation procedures to forestall deprivations by state actors bent upon departing from, or indifferent to, complying with established practices. Unsurprisingly, the Court is vague regarding how its proffered procedures would prevent the deprivation Burch alleges, and why the safeguards would not form merely one more set of procedural protections that state employees could willfully, recklessly, and wantonly subvert. Indeed, Burch alleges that, presented with the clearest evidence of his incompetence, petitioners nonetheless wantonly or recklessly denied him the protections of the State's admission procedures and requirements. The state actor so indifferent to guaranteed protections would be no more prevented from working the deprivation by additional procedural requirements than would the mail handler in *Parratt* or the prison guard in *Hudson.* In those cases, the State could have, and no doubt did, provide a range of predeprivation requirements and safeguards guiding both prison searches and care of packages.

Even indulging the Court's belief that the proffered safeguards would provide "some" benefit, *Parratt* and *Hudson* extend beyond circumstances in which procedural safeguards would have had "negligible" value. In *Parratt* and *Hudson* additional measures would conceivably have had some benefit in preventing the alleged deprivations. A practice of barring individual or unsupervised shakedown searches, a procedure of always pairing or monitoring guards, or a requirement that searches be conducted according to "an established policy" might possibly have helped to prevent the type of deprivation considered in *Hudson.* More sensible staffing practices, better training, or a more rigorous tracking procedure may have averted the deprivation at issue in *Parratt.* In those cases, like this one, the State knew the exact context in which the wrongful deprivation would occur. Yet the possibility of implementing such marginally beneficial measures, in light of the type of alleged deprivation, did not alter the analysis. The State's inability to foresee and to forestall the wrongful departure from established procedures renders additional predeprivation measures "impracticable" and not required by the dictates of due process.

Every command to act imparts the duty to exercise discretion in accord with the command and affords the opportunity to abuse that discretion. The *Mathews* test measures whether the State has sufficiently constrained discretion in the usual case, while the *Parratt* doctrine requires the State to provide a remedy for any wrongful abuse. The Court suggests that this case differs from *Parratt* and *Hudson* because petitioners possessed a sort of delegated power. Yet petitioners no more had the delegated power to depart from the admission procedures and requirements than did the guard in *Hudson* to exceed the limits of his established search and seizure authority, or the prison official in *Parratt* wrongfully to withhold or misdeliver mail. Petitioners' delegated duty to act in accord with Florida's admission procedures is akin to the mail handler's duty to follow and implement the procedures surrounding delivery of packages, or the guard's duty to conduct the search properly. In the appropriate circumstances and pursuant to established procedures, the guard in *Hudson* was charged with seizing property pursuant to a search. The official in *Parratt* no doubt possessed some power to withhold certain packages from prisoners. *Parratt* and *Hudson* distinguish sharply between deprivations caused by unauthorized acts and those occasioned by established state procedures. The delegation argument blurs this line and ignores the unauthorized nature of petitioners' alleged departure from established practices.

* * * *

I respectfully dissent.

DISCUSSION AND QUESTIONS

What are the standards for determining whether a procedural due process claim is viable after *Zinermon*? The distinction between "established state procedure," which is governed by the *Mathews* test, and "random, unauthorized" deprivations, governed by *Parratt*, no longer guides the analysis in all cases. At least according to the dissent in *Zinermon*, the *Parratt* standard no longer applies when random, unauthorized deprivations are committed by individuals exercising "broadly delegated power that carries with it pervasive risk of wrongful deprivation." This means the deprivation is actionable under § 1983 regardless of whether state law otherwise provides the plaintiff a remedy.

The majority comes close to impugning the adequacy of state procedures for voluntary commitment—which would require application of the *Mathews* test. The Court observes, "[W]e cannot say that predeprivation process was impossible here. Florida already has an established procedure for involuntary placement. The problem is only to ensure that this procedure is afforded to all patients who cannot be admitted voluntarily, both those who are unwilling and those who are unable to give consent." Burch, however, did not challenge the constitutionality of Florida commitment law. Any damages claim against the state would have been barred by sovereign immunity.

Does *Zinermon* impose liability on government employees because their state has failed to sufficiently guide their exercise of power? Are employees now charged with "fashioning effective procedures or ensuring that required procedures are not routinely evaded" on pain of personal liability? Is this fair? Does the fact that state employees were alleged to have acted with "willful, wanton, and reckless disregard" of Burch's rights mollify your concerns about their legal responsibility?

By the way, should the individual defendants who violated Burch's constitutional rights nonetheless prevail because due process law was not "clearly established" when they acted?

PROBLEM 9-6

No Holds Barred

Max Goldberg was assistant principal at Newport High School. One day he was asked by a twelfth-grade teacher to come to her classroom and break up an altercation between two youths. Max immediately went to the classroom and intervened between the two boys. One youth, Lee Lesnar, continued to taunt both Max and the other boy involved in the altercation. Max eventually decided he needed to take Lee to the principal's office and call his parents. Lee refused to accompany Max, leading Max to apply an arm hold that enabled him to force Lee down the hall to the principal's office.

Max then called Lee's parents. Lee's father, B.J., soon arrived. But rather than supporting Max, B.J. began defending his son and arguing with Max. When the argument escalated, B.J. attempted to kick Max using one of the techniques he had learned in his study of Tae Kwon Do. Max responded by grabbing B.J.'s leg and applying a "knee bar" he had learned while studying jiu-jitsu. As a consequence, B.J.'s knee was severely injured. It appears in retrospect that Max could have restrained B.J. without inflicting serious injury.

B.J. and his son have now filed suit against Max and the school system. Each plaintiff alleges (1) a substantive due process claim, and (2) a claim for assault and battery under state tort law. B.J.'s son has also alleged (3) a separate federal claim against Max, arguing that Max used excessive force in "seizing" Lee and taking him to the principal's office.

You may assume case precedent recognizes students have a Fourth Amendment right to be free of the use of excessive force when school administrators restrain them to enforce school disciplinary rules. *See, e.g, Shuman v. Penn Manor Sch. Dist.*, 422 F.3d 141 (3d Cir. 2005). You may also assume that Max and the school system enjoy no immunity from damages under state tort law.

Discuss what problems, if any, the plaintiffs may encounter in attempting to recover damages from the defendants under the substantive due process claim.

6. *Which Federal Statutory Rights Are Enforceable Under Section 1983?*

Section 1983 provides a remedy for rights secured by the "Constitution or laws" of the United States. Among the important issues the Court has addressed when interpreting and applying this phraseology are (1) does the term "laws" encompass *statutory* law and, if so, what types of statutes? and (2) when does a covered law establish "rights" enforceable under § 1983?

The meaning of "laws." In *Maine v. Thiboutot*, 448 U.S. 1 (1980), the Court expansively interpreted the term "laws" to include federal statutes as well as the Constitution. Further, the Court refused to limit enforcement of statutory claims to those securing "civil rights" or "equal protection." *Id.* at 7-8. In *Thiboutot*, the Court authorized a § 1983 remedy to enforce provisions of the Social Security Act, and also held that § 1988 attorney's fees are recoverable in such actions.

The consequences of the ruling in *Thiboutot* were alarming to dissenting Justice Powell, who identified literally hundreds of federal statutes whose violation by government actors was now actionable under § 1983. In essence, the Court's ruling amended the remedial provisions of numerous federal statutes to create remedies not specifically considered by Congress. Justice Powell was particularly concerned with the numerous federal-state programs for the administration of welfare-type benefits. Implementation of *Thiboutot* seems to affirm that such programs have been the target of most § 1983 claims invoking federal statutes. *See* Harold S. Lewis, Jr. & Elizabeth J. Norman, Civil Rights Law and Practice 293 (2d ed. 2004).

REVIEW AND CONSOLIDATION

Securing Due Process Through Section 1983

- *State action* implicating constitutional due process protections, and action "*under color of state law*" implicating § 1983, include
  - formal governmental action at the state[20] or local level; and
  - most random, unauthorized action by state or local government officials.
  - Plaintiffs are generally not required to exhaust state remedies before suing under § 1983; nor do state remedies preempt the § 1983 remedy.
- *Substantive due process* protects against certain forms of state action regardless of what procedures government affords. Substantive due process includes
  - constitutional protections made applicable through the Fourteenth Amendment, for example, "incorporated" Bill of Rights protections; and
  - the right to be free from certain forms of "arbitrary or conscience-shocking" state action.
- *Procedural due process* forbids state action that deprives a person of "life, liberty or property" without "due process of law." A violation of procedural due process may occur through:
  - established state procedures; or
  - random, unauthorized behavior of government officials.
- When a procedural due process claim is based on *random, unauthorized* behavior
  - the deprivation must be intentional (or perhaps the result of gross negligence or recklessness); and
  - remedies under state law must be constitutionally inadequate (a requirement whose meaning remains unclear).

One year after *Thiboutot*, the Court announced two important limits to the use of § 1983 to enforce statutory claims. First, a court must consider whether a particular statute's remedial scheme (particularly, one providing more limited remedies than those authorized by § 1983) is the "exclusive remedy" for its enforcement, thereby preempting use of § 1983. *See Middlesex Cnty. Sewerage Auth. v. National Sea Clammers Ass'n* 453 U.S. 1 (1981). In *Sea Clammers*, Justice Powell wrote for the majority in holding that federal statutes regulating water pollution provided a "comprehensive" remedy preempting § 1983, even though these statutes authorized prospective relief, and not damages for past violations. Nor did these statutes explicitly preempt use of § 1983 to enforce their provisions.

20. Recall, however, that the state itself is not a person within the meaning of § 1983.

Later Court decisions seemed to recognize a "rebuttable presumption" that § 1983 can be used to enforce federal statutory rights. *See, e.g., Blessing v. Freestone*, 520 U.S. 329, 341 (1997). To rebut this presumption, a party was required to identify evidence that Congress specifically considered and rejected remedies under § 1983, or that Congress enacted a "comprehensive enforcement scheme that is incompatible with individual enforcement under § 1983." *Id.* However, in *City of Rancho Palos Verdes v. Abrams*, 544 U.S. 113 (2005), the majority opinion of Justice Scalia indicated that the burden of rebutting such a presumption is usually not very difficult to satisfy. *Id.* at 121. According to the Court, a statute's creation of an "express, private" remedy "ordinarily" signals that Congress intended to foreclose more expansive remedies under § 1983. At the same time, the majority refused to adopt a per se rule that a statute's creation of an express remedy "conclusive[ly]" demonstrates Congress' rejection of a § 1983 remedy. According to the Court, the "ordinary inference that the remedy provided in the statute is exclusive can surely be overcome by textual indication, express or implicit, that the remedy is to complement, rather than supplant, § 1983." *Id.* at 122.

To date, the Court has found a statutory remedy to be exclusive when it provides some form of comprehensive *judicial* remedy. When a federal statute contains no remedy, or the remedy is purely administrative, the Court has declined to find a § 1983 remedy preempted. *See, e.g. Golden State Transit Corp. v. City of Los Angeles*, 493 U.S. 103 (1989); *Wright v. City of Roanoke*, 479 U.S. 418 (1987).

A variation on this problem arises when § 1983 is used to enforce constitutional rights that overlap with federal statutory rights. For example, § 1983 can be used to sue local government employers who engage in job discrimination based on gender or race, based on the Equal Protection Clause of the Fourteenth Amendment. At the same time, Congress has enacted Title VII, which also prohibits gender and racial discrimination in both private and public employment. But Title VII requires that employees act expeditiously in complaining about job discrimination and also requires that they first exhaust administrative remedies (e.g., complaining to the EEOC) before filing suit in court.

Most lower courts agree that Title VII does not affect use of § 1983 to enforce employment discrimination claims based on the *Constitution. See, e.g., Johnson v. City of Fort Lauderdale*, 148 F.3d 1228, 1231 (11th Cir. 1998); 3 Employment Discrimination Coordinator § 114A:8 (2014). For example, a plaintiff may assert a § 1983 claim against individual supervisors who engage in job discrimination based on the Constitution, even though the Title VII remedy limits liability to the public employers and denies relief against individual supervisors. *See, e.g., Banks v. State Univ. of N.Y.*, 2007 WL 895505 (W.D.N.Y. 2007). At the same time, a claim based on rights afforded by a federal *statute* may be subject to the remedial rules found in that statute rather than those set forth in § 1983. *See, e.g., Grey v. Wilburn*, 270 F.3d 607 (8th Cir. 2001).

In *Fitzgerald v. Barnstable School Committee*, 555 U.S. 246 (2009), the Court held that Title IX is not the exclusive mechanism for suing for gender discrimination (sexual harassment) in public schools. The Court reasoned that Title IX is not a "comprehensive remedial scheme" for enforcing gender equality in the schools. *Id.* at 258. For example, Title IX does not authorize suit against school officials and other individuals. In light of these and other concerns, the Court held that

§ 1983 can be used to enforce the Equal Protection Clause even when an alternative remedy might exist under Title IX.

The existence of legal "rights." The use of § 1983 to enforce federal statutes (and occasionally constitutional provisions) has been further restricted by the Court's increased scrutiny of whether a law actually creates "rights" enforceable by the individual plaintiff. *See Pennhurst State Sch. & Hosp. v. Halderman*, 451 U.S. 1 (1981). A recent example of this scrutiny is the Court's decision in *Gonzaga University v. Doe*, excerpted below.

GONZAGA UNIVERSITY v. DOE

536 U.S. 273 (2002)

[A former student sued the university because of alleged violations of the Family Educational Rights and Privacy Act of 1974 (FERPA). FERPA prevents disclosure of a student's educational records unless the university has obtained proper consent. Gonzaga University disclosed the plaintiff's records without consent, preventing him from obtaining a state teaching certificate. Because the university was arguably acting "under color" of state law, the plaintiff sued under § 1983 to enforce rights allegedly conferred by FERPA.]

CHIEF JUSTICE REHNQUIST delivered the opinion of the Court.

The question presented is whether a student may sue a private university for damages under 42 U.S.C. § 1983 to enforce provisions of the Family Educational Rights and Privacy Act of 1974 (FERPA or Act), which prohibit the federal funding of educational institutions that have a policy or practice of releasing education records to unauthorized persons. We hold such an action foreclosed because the relevant provisions of FERPA create no personal rights to enforce under 42 U.S.C. § 1983.

Respondent John Doe is a former undergraduate in the School of Education at Gonzaga University, a private university in Spokane, Washington. He planned to graduate and teach at a Washington public elementary school. Washington at the time required all of its new teachers to obtain an affidavit of good moral character from a dean of their graduating college or university. In October 1993, Roberta League, Gonzaga's "teacher certification specialist," overheard one student tell another that respondent engaged in acts of sexual misconduct against Jane Doe, a female undergraduate. League launched an investigation and contacted the state agency responsible for teacher certification, identifying respondent by name and discussing the allegations against him. Respondent did not learn of the investigation, or that information about him had been disclosed, until March 1994, when he was told by League and others that he would not receive the affidavit required for certification as a Washington schoolteacher.

Respondent then sued Gonzaga and League (petitioners) in state court. He alleged violations of Washington tort and contract law, as well as a pendent violation of § 1983 for the release of personal information to an "unauthorized person" in violation of FERPA. A jury found for respondent on all counts, awarding him $1,155,000, including $150,000 in compensatory damages and $300,000 in punitive damages on the FERPA claim.

* * * *

Congress enacted FERPA under its spending power to condition the receipt of federal funds on certain requirements relating to the access and disclosure of student educational records. The Act directs the Secretary of Education to withhold federal funds from any public or private "educational agency or institution" that fails to comply with these conditions. As relevant here, the Act provides:

> No funds shall be made available under any applicable program to any educational agency or institution which has a policy or practice of permitting the release of education records (or personally identifiable information contained therein . . .) of students without the written consent of their parents to any individual, agency, or organization."

20 U.S.C. § 1232g(b)(1).

The Act directs the Secretary of Education to enforce this and other of the Act's spending conditions. The Secretary is required to establish an office and review board within the Department of Education for "investigating, processing, reviewing, and adjudicating violations of [the Act]." Funds may be terminated only if the Secretary determines that a recipient institution "is failing to comply substantially with any requirement of [the Act]" and that such compliance "cannot be secured by voluntary means."

Respondent contends that this statutory regime confers upon any student enrolled at a covered school or institution a federal right, enforceable in suits for damages under § 1983, not to have "education records" disclosed to unauthorized persons without the student's express written consent. But we have never before held, and decline to do so here, that spending legislation drafted in terms resembling those of FERPA can confer enforceable rights.

* * * *

[T]here is no question that FERPA's nondisclosure provisions fail to confer enforceable rights. To begin with, the provisions entirely lack the sort of "rights-creating" language critical to showing the requisite congressional intent to create new rights. Unlike the individually focused terminology of Titles VI and IX ("No person . . . shall . . . be subjected to discrimination"), FERPA's provisions speak only to the Secretary of Education, directing that "[n]o funds shall be made available" to any "educational agency or institution" which has a prohibited "policy or practice." This focus is two steps removed from the interests of individual students and parents and clearly does not confer the sort of "individual entitlement" that is enforceable under § 1983.

* * * *

FERPA's nondisclosure provisions further speak only in terms of institutional policy and practice, not individual instances of disclosure. Therefore . . . they have an "aggregate" focus, they are not concerned with "whether the needs of any particular person have been satisfied," and they cannot "give rise to individual rights. . . ." Recipient institutions can further avoid termination of funding so long as they "comply substantially" with the Act's requirements. . . .

Our conclusion that FERPA's nondisclosure provisions fail to confer enforceable rights is buttressed by the mechanism that Congress chose to provide for enforcing those provisions. Congress expressly authorized the Secretary of Education to "deal with violations" of the Act, and required the Secretary to "establish or designate [a] review board" for investigating and adjudicating such violations. Pursuant to these provisions, the Secretary created the Family Policy Compliance Office (FPCO) "to act as the Review Board required under the Act [and] to enforce the Act with respect to all applicable programs." The FPCO permits students and parents who suspect a violation of the Act to file individual written complaints. If a complaint is timely and contains required information, the FPCO will initiate an investigation, notify the educational institution of the charge, and request a written response. If a violation is found, the FPCO distributes a notice of factual findings and a "statement of the specific steps that the agency or institution must take to comply" with FERPA. . . .

* * * *

In sum, if Congress wishes to create new rights enforceable under § 1983, it must do so in clear and unambiguous terms — no less and no more than what is required for Congress to create new rights enforceable under an implied private right of action. FERPA's nondisclosure provisions contain no rights-creating language, they have an aggregate, not individual, focus, and they serve primarily to direct the Secretary of Education's distribution of public funds to educational institutions. They therefore create no rights enforceable under § 1983.

[Concurring and dissenting opinions are omitted.]

DISCUSSION AND QUESTIONS

It often comes as a surprise to students — and clients — that the violation of a federal statutory duty does not confer any "rights" on persons protected by the statute. Isn't it apparent that Congress enacted FERPA to protect the privacy of students' education records? After all, the Court points out that students or parents who suspect a violation of FERPA can file individual complaints and initiate a federal investigation of the offending institution. Doesn't this suggest that students have some form of enforceable "rights"? Or is there a distinction between federal protection and federal rights?

Perhaps the Court's opinion is best understood by focusing on its use of the term "enforceable rights" under § 1983. FERPA protects the privacy interests of students in the "aggregate" by requiring that universities "substantially" comply with the statute. But it stops short of protecting students individually. Even if a university has violated FERPA, it risks losing federal funding only if it has a "policy or practice" (the Court's language) of violating the Act. Apparently, individual violations of FERPA are tolerated if the university "substantially" complies with its obligations.

The Court's conclusion in *Gonzaga University* relates to another issue that has generated great controversy in the Court in recent decades — whether the Court should recognize "implied rights of action" under federal statutes that fail to grant injured parties an explicit remedy. We will return to this part of the Court's opinion in Chapter 11. For the present, note that when a federal statute creates "rights" that have been violated by a state or local *government* official, § 1983 may provide an express remedy. The question a court must address is not whether to recognize an "implied" remedy; rather a court must determine whether the express remedy provided by § 1983 has been preempted by Congress.

For a recent application of *Gonzaga* to the issue whether aggrieved persons have enforceable "rights" under the Medicaid Act, consider *Equal Access for El Paso, Inc. v. Hawkins,* 509 F.3d 697 (5th Cir. 2007). In *Hawkins,* the Fifth Circuit held that "equal access" provisions of the Medicaid Act failed to "unambiguously confer[]" rights on the plaintiffs. In comparison, courts have found enforceable rights in those provisions of the Medicaid Act that refer to "individuals" or "families."[21]

7. *When May a Party Recover Attorney's Fees in a Section 1983 Suit?*

We conclude our study with an overview of 42 U.S.C. § 1988, which is the statute authorizing recovery of attorney's fees in actions based on § 1983. The study of attorney's fees is sometimes minimized in law school, as if it were a remedial technicality to be addressed at the end of a lawsuit. But the viability of many constitutional and civil rights claims comes down to whether the plaintiff's lawyer has a realistic prospect of recovering her fees. Public interest groups and private lawyers performing *pro bono* work are not adequate to ensure vigorous enforcement of the Constitution. Vigorous enforcement depends appreciably on assuring lawyers that their substantial investment of time and money in a § 1983 action will be remunerated.

Section 1988(b) provides in relevant part: "In an action or proceeding to enforce a provision of . . . section 1983 . . . the court, in its discretion, may allow the prevailing party . . . a reasonable attorney's fee as part of costs." Interpretation of this statute has generated as much litigation as other issues we have examined in our study of § 1983. We will consider some of the more important interpretive issues raised by § 1988.

"In an action or proceeding to enforce" section 1983. Most legal grievances never result in the filing of lawsuit, and most lawsuits never reach final judgment. *See, e.g.,* Ahmed E. Taha, *Data and Selection Bias: A Case Study,* 75 UMKC L. Rev. 171, 172 (2006). One reason grievances may never result in a lawsuit is that the aggrieved party takes advantage of pre-suit dispute resolution mechanisms like administrative proceedings. With the exception of state prisoners, *see* 42 U.S.C. § 1997e, § 1983 plaintiffs are not required to exhaust administrative proceedings prior to filing suit. *See Patsy v. Board of Regents,* 457 U.S. 496 (1982). But aggrieved parties often prefer to pursue administrative proceedings before filing suit because such proceedings may offer an informal, less-costly way for parties to resolve a dispute and may spare undesired publicity.

What if administrative proceedings succeed and the lawyer representing a complainant "prevails" without having to file suit? Are administrative proceedings the type of "proceeding" encompassed by § 1988(b)? In *North Carolina Department of Transportation v. Crest Street Community Council,* 479 U.S. 6 (1986), the Court answered "no." The Court held that an absolute prerequisite for the recovery of fees is the filing of a judicial action seeking relief on the merits. Administrative proceedings and their like do not qualify as "an action or proceeding" to enforce § 1983.

21. *See* Anne M. Dwyer, *Ensuring Equal Access: Rethinking Enforcement of Medicaid's Equal Access Provision,* 97 Minn. L. Rev. 2320, 2332 (2013).

The rule in *Crest* may penalize the lawyer who succeeds in resolving a dispute extra-judicially. Pre-suit success on the merits usually precludes filing a suit, since the dispute is now moot. Further, *Crest*'s requirement that a suit seek "relief on the merits" to qualify for attorney's fees means that a subsequent suit seeking only attorney's fees will not suffice.

If a lawyer assists the client in pursuing administrative proceedings, but the dispute is not resolved, the lawyer may still be unable to recover fees related to these proceedings if the client later prevails at trial. In *Webb v. Dyer County Board of Education*, 471 U.S. 234 (1985), the Court uphold a trial court's denial of attorney's fees to a plaintiff who prevailed at trial after first pursuing an administrative remedy. Because the administrative proceedings (to which the plaintiff's lawyer devoted years) were "optional" according to *Patsy v. Board of Regents*, the trial court properly denied fees for those proceedings. The Court did suggest that fees might sometimes be awarded for administrative work that was "both useful and of a type ordinarily necessary to advance the civil rights litigation to the stage it reached." But such a partial award of fees falls within the trial court's discretion.

The lawyer considering whether to pursue optional administrative proceedings may sometimes face an apparent conflict of interests. If the lawyer needs to recover attorney's fees under § 1988 to fund the litigation, the lawyer may be less inclined to pursue optional administrative proceedings or to resolve the dispute in those proceedings. However, the client's best interests may lie in an administrative resolution. Would it be ethical for a lawyer to include a provision in her contract obligating the client to make adequate provision for the payment of fees before voluntarily resolving a dispute? For a thorough examination of this issue, see Neil M. Goldstein, *Preserving Fee-Shifting After* Evan v. Jeff D.: *Joint Attorney/Client Control of Settlements*, 11 Indus. L.J. 267 (1989). Goldstein concludes that client agreements to preserve adequate compensation for attorneys do not violate ethical rules governing lawyers.

"In [the court's] discretion." While the trial court has considerable discretion in determining the amount of attorney's fees to be awarded (as discussed later), it has little discretion to decide *whether* to award fees to the party prevailing at trial. Barring exceptional circumstances, a prevailing plaintiff must be awarded fees. *See Newman v. Piggie Park Enters., Inc.*, 390 U.S. 400 (1968) (applying a civil rights fee statute on which § 1988 is patterned). But a prevailing defendant is entitled to fees only if the plaintiff's claims were "frivolous, unreasonable or without foundation." *See Hughes v. Rowe*, 449 U.S. 5, 14 (1980). To assess fees against a plaintiff based solely on the fact he did not prevail at trial "would substantially add to the risks inhering in most litigation and would undercut the efforts of Congress to promote the vigorous enforcement of the provisions" of § 1983. *Id.* As the Court emphasized in *Hughes*, dismissal of a plaintiff's complaint for failure to state a claim does not necessarily entail that the complaint was frivolous.

There is one important exception to the rule that prevailing plaintiffs may recover their fees. When the losing defendant has previously made an offer of judgment under Federal Rule of Civil Procedure 68, and the plaintiff has failed to secure a judgment at trial more favorable than the offer, the plaintiff cannot recover fees or costs incurred after rejection of the offer. *See Marek v. Chesney*, 473 U.S. 1 (1985).

Becoming a "prevailing" plaintiff.[22] Once suit has been filed, the plaintiff has control over whether to accept a monetary settlement in lieu of a verdict. If a settlement offer does not sufficiently compensate the plaintiff for his damages, attorney's fees, and other litigation costs, the plaintiff can simply demand a trial. Assuming the plaintiff prevails at trial, § 1988 authorizes the court to award fees and costs.

A plaintiff's control over the outcome of litigation may decrease when equitable relief, like an injunction, is sought. In some circumstances, the defendant may voluntarily alter its legal policies or its behavior, and this may "moot" the controversy, requiring dismissal of the suit. In Chapter 2, we address the defendant's power to moot a controversy by voluntarily changing its policies or behavior. That power is closely circumscribed: "It is well settled that a defendant's voluntary cessation of a challenged practice does not deprive a federal court of its power to determine the legality of the practice" unless it is "absolutely clear that the allegedly wrongful behavior could not reasonably be expected to recur." *Friends of the Earth, Inc. v. Laidlaw Envtl. Servs., Inc.*, 528 U.S. 167, 189 (2000) (discussed in Chapter 2). But defendants enjoy a limited power to moot a suit by voluntary action if they satisfy the court that there is no reasonable prospect that the challenged action will recur.

The question arises: if a defendant succeeds in mooting a suit by a voluntary change in policy or conduct, can the plaintiff nonetheless recover attorney's fees as the "prevailing party"? Most federal circuits to consider this issue prior to 2001 agreed that, if a plaintiff's suit was the "catalyst" for the defendant's change, the plaintiff is a prevailing party entitled to recover fees. (Recall that the plaintiff must have filed suit before the defendant changed its position or else there is no predicate "proceeding" for awarding any fees.) In the following case, a sharply divided Supreme Court rejected the catalyst theory. Consider the justices' differing reasons for rejecting or perpetuating the catalyst theory, and the likely implications of the Court's ruling.

BUCKHANNON BOARD & CARE HOME, INC. v. WEST VIRGINIA DEPARTMENT OF HEALTH & HUMAN RESOURCES

523 U.S. 598 (2001)

Chief Justice Rehnquist delivered the opinion of the Court.

Numerous federal statutes allow courts to award attorney's fees and costs to the "prevailing party." The question presented here is whether this term includes a party that has failed to secure a judgment on the merits or a court-ordered consent decree, but has nonetheless achieved the desired result because the lawsuit brought about a voluntary change in the defendant's conduct. We hold that it does not.

Buckhannon Board and Care Home, Inc., which operates care homes that provide assisted living to their residents, failed an inspection by the West Virginia Office of the State Fire Marshal because some of the residents were

22. Based on legislative history, the Court has determined that a prevailing defendant is not entitled to recover its attorney's fee unless the plaintiff's claims are frivolous. *See, e.g., Hughes v. Rowe*, 449 U.S. 5 (1980). In *Fox v. Vice*, 131 S. Ct. 2205 (2011), the Court held that, when a plaintiff's suit involves both frivolous and non-frivolous claims, a court may grant reasonable fees to the defendant, but only for costs that the defendant would not have incurred but for the frivolous claims.

incapable of "self-preservation" as defined under state law. On October 28, 1997, after receiving cease and desist orders requiring the closure of its residential care facilities within 30 days, Buckhannon Board and Care Home, Inc., on behalf of itself and other similarly situated homes and residents (hereinafter petitioners), brought suit in the United States District Court for the Northern District of West Virginia against the State of West Virginia, two of its agencies, and 18 individuals (hereinafter respondents), seeking declaratory and injunctive relief that the "self-preservation" requirement violated the Fair Housing Amendments Act of 1988 (FHAA), and the Americans with Disabilities Act of 1990 (ADA).

Respondents agreed to stay enforcement of the cease-and-desist orders pending resolution of the case and the parties began discovery. In 1998, the West Virginia Legislature enacted two bills eliminating the "self-preservation" requirement, and respondents moved to dismiss the case as moot. The District Court granted the motion, finding that the 1998 legislation had eliminated the allegedly offensive provisions and that there was no indication that the West Virginia Legislature would repeal the amendments.

Petitioners requested attorney's fees as the "prevailing party" under the FHAA ("[T]he court, in its discretion, may allow the prevailing party . . . a reasonable attorney's fee and costs"), and ADA, ("[T]he court . . . , in its discretion, may allow the prevailing party . . . a reasonable attorney's fee, including litigation expenses, and costs"). Petitioners argued that they were entitled to attorney's fees under the "catalyst theory," which posits that a plaintiff is a "prevailing party" if it achieves the desired result because the lawsuit brought about a voluntary change in the defendant's conduct. Although most Courts of Appeals recognize the "catalyst theory," the Court of Appeals for the Fourth Circuit rejected it in [an earlier case]. The District Court accordingly denied the motion and, for the same reason, the Court of Appeals affirmed in an unpublished, *per curiam* opinion. To resolve the disagreement amongst the Courts of Appeals, we granted certiorari, and now affirm.

In designating those parties eligible for an award of litigation costs, Congress employed the term "prevailing party," a legal term of art. Black's Law Dictionary, 1145 (7th ed. 1999), defines "prevailing party" as "[a] party in whose favor a judgment is rendered, regardless of the amount of damages awarded—in certain cases, the court will award attorney's fees to the prevailing party, also termed *successful party*." This view that a "prevailing party" is one who has been awarded some relief by the court can be distilled from our prior cases.

In *Hanrahan v. Hampton*, 446 U.S. 754, 758 (1980), we reviewed the legislative history of § 1988 and found that "Congress intended to permit the interim award of counsel fees only when a party has prevailed on the merits of at least some of his claims." Our "[r]espect for ordinary language requires that a plaintiff receive at least some relief on the merits of his claim before he can be said to prevail. We have held that even an award of nominal damages suffices under this test."

In addition to judgments on the merits, we have held that settlement agreements enforced through a consent decree may serve as the basis for an award of attorney's fees. Although a consent decree does not always include an admission of liability by the defendant, it nonetheless is a court-ordered "chang[e] [in] the legal relationship between [the plaintiff] and the defendant." These decisions, taken together, establish that enforceable judgments on the merits and court-ordered consent decrees create the "material alteration of the legal relationship of the parties" necessary to permit an award of attorney's fees.

We think, however, the "catalyst theory" falls on the other side of the line from these examples. It allows an award where there is no judicially sanctioned change in the legal relationship of the parties. Even under a limited form of the "catalyst theory," a plaintiff could recover attorney's fees if it established that the "complaint had sufficient merit to withstand a motion to dismiss for lack of jurisdiction or failure to state a claim on which relief may be granted." This is not the type of legal merit that our prior decisions, based upon plain language and congressional intent, have found necessary. A defendant's voluntary change in conduct, although perhaps accomplishing what the plaintiff sought to achieve by the lawsuit, lacks the necessary judicial *imprimatur* on the change. Our precedents thus counsel against holding that the term "prevailing party" authorizes an award of attorney's fees *without* a corresponding alteration in the legal relationship of the parties.

Petitioners assert that the "catalyst theory" is necessary to prevent defendants from unilaterally mooting an action before judgment in an effort to avoid an award of attorney's fees. They also claim that the rejection of the "catalyst theory" will deter plaintiffs with meritorious but expensive cases from bringing suit. We are skeptical of these assertions, which are entirely speculative and unsupported by any empirical evidence.

Petitioners discount the disincentive that the "catalyst theory" may have upon a defendant's decision to voluntarily change its conduct, conduct that may not be illegal. "The defendants' potential liability for fees in this kind of litigation can be as significant as, and sometimes even more significant than, their potential liability on the merits," and the possibility of being assessed attorney's fees may well deter a defendant from altering its conduct.

And petitioners' fear of mischievous defendants only materializes in claims for equitable relief, for so long as the plaintiff has a cause of action for damages, a defendant's change in conduct will not moot the case. Even then, it is not clear how often courts will find a case mooted: "It is well settled that a defendant's voluntary cessation of a challenged practice does not deprive a federal court of its power to determine the legality of the practice" unless it is "absolutely clear that the allegedly wrongful behavior could not reasonably be expected to recur." If a case is not found to be moot, and the plaintiff later procures an enforceable judgment, the court may of course award attorney's fees. Given this possibility, a defendant has a strong incentive to enter a settlement agreement, where it can negotiate attorney's fees and costs.

We have also stated that "[a] request for attorney's fees should not result in a second major litigation," and have accordingly avoided an interpretation of the fee-shifting statutes that would have "spawn[ed] a second litigation of significant dimension." Among other things, a "catalyst theory" hearing would require analysis of the defendant's subjective motivations in changing its conduct, an analysis that "will likely depend on a highly factbound inquiry and may turn on reasonable inferences from the nature and timing of the defendant's change in conduct." Although we do not doubt the ability of district courts to perform the nuanced "three thresholds" test required by the "catalyst theory"—whether the claim was colorable rather than groundless; whether the lawsuit was a substantial rather than an insubstantial cause of the defendant's change in conduct; whether the defendant's change in conduct was motivated by the plaintiff's threat of victory rather than threat of expense—it is clearly not a formula for "ready administrability."

Given the clear meaning of "prevailing party" in the fee-shifting statutes, we need not determine which way these various policy arguments cut. In *Alyeska*, we said that Congress had not "extended any roving authority to the Judiciary to allow counsel fees as costs or otherwise whenever the courts might deem them warranted." To disregard the clear legislative language and the holdings of our prior cases on the basis of such policy arguments would be a similar assumption of a "roving authority." For the reasons stated above, we hold that the "catalyst theory" is not a permissible basis for the award of attorney's fees under the FHAA and ADA.

[Justice Scalia's concurring opinion is omitted.]

JUSTICE GINSBURG, with whom JUSTICE STEVENS, JUSTICE SOUTER, and JUSTICE BREYER join, dissenting.

[The following excerpt omits the dissent's discussion of (1) whether legislative history supports the catalyst theory and (2) whether prevailing circuit court opinion requires deference.]

In opposition to the argument that defendants will resist change in order to stave off an award of fees, one could urge that the catalyst rule may lead defendants promptly to comply with the law's requirements: the longer the litigation, the larger the fees. Indeed, one who knows noncompliance will be expensive might be encouraged to conform his conduct to the legal requirements before litigation is threatened. No doubt, a mootness dismissal is unlikely when recurrence of the controversy is under the defendant's control. But, as earlier observed, why should this Court's fee-shifting rulings drive a plaintiff prepared to accept adequate relief, though out-of-court and unrecorded, to litigate on and on? And if the catalyst rule leads defendants to negotiate not only settlement terms but also allied counsel fees, is that not a consummation to applaud, not deplore?

As to the burden on the court, is it not the norm for the judge to whom the case has been assigned to resolve fee disputes (deciding whether an award is in order, and if it is, the amount due), thereby clearing the case from the calendar? If factfinding becomes necessary under the catalyst rule, is it not the sort that "the district courts, in their factfinding expertise, deal with on a regular basis"? Might not one conclude overall, as Courts of Appeals have suggested, that the catalyst rule "saves judicial resources," by encouraging "plaintiffs to discontinue litigation after receiving through the defendant's acquiescence the remedy initially sought"?

* * * *

DISCUSSION AND QUESTIONS

In *Buckhannon*, the trial court found no reasonable prospect that the state legislature would later re-institute its challenged law governing nursing homes. Consequently, it found the suit was mooted by the change in state law and dismissed the suit. This precluded the plaintiffs from prevailing through a court judgment and recovering attorney's fees.

In some sense, rejection of the catalyst theory promotes compliance with federal law because it provides the defendant an incentive to avoid payment of costly fees. If the defendant changes its legal policies or behavior, and the court finds no reasonable risk the defendant might recidivate, the defendant has avoided costly litigation while providing plaintiffs and those similarly situated what they wanted at the outset of the suit. Is there a response to this contention? Can one argue that the absence of the catalyst theory may ultimately undermine compliance with federal law?

Now assume that, contrary to the trial court's ruling *Buckhannon,* a defendant's attempt to moot a lawsuit by changing its policy usually fails. Will the absence of a catalyst theory have any effect on the defendant's willingness to voluntarily change its position? Do the strict limits on a defendant's power to moot a lawsuit diminish the impact of the Court's holding in *Buckhannon*?

Finally, consider the position of the plaintiff who learns that a defendant is willing to change its policy and settle the case. Of course, if the defendant agrees to pay the plaintiff's attorney's fees, the plaintiff has strong incentive to accept the proposed settlement. But what if the defendant refuses to pay fees? Should the plaintiff refuse to settle and argue to the court that, even if the defendant voluntarily changes its policy, the suit is not moot? Should the plaintiff's attorney, foreseeing such a development, include a provision in the client's contract obligating the client to make provision for payment of fees before settling a suit?

Think about the implications of *Buckhannon* as you consider the following problem.

PROBLEM 9-7

To Settle or Not to Settle

Let's return again to the Reference Problem and the youth curfew ordinance. Assume that several local youths and their parents have brought suit to have the ordinance declared unconstitutional and enjoin its enforcement. Also, at least one suit is pending in which a local youth arrested for violating the ordinance has sued for damages. The city council has convened to consider how it should respond to the suit.

The city's attorney advises the council that it is unclear whether courts will ultimately invalidate the ordinance. "There are arguments on both sides of the issue, although I still believe we have the better arguments." One councilwoman proposes that the city repeal the curfew ordinance. She observes, "I'm not sure the minor reduction in juvenile crime justifies what this ordinance might cost us in damages and fees down the road." Another councilman disagrees: "Many of my constituents have called me in support of the ordinance. It is good policy worth defending. What kind of representatives are we if we cave in as soon as someone files a lawsuit?"

The city council decides to ask the city's attorney for a formal opinion discussing possible responses to the pending suits.

You work for the city's attorney. She asks that you advise her on the financial implications of the pending suits. You are to consider both the risk of damages and the risk of fees. Based on the law you have studied to this point in the chapter, offer your opinion on these risks and whether they might be reduced by city action.

Another issue that has arisen in determining whether a plaintiff is the prevailing party is how courts should treat the plaintiff who has (1) won on some issues but not others, or (2) won on supplemental state-law claims that overlap with federal claims.

At the outset of a suit, a plaintiff's lawyer will want to consider all plausible claims, weak and strong, federal and state. The lawyer will usually want to assert all plausible claims because omission of a viable claim typically results in its forfeiture once the case goes to final judgment. *See, e.g., Allen v. McCurry*, 449 U.S. 90 (1980) (principles of res judicata and full faith and credit apply to § 1983 claims). But the lawyer must also consider whether success on state-law claims may undermine her later entitlement to fees under § 1988.

The Supreme Court has ruled that a plaintiff must attain success on a "significant issue" before acquiring the status of a "prevailing party." *See Texas State Teachers Ass'n v. Garland Indep. Sch. Dist.*, 489 U.S. 782 (1989). "Slight" or *de minimis* success in the suit is not enough. *See Hewitt v. Helms*, 482 U.S. 755 (1987). In suits seeking equitable relief, the plaintiff must achieve relief that modifies the defendant's behavior in a manner directly benefiting the plaintiff. *See Farrar v. Hobby*, 506 U.S. 103 (1992). In suits seeking monetary relief, an award of "nominal" damages may make the plaintiff a "prevailing" party, but "the only reasonable fee is usually no fee at all." *Id.* at 113.

Assuming the plaintiff has won relief on a "significant issue," does it matter that the issue is based on state law? In *Maher v. Gagne*, 448 U.S. 122 (1980), the Court indicated that a party can be a "prevailing" party under federal fee statutes even if he succeeds based on state-law claims. Provided the federal claims asserted by the plaintiff are sufficiently "substantial," the plaintiff may recover fees for succeeding on non-fee claims that are factually related to fee claims. *Id.* at 132-33. Among other things, this may permit the trial court to resolve the case without unnecessarily addressing constitutional issues. *Id.* However, if the plaintiff prevails on non-fee claims that are *unrelated* to those claims qualifying for fees under federal law, the plaintiff will not be a "prevailing" party for fee purposes. *See Smith v. Robinson*, 468 U.S. 992, 1006 (1984). In any event, if the plaintiff's federal claims are actually rejected, a victory on state claims will not normally suffice to make the plaintiff a prevailing party under federal fee statutes. *See, e.g.*, Robert L. Rossi, 1 Attorneys' Fees § 10:23 (2007).

A "reasonable attorney's fee." The determination of a "reasonable" attorney's fee is left to the trial court's discretion. We will not attempt to summarize the extensive literature on fee determinations. Instead, we offer several important doctrinal observations concerning fees.

First, the fee is usually based on the "lodestar" formula, calculated by multiplying the number of hours invested by a lawyer times a reasonable billing rate. The Court has rejected the use of "fee enhancers," such as multiplying the lodestar calculation to allow for the risk a lawyer has assumed in prosecuting a case. *See City of Burlington v. Dague*, 505 U.S. 557 (1992). In *Penny v. Kenny A. ex rel. Winn*, 130 S. Ct. 1662 (2010), the Court affirmed that the "lodestar" formula is usually the proper method for compensating successful lawyers. The Court stated that only in "rare" or "exceptional" circumstances should lower courts enhance the lodestar recovery based on a lawyer's superior performance. *Id.* at 1674. Because a lawyer's fee is based on hours reasonably expended on compensable claims, it is important that the lawyer keep good time records. A lawyer's records should set out the subject matter of work performed "with sufficient particularity so that the court can assess the time claimed for each activity." *Norman v. Housing Auth.*, 836 F.2d 1292, 1303 (11th Cir. 1988).

What if the plaintiff's lawyer invests very substantial time in a case but the jury awards damages appreciably less than the lawyer's fee? Does the lawyer run the risk that a less-than-desired award of damages will undermine recovery of the lawyer's full fee? This issue arose in *City of Riverside v. Rivera*, 477 U.S. 561 (1986). In a suit against the city and several police officers alleging Fourth Amendment claims as well as state-law claims, the plaintiffs were awarded $33,350 in compensatory and punitive damages: $13,300 of the award was for the federal claims, and $20,050 was for the state-law claims. The trial court awarded the plaintiffs' lawyers *$245,456* in attorney's fees, which the court found "reasonable."

The defendants argued that attorney's fees awarded under § 1988 suits should be proportionate to the damages recovered. The Court rejected a proportionality requirement:

> Because damages awards do not reflect fully the public benefit advanced by civil rights litigation, Congress did not intend for fees in civil rights cases, unlike most private law cases, to depend on obtaining substantial monetary relief. Rather, Congress made clear that it "intended that the amount of fees awarded under [§ 1988] be governed by the same standards which prevail in other types of equally complex Federal litigation, such as antitrust cases and not be reduced because the rights involved may be nonpecuniary in nature."
>
> A rule of proportionality would make it difficult, if not impossible, for individuals with meritorious civil rights claims but relatively small potential damages to obtain redress from the courts. This is totally inconsistent with Congress' purpose in enacting § 1988. Congress recognized that private-sector fee arrangements were inadequate to ensure sufficiently vigorous enforcement of civil rights. In order to ensure that lawyers would be willing to represent persons with legitimate civil rights grievances, Congress determined that it would be necessary to compensate lawyers for all time reasonably expended on a case.

Id. at 575-76.

Still other important issues concerning a fee award arise when the client's contract contains a contingent-fee provision. Lawyers representing § 1983 plaintiffs often include such provisions in their contract when damages are sought. The Court has determined that the agreed-to contingent fee operates independently of the plaintiff's statutory fee. In particular, the losing defendant cannot avoid paying the "lodestar" fee earned by the plaintiff's lawyer based on the claim that the lawyer agreed to a contingent fee that works out to be less. Therefore, the plaintiff's lawyer can request payment of a lodestar fee despite the fact that her contingent share of awarded damages would be less. *See Blanchard v. Bergerson*, 489 U.S. 87, 88 (1989). There is thus no risk that by agreeing to a contingent fee the lawyer has undermined a future claim to full statutory fees.

Similarly, the plaintiff cannot avoid paying a contingent fee by pointing out that this fee exceeds a court-awarded fee. *See Venegas v. Mitchell*, 495 U.S. 82, 83-84 (1990). According to the Court in *Venegas*, the fee statute does not abrogate a lawyer and client's right to agree to a contingent fee. Of course, if the plaintiff's lawyer is awarded a statutory fee, the recovery of a contingent fee will ordinarily be reduced by the amount the defendant pays.

Recovering attorney's fees from the state. Earlier we discussed the use of *Ex parte Young* suits against state officials in their "official" capacity to obtain equitable relief that is essentially against the state. A common *Ex parte Young* action seeks a declaration that state law is unconstitutional and an injunction forbidding the official sued from enforcing the law. See Chapter 8.

In *Hutto v. Finney*, 437 U.S. 678 (1978), the Court affirmed that a state may be ordered to pay attorney's fees under § 1988 in *Ex parte Young* actions. According to the Court, Congress properly exercised its power under the Fourteenth Amendment when it authorized awards of costs and fees against the state. Any Eleventh Amendment immunity enjoyed by the state was abrogated upon enactment of § 1988.

8. *Does Section 1983 Law Vary When Applied by a State Court?*

You will not be surprised to learn that § 1983 suits can be filed in state court and that state courts are obligated to hear such suits. A unanimous Court affirmed these principles in *Howlett v. Rose*, 496 U.S. 356 (1990). Nor can a state refuse to exercise jurisdiction over § 1983 claims by adopting a "non-discriminatory" rule that precludes both federal and state courts from entertaining specific types of litigation. In *Haywood v. Drown*, 556 U.S. 729 (2009), the Court held that New York could not prohibit its courts from hearing all damages claims—including claims brought under § 1983—against corrections officers. Even though New York law "equally" denied its courts jurisdiction based on either state or federal law, the Court held the law was preempted by the Supremacy Clause:

> Our holding addresses only the unique scheme adopted by the State of New York—a law designed to shield a particular class of defendants (correction officers) from a particular type of liability (damages) brought by a particular class of plaintiffs (prisoners). Based on the belief that damages suits against correction officers are frivolous and vexatious, [New York law] is effectively an immunity statute cloaked in jurisdictional garb. Finding this scheme unconstitutional merely confirms that the Supremacy Clause cannot be evaded by formalism.

Id. at 741-42.

Today, a significant amount of § 1983 litigation occurs in state court, and counsel should never overlook the possibility that a state court forum may have legal or practical benefits. *See generally* STEVEN STEINGLASS, SECTION 1983 LITIGATION IN STATE COURTS (2005). It has been said that plaintiffs suing in state court based on federal claims "take state courts as they find them." *See* Henry P. Monaghan, *Third Party Standing*, 84 COLUM. L. REV. 277, 294 n.93 (1984). This aphorism captures the idea that state courts may normally apply their own jurisdictional and procedural law regardless of the presence of federal claims in a suit. But state procedures may not "unnecessarily burden" or "interfere" with the enforcement of federal law. *See, e.g., Johnson v. Fankell*, 520 U.S. 911, 921 (1997). The uncommon situation where preemption occurs arose in *Felder v. Casey*, 487 U.S. 131, 134 (1998).

In *Felder*, the Court held that the state court could not apply its own version of an "exhaustion" requirement to a claim based on § 1983. State law required that plaintiffs suing a government entity give the entity notice of their intention to sue and defer filing suit until the entity had several months to consider the claim. Although this notice-of-claim requirement applied equally to claims based on state and federal law, the Court concluded that it unduly burdened enforcement of § 1983 claims and conflicted with the Court's ruling in *Patsy v. Board of Regents*, 457 U.S. 496 (1982), where the Court held that plaintiffs need not comply with pre-suit administrative exhaustion requirements created by state law. The Court also found the state notice-of-claim provision to be "outcome determinative."

Nonetheless, the Court emphasized in its later decision, *Johnson v. Fankell*, 520 U.S. 911 (1997), that preemption of state procedural law is the exception. In *Fankell*, the Court held that state courts were not required to provide interlocutory review of orders denying a defense of qualified immunity. Because qualified immunity is "suit immunity," an official's ability to seek interlocutory review of the rejection of qualified immunity would seem to be an important aspect of the § 1983 remedy. The fact that the Court rejected the defendant's arguments in *Fankell* stresses the heavy burden borne by those who would displace state procedural law.

Although preemption of state procedural law is exceptional, it does occur, and counsel should be alert to the possibility that a preemption claim might be viable and advantageous. For example, Florida procedural law precludes a party from pleading a punitive damages remedy without first proffering proof in support of the remedy and obtaining court permission. *See* Fla. Stat. § 768.72. One state court has ruled that this statute cannot be applied to a claim based on § 1983. *See Sanchez v. Degoria*, 733 So. 2d 1103, 1107 (Fla. Dist. Ct. App. 1999). Similarly, Florida's equivalent of the federal "offer of judgment" rule permits a defendant not only to stop the accrual of a plaintiff's recoverable attorney's fees but actually also to shift the defendant's fees to the plaintiff. *See* Fla. R. Civ. P. 1.442. A Florida state court has concluded that this use of the rule is impermissible when suit is based on § 1983. *See Moran v. City of Lakeland*, 694 So. 2d 886 (Fla. Dist. Ct. App. 1997).

A final note on section 1983 litigation. Having been introduced to § 1983 in this chapter, you can appreciate that this "remedial" statute is central to much contemporary constitutional litigation. Even a lawyer well versed in modern constitutional interpretation cannot begin to assess the wisdom of litigation without understanding how § 1983 shapes the lawsuit.

Suits under § 1983 have played a prominent role in the development of federal courts doctrine. In the next chapter we examine how § 1983 litigation has been central to the Court's development of one variety of the "abstention" doctrine.

Before leaving our study of § 1983, reflect on the liability scheme devised by Congress and the Court, and how it might be improved.

EXPLORING DOCTRINE

A New Remedial Framework for Redressing Constitutional Violations

We have now examined the circumstances under which individual officials and the governments they represent must pay damages for violations of federal law. The extensive commentary on § 1983 suggests that few are enthused by the liability scheme that has evolved in past decades.

Assume you are chief aide to a prominent state legislator. The legislator would like to devise a liability scheme for enforcing your state's constitution, which confers most of the individual rights afforded by the U.S. Constitution. You have been asked to develop a state-law counterpart to § 1983, but one that more fairly and effectively allocates liability among government entities and those they employ. You should be specific about the standards for assessing individual and government liability. One suggestion would have government assume liability for all constitutional wrongs committed during an employee's "course of employment" (respondeat superior) unless the employee has acted "willfully, maliciously, or in bad faith."

Describe the principal components of the remedial scheme you would recommend for enforcing the state's constitution. Explain what inadequacies in § 1983 your proposal would correct. Assess whether the suggested proposal for respondeat superior liability has merit.

By the way, you need not fear personal liability if you botch the job. Courts appear to recognize that you have derivative legislative immunity for your work as a state legislative aide. *See Romero-Barcelo v. Hernandez-Agosto*, 75 F.3d 23 (1st Cir. 1996).

D. SOME ADDITIONAL PROBLEMS

PROBLEM 9-8

Necessary Force?

The parents of Paul Price have sued the City of Castle Rock and its police officer, Tom Tiger, in Maine state court. Paul Price was fatally shot by Tiger during a routine traffic stop. Tiger's testimony indicates that Price was stopped one evening because the left taillight on his vehicle was not illuminated. When Tiger approached the driver's side of the car, he observed Price rolling down the window and "pointing an eight-inch long, dark object at me." Believing Price was aiming a gun at him, Price fired one shot at Price, resulting in his death. It turns out that Price was extending his wallet, which contained his license.

Price's parents have asserted two claims against Tiger: (1) a Fourth Amendment claim for Tiger's use of allegedly unconstitutional deadly force, and (2) a state tort claim for assault and battery. Price's parents have asserted similar claims against the city.

Tiger's summary judgment motion. Before trial, Tiger moved for summary judgment on the plaintiffs' Fourth Amendment claim based on the defense of qualified immunity. According to current Court interpretation, the Fourth Amendment authorizes an officer's use of deadly force only if he has "probable cause" to believe a person poses "an immediate threat of serious physical injury or death." *See Tennessee v. Garner*, 471 U.S. 1 (1985). To support his motion for summary judgment, Tiger submits (a) his own affidavit reciting the circumstances leading him to fear Price was aiming a gun at him as he approached the car; and (b) the affidavit of an expert in police investigation techniques, stating that "under the poor lighting conditions encountered by Tiger it was eminently reasonable to mistake the suspect's wallet for a weapon."

In response to Tiger's motion for summary judgment, the plaintiffs produce the affidavit of their own expert in police practices. Their expert states, "Officer Tiger had obvious means to avoid any supposed threat. Because the suspect was still in his car, Officer Tiger could have simply stepped toward the rear of the car and avoided any threat from the phantom weapon. He then could have focused his flashlight on the suspect's wallet and readily identified its nature. What is more, no reasonable officer would have mistaken a wallet with the dimensions of the suspect's wallet for a weapon."

Before the trial court ruled on Tiger's motion, Tiger provided a recent opinion of a federal district court in Georgia reciting "the well established principle that law enforcement officers have no duty to retreat when confronting criminal suspects. The imposition of a duty to retreat is patently inconsistent with the essential mission of law enforcement."

(1) How should the court rule on Tiger's motion for summary judgment based on your knowledge of qualified immunity?
(2) What can Tiger do, if anything, if the trial court denies his motion and state appellate rules provide him no right to seek interlocutory review?

The city's summary judgment motion. The City of Castle Rock also moved for summary judgment based on the argument that, regardless of whether Officer Tiger violated Price's constitutional rights, the city is not liable for the violation under Supreme Court precedent governing municipal liability. In support of its motion, the city provided the following supporting evidence:

- The police department's training manual specifically requires that an officer "have reasonable belief that a suspect is armed and dangerous" before using deadly force.
- After the sole prior incident involving a city officer's use of deadly force in the past 20 years, the officer was required to defend his actions before an "internal review board," which found the officer had properly used deadly force.
- Officer Tiger received more than ten hours of training in the law and procedures involved with the use of deadly force.

The plaintiffs responded to the city's motion as follows. First, the plaintiffs pointed out that the department's training manual requires an officer to have "reasonable belief" that a suspect is armed and dangerous. However, *Tennessee v. Garner* requires "probable cause," not "reasonable belief." Second, the plaintiffs proffer their own expert's testimony that, after reviewing records concerning the sole contemporary incident involving a city officer's use of deadly force, he believes the city "ignored evidence the officer lacked probable cause to use deadly force. It is difficult for me to conclude the department's internal investigation was thorough or objective."

Before the trial court rules on the city's motion, the city submits a supplemental affidavit of Officer Tiger stating, "I have always understood the department's requirement of a 'reasonable belief' that deadly force is threatened to be the same as requiring 'probable cause' of a threat."

(1) What forms of municipal "policy" do the plaintiffs argue to support their claim of city liability?
(2) Should the court grant the city's motion for summary judgment?

A few more questions.

(1) Based on the information provided above, does Tiger have strong grounds for seeking summary judgment if the plaintiffs' complaint requests an award of *punitive* damages?
(2) Based on the information provided above, do the plaintiffs have grounds for seeking to amend their complaint to add a claim for denial of *due process*? (Note: this claim would be *in addition* to existing claims based on Fourth Amendment rights "incorporated" through the Due Process Clause.) Would your answer to this question change at all if you learned that, under state law, the defendants were immune from damages for the allegedly wrongful shooting?

CHAPTER 10

Protecting State Courts from Interference by Federal Courts

A. A REFERENCE PROBLEM

In this chapter we consider how federal statutes and judicially created abstention doctrine protect state courts from various forms of interference by federal courts. The Reference Problem below introduces many of those protections.

* * * *

Since the Supreme Court's decisions recognizing citizens' Second Amendment right to bear arms,[1] governmental bodies have faced uncertainties when regulating handgun possession. One uncertainty is the scope of their power to regulate the carrying of concealed weapons.

Assume that the City of Tombstone exercises its power under state statutes to regulate the carrying of concealed firearms. Although the state itself issues concealed-carry permits to persons who pass a test and meet statewide licensing criteria, cities can adopt additional "reasonable requirements" for persons who wish to carry concealed weapons within the city limits. Tombstone thus restricts the carrying of concealed weapons to persons who have obtained an additional permit from the city police department. To obtain this additional permit, the applicant must show "good cause" for carrying a concealed weapon within the city limits. Tombstone's ordinance states that "good cause" means "a set of circumstances that distinguish a person from the mainstream and cause him or her to be placed in harm's way." Thus, an applicant must show that circumstances create a special, pressing need for personal protection, and the ordinance specifically states that "a general concern for one's personal safety alone is not considered good cause."[2] Based on its good-cause requirement, Tombstone denies most applications for a permit.

Doug Holliday operates a business in Tombstone called Total Defense Systems. One service Holliday offers is a course in the safe and lawful use of concealed weapons; persons applying for a concealed-carry permit from the state are required to take such a course. Another important service is training persons in the efficient use of concealed weapons for self-defense. This usually involves introducing persons to techniques for withdrawing the weapon from a concealed position and using it.

Holliday's business had operated successfully for more than ten years when Tombstone first adopted its concealed-carry ordinance. Soon after adoption of the ordinance, an undercover police officer attended one of Holliday's training sessions and observed that Holliday and his students carried concealed weapons and withdrew them as part of their training. At that point, the officer identified himself and wrote a citation charging Holliday with violation of Tombstone's ordinance. None of the students were charged, but the officer warned them that they could not continuing carrying concealed weapons in Tombstone without obtaining a city permit.

Holliday eventually paid a small fine for violating Tombstone's ordinance but publicly declared that it was "blatantly unconstitutional" and that he would sue Tombstone if it continued to harass citizens and businesses. When the city learned that Holliday was continuing to hold classes in weapon use, it filed an injunctive action in state court seeking to enforce its ordinance against Holliday's business and to have that business declared a public nuisance. Holliday retained a lawyer to defend him, and his main defense was that the ordinance violated his Second Amendment right to bear arms. The trial court rejected Holliday's constitutional defense in pretrial proceedings. But the City's suit against Holliday continues and will likely be tried in the coming year.

1. *See McDonald v. City of Chicago*, 561 U.S. 742 (2010); *District of Columbia v. Heller*, 554 U.S. 670 (2008).

2. Much of this hypothetical ordinance is based on an ordinance adopted by the County of San Diego and struck down by a divided panel in *Peruta v. County of San Diego*, 742 F.3d 1144 (9th Cir. 2014).

The trial court's ruling rejecting Holliday's constitutional defense has received much attention in the press. Holliday's business has suffered appreciable losses as customers have dwindled. Another local business offering services similar to Holliday's—Masterson's Firearms Training—has likewise suffered substantial business losses. When Masterson heard of the court's ruling in the action against Holliday, he immediately ceased offering training in the use of concealed weapons. And although Masterson hasn't been threatened with legal action by the city, he has erected large signs on his business property condemning the city's "armed assault on citizens' Second Amendment rights."

Holliday's and Masterson's businesses are members of a statewide association that promotes the use of concealed weapons and opposes laws that restrict the carrying of such weapons. The association has agreed to fund a federal suit challenging Tombstone's ordinance. Among other things, the association is concerned that other cities in the state are considering the adoption of ordinances similar to Tombstone's.

Holliday and Masterson have now sued Tombstone in federal court and seek the following forms of relief: (1) a declaration that Tombstone's ordinance violates the Second Amendment to the U.S. Constitution; (2) an injunction forbidding continued enforcement of the ordinance; (3) declaratory and injunctive relief based on the state's constitution, which also grants citizens the right to bear arms; (4) damages for their businesses' economic losses; and (5) damages for the fine Holliday paid when he was first cited for violating the ordinance.

Counsel for Tombstone intends to defend its ordinance but is concerned that the federal suit against it has been assigned to Judge Bean. Bean is an ex-Army Ranger, avid sportsman, and marksman. Tombstone's counsel believes their prospects will be much improved if the constitutional issues are resolved in state trial and appellate courts. So Tombstone files a motion in federal court in which it argues (1) further proceedings in federal court will violate the federal Anti-Injunction Act, which forbids federal court interference with pending state court proceedings; (2) the federal court should abstain from proceeding while litigation related to the Tombstone ordinance is pending in state court; (3) the federal court is precluded from ruling on Holliday's challenge to the ordinance's constitutionality now that a state court has rejected that same challenge; and (4) in any event, the federal court should refrain from deciding the federal constitutional issue until state courts have had the opportunity to consider whether the ordinance violates the state constitution.

* * * *

The Reference Problem illustrates the tangle of issues that can arise when federal courts are asked to adjudicate controversies that are related to proceedings pending in state court. Some of the important issues we will address in this chapter include the following:

- Does the Anti-Injunction Act prohibit a federal court from directly enjoining a pending state court action? Does the Act also prohibit a federal court from granting less intrusive forms of relief? Are there exceptions to the Act that might be useful to federal plaintiffs like those described in the Reference Problem?
- How does the abstention doctrine developed by the Supreme Court supplement the protections afforded state courts by the Anti-Injunction Act?

Does the Court's recognition of additional protections for state courts usurp Congress' power to regulate federal court jurisdiction?

- What federalism values are served by the various abstention doctrines? To what extent does abstention compromise enforcement of supreme federal law? How much discretion do federal courts have in deciding whether to abstain? What are the practical consequences of federal court abstention for the affected parties?

B. CONTEXT AND BACKGROUND

In Chapter 3 we considered Congress' broad power to confer Article III jurisdiction on federal courts, as well as its power to withhold jurisdiction. We concluded that Congress' power is subject to few restraints, and those are specifically derived from the Constitution.

A century ago the Court reiterated that Congress' conferral of federal court jurisdiction cannot be overridden by the Court itself: "We have no more right to decline the exercise of jurisdiction which is given, than to usurp that which is not given." *Ex parte Young*, 209 U.S. 123, 143 (1908).[3] If this comment were literally true, our study of restraints on federal court jurisdiction would largely be an exercise in statutory interpretation. But we discover in this chapter that *Ex parte Young* cannot be read literally. While Congress has enacted important statutory restraints to protect the sovereign interests of state courts, the Court has supplemented these restraints through its recognition of various "abstention" doctrines. In fact, judicially created abstention often eclipses the importance of statutory limits. This is especially true in the setting we highlight in this chapter—where federal courts are asked to enforce the Constitution by restraining unlawful state action.

1. *Tension in the Exercise of Jurisdiction by Federal and State Courts*

Our constitutional scheme of judicial power creates the potential for tension and conflict between federal and state courts. Much of the jurisdiction exercised by federal courts is shared concurrently with state courts. As we will see later, litigants often have the power to select the court in which to resolve their disputes, even when the other disputants have selected another court. Further, as we learned in Chapter 9, § 1983 grants federal courts the power to scrutinize the constitutionality of state action, including the conduct of state judges.

Given the constitutional scheme of federal and state court power, federal courts may be asked to exercise their power in ways that interfere with state courts. The materials in this chapter address various forms of potential interference, three of which receive special emphasis: (1) interference with the role of state courts as *expositors* of state law; (2) interference with the role of state

3. The Court recently remarked that "there is surely a starting presumption that when jurisdiction is conferred, a court may not decline to exercise it," although this generalization requires some "fine tuning." *See Union Pac. R.R. Co. v. Brotherhood of Locomotive Eng'rs & Trainmen*, 130 S. Ct 584, 590 (2009). The Court noted that this presumption applies equally to administrative agencies exercising adjudicative authority.

courts as efficient *dispute resolution tribunals*, particularly disputes affecting important state interests; and (3) diminution of the perceived *integrity* of state courts by casting aspersion on their ability or willingness to enforce federal law.

State courts as expositors of state law. At this point in your legal study you fully appreciate the role of courts as expositors of the law. You know that, under our constitutional scheme, the ultimate expositor of a sovereign's law is the sovereign's courts, especially its supreme court. In the case of state law, this important role is best served when litigation requiring interpretation of a state's law occurs in that state's courts. Yet federal courts are routinely required to interpret state law. As we learned in Chapters 6 and 7, federal courts frequently interpret state law when they exercise diversity-of-citizenship jurisdiction and supplemental jurisdiction. And they often interpret state law when they assess the constitutionality of state action and state law. Because a federal court's interpretation of state law is not directly reviewable by state courts,[4] misinterpretations of state law may go uncorrected and the resulting bad precedent may live on until state courts revisit precedent in separate litigation.

The question arises: Are there situations in which federal courts should decline to exercise jurisdiction over a state-law issue and, instead, permit the controversy to be resolved in state court? In this chapter we consider how *Pullman* and *Burford* abstention may require federal courts to defer resolution of state-law issues to state courts. As you can imagine, such abstention is closely circumscribed. Otherwise, abstention could seriously disrupt the functioning of federal courts in their routine exercise of diversity-of-citizenship and supplemental jurisdiction, and abstention could compromise their important role as arbiters of constitutional challenges to state law and state action.

State courts as efficient dispute resolution tribunals. Another important role of state courts is that of dispute resolution. Like federal courts, state courts have limited resources and prefer to use those resources to provide the most comprehensive resolution of controversies. This is especially true when the controversy touches upon important state interests (e.g., regulation of scarce resources like water or minerals) or when the state has developed a special administrative and judicial scheme to resolve broad-ranging controversies that require a coordinated solution. We consider how doctrines like *Burford* abstention accommodate a state's interest in resolving such controversies.

We also consider how the dispute resolution role of state courts is promoted by requiring federal courts to respect the ultimate *decisions* of state courts. As we will see, the Full Faith and Credit Clause of the Constitution provides important protection for state court proceedings that have resulted in final decisions, even final decisions that arguably compromise a party's rights under federal law.

Protecting the integrity of state courts. You may recall from Chapter 1 that the Framers of the Constitution declined to mandate the creation of federal trial courts, in part based on the belief that state courts were adequate to enforce

4. The principal method by which state courts advise federal courts on the meaning of state law is through the answering of certified questions (they do not "review" federal court interpretations of state law). State laws vary as to whether, and how, certified questions are answered by state supreme courts. For example, some states will answer certified questions transmitted from both trial and appellate courts, *see, e.g.*, Colo. R. App. P. 22.1, while others will review questions transmitted by only federal appellate courts, *see, e.g.*, Fla. R. App. P. 9.150.

federal law so long as Supreme Court review was available. This trust in state courts is shored up by the mandated supremacy of federal law in state court proceedings and the oath state court judges take to uphold federal law.

Even though trust in state government and state courts eroded after the Civil War, the modern Court has affirmed that federal courts should still show great respect for the constitutional role of state courts. As we will see, this deference, or "comity," is appropriate even when there is reason to suspect that state actors may be violating federal law. One form of comity, identified with "*Younger*" abstention, has become an important check on the exercise of federal jurisdiction when the would-be federal plaintiff has been previously haled into state court, often as a criminal defendant.

All these argued forms of interference with state courts are controversial. Critics contend that the alleged interference is specifically contemplated by our constitutional scheme of federal court jurisdiction. They also emphasize that much of this interference appears acceptable to Congress, as evidenced by the absence of legislation affirming judicially created abstention. Critics also question whether the abstention doctrines truly accomplish what they purport to accomplish. We evaluate some of these criticisms in later discussion.

2. *Plan of Coverage*

We begin the chapter by considering the Anti-Injunction Act, Congress' most comprehensive restraint on federal court interference with state court proceedings. First, we consider what federal court action is barred by the Act and in what circumstances. We then consider how the Court has interpreted the three exceptions to the Act's prohibitions. These exceptions authorize injunctive relief when (a) expressly authorized by Congress; (b) necessary for exercise of a federal court's jurisdiction; or (c) necessary to protect or effectuate a court's judgments. As we discover, two of the exceptions usually have little practical impact on the exercise of federal court jurisdiction. The third exception, on the other hand, *appears* to preserve an important role for federal courts in preventing the abuse of state power to deny parties their constitutional protections. But we will learn that judicially created abstention doctrine compromises this important role.

We then consider several of the abstention doctrines, with special emphasis on those involving federal court challenges to allegedly unconstitutional state action.[5] We first examine *Pullman* abstention. *Pullman* abstention may apply when a federal court entertains a constitutional challenge to state law whose meaning is unclear. Under *Pullman* abstention, if state court clarification of the law's meaning might moot the constitutional challenge, federal courts are usually required to abstain. Such abstention serves both federal and state purposes: the federal court avoids ruling on the constitutional challenge while permitting a state court to interpret its own law. We consider in more detail the circumstances where *Pullman* abstention is proper, the procedures used to implement *Pullman* abstention, and the possible impact of abstention on the course of federal court litigation.

5. The term "state action" encompasses the laws and conduct of both state and local governments unless specifically qualified in discussion. See Chapter 9 (discussing broader use of the term "state" in constitutional litigation).

Next we consider *Younger* abstention. This form of abstention usually arises when a federal plaintiff seeks to restrain proceedings in state court that allegedly threaten his constitutional rights. The classic example is a plaintiff's attempt to enjoin a pending prosecution in state court that violates, in some way, the Constitution. We consider the critical importance of the timing of federal and state proceedings, and how many putative federal plaintiffs lose their federal forum because state proceedings have already begun or are imminent. We also consider the importance of a federal plaintiff's standing and the ripeness of a controversy in determining whether the plaintiff can sometimes avoid the restrictions of *Younger* abstention. Finally, we consider how *Younger* abstention has been extended to prevent federal interference with state civil proceedings, even proceedings to which the state is not a party.

Resolution of the issues raised by the Reference Problem largely turns on correct application of the *Pullman* and *Younger* abstention doctrines. But we also consider, briefly, a few other forms of abstention doctrine that apply in other settings. In particular, we consider how *Burford* abstention may be implicated when state courts adjudicate disputes involving important state interests, particularly disputes requiring the interpretation of unsettled state law. Finally, we consider how a doctrine often referred to as *Colorado River* abstention provides federal courts a very limited authority to avoid adjudicating some disputes that are being adjudicated simultaneously in state court.

To conclude this chapter, we note the importance of the Full Faith and Credit Clause of Article IV of the Constitution in protecting state court judgments from federal interference. As we learn, the strongest protection of state court proceedings arises when those proceedings have produced a final judgment. Even when federal court suits pose important questions of constitutional law, a federal court may be precluded from addressing factual or legal issues previously resolved — correctly or incorrectly — in state court.

C. THE LAW AND PROBLEMS

1. *The Anti-Injunction Act*

Congress has enacted several statutes that prevent federal courts from exercising jurisdiction to interfere with the enforcement of state law. For example, the Tax Injunction Act, 28 U.S.C. § 1341, prevents district courts from interfering with the levy or collection of state taxes, provided state courts give the aggrieved person a "plain, speedy and efficient remedy." A similar statute, 26 U.S.C. § 7461, forbids enjoining the collection of a federal tax and was considered by the Court when it upheld the constitutionality of the Affordable Care Act in 2012.[6] Yet another statute, the Johnson Act, 28 U.S.C. § 1342, prevents district courts from interfering with the decisions of state agencies setting public utility rates, again with the caveat that state courts offer the aggrieved person a "plain, speedy and efficient remedy."

We focus on the most broad-ranging statutory restriction on federal court jurisdiction, the Anti-Injunction Act, 28 U.S.C. § 2283. The Act is a surprisingly

6. *National Fed'n of Indep. Bus. v. Sebelius*, 132 S. Ct. 2566 (2012).

succinct statement of the federal courts' limited power to enjoin state court proceedings:

> A court of the United States may not grant an injunction to stay proceedings in a State court except as expressly authorized by Act of Congress, or where necessary in aid of its jurisdiction, or to protect or effectuate its judgments.

Congress first enacted limits on federal injunctive power in 1793, although Congress' original purpose remains obscure. *See Mitchum v. Foster*, 407 U.S. 225, 232 (1972). Modern versions of the Act are intended to prevent "needless friction" and "conflict" between state and federal courts, and it is these modern versions that have been most vigorously enforced by the Supreme Court. *See, e.g., Toucy v. New York Life Ins. Co.*, 314 U.S. 118 (1941); *Amalgamated Clothing Workers of Am. v. Richman Bros.*, 348 U.S. 511, 514-516 (1955).

a. What the Act Prohibits

The Act creates an "absolute prohibition against enjoining state court proceedings, unless the injunction falls within one of three specifically defined exceptions." *Mitchum*, 407 U.S. at 229. The scope of the Act's prohibition has been elaborated by the Court in several decisions.

First, while the Act seems to literally prohibit injunctions against state court proceedings themselves, it has been interpreted to also prohibit injunctions against *parties* involved in state court proceedings. This means a federal plaintiff cannot circumvent the Act by seeking an injunction against a state court litigant, rather than the state court itself. *See Atlantic Coast Line R.R. Co. v. Brotherhood of Locomotive Eng'rs*, 398 U.S. 281, 286 (1970). It also means a criminal defendant cannot stop his state court prosecution by seeking federal court relief against the prosecutor.

Second, the Act prevents interference with *pending* state court proceedings, not proceedings yet to be commenced. *See Dombrowski v. Pfister*, 380 U.S. 479, 484 n.2 (1965). In other words, a federal plaintiff can seek to enjoin a plaintiff or prosecutor from *initiating* a state court action, provided requirements like standing and ripeness are satisfied. But once state proceedings have commenced, the Act's prohibition comes into play. Further, the Act continues to apply even after the trial has ended by prohibiting interference with the *enforcement* of any judgment resulting from the state court proceeding. *See County of Imperial v. Munoz*, 449 U.S. 54, 59 (1980) (even though state court proceedings have concluded, a federal court cannot enjoin enforcement of an injunction issued by the state court).

Third, the Act does *not* prohibit a person who is a "stranger" to state court proceedings, that is, a person neither a party nor in privity with a party, from obtaining federal court relief that ultimately interferes with those proceedings. *See Hale v. Bimco Trading, Inc.*, 306 U.S. 375 (1939). This limit on the scope of the Act can be quite important when the constitutionality of state law or state action is challenged. Consider, for example, the situation where a newly enacted state law prohibits physicians from giving terminally ill patients general information on methods for suicide. Assume that Dr. Krevakian is being prosecuted in Madison County for violating this law. Assume further that another physician practicing in Jefferson County, Dr. Bright, wishes to continue advising patients about suicide methods but has not yet violated state law. If Dr. Bright seeks to enjoin Jefferson County from enforcing this allegedly unconstitutional law in federal court, the Anti-Injunction Act will not prohibit the suit simply because a state prosecution is pending against Dr. Krevakian. Dr. Bright is a "stranger" to the prosecution in Madison County. Even if a federal court judgment invalidating state law might cause Jefferson County to drop its prosecution against Dr. Krevakian,[7] this incidental effect does not implicate the Anti-Injunction Act in Dr. Bright's suit.

Finally, the Anti-Injunction Act does not apply to suits brought by the United States or its agencies. *See, e.g., Leiter Minerals, Inc. v. United States*, 352 U.S. 220 (1957); *NLRB v. Nash-Finch Co.*, 404 U.S. 138 (1971). In *Leiter*, the Court was unwilling to impute to Congress an intent to "frustrate[] . . . superior federal interests" that are at stake when the United States itself seeks to restrain improper state court proceedings. 352 U.S. at 226.

The Act prohibits injunctions but does not specifically address requests for *declaratory* relief that would essentially declare that pending state proceedings are unlawful. In other settings, however, the Supreme Court has concluded that declaratory relief is just as offensive as injunctive relief. *See, e.g., California v. Grace Brethren Church*, 457 U.S. 393, 407-11 (1982) (construing the Tax Injunction Act); *Samuels v. Mackell*, 401 U.S. 66 (1971) (extending *Younger* abstention to federal suits seeking to declare a state court prosecution unconstitutional). Consequently, most courts to decide the issue have concluded that the Act also bans declaratory relief that would declare the unlawfulness of pending state proceedings. *See, e.g., Silent Drive, Inc. v. Strong Indus., Inc.*, 326 F.3d 1194, 1203 n.2 (Fed. Cir. 2003).

b. Express Exceptions to the Act

The Act states what seems to be obvious: Congress can "expressly authorize" exceptions to its own statutory prohibition. The issue raised by this provision is, when does a particular federal statute constitute Congress' express authorization of injunctive relief?

It is now clear that a federal statute need not expressly refer to the Act in order to be an express exception to it. Examples of express exceptions include federal statutes authorizing injunctive relief against state courts (a) when a case has been removed to federal court; (b) when a federal court is adjudicating an interpleader action; (c) when a federal bankruptcy court is adjudicating a bankruptcy; and (d) when a federal court is asked to provide "habeas corpus" relief to persons detained under the authority of state courts. *See* 28 U.S.C. § 1446(d) (removal); 28 U.S.C. § 2361 (interpleader); 11 U.S.C. § 362 (bankruptcy); 28 U.S.C. § 2251 (habeas corpus).

But what of the situation where a federal statute authorizes equitable relief generally but does not specifically authorize equitable relief against state courts as such? The most important case presenting this issue is *Mitchum v. Foster*, 407 U.S. 225 (1972). *Mitchum* posed the question, is 42 U.S.C. § 1983 an express exception to the Act?

7. The stare decisis effect of the decision in Dr. Krevakian's suit may well bring an end to similar prosecutions in the state.

To appreciate the Court's opinion, excerpted below, it helps to recall our prior study of § 1983, as well as to foreshadow later discussion of abstention doctrine. We learned in Chapter 9 that § 1983 is a generic remedy against state action that violates federal law, especially the Constitution. Section 1983 authorizes a "suit in equity" to restrain violations of federal law, and 42 U.S.C. § 1343 confers federal court jurisdiction to entertain such suits. But neither statute expressly authorizes injunctive relief against state courts. At the same time, the Court has stated that § 1983 is premised on a suspicion that state courts cannot always be trusted to enforce federal law. One of the consequences of this suspicion is that state judges enjoy no absolute immunity from suits seeking injunctive relief under § 1983. But does the Anti-Injunction Act permit a federal court to issue such relief once proceedings in state court have commenced? *Mitchum* answers this question.

Mitchum was decided one year after *Younger v. Harris*, 401 U.S. 37 (1971), which inaugurated a new form of abstention that generally prohibits federal courts from enjoining state court criminal proceedings. We consider *Younger* abstention in much greater detail later in this chapter. But for present purposes, consider that a court-made rule requiring federal courts to abstain from enjoining state courts only becomes necessary if the Act permits federal court injunctions in the first instance. In *Younger* the Court had assumed without deciding that § 1983 was an "express" exception to the Act. *Mitchum* finally resolved the issue.

In *Mitchum*, a Florida state court issued a preliminary order closing Mitchum's adult book store because it constituted a public nuisance. After unsuccessfully opposing the order in state court, Mitchum filed suit in federal court for injunctive and declaratory relief under § 1983. In that suit he argued that the state prosecutor and state court were violating his rights under the First and Fourteenth Amendments. A panel of federal judges eventually concluded his suit was barred by the Anti-Injunction Act because it did not come within one of the Act's exceptions. On review, the Supreme Court concluded that § 1983 was an "express" exception to the Act.

MITCHUM v. FOSTER

407 U.S. 225 (1971)

MR. JUSTICE STEWART delivered the opinion of the Court. . . .

In *Younger*, this Court emphatically reaffirmed the fundamental policy against federal interference with state criminal prosecutions. It made clear that even the possible unconstitutionality of a statute "on its face" does not in itself justify an injunction against good-faith attempts to enforce it. At the same time, however, the Court clearly left room for federal injunctive intervention in a pending state court prosecution in certain exceptional circumstances—where irreparable injury is both great and immediate, where the state law is flagrantly and patently violative of express constitutional prohibitions, or where there is a showing of bad faith, harassment, or . . . other unusual circumstances that would call for equitable relief.

* * * *

While the Court in *Younger* and its companion cases expressly disavowed deciding the question now before us—whether section 1983 comes within the "expressly authorized" exception of the anti-injunction statute, it is evident that our decisions in those cases cannot be disregarded in deciding this question. In the first place, if section 1983 is not within the statutory exception, then the anti-injunction statute would have absolutely barred the injunction issued in *Younger*, as the appellant in that case argued, and there would have been no occasion whatever for the Court to decide that case upon the 'policy' ground of "Our Federalism." Secondly, if section 1983 is not within the "expressly authorized" exception of the anti-injunction statute, then we must overrule *Younger* and its companion cases insofar as they recognized the permissibility of injunctive relief against pending criminal prosecutions in certain limited and exceptional circumstances.

* * * *

In the first place, it is evident that, in order to qualify under the "expressly authorized" exception of the anti-injunction statute, a federal law need not contain an express reference to that statute. Indeed, none of the previously recognized statutory exceptions contains any such reference. Secondly, a federal law need not expressly authorize an injunction of a state court proceeding in order to qualify as an exception. . . . Thirdly, it is clear that, in order to qualify as an "expressly authorized" exception to the anti-injunction statute, an Act of Congress must have created a specific and uniquely federal right or remedy, enforceable in a federal court of equity, that could be frustrated if the federal court were not empowered to enjoin a state court proceeding. This is not to say that in order to come within the exception an Act of Congress must, on its face and in every one of its provisions, be totally incompatible with the prohibition of the anti-injunction statute. The test, rather, is whether an Act of Congress, clearly creating a federal right or remedy enforceable in a federal court of equity, could be given its intended scope only by the stay of a state court proceeding.

* * * *

It is clear from the legislative debates surrounding passage of section 1983's predecessor that the Act was intended to enforce the provisions of the Fourteenth Amendment "against State action, . . . whether that action be executive, legislative, or judicial." Proponents of the legislation noted that state courts were being used to harass and injure individuals, either because the state courts were powerless to stop deprivations or were in league with those who were bent upon abrogation of federally protected rights. . . . [L]egislative history makes evident that Congress clearly conceived that it was altering the relationship between the States and the Nation with respect to the protection of federally created rights; it was concerned that state instrumentalities could not protect those rights; it realized that state officers might, in fact, be antipathetic to the vindication of those rights; and it believed that these failings extended to the state courts.

Section 1983 was thus a product of a vast transformation from the concepts of federalism that had prevailed in the late 18th century when the anti-injunction statute was enacted. The very purpose of section 1983 was to interpose the federal courts between the States and the people, as guardians of the people's federal rights — to protect the people from unconstitutional action under color of state law, "whether that action be executive, legislative, or judicial." In carrying out that purpose, Congress plainly authorized the federal courts to issue injunctions in section 1983 actions, by expressly authorizing a "suit in equity" as one of the means of redress. And this Court long ago recognized that federal injunctive relief against a state court proceeding can in some circumstances be essential to prevent great, immediate, and irreparable loss of a person's constitutional rights.

In so concluding, we do not question or qualify in any way the principles of equity, comity, and federalism that must restrain a federal court when asked to enjoin a state court proceeding. These principles, in the context of state criminal prosecutions, were canvassed at length last Term in *Younger v. Harris* and its companion cases. They are principles that have been emphasized by this Court many times in the past. Today we decide only that the District Court in this case was in error in holding that, because of the anti-injunction statute, it was absolutely without power in this section 1983 action to enjoin a proceeding pending in a state court under any circumstances whatsoever.

* * * *

MR. CHIEF JUSTICE BURGER [concurring]

I concur in the opinion of the Court and add a few words to emphasize what the Court is and is not deciding today as I read the opinion. The Court holds only that 28 U.S.C. section 2283, which is an absolute bar to injunctions against state court proceedings in most suits, does not apply to a suit brought under 42 U.S.C. section 1983 seeking an injunction of state proceedings. But, as the Court's opinion has noted, it does nothing to "question or qualify in any way the principles of equity, comity, and federalism that must restrain a federal court when asked to enjoin a state court proceeding." In the context of pending state criminal proceedings, we held in Younger v. Harris that these principles allow a federal court properly to issue an injunction in only a narrow class of circumstances. We have not yet reached or decided exactly how great a restraint is imposed by these principles on a federal court asked to enjoin state civil proceedings. Therefore, on remand in this case, it seems to me the District Court, before reaching a decision on the merits of appellant's claim, should properly consider whether general notions of equity or principles of federalism, similar to those invoked in *Younger*, prevent the issuance of an injunction against the state "nuisance abatement" proceedings in the circumstances of this case.

DISCUSSION

Express exceptions under Mitchum. The Court reiterated in *Mitchum* that a federal statute may create an express exception to the Act even though it neither mentions the Act nor specifically authorizes an injunction against state courts. According to the Court, a statute that gives federal courts the power to grant equitable relief may be an express exception to the Act if the statute creates a "unique" right or remedy whose purposes would be frustrated if federal courts lacked the power to enjoin state courts.

Applying this criterion, the Court examined the legislative history of § 1983. This history showed that Congress was specifically concerned with the power of state courts to perpetrate or condone violations of federal law. The very action "under color of state law" targeted by Congress included the action of state courts. If § 1983 were not an express exception to the Anti-Injunction Act, one of the section's primary goals could be thwarted.

Mitchum raises the question, when will legislative history suffice to establish an express exception to the Anti-Injunction Act? Section 1983 was truly a unique federal remedy enacted against a background of state court indifference, or worse, to federal rights. In addition, § 1983 was enacted at a time (1871) when Congress may not have fully appreciated the need to "expressly" authorize state court injunctions. The express exception was not codified until 1948, and § 1983 was enacted at a time when the Supreme Court had not yet specifically relied on the Anti-Injunction Act in rendering any decision. *See Watson v. Jones*, 13 Wall. (80 U.S.) 679 (1872). Consequently, § 1983 presented a particularly strong case for inferring an express exception. Contemporary statutes may present a different question.

The Court has construed the Act's express exception in only one case since *Mitchum* was decided. In *Vendo Co. v. Lektro-Vend Corp.*, 433 U.S. 623 (1977), the Court considered whether federal antitrust laws create an express exception when state courts are used for anti-competitive purposes. In *Vendo* a federal court injunction was obtained to prevent enforcement of a state court judgment that, according to the Seventh Circuit, violated the Clayton Act.

In *Vendo*, the Court reversed an injunction approved by the Seventh Circuit, even though a majority of justices concluded that the Clayton Act constituted an express exception in at least *some* circumstances. Justice Rehnquist's plurality opinion on behalf of three justices thought *Mitchum* distinguishable based on § 1983's exceptional legislative history. *Id.* at 634. Absent such legislative history, the plurality thought any threat to federal policy resulting from state court proceedings could be addressed by Supreme Court review. Two other justices, joining in the plurality's decision to overturn the federal injunction in *Vendo*, believed that a federal court has the power to enjoin state court proceedings only if they were part of a "pattern of baseless repetitive claims." *Id.* at 643-44. These justices did not indicate that an express exception to the Act requires supporting legislative history like that in *Mitchum*. Finally, the dissenting justices concluded that Congress' intent to eliminate anti-competitive conduct in "all forms" implied an express exception to the Anti-Injunction Act, even while admitting that the legislative history of antitrust laws did not specifically contemplate that state courts might contribute to anti-competitive behavior. *Id.* at 648 n.30.

Vendo, consequently, leaves open the question whether an express exception to the Act can be found when there is neither (a) express statutory authorization of injunctions against state court proceedings, nor (b) legislative history indicating Congress specifically anticipated such injunctions. In the intervening decades since *Vendo*, the Court has provided no further guidance. Lower federal courts remain divided on how to interpret the Act's express exception. *Compare, e.g., General Motors Corp. v. Buha*, 623 F.2d 455 (6th Cir. 1980) (finding that ERISA constitutes an express exception to the Act), *with Employers Resource Management Co. v. Shannon*, 65 F.3d 1126 (4th Cir. 1995) (rejecting view that ERISA constitutes an express exception), *and Trustees of Carpenters' Health & Welfare Trust Fund of St. Louis v. Darr*, 694 F.3d 803 (7th Cir. 2012) (holding that ERISA is not an express exception to the Act in most situations).

Mitchum and Younger abstention. The Court in *Mitchum* recognized a certain amount of tension between its ruling that § 1983 is an express exception to the Anti-Injunction Act, and its prior ruling in *Younger* that courts should abstain when asked to enjoin ongoing state criminal proceedings. But the Court found that § 1983 served such a purpose despite the limits imposed by *Younger* abstention. As the Court pointed out, *Younger* does not preclude an injunction under § 1983 when "exceptional circumstances" are present. For example, § 1983 might support an injunction against state court proceedings if "state law is flagrantly and patently violative of express constitutional prohibitions, or where there is a showing of bad faith, harassment, or . . . other unusual circumstances that would call for equitable relief." In addition, *Younger* specifically limits injunctions of state court *criminal* proceedings. *Mitchum,* however, was a civil case based on state nuisance law.

We soon explore the development of *Younger* abstention and consider how often, as a practical matter, "exceptional circumstances" actually arise. We also consider the extension of *Younger* to civil proceedings, including proceedings like those filed by the prosecutor in *Mitchum.* As we explore these materials, keep one important question in mind: Does the safety valve provided by § 1983 amount to anything given the Court's extension of *Younger* abstention?

c. Exceptions to the Act to Protect Federal Court Jurisdiction or Judgments

The Anti-Injunction Act also permits a federal court to enjoin state proceedings when "necessary in aid of its jurisdiction, or to protect or effectuate its judgments." Both exceptions have a definite, limited meaning according to the Court.

i. Injunctions "in Aid of" Federal Court Jurisdiction

This exception to the Act currently has two undisputed applications.[8] First, when a case has been removed from state to federal court, the federal court has power to enjoin a state court that continues to exercise jurisdiction despite receiving notice of removal. Notice of removal is provided to the state court under 28 U.S.C. § 1446(d), which declares that the state court "shall proceed no further unless and until the case is remanded." The "in aid of" exception appears to be redundant of the "express" exception, since § 1446 clearly fits within the Court's interpretation of the latter exception.

The second application of the "in aid of" jurisdiction exception occurs when a federal court exercises *in rem* or *quasi in rem* jurisdiction based on its control of property. Provided a federal court obtains control of the property ("res") before a state court does, it has authority to enjoin subsequent state court proceedings to protect its exercise of jurisdiction. In other words, the federal court has a form of exclusive jurisdiction over the property.[9]

We soon consider whether the "in aid of" jurisdiction exception can be construed more broadly than the two applications mentioned above. But to consider this broader construction properly, we must first take a brief detour and

8. In 1995, Congress enacted the Private Securities Litigation Reform Act to curb perceived abuses in the filing of suits under federal securities laws. One provision of this statute directs a federal court to stay discovery proceedings while the plaintiff's complaint is scrutinized under the statute's heightened pleading requirements. *See* 15 U.S.C. § 78u-4(b)(3)(D). To ensure that plaintiffs not circumvent discovery limitations by pursuing discovery in state court, the statute states: "Upon a proper showing, a court may stay discovery proceedings in any private action in a State court, as necessary in aid of its jurisdiction, or to protect or effectuate its judgments."

9. Similarly, a state court has the authority to enjoin federal proceedings—a unique power—if a federal court attempts to exercise jurisdiction over property already serving as the jurisdictional basis for exercise of state court power. *See Donovan v. City of Dallas,* 377 U.S. 408, 412 (1964).

examine the Act's third exception, giving federal courts the power to enjoin state courts to "protect or effectuate" the federal courts' judgments. After we briefly examine the core meaning of this third exception, we consider how litigants have attempted to use in tandem the second and third exceptions to expand the federal courts' injunctive power.

ii. Injunctions to "Protect or Effectuate" Federal Judgments

This third exception is commonly referred to as the "relitigation" exception. It permits federal courts to enjoin state court proceedings to protect an existing federal *judgment.* The relitigation exception builds on the doctrine commonly called "collateral estoppel," now referred to in federal court as "issue preclusion." *See Chick Kam Choo v. Exxon Corp.*, 486 U.S. 140, 147 (1988). Under issue preclusion, a party to a prior judgment is not permitted to relitigate issues previously decided in the prior suit. The relitigation exception gives federal courts the authority to enjoin a state court action that threatens the issue-preclusive effect of an existing federal judgment.

In *Smith v. Bayer Corp.*, 131 S. Ct. 2368 (2011), the Court stressed that the relitigation exception can be invoked only when "preclusion is clear beyond peradventure." *Smith* involved a consumer's attempt in state court to obtain certification of a class action under West Virginia's class action rule, when another consumer had previously been denied certification of a similar proposed class by a federal court applying the federal class action rule (Rule 23). The Court held that the lower federal court lacked the power to enjoin the second attempted class action in state court for two reasons. First, plaintiff Smith was not the same plaintiff, or in privity with the same plaintiff, who was earlier denied certification by the federal court. To the contrary, because the earlier federal court denied certification, the plaintiff in that case was denied the opportunity to represent other consumers like Smith. Second, the West Virginia courts had previously stated that they might not interpret the state class action rule in the same manner as Federal Rule 23 is interpreted. For this reason, the class certification decision under state law did not present the identical issue earlier presented to the federal court.

The doctrine of issue preclusion is often examined closely in courses such as Civil Procedure and Conflict of Laws. We will not duplicate this coverage. Suffice it to say that the relitigation exception generally protects a party relying on a federal judgment from having to incur the time, expense, and risk of litigating in state court matters that have been conclusively resolved in a prior federal court suit.

Challenging issues sometimes arise in determining what forms of federal "judgments" are protected by the relitigation exception. In most disputes,[10] two important requirements must be satisfied before a federal judgment qualifies for protection under the relitigation exception: (1) the federal judgment must be "final"; and (2) the judgment must be "on the merits." This means a federal court may not normally use the relitigation exception until a federal suit has resulted in a final judgment that disposes of the merits of a controversy. When a federal court disposes of a suit on procedural grounds not related to the

10. We are simplifying preclusion doctrine for present discussion and again refer you to the more comprehensive treatment offered in other courses.

merits of a controversy, the relitigation exception does not apply. *See Chick Kam Choo, supra* (federal court dismissal of a suit on forum non conveniens grounds is not "on the merits" and does not implicate the relitigation exception).

The requirement of a final judgment on the merits limits a federal court's power to address a situation that arises surprisingly often in modern litigation. This is the situation where a dispute leads to lawsuits in different courts. Such "parallel" proceedings are generally permitted even though they result in the duplication of litigation activity in two or more courts, and even though they raise the possibility that one court will issue a final judgment precluding further litigation in the other court. Consider, for example, a dispute between an insurer and its insured. Suppose the insured files suit against the insurer in state court, seeking to recover benefits under an insurance policy. Suppose further that the insurer files its own suit in federal court seeking a declaration that the insurance policy does not cover the insured's loss.[11] Under the doctrine of issue preclusion, when one of the courts finally adjudicates the coverage issue, the other court may not relitigate that issue. This may prompt a "race to judgment" and create the very real possibility that one court will waste its time adjudicating a dispute that is eventually preempted by the other court's judgment.

If two parallel suits are pending in the federal court system, the two federal courts may employ a variety of devices to avoid or limit duplication. For example, one of the suits may be transferred and consolidated with the other suit. But there is no mechanism for consolidating suits filed in both state and federal court, even if the courts agree this is a good idea.

In *Atlantic Coast Line,* discussed below, a union argued for an expansive interpretation of both the relitigation exception and the "in aid of" jurisdiction exception to help it avoid parallel, conflicting proceedings in state and federal court. *Atlantic Coast Line* is a very complicated case, but it offers important insights into the meaning of both the relitigation and "in aid of" jurisdiction exceptions.

The dispute in *Atlantic Coast Line* arose out of the union's picketing of railroad facilities owned by Atlantic Coast Line Railroad, or "ACL." ACL first attempted to enjoin the picketing through a federal court injunction. When a federal judge denied ACL's request, the railroad filed a similar action in Florida state court. ACL succeeded in state court, as a state judge enjoined the union's picketing at one of the railroad's facilities, the "Moncrief Yard." But in the meantime, the United States Supreme Court had reversed a Florida court injunction of picketing at a *second* facility adjacent to the Moncrief Yard, the "Jacksonville Terminal." (As we said, the disputes underlying *Atlantic Coast Line* are very complicated!) According to the Supreme Court's decision in the Jacksonville Terminal dispute, federal law prohibited state court injunctions against union picketing.

In light of the Supreme Court's decision in the Jacksonville Terminal case, the union asked the Florida court to reverse its decision in the Moncrief Yard case. The state court refused and concluded that the Supreme Court's decision in the Jacksonville Terminal dispute was not controlling. Instead of seeking review of the state court's refusal in the Supreme Court, the union asked a *lower* federal court to enjoin continued enforcement of the state court's injunction. The union argued that the federal court had authority to enjoin the state court

11. You might be thinking, why doesn't the insurer desiring a federal forum simply remove to federal court? Sometimes this is possible. But other times the defendant insurer may lack this option. For example, there may be diversity of citizenship between the insured and the insurer, but the insured may join the insurer's non-diverse agent in the state court suit and destroy complete diversity.

injunction based on both the relitigation exception and the "in aid of" jurisdiction exception. The lower federal courts agreed. At this point the dispute moved to the Supreme Court, resulting in the *Atlantic Coast Line* opinion we now consider.

It might seem, at first glance, that the Florida state court had flouted the prior federal court decision refusing to enjoin union picketing. But in *Atlantic Coast Line* the Supreme Court reviewed the proceedings leading to the federal court's decision and concluded that the federal court had *not* litigated and decided the *same* issue later decided by the Florida state court. According to the Court, the federal court denied ACL's request for an injunction against union picketing at the Moncrief Yard facility because federal statutes prohibited a *federal* court from enjoining union picketing. But the issue presented in state court was whether federal law prohibited a *state* court from enjoining picketing. Thus, ACL was not "relitigating" the issue previously decided by the federal court. As you will see in the excerpt from *Atlantic Coast Line* presented below, the dissent sharply disagreed with the majority's depiction of what had been decided by the federal district court.

But what of the subsequent decision of the Supreme Court in the Jacksonville Terminal dispute, concluding that union picketing at that terminal was protected by federal law? The Court in *Atlantic Coast Line* entertained the possibility that the state court had erred when it found the Supreme Court's earlier decision in the Jacksonville Terminal dispute was not controlling in the Moncrief Yard dispute. But according to the Court, if the union disagreed with the state court's finding that the Court's earlier decision was not controlling in the Moncrief Yard dispute, it had the option of seeking review by the Court. Having failed to seek such review, the Florida court's decision on that issue was final.

Atlantic Coast Line illustrates the fine distinctions that must be drawn in applying the relitigation exception, where much turns on how precisely a court defines the scope of previously litigated issues. But the case also says something important about the "in aid of" jurisdiction exception. The union argued also in *Atlantic Coast Line* that the federal court that originally denied ACL's request to enjoin union picketing had the power to stop ACL from making an end run in state court under the guise of raising new issues to support an injunction. Here is the Court's response to that argument.

ATLANTIC COAST LINE RAILROAD CO. v. BROTHERHOOD OF LOCOMOTIVE ENGINEERS

398 U.S. 281 (1970)

MR. JUSTICE BLACK delivered the opinion of the Court.

* * * *

[A] federal court does not have inherent power to ignore the limitations of [the Anti-Injunction Act] and to enjoin state court proceedings merely because those proceedings interfere with a protected federal right or invade an area preempted by federal law, even when the interference is unmistakably clear. This rule applies regardless of whether the federal court itself has jurisdiction over the controversy, or whether it is ousted from jurisdiction for the same reason that the state court is. . . . This conclusion is required because Congress itself set forth the only exceptions to the statute, and those exceptions do not include this situation. [I]f the District Court does have jurisdiction, it is not enough that the requested injunction is related to that jurisdiction, but it must be "necessary in aid of" that jurisdiction. While this language is admittedly broad, we conclude that it implies something similar to the concept of injunctions to "protect or effectuate" judgments. Both exceptions to the general prohibition of [the Act] imply that some federal injunctive relief may be necessary to prevent a state court from so interfering with a federal court's consideration or disposition of a case as to seriously impair the federal court's flexibility and authority to decide that case. Third, no such situation is presented here. Although the federal court did have jurisdiction of the railroad's complaint based on federal law, the state court also had jurisdiction over the complaint based on state law and the union's asserted federal defense as well. While the railroad could probably have based its federal case on the pendent state law claims as well, it was free to refrain from doing so and leave the state law questions and the related issue concerning preclusion of state remedies by federal law to the state courts. Conversely, although it could have tendered its federal claims to the state court, it was also free to restrict the state complaint to state grounds alone. In short, the state and federal courts had concurrent jurisdiction in this case, and neither court was free to prevent either party from simultaneously pursuing claims in both courts. Therefore the state court's assumption of jurisdiction over the state law claims and the federal preclusion issue did not hinder the federal court's jurisdiction so as to make an injunction necessary to aid that jurisdiction. Nor was an injunction necessary because the state court may have taken action which the federal court was certain was improper under the Jacksonville Terminal decision. Again, lower federal courts possess no power whatever to sit in direct review of state court decisions. If the union was adversely affected by the state court's decision, it was free to seek vindication of its federal right in the Florida appellate courts and ultimately, if necessary, in this Court. Similarly if, because of the Florida Circuit Court's action, the union faced the threat of immediate irreparable injury sufficient to justify an injunction under usual equitable principles, it was undoubtedly free to seek such relief from the Florida appellate courts, and might possibly in certain emergency circumstances seek such relief from this Court as well. Unlike the Federal District Court, this Court does have potential appellate jurisdiction over federal questions raised in state court proceedings, and that broader jurisdiction allows this Court correspondingly broader authority to issue injunctions "necessary in aid of its jurisdiction."

This case is by no means an easy one. The arguments in support of the union's contentions are not insubstantial. But whatever doubts we may have are strongly affected by the general prohibition of [the Act.] Any doubts as to the propriety of a federal injunction against state court proceedings should be resolved in favor of permitting the state courts to proceed in an orderly fashion to finally determine the controversy. The explicit wording of [the Act] itself implies as much, and the fundamental principle of a dual system of courts leads inevitably to that conclusion.

[Justice Harlan's concurrence is omitted.]

Mr. Justice Brennan, with whom Mr. Justice White joins, dissenting.

My disagreement with the Court in this case is a relatively narrow one. I do not disagree with much that is said concerning the history and policies underlying [the Act.] Nor do I dispute the Court's holding . . . that federal courts do not have authority to enjoin state proceedings merely because it is asserted that the state court is improperly asserting jurisdiction in an area preempted by federal law or federal procedures. Nevertheless in my view the District Court has discretion to enjoin the state proceedings in the present case because it acted pursuant to an explicit exception to the prohibition of [the Act], that is, 'to protect or effectuate (the District Court's) judgments.'

In my view, what the District Court decided in 1967 was that BLE had a federally protected right to picket at the Moncrief Yard and, by necessary implication, that this right could not be subverted by resort to state proceedings. I find it difficult indeed to ascribe to the District Judge the views that the Court now says he held, namely, that ACL, merely by marching across the street to the state court, could render wholly nugatory the District Judge's declaration that BLE had a federally protected right to strike at the Moncrief Yard.

Moreover, it is readily apparent from the District Court's 1969 order enjoining the state proceedings that the District Judge viewed his 1967 order as delineating the rights of the respective parties, and, more particularly, as establishing BLE's right to conduct the picketing in question under paramount federal law. This interpretation should be accepted as controlling, for certainly the District Judge is in the best position to render an authoritative interpretation of his own order. In the 1969 injunction order, after . . . concluding that the District Court could grant injunctive relief 'in aid of its jurisdiction,' the court alternatively held that it had power to stay the state court proceedings so as to effectuate its 1967 order.

* * * *

In justifying its . . . construction of the District Court's orders, the Court takes the position that any doubts concerning the propriety of an injunction against state proceedings should be resolved against the granting of injunctive relief. Unquestionably [the Act] manifests a general design on the part of Congress that federal courts not precipitately interfere with the orderly determination of controversies in state proceedings. However, this policy of nonintervention is by no means absolute, as the explicit exceptions in [the Act] make entirely clear. Thus, [the Act] evinces a congressional intent that resort to state proceedings not be permitted to undermine a prior judgment of a federal court. But that is exactly what has occurred in the present case. Indeed, the federal determination that BLE may picket at the Moncrief Yard has been rendered wholly ineffective by the state injunction. The crippling restrictions that the Court today places upon the power of the District Court to effectuate and protect its orders are totally inconsistent with both the plain language of [the Act] and the policies underlying that statutory provision.

Accordingly, I would affirm the judgment of the Court of Appeals sustaining the District Court's grant of injunctive relief against petitioner's giving effect to, or availing itself of, the benefit of the state court injunction.

DISCUSSION AND QUESTIONS

Parallel proceedings after Atlantic Coast Line. Notice that both the majority and the dissent seem to agree that "the state and federal courts had concurrent jurisdiction in this case, and neither court was free to prevent either party from simultaneously pursuing claims in both courts." The dissent's point of disagreement concerns what was decided by the federal district court, and whether that court had the power to enjoin state proceedings to "protect" its earlier judgment. Consequently, the "in aid of" jurisdiction exception seems to have little utility in preventing the duplication and conflict that may result from parallel proceedings in state and federal court. *Atlantic Coast Line* affirms that the Anti-Injunction Act largely prevents federal courts from addressing the problem of parallel litigation by enjoining state proceedings. The only exception to this rule is the uncommon situation where federal jurisdiction is based on *in rem* jurisdiction.

Consider the union's response to the original federal court action filed by ACL to enjoin union picketing. Is there anything the union could have done to make *sure* the federal court addressed its right to picket free of state court, as well as federal court, interference? Could the union have actually raised the issue of its right to picket without state court interference? How?

At the end of this chapter we briefly address another federal court strategy for avoiding duplicative litigation—abstaining from the exercise of federal jurisdiction in deference to parallel state court proceedings. As we will learn, this strategy has limited utility and would not have been an option in situations like that faced by the federal court in *Atlantic Coast Line.*

Asserting the relitigation exception to enjoin state court proceedings. The relitigation exception recognizes that state courts must respect federal courts' resolution of issues. As we learn later in this chapter, this respect is reciprocal, and federal courts must defer to the judgments of state courts as well. Respect for state court judgments is specifically mandated by the "full faith and credit" requirement of Article IV of the Constitution and 28 U.S.C. § 1738.

The mutual respect accorded federal and state court judgments results in a seemingly anomalous rule. According to the Court, if a state court is asked to halt its own proceedings in deference to a prior federal judgment, and the state court rejects the argument that the federal judgment is preclusive, the state court's ruling on preclusion is *itself* entitled to full faith and credit. *See Parsons Steel, Inc. v. First Ala. Bank*, 474 U.S. 518 (1986). Even if the state court improperly rejects a litigant's argument that a prior federal court decision precludes reconsideration of an issue, the state's decision is binding—subject to the appellate review in state court and possible review in the United States Supreme Court. Thus, a federal court cannot step in and order a state court to respect its judgments once the state court has decided differently. As the Court observed in *Parsons Steel*, the relitigation exception is "limited to those situations in which the state court has not yet ruled on the merits of the res judicata issue." *Id.* at 524.

The Court's decision in *Parsons Steel* compels a party who wishes to rely on a prior federal judgment to make a strategic choice. If the party chooses to assert its preclusion argument in state court, it is bound by that court's ruling unless it is reversed on appeal. If the party wishes to have a federal court determine the preclusive effect of its own judgment, it must return to federal court and seek injunctive relief prior to disposition of the case in state court. Whichever court is asked to rule on the preclusion issue, its decision should be preclusive on the preclusion issue! Because it is reasonable to assume that state courts will usually accord federal court judgments the proper preclusive effect, most litigants will be willing to argue the preclusion issue in state court.

PROBLEM 10-1

Securing Federal Court Relief Consistent with the Anti-Injunction Act

Assume that a few years ago Congress enacted legislation to address perceived problems with suits challenging the alleged harmful effects of prescription drugs. Legislative history reveals Congress' concern with "indulgent, scientifically un-rigorous" standards for the admission of medical testimony employed by several state courts. One special concern was "scientifically unreliable" testimony in suits seeking to recover damages from the manufacturers of drugs and physicians who prescribe them.

Based on the report of its committee, Congress passed the "Sound Science in Pharmacology Act." The SSPA does not change the applicable substantive law governing suits against drug manufacturers and physicians — state law still determines liability standards and the scope of recoverable damages. But the SSPA gives federal courts non-exclusive jurisdiction in suits alleging negligence by drug manufacturers or prescribing physicians (subject to additional definitions and limits not relevant to the question). The SSPA also grants defendants sued in state court the right to remove their case to federal court. Defendants exercising their right to remove are governed by all procedures set forth in 28 U.S.C. §§ 1446-1449.

Legislative history accompanying the SSPA indicates Congress' expectation that suits filed in or removed to federal court will be resolved using the "more rigorous" standards for the admissibility of scientific evidence applied by federal courts. The SSPA also grants federal courts express authority to exercise "traditional equitable remedial powers," including the right to grant declaratory relief.

Consider this hypothetical federal statute and its legislative history in resolving the following two problems:

(a) Dr. Gould was sued several months ago in Texas state court for allegedly prescribing a cholesterol-controlling drug without disclosing a risk identified by recent research, namely, that use of the drug can precipitate a stroke. The drug's manufacturer, Merkle Corporation, was also sued but settled immediately after the case was filed. Unfortunately, Dr. Gould's lawyer overlooked the 30-day deadline for removal set forth in 28 U.S.C. § 1446. Also unfortunate for Dr. Gould, Texas state courts are well known for their liberal, even "indulgent" standards governing the admissibility of scientific evidence (again, this is a hypothetical). Dr. Gould's lawyers have strong reason to suspect, based on recent Texas court decisions, that the state court will admit medical testimony linking the suspect drug to the plaintiff's injuries even though that same testimony has been repeatedly excluded by federal courts applying the *Daubert* standard. Based on your study of the Anti-Injunction Act, does a federal court have authority to enjoin the pending Texas court suit based on the SSPA?

(b) Assume in answering this question that a federal district court in Texas recently issued a declaratory judgment in a suit filed by Merkle Corporation. In that suit, Merkle obtained a declaration that the drug challenged in the pending Gould negligence action is "medically safe insofar as there is no reliable scientific evidence linking [the drug] to the occurrence of strokes." Does this federal declaratory judgment improve Dr. Gould's chances of obtaining injunctive relief against the Texas court action pending against him?

FIGURE 10-1

Does the Anti-Injunction Act Prohibit Federal Court Relief?

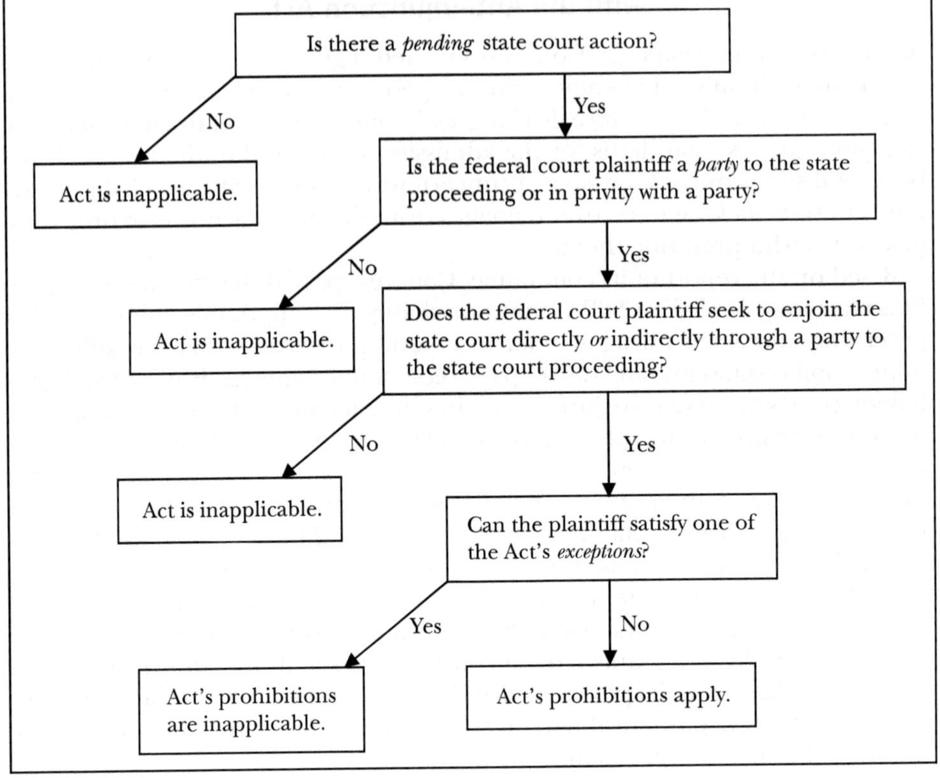

2. *Pullman* Abstention

In the Anti-Injunction Act, Congress has crafted a fairly comprehensive policy governing federal court interference with state court proceedings. But the Act is not the last word on federal court interference. We now consider several important forms of "abstention" developed by the federal courts without specific mandate from Congress. The term "abstention" encompasses "judicially created rules whereby federal courts may not decide some matter before them even though all jurisdictional and justiciability requirements are met." ERWIN CHEMERINSKY, FEDERAL JURISDICTION 811 (Aspen 6th ed. 2012).

Pullman abstention is one of the oldest forms of abstention authorized by the Court. As you read the decision in *Railroad Commission of Texas v. Pullman Co.*, consider the Court's rationale for this form of abstention and how it is to be implemented by federal district courts.

RAILROAD COMMISSION OF TEXAS v. PULLMAN COMPANY

312 U.S. 157 (1943)

MR. JUSTICE FRANKFURTER delivered the opinion of the Court.

In those sections of Texas where the local passenger traffic is slight, trains carry but one sleeping car. These trains, unlike trains having two or more sleepers, are without a Pullman conductor; the sleeper is in the charge of a porter who is subject to the train conductor's control. As is well known, porters on Pullmans are colored and conductors are white. Addressing itself to this situation, the Texas Railroad Commission after due hearing ordered that "no sleeping car shall be operated on any line of railroad in the State of Texas . . . unless such cars are continuously in the charge of an employee . . . having the rank and position of Pullman conductor." Thereupon, the Pullman Company and the railroads affected brought this action in a federal district court to enjoin the Commission's order. Pullman porters were permitted to intervene as complainants, and Pullman conductors entered the litigation in support of the order. Three judges having been convened, the court enjoined enforcement of the order. From this decree, the case came here directly.

The Pullman Company and the railroads assailed the order as unauthorized by Texas law as well as violative of the Equal Protection, the Due Process and the Commerce Clauses of the Constitution. . . .

The complaint of the Pullman porters undoubtedly tendered a substantial constitutional issue. It is more than substantial. It touches a sensitive area of social policy upon which the federal courts ought not to enter unless no alternative to its adjudication is open. Such constitutional adjudication plainly can be avoided if a definitive ruling on the state issue would terminate the controversy. It is therefore our duty to turn to a consideration of questions under Texas law.

The Commission found justification for its order in [Texas statutes]. It is common ground that if the order is within the Commission's authority its subject matter must be included in the Commission's power to prevent "unjust discrimination . . . and to prevent any and all other abuses" in the conduct of railroads. Whether arrangements pertaining to the staffs of Pullman cars are covered by the Texas concept of 'discrimination' is far from clear. What practices of the railroads may be deemed to be "abuses" subject to the Commission's correction is equally doubtful. Reading the Texas statutes and the Texas decisions as outsiders without special competence in Texas law, we would have little confidence in our independent judgment regarding the application of that law to the present situation. The lower court did deny that the Texas statutes sustained the Commission's assertion of power. And this represents the view of an able and experienced circuit judge of the circuit which includes Texas and of two capable district judges trained in Texas law. Had we or they no choice in the matter but to decide what is the law of the state, we should hesitate long before rejecting their forecast of Texas law. But no matter how seasoned the judgment of the district court may be, it cannot escape being a forecast rather than a determination. The last word on the meaning of [Texas law], and therefore the last word on the statutory authority of the Railroad Commission in this case, belongs neither to us nor to the district court but to the supreme court of Texas. In this situation a federal court of equity is asked to decide an issue by making a tentative answer which may be displaced tomorrow by a state adjudication. The reign of law is hardly promoted if an unnecessary ruling of a federal court is thus supplanted by a controlling decision of a state court. The resources of equity are equal to an adjustment that will avoid the waste of a tentative decision as well as the friction of a premature constitutional adjudication.

An appeal to the chancellor is an appeal to the "exercise of the sound discretion, which guides the determination of courts of equity." The history of equity jurisdiction is the history of regard for public consequences in employing the extraordinary remedy of the injunction. There have been as many and as variegated applications of this supple principle as the situations that have brought it into play. Few public interests have a higher claim upon the discretion of a federal chancellor than the avoidance of needless friction with state policies, whether the policy relates to the enforcement of the criminal law, or the administration of a specialized scheme for liquidating embarrassed business enterprises, or the final authority of a state court to interpret doubtful regulatory laws of the state. These cases reflect a doctrine of abstention appropriate to our federal system whereby the federal courts, "exercising a wise discretion," restrain their authority because of "scrupulous regard for the rightful independence of the state governments" and for the smooth working of the federal judiciary. This use of equitable powers is a contribution of the courts in furthering the harmonious relation between state and federal authority without the need of rigorous congressional restriction of those powers.

Regard for these important considerations of policy in the administration of federal equity jurisdiction is decisive here. If there was no warrant in state law for the Commission's assumption of authority there is an end of the litigation; the constitutional issue does not arise. The law of Texas appears to furnish easy and ample means for determining the Commission's authority. [Texas statutory law] gives a review of such an order in the state courts. Or, if there are difficulties in the way of this procedure of which we have not been apprised, the issue of state law may be settled by appropriate action on the part of the State to enforce obedience to the order. In the absence of any showing that these obvious methods for securing a definitive ruling in the state courts cannot be pursued with full protection of the constitutional claim, the district court should exercise its wise discretion by staying its hands.

We therefore remand the cause to the district court, with directions to retain the bill pending a determination of proceedings, to be brought with reasonable promptness, in the state court in conformity with this opinion.

DISCUSSION AND QUESTIONS

Argued rationales for Pullman abstention. The Court offers three rationales to support *Pullman* abstention. First, abstention avoids "needless friction" between federal and state courts by giving state courts the first opportunity to assess the validity and meaning of their own laws based on state-law grounds. Second, abstention permits federal courts to avoid giving "tentative" interpretations of state law that may later be reversed by state courts. Third, abstention permits federal courts to "avoid" difficult and sensitive constitutional rulings. In considering these rationales, think back to the forms of "interference" with state courts identified in the introduction to this chapter. Which are implicated by *Pullman* abstention?

The Court's rationales for *Pullman* abstention have been criticized as overbroad, unconvincing, and inconsistent with the adjudicative obligations imposed on federal courts by Congress. *See, e.g.*, Martha Field, *Abstention in Constitutional Cases: The Scope of* Pullman *Abstention Doctrine*, 122 U. PA. L. REV. 1071, 1084-1172 (1974) (arguing for a more fine-tuned, limited use of *Pullman* abstention). Professor Field does not see a substantial threat of "interference" with state courts unless either (1) state law is especially unclear, or (2) an incorrect interpretation of state law by a federal court could interfere with "an important state program." *Id.* at 1090-95. Other commentators question whether federal courts should ever defer to state courts and permit them to interpret state law when a federal constitutional issue looms in the background. *See Developments in the Law: Section 1983 and Federalism*, 90 HARV. L. REV. 1250, 1255 (1977).

Even if a federal court's interpretation of uncertain state law does not jeopardize "an important state program," can it be said that some form of "friction" or interference with state courts is a risk anytime a federal court is asked to strike down state law as unconstitutional? Is such friction or interference implicit in the federal courts' obligation to invalidate unconstitutional state law? Does *Pullman* abstention sensibly reduce some of this friction by giving state courts the chance to police their own laws on state-law grounds?

The Court also justifies *Pullman* abstention by referring to its long-standing policy of avoiding unnecessary constitutional rulings. *See* Ashwander v. Tennessee Valley Auth., 297 U.S. 288, 346-47 (1936) (Brandeis, J., concurring). But do you see a means by which a federal court could enforce this policy while continuing to adjudicate a dispute involving both state and federal issues? If so, does this policy truly support *Pullman* abstention?

Determining when Pullman abstention is required. The Court has stated that *Pullman* abstention is appropriate when (1) there is an unsettled issue of state law, and (2) state law is "fairly subject to an interpretation which will render unnecessary or substantially modify the federal constitutional question." *See, e.g., City of Houston v. Hill*, 482 U.S. 451, 468 (1987). Applying these criteria requires the exercise of judgment, which means it is sometimes difficult to predict whether a federal court will invoke *Pullman* abstention.

The meaning of state law may be clear even though it has not been construed by a state's courts. *See, e.g., Thornburgh v. American Coll. of Obstetricians*, 476 U.S. 747, 756 (1986). Further, the Court has indicated that, when state law clearly violates the U.S. Constitution, a federal court need not abstain to permit a state court to scrutinize that law under provisions of a state constitution paralleling those found in the U.S. Constitution. *See Wisconsin v. Constantineau*, 400 U.S. 433 (1971) (declining to abstain so that state courts could apply the state's constitutional counterpart to the Due Process Clause). *Constantineau* affirms an important limitation on *Pullman* abstention given the widespread duplication of federal constitutional provisions concerning due process, equal protection, and free speech in state constitutions. Can you see why the Court is reluctant to extend *Pullman* abstention to this context?

At the same time, *Constantineau* does not preclude use of *Pullman* abstention in all cases where the unclear state law is a state constitutional provision. For example, when a state's constitution creates unique protections not redundant of those found in the U.S. Constitution, *Pullman* abstention may still be appropriate. *See Reetz v. Bozanich*, 397 U.S. 82, 87 (1970) (abstention was proper to permit Alaska courts to construe provisions of the state constitution addressing the state's unique fishing resources).

The standard for determining when state law is sufficiently unclear to justify *Pullman* abstention is, so to speak, unclear. Professor Field has criticized the subjectivity of this standard and how it invites judges and justices to manipulate case outcomes. She observes:

> The principal standard for abstention, which relates to unclarity in the state issue, is so much a question of degree and is so subjective that misuse of the abstention

> doctrine cannot be detected with any assurance and also cannot be controlled effectively. Yet, an examination of a series of abstention decisions does suggest that in situations in which the enunciated tests apply equally, abstention is sometimes ordered and is sometimes not, and that federal judicial views concerning the merits of the federal cause of action are often the impetus for an abstention ruling, quite apart from the need for clarification of state law. A Justice committed to environmental controls who generally opposes abstention, for example, may be the first to abstain in an environmental case in which the lower court ruling was unfavorable to the environmental lists. The lack of clarity in state law he detects to justify the abstention seems largely illusory. Abstention then becomes merely a device to set aside a lower court ruling thought undesirable for reasons having no relation to the abstention doctrine.

122 U. Pa. L. Rev. at 602-03.

There is also ambiguity in the second criterion for *Pullman* abstention—whether a state court's interpretation of state law might moot or substantially modify the federal constitutional question. The Court's decision in *Baggett v. Bullitt*, 377 U.S. 360 (1964), provides guidance in at least one important situation, when state law is challenged as unconstitutionally vague. In *Baggett*, the Court found abstention improper when plaintiffs challenged the constitutionality of a state law requiring loyalty oaths from state employees. According to the Court, the vagueness of state law could not be eliminated by the single interpretation of one state court; rather, elimination of the law's vagueness would require "extensive adjudications, under the impact of a variety of factual situations. . . ." *Id.* at 377. *See also City of Houston v. Hill*, 482 U.S. 451, 467-68 (1987) (expressing the Court's reluctance to authorize *Pullman* abstention in cases "involving facial challenges based on the First Amendment" because delay may chill exercise of a constitutional right).

In *Pullman*, the Court supported its conclusion that abstention was appropriate because the case presented "a sensitive area of social policy." The Court has subsequently failed to elaborate on how this consideration should influence the decision whether to abstain. Some courts construe this aspect of *Pullman* to require consideration of a third criterion when deciding whether to abstain. The Third Circuit, for example, asks whether abstention is appropriate because a federal court's interpretation of state law might disrupt "important state policies." *D'Iorio v. County of Delaware*, 592 F.2d 681, 686 (3d Cir. 1978). The Ninth Circuit has stated that *Pullman* abstention is justified when a federal court is asked to resolve a "sensitive area of social policy" best left to the states. *Fireman's Fund Ins. Co. v. City of Lodi, Cal.*, 302 F.3d 928, 939 (9th Cir. 2002). Introduction of a third criterion in the *Pullman* analysis may foster the federalism concerns underlying the doctrine, but this criterion also interjects yet more subjectivity and unpredictability.

A final question arises concerning application of *Pullman* abstention: If the *Pullman* criteria seem applicable, *must* a federal court abstain, or does it retain discretion in deciding whether to abstain? The Court has given mixed signals on this question but seems to consider *Pullman* abstention a discretionary doctrine. *See* Chemerinsky, *supra*, at 823.

The procedures for invoking Pullman abstention. *Pullman* abstention can be invoked either by a party or by the court *sua sponte*. *See Bellotti v. Baird*, 428 U.S. 132 (1976). But how is abstention actually implemented? Recall that

Pullman abstention is intended to provide state courts the opportunity to invalidate state law on state-law grounds, while permitting federal courts to avoid federal constitutional rulings until necessary. *Pullman* thus contemplates that further federal court proceedings may sometimes be needed. How do the parties process a case that involves the courts of two independent sovereigns? And what choices do the parties have once abstention is ordered?

Much of the procedure of *Pullman* abstention was resolved by the Court in *England v. Louisiana State Board of Medical Examiners*, 375 U.S. 411 (1964). In *England*, a federal court abstained when asked by a group of chiropractors to declare unconstitutional a state law limiting their practice. According to the federal court, it was unclear whether the state law even applied to the profession. When the chiropractors subsequently asserted their claims—both state and federal—in state court, they lost. Then, instead of seeking review in the United States Supreme Court, the chiropractors returned to federal court. But the federal court concluded that, because state courts had resolved the federal constitutional claims, it was bound by their decision and had to dismiss the plaintiffs' case.

In discussing the "relitigation" exception to the Anti-Injunction Act, we saw that federal and state courts must usually defer to each other's final rulings on legal issues. See *supra* pp. ____. How, then, does a party whose case has been diverted to state court based on *Pullman* abstention handle federal claims during the course of the state proceeding? *England* gives an answer.

ENGLAND v. LOUISIANA STATE BOARD OF MEDICAL EXAMINERS

375 U.S. 411 (1964)

MR. JUSTICE BRENNAN delivered the opinion of the Court.

* * * *

There are fundamental objections to any conclusion that a litigant who has properly invoked the jurisdiction of a Federal District Court to consider federal constitutional claims can be compelled, without his consent and through no fault of his own, to accept instead a state court's determination of those claims. Such a result would be at war with the unqualified terms in which Congress, pursuant to constitutional authorization, has conferred specific categories of jurisdiction upon the federal courts, and with the principle that "When a Federal court is properly appealed to in a case over which it has by law jurisdiction, it is its duty to take such jurisdiction. . . . The right of a party plaintiff to choose a Federal court where there is a choice cannot be properly denied." Nor does anything in the abstention doctrine require or support such a result. Abstention is a judge-fashioned vehicle for according appropriate deference to the "respective competence of the state and federal court systems." Its recognition of the role of state courts as the final expositors of state law implies no disregard for the primacy of the federal judiciary in deciding questions of federal law. Accordingly, we have on several occasions explicitly recognized that abstention "does not, of course, involve the abdication of federal jurisdiction, but only the postponement of its exercise."

It is true that, after a postabstention determination and rejection of his federal claims by the state courts, a litigant could seek direct review in this Court. But such review, even when available by appeal rather than only by discretionary with of certiorari, is an inadequate substitute for the initial District Court determination. . . . This is true as to issues of law; it is especially true as to issues of fact. Limiting the litigant to review here would deny him the benefit of a federal trial court's role in constructing a record and making fact findings. How the facts are found will often dictate the decision of federal claims. "It is the typical, not the rare, case in which constitutional claims turn upon the resolution of contested factual issues." "There is always in litigation a margin of error, representing error in factfinding. . . ." Thus in cases where, but for the application of the abstention doctrine, the primary fact determination would have been by the District Court, a litigant may not be unwillingly deprived of that determination. The possibility of appellate review by this Court of a state court determination may not be substituted, against a party's wishes, for his right to litigate his federal claims fully in the federal courts.

We [have] also made clear, however, that a party may elect to forgo that right. . . . We fashioned the rule recognizing such an election because we saw no inconsistency with the abstention doctrine in allowing a litigant to decide, once the federal court has abstained and compelled him to proceed in the state courts in any event, to abandon his original choice of a federal forum and submit his entire case to the state courts, relying on the opportunity to come here directly if the state decision on his federal claims should go against him. Such a choice by a litigant serves to avoid much of the delay and expense to which application of the abstention doctrine inevitably gives rise; when the choice is voluntarily made, we see no reason why it should not be given effect.

[The Court then explained that, while the plaintiff must alert the state court to the existence of federal constitutional issues so that it can construe state law in light of the pending federal issues, it is not required to submit the federal issues to the state court for resolution. *See Government & Civic Emps. Organizing Comm. (C.I.O.) v. Windsor*, 353 U.S. 364 (1957).]

We recognize that in the heat of litigation a party may find it difficult to avoid doing more than is required by *Windsor*. This would be particularly true in the typical case, such as the instant one, where the state courts are asked to construe a state statute against the backdrop of a federal constitutional challenge. The litigant denying the statute's applicability may be led not merely to state his federal constitutional claim but to argue it, for if he can persuade the state court that application of the statute to him would offend the Federal Constitution, he will ordinarily have persuaded it that the statute should not be construed as applicable to him. In addition, the parties cannot prevent the state court from rendering a decision on the federal question if it chooses to do so; and even if such a decision is not explicit, a holding that the statute is applicable may arguably imply, in view of the constitutional objections to such a construction, that the court considers the constitutional challenge to be without merit. Despite these uncertainties arising from application of *Windsor*—which decision, we repeat, does not require that federal claims be actually litigated in the state courts—a party may readily forestall any conclusion that he has elected not to return to the District Court. He may accomplish this by making on the state record the "reservation to the disposition of the entire case by the state courts" that we referred to in [prior decisions]. That is, he may inform the state courts that he is exposing his federal claims there only for the purpose of complying with *Windsor*, and that he intends, should the state courts hold against him on the question of state law, to return to the District Court for disposition of his federal contentions. Such an explicit reservation is not indispensable; the litigant is in no event to be denied his right to return to the District Court unless it clearly appears that he voluntarily did more than *Windsor* required and fully litigated his federal claims in the state courts. When the reservation has been made, however, his right to return will in all events be preserved.

[The concurring opinion of Justice Douglas and the opinion of Justice Black, concurring in part and dissenting in part, are omitted.]

DISCUSSION

England indicates that a federal plaintiff subject to *Pullman* abstention has the choice of (1) submitting all claims, state or federal, to the state court for final resolution; or (2) submitting only state claims to the state court, while alerting the court to the existence of federal constitutional claims that have been reserved for ultimate resolution, if necessary, in federal court.[12]

Pullman abstention cannot work if the state court refuses to litigate the state-law issues. In the past, some state courts refused to litigate state-law issues based on the view that their decision would be an "advisory" opinion not permitted under state law. This appears to be less of a problem today. In addition, many state courts have the power to answer "certified" questions of state law forwarded by a federal district court. When this mechanism exists, it can simplify implementation of *Pullman* and spare the plaintiff the need to commence a separate state court suit.

The procedures for implementing *Pullman* abstention have been properly criticized as costly, time-consuming, and a delaying tactic for defendants. A federal plaintiff may be required to litigate state-law issues in state trial court; appeal adverse rulings on those issues (or defend against an opponent's appeal) in state court; return to lower state courts after an appeal; and, still later, return to federal court if the state courts' resolution of the case is unsatisfactory. Professor Currie has observed that *Pullman* has "a Bleak House aspect that in my mind is too high a price to pay for the gains in avoiding error, friction, and constitutional questions." David Currie, *The Federal Courts and the American Law Institute (Part II)*, 36 U. Chi. L. Rev. 268, 317 (1969).

PROBLEM 10-2

Invoking and Implementing Pullman Abstention

Assume you serve as a judicial clerk to a federal district judge in Oregon. The judge has asked your opinion concerning whether *Pullman* abstention is appropriate in a case assigned to her.

Two men have challenged an Oregon statute prohibiting marriage between persons of the same gender.[13] They allege that the statute violates numerous provisions of the Oregon Constitution. They also allege that the statute violates the Due Process and Equal Protection Clauses of the U.S. Constitution.

12. On occasion, the federal plaintiff might be permitted to assert some, but not all, federal claims in state court. If that tack is permissible, the plaintiff will be permitted later to assert in federal court those claims not decided by the state court. *See generally San Remo Hotel, L.P. v. City & Cnty. of S.F.*, 545 U.S. 323, 336 (2005).

13. The law on which this problem is based is fictionalized.

The plaintiffs rely in part on a recent Oregon trial court decision declaring that the Oregon Constitution prohibits statutory bans on same-sex marriage. That case is currently on appeal to an Oregon intermediate appellate court. In support of their federal constitutional claims, the plaintiffs rely on a recent decision of a federal district court in New York, which found unconstitutional that state's statutory ban on same-sex marriages.

The Ninth Circuit, encompassing Oregon, has stated that *Pullman* abstention is appropriate where (1) the plaintiffs' complaint touches a sensitive area of social policy upon which the federal court ought not to enter unless no alternative to its adjudication is open; (2) federal constitutional adjudication plainly can be avoided if a definitive ruling on the state issue would terminate the controversy; and (3) the possibly determinative issue of state law is doubtful. At this point, the defendants in the pending case have not requested that your judge abstain under *Pullman*.

By the way, you may assume Oregon has no mechanism permitting federal district courts to certify questions to Oregon state courts.

What advice would you give the judge?

REVIEW AND CONSOLIDATION

Pullman Abstention

✦ A federal court *may* abstain from deciding a question of state law when
- there is substantial uncertainty as to the meaning of state law; and
- state law is "fairly subject to an interpretation" that could moot the need for a resolution of a pending issue of constitutional law.

✦ Some federal courts also construe *Pullman* to require consideration of additional factors such as whether a federal court proceeding might disrupt "important state policies" or touch on "a sensitive area of social policy."

✦ Courts are more reluctant to invoke *Pullman* abstention when state law is challenged as unconstitutionally vague or when state law threatens to chill the exercise of First Amendment activity.

✦ Procedural aspects of *Pullman* abstention include the following:
- The abstention issue can be raised by any party or by the court.
- When abstention is ordered, the federal court retains jurisdiction to rule on constitutional issues not mooted by the state court's interpretation of state law *unless* the parties agree to submit all issues to the state court.
- Either party has the option in state court of "reserving" federal constitutional issues for decision by the federal court.
- If the parties choose to litigate federal constitutional issues in state court, the state court's judgment on those issues is binding on the federal court.
- As an alternative to formal *Pullman* abstention, a federal court may certify a state-law issue to the state's supreme court when authorized by state law.

3. *Younger Abstention*

We have seen that the Anti-Injunction Act does not prohibit federal courts from enjoining the *commencement* of state court proceedings. Provided a federal plaintiff satisfies justiciability requirements, he may seek a federal court injunction to prevent the initiation of proceedings in state court. The famous case of *Ex parte Young* affirms the power of federal courts to act when a person fears prosecution under unconstitutional state law. *Ex parte Young* states that federal injunctive relief is proper when state authorities "are about to commence proceedings, either of a civil or criminal nature, to enforce against parties affected an unconstitutional act, violating the Federal Constitution." 209 U.S. 123, 156 (1908).

However, the power of federal courts to prevent the commencement of unlawful prosecutions has long been tempered by principles of equity and federalism. As the Court observed in *Dombrowski v. Pfister*, 380 U.S. 479, 484-85 (1965), "the Court has recognized that federal interference with a State's good-faith administration of its criminal laws is peculiarly inconsistent with our federal framework. It is generally to be assumed that state courts and prosecutors will observe constitutional limitations as expounded by this Court, and that the mere possibility of erroneous initial application of constitutional standards will usually not amount to the irreparable injury necessary to justify a disruption of orderly state proceedings." Still, as *Dombrowski* illustrated, equitable and federalism restraints can be overcome when state authorities seek to enforce overly broad state laws that chill the exercise of First Amendment rights. In *Dombrowski*, the Court upheld injunctive relief against state court proceedings when the federal plaintiffs—civil rights activists in Louisiana who had been repeatedly arrested and harassed by state officials—challenged state law regulating "subversive" and communist activities. (The key facts in *Dombrowski* are recited in *Younger* below.)

After *Dombrowski*, plaintiffs filed hundreds of cases in federal court, seeking to enjoin state court proceedings. *See* Frank Maraist, *Federal Injunctive Relief Against State Court Proceedings: The Significance of* Dombrowski, 48 Tex. L. Rev. 535, 606 (1970). Arguments that state laws were "overbroad" and induced a "chilling effect" came to be slogans of civil rights activists. *See* Owen Fiss, Dombrowski, 86 Yale L.J. 1103, 1116 (1977). In *Younger v. Harris*, the Court had a further opportunity to elaborate on the equitable and federalism principles governing state court injunctions.

YOUNGER v. HARRIS

401 U.S. 37 (1971)

Mr. Justice Black delivered the opinion of the Court.

Appellee, John Harris, Jr., was indicted in a California state court, charged with violation of the . . . California Criminal Syndicalism Act. He then filed a complaint in the Federal District Court, asking that court to enjoin the appellant, Younger, the District Attorney of Los Angeles County, from prosecuting him, and alleging that the prosecution and even the presence of the Act inhibited him in the exercise of his rights of free speech and press, rights guaranteed him by the First and Fourteenth Amendments. Appellees Jim

Dan and Diane Hirsch intervened as plaintiffs in the suit, claiming that the prosecution of Harris would inhibit them as members of the Progressive Labor Party from peacefully advocating the program of their party, which was to replace capitalism with socialism and to abolish the profit system of production in this country. Appellee Farrell Broslawsky, an instructor in history at Los Angeles Valley College, also intervened claiming that the prosecution of Harris made him uncertain as to whether he could teach about the doctrines of Karl Marx or read from the Communist Manifesto as part of his classwork. All claimed that unless the United States court restrained the state prosecution of Harris each would suffer immediate and irreparable injury. A three-judge Federal District Court, . . . held that it had jurisdiction and power to restrain the District Attorney from prosecuting, held that the State's Criminal Syndicalism Act was void for vagueness and overbreadth in violation of the First and Fourteenth Amendments, and accordingly restrained the District Attorney from "further prosecution of the currently pending action against plaintiff Harris for alleged violation of the Act."

* * * *

Appellee Harris has been indicted, and was actually being prosecuted by California for a violation of its Criminal Syndicalism Act at the time this suit was filed. He thus has an acute, live controversy with the State and its prosecutor. But none of the other parties plaintiff in the District Court, Dan, Hirsch, or Broslawsky, has such a controversy. None has been indicted, arrested, or even threatened by the prosecutor. . . . Whatever right Harris, who is being prosecuted under the state syndicalism law may have, Dan, Hirsch, and Broslawsky cannot share it with him. If these three had alleged that they would be prosecuted for the conduct they planned to engage in, and if the District Court had found this allegation to be true — either on the admission of the State's district attorney or on any other evidence — then a genuine controversy might be said to exist. But here appellees Dan, Hirsch, and Broslawsky do not claim that they have ever been threatened with prosecution, that a prosecution is likely, or even that a prosecution is remotely possible. They claim the right to bring this suit solely because, in the language of their complaint, they "feel inhibited." We do not think this allegation even if true, is sufficient to bring the equitable jurisdiction of the federal courts into play to enjoin a pending state prosecution. A federal lawsuit to stop a prosecution in a state court is a serious matter. And persons having no fears of state prosecution except those that are imaginary or speculative, are not to be accepted as appropriate plaintiffs in such cases. Since Harris is actually being prosecuted under the challenged laws, however, we proceed with him as a proper party.

Since the beginning of this country's history Congress has, subject to few exceptions, manifested a desire to permit state courts to try state cases free from interference by federal courts. In 1793 an Act unconditionally provided: "[N]or shall a writ of injunction be granted to stay proceedings in any court of a state. . . ." A comparison of the 1793 Act with 28 U.S.C. section 2283 [the Anti-Injunction Act], its present-day successor, graphically illustrates how few and minor have been the exceptions granted from the flat, prohibitory language of the old Act. During all this lapse of years from 1793 to 1970 the statutory exceptions to the 1793 congressional enactment have been only three; (1) "except as expressly authorized by Act of Congress"; (2) "where necessary in aid of its jurisdiction"; and (3) "to protect or effectuate its judgments." In addition, a judicial exception to the longstanding policy evidenced by the statute has been made where a person about to be prosecuted in a state court can show that he will, if the proceeding in the state court is not enjoined, suffer irreparable damages. *See Ex parte Young.* The precise reasons for this longstanding public policy against federal court interference with state court proceedings have never been specifically identified but the primary sources of the policy are plain. One is the basic doctrine of equity jurisprudence that courts of equity should not act, and particularly should not act to restrain a criminal prosecution, when the moving party has an adequate remedy at law and will not suffer irreparable injury if denied equitable relief. The doctrine may originally have grown out of circumstances peculiar to the English judicial system and not applicable in this country, but its fundamental purpose of restraining equity jurisdiction within narrow limits is equally important under our Constitution, in order to prevent erosion of the role of the jury and avoid a duplication of legal proceedings and legal sanctions where a single suit would be adequate to protect the rights asserted. This underlying reason for restraining courts of equity from interfering with criminal prosecutions is reinforced by an even more vital consideration, the notion of "comity," that is, a proper respect for state functions, a recognition of the fact that the entire country is made up of a Union of separate state governments, and a continuance of the belief that the National Government will fare best if the States and their institutions are left free to perform their separate functions in their separate ways. This, perhaps for lack of a better and clearer way to describe it, is referred to by many as "Our Federalism," and one familiar with the profound debates that ushered our Federal Constitution into existence is bound to respect those who remain loyal to the ideals and dreams of "Our Federalism." The concept does not mean blind deference to "States' Rights" any more than it means centralization of control over every important issue in our National Government and its courts. The Framers rejected both these courses. What the concept does represent is a system in which there is sensitivity to the legitimate interests of both State and National Governments, and in which the National Government, anxious though it may be to vindicate and protect federal rights and federal interests, always endeavors to do so in ways that will not unduly interfere with the legitimate activities of the . . . States. It should never be forgotten that this slogan, "Our Federalism," born in the early struggling days of our Union of States, occupies a highly important place in our Nation's history and its future.

This brief discussion should be enough to suggest some of the reasons why it has been perfectly natural for our cases to repeat time and time again that the normal thing to do when federal courts are asked to enjoin pending proceedings in state courts is not to issue such injunctions.

* * * *

In [prior] cases the Court stressed the importance of showing irreparable injury, the traditional prerequisite to obtaining an injunction. In addition, however, the Court also made clear that in view of the fundamental policy against federal interference with state criminal prosecutions, even irreparable injury is insufficient unless it is "both great and immediate." Certain types of injury, in particular, the cost, anxiety, and inconvenience of having to defend against a single criminal prosecution, could not by themselves be considered "irreparable" in the special legal sense of that term. Instead, the threat to the plaintiff's federally protected rights must be one that cannot be eliminated by his defense against a single criminal prosecution.

* * * *

This is where the law stood when the Court decided Dombrowski v. Pfister, and held that an injunction against the enforcement of certain state criminal statutes could properly issue under the circumstances presented in that case. In *Dombrowski,* unlike many of the earlier cases denying injunctions, the complaint made substantial allegations that: "the threats to enforce the statutes against appellants are not made with any expectation of securing valid convictions, but rather are part of a plan to employ arrests, seizures, and threats of prosecution under color of the statutes to harass appellants and discourage them and their supporters from asserting and attempting to vindicate the constitutional rights of Negro citizens of Louisiana." The appellants in *Dombrowski* had offered to prove that their offices had been raided and all their files and records seized pursuant to search and arrest warrants that were later summarily vacated by a state judge for lack of probable cause. They also offered to prove that despite the state court order quashing the warrants and suppressing the evidence seized, the prosecutor was continuing to threaten to initiate new prosecutions of appellants under the same statutes, was holding public hearings at which photostatic copies of the illegally seized documents were being used, and was threatening to use other copies of the illegally seized documents to obtain grand jury indictments against the appellants on charges of violating the same statutes. These circumstances, as viewed by the Court, sufficiently establish the kind of irreparable injury, above and beyond that associated with the defense of a single prosecution brought in good faith, that had always been considered sufficient to justify federal intervention. Indeed . . . the Court in *Dombrowski* went on to say: "But the allegations in this complaint depict a situation in which defense of the State's criminal prosecution will not assure adequate vindication of constitutional rights. They suggest that a substantial loss of or impairment of freedoms of expression will occur if appellants must await the state court's disposition and ultimate review in this Court of any adverse determination. These allegations, if true, clearly show irreparable injury."

It is against the background of these principles that we must judge the propriety of an injunction under the circumstances of the present case. Here a proceeding was already pending in the state court, affording Harris an opportunity to raise his constitutional claims. There is no suggestion that this single prosecution against Harris is brought in bad faith or is only one of a series of repeated prosecutions to which he will be subjected. In other words, the injury that Harris faces is solely "that incidental to every criminal proceeding brought lawfully and in good faith," and therefore under the settled doctrine we have already described he is not entitled to equitable relief "even if such statutes are unconstitutional." [The District Court, however, thought that the *Dombrowski* decision substantially broadened the availability of injunctions against state criminal prosecutions and that under that decision the federal courts may give equitable relief, without regard to any showing of bad faith or harassment, whenever a state statute is found "on its face" to be vague or overly broad, in violation of the First Amendment. We recognize that there are some statements in the *Dombrowski* opinion that would seem to support this argument. But, as we have already seen, such statements were unnecessary to the decision of that case, because the Court found that the plaintiffs had alleged a basis for equitable relief under the long-established standards. In addition, we do not regard the reasons adduced to support this position as sufficient to justify such a substantial departure from the established doctrines regarding the availability of injunctive relief.] It is undoubtedly true, as the Court stated in *Dombrowski,* that "(a) criminal prosecution under a statute regulating expression usually involves imponderables and contingencies that themselves may inhibit the full exercise of First Amendment freedoms." But this sort of "chilling effect," as the Court called it, should not by itself justify federal intervention. In the first place, the chilling effect cannot be satisfactorily eliminated by federal injunctive relief. In *Dombrowski* itself the Court stated that the injunction to be issued there could be lifted if the State obtained an "acceptable limiting construction" from the state courts. The Court then made clear that once this was done, prosecutions could then be brought for conduct occurring before the narrowing construction was made, and proper convictions could stand so long as the defendants were not deprived of fair warning. The kind of relief granted in *Dombrowski* thus does not effectively eliminate uncertainty as to the coverage of the state statute and leaves most citizens with virtually the same doubts as before regarding the danger that their conduct might eventually be subjected to criminal sanctions. The chilling effect can, of course, be eliminated by an injunction that would prohibit any prosecution whatever for conduct occurring prior to a satisfactory rewriting of the statute. But the States would then be stripped of all power to prosecute even the socially dangerous and constitutionally unprotected conduct that had been covered by the statute, until a new statute could be passed by the state legislature and approved by the federal courts in potentially lengthy trial and appellate proceedings. Thus, in *Dombrowski* itself the Court carefully reaffirmed the principle that even in the direct prosecution in the State's own courts, a valid narrowing construction can be applied to conduct occurring prior to the date when the narrowing construction was made, in the absence of fair warning problems.

Moreover, the existence of a "chilling effect," even in the area of First Amendment rights, has never been considered a sufficient basis, in and of itself, for prohibiting state action. Where a statute does not directly abridge free speech, but—while regulating a subject within the State's power—tends to have the incidental effect of inhibiting First Amendment rights, it is well settled that the statute can be upheld if the effect on speech is minor in relation to the need for control of the conduct and the lack of alternative means for doing so. Just as the incidental "chilling effect" of such statutes does not automatically render them unconstitutional, so the chilling effect that admittedly can result from the very existence of certain laws on the statute books does not in itself justify prohibiting the State from carrying out the important and necessary task of enforcing these laws against socially harmful conduct that the State believes in good faith to be punishable under its laws and the Constitution.

* * * *

For these reasons, fundamental not only to our federal system but also to the basic functions of the Judicial Branch of the National Government under our Constitution, we hold that the *Dombrowski* decision should not be regarded as having upset the settled doctrines that have always confined very narrowly the availability of injunctive relief against state criminal prosecutions. We do not think that opinion stands for the proposition that a federal court can properly enjoin enforcement of a statute solely on the basis of a showing that the statute "on its face" abridges First Amendment rights. There may, of course, be extraordinary circumstances in which the necessary irreparable injury can be shown even in the absence of the usual prerequisites of bad faith and harassment. "It is of course conceivable that a statute might be flagrantly and patently violative of express constitutional prohibitions in every clause, sentence and paragraph, and in whatever manner and against whomever an effort might be made to apply it." Other unusual situations calling for federal intervention might also arise, but there is no point in our attempting now to specify what they might be. It is sufficient for purposes of the present case to hold, as we do, that the possible unconstitutionality of a statute "on its face" does not in itself justify an injunction against good-faith attempts to enforce it, and that appellee Harris has failed to make any showing of bad faith, harassment, or any other unusual circumstance that would call for equitable relief. Because our holding rests on the absence of the factors necessary under equitable principles to justify federal intervention, we have no occasion to consider whether [the Anti-Injunction Act] would in and of itself be controlling under the circumstances of this case.

The judgment of the District Court is reversed, and the case is remanded for further proceedings not inconsistent with this opinion.

MR. JUSTICE BRENNAN with whom MR. JUSTICE WHITE and MR. JUSTICE MARSHALL join, concurring in the result.

I agree that the judgment of the District Court should be reversed. Appellee Harris had been indicted for violations of the California Criminal Syndicalism Act before he sued in federal court. He has not alleged that the prosecution was brought in bad faith to harass him. His constitutional contentions may be adequately adjudicated in the state criminal proceeding, and federal intervention at his instance was therefore improper.

Appellees Hirsch and Dan have alleged that they "feel inhibited" by the statute and the prosecution of Harris from advocating the program of the Progressive Labor Party. Appellee Broslawsky has alleged that he "is uncertain" whether as an instructor in college history he can under the statute give instruction relating to the Communist Manifesto and similar revolutionary works. None of these appellees has stated any ground for a reasonable expectation that he will actually be prosecuted under the statute for taking the actions contemplated. [The court below expressly declined to rely on any finding "that . . . Dan, Hirsch or Broslawsky stand[s] in any danger of prosecution by the [State], because of the activities that they ascribed to themselves in the complaint. It is true, as the court below pointed out, that "[w]ell-intentioned prosecutors and judicial safeguards do not neutralize the vice of a vague law," but still there must be a live controversy under Art. III. No threats of prosecution of these appellees are alleged.] Although Dan and Hirsch have alleged that they desire to advocate doctrines of the Progressive Labor Party, they have not asserted that their advocacy will be of the same genre as that which brought on the prosecution of Harris. In short, there is no reason to think that California has any ripe controversy with them.

DISCUSSION AND QUESTIONS

The core meaning of Younger. In *Younger*, the Court inaugurated a new abstention doctrine that generally prohibits federal courts from enjoining *pending* state prosecutions. Unlike *Pullman* abstention, where federal proceedings are normally stayed to await the outcome of state proceedings, *Younger* typically requires dismissal of the federal suit. *Younger* abstention applies even though the federal plaintiff otherwise satisfies jurisdictional and justiciability requirements. And as mentioned in earlier discussion of the Anti-Injunction Act, *Younger* abstention restricts federal court power over state courts even though § 1983 is an "express" exception to the Act. Further, as the Court affirmed in a companion case to *Younger*, *Samuels v. Mackell*, 401 U.S. 66 (1971), a federal court may not circumvent this new abstention doctrine by granting declaratory rather than injunctive relief.

Younger abstention is not limited to the situation where the putative federal plaintiff is being prosecuted in state court for allegedly constitutionally protected activity (as in *Younger*). It applies as well when a state court prosecution is allegedly tainted because of the state's use of unconstitutional procedure. For example, in another companion case to *Younger*, *Perez v. Ledesma*, 401 U.S. 82 (1971), the Court required abstention when a federal court was asked to enjoin a state prosecutor's use of unconstitutionally obtained evidence. *Perez* signaled that *Younger* abstention would operate to prevent federal courts from policing pending state court proceedings to ensure compliance with emerging rules governing the constitutionality of searches and seizures.

At the same time, the Court in *Younger* acknowledged exceptions to its new abstention doctrine when "extraordinary circumstances" are present. Such extraordinary circumstances include (1) a bad-faith prosecution, (2) a challenge to patently unconstitutional state law, or (3) the absence of an adequate state forum in which the putative federal plaintiff can raise his constitutional challenge. *Younger* made clear, however, that allegations of overbreadth or "chilling effect" do not create "extraordinary circumstances" justifying equitable relief against a pending state prosecution. *Younger* also emphasized that the cost, anxiety, and inconvenience of having to defend oneself in state court are not "irreparable harm" justifying injunctive relief.

The case of *Dombrowski v. Pfister* illustrates the Court's restrictive understanding of what constitutes a bad-faith prosecution. The Court in *Younger* emphasized that the *Dombrowski* plaintiffs alleged a pattern of arrest and indictment even though the state had no actual intent to prosecute. Further, this pattern was accompanied by other forms of harassment calculated to deter the plaintiffs from basic civil-rights advocacy. The plaintiff could not demonstrate such egregious circumstances in *Younger*. Nor have other plaintiffs satisfied this standard in later cases to come before the Court. Since *Younger* the Court has rejected all claims of bad-faith prosecution. *See, e.g.*, *Hicks v. Miranda*, 422 U.S. 332, 350-51 (1975).

Federal plaintiffs alleging that state law is "patently unconstitutional" have also fared poorly before the Court. As Justice Stevens observed when dissenting in *Trainor v. Hernandez*, 431 U.S. 434, 462 (1977), "the Court seems to be saying that the 'patently and flagrantly unconstitutional' exception to *Younger*-type abstention is unavailable whenever a statute has a legitimate title, or a legitimate severability clause, or some other equally innocuous provision." *See also* Douglas Laycock, *Federal Interference with State Prosecutions: The Need for Prospective Relief*, 1977 Sup. Ct. Rev. 193, 198 ("This exception has become meaningless since *Trainor v. Hernandez*.") We will return to this point later.

According to Professor Fiss, "[a]s a practical matter . . . the universe of bad-faith harassment claims that can be established is virtually empty." *See* Owen Fiss, Dombrowski, 86 Yale L.J. 1103, 1115 (1977).

Justifications for Younger abstention. The Supreme Court was unanimous in ordering abstention in *Younger*. Justice Black identified several justifications for abstention, many of them interrelated. First, he noted that a long-standing principle of equity disfavored injunctions of state criminal proceedings. Second, he explained that state courts will usually provide defendants an adequate forum in which to assert their federal defenses—barring "extraordinary circumstances." Third, he emphasized that "comity" and "Our Federalism" demand respect for state court proceedings. Fourth, he remarked how federal court injunctions of state criminal prosecutions might interfere with "legitimate activities" of the states—that is, operation of the states' criminal justice system.

Younger has been sorely criticized in the literature. "Many forests have been leveled printing articles in opposition to and in support of *Younger* abstention." Daniel Jordan Simon, *Abstention Preemption: How the Federal Courts Have Opened the Door to the Eradication of "Our Federalism,"* 99 Nw. U. L. Rev. 1355, 1357 (2005). In reviewing that literature, Professor Chemerinsky identifies these principal criticisms:

- *Younger* abstention violates separation-of-powers doctrine, by limiting federal court jurisdiction without authorization by Congress and, arguably, contravening Congress' authorization of injunctive relief against state courts through § 1983;
- The Court mistakenly assumes there is "parity" between state and federal courts when it concludes that state courts can be trusted to enforce federal law at the behest of state criminal defendants;
- The Court mistakenly assumes state criminal proceedings provide an adequate, alternative forum for the resolution of important constitutional issues; contrary to the Court's assumption, criminal defendants cannot usually obtain widespread, prospective relief even if they prevail on their constitutional claims; and
- There is little if any empirical support for the Court's conclusion that state judges would be affronted by federal injunctive relief against allegedly unconstitutional state proceedings; to the contrary, state judges may never learn that a pending criminal prosecution has been diverted to federal court and, if they do, will both respect the federal courts' right to construe federal law and welcome the reduction in their criminal docket.

Chemerinsky, *supra*, at 858-60.

Assume the current Court repudiated the *Younger* doctrine. What effect would the greater availability of federal injunctive relief likely have on criminal prosecutions in state court? Would there be appreciable interference with the states' criminal justice systems? How often would state criminal defendants asserting federal defenses choose to file separate actions in federal court to halt their prosecution? Who would represent these defendants in federal proceedings (presumably not state public defenders)? Would the availability of a federal forum induce defendants to file federal suits in order to frustrate or delay their state court prosecutions?

If the *Younger* doctrine were repealed, would state court judges be offended by the intervention of federal courts? Do you agree with Professor Chemerinsky's comment that state court judges might even welcome federal courts' assumption of some of their workload?

Much of the controversy generated by *Younger* abstention relates to the "parity" debate highlighted in other chapters. *Younger* provides us an opportunity to reconsider the parity debate in another legal setting.

EXPLORING DOCTRINE

The Case for Twenty-first Century "Comity"

Younger was decided in a milieu quite different from the present one. The Cold War sharpened fears of the spread of Communist ideology, and government sometimes responded to the perceived threat by suppressing political expression (as in *Younger*). As well, fear and suppression were sometimes the response to protests against the unpopular Vietnam War (*Steffel v. Thompson, infra*). Finally, state and local government officials were often in the forefront of public opposition to one of the most dramatic transformations in American legal history—the end of racial segregation and discrimination (as in *Dombrowski*).

Whatever your misgivings about *Younger* abstention circa 1971, does the doctrine now reflect a well-justified trust that state court judges will enforce the U.S. Constitution? Or do you still find reason to apprehend that state courts will not provide an "adequate" forum for the enforcement of constitutional rights in criminal proceedings? If you do have misgivings, in what types of criminal prosecutions do you apprehend that state courts cannot be trusted to enforce constitutional rights as vigilantly as federal courts do?

a. *Younger* Abstention, Standing, and Anticipatory Federal Relief

All the justices writing in *Younger* agreed that, with the exception of John Harris, the plaintiffs lacked standing. Because "none has been indicted, arrested, or even threatened by the prosecutor," the Court found their feared encounters with the state were conjectural and not ripe for decision.

The facts of *Younger* highlight a possible dilemma for persons apprehensive about whether their planned activities might subject them to prosecution. The feared confrontation with state authority must ripen to the point where the person can qualify for federal court relief. But if the controversy has ripened to the point where the person has actually been arrested for engaging in conduct, the controversy cannot be adjudicated by a federal court.

The next case, *Steffel v. Thompson*, illustrates how the ripeness/abstention dilemma can sometimes be avoided. It also affirms that *Younger* abstention, like the Anti-Injunction Act, does not bar federal court relief when the court acts prior to the commencement of state court proceedings.

STEFFEL v. THOMPSON

415 U.S. 452 (1974)

MR. JUSTICE BRENNAN delivered the opinion of the Court.

. . . This case presents the important question . . . whether declaratory relief is precluded when a state prosecution has been threatened, but is not pending, and a showing of bad-faith enforcement or other special circumstances has not been made. Petitioner, and others, filed a complaint in the District Court for the Northern District of Georgia, invoking 42 U.S.C. § 1983. The complaint requested a declaratory judgment that [a Georgia criminal-trespass statute] was being applied in violation of petitioner's First and Fourteenth Amendment rights, and an injunction restraining respondents — the Solicitor of the Civil and Criminal Court of DeKalb County, the chief of the DeKalb County Police, the owner of the North DeKalb Shopping Center, and the manager of that shopping center — from enforcing the statute so as to interfere with petitioner's constitutionally protected activities.

The parties stipulated to the relevant facts: On October 8, 1970, while petitioner and other individuals were distributing handbills protesting American involvement in Vietnam on an exterior sidewalk of the North DeKalb Shopping Center, shopping center employees asked them to stop handbilling and leave. They declined to do so, and police officers were summoned. The officers told them that they would be arrested if they did not stop handbilling. The group then left to avoid arrest. Two days later petitioner and a companion returned to the shopping center and again began handbilling. The manager of the center called the police, and petitioner and his companion were once again told that failure to stop their handbilling would result in their arrests. Petitioner left to avoid arrest. His companion stayed, however, continued handbilling, and was arrested and subsequently arraigned on a charge of criminal trespass.[14]

At the threshold we must consider whether petitioner presents an "actual controversy," a requirement imposed by Art. III of the Constitution and the express terms of the Federal Declaratory Judgment Act. . . .

Unlike three of the appellees in Younger v. Harris, petitioner has alleged threats of prosecution that cannot be characterized as "imaginary or speculative." He has been twice warned to stop handbilling that he claims is constitutionally protected and has been told by the police that if he again handbills at the shopping center and disobeys a warning to stop he will likely be prosecuted. The prosecution of petitioner's handbilling companion is ample demonstration that petitioner's concern with arrest has not been "chimerical." In these circumstances, it is not necessary that petitioner first expose himself to actual arrest or prosecution to be entitled to challenge a statute that he claims deters the exercise of his constitutional rights. Moreover, petitioner's challenge is to those specific provisions of state law which have provided the basis for threats of criminal prosecution against him.

Sensitive to principles of equity, comity, and federalism, we recognized in *Younger v. Harris* that federal courts should ordinarily refrain from enjoining ongoing state criminal prosecutions. We were cognizant that a pending state proceeding, in all but unusual cases, would provide the federal plaintiff with the necessary vehicle for vindicating his constitutional rights, and, in that circumstance, the restraining of an ongoing prosecution would entail an unseemly failure to give effect to the principle that state courts have the solemn responsibility, equally with the federal courts "to guard, enforce, and protect every right granted or secured by the constitution of the United States. . . . In *Samuels v. Mackell*, the Court also found that the same principles ordinarily would be flouted by issuance of a federal declaratory judgment when a state

14. [Footnote 3 in Court's opinion.] "We were advised at oral argument that the trial of petitioner's companion, Sandra Lee Becker, has been stayed pending decision of this case."

proceeding was pending, since the intrusive effect of declaratory relief "will result in precisely the same interference with and disruption of state proceedings that the long-standing policy limiting injunctions was designed to avoid."

Neither *Younger* nor *Samuels* . . . decided the question whether federal intervention might be permissible in the absence of a pending state prosecution. In *Younger*, the Court said: "We express no view about the circumstances under which federal courts may act when there is no prosecution pending in state courts at the time the federal proceeding is begun." . . .

These reservations anticipated the Court's recognition that the relevant principles of equity, comity, and federalism "have little force in the absence of a pending state proceeding." When no state criminal proceeding is pending at the time the federal complaint is filed, federal intervention does not result in duplicative legal proceedings or disruption of the state criminal justice system; nor can federal intervention, in that circumstance, be interpreted as reflecting negatively upon the state court's ability to enforce constitutional principles. In addition, while a pending state prosecution provides the federal plaintiff with a concrete opportunity to vindicate his constitutional rights, a refusal on the part of the federal courts to intervene when no state proceeding is pending may place the hapless plaintiff between the Scylla of intentionally flouting state law and the Charybdis of forgoing what he believes to be constitutionally protected activity in order to avoid becoming enmeshed in a criminal proceeding. When no state proceeding is pending and thus considerations of equity, comity, and federalism have little vitality, the propriety of granting federal declaratory relief may properly be considered independently of a request for injunctive relief.

[The Court goes on to observe that Steffel was currently seeking only declaratory relief, and that possible limits on a federal court's power to enjoin state court proceedings—in particular the requirement that Steffel show an immediate threat of irreparable injury—did not apply to actions seeking declaratory relief. The Court also observed that "Congress plainly intended declaratory relief to act as an alternative to the strong medicine of the injunction and to be utilized to test the constitutionality of state criminal statutes in cases where injunctive relief would be unavailable. . . ." Finally, the Court observed that "the pending prosecution of petitioner's handbilling companion does not affect petitioner's action for declaratory relief."]

* * * *

We therefore hold that, regardless of whether injunctive relief may be appropriate, federal declaratory relief is not precluded when no state prosecution is pending and a federal plaintiff demonstrates a genuine threat of enforcement of a disputed state criminal statute, whether an attack is made on the constitutionality of the statute on its face or as applied.

MR. JUSTICE STEWART, with whom THE CHIEF JUSTICE joins, concurring.

. . . Our decision today must not be understood as authorizing the invocation of federal declaratory judgment jurisdiction by a person who thinks a state criminal law is unconstitutional, even if he genuinely feels "chilled" in his freedom of action by the law's existence, and even if he honestly entertains the subjective belief that he may now or in the future be prosecuted under it. . . . The petitioner in this case has succeeded in objectively showing that the threat of imminent arrest, corroborated by the actual arrest of his companion, has created an actual concrete controversy between himself and the agents of the State. He has, therefore, demonstrated "a genuine threat of enforcement of a disputed state criminal statute." Cases where such a "genuine threat" can be demonstrated will, I think, be exceedingly rare.

MR. JUSTICE WHITE, concurring.

[Justice White wrote to emphasize his disagreement with comments of Justice Rehnquist, reproduced below.] . . . I would anticipate that a final declaratory judgment entered by a federal court holding particular conduct of the federal plaintiff to be immune on federal constitutional grounds from prosecution under state law should be accorded res judicata effect in any later prosecution of that very conduct. There would also, I think, be additional circumstances in which the federal judgment should be considered as more than a mere precedent bearing on the issue before the state court. Neither can I at this stage agree that the federal court, having rendered a declaratory judgment in favor of the plaintiff, could not enjoin a later state prosecution for conduct that the federal court has declared immune. The Declaratory Judgment Act itself provides that a "declaration shall have the force and effect of a final judgment or decree" . . . and provides for "[f]urther necessary or proper relief . . . against any adverse party whose rights have been determined by such judgment," and it would not seem improper to enjoin local prosecutors who refuse to observe adverse federal judgments.

Finally, I would think that a federal suit challenging a state criminal statute on federal constitutional grounds could be sufficiently far along so that ordinary consideration of economy would warrant refusal to dismiss the federal case solely because a state prosecution has subsequently been filed and the federal question may be litigated there.

MR. JUSTICE REHNQUIST, with whom THE CHIEF JUSTICE joins, concurring.

. . . Because the opinion today may possibly be read by resourceful counsel as commencing a new and less restrictive curve in this path of adjudication, I feel it is important to emphasize what the opinion does and does not say.

To begin with, it seems appropriate to restate the obvious: the Court's decision today deals only with declaratory relief and with threatened prosecutions. The case provides no authority for the granting of any injunctive relief nor does it provide authority for the granting of any relief at all when prosecutions are pending. The Court quite properly leaves for another day whether the granting of a declaratory judgment by a federal court will have any subsequent res judicata effect or will perhaps support the issuance of a later federal injunction. But since possible resolutions of those issues would substantially undercut the principles of federalism reaffirmed in Younger v. Harris, 401 U.S. 37 (1971), and preserved by the decision today, I feel it appropriate to add a few remarks.

First, the legislative history of the Declaratory Judgment Act and the Court's opinion in this case both recognize that the declaratory judgment procedure is an alternative to pursuit of the arguably illegal activity. There is nothing in the Act's history to suggest that Congress intended to provide persons wishing to violate state laws with a federal shield behind which they could carry on their contemplated conduct. Thus I do not believe that a federal plaintiff in a declaratory judgment action can avoid, by the mere filing of a complaint, the principles so firmly expressed in *Samuels* [*v. Mackel*, where the Court held that federal courts may not issue declaratory relief if a state criminal prosecution is pending]. The plaintiff who continues to violate a state statute after the filing of his federal complaint does so both at the risk of state prosecution and at the risk of dismissal of his federal lawsuit. For any arrest prior to resolution of the federal action would constitute a pending prosecution and bar declaratory relief under the principles of *Samuels*.

Second, I do not believe that today's decision can properly be raised to support the issuance of a federal injunction based upon a favorable declaratory judgment. The Court's description of declaratory relief as "a milder alternative to the injunction remedy," having a "less intrusive effect on the administration of state criminal laws" than an injunction, indicates to me critical distinctions which make declaratory relief appropriate where injunctive relief would not be. It would all but totally obscure these important distinctions if a successful application for declaratory relief came to be regarded, not as the conclusion of a lawsuit but as a giant step toward obtaining an injunction against a subsequent criminal prosecution.

* * * *

A declaratory judgment is simply a statement of rights, not a binding order supplemented by continuing sanctions. State authorities may choose to be guided by the judgment of a lower federal court, but they are not compelled to follow the decision by threat of contempt or other penalties. If the federal plaintiff pursues the conduct for which he was previously threatened with arrest and is in fact arrested, he may not return the controversy to federal court, although he may, of course, raise the federal declaratory judgment in the state court for whatever value it may prove to have. In any event, the defendant at that point is able to present his case for full consideration by a state court charged, as are the federal courts, to preserve the defendant's constitutional rights. Federal interference with this process would involve precisely the same concerns discussed in *Younger* and recited in the Court's opinion in this case.

* * * *

DISCUSSION AND QUESTIONS

Steffel allows a federal court to issue declaratory relief addressing the constitutionality of a plaintiff's intended conduct provided the plaintiff demonstrates a sufficiently developed controversy. Steffel showed a developed controversy because he had been specifically threatened with arrest and prosecution if he did not desist from leafleting at the shopping center. Further, his confederate (Becker) had been arrested and her prosecution was pending. How often will the federal plaintiff have such a strong case for standing? Justice Stewart, concurring, comments that cases of "genuine threat" like Steffel's will be "exceedingly rare." Would Steffel have met standing requirements if he had not been personally threatened with arrest? If Becker had not been arrested? If both he and Becker had left the shopping center and no one was arrested?

The fact that criminal charges were pending against Becker created a seemingly insuperable barrier to Becker's access to federal court. But what options did Becker have once criminal proceedings against her ended? Would Becker then be permitted to bring a federal court action seeking a declaration that she has a constitutional right to leaflet at the shopping center *in the future*? Assuming her federal court complaint did not address the lawfulness of prior conduct for which she had already been prosecuted, *Younger* abstention would not seem to be a problem. But would Becker have standing to litigate the lawfulness of future conduct of the same or similar nature?

Becker's past prosecution might, or might not, be adequate to satisfy standing and equitable requirements for federal relief. For example, in *Juidice v. Vail*, 430 U.S. 327 (1977), the Court considered the standing of persons previously subjected to criminal contempt sanctions under state judgment-collection procedures. Because some of these judgment debtors had now paid the outstanding judgments against them and criminal sanctions had ended, the Court found they lacked standing to challenge possible future application of criminal sanctions against them. *Id.* at 333 n.8 ("holding that since the complaint does not allege the likelihood, or even the possibility, of future contempt orders," persons previously subject to contempt sanctions lacked standing to obtain prospective relief).

But in *Wooley v. Maynard*, 430 U.S. 705 (1977), the Court upheld injunctive relief on behalf of the federal plaintiffs, who had been subject to three prosecutions over the course of five weeks, all for the same behavior — covering over the New Hampshire state motto, "Live Free or Die," on their license plate. The plaintiffs made clear that they did not seek to "annul" the results of prior state proceedings. *Id.* at 710. Although the Court recited the principle that federal courts should normally refrain from enjoining the enforcement of state criminal statutes, the threat of "repeated prosecutions in the future" justified the plaintiffs' request for equitable relief. *Id.* at 712.

In light of *Juidice* and *Wooley*, would Becker have standing to secure federal protection from future prosecution based on one prior prosecution of similar conduct?

Notice that Becker's pending prosecution had no effect on Steffel's ability to obtain federal declaratory relief, other than to strengthen his standing argument. Even though the state court had stayed criminal proceedings against confederate Becker pending resolution of Steffel's federal court action, the Court did not find that possible indirect interference with state proceedings raised any of the concerns addressed by *Younger* abstention.

The exchange between Justices White and Rehnquist highlights issues not resolved by the majority. Justice White believed that a federal judgment declaring the plaintiff's conduct to be protected would be "res judicata" if the state later prosecutes the plaintiff for engaging in "that very conduct." Similarly, Justice White expressed support for a federal court's issuing additional, injunctive relief if the state courts refuse to honor the prior declaratory judgment.

Justice Rehnquist, on the other hand, focused on the situation of a federal plaintiff who seeks declaratory relief while continuing to engage in the conduct prompting his request for relief. According to Justice Rehnquist, if the state chooses to file charges against the federal plaintiff for continuing conduct, *Younger* and *Samuels* require the federal court to halt its proceedings. In addition, Justice Rehnquist construed a federal declaratory judgment as "simply a statement of rights" without "binding" effect on state officials. State officials may choose to defer to the judgment, but deference is not required. Does Justice Rehnquist's view simply reflect proper deference to state law and courts under the *Younger* doctrine? Or has he trivialized the majority's decision in *Steffel*?

b. *Hicks v. Miranda* and a "Race to the Court"

Justice Rehnquist's concurrence in *Steffel* emphasized his view that persons seeking federal declaratory relief should not assume that the filing of a federal action immunizes them from prosecution for future conduct. But what of the situation where a federal plaintiff has *already* engaged in conduct the state thinks criminal, and the state has not yet filed charges at the time the plaintiff files suit in federal court? If the state responds to the federal suit by filing charges, does *Younger* abstention prevent further federal proceedings? To illustrate, what if, following Steffel's filing of his federal suit, the state had filed charges of criminal trespass against Steffel for his *original* leafleting activity at the shopping mall?

The Court addressed such a scenario in *Hicks v. Miranda*, 422 U.S. 332 (1975). *Hicks* arose out of an adult theatre owner's decision to show the then-controversial movie *Deep Throat*. Believing the movie to be obscene, law enforcement seized copies of the film and arrested two theatre employees—but not the theatre owner, Vincent Miranda. The state also commenced civil proceedings to have the film declared obscene. Miranda, doing business as the Pussycat Theatre, was named as a party to these proceedings. A state court eventually decided *Deep Throat* was obscene and ordered seizure of all copies of the film possessed by the theatre.

Miranda declined to appeal the state court decision ordering seizure of his films, telling the state court he was "reserving" his constitutional challenges for determination by a federal court.[15] Instead, Miranda filed suit in federal court, seeking a declaratory judgment that state obscenity law was unconstitutional and an injunction ordering return of all copies of the film. Miranda initially sought a temporary restraining order (TRO), which the federal court denied. Later, a federal court panel declared state law unconstitutional and ordered the films' return.

The Supreme Court held that the federal court erred when it failed to abstain under *Younger*. The Court observed:

> When [the plaintiffs] filed their federal complaint, no state criminal proceedings were pending against appellees by name; but two employees of the theater had been charged and four copies of "Deep Throat" belonging to appellees had been seized, were being held, and had been declared to be obscene and seizable by the Superior Court. Appellees had a substantial stake in the state proceedings, so much so that they sought federal relief, demanding that the state statute be declared void and their films be returned to them. Obviously, their interests and those of their employees were intertwined and, as we have pointed out, the federal action sought to interfere with the pending state prosecution. Absent a clear showing that appellees, whose lawyers also represented their employees, could not seek the return of their property in the state proceedings and see to it that their federal claims were presented there, the requirements of *Younger v. Harris* could not be avoided on the ground that no criminal prosecution was pending against appellees on the date the federal complaint was filed.

Id. at 349.

In addition to finding that Miranda's federal suit was "intertwined" with the pending state proceedings against his film and his employees, the Court ruled that *Younger* abstention applied because *one day* after the federal court complaint was served, state officials joined the owner to the criminal proceedings pending against his employees. The Court commented:

> What is more, on the day following the completion of service of the complaint, appellees were charged along with their employees in Municipal Court. Neither

15. Miranda relied on *England v. Louisiana State Board of Medical Examiners*. As we have seen, this reservation applies when *Pullman* abstention is implemented, which was not the case in *Hicks*.

> *Steffel v. Thompson* nor any other case in this Court has held that for *Younger v. Harris* to apply, the state criminal proceedings must be pending on the day the federal case is filed. Indeed, the issue has been left open; and we now hold that where state criminal proceedings are begun against the federal plaintiffs after the federal complaint is filed but before any proceedings of substance on the merits have taken place in the federal court, the principles of *Younger v. Harris* should apply in full force. Here, appellees were charged on January 15, prior to answering the federal case and prior to any proceedings whatsoever before the three-judge court. Unless we are to trivialize the principles of *Younger v. Harris*, the federal complaint should have been dismissed on the appellants' motion absent satisfactory proof of those extraordinary circumstances. . . .

Id. at 349-50.

The dissent sharply rebuked the majority for making *Younger* abstention contingent on which side wins the race to the courthouse. It observed:

> The Court's new rule creates a reality which few state prosecutors can be expected to ignore. It is an open invitation to state officials to institute state proceedings in order to defeat federal jurisdiction. One need not impugn the motives of state officials to suppose that they would rather prosecute a criminal suit in state court than defend a civil case in a federal forum. Today's opinion virtually instructs state officials to answer federal complaints with state indictments. . . .

Id. at 357.

Hicks does not elaborate on what "proceedings of substance on the merits" are sufficient to permit a federal court to continue once the state commences its own proceedings in state court. Miranda's request for a TRO from the federal court in *Hicks* was not enough activity to circumvent *Younger* abstention. But in a later decision, the Court indicated that a federal court's grant of a preliminary injunction against state officials *was* sufficient action to permit the federal court to continue with its proceedings. *See Hawaii Hous. Auth. v. Midkiff*, 467 U.S. 229, 238 (1984).

The Court's decision in *Doran v. Salem Inn, Inc.*, 422 U.S. 922 (1975), provides further guidance on the machinations of seeking federal court relief in the shadow of *Younger* abstention. In *Doran*, a town had recently enacted an ordinance prohibiting topless dancing. Three local bar owners, who had previously featured topless dancing, sued in federal court to prevent enforcement of the ordinance. In the meantime, they discontinued topless dancing. The bar owners' initial request for a federal TRO was denied. At that point, one of the three owners resumed topless dancing at its bar. The state then filed criminal charges against the bar and its dancers in state court.

The federal court eventually issued a preliminary injunction prohibiting enforcement of the local ordinance. In opposing the preliminary injunction, the state argued that *Younger* barred the plaintiffs' request, especially the request of the plaintiff now being prosecuted in state court. The federal court disagreed, finding that the pending state prosecutions had no effect on the two plaintiffs not parties to the prosecutions. The court also decided it would be "anomalous" not to go ahead and grant relief to the third plaintiff, despite the prosecution pending against it in state court.

Justice Rehnquist, writing for the Court, affirmed the federal court's entry of a preliminary injunction on behalf of the two plaintiffs *not* involved in the state court proceedings. Responding to the state's argument that there was a sufficient relationship between these two plaintiffs and the third plaintiff being prosecuted, the Court observed, "While there plainly may be some circumstances in which legally distinct parties are so closely related that they should all be subject to the *Younger* considerations which govern any one of them, this is not such a case; while respondents are represented by common counsel, and have similar business activities and problems, they are apparently unrelated in terms of ownership, control, and management." *Id.* at 928-29.

Justice Rehnquist then turned to the question whether *Steffel*'s authorization of declaratory relief concerning the lawfulness of proposed conduct permitted the granting of a preliminary injunction. The Court agreed that preliminary injunctive relief was permissible:

> We now hold that on the facts of this case the issuance of a preliminary injunction is not subject to the restrictions of *Younger*. The principle underlying *Younger* and *Samuels* is that state courts are fully competent to adjudicate constitutional claims, and therefore a federal court should, in all but the most exceptional circumstances, refuse to interfere with an ongoing state criminal proceeding. In the absence of such a proceeding, however, as we recognized in *Steffel*, a plaintiff may challenge the constitutionality of the state statute in federal court, assuming he can satisfy the requirements for federal jurisdiction.

Id. at 930.

The Court also emphasized that the federal court's preliminary injunction would *not* affect the state's pending prosecution of the third bar, nor would it affect other bars not parties to the federal proceedings. "[N]either declaratory nor injunctive relief can directly interfere with enforcement of contested statutes or ordinances except with respect to the particular federal plaintiffs, and the State is free to prosecute others who may violate the statute." *Id.* at 931.

The Court in *Doran* refrained from deciding whether the federal court could ultimately issue a permanent injunction against the state, or instead had to limit any permanent relief to a declaratory judgment. In *Wooley v. Maynard*, 430 U.S. 705 (1977), however, the Court upheld issuance of a permanent injunction on behalf of a Jehovah's Witness who had been repeatedly prosecuted for covering up the motto on a New Hampshire license plate, "Live free or die." Although some commentators find *Wooley* distinguishable as an instance of "bad faith" prosecution, lower courts generally construe *Wooley* as an endorsement of permanent injunctions to restrain future state prosecutions. CHEMERINSKY, *supra*, at 872.

PROBLEM 10-3

Navigating Through Younger *Abstention*

Recall the basic dispute in *Steffel v. Thompson*. Assume that Steffel and his companion, Becker (the one who was arrested), were officers in an activist organization, Stop the War Now! After Steffel filed his suit seeking declaratory relief, he moved for a preliminary injunction. The federal court denied his motion, while commenting that "the court's decision does not reflect its opinion as to the plaintiff's ultimate prospects of obtaining permanent relief. To the contrary, the court notes that, upon further proof and proceedings, plaintiff

Steffel may well secure the permanent declaratory relief he requests in his complaint."

Shortly after the federal court denied Steffel's request for preliminary relief, the owner of the shopping center where he and Becker handed out their leaflets had the state file charges against Steffel for criminal trespass, essentially adding him as a co-defendant in Becker's pending prosecution. Before the criminal case against Steffel and Becker went to trial, Steffel secured a declaratory judgment from the federal court declaring that his leafleting activity at the shopping center was constitutionally protected.

Part A:

Steffel's federal court case is now on appeal. The State argues:

(1) The federal court should have abstained because the state filed criminal charges against Steffel before the federal court issued any relief; and
(2) The federal court should have abstained because Steffel and Becker's cases were so intertwined that federal relief will inevitably affect Becker's pending prosecution.

Evaluate the State's chances of prevailing with its arguments.

Part B:

Assume that, after the federal district court entered the declaratory judgment Steffel requested, Becker filed her own action in the same federal court. She argues:

(1) The state is now conducting a bad-faith prosecution and, under *Younger*, the federal court is not barred from enjoining her continued prosecution; and
(2) Under the "relitigation" exception to the Anti-Injunction Act, the federal court may enjoin Becker's state prosecution because the federal court has previously adjudged leafleting activity at the shopping center to be protected under the Constitution.

Evaluate Becker's chances of prevailing with her arguments.

c. *Younger*'s Impact on Federal Court Suits Seeking Damages

The classic *Younger* problem arises when a state criminal defendant asks a federal court to pass on the constitutionality of his prosecution. As we have seen, the Supreme Court believes that principles of equity and federalism require that the criminal defendant assert his constitutional defenses in state court. The Court assumes parity between federal and state courts, leaving criminal defendants to vindicate their interests in state court.

In some cases, however, a person arguing that his constitutional rights have been violated by state officials may choose to go on the offensive. Section 1983, as we have seen, authorizes a suit for damages when state officials have violated a person's constitutional rights (assuming the officials enjoy no absolute immunity from damages). For example, a person who believes he was subjected to an unconstitutional search or seizure may not only object to his prosecution in state court (e.g., at a suppression hearing), he may sue the offending officials for damages in federal court.[16]

The question arises: must a federal court dismiss a damages action based on *Younger* abstention when the plaintiff's complaint requires a ruling on the constitutionality of state conduct that underlies a pending prosecution in state court? If *Samuels v. Mackel* prohibits declaratory relief when a criminal prosecution is pending in state court, shouldn't it also prohibit monetary relief requiring a ruling—the equivalent of a declaratory judgment—on the constitutionality of the state's conduct?

In *Deakins v. Monaghan*, 484 U.S. 193 (1988), the Court declined to consider *Younger*'s impact on federal court suits seeking damages. But the Court did rule that a federal district court should have *stayed* the plaintiff's damages action rather than dismissing it, at least where the plaintiff's damages claims could not be adjudicated in pending state proceedings. *Id.* at 202.

Federal courts appear not to have reached a consensus about how *Younger* affects suits seeking damages.[17] Some circuits interpret *Deakins* as supporting the extension of *Younger* abstention to damages actions, while others don't. In situations where the plaintiff's damages action would require a finding that implicates the validity of his prior state court conviction, the Court has held that the damages action can't proceed until the prior conviction has been overturned. *See Heck v. Humphrey*, 512 U.S. 477 (1994)

It also remains unsettled what preclusive effect a state court's ruling on the underlying constitutional issue will have on a damages action pending in federal court. Arguably, if state preclusion law would preclude relitigation of the constitutional issue in a subsequent state court action for damages, the same preclusive effect is required in a federal court action for damages. *See, e.g., Nelson v. Murphy*, 44 F.3d 497, 502-03 (7th Cir. 1995) (state preclusion rules apply to preclude § 1983 damages claims when a federal court has stayed its proceedings under *Younger*). But does this outcome effectively transform a federal court's stay into a form of "abstention," at least regarding the underlying constitutional issue? That is, the state court makes the final decision regarding the constitutional issue, as it does when conventional *Younger* abstention is invoked. (As an aside, can you see why *Pullman* abstention and an *England* reservation do not help the federal plaintiff in this situation?)

d. *Younger* Abstention and State Civil Proceedings

Younger abstention derives in part from "the fundamental policy against federal interference with state criminal proceedings." 401 U.S. at 46. Although controversial, *Younger* abstention seems to have strongest footing when federal courts are asked to enjoin state criminal proceedings. After all, states have a compelling interest in securing compliance with criminal law by punishing transgressions. Further, modern state criminal procedures almost always provide defendants the opportunity to challenge the constitutionality of their

16. Of course, some constitutional claims factually related to a state court prosecution may have no bearing on the constitutionality of the prosecution itself. For example, a claim that police officers used excessive force in making an arrest will not directly affect the legality of an ensuing prosecution for the crime prompting the arrest.

17. *See* Martin A. Schwartz, Section 1983 Litigation Claims and Defenses § 14.03 (2014).

prosecution, whether by challenging the substance of criminal charges or by challenging the procedures used by the state to secure a conviction.

Federal interference with pending civil proceedings in state court may raise different concerns. For one thing, the state is not a party to most civil litigation, and the costs of federal intervention are borne largely by private parties. At the same time, federal intervention in civil proceedings might still be construed as an affront to the integrity of state courts, justifying some form of "comity" restraint.

In the decade following *Younger*, the Court was asked to extend abstention to a variety of civil proceedings. In most cases the Court agreed that *Younger* abstention should be extended to the judicial and quasi-judicial proceedings before it. We now examine several of these cases.

A note of explanation: There is no satisfying organization of *Younger* abstention cases in the civil setting. These cases turn on several factors — the presence of the state as a litigant, the type of state interest jeopardized by intervention, the impact of intervention on state court procedures, and the availability of alternative methods for raising constitutional issues in state proceedings — that cannot be convincingly reconciled into clear patterns. The organization of these cases offered below is merely an attempt to assist the presentation of unruly material.

i. Civil Proceedings Where the State Is a Party[18]

Younger was first extended to civil proceedings in *Huffman v. Pursue, Ltd.*, 420 U.S. 592 (1975). In *Huffman*, the state had filed a civil nuisance proceeding to shut down an adult theatre allegedly showing obscene films. The state court ordered the theatre closed, and its owner declined to seek review in state appellate courts. Instead, the owner filed a federal court suit challenging the constitutionality of state law. A federal district court eventually ruled state law was vague and vacated, in part, the state court's order closing the theatre.

In *Huffman*, the Court reversed the federal court order based on *Younger* abstention. Justice Rehnquist, writing for the majority, commented:

> *Younger* . . . rests upon the traditional reluctance of courts of equity, even within a unitary system, to interfere with a criminal prosecution. Strictly speaking, this element of *Younger* is not available to mandate federal restraint in civil cases. But whatever may be the weight attached to this factor in civil litigation involving private parties, we deal here with a state proceeding which in important respects is more akin to a criminal prosecution than are most civil cases. The State is a party to the Court of Common Pleas proceeding, and the proceeding is both in aid of and closely related to criminal statutes which prohibit the dissemination of obscene materials. Thus, an offense to the State's interest in the nuisance litigation is likely to be every bit as great as it would be were this a criminal proceeding. Similarly, while in this case the District Court's injunction has not directly disrupted Ohio's criminal justice system, it has disrupted that State's efforts to protect the very interests which underlie its criminal laws and to obtain compliance with precisely the standards which are embodied in its criminal laws.

18. We use the term "state" as it is used in § 1983 litigation to signify both state and local governmental actors.

Id. at 604.

The Court also rejected the theatre's argument that, because the state proceeding has already ended and a final judgment entered, a federal court injunction would not interfere with a "pending" state proceeding as occurred in *Younger.* According to the Court, federal intervention post-trial is just as disruptive of state interests as intervention at an earlier stage. *Id.* at 608-09. Note that this interpretation of *Younger* abstention mirrors interpretation of the Anti-Injunction Act, which also forbids interference with state proceedings that have resulted in a final judgment.

Justice Brennan, writing for the dissenting justices in *Huffman,* commented that the majority's ruling was "obviously only the first step toward extending to state civil proceedings generally" the *Younger* doctrine. *Id.* at 613. The dissent objected to the extension of *Younger* to the civil setting based in part on historical practice and in part on the more limited protections afforded defendants in civil proceedings:

> The extension [of *Younger*] also threatens serious prejudice to the potential federal-court plaintiff not present when the pending state proceeding is a criminal prosecution. That prosecution does not come into existence until completion of steps designed to safeguard him against spurious prosecution—arrest, charge, information, or indictment. In contrast, the civil proceeding, as in this case, comes into existence merely upon the filing of a complaint, whether or not well founded. To deny by fiat of this Court the potential federal plaintiff a federal forum in that circumstance is obviously to arm his adversary (here the public authorities) with an easily wielded weapon to strip him of a forum and a remedy that federal statutes were enacted to assure him.

Id. at 615.

Recall the decision in *Mitchum v. Foster,* where the Court held that § 1983 is an express exception to the Anti-Injunction Act. *Mitchum,* like *Huffman,* involved a state civil proceeding brought to shut down the operation of an adult theatre under state nuisance law. Does the outcome in *Huffman* suggest that *Mitchum* could be resolved today based on abstention doctrine alone?

In *Trainor v. Hernandez,* 431 U.S. 434 (1977), reproduced below, the Court applied *Younger* abstention to prevent interference with a civil proceeding brought by the state's Department of Public Aid. The state accused the Hernandezes of welfare fraud and, in lieu of filing criminal charges against them, filed a civil action to recover monies wrongfully obtained from the state. So far, the case looked similar to *Huffman.* But several factors distinguished *Trainor* from *Huffman.* First, the federal plaintiffs did *not* attempt to enjoin the state's civil action to recover wrongfully obtained monies; instead, they challenged the state's use of civil attachment procedures to freeze their bank account prior to entry of a state court judgment in the fraud action. Second, the state attachment law whose enforcement they sought to enjoin was equally available to private and governmental claimants. The Hernandezes attempted to represent a class of all debtors potentially subject to state attachment law, regardless of whether their property was attached by state officials or private creditors. For that reason, the Hernandezes sought relief not only against the state Department of Public Aid, but also against state sheriffs and court clerks who administered state attachment procedures on behalf of private and public claimants. Third, the Hernandezes questioned whether they could even assert their challenge to the constitutionality of state law in the pending attachment proceedings.

TRAINOR v. HERNANDEZ

431 U.S. 434 (1977)

Mr. Justice White delivered the opinion of the Court.

The Illinois Department of Public Aid (IDPA) filed a lawsuit in the Circuit Court of Cook County, Ill., on October 30, 1974, against appellees Juan and Maria Hernandez, alleging that they had fraudulently concealed assets while applying for and receiving public assistance. Such conduct is a crime under Illinois law. The IDPA, however, proceeded civilly and sought only return of the money alleged to have been wrongfully received. The IDPA simultaneously instituted an attachment proceeding against appellees' property. Pursuant to the Illinois Attachment Act (Act), the IDPA filed an affidavit setting forth the nature and amount of the underlying claim and alleging that the appellees had obtained money from the IDPA by fraud. The writ of attachment was issued automatically by the clerk of the court upon receipt of this affidavit. The writ was then given to the sheriff who executed it . . . on money belonging to appellees in a credit union. Appellees received notice of the attachment, freezing their money in the credit union . . . when they received the writ, the complaint, and the affidavit in support of the writ. . . . Appellees appeared in court and were informed that the matter would be continued. . . . Appellees never filed an answer either to the attachment or to the underlying complaint. They did not seek a prompt hearing nor did they attempt to quash the attachment on the ground that the procedures surrounding its issuance rendered it and the Act unconstitutional. Instead appellees filed the instant lawsuit in the United States District Court . . . seeking, inter alia, return of the attached money. The federal complaint alleged that the appellees' property had been attached pursuant to the Act and that the Act was unconstitutional in that it provided for the deprivation of debtors' property without due process of law. Appellees as plaintiffs sought to represent a class of those "who have had or may have their property attached without notice or hearing upon the creditor's mere allegation of fraudulent conduct pursuant to the Illinois Attachment Act." They named as defendants appellants Trainor and O'Malley, officials of the IDPA, and sought declaration of a defendant class made up of all the court clerks in the Circuit Courts of Illinois, and of another defendant class of all sheriffs in Illinois. They sought an injunction against Trainor and O'Malley forbidding them to seek attachments under the Act and an injunction against the clerks and sheriffs forbidding them to issue or serve writs of attachment under the Act. Appellees also sought preliminary relief in the form of an order directing the Sheriff of Cook County to release the property which had been attached.

[The Court next described how the federal district court certified the class the plaintiffs sought to represent, and issued injunctive relief against, among others, all state sheriffs and court clerks involved with administering the state's attachment law.]

* * * *

An action against appellees was pending in state court when they filed their federal suit. The state action was a suit by the State to recover from appellees welfare payments that allegedly had been fraudulently obtained. The writ of attachment issued as part of that action. [The District Court thought that *Younger* policies were irrelevant because suits to recover money and writs of attachment were available to private parties as well as the State; it was only because of the coincidence that the State was a party that the suit was "arguably" in aid of the criminal law. But the fact remains that the State was a party to the suit in its role of administering its public-assistance programs.] Both the suit and the accompanying writ of attachment were brought to vindicate important state policies such as safeguarding the fiscal integrity of those programs. The state authorities also had the option of vindicating these policies through criminal prosecutions. Although . . . the State's interest here is "[p]erhaps . . . not quite as important as is the State's interest in the enforcement of its criminal laws . . . or even its interest in the maintenance of a quasi-criminal proceeding . . . ," the principles of *Younger* and *Huffman* are broad enough to apply to interference by a federal court with an ongoing civil enforcement action such as this, brought by the State in its sovereign capacity.

For a federal court to proceed with its case rather than to remit appellees to their remedies in a pending state enforcement suit would confront the State with a choice of engaging in duplicative litigation, thereby risking a temporary federal injunction, or of interrupting its enforcement proceedings pending decision of the federal court at some unknown time in the future. It would also foreclose the opportunity of the state court to construe the challenged statute in the face of the actual federal constitutional challenges that would also be pending for decision before it, a privilege not wholly shared by the federal courts. Of course, in the case before us the state statute was invalidated and a federal injunction prohibited state officers from using or enforcing the attachment statute for any purpose. The eviscerating impact on many state enforcement actions is readily apparent.[19] This disruption of suits by the State in its sovereign capacity, when combined with the negative reflection on the State's ability to adjudicate federal claims that occurs whenever a federal court enjoins a pending state proceeding, leads us to the conclusion that the interests of comity and federalism on which *Younger* and *Samuels v. Mackell* primarily rest apply in full force here. The pendency of the state-court action called for restraint by the federal court and for the dismissal of appellees' complaint unless extraordinary circumstances were present warranting federal interference or unless their state remedies were inadequate to litigate their federal due process claim.

No extraordinary circumstances warranting equitable relief were present here. There is no suggestion that the pending state action was brought in bad faith or for the purpose of harassing appellees. [Nor does] this case come[] within the exception that we said in *Younger* might exist where a state statute is "flagrantly and patently violative of express constitutional prohibitions

19. [Footnote 9 in Court's opinion.] Appellees argue that the injunction issued below in no way interfered with a pending state case. They point to the fact that only the attachment proceeding was interfered with [and] the underlying fraud action may continue unimpeded, and claim that the attachment proceeding is not a court proceeding within the doctrine of *Younger* and *Huffman*. . . . In this case the attachment was issued by a court clerk and is very much a part of the underlying action for fraud. Moreover, the attachment in this case contained a return date on which the parties were to appear in court and at which time the appellees would have had an opportunity to contest the validity of the attachment. Thus the attachment proceeding was "pending" in the state courts within the *Younger* and *Huffman* doctrine at the time of the federal suit.

in every clause, sentence and paragraph, and in whatever manner and against whomever an effort might be made to apply it."

As for whether appellees could have presented their federal due process challenge to the attachment statute in the pending state proceeding, that question, if presented below, was not addressed by the District Court, which placed its rejection of *Younger* and *Huffman* on broader grounds. The issue is heavily laden with local law, and we do not rule on it here in the first instance.[20]

The grounds on which the District Court refused to apply the principles of *Younger* and *Huffman* were infirm; it was therefore error, on those grounds, to entertain the action on behalf of either the named or the unnamed plaintiffs and to reach the issue of the constitutionality of the Illinois attachment statute.[21]

The judgment is therefore reversed. . . .

[Justice Blackmun's concurrence is omitted.]

MR. JUSTICE BRENNAN, with whom MR. JUSTICE MARSHALL joins, dissenting.

The Court continues on, to me, the wholly improper course of extending *Younger* principles to deny a federal forum to plaintiffs invoking 42 U.S.C. §1983 for the decision of meritorious federal constitutional claims when a civil action that might entertain such claims is pending in a state court. Because I am of the view that the decision patently disregards Congress' purpose in enacting section 1983 to open federal courts to the decision of such claims without regard to the pendency of such state civil actions and because the decision indefensibly departs from prior decisions of this Court, I respectfully dissent.

* * * *

In this case the federal plaintiffs seek an injunction only against the use of statutory attachment proceedings which, properly speaking, are not part of the pending civil suit at all. The relief granted here in no way interfered with or prevented the State from proceeding with its suit in state court. It merely enjoined the use of an unconstitutional mechanism for attaching assets from which the State hoped to satisfy its judgment if it prevailed on the merits of the underlying lawsuit. To say that the interest of the State in continuing to use an unconstitutional attachment mechanism to insure payment of a liability not yet established brings into play "in full force" "all the interests of comity and federalism" present in a state criminal prosecution is simply wrong. . . .

The application of *Younger* principles here is also inappropriate because even in the underlying lawsuit the State seeks only a civil recovery of money allegedly fraudulently received. The Court relies on the State's fortuitous presence as a plaintiff in the state-court suit to conclude that the suit is closely related to a criminal suit, but I am hard pressed to understand why the "mere happenstance," that the State of Illinois rather than a private party invoked the Attachment Act makes this so. The Court's reliance on the presence of the State here

20. [Footnote 10 in Court's opinion.] The parties are in disagreement on this issue, the State squarely asserting, and the appellees denying, that the federal due process claim could have been presented and decided in the pending attachment proceeding. Mr. Justice Stevens, in dissent, offers additional reasons not relied on by appellees and not addressed by the State for concluding that the state suit did not offer an adequate forum for litigating the federal claim. We do not resolve these conflicting views.

21. [Footnote 11 in Court's opinion.] Appellees have argued here that the relief granted in favor of other class members is not barred by *Younger* and *Huffman* because state cases were not pending against some of them. Since the class should never have been certified, we need not address this argument.

may suggest that it might view differently an attachment under the same Act at the instance of a private party, but no reason is advanced why the State as plaintiff should enjoy such an advantage in its own courts over the ordinary citizen plaintiff. Under any analysis, it seems to me that this solicitousness for the State's use of an unconstitutional ancillary proceeding to a civil lawsuit is hardly compelled by the great principles of federalism, comity, and mutual respect between federal and state courts that account for *Younger* and its progeny.

* * * *

Even assuming, arguendo, the applicability of *Younger* principles, I agree with the District Court that the Illinois Attachment Act falls within one of the established exceptions to those principles. As an example of an "extraordinary circumstance" that might justify federal-court intervention, *Younger* referred to a statute that "might be flagrantly and patently violative of express constitutional prohibitions in every clause, sentence and paragraph, and in whatever manner and against whomever an effort might be made to apply it." Explicitly relying on this exception to *Younger*, the District Court held that the Illinois Act is "patently and flagrantly violative of the constitution." The Court holds that this finding is insufficient to bring this case within the *Younger* exception. . . . [Justice Brennan then explained how, under Court precedent, Illinois attachment law failed to provide essential constitutional safeguards and was therefore "flagrantly and patently violative of express constitutional prohibitions" under the relevant decisions of this Court.]

* * * *

MR. JUSTICE STEVENS, dissenting.

* * * *

Today the Court seems to be saying that the "patently and flagrantly unconstitutional" exception to *Younger*-type abstention is unavailable whenever a statute has a legitimate title, or a legitimate severability clause, or some other equally innocuous provision. . . . In effect, this treatment preserves an illusion of flexibility in the application of a *Younger*-type abstention, but it actually eliminates one of the exceptions from the doctrine. For the typical constitutional attack on a statute focuses on one, or a few, objectionable features. Although . . . it is conceivable that there are some totally unconstitutional statutes, the possibility is quite remote. More importantly, the Court has never explained why all sections of any statute must be considered invalid in order to justify an injunction against a portion that is itself flagrantly unconstitutional. Even if this Court finds the constitutional issue less clear than did the District Court, I do not understand what governmental interest is served by refusing to address the merits at this stage of the proceedings.

The Court explicitly does not decide "whether *Younger* principles apply to all civil litigation." Its holding in this case therefore rests squarely on the fact that the State, rather than some other litigant, is the creditor that invoked the Illinois attachment procedure. This rationale cannot be tenable unless principles of federalism require greater deference to the State's interest in collecting its own claims than to its interest in providing a forum for other creditors in the community. It would seem rather obvious to me that the amount [is] of far less concern to the sovereign than the integrity of its own procedures. Consequently, the fact that a State is a party to a pending proceeding should make it less objectionable to have the constitutional issue adjudicated in a federal forum than if only private litigants were involved. I therefore find it hard to accept the Court's contrary evaluation as a principled application of the majestic language in Mr. Justice Black's *Younger* opinion.

* * * *

The Court's decision to remand this litigation to the District Court to decide whether the Illinois attachment procedure provides a debtor with an appropriate forum in which to challenge the constitutionality of the Illinois attachment procedure is ironic. For that procedure includes among its undesirable features a set of rules which effectively foreclose any challenge to its constitutionality in the Illinois courts.

Although it is true that [Illinois law] allows the defendant to file a motion to quash the attachment, the purpose of such a motion is to test the sufficiency and truth of the facts alleged in the affidavit or the adequacy of the attachment bond. [Illinois law] precludes consideration of any other issues. Even if contrary to a fair reading the statute might be construed to allow consideration of a constitutional challenge on a motion to quash, a trial judge may summarily reject such a challenge without fear of reversal; for an order denying such a motion is interlocutory and nonappealable. The ruling on the validity of an attachment does not become final until the underlying tort or contract claim is resolved. At that time, the attachment issue will, of course, be moot because the prevailing party will then be entitled to the property regardless of the validity of the attachment.

. . . [A] principled application of the rationale of *Younger v. Harris* forecloses abstention in cases in which the federal challenge is to the constitutionality of the state procedure itself. Since this federal plaintiff raised a serious question about the fairness of the Illinois attachment procedure, and since that procedure does not afford a plain, speedy, and efficient remedy for his federal claim, it necessarily follows that *Younger* abstention is inappropriate. . . .

DISCUSSION AND QUESTIONS

Trainor prohibited the Hernandezes from obtaining federal court relief against state attachment procedures because a state suit was pending against them. The Court also concluded that, since the Hernandezes could not obtain individual relief, they could not represent a class of persons that included many persons not subject to *Younger* abstention. Does this mean those persons not subject to *Younger* could independently seek a federal injunction against enforcement of state attachment law? In what circumstances would others be permitted to seek injunctive relief? For example, would debtors who have been subject to state attachment procedures in the past have standing to challenge their use in *future* debt-collection actions? Would debtors currently subject to state attachment procedures in suits brought by *private* creditors be limited by *Younger*? What if such debtors sought to represent a class consisting of *all* persons potentially subject to state attachment procedures, including persons who might have those procedures used against them by governmental creditors?

The state attachment procedure challenged in *Trainor* seemed clearly unconstitutional under the Court's due process precedent. Even if one agrees with the majority's extension of *Younger* to civil proceedings like those in *Trainor*, one must accept that abstention here requires deference to state action that is hardly commendable. The majority emphasized that the state court action was "brought by the State in its sovereign capacity," and that "the suit and the accompanying writ of attachment were brought to vindicate important state policies such as safeguarding the fiscal integrity" of state public-assistance programs. True, but does the state's interest trump regardless of whether the state attempts to promote that interest through unconstitutional procedures? Does *Trainor* imply that the merits of the constitutional challenge are irrelevant to the abstention question?

The dissenting opinions criticize the majority's disregard of the patent unconstitutionality of state law. According to the dissenters, the majority creates an insuperable barrier to federal court review by approving federal court action only if state law violates the constitution in "every clause, sentence and paragraph." Is the majority's position as absurd as the dissenters suggest? Will a state law ever be patently unconstitutional under this standard? Consider the following Problem.

PROBLEM 10-4

Identifying Thoroughly Unconstitutional State Law

The First Amendment generally protects politically seditious speech unless it poses a clear and present danger of inciting unlawful behavior. Can you imagine a state or local law that might violate the First Amendment "in every clause, sentence and paragraph, and in whatever manner and against whomever an effort might be made to apply it"? Try writing a simple law that meets this standard.

By the way, how likely is it that a contemporary legislature would enact such a law? Is our quest for such a law better directed toward antiquated laws that have escaped the attention of government? Does government ever attempt to enforce such laws? To assist you in this quest, take a look at the website http://www.dumblaws.com.

The adequacy of an alternative forum. In *Trainor*, Justice Stevens (a former member of the Illinois bar) argued the federal plaintiffs lacked an "adequate forum" to assert their constitutional challenge to state attachment procedures. According to Justice Stevens, a state judge had authority to ignore the constitutional challenge or, if the judge entertained their challenge and rejected it, her decision could not be reviewed until the end of the underlying civil suit. The majority, of course, declined to address the issue on the record presented to it.

The issue of what constitutes an "adequate" state forum arose again in *Moore v. Sims*, 442 U.S. 415 (1979). *Moore* involved one of the most contentious and important issues that can arise in "civil" proceedings — under what circumstances can the state summarily remove children from their parents' custody? The state and federal proceedings involved in *Moore* are complex and convoluted. Suffice it to say that a federal district court issued a preliminary injunction prohibiting the state from using its procedures to take custody of the federal plaintiffs' children until the district court had full opportunity to scrutinize the constitutionality of the state law. The plaintiffs' children had been previously taken from them for 42 days, apparently without affording the parents a hearing, but the children had later been returned to their parents. Among the district court's constitutional concerns were possible inadequacies in providing parents notice and a timely opportunity to contest removal of their children.

The Court invoked *Younger* abstention based on the "important state interests" advocated by the state in the child custody proceedings. *Id.* at 423. According to the Court, the pertinent inquiry was "whether the state proceedings afford an adequate opportunity to raise the constitutional claims, and Texas law appears to raise no procedural barriers." *Id.* at 430. The district court had found *Younger* abstention inapplicable because the state seized and detained the plaintiffs' children without holding an immediate hearing at which the parents could argue their objections. But the majority, in an opinion authored by Justice Rehnquist, disagreed. Further, the majority emphasized that the plaintiffs' children were now in their parents' custody and would remain so until a state court conducted a hearing to consider the state's pending request to regain custody of the children.

Justice Stevens, dissenting, accused the majority of ignoring the gravamen of the plaintiffs' suit. According to Justice Stevens, the Sims sought federal relief primarily to test the constitutionality of the *original* seizure of their children. As he summarized the Simses' plight:

> The three Sims children were taken into custody by the Harris County Child Welfare Unit on March 25, 1976, based on a telephone report that one of the children was possibly the victim of child abuse. After "diligent" but unsuccessful efforts by the parents to be heard in state court, they finally went to federal court where, 42 days after they lost custody of their children, the Simses were heard for the first time in a court of law and their children were returned to them. In due course, the federal court held that the state statutory procedures were defective because they did not provide for adequate notice to the parents, and did not provide for an adequate hearing whenever the State sought to retain custody for more than 10 days. Although other portions of the District Court decision as to the State's procedures are challenged by the appeal in this Court, the appellants have not questioned these aspects of the District Court's judgment. It is therefore undisputed that the Texas procedures did not afford the parents a fair opportunity to vindicate their rights.

Id. at 441-42.

The decision in *Moore v. Sims* raises troubling questions about how far the Court will go to find that state procedures are "adequate" to justify *Younger* abstention. Even assuming the majority was correct in concluding that the Simses could assert their constitutional challenges in state court, its opinion indicates quite modest scrutiny of the question whether state procedures are adequate.

Administrative proceedings. Administrative bodies (e.g., agencies, commissions) may be used to carry out a variety of executive, legislative, and judicial functions. After *Moore v. Sims*, the Court had several opportunities to address those circumstances where administrative proceedings enjoy some form of protection under *Younger*.

The Court's decision in *Middlesex County Ethics Committee v. Garden State Bar Ass'n*, 457 U.S. 423 (1982), is of special interest to aspiring lawyers. In *Middlesex*, a lawyer was investigated by a state bar ethics committee after he criticized a judge's behavior as "legalized lynching" by a "kangaroo court." *Id.* at 428. He then turned his criticisms toward the ethics committee by filing a federal court action seeking to enjoin the committee's alleged violation of his First Amendment rights.

The Court in *Middlesex* appeared to announce a discrete test for assessing the applicability of *Younger* abstention to civil proceedings. The Court observed: "The question in this case is threefold: *first*, do state bar disciplinary hearings within the constitutionally prescribed jurisdiction of the State Supreme Court constitute an ongoing state judicial proceeding; *second*, do the proceedings implicate important state interests; and *third*, is there an adequate opportunity in the state proceedings to raise constitutional challenges." *Id.* at 432.

The Court held that *Younger* abstention prevented federal interference with the committee's proceedings because the committee was an "arm" of the state supreme court engaged in a "judicial" function akin to that of a "special master." *Id.* at 433-34. Further, the committee was adjudicating the state's "extremely important interest in maintaining and assuring the professional conduct of the attorneys it licenses." Finally, state law provided the federal plaintiff an "adequate opportunity" to assert his constitutional challenge. Even though state law in existence at the time the committee conducted its hearing was ambiguous about the committee's authority to entertain constitutional challenges, the Court was willing to consider the fact that the state supreme court had specifically granted the committee such authority while the case was pending, and even granted aggrieved lawyers the right to interlocutory review in the supreme court itself. *Id.* at 436-37.

Middlesex affirms that *Younger* abstention can be applied to protect state administrative proceedings of a quasi-judicial nature. In a later case, *Ohio Civil Rights Commission v. Dayton Christian Schools*, 477 U.S. 619 (1986), the commission had filed a complaint initiating administrative proceedings against a church-run school. The school had declined to renew a teacher's contract based on its policy requiring pregnant teachers to stay at home with their children. When the teacher contacted a lawyer to challenge the school's action, she was terminated for violating another contract term requiring internal resolution of disputes.

The church-run school responded to the commission's complaint against it by filing suit in federal court. The school claimed that the commission's investigation of its policies violated its rights under the religion clauses of the First Amendment. Eventually, a federal circuit court agreed with the school.

Applying the three-part test from *Middlesex*, the Court concluded that abstention was required. First, the Court found that the commission's administrative proceedings were "judicial in nature." *Id.* at 627. Second, it found that the proceedings addressing gender discrimination served an "important state interest." *Id.* at 628. Finally, the Court concluded that state law provided the federal plaintiff an adequate opportunity to assert its constitutional defenses. Even if the commission itself lacked authority to address constitutional issues, it was sufficient "that constitutional claims may be raised in state-court judicial *review* of the administrative proceeding." *Id.* at 629 (emphasis added).

In *New Orleans Public Service, Inc. v. Council of City of New Orleans* (*NOPSI*), 491 U.S. 350 (1989), the Court made clear that the presence of government in civil litigation is not sufficient, standing alone, to require *Younger* abstention. In *NOPSI*, the city council had denied a public utility the full rate increase it requested and rejected the utility's argument that this denial violated the Constitution (based on federal preemption). The city council then filed a declaratory judgment action in state court to have its rate decision affirmed, while the utility filed its own suit in federal court, challenging that decision. The lower federal court abstained based in part on *Younger.*

The Supreme Court reversed, with Justice Scalia writing for the majority. The Court considered whether *Younger* abstention was required in deference to *either* the city council's rate-approval proceedings or the state court's review of that city council's decision. The Court refused to extend *Younger* to the city council's proceedings, finding they were not judicial in nature as required by *Younger. Id.* at 370. As for the pending state court proceeding reviewing the council's decision, the Court concluded that this concededly judicial proceeding was not protected by *Younger*:

> Although our concern for comity and federalism has led us to expand the protection of *Younger* beyond state criminal prosecutions, to civil enforcement proceedings, and even to civil proceedings involving certain orders that are uniquely in furtherance of the state courts' ability to perform their judicial functions, *it has never been suggested that* Younger *requires abstention in deference to a state judicial proceeding reviewing legislative or executive action.* Such a broad abstention requirement would make a mockery of the rule that only exceptional circumstances justify a federal court's refusal to decide a case in deference to the States.

Id. at 367-68 (emphasis added).

ii. Civil Proceedings Between Private Parties

So far we have examined cases where the state, in some capacity, was a party to the pending state proceeding. The presence of the state underscores the Court's concern that "important state interests" might be jeopardized by federal interference.

The presence of the state as a party in most of the Court's *Younger* abstention cases also reflects another aspect of this form of abstention. Recall that *Younger* abstention acquired importance when the Court decided (or, initially, assumed) that § 1983 is an "express" exception to the Anti-Injunction Act. As we learned in Chapter 9, § 1983 provides a remedy for violations of federal law that occur "under color of state law," a phrase usually synonymous with "state action." Consequently, one would expect that the state (broadly defined to include local government actors as well) will be a party to most civil proceedings protected by *Younger* abstention.

But purely private litigation can sometimes elicit state action that violates the Constitution. This occurred in *Juidice v. Vail*, 430 U.S. 327 (1977), where the Court first extended *Younger* abstention to prevent interference with civil litigation to which the state (i.e., government) was not a party.

In *Juidice*, judgment creditors sought to depose judgment debtors to learn what assets they might have to satisfy the judgments. When the debtors did not appear for discovery, the judgment creditors obtained court orders compelling the debtors to cooperate. When the debtors still did not appear, state judges issued contempt orders, resulting in most of the debtors' imprisonment. The debtors subsequently sought federal court injunctive relief against the *sheriffs* charged with serving process related to the contempt sanctions. They alleged that state contempt procedures denied them procedural due process.

The Supreme Court held that *Younger* abstention prevented federal court interference with the state's enforcement of its contempt procedures even though the underlying dispute involved solely private parties:

> A State's interest in the contempt process, through which it vindicates the regular operation of its judicial system, so long as that system itself affords the opportunity to pursue federal claims within it, is surely an important interest. Perhaps it is not quite as important as is the State's interest in the enforcement of its criminal laws [as in *Younger*] or even its interest in the maintenance of a quasi-criminal proceeding such as was involved in *Huffman.* But we think it is of sufficiently great import to require application of the principles of those cases. The contempt power lies at the core of the administration of a State's judicial system. Whether disobedience of a court-sanctioned subpoena, and the resulting process leading to a finding of contempt of court, is labeled civil, quasi-criminal, or criminal in nature, we think the salient fact is that federal-court interference with the State's contempt process is "an offense to the State's interest . . . likely to be every bit as great as it would be were this a criminal proceeding." Moreover, such interference with the contempt process not only "unduly interfere[s] with the legitimate activities of the Stat[e]," but also "can readily be interpreted 'as reflecting negatively upon the state courts' ability to enforce constitutional principles.[']"

Id. at 335-36.

The Court next considered the application of *Younger* to civil litigation between purely private parties in *Pennzoil Co. v. Texaco, Inc.*, 481 U.S. 1 (1987). Pennzoil had obtained a Texas state court judgment against Texaco for more than $10 billion in damages. In order to prevent collection of the judgment while an appeal was pending, Texaco was required by state law to post a supersedeas bond of more than $13 billion—a requirement Texaco could not satisfy, meaning that Pennzoil could seriously damage Texaco's business by seeking to enforce the judgment before the appeal was resolved. Texaco then brought suit in a federal district court in New York, among other things, to enjoin Pennzoil from enforcing the Texas state bond requirement. The federal court granted relief for Texaco.

Texaco's challenge to state bond requirements was cast as a federal claim based on 42 U.S.C. § 1983 and the Due Process Clause. The requisite "state action" was premised on the fact that Pennzoil was required to engage in joint action with Texas state officials, including court personnel, to enforce state bond requirements. *See Texaco, Inc. v. Pennzoil Co.*, 784 F.2d 1133, 1145-46 (2d Cir. 1986). Finding sufficient collaboration between Pennzoil and state officials, the Second Circuit concluded that Pennzoil was subject to suit under federal law. *Id.* Pennzoil was enjoined from enforcing Texas law, as were other unnamed parties acting "in concert" with Pennzoil.

The Court concluded that its prior decision in *Juidice v. Vail* required that the lower federal court abstain:

> The reasoning of *Juidice* controls here. That case rests on the importance to the States of enforcing the orders and judgments of their courts. There is little difference between the State's interest in forcing persons to transfer property in response to a court's judgment and in forcing persons to respond to the court's process on pain of contempt. Both *Juidice* and this case involve challenges to the

> processes by which the State compels compliance with the judgments of its courts. Not only would federal injunctions in such cases interfere with the execution of state judgments, but they would do so on grounds that challenge the very process by which those judgments were obtained. So long as those challenges relate to pending state proceedings, proper respect for the ability of state courts to resolve federal questions presented in state-court litigation mandates that the federal court stay its hand.

Id. at 13-14.

The majority in *Pennzoil* disputed Justice Stevens's suggestion in his dissent that *Younger* now extended to *any* civil proceeding. The majority emphasized that it was specifically relying on "the State's interest in protecting the authority of the judicial system, so that its orders and judgments are not rendered nugatory." *Id.* at 14 n.12.

A more limited view of *Younger*'s application to private-party litigation was also affirmed in *New Orleans Public Service, Inc. v. Council of City of New Orleans*, 491 U.S. 350 (1989), a case discussed earlier. In *New Orleans Public Service*, the Court characterized *Juidice* and *Pennzoil* as cases extending *Younger* to "civil proceedings involving certain orders that are uniquely in furtherance of the state courts' ability to perform their judicial functions." *Id.* at 368.

More recently, in *Sprint Communications Inc. v. Jacobs*, 134 S. Ct. 584 (2014), the Court emphasized that *Younger* abstention seldom applies when federal courts are asked to take action that might interfere with parallel, private litigation in state court. In *Sprint*, the federal district court invoked *Younger* abstention to prevent interference with state court review of an administrative decision that addressed a controversy between private corporations. The Court reversed and affirmed that *Younger* applies solely to state civil proceedings that are "akin to criminal prosecutions" or that "implicate a State's interest in enforcing the orders and judgments of its courts." *Id.* at 592-93.

PROBLEM 10-5

Younger *Abstention and Private-Party Litigation*

Stewart and Amanda are former officers in a land development company, Gulf American, Inc. When Gulf American filed for bankruptcy in 2007, land purchasers learned that the bankruptcy may have been precipitated by the fraud of Stewart and Amanda. Several land purchasers filed common-law fraud actions in Mississippi state court against Stewart and Amanda. Stewart and Amanda are also being investigated by the state's attorney general, who has not yet decided whether to file criminal charges against them.

Recently, plaintiffs' counsel in the state civil action deposed Stewart. He was asked detailed questions about his conduct with Gulf American, some of them prompting Stewart to object and assert the Fifth Amendment privilege against self-incrimination. Eventually, plaintiffs' counsel filed a motion asking the supervising state court judge to protect Stewart from answering some of the questions objected to during his deposition. The judge upheld a few of Stewart's objections but denied others. In particular, she ruled that Stewart had to answer questions pertaining to two land transactions (the "Bleakacre" transactions) but did not have to answer questions related to other land transactions.

Stewart had the option of seeking interlocutory review in state appellate court, but instead filed suit in federal court, seeking declaratory and injunctive relief.

He was joined in his suit by Amanda. Stewart and Amanda ask the federal court to consider the constitutionality of the state court's order requiring Stewart to answer questions concerning the Bleakacre transactions. Stewart asks the federal court to issue an order barring plaintiffs' counsel from asking questions concerning the Bleakacre transactions. Amanda seeks a similar order.

The state court plaintiffs, the only named defendants in the federal court action, argue that both the Anti-Injunction Act and *Younger* abstention prevent federal court interference with discovery in the state court. They also argue that Amanda lacks standing to obtain federal court relief.

Will the federal court uphold the state court plaintiffs' objections?

REVIEW AND CONSOLIDATION

Younger Abstention

- ✦ *Younger* abstention, as originally inaugurated, prevents a federal court from enjoining a criminal prosecution pending in state court.
- ✦ *Younger* abstention also prevents a federal court from granting declaratory relief in situations where injunctive relief is prohibited.
- ✦ Most lower courts conclude that *Younger* abstention is not required when a federal court plaintiff seeks damages arising from conduct addressed in a pending state criminal prosecution. The Court has suggested, however, that it may be appropriate for a federal court to stay its proceedings until the state court action is completed.
- ✦ The Court ostensibly recognizes exceptions to *Younger* abstention in "extraordinary circumstances." These include (1) a bad-faith prosecution in state court, (2) a challenge to patently unconstitutional state law, or (3) the absence of an adequate state forum in which federal plaintiffs can raise their constitutional challenge. These exceptions are rarely, if ever, satisfied.
- ✦ *Younger* abstention does not prevent a person who otherwise satisfies standing requirements from seeking federal equitable relief against future state court proceedings. However, if the state commences proceedings against that person before the federal court has completed "proceedings of substance on the merits," *Younger* may bar further federal court action.
- ✦ *Younger* abstention prevents federal court interference with certain civil proceedings pending in state court. These include
  - judicial or quasi-judicial proceedings to which the state is a party and involving "important state interests"; and
  - some state court proceedings between private parties to the extent that a federal court plaintiff challenges the enforcement of orders important to the state court's performance of "judicial functions."

4. *Other Forms of Abstention*

We have considered two important forms of abstention, *Pullman* and *Younger* abstention, that have special importance in federal court suits raising constitutional issues. *Pullman* abstention provides state courts the opportunity to construe unsettled state law while permitting the parties to return to federal court and litigate federal constitutional issues once state-law issues are resolved. *Younger* abstention, on the other hand, results in dismissal of a federal court suit, based on the assumption that state courts are almost always adequate to resolve both federal and state-law issues.

There are yet other forms of abstention, although commentators do not agree on how many of these forms exist. *See, e.g.*, Leonard Birdsong, *Comity and Our Federalism in the Twenty-first Century: The Abstention Doctrines Will Always Be with Us— Get Over It!*, 36 Creighton L. Rev. 375, 376 (2003). These other abstention forms can be classified in different ways and sometimes are referred to by different names in the literature. In this last section of this chapter, we provide a brief introduction to these other forms of abstention based on a classification scheme we find useful.

a. "*Burford*" Abstention

Burford abstention, which traces to the Court's decision in *Burford v. Sun Oil Co.*, 319 U.S. 315 (1943), is sometimes referred to as "administrative" abstention, even though it extends to interference with proceedings in both state agencies and state courts. In *Burford*, Sun Oil brought a federal court suit to enjoin the decision of a Texas state commission authorizing Burford to drill several oil wells. Sun Oil challenged the commission's order based on both constitutional and state-law grounds.

The Supreme Court held that the district court should have dismissed the case. The Court emphasized several factors requiring dismissal: (1) the presence of numerous unsettled issues concerning the interpretation of state law; (2) the existence of a complex dispute resolution system involving a state commission and centralized review in select state courts, whose judges had special expertise in the regulated field; (3) the need for centralized, consistent decisions regarding a natural resource shared among various oil well owners; and (4) the importance of oil and gas to the state's economy. The Court specifically observed that, in the past, federal and state court proceedings had led to conflicting rulings. *Id.* at 328-30.

The Court later explained the basis for its decision in *Burford* this way: "We ultimately concluded . . . that dismissal was appropriate because the availability of an alternative, federal forum threatened to frustrate the purpose of the complex administrative system that Texas had established." *Quackenbush v. Allstate Ins. Co.*, 517 U.S. 706, 725 (1996). In still another decision, the Court stressed that *Burford* abstention supports dismissal only in "extraordinary circumstances" where (1) a federal suit presents "difficult questions of state law bearing on policy problems of substantial public import whose importance transcends the result in the case then at bar," or (2) a decision by the federal court "would be disruptive of state efforts to establish a coherent policy with respect to a matter of substantial public concern." *New Orleans Pub. Serv., Inc. v. Council of City of New Orleans*, 491 U.S. 350, 361 (1989). At the same time, the Court has acknowledged there is no "formulaic test" for determining when *Burford* abstention is required. *Quackenbush, supra*, 517 U.S. at 727-28.

As described by the Court, *Burford* abstention can involve aspects of *Pullman* abstention ("difficult questions of state law") and *Younger* abstention (state interests of "substantial public import"). But unlike *Pullman* abstention, *Burford* abstention is not based on a federal court's interest in avoiding the decision of constitutional questions. And unlike *Younger* abstention, *Burford* abstention may be appropriate even though a federal court is not being asked to enjoin or declare unlawful proceedings pending in state court. In addition, *Burford* abstention is specifically reserved for "extraordinary circumstances," in contrast to *Pullman* and *Younger*, where abstention is more regularly invoked.

Proper application of *Burford* remains controversial, in part because of the seeming inconsistencies in the Court's own application of the doctrine. The most oft-cited examples of such inconsistency are the Court's decisions in *Louisiana Power & Light Co. v. City of Thibodaux*, 360 U.S. 25 (1959), and *County of Allegheny v. Frank Mashuda Co.*, 360 U.S. 185 (1959), which were handed down by the Court on the same day.

In *Thibodaux*, the Court affirmed a lower court's decision staying litigation that had been removed from state court. A city had commenced eminent domain proceedings in state court to take property owned by a utility. When the utility removed the case to federal court based on diversity of citizenship, the district court stayed further proceedings to permit the state court to decide whether the city had authority under state law to effect the taking. Note that no party raised a federal constitutional claim, and so *Pullman* abstention was not applicable. The Court affirmed the district court's stay because of the "special and peculiar nature" of eminent domain proceedings and the sensitive question of how eminent domain power was allocated between state and local government. *Id.* at 27-28. The Court expressed deference to the opinion of the federal judge—who was knowledgeable in state law—that the legal issue of the city's eminent domain authority was best resolved by the state courts.

Yet on the same day, in *Mashuda*, the Court reversed a federal court decision dismissing a suit brought by a landowner whose land had been taken by the city through its eminent domain power and then leased to private parties. The owner commenced a federal diversity action challenging the taking based on state law that unambiguously prohibited government from using its eminent domain power for private purposes. The Court found abstention improper for several reasons. First, the federal court was not invoking abstention to avoid deciding a constitutional question (*Pullman*). Second, the Court saw no threat of disruption to state administrative processes serving important state needs (*Burford*). Finally, the Court found that the city's exercise of eminent domain power raised no "mystical" issues of "sovereignty" requiring federal court deference.

Most members of the Court seemed to agree that *Thibodaux* and *Mashuda* required the same resolution under abstention doctrine, although they disagreed about what resolution was proper. The pivotal concurring opinion of Justice Stewart in *Thibodaux* distinguished the two cases based on (1) the fact that the district court had dismissed rather than stayed the proceedings in *Mashuda*, and (2) the fact that the meaning of state law was undisputed in *Mashuda*. 360 U.S. at 31 (Stewart, J., concurring). The Court would later observe, however, that the critical distinction between the cases was the district courts' differing decisions to dismiss (*Mashuda*) or stay (*Thibodaux*). *See Quackenbush v. Allstate Ins. Co.*, 517 U.S. 706, 721 (1996).

In still another decision, *Kaiser Steel Corp. v. W.S. Ranch Co.*, 391 U.S. 593 (1968), the Court issued a *per curiam* opinion *requiring* a district court to stay proceedings in a diversity-of-citizenship suit challenging a state's condemnation of private property for the purpose of granting another property owner access to water. The Court emphasized that the case presented a "novel" question concerning the meaning of New Mexico's constitution that was of "vital concern" to the state's use of scarce natural resources. *Id.* at 594.

The current *Burford* doctrine *appears* to authorize stays (and occasionally dismissals as in *Burford*) when a federal suit raises unsettled issues of state law pertaining to subjects of "substantial" importance to state or local government. The importance of an issue to government may be indicated by its creation of a specialized administrative and judicial scheme to provide "coherent" resolutions of disputes, as in *Burford*, but this is not a *sine qua non* for abstention (*see Thibodaux*). This form of abstention may be invoked in cases premised on either federal question or diversity-of-citizenship jurisdiction. But as the Court has repeatedly stated, such abstention is reserved for "extraordinary circumstances" and should not be regularly exercised.

All that said, "generalizations about *Burford* abstention are dangerous." William E. Ryckman, *Land Use Litigation, Federal Jurisdiction, and the Abstention Doctrines*, 69 Cal. L. Rev. 377 (1981). In applying this unruly doctrine, there is no substitute for close analysis of case precedent, including precedent in one's particular federal circuit. But the following criteria appear to be relevant under Court precedent:

REVIEW AND CONSOLIDATION

Criteria for Assessing the Propriety of Burford Abstention

- ✦ Does the federal case present unsettled state-law issues?
- ✦ Do the unsettled state-law issues concern matters of substantial importance to local or state government?
- ✦ Does the federal case address a type of dispute that requires coherent, consistent resolution by federal and state courts?
- ✦ Has the state developed a unitary administrative judicial scheme for resolving the type of dispute presented?
- ✦ Has the federal court stayed or dismissed its proceedings?

b. *Colorado River* Abstention

"*Colorado River*" abstention addresses a problem we briefly examined in our study of the Anti-Injunction Act. This is the problem of "parallel" or "duplicative" lawsuits, where litigation in both state and federal court seems to address overlapping factual or legal issues. As we saw, none of the exceptions to the Anti-Injunction Act authorizes a federal court to enjoin state proceedings simply because the state court may be adjudicating issues also before the federal court. The only occasions when a federal court can enjoin duplicative state proceedings are the rare situations when (1) the federal court was first to acquire jurisdiction over property and the state court attempts to adjudicate interests in the same property; or (2) the federal court has previously issued a final judgment and a state court tries to "relitigate" issues already decided by the federal court.

Colorado River abstention provides federal courts another, limited tack for avoiding parallel litigation where they lack power to enjoin a state court—the federal court can abstain and defer to the state court. Like *Burford* abstention, *Colorado River* abstention is reserved for "exceptional circumstances." 424 U.S. 800, 818 (1976). Yet *Colorado River* abstention seems to be even more exceptional than *Burford* abstention. As one federal circuit court has observed, *Colorado River* abstention "is permissible in fewer circumstances than are the other abstention doctrines, which themselves carve out only slender exceptions to the robust duty to exercise jurisdiction." *Ambrosia Coal & Constr. Co. v. Page Morales*, 368 F.3d 1320, 1331 (11th Cir. 2004).

The case of *Colorado River* arose out of a suit filed by the United States seeking a declaration of water rights in the Colorado River. The United States filed suit in federal court and named more than 1,000 defendants. One of those defendants then filed suit in state court naming the United States as a defendant, pursuant to a rare statutory waiver of the United States' sovereign immunity from suit in state court. *See* 43 U.S.C. § 666. In light of the pending state court action addressing the United States' water rights, the federal district court dismissed the United States' suit.

The Supreme Court upheld the district court's dismissal. In the following excerpts from the Court's opinion, consider how the Court describes (1) the federal courts' obligation to exercise jurisdiction conferred on them by Congress; (2) the curtailment of that obligation through existing abstention doctrine (which the Court finds inapplicable); and (3) the special facts that support dismissal in *Colorado River*. An explanatory note: the Court does not announce a new form of "abstention" as such. But the Court ultimately affirms the lower court based on what has come to be called "*Colorado River*" abstention by most commentators, many lower courts, and some Supreme Court justices.

COLORADO RIVER WATER CONSERVATION DISTRICT v. UNITED STATES

424 U.S. 800 (1976)

MR. JUSTICE BRENNAN delivered the opinion of the Court.

* * * *

Abstention from the exercise of federal jurisdiction is the exception, not the rule. "The doctrine of abstention, under which a District Court may decline to exercise or postpone the exercise of its jurisdiction, is an extraordinary and narrow exception to the duty of a District Court to adjudicate a controversy properly before it. Abdication of the obligation to decide cases can be justified under this doctrine only in the exceptional circumstances where the order to the parties to repair to the state court would clearly serve an important countervailing interest." "[I]t was never a doctrine of equity that a federal court should exercise its judicial discretion to dismiss a suit merely because a State court could entertain it." Our decisions have confined the circumstances appropriate for abstention to three general categories.

(a) Abstention is appropriate "in cases presenting a federal constitutional issue which might be mooted or presented in a different posture by a state court determination of pertinent state law." [The Court cites *Pullman* among other cases.] This case, however, presents no federal constitutional issue for decision.

(b) Abstention is also appropriate where there have been presented difficult questions of state law bearing on policy problems of substantial public import whose importance transcends the result in the case then at bar. *Louisiana Power & Light Co. v. City of Thibodaux,* for example, involved such a question. In particular, the concern there was with the scope of the eminent domain power of municipalities under state law. In some cases, however, the state question itself need not be determinative of state policy. It is enough that exercise of federal review of the question in a case and in similar cases would be disruptive of state efforts to establish a coherent policy with respect to a matter of substantial public concern. In Burford v. Sun Oil Co., for example, the Court held that a suit seeking review of the reasonableness under Texas state law of a state commission's permit to drill oil wells should have been dismissed by the District Court. The reasonableness of the permit in that case was not of transcendent importance, but review of reasonableness by the federal courts in that and future cases, where the State had established its own elaborate review system for dealing with the geological complexities of oil and gas fields, would have had an impermissibly disruptive effect on state policy for the management of those fields.

The present case clearly does not fall within this second category of abstention. While state claims are involved in the case, the state law to be applied appears to be settled. No questions bearing on state policy are presented for decision. Nor will decision of the state claims impair efforts to implement state policy as in *Burford.* To be sure, the federal claims that are involved in the case go to the establishment of water rights which may conflict with similar rights based on state law. But the mere potential for conflict in the results of adjudications, does not, without more, warrant staying exercise of federal jurisdiction. The potential conflict here, involving state claims and federal claims, would not be such as to impair impermissibly the State's effort to effect its policy respecting the allocation of state waters. Nor would exercise of federal jurisdiction here interrupt any such efforts by restraining the exercise of authority vested in state officers.

(c) Finally, abstention is appropriate where, absent bad faith, harassment, or a patently invalid state statute, federal jurisdiction has been invoked for the purpose of restraining state criminal proceedings [citing *Younger v. Harris* among other cases]. Like the previous two categories, this category also does not include this case. We deal here neither with a criminal proceeding nor such a nuisance proceeding. . . . We also do not deal with an attempt to restrain such actions or to seek a declaratory judgment as to the validity of a state criminal law under which criminal proceedings are pending in a state court.

Although this case falls within none of the abstention categories, there are principles unrelated to considerations of proper constitutional adjudication and regard for federal-state relations which govern in situations involving the contemporaneous exercise of concurrent jurisdictions, either by federal courts or by state and federal courts. These principles rest on considerations of "[w]ise judicial administration, giving regard to conservation of judicial resources and comprehensive disposition of litigation." Generally, as between state and federal courts, the rule is that "the pendency of an action in the state court is no bar to proceedings concerning the same matter in the Federal court having jurisdiction. . . ." As between federal district courts, however, though no precise rule has evolved, the general principle is to avoid duplicative litigation. This difference in general approach between state-federal concurrent jurisdiction and wholly federal concurrent jurisdiction stems from the virtually unflagging obligation of the federal courts to exercise the jurisdiction given them. Given this obligation, and the absence of weightier considerations of constitutional adjudication and state-federal relations, the circumstances permitting the dismissal of a federal suit due to the presence of a concurrent state proceeding for reasons of wise judicial administration are considerably more limited than the circumstances appropriate for abstention. The former circumstances, though exceptional, do nevertheless exist.

It has been held, for example, that the court first assuming jurisdiction over property may exercise that jurisdiction to the exclusion of other courts. In assessing the appropriateness of dismissal in the event of an exercise of concurrent jurisdiction, a federal court may also consider such factors as the inconvenience of the federal forum, and the order in which jurisdiction was obtained by the concurrent forums. No one factor is necessarily determinative; a carefully considered judgment taking into account both the obligation to exercise jurisdiction and the combination of factors counseling against that exercise is required. Only the clearest of justifications will warrant dismissal.

Turning to the present case, a number of factors clearly counsel against concurrent federal proceedings. The most important of these is the McCarran Amendment[22] itself. The clear federal policy evinced by that legislation is the avoidance of piecemeal adjudication of water rights in a river system. This policy is akin to that underlying the rule requiring that jurisdiction be yielded to the court first acquiring control of property, for the concern in such instances is with avoiding the generation of additional litigation through permitting inconsistent dispositions of property. This concern is heightened with respect to water rights, the relationships among which are highly interdependent. Indeed, we have recognized that actions seeking the allocation of water essentially involve the disposition of property and are best conducted in unified proceedings. The consent to jurisdiction given by the McCarran Amendment bespeaks a policy that recognizes the availability of comprehensive state systems for adjudication of water rights as the means for achieving these goals.

As has already been observed, the Colorado Water Rights Determination and Administration Act established such a system for the adjudication and management of rights to the use of the State's waters. As the Government concedes, the Act established a single continuous proceeding for water rights adjudication . . . that "reaches all claims, perhaps month by month but inclusively in the totality." Additionally, the responsibility of managing the State's waters, to the end that they be allocated in accordance with adjudicated water rights, is given to the State Engineer.

* * * *

The judgment of the Court of Appeals is reversed and the judgment of the District Court dismissing the complaint is affirmed for the reasons here stated.

22. In the McCarran Act, Congress consented to suits against the United States in certain state court proceedings involving the adjudication of rights to use river waters.

Mr. Justice Stewart, with whom Mr. Justice Blackmun and Mr. Justice Stevens concur, dissenting.

The Court says that the United States District Court for the District of Colorado clearly had jurisdiction over this lawsuit. I agree. The Court further says that the McCarran Amendment "in no way diminished" the District Court's jurisdiction. I agree. The Court also says that federal courts have a "virtually unflagging obligation . . . to exercise the jurisdiction given them." I agree. And finally, the Court says that nothing in the abstention doctrine "in any of its forms" justified the District Court's dismissal of the Government's complaint. I agree. These views would seem to lead ineluctably to the conclusion that the District Court was wrong in dismissing the complaint. Yet the Court holds that the order of dismissal was "appropriate." With that conclusion I must respectfully disagree.

In holding that the United States shall not be allowed to proceed with its lawsuit, the Court relies principally on cases reflecting the rule that where "control of the property which is the subject of the suit (is necessary) in order to proceed with the cause and to grant the relief sought, the jurisdiction of one court must of necessity yield to that of the other." But as [case law] make[s] clear, this rule applies only when exclusive control over the subject matter is necessary to effectuate a court's judgment. Here the federal court did not need to obtain In rem or Quasi in rem jurisdiction in order to decide the issues before it. The court was asked simply to determine as a matter of federal law whether federal reservations of water rights had occurred, and, if so, the date and scope of the reservations. The District Court could make such a determination without having control of the river.

* * * *

The Court's principal reason for deciding to close the doors of the federal courthouse to the United States in this case seems to stem from the view that its decision will avoid piecemeal adjudication of water rights. To the extent that this view is based on the special considerations governing In rem proceedings, it is without precedential basis. To the extent that the Court's view is based on the realistic practicalities of this case, it is simply wrong, because the relegation of the Government to the state courts will not avoid piecemeal litigation.

The Colorado courts are currently engaged in two types of proceedings under the State's water-rights law. First, they are processing new claims to water based on recent appropriations. Second, they are integrating these new awards of water rights with all past decisions awarding such rights into one all-inclusive tabulation for each water source. The claims of the United States that are involved in this case have not been adjudicated in the past. Yet they do not involve recent appropriations of water. In fact, these claims are wholly dissimilar to normal state water claims, because they are not based on actual beneficial use of water but rather on an intention formed at the time the federal land use was established to reserve a certain amount of water to support the federal reservations. The state court will, therefore, have to conduct separate proceedings to determine these claims. And only after the state court adjudicates the claims will they be incorporated into the water source tabulations. If this suit were allowed to proceed in federal court the same procedures would be followed, and the federal court decree would be incorporated into the state tabulation, as other federal court decrees have been incorporated in the past. Thus, the same process will occur regardless of which forum considers these claims. Whether the virtually identical separate proceedings take place in a federal court or a state court, the adjudication of the claims will be neither more nor less "piecemeal." Essentially the same process will be followed in each instance.

As the Court says, it is the virtual "unflagging obligation" of a federal court to exercise the jurisdiction that has been conferred upon it. Obedience to that obligation is particularly "appropriate" in this case, for at least two reasons.

First, the issues involved are issues of federal law. A federal court is more likely than a state court to be familiar with federal water law and to have had experience in interpreting the relevant federal statutes, regulations, and Indian treaties. Moreover, if tried in a federal court, these issues of federal law will be reviewable in a federal appellate court, whereas federal judicial review of the state courts' resolution of issues of federal law will be possible only on review by this Court in the exercise of its certiorari jurisdiction.

Second, some of the federal claims in this lawsuit relate to water reserved for Indian reservations. It is not necessary to determine that there is no state-court jurisdiction of these claims to support the proposition that a federal court is a more appropriate forum than a state court for determination of questions of life-and-death importance to Indians. This Court has long recognized that "[t]he policy of leaving Indians free from state jurisdiction and control is deeply rooted in the Nation's history."

The Court says that "[o]nly the clearest of justifications will warrant dismissal" of a lawsuit within the jurisdiction of a federal court. In my opinion there was no justification at all for the District Court's order of dismissal in this case.

I would affirm the judgment of the Court of Appeals.

[The dissent of Justice Stevens is omitted. In his dissent, Justice Stevens commented on the "anomalous" result reached by the majority, preventing the United States from litigating a federal claim in federal court.]

DISCUSSION AND QUESTIONS

The dispute in *Colorado River*, like that in *Burford*, involved litigation over important state resources. Why does the Court conclude *Burford* abstention is inapplicable? Could the Court have tweaked *Burford* abstention to accommodate the facts of *Colorado River* and so avoided inaugurating a new form of abstention? How?

The Court emphasizes the McCarran Act's policy favoring unitary resolution of competing claims to water rights. At the same time, the Court notes that state and federal courts have concurrent jurisdiction over water claims of the United States. In *Colorado River*, the United States chose a federal court, and only later did some of the federal court defendants choose to commence parallel litigation in state court. Yet the Court defers to state court, in part because of its comprehensive scheme for adjudicating water rights. After *Colorado River*, do parties disputing water rights claims of the United States have the ultimate choice of forum (at least in Colorado)?

The Supreme Court has considered the scope of *Colorado River* abstention in other cases. *See, e.g., Will v. Calvert Fire Ins. Co.*, 437 U.S. 655 (1978). The most important decision since *Colorado River* is *Moses H. Cone Memorial Hospital v. Mercury Construction Co.*, 460 U.S. 1 (1983). *Moses Cone* addresses the application of *Colorado River* abstention[23] to a more conventional dispute between private parties. In *Moses H. Cone*, a hospital sued a construction company in state court for a declaratory judgment that it owed the construction company no additional monies under a contract, and for a declaration that the arbitration clause in the contract was no longer enforceable. In response to the hospital's suit, the construction company filed its own suit in federal court based on diversity of citizenship and sought to compel arbitration under the United States Arbitration Act. The federal district court stayed its proceedings because the federal and state suits addressed the same issue, namely, whether the hospital was obligated to arbitrate the dispute.

The Court held that the district court's stay of proceedings was improper because the case did not raise the "exceptional circumstances" required by *Colorado River*. According to the Court, *Colorado River* requires a balancing of factors whose weight varies with the facts of the dispute, and the presumption is against deferring to state court. The Court commented, "[T]he decision whether to dismiss a federal action because of parallel state-court litigation does not rest on a mechanical checklist, but on a careful balancing of the important factors as they apply in a given case, with the balance heavily weighted in favor of the exercise of jurisdiction. The weight to be given to any one factor may vary greatly from case to case, depending on the particular setting of the case." *Id.* at 16.

The Court concluded that the *Colorado River* factors actually supported exercise of federal jurisdiction rather than discouraging it. *Id.* at 19-20. In addition, the Court added two other factors a court should consider when deciding whether to abstain. First, when federal law provides the rule of decision, as in *Moses Cone*, exercise of federal jurisdiction is encouraged. *Id.* at 23-24. Second, a federal district court should consider whether state court provides an "adequate" forum for enforcement of federal law. In *Moses Cone*, it was unclear whether federal law required a state court, as distinct from a federal court, to compel arbitration. *Id.* at 26-27. If federal law did not require state courts to compel arbitration, the Court reasoned in somewhat circular fashion, a state court might be an inadequate forum.

Finally, the Court rejected the argument that *Colorado River* was distinguishable because the lower federal court in *Moses Cone* had stayed its proceedings, rather than dismissing them, as in *Colorado River*. The Court observed that *Colorado River* contemplates that a federal court "will have nothing further to do in resolving any substantive part of the case, whether it stays or dismisses." *Id.* at 28.

Another example of the Supreme Court's use of "comity" doctrine to avoid interference with state government is found in *Levin v. Commerce Energy, Inc.*, 560 U.S. 413 (2010). In *Levin*, the Court invoked comity doctrine and upheld a district court's dismissal of a suit brought against the Ohio Tax Commissioner. The plaintiffs alleged that the state had imposed discriminatory taxes in violation of the Equal Protection and Commerce Clauses. The Court, in an opinion by Justice Ginsburg, held that comity required that the plaintiffs litigate their constitutional claims in state court, which provided an "adequate" forum.

Justice Ginsburg remarked that, even though the district court otherwise had jurisdiction over the plaintiffs' suit, comity doctrine "counseled" the court to

23. Justice Brennan, who authored *Moses Cone*, still refrained from describing the *Colorado River* doctrine as a form of "abstention."

resist exercising that jurisdiction. *Id.* at 421. Quoting from *Younger v. Harris*, the Court wrote that comity doctrine reflects:

> a proper respect for state functions, a recognition of the fact that the entire country is made up of a Union of separate state governments, and a continuance of the belief that the National Government will fare best if the States and their institutions are left free to perform their separate functions in separate ways.

Id. (citations omitted).

PROBLEM 10-6

A Case of Duplicative Litigation

Two years ago the Wyoming legislature[24] enacted a law entitled, "The Preservation of Scenic and Recreational Resources Act" (the Act). The Act was passed in response to the over-development of lands along Wyoming rivers. The legislature found that private landowners were erecting buildings, fences, and other structures along the state's scenic rivers, with the consequences that (a) public views of riparian environments were being diminished or degraded; (b) public access to state rivers for boating and fishing was being restricted; and (c) discharge of fertilizers and other pollutants into rivers was increasing. To combat these problems, the legislature authorized counties to enact ordinances restricting building and development along state rivers.

Last year Teton County enacted an ordinance in reliance on the Act. Among other things, the ordinance prohibits the construction of any building, fence, or other structure within 200 feet of state rivers. While the ordinance "grandfathers" in existing structures, it prevents completion of existing construction on which there has been only "nominal work."

Teton County, like a few other counties in Wyoming, has attempted to enforce its new ordinance rigorously. Several suits brought by Teton County are currently pending in the state trial court encompassing Teton County. In those suits, defending landowners are challenging the constitutionality of Teton County's new ordinance.

Recently, Teton County brought another suit in the local state court, this one to enjoin Bridger Lodge, a private company that operates a lodge along the Snake River, from continuing with plans to construct several new lodging units within 100 feet of the river. As soon as the county filed suit, Bridger Lodge filed suit in federal court asking the court to declare that the county's ordinance (1) exceeded the authority granted the county under the Act, and (2) violated the Wyoming Constitution by "taking private property without just compensation." Jurisdiction is based on diversity of citizenship because Bridger Lodge is incorporated in Delaware and has its principal executive headquarters in California (it operates other lodging facilities in the western United States). Suit was filed in the federal district court in Casper, Wyoming. Although the federal court is almost 300 miles from the state court in Teton County, no other federal court is nearer to Teton County.

The County has now asked the federal court to stay or dismiss Bridger Lodge's case. The County emphasizes these points: (a) there is substantial uncertainty

24. The law and facts in this problem are fictionalized.

about the meaning of the state Act and whether the county ordinance exceeds statutory authorization; (b) several cases are already pending in Wyoming state court that raise substantially the same issues raised by Bridger Lodge; and (c) because the Wyoming Supreme Court is the sole appellate court for pending cases (there are no intermediate appellate courts), the proper interpretation of the Act will likely be addressed and conclusively resolved within one to two years when pending cases are eventually appealed to the Wyoming Supreme Court.

Consider these questions:

(1) Should the federal court stay or dismiss Bridger Lodge's suit based on any of the abstention doctrines we have studied?
(2) Does your answer to question 1 change if Bridger Lodge asserts a federal constitutional challenge in the pending federal action?

REVIEW AND CONSOLIDATION

Criteria for Assessing the Propriety of Colorado River Abstention

- ✦ Is there a pending state court proceeding where issues raised in the federal court action can be fully addressed?
- ✦ Does the pending federal court action present a federal issue?
- ✦ Would exercise of federal jurisdiction duplicate proceedings pending in state court?
- ✦ Is there a federal statutory policy disfavoring piecemeal resolution of the dispute in separate federal and state proceedings?
- ✦ How far have proceedings in federal court advanced? Were federal court proceedings commenced prior to state court proceedings?
- ✦ How convenient is the federal forum compared to the alternative state forum?

5. *A Final Note on "Full Faith and Credit"*

We have examined statutory and court-made law intended to protect state courts and state interests from interference by federal courts. Sometimes the protective method brings to an end a federal court's involvement with the plaintiff's dispute, as is the case with *Younger* abstention. At other times, federal court involvement with a dispute is only postponed (e.g., stayed), and the court may later be asked to resolve aspects of the dispute (e.g., resolving constitutional issues not resolved in state court when *Pullman* abstention is invoked).

If a federal court is asked to resolve some aspect of a dispute after a state court has resolved other aspects, a question sometimes arises—what effect does state court adjudication have on subsequent federal litigation? That question leads to final consideration of one other protection for state court proceedings — the requirement that federal courts give preclusive effect to state court judgments.

Article IV of the United States Constitution demands that "Full Faith and Credit shall be given in each State to the public Acts, Records, and judicial Proceedings of every other State. And the Congress may by general Laws prescribe the Manner in which such Acts, Records and Proceedings shall be proved, and the Effect thereof." Congress has implemented the Full Faith and Credit Clause through 28 U.S.C. § 1738. Section 1738 provides that "judicial proceedings . . . shall have the same full faith and credit in every court within the United States and its Territories and Possessions as they have by law or usage in the courts of such State. . . ."

The full faith and credit given to state judgments has long been understood to encompass the doctrines of issue preclusion (aka collateral estoppel) and claim preclusion (aka res judicata). *See San Remo Hotel, L.P. v. City & Cnty. of S.F.*, 545 U.S. 323, 336 (2005). As the Court has characterized collateral estoppel, "once a court has decided *an issue of fact or law necessary to its judgment,* that decision may preclude relitigation of the issue in a suit on a different cause of action involving a party to the first case." *Allen v. McCurry*, 449 U.S. 90, 94 (1980) (emphasis added). Under the doctrine of res judicata, "a final judgment on the merits of an action precludes the parties or their privies from relitigating issues that were or could have been raised in that action." *Id.* After a state court has entered final judgment in a dispute, Full Faith and Credit requires that other courts — federal or state — give that judgment the same preclusive effect that it would be given by the state court that rendered it.[25]

The Supreme Court has repeatedly affirmed that a plaintiff's right to invoke federal jurisdiction does not entail the right to have a federal court decide matters already resolved by a state court. In *Allen v. McCurry, supra,* the Court rejected the argument that a plaintiff seeking to assert claims under 42 U.S.C. § 1983 can relitigate issues previously determined in a state court criminal proceeding. In support of its decision, the Court invoked the principle of "comity" recognized in *Younger.* 449 U.S. at 96 ("Res judicata and collateral estoppel not only reduce unnecessary litigation and foster reliance on adjudication but also promote the comity between state and federal courts that has been recognized as a bulwark of the federal system.").

In *Migra v. Warren City School District Board of Education,* 465 U.S. 75 (1984), the Court affirmed that full faith and credit had to be given to the "res judicata" effect of a state court judgment even though a federal plaintiff may forfeit altogether her right to assert a constitutional claim under § 1983. In *Migra,* the federal plaintiff had previously sued the defendant in state court based on state-law claims, but had failed to assert her constitutional claims. The Court affirmed that the resulting state court judgment precluded a federal court from adjudicating constitutional claims if, under the preclusion law of the state, the plaintiff would have forfeited her constitutional claims by failing to assert them in state court. *Id.* at 85.

The Court's decisions in *Allen v. McCurry* and *Migra v. Warren City School District Board of Education* emphasize that, while a federal court may sometimes resolve issues in a case that have already been heard by a state court, it cannot ignore the

25. Although the Full Faith and Credit Clause literally protects state court judgments, not those of federal courts, an analogous form of protection is given federal court judgments. *See* 18B Charles Allen Wright et al., Federal Practice and Procedure ' 4468 (2014).

preclusive effect of state court proceedings if they result in a final judgment prior to conclusion of the federal action.

Recently the Court had occasion to address how preclusion law operates when a court invokes *Pullman* abstention. You will recall that, when a federal court invokes *Pullman* abstention to avoid deciding a constitutional question, either party is permitted to "reserve" the constitutional question for ultimate decision by the federal court (assuming it is not mooted by the state court's interpretation of state law). *See, e.g., England v. Louisiana State Bd. of Med. Exam'rs*, 375 U.S. 411 (1964). In *San Remo Hotel, L.P. v. City & County of San Francisco*, 545 U.S. 323 (2005), the Court held that a federal plaintiff was precluded by a state court judgment when it actually argued in state court the federal constitutional claim it purportedly had "reserved" for federal court consideration under *Pullman.* In state court, the plaintiff had "broadened" the scope of its case by essentially arguing the elements of a federal "takings" claim. *Id.* at 341. According to the Court, the plaintiff's "gratuitous" litigation of the takings claim in state court, resulting in a state court ruling, prevented relitigation of that claim in federal court.

Consequently, a party's right to litigate a federal claim in federal court does not entail the right to relitigate that claim once it has been resolved in state court. Nor can a party disregard state law requiring it to "use or lose" federal claims—with the limited exception of a claim reserved under *Pullman.* Full faith and credit requires that federal courts give a state court judgment the same respect that the state's courts would, even if the judgment contains error in the application or interpretation of federal law.[26] Emphasizing the value of finality mandated by full faith and credit, the Court has observed that "it is just as important that there should be a place to end as that there should be a place to begin litigation." *Stoll v. Gottlieb*, 305 U.S. 165, 172 (1938).

D. SOME ADDITIONAL PROBLEMS

PROBLEM 10-7

Admission to the Bar

Chloe Granger is a professor of law at State University College of Law. She is also a member of the State Bar and occasionally advises or represents students seeking admission to the Bar.

Chloe has become very concerned by the State Bar's handling of "character and fitness" applications by students with histories of psychological problems. Chloe has advised or represented five or six students whose application to the bar was delayed or denied because the students admitted having episodes of clinical depression in the past. She has learned that the bar has an unwritten policy of requiring that all persons with a history of depression either (1) show they are currently receiving psychological counseling, or (2) show they are currently taking medication for depression.

26. *See* Michael Finch & Jerome Kasriel, *Federal Court Correction of State Court Error: The Singular Case of Interstate Custody Disputes*, 48 Ohio St. L.J. 927, 968 (1987).

One of Chloe's former clients, Alfred, was denied admission to the bar because he was neither receiving counseling nor taking medication for a "mild" but persistent diagnosis of depression. Chloe appealed Alfred's case to the State Supreme Court, which has authority to review admissions decisions of the Bar Admissions Committee. The Committee is considered to be an agency of the Supreme Court. The Supreme Court affirmed the Committee's decision on Alfred but invited him to reapply to the bar "upon satisfactory proof that current psychological conditions are being addressed."

Another of Chloe's clients, Dora, has an application to the bar currently pending. She has been summoned to appear at a hearing before the Bar Admissions Committee next month. She has been informed that the Committee wishes to inquire about the "psychological diagnoses" disclosed in her application. In that application, Dora disclosed that she suffered from clinical depression. However, Dora is opposed on religious grounds to both psychological and medical counseling, and is also opposed to taking medication for her depression. She believes that spiritual solutions to her depression are the only options permitted by her church's tenets of faith.

Chloe would like to file suit in federal court to enjoin, or have declared unlawful, the State Bar's policy toward the admission of persons with clinical depression. She believes that the policy violates the federal Americans with Disabilities Act (ADA) and, in the case of Dora, violates her First Amendment right to religious freedom. Assume that the ADA provides that "an action to recover equitable relief may be maintained against a defendant in any Federal or State court of competent jurisdiction. . . ."

What problems might Chloe encounter if she sues the State Bar to obtain relief on behalf of Alfred and Dora? Please consider possible obstacles imposed by the Anti-Injunction Act, abstention doctrine, and standing.

PROBLEM 10-8

Who's Calling?

Under Indiana statutes, it is generally unlawful for commercial operations to conduct phone solicitation through automatic dialing. It is also unlawful for persons or organizations to engage such commercial operations. In the fall of 2008, the Indiana public interest organization Stop Confiscatory Taxes (SCT) hired a company called "FreeEats, Inc." to make automated calls to voters immediately prior to the November presidential elections. FreeEats conducts business in all 50 states.

Shortly after FreeEats began making automated calls to Indiana residents on behalf of SCT, the State of Indiana filed suit in state court to enjoin SCT from using automated phone dialing and to recover civil penalties prescribed by Indiana law. Two days later, FreeEats filed a federal court suit seeking injunctive and declaratory relief against state officials based on the alleged unconstitutionality of Indiana law. FreeEats also requested a preliminary injunction against the State of Indiana, and emphasized that the pending election was only seven days away.

The State of Indiana responded to FreeEats's federal suit by filing a motion to dismiss the suit based on *Pullman* abstention and a response in opposition to FreeEats's motion for a preliminary injunction. The state emphasizes that FreeEats is "in privity" with SCT; that SCT can assert an objection to the constitutionality of Indiana law by way of an affirmative defense or counterclaim in the state proceeding; and that FreeEats can intervene in the pending state court action against SCT.

(1) Should the federal court abstain? What issues are raised concerning possible application of *Younger* abstention?
(2) If the State of Indiana joins FreeEats as a defendant to its state court action against SCT two days after being served with FreeEats's federal court motion for preliminary injunctive relief, is the state's argument for *Pullman* abstention strengthened?

CHAPTER 11

Federal Courts' Power to Make Federal Law

A. A REFERENCE PROBLEM

The Senate Judiciary Committee has been asked to consider a proposal intended to restrain members of the federal judiciary from "legislating from the bench."[1] Although advocates of the proposal recognize that the most effective restraint on judicial legislation is the appointment of judges who disavow such a power, they appreciate that judges' views of their power sometimes evolve when they ascend to the bench.

One component of the new proposal addresses the common-lawmaking power of federal judges. Such "common law" includes any judicially developed legal rule "where the authority for [the] federal rule is not explicitly or clearly found in federal statutory or constitutional command."[2] To restrain the development of such common law, the proposal provides as follows:

- Except where specifically authorized by an Act of Congress, the federal judiciary shall not adopt or apply federal "common law" rules (defined by the standard quoted above) when exercising its power under federal jurisdictional statutes.
- In any case where rules of decision are not expressly provided by the Constitution, federal statutes, or lawful administrative regulations, a federal court exercising original jurisdiction is to apply the law of the state encompassing the federal district.
- Nothing in the proposal affects the federal courts' power to develop common-law rules in select areas where they have continued to exercise such a power following the Court's decision in *Erie Railroad Co. v. Tompkins.* These areas are specifically defined to include disputes "concerned with the rights and obligations of the United States, interstate and international disputes implicating the conflicting rights of States or . . . relations with foreign nations, and admiralty cases."[3]

You serve as legislative counsel to Senator Wiseman. The senator, a lawyer, confesses to you that she is not sure what, exactly, is intended by the proposal or what impact it would have on federal court adjudication. She understands that there is "limited" common-lawmaking power after *Erie,* but the proposal seems to accept that form of common law as legitimate. Consequently, she asks you to advise her concerning (1) what impact, if any, the proposal would have on the federal courts' power to develop decisional rules, and (2) whether there are either constitutional or pragmatic concerns raised by the proposal.

* * * *

The Reference Problem raises one aspect of "judicial lawmaking" that receives little attention from politicians or the public. But the "common

1. *Cf.* George W. Bush, President of the United States, State of the Union Address by the President (Jan. 31, 2006), http://www.whitehouse.gov/stateoftheunion/2006 ("I will continue to nominate men and women who understand that judges must be servants of the law, and not legislate from the bench.").
2. *See* Henry P. Monaghan, *The Supreme Court, 1974 Term— Foreword: Constitutional Common Law,* 89 Harv. L. Rev. 1, 33 (1975).
3. *Texas Indus., Inc. v. Radcliff Materials, Inc.,* 451 U.S. 630, 641 (1981).

lawmaking" power of federal jurists, as defined in the problem, remains one of the most contentious issues confronted by the contemporary Court. It is also an issue whose resolution may well turn on the next few justices appointed.

Some of the important issues concerning the federal courts' lawmaking powers that we address in this chapter are

- What is the historical meaning of "common law," and how has it evolved over the first two centuries of the federal courts' existence?
- Does the Constitution provide meaningful limits on the federal courts' power to devise rules of decision? What is the role of federalism and separation-of-powers doctrine in enunciating those limits?
- Has Congress recognized the common-lawmaking power of federal courts and, if so, when has it authorized exercise of this power?
- Do current divisions on the Court reflect disagreement about the very existence of common-lawmaking power or, instead, about when the power should be used?
- Does the federal courts' common-lawmaking power vary depending on whether courts are adjudicating statutory or constitutional law?
- In the many situations where a federal statutory scheme fails to dictate the rule for resolving a discrete legal issue arising under the scheme, should federal courts develop a rule of decision or, instead, select a decisional rule from state law?

As you consider these questions, we believe you will come to appreciate that the phenomenon of "federal common law" may be richer and more varied than is sometimes appreciated after study of *Erie* in the first year of law school. We also believe you will begin to see that *Erie* does not come close to settling the issue of the federal courts' power to "make" law.

B. CONTEXT AND BACKGROUND

> Federal courts, unlike state courts, are not general common law courts and do not possess a general power to develop and apply their own rules of decision.[4]

> At the very least, effective Constitutionalism requires recognition of power in the federal courts to declare, as a matter of common law or 'judicial legislation,' rules which may be necessary to fill in interstitially or otherwise effectuate the statutory patterns enacted in the large by Congress.[5]

1. *The Common-Law Tradition in the Framers' Era*

Contemporary lawyers can scarcely imagine the state of eighteenth-century "law" and the role courts played in developing that law. "For Americans of the post-Revolutionary generation, there was scarcely any question that the courts would supply a major portion of the standards for behavior. Nor could there be

4. Milwaukee v. Illinois, 451 U.S. 304, 312 (1981).
5. *United States v. Little Lake Misere Land Co.*, 412 U.S. 580, 593 (1973).

any doubt that the common law of England, at least as it was seen through colonial eyes, was the reference point for legal analysis."[6] Even before states enacted "reception statutes" formally adopting the common law of England as part of their own jurisprudence, this common law provided the principles and procedures by which most cases were adjudicated. Further, state courts felt free to exercise "common-law jurisdiction" without awaiting legislative action conferring such jurisdiction.

English common law, which Blackstone described as law derived from established custom, was often ill-suited to the social and economic environment of post-war America. It was especially unappealing insofar as it reflected monarchical and feudal political relations against which the colonies had rebelled. Yet this common-law heritage would be indispensable to the early American legal system, which had sparse legislative guidance in resolving legal disputes.[7]

At the same time, eighteenth-century observers appreciated that there was no monolithic body of "common law" uniformly applied by all nations.[8] To the contrary, each state had a say in which parts of the common law would apply in its territory. As Justice Chase observed:

> When the American colonies were first settled by our ancestors, it was held, as well by the settlers, as by the judges and lawyers of England, that they brought hither, as a birth-right and inheritance, so much of the common law as was applicable to their local situation and change of circumstances. But each colony judged for itself what parts of the common law were applicable to its new condition; and in various modes by legislative acts, by judicial decisions, or by constant usage, adopted some parts, and rejected others. Hence, he who shall travel through the different states, will soon discover, that the whole of the common law of England has been nowhere introduced; that some states have rejected what others have adopted; and that there is, in short, a great and essential diversity in the subjects to which the common law is applied, as well as in the extent of its application.[9]

For the new American states, common law played many roles in the development of their jurisprudence. First, common law often provided the only legal rules governing a dispute because there was no relevant state legislation. Second, even when legislation existed, it was interpreted according to rules and presumptions derived from the common law. Finally, state legislation was inevitably "interstitial" and incomplete, and it operated against the background of common-law rules. This is reflected in the principle of statutory construction that presumes state legislation does not alter the common law unless legislative intent is clear.[10] Even today, much state law is a pastiche of statutory and common-law rules.

6. Stewart Jay, *Origins of Federal Common Law, Part II*, 133 U. Pa. L. Rev. 1231, 1236 (1985) (hereinafter Jay, part II).

7. *See* Mary Tachau, Federal Courts in the Early Republic Kentucky 1789-1816, at 78 (1978) ("From the established settlements of Massachusetts, New York, and Virginia, to the frontiers of the Indiana and Michigan Territories, it was English law and legal forms that defined American jurisprudence. There may well have been widespread impatience with the technicalities that often made justice expensive and inaccessible, and certainly there were scattered incidents of local resistance to the courts. But the fathers and sons of the American Revolution concentrated on trying to make the old system more responsive, instead of destroying it or creating a more rational system.").

8. Julius Goebel, *Ex Parte Clio*, 54 Colum. L. Rev. 450, 457 (1954).

9. *United States v. Worrall*, 28 F. Cas. 774, 779 (C.C.D. Pa. 1798).

10. *See generally* Norman J. Singer, 2B Sutherland Statutory Construction ' 50:1 (6th ed. 2007).

But what role did the common-law tradition play in the newly created *federal courts*? The federal courts, after all, were courts of limited jurisdiction in the service of a sovereign whose own powers were delegated by the states and carefully limited. Further, neither the Constitution nor federal statutes have ever authorized the "reception" of English common law.[11] Given these limitations, did the Framers envision that federal courts would exercise common-law powers similar to those exercise by the state courts?

2. *The Political Struggle over the Role of Common Law in Early Federal Courts*

Professor Stewart Jay has chronicled the intense political struggle between Federalists and Republicans over the role that common law was to play in the new federal courts.[12] This struggle was part of a larger conflict concerning how weak or how strong the new national government should be.

The story of federal common law told in courses such as Civil Procedure typically begins with *Swift v. Tyson,* 41 U.S. 1, 16 Pet. 1 (1842), after which it moves to its denouement in *Erie Railroad Co. v. Tompkins,* 304 U.S. 64 (1938). But this version overlooks a critical episode in the early life of the federal court system, one that had much to say about the constitutional structure of that system. This episode concerned the power of federal courts to punish common-law crimes, culminating in the foundational decision in *United States v. Hudson,* 11 U.S. (7 Cranch) 32 (1812).

As Professor Jay explains, the virtually unanimous opinion of the Federalist bench—who dominated the federal courts in the latter part of the eighteenth century—was that federal courts had the power to punish violations of common-law crimes and had the related power to exercise "common-law jurisdiction" over such prosecutions without express authorization from Congress.[13] The unwritten "law of nations" had become part of the law of the United States at its formation.[14] Federalists maintained that the power to exercise common-law authority in criminal law was an implicit attribute of the new federal courts.[15] Federalist judges would come to use that power to prosecute violators of common-law crimes, quite often their Republican political opponents or their media surrogates.[16]

In contrast, Republicans believed that states, alone, were the true "sovereigns" that had received common-law powers. As Thomas Jefferson observed with foreboding, "Of all the doctrines which have ever been broached by the federal government, the novel one, of the common law being in force & cognizable as an existing law in their courts, is to me the most formidable." Jefferson apprehended that, if common-law authority—which extended to virtually all legal subjects, from crimes to estates—were conferred on federal courts, state

11. The large majority of states have expressly adopted the common law of England. *See* Ford W. Hall, *The Common Law: An Account of Its Reception in the United States,* 4 VAND. L. REV. 791, 799 (1951).
12. *See* Stewart Jay, *Origins of Federal Common Law, Part I,* 133 U. PA. L. REV. 1003 (1985) (hereinafter Jay, part I); Jay, part II, *supra* note 6.
13. *See* Jay, part I, *supra* note 12, at 1016-17.
14. *See id.* at 1040.
15. *See id.* at 1071.
16. *Id.* at 1082-83.

courts would soon be "shut up."[17] Republicans argued that there was no constitutional authority for the national government's assumption of such vast legal authority.

In addition to raising federalism concerns, Republicans also contended that the federal courts' exercise of a federal common-law authority would violate separation-of-powers principles. There was growing appreciation for the role that judges played in "discovering" common-law rules, especially given the lack of case reports.[18] Republicans voiced a surprisingly contemporary sounding criticism, that "adopting the common law is only another name for legislation" with "extremely dangerous" consequences since judges are not elected by the people.[19] As Professor Jay summarizes Republican fears, "[F]ederal judges, unelected, unaccountable and yet thoroughly partisan, were seen as using common law jurisdiction to transfer the political authority of the states to Federalist conspirators."[20]

The Supreme Court eventually vindicated the Republican position in 1812— by which time Republican appointees were in the majority—when it rejected the claim that federal courts have jurisdiction to prosecute common-law crimes. *See United States v. Hudson & Goodwin,* 11 U.S. (7 Cranch) 32 (1812). In *Hudson,* the Court rejected common-law criminal jurisdiction based on both federalism and separation-of-powers concerns.

> The powers of the general Government are made up of concessions from the several states—whatever is not expressly given to the former, the latter expressly reserve. The judicial power of the United States is a constituent part of those concessions,—that power is to be exercised by Courts organized for the purpose, and brought into existence by an effort of the legislative power of the Union. Of all the Courts which the United States may, under their general powers, constitute, one only, the Supreme Court, possesses jurisdiction derived immediately from the constitution, and of which the legislative power cannot deprive it. All other Courts created by the general Government possess no jurisdiction but what is given them by the power that creates them, and can be vested with none but what the power ceded to the general Government will authorize them to confer.

Id. at 33.

The Court also rejected the contention that federal courts have a common-law power to define what conduct is criminal: "The legislative authority of the Union must first make an act a crime, affix a punishment to it, and declare the Court that shall have jurisdiction of the offence." *Id.* at 34. In other words, *Hudson* vindicated in at least one context the Republican view that federal lawmaking authority was limited and vested in elected members of the legislative branch.

17. Letter from Thomas Jefferson to Edmund Randolph (Aug. 18, 1799), *reprinted in* 9 The Works of Thomas Jefferson 73 (P. Ford ed., 1905). Part of this fear was based on the fact that federal courts with authority to apply the common law would, based on historical practice, also have a "common law" jurisdiction over cases arising under the common law. "For, if it be true that the common law of England, has been adopted by the United States in their national, or federal capacity, the jurisdiction of the federal courts must be co-extensive with it; or, in other words, unlimited: so also, must be the jurisdiction, and authority of the other branches of the federal government; that is to say, their powers respectively must be, likewise, unlimited." Tucker, app. to 1 W. Blackstone, Commentaries 380 note E (S. Tucker ed., 1803).

18. *See* Jay, part I, *supra* note 12, at 1057-58, 1062.

19. 11 Annals of Cong. 713 (1802) (statement of Rep. Macon).

20. *See* Jay, part I, *supra* note 12, at 1111.

Federal judges lacked the authority to develop rules of criminal common law, at least until authorized by Congress.

3. *The Continuing Role for Common Law in Federal Courts*

The contemporary Court has construed *Hudson* more broadly than its holding literally commands. For example, in Milwaukee v. Illinois, 451 U.S. 304, 312 (1981), the Court cited *Hudson* for the proposition that "federal courts, unlike state courts, are not general common law courts and do not possess a general power to develop and apply their own rules of decision." But what does the Court mean when it observes that federal courts are not "general" common-law courts and lack "general" power to develop rules of decision? And if *Hudson* somehow affirms these principles, what are we to make of the subsequent decision in *Swift v. Tyson*, which inaugurated an era when federal courts "assumed, in the broad field of 'general law,' the power to declare rules of decision"? *Erie R.R. Co. v. Tompkins*, 304 U.S. 64, 72 (1938).

In this chapter we explore several issues raised by *Hudson, Swift, Erie,* and yet other decisions touching upon the federal courts' common-law powers. The rulemaking[21] power of federal courts inevitably takes us back to "our abiding political problem,"[22] how to allocate power between federal and state government. Each time the federal courts exercise authority to develop rules of decision, they arguably compromise the authority of state legislatures and state courts to devise their own rules. This is a core federalism concern that has pervaded the issue of federal common law since the nation's inception—as evidenced by the controversy over common-law crimes in *Hudson,* which eighteenth-century Republicans viewed as a Federalist plot to "install a consolidated national government through incorporation of British common law."[23]

Related to the federalism concern about allocation of political power between the national and state governments is the issue of separation of powers. As mentioned earlier, eighteenth-century Republicans protested that common-law development was often akin to "legislation," and insisted that federal legislative authority belonged to elected members of Congress. Republicans shared apprehensions that the new federal judiciary—appointed by the Federalist Party throughout the national government's first decade of operation—would use common-lawmaking powers to usurp Congress' power and, indirectly, to circumvent the states' power to control Congress.

"Common law" in the twenty-first century bears little apparent resemblance to the common law of concern to Federalists and Republicans. At least after *Erie,* modern legal thinking is pervaded by positivism and the belief that all law exists because it has some specific governmental authority behind it. As Justice Holmes observed, "The common law . . . is not the common law generally but the law of

21. In this chapter, references to the "rulemaking" authority of federal courts encompass the courts' power to make "rules of decision" (which can usually be characterized as "substantive" rules). The term "rulemaking" does not refer to the federal courts' power to develop "procedural" rules—today a relatively uncontroversial subject—unless specifically explained in that way. You have previously addressed the procedural rulemaking power of federal courts in Civil Procedure, and we will not return to that discussion.

22. Felix Frankfurter, *Distribution of Judicial Power Between United States and State Courts,* 13 Cornell L.Q. 499, 500 (1928).

23. *See* Jay, part II, *supra* note 6, at 1323.

that State existing by the authority of that State without regard to what it may have been in England or anywhere else."[24]

But as we learn in *Swift*, well into the nineteenth century many jurists believed that certain bodies of law existed apart from specific legal authorities and their task was to discover that law through reasoning processes familiar to common-law judges. At times, the non-positivist law derived from custom—whether English or international—and at other times the law derived from immutable moral principles thought to be metaphysical fixtures of the known universe, what is sometimes referred to as "natural law." This view of the law is now unconvincing to most of us. But we should not too readily lapse into a cynicism that views the common-law process of our predecessors as a mere cover for the manipulation and control of political power. As we will see, eighteenth- and nineteenth-century jurists took seriously the notion that some core legal principles were not subject to political manipulation, even that of their own political parties.

As used today, the term "common law" is both ambiguous and controversial. Sometimes common law is referred to as "judge-made" law, even by careful legal scholars.[25] The Court seems to share this understanding, as it has explained that common law is "a rule of decision that amounts, not simply to an interpretation of a federal statute or a properly promulgated administrative rule, but, rather, to the judicial 'creation' of a special federal rule of decision." *Atherton v. FDIC*, 519 U.S. 213, 218 (1997). But this immediately raises the issue, what distinguishes judge-made *interpretations* of positive-law from "common law"? After all, the Court has obviously "made" law when it interprets terms like "due process" and "cruel and unusual punishment" in contexts beyond the contemplation of the Constitution's Framers. Acknowledging this problem, most commentators adopt a pragmatic notion of common law that includes "federal rules of decision where the authority for a federal rule is not explicitly or clearly found in federal statutory or constitutional command."[26] That notion will have to suffice for us as well.

Our understanding of the nature and scope of common law has very real consequences. For example, if judicially developed rules like the exclusionary rule or the requirement of *Miranda* warnings result from constitutional *interpretation*, Congress and the states may be powerless to revise those interpretations. On the other hand, if such rules are viewed as some form of common law, there is little doubt that Congress can amend the rules in the same fashion that state legislatures modify the common-law rulings of state courts.

Perhaps the most important issue concerning the federal courts' power to develop non-textual rules arises in constitutional litigation. As we learned in Chapter 9, the Constitution seldom authorizes remedies to enforce the rights it confers. But does the Constitution's silence mean that persons whose rights have been violated lack the traditional remedy for vindicating violations, compensatory damages? Is such a remedy contingent on congressional action? Is it

24. *Black & White Taxicab & Transfer Co. v. Brown & Yellow Taxicab & Transfer Co.*, 276 U.S. 518, 533-34 (1928) (Holmes, J., dissenting).

25. *See, e.g.*, Henry P. Monaghan, *The Supreme Court, 1974 Term—Foreword: Constitutional Common Law*, 89 HARV. L. REV. 1, 33 (1975).

26. *See id. See also* Martha A. Field, *Sources of Law: The Scope of Federal Common Law*, 99 HARV. L. REV. 881, 890 (1986) ("[F]ederal common law . . . refer[s] to any rule of federal law created by a court . . . when the substance of that rule is not clearly suggested by federal enactments—constitutional or congressional.").

contingent on the existence of a state statutory or common-law remedy? Or, in the case of the Constitution, do federal courts enjoy the same common-law remedial power state courts do? Is it even possible that the Constitution *itself* implies the existence of some remedies to render its protections meaningful?

As you can already see, questions involving the federal courts' rulemaking powers are by no means obsolete or trivial after *Erie*.

4. *Plan of Coverage*

We begin this chapter by briefly considering the evolution in federal common-lawmaking authority from *Swift* to *Erie*, an evolution that occurred in the context of diversity jurisdiction. As we learn, the Court in *Swift* avoided the constitutional issue raised in *Hudson*—can federal courts exercise common-lawmaking authority as state courts do in the absence of specific constitutional or congressional authorization?—by positing the existence of a transnational commercial law that traces its authority to neither federal nor state government. The Court's tack in *Swift*, we discover, was not only well supported by eighteenth-century conceptions of commercial law, but also provided the historical basis for several forms of common law that remain intact after *Erie*.

We then briefly consider how *Erie* reconceptualizes common law and largely vindicates the Republicans' position in *Hudson*. We also consider the constitutional theories animating the *Erie* decision, which prove important when the Court later exercises common-lawmaking power outside the context of diversity jurisdiction.

Next we examine those forms of "specific" federal common law that survive *Erie*. First, we examine those forms of common law whose existence has been inferred from the Constitution's jurisdictional grants and its structure. These include disputes in admiralty, disputes between states, and disputes implicating foreign relations. Second, we look at a fourth form of specific common law, that which applies in determining the proprietary rights and duties of the United States. As we learn, the Court's decision to recognize this broad-ranging form of common-law authority overturns the approach that applied through most of the nation's history, when the United States "did business" within the same framework of state laws used by private business. But as we also discover, the Court has revived much of its earlier practice by the anomalous decision to "borrow" state law in defining federal common law. After considering the federal courts' power to develop common law to govern proprietary interests of the United States, we also briefly examine whether this power includes the power to regulate the rights and duties of private parties operating in the shadow of the federal government.

We next consider express or implied congressional authorization of common-lawmaking authority. Contrary to a popular impression that federal courts act unlawfully when they "make law," we learn that Congress has at times authorized judicial lawmaking. At yet other times, Congress has apparently legislated with the expectation that federal courts will fill "gaps" in its law by developing "interstitial" legal rules.

The next form of common-lawmaking power we examine builds on prior discussion, including discussion of the federal courts' "interstitial" lawmaking authority to promote congressional intent. We review the federal courts' power to develop remedial rules for the enforcement of statutory rights. We first consider the courts' relatively uncontroversial exercise of rulemaking power to flesh out the details of federal statutory remedies, as when the courts devise the judicial equivalent of "statutes of limitation" to govern enforcement of federal statutory claims. We then turn to the far more controversial exercise of the courts' rulemaking power to develop monetary remedies to enforce statutory rights. As we learn, the Court exercised a fairly broad remedial power for more than a decade, beginning in the mid-1960s, based on the assumption that the power to devise a damages remedy was intrinsic to the federal courts' exercise of jurisdiction. We then study how the Court's position has evolved to one in which a statutory damages remedy is presumed unavailable absent compelling evidence that Congress intended such a remedy.

Finally, we examine a parallel evolution in federal courts' power to develop monetary remedies to enforce *constitutional* rights that have been violated by federal officials. As with the remedial power to enforce federal statutes, the power to enforce constitutional rights through appropriate monetary remedies was assumed by the Court well into the 1970s (within announced limits). But the Court's presumption in favor of monetary remedies for constitutional violations has been rejected in more recent decades. Increasingly the Court has relied on the "exceptions" recognized in prior cases effectively to eliminate monetary remedies for most constitutional violations by federal officials. In most cases, the Court has found that alternative, limited remedies developed by Congress preclude the recognition of a judicially developed damages remedy. The result for persons whose constitutional rights have been violated is often a sharply curtailed opportunity to vindicate their rights, and sometimes no opportunity at all. We consider whether the Court has acted consistent with a proper understanding of the limits of its lawmaking power under the Constitution or whether, instead, the Court has failed in its obligation to enforce the Constitution.

C. THE LAW AND PROBLEMS

1. *From Swift to Erie*

Swift v. Tyson. In theory, the Court's decision in *United States v. Hudson* might have preempted the century-long "*Swift* regime," during which federal courts developed their own rules of decision for diversity suits. According to the modern Court, *Hudson* supports the same principle as *Erie*—namely, that federal courts lack a general power to develop rules of decision.[27] Defense counsel in *Swift* was well aware of the implications of *Hudson* and relied on that decision to challenge the plaintiff's contention that state common-law rules could be replaced by the federal courts' own version of common law.

You will recall from Civil Procedure that *Swift* presented an issue of contract law—whether a party who had accepted a note in payment of a preexisting debt was a "holder in due course" not subject to an underlying defense of fraud. According to the New York courts, the plaintiff was not a holder in due course and the underlying fraud defense prevented his recovery. According to federal precedent, the plaintiff was a holder in due course and could recover on the note.

27. *See* Milwaukee v. Illinois, 451 U.S. 304, 312 (1981).

When this diversity dispute was appealed to the Supreme Court, the plaintiff asked that the Court follow the federal view of contract law and permit recovery. The plaintiff argued, among other things, that (1) the Court plainly had jurisdiction to decide the issue based on diversity (recall that "common law" jurisdiction was found lacking in *Hudson*); (2) the issue was one of "general" commercial law requiring the Court to apply its own conscience and judgment; and (3) deference to state common-law precedent would undermine national commerce and the Court's own integrity by producing "vacillating" rulings tethered to the inconsistent interpretations of state courts. *Swift v. Tyson*, 41 U.S. 1, 3-6 (1842). The plaintiff also argued that the Court was not obligated to follow state court interpretations of the common law under the command of the Rules of Decision Act (RDA). The RDA, still part of the U.S. Code, provides:

> The laws of the several states, except where the Constitution or treaties of the United States or Acts of Congress otherwise require or provide, shall be regarded as rules of decision in civil actions in the courts of the United States, in cases where they apply.

28 U.S.C. § 1652. According to plaintiff's counsel, the RDA's reference to "laws of the several states" means "nothing else than the written constitutional system and statutes of such states." *Id.* at 8-9. In other words, the RDA signaled Congress' belief that federal courts were not bound by common-law rules developed by local state courts.

Defense counsel argued that the RDA compelled application of the "decisions of the courts of [the states]," as well as their positive law provisions. *Id.* at 10. In addition, defense counsel cited *Hudson* for the proposition that the United States had never adopted the common law to provide an independent body of decisional rules to govern federal courts: "The common law has never been otherwise adopted, nor have the courts power to create or adopt laws—they must administer the law as existing." *Id.* at 11. Further, the defense asserted that the common law had not been adopted by implication as part of federal jurisprudence. Consequently, in the absence of a congressional act specifically adopting the common law as part of the larger body of federal law, the defendant argued that federal courts had no authority to displace state law under the RDA.

The Supreme Court readily dismissed the RDA's command, as well as the seeming conflict between federal and state common law. The Court concluded that the general, commercial law issue posed in *Swift* was governed by neither "federal" nor "state" common law. In its famous description of the "non-written" law applicable in *Swift*, the Court remarked:

> It is observable, that the courts of New York do not found their decisions upon this point, upon any local statute, or positive, fixed or ancient local usage; but they deduce the doctrine from the general principles of commercial law. It is however, contended that the [RDA], furnishes a rule obligatory upon this court to follow the decisions of the state tribunals in all cases to which they apply. That section provides "that the laws of the several states, except where the constitution, treaties or statutes of the United States shall otherwise require or provide, shall be regarded as rules of decision, in trials at common law, in the courts of the United States, in cases where they apply." In order to maintain the argument, it is essential, therefore, to hold, that the word "laws," in this section, includes within the scope of its meaning,

the decisions of the local tribunals. *In the ordinary use of language, it will hardly be contended, that the decisions of courts constitute laws. They are, at most, only evidence of what the laws are, and are not, of themselves, laws.* They are often re-examined, reversed and qualified by the courts themselves, whenever they are found to be either defective, or ill-founded, or otherwise incorrect. The laws of a state are more usually understood to mean the rules and enactments promulgated by the legislative authority thereof, or long-established local customs having the force of laws. In all the various cases, which have hitherto come before us for decision, this court have uniformly supposed, that the true interpretation of the [RDA] limited its application to state laws, strictly local, that is to say, to the positive statutes of the state, and the construction thereof adopted by the local tribunals, and to rights and titles to things having a permanent locality, such as the rights and titles to real estate, and other matters immovable and intra-territorial in their nature and character. *It never has been supposed by us, that the section did apply, or was designed to apply, to questions of a more general nature, not at all dependent upon local statutes or local usages of a fixed and permanent operation, as, for example, to the construction of ordinary contracts or other written instruments, and especially to questions of general commercial law, where the state tribunals are called upon to perform the like functions as ourselves, that is, to ascertain, upon general reasoning and legal analogies, what is the true exposition of the contract or instrument, or what is the just rule furnished by the principles of commercial law to govern the case.* And we have not now the slightest difficulty in holding, that this section, upon its true intendment and construction, is strictly limited to local statutes and local usages of the character before stated, and does not extend to contracts and other instruments of a commercial nature, the true interpretation and effect whereof are to be sought, not in the decisions of the local tribunals, but in the general principles and doctrines of commercial jurisprudence. Undoubtedly, the decisions of the local tribunals upon such subjects are entitled to, and will receive, the most deliberate attention and respect of this court; but they cannot furnish positive rules, or conclusive authority, by which our own judgments are to be bound up and governed. *The law respecting negotiable instruments may be truly declared in the languages of Cicero, adopted by Lord MANSFIELD . . . to be in a great measure, not the law of a single country only, but of the commercial world.*

Id. at 18-19 (emphasis added).

DISCUSSION AND QUESTIONS

If the common law used by early American courts is envisioned as a homogeneous form of law, it is difficult to reconcile *Hudson* and *Swift.* After all, there is no obvious reason why the common law of crimes in *Hudson* should be viewed differently from the common law of commerce addressed in *Swift.* If there is a body of common law that exists apart from the "decisions of courts" (*Swift*), why wasn't it applied in *Hudson*? Even more so than in *Swift, Hudson* involved a legal issue that did not seem to depend on "local statutes or usages," namely, the rules of libel applicable to falsehoods uttered against the President of the United States. Did *Hudson* arguably err in requiring that criminal common law be specifically adopted as "federal" law before it could be enforced by the federal courts?

Or was the error made in *Swift*? According to the leading Republican interpretation of common law during the Framers' era, ferreting out the meaning of common law is inherently a "legislative" task. Further, the common law inherited by the American states was transitional and inevitably revised by each state to conform to its own perceived needs. Yet *Swift* seems to attribute a universality and transcendence to commercial common law at odds with the Republican view reflected in *Hudson.*

Perhaps the mistake in comparing *Hudson* and *Swift* is to assume there is a single vision of the common law underlying the two decisions. As Professor Jay has cautioned, "there was no coherent concept in the early nineteenth century of 'federal common law' as we now make use of that expression."[28] *Swift* may reflect a quite different *version* of the "common law" than the Court addressed in *Hudson. Swift* recognizes a form of non-positive law applicable to interstate and international commercial disputes based on international custom or the "law of nations."[29] As Professor Jay observes, general commercial law seemed more akin to *international law* than English common law: "Due to its supposedly international character, the law merchant was often treated by English legal writers as distinct from the common law of England."[30] Although assimilated into the English common law, general commercial law principles had a distinctly transnational cast not subject to parochial revision by each state. Perhaps this helps explain why, despite the Court's prior decision in *Hudson,* there was not a strong Republican reaction to the decision in *Swift.*[31] Indeed, other than Justice Story, the justices on the bench that decided *Swift* were Republican appointees.

Other scholars have remarked on how the *Swift* view of unwritten commercial law was neither anomalous nor particularly controversial at the time. Professor Bradford Clark has recently commented:

> *Swift* was arguably defensible when decided because state and federal courts alike considered questions of general commercial law at the time to be governed by the law merchant, a branch of the law of nations. In the early nineteenth century, both sets of courts "considered themselves to be deciding questions under a general law merchant that was neither distinctively state nor federal." On this understanding, the courts of each sovereign felt free to exercise independent judgment to ascertain applicable customs and, when necessary, to reach conclusions contrary to those of the other. Taken in historical context, the *Swift* Court arguably did no more than what New York law instructed it to do—i.e., to exercise independent judgment to ascertain the applicable rule of customary commercial law.[32]

Swift's interpretation of the RDA has also been supported by contemporary analysis of congressional history.[33] For example, Professor Patrick Borchers argues that Congress intended in the RDA that federal courts apply a developing "American" version of general common law (not the version of any particular state), which was evolving into something quite different from the English

28. *See* Jay, part I, *supra* note 12, at 1010.

29. *See* Bradford R. Clark, *Federal Common Law: A Structural Reinterpretation,* 144 U. Pa. L. Rev. 1245, 1279-80 (1996).

30. *See* Jay, part II, *supra* note 6, at 1278. The law merchant was "a particular system of customs . . . which, however different from . . . the common law, is . . . allowed, for the benefit of trade," and "which all nations agree in and take notice of." 1 William Blackstone, Commentaries *75, *264.

31. *See* Jay, part II, *supra* note 6, at 1276 ("For a considerable period in early American judicial history, the federal courts were free to develop a common law for civil cases, particularly in the commercial field, without provoking serious objections of the sort raised in *Hudson.*").

32. Bradford R. Clark, Erie*'s Constitutional Source,* 95 Cal. L. Rev. 1289, 1292-93 (2007).

33. *See, e.g.,* Wilfred J. Ritz, Rewriting the History of the Judiciary Act of 1789, at 8-12, 126-48 (Holt & LaRue eds., 1990).

common law to which it traced its lineage.[34] In fact, Professor Borchers asserts that federal courts had followed the approach eventually affirmed in *Swift* from the time they began exercising diversity jurisdiction.[35] *Swift* was thus "merely a garden-variety exposition of the prevailing view of the law applicable in diversity cases."[36]

One consequence of *Swift*'s "transnational" view of general commercial law was that federal court precedent had no binding effect on *state* courts. Because federal courts were not interpreting "federal" law when they discerned general commercial law rules, their interpretations did not bind the states under the Supremacy Clause.[37] As we learn later, the contemporary view of common law developed by federal courts restores it to its place among the pantheon of supreme federal laws binding on the states.

The trajectory of *Swift*'s expansion and eventual rejection in *Erie* will be familiar to you from Civil Procedure. By the time of the *Erie* decision, legal positivism had largely eroded the jurisprudential foundation of *Swift*, whether common law was interpreted as a transnational set of customs or an emanation of natural law. As Justice Holmes famously derided *Swift*'s concept of the common law, "the common law is not a brooding omnipresence in the sky, but the articulate voice of some sovereign or quasi sovereign that can be identified." Southern Pac. Co. v. Jensen, 244 U.S. 205, 222 (1917) (Holmes, J., dissenting).

Swift might have enjoyed a longer life had federal judges not extended their common-law powers well beyond the interstate commercial setting presented in *Swift*. However, federal judges ensured the disreputability of *Swift* when they discerned common-law rules to govern legal issues that seemed distinctly local, and not international. For example, in *City of Chicago v. Robbins*, 67 U.S. 418, 429 (1862), the Court did not hesitate to disregard state court precedent in announcing its own common-law rule to govern a municipality's liability for poorly maintained streets—"where private rights are to be determined by the application of common law rules alone, this Court, although entertaining for State tribunals the highest respect, does not feel bound by their decisions." As *Robbins* illustrates, *Swift*'s avowed deference to state law on "local" issues seemed often a hollow concession. In addition, the *Swift* doctrine led to dreaded "forum shopping," in part because the hoped-for convergence in federal and state court interpretation of the common law never occurred. State courts, which were not bound by the common-law rulings of federal courts, often exercised their independence to ignore federal precedent. Consequently, a litigant's selection of a federal forum in diversity actions could be tantamount to a selection of the substantive legal rules to govern the suit.

The citation of *Erie* has become almost obligatory in modern decisions discussing the authority of federal courts to develop common-law rules of decision. Excerpted below are the critical parts of the majority's opinion in *Erie* explaining why the *Swift* doctrine was overturned after almost a century of operation. Recall that the Court in *Erie* was asked whether a federal court exercising diversity jurisdiction should apply state negligence law or develop its own "general

34. *See* Patrick Borchers, *The* Origins of Diversity Jurisdiction, the Rise of Legal Positivism, and a Brave New World for Erie and Klaxon, 72 TEX. L. REV. 79, 109-10 (1993).

35. *See id.* at 112-14.

36. *Id.* at 114.

37. *See* William A. Fletcher, *The* General Common Law and Section 34 of the Judiciary Act of 1789: The Example of Marine Insurance, 97 HARV. L. REV. 1513, 1516 (1984).

law" rule to govern liability. Consider what these excerpts say about the federal courts' authority to develop such rules of decision.

ERIE RAILROAD CO. v. TOMPKINS

304 U.S. 64 (1938)

MR. JUSTICE BRANDEIS delivered the opinion of the Court.

The question for decision is whether the oft-challenged doctrine of *Swift v. Tyson* shall now be disapproved.

* * * *

The Erie had contended that application of the Pennsylvania rule was required, among other things, by section 34 of the Federal Judiciary Act of September 24, 1789, which provides: "The laws of the several States, except where the Constitution, treaties, or statutes of the United States otherwise require or provide, shall be regarded as rules of decision in trials at common law, in the courts of the United States, in cases where they apply."

Because of the importance of the question whether the federal court was free to disregard the alleged rule of the Pennsylvania common law, we granted certiorari.

First. *Swift v. Tyson* held that federal courts exercising jurisdiction on the ground of diversity of citizenship need not, in matters of general jurisprudence, apply the unwritten law of the state as declared by its highest court; that they are free to exercise an independent judgment as to what the common law of the state is — or should be.

The Court in applying the rule of section 34 to equity cases, in Mason v. United States, 260 U.S. 545, 559, said: "The statute, however, is merely declarative of the rule which would exist in the absence of the statute. The federal courts assumed, in the broad field of 'general law,' the power to declare rules of decision which Congress was confessedly without power to enact as statutes. Doubt was repeatedly expressed as to the correctness of the construction given section 34, and as to the soundness of the rule which it introduced. But it was the more recent research of a competent scholar, who examined the original document, which established that the construction given to it by the Court was erroneous; and that the purpose of the section was merely to make certain that, in all matters except those in which some federal law is controlling, the federal courts exercising jurisdiction in diversity of citizenship cases would apply as their rules of decision the law of the state, unwritten as well as written.

Criticism of the doctrine became widespread after the decision of Black & White Taxicab & Transfer Co. v. Brown & Yellow Taxicab & Transfer Co., 276 U.S. 518. There, Brown & Yellow, a Kentucky corporation owned by Kentuckians, and the Louisville & Nashville Railroad, also a Kentucky corporation, wished that the former should have the exclusive privilege of soliciting passenger and baggage transportation at the Bowling Green, Ky., Railroad station; and that the Black & White, a competing Kentucky corporation, should be prevented from interfering with that privilege. Knowing that such a contract would be void under the common law of Kentucky, it was arranged that the Brown & Yellow reincorporate under the law of Tennessee, and that the contract with the railroad should be executed there. The suit was then brought by the Tennessee corporation in the federal court for Western Kentucky to enjoin competition by the Black & White; an injunction issued by the District Court was sustained by the Court of Appeals; and this Court, citing many decisions in which the doctrine of *Swift & Tyson* had been applied, affirmed the decree.

On the other hand, the mischievous results of the doctrine had become apparent. Diversity of citizenship jurisdiction was conferred in order to prevent apprehended discrimination in state courts against those not citizens of the state. *Swift v. Tyson* introduced grave discrimination by noncitizens against citizens. It made rights enjoyed under the unwritten "general law" vary according to whether enforcement was sought in the state or in the federal court; and the privilege of selecting the court in which the right should be determined was conferred upon the noncitizen. Thus, the doctrine rendered impossible equal protection of the law. In attempting to promote uniformity of law throughout the United States, the doctrine had prevented uniformity in the administration of the law of the state.

The discrimination resulting became in practice far-reaching. This resulted in part from the broad province accorded to the so-called "general law" as to which federal courts exercised an independent judgment. In addition to questions of purely commercial law, "general law" was held to include the obligations under contracts entered into and to be performed within the state, the extent to which a carrier operating within a state may stipulate for exemption from liability for his own negligence or that of his employee; the liability for torts committed within the state upon persons resident or property located there, even where the question of liability depended upon the scope of a property right conferred by the state; and the right to exemplary or punitive damages. Furthermore, state decisions construing local deeds, mineral conveyances, and even devises of real estate, were disregarded.

* * * *

Second. Experience in applying the doctrine of *Swift v. Tyson* had revealed its defects, political and social; and the benefits expected to flow from the rule did not accrue. Persistence of state courts in their own opinions on questions of common law prevented uniformity; and the impossibility of discovering a satisfactory line of demarcation between the province of general law and that of local law developed a new well of uncertainties.

The injustice and confusion incident to the doctrine of *Swift v. Tyson* have been repeatedly urged as reasons for abolishing or limiting diversity of citizenship jurisdiction. Other legislative relief has been proposed. If only a question of statutory construction were involved, we should not be prepared to abandon a doctrine so widely applied throughout nearly a century. But the unconstitutionality of the course pursued has now been made clear, and compels us to do so.

Except in matters governed by the Federal Constitution or by acts of Congress, the law to be applied in any case is the law of the state. And whether the law of the state shall be declared by its Legislature in a statute or by its highest court in a decision is not a matter of federal concern. There is no federal general common law. Congress has no power to declare substantive rules of common law applicable in a state whether they be local in their nature or 'general,' be they commercial law or a part of the law of torts. And no clause in the Constitution purports to confer such a power upon the federal courts. As stated by Mr. Justice Field when protesting in Baltimore & Ohio R.R. Co. v. Baugh, 149 U.S. 368, 401, against ignoring the Ohio common law of fellow-servant liability:

> I am aware that what has been termed the general law of the country — which is often little less than what the judge advancing the doctrine thinks at the time should be the general law on a particular subject — has been often advanced in judicial opinions of this court to control a conflicting law of a state. I admit that learned judges have fallen into the habit of repeating this doctrine as a convenient mode of brushing aside the law of a state in conflict with their views. And I confess that, moved and governed by the authority of the great names of those judges, I have, myself, in many instances, unhesitatingly and confidently, but I think now erroneously, repeated the same doctrine. But, notwithstanding the great names which may be cited in favor of the doctrine, and notwithstanding the frequency with which the doctrine has been reiterated, there stands, as a perpetual protest against its repetition, the constitution of the United States, which recognizes and preserves the autonomy and independence of the states, — independence in their legislative and independence in their judicial departments. Supervision over either the legislative or the judicial action of the states is in no case permissible except as to matters by the constitution specifically authorized or delegated to the United States. Any interference with either, except as thus permitted, is an invasion of the authority of the state, and, to that extent, a denial of its independence.

The fallacy underlying the rule declared in *Swift v. Tyson* is made clear by Mr. Justice Holmes. The doctrine rests upon the assumption that there is "a transcendental body of law outside of any particular State but obligatory within it unless and until changed by statute," that federal courts have the power to use their judgment as to what the rules of common law are; and that in the federal courts "the parties are entitled to an independent judgment on matters of general law":

> "But law in the sense in which courts speak of it today does not exist without some definite authority behind it. The common law so far as it is enforced in a State, whether called common law or not, is not the common law generally but the law of that State existing by the authority of that State without regard to what it may have been in England or anywhere else. * * *
>
> "The authority and only authority is the State, and if that be so, the voice adopted by the State as its own (whether it be of its Legislature or of its Supreme Court) should utter the last word."

Thus the doctrine of *Swift v. Tyson* is, as Mr. Justice Holmes said, "an unconstitutional assumption of powers by the Courts of the United States which no lapse of time or respectable array of opinion should make us hesitate to correct." In disapproving that doctrine we do not hold unconstitutional section 34 of the Federal Judiciary Act of 1789 or any other act of Congress. We merely declare that in applying the doctrine this Court and the lower courts have invaded rights which in our opinion are reserved by the Constitution to the several states.

DISCUSSION AND QUESTIONS

The rationales for overturning Swift. The Court offers three reasons for overruling *Swift.* First, it relies on "more recent research" purportedly showing that the RDA contemplated deference to state common law as well as state positive law. *Swift* was thus based on a misinterpretation of the statute. In fact, Professor

Martin Redish argues that, under *Erie*'s interpretation of the RDA, federal common law should be generally prohibited.[38]

But the Court's "potent" interpretation of the RDA has not devastated the continued development of common law.[39] As Professor Merrill observes, the Court has largely disregarded the RDA in later pronouncements about federal common lawmaking.[40] Further, by its terms the RDA requires application of state law unless "the Constitution or treaties of the United States or Acts of Congress otherwise require or provide." As we learn in later discussion, much of the federal common law affirmed after *Erie* is traceable, albeit loosely, to some constitutional or statutory source. This provides plausible ground for avoiding the mandate of the RDA. Finally, post-*Erie* scholarship raises substantial doubt about the Court's revised interpretation of the RDA in *Erie*. Even if this interpretation has not yet been reversed by the Court, its shakiness may give reason to avoid using it as the basis for challenging later development of federal common law.[41]

A second reason why the Court chose to overturn *Swift* was the perceived "injustice and confusion" resulting from the fact that federal and state courts continued to disagree about the proper interpretation of the common law in the *Swift* era. Among other things, this divergence in common-law interpretation led to widespread forum shopping and "unequal" treatment of similarly situated litigants based solely on the fortuity of diverse citizenship. Recall that this injustice and confusion occurred because, under the *Swift* regime, federal interpretations of common law were not binding on state courts under the Supremacy Clause since federal courts were not purporting to interpret "federal" law.

It is the third justification for overruling *Swift* that has greatest relevance to modern federal common law. According to the Court, "Except in matters governed by the Federal Constitution or by acts of Congress, the law to be applied in any case is the law of the state." Under this interpretation of federal power, the RDA becomes secondary because the Constitution itself directs that state law—whether legislative or judge-made—be applied when there is no constitutional or statutory rule of decision. Further, the Court indicates that its constitutional holding restricts *Congress* as well as the courts. The Court remarks, "Congress has no power to declare substantive rules of common law applicable in a state whether they be local in their nature or 'general,' be they commercial law or a part of the law of torts. And no clause in the Constitution purports to confer such a power upon the federal courts." The Court's reference to Congress' lack of power to "declare substantive rules of common law" is somewhat confusing since we normally think of Congress' declared rules as legislation, not common law.

The precise constitutional foundation of *Erie* remains unsettled to this day. The scholarly literature, which presents highly varied interpretations of *Erie*'s constitutional basis, is extensive.[42] One of the principal fracture lines in the

38. *See* Martin H. Redish, Federal Common Law, Political Legitimacy, and the Interpretive Process: An "Institutionalist" Perspective, 83 NW. U. L. REV. 761 (1989).

39. Thomas W. Merrill, *The* Common Law Powers of Federal CourtS, 52 U. CHI. L. REV. 1, 31-32 (1985).

40. *See id.*

41. In another context we will examine, where federal courts "borrow" state law to fill out the remedial gaps of federal law, the Court has not hewed strictly to the view that the RDA mandates application of state law in the absence of positive federal law. *See, e.g., Lampf, Pleva, Lipkind, Prupis & Petigrow v. Gilbertson*, 501 U.S. 350, 355-56 (1991).

42. A *small* sample of some of the more influential articles includes Alfred Hill, *The* Erie *Doctrine and the Constitution*, 53 Nw. U. L. Rev. 427 (1958); John Hart Ely, *The* Irrepressible Myth of Erie, 87 HARV. L. REV. 693 (1974); Paul J. Mishkin, Some Further Last Words on Erie—The Thread, 87 HARV. L. REV. 1682 (1974); Henry P. Monaghan, *Book Review*, 87 HARV. L. REV. 889 (1974);

literature is whether *Erie* affirms a broad restraint on all federal power, both legislative and judicial, or whether *Erie* recognizes special limits on the lawmaking power of *courts*. Under the first view, *Erie* recognizes an important federalism restraint on federal power but one not unique to common lawmaking. Under the second view, *Erie* recognizes special restraints on the judiciary extending beyond federalism concerns and embracing separation-of-powers concerns.

The first view, interpreting *Erie* as a general federalism restraint on national power, has been stated as follows:

> As the general structure of the Constitution and the tenth amendment make clear, the framers anticipated that the federal government would exercise only specifically enumerated powers. All other powers were reserved to the states or the people. The federal judiciary, as a branch of the federal government, is also limited by this specific enumeration of powers. Thus, any assertion by the judiciary of a general power to make law would encroach upon the powers reserved to the states. This, in a nutshell, is the constitutional thesis of *Erie*.[43]

In other words, the *Swift* regime was unconstitutional "because nothing in the Constitution provided the central government with a general lawmaking authority of the sort the Court had been exercising under *Swift*.[44]

Many other scholars conclude, however, that *Erie* stands for another proposition — that there are unique limits on the power of federal courts to develop rules of decision without congressional authorization. Professor Henry Monaghan writes:

> Because there is both residual and concurrent lawmaking power in the states, "[f]ederal intervention has been thought of as requiring special justification, and the decision that such justification has been shown, being essentially discretionary, has belonged in most cases to Congress." [Citation omitted.] *Erie* fully reflects that perception. It recognizes that federal judicial power to displace state law is not coextensive with the scope of dormant congressional power.[45]

Under this view, the federal judiciary is viewed as "an organ of limited powers within a government of limited powers."[46] As the Court has stated, "[T]he federal lawmaking power is vested in the legislative, not the judicial, branch of government."[47]

Even if *Erie* is not explicit about separation-of-powers concerns, the Court has indicated that these concerns underlie the decision. For example, the Court remarked in City of Milwaukee v. Illinois, 451 U.S. 304, 312-13 (1981):

Martha A. Field, Sources of Law: The Scope of Federal Common Law, 99 HARV. L. REV. 881 (1986); Thomas W. Merrill, *The* Common Law Powers of Federal Courts, 52 U. CHI. L. REV. 1, 5 (1985); Martin H. Redish, Federal Common Law, Political Legitimacy, and the Interpretive Process: An "Institutionalist" Perspective, 83 NW. U. L. REV. 761, 765 (1989); Bradford R. Clark, Federal Common Law: A Structural Reinterpretation, 144 U. PA. L. REV. 1245 (1996).

43. *See* Merrill, *supra* note 42, at 13-14.

44. *See* Ely, *supra* note 42, at 703-04.

45. Henry P. Monaghan, *The Supreme Court, 1974 Term — Foreword: Constitutional Common Law*, 89 HARV. L. REV. 1, 13 (1975).

46. Note, *The Competence of Federal Courts to Formulate Rules of Decision*, 77 HARV. L. REV. 1084, 1085 (1964).

47. Northwest Airlines v. Transport Workers Union, 451 U.S. 77, 95 (1981).

> Federal courts, unlike state courts, are not general common law courts and do not possess a general power to develop and apply their own rules of decision. [Citations omitted.] The enactment of a federal rule in an area of national concern, and the decision whether to displace state law in doing so, is generally made not by the federal judiciary, purposefully insulated from democratic pressures, but by the people through their elected representatives in Congress. *Erie* recognized as much. . . .

As you will recognize, the Court's concerns with judicial rulemaking are similar to those expressed by early Republicans, who viewed much common lawmaking as legislative action.

The Court in *Erie* does not identify any specific constitutional provision or precedent to support its conclusion. Nonetheless, the history of federal common law, both before and after *Erie,* confirms that several constitutional considerations are raised whenever federal courts assert common-lawmaking authority. What is the source of the federal courts' power to make common law? How does the exercise of that power encroach on the traditional prerogatives of state lawmakers? How does it encroach on constitutional prerogatives of Congress? These questions hover over our discussion of federal common law in the remainder of this chapter.

Before considering contemporary federal common law, let's reflect on the possible implications of *Hudson, Swift,* and *Erie* in the context of a hypothetical problem.

PROBLEM 11-1

Congress, the Courts, and Common-Lawmaking Authority

Assume that, in the distant future of American politics, Congress decides to make fuller use of the federal courts' perceived competence in the realm of remedial law. According to a congressional report, there are great inconsistencies and even irrationality in the present hodgepodge of remedial provisions that accompany federal statutes. The report favorably comments on the federal courts' relatively superior expertise in devising remedies to redress discrete violations of federal law. As a consequence, the report recommends that the federal courts become greater "partners in the elaboration of federal remedial schemes."

Based on the report, Congress enacts legislation stating, "Except where otherwise provided in federal legislation, the federal courts shall have the common law power to develop remedial provisions to enforce statutory rights created by Congress. This power includes the power to authorize the recovery of all forms of monetary relief known to the common law, as well as the right to authorize recovery of attorney's fees."

Based on our limited study of the history of federal common law to this point in the chapter, do you believe the proposed legislation would survive a constitutional challenge? What constitutional problems, if any, do you find in the legislation? In considering potential problems, reflect on the meaning of *Hudson* and *Erie,* which remain leading precedents on the federal courts' common-lawmaking power.

2. *Enclaves of Federal Common-Lawmaking Power Derived from Constitutional Jurisdiction and Structure*

Although *Erie* rejected the existence of "federal general common law," it did not cast doubt on more specific forms of federal common law pre-dating *Erie.* As the Court explained in *Texas Industries, Inc. v. Radcliff Materials, Inc.*, 451 U.S. 630, 640 (1981),

> There is, of course, "no federal general common law." Nevertheless, the Court has recognized the need and authority in some limited areas to formulate what has come to be known as "federal common law." These instances are "few and restricted," and fall into essentially two categories: those in which a federal rule of decision is "necessary to protect uniquely federal interests," and those in which Congress has given the courts the power to develop substantive law.

Even though *Texas Industries* announced two "categories" of federal common law that persist after *Erie,* these categories do not greatly assist our ability to define or predict when federal common law is appropriate.[48] As Professor Chemerinsky has remarked, there is ultimately no "coherent body of legal principles"[49] to bring order to this subject. In the remainder of this chapter we will occasionally refer to these categories, but we will use them as the basic organizational structure for discussion.

Several forms of federal common law that "protect uniquely federal interests" share the characteristic that they derive from a constitutional grant of federal court *jurisdiction,* supplemented by concepts of constitutional structure. These forms of common law—applicable to disputes in admiralty, conflicts between states, and disputes involving relations with foreign nations—give federal courts the power to devise decisional rules over broad *subject areas.* These "enclaves" of federal court power contrast with other forms of common lawmaking we examine in later discussion, where the courts' power is often thought to be more "interstitial" or issue specific.

Common-lawmaking authority derived from a grant of jurisdiction appears anomalous. In most other contexts, the Court has rejected arguments that the federal courts' authority to exercise jurisdiction entails a corresponding authority to develop federal common law. For example, the Court in *Erie* implicitly rejected the position that Article III's grant of diversity jurisdiction granted a federal court power to develop common law. In other situations, the Court has been more explicit: "The vesting of jurisdiction in the federal courts does not in and of itself give rise to authority to formulate federal common law."[50] Despite such sweeping pronouncements, however, common-lawmaking authority in admiralty litigation,[51] in disputes between

48. In *Texas Industries, Inc. v. Radcliff Materials, Inc.*, 451 U.S. 630, 641 (1981), the Court explained that the first category, derived from "uniquely federal interests," includes "such narrow areas as those concerned with the rights and obligations of the United States, interstate and international disputes implicating the conflicting rights of States or our relations with foreign nations, and admiralty cases." These examples are often identified as the forms of special common law existing after *Erie,* but they are not exhaustive, as we will learn.

49. Erwin Chemerinsky, Federal Jurisdiction 384 (Aspen 6th ed. 2012).

50. *Texas Indus., Inc. v. Radcliff Materials, Inc.*, 451 U.S. 630, 640-41 (1981); *see also United States v. Little Lake Misere Land Co*, 412 U.S. 580, 591 (1973) (rejecting the contention that constitutional jurisdiction over disputes involving the United States entails the power to develop federal common law).

51. *See, e.g.*, Moragne v. States Marine Lines, Inc., 398 U.S. 375, 381-403 (1970).

states,[52] and to a lesser extent in disputes implicating foreign relations,[53] is closely related to constitutional grants of federal court jurisdiction.[54]

a. Admiralty

Today, the closest thing to some form of "general" federal common law is the law of admiralty. Much litigation that arises under admiralty and maritime jurisdiction is governed by federal common law.[55] Further, admiralty law preempts a great deal of state law based on the courts' conclusion that state law "works material prejudice to the characteristic features of the general maritime law or interferes with the proper harmony and uniformity of that law in its international and interstate relations."[56] The common law of admiralty is squarely founded on Article III's grant of jurisdiction.[57] As the Court has commented, "[w]ith admiralty jurisdiction . . . comes the application of substantive admiralty law."[58]

In theory, *Erie* might have decimated the common law of admiralty as it did the "law merchant" recognized in *Swift*. In the eighteenth and nineteenth centuries, both admiralty and the law merchant were subdivisions of the same "law of nations," and thus owed their authority to neither federal nor state government.[59] Ironically, Justice Holmes's derisive reference to the "brooding omnipresence" theory of stateless common law, quoted in *Erie*, was originally directed at admiralty law.[60] Yet admiralty law, unlike general commercial law, was preserved after *Erie*, albeit as a form of "federal" common law and not a more abstract "law of nations."

Some commentators argue that current maritime common law presents the same constitutional concerns identified in *Erie* and should be limited or even rejected.[61] But admiralty common law does not raise the breadth of concerns raised by the "general" common law inaugurated by *Swift*, which eventually extended far beyond the "law merchant" or rules of international commerce. Admiralty law can be viewed as a more limited enclave of common law posing much less threat to the general jurisprudence of the states. Further, the need for strong federal authority in maritime law was largely conceded during the constitutional debates. The Framers seemed to agree there was special need for uniformity in the decisional rules governing admiralty disputes given its

52. *See, e.g.*, Hinderlider v. La Plata River & Cherry Creek Ditch Co., 304 U.S. 92, 110 (1938) (decided the same day as *Erie*).

53. *See, e.g.*, Banco Nacional de Cuba v. Sabbatino, 376 U.S. 398, 421-27 (1964).

54. The Court has also affirmed that federal law exclusively governs relations with American Indians, and that questions of Indian relations are occasionally governed by federal common law. *See County of Oneida v. Oneida Indian Nation*, 470 U.S. 226, 233-36 (1985). More often, federal legislation governs issues involving Indian relations.

55. *See* Clark, *supra* note 42, at 1332.

56. Southern Pac. Co. v. Jensen, 244 U.S. 205, 216 (1917).

57. *See, e.g.*, Martin H. Redish, Federal Jurisdiction: Tensions in the Allocation of Judicial Power 122 (2d ed. 1990) ("It is well accepted . . . that the provisions of Article III, section 2 of the Constitution extending the federal judicial power to [admiralty and interstate cases] vest the federal judiciary with authority to develop its own substantive legal principles in cases falling within these areas.").

58. East River S.S. Corp. v. Transamerica Delaval Inc., 476 U.S. 858, 864 (1986)).

59. *See, e.g.*, Clark, *supra* note 42, at 1280-81.

60. Southern Pac. Co. v. Jensen, 244 U.S. 205, 222 (1917) (Holmes, J., dissenting).

61. *See* Clark, *supra* note 42, at 1360.

centrality in the nation's developing commerce.[62] As one commentator has observed concerning the consensus support for admiralty jurisdiction, "Amid all the questions on which our ancestors wrangled this is one of the few that was conceded to the common government without a groan."[63]

In addition, separation-of-powers concerns are minimized in admiralty law. Significantly, while Article III confers admiralty jurisdiction on the federal courts, the Constitution fails to grant Congress a corresponding legislative authority under Article I.[64] Consequently, any argument that the Court usurps legislative authority in developing admiralty law fails to gain traction.

b. Disputes Between States

Article III, section 2, of the Constitution authorizes federal jurisdiction over controversies "between two or more states," and grants the Supreme Court original jurisdiction (trial jurisdiction) in suits where a state is a party. Based on this grant, Congress has conferred original and exclusive jurisdiction on the Court in state-versus-state controversies. *See* 28 U.S.C. § 1251(a). The Court has exercised this jurisdiction frequently in suits between states over boundary disputes, water rights, interstate pollution, and alleged discrimination in commercial and tax matters.[65]

More than a century ago, the Court recognized that the rules it develops to resolve disputes between states are akin to "interstate common law."[66] The development of this federal common law appears necessary since a particular state's law cannot be fairly applied to its disputes with a neighboring state.[67]

Nor does the Court's development of common-law rules constitute any appreciable compromise of separation-of-powers principles.[68] In the most important type of dispute between states—that involving disputed state boundaries—Congress is restricted by the Constitution from legislating a decisional rule.[69] In other settings, where Congress enjoys greater legislative authority, the Court has often shown restraint in exercising its common-lawmaking power, observing that "it is for Congress, not federal courts, to articulate the appropriate standards to be applied as a matter of federal law."[70]

62. *See* Ernest A. Young, *Preemption at Sea*, 67 GEO. WASH. L. REV. 273, 325-27 (1999) ("The history suggests . . . that the general maritime law and the general commercial law were jurisprudentially identical, and that the Framers viewed neither as "federal" in the sense we think of today."). *See also* Clark, *supra* note 42, at 1348 ("Although in the present day the interests appear largely indistinguishable in both classes of cases, a uniform law was apparently one reason for the establishment of the admiralty jurisdiction in 1789, while the diversity jurisdiction is generally regarded as intended only to insure unbiased protection against the provincialism of state courts in the administration of their own laws in cases involving citizens of other states.").

63. Frederick Bauman, *Admiralty and Maritime Jurisdiction*, 36 AM. L. REV. 182, 186 (1902).

64. *See* Young, *supra*, note 62, at 281.

65. CHEMERINSKY, *supra* note 49, at 698-99.

66. *Kansas v. Colorado*, 206 U.S. 46, 98 (1907).

67. *See Texas Indus., Inc. v. Radcliff Materials, Inc.*, 451 U.S. 630, 641 (1981).

68. Professor Bradford Clark argues that this form of common law does raise constitutional concerns, but he largely resolves these concerns by pointing to a quasi-constitutional principle of the "absolute equality" of the states, as well as to international law. *See* Clark, *supra* note 42, at 1328-29.

69. *See* Clark, *supra* note 42, at 1367 ("Congress is without power to legislate a new border between states"); U.S. CONST. art. I, § 8, cl. 17.

70. *Milwaukee v. Illinois*, 451 U.S. 304, 316 (1981).

c. Foreign Relations[71]

At least in theory, one of the most important "enclaves of federal judge-made law" is that governing international disputes involving relations with foreign nations.[72] In *Banco Nacional de Cuba v. Sabbatino,* 376 U.S. 398 (1964), the Court held that federal common law applied to determine the rights of the nation of Cuba to property it appropriated after the Cuban revolution. In choosing to follow the "act of state" doctrine, which prohibits one nation from inquiring into the validity of another nation's public acts within its borders, the Court rejected the contention that *Erie* precluded the application of federal common law: "It seems fair to assume that the Court did not have rules like the act of state doctrine in mind when it decided *Erie R. Co. v. Tompkins.*"[73] The Court reached this conclusion even though legal rules like the act of state doctrine derive from the same "law of nations" that underlay the discredited law merchant applied in *Swift.*[74]

Sabbatino's recognition of a federal common-lawmaking power in disputes involving international relations is largely uncontroversial[75] and arguably raises no substantial constitutional concerns. Under the Constitution, political power in foreign relations is vested exclusively in the federal government—primarily Congress but also the President.[76] Further, the Constitution contains numerous provisions disabling the states from regulating foreign relations.[77] Consequently, the Court has not hesitated to conclude that *Erie* is irrelevant to matters entrusted by the Constitution to the national government: "the *Erie* decision, which related only to the law to be applied in exercise of that jurisdiction, had no effect, and was intended to have none, to bring within the governance of state law matters exclusively federal, because made so by constitutional or valid congressional command, or others so vitally affecting interests, powers and relations of the Federal Government as to require uniform national disposition rather than diversified state rulings."[78]

Insofar as *Sabbatino* recognizes the power of federal courts to apply rules not specifically endorsed by the legislative and executive branches, it might raise separation-of-powers concerns. In fact, Congress acted quickly to overturn *Sabbatino*'s rule. Since *Sabbatino,* the Court's use of this power has been "relatively infrequent,"[79] perhaps signaling the Court's reluctance to encroach on the constitutional prerogatives of Congress and the President. However, lower federal courts have used this common-lawmaking power with greater frequency,

71. In *Banco Nacional de Cuba v. Sabbatino,* 376 U.S. 398, 427 n.25 (1964), the Court based its exercise of common-law power on a number of "indirect" sources, including jurisdictional provisions of the Constitution and the federal code. *See also* Jay Tidmarsh & Brian J. Murphy, *A Theory of Federal Common Law,* 100 Nw. U. L. Rev. 585, 623 (2006) ("The claim for a federal common law of international relations relies heavily on the ninth jurisdictional grant, the grant of jurisdiction in controversies 'between a State, or the Citizens thereof, and foreign States, Citizens, or Subjects.'").

72. *Banco Nacional de Cuba v. Sabbatino,* 376 U.S. 398, 426 (1964).

73. *Id.* at 425.

74. *See* Clark, *supra* note 42, at 1282, 1297, 1301.

75. *See* Jack L. Goldsmith, *Federal Courts, Foreign Affairs, and Federalism,* 83 Va. L. Rev. 1617, 1632 (1997) ("[T]here is a remarkable consensus about the legitimacy of the federal common law of foreign relations.").

76. *See* Clark, *supra* note 42, at 1294-99.

77. *See id.* at 1295-96.

78. United States v. Standard Oil Co., 332 U.S. 301, 307 (1947). Professor Goldsmith, however, sharply disputes the prevailing view that foreign relations are trusted exclusively to the national government. *See* Goldsmith, *supra* note 75, at 1664.

79. *See* Goldsmith, *supra* note 75, at 1632.

leading a few dissenting scholars to question the continuing wisdom and constitutionality of this power.[80] Whether the Court will ultimately rein in the lower federal courts in deference to the legislative and executive branches remains to be seen.[81]

3. *An Enclave of Federal Common Law to Protect the Proprietary Interests of the United States*

One might argue that legal disputes involving the United States provide especially strong justification for the development of federal common law. First, the United States enjoys a broad immunity from state regulation, a principle established in *McCulloch v. Maryland,* 17 U.S. (4 Wheat.) 316, 436 (1819): "[T]he states have no power, by taxation or otherwise, to retard, impede, burden, or in any manner control, the operations of the constitutional laws enacted by congress to carry into execution the powers vested in the general government." Second, Article III, section 2, authorizes federal court jurisdiction over suits to which the United States is a party. Third, the United States enjoys a broad sovereign immunity preventing it from being sued without its consent; this effectively precludes state courts from exercising jurisdiction over the United States except where specially authorized by Congress.[82] Consequently, state courts would seem to have little power or opportunity to develop jurisprudence pertaining to the national government.

But the United States, like other governments, sometimes engages in conduct that appears less "governmental" and more like the conduct engaged in by private parties — what is usually described as "proprietary" activity. Like private proprietors, the United States frequently engages in conventional business activity like entering into contracts (e.g., purchasing goods or equipment) and acquiring, using, and selling property (e.g., renting office space or selling unwanted federal lands). Obviously, there must be some body of legal rules to govern its proprietary transactions. Congress could enact of body of such rules to govern the United States' proprietary activity, but it never has. As a consequence, the federal courts early faced the question of what law governed the rights and duties of the United States when they exercised jurisdiction over the national government's proprietary disputes.

When the United States first began engaging in proprietary activity, it rarely claimed that its sovereignty entitled it to its own special commercial law in displacement of state law.[83] To the contrary, the United States frequently *urged* its right to have its proprietary activity governed by state law. In *Cotton v. United States,* 52 U.S. (How.) 229 (1850), a defendant who had unlawfully taken timber

80. *See id.* at 1680-98. For a related argument that litigants are now exploiting the common law of foreign relations to their advantage in private litigation, see Lumen N. Mulligan, *No Longer Safe at Home: Preventing the Misuse of Federal Common Law of Foreign Relations as a Defense Tactic in Private Transnational Litigation,* 100 MICH. L. REV. 2408 (2002).

81. The Court has demonstrated considerable deference to the President's foreign affairs power in recent decisions by preempting state law perceived to be inconsistent with the exercise of that power. *See, e.g., American Ins. Ass'n v. Garamendi,* 539 U.S. 396 (2003).

82. *See generally* CHEMERINSKY, *supra* note 49, at 657.

83. The notion that a government surrenders part of its sovereignty when it enters into the private world of commerce is reflected in modern federal law. Under the Foreign Sovereign Immunity Act, a foreign nation waives its immunity from suit when the suit arises from its "commercial" activities. *See* 28 U.S.C. ' 1605(a)(2).

from federal land argued that the sole civil remedy available to the United States was a remedy enacted by Congress, but that Congress had not yet enacted such a remedy. But at the urging of the United States, the Court held that "as an owner of property in almost every State of the Union, [the United States has] the same right to have it protected by the local laws that other persons have." *Id.* at 231. In support of its conclusion, the Court cited earlier precedent concerning the United States' rights in negotiable instruments; according to the Court, the federal government enjoys "all the rights and incur[s] all the responsibilities of other persons who are parties to such instruments." *Id.* at 232.

Although there is some contrary precedent,[84] the prevailing approach through the early twentieth century was to apply state law to the proprietary transactions of the United States.[85] The national government conducted its business on the same terms as private proprietors did or, as the Court stated in *Clearfield Trust*, below, "the United States does business on business terms." Implicit in the Court's approach is the conclusion that neither federal jurisdiction over disputes involving the United States, nor some "amorphous doctrine of national sovereignty," generally authorizes the creation of federal common law to govern federal proprietary activity.[86]

The pivotal decision, broadly read as inaugurating a new form of federal common law to govern proprietary activities of the United States, is *Clearfield Trust Co. v. United States*, 318 U.S. 363 (1943). In *Clearfield*, the Court endorsed a federal common law governing the United States' proprietary activity despite the defendant's argument that *Erie* (issued just five years earlier) required application of state common law.

CLEARFIELD TRUST CO. v. UNITED STATES

318 U.S. 744 (1943)

MR. JUSTICE DOUGLAS delivered the opinion of the Court.

On April 28, 1936, a check was drawn on the Treasurer of the United States through the Federal Reserve Bank of Philadelphia to the order of Clair A. Barner in the amount of $24.20. It was dated at Harrisburg, Pennsylvania and was drawn for services rendered by Barner to the Works Progress Administration. The check was placed in the mail addressed to Barner at his address in Mackeyville, Pa. Barner never received the check. Some unknown person obtained it in a mysterious manner and presented it to the J.C. Penney Co. store in Clearfield, Pa., representing that he was the payee and identifying himself to the satisfaction of the employees of J.C. Penney Co. He endorsed the check in the name of Barner and transferred it to J.C. Penney Co. in exchange for cash and merchandise. Barner never authorized the endorsement nor participated in the proceeds of the check. J.C. Penney Co. endorsed the check over to the Clearfield Trust Co. which accepted it as agent for the purpose of collection and endorsed it as

84. *See, e.g., Duncan v. United States*, 32 (7 Pet.) 435 (1833) (applying general-common-law principles to determine liability under federally issued bonds).

85. *See United States v. Little Lake Misere Land Co.*, 412 U.S. 580, 591-92 (1973) (pre-*Erie* precedent suggesting that "the United States, while protected by the Constitution from discriminatory state action, and perhaps certain other special forms of state control, was nevertheless governed generally in its ordinary proprietary relations by state law," citing Henry M. Hart, Jr., *The Relations Between State and Federal Law*, 54 COLUM. L. REV. 489, 533 (1954)).

86. *See Little Lake Misere, supra*, 412 U.S. at 591, 592 n.10.

follows: "Pay to the order of Federal Reserve Bank of Philadelphia, Prior Endorsements Guaranteed." Clearfield Trust Co. collected the check from the United States through the Federal Reserve Bank of Philadelphia and paid the full amount thereof to J.C. Penney Co. Neither the Clearfield Trust Co. nor J.C. Penney Co. had any knowledge or suspicion of the forgery. Each acted in good faith. On or before May 10, 1936, Barner advised the timekeeper and the foreman of the W.P.A. project on which he was employed that he had not received the check in question. This information was duly communicated to other agents of the United States and on November 30, 1936, Barner executed an affidavit alleging that the endorsement of his name on the check was a forgery. No notice was given the Clearfield Trust Co. or J.C. Penney Co. of the forgery until January 12, 1937, at which time the Clearfield Trust Co. was notified. The first notice received by Clearfield Trust Co. that the United States was asking reimbursement was on August 31, 1937.

This suit was instituted in 1939 by the United States against the Clearfield Trust Co. The cause of action was based on the express guaranty of prior endorsements made by the Clearfield Trust Co. The District Court held that the rights of the parties were to be determined by the law of Pennsylvania and that since the United States unreasonably delayed in giving notice of the forgery to the Clearfield Trust Co., it was barred from recovery. It accordingly dismissed the complaint. On appeal the Circuit Court of Appeals reversed. The case is here on a petition for a writ of certiorari which we granted because of the importance of the problems raised and the [inter-circuit] conflict. . . .

We agree with the Circuit Court of Appeals that the rule of Erie R. Co. v. Tompkins does not apply to this action. The rights and duties of the United States on commercial paper which it issues are governed by federal rather than local law. When the United States disburses its funds or pays its debts, it is exercising a constitutional function or power. This check was issued for services performed under the Federal Emergency Relief Act of 1935. The authority to issue the check had its origin in the Constitution and the statutes of the United States and was in no way dependent on the laws of Pennsylvania or of any other state. The duties imposed upon the United States and the rights acquired by it as a result of the issuance find their roots in the same federal sources. In absence of an applicable Act of Congress it is for the federal courts to fashion the governing rule of law according to their own standards.

* * * *

In our choice of the applicable federal rule we have occasionally selected state law. But reasons which may make state law at times the appropriate federal rule are singularly inappropriate here. The issuance of commercial paper by the United States is on a vast scale and transactions in that paper from issuance to payment will commonly occur in several states. The application of state law, even without the conflict of laws rules of the forum, would subject the rights and duties of the United States to exceptional uncertainty. It would lead to great diversity in results by making identical transactions subject to the vagaries of the laws of the several states. The desirability of a uniform rule is plain. And while the federal law merchant developed for about a century under the regime of Swift v. Tyson, 16 Pet. 1, represented general commercial law rather than a choice of a federal rule designed to protect a federal right, it nevertheless stands as a convenient source of reference for fashioning federal rules applicable to these federal questions.

* * * *

If it is shown that the drawee on learning of the forgery did not give prompt notice of it and that damage resulted, recovery by the drawee is barred. The fact that the drawee is the United States and the laches those of its employees are not material. The United States as drawee of commercial paper stands in no different light than any other drawee. As stated in United States v. National Exchange Bank, 270 U.S. 527, 534, "The United States does business on business terms." It is not excepted from the general rules governing the rights and duties of drawees "by the largeness of its dealings and its having to employ agents to do what if done by a principal in person would leave no room for doubt." But the damage occasioned by the delay must be established and not left to conjecture. Cases such as *Market St. Title & Trust Co. v. Chelten Trust Co., supra,* place the burden on the drawee of giving prompt notice of the forgery—injury to the defendant being presumed by the mere fact of delay. But we do not think that he who accepts a forged signature of a payee deserves that preferred treatment. It is his neglect or error in accepting the forger's signature which occasions the loss. He should be allowed to shift that loss to the drawee only on a clear showing that the drawee's delay in notifying him of the forgery caused him damage. No such damage has been shown by Clearfield Trust Co. who so far as appears can still recover from J.C. Penney Co.

Affirmed.

DISCUSSION AND QUESTIONS

Justifications for developing federal common law under Clearfield Trust. *Clearfield Trust* is often cited for the authority of federal courts to develop common law to govern questions involving the "rights and obligations of the United States,"[87] or the "proprietary" rights of the United States.[88] Given the decision's importance, we might ask whether the Court adequately justifies its recognition of this new area of federal common law so soon after *Erie.*

Does the fact that the United States was "exercising a constitutional function," or that its check "had its origins" in federal law, explain why federal common law governs the issue of liability on a stolen check? Isn't it axiomatic that the United States' conduct arises from the performance of a "constitutional" function? This observation supports the constitutionality of the federal programs involved, and would also support Congress' enactment of legislation governing forged checks. But does it really support the Court's conclusion that it has authority to develop a federal *common law*? If the constitutional origins of a federal program are alone sufficient to support creation of federal common law, does this mean that the federal courts have power to develop all rules of decision to govern the United States' activity when Congress has not enacted its own rule?

Why didn't the Court simply hold that federal common law governs the rights and duties of the United States? Does the opinion suggest any reason why this broad interpretation of federal common law is inapplicable?

The federal courts' power to develop common law under *Clearfield Trust* has been described by the Court as a power derived from "uniquely federal

87. *Texas Indus., Inc. v. Radcliff Materials, Inc.*, 451 U.S. 630, 640 (1981).
88. *See* CHEMERINSKY, *supra* note 49, at 390.

interests."[89] Is the phrase "unique federal interests," at least as applied in *Clearfield Trust,* simply another way of saying the United States is a party? If the presence of the United States as a party is sufficient to justify development of a new form of common law, why did the Court usually decline to develop such common law in the first century or so of the United States' existence? Could one argue that *Clearfield Trust* reflects the dramatic expansion of the federal government in the New Deal era (the worker whose check was stolen was employed by the new Works Project Administration)? Or does *Clearfield Trust* instead reflect a dramatic expansion in the Court's view of federal power (including its own) at the states' loss?

"Interstitial" lawmaking and federal programs. Another clue to the Court's recognition of common-lawmaking authority in *Clearfield Trust* is found in its later opinion, *United States v. Little Lake Misere Land Co.*, 412 U.S. 580 (1973). In *Lake Misere,* the Court applied federal law to govern the rights of the United States in land acquired under the Migratory Bird Conservation Act. The Court rejected the contention that state law governed, which would have abrogated rights spelled out in the contract of purchase and arguably permitted future mineral extraction on protected federal lands. In reaching its conclusion, the Court remarked on the special need for federal courts to engage in "interstitial lawmaking" when federal legislation is incomplete:

> Here, the choice-of-law task is a federal task for federal courts, as defined by *Clearfield Trust Co. v. United States.* Since *Erie,* and as a corollary of that decision, we have consistently acted on the assumption that dealings which may be "ordinary" or "local" as between private citizens raise serious questions of national sovereignty when they arise in the context of a specific constitutional or statutory provision; particularly is this so when transactions undertaken by the Federal Government are involved, as in this case. In such cases, the Constitution or Acts of Congress "require" otherwise than that state law govern of its own force.
>
> There will often be no specific federal legislation governing a particular transaction to which the United States is a party; here, for example, no provision of the Migratory Bird Conservation Act guides us to choose state or federal law in interpreting federal land acquisition agreements under the Act. But silence on that score in federal legislation is no reason for limiting the reach of federal law. . . . To the contrary, the inevitable incompleteness presented by all legislation means that interstitial federal lawmaking is a basic responsibility of the federal courts. "At the very least, effective Constitutionalism requires recognition of power in the federal courts to declare, as a matter of common law or 'judicial legislation,' rules which may be necessary to fill in interstitially or otherwise effectuate the statutory patterns enacted in the large by Congress. In other words, it must mean recognition of federal judicial competence to declare the governing law in an area comprising issues substantially related to an established program of government operation."
>
> This, then, is what has aptly been described as the "first" of the two holdings of *Clearfield Trust Co. v. United States,* that the right of the United States to seek legal redress for duly authorized proprietary transactions "is a federal right, so that the courts of the United States may formulate a rule of decision."

Id. at 592-93.

89. *See Boyle v. United Techs. Corp.*, 487 U.S. 500, 504-05 (1988).

Lake Misere refines the Court's explanation of its common-lawmaking power in *Clearfield Trust* by positing some *institutional necessity*. Courts must sometimes develop rules of decision because Congress lacks the institutional capacity to fully spell out those rules. Courts develop "interstitial" rules not because a federal program is rooted in the Constitution but because Congress depends on the courts to "effectuate . . . statutory patterns." Judicial rulemaking is "a basic responsibility of the federal courts."

According to Professor Mishkin, Congress (or probably any legislative body) is institutionally incapable of drafting comprehensive legislation that provides rules to govern every imaginable situation. The inevitable incompleteness of legislation necessitates that federal courts sometimes develop rules consistent with legislative policy, rather than simply filling the gap with local state law. The federal courts' role in supplemental lawmaking exists despite separation-of-powers concerns:

> To be sure, within the central structure, those powers are granted to the Congress, and, for various good reasons such grants cannot be taken directly to authorize judicial law-making of equal scope. At the same time, the separation of powers cannot be watertight; exclusive reliance upon statutory provision for the solution of all problems is futile. Beyond the political realities which will at times compel congressional by-passing of any issue — thus leaving it open until pending litigation forces court resolution — lie such simpler pressures as shortness of time and, perhaps most important, the severe limits of human foresight. Together, these factors combine to make the concept of statutory enactment as a totally self-sufficient and exclusive legislative process entirely unreal.[90]

As we learn later, "interstitial"[91] lawmaking by the federal courts occurs in contexts where the United States is not a party. Clearly Professor Mishkin's description of this lawmaking power suggests it has broad application across all types of statutory programs. But other commentators argue that the Court should exercise restraint when filling the gaps in federal legislation. Consider the following comments of Professor Monaghan:

> Specialized federal common law exists despite the fact that the allocation of law-making competence in our federal system imposes severe limits on the federal judicial authority to displace state law. The limited powers of the national government were, with some exceptions, granted to Congress, ordinarily leaving to its discretion — and not the courts' — the decision of whether and how these powers were to be exercised. Moreover, national powers are interstitial powers, exercised "against the background of the total corpus juris of the states. . . ." When exercised, they may therefore alter or reverse preexisting state policy. Thus, when a federal court announces a federal rule of decision in an area of plenary congressional competence, it exercises an initiative normally left to Congress, ousts state law, and yet acts without the political checks on national power created by state representation in Congress.
>
> Because there is both residual and concurrent lawmaking power in the states, "[f]ederal intervention has been thought of as requiring special justification, and

90. Paul J. Mishkin, *The Variousness of "Federal Law": Competence and Discretion in the Choice of National and State Rules for Decision*, 105 U. Pa. L. Rev. 797, 800 (1957).

91. The term "interstitial" is commonly used in discussion of federal common law. It simply refers to the space, or gap, between two things.

the decision that such justification has been shown, being essentially discretionary, has belonged in most cases to Congress."[92]

As Professor Monaghan observes, there is another way to fill the interstices of federal law—by applying state law. Prior to *Clearfield Trust* the prevailing view appeared to be that the "background of the total corpus juris of the states" usually was sufficient to provide rules of decision regarding the United States' proprietary activities. This approach still has many adherents on the Court.[93]

Although the form of federal common law inaugurated by *Clearfield Trust* is still recognized by the Court, the "corpus juris" of state law has reestablished its prominence in suits involving the United States' proprietary rights. In *United States v. Kimbell Foods, Inc.*, excerpted below, the Court was asked to apply federal common law to determine the relative priority of federal agency liens on private property. The Court had occasion to address the two questions raised in *Clearfield Trust*: (1) when do federal courts have a specialized power to develop common law, and (2) how do courts exercising that power determine the content of the new common-law rule? As you read the opinion, consider how state law re-insinuates itself into disputes involving the proprietary rights of the United States. Ask whether the "borrowing" of state law to determine the content of "federal" common law undermines the rationale of *Clearfield Trust.*

UNITED STATES v. KIMBELL FOODS, INC.

440 U.S. 715 (1979)

MR. JUSTICE MARSHALL delivered the opinion of the Court.

We granted certiorari in these cases to determine whether contractual liens arising from certain federal loan programs take precedence over private liens, in the absence of a federal statute setting priorities. To resolve this question, we must decide first whether federal or state law governs the controversies; and second, if federal law applies, whether this Court should fashion a uniform priority rule or incorporate state commercial law. We conclude that the source of law is federal, but that a national rule is unnecessary to protect the federal interests underlying the loan programs. Accordingly, we adopt state law as the appropriate federal rule for establishing the relative priority of these competing federal and private liens.

I

[The Court recites the complex events leading to Kimbell Foods's action to recover monies owed to it by the debtor supermarket. The ultimate issue confronting the federal district court was whether Kimbell Foods's secured interest in the supermarket's inventory and equipment, now converted to cash in an

92. *See* Monaghan, *supra* note 42, at 11.

93. *See O'Melveny & Myers v. FDIC*, 512 U.S. 79, 85 (1994) ("[M]atters left unaddressed in such a scheme are presumably left subject to the disposition provided by state law.")

escrow fund, was superior to the Small Business Administration's (SBA's) later-acquired security interest in the same property.]

Kimbell thereafter brought the instant action to foreclose on its lien, claiming that its security interest in the escrow fund was superior to the SBA's. The District Court held for the Government. On determining that federal law controlled the controversy, the court applied principles developed by this Court to afford federal statutory tax liens special priority over state and private liens where the governing statute does not specify priorities.

* * * *

The Court of Appeals reversed. It agreed that federal law governs the rights of the United States under its SBA loan program, and that the "first in time, first in right" priority principle should control the competing claims. However, the court refused to extend the choateness rule[94] to situations in which the Federal Government was not an involuntary creditor of tax delinquents, but rather a voluntary commercial lender. Instead, it fashioned a new federal rule for determining which lien was first in time, and concluded that "in the context of competing state security interests arising under the U.C.C.," the first to meet UCC perfection requirements achieved priority.

* * * *

II

This Court has consistently held that federal law governs questions involving the rights of the United States arising under nationwide federal programs. As the Court explained in *Clearfield Trust Co. v. United States*:

> When the United States disburses its funds or pays its debts, it is exercising a constitutional function or power. . . . The authority [to do so] had its origin in the Constitution and the statutes of the United States and was in no way dependent on the laws [of any State]. The duties imposed upon the United States and the rights acquired by it . . . find their roots in the same federal sources. In absence of an applicable Act of Congress it is for the federal courts to fashion the governing rule of law according to their own standards.

Guided by these principles, we think it clear that the priority of liens stemming from federal lending programs must be determined with reference to federal law. The SBA and FHA unquestionably perform federal functions within the meaning of *Clearfield*. Since the agencies derive their authority to effectuate loan transactions from specific Acts of Congress passed in the exercise of a "constitutional function or power," their rights, as well, should derive from a federal source. When Government activities "aris[e] from and bea[r] heavily upon a federal . . . program," the Constitution and Acts of Congress "'require' otherwise than that state law govern of its own force." United States v. Little Lake Misere Land Co. In such contexts, federal interests are sufficiently implicated to warrant the protection of federal law.

That the statutes authorizing these federal lending programs do not specify the appropriate rule of decision in no way limits the reach of federal law. It is

94. The choateness rule prevented Kimbell Foods from perfecting a security interest for its future advances to the grocery.

precisely when Congress has not spoken "'in an area comprising issues substantially related to an established program of government operation,'" [quoting Mishkin] that *Clearfield* directs federal courts to fill the interstices of federal legislation "according to their own standards." Federal law therefore controls the Government's priority rights. The more difficult task, to which we turn, is giving content to this federal rule.

III

Controversies directly affecting the operations of federal programs, although governed by federal law, do not inevitably require resort to uniform federal rules. Whether to adopt state law or to fashion a nationwide federal rule is a matter of judicial policy "dependent upon a variety of considerations always relevant to the nature of the specific governmental interests and to the effects upon them of applying state law."[95]

Undoubtedly, federal programs that "by their nature are and must be uniform in character throughout the Nation" necessitate formulation of controlling federal rules. Conversely, when there is little need for a nationally uniform body of law, state law may be incorporated as the federal rule of decision. Apart from considerations of uniformity, we must also determine whether application of state law would frustrate specific objectives of the federal programs. If so, we must fashion special rules solicitous of those federal interests. Finally, our choice-of-law inquiry must consider the extent to which application of a federal rule would disrupt commercial relationships predicated on state law.

The Government argues that effective administration of its lending programs requires uniform federal rules of priority. It contends further that resort to any rules other than first in time, first in right and choateness would conflict with protectionist fiscal policies underlying the programs. We are unpersuaded that, in the circumstances presented here, nationwide standards favoring claims of the United States are necessary to ease program administration or to safeguard the Federal Treasury from defaulting debtors. Because the state commercial codes "furnish convenient solutions in no way inconsistent with adequate protection of the federal interest[s]," we decline to override intricate state laws of general applicability on which private creditors base their daily commercial transactions.

Incorporating state law to determine the rights of the United States as against private creditors would in no way hinder administration of the SBA and FHA loan programs. [In *United States v. Yazell*, 382 U.S. 341 (1966), this Court rejected the argument, similar to the Government's here, that a need for uniformity precluded application of state coverture rules to an SBA loan contract. Because SBA operations were "specifically and in great detail adapted to state law," the federal interest in supplanting "important and carefully evolved state arrangements designed to serve multiple purposes" was minimal. Our conclusion that compliance with state law would produce no hardship on the agency

95. [Footnote 21 in Court's opinion.] As explained by one commentator: "Whether state law is to be incorporated as a matter of federal common law . . . involves the . . . problem of the relationship of a particular issue to a going federal program. The question of judicial incorporation can only arise in an area which is sufficiently close to a national operation to establish competence in the federal courts to choose the governing law, and yet not so close as clearly to require the application of a single nationwide rule of substance." [Citation to Mishkin omitted.]

was also based on the SBA's practice of "individually negotiat[ing] in painfully particularized detail" each loan transaction. These observations apply with equal force here and compel us again to reject generalized pleas for uniformity as substitutes for concrete evidence that adopting state law would adversely affect administration of the federal programs.

Although the SBA Financial Assistance Manual on which this Court relied in *Yazell* is no longer "replete with admonitions to follow state law carefully," SBA employees are still instructed to, and indeed do, follow state law. In fact, a fair reading of the SBA Financial Assistance Manual indicates that the agency assumes its security interests are controlled to a large extent by the commercial law of each State. Similarly, FHA regulations expressly incorporate state law. They mandate compliance with state procedures for perfecting and maintaining valid security interests, and highlight those rules that differ from State to State. To ensure that employees are aware of new developments, the FHA also issues "State supplements" to "reflect any State statutory changes in its version of the UCC." Contrary to the Government's claim that the FHA complies only with state procedural rules, the agency's reliance on state law extends to substantive requirements as well. Indeed, applicable regulations suggest that state rules determine the priority of FHA liens when federal statutes or agency regulations are not controlling.

Thus, the agencies' own operating practices belie their assertion that a federal rule of priority is needed to avoid the administrative burdens created by disparate state commercial rules. The programs already conform to each State's commercial standards. By using local lending offices and employees who are familiar with the law of their respective localities, the agencies function effectively without uniform procedures and legal rules.

Nevertheless, the Government maintains that requiring the agencies to assess security arrangements under local law would dictate close scrutiny of each transaction and thereby impede expeditious processing of loans. We disagree. Choosing responsible debtors necessarily requires individualized selection procedures, which the agencies have already implemented in considerable detail. Each applicant's financial condition is evaluated under rigorous standards in a lengthy process. Agency employees negotiate personally with borrowers, investigate property offered as collateral for encumbrances, and obtain local legal advice on the adequacy of proposed security arrangements. In addition, they adapt the terms of every loan to the parties' needs and capabilities. Because each application currently receives individual scrutiny, the agencies can readily adjust loan transactions to reflect state priority rules, just as they consider other factual and legal matters before disbursing Government funds. As we noted in United States v. Yazell, these lending programs are distinguishable from "nationwide act[s] of the Federal Government, emanating in a single form from a single source." Since there is no indication that variant state priority schemes would burden current methods of loan processing, we conclude that considerations of administrative convenience do not warrant adoption of a uniform federal law.

The Government argues that applying state law to these lending programs would undermine its ability to recover funds disbursed and therefore would conflict with program objectives. In the Government's view, it is difficult "to identify a material distinction between a dollar received from the collection of taxes and a dollar returned to the Treasury on repayment of a federal loan." Therefore, the agencies conclude, just as "the purpose of the federal tax lien statute to insure prompt and certain collection of taxes" justified our imposition of the first-in-time and choateness doctrines in the tax lien context, the federal interest in recovering on loans compels similar legal protection of the agencies' consensual liens. However, we believe significant differences between federal tax liens and consensual liens counsel against unreflective extension of rules that immunize the United States from the commercial law governing all other voluntary secured creditors. These differences persuade us that deference to customary commercial practices would not frustrate the objectives of the lending programs.

That collection of taxes is vital to the functioning, indeed existence, of government cannot be denied. Congress recognized as much over 100 years ago when it authorized creation of federal tax liens. The importance of securing adequate revenues to discharge national obligations justifies the extraordinary priority accorded federal tax liens through the choateness and first-in-time doctrines. By contrast, when the United States operates as a moneylending institution under carefully circumscribed programs, its interest in recouping the limited sums advanced is of a different order. Thus, there is less need here than in the tax lien area to invoke protective measures against defaulting debtors in a manner disruptive of existing credit markets.

To equate tax liens with these consensual liens also misperceives the principal congressional concerns underlying the respective statutes. The overriding purpose of the tax lien statute obviously is to ensure prompt revenue collection. The same cannot be said of the SBA and FHA lending programs. They are a form of social welfare legislation, primarily designed to assist farmers and businesses that cannot obtain funds from private lenders on reasonable terms. We believe that had Congress intended the private commercial sector, rather than taxpayers in general, to bear the risks of default entailed by these public welfare programs, it would have established a priority scheme displacing state law. Far from doing so, both Congress and the agencies have expressly recognized the priority of certain private liens over the agencies' security interests, thereby indicating that the extraordinary safeguards applied in the tax lien area are unnecessary to maintain the lending programs.

The Government's ability to safeguard its interests in commercial dealings further reveals that the rules developed in the tax lien area are unnecessary here, and that state priority rules would not conflict with federal lending objectives. The United States is an involuntary creditor of delinquent taxpayers, unable to control the factors that make tax collection likely. In contrast, when the United States acts as a lender or guarantor, it does so voluntarily, with detailed knowledge of the borrower's financial status. The agencies evaluate the risks associated with each loan, examine the interests of other creditors, choose the security believed necessary to assure repayment, and set the terms of every agreement. By carefully selecting loan recipients and tailoring each transaction with state law in mind, the agencies are fully capable of establishing terms that will secure repayment.

The Government nonetheless argues that its opportunity to evaluate the credit worthiness of loan applicants provides minimal safety. Because the SBA and FHA make loans only when private lenders will not, the United States believes that its security interests demand greater protection than ordinary commercial arrangements. We find this argument unconvincing. The lending agencies do not indiscriminately distribute public funds and hope that reimbursement will follow. SBA loans must be "of such sound value or so secured as reasonably to assure repayment." The FHA operates under a similar restriction. Both agencies have promulgated exhaustive instructions to ensure that loan recipients are financially reliable and to prevent improvident loans. The Government therefore is in substantially the same position as private lenders, and the special status it seeks is unnecessary to safeguard the public fisc. Moreover, Congress' admonitions to extend loans judiciously supports the view that it did not intend to confer special privileges on agencies that enter the commercial field. Accordingly, we agree with the Court of Appeals that "[a]s a quasi-commercial lender, [the Government] does not require . . . the special priority which it compels as sovereign" in its tax-collecting capacity.

* * * *

In structuring financial transactions, businessmen depend on state commercial law to provide the stability essential for reliable evaluation of the risks involved. However, subjecting federal contractual liens to the doctrines developed in the tax lien area could undermine that stability. Creditors who justifiably rely on state law to obtain superior liens would have their expectations thwarted whenever a federal contractual security interest suddenly appeared and took precedence.

Considerable uncertainty would also result from the approach used in the opinions below. Developing priority rules on a case-by-case basis, depending on the types of competing private liens involved, leaves creditors without the definite body of law they require in structuring sound business transactions. Because the ultimate consequences of altering settled commercial practices are so difficult to foresee, we hesitate to create new uncertainties, in the absence of careful legislative deliberation. Of course, formulating special rules to govern the priority of the federal consensual liens in issue here would be justified if necessary to vindicate important national interests. But neither the Government nor the Court of Appeals advanced any concrete reasons for rejecting well-established commercial rules which have proven workable over time. Thus, the prudent course is to adopt the readymade body of state law as the federal rule of decision until Congress strikes a different accommodation.

Accordingly, we hold that, absent a congressional directive, the relative priority of private liens and consensual liens arising from these Government lending programs is to be determined under nondiscriminatory state laws.

DISCUSSION AND QUESTIONS

Interstitial lawmaking to govern the United States' proprietary interests. The Court does not hesitate in concluding that federal common law governs "questions involving the rights of the United States arising under nationwide federal programs." Because the SBA and FHA "derive their authority to effectuate loan transactions from specific Acts of Congress passed in the exercise of a 'constitutional function or power,' their rights, as well, should derive from a federal source." Does the Court add anything to the brief discussion of its authority to make common law in *Clearfield Trust*?

At the same time, the Court in *Kimbell Foods* draws support from Professor Mishkin's theory of interstitial lawmaking power regarding issues "substantially related to an established program of government operation." This approach is arguably more issue specific, requiring the Court to consider whether the United States requires a federal common-law rule to govern the issue in dispute. The question arises: Are there situations where federal courts might decline to develop a common-law rule to govern the United States' proprietary interests because the specific issue does not require a "federal" rule?

The Court's decision in *United States v. Yazell*, 382 U.S. 341 (1966), is sometimes cited as an exceptional example of the Court's willingness to decline making a common-law rule to govern the United States' proprietary activity.[96] In *Yazell*, the SBA had entered into a loan with a man, and with his wife, Mrs. Yazell, as cosigner. Under state law at the time, Ms. Yazell was prevented from obligating herself for her husband's debt. The SBA knew of this restriction when Ms. Yazell signed the loan, and yet sought to take "unconscionable advantage" of her by insisting she obligate herself despite state law. *See id.* at 346.

In *Yazell*, the Court refused to fashion a federal common-law rule to circumvent the wife's defense under state law. The Court explained that under *Clearfield Trust* and other precedent, "decisions applying 'federal law' to supersede state law typically relate to programs and actions which by their nature are and must be uniform in character throughout the Nation." *Id.* at 507. The loan transaction involving Ms. Yazell arose from an "individually negotiated contract" in which the SBA had notice of the potential impact of state law. The Court remarked that, at least in the area of "family and family-property arrangements," federal courts should not override state law in the absence of "clear and substantial" federal interests. *Id.*

Although *Yazell* is sometimes cited to illustrate that development of a federal rule to govern the United States' proprietary interests is not inevitable, the Court actually avoided the issue. The Court specifically declined to say whether it was (a) *applying* state law, or (b) developing a federal common-law rule that *adopted* state law. The Court remarked, "it is unnecessary to decide in the present case whether the Texas law of coverture should apply *ex proprio vigore*— on the theory that the contract here was made pursuant and subject to this provision of state law—or by "adoption" as a federal principle. . . ." *Id.* at 357.

In any event, in later cases the Court seems to have tempered its earlier statements in cases like *Clearfield Trust*, where it implied a broad rulemaking power whenever federal courts address "questions involving the rights of the United States arising under nationwide federal programs." For example, in *O'Melveny & Myers v. FDIC*, 512 U.S. 79, 87 (1994), the Court emphasized the need for some "significant conflict" between federal policy and state law as a prerequisite to developing federal common law: "Our cases uniformly require the existence of such a conflict as a precondition for recognition of a federal rule of decision." In support of this position, the Court in *O'Melveny* relied on its decision in *Kimbell Foods*.

Choosing the appropriate federal rule. In reaching its decision to apply state lien priority law in *United States v. Yazell*, the Court identified three relevant criteria: (1) the need for uniformity in the federal program, (2) whether application of state law would frustrate specific objectives of the federal program; and (3) the extent to which application of a federal rule would disrupt commercial relationships predicated on state law. The Court in *Yazell* concluded that these criteria failed to justify displacement of state law.

The Court in *Kimbell Foods* also concluded that state law should determine the rights of the United States, although the Court expressly "adopted" state law as

96. *See, e.g.*, CHEMERINSKY, *supra* note 49, at 392.

the "federal" common-law rule. In deferring to state law, the Court "declined to override intricate state laws of general applicability on which private creditors base their daily commercial transactions." One is reminded of the Court's observation in *Clearfield Foods* that "the United States does business on business terms." The Court in *Kimbell Foods* rejected the argument that federal agencies would be harmed by having to contour lending transactions to state law. The Court emphasized that conformity to state law is already an important aspect of agency transactions. According to the Court, the "administrative convenience" of federal agencies is not sufficient reason for displacing state law.

Nor did the Court accept the government's contention that uniform federal law is needed to facilitate the collection of loans. The government attempted to analogize to the collection of federal revenues through tax liens, apparently in an effort to show that its interests were not purely "proprietary." The Court disagreed: "when the United States operates as a moneylending institution under carefully circumscribed programs, its interest in recouping the limited sums advanced is of a different order. Thus, there is less need here than in the tax lien area to invoke protective measures against defaulting debtors in a manner disruptive of existing credit markets." 440 U.S. 715, 734. In *O'Melveny & Myers v. FDIC*, 512 U.S. 79, 88 (1994), the Court disparaged the government's alleged interest in the development of federal common law to enhance collection of federal revenues, referring to the argument as a "more money" rationale.

Finally, in *Kimbell Foods* the Court expressed concerns about how the lien priority rule argued by the government might affect commercial interests otherwise relying on state law (largely derived from the Uniform Commercial Code). "We hesitate to create new uncertainties, in the absence of careful legislative deliberation. Of course, formulating special rules to govern the priority of the federal consensual liens in issue here would be justified if necessary to vindicate important national interests. But neither the Government nor the Court of Appeals advanced any concrete reasons for rejecting well-established commercial rules which have proven workable over time. Thus, the prudent course is to adopt the readymade body of state law as the federal rule of decision until Congress strikes a different accommodation." *Id.* at 739-40.

Reflect on the perceived need for a federal rule in *Clearfield Trust*, the case that launched this version of federal common law. The rule adopted in *Clearfield Trust* excused the United States from giving timely notice to an endorsee bank that the check it honored had been forged. Despite learning earlier of the forgery, the United States delayed six months in notifying the bank and delayed yet another six months in demanding reimbursement from the bank.[97] But the Court refused to apply state law and instead required that the bank show that it was prejudiced by the delayed notice of the United States. What strong federal policy was served by the Court's development of a federal rule in *Clearfield Trust*? Since the United States could have satisfied state law by timely notifying the bank, did it have any greater need for a uniform federal rule of notification than the agencies in *Kimbell Foods* had for a uniform rule of lien priorities?[98] Does the Court's ready development of a federal rule in *Clearfield*

97. The underlying facts of the dispute are described in Mishkin, *supra* note 42, at 828-29.

98. Professor Mishkin, whose strong support of common-lawmaking authority in *Clearfield Trust* has clearly influenced the Court, concluded that there was no need for a uniform federal rule in that particular case. *See id.* at 828-32.

Trust suggest the Court was already disposed to federalize the proprietary interests of the United States?

Clearfield methodology re-rationalized? More recently, the Court has suggested that *Clearfield Trust* may have over-complicated the inquiry whether to replace state law with federal common law. In cases like *Clearfield Trust* and *Kimbell Foods,* the Court first asks whether a "federal" rule should govern the issue in dispute. When the United States' proprietary interests are at stake, the Court almost always concludes a federal rule should govern. But then the Court must consider the content of the federal rule. And increasingly the Court has adopted local state law for content. The consequence of adopting state law to provide content to the "federal" rule *seems* to lead to the same result as simply declining to develop a federal rule at all.

In *Empire Health Assurance, Inc. v. McVeigh,* 547 U.S. 677 (2006), the Court offered a simplified version of the *Clearfield Trust* questions, one that suggests the two questions can be collapsed into one: "whether the relevant federal interest warrants displacement of state law."

> Referring simply to "the displacement of state law," the Court recognized that prior cases had treated discretely (1) the competence of federal courts to formulate a federal rule of decision, and (2) the appropriateness of declaring a federal rule rather than borrowing, incorporating, or adopting state law in point. The Court preferred "the more modest terminology," questioning whether "the distinction between displacement of state law and displacement of federal law's incorporation of state law ever makes a practical difference."[99]

The Court's comments in *McVeigh* suggest much greater reluctance than in prior cases to displace state law when the United States' proprietary interests are at stake. *McVeigh* does not directly question the power of federal courts to develop federal common law under *Clearfield Trust,* but it does suggest that this power is to be exercised based on an assessment of the "relevant federal interest." In contrast to the Court's approach to common lawmaking in areas like admiralty and disputes between states, *McVeigh* indicates that federal common law should not *presumptively* dominate the law governing federal proprietary activities. Does *McVeigh* imply that the "interstitial" approach to common lawmaking advocated by Professor Mishkin has now prevailed in disputes involving the United States' proprietary interests? Has the Court's disposition to develop an independent body of "federal" law evolved since *Clearfield Trust?*

PROBLEM 11-2

The Innocent Spouse

Mitchell Marks was convicted in federal court for possession and distribution of cocaine. Afterward, the United States commenced a civil forfeiture proceeding to acquire real property used by Mitchell in committing his criminal acts. His wife, Leah, intervened in the proceeding and argued that, as an "innocent spouse" as defined by federal law, her interest in the realty was not forfeited

99. *Id.* at 691-92.

to the government. Further, she argued that under Michigan law she and her husband held the real estate as a "tenants by the entirety," and that Michigan law gave her an "undivided" interest in the real estate in its entirety. Consequently, she argued that federal statutes exempting forfeiture of the "property" of an innocent spouse extended to her interest in *all* the property, even though her husband likewise owned an "undivided" interest in the property.

The United States disagreed. It argued that "a federal common law of forfeiture is needed to effectuate the goals and purposes of the federal forfeiture scheme. Forfeiture statutes serve the ends of law enforcement by preventing further illicit use of the property and by imposing an economic penalty, thereby rendering illegal behavior unprofitable. Drug dealers will circumvent the impact of the forfeiture statutes by investing their assets in property such as entireties property which may be shielded from forfeiture by reason of the nature of the property interest under state law." Although the government did not contend that Mitchell had actually attempted to shield property by acquiring it with Leah as tenants by the entirety, it argued that a uniform federal rule would promote consistent law enforcement throughout the nation. It contended that an appropriate federal common-law rule would recognize that innocent spouses like Leah are entitled to an exemption for only one-half of property jointly owned with a convicted felon.

Should the federal court develop a federal common-law rule to determine the extent of Leah's protected property interest? If it does, should it simply adopt local (Michigan) state law or should it develop a uniform national rule?

The penumbra of Clearfield Trust: Can private parties benefit from the common law governing federal proprietary interests? *Clearfield Trust* did not address one important issue raised by its ruling: did the bank that honored the forged check but lost to the United States have its *own* federal common-law right to recover its losses from J.C. Penney, the store that originally cashed the forged check? Stated generically, does federal common law govern the legal relations of *private* parties who act on the periphery of the United States' proprietary activities?

In *Bank of America v. Parnell*, 352 U.S. 29 (1956), the Court declined to extend its power under *Clearfield Trust* to private-party disputes. In *Parnell*, a federal circuit court had concluded that *Clearfield Trust* required application of federal common law in a suit filed by the corporate plaintiff against private parties who had allegedly stolen or honored federally guaranteed bearer bonds. Although originally named as a defendant, the Federal Reserve Bank was dismissed from the case before trial. The key legal issue was whether the private defendants had honored the bonds in good faith.

The Court held that state law governed the issue whether the private defendants had acted in good faith. According to the Court,

> Securities issued by the Government generate immediate interests of the Government. These were dealt with in *Clearfield Trust.* But they also radiate interests in transactions between private parties. *The present litigation is purely between private parties and does not touch the rights and duties of the United States.* The only possible interest of the United States in a situation like the one here, exclusively involving the transfer of Government paper between private persons, is that the floating of securities of the United States might somehow or other be adversely affected by the local rule of a particular State regarding the liability of a converter. This is far too

> speculative, far too remote a possibility to justify the application of federal law to transactions essentially of local concern.
>
> *We do not mean to imply that litigation with respect to Government paper necessarily precludes the presence of a federal interest, to be governed by federal law, in all situations merely because it is a suit between private parties,* or that it is beyond the range of federal legislation to deal comprehensively with Government paper. We do not of course foreclose such judicial or legislative action in appropriate situations by concluding that this controversy over burden of proof and good faith represents too essentially a private transaction not to be dealt with by the local law of Pennsylvania where the transactions took place.

Id. at 33-34 (emphasis added).

In *Miree v. DeKalb County*, 433 U.S. 25 (1977), the Court reaffirmed the approach taken in *Parnell* by refusing to develop federal common law to govern a dispute between victims of a plane crash and the municipality that operated an airport. The plaintiffs argued they were entitled to recover as third-party beneficiaries of a contract between the municipality and the Federal Aviation Administration. The FAA contract allegedly required that the municipality comply with safety measures that would have prevented the crash.

The Court in *Miree* refused to develop a common-law rule and also concluded that any federal interest implicated by the dispute was too remote to justify development of such a rule. The Solicitor General had informed the Court that resolution of the private-party dispute would have *no* effect on the plaintiffs' separate claim against the United States under federal law (the Federal Tort Claims Act (FTCA), 28 U.S.C. § 1346). The Court concluded:

> The question of whether petitioners may sue respondent does not require decision under federal common law since the litigation is among private parties and no substantial rights or duties of the United States hinge on its outcome. On the other hand, nothing we say here forecloses the applicability of federal common law in interpreting the rights and duties of the United States under federal contracts.

433 U.S. at 31.

The Court acknowledged that the absence of the United States as a litigant did not preclude it from fashioning a common-law rule. But to justify such rulemaking, the Court required a strong showing that state law was in "significant conflict" with federal policy:

> "In deciding whether rules of federal common law should be fashioned, normally the guiding principle is that a significant conflict between some federal policy or interest and the use of state law in the premises must first be specifically shown. It is by no means enough that, as we may assume, Congress could under the Constitution readily enact a complete code of law governing transactions in federal mineral leases among private parties. Whether latent federal power should be exercised to displace state law is primarily a decision for Congress."

Id. at 31-32. Is the Court's approach in *Miree* an example of Professor Mishkin's issue-specific interstitial lawmaking?

The Court's later decision *Boyle v. United Technologies Corp.*, 487 U.S. 500 (1988), illustrates the less common situation where the strength of federal policy supports displacement of state law in private-party litigation. *Boyle* presented the question whether state law should govern the liability of a private contractor who provided the U.S. military equipment in conformity with federal specifications.

The defendant had provided helicopters to the Navy whose defectively designed escape hatch had led to the death of a pilot. Based on Virginia state law, a jury found the military contractor liable for its defective design.

On appeal, a divided Supreme Court held that state law was displaced and, as a matter of federal common law, the defendant was not liable. In reaching its decision, the majority was required to explain why, despite the absence of federal statutory defense and the absence of the United States as a party to the case, federal law displaced state law. The sharp disagreement between the majority and the dissent illuminates some of the contemporary features of both federal common law and preemption doctrine.

Under modern preemption doctrine, state law may be preempted in three situations. First Congress may *expressly* preempt state law, a form of preemption we return to later. Second, Congress may *impliedly* preempt state law by "occupying a field" of legal regulation. Third, federal law may preempt state law because there is "irreconcilable conflict" between the laws.[100] The third form of preemption usually turns on an analysis of the specific laws and specific issue presented to the court. This is the form of preemption argued in *Boyle.*

Some additional background information will help in your reading of *Boyle.* First, although the United States has waived its sovereign immunity for the negligence of federal employees under the FTCA, the Court has interpreted the Act to deny a cause of action for military personnel injured during the course of military service. This immunity is styled the "*Feres* doctrine." *See Feres v. United States,* 340 U.S 135 (1950). But the doctrine does not directly apply to suits against private parties like military contractors. Second, even when the United States is otherwise liable under the FTCA, liability does not extend to negligence related to officials' "discretionary" functions. *See* 28 U.S.C. § 2680(a).

BOYLE v. UNITED TECHNOLOGIES CORP.

487 U.S. 500 (1988)

JUSTICE SCALIA delivered the opinion of the Court.

* * * *

Petitioner's broadest contention is that, in the absence of legislation specifically immunizing Government contractors from liability for design defects, there is no basis for judicial recognition of such a defense. We disagree. In most fields of activity, to be sure, this Court has refused to find federal preemption of state law in the absence of either a clear statutory prescription, or a direct conflict between federal and state law. But we have held that a few areas, involving "uniquely federal interests," are so committed by the Constitution and laws of the United States to federal control that state law is pre-empted and replaced, where necessary, by federal law of a content prescribed (absent explicit statutory directive) by the courts — so-called "federal common law." [Citing, among other cases, *Kimbell Foods, Clearfield Trust,* and *Sabbatino.*]

The dispute in the present case borders upon two areas that we have found to involve such "uniquely federal interests." We have held that obligations to and rights of the United States under its contracts are governed exclusively by federal law. The present case does not involve an obligation to the United States under

100. *See generally Barnett Bank of Marion Cnty., N.A. v. Nelson,* 517 U.S. 25, 31 (1996).

its contract, but rather liability to third persons. That liability may be styled one in tort, but it arises out of performance of the contract.

Another area that we have found to be of peculiarly federal concern, warranting the displacement of state law, is the civil liability of federal officials for actions taken in the course of their duty. We have held in many contexts that the scope of that liability is controlled by federal law. The present case involves an independent contractor performing its obligation under a procurement contract, rather than an official performing his duty as a federal employee, but there is obviously implicated the same interest in getting the Government's work done.

We think the reasons for considering these closely related areas to be of "uniquely federal" interest apply as well to the civil liabilities arising out of the performance of federal procurement contracts. We have come close to holding as much. In Yearsley v. W.A. Ross Construction Co., 309 U.S. 18 (1940), we rejected an attempt by a landowner to hold a construction contractor liable under state law for the erosion of 95 acres caused by the contractor's work in constructing dikes for the Government. We said that "if [the] authority to carry out the project was validly conferred, that is, if what was done was within the constitutional power of Congress, there is no liability on the part of the contractor for executing its will." The federal interest justifying this holding surely exists as much in procurement contracts as in performance contracts; we see no basis for a distinction.

Moreover, it is plain that the Federal Government's interest in the procurement of equipment is implicated by suits such as the present one — even though the dispute is one between private parties. It is true that where "litigation is purely between private parties and does not touch the rights and duties of the United States" federal law does not govern. Thus, for example, in Miree v. DeKalb County, which involved the question whether certain private parties could sue as third-party beneficiaries to an agreement between a municipality and the Federal Aviation Administration, we found that state law was not displaced because "the operations of the United States in connection with FAA grants such as these . . . would [not] be burdened" by allowing state law to determine whether third-party beneficiaries could sue, and because "any federal interest in the outcome of the [dispute] before us '[was] far too speculative, far too remote a possibility to justify the application of federal law to transactions essentially of local concern.'" But the same is not true here. The imposition of liability on Government contractors will directly affect the terms of Government contracts: either the contractor will decline to manufacture the design specified by the Government, or it will raise its price. Either way, the interests of the United States will be directly affected.

That the procurement of equipment by the United States is an area of uniquely federal interest does not, however, end the inquiry. That merely establishes a necessary, not a sufficient, condition for the displacement of state law. Displacement will occur only where, as we have variously described, a "significant conflict" exists between an identifiable "federal policy or interest and the [operation] of state law," or the application of state law would "frustrate specific objectives" of federal legislation [citing *Kimbell Foods*]. The conflict with federal policy need not be as sharp as that which must exist for ordinary pre-emption when Congress legislates "in a field which the States have traditionally occupied." Or to put the point differently, the fact that the area in question is one of unique federal concern changes what would otherwise be a conflict that cannot produce pre-emption into one that can. But conflict there must be. In some cases, for example where the federal interest requires a uniform rule, the entire body of state law applicable to the area conflicts and is replaced by federal rules. See, e.g., *Clearfield Trust* (rights and obligations of United States with respect to commercial paper must be governed by uniform federal rule). In others, the conflict is more narrow, and only particular elements of state law are superseded. See, e.g., *Little Lake Misere Land Co.* (even assuming state law should generally govern federal land acquisitions, particular state law at issue may not).[101]

In *Miree*, the suit was not seeking to impose upon the person contracting with the Government a duty contrary to the duty imposed by the Government contract. Rather, it was the contractual duty itself that the private plaintiff (as third-party beneficiary) sought to enforce. Between *Miree* and the present case, it is easy to conceive of an intermediate situation, in which the duty sought to be imposed on the contractor is not identical to one assumed under the contract, but is also not contrary to any assumed. If, for example, the United States contracts for the purchase and installation of an air conditioning-unit, specifying the cooling capacity but not the precise manner of construction, a state law imposing upon the manufacturer of such units a duty of care to include a certain safety feature would not be a duty identical to anything promised the Government, but neither would it be contrary. The contractor could comply with both its contractual obligations and the state-prescribed duty of care. No one suggests that state law would generally be pre-empted in this context.

The present case, however, is at the opposite extreme from *Miree*. Here the state-imposed duty of care that is the asserted basis of the contractor's liability (specifically, the duty to equip helicopters with the sort of escape-hatch mechanism petitioner claims was necessary) is precisely contrary to the duty imposed by the Government contract (the duty to manufacture and deliver helicopters with the sort of escape-hatch mechanism shown by the specifications). Even in this sort of situation, it would be unreasonable to say that there is always a "significant conflict" between the state law and a federal policy or interest. If, for example, a federal procurement officer orders, by model number, a quantity of stock helicopters that happen to be equipped with escape hatches opening outward, it is impossible to say that the Government has a significant interest in that particular feature. That would be scarcely more reasonable than saying that a private individual who orders such a craft by model number cannot sue for the manufacturer's negligence because he got precisely what he ordered.

In its search for the limiting principle to identify those situations in which a "significant conflict" with federal policy or interests does arise, the Court of Appeals, in the lead case upon which its opinion here relied, identified as the source of the conflict the *Feres* doctrine, under which the Federal Tort Claims Act (FTCA) does not cover injuries to Armed Services personnel in the course of

101. [Footnote 3 in Court's opinion.] We refer here to the displacement of state law, although it is possible to analyze it as the displacement of federal-law reference to state law for the rule of decision. Some of our cases appear to regard the area in which a uniquely federal interest exists as being entirely governed by federal law, with federal law deigning to "borro[w]," or "incorporat[e]" or "adopt," United States v. Kimbell Foods, Inc., state law except where a significant conflict with federal policy exists. We see nothing to be gained by expanding the theoretical scope of the federal pre-emption beyond its practical effect, and so adopt the more modest terminology. If the distinction between displacement of state law and displacement of federal law's incorporation of state law ever makes a practical difference, it at least does not do so in the present case.

military service. Military contractor liability would conflict with this doctrine, the Fourth Circuit reasoned, since the increased cost of the contractor's tort liability would be added to the price of the contract, and "[s]uch pass-through costs would . . . defeat the purpose of the immunity for military accidents conferred upon the government itself." Other courts upholding the defense have embraced similar reasoning. We do not adopt this analysis because it seems to us that the *Feres* doctrine, in its application to the present problem, logically produces results that are in some respects too broad and in some respects too narrow. Too broad, because if the Government contractor defense is to prohibit suit against the manufacturer whenever *Feres* would prevent suit against the Government, then even injuries caused to military personnel by a helicopter purchased from stock (in our example above), or by any standard equipment purchased by the Government, would be covered. Since *Feres* prohibits all service-related tort claims against the Government, a contractor defense that rests upon it should prohibit all service-related tort claims against the manufacturer — making inexplicable the three limiting criteria for contractor immunity (which we will discuss presently) that the Court of Appeals adopted. On the other hand, reliance on *Feres* produces (or logically should produce) results that are in another respect too narrow. Since that doctrine covers only service-related injuries, and not injuries caused by the military to civilians, it could not be invoked to prevent, for example, a civilian's suit against the manufacturer of fighter planes, based on a state tort theory, claiming harm from what is alleged to be needlessly high levels of noise produced by the jet engines. Yet we think that the character of the jet engines the Government orders for its fighter planes cannot be regulated by state tort law, no more in suits by civilians than in suits by members of the Armed Services.

There is, however, a statutory provision that demonstrates the potential for, and suggests the outlines of, "significant conflict" between federal interests and state law in the context of Government procurement. In the FTCA, Congress authorized damages to be recovered against the United States for harm caused by the negligent or wrongful conduct of Government employees, to the extent that a private person would be liable under the law of the place where the conduct occurred. 28 U.S.C. § 1346(b). It excepted from this consent to suit, however,

> "[a]ny claim . . . based upon the exercise or performance or the failure to exercise or perform a discretionary function or duty on the part of a federal agency or an employee of the Government, whether or not the discretion involved be abused." 28 U.S.C. § 2680(a).

We think that the selection of the appropriate design for military equipment to be used by our Armed Forces is assuredly a discretionary function within the meaning of this provision. It often involves not merely engineering analysis but judgment as to the balancing of many technical, military, and even social considerations, including specifically the trade-off between greater safety and greater combat effectiveness. And we are further of the view that permitting "second-guessing" of these judgments, through state tort suits against contractors would produce the same effect sought to be avoided by the FTCA exemption. The financial burden of judgments against the contractors would ultimately be passed through, substantially if not totally, to the United States itself, since defense contractors will predictably raise their prices to cover, or to insure against, contingent liability for the Government-ordered designs. To put the point differently: It makes little sense to insulate the Government against financial liability for the judgment that a particular feature of military equipment is necessary when the Government produces the equipment itself, but not when it contracts for the production. In sum, we are of the view that state law which holds Government contractors liable for design defects in military equipment does in some circumstances present a "significant conflict" with federal policy and must be displaced.

Liability for design defects in military equipment cannot be imposed, pursuant to state law, when (1) the United States approved reasonably precise specifications; (2) the equipment conformed to those specifications; and (3) the supplier warned the United States about the dangers in the use of the equipment that were known to the supplier but not to the United States. The first two of these conditions assure that the suit is within the area where the policy of the "discretionary function" would be frustrated—i.e., they assure that the design feature in question was considered by a Government officer, and not merely by the contractor itself. The third condition is necessary because, in its absence, the displacement of state tort law would create some incentive for the manufacturer to withhold knowledge of risks, since conveying that knowledge might disrupt the contract but withholding it would produce no liability. We adopt this provision lest our effort to protect discretionary functions perversely impede them by cutting off information highly relevant to the discretionary decision.

* * * *

Accordingly, the judgment is vacated and the case is remanded.

JUSTICE BRENNAN, with whom JUSTICE MARSHALL and JUSTICE BLACKMUN join, dissenting.

* * * *

In my view, this Court lacks both authority and expertise to fashion such a rule, whether to protect the Treasury of the United States or the coffers of industry. Because I would leave that exercise of legislative power to Congress, where our Constitution places it, I would reverse the Court of Appeals and reinstate petitioner's jury award.

* * * *

In pronouncing that "[t]here is no federal general common law," *Erie* put to rest the notion that the grant of diversity jurisdiction to federal courts is itself authority to fashion rules of substantive law. As the author of today's opinion for the Court pronounced for a unanimous Court just two months ago, "we start with the assumption that the historic police powers of the States were not to be superseded . . . unless that was the clear and manifest purpose of Congress." Just as "[t]here is no federal pre-emption in *vacuo,* without a constitutional text or a federal statute to assert it," federal common law cannot supersede state law in *vacuo* out of no more than an idiosyncratic determination by five Justices that a particular area is "uniquely federal."

Accordingly, we have emphasized that federal common law can displace state law in "few and restricted" instances. "[A]bsent some congressional authorization to formulate substantive rules of decision, federal common law exists only in such narrow areas as those concerned with the rights and obligations of the United States, interstate and international disputes implicating conflicting rights of States or our relations with foreign nations, and admiralty cases." "The enactment of a federal rule in an area of national concern, and the decision whether to displace state law in doing so, is generally made not by the federal judiciary, purposefully insulated from democratic pressures, but by the people through their elected representatives in Congress." State laws "should be overridden by the federal courts only where clear and substantial interests of the National Government, which cannot be served consistently with respect for such state interests, will suffer major damage if the state law is applied."

Congress has not decided to supersede state law here (if anything, it has decided not to) and the Court does not pretend that its newly manufactured "Government contractor defense" fits within any of the handful of "narrow areas," of "uniquely federal interests" in which we have heretofore done so. Rather, the Court creates a new category of "uniquely federal interests" out of a synthesis of two whose origins predate *Erie* itself: the interest in administering the "obligations to and rights of the United States under its contracts," and the interest in regulating the "civil liability of federal officials for actions taken in the course of their duty." This case is, however, simply a suit between two private parties. We have steadfastly declined to impose federal contract law on relationships that are collateral to a federal contract, or to extend the federal employee's immunity beyond federal employees. And the Court's ability to list 2, or 10, inapplicable areas of "uniquely federal interest" does not support its conclusion that the liability of Government contractors is so "clear and substantial" an interest that this Court must step in lest state law does "major damage."

The proposition that federal common law continues to govern the "obligations to and rights of the United States under its contracts" is nearly as old as *Erie* itself. Federal law typically controls when the Federal Government is a party to a suit involving its rights or obligations under a contract, whether the contract entails procurement, a conveyance of property, or a commercial instrument issued by the Government, or assigned to it. Any such transaction necessarily "radiate[s] interests in transactions between private parties." But it is by now established that our power to create federal common law controlling the Federal Government's contractual rights and obligations does not translate into a power to prescribe rules that cover all transactions or contractual relationships collateral to Government contracts.

* * * *

Here, as in *Miree, Parnell,* and *Wallis,* a Government contract governed by federal common law looms in the background. But here, too, the United States is not a party to the suit and the suit neither "touch[es] the rights and duties of the United States," nor has a "direct effect upon the United States or its Treasury," The relationship at issue is at best collateral to the Government contract. We have no greater power to displace state law governing the collateral relationship in the Government procurement realm than we had to dictate federal rules governing equally collateral relationships in the areas of aviation, Government-issued commercial paper, or federal lands.

That the Government might have to pay higher prices for what it orders if delivery in accordance with the contract exposes the seller to potential liability, does not distinguish this case. Each of the cases just discussed declined to extend the reach of federal common law despite the assertion of comparable interests that would have affected the terms of the Government contract—whether its price or its substance—just as "directly" (or indirectly). Third-party beneficiaries can sue under a county's contract with the FAA, for example, even though—as the Court's focus on the absence of "direct effect on the United States or its Treasury," suggests—counties will likely pass on the costs to the Government in future contract negotiations. Similarly, we held that state law may govern the circumstances under which stolen federal bonds can be recovered, notwithstanding Parnell's argument that "the value of bonds to the first purchaser and hence their salability by the Government would be materially affected." As in each of the cases declining to extend the traditional reach of federal law of contracts beyond the rights and duties of the Federal Government, "any federal interest in the outcome of the question before us 'is far too speculative, far too remote a possibility to justify the application of federal law to transactions essentially of local concern."

At bottom, the Court's analysis is premised on the proposition that any tort liability indirectly absorbed by the Government so burdens governmental functions as to compel us to act when Congress has not. That proposition is by no means uncontroversial. The tort system is premised on the assumption that the imposition of liability encourages actors to prevent any injury whose expected cost exceeds the cost of prevention. If the system is working as it should, Government contractors will design equipment to avoid certain injuries (like the deaths of soldiers or Government employees), which would be certain to burden the Government. The Court therefore has no basis for its assumption that tort liability will result in a net burden on the Government (let alone a clearly excessive net burden) rather than a net gain.

Perhaps tort liability is an inefficient means of ensuring the quality of design efforts, but "[w]hatever the merits of the policy" the Court wishes to implement, "its conversion into law is a proper subject for congressional action, not for any creative power of ours." It is, after all, "Congress, not this Court or the other federal courts, [that] is the custodian of the national purse. By the same token [Congress] is the primary and most often the exclusive arbiter of federal fiscal affairs. And these comprehend, as we have said, securing the treasury or the Government against financial losses however inflicted . . ." If Congress shared the Court's assumptions and conclusion it could readily enact "A BILL [t]o place limitations on the civil liability of government contractors to ensure that such liability does not impede the ability of the United States to procure necessary goods and services." It has not.

Were I a legislator, I would probably vote against any law absolving multibillion dollar private enterprises from answering for their tragic mistakes, at least if that law were justified by no more than the unsupported speculation that their liability might ultimately burden the United States Treasury. Some of my colleagues here would evidently vote otherwise (as they have here), but that should not matter here. We are judges not legislators, and the vote is not ours to cast.

I respectfully dissent.

JUSTICE STEVENS, dissenting.

When judges are asked to embark on a lawmaking venture, I believe they should carefully consider whether they, or a legislative body, are better equipped to perform the task at hand. There are instances of so-called interstitial lawmaking that inevitably become part of the judicial process. But when we are asked to create an entirely new doctrine—to answer "questions of policy on which Congress has not spoken,"—we have a special duty to identify the proper decisionmaker before trying to make the proper decision.

When the novel question of policy involves a balancing of the conflicting interests in the efficient operation of a massive governmental program and the protection of the rights of the individual—whether in the social welfare context, the civil service context, or the military procurement context—I feel very deeply that we should defer to the expertise of the Congress.

* * * *

DISCUSSION AND QUESTIONS

To begin with, consider the following questions concerning the decision in *Boyle*:

1. What is the federal rule announced in *Boyle*? In stating the rule, make sure you are clear about whether *Boyle* (a) announces a limited federal cause of action against military contractors, or (b) announces a federal defense to causes of action derived from some other source.
2. Can you identify in *Boyle* a structured answer to the question, when do federal courts have authority to develop common-law rules? Do the majority and dissent agree on the answer but disagree on how it applies to the controversy at issue?

The majority in *Boyle* describes the issue as largely one of federal "preemption." The dissent is more explicit that the issue is one of common-lawmaking authority. How do preemption and common lawmaking differ? *Do* they ultimately differ?

The dissent quotes Justice Scalia in an earlier opinion where he commented, "[W]e start with the assumption that the historic police powers of the States were not to be superseded . . . unless that was the clear and manifest purpose of Congress." Justice Scalia is well known as an advocate of the view that the Court's principal task in interpreting legislation is to enforce the meaning of statutory text. Has Justice Scalia been true to his philosophy in *Boyle*? Should he have simply emphasized his misgivings about the imposition of state-law liability on military contractors and pointed out the need for *congressional* legislation immunizing them?

At the same time, is the dissent insisting on some clear declaration of common-lawmaking authority while overlooking the absence of such a declaration in prior decisions? Were the "uniquely federal interests" present in *Clearfield Trust* and *Kimbell Foods* more compelling than those in *Boyle*?

Since *Boyle*, the Court has been highly reluctant to develop federal common law when the rights and duties of the United States are collateral to a legal dispute. For example, in *Atherton v. FDIC*, 519 U.S. 213 (1997), the Court declined to develop federal common-law rules to govern the liability of officers and directors of federally insured savings institutions. The majority's summary description of the relative role of state law and federal common law is revealing:

> This Court has recently discussed what one might call "federal common law" in the strictest sense, *i.e.*, a rule of decision that amounts, not simply to an interpretation of a federal statute or a properly promulgated administrative rule, but, rather, to the judicial "creation" of a special federal rule of decision. The Court has said that "cases in which judicial creation of a special federal rule would be justified . . . are . . . 'few and restricted.'" Whether latent federal power should be exercised to displace state law is primarily a decision for Congress, not the federal courts. Nor does the

> existence of related federal statutes automatically show that Congress intended courts to create federal common law rules, for Congress acts . . . against the background of the total *corpus juris* of the states. . . . Thus, normally, when courts decide to fashion rules of federal common law, the guiding principle is that a significant conflict between some federal policy or interest and the use of state law . . . must first be specifically shown. Indeed, such a "conflict" is normally a "precondition."

Id. at 218.

PROBLEM 11-3

Who's in Charge?

In 2006, a regional office of the Federal General Services Administration (GSA) contracted with Wheeled Coach to provide ambulances to service VA hospitals in several midwest states. Wheeled Coach provided the ambulances, which were modified in significant ways to comply with the VA's specified requirements.

In 2008, a patient was injured when a VA ambulance collided with an automobile in Kansas City, Kansas. The patient subsequently sued Wheeled Coach under Kansas law, arguing that the company's failure to comply with Kansas's statutes regulating air bags on emergency vehicles constituted "negligence per se." Wheeled Coach has now moved to dismiss the suit based on the argument that it fully complied with the VA's contractual requirements and they said nothing about air bag requirements. Based on the Court's decision in *Boyle,* Wheeled Coach argues that it has a federal common-law, "contractor" defense to the plaintiff's claim.

Does *Boyle* support the defense alleged by Wheeled Coach?

REVIEW AND CONSOLIDATION

"Conventional" Enclaves of Federal Common Law

Common-lawmaking authority is most settled in these areas:

- Disputes in admiralty
- Disputes between states
- Disputes affecting foreign relations
- Disputes involving the United States' proprietary rights

Regarding common lawmaking when the United States' proprietary rights are in dispute, unresolved issues include the following:

- Is the Court's current working presumption—that state law governs the United States' proprietary rights unless it conflicts with a demonstrable federal interest—itself working?
- When the Court applies state law, is it "adopting" state law as the federal rule or simply applying state law? Does the suggested difference matter?

4. *Congressional Directives on Choosing the Applicable Rule of Decision*

We have seen a variety of perspectives on the relationship of federal statutes and state law. The working presumption, according to the Court, is that state law continues to operate even when federal law addresses the same subject. Further, state law is often adopted to fill in gaps found in federal law (i.e., interstitial lawmaking). In some situations, however, state law is preempted by federal law based on the conclusion that state law is incompatible with federal policy. When state law is preempted, federal courts may be called on to develop a distinct federal common-law rule to effectuate statutory policy.

Throughout its history, the Court has acknowledged Congress' ultimate authority to *choose* how its laws interface with state law. Congress sometimes exercises that authority by giving explicit directions about the interrelationship between federal and state law. At other times, the Court concludes that Congress has exercised this authority by implication. Let's consider examples of how Congress has expressly or impliedly given directives on the use of state law.

a. Preempting, Saving, and Adopting State Law

Congress sometimes declares expressly the extent to which its enactments *preempt* related state law.[102] Consider 15 U.S.C. § 4406(b), regulating smokeless tobacco. Section 4406(b) provides that "no statement relating to the use of smokeless tobacco products and health . . . shall be required by any State or local statute or regulation to be included on any package or in any advertisement" other than the statement specifically endorsed by Congress. At the same time, § 4406(c) declares that "nothing in this chapter shall relieve any person from liability at common law or under State statutory law to any other person." This "savings" provision in § 4406(c) is perhaps the most frequent type of reference to state common law found in federal statutes.[103]

At other times, Congress expressly *adopts* state law to accomplish its legislative goals. For example, Congress has directed that courts use state law when enforcing federal civil rights laws. Title 42 U.S.C. § 1988(a) states that, when federal laws are "not adapted" to the purposes of civil rights enforcement or are "deficient," "the common law, as modified and changed by the constitution and statutes of the State" where a case is pending "shall govern" "so far as the same is not inconsistent" with federal law.[104] Another example is the FTCA, discussed in *Boyle v. United Technologies.* The FTCA states that the United States is liable for the negligence of its employees acting within the scope of their employment "if a private person would be liable . . . in accordance with the law of the place [i.e., state] where the act or omission occurred." 28 U.S.C. § 2672.

102. *See, e.g.*, 15 U.S.C. § 78bb(4)(1) (preempting certain class actions for securities fraud based on "the statutory or common law of any State or subdivision"); 17 U.S.C. § 301 (preempting state common law governing federal copyright).

103. *See, e.g.*, 15 U.S.C. § 2072 (providing that statutory liability for violations of consumer product safety requirements does not preempt "other remedies provided by common law or under Federal or State law").

104. See Chapter 10.

Another illustration of congressional adoption of state common law is found in the Federal Rules of Evidence. Rule 501 states that, "in civil actions and proceedings, with respect to an element of a claim or defense as to which State law supplies the rule of decision, the privilege of a witness, person, government, State, or political subdivision thereof shall be determined in accordance with State law." Congress' borrowing of state law under Rule 501 reflects deference to federalism concerns: "the rationale underlying the proviso is that federal law should not supersede that of the States in substantive areas such as privilege absent a compelling reason."[105]

b. Express Authorization of Federal Common Lawmaking

In a small number of settings, Congress has expressly declared that the federal courts are to develop federal common law to implement federal statutes. Federal Rule of Evidence 501 again provides a useful illustration. When applying substantive federal law, federal courts are told that the privileges enjoyed by parties and witnesses are to be governed "by the principles of the common law as they may be interpreted by the courts of the United States in the light of reason and experience." Rule 501 affirms prior federal court practice, where the law of privilege was developed by federal courts through common-law rules.[106]

Another example of the express authorization of federal common lawmaking is found in statutes criminalizing violations of federal clean air standards. Title 42 U.S.C. § 4213(d) states that "all general defenses, affirmative defenses, and bars to prosecution that may apply with respect to other Federal criminal offenses may apply and shall be determined by the courts of the United States according to the principles of common law as they may be interpreted in the light of reason and experience." Although not frequent, other acts of Congress call for application of the "principles of common law" when interpreting federal statutes.[107]

One of the most controversial authorizations of "interstitial" federal common-lawmaking power is that found in 42 U.S.C. § 1988. Section 1988(a), referred to earlier, authorizes application of local common law to suits under § 1983 against local and state governmental defendants, except where this common law is inconsistent with federal policy.[108] The Court has explained how § 1988 is intended to operate:

> The century-old Civil Rights Acts do not contain every rule of decision required to adjudicate claims asserted under them. In the absence of specific guidance, Congress has directed federal courts to follow a three-step process to borrow an

105. *See* Committee report accompanying Federal Rule of Evidence 501.

106. *See, e.g., Stein v. Bowman*, 38 U.S. 209 (1839).

107. *See also* 12 U.S.C. § 1789(a)(1) (federal common law to govern agency actions to enforce laws governing federal credit unions"); 12 U.S.C. § 2279aa-14(2) (agency actions to enforce federal farm-credit laws, "to the extent applicable, shall be deemed to be governed by Federal common law"); 42 U.S.C. § 6928(f)(4) (criminal prosecution to enforce hazardous waste management laws "shall be determined by the courts of the United States according to the principles of common law as they may be interpreted in the light of reason and experience").

108. Section 1988 provides that, when federal law does not provide an adequate governing rule, "the common law, as modified and changed by the constitution and statutes of the State wherein the court having jurisdiction of such civil or criminal cause is held, so far as the same is not inconsistent with the Constitution and laws of the United States, shall be extended to and govern the said courts in the trial and disposition of the cause. . . ."

> appropriate rule. First, courts are to look to the laws of the United States "so far as such laws are suitable to carry [the civil and criminal civil rights statutes] into effect." If no suitable federal rule exists, courts undertake the second step by considering application of state "common law, as modified and changed by the constitution and statutes" of the forum State. A third step asserts the predominance of the federal interest: courts are to apply state law only if it is not "inconsistent with the Constitution and laws of the United States.

Burnett v. Grattan, 486 U.S. 42, 47 (1984).

As discussed in Chapter 10, the Court's use of state common law under § 1988 defies predictability. At times, the Court has considered legislative history and nineteenth-century common law to infer congressional intent, thus developing a federal rule purportedly based on an "interpretation" of federal law. At other times, the Court has adopted local state common law to "fill the gaps" in § 1983. And yet at other times, the Court has self-consciously developed a rule of decision based on its conception of sound policy, that is, it has developed federal common law. Thus, this important area of "interstitial" law development is often controversial and unpredictable, notwithstanding the Court's assertion that it follows a specific methodology like that described in *Burnett.*[109]

c. Implied Authorization of Federal Common Lawmaking

Even in the absence of express authorization to develop common-law rules, the Court has occasionally inferred such authorization. The leading case is *Textile Workers Union of America v. Lincoln Mills*, 353 U.S. 448 (1957).[110] In *Lincoln Mills* the Court examined the legislative history of section 301 of the Taft-Hartley Act, which confers federal jurisdiction over labor-management contracts affecting interstate commerce, and concluded that Congress intended that federal courts develop common law to implement statutory policy. Perhaps significantly, the majority opinion in *Lincoln Mills* was written by Justice Douglas, who also wrote the majority opinion in *Clearfield Trust.* As in *Clearfield Trust,* Justice Douglas showed little hesitation in finding authority to develop common-law rules: "It is not uncommon for federal courts to fashion federal law where federal rights are concerned. See *Clearfield Trust Co. v. United States.* . . . Congress has indicated by § 301(a) the purpose to follow that course here." 353 U.S. at 457. In dissent, Justice Frankfurter sharply criticized the majority's conclusion that a "clear" authorization to develop federal common law emerged from "the somewhat, to say the least, cloudy and confusing legislative history. This is more than can be fairly asked even from the alchemy of construction." *Id.* at 462.

Another highly significant area of federal common lawmaking today exists under ERISA (the Employee Retirement and Income Security Act). In ERISA, Congress expressly stated that its provisions governing employee benefit plans

109. *See generally,* Seth F. Kreimer, *The Source of Law in Civil Rights Actions: Some Old Light on Section 1988,* 133 U. Pa. L. Rev. 601 (1985). One of the conceptual difficulties with the "borrowing" of local state law is that the Congress enacting § 1983 had grave misgivings about the states' propensity to enforce federal law. *See id.* at 616. For this reason, Professor Kreimer argues that "[t]he 1871 Congress itself manifested a preference for the common law power of federal courts to adjust the framework of the law to meet the problems of the changing society." *Id.* at 633.

110. *Textile Workers* is discussed more fully in Chapter 5.

"shall supersede any and all state laws" pertaining to such plans,[111] while "saving" state law governing "insurance, banking, or securities."[112] In *Pilot Life Insurance Co. v. Dedeaux,* 482 U.S. 44, 55-56 (1987), the Court concluded that ERISA authorized the development of a federal common law of rights and duties. The Court heavily relied on legislative history, in which members of Congress repeatedly observed that ERISA was to be construed similarly to section 301 of the Taft-Hartley Act, the statute found to authorize common lawmaking in *Lincoln Mills. See id.* at 54-57.

The Court has found an implied common-lawmaking authority under the Sherman Antitrust Act, which broadly prohibits, *inter alia,* "restraints on trade." 15 U.S.C. § 1. As the Court remarked in *National Society of Professional Engineers v. United States,* 435 U.S. 679, 688 (1978), "Congress . . . did not intend the text of the Sherman Act to delineate the full meaning of the statute or its application in concrete situations. The legislative history makes it perfectly clear that it expected the courts to give shape to the statute's broad mandate by drawing on common law tradition."[113]

Finally, in *Kiobel v. Royal Dutch Petroleum Co.,* 133 S. Ct. 1659 (2013), the Court affirmed that Congress conferred a limited common-lawmaking power on federal district courts when it granted them "original jurisdiction of any civil action by an alien for a tort only, committed in violation of the law of nations or a treaty of the United States." 28 U.S.C. § 1350. This statute, known as the Alien Tort Statute, gave the courts power to recognize a cause of action to recover for violations of a "modest" number of international law violations. 133 S. Ct. at 1663. But in *Kiobel,* the Court held that Congress did not intend that the courts recognize a cause of action for claims arising from conduct outside United States' territory.

The federal courts' common-lawmaking authority under the Taft-Hartley Act, ERISA, the Sherman Act, and the Alien Tort Statute goes beyond the type of issue-specific "interstitial" rulemaking referred to earlier. Common lawmaking under these important federal laws shares two characteristics distinguishing it from conventional "interstitial" lawmaking. First, the authority to develop common law is traced to specific evidence of congressional intent, most often legislative history. Second, the inferred congressional authorization extends to common lawmaking covering a wide subject area, not a mere "gap filling."

American Electric Power Co. v. Connecticut, 131 S. Ct. 2527 (2011), illustrates how, in other statutory settings, federal legislation preempts the federal courts' authority to make common law. In *American Electric,* the Court rejected the

111. 29 U.S.C. § 1144(a).

112. 29 U.S.C. § 1144(b)(2)(A).

113. The most recent example of inferred congressional authorization of common law is *Sosa v. Alvarez-Machain,* 542 U.S. 692 (2004). In *Sosa,* the Court considered whether the Alien Tort Statute, 28 U.S.C. § 1350, a jurisdictional statute included in the Judiciary Act of 1789, authorized relief on behalf of a Mexican national who had been kidnapped by federal authorities to be tried based on his involvement in the murder of a DEA agent. The Court concluded that the first Congress had authorized jurisdiction under this statute to enforce a limited number of rights recognized by the "law of nations" (a form of common law in the *Swift* sense of the term). The Court further concluded that it had a tightly constrained power to develop common-law rules to implement the Alien Tort Statute, based in large part on "the current state of international law." *Id.* at 733. In the course of its opinion, the Court took pains to emphasize—in response to the concurring opinion of Justice Scalia—that *Erie* permits "limited enclaves in which federal courts may derive some substantive law in a common law way." *Id.* at 729.

attempt by numerous plaintiffs (including states) to maintain a federal common-law action against electric companies whose emissions of carbon dioxide allegedly contributed to global warming and constituted an interstate nuisance. The Court held that the Clean Air Act delegated control over such emissions to the EPA, thus preempting judicial recognition of common-law claims. At the same time, the Court declined to decide whether the statutory scheme also preempted state law.

EXPLORING DOCTRINE

The Significance of Congressional Authorization

In this subsection we have identified examples of Congress' express and implied directions concerning the rules of decision to be applied when implementing federal legislation. In these examples, Congress has given guidance on such issues as the borrowing of state law, the preemption of state law, and the development of federal common law.

Do these examples of congressional direction have any implications for the federal courts' willingness to infer common-lawmaking authority *without* such direction? Could it be argued that, lacking some form of congressional direction, the federal courts should simply refer to state law, the background "corpus juris" against which Congress legislates? Or is Professor Mishkin correct when he argues that Congress is institutionally incapable of foreseeing all issues that might arise under statutory schemes, thus making it the "responsibility" of federal courts to fill unexpected gaps even where Congress has not authorized such gap filling?

REVIEW AND CONSOLIDATION

Common Lawmaking to Implement Federal Statutes

In addition to exercising their authority to develop common law in designated "enclaves," federal courts may be called upon to develop rules to implement specific federal statutes. This power may be based on

- Express congressional authorization,
- Implied congressional authorization, or
- Perceived necessity (i.e., Mishkin's "interstitial" lawmaking).

The distinction between "interstitial" lawmaking and statutory construction or interpretation is not always clear. Indeed, the very distinction remains controversial.

5. *Federal Court Authority to Develop Remedial Provisions for the Enforcement of Federal Statutes*

The federal courts have often been called upon to engage in interstitial law-making when filling in the *remedial* gaps in federal statutes. Federal statutes frequently fail to address specific remedial issues that arise in the statutes' implementation. Examples of remedial gaps include the failure to specify how much time a plaintiff has to file a claim under federal law, what pre-suit action is required before filing a claim,[114] which party bears the burden of proof on statutory elements,[115] and what standard of care governs compliance with statutory duties.[116]

It is undisputed that the remedial rules to be applied when implementing *federal* statutes are "federal" in nature, whether the rules are derived from state law or some other source.[117] *Erie*'s concern with the federal courts' authority to displace "substantive" state law is not relevant. The issues that typically arises when federal courts are asked to fill a remedial gap in federal statutes are *whether* and *how* to fill the gap.

Sometimes the Court employs rules of statutory construction and finds, by inference, that a statute actually contains a rule to fill the remedial gap.[118] At other times the Court fills the remedial gap by discovering the appropriate rule in some related federal law (e.g., a statute or procedural rule).[119] But where the gap cannot be filled by interpretation or construction of a federal statute, the Court often engages in some form of common lawmaking.[120]

When developing a remedial rule federal courts frequently recite a principle we have already examined, that Congress legislates "against the background of the total corpus juris of the states. . . ."[121] The working presumption is that state law will be adopted as the pertinent federal rule. Consider the Court's comments in *Kamen v. Kemper Financial Services, Inc.*, 500 U.S. 90, 98 (1991), made in the course of developing a "federal" remedial rule:

> It does not follow, however, that the content of such a rule must be wholly the product of a federal court's own devising. Our cases indicate that a court should endeavor to fill the interstices of federal remedial schemes with uniform federal rules only when the scheme in question evidences a distinct need for nationwide legal standards, see, *e.g.* Clearfield Trust Co. v. United States, or when express provisions in analogous statutory schemes embody congressional policy choices readily applicable to the matter at hand, see, *e.g.*, Boyle v. United Technologies

114. *See Kamen v. Kemper Fin. Servs., Inc.*, 500 U.S. 90 (1991).
115. *See Schaffer v. Weast*, 546 U.S. 49 (2005).
116. *See Atherton v. FDIC*, 519 U.S. 213 (1997).
117. *See, e.g., Kamen, supra*, 500 U.S. at 97.
118. For example, in *Schaffer, supra*, the Court concluded that Congress intended for courts to apply the traditional burden-of-proof requirement, which places that burden on the party seeking relief. 546 U.S. 57-58 ("Absent some reason to believe that Congress intended otherwise . . . we will conclude that the burden of persuasion lies where it usually falls, upon the party seeking relief.").
119. For example, in *Kamen, supra*, the Court had to determine whether Federal Rule 23.1, governing the pre-suit requirements in derivative actions, mandates that shareholders make a demand on a corporation before commencing a derivative action. The Court concluded that Rule 23.1 "does not create a demand requirement of any particular dimension," and so had to develop a common-law rule to govern the issue. 500 U.S. at 96-97.
120. Even when engaged in common lawmaking, the Court will frequently refer to inferred congressional intent to support either its exercise of lawmaking authority or its choice of the applicable rule. We examine this point shortly when we consider implied causes of action.
121. *Wallis v. Pan Am. Petroleum Corp.*, 384 U.S. 63, 68 (1963).

> Corp. Otherwise, we have indicated that federal courts should "incorporat[e] [state law] as the federal rule of decision," unless "application of [the particular] state law [in question] would frustrate specific objectives of the federal programs." *United States v. Kimbell Foods, Inc.* The presumption that state law should be incorporated into federal common law is particularly strong in areas in which private parties have entered legal relationships with the expectation that their rights and obligations would be governed by state-law standards.

Notice how the Court assimilates common-law precedent involving the United States' proprietary interests when discussing remedial rulemaking.

a. Statutes of Limitation

One of the recurring remedial issues confronted by the Court is the choice of a limitations period to govern how much time a party has to sue under federal law. As mentioned, the Court routinely infers that Congress wanted the courts to apply state law when "fashioning remedial details." When fashioning limitations rules the Court has "generally concluded that Congress intended that the courts apply the most closely analogous statute of limitations under state law."[122]

On some occasions, however, the Court concludes that state limitations law is unsuitable and instead adopts the limitations period found in a separate statute. The adoption of state limitations law may be unsuitable when there is need for a uniform limitations period or where application of state law would undermine federal policy in some other respect. For example, in Lampf, Pleva, Lipkind, Prupis & Petigrow v. Gilbertson, 501 U.S. 350 (1991), the Court adopted an analogous federal statute of limitations to govern securities fraud suits under Rule 10b-5 of the Securities Exchange Act of 1934. The Court declined to borrow state law because, among other things, (1) Rule 10b-5 addressed such diverse legal claims that a single state limitations statute was not well suited to the enforcement of federal law; (2) the diversity of federal claims remediable under Rule 10b-5 might lead to the application of differing state limitations periods within a single jurisdiction; and (3) violations of Rule 10b-5 are often "interstate" phenomena, presenting the possibility that plaintiffs could forum shop to obtain the most favorable state limitations period. *Id.* at 357.

In 1990, Congress responded to the seemingly intractable issue of how courts should develop limitations law for federal statutes by enacting a generic solution, 28 U.S.C. § 1658. This statute provides a single four-year statute of limitations for subsequently enacted statutes that lack a limitations provision. Congress even attempted to rectify what it considered to be an errant choice of the limitations period in *Lampf, supra.* In response to *Lampf,* Congress reinstated lawsuits dismissed before the decision was issued if those suits otherwise satisfied state limitations laws that might have applied. Congress' attempt to essentially overrule the Court's decision in *Lampf* was struck down in *Plaut v. Spendthrift Farms, Inc.*, 514 U.S. 211 (1995). The Court concluded in *Plaut* that Congress had violated separation of powers insofar as it attempted to reopen retroactively judgments that had been entered before § 1658 created its fall-back

122. *DelCostello v. International Bhd. of Teamsters*, 462 U.S. 151, 158 (1983).

limitations period. *Plaut* illustrates that, in at least one unique setting,[123] federal common-law rules are not ultimately subject to congressional control.

b. Implied Causes of Action

Sometimes a federal court adjudicating a dispute has no choice but to fill a remedial gap. For example, necessity dictates that a trial court allocate the burden of proof when trying a case under federal law regardless of whether Congress has considered the issue. But more often interstitial lawmaking is not strictly "necessary." For example, federal courts can simply decline to impose a limitations period on the filing of a federal claim when a statute is silent, a tack the Court has occasionally taken.[124] Similarly, federal courts can simply decline to grant a remedy requested by the plaintiff when Congress has not specifically authorized that remedy.

Probably the most controversial issue to arise concerning interstitial remedial rulemaking is whether courts should grant a *monetary* remedy when a federal statute is silent on the subject. In a variety of settings, federal statutes impose duties but fail to specifically authorize legal remedies for those persons injured when those duties are violated. Examples of such duties that lack a private enforcement mechanism include many criminal laws, regulatory laws, and a variety of social welfare programs. Such statutes typically authorize enforcement action by federal *officials*—like the Justice Department or an administrative agency—but are either silent about remedies available to injured persons or grant injured persons a very limited remedy (e.g., filing an administrative complaint). As mentioned, the most significant omission the Court has addressed in past decades is the absence of any remedy authorizing the recovery of monetary damages. The question whether the Court should authorize a monetary remedy not specifically authorized by statute is often referred to as the problem of the "implied cause of action," although it often might be more usefully described as the problem of an "implied remedy."[125]

The earliest Court recognition of some version of an implied cause of action is *Texas & Pacific Railway v. Rigsby*, 241 U.S. 33 (1916). In *Rigsby*, the Court permitted an injured railroad worker to maintain an action in negligence based on the railroad's violation of a federal criminal statute governing safety standards. The plaintiff's cause of action was strictly speaking a negligence *per se* action in which federal law provided an enforceable duty and state negligence law provided the remedy. Nonetheless, the Court announced a broader view of its power to authorize a remedy for the violation of federal law:

> A disregard of the command of the statute is a wrongful act, and where it results in damage to one of the class for whose especial benefit the statute was enacted, the right to recover the damages from the party in default is implied, according to a doctrine of the common law. . . . [Citation and internal quotation omitted.] So, in

123. The Court in *Plaut* could find no prior situation where Congress had attempted to reopen final judgments to apply subsequently enacted law.

124. See note __, *supra.*

125. A "cause of action" typically requires at least two things—a "right" that the plaintiff claims has been violated and a "remedy" the plaintiff demands to rectify the violation. Many of the "implied cause of action" cases turn on whether the court should authorize a remedy, although an appreciable minority of these cases turn on whether federal law affords the plaintiff a "right."

> every case, where a statute enacts, or prohibits a thing for the benefit of a person, he shall have a remedy upon the same statute for the thing enacted for his advantage, or for the recompense of a wrong done to him contrary to the said law. This is but an application of the maxim, *Ubi jus ibi remedium* [where there is a right, there is a remedy].

Id. at 39-40.

Beginning in the 1960s, the Court interpreted precedent like *Rigsby* as authority for federal courts to "grant all necessary remedial relief" when exercising their jurisdiction to enforce specific federal statutes. *See J.I. Case Co. v. Borak*, 377 U.S. 426 (1964). In *Borak*, the Court permitted a shareholder who had suffered economic losses as a result of the issuance of a misleading proxy statement to seek damages. Although federal securities law gave the Securities and Exchange Commission authority to enforce its provisions, that law did not authorize suit by a private party to recover damages. Nonetheless, the Court concluded that "private enforcement of the proxy rules provides a necessary supplement to Commission action." *Id.* at 432. According to the Court, "It is for the federal courts to adjust their remedies so as to grant the necessary relief where federally secured rights are invaded." *Id.* at 433.

The Court's unanimous opinion in *Borak* appeared to affirm a broad authority to develop common-law remedies both (1) to *compensate* persons injured by violations of federal law, and (2) to provide additional *deterrence* to violations of federal law. This authority could be exercised without identifying express or implied congressional authorization of rulemaking power. In the decade following *Borak*, both the lower federal courts and the Supreme Court authorized private causes of action in a variety of contexts.[126]

But by 1975, the newly emergent Burger Court began to recede from the broader statements in *Borak*. In *Cort v. Ash*, 422 U.S. 66 (1975), the Court announced a four-part test for determining whether a private cause of action should be recognized, one that gave greater prominence to legislative intent. Purporting to synthesize prior precedent, a unanimous Court held:

> In determining whether a private remedy is implicit in a statute not expressly providing one, several factors are relevant. First, is the plaintiff one of the class for whose especial benefit the statute was enacted, that is, does the statute create a federal right in favor of the plaintiff? Second, is there any indication of legislative intent, explicit or implicit, either to create such a remedy or to deny one? Third, is it consistent with the underlying purposes of the legislative scheme to imply such a remedy for the plaintiff? And finally, is the cause of action one traditionally relegated to state law, in an area basically the concern of the States, so that it would be inappropriate to infer a cause of action based solely on federal law?

Id. at 78 (internal citations and quotations marks omitted).

In *Cort*, the Court denied the plaintiff a damages remedy under a federal criminal statute that contained no mechanisms for civil enforcement. At the same time, the Court did not specifically *require* that a remedy be based on inferred congressional intent; such intent was one of four factors to be considered.

126. This history is briefly recounted in Tamar Frankel, *Implied Rights of Action*, 67 VA. L. REV. 553, 560-61 (1981).

After *Cort,* the Court generally showed much greater reluctance to infer private causes of action.[127] But not always. In *Cannon v. University of Chicago,* 441 U.S. 677 (1979), the Court recognized an implied cause of action under Title IX,[128] prohibiting gender discrimination in federally funded programs for higher education. Viewing its task as one of "statutory construction," the Court was influenced by its conclusion that *Congress* was aware of pre-*Cort* era precedent when it enacted Title IX, and presumably intended or at least expected that the statute would be interpreted to create an implied right of action. *See id.* at 699 (it is "realistic to presume that Congress was thoroughly familiar with these unusually important precedents from this and other federal courts and that it expected its enactment to be interpreted in conformity with them"). Thus, *Cannon* suggested that Congress enacted statutes with a working knowledge of the Court's precedent, which implied that statutes enacted during the period when the Court more liberally recognized implied causes of action might be treated differently from statutes enacted during a more conservative period.

The Court's opinion in *Cannon,* unlike those in *Borak* and *Cort,* was not unanimous. Two justices disputed the Court's application of the *Cort* factors. Justice Powell in dissent argued that "Congress recognizes that the creation of private actions is a legislative function and frequently exercises it. When Congress chooses not to provide a private civil remedy, federal courts should not assume the legislative role of creating such a remedy and thereby enlarge their jurisdiction." *Id.* at 730-31.

In *Touche Ross & Co. v. Redington,* 442 U.S. 560 (1979), the Court made clear that it lacked authority to recognize an implied cause of action based on an *inherent* judicial power to remedy statutory violations, which was more or less the *Borak* view.[129] With the exception of two justices, the Court affirmed that "the question of the existence of a statutory cause of action is, of course, one of statutory construction. As we recently have emphasized, the fact that a federal statute has been violated and some person harmed does not automatically give rise to a private cause of action in favor of that person. Instead, our task is limited solely to determining whether Congress intended to create [a] private right of action." *Id.* at 568.

In *Alexander v. Sandoval,* 532 U.S. 275, 286-87 (2001), a divided Court illustrated one of the principal fault lines in the implied-cause doctrine. In *Sandoval,* a bare majority rejected an implied cause of action under *federal regulations* issued pursuant to Title VI, which prohibits racial discrimination by recipients of federal funds.[130] Those regulations proscribed both "disparate treatment" discrimination (improper motive) and "disparate impact" discrimination (practices having a disparate impact on a protected group without evidence that the practices were adopted with an improper motive). Although Title VI does not extend to disparate impact discrimination, the Court was willing to assume that the federal regulations were validly issued and disparate impact discrimination was lawfully proscribed.

127. *See, e.g.,* Chrysler Corp. v. Brown, 441 U.S. 281 (1979); Piper v. Chris-Craft Indus., 430 U.S. 1 (1977).

128. 20 U.S.C. § 1681(a).

129. *See also Transamerica Mortg. Advisors, Inc. v. Lewis,* 444 U.S. 11, 15 (1979) ("While some opinions of the Court have placed considerable emphasis upon the desirability of implying private rights of action in order to provide remedies thought to effectuate the purposes of a given statute, *e.g., J.I. Case Co. v. Borak,* what must ultimately be determined is whether Congress intended to create the private remedy asserted.").

130. 42 U.S.C. §§ 2000d *et seq.*

All members of the Court agreed that the question of an implied remedy ultimately turned on congressional intent. But the justices disagreed about what role the Court's *own* history in developing implied-cause doctrine played in assessing congressional intent.

The majority, in an opinion written by Justice Scalia, rejected an implied cause of action to enforce the administrative regulations proscribing disparate impact discrimination. Here is how Justice Scalia summarized the Court's precedent:

> Like substantive federal law itself, private rights of action to enforce federal law must be created by Congress. The judicial task is to interpret the statute Congress has passed to determine whether it displays an intent to create not just a private right but also a private remedy. Statutory intent on this latter point is determinative. Without it, a cause of action does not exist and courts may not create one, no matter how desirable that might be as a policy matter, or how compatible with the statute.

Id. at 286-87.

In assessing "statutory intent," the Court also found unpersuasive the argument that Congress' reenactment of a statute in the pre-*Cort* era implied approval of a broader judicial power to infer a cause of action.

Writing for the four dissenting justices, Justice Stevens harshly rebuked the majority's "evident antipathy toward implied rights of action" and dismissal of such rights as "common law judicial activism." *Id.* at 311, 315 (Stevens, J., dissenting). While recognizing that implied causes of action turn on "statutory construction" not mere "policy," the dissent argued that the *Cort* factors still remained important tools for discovering Congress' intent. *Id.* at 312. One of those factors, the dissent argued, was the "contemporary legal context" in which Congress enacted legislation: "the objective manifestations of congressional intent to create a private right of action must be measured in light of the enacting Congress' expectations as to how the judiciary might evaluate the question." *Id.*[131]

Most recently, the Court has declined to extend what is perhaps the most important implied right of action it has recognized—the right to sue under Rule 10b-5 for fraud and misrepresentation related to the purchase of securities.[132] In *Stoneridge Investment Partners, LLC v. Scientific-Atlanta*, 552 U.S. 148, (2008), the Court expressed a very restrictive view of the federal courts' authority to develop implied causes of action. Writing for the 5-3 majority in *Stoneridge*, Justice Kennedy observed:

> The § 10(b) private cause of action is a judicial construct that Congress did not enact in the text of the relevant statutes. Though the rule once may have been otherwise, see J.I. Case Co. v. Borak, it is settled that there is an implied cause of action only if the underlying statute can be interpreted to disclose the intent to create one. This is for good reason. In the absence of congressional intent the Judiciary's recognition of an implied private right of action "necessarily extends its authority to embrace a dispute Congress has not assigned it to resolve. This runs contrary to the established principle that '[t]he jurisdiction of the federal

131. "At the time Congress was considering Title VI, it was normal practice for the courts to infer that Congress intended a private right of action whenever it passed a statute designed to protect a particular class that did not contain enforcement mechanisms which would be thwarted by a private remedy." 532 U.S. at 314.

132. *See* 15 U.S.C. § 78j(b); SEC Rule 10b-5, 17 C.F.R. § 240.10b-5.

courts is carefully guarded against expansion by judicial interpretation . . . ,' and conflicts with the authority of Congress under Art. III to set the limits of federal jurisdiction." The determination of who can seek a remedy has significant consequences for the reach of federal power. Concerns with the judicial creation of a private cause of action caution against its expansion. The decision to extend the cause of action is for Congress, not for us. Though it remains the law, the § 10(b) private right should not be extended beyond its present boundaries.[133]

Justice Stevens, writing for three dissenting justices, reprised his dissent in *Sandoval*:

During the first two centuries of this Nation's history much of our law was developed by judges in the common law tradition. A basic principle animating our jurisprudence was enshrined in state constitution provisions guaranteeing, in substance, that "every wrong shall have a remedy." Fashioning appropriate remedies for the violation of rules of law designed to protect a class of citizens was the routine business of judges. See *Marbury v. Madison.* While it is true that in the early days state law was the source of most of those rules, throughout our history—until 1975—the same practice prevailed in federal courts with regard to federal statutes that left questions of remedy open for judges to answer. In Texas & Pacific R. Co. v. Rigsby, this Court stated the following: "A disregard of the command of the statute is a wrongful act, and where it results in damage to one of the class for whose especial benefit the statute was enacted, the right to recover the damages from the party in default is implied, according to a doctrine of the common law expressed in . . . these words: 'So, in every case, where a statute enacts, or prohibits a thing for the benefit of a person, he shall have a remedy upon the same statute for the thing enacted for his advantage, or for the recompense of a wrong done to him contrary to the said law.'"

* * * *

During the late 1940's, the 1950's, the 1960's and the early 1970's there was widespread, indeed almost general, recognition of implied causes of action for damages under many provisions of the Securities Exchange Act, including not only the antifraud provisions, but many others.

* * * *

In light of the history of court-created remedies and specifically the history of implied causes of action under § 10(b), the Court is simply wrong when it states that Congress did not impliedly authorize this private cause of action "when it first enacted the statute." Courts near in time to the enactment of the securities laws recognized that the principle in *Rigsby* applied to the securities laws. Congress enacted § 10(b) with the understanding that federal courts respected the principle that every wrong would have a remedy. Today's decision simply cuts back further on Congress' intended remedy.

552 U.S. at 176-80, 128 S. Ct. at 779-82.

DISCUSSION AND QUESTIONS

Rights without remedies. Judicial "lawmaking" has, of course, become an important point of contention in the nation's politics. Justice Powell, dissenting

133. 552 U.S. at 164-65, 128 S. Ct. at 772-73. (Justice Breyer did not participate in the decision.)

in *Cannon*, observed that "the creation of private actions is a legislative function." Is there something distinctive about creating a private right of action that distinguishes it from other types of common lawmaking the Court finds permissible? Why is this not viewed as simply another form of "interstitial" rulemaking where federal courts fill the gap to promote their perceptions of statutory policy? What is the qualitative difference, for example, between a court's developing a statute of limitations and its development of an implied remedy? Is Justice Powell's view of a strict limitation on the power of federal courts to exercise "legislative" power a reflection of "formalism," that is, the belief that the Constitution strictly divides powers between the legislative and judicial branches?[134] Or does Justice Powell's view reflect an important pragmatic difference between implied causes of action and other forms of interstitial lawmaking power?

Dissenting in *Sandoval*, Justice Stevens invoked the "basic principle animating our jurisprudence" that "'every wrong shall have a remedy.'" This principle certainly has strong appeal as a principle of justice. But it cannot be understood as a *requirement* of federal statutory enforcement. For example, we learned in Chapter 10 that there are many occasions when a person suffers a wrong under federal law (both statutes and the Constitution) but ultimately has no remedy against state and local government actors. Consequently, the maxim that every wrong should be remedied may be a sound principle of statutory construction, but it cannot be taken literally as a commandment that federal courts develop a remedy.[135]

In *Sandoval*, the Court was asked to recognize an implied right of action to enforce *administrative regulations* proscribing "disparate impact" discrimination, even though the federal statute implemented by the administrative regulations, Title VI, only proscribes "disparate treatment" discrimination. The Court assumed the regulations were a lawful exercise of the agency's authority to enforce Title VI but concluded that "language in a regulation may invoke a private right of action that Congress through statutory text created, but it may not create a right that Congress has not." 128 S. Ct. at 291. Justice Stevens, dissenting, observed that Title VI authorized administrative adoption of "prophylactic" rules like that prohibiting disparate impact discrimination. *Id.* at 305. He also cited to the *Chevron* doctrine, "that when the agencies charged with administering a broadly worded statute offer regulations interpreting that statute or giving concrete guidance as to its implementation, we treat their interpretation of the statute's breadth as controlling unless it presents an unreasonable construction of the statutory text." *Id.* at 309 (citing *Chevron U.S.A. Inc. v. Natural Res. Def. Council, Inc.*, 467 U.S. 837 (1984)). According to Justice Stevens, "there is simply no logical or legal justification for differentiating between actions to enforce the regulations and actions to enforce the statutory text." *Id.* at 310 n.20.

134. *See generally* NEAL DEVINS & LOUIS FISHER, THE DEMOCRATIC CONSTITUTION 77 (2004) ("Under the best of conditions, the Supreme Court offers limited help in resolving basic disputes over separation of powers. . . . [D]uring recent decades, the Court has slipped back and forth in its search for principles, sometimes embracing a functional and pragmatic approach and switching later to a strict, formalist model.").

135. *See, e.g.*, Ryan D. Newman, *From* Bivens *to* Malesko *and Beyond: Implied Constitutional Remedies and the Separation of Powers*, 85 TEX. L. REV. 471, 471 (2006) ("The idea that for every violation of a legal right there must be a remedy is more normative than descriptive primarily because many violations go unremedied.").

Do you agree that, if the Court otherwise concludes that an agency interpretation of a statute is reasonable, it should apply implied-rights doctrine equally to both regulations and the authorizing statute? Or does separation of powers assume greater force when the courts are asked to infer a remedy based on a regulation that itself is an inference from congressional intent?

The importance of identifying a statutory "right." In *Sandoval,* the Court reiterated the distinction between federal statutes that impose duties and statutes that also confer rights on injured persons. The Court observed, "Statutes that focus on the person regulated rather than the individuals protected create no implication of an intent to confer rights on a particular class of persons." In recent decades the Court has often explored whether statutory language creates enforceable "rights." Among other things, the Court scrutinizes whether a statute identifies a "benefited class" of persons that include the plaintiff. Titles VI and IX clearly identify a class of persons benefited by their proscriptions by stating, "no *person* . . . shall . . . be subjected to discrimination." In contrast, many federal statutes focus solely on "the person regulated," thus imposing federal duties without recognizing correlative "rights" for injured persons. For example, in *Gonzaga University v. Doe,* 536 U.S. 273 (2002), the Court refused to find that the Family Educational Rights and Privacy Act (FERPA) created rights on behalf of students whose protected educational records were disclosed in violation of the statute. FERPA states that "[n]o funds shall be made available" to any "educational agency or institution" that has a prohibited "policy or practice." Because the statute imposes duties on educational institutions without also using "rights-creating" language that encompasses students whose educational records have been compromised, the Court in *Gonzaga* concluded that FERPA could not be enforced through the remedies otherwise available under § 1983.[136]

The discovery of "rights-creating" language in a statute is not, alone, sufficient to carry the plaintiff's burden under the Court's current approach emphasizing specific legislative intent. But without such language, the plaintiff has no chance of carrying this burden.

The current emphasis on legislative intent. All members of the Court appear to agree that the issue of implied remedies turns on legislative intent in some form. This is a significant change from the earlier approach in cases like *Rigsby,* where the Court presumed it had common-lawmaking power to infer private remedies under federal statutes. Distinguished jurists have assumed, at least during an earlier era, that federal courts have an implied authority to develop remedies to enforce federal statutes:

> A duty declared by Congress does not evaporate for want of a formulated sanction. When Congress has left the matter at large for judicial determination, our function is to decide what remedies are appropriate in the light of the statutory language and purpose and of the traditional modes by which courts compel performance of legal obligations. If civil liability is appropriate to effectuate the purposes of a statute, courts are not denied this traditional remedy because it is not specifically authorized.

136. See Chapter 10.

Montana-Dakota Utils. Co. v. Northwestern Pub. Serv. Co., 341 U.S. 246, 261 (1951) (Frankfurter, J., dissenting) (citations omitted).

The position that federal courts have a general implied authority to implement federal statutes by developing remedies appears to be shared by no current justice. All members of the Court concur in the need for some form of statute-specific congressional authorization of the power to devise a private remedy. The principal difference among justices now seems to be what evidence of congressional intent is required to support an implied right of action.

A slim majority on the current Court requires a fairly compelling demonstration that Congress authorized creation of a cause of action. Is that a workable requirement, or does it inevitably preclude the recognition of implied remedies (with the exception of implied remedies that have been "grandfathered" in by the Court)? Consider Justice Scalia's professed distrust of legislative history. As he recently commented in his concurring opinion in *Zedner v. United States*, 547 U.S. 489, 511 (2006), "[T]he use of legislative history is illegitimate and ill advised in the interpretation of any statute—and especially a statute that is clear on its face."[137] Similarly, in *Sandoval* Justice Scalia wrote that, even if Congress re-enacts legislation without expressly disapproving prior Court interpretation, as a "general matter" Congress' inaction "deserves . . . little weight" in the interpretive process. 532 U.S. at 292.

If an appreciable number of justices actually believe legislative history is unavailing in the face of clear statutory language,[138] what are the prospects of persuading the Court to recognize an "implied" cause of action? Might this mistrust of legislative history help explain the modern Court's "antipathy," as Justice Stevens described it, to implied remedies?

Is it incongruous to search for congressional authorization of an implied remedy when Congress has obviously omitted the remedy from a statute? Professor Martha Field argues that it is not:

> Because of Congress' unwillingness and inability to foresee all questions and situations that may arise in relation to its enactments . . . the only way our system can produce sensible and sensitive results across the board is to allow courts to follow their current approach [referring to the approach in *Cort v. Ash*]. It is proper for courts to ask, both on the authorization and on the content issues, what Congress . . . *would have wanted* if they had adverted to the problem before the Court and had known the facts and circumstances known to the Court.[139]

In other words, Professor Field believes that the proper search is for the "constructive" intent of Congress—what it "would have wanted" had it squarely considered the issue later considered by a federal court. This is distinguished from the current approach of a majority of justices, who search for the "specific" intent of Congress, that is, whether Congress specifically contemplated that federal courts would infer a remedy. Professor Field's emphasis on constructive intent reflects the view that, in most cases, Congress simply "did not foresee the

137. Justice Thomas also appears to share this view in situations where the text of a statute is clear. *See generally* Jordan Wilder Connors, *Treating Like Subdecisions Alike: The Scope of Stare Decisis as Applied to Judicial Methodology*, 108 COLUM. L. REV. 681, 706 (2008).

138. Both Justices Powell and Rehnquist agreed in *Cannon* that the Court should not infer a private cause of action "absent the most compelling evidence that Congress in fact intended such an action to exist." 441 U.S. at 749 (Powell, J., dissenting); *id.* at 718 (Rehnquist, J., concurring).

139. *See* Field, *supra* note 42, at 945.

problem" of whether a particular statutory remedy was appropriate.[140] The notion that federal courts have authority to address problems overlooked by Congress during the legislative process is, of course, at the heart of their "interstitial" lawmaking powers.

The argument for using constructive legislative intent is often supported by another consideration—the presumption that Congress is aware of the "contemporary legal context" when it enacts laws. This presumption has figured significantly in recent Court controversies about implied causes of action—as evidenced by the decisions in *Sandoval* and *Stoneridge*. Particularly with statutes enacted in the pre-*Cort* era, Congress may have assumed the federal courts would supplement its legislation to accommodate its enforcement by private parties. Many scholars agree with Professor Field that it is mistaken to assume that "congressional silence reflects an intention to foreclose judicial creation" of private remedies. "It is equally plausible that Congress enacts legislation "in contemplation of possible private enforcement."[141]

The Court's misgivings about its power to infer private remedies. The Court's contraction of its power to develop statutory remedies has had few academic defenders. The literature over the past 25 years has been overwhelmingly critical.[142] This contrasts with the views of the justices themselves, almost all of whom have "subscribed to an opinion raising questions in one or another context about the common law functions of federal courts."[143] Professor Peter Strauss has remarked that the justices' misgivings about their power to develop common law are more "instinctual than intellectual."[144] Some support for this view can be found in offhand remarks made during oral argument before the Court. For example, during argument in *Stoneridge* Chief Justice Roberts is said to have remarked that "Rule 10(b)(5) is a private cause of action that we made up. . . . [W]e do not do that anymore. . . ."[145]

If the Court's reluctance to recognize implied remedies is somehow based on political "instinct," that instinct may be influenced by the perception that an earlier Court was promoting a political agenda. In 1984, Professor George Brown commented that "the implied rights debate can be seen in a broader context as part of the debate over judicial activism."[146] Consistent with this view is Justice Powell's dissent in *Cannon*, where he took pains to identify "no less than 20 decisions by the Courts of Appeals [that] have implied private actions from federal statutes" in a brief four-year period.[147]

140. *See* George D. Brown, *Of Activism and* Erie—*The Implication Doctrine's Implication for the Nature and Role of the Federal Courts*, 69 Iowa L. Rev. 617, 629 (1984).

141. *See* Richard B. Stewart & Cass Row Sunstein, *Public Programs and Private Rights*, 95 Harv. L. Rev. 1193, 1291 (1982).

142. The articles by Professors Field and Frankel illustrate criticism of the Court's decision through the early-1980s. More contemporary criticism is illustrated by Andrew M. Siegel, *The Court Against the Courts: Hostility to Litigation as an Organizing Theme in the Rehnquist Court's Jurisprudence*, 84 Tex. L. Rev. 1097 (2006), and Peter L. Strauss, *Courts or Tribunals: Federal Courts and the Common Law*, 53 Ala. L. Rev. 891 (2002). Professor Brown, *supra* note 140, is the exceptional scholar who defends the Court.

143. *See* Strauss, *supra* note 142, at 924.

144. *See id.*

145. *Roundtable Discussion, An Enigmatic Court? Examining the Roberts Court as It Begins Year Three*, 35 Pepp. L. Rev. 547, 565 (2008) (comment of Professor Kmiec).

146. *See* Brown, *supra* note 140, at 649.

147. 441 U.S. at 741.

An alternative, perhaps complementary interpretation of the Court's reluctance to infer statutory remedies is that the Court has developed misgivings about the federal courts' *competence* to make the policy choices involved in implying remedies. Some justices have expressed this concern.[148] There may be some basis for this view in the area of implied remedies to enforce securities laws. For example, Professor Tamar Frankel — otherwise an advocate of the Court's remedial power — commented in 1981 that the expansion of implied causes under federal securities law might have altered the Court's receptivity to implied remedies.[149] Such expansion included the proliferation of class actions to enforce securities laws, and this litigation was believed to have an impact on the securities markets. Perceptions of litigation abuse eventually prompted Congress, in the 1990s, to enact unique requirements for such litigation[150] and to preempt class actions in state court and class actions under state law.[151]

But the Court's retrenchment of implied-remedy doctrine ultimately seems founded on misgivings about the Court's authority more than its competence. Justice Powell's dissenting opinion in *Cannon* still provides the fullest statement of the view that the Congress alone has constitutional authority to craft statutory remedies. According to Justice Powell, when the Court exercises lawmaking power,

> It . . . invites Congress to avoid resolution of the often controversial question whether a new regulatory statute should be enforced through private litigation. Rather than confronting the hard political choices involved, Congress is encouraged to shirk its constitutional obligation and leave the issue to the courts to decide. When this happens, the legislative process with its public scrutiny and participation has been bypassed, with attendant prejudice to everyone concerned. Because the courts are free to reach a result different from that which the normal play of political forces would have produced, the intended beneficiaries of the legislation are unable to ensure the full measure of protection their needs may warrant. For the same reason, those subject to the legislative constraints are denied the opportunity to forestall through the political process potentially unnecessary and disruptive litigation. Moreover, the public generally is denied the benefits that are derived from the making of important societal choices through the open debate of the democratic process. The Court's implication doctrine encourages, as a corollary to the political default by Congress, an increase in the governmental power exercised by the federal judiciary.

148. *See* Bivens v. Six Unknown Named Agents of the Fed. Bureau of Narcotics, 403 U.S. 388, 412 (1971) (Burger, C.J., dissenting) ("Legislation is the business of the Congress, and it has the facilities and competence for that task — as we do not."). Many scholars dispute the assertion that the Court lacks institutional competence to infer statutory remedies. *See, e.g.*, George D. Brown, Letting Statutory Tails Wag Constitutional Dogs — Have the Bivens Dissenters Prevailed?, 64 IND. L.J. 263, 284 (1989). *See generally* Susan Bandes, REINVENTING BIVENS: THE SELF-EXECUTING CONSTITUTION, 68 S. CAL. L. REV. 289, 320 (1995) (concluding the dispute over the courts' competence is unresolvable).

149. *See* Frankel, *supra* note 126, at 570 ("Private enforcement of the securities acts represents a peculiar combination of private motives and public goals. Although the *Borak* Court justified private rights of action for securities violations as necessary deterrents, private litigation takes the form of compensatory proceedings, i.e., traditional tort suits. The impact of such proceedings on the functioning of the securities markets is, of course, an empirical question, and existing studies support no firm conclusions. Nonetheless, analysis and reflection suggest that such private compensatory actions (especially in the form of class actions) are ill-suited to the deterrence system of the securities laws and may hamper the central purposes of those statutes."). *But see* Brown, *supra* note141, at 636 (arguing that this theory is "dubious" and does not adequately account for the general retraction in implied-rights doctrine.)

150. *See* Private Securities Litigation Reform Act of 1995, Pub. L. No. 104-67 (codified in various sections of Title 15). The Act included reforms limiting the recoverable damages in securities litigation and also limiting the recovery of attorney's fees.

151. *See Merrill Lynch, Pierce, Fenner, & Smith, Inc. v. Dabit*, 547 U.S. 71 (2006).

> The dangers posed by judicial arrogation of the right to resolve general societal conflicts have been manifest to this Court throughout its history.
>
> It is true that the federal judiciary necessarily exercises substantial powers to construe legislation, including, when appropriate, the power to prescribe substantive standards of conduct that supplement federal legislation. But this power normally is exercised with respect to disputes over which a court already has jurisdiction, and in which the existence of the asserted cause of action is established. Implication of a private cause of action, in contrast, involves a significant additional step. By creating a private action, a court of limited jurisdiction necessarily extends its authority to embrace a dispute Congress has not assigned it to resolve. This runs contrary to the established principle that the jurisdiction of the federal courts is carefully guarded against expansion by judicial interpretation and conflicts with the authority of Congress under Art. III to set the limits of federal jurisdiction.

441 U.S. at 743-47 (internal citations and quotation marks omitted).

Justice Powell's conception of the legislative process plainly conflicts with that of Professor Field. Professor Field believes that "Congress' unwillingness and inability" to address remedial issues justifies the courts' development of "sensible and sensitive results." Justice Powell, in contrast, considers Congress' responsibility to resolve important remedial issues to be a non-delegable duty. And when federal courts take it upon themselves to fill important remedial gaps, they induce Congress to avoid its legislative duty.

Which view do you find more persuasive? If one adopts Professor Field's view, how does one develop workable limits on the courts' lawmaking power? On the other hand, if one adopts Justice Powell's view, how does one legitimize the federal courts' well-established power to develop "interstitial" rules in other contexts? Justice Powell comments on how recognition of implied rights of action extends a federal court's jurisdiction by giving it "authority to embrace a dispute Congress has not assigned it to resolve."[152] Does this sufficiently distinguish the precedent we have considered where the Court engages in interstitial lawmaking? Do you agree with Justice Powell that there is just something different about devising a monetary remedy to enforce federal statutes?

Are Justice Powell's concerns mitigated by the fact that Congress can always correct errant rulemaking by the courts? Some scholars have also argued that Congress' power to revise judicially created rules vitiates any residual concern with separation of powers.[153] Are you persuaded? Or does normal legislative inertia (including the filibuster power exercisable by a minority in the Senate) dilute Congress' practical checks on judicial rulemaking? If you share Justice Powell's concerns about congressional delegation of legislative power, do these concerns extend as well to *express* delegations of rulemaking power? No one on the Court appears to dispute its power to make rules when Congress authorizes judicial rulemaking. But doesn't the Court's exercise of delegated rulemaking power also threaten the "open debate of the democratic process" that otherwise would occur in Congress? If so, have opponents of implied remedies acted consistently with their philosophy of legislative power?

152. If a plaintiff has no available remedy under federal law, her suit will be dismissed for "failure to state a claim" under Federal Rule of Civil Procedure 8(a)(3).

153. *See, e.g.*, Monaghan, *supra* note 42, at 34 (making this observation in the context of the courts' exercise of "constitutional" common-lawmaking power). *See also* Guido Calabresi, A Common Law for the Age of Statutes 120-23 (1982).

PROBLEM 11-4

Return to Sender

In May of 2008, June Jones received in the mail a collection of CDs entitled "Romantic Moments through the Ages." The CDs were recordings by a studio orchestra of numerous well-known songs and excerpts from classical compositions. Featured recordings included, for example, the theme from *Love Story*, selections from *La Boheme*, and songs by the Carpenters. June had never requested the CDs and did not care for most of the music on them. She gave the CDs to a local thrift shop.

The company that mailed the CDs, Enchantment, Inc. (Enchantment), soon sent June a bill for $49. She emailed the company and, after waiting weeks for a response, was told that she needed to pay for the CDs in "10 business days" or else face "damage to your credit." June paid for the CDs and then saw a lawyer.

39 U.S.C. § 3009 provides in pertinent part:

> [T]he mailing of unordered merchandise or of communications constitutes an unfair method of competition and an unfair trade practice. . . . Any merchandise mailed in violation of [this provision] may be treated as a gift by the recipient, who shall have the right to retain, use, discard, or dispose of it in any manner he sees fit without any obligation whatsoever to the sender. . . . No mailer of any merchandise mailed in violation of [this provision] shall mail to any recipient of such merchandise a bill for such merchandise or any dunning communications.[154]

The statute specifically authorizes the Federal Trade Commission to enforce its provisions through administrative action, including the issuance of injunctions and civil fines. The statute's legislative history is silent about whether aggrieved persons have an implied cause of action.

June's lawyer has commenced a class action in federal court on behalf of June and others who received unsolicited mailings from Enchantment. The plaintiffs' complaint alleges an implied cause of action under the above-quoted statute. The plaintiffs demand damages, including (a) restitution of any monies paid by plaintiffs for unsolicited merchandise, and (b) damages for economic losses suffered by plaintiffs (e.g., adverse credit ratings for those who refused to pay for unsolicited merchandise).

In support of their claimed cause of action under the statute, the plaintiffs argue that the statute plainly confers "rights" on them. They further argue that the statute contains "no suggestion that its beneficiaries must rely exclusively on that overworked FTC for the vindication of their rights." Finally, they point out that the statutory protections afforded them were enacted by Congress in 1971, several years before the Court announced its more restrictive approach to implied statutory causes of action in *Cort v. Ash.*[155]

Do the plaintiffs have a viable argument for recognition of an implied cause of action? Why or why not?

---

154. Such statutes are common under state law also and are often known as Unsolicited Merchandise statutes. For this problem, assume we are dealing only with the FTC statutes.

155. The statutory protections were actually added in 1999, but we have altered the enactment date for purposes of the Problem.

6. *Federal Court Authority to Develop "Constitutional Common Law" Rules*

As we learned in Chapter 10, the Constitution confers numerous rights on "the people" but is largely silent about the enforcement of those rights. In the case of local and state government actors, Congress has enacted remedies for the enforcement of constitutional rights through such statutes as 42 U.S.C. § 1983. But Congress has not enacted legislation comparable to § 1983 to enforce constitutional rights against federal government violators. Further, Congress has not exercised its exclusive authority[156] to waive the United States' sovereign immunity in suits to enforce the Bill of Rights, even though many of those rights protect against improper conduct by the federal government.

The Court has long recognized that plaintiffs may sue federal officials to obtain *equitable* (e.g., injunctive) relief when those officials engage in "ultra vires" conduct lacking constitutional or statutory authorization.[157] Thus, the Court has recognized the equivalent of an "*Ex parte Young*" action[158] to restrain unconstitutional conduct by federal officers.[159]

But does the federal courts' power to enjoin unconstitutional conduct by a federal official entail the power to *award damages* resulting from such conduct? If such a power exists, does it derive from the Constitution itself or is it an implicit power similar to that exercised by the federal courts when granting equitable relief? And to what extent is the federal courts' power to recognize monetary relief for violations of the Constitution subject to Congress' control?

In the final section of this chapter, we consider the contemporary Court's answer to these questions, or at least to most of them. It will soon be apparent to you that these questions are akin to those discussed in the previous section when addressing implied statutory remedies. At the same time, we must ask whether precedent concerning implied statutory remedies is really apt when discussing constitutional remedies. Consider the following suggested distinctions between statutory and constitutional remedies, and whether they have bearing on the federal courts' rulemaking authority.

156. *See, e.g., Lane v. Pena*, 518 U.S. 187 (1996) (Congress must explicitly waive sovereign immunity before the United States can be sued in federal court).

157. *See, e.g., Larson v. Domestic & Foreign Commerce Corp.*, 337 U.S. 682, 689 (1949) (conduct not authorized by federal law is "individual not sovereign" action, which courts may restrain).

158. This action is discussed in Chapter 8.

159. *See, e.g., Bell v. Hood*, 327 U.S. 678, 684 (1946) ("[I]t is established practice for this Court to sustain the jurisdiction of federal courts to issue injunctions to protect rights safeguarded by the Constitution."). *Elgin v. Department of the Treasury*, 132 S. Ct. 2126 (2012), illustrates possible limits on the federal courts' power to restrain the unconstitutional action of federal officials. In *Elgin*, the Court held that federal employees challenging the constitutionality of the Military Selective Service Act had to proceed administratively under federal civil-service statutes, which provided the exclusive remedy for their constitutional claims. Because Congress channeled review of federal employees' claims through administrative proceedings, federal district courts could not exercise their general authority under 28 U.S.C. § 1331 to enjoin alleged violations of the Constitution. Federal administrative procedures provided the plaintiffs their exclusive remedy even though their constitutional claims might not be considered until appellate review was later sought in the Federal Circuit. *Id.* at 2139. The three dissenting justices agreed that the federal courts' power to restrain unconstitutional federal action under § 1331 might be limited when Congress provides an exclusive administrative remedy, but concluded that Congress never intended for administrative procedures to preempt the federal courts' power. *Id.* at 2147.

EXPLORING DOCTRINE

Distinctions Between Statutory and Constitutional Remedies

- The Supreme Court is the ultimate expositor of the Constitution's meaning.
- Congress has plenary power over the remedies authorized in federal statutes; its power to alter remedies authorized by the Constitution may be limited.
- Congress has regular opportunity to revisit the issue of statutory remedies in light of contemporary developments; such an opportunity is not available for amending the Constitution except through its exceedingly cumbersome amendment mechanisms.
- Most implied constitutional remedies are used to redress wrongs committed by officials of the United States. Most implied statutory remedies, in contrast, are asserted against private actors.

a. Before *Bivens*

The seminal case concerning implied damages remedies for constitutional violations by federal officials is *Bivens v. Six Unknown Named Agents of the Federal Bureau of Narcotics*, 403 U.S. 388 (1971). Indeed, actions seeking such a remedy have come to be called "*Bivens*" actions in the literature. Before considering *Bivens*, it is useful to consider the legal context in which the case was decided.

First, prior to *Bivens*, the Court had recognized that federal officials could be sued for conduct considered tortious under *state* law. At the same time, the Court affirmed that *federal common law* might apply in determining what defenses were appropriate if the official's conduct occurred while acting within the scope of federal employment. For example, in *Howard v. Lyons*, 360 U.S. 593 (1959), the Court held that a federal common law of privilege would apply when a naval commander was sued under state law for allegedly defaming the plaintiff. Citing *Clearfield Trust*, the Court held that any privilege enjoyed by the commander was one of "peculiarly federal concern" that was to be "judged by federal standards, to be formulated by the courts in the absence of legislative action by Congress." *Id.* at 597.

Second, *Bivens* was decided at a time when the Court had recognized its broadest power to develop "implied" statutory remedies. The leading precedent at this time was *J.I. Case Co. v. Borak*, 377 U.S. 426 (1964), where the Court unanimously recognized its power to infer statutory remedies unless prohibited by Congress. In *Borak*, the Court announced that federal courts have a broad power to "adjust their remedies so as to grant the necessary relief where federally secured rights are invaded." *Id.* at 433.

Third, prior to *Bivens* the Court had issued its controversial decision in *Miranda v. Arizona*, 384 U.S. 486 (1966), enforcing the Fifth Amendment protection against self-incrimination[160] by requiring that states give "*Miranda*" warnings before commencing custodial interrogations of criminal suspects. In *Miranda*, the Court indicated that the specific warnings it required were not directly compelled by its interpretation of the Constitution:

> It is impossible for us to foresee the potential alternatives for protecting the privilege which might be devised by Congress or the States in the exercise of their creative rule-making capacities. *Therefore we cannot say that the Constitution necessarily requires adherence to any particular solution for the inherent compulsions of the interrogation process as it is presently conducted.* Our decision in no way creates a constitutional straitjacket which will handicap sound efforts at reform, nor is it intended to have this effect. We encourage Congress and the States to continue their laudable search for increasingly effective ways of protecting the rights of the individual while promoting efficient enforcement of our criminal laws. However, unless we are shown other procedures which are at least as effective in apprising accused persons of their right of silence and in assuring a continuous opportunity to exercise it, the following safeguards must be observed.[161]

Although *Miranda* did not commit the Court to a "particular solution," the Court indicated that any substitute solution by Congress or the states had to be "at least as effective" as the Court's own rule. The Court's flexible approach in *Miranda* contrasted with its prior decision in *Mapp v. Ohio*, 367 U.S. 643 (1961). In *Mapp*, the Court applied the "exclusionary rule" to the states, prohibiting the introduction of evidence seized in violation of the Constitution. But the Court's ruling in *Mapp* contained no invitation to Congress or the states to develop an effective alternative. To the contrary, the Court concluded that "the exclusionary rule is an essential part of both the Fourth and Fourteenth Amendments." *Id.* at 657. Consequently, the *Miranda* warning, not directly required by the Constitution, implemented *Mapp*'s exclusionary rule, which seemed mandated by the Constitution.[162] *Miranda* thus suggested the Court would exercise a power to enforce the Constitution through remedial rules that *might* be subject to modification by Congress and even the states. This suggested to some scholars that the Court was engaged in the development of "constitutional common law."[163]

Some 25 years before *Bivens* was decided, the Court had strongly implied it had authority to develop monetary remedies to enforce constitutional rights against federal officials. In *Bell v. Hood*, 327 U.S. 678, 684 (1946), the Court suggested that its firmly established power to grant equitable relief entailed a related power to award damages: "[W]here federally protected rights have been invaded, it has been the rule from the beginning that courts will be alert to adjust their remedies so as to grant the necessary relief." In *Bivens*, the Court was asked to implement the power it had recognized in *Bell v. Hood.*

160. This privilege, found in the Fifth Amendment, was applied to the states through the Fourteenth Amendment in *Malloy v. Hogan*, 378 U.S. 1 (1964).

161. 384 U.S. at 467 (emphasis added).

162. The Court appears to have receded from *Mapp* in a later decision, *United States v. Leon*, 468 U.S. 897 (1984).

163. *See, e.g.*, Monaghan, *supra* note 42, at 2-4.

b. From *Bivens* to *Carlson*

In *Bivens,* the Court affirmed its power to develop a monetary remedy when constitutional rights are violated by a federal official. Few decisions match *Bivens* in the breadth of discussion concerning the remedial powers of federal courts when constitutional rights are violated. As you read the decision, notice how it builds on cases and themes we examined earlier, including the common-lawmaking powers of federal courts and the relative role of Congress and the courts in devising remedies.

BIVENS v. SIX UNKNOWN NAMED AGENTS OF THE FEDERAL BUREAU OF NARCOTICS

403 U.S. 388 (1971)

MR. JUSTICE BRENNAN delivered the opinion of the Court.

The Fourth Amendment provides that:

> "The right of the people to be secure in their persons, houses, papers, and effects, against unreasonable searches and seizures, shall not be violated. * * *"

In Bell v. Hood, 327 U.S. 678 (1946), we reserved the question whether violation of that command by a federal agent acting under color of his authority gives rise to a cause of action for damages consequent upon his unconstitutional conduct. Today we hold that it does.

This case has its origin in an arrest and search carried out on the morning of November 26, 1965. Petitioner's complaint alleged that on that day respondents, agents of the Federal Bureau of Narcotics acting under claim of federal authority, entered his apartment and arrested him for alleged narcotics violations. The agents manacled petitioner in front of his wife and children, and threatened to arrest the entire family. They searched the apartment from stem to stern. Thereafter, petitioner was taken to the federal courthouse in Brooklyn, where he was interrogated, booked, and subjected to a visual strip search.

On July 7, 1967, petitioner brought suit in Federal District Court. In addition to the allegations above, his complaint asserted that the arrest and search were effected without a warrant, and that unreasonable force was employed in making the arrest; fairly read, it alleges as well that the arrest was made without probable cause. Petitioner claimed to have suffered great humiliation, embarrassment, and mental suffering as a result of the agents' unlawful conduct, and sought $15,000 damages from each of them. The District Court, on respondents' motion, dismissed the complaint on the ground, *inter alia,* that it failed to state a cause of action. The Court of Appeals affirmed on that basis. We reverse.

Respondents do not argue that petitioner should be entirely without remedy for an unconstitutional invasion of his rights by federal agents. In respondents' view, however, the rights that petitioner asserts — primarily rights of privacy — are creations of state and not of federal law. Accordingly, they argue, petitioner may obtain money damages to redress invasion of these rights only by an action in tort, under state law, in the state courts. In this scheme the Fourth Amendment would serve merely to limit the extent to which the agents could defend the state law tort suit by asserting that their actions were a valid exercise of federal power: if the agents were shown to have violated the Fourth Amendment, such a defense would be lost to them and they would stand before the state law merely as private individuals. . . .

We think that respondents' thesis rests upon an unduly restrictive view of the Fourth Amendment's protection against unreasonable searches and seizures by federal agents, a view that has consistently been rejected by this Court. Respondents seek to treat the relationship between a citizen and a federal agent unconstitutionally exercising his authority as no different from the relationship between two private citizens. In so doing, they ignore the fact that power, once granted, does not disappear like a magic gift when it is wrongfully used. An agent acting—albeit unconstitutionally—in the name of the United States possesses a far greater capacity for harm than an individual trespasser exercising no authority other than his own. Accordingly, as our cases make clear, the Fourth Amendment operates as a limitation upon the exercise of federal power regardless of whether the State in whose jurisdiction that power is exercised would prohibit or penalize the identical act if engaged in by a private citizen. It guarantees to citizens of the United States the absolute right to be free from unreasonable searches and seizures carried out by virtue of federal authority. And "where federally protected rights have been invaded, it has been the rule from the beginning that courts will be alert to adjust their remedies so as to grant the necessary relief."

First. Our cases have long since rejected the notion that the Fourth Amendment proscribes only such conduct as would, if engaged in by private persons, be condemned by state law. . . .

Second. The interests protected by state laws regulating trespass and the invasion of privacy, and those protected by the Fourth Amendment's guarantee against unreasonable searches and seizures, may be inconsistent or even hostile. Thus, we may bar the door against an unwelcome private intruder, or call the police if he persists in seeking entrance. The availability of such alternative means for the protection of privacy may lead the State to restrict imposition of liability for any consequent trespass. A private citizen, asserting no authority other than his own, will not normally be liable in trespass if he demands, and is granted, admission to another's house. But one who demands admission under a claim of federal authority stands in a far different position. The mere invocation of federal power by a federal law enforcement official will normally render futile any attempt to resist an unlawful entry or arrest by resort to the local police; and a claim of authority to enter is likely to unlock the door as well. . . . Nor is it adequate to answer that state law may take into account the different status of one clothed with the authority of the Federal Government. For just as state law may not authorize federal agents to violate the Fourth Amendment, neither may state law undertake to limit the extent to which federal authority can be exercised. The inevitable consequence of this dual limitation on state power is that the federal question becomes not merely a possible defense to the state law action, but an independent claim both necessary and sufficient to make out the plaintiff's cause of action.

Third. That damages may be obtained for injuries consequent upon a violation of the Fourth Amendment by federal officials should hardly seem a surprising proposition. Historically, damages have been regarded as the ordinary remedy for an invasion of personal interests in liberty. Of course, the Fourth Amendment does not in so many words provide for its enforcement by an award of money damages for the consequences of its violation. But "it is . . . well settled that where legal rights have been invaded, and a federal statute provides for a general right to sue for such invasion, federal courts may use any available remedy to make good the wrong done." The present case involves no special factors counseling hesitation in the absence of affirmative action by Congress. We are not dealing with a question of "federal fiscal policy," as in United States v. Standard Oil Co., 332 U.S. 301, 311 (1947). In that case we refused to infer from the Government-soldier relationship that the United States could recover damages from one who negligently injured a soldier and thereby caused the Government to pay his medical expenses and lose his services during the course of his hospitalization. Noting that Congress was normally quite solicitous where the federal purse was involved, we pointed out that "the United States [was] the party plaintiff to the suit. And the United States has power at any time to create the liability." Nor are we asked in this case to impose liability upon a congressional employee for actions contrary to no constitutional prohibition, but merely said to be in excess of the authority delegated to him by the Congress. Finally, we cannot accept respondents' formulation of the question as whether the availability of money damages is necessary to enforce the Fourth Amendment. For we have here no explicit congressional declaration that persons injured by a federal officer's violation of the Fourth Amendment may not recover money damages from the agents, but must instead be remitted to another remedy, equally effective in the view of Congress. The question is merely whether petitioner, if he can demonstrate an injury consequent upon the violation by federal agents of his Fourth Amendment rights, is entitled to redress his injury through a particular remedial mechanism normally available in the federal courts. *Cf. J.I. Case Co. v. Borak.* "The very essence of civil liberty certainly consists in the right of every individual to claim the protection of the laws, whenever he receives an injury." *Marbury v. Madison.* Having concluded that petitioner's complaint states a cause of action under the Fourth Amendment, we hold that petitioner is entitled to recover money damages for any injuries he has suffered as a result of the agents' violation of the Amendment.

In addition to holding that petitioner's complaint had failed to state facts making out a cause of action, the District Court ruled that in any event respondents were immune from liability by virtue of their official position. This question was not passed upon by the Court of Appeals, and accordingly we do not consider it here. The judgment of the Court of Appeals is reversed and the case is remanded for further proceedings consistent with this opinion.

So ordered.

MR. JUSTICE HARLAN, concurring in the judgment.

My initial view of this case was that the Court of Appeals was correct in dismissing the complaint, but for reasons stated in this opinion I am now persuaded to the contrary. Accordingly, I join in the judgment of reversal.

* * * *

I

I turn first to the contention that the constitutional power of federal courts to accord Bivens damages for his claim depends on the passage of a statute creating a "federal cause of action." Although the point is not entirely free of ambiguity, I do not understand either the Government or my dissenting Brothers to maintain that Bivens' contention that he is entitled to be free from the type of official conduct prohibited by the Fourth Amendment depends on a decision by the State in which he resides to accord him a remedy. Such a position would be incompatible with the presumed availability of federal equitable relief, if a proper showing can be made in terms of the ordinary principles governing equitable remedies. However broad a federal court's discretion concerning equitable remedies, it is absolutely clear . . . that in a nondiversity suit a federal court's power to grant even equitable relief depends on the presence of a substantive right derived from federal law.

Thus the interest which Bivens claims—to be free from official conduct in contravention of the Fourth Amendment—is a federally protected interest. Therefore, the question of judicial power to grant Bivens damages is not a problem of the "source" of the "right"; instead, the question is whether the power to authorize damages as a judicial remedy for the vindication of a federal constitutional right is placed by the Constitution itself exclusively in Congress' hands.

II

The contention that the federal courts [cannot recognize a remedy for a violation of constitutional rights] until Congress explicitly authorizes the remedy cannot rest on the notion that the decision to grant compensatory relief involves a resolution of policy considerations not susceptible of judicial discernment. Thus, in suits for damages based on violations of federal statutes lacking any express authorization of a damage remedy, this Court has authorized such relief where, in its view, damages are necessary to effectuate the congressional policy underpinning the substantive provisions of the statute. *J.I. Case Co. v. Borak.*[164]

If it is not the nature of the remedy which is thought to render a judgment as to the appropriateness of damages inherently "legislative," then it must be the nature of the legal interest offered as an occasion for invoking otherwise appropriate judicial relief. But I do not think that the fact that the interest is protected by the Constitution rather than statute or common law justifies the assertion that federal courts are powerless to grant damages in the absence of explicit congressional action authorizing the remedy. Initially, I note that it would be at least anomalous to conclude that the federal judiciary—while competent to choose among the range of traditional judicial remedies to implement statutory and common law policies, and even to generate substantive rules governing primary

164. [Footnote 4 in Justice Harlan's concurring opinion.] The *Borak* case is an especially clear example of the exercise of federal judicial power to accord damages as an appropriate remedy in the absence of statutory authorization of a federal cause of action. There we "implied" . . . a private cause of action for damages for violation of § 14(a) of the Securities Exchange Act of 1934. We did so in an area where federal regulation has been singularly comprehensive and elaborate administrative enforcement machinery had been provided. The exercise of judicial power involved in *Borak* simply cannot be justified in terms of statutory construction, nor did the *Borak* Court purport to do so. The notion of "implying" a remedy, therefore, as applied to cases like *Borak*, can only refer to a process whereby the federal judiciary exercises a choice among traditionally available judicial remedies according to reasons related to the substantive social policy embodied in an act of positive law.

behavior in furtherance of broadly formulated policies articulated by statute or Constitution [citing *Lincoln Mills* and *Clearfield Trust*] — is powerless to accord a damages remedy to vindicate social policies which, by virtue of their inclusion in the Constitution, are aimed predominantly at restraining the Government as an instrument of the popular will.

More importantly, the presumed availability of federal equitable relief against threatened invasions of constitutional interests appears entirely to negate the contention that the status of an interest as constitutionally protected divests federal courts of the power to grant damages absent express congressional authorization. Congress provided specially for the exercise of equitable remedial powers by federal courts in part because of the limited availability of equitable remedies in state courts in the early days of the Republic. And this Court's decisions make clear that, at least absent congressional restrictions, the scope of equitable remedial discretion is to be determined according to the distinctive historical traditions of equity as an institution. The reach of a federal district court's "inherent equitable powers," is broad indeed; nonetheless, the federal judiciary is not empowered to grant equitable relief in the absence of congressional action extending jurisdiction over the subject matter of the suit.

If explicit congressional authorization is an absolute prerequisite to the power of a federal court to accord compensatory relief regardless of the necessity or appropriateness of damages as a remedy simply because of the status of a legal interest as constitutionally protected, then it seems to me that explicit congressional authorization is similarly prerequisite to the exercise of equitable remedial discretion in favor of constitutionally protected interests. Conversely, if a general grant of jurisdiction to the federal courts by Congress is thought adequate to empower a federal court to grant equitable relief for all areas of subject-matter jurisdiction enumerated therein, then it seems to me that the same statute is sufficient to empower a federal court to grant a traditional remedy at law. Of course, the special historical traditions governing the federal equity system might still bear on the comparative appropriateness of granting equitable relief as opposed to money damages. That possibility, however, relates, not to whether the federal courts have the power to afford one type of remedy as opposed to the other, but rather to the criteria which should govern the exercise of our power. To that question, I now pass.

III

The major thrust of the Government's position is that, where Congress has not expressly authorized a particular remedy, a federal court should exercise its power to accord a traditional form of judicial relief at the behest of a litigant, who claims a constitutionally protected interest has been invaded, only where the remedy is "essential," or "indispensable for vindicating constitutional rights." While this "essentially" test is most clearly articulated with respect to damage remedies, apparently the Government believes the same test explains the exercise of equitable remedial powers. It is argued that historically the Court has rarely exercised the power to accord such relief in the absence of an express congressional authorization and that "[i]f Congress had thought that federal officers should be subject to a law different than state law, it would have had no difficulty in saying so, as it did with respect to state officers. . . ." Although conceding that the standard of determining whether a damage remedy should be utilized to effectuate statutory policies is one of "necessity" or "appropriateness," see J.I. Case Co. v. Borak, the government contends that questions concerning congressional discretion to modify judicial remedies relating to constitutionally protected interests warrant a more stringent constraint on the exercise of judicial power with respect to this class of legally protected interests.

These arguments for a more stringent test to govern the grant of damages in constitutional cases[165] seem to be adequately answered by the point that the judiciary has a particular responsibility to assure the vindication of constitutional interests such as those embraced by the Fourth Amendment. To be sure, "it must be remembered that legislatures are ultimate guardians of the liberties and welfare of the people in quite as great a degree as the courts." But it must also be recognized that the Bill of Rights is particularly intended to vindicate the interests of the individual in the face of the popular will as expressed in legislative majorities; at the very least, it strikes me as no more appropriate to await express congressional authorization of traditional judicial relief with regard to these legal interests than with respect to interests protected by federal statutes.

The question then, is, as I see it, whether compensatory relief is "necessary" or "appropriate" to the vindication of the interest asserted. *Cf.* J.I. Case Co. v. Borak. In resolving that question, it seems to me that the range of policy considerations we may take into account is at least as broad as the range of a legislature would consider with respect to an express statutory authorization of a traditional remedy. In this regard I agree with the Court that the appropriateness of according Bivens compensatory relief does not turn simply on the deterrent effect liability will have on federal official conduct. Damages as a traditional form of compensation for invasion of a legally protected interest may be entirely appropriate even if no substantial deterrent effects on future official lawlessness might be thought to result. Bivens, after all, has invoked judicial processes claiming entitlement to compensation for injuries resulting from allegedly lawless official behavior, if those injuries are properly compensable in money damages. I do not think a court of law—vested with the power to accord a remedy—should deny him his relief simply because he cannot show that future lawless conduct will thereby be deterred.

And I think it is clear that Bivens advances a claim of the sort that, if proved, would be properly compensable in damages. The personal interests protected by the Fourth Amendment are those we attempt to capture by the notion of "privacy"; while the Court today properly points out that the type of harm which officials can inflict when they invade protected zones of an individual's life are different from the types of harm private citizens inflict on one another, the experience of judges in dealing with private trespass and false imprisonment claims supports the conclusion that courts of law are capable of making the types of judgment concerning causation and magnitude of injury necessary to accord meaningful compensation for invasion of Fourth Amendment rights.

On the other hand, the limitations on state remedies for violation of common law rights by private citizens argue in favor of a federal damages remedy. The

165. [Footnote 7 in Justice Harlan's concurrence.] I express no view on the Government's suggestion that congressional authority to simply discard the remedy the Court today authorizes might be in doubt; nor do I understand the Court's opinion today to express any view on that particular question.

injuries inflicted by officials acting under color of law, while no less compensable in damages than those inflicted by private parties, are substantially different in kind. It seems to me entirely proper that these injuries be compensable according to uniform rules of federal law, especially in light of the very large element of federal law which must in any event control the scope of official defenses to liability. [*Howard v. Lyons.*] Certainly, there is very little to be gained from the standpoint of federalism by preserving different rules of liability for federal officers dependent on the State where the injury occurs.

Putting aside the desirability of leaving the problem of federal official liability to the vagaries of common law actions, it is apparent that some form of damages is the only possible remedy for someone in Bivens' alleged position. It will be a rare case indeed in which an individual in Bivens' position will be able to obviate the harm by securing injunctive relief from any court. However desirable a direct remedy against the Government might be as a substitute for individual official liability, the sovereign still remains immune to suit. Finally, assuming Bivens' innocence of the crime charged, the "exclusionary rule" is simply irrelevant. For people in Bivens' shoes, it is damages or nothing.

The only substantial policy consideration advanced against recognition of a federal cause of action for violation of Fourth Amendment rights by federal officials is the incremental expenditure of judicial resources that will be necessitated by this class of litigation. There is, however, something ultimately self-defeating about this argument. For if, as the Government contends, damages will rarely be realized by plaintiffs in these cases because of jury hostility, the limited resources of the official concerned, etc., then I am not ready to assume that there will be a significant increase in the expenditure of judicial resources on these claims. Few responsible lawyers and plaintiffs are likely to choose the course of litigation if the statistical chances of success are truly *de minimis*. And I simply cannot agree with my Brother Black that the possibility of "frivolous" claims—if defined simply as claims with no legal merit—warrants closing the courthouse doors to people in Bivens' situation. There are other ways, short of that, of coping with frivolous lawsuits.

On the other hand, if—as I believe is the case with respect, at least, to the most flagrant abuses of official power—damages to some degree will be available when the option of litigation is chosen, then the question appears to be how Fourth Amendment interests rank on a scale of social values compared with, for example, the interests of stockholders defrauded by misleading proxies. *See J.I. Case Co. v. Borak.* Judicial resources, I am well aware, are increasingly scarce these days. Nonetheless, when we automatically close the courthouse door solely on this basis, we implicitly express a value judgment on the comparative importance of classes of legally protected interests. And current limitations upon the effective functioning of the courts arising from budgetary inadequacies should not be permitted to stand in the way of the recognition of otherwise sound constitutional principles.

Of course, for a variety of reasons, the remedy may not often be sought. And the countervailing interests in efficient law enforcement of course argue for a protective zone with respect to many types of Fourth Amendment violations. But, while I express no view on the immunity defense offered in the instant case, I deem it proper to venture the thought that at the very least such a remedy would be available for the most flagrant and patently unjustified sorts of police conduct. Although litigants may not often choose to seek relief, it is important, in a civilized society, that the judicial branch of the Nation's government stand ready to afford a remedy in these circumstances. It goes without saying that I intimate no view on the merits of petitioner's underlying claim.

For these reasons, I concur in the judgment of the Court.

MR. CHIEF JUSTICE BURGER, dissenting.

I dissent from today's holding which judicially creates a damage remedy not provided for by the Constitution and not enacted by Congress. We would more surely preserve the important values of the doctrine of separation of powers—and perhaps get a better result—by recommending a solution to the Congress as the branch of government in which the Constitution has vested the legislative power. Legislation is the business of the Congress, and it has the facilities and competence for that task—as we do not.

* * * *

The problems of both error and deliberate misconduct by law enforcement officials call for a workable remedy. Private damage actions against individual police officers concededly have not adequately met this requirement, and it would be fallacious to assume today's work of the Court in creating a remedy will really accomplish its stated objective. There is some validity to the claims that juries will not return verdicts against individual officers except in those unusual cases where the violation has been flagrant or where the error has been complete, as in the arrest of the wrong person or the search of the wrong house. There is surely serious doubt, for example, that a drug peddler caught packing his wares will be able to arouse much sympathy in a jury on the ground that the police officer did not announce his identity and purpose fully or because he failed to utter a "few more words." Jurors may well refuse to penalize a police officer at the behest of a person they believe to be a "criminal" and probably will not punish an officer for honest errors of judgment. In any event an actual recovery depends on finding non-exempt assets of the police officer from which a judgment can be satisfied.

I conclude, therefore, that an entirely different remedy is necessary but it is one that in my view is as much beyond judicial power as the step the Court takes today. Congress should develop an administrative or quasi-judicial remedy against the government itself to afford compensation and restitution for persons whose Fourth Amendment rights have been violated. The venerable doctrine of *respondeat superior* in our tort law provides an entirely appropriate conceptual basis for this remedy. If, for example, a security guard privately employed by a department store commits an assault or other tort on a customer such as an improper search, the victim has a simple and obvious remedy—an action for money damages against the guard's employer, the department store. Such a statutory scheme would have the added advantage of providing some remedy to the completely innocent persons who are sometimes the victims of illegal police conduct—something that the suppression doctrine, of course, can never accomplish.

A simple structure would suffice. For example, Congress could enact a statute along the following lines:

(a) a waiver of sovereign immunity as to the illegal acts of law enforcement officials committed in the performance of assigned duties;

(b) the creation of a cause of action for damages sustained by any person aggrieved by conduct of governmental agents in violation of the Fourth Amendment or statutes regulating official conduct;
(c) the creation of a tribunal, quasijudicial in nature or perhaps patterned after the United States Court of Claims to adjudicate all claims under the statute;
(d) a provision that this statutory remedy is in lieu of the exclusion of evidence secured for use in criminal cases in violation of the Fourth Amendment; and
(e) a provision directing that no evidence, otherwise admissible, shall be excluded from any criminal proceeding because of violation of the Fourth Amendment.

Once the constitutional validity of such a statute is established, it can reasonably be assumed that the States would develop their own remedial systems on the federal model. Indeed there is nothing to prevent a State from enacting a comparable statutory scheme without waiting for the Congress. Steps along these lines would move our system toward more responsible law enforcement on the one hand and away from the irrational and drastic results of the suppression doctrine on the other. Independent of the alternative embraced in this dissenting opinion, I believe the time has come to re-examine the scope of the exclusionary rule and consider at least some narrowing of its thrust so as to eliminate the anomalies it has produced.

In a country that prides itself on innovation, inventive genius, and willingness to experiment, it is a paradox that we should cling for more than a half century to a legal mechanism that was poorly designed and never really worked. I can only hope now that the Congress will manifest a willingness to view realistically the hard evidence of the half-century history of the suppression doctrine revealing thousands of cases in which the criminal was set free because the constable blundered and virtually no evidence that innocent victims of police error—such as petitioner claims to be—have been afforded meaningful redress.

Mr. Justice Black, dissenting.

There can be no doubt that Congress could create a federal cause of action for damages for an unreasonable search in violation of the Fourth Amendment. Although Congress has created such a federal cause of action against state officials acting under color of state law, it has never created such a cause of action against federal officials. For us to do so is, in my judgment, an exercise of power that the Constitution does not give us.

Even if we had the legislative power to create a remedy, there are many reasons why we should decline to create a cause of action where none has existed since the formation of our Government. The courts of the United States as well as those of the States are choked with lawsuits. The number of cases on the docket of this Court have reached an unprecedented volume in recent years. A majority of these cases are brought by citizens with substantial complaints—persons who are physically or economically injured by torts or frauds or governmental infringement of their rights; persons who have been unjustly deprived of their liberty or their property; and persons who have not yet received the equal opportunity in education, employment, and pursuit of happiness that was the dream of our forefathers. Unfortunately, there have also been a growing number of frivolous lawsuits, particularly actions for damages against law enforcement officers whose conduct has been judicially sanctioned by state trial and appellate courts and in many instances even by this Court. My fellow Justices on this Court and our brethren throughout the federal judiciary know only too well the time-consuming task of conscientiously poring over hundreds of thousands of pages of factual allegations of misconduct by police, judicial, and corrections officials. Of course, there are instances of legitimate grievances, but legislators might well desire to devote judicial resources to other problems of a more serious nature.

We sit at the top of a judicial system accused by some of nearing the point of collapse. Many criminal defendants do not receive speedy trials and neither society nor the accused are assured of justice when inordinate delays occur. Citizens must wait years to litigate their private civil suits. Substantial changes in correctional and parole systems demand the attention of the lawmakers and the judiciary. If I were a legislator I might well find these and other needs so pressing as to make me believe that the resources of lawyers and judges should be devoted to them rather than to civil damage actions against officers who generally strive to perform within constitutional bounds. There is also a real danger that such suits might deter officials from the proper and honest performance of their duties.

All of these considerations make imperative careful study and weighing of the arguments both for and against the creation of such a remedy under the Fourth Amendment. I would have great difficulty for myself in resolving the competing policies, goals, and priorities in the use of resources, if I thought it were my job to resolve those questions. But that is not my task. The task of evaluating the pros and cons of creating judicial remedies for particular wrongs is a matter for Congress and the legislatures of the States. Congress has not provided that any federal court can entertain a suit against a federal officer for violations of Fourth Amendment rights occurring in the performance of his duties. A strong inference can be drawn from creation of such actions against state officials that Congress does not desire to permit such suits against federal officials. Should the time come when Congress desires such lawsuits, it has before it a model of valid legislation, 42 U.S.C. § 1983, to create a damage remedy against federal officers. Cases could be cited to support the legal proposition which I assert, but it seems to me to be a matter of common understanding that the business of the judiciary is to interpret the laws and not to make them.

I dissent.

MR. JUSTICE BLACKMUN, dissenting.

I, too, dissent. I do so largely for the reasons expressed in Chief Judge Lumbard's thoughtful and scholarly opinion for the Court of Appeals. But I also feel that the judicial legislation, which the Court by its opinion today concededly is effectuating, opens the door for another avalanche of new federal cases. Whenever a suspect imagines, or chooses to assert, that a Fourth Amendment right has been violated, he will now immediately sue the federal officer in federal court. This will tend to stultify proper law enforcement and to make the day's labor for the honest and conscientious officer even more onerous and more critical. Why the Court moves in this direction at this time of our history, I do not know. The Fourth Amendment was adopted in 1791, and in all the intervening years neither the Congress nor the Court has seen fit to take this step. I had thought that for the truly aggrieved person other quite adequate remedies have always been available. If not, it is the Congress and not this Court that should act.

DISCUSSION AND QUESTIONS

The power to recognize a monetary remedy for constitutional violations. Both the majority and concurrence found support for their remedial power in (1) the federal courts' historical power to grant equitable relief, and (2) the Court's prior recognition, in *Borak*, of its power to grant monetary relief when "necessary" to promote the purposes of federal statutes. Justice Harlan concluded that the courts' historical power to develop equitable remedies is compelling proof of the courts' power to award monetary relief: "if a general grant of jurisdiction to the federal courts by Congress is thought adequate to empower a federal court to grant equitable relief for all areas of subject-matter jurisdiction enumerated therein, then it seems to me that the same statute is sufficient to empower a federal court to grant a traditional remedy at law."

At least regarding the federal courts' power to recognize a monetary remedy, is there an adequate answer to Justice Harlan's conclusion? Stated differently, is there a principled basis for distinguishing the courts' historical power to develop equitable remedies and its power to award damages? What about Justice Blackmun's observation that, since 1791 (when the Bill of Rights became effective), neither the Court nor Congress has exercised a power to develop monetary remedies for constitutional violations? Does that observation adequately answer Justice Harlan's reliance on historical practice?

Insofar as the majority relied on *Borak* and its power to infer statutory remedies, has the Court's subsequent rejection of *Borak* and its current insistence on congressional authorization of statutory remedies (expressly or by implication) undermined part of *Bivens*'s foundation? Does *Bivens* reflect a view of the Court's power that has become obsolescent?

On the other hand, should the Court have *greater* power when developing remedies to enforce the Constitution? After all, to the extent that "intent" is relevant, the Framers' intent and not that of Congress is what matters.[166] Granted, debates about the Framers' intent are notoriously difficult to resolve, and courts may have to speculate about the "constructive" intent of the Framers — that is, what they would have intended if faced with the specific remedial issue confronted by modern courts.[167] But if one accepts that constructive intent is a valid tool for constitutional interpretation, does this render less important what Congress thinks proper?

The three dissenting justices argued that the Court lacks power to develop a monetary remedy to enforce the Constitution because this violates the constitutional separation of powers. They articulated a view we have heard articulated earlier by Justice Powell when considering implied statutory causes, namely, that developing monetary remedies is a "legislative" function. As Justice Burger commented, "legislation is the business of the Congress, and it has the facilities and competence for that task — as we do not." Justice Blackmun styled the majority's ruling "judicial legislation." But these justices did not join issue

166. The concept of the "Framers' intent" is, admittedly, fraught with ambiguity. For example, in *District of Columbia v. Heller*, 128 S. Ct. 2783 (2008), which affirmed a citizen's general Second Amendment right to keep and bear weapons, the majority emphasized the *historical* understanding of the Second Amendment's language and minimized the relevance of "legislative history" attending adoption of the amendment. *See, e.g., id.* at 2797-99, 2804. In any event, when assessing the existence of implied remedies under the Constitution, the focus shifts from Congress' contemporary understanding to eighteenth-century understandings of remedies.

167. Recall Professor Field's discussion of constructive intent regarding statutes.

with Justice Harlan, who provided an extended discussion of the Court's authority to devise a remedy for Bivens.

Are concerns about judicial "legislation" as important when constitutional rights are at issue? Consider the "legislative" processes leading to the enactment of statutes and the adoption of constitutional provisions. Can one usefully analogize from one context to the other? Is it relevant that the Fourteenth Amendment, section 5, specifically grants Congress the authority to enforce its provisions, while there is no similar grant in the Bill of Rights? Is it relevant that the Court has long considered itself the ultimate expositor of the Constitution's meaning?

Constitutional common lawmaking? The majority in *Bivens* declined to address whether Congress had the ultimate power to control constitutional remedies. Justice Brennan specifically noted that Congress has not attempted to withdraw the Court's remedial power by devising a constitutional remedy that is "equally effective in the view of Congress." What was Justice Brennan implying by this reference to congressional power over remedial issues? Did he imply that Congress might have the authority to preempt a judicial remedy *if* its own remedy is "equally effective"? Does the Constitution require some minimally effective remedy, whether created by Congress or the courts?

Professor Henry Monaghan has interpreted *Bivens*, as well as *Mapp v. Ohio* and *Miranda v. Arizona*, as examples of "constitutional common law." Professor Monaghan argues that the Court has devised in these and similar cases "a substructure of substantive, procedural, and remedial rules drawing their inspiration and authority from, but not required by, various constitutional provisions; in short, a constitutional common law subject to amendment, modification, or even reversal by Congress."[168] Professor Monaghan is careful to emphasize that the Court has not characterized its actions as "constitutional common law," but he nonetheless believes this is a fair description of many of the Court's decisions.

Professor Monaghan argues that this approach to understanding decisions like *Bivens* has several advantages. First it "enables the Court to act interstitially in protecting private rights, [and] also . . . provides the Court with a means for involving Congress in the continuing process of defining the content and consequences of individual liberties."[169] Second, by construing decisions like *Bivens* as a form of "common law" rather than constitutional interpretation, the Court has more flexibility in altering precedent and maintaining institutional integrity:

> So long as the rules are thought to be constitutional in character . . . pressures for change can be accommodated only through an express overruling of prior doctrine, or the whittling away of an original holding through spurious "distinctions" or through such devices as doctrines of waiver, standing, and harmless error. None of these tactics is without its institutional costs—both in terms of a break in the continuity of constitutional doctrine and in a departure from the norm of principled adjudication.[170]

Finally, a "common law" interpretation of decisions like *Bivens* enhances the political process for protecting individual liberties:

168. *See* Monaghan, *supra* note 42, at 3-4.
169. *Id.* at 27.
170. *Id.*

> Extending individual liberty on a common law basis therefore triggers an important shift in the political process. The Court, in effect, opens a dialogue with Congress, but one in which the factor of inertia is now on the side of individual liberty. For instead of requiring an affirmative act by Congress and the President to protect individual liberty, such an act is necessary to deny it. Even so, constitutional common law contains built-in safeguards — where the Court's rule is perceived to have gone too far, it can be rejected or modified by the political process without the necessity of a constitutional amendment.[171]

Is *Bivens* properly interpreted as a form of common lawmaking? How is your answer affected by these comments made by the majority and Justice Harlan:

- The majority acknowledged that Congress could replace the Court's remedy with one it considered "equally effective."
- The majority emphasized that it was merely applying a "normal" remedy applied in other settings, and rejected "respondents' formulation of the question as whether the availability of money damages is necessary to enforce the Fourth Amendment."
- Justice Harlan concluded that Congress' "general grant of jurisdiction" entailed the power to afford a "traditional remedy."

Other scholars have disputed Professor Monaghan's interpretation of *Bivens.* For example, Professors Schrock and Welsh argue that the Court concluded in *Bivens* "that for persons circumstanced as was Mr. Bivens, the constitutional guarantee embraces a right of action — the right to damages ascribed to Bivens derives from the fourth amendment itself."[172] Further, they raise doubts about the legitimacy of "constitutional common law" based on federalism, separation of powers, and the enforcement of civil liberties.

The Supreme Court's interpretation of its more controversial precedent governing police misconduct has been confusing. In *Dickerson v. United States,* 530 U.S. 428, 443 (2000), the Court rejected the argument that *Miranda* warnings are a form of common law subject to revision by Congress. The Court concluded that "*Miranda* announced a constitutional rule that Congress may not supersede legislatively."

But in *Davis v. United States,* 131 S. Ct. 2419, 2426 (2011), the Court stated that the exclusionary rule is a "'prudential' doctrine created by this Court to 'compel respect for the constitutional guaranty.'" The Court declined to apply the rule when police officers relied on binding circuit court precedent to conduct an automobile search, and that precedent was later overturned by the Court. The Court concluded that the exclusionary rule's deterrent effect would not be served when police performed "a search in objectively reasonable reliance on binding judicial precedent." Six justices of the Court wrote this about the exclusionary rule: "The [Fourth] Amendment says nothing about suppressing evidence obtained in violation of this command. That rule — the exclusionary rule — is a 'prudential' doctrine created by this Court to 'compel respect for the constitutional guaranty.' Exclusion is 'not a personal constitutional right,' nor is it designed to 'redress the injury' occasioned by an unconstitutional search." *Id.* at 2426.

171. *Id.* at 29.

172. *See* Thomas S. Schrock & Robert C. Welsh, *Reconsidering the Constitutional Common Law,* 91 Harv. L. Rev. 1118, 1136 (1978).

As you consider the Court's decisions after *Bivens*, keep in mind the dispute about whether *Bivens* is constitutional interpretation, constitutional common law, or a derivation from jurisdictional statutes (as Justice Harlan suggested). Which view is more consistent with the Court's application of *Bivens* in later cases?

The role of state law. The Court rejected the defendants' contention that state law provided Bivens whatever relief he was entitled to. According to the Court, state tort law does not protect the identical interests protected by the Fourth Amendment. Further, a federal law enforcement official's authority to act inevitably poses federal questions, including the appropriate defenses to state-law claims. *See Howard v. Lyons*, 360 U.S. 593 (1959). Consequently, any state-law claim against a federal official will be interlarded with federal defenses. This, according to Justice Harlan, suggests that federal officials should operate under uniform federal rules and not be subject to "the vagaries of common law actions" in each state.

Although one might infer from *Bivens* that state law is now irrelevant in suits to enforce constitutional claims, this is not the case. Within three years of *Bivens*, Congress amended the FTCA and extended the respondeat superior liability of the United States "for any claim arising . . . out of assault, battery, false imprisonment, false arrest, abuse of process, or malicious prosecution" committed by federal "investigative or law enforcement officers." *See* 28 U.S.C. § 2680(h). Section 2674 of the FTCA renders the United States liable for such claims if, under the law of the state where the officer's conduct occurred, a private person would be liable. In an appreciable number of situations, state law affords injured persons protections that overlap with constitutional protections. Where state and federal law overlap, the FTCA permits the injured person to elect remedies, choosing to sue either the United States under the FTCA or the officer under *Bivens*. *See* 28 U.S.C. § 2679(b)(2) (FTCA remedy is not exclusive when claim arises from "a violation of the Constitution of the United States").

Do these later congressional amendments to the FTCA ratify the Court's understanding of its power in *Bivens*? As we have learned in the previous section, the Court has never doubted its authority to exercise a delegated rulemaking power. Does the FTCA constitute some form of delegation, or at least a ratification of the Court's belief it has the power to develop constitutional remedies?

Judicial discretion to recognize a constitutional remedy. Justice Harlan's concurrence explicitly separated two questions: whether the Court has authority to recognize a monetary remedy for constitutional violations, and what criteria should govern the exercise of that power. Justice Harlan's approach is similar to the Court's approach in *Clearfield Trust*, where the Court distinguished the issue of its authority to develop common law and the issue of whether and how it should formulate the common-law rule.

Both the majority and Justice Harlan dispose of the defendants' attempts to establish certain prerequisites for inferring a constitutional remedy. For example, Justice Harlan rejected the argument that an implied remedy is appropriate only when needed to deter constitutional violations. He focused, instead, on the interests of Mr. Bivens, for whom "it [was] damages or nothing." The majority mentioned the *absence* of two factors that, it suggests, might have influenced its decision if present. First, the Court noted that there were no "special factors" counseling caution in granting Mr. Bivens damages. Second, the Court noted that Congress has not enacted an alternative remedy with "explicit" directions that it be the exclusive remedy. As we soon see, these factors take on critical importance in later decisions.

The Court in *Bivens* also rejected the contention that it lacked institutional "competence" to devise constitutional remedies. Justice Harlan responded to challenges to the Court's competence by citing to the Court's similar exercise of remedial powers in other common-law contexts and in *Borak*. Dissenting justices, on the other hand, raised several policy concerns they thought best suited to congressional resolution, including the impact of *Bivens* actions on the federal courts' workload, and the possibility that *Bivens* actions might overdeter law enforcement activity.

Reflect on our study, in Chapter 10, of constitutional claims against state- and local-government officials under § 1983. As we learned in that chapter, the Court has developed a highly sophisticated body of federal law to govern such suits, ranging from liability standards to immunities.[173] Although the Court has attempted to attribute many of its rulings to legislative history, it is difficult to avoid the conclusion that the ultimate foundation of many Court rulings is perceived policy. In fact, the Court—including conservative justices—has acknowledged its policymaking role.

Does the Court's quite extensive role in developing rules to govern claims under § 1983 undermine the argument that it lacks competence to do the same under *Bivens*? That is, assuming the Court has authority to develop constitutional remedies, does § 1983 jurisprudence answer doubts about its competence?

Davis v. Passman. In *Davis v. Passman*,[174] decided eight years after *Bivens*, the Court affirmed a damages remedy on behalf of a congressional aide who was terminated by Congressman Passman because the congressman thought he needed "a man" to serve as his administrative aide. 442 U.S. at 230. At the time, neither Title VII nor state law provided the plaintiff a remedy for gender discrimination.[175] The aide sued Congressman Passman under the Fifth Amendment's Due Process Clause, and argued that she was entitled to recover damages for her termination. The court of appeals disagreed, concluding that an implied remedy was precluded based on the Court's standard for inferring statutory remedies, which the Court announced four years earlier in *Cort v. Ash*, 422 U.S. 66 (1975). Nor did the circuit court believe that a damages remedy was "constitutionally compelled." 442 U.S. at 233.

The Supreme Court reversed and held (1) that the plaintiff "had a cause of action under the Fifth Amendment," and (2) that the only remaining question was whether it was "appropriate" to recognize a damages remedy to redress her injury. The Court, in an opinion by Justice Brennan, the author of the majority opinion in *Bivens*, found that a damages remedy was "judicially manageable," and also found that Congress had not impliedly rejected a remedy against members of Congress when it failed to extend Title VII to congressional employees. As in *Bivens*, the Court mentioned but had no occasion to determine whether,

173. As discussed in Chapter 10, the Court has often interchanged its rulings under § 1983 and *Bivens*, as when it elaborates on the doctrine of qualified immunity.

174. 442 U.S. 228 (1979).

175. Congress would extend employment discrimination laws to itself in the years following *Davis*.

"were Congress to create equally effective alternative remedies, the need for damages relief might be obviated." *Id.* at 248.

Four justices dissented. Justice Powell, who that same Term had issued his strong dissent in *Cannon v. University of Chicago*, 441 U.S. 667 (1979), contested the majority's suggestion that a *Bivens* remedy "must" be recognized by the courts unless an "equally effective" remedy is available to a plaintiff. 442 U.S. at 252 (Powell, J., dissenting). Justice Powell believed that separation of powers counseled the Court to refrain from authorizing a damages remedy against a member of Congress. At the same time, Justice Powell did *not* dispute that the Court had authority to develop a monetary remedy under *Bivens*. He agreed that the Court "necessarily has wider latitude in interpreting the Constitution than it does in construing a statute," and that it has a "greater responsibility" for enforcing constitutional rights than statutory rights. *Id.* at 252 n.1. Perhaps this helps explain why Justice Powell did not allude to the Court's precedent inferring statutory remedies.

Carlson v. Green. In *Carlson v. Green*, 446 U.S. 14 (1980), the Court considered whether to recognize a *Bivens* remedy on behalf of the estate of a federal prisoner who had allegedly died because he was subjected to "cruel and unusual punishment" (inadequate medical care) in violation of the Eighth Amendment. In *Carlson*, the Court addressed for the first time the situation of a plaintiff who had an alternative remedy under federal law, a negligence claim under the FTCA. *Id.* at 16. In the majority opinion, written by Justice Brennan, the Court held that the estate could recover damages based on the constitutional violation.

Justice Brennan began his opinion by affirming the Court's authority to recognize a damages remedy despite the absence of statutory authorization. The remedy could be "defeated" in two situations, which *Bivens* had foreshadowed. A monetary remedy would not be authorized

1. when defendants demonstrate special factors counseling hesitation in the absence of affirmative action by Congress," or
2. "when defendants show that Congress has provided an alternative remedy which it explicitly declared to be a *substitute* for recovery directly under the Constitution and viewed as equally effective."

Id. at 19-20. Justice Brennan found no "special factors" defeating a remedy against federal health care providers. Nor did he find that Congress, through the FTCA, had developed an exclusive remedy it deemed "equally effective" as a *Bivens* remedy. Justice Brennan mentioned, among other things, that Congress had expressly declined to make the FTCA an exclusive remedy for the "intentional" torts of federal officials. *Id.* at 20. Justice Brennan also determined that the FTCA was not "equally effective" as a *Bivens* remedy, since it (a) did not impose liability on the official wrongdoer, thus reducing the "deterrent" effect of the remedy; (b) did not provide for trial by jury; and (c) did not permit the recovery of punitive damages. Finally, because the FTCA incorporates state-law liability rules, it does not promote the federal interest in having a "uniform" rule of constitutional liability. *Id.* at 21-23.

Justice Powell concurred in the judgment, agreeing that the FTCA did not provide and was not intended to provide a remedy to replace *Bivens* remedies. But he took exception to the majority's description of the appropriate methodology for inferring a constitutional remedy. According to Justice Powell, "We are concerned here with inferring a right of action for damages directly from the Constitution." *Id.* at 26 (Powell, J., concurring). When inferring such a right of action, the Court must exercise a "principled discretion." Justice Powell argued that there seemed to be little discretion left in the majority's view, since it appeared that a statutory remedy precluded a *Bivens* remedy only when Congress *explicitly* stated that its "equally effective" statutory remedy was exclusive. *Id.* at 27.

Justice Rehnquist dissented, arguing that the Court took a "wrong turn" in *Bivens. Id.* at 32. Justice Rehnquist agreed with Justice Powell that "*Bivens* inferred a constitutional damages remedy from the Fourth Amendment." *Id.* at 35. But he now believed that *Bivens* should be overturned. Justice Rehnquist argued that *Bivens* had erred in recognizing a judicial power to develop a monetary remedy for constitutional violations. He argued that the two main supports for this power enunciated by Justice Harlan in his *Bivens* concurrence were flawed. First, he rejected the contention that Congress' conferral of "arising under" jurisdiction entailed the power to develop remedies.[176] Section 1983, Justice Rehnquist noted, illustrated that Congress exercises its power to confer remedial authority on the federal courts independent of its conferral of jurisdiction. *Id.* at 39-40.

Second, Justice Rehnquist contended that *Bivens* was based on the now-obsolete view of the courts' remedial powers that prevailed under *Borak*, prior to the Court's decision in *Cort v. Ash.* According to Justice Rehnquist, it had "become clear since *Bivens* that there is nothing left of the rationale of *Borak.*" *Id.* at 41 n.5.

In conclusion, Justice Rehnquist stated, "In my view the authority of federal courts to fashion remedies based on the 'common law' of damages for constitutional violations likewise falls within the legislative domain, and does not exist where not conferred by Congress." *Id.* at 38. In sharp distinction to the majority's position, Justice Rehnquist saw no difference between the decision to infer a constitutional remedy and the decision to infer a statutory one.

c. The Contraction of Implied Constitutional Remedies After *Carlson*

In a series of decisions since *Carlson*, the Court has refused to recognize a *Bivens* remedy in other contexts. But the Court has not overturned *Bivens.* Instead, it has at least purported to work within the methodological framework of prior decisions in refusing to extend *Bivens* to other contexts.

Bush v. Lucas. In *Bush v. Lucas*, 462 U.S. 367 (1983), the Court refused to recognize an implied damages remedy under the First Amendment on behalf of a federal employee who alleged he was demoted because he made public statements criticizing NASA. Although Bush pursued civil service remedies before a federal agency and was reinstated with back pay, he simultaneously sued his supervisors for violations of state defamation law and the First Amendment.

176. Recall that Justice Harlan wrote in *Bivens* that "if a general grant of jurisdiction to the federal courts by Congress is thought adequate to empower a federal court to grant equitable relief for all areas of subject-matter jurisdiction enumerated therein, then it seems to me that the same statute is sufficient to empower a federal court to grant a traditional remedy at law."

Bush sought damages for the noneconomic injuries resulting from his demotion ("emotional and dignitary harms") as well as attorney's fees, neither of which was recoverable in his administrative action.

The Court held that statutory civil service remedies preempted the Court's power to grant Bush further relief under *Bivens.* Justice Stevens, writing for the majority, accepted that Congress had neither authorized nor preempted a *Bivens* remedy. He also accepted that, in civil service legislation, "Congress has provided a less than complete remedy for the wrong." *Id.* at 373. Justice Stevens further recognized that, were the Court writing "on a clean slate," it could either (1) affirm its "common law" power to develop an appropriate constitutional remedy, or (2) refuse to recognize any remedy not provided by Congress. But Court precedent appeared to "establish our power to grant relief that is not expressly authorized by statute," while counseling "that such power is to be exercised in the light of relevant policy determinations made by the Congress." *Id.* Somewhat confusingly, Justice Stevens announced that the Court's remedial power derived from its jurisdictional power,[177] while also stating that "the Constitution itself supports a private cause of action for damages against a federal official." *Id.* at 374.

Justice Stevens wrote that Congress' "elaborate remedial scheme" based on its careful consideration of "conflicting policy considerations" should not be augmented by a judicially developed remedy. Congress was in a "better position" to weigh workplace efficiency against the rights of federal employees, particularly given its ability to inform itself through "factfinding procedures" not available to the courts. *Id.* at 389. Justices Marshall and Blackmun concurred, finding "special factors" justified Court deference to Congress' "comprehensive scheme." *Id.* at 390. They also concluded that civil service relief was no less "effective" than a *Bivens* remedy might be. *Id.* at 391.

Schweiker v. Chilicky.[178] In *Schweiker v. Chilicky,* 487 U.S. 412 (1988), a divided Court refused to recognize a *Bivens* remedy against administrative officials who wrongfully denied Social Security benefits to an estimated 200,000 claimants. Eventually Congress intervened and adopted emergency legislation to correct the offending administrative processes and restore wrongfully denied benefits. Nonetheless, persons who had suffered as the result of the denial of Social Security benefits sued federal officials under the Fifth Amendment's Due Process Clause.

As in *Bush v. Lucas,* the Court concluded that "special factors" counseled against recognizing a *Bivens* remedy, especially because Congress had enacted an alternative remedial scheme it believed "*adequate.*" *Id.* at 423. The Court recognized that the alternative scheme failed to compensate claimants for the noneconomic damages resulting from the wrongful denial of benefits, and also failed to deter official misconduct through the imposition of personal liability. Nonetheless, the Court found that Congress had provided "meaningful safeguards [and] remedies for aggrieved claimants. *Id.* at 425. In a showing of great

177. *See also id.* at 378 ("The federal courts' statutory jurisdiction to decide federal questions confers adequate power to award damages to the victim of a constitutional violation.").

178. Before *Schweiker,* the Court refused to give a *Bivens* remedy to military personnel who alleged discriminatory treatment by their superiors. *See Chappell v. Wallace,* 462 U.S. 296 (1983). The Court based its decision on "special factors" that required deference to the military's distinct system of military justice. In *United States v. Stanley,* 483 U.S. 669 (1987), the Court affirmed that *Bivens* suits are categorically precluded when they arise from military service.

deference to the institutional competence of Congress, the Court remarked that "[w]hether or not we believe that its response was the best response, Congress is the body charged with making the inevitable compromises required in the design of a massive and complex welfare benefits program." *Id.* at 429.

The dissent, authored by Justice Brennan, argued that the deference shown to Congress in prior decisions involving federal civil service and military service ("special factors") was not appropriate to disputes filed by private citizens. Justice Brennan also emphasized there was no indication that Congress *intended* its alternative remedial scheme to preempt a *Bivens* remedy. Further, the remedy provided by Congress simply failed to address the injuries alleged by the claimaints.

Correctional Services Corp. v. Malesko. In *Correctional Services Corp. v. Malesko,* 534 U.S. 61 (2001), the Court considered whether a *Bivens* remedy might be inferred against private, federal contractors operating a halfway house on behalf of the Federal Bureau of Prisons. Justice Rehnquist, writing for the majority in *Malesko,* rejected any extension of *Bivens* remedies to private entities. His remarks concerning *Bivens* remedies, if implemented in future decisions, would seem to foreclose most if not all future applications of *Bivens.*

First, Justice Rehnquist observed, "Our authority to imply a new constitutional tort, not expressly authorized by statute, is anchored in our general jurisdiction to decide all cases 'arising under the Constitution, laws, or treaties of the United States.' 28 U.S.C. § 1331." *Id.* at 66. If *Bivens* remedies are not "anchored" in the Constitution itself, there may be no constitutional barrier to eliminating them.

Second, Justice Rehnquist summarized *Bivens* precedent quite narrowly:

> In 30 years of *Bivens* jurisprudence we have extended its holding only twice, to provide an otherwise nonexistent cause of action against *individual officers* alleged to have acted unconstitutionally, or to provide a cause of action for a plaintiff who lacked *any alternative remedy* for harms caused by an individual officer's unconstitutional conduct. Where such circumstances are not present, we have consistently rejected invitations to extend *Bivens*. . . .

Id. at 70 (emphasis in original). Justice Rehnquist's reference to the lack of "any alternative remedy" contrasts with earlier opinions of the Court suggesting a *Bivens* remedy might give way to an "equally effective" remedy authorized by Congress.

Third, Justice Rehnquist remarked that "[t]he purpose of *Bivens* is to deter individual federal officers from committing constitutional violations." *Id.* at 70. Still later in his opinion, Justice Rehnquist added that *Bivens* is concerned "solely with deterring the unconstitutional acts of individual officers." *Id.* at 71. This interpretation of the purpose of *Bivens* remedies contrasts with the Court's statements in earlier decisions, emphasizing that such remedies ensure "the vindication of the interest asserted" by the victim of a constitutional violation and "make good the wrong done." *See, e.g., Bivens, supra.*[179]

Justice Stevens, writing for the four dissenting justices, rebuked the majority for its antipathy toward *Bivens.* According to Justice Stevens, "the driving force

179. *See, e.g.,* Susan Bandes, Reinventing Bivens: The Self-Executing Constitution, 68 S. Cal. L. Rev. 289, 304 (1995) ("*Bivens* stands for the proposition that the existence of remedies for others is beside the point: The particular plaintiff before the court is entitled to adequate relief.").

behind the Court's decision is a disagreement with the holding in *Bivens* itself." Arguing for the institutional value of *stare decisis*, Justice Stevens concluded:

> [A] rule that has been such a well-recognized part of our law for over 30 years should be accorded full respect by the Members of this Court, whether or not they would have endorsed that rule when it was first announced. For our primary duty is to apply and enforce settled law, not to revise that law to accord with our own notions of sound policy.

Id. at 83.

Wilkie v. Robbins. A more recent application of the *Bivens* doctrine is *Wilkie v. Robbins*, 551 U.S. 537 (2007), which one commentator argues is an "unprecedented" decision denying the plaintiff any relief despite a constitutional violation.[180] In *Wilkie*, a private landowner and operator of a guest ranch sued officials of the Federal Bureau of Land Management (BLM). He alleged that BLM officials engaged in a campaign of harassment and coercion when he refused to grant the BLM an easement across his property in Wyoming. Justice Ginsburg's partial concurrence in *Wilkie* succinctly described the plaintiff's plight:

> Bureau of Land Management (BLM) officials in Wyoming made a careless error. They failed to record an easement obtained for the United States along a stretch of land on the privately owned High Island Ranch. Plaintiff-respondent Frank Robbins purchased the ranch knowing nothing about the easement granted by the prior owner. Under Wyoming law, Robbins took title to the land free of the easement. BLM officials, realizing their mistake, demanded from Robbins an easement—for which they did not propose to pay—to replace the one they carelessly lost. Their demand, one of them told Robbins, was nonnegotiable. Robbins was directed to provide the easement, or else. When he declined to follow that instruction, the BLM officials mounted a seven-year campaign of relentless harassment and intimidation to force Robbins to give in. They refused to maintain the road providing access to the ranch, trespassed on Robbins' property, brought unfounded criminal charges against him, canceled his special recreational use permit and grazing privileges, interfered with his business operations, and invaded the privacy of his ranch guests on cattle drives.

551 U.S. at 568-69 (Ginsburg, J., concurring in part and dissenting in part).

Robbins sued BLM officials alleging a *Bivens* claim under the Fifth Amendment as well as a claim under RICO.[181] The substantive constitutional issue framed by the plaintiff was this: "[C]an government officials avoid the Fifth Amendment's prohibition against taking property without just compensation by using their regulatory powers to harass, punish, and coerce a private citizen into giving the Government his property without payment?" 551 U.S. at 556 n.8.

Consider how the Court describes and applies its power under *Bivens*. Notice that the majority opinion in *Wilkie* was written by Justice Souter, one of four dissenting justices in *Malesko*. Notice also that *Wilkie* provided Chief Justice Roberts and Justice Alito their first opportunity to consider application of a *Bivens* remedy.

180. Laurence H. Tribe, *Death by a Thousand Cuts: Constitutional Wrongs Without Remedies After* Wilkie v. Robbins, 2007 Cato Sup. Ct. Rev. 23, 25.

181. 18 U.S.C. §§ 1961-1968.

WILKIE v. ROBBINS

551 U.S. 537 (2007)

JUSTICE SOUTER delivered the opinion of the Court.

* * * *

The first question is whether to devise a new *Bivens* damages action for retaliating against the exercise of ownership rights, in addition to the discrete administrative and judicial remedies available to a landowner like Robbins in dealing with the Government's employees. Bivens held that the victim of a Fourth Amendment violation by federal officers had a claim for damages, and in the years following we have recognized two more nonstatutory damages remedies, the first for employment discrimination in violation of the Due Process Clause, *Davis v. Passman*, and the second for an Eighth Amendment violation by prison officials, *Carlson v. Green*. But we have also held that any freestanding damages remedy for a claimed constitutional violation has to represent a judgment about the best way to implement a constitutional guarantee; it is not an automatic entitlement no matter what other means there may be to vindicate a protected interest, and in most instances we have found a *Bivens* remedy unjustified. We have accordingly held against applying the *Bivens* model to claims of First Amendment violations by federal employers, Bush v. Lucas, harm to military personnel through activity incident to service, United States v. Stanley, Chappell v. Wallace, and wrongful denials of Social Security disability benefits, *Schweiker v. Chilicky*. We have seen no case for extending *Bivens* to claims against federal agencies, F.D.I.C. v. Meyer, 510 U.S. 471 (1994), or against private prisons, Correctional Services Corp. v. Malesko, 534 U.S. 61 (2001).

Whatever the ultimate conclusion, however, our consideration of a *Bivens* request follows a familiar sequence, and on the assumption that a constitutionally recognized interest is adversely affected by the actions of federal employees, the decision whether to recognize a *Bivens* remedy may require two steps. In the first place, there is the question whether any alternative, existing process for protecting the interest amounts to a convincing reason for the Judicial Branch to refrain from providing a new and freestanding remedy in damages. But even in the absence of an alternative, a *Bivens* remedy is a subject of judgment: "the federal courts must make the kind of remedial determination that is appropriate for a common law tribunal, paying particular heed, however, to any special factors counselling hesitation before authorizing a new kind of federal litigation." [Citing *Bush v. Lucas.*]

[The Court then reviewed Robbins's legal history and concluded that he could have vindicated his rights in a variety of state and federal judicial and administrative proceedings, some of which had already occurred. At the same time, the Court recognized that Robbins would have to assert his interests in a variety of proceedings.]

This state of the law gives Robbins no intuitively meritorious case for recognizing a new constitutional cause of action, but neither does it plainly answer no to the question whether he should have it. Like the combination of public and private land ownership around the ranch, the forums of defense and redress open to Robbins are a patchwork, an assemblage of state and federal, administrative and judicial benches applying regulations, statutes and common law rules. It would be hard to infer that Congress expected the Judiciary to stay its *Bivens* hand, but equally hard to extract any clear lesson that *Bivens* ought to spawn a new claim. Compare Bush (refusing to create a *Bivens* remedy when faced with "an elaborate remedial system that has been constructed step by step, with careful attention to conflicting policy considerations"); and Schweiker ("Congress chose specific forms and levels of protection for the rights of persons affected"), with Bivens, (finding "no explicit congressional declaration that persons injured [in this way] may not recover money damages from the agents, but must instead be remitted to another remedy, equally effective in the view of Congress").

[Having recognized that there was no single remedial scheme in which Robbins could vindicate his interests, much less a congressionally authorized scheme, the Court considered whether "special factors" cautioned against granting a *Bivens* remedy. The Court grappled with the issue of how Robbins's Fifth Amendment claim might actually be implemented given the variety of ways in which he was allegedly harassed by federal officials. Concluding that a *Bivens* action to enforce the type of constitutional claim advocated by Robbins would likely be unmanageable, the Court made the following comments:]

[A] *Bivens* action to redress retaliation against those who resist Government impositions on their property rights would invite claims in every sphere of legitimate governmental action affecting property interests, from negotiating tax claim settlements to enforcing Occupational Safety and Health Administration regulations. Exercising any governmental authority affecting the value or enjoyment of property interests would fall within the *Bivens* regime, and across this enormous swath of potential litigation would hover the difficulty of devising a "too much" standard that could guide an employee's conduct and a judicial factfinder's conclusion.

The point here is not to deny that Government employees sometimes overreach, for of course they do, and they may have done so here if all the allegations are true. The point is the reasonable fear that a general *Bivens* cure would be worse than the disease.

In sum, defendants were acting in the name of the Bureau, which had the authority to grant (and had given) Robbins some use of public lands under its control and wanted a right-of-way in return. Defendants bargained hard by capitalizing on their discretionary authority and Robbins's violations of various permit terms, though truculence was apparent on both sides. One of the defendants, at least, clearly crossed the line into impermissible conduct in breaking into Robbins's lodge, although it is not clear from the record that any other action by defendants was more serious than garden-variety trespass, and the Government has successfully defended every decision to eliminate Robbins's permission to use public lands in the ways he had previously enjoyed. Robbins had ready at hand a wide variety of administrative and judicial remedies to redress his injuries. The proposal, nonetheless, to create a new *Bivens* remedy to redress such injuries collectively on a theory of retaliation for exercising his property right to exclude, or on a general theory of unjustifiably burdening his rights as a property owner, raises a serious difficulty of devising a workable cause of action. A judicial standard to identify illegitimate pressure going beyond legitimately hard bargaining would be endlessly knotty to work out, and a general provision for tortlike liability when Government employees are unduly zealous in pressing a governmental interest affecting property would invite an onslaught of *Bivens* actions.

We think accordingly that any damages remedy for actions by Government employees who push too hard for the Government's benefit may come better, if at all, through legislation. Congress is in a far better position than a court to evaluate the impact of a new species of litigation against those who act on the public's behalf. And Congress can tailor any remedy to the problem perceived, thus lessening the risk of raising a tide of suits threatening legitimate initiative on the part of the Government's employees.

[The Court's discussion of Robbins's RICO claim, which was rejected, is omitted.]

JUSTICE THOMAS, with whom JUSTICE SCALIA joins, concurring.

The Court correctly concludes that *Bivens* does not supply a cause of action in this case. I therefore join its opinion. I write separately because I would not extend *Bivens* even if its reasoning logically applied to this case. *Bivens* is a relic of the heady days in which this Court assumed common law powers to create causes of action. Accordingly, in my view, *Bivens* and its progeny should be limited "to the precise circumstances that they involved."

JUSTICE GINSBURG, with whom JUSTICE STEVENS joins, concurring in part and dissenting in part.

* * * *

Robbins commenced this lawsuit to end the incessant harassment and intimidation he endured. He asserted that the Fifth Amendment's Takings Clause forbids government action calculated to acquire private property coercively and cost-free. He further urged that federal officials dishonor their constitutional obligation when they act in retaliation for the property owner's resistance to an uncompensated taking. In support of his claim for relief, Robbins relied on *Bivens*. The Court recognizes that the "remedy" to which the Government would confine Robbins—a discrete challenge to each offending action as it occurs—is inadequate. A remedy so limited would expose Robbins' business to "death by a thousand cuts." Nevertheless, the Court rejects his claim, for it fears the consequences. Allowing Robbins to pursue this suit, the Court maintains, would open the floodgates to a host of unworthy suits "in every sphere of legitimate governmental action affecting property interests."

* * * *

Some Members of this Court consider *Bivens* a dated precedent [quoting the concurrence of Justices Scalia and Thomas]. But the Court has so far adhered to *Bivens*' core holding: Absent congressional command or special factors counseling hesitation, "victims of a constitutional violation by a federal agent have a right to recover damages against the official in federal court despite the absence of any statute conferring such a right." *Carlson*.

The Court does not hold that Robbins' *Bivens* suit is precluded by a carefully calibrated administrative regime like those at issue in *Bush, Chilicky, Chappell,* or Stanley, nor could it. As the Court recognizes, Robbins has no alternative remedy for the relentless torment he alleges. True, Robbins may have had discrete remedies for particular instances of harassment. But, in these circumstances, piecemeal litigation, the Court acknowledges, cannot forestall "death by a thousand cuts." For plaintiffs in Robbins' shoes, "it is damages or nothing." Despite the Court's awareness that Robbins lacks an effective alternative remedy, it nevertheless bars his suit. The Court finds, on the facts of this case, a special factor counseling hesitation quite unlike any we have recognized before.

Allowing Robbins to seek damages for years of harassment, the Court says, "would invite an onslaught of *Bivens* actions," with plaintiffs pressing claims "in every sphere of legitimate governmental action affecting property interests." The "floodgates" argument the Court today embraces has been rehearsed and rejected before.

* * * *

The Court's opinion is driven by the "fear" that a "*Bivens* cure" for the retaliation Robbins experienced may be "worse than the disease." This concern seems to me exaggerated. Robbins' suit is predicated upon the agents' vindictive motive, and the presence of this element in his claim minimizes the risk of making everyday bureaucratic overreaching fare for constitutional litigation. Indeed, one could securely forecast that the flood the Court fears would not come to pass. In *Passman*, the Courts said that it did not "perceive the potential for . . . a deluge," because, under 42 U.S.C. § 1983, "a damages remedy [was] already available to redress injuries such as petitioner's when they occur under color of state law." A similar sideglance could be cast here. Because we have no reason to believe that state employees are any more or less respectful of Fifth Amendment rights than federal agents, § 1983 provides a controlled experiment. If numerous *Bivens* claims would eventuate were courts to entertain claims like Robbins', then courts should already have encountered endeavors to mount Fifth Amendment Takings suits under § 1983. But the Court of Appeals, the Solicitor General, and Robbins all agree that there are no reported cases on charges of retaliation by state officials against the exercise of Takings Clause rights.

* * * *

Thirty-six years ago, the Court created the *Bivens* remedy. In doing so, it assured that federal officials would be subject to the same constraints as state officials in dealing with the fundamental rights of the people who dwell in this land. Today, the Court decides that elaboration of *Bivens* to cover Robbins' case should be left to Congress. The *Bivens* analog to § 1983, however, is hardly an obscure part of the Court's jurisprudence. If Congress wishes to codify and further define the *Bivens* remedy, it may do so at anytime. Unless and until Congress acts, however, the Court should not shy away from the effort to ensure that bedrock constitutional rights do not become "merely precatory."

DISCUSSION AND QUESTIONS

Justice Souter, speaking for seven members of the Court, observes that "even in the absence of an alternative, a *Bivens* remedy is a subject of judgment: the federal courts must make the kind of remedial determination that is appropriate for a common law tribunal." Consider how this contrasts with prior opinions. For example, *Davis v. Passman* accords the Court far less discretion in declining to recognize a *Bivens* remedy. As described by concurring Justice Powell, a *Bivens* remedy "must" be recognized by the courts unless an "equally effective" remedy is available to a plaintiff. 442 U.S. at 252.

Justice Souter also emphasized the importance of whether a new *Bivens* remedy is a "workable" cause of action. Because of doubts that Robbins's claimed cause of action would be "workable" in the administrative environment, the Court concluded that Congress had superior competence to devise an appropriate remedy.

According to Harvard Professor Laurence Tribe, who represented Robbins pro bono in *Wilkie*, the Court's decision was unprecedented. He observes, "[F]or the first time since *Bivens* [the Court] held, without any indication from Congress that it disfavored the application of a *Bivens* remedy in such circumstances, that a private citizen could not sue a government official for a constitutional violation, even in the absence of any alternative to such a suit that would operate to deter that kind of violation or at least redress it when deterrence failed."[182] According to Professor Tribe, not only did the Court leave Robbins without an effective remedy, the Court announced that the decision to recognize a constitutional remedy is one of "judgment." The result is a seeming "unbridled" judicial discretion that, in its own right, raises questions about the legitimacy of the Court's power.[183]

Do you agree with Professor Tribe that the Court's *Bivens* power is now a fully discretionary power with no principled limitations?

Notice that, in one important sense, *Wilkie* cannot be classified as a "conservative" decision, since it rejected the claims of a rancher whose private property interests were compromised by very "activist" federal officials. Yet, while the majority conceded that Robbins's constitutional rights may have been violated, they declined to provide him a viable forum for litigating his assembly of claims. Oddly, members of the Court not known for their "conservative" dispositions—Justices Ginsburg and Stevens—showed greatest sympathy for Robbins's plight.

In *Hui v. Castaneda*, 130 S. Ct. 1845 (2010), newly appointed Justice Sotomayor wrote for a unanimous Court in refusing to authorize a *Bivens* remedy against officers and employees of the Public Health Service based on their alleged violation of an immigration detainee's Fifth and Eighth Amendment rights. The detainee's survivors had sued the individual federal officials for medical negligence in failing to diagnose metastatic cancer. The Court held that the survivors' exclusive remedy was to sue the United States under the FTCA. The Court reasoned that its inquiry "begins and ends" with the express language of a federal statute making suit against the United States the "exclusive" remedy for medical negligence and granting public health officials immunity from suit. *Id.* at 1850.

The Ninth Circuit had recognized a *Bivens* remedy in reliance on *Carlson v. Green*. The Ninth Circuit pointed out that (1) the FTCA remedy was "not equally effective as a *Bivens* remedy"; and (2) no "special factors" militated against inferring a *Bivens* remedy against public health officials. *Id.* The Supreme Court found this reasoning unpersuasive given the clear statutory language immunizing public health personnel:

> In construing [the federal statute], we are mindful of the confines of our judicial role. Respondents' amici caution that providing special immunity for [Public Health Service] personnel is contrary to the public interest. Respondents likewise contend that allowing *Bivens* claims against [public health] personnel is necessary to ensure an adequate standard of care in federal detention facilities, and they further urge that permitting such actions would not endanger [the Public Health Service's] institutional interests as it would simply place PHS personnel in the same

182. Laurence H. Tribe, *Death by a Thousand Cuts: Constitutional Wrongs Without Remedies After* Wilkie v. Robbins, 2007 Cato Sup. Ct. Rev. 23, 25.

183. *See id.* at 71.

> position as other federal employees who perform similar functions. We are required, however, to read the statute according to its text. Because [the statute] plainly precludes a *Bivens* action against petitioners for the harms alleged in this case, we reverse the judgment of the Ninth Circuit. . . .

Id. at 1854-55.

One year before *Castaneda* was decided, the Court was asked to recognize a *Bivens* remedy against federal officials in *Ashcroft v. Iqbal*, 556 U.S. 662 (2009). The plaintiff alleged that federal officials—including former Attorney General Ashcroft—had violated his rights under the Free Exercise Clause of the First Amendment. Although the majority avoided ruling on the *Bivens* question, it reiterated the Court's reluctance to expand *Bivens*:

> Because implied causes of action are disfavored, the Court has been reluctant to extend *Bivens* liability "to any new context or new category of defendants." That reluctance might well have disposed of respondent's First Amendment claim of religious discrimination. For while we have allowed a *Bivens* action to redress a violation of the equal protection component of the Due Process Clause of the Fifth Amendment, we have not found an implied damages remedy under the Free Exercise Clause. Indeed, we have declined to extend *Bivens* to a claim sounding in the First Amendment [citing *Bush v. Lucas*, summarized in the text at page ***]. Petitioners do not press this argument, however, so we assume, without deciding, that respondent's First Amendment claim is actionable under *Bivens*.

Id. at 675 (citations omitted).

Finally, in *Minecci v. Pollard*, 132 S. Ct. 617 (2012), the Court refused to recognize a *Bivens* remedy to enforce Eighth Amendment rights against employees of a private company operating a prison on behalf of the United States. The Court affirmed its approach to *Bivens* as stated in *Wilkie v. Robbins* and concluded that state tort law provided an "alternative, existing process" sufficient to protect the plaintiff's constitutional interests. *Id.* at 623. The Court recognized that state law capped the damages recoverable by the plaintiff and also denied damages for emotional injury but nonetheless found the state-law remedies adequate.

PROBLEM 11-5

A Fit Punishment?

Montana Quality Food Processing, Inc. (MQF) recently went out of business. MQF has a simple explanation for its business failure—an official of the Federal Food and Drug Administration (FDA) retaliated against the small company when its owner made numerous complaints about the official's failure to contain outbreaks of E. coli bacteria by more careful monitoring of large meat suppliers, like ConAgra.

In 2001, an FDA official named Munster identified the presence of E. coli bacteria in meat processed by MQF. MQF carefully reviewed its operations and determined that the tainted meat had been supplied by ConAgra. MQF reported this to Munster and urged that the FDA institute procedures for isolating and monitoring meat supplies received from large suppliers like ConAgra. Munster ignored MQF's request. Further, Munster threatened to suspend meat inspections at MQF's facilities in Shelby, Montana, which would have immediately resulted in a shutdown of MQF's business. According to Munster, "you need to address the problem locally rather than pointing the finger at someone else."

MQF complied with Munster's requests, at great cost. MQF also contacted Montana's U.S. senators and congressman. These representatives urged Munster and the FDA to "take seriously" MQF's concerns. But the main consequence of the intervention was yet greater regulation and inspection at MQF's facilities.

MQF commenced administrative proceedings against the FDA, alleging that Munster's actions were retaliatory in violation of the First Amendment. Under federal law, MQF could seek both injunctive and declaratory relief in the agency proceedings, but no damages.

Eventually, other FDA officials were able to verify that ConAgra was, in fact, the source of E. coli–infected meat supplies. But by that time, MQF had gone out of business. Its administrative action was dismissed as "moot."

MQF has now filed a *Bivens* action against Munster in the United States District Court for the District of Montana. In support of its action, MQF argues (1) it has no alternative remedy for monetary relief under federal statutes; and (2) unlike the situation in *Wilkie v. Robbins*, MQF is challenging the specific wrongful actions of a single federal official, making resolution of his claim "far more manageable."

Discuss whether MQF has a plausible argument for recovering under *Bivens*. If you need additional information, please explain what you need.

d. Concluding Observations on *Bivens* Remedies

More recent decisions have led some observers to conclude the Court has overturned *Bivens* without saying so. Even though the Court has yet to embrace the stronger language used by Justices Scalia and Thomas in cases like *Malesko* and *Wilkie*, it appears the *Bivens* remedy is a "mere shadow of its former self"[184] that is "destined to fade away."[185] Professor Tribe now believes that "the *Bivens* doctrine is . . . on life support with little prospect of recovery."[186]

Yet one observation gives us pause in writing obituaries for the federal courts' rulemaking power. Over the past two decades, most of the Court's important decisions concerning constitutional and statutory remedies turn on the vote of a *single* justice. Further, it is apparent that *stare decisis* is less influential in Court decisions concerning common-lawmaking power—the contraction of the broad power recognized in cases like *Bivens* and *Borak* forcefully demonstrates this. With small changes in the Court's membership, we could see significant changes in the Court's view of its common-lawmaking power.

184. *See* Newman, *supra* note 135, at 472.

185. David L. Shapiro, *The Role of Precedent in Constitutional Adjudication: An Introspection*, 86 Tex. L. Rev. 929, 941 n.41 (2008)

186. *See* Tribe, *supra* note 182, at 26.

EXPLORING DOCTRINE

What Methodology Does the Court Actually Use When Deciding Whether to Recognize a Bivens Remedy?

When you reflect on the Court's opinions from *Bivens* to *Wilkie*, can you confidently predict what methodology the Court will use when deciding whether to recognize a *Bivens* remedy? In particular, how do you answer the following questions?:

- Who bears the burden of establishing/refuting a *Bivens* remedy? Does the Court begin with a presumption that damages are available to rectify a constitutional violation, or does it begin with the presumption they are not available?
- After *Wilkie*, must a defendant show that the plaintiff has an "adequate" or "equally effective" federal remedy in order to avoid recognition of a *Bivens* remedy? Further, will the Court now consider the plaintiff's alternative remedies under state law?
- How does *Wilkie* contribute to the Court's understanding of what is meant by "special factors" militating against recognition of a *Bivens* remedy?
- After *Wilkie*, do you have a better sense of whether *Bivens* remedies are based on (a) constitutional interpretation, (b) the federal courts' common-lawmaking power, or (c) the federal courts' jurisdictional power?

D. SOME ADDITIONAL PROBLEMS

PROBLEM 11-6

Beneath the Waves

In 2007, AT&T sued the owners of the M/V *Cape Fear*, a fishing vessel, for damage caused to an underwater communications cable extending from Lands End, England, to Tuckertown, New Jersey. While the M/V *Cape Fear* was dragging fishing gear along the ocean floor off the Jersey shore, it severed the communications cable in several places. AT&T spent more than $3 million to repair the damage.

AT&T alleged three claims in its federal court complaint. First, it alleged a claim under federal maritime law. Second, it alleged an implied cause of action under the Submarine Cable Act of 1888 (the Cable Act). Third, it alleged a claim under state negligence law, based on the allegation that violation of the Cable

Act was "negligence per se" according to applicable state court precedent. In its answer to the complaint, Cape Fear alleged (1) the claim under federal maritime law was subject to a liability limit equal to the value of the M/V *Cape Fear*, which is approximately $1million; (2) AT&T has no implied right of action under the Cable Act; and (3) federal law preempts the state-law claim for negligence per se. Assume the parties agree that, if the Cable Act provides an implied cause of action, liability limits applicable to count one, the maritime claim, will not apply to the implied cause of action.

Although this hypothetical arises in part under federal maritime law, you may assume that maritime law does *not* alter the analysis otherwise applicable when assessing the implied-cause and preemption issues.

The district court is later asked to dismiss AT&T's claims under the Cable Act (count two) and state negligence law (count three). The district court refuses based on its conclusions that the Cable Act supports an implied cause of action and does not preempt state-law remedies. In support of its conclusions, the court observes that

- Under the Cable Act it is a misdemeanor to "damage a submarine cable by culpable negligence."
- The Act states that "the penalties provided in this chapter for the breaking or injury of a submarine cable shall not be a bar to a suit for damages on account of such breaking or injury."
- The Act also states that the district courts "shall have jurisdiction over all offenses against this chapter and of all suits of a civil nature arising" under the Act.
- In 1888, when the Cable Act was enacted, "courts frequently inferred private rights of action from criminal statutes and we should presume that Congress expected the courts to do so here." In support of this point, the district court cites *Texas & Pacific Railway Co. v. Rigsby* (discussed earlier at page ***).
- Finally, Congress specifically preserved civil remedies under state law, thus rebutting Cape Fear's preemption argument.

Based on our study of implied causes of action and preemption, do you believe the owners of the M/V *Cape Fear* have a good chance of getting the district court reversed on appeal?

PROBLEM 11-7

Honor Among Thieves

Arizona Industries (AI) was sued in 2008 for price fixing in violation of the Sherman Act, 15 U.S.C. § 1. Because another company, Raddly Industries, had participated with AI in the alleged price fixing, AI impleaded Raddly to obtain contribution in the event it was held liable under the Sherman Act. Even after Raddly was impleaded, the original antitrust plaintiff declined to assert a claim against Raddly.

Raddly moves to dismiss AI's claim for contribution. It argues that the Sherman Act does not authorize an action for contribution among conspirators. To the contrary, the Sherman Act imposes joint and several liability on conspirators and also authorizes recovery of treble damages. According to Raddly—which vigorously denies it engaged in price fixing—the Sherman Act is "strong medicine" that imposes liability on *any* violator and does not permit a violator to mitigate its losses by seeking contribution from alleged coconspirators. Further, Raddly contends that the Sherman Act contains no legislative history indicating Congress intended to permit claims for contribution.

AI responds that it is unfair to permit Raddly to avoid liability simply because the victim of an antitrust violation chooses to sue only one of several conspirators. AI also argues that by recognizing its right to obtain contribution from Raddly, the court will enhance deterrence of antitrust behavior. Finally, AI argues that the Supreme Court has previously recognized the power of federal courts to develop "common law" to implement the Sherman Act.

The district court dismisses AI's claim for contribution. The court makes these points to support its conclusion: (1) the Sherman Act does not expressly authorize a right of action for contribution; (2) no legislative history supports a claim for contribution; (3) the Act reflects an intent to punish antitrust conspirators like AI, not to relieve their punishment through contribution; and (4) the common-lawmaking authority previously announced by the Court only extends to defining *violations* of the Act, not to devising new causes of action.

Based on our study of implied causes of action, do you believe AI has a good chance of getting the district court reversed on appeal?

CHAPTER 12

The Original Jurisdiction of the Supreme Court and Appellate Jurisdiction in the Federal Courts

A. A REFERENCE PROBLEM

In this chapter, we consider the Supreme Court's original jurisdiction and appellate jurisdiction in the federal courts. Our focus is the Supreme Court's appellate jurisdiction over state court decisions. The following Reference Problem introduces many of the concepts we explore.

* * * *

Cellular Static

Ashby Darlington is a prep school dropout with an accumulating rap sheet of drug-related offenses. On a hunch, police officers in Pittsburgh, Pennsylvania, investigating a drug ring, interviewed Darlington in connection with a drug transaction resulting in a murder near Pittsburgh's Shady Side neighborhood. During the interview, Darlington offered an alibi, suggesting that he had not been in the Pittsburgh metro area during the murder. Afterwards, police sought historical records on Darlington's cell phone number from cell phone companies operating towers in the area. With this information, it is possible to ascertain whether a given cell phone was used in the geographic area of a given cell tower. The police found that Darlington's cell phone had, in fact, been used in the area of, and contemporaneous with, the murder. The police and their contacts at the cell phone companies were unaware that the Pennsylvania legislature had recently passed, and the governor signed, the "Cell Phone Privacy Act," requiring a valid warrant predicated on probable cause before cell phone tower information could be released to law enforcement.

The police officers then sought a warrant to search Darlington's apartment. The warrant was based, in large measure, on the discrepancy between Darlington's interview and his cell phone location records. During that search, the police found drugs and the weapon used in the murder. During his Pennsylvania state court trial, Darlington moved to suppress the evidence obtained during the search of his apartment on the ground that there was no warrant issued for, and no probable cause to support, the police's receipt of his cell phone information from cell tower operators. He cited (1) the Cell Phone Privacy Act, arguing that its remedy must be evidence suppression; and (2) a recent case from the United States District Court for the Western District of Pennsylvania that held that the Fourth Amendment of the U.S. Constitution prohibits obtaining records that show where customers used their cell phones in the absence of a warrant supported by probable cause. The trial judge denied Darlington's motions, and Darlington was convicted of murder and received a life sentence without parole.

On Darlington's appeal, the Pennsylvania Supreme Court reversed, holding that the Cell Phone Privacy Act had been violated and, based on a review of the policy informing the statute and Pennsylvania precedent, that suppression was the proper remedy for such a violation. The court also noted that the "recent opinion of a federal district court in the Western District of Pennsylvania also comports with our view of Darlington's appeal under Fourth Amendment analysis."

The Pennsylvania Commonwealth's Attorney has now filed a petition for certiorari in the United States Supreme Court.

Does the Supreme Court have jurisdiction? Why or why not?

* * * *

As you think about your response, consider the following questions raised (some not so obviously) by the problem:

- How would your analysis change if Pennsylvania law did not require suppression as a remedy for a violation of the Cell Phone Privacy Act?
- Could Darlington have challenged the state court conviction by appealing to the Pennsylvania federal district court, seeking vindication in light of its recent favorable jurisprudence?
- What are the federalism concerns? Is it possible for the state to grant more rights than the U.S. Constitution does?
- How can the Pennsylvania courts insulate their decisions from Supreme Court review?

You will probably not be able to answer most of these questions now. You should be able to do so at the conclusion of this chapter.

B. CONTEXT AND BACKGROUND

This chapter explores the Supreme Court's original and appellate jurisdiction. It focuses on the Court's review of state court opinions because this area implicates a primary theme of federal jurisdiction — federalism. We examine the Supreme Court's constitutional and statutory authority and explore when the Court should refrain from reviewing state court decisions. We analyze the "final judgment rule" — the notion that the Supreme Court may review only the final judgment of a federal court of appeals or the final judgment of the highest court of a state — and explore the various exceptions to the rule. We also devote our attention to the doctrinal position that the Supreme Court may not review state court opinions when "adequate and independent state grounds" support the state court decision. The chapter concludes with consideration of the *Rooker-Feldman* doctrine, which significantly curtails review of state court judgments by lower federal courts.

C. THE LAW AND PROBLEMS

1. *Supreme Court Original Jurisdiction*

The judicial power of the federal courts includes nine types of cases as outlined in Article III, section 2, clause 1. The Supreme Court lacks the authority to hear any matter, under its original or appellate jurisdiction, *unless* the case fits within these nine listed categories of federal judicial power. To determine which cases the Court may hear pursuant to its original jurisdiction, the next clause of Article III of the Constitution provides the foundation and limits.

Yet, as discussed in Chapter 3, we must remain cognizant of Congress' role in enacting statutory jurisdictional authority. As you review the relevant constitutional text, consider whether congressional action is required to vest the original jurisdiction described in Article III and whether Congress may enlarge or decrease the Supreme Court's constitutionally defined original jurisdiction.

Clause 2 of Article III, section 2, sets forth the Supreme Court's original jurisdiction. The Court possesses trial jurisdiction over the cases within its Article III original jurisdiction. The Constitution provides that the Supreme Court shall have original jurisdiction "in all cases affecting ambassadors, other public ministers and consuls, and those in which the State shall be a party." The remainder of clause 2 states that "in all other cases before mentioned" — that is, the remaining types of cases within federal court judicial power listed in clause 1, the Supreme Court "shall have appellate jurisdiction."

Extensive scholarly emphasis, jurisprudence, and public awareness exist regarding the Supreme Court's appellate jurisdiction. Much less attention focuses on the Court's original jurisdiction. Common conceptions of the Supreme Court are of its role as the Court of last resort, not the Court of first resort. One simple reason for the primacy of the Supreme Court's review function is that the Supreme Court rarely exercises its original jurisdiction.

Also, the Court utilizes its review function to ensure supremacy and uniformity of interpretations of federal authority. Assertion of the Supreme Court's original jurisdiction, although rare, remains an important and curious function. The special significance exists because, when asserting original jurisdiction, the Court operates as the trial court. What is the scope of the Supreme Court's power to hear cases in the first instance?

May the Supreme Court hear matters that lie beyond Article III, section 2, clause 2? Recall that in *Marbury v. Madison* (see Chapter 1) Marbury requested the Court, sitting as a trial court, to issue a writ of mandamus against a federal officer—to force the federal officer to issue the commission. The Judiciary Act of 1789 authorized original jurisdiction over cases requesting a writ of mandamus against a federal government officer. Article III, however, did not include such a controversy in its list of matters for original jurisdiction. Chief Justice Marshall concluded that the original jurisdiction set forth in Article III is an exhaustive list. He thus reasoned that Congress cannot expand the Court's original jurisdiction beyond Article III's strictures.

Recall Professor Chemerinsky's exploration of whether Article III constitutes a floor versus a ceiling regarding the jurisdiction it outlines for the federal courts (see Chapter 3, Figure 3.1). Under Chief Justice Marshall's view, Article III's enumeration of the Court's original jurisdiction constitutes a ceiling—it provides the maximum level of the Court's potential trial court jurisdiction. Thus, it would be unconstitutional for Congress to enlarge this jurisdiction. Recall the disposition of the *Marbury* case—the Court dismissed Marbury's request for a writ of mandamus because the Court lacked the authority to hear the case. The Supreme Court held that this provision embodied an unconstitutional extension of Article III's articulation of original jurisdiction. Thus, the Supreme Court declared that it did not possess constitutional power to hear the suit. *Marbury*'s reasoning regarding the exhaustive nature of Article III's grant of original jurisdiction remains governing precedent today. Accordingly, Congress cannot expand the original jurisdiction of the Court beyond Article III's stipulated enumerations.

Should Congress be able to narrow the Supreme Court's original jurisdiction? What if Congress had never enacted a statute authorizing the Court's original jurisdiction? In other words, is the Article III jurisdictional grant of the Court's original jurisdiction self-executing, such that the Court could opt to hear a case within the constitutional grant, despite the lack of a statutory authorization? The orthodox view of scholars supported by Supreme Court jurisprudence is that Article III's grant of original jurisdiction for the Supreme Court is self-executing. The consequence of this reasoning is that the jurisdictional statutes that Congress passes are unnecessary. Under *Marbury*, Congress cannot expand the Supreme Court's original jurisdiction beyond Article III's enumeration, and under conventional wisdom, Congress also lacks the power to diminish the Court's power to hear the constitutionally enumerated cases.

Although a congressional grant of jurisdictional authority is deemed superfluous for the Supreme Court's original jurisdiction, Congress has passed and continues to pass jurisdictional statutes. Interestingly, Congress flexes its muscle by establishing which types of Supreme Court original jurisdiction may be concurrent with jurisdiction in lower federal courts or state courts. For example, Congress provides for the Supreme Court's original jurisdiction in 28 U.S.C. § 1251:

(a) The Supreme Court shall have *original and exclusive jurisdiction* of all controversies between two or more States.

(b) The Supreme Court shall have *original but not exclusive* jurisdiction of:

(1) All actions or proceedings to which ambassadors, other public ministers, consuls, or vice consuls of foreign states are parties;
(2) All controversies between the United States and a State;
(3) All actions or proceedings by a State against the citizens of another State or against aliens.[1]

Accordingly, Congress dictates that lower federal courts cannot hear cases "between two or more states" — only the Supreme Court possesses trial jurisdiction over such a matter.[2] In contrast, Congress authorizes nonexclusive original jurisdiction over cases (i) "to which ambassadors, other public ministers, consuls, or vice consuls of foreign states are parties;" (ii) "between the United States and a State;" and (iii) by a State against the citizens of another State or against aliens." The trial of any controversy within these three categories *may* occur in the Supreme Court or in a federal district court. Note, however, that the Court may decline jurisdiction and require that the case be tried in a lower federal court or in a state court. If a lower federal court handles the case, the Supreme Court possesses appellate jurisdiction over the decision.

As a result of Congress' jurisdictional statute, the Court's trial jurisdiction is exclusive only over cases between two or more states, and the parties must be the states themselves, not local governmental bodies. Historical support for this exclusivity stems from the national interest in deterring states from resorting to violence against one another. Border disputes and controversies over water rights also create the need for a forum that could be sufficiently impartial. The Supreme Court is seen as the best able body to resolve disputes between states with the level of independence required. In contrast, the state courts would have an impermissible vested interest in the case's resolution. Even lower federal courts may have biases because such courts sit within states and have judges who often served as local lawyers before ascending to the federal bench. Congress, therefore, assigned exclusive original jurisdiction to the Supreme Court for cases between state governments. Despite this exclusive jurisdiction, the Supreme Court has not felt required to hear such matters. In fact, the Court has exercised discretion to refuse original jurisdiction in suits between states, and it has reasoned that declining jurisdiction is essential to preserve "the most effective functioning of this Court within the federal system."[3] Thus, the Court might decline jurisdiction if it perceives there is insufficient federal interest. When might inadequate federal interests exist in a case between states? What other judicial arena would be available to the disaffected state governments?

Consider Problem 12-1.

1. 28 U.S.C. § 1251 (emphasis added).
2. According to Supreme Court jurisprudence, the Eleventh Amendment sovereign immunity principles do not prohibit a state from suing another state in the Supreme Court. *See, e.g.*, *Virginia v. West Virginia*, 206 U.S. 290, 319 (1907) (finding no Eleventh Amendment bar because, when states joined the union, they consented to suits by other states before the Supreme Court).
3. *Texas v. New Mexico*, 462 U.S. 554, 570 (1983).

PROBLEM 12-1

Grid Iron Gridlock

Students of West Virginia University were looking forward to their upcoming football game, which pitted the Mountaineers against the California Golden Bears. The game was set for the third week of the season. As the season approached, the California Golden Bears received an offer to play on the same date against a top ten team on national television. California accepted this new offer and, in doing so, breached the contract it had with West Virginia University. After much public outcry, the Governor of West Virginia announces that the State of West Virginia is filing suit against the State of California for breach of contract. The West Virginia Governor files this suit in the United States Supreme Court, pursuant to Article III.

Can the Supreme Court exercise jurisdiction? Must the Court exercise jurisdiction? Consider whether any alternative forums exist.

As Problem 12-1 demonstrates, states may invoke Article III jurisdiction regarding matters of import to the state for which they seek hearing in an independent tribunal. The Court balances Congress' authorization of exclusive original jurisdiction with the Court's interest in protecting its proper role within the federal system. Determining the proper role may be difficult when the federal interests are nonexistent, yet the consequences of refusing jurisdiction are harsh.

Controversies between states constitute the bulk of the Supreme Court's exercise of its original jurisdiction, and these matters remain rare. Accordingly, the lion's share of the Court's energy has been consistently devoted to appellate review.

2. *Supreme Court Appellate Review*

Extensive historical machinations existed regarding the procedural route of access to the United States Supreme Court. Since 1988, however, when Congress altered its federal statutes governing the Supreme Court's appellate jurisdiction, much of the complexity evaporated. With these changes, Congress essentially eliminated mandatory appellate jurisdiction. The statutory amendments to 28 U.S.C. § 1257 provided that all state court decisions would be reviewable only by the certiorari method.

Appellate jurisdiction previously was divided between review by appeal and review by writ of certiorari. Historically, then, appeal was a matter of right,[4] while certiorari was exclusively a discretionary vehicle of the Court. Yet the Court often exercised discretion with appeals as a matter of right by dismissing such cases based on the judgment below or summarily affirmed without full briefing or

4. During the bulk of the twentieth century, the Supreme Court reviewed on appeal final judgments from state courts if the state court opinion invalidated a federal statute or insulated a state statute from a federal constitutional challenge. Regarding lower federal court decisions, the appeal process functioned similarly: A party could appeal to the Supreme Court a final judgment of the federal court when the court invalidated a state statute or ruled that a federal statute was unconstitutional in a civil proceeding in which the government was a party.

argument. *See, e.g., Zucht v. King*, 260 U.S. 174 (1922). Currently, however, mandatory appellate jurisdiction has all but vanished,[5] and certiorari is the name of the game. Thus, much lies in the discretion of the Court. In recent years, the Supreme Court tends to hear and decide approximately 75 cases per year. This is a significant reduction from even the Court's 1980 docket—often double the caseload of more recent terms. This decrease in the Court's productivity is in sharp contrast with the growth of lower federal courts, the increased numbers of rulings in state and federal courts, and the steady influx of writs of certiorari. See Chapter 1. Regarding the Court's selection method, critics see flaws in the process, the number of denials, and the types of cases selected. In this chapter, examine the Court's interpretation of jurisdictional principles in its decision to hear certain cases but to deny jurisdiction to others. Recall that the Court applies similar gatekeeping functions using justiciability and abstention doctrines. Accordingly, as you read, consider whether the existing jurisdictional rules foster sufficient access to the Court for controversies meriting the Court's attention, and pay particular attention to cases implicating the Court's essential functions.

The Supreme Court's contemporary role is largely to serve as the ultimate tribunal in the American judicial system. A critical component of the Court's function follows Chief Justice Marshall's declaration from *Marbury*: "it is emphatically the province and duty of the judicial department to say what the law is." The Supreme Court provides the ultimate interpretations of federal law and ensures uniformity in interpretations by resolving conflicting opinions among the state and federal courts. Thus, among the Supreme Court's essential functions is to provide the ultimate exposition of constitutional law and to ensure that our constitutional protections have the same meaning throughout the country.

The Court also serves as the enforcer of the Supremacy Clause. Otherwise, state courts might be free to ignore Supreme Court precedent. The force of *Marbury* has only strengthened since its ruling. Now the Supreme Court is the authoritative interpreter of the Constitution and correspondingly must protect its rulings against disregard by state courts. The Supreme Court has reinforced its essential role of ultimate arbiter of constitutional law, as articulated in *Marbury*, as "permanent and indispensable" to our constitutional system of government. *See Cooper v. Aaron*, 358 U.S. 1, 19 (1958). Note also that such state court rulings are generally unreviewable in lower federal courts (*see Rooker-Feldman* doctrine in section C.3). Accordingly, the Supreme Court secures enforcement of the Supremacy Clause as to state courts through its appellate jurisdiction over state court decisions.

As you read about the scope and limits of the Supreme Court's power, consider how the jurisdictional doctrines help or hinder the Court's proper functioning within our constitutional democracy. Evaluate the promotion of interpretation, uniformity, and supremacy, while remaining cognizant of the risks of encroachment on a state's legitimate spheres of authority. Last, retain focus on the consequences of the Court's refusal of jurisdiction in terms of

5. Mandatory appeals remain a limited component of the Supreme Court's role. For example, remaining categories of mandatory appeals include the slim group of cases decided by three-judge district court panels pursuant to 28 U.S.C. § 1253 (authorizing direct appeals from three-judge district court decisions granting or denying injunctive relief), as well as groups of cases specially designated by statute.

whether an alternative forum exists and whether any related parity concerns exist with regard to a state versus a federal tribunal.

a. Review of Final Judgments of a State's Highest Court

As a preliminary question, does the United States Supreme Court possess the power to review opinions of state courts? Such review poses serious federalism concerns given that the Supreme Court might overrule the state court's interpretations and holding. One might expect the Constitution to address the issue, but it does not explicitly provide for the Supreme Court's review of state court decisions. Instead, the Judiciary Act of 1789 so provided.

Although the procedural path has evolved, the Supreme Court has retained the power to review certain state court decisions. Section 25 of the Act provided such review by writ of error to the state's highest court in certain circumstances. Notably, section 25 did not extend jurisdiction coextensive with Article III's jurisdiction. Rather, section 25 limited the Supreme Court's power to review only state court rulings *against* federal law or federal government interests. The Judiciary Act of 1789 specifically provided for Supreme Court review of decisions from the highest court of a state where the state court decision

> question[s] the validity of a treaty or statute of, or an authority exercised under the United States, and the decision is against their validity; or . . . question[s] the validity of a statute of, or an authority exercised under any State, on the ground of their being repugnant to the constitution, treaties or laws of the United States, and the decision is in favour of such their validity, or . . . question[s] the construction of any clause of the constitution, or of a treaty, or statute of, or commission held under the United States, and the decision is against the title, right, privilege or exemption specially set up or claimed by either party, under such clause of the said Constitution, treaty, statute or commission. . . .[6]

Further, Congress explicitly provided in section 25 that such state court decisions "may be re-examined and reversed or affirmed in the Supreme Court of the United States upon a writ of error. . . ."

How does the federal statutory authorization interplay with Article III? The Supreme Court clarified its constitutional foundation for reviewing state court decisions in a number of early decisions, including *Martin v. Hunter's Lessee.* As you examine this material, consider the source and the proper scope of the Court's power.

i. Supreme Court's Power to Review State Court Decisions

In the following case, *Martin v. Hunter's Lessee,* the Court (i) establishes its power to review state court judgments, (ii) articulates how such review fosters the Court's essential functions of ensuring supremacy and uniformity of federal law interpretations, and (iii) reasons that the Constitution mandates that Congress had to create at least some lower federal courts. The argument that

6. Act of Sept. 24, 1789, ch. 20, 1 Stat. 73, 85-87.

Congress' creation of lower federal courts is constitutionally required is relevant to Chapter 3's study of congressional control over federal court jurisdiction. This chapter focuses on the Supreme Court's review of state courts and how such review helps foster the Court's essential functions.

MARTIN v. HUNTER'S LESSEE

14 U.S. (1 Wheat.) 304 (1816)

JUSTICE STORY delivered the opinion of the court.

[In an ownership dispute over land in Virginia, Mr. Martin claimed title pursuant to an inheritance from Lord Fairfax, a British citizen. Two treaties between the United States and England protected ownership rights of British citizens who owned land in the United States. Mr. Hunter asserted, and the Virginia Court of Appeals agreed, that Mr. Martin lacked a valid claim because Virginia had taken and disposed of the land prior to the treaties' effective dates. The Supreme Court held that, pursuant to the treaty rights, Lord Fairfax owned and validly bequeathed the land to Mr. Martin. The Virginia Court of Appeals rejected the Supreme Court's power to review state court decisions and accordingly refused compliance with the Court's mandate.]

This is a writ of error from the court of appeals of Virginia, founded upon the refusal of that court to obey the mandate of this court, requiring the judgment rendered in this very cause, at February term, 1813, to be carried into due execution. The following is the judgment of the court of appeals rendered on the mandate: "The court is unanimously of opinion, that the appellate power of the supreme court of the United States does not extend to this court, under a sound construction of the constitution of the United States; that so much of the 25th section of the act of congress to establish the judicial courts of the United States, as extends the appellate jurisdiction of the supreme court to this court, is not in pursuance of the constitution of the United States; that the writ of error, in this cause, was improvidently allowed under the authority of that act; that the proceedings thereon in the supreme court were, *coram non judice*, in relation to this court, and that obedience to its mandate be declined by the court."

* * * *

The constitution of the United States was ordained and established, not by the states in their sovereign capacities, but emphatically, as the preamble of the constitution declares, by "the people of the United States." There can be no doubt that it was competent to the people to invest the general government with all the powers which they might deem proper and necessary; to extend or restrain these powers according to their own good pleasure, and to give them a paramount and supreme authority. As little doubt can there be, that the people had a right to prohibit to the states the exercise of any powers which were, in their judgment, incompatible with the objects of the general compact; to make the powers of the state governments, in given cases, subordinate to those of the nation, or to reserve to themselves those sovereign authorities which they might not choose to delegate to either. The constitution was not, therefore, necessarily carved out of existing state sovereignties, nor a surrender of powers already existing in state institutions, for the powers of the states depend upon their own constitutions; and the people of every state had the right to modify and restrain them, according to their own views of the policy or principle. On the other hand, it is perfectly clear that the sovereign powers vested in the state governments, by their respective constitutions, remained unaltered and unimpaired, except so far as they were granted to the government of the United States.

These deductions do not rest upon general reasoning, plain and obvious as they seem to be. They have been positively recognised by one of the articles in amendment of the constitution, which declares, that "the powers not delegated to the United States by the constitution, nor prohibited by it to the states, are reserved to the states respectively, or *to the people.*" The government, then, of the United States, can claim no powers which are not granted to it by the constitution, and the powers actually granted, must be such as are expressly given, or given by necessary implication. . . .

* * * *

The third article of the constitution is that which must principally attract our attention. The 1st section declares, "the judicial power of the United States shall be vested in one supreme court, and in such other inferior courts as the congress may, from time to time, ordain and establish." The 2d section declares, that "the judicial power shall extend to all cases in law or equity, arising under this constitution, the laws of the United States, and the treaties made, or which shall be made, under their authority; to all cases affecting ambassadors, other public ministers and consuls; to all cases of admiralty and maritime jurisdiction; to controversies to which the United States shall be a party; to controversies between two or more states; between a state and citizens of another state; between citizens of different states; between citizens of the same state, claiming lands under the grants of different states; and between a state or the citizens thereof, and foreign states, citizens, or subjects." It then proceeds to declare, that "in all cases affecting ambassadors, other public ministers and consuls, and those in which a state shall be a party, the supreme court shall have original jurisdiction. In all the other cases before mentioned the supreme court shall have appellate jurisdiction, both as to law and fact, with such exceptions, and under such regulations, as the congress shall make."

Such is the language of the article creating and defining the judicial power of the United States. It is the voice of the whole American people solemnly declared, in establishing one great department of that government which was, in many respects, national, and in all, supreme. It is a part of the very same instrument which was to act not merely upon individuals, but upon states; and to deprive them altogether of the exercise of some powers of sovereignty, and to restrain and regulate them in the exercise of others.

Let this article be carefully weighed and considered. The language of the article throughout is manifestly designed to be mandatory upon the legislature. Its obligatory force is so imperative, that congress could not, without a violation of its duty, have refused to carry it into operation. The judicial power of the United States shall be vested (not may be vested) in one supreme court, and in such inferior courts as congress may, from time to time, ordain and establish. Could congress have lawfully refused to create a supreme court, or to vest in it the constitutional jurisdiction? "The judges, both of the supreme and inferior courts, shall hold their offices during good behaviour, and shall, at stated times, receive, for their services, a compensation which shall not be diminished during their continuance in office." Could congress create or limit any other tenure of the judicial office? Could they refuse to pay, at stated times, the stipulated salary, or diminish it during the continuance in office? But one answer can be given to these questions: it must be in the negative. The object of the constitution was to establish three great departments of government; the legislative, the executive, and the judicial departments. The first was to pass laws, the second to approve and execute them, and the third to expound and enforce them. Without the latter, it would be impossible to carry into effect some of the express provisions of the constitution. How, otherwise, could crimes against the United States be tried and punished? How could causes between two states be heard and determined? The judicial power must, therefore, be vested in some court, by congress; and to suppose that it was not an obligation binding on them, but might, at their pleasure, be omitted or declined, is to suppose that, under the sanction of the constitution, they might defeat the constitution itself; a construction which would lead to such a result cannot be sound.

* * * *

If, then, it is a duty of congress to vest the judicial power of the United States, it is a duty to vest the whole judicial power. The language, if imperative as to one part, is imperative as to all. If it were otherwise, this anomaly would exist, that congress might successively refuse to vest the jurisdiction in any one class of cases enumerated in the constitution, and thereby defeat the jurisdiction as to all; for the constitution has not singled out any class on which congress are bound to act in preference to others.

The next consideration is as to the courts in which the judicial power shall be vested. It is manifest that a supreme court must be established; but whether it be equally obligatory to establish inferior courts, is a question of some difficulty. If congress may lawfully omit to establish inferior courts, it might follow, that in some of the enumerated cases the judicial power could nowhere exist. The supreme court can have original jurisdiction in two classes of cases only, viz. in cases affecting ambassadors, other public ministers and consuls, and in cases in which a state is a party. Congress cannot vest any portion of the judicial power of the United States, except in courts ordained and established by itself; and if in any of the cases enumerated in the constitution, the state courts did not then possess jurisdiction, the appellate jurisdiction of the supreme court (admitting that it could act on state courts) could not reach those cases, and, consequently, the injunction of the constitution, that the judicial power "shall be vested," would be disobeyed. It would seem, therefore, to follow, that congress are bound to create some inferior courts, in which to vest all that jurisdiction which, under the constitution, is exclusively vested in the United States, and of which the supreme court cannot take original cognizance. They might establish one or more inferior courts; they might parcel out the jurisdiction among such courts, from time to time, at their own pleasure. But the whole judicial power of the United States should be, at all times, vested either in an original or appellate form, in some courts created under its authority.

This construction will be fortified by an attentive examination of the second section of the third article. The words are "the judicial power shall extend." [W]e are of opinion that the words are used in an imperative sense. They import an absolute grant of judicial power. They cannot have a relative signification applicable to powers already granted; for the American people had not made any previous grant. The constitution was for a new government, organized with new substantive powers, and not a mere supplementary charter to a government already existing. The confederation was a compact between states; and its structure and powers were wholly unlike those of the national government. The constitution was an act of the people of the United States to supercede the confederation, and not to be ingrafted on it, as a stock through which it was to receive life and nourishment.

* * * *

[T]he next question is as to the cases to which it shall apply. The answer is found in the constitution itself. The judicial power shall extend to all the cases enumerated in the constitution. As the mode is not limited, it may extend to all such cases, in any form, in which judicial power may be exercised. It may, therefore, extend to them in the shape of original or appellate jurisdiction, or both; for there is nothing in the nature of the cases which binds to the exercise of the one in preference to the other.

In what cases (if any) is this judicial power exclusive, or exclusive at the election of congress? It will be observed that there are two classes of cases enumerated in the constitution, between which a distinction seems to be drawn. The first class includes cases arising under the constitution, laws, and treaties of the United States; cases affecting ambassadors, other public ministers and consuls, and cases of admiralty and maritime jurisdiction. In this class the expression is, and that the judicial power shall extend to all cases; but in the subsequent part of the clause which embraces all the other cases of national cognizance, and forms the second class, the word "all" is dropped seemingly *ex industria*. Here the judicial authority is to extend to controversies (not to all controversies) to which the United States shall be a party. . . .

The vital importance of all the cases enumerated in the first class to the national sovereignty, might warrant such a distinction. In the first place, as to cases arriving under the constitution, laws, and treaties of the United States. Here the state courts could not ordinarily possess a direct jurisdiction. The jurisdiction over such cases could not exist in the state courts previous to the adoption of the constitution, and it could not afterwards be directly conferred on them; for the constitution expressly requires the judicial power to be vested in courts ordained and established by the United States. This class of cases would embrace civil as well as criminal jurisdiction, and affect not only our internal policy, but our foreign relations. It would, therefore, be perilous to restrain it in any manner whatsoever, inasmuch as it might hazard the national safety. . . .

* * * *

[T]here is, certainly, vast weight in the argument which has been urged, that the constitution is imperative upon congress to vest all the judicial power of the United States, in the shape of original jurisdiction, in the supreme and inferior courts created under its own authority. At all events, whether the one construction or the other prevail, it is manifest that the judicial power of the United States is unavoidably, in some cases, exclusive of all state authority, and in all others, may be made so at the election of congress. . . .

But, even admitting that the language of the constitution is not mandatory, and that congress may constitutionally omit to vest the judicial power in courts of the United States, it cannot be deemed that when it is vested, it may be exercised to the utmost constitutional extent.

[A]ppellate jurisdiction is given by the constitution to the supreme court in all cases where it has not original jurisdiction; subject, however, to such exceptions and regulations as congress may prescribe. It is, therefore, capable of embracing every case enumerated in the constitution, which is not exclusively to be decided by way of original jurisdiction. But the exercise of appellate jurisdiction is far from being limited by the terms of the constitution to the supreme court. There can be no doubt that congress may create a succession of inferior tribunals, in each of which it may vest appellate as well as original jurisdiction. The judicial power is delegated by the constitution in the most general terms, and may, therefore, be exercised by congress under every variety of form, of appellate or original jurisdiction. And as there is nothing in the constitution which restrains or limits this power, it must, therefore, in all other cases, subsist in the utmost latitude of which, in its own nature, it is susceptible.

As, then, by the terms of the constitution, the appellate jurisdiction is not limited as to the supreme court, and as to this court it may be exercised in all other cases than those of which it has original cognizance, what is there to restrain its exercise over state tribunals in the enumerated cases? The appellate power is not limited by the terms of the third article to any particular courts. The words are, "the judicial power (which includes appellate power) shall extend to all cases," and "in all other cases before mentioned the supreme court shall have appellate jurisdiction." It is the case, then, and not the court, that gives the jurisdiction. If the judicial power extends to the case, it will be in vain to search in the letter of the constitution for any qualification as to the tribunal where it depends. It is incumbent, then, upon those who assert such a qualification to show its existence by necessary implication. If the text be clear and distinct, no restriction upon its plain and obvious import ought to be admitted, unless the inference be irresistible.

If the constitution meant to limit the appellate jurisdiction to cases pending in the courts of the United States, it would necessarily follow that the jurisdiction of these courts would, in all the cases enumerated in the constitution, be exclusive of state tribunals. How otherwise could the jurisdiction extend to all cases arising under the constitution, laws, and treaties of the United States, or to all cases of admiralty and maritime jurisdiction? If some of these cases might be entertained by state tribunals, and no appellate jurisdiction as to them should exist, then the appellate power would not extend to all, but to some, cases. If state tribunals might exercise concurrent jurisdiction over all or some of the other classes of cases in the constitution without control, then the appellate jurisdiction of the United States might, as to such cases, have no real existence, contrary to the manifest intent of the constitution. Under such circumstances, to give effect to the judicial power, it must be construed to be exclusive; and this not only when the *casus foederis* should arise directly, but when it should arise, incidentally, in cases pending in state courts. This construction would abridge the jurisdiction of such court far more than has been ever contemplated in any act of congress.

On the other hand, if, as has been contended, a discretion be vested in congress to establish, or not to establish, inferior courts at their own pleasure, and congress should not establish such courts, the appellate jurisdiction of the supreme Court would have nothing to act upon, unless it could act upon cases pending in the state courts. Under such circumstances it must be held that the appellate power would extend to state courts; for the constitution is peremptory that it shall extend to certain enumerated cases, which cases could exist in no other courts. Any other construction, upon this supposition, would involve this strange contradiction, that a discretionary power vested in congress, and which they might rightfully omit to exercise, would defeat the absolute injunctions of the constitution in relation to the whole appellate power.

But it is plain that the framers of the constitution did contemplate that cases within the judicial cognizance of the United States not only might but would arise in the state courts, in the exercise of their ordinary jurisdiction. With this view the sixth article declares, that "this constitution, and the laws of the United States which shall be made in pursuance thereof, and all treaties made, or which shall be made, under the authority of the United States, shall be the supreme law of the land, and the judges in every state shall be bound thereby, any thing in the constitution or laws of any state to the contrary notwithstanding." It is obvious that this obligation is imperative upon the state judges in their official, and not merely in their private, capacities. From the very nature of their judicial duties they would be called upon to pronounce the law applicable to the case in judgment. They were not to decide merely according to the laws or constitution of the state, but according to the constitution, laws and treaties of the United States — "the supreme law of the land."

* * * *

It must, therefore, be conceded that the constitution not only contemplated, but meant to provide for cases within the scope of the judicial power of the United States, which might yet depend before state tribunals. It was foreseen that in the exercise of their ordinary jurisdiction, state courts would incidentally take cognizance of cases arising under the constitution, the laws, and treaties of the United States. Yet to all these cases the judicial power, by the very terms of the constitution, is to extend. It cannot extend by original jurisdiction if that was already rightfully and exclusively attached in the state courts, which (as has been already shown) may occur; it must, therefore, extend by appellate jurisdiction, or not at all. It would seem to follow that the appellate power of the United States must, in such cases, extend to state tribunals; and if in such cases, there is no reason why it should not equally attach upon all others within the purview of the constitution.

It has been argued that such an appellate jurisdiction over state courts is inconsistent with the genius of our governments, and the spirit of the constitution. That the latter was never designed to act upon state sovereignties, but only upon the people, and that if the power exists, it will materially impair the sovereignty of the states, and the independence of their courts. We cannot yield to the force of this reasoning; it assumes principles which we cannot admit, and draws conclusions to which we do not yield our assent.

It is a mistake that the constitution was not designed to operate upon states, in their corporate capacities. It is crowded with provisions which restrain or annul the sovereignty of the states in some of the highest branches of their prerogatives. The tenth section of the first article contains a long list of disabilities and prohibitions imposed upon the states. Surely, when such essential portions of state sovereignty are taken away, or prohibited to be exercised, it cannot be correctly asserted that the constitution does not act upon the states. The language of the constitution is also imperative upon the states as to the performance of many duties. It is imperative upon the state legislatures to make laws prescribing the time, places, and manner of holding elections for senators and representatives, and for electors of president and vice-president. And in these, as well as some other cases, congress have a right to revise, amend, or supercede the laws which may be passed by state legislatures. When, therefore, the states are stripped of some of the highest attributes of sovereignty, and the same are given to the United States; when the legislatures of the states are, in some respects, under the control of congress, and in every case are, under the constitution, bound by the paramount authority of the United States; it is certainly difficult to support the argument that the appellate power over the decisions of state courts is contrary to the genius of our institutions. The courts of the United States can, without question, revise the proceedings of the executive and legislative authorities of the states, and if they are found to be contrary to the constitution, may declare them to be of no legal validity. Surely the exercise of the same right over judicial tribunals is not a higher or more dangerous act of sovereign power.

Nor can such a right be deemed to impair the independence of state judges. It is assuming the very ground in controversy to assert that they possess an absolute independence of the United States. In respect to the powers granted to the United States, they are not independent; they are expressly bound to obedience by the letter of the constitution; and if they should unintentionally transcend their authority, or misconstrue the constitution, there is no more reason for giving their judgments an absolute and irresistible force, than for giving it to the acts of the other co-ordinate departments of state sovereignty.

The argument urged from the possibility of the abuse of the revising power, is equally unsatisfactory. It is always a doubtful course, to argue against the use or existence of a power, from the possibility of its abuse. It is still more difficult, by such an argument, to ingraft upon a general power a restriction which is not to be found in the terms in which it is given. From the very nature of things, the absolute right of decision, in the last resort, must rest somewhere — wherever it may be vested it is susceptible of abuse. In all questions of jurisdiction the inferior, or appellate court, must pronounce the final judgment; and common sense, as well as legal reasoning, has conferred it upon the latter.

It has been further argued against the existence of this appellate power, that it would form a novelty in our judicial institutions. This is certainly a mistake. In the articles of confederation, an instrument framed with infinitely more deference to state rights and state jealousies, a power was given to congress to establish "courts for revising and determining, finally, appeals in all cases of captures." It is remarkable, that no power was given to entertain original jurisdiction in such cases; and, consequently, the appellate power (although not so expressed in terms) was altogether to be exercised in revising the decisions of state tribunals. This was, undoubtedly, so far a surrender of state sovereignty; but it never was supposed to be a power fraught with public danger, or destructive of the independence of state judges. On the contrary, it was supposed to be a power indispensable to the public safety, inasmuch as our national rights might otherwise be compromitted, and our national peace been dangered. Under the present constitution the prize jurisdiction is confined to the courts of the United States; and a power to revise the decisions of state courts, if they should assert jurisdiction over prize causes, cannot be less important, or less useful, than it was under the confederation.

* * * *

It is further argued, that no great public mischief can result from a construction which shall limit the appellate power of the United States to cases in their own courts: first, because state judges are bound by an oath to support the constitution of the United States, and must be presumed to be men of learning and integrity; and, secondly, because congress must have an unquestionable right to remove all cases within the scope of the judicial power from the state courts to the courts of the United States, at any time before final judgment, thought not after final judgment. As to the first reason—admitting that the judges of the state courts are, and always will be, of as much learning, integrity, and wisdom, as those of the courts of the United States, (which we very cheerfully admit,) it does not aid the argument. It is manifest that the constitution has proceeded upon a theory of its own, and given or withheld powers according to the judgment of the American people, by whom it was adopted. We can only construe its powers, and cannot inquire into the policy or principles which induced the grant of them. The constitution has presumed (whether rightly or wrongly we do not inquire) that state attachments, state prejudices, state jealousies, and state interests, might some times obstruct, or control, or be supposed to obstruct or control, the regular administration of justice. Hence, in controversies between states; between citizens of different states; between citizens claiming grants under different states; between a state and its citizens, or foreigners, and between citizens and foreigners, it enables the parties, under the authority of congress, to have the controversies heard, tried, and determined before the national tribunals. No other reason than that which has been stated can be assigned, why some, at least, of those cases should not have been left to the cognizance of the state courts. In respect to the other enumerated cases—the cases arising under the constitution, laws, and treaties of the United States, cases affecting ambassadors and other public ministers, and cases of admiralty and maritime jurisdiction—reasons of a higher and more extensive nature, touching the safety, peace, and sovereignty of the nation, might well justify a grant of exclusive jurisdiction.

This is not all. A motive of another kind, perfectly compatible with the most sincere respect for state tribunals, might induce the grant of appellate power over their decisions. That motive is the importance, and even necessity of uniformity of decisions throughout the whole United States, upon all subjects within the purview of the constitution. Judges of equal learning and integrity, in different states, might differently interpret a statute, or a treaty of the United States, or even the constitution itself: If there were no revising authority to control these jarring and discordant judgments, and harmonize them into uniformity, the laws, the treaties, and the constitution of the United States would be different in different states, and might, perhaps, never have precisely the same construction, obligation, or efficacy, in any two states. The public mischiefs that would attend such a state of things would be truly deplorable; and it cannot be believed that they could have escaped the enlightened convention which formed the constitution. What, indeed, might then have been only prophecy, has now become fact; and the appellate jurisdiction must continue to be the only adequate remedy for such evils.

There is an additional consideration, which is entitled to great weight. The constitution of the United States was designed for the common and equal benefit of all the people of the United States. The judicial power was granted for the same benign and salutary purposes. It was not to be exercised exclusively for the benefit of parties who might be plaintiffs, and would elect the national forum, but also for the protection of defendants who might be entitled to try their rights, or assert their privileges, before the same forum. Yet, if the construction contended for be correct, it will follow, that as the plaintiff may always elect the state court, the defendant may be deprived of all the security which the constitution intended in aid of his rights. Such a state of things can, in no respect, be considered as giving equal rights. To obviate this difficulty, we are referred to the power which it is admitted congress possess to remove suits from state courts to the national courts. . . .

* * * *

On the whole, the court are of opinion, that the appellate power of the United States does extend to cases pending in the state courts; and that the 25th section of the judiciary act, which authorizes the exercise of this jurisdiction in the specified cases, by a writ of error, is supported by the letter and spirit of the constitution. . . .

Strong as this conclusion stands upon the general language of the constitution, it may still derive support from other sources. It is an historical fact, that this exposition of the constitution, extending its appellate power to state courts, was, previous to its adoption, uniformly and publicly avowed by its friends, and admitted by its enemies, as the basis of their respective reasonings, both in and out of the state conventions. It is an historical fact, that at the time when the judiciary act was submitted to the deliberations of the first congress, composed, as it was, not only of men of great learning and ability, but of men who had acted a principal part in framing, supporting, or opposing that constitution, the same exposition was explicitly declared and admitted by the friends and by the opponents of that system. It is an historical fact, that the supreme court of the United States have, from time to time, sustained this appellate jurisdiction in a great variety of cases, brought from the tribunals of many of the most important states in the union, and that no state tribunal has ever breathed a judicial doubt on the subject, or declined to obey the mandate of the supreme court, until the present occasion. . . .

The next question which has been argued, is, whether the case at bar be within the purview of the 25th section of the judiciary act, so that this court may rightfully sustain the present writ of error. This section, stripped of passages unimportant in this inquiry, enacts, in substance, that a final judgment or decree in any suit in the highest court of law or equity of a state, where is drawn in question the validity of a treaty or statute of, or an authority excised under, the United States, and the decision is against their validity. . . .

That the present writ of error is founded upon a judgment of the court below, which drew in question and denied the validity of a statute of the United States, is incontrovertible, for it is apparent upon the face of the record. . . . The case, then, falls directly within the terms of the act. It is a final judgment in a suit in a state court, denying the validity of a statute of the United States; and unless a distinction can be made between proceedings under a mandate, and proceedings in an original suit, a writ of error is the proper remedy to revise that judgment. . . .

* * * *

But it is contended, that the former judgment of this court was rendered upon a case not within the purview of this section of the judicial act, and that as it was pronounced by an incompetent jurisdiction, it was utterly void, and cannot be a sufficient foundation to sustain any subsequent proceedings. . . . The question now litigated is not upon the construction of a treaty, but upon the constitutionality of a statute of the United States, which is clearly within our jurisdiction.

[I]n ordinary cases a second writ of error has never been supposed to draw in question the propriety of the first judgment. . . .

In this case, however, from motives of a public nature, we are entirely willing to wave all objections, and to go back and re-examine the question of jurisdiction as it stood upon the record formerly in judgment. We have great confidence that our jurisdiction will, on a careful examination, stand confirmed as well upon principle as authority. [The Court analyzed the particular circumstances of the instant case.] Under such circumstances it was strictly a suit where was drawn in question the construction of a treaty, and the decision was against the title specially set up or claimed by the defendant. It would fall, then, within the very terms of the act.

The objection urged at the bar is, that this court cannot inquire into the title, but simply into the correctness of the construction put upon the treaty by the court of appeals; and that their judgment is not re-examinable here, unless it appear on the face of the record that some construction was put upon the treaty. If, therefore, that court might have decided the case upon the invalidity of the title, (and, *non constat,* that they did not,) independent of the treaty, there is an end of the appellate jurisdiction of this court. In support of this objection much stress is laid upon the last clause of the section, which declares, that no other cause shall be regarded as a ground of reversal than such as appears *on the face* of the record and *immediately* respects the construction of the treaty, &c., in dispute.

If this be the true construction of the section, it will be wholly inadequate for the purposes which it professes to have in view, and may be evaded at pleasure. But we see no reason for adopting this narrow construction; and there are the strongest reasons against it, founded upon the words as well as the intent of the legislature. What is the case for which the body of the section provides a remedy by writ of error? The answer must be in the words of the section, a suit where is drawn in question the construction of a treaty, and the decision is against *the title set up by the party.* It is, therefore, the decision against the title set up with reference to the treaty, and not the mere abstract construction of the treaty itself, upon which the statute intends to found the appellate jurisdiction. . . .

The restraining clause was manifestly intended for a very different purpose. It was foreseen that the parties might claim under various titles, and might assert various defences, altogether independent of each other. The court might admit or reject evidence applicable to one particular title, and not to all, and in such cases it was the intention of congress to limit what would otherwise have unquestionably attached to the court, the right of revising all the points involved in the cause. It therefore restrains this right to such errors as respect the questions specified in the section; and in this view, it has an appropriate sense, consistent with the preceding clauses. We are, therefore, satisfied, that, upon principle, the case was rightfully before us, and if the point were perfectly new, we should not hesitate to assert the jurisdiction.

* * * *

We have not thought it incumbent on us to give any opinion upon the question, whether this court have authority to issue a writ of mandamus to the court of appeals to enforce the former judgments, as we do not think it necessarily involved in the decision of this cause.

It is the opinion of the whole court, that the judgment of the court of appeals of Virginia, rendered on the mandate in this cause, be reversed, and the judgment of the district court, held at Winchester, be, and the same is hereby affirmed.

JUSTICE JOHNSON [concurring].

It will be observed in this case, that the court disavows all intention to decide on the right to issue compulsory process to the state courts; thus leaving us, in my opinion, where the constitution and laws place us — supreme over persons and cases as far as our judicial powers extend, but not asserting any compulsory control over the state tribunals.

* * * *

I view this question as one of the most momentous importance; as one which may affect, in its consequences, the permanence of the American union. It presents an instance of collision between the judicial powers of the union, and one of the greatest states in the union, on a point the most delicate and difficult to be adjusted. On the one hand, the general government must cease to exist whenever it loses the power of protecting itself in the exercise of its constitutional powers. . . .

On the other hand, so firmly am I persuaded that the American people can no longer enjoy the blessings of a free government, whenever the state sovereignties shall be prostrated at the feet of the general government, nor the proud consciousness of equality and security, any longer than the independence of judicial power shall be maintained consecrated and intangible, that I could borrow the language of a celebrated orator, and exclaim, "I rejoice that Virginia has resisted."

Yet here I must claim the privilege of expressing my regret, that the opposition of the high and truly respected tribunal of that state had not been marked with a little more moderation. The only point necessary to be decided in the case then before them was, "whether they were bound to obey the mandate emanating from this court?" But in the judgment entered on their minutes, they have affirmed that the case was, in this court, *coram non judice*, or, in other words, that this court had not jurisdiction over it.

This is assuming a truly alarming latitude of judicial power. Where is it to end? It is an acknowledged principle of, I believe, every court in the world, that not only the decisions, but every thing done under the judicial process of courts, not having jurisdiction, are, ipso facto, void. Are, then, the judgments of this court to be reviewed in every court of the union? And is every recovery of money, every change of property, that has taken place under our process, to be considered as null, void, and tortious?

We pretend not to more infallibility than other courts composed of the same frail materials which compose this. It would be the height of affectation to close our minds upon the recollection that we have been extracted from the same seminaries in which originated the learned men who preside over the state tribunals. But there is one claim which we can with confidence assert in our own name upon those tribunals — the profound, uniform, and unaffected respect which this court has always exhibited for state decisions, give us strong pretensions to judicial comity. And another claim I may assert, in the name of the American people; in this court, every state in the union is represented; we are constituted by the voice of the union, and when decisions take place, which nothing but a spirit to give ground and harmonize can reconcile, ours is the superior claim upon the comity of the state tribunals. . . .

* * * *

[D]oes the judicial power of the United States extend to the revision of decisions of state courts, in cases arising under treaties? But, in order to generalize the question, and present it in the true form in which it presents itself in this case, we will inquire whether the constitution sanctions the exercise of a revising power over the decisions of state tribunals in those cases to which the judicial power of the United States extends?

And here it appears to me that the great difficulty is on the other side. That the real doubt is, whether the state tribunals can constitutionally exercise jurisdiction in any of the cases to which the judicial power of the United States extends.

Some cession of judicial power is contemplated by the third article of the constitution: that which is ceded can no longer be retained. In one of the circuit courts of the United States, it has been decided (with what correctness I will not say) that the cession of a power to pass an uniform act of bankruptcy, although not acted on by the United States, deprives the states of the power of passing laws to that effect. With regard to the admiralty and maritime jurisdiction, it would be difficult to prove that the states could resume it, if the United States should abolish the courts vested with that jurisdiction; yet, it is blended with the other cases of jurisdiction, in the second section of the third article, and ceded in the same words. But it is contended that the second section of the third article contains no express cession of jurisdiction; that it only vests a power in congress to assume jurisdiction to the extent therein expressed. And under this head arose the discussion on the construction proper to be given to that article.

* * * *

[I]t is argued that a power to assume jurisdiction to the constitutional extent, does not necessarily carry with it a right to exercise appellate power over the state tribunals.

* * * *

But we know that by the 3d article of the constitution, judicial power, to a certain extent, is vested in the general government, and that by the same instrument, power is given to pass all laws necessary to carry into effect the provisions of the constitution. At present it is only necessary to vindicate the laws which they have passed affecting civil cases pending in state tribunals.

* * * *

The absolute necessity that there was for congress to exercise something of a revising power over cases and parties in the state courts, will appear from this consideration.

Suppose the whole extent of the judicial power of the United States vested in their own courts, yet such a provision would not answer all the ends of the constitution, for two reasons:

1st. Although the plaintiff may, in such case, have the full benefit of the constitution extended to him, yet the defendant would not; as the plaintiff might force him into the court of the state at his election.

2dly. Supposing it possible so to legislate as to give the courts of the United States original jurisdiction in all cases arising under the constitution, laws, &c., in the words of the 2d section of the 3d article, (a point on which I have some doubt, and which in time might, perhaps, under some quo minus fiction, or a willing construction, greatly accumulate the jurisdiction of those courts,) yet a very large class of cases would remain unprovided for. Incidental questions would often arise, and as a court of competent jurisdiction in the principal case must decide all such questions, whatever laws they arise under, endless might be the diversity of decisions throughout the union upon the constitution, treaties, and laws, of the United States; a subject on which the tranquillity of the union, internally and externally, may materially depend.

* * * *

[Chief Justice Marshall did not participate in the decision because he had contracted to purchase a significant portion of the Fairfax estate at issue in the litigation.]

DISCUSSION AND QUESTIONS

Martin v. Hunter's Lessee presented a pivotal moment in the Court's jurisprudence regarding the role of the Court vis-à-vis state courts. The federalism tension was palpable given the Virginia Court of Appeals' disobeying the Supreme Court's earlier substantive ruling. Thus, the Supreme Court had to proceed with a delicate yet firm voice. Justice Story did so by cogently establishing constitutional grounding for the Court's authority to review state court judgments.

In Justice Story's estimation, the Constitution presumed such review. Specifically, Justice Story reasoned that without authority to review state court decisions, the Court's role would be limited to hearing a narrow set of cases under its original jurisdiction. Further, Article III's pronouncements regarding the Supreme Court's appellate authority would be meaningless given that Article III provided Congress the discretion to decline to create lower federal courts. Based on your reading of Article III, is Justice Story's logic persuasive? What further support does Justice Story provide for the Supreme Court's authority?

How did the Court handle the parity issue? Did Justice Story view state court judges as competent, intelligent, and capable of judicial independence? Take a moment to explore what, if any, harms might have resulted if the Court had agreed with the Virginia Court of Appeals that the Court lacked the authority to review state court judgments. Justice Story deemed the Court's review of state court judgments as not only constitutionally justified, but also necessary to safeguard uniformity in the interpretation of federal law. Should ensuring uniform interpretation of federal law warrant a broad view of the Supreme Court's authority to review state court judgments?

The Supreme Court's power to review state court decisions, however, is not without limits. These doctrines of restraint include the "final judgment rule" and the "adequate and independent state grounds doctrine." The following sections explore the parameters of the Court's review of state court rulings.

ii. The Final Judgment Rule and Its Exceptions

Congressional authorization for Supreme Court review of state court decisions has been consistent, but it is not without restrictions on the scope of the Court's power. Pursuant to 28 U.S.C. § 1257, Supreme Court review is limited to only the "final" judgments of state courts. The state court decision must be "rendered by the highest court of a State in which a decision could be had." Further, the ruling must be a final judgment or decree of the highest state court.

Such restrictions aim to protect the Supreme Court's proper functioning within our federal system. For the Court to maintain optimal functioning, it must avoid unnecessary federalism tensions. The final judgment rule reduces tension with state courts by limiting the scope of the Supreme Court's review authority over state court decisions. The final judgment rule also facilitates judicial efficiency by ensuring that judicial resources are not wasted via piecemeal proceedings. It thereby streamlines judicial resolution. In this way, the final judgment rule is similar to justiciability doctrines like ripeness and mootness (see Chapter 2) — proper timing of the challenge within the life of the controversy and its relevant proceedings is essential. Otherwise, potential litigants would waste the scarce and important resource of the Court's time. Further, recall that not only must the time be right for the review, but also the controversy must be the right category of case.

The requirement of finality appears a simple distinction, but the Court has developed nuanced interpretations of finality's meaning in cases where a final judgment is technically lacking but practically apparent. In other words, the final judgment hurdle will be cleared, despite the fact that the state court has not entered the final judgment, if the state court decision is practically complete such that there is nothing further that must be done in state court and the substantive outcome is apparent.

A further complexity arises in the final judgment jurisprudence from the Court's treatment of appealability under the statute. The Court has developed significant exceptions that may devour the intended limitations. An examination of the existing exceptions follows in *Cox Broadcasting Co. v. Cohn.* Preceding *Cox Broadcasting,* the Court, for example, recognized an exception to the final judgment rule for matters in which the state court ordered a transfer of property, without issuing a final judgment, because an accounting of profits was left as the only remaining task in state court. *See Radio Station WOW, Inc. v. Johnson,* 326 U.S. 120 (1945). The *Cox Broadcasting* Court discusses *Radio Station WOW* among other exceptions to the final judgment rule. Are such exceptions appropriate? At what point does the final judgment limitation disappear?

Consider the final judgment rule and its exceptions in the next case.

COX BROADCASTING CO. v. COHN

420 U.S. 469 (1975)

JUSTICE WHITE delivered the opinion of the Court.

The issue before us in this case is whether, consistently with the First and Fourteenth Amendments, a State may extend a cause of action for damages for invasion of privacy caused by the publication of the name of a deceased rape victim which was publicly revealed in connection with the prosecution of the crime.

I

In August 1971, appellee's 17-year-old daughter was the victim of a rape and did not survive the incident. Six youths were soon indicted for murder and rape. Although there was substantial press coverage of the crime and of subsequent developments, the identity of the victim was not disclosed pending trial, perhaps because of Ga. Code Ann. § 26-9901 (1972), which makes it a misdemeanor to publish or broadcast the name or identity of a rape victim. In April 1972, some eight months later, the six defendants appeared in court. Five pleaded guilty to rape or attempted rape, the charge of murder having been dropped. The guilty pleas were accepted by the court, and the trial of the defendant pleading not guilty was set for a later date.

In the course of the proceedings that day, appellant Wasell, a reporter covering the incident for his employer, learned the name of the victim from an examination of the indictments which were made available for his inspection in the courtroom. That the name of the victim appears in the indictments and that the indictments were public records available for inspection are not disputed. Later that day, Wassell broadcast over the facilities of station WSB-TV, a television station owned by appellant Cox Broadcasting Corp., a news report concerning the court proceedings. The report named the victim of the crime and was repeated the following day.

In May 1972, appellee brought an action for money damages against appellants, relying on § 26-9901 and claiming that his right to privacy had been invaded by the television broadcasts giving the name of his deceased daughter. Appellants admitted the broadcasts but claimed that they were privileged under both state law and the First and Fourteenth Amendments. The trial court, rejecting appellants' constitutional claims and holding that the Georgia statute gave a civil remedy to those injured by its violation, granted summary judgment to appellee as to liability, with the determination of damages to await trial by jury.

On appeal, the Georgia Supreme Court, in its initial opinion, held that the trial court had erred in construing § 26-9901 to extend a civil cause of action for invasion of privacy and thus found it unnecessary to consider the constitutionality of the statute. The court went on to rule, however, that the complaint stated a cause of action "for the invasion of the appellee's right of privacy, or for the tort of public disclosure"—a "common law tort exist[ing] in this jurisdiction without the help of the statute that the trial judge in this case relied on." Although the privacy invaded was not that of the deceased victim, the father was held to have stated a claim for invasion of his own privacy by reason of the publication of his daughter's name. The court explained, however, that liability did not follow as a matter of law and that summary judgment was improper; whether the public disclosure of the name actually invaded appellee's "zone of privacy," and if so, to what extent, were issues to be determined by the trier of fact. Also, "in formulating such an issue for determination by the fact-finder, it is reasonable to require the appellee to prove that the appellants invaded his privacy with willful or negligent disregard for the fact that reasonable men would find the invasion highly offensive." The Georgia Supreme Court did agree with the trial court, however, that the First and Fourteenth Amendments did not, as a matter of law, require judgment for appellants. . . .

Upon motion for rehearing the Georgia court countered the argument that the victim's name was a matter of public interest and could be published with impunity by relying on § 26-9901 as an authoritative declaration of state policy that the name of a rape victim was not a matter of public concern. This time the court felt compelled to determine the constitutionality of the statute and sustained it as a "legitimate limitation on the right of freedom of expression contained in the First Amendment." . . . We conclude that the Court has jurisdiction, and reverse the judgment of the Georgia Supreme Court.

II

* * * *

Since 1789, Congress has granted this Court appellate jurisdiction with respect to state litigation only after the highest state court in which judgment could be had has rendered a "[f]inal judgment or decree." Title 28 U.S.C. § 1257 retains this limitation on our power to review cases coming from state courts. The Court has noted that "[c]onsiderations of English usage as well as those of judicial policy" would justify an interpretation of the final-judgment rule to preclude review "where anything further remains to be determined by a State court, no matter how dissociated from the only federal issue that has finally been adjudicated by the highest court of the State." Radio Station WOW, Inc. v. Johnson, 326 U.S. 120, 124 (1945). But the Court there observed that the rule had not been administered in such a mechanical fashion and that there were circumstances in which there has been "a departure from this requirement of finality for federal appellate jurisdiction."

These circumstances were said to be "very few"; but as the cases have unfolded, the Court has recurringly encountered situations in which the highest court of a State has finally determined the federal issue present in a particular case, but in which there are further proceedings in the lower state courts to come. There are now at least four categories of such cases in which the Court has treated the decision on the federal issue as a final judgment for the purposes of 28 U.S.C. § 1257 and has taken jurisdiction without awaiting the completion of the additional proceedings anticipated in the lower state courts. In most, if not all, of the cases in these categories, these additional proceedings would not require the decision of other federal questions that might also require review by the Court at a later date,[7] and immediate rather than delayed review would be the best way to avoid "the mischief of economic waste and of delayed justice," Radio Station WOW, as well as precipitate interference with state litigation.[8] In the cases in the first two categories considered below, the federal issue would not be mooted or otherwise affected by the proceedings yet to be had because those proceedings have little substance, their outcome is certain, or they are wholly unrelated to the federal question. In the other two categories, however, the federal issue would be mooted if the petitioner or appellant seeking to bring the action here prevailed on the merits in the later state-court proceedings, but

7. [Footnote 6 in Court's opinion.] Eminent domain proceedings are of the type that may involve an interlocutory decision as to a federal question with another federal question to be decided later. "For in those cases the federal constitutional question embraces not only a taking but a taking on payment of just compensation. A state judgment is not final unless it covers both aspects of that integral problem."

8. [Footnote 7 in Court's opinion.] *Gillespie v. United States Steel Corp.*, 379 U.S. 148 (1964), arose in the federal courts and involved the requirement of 28 U.S.C. § 1291 that judgments of district courts be final if they are to be appealed to the courts of appeals. In the course of deciding that the judgment of the District Court in the case had been final, the Court indicated its approach to finality requirements: "And our cases long have recognized that whether a ruling is 'final' within the meaning of § 1291 is frequently so close a question that decision of that issue either way can be supported with equally forceful arguments, and that it is impossible to devise a formula to resolve all marginal cases coming within what might well be called the 'twilight zone' of finality. Because of this difficulty this Court has held that the requirement of finality is to be given a 'practical rather than a technical construction.' *Cohen v. Beneficial Industrial Loan Corp.*, [337 U.S. 541, 546]. *Dickinson v. Petroleum Conversion Corp.*, 338 U.S. 507, 511, pointed out that [Further,] in deciding the question of finality the most important competing considerations are 'the inconvenience and costs of piecemeal review on the one hand and the danger of denying justice by delay on the other.'"

there is nevertheless sufficient justification for immediate review of the federal question finally determined in the state courts.

In the first category are those cases in which there are further proceedings—even entire trials—yet to occur in the state courts but where for one reason or another the federal issue is conclusive or the outcome of further proceedings preordained. In these circumstances, because the case is for all practical purposes concluded, the judgment of the state court on the federal issue is deemed final. In Mills v. Alabama, 384 U.S. 214 (1966), for example, a demurrer to a criminal complaint was sustained on federal constitutional grounds by a state trial court. The State Supreme Court reversed, remanding for jury trial. This Court took jurisdiction on the reasoning that the appellant had no defense other than his federal claim and could not prevail at trial on the facts or any nonfederal ground. To dismiss the appeal "would not only be an inexcusable delay of the benefits Congress intended to grant by providing for appeal to this Court, but it would also result in a completely unnecessary waste of time and energy in judicial systems already troubled by delays due to congested dockets."

Second, there are cases such as *Radio Station WOW* and Brady v. Maryland, 373 U.S. 83 (1963), in which the federal issue, finally decided by the highest court in the State, will survive and require decision regardless of the outcome of future state-court proceedings. In *Radio Station WOW*, the Nebraska Supreme Court directed the transfer of the properties of a federally licensed radio station and ordered an accounting, rejecting the claim that the transfer order would interfere with the federal license. The federal issue was held reviewable here despite the pending accounting on the "presupposition . . . that the federal questions that could come here have been adjudicated by the State court, and that the accounting which remains to be taken could not remotely give rise to a federal question . . . that may later come here. . . ." The judgment rejecting the federal claim and directing the transfer was deemed "dissociated from a provision for an accounting even though that is decreed in the same order." Nothing that could happen in the course of the accounting, short of settlement of the case, would foreclose or make unnecessary decision on the federal question. Older cases in the Court had reached the same result on similar facts. In the latter case, the Court, in an opinion by Mr. Chief Justice Taney, stated that the Court had not understood the final-judgment rule "in this strict and technical sense, but has given [it] a more liberal, and, as we think, a more reasonable construction, and one more consonant to the intention of the legislature."

In the third category are those situations where the federal claim has been finally decided, with further proceedings on the merits in the state courts to come, but in which later review of the federal issue cannot be had, whatever the ultimate outcome of the case. Thus, in these cases, if the party seeking interim review ultimately prevails on the merits, the federal issue will be mooted; if he were to lose on the merits, however, the governing state law would not permit him again to present his federal claims for review. The Court has taken jurisdiction in these circumstances prior to completion of the case in the state courts. California v. Stewart, 384 U.S. 436 (1966) (decided with *Miranda v. Arizona*), epitomizes this category. There the state court reversed a conviction on federal constitutional grounds and remanded for a new trial. Although the State might have prevailed at trial, we granted its petition for certiorari and affirmed, explaining that the state judgment was "final" since an acquittal of the defendant at trial would preclude, under state law, an appeal by the State.

A recent decision in this category is North Dakota State Board of Pharmacy v. Snyder's Drug Stores, Inc., 414 U.S. 156 (1973), in which the Pharmacy Board rejected an application for a pharmacy operating permit relying on a state statute specifying ownership requirements which the applicant did not meet. The State Supreme Court held the statute unconstitutional and remanded the matter to the Board for further consideration of the application, freed from the constraints of the ownership statute. The Board brought the case here, claiming that the statute was constitutionally acceptable under modern cases. After reviewing the various circumstances under which the finality requirement has been deemed satisfied despite the fact that litigation had not terminated in the state courts, we entertained the case over claims that we had no jurisdiction. The federal issue would not survive the remand, whatever the result of the state administrative proceedings. The Board might deny the license on state-law grounds, thus foreclosing the federal issue, and the Court also ascertained that under state law the Board could not bring the federal issue here in the event the applicant satisfied the requirements of state law except for the invalidated ownership statute. Under these circumstances, the issue was ripe for review.[9]

Lastly, there are those situations where the federal issue has been finally decided in the state courts with further proceedings pending in which the party seeking review here might prevail on the merits on nonfederal grounds, thus rendering unnecessary review of the federal issue by this Court, and where reversal of the state court on the federal issue would be preclusive of any further litigation on the relevant cause of action rather than merely controlling the nature and character of, or determining the admissibility of evidence in, the state proceedings still to come. In these circumstances, if a refusal immediately to review the state court decision might seriously erode federal policy, the Court has entertained and decided the federal issue, which itself has been finally determined by the state courts for purposes of the state litigation.

In Construction Laborers v. Curry, 371 U.S. 542 (1963), the state courts temporarily enjoined labor union picketing over claims that the National Labor Relations Board had exclusive jurisdiction of the controversy. The Court took jurisdiction for two independent reasons. First, the power of the state court to proceed in the face of the preemption claim was deemed an issue separable from the merits and ripe for review in this Court, particularly "when postponing review would seriously erode the national labor policy requiring the subject matter of respondents' cause to be heard by the . . . Board, not by the state courts." Second, the Court was convinced that in any event the union had no defense to the entry of a permanent injunction other than the preemption claim that had already been ruled on in the state courts. Hence the case was for all practical purposes concluded in the state tribunals.

In Mercantile National Bank v. Langdeau, 371 U.S. 555 (1963), two national banks were sued, along with others, in the courts of Travis County, Tex. The claim asserted was conspiracy to defraud an insurance company. The banks as a preliminary matter asserted that a special federal venue statute immunized them from suit in Travis County and that they could properly be sued only in another

9. [Footnote 10 in Court's opinion.] *Cohen v. Beneficial Industrial Loan Corp.*, 337 U.S. 541 (1949), was a diversity action in the federal courts in the course of which there arose the question of the validity of a state statute requiring plaintiffs in stockholder suits to post security for costs as a prerequisite to bringing the action. The District Court held the state law inapplicable, the Court of Appeals reversed, and this Court, after granting certiorari, held that the issue of security for costs was separable from and independent of the merits and that if review were to be postponed until the termination of the litigation, "it will be too late effectively to review the present order and the rights conferred by the statute, if it is applicable, will have been lost, probably irreparably."

county. Although trial was still to be had and the banks might well prevail on the merits, the Court, relying on *Curry*, entertained the issue as a "separate and independent matter, anterior to the merits and not enmeshed in the factual and legal issues comprising the plaintiff's cause of action." Moreover, it would serve the policy of the federal statute "to determine now in which state court appellants may be tried rather than to subject them . . . to long and complex litigation which may all be for naught if consideration of the preliminary question of venue is postponed until the conclusion of the proceedings." Miami Herald Publishing Co. v. Tornillo, 418 U.S. 241 (1974), is the latest case in this category. There a candidate for public office sued a newspaper for refusing, allegedly contrary to a state statute, to carry his reply to the paper's editorial critical of his qualifications. The trial court held the act unconstitutional, denying both injunctive relief and damages. The State Supreme Court reversed, sustaining the statute against the challenge based upon the First and Fourteenth Amendments and remanding the case for a trial and appropriate relief, including damages. The newspaper brought the case here. We sustained our jurisdiction, relying on the principles elaborated in the North Dakota case and observing:

> Whichever way we were to decide on the merits, it would be intolerable to leave unanswered, under these circumstances, an important question of freedom of the press under the First Amendment; an uneasy and unsettled constitutional posture of § 104.38 could only further harm the operation of a free press.

In light of the prior cases, we conclude that we have jurisdiction to review the judgment of the Georgia Supreme Court rejecting the challenge under the First and Fourteenth Amendments to the state law authorizing damage suits against the press for publishing the name of a rape victim whose identity is revealed in the course of a public prosecution. The Georgia Supreme Court's judgment is plainly final on the federal issue and is not subject to further review in the state courts. Appellants will be liable for damages if the elements of the state cause of action are proved. They may prevail at trial on nonfederal grounds, it is true, but if the Georgia court erroneously upheld the statute, there should be no trial at all. Moreover, even if appellants prevailed at trial and made unnecessary further consideration of the constitutional question, there would remain in effect the unreviewed decision of the State Supreme Court that a civil action for publishing the name of a rape victim disclosed in a public judicial proceeding may go forward despite the First and Fourteenth Amendments. Delaying final decision of the First Amendment claim until after trial will "leave unanswered . . . an important question of freedom of the press under the First Amendment," "an uneasy and unsettled constitutional posture [that] could only further harm the operation of a free press." On the other hand, if we now hold that the First and Fourteenth Amendments bar civil liability for broadcasting the victim's name, this litigation ends. Given these factors—that the litigation could be terminated by our decision on the merits and that a failure to decide the question now will leave the press in Georgia operating in the shadow of the civil and criminal sanctions of a rule of law and a statute the constitutionality of which is in serious doubt—we find that reaching the merits is consistent with the pragmatic approach that we have followed in the past in determining finality.

[In Part III, the Court determined that the freedom of the press protection provided in the First and Fourteenth Amendments prohibited the State of

Georgia from making the broadcast subject to civil liability for publicizing the victim's name. The Court reasoned that the Constitution barred Georgia from imposing sanctions on the publication of truthful information available on the public record.]

[Chief Justice Burger concurs in the judgment. The concurring opinions of Justice Douglas and Justice Powell are omitted.]

JUSTICE REHNQUIST, dissenting.

[T]his Court has steadily discovered new exceptions to the finality requirement, such that they can hardly any longer be described as "very few." . . . Although the Court's opinion today does accord detailed consideration to this problem, I do not believe that the reasons it expresses can support its result.

I

The Court has taken what it terms a "pragmatic" approach to the finality problem presented in this case. In so doing, it has relied heavily on Gillespie v. United States Steel Corp., 379 U.S. 148 (1964). As the Court acknowledges, *Gillespie* involved 28 U.S.C. § 1291, which restricts the appellate jurisdiction of the federal courts of appeals to "final decisions of the district courts." Although acknowledging this distinction, the Court accords it no importance and adopts *Gillespie*'s approach without any consideration of whether the finality requirement for this Court's jurisdiction over a "judgment or decree" of a state court is grounded on more serious concerns than is the limitation of court of appeals jurisdiction to final "decisions" of the district courts. I believe that the underlying concerns are different, and that the difference counsels a more restrictive approach when § 1257 finality is at issue.

According to *Gillespie*, the finality requirement is imposed as a matter of minimizing "the inconvenience and costs of piecemeal review." This proposition is undoubtedly sound so long as one is considering the administration of the federal court system. Were judicial efficiency the only interest at stake there would be less inclination to challenge the Court's resolution in this case, although, as discussed below, I have serious reservations that the standards the Court has formulated are effective for achieving even this single goal. The case before us, however, is an appeal from a state court, and this fact introduces additional interests which must be accommodated in fashioning any exception to the literal application of the finality requirement. I consider § 1257 finality to be but one of a number of congressional provisions reflecting concern that uncontrolled federal judicial interference with state administrative and judicial functions would have untoward consequences for our federal system. This is by no means a novel view of the § 1257 finality requirement. In Radio Station WOW, Mr. Justice Frankfurter's opinion for the Court explained the finality requirement as follows:

> This requirement has the support of considerations generally applicable to good judicial administration. It avoids the mischief of economic waste and of delayed justice. Only in very few situations, where intermediate rulings may carry serious public consequences, has there been a departure from this requirement of finality for federal appellate jurisdiction. This prerequisite to review derives added force when the jurisdiction of this Court is invoked to upset the decision of a State court.

> Here we are in the realm of potential conflict between the courts of two different governments. And so, ever since 1789, Congress has granted this Court the power to intervene in State litigation only after "the highest court of a State in which a decision in the suit could be had" has rendered a "final judgment or decree." This requirement is not one of those technicalities to be easily scorned. It is an important factor in the smooth working of our federal system.

* * * *

[W]e have in recent years emphasized and re-emphasized the importance of comity and federalism in dealing with a related problem, that of district court interference with ongoing state judicial proceedings. See Younger v. Harris, 401 U.S. 37. Because these concerns are important, and because they provide "added force" to § 1257's finality requirement, I believe that the Court has erred by simply importing the approach of cases in which the only concern is efficient judicial administration.

II

But quite apart from the considerations of federalism which counsel against an expansive reading of our jurisdiction under § 1257, the Court's holding today enunciates a virtually formless exception to the finality requirement, one which differs in kind from those previously carved out. By contrast, *Construction Laborers v. Curry* and *Mercantile National Bank v. Langdeau* are based on the understandable principle that where the proper forum for trying the issue joined in the state courts depends on the resolution of the federal question raised on appeal, sound judicial administration requires that such a question be decided by this Court, if it is to be decided at all, sooner rather than later in the course of the litigation. Organization for a Better Austin v. Keefe, 402 U.S. 415 (1971), and *Mills v. Alabama* rest on the premise that where as a practical matter the state litigation has been concluded by the decision of the State's highest court, the fact that in terms of state procedure the ruling is interlocutory should not bar a determination by this Court of the merits of the federal question.

Still other exceptions, as noted in the Court's opinion, have been made where the federal question decided by the highest court of the State is bound to survive and be presented for decision here regardless of the outcome of future state-court proceedings, *Radio Station WOW*; Brady v. Maryland, 373 U.S. 83 (1963), and for the situation in which later review of the federal issue cannot be had, whatever the ultimate outcome of the subsequent proceedings directed by the highest court of the State, California v. Stewart, 384 U.S. 436 (1966). While the totality of these exceptions certainly indicates that the Court has been willing to impart to the language "final judgment or decree" a great deal of flexibility, each of them is arguably consistent with the intent of Congress in enacting § 1257, if not with the language it used, and each of them is relatively workable in practice.

To those established exceptions is now added one so formless that it cannot be paraphrased, but instead must be quoted:

> Given these factors — that the litigation could be terminated by our decision on the merits and that a failure to decide the question now will leave the press in

Georgia operating in the shadow of the civil and criminal sanctions of a rule of law and a statute the constitutionality of which is in serious doubt—we find that reaching the merits is consistent with the pragmatic approach that we have followed in the past in determining finality.

There are a number of difficulties with this test. One of them is the Court's willingness to look to the merits. It is not clear from the Court's opinion, however, exactly how great a look at the merits we are to take. On the one hand, the Court emphasizes that if we reverse the Supreme Court of Georgia the litigation will end, and it refers to cases in which the federal issue has been decided "arguably wrongly." On the other hand, it claims to look to the merits "only to the extent of determining that the issue is substantial." If the latter is all the Court means, then the inquiry is no more extensive than is involved when we determine whether a case is appropriate for plenary consideration; but if no more is meant, our decision is just as likely to be a costly intermediate step in the litigation as it is to be the concluding event. If, on the other hand, the Court really intends its doctrine to reach only so far as cases in which our decision in all probability will terminate the litigation, then the Court is reversing the traditional sequence of judicial decisionmaking. Heretofore, it has generally been thought that a court first assumed jurisdiction of a case, and then went on to decide the merits of the questions it presented. But henceforth in determining our own jurisdiction we may be obliged to determine whether or not we agree with the merits of the decision of the highest court of a State.

* * * *

But the greatest difficulty with the test enunciated today is that it totally abandons the principle that constitutional issues are too important to be decided save when absolutely necessary, and are to be avoided if there are grounds for decision of lesser dimension. The long line of cases which established this rule makes clear that it is a principle primarily designed, not to benefit the lower courts, or state-federal relations, but rather to safeguard this Court's own process of constitutional adjudication.

"[This] Court will not 'anticipate a question of constitutional law in advance of the necessity of deciding it.'" . . . In this case there has yet to be an adjudication of liability against appellants, and unlike the appellant in *Mills v. Alabama*, they do not concede that they have no nonfederal defenses. Nonetheless, the Court rules on their constitutional defense. Far from eschewing a constitutional holding in advance of the necessity for one, the Court construes § 1257 so that it may virtually rush out and meet the prospective constitutional litigant as he approaches our doors.

* * * *

I would dismiss for want of jurisdiction.

DISCUSSION AND QUESTIONS

The majority in *Cox Broadcasting* holds that the Court possesses appellate jurisdiction pursuant to § 1257, despite the fact that the state supreme court had remanded the matter for plenary trial. Is finality still required? Did the

Court persuade you of the justification for its review? Should the claim fit within the fourth category of exceptions?

The Supreme Court, in *Cox Broadcasting*, stretches the principles of finality with an expansive interpretation and broad exceptions. Are you convinced by the Court's reasoning? What goals may be lost if the requirement of finality vanishes? In other words, when the Court claims the power to review a state court judgment despite the absence of technical finality, does the Court encroach unnecessarily on the state's sovereignty? Consider the motivations of the Court as to why it would want to render cases like *Cox Broadcasting* reviewable. Are there federal interests at stake that warrant the expansion of the exceptions to finality?

In *Cox Broadcasting*, the Court determined that finality existed because the federal issue was "plainly final" and "not subject to further review in the state courts." Yet, as the Court recognized, it is possible that the defendants could have won on the merits in the remanded state trial. The state court could have rendered its decision on non-federal grounds given that the state court had already rejected the defendants' First Amendment defense. If the state court had so ruled, would the Supreme Court have been able to review the state court judgment? The Supreme Court expressed concern for the potentially viable First Amendment claims of the defendants. If a valid First Amendment defense existed, the Court noted that no trial should occur. Does protection of the interpretation of the First Amendment warrant expanding finality principles as the Court did in *Cox Broadcasting*?

REVIEW AND CONSOLIDATION

Four Exceptions to the Final Judgment Rule—Warranting Supreme Court Review?

1. Practical Finality ➔ case where a technical final judgment is absent, but as a practical matter, nothing remains to be done in the state court such that the outcome of remaining state proceedings is clear.
2. Survivable Federal Issue ➔ case where "the federal issue, finally decided by the highest court in the State, will survive and require decision regardless of the outcome of future state-court proceedings."
3. Federal Issue Ripe Only Now, but Moot Later ➔ case where the Supreme Court only has this one bite at the federal issue because if the Court does not review the case now, it will never be able to review the state court's decision on federal issues.
4. Federal Policy Import ➔ case where (i) the state court has issued a final decision on a federal issue, (ii) reversal of the court's ruling on the federal issue would preclude any further litigation, and (iii) "the state-court decision might seriously erode federal policy" if the Court does not review the case immediately.

iii. The Adequate and Independent State Grounds Doctrine

The Supreme Court lacks the power to review state court decisions on state-law grounds. Although the Constitution does not explicitly prohibit such review, Supreme Court precedent supports this limitation. In applying this bar, the Court has articulated the adequate and independent state grounds doctrine. The doctrine further protects federalism principles by curtailing review. Examine the following case to explore the roots of the restriction and its policy rationale.

MURDOCK v. CITY OF MEMPHIS

187 U.S. (20 Wall.) 590 (1875)

[Murdock's ancestors, in 1844, conveyed land to the City of Memphis for use as a federal navy depot. Pursuant to the deed of sale, the land would revert to the grantors or their heirs if the United States failed to use the land as a navy depot. During 1844, Memphis conveyed the land to the federal government, and the United States made improvements but did not use the land as a naval depot. After ten years, the United States abandoned the property and returned the land to Memphis. Murdock sued Memphis, in Tennessee state court, for the return of the property pursuant to the deed's terms — a state-law claim. Murdock also argued that the federal law requiring the transfer of the land back to Memphis should constitute a directive to Memphis to hold the land in a constructive trust for Murdock, the true owner. In the Tennessee state courts, Murdock lost under both theories. He then sought Supreme Court review. Murdock contended that Congress' 1867 Act amended section 25 of the Judiciary Act of 1789 and, in so doing, established the Court's power to review both the state and federal arguments.

Section 25 of the Judiciary Act of 1789 reads:

> That a final judgment or decree in any suit, in the highest court of law or equity of a State in which a decision in the suit could be had, where is drawn in question the validity of a treaty or statute of, or an authority exercised under the United States, and the decision is against their validity; or where is drawn in question the validity of a statute of, or an authority exercised under any State, on the ground of their being repugnant to the Constitution, treaties, or laws of the United States, and the decision is in favor of such their validity, or where is drawn in question the construction of any clause of the Constitution, or of a treaty or statute of, or commission held under the United States, and the decision is against the title, right, privilege, or exemption specially set up or claimed by either party, under such clause of the said Constitution, treaty, statute, or commission, may be re-examined and reversed or affirmed in the Supreme Court of the United States upon a writ of error, the citation being signed by the chief justice, or judge, or chancellor of the court rendering or passing the judgment or decree complained of, or by a justice of the Supreme Court of the United States, in the same manner and under the same regulations, and the writ shall have the same effect as if the judgment or decree complained of had been rendered or passed in a Circuit Court, and the proceeding upon the reversal shall also be the same, except that the Supreme Court, instead of remanding the cause for a final decision, as before provided, may at their discretion, if the cause shall have been once remanded before, proceed to a final decision of the same and award execution. But no

> other error shall be assigned or regarded as a ground of reversal in any such case as aforesaid than such as appears on the face of the record and immediately respects the before-mentioned questions of validity or construction of the said Constitution, treaties, statutes, commissions, or authorities in dispute.

The second section of the Judiciary Act of 1867 provides:

> That a final judgment or decree in any suit in the highest court of a State in which a decision in the suit could be had, where is drawn in question the validity of a treaty or statute of or an authority exercised under the United States, and the decision is against their validity, or where is drawn in question the validity of a statute of or an authority exercised under any State, on the ground of their being repugnant to the Constitution, treaties, or laws of the United States, and the decision is in favor of such their validity, or where any title, right, privilege, or immunity is claimed under the Constitution, or any treaty or statute of, or commission held, or authority exercised, under the United States, and the decision is against the title, right, privilege, or immunity specially set up or claimed by either party under such Constitution, treaty, statute, commission, or authority, may be re-examined and reversed or affirmed in the Supreme Court of the United States, upon a writ of error, the citation being signed by the chief justice, or judge, or chancellor of the court rendering or passing the judgment or decree complained of, or by a justice of the Supreme Court of the United States, in the same manner, and under the same regulations, and the writ shall have the same effect as if the judgment or decree complained of had been rendered or passed in a court of the United States; and the proceeding upon the reversal shall also be the same, except that the Supreme Court may, at their discretion, proceed to a final decision of the same, and award execution or remand the same to an inferior court.

After the Court set forth the two sections of the Act, it provided pertinent legislative history:

> The published proceedings of the two houses of Congress show that the bill, which subsequently became a law, was reported by a committee which had been instructed "to inquire and report what legislation was necessary to enable the courts of the United States to enforce the freedom of the wives and children of soldiers of the United States, under the joint resolution of Congress of March 3d, 1865, and the liberty of all persons under the operation of the constitutional amendment abolishing slavery." The bill, so far as the point now under consideration is concerned, was not the subject of special comment. The effect of it was declared by the member of the House of Representatives who reported it from the committee, to be "to enlarge the privilege of the writ of habeas corpus." In the Senate an inquiry was made "whether the second section was drawn on the same principle as the twenty-fifth section of the Judiciary Act of 1789." The reply was, "It is a little broader than the Judiciary Act. It is of a similar character."]

JUSTICE MILLER delivered the opinion of the court.

* * * *

The questions propounded by the court for discussion by counsel were these:

1. Does the second section of the act of February 5th, 1867, repeal all or any part of the twenty-fifth section of the act of 1789, commonly called the Judiciary Act?

[The Court found that section 25 of the 1789 was repealed by section 2 of the 1867 Act.]

2. Is it the true intent and meaning of the act of 1867, above referred to, that when this court has jurisdiction of a case, by reason of any of the questions therein mentioned, it shall proceed to decide all the questions presented by the record which are necessary to a final judgment or decree?

[Section 25 "in express terms limited the power of the Supreme Court in reversing the judgment of a State court, to errors apparent on the face of the record and which respected questions, that for the sake of brevity, though not with strict verbal accuracy, we shall call Federal questions, namely, those in regard to the validity of construction of the Constitution, treaties, statutes, commissions, or authority of the Federal government."]

3. If this question be answered affirmatively, does the Constitution of the United States authorize Congress to confer such a jurisdiction on this court?

* * * *

[Murdock's] argument may be thus stated: 1. That the Constitution declares that the judicial power of the United States shall extend to *cases* of a character which includes the questions described in the section, and that by the word *case*, is to be understood all of the case in which such a question arises. 2. That by the fair construction of the act of 1789 in regard to removing those cases to this court, the power and the duty of re-examining the whole case would have been devolved on the court, but for the restriction of the clause omitted in the act of 1867; and that the same language is used in the latter act regulating the removal, but omitting the restrictive clause. And, 3. That by re-enacting the statute in the same terms as to the removal of cases from the State courts, without the restrictive clause, Congress is to be understood as conferring the power which that clause prohibited.

We will consider the last proposition first.

What were the precise motives which induced the omission of this clause it is impossible to ascertain with any degree of satisfaction. In a legislative body like Congress, it is reasonable to suppose that among those who considered this matter at all, there were varying reasons for consenting to the change. No doubt there were those who, believing that the Constitution gave no right to the Federal judiciary to go beyond the line marked by the omitted clause, thought its presence or absence immaterial; and in a revision of the statute it was wise to leave it out, because its presence implied that such a power was within the competency of Congress to bestow. There were also, no doubt, those who believed that the section standing without that clause did not confer the power which it prohibited, and that it was, therefore, better omitted. It may also have been within the thought of a few that all that is now claimed would follow the repeal of the clause. But if Congress, or the framers of the bill, had a clear purpose to enact affirmatively that the court *should consider* the class of errors which that clause forbid, nothing hindered that they should say so in positive terms; and in reversing the policy of the government from its foundation in one of the most important subjects on which that body could act, it is reasonably to be expected that Congress would use plain, unmistakable language in giving expression to such intention.

There is, therefore, no sufficient reason for holding that Congress, by repealing or omitting this restrictive clause, intended to enact affirmatively the thing which that clause had prohibited.

* * * *

There is, therefore, nothing in the language of the act, . . . which in express terms defines the extent of the re-examination which this court shall give to such cases.

But we have not yet considered the most important part of the statute, namely, that which declares that it is only upon the existence of certain questions in the case that this court can entertain jurisdiction at all. Nor is the mere existence of such a question in the case sufficient to give jurisdiction — the question must have been *decided* in the State court. Nor is it sufficient that such a question was raised and was decided. It must have been decided in a certain way, that is, against the right set up under the Constitution, laws, treaties, or authority of the United States. The Federal question may have been erroneously decided. It may be quite apparent to this court that a wrong construction has been given to the Federal law, but if the right claimed under it by plaintiff in error has been conceded to him, this court cannot entertain jurisdiction of the case, so very careful is the statute, both of 1789 and of 1867, to narrow, to limit, and define the jurisdiction which this court exercises over the judgments of the State courts. Is it consistent with this extreme caution to suppose that Congress intended, when those cases came here, that this court should not only examine those questions, but all others found in the record? — questions of common law, of State statutes, of controverted facts, and conflicting evidence. Or is it the more reasonable inference that Congress intended that the cases should be brought here that *those questions* might be decided and *finally* decided by the court established by the Constitution of the Union, and the court which has always been supposed to be not only the most appropriate but the only proper tribunal for their final decision? No such reason nor any necessity exists for the decision by this court of other questions in those cases. The jurisdiction has been exercised for nearly a century without serious inconvenience to the due administration of justice. The State courts are the appropriate tribunals, as this court has repeatedly held, for the decision of questions arising under their local law, whether statutory or otherwise. And it is not lightly to be presumed that Congress acted upon a principle which implies a distrust of their integrity or of their ability to construe those laws correctly.

Let us look for a moment into the effect of the proposition contended for upon the cases as they come up for consideration in the conference-room. If it is found that no such question is raised or decided in the court below, then all will concede that it must be dismissed for want of jurisdiction. But if it is found that the Federal question was raised and was decided against the plaintiff in error, then the first duty of the court obviously is to determine whether it was correctly decided by the State court. Let us suppose that we find that the court below was right in its decision on that question. What, then, are we to do? Was it the intention of Congress to say that while you can only bring the case here on account of this question, yet when it is here, though it may turn out that the plaintiff in error was wrong on that question, and the judgment of the court below was right, though he has wrongfully dragged the defendant into this court by the allegation of an error which did not exist, and without which the case could not rightfully be here, he can still insist on an inquiry into all the other matters which were litigated in the case? This is neither reasonable nor just.

In such case both the nature of the jurisdiction conferred and the nature and fitness of things demand that, no error being found in the matter which authorized the re-examination, the judgment of the State court should be affirmed, and the case remitted to that court for its further enforcement.

The whole argument we are combating, however, goes upon the assumption that when it is found that the record shows that one of the questions mentioned has been decided against the claim of the plaintiff in error, this court has jurisdiction, and that jurisdiction extends to the whole case. If it extends to the whole case then the court must re-examine the whole case, and if it re-examines it must decide the whole case. It is difficult to escape the logic of the argument if the first premise be conceded. But it is here the error lies. We are of opinion that upon a fair construction of the whole language of the section the jurisdiction conferred is limited to the decision of the questions mentioned in the statute, and, as a necessary consequence of this, to the exercise of such powers as may be necessary to cause the judgment in that decision to be respected.

* * * *

It requires a very bold reach of thought, and a readiness to impute to Congress a radical and hazardous change of a policy vital in its essential nature to the independence of the State courts, to believe that that body contemplated, or intended, what is claimed, by the mere omission of a clause in the substituted statute, which may well be held to have been superfluous, or nearly so, in the old one.

Another consideration, not without weight in seeking after the intention of Congress, is found in the fact that where that body has clearly shown an intention to bring the whole of a case which arises under the constitutional provision as to its subject-matter under the jurisdiction of a Federal court, it has conferred its cognizance on Federal courts of original jurisdiction and not on the Supreme Court.

* * * *

It is not difficult to discover what the purpose of Congress in the passage of this law was. . . . [W]hatever conflict of opinion might exist in [state] courts on other subjects, the rights which depended on the Federal laws should be the same everywhere, and that their construction should be uniform. This could only be done by conferring upon the Supreme Court of the United States — the appellate tribunal established by the Constitution — the right to decide these questions finally and in a manner which would be conclusive on all other courts, State or National. This was the first purpose of the statute, and it does not require that, in a case involving a variety of questions, any other should be decided than those described in the act.

Secondly. It was no doubt the purpose of Congress to secure to every litigant whose rights depended on any question of Federal law that that question should be decided for him by the highest Federal tribunal if he desired it, when the decisions of the State courts were against him on that question. That rights of this character, guaranteed to him by the Constitution and laws of the Union, should not be left to the exclusive and final control of the State courts.

There may be some plausibility in the argument that these rights cannot be protected in all cases unless the Supreme Court has final control of the whole case. But the experience of eighty-five years of the administration of the law under the opposite theory would seem to be a satisfactory answer to the argument. It is not to be presumed that the State courts, where the rule is clearly laid down to them on the Federal question, and its influence on the case fully seen, will disregard or overlook it, and this is all that the rights of the party claiming under it require. Besides, by the very terms of this statute, when the Supreme Court is of opinion that the question of Federal law is of such relative importance to the whole case that it should control the final judgment, that court is authorized to render such judgment and enforce it by its own process. It cannot, therefore, be maintained that it is in any case necessary for the security of the rights claimed under the Constitution, laws, or treaties of the United States that the Supreme Court should examine and decide other questions not of a Federal character.

And we are of opinion that the act of 1867 does not confer such a jurisdiction.

This renders unnecessary a decision of the question whether, if Congress had conferred such authority, the act would have been constitutional. It will be time enough for this court to inquire into the exercise it in language which that body has attempted to exercise it in language which makes such an intention so clear as to require it.

* * * *

It is proper, in this first attempt to construe this important statute as amended, to say a few words on another point. What shall be done by this court when the question has been found to exist in the record, and to have been decided against the plaintiff in error, and *rightfully* decided, we have already seen, and it presents no difficulties.

But when it appears that the Federal question was decided erroneously against the plaintiff in error, we must then reverse the case undoubtedly, if there are no other issues decided in it than that. It often has occurred, however, and will occur again, that there are other points in the case than those of Federal cognizance, on which the judgment of the court below may stand; those points being of themselves sufficient to control the case.

Or it may be, that there are other issues in the case, but they are not of such controlling influence on the whole case that they are alone sufficient to support the judgment.

It may also be found that notwithstanding there are many other questions in the record of the case, the issue raised by the Federal question is such that its decision must dispose of the whole case.

In the two latter instances there can be no doubt that the judgment of the State court must be reversed, and under the new act this court can either render the final judgment or decree here, or remand the case to the State court for that purpose.

But in the other cases supposed, why should a judgment be reversed for an error in deciding the Federal question, if the same judgment must be rendered on the other points in the case? And why should this court reverse a judgment which is right on the whole record presented to us; or where the same judgment will be rendered by the court below, after they have corrected the error in the Federal question?

We have already laid down the rule that we are not authorized to examine these other questions for the purpose of deciding whether the State court ruled correctly on them or not. We are of opinion that on these subjects not embraced in the class of questions stated in the statute, we must receive the decision of the State courts as conclusive.

But when we find that the State court had decided the Federal question erroneously, then to prevent a useless and profitless reversal, which can do the plaintiff in error no good, and can only embarrass and delay the defendant, we must so far look into the remainder of the record as to see whether the decision of the Federal question alone is sufficient to dispose of the case, or to require its reversal; or on the other hand, whether there exist other matters in the record actually decided by the State court which are sufficient to maintain the judgment of that court, notwithstanding the error in deciding the Federal question. In the latter case the court would not be justified in reversing the judgment of the State court.

But this examination into the points in the record other than the Federal question is not for the purpose of determining whether they were correctly or erroneously decided, but to ascertain if any such have been decided, and their sufficiency to maintain the final judgment, as decided by the State court.

Beyond this we are not at liberty to go, and we can only go this far to prevent the injustice of reversing a judgment which must in the end be reaffirmed, even in this court, if brought here again from the State court after it has corrected its error in the matter of Federal law.

Finally, we hold the following propositions on this subject as flowing from the statute as it now stands:

1. That it is essential to the jurisdiction of this court over the judgment of a State court, that it shall appear that one of the questions mentioned in the act must have been raised, and presented to the State court.
2. That it must have been decided by the State court, or that its decision was necessary to the judgment or decree, rendered in the case.
3. That the decision must have been against the right claimed or asserted by plaintiff in error under the Constitution, treaties, laws, or authority of the United States.
4. These things appearing, this court has jurisdiction and must examine the judgment so far as to enable it to decide whether this claim of right was correctly adjudicated by the State court.
5. If it finds that it was rightly decided, the judgment must be affirmed.
6. If it was erroneously decided against plaintiff in error, then this court must further inquire, whether there is any other matter or issue adjudged by the State court, which is sufficiently broad to maintain the judgment of that court, notwithstanding the error in deciding the issue raised by the Federal question. If this is found to be the case, the judgment must be affirmed without inquiring into the soundness of the decision on such other matter or issue.
7. But if it be found that the issue raised by the question of Federal law is of such controlling character that its correct decision is necessary to any final judgment in the case, or that there has been no decision by the State court of any other matter or issue which is sufficient to maintain the judgment of that court without regard to the Federal question, then this court will reverse the judgment of the State court, and will either render such judgment here as the State court should have rendered, or remand the case to that court, as the circumstances of the case may require.

Applying the principles here laid down to the case now before the court, we are of opinion that this court has jurisdiction, and that the judgment of the Supreme Court of Tennessee must be affirmed.

* * * *

[The Court concluded that Murdock could not establish any federal right to the land.]

AFFIRMED.

JUSTICE CLIFFORD, with whom concurred JUSTICE SWAYNE, dissenting:

I dissent from so much of the opinion of the court as denies the jurisdiction of this court to determine the whole case, where it appears that the record presents a Federal question and that the Federal question was erroneously decided to the prejudice of the plaintiff in error; as in that state of the record it is, in my judgment, the duty of this court, under the recent act of Congress, to decide the whole merits of the controversy, and to affirm or reverse the judgment of the State court. Tested by the new law it would seem that it must be so, as this court cannot in that state of the record dismiss the writ of error, nor can the court reverse the judgment without deciding every question which the record presents.

Where the Federal question is rightly decided the judgment of the State court may be affirmed, upon the ground that the jurisdiction does not attach to the other questions involved in the merits of the controversy; but where the Federal question is erroneously decided the whole merits must be decided by this court, else the new law, which it is admitted repeals the twenty-fifth section of the Judiciary Act, is without meaning, operation, or effect, except to repeal the prior law.

* * * *

JUSTICE BRADLEY, dissenting:

. . . I deem it very doubtful whether the court has any jurisdiction at all over this particular case. . . . Proving that the government did not appropriate the land for a navy yard is a very different thing from setting up a claim to the land under an act of Congress.

I think, therefore, that in this case there was no title or right claimed by the appellants under any statute of, or authority exercised under, the United States; and consequently that there was no decision against any such title; and, therefore, that this court has no jurisdiction.

But supposing, as the majority of the court holds, that it has jurisdiction, I cannot concur in the conclusion that we can only decide the Federal question raised by the record. If we have jurisdiction at all, in my judgment we have jurisdiction of the *case*, and not merely of a *question* in it. . . .

Now, Congress, in the act of 1867, when revising the twenty-fifth section of the Judiciary Act, whilst following the general frame and modes of expression of that section, omitted the clause above referred to, which restricted the court to a consideration of the Federal questions. This omission cannot be regarded as having no meaning. The clause by its presence in the original act meant something, and effected something. It had the effect of restricting the consideration of the court to a certain class of question as a ground of reversal, which restriction would not have existed without it. The omission of the clause, according to a well-settled rule of construction, must necessarily have the effect of removing the restriction which it effected in the old law.

In my judgment, therefore, if the court had jurisdiction of the case, it was bound to consider not only the Federal question raised by the record, but the whole case. As the court, however, has decided otherwise, it is not proper that I should express any opinion on the merits.

[Chief Justice Waite was appointed after reargument and took no part in the judgment.]

DISCUSSION AND QUESTIONS

The *Murdock* Court made clear that it lacked power to review state court rulings on state law. In the Court's articulation of the adequate and independent state ground doctrine, two grounds arise: (i) substantive state law and (ii) procedural state law. Substantive state law is implicated when the state court opinion rests on both federal and non-federal grounds, and the Supreme Court determines that the non-federal ground, by itself, would support the state court judgment. Support for this rule exists in the prohibition against issuing advisory opinions (see Chapter 2). *See Herb v. Pitcairn,* 324 U.S. 117 (1945). In other words, the Supreme Court's review to articulate its interpretation of federal grounds is unnecessary because the state court decision is justified on the state's substantive law standing alone.

Under the procedural subcategory, the Supreme Court will decline review when the state court does not adjudicate a federal issue because the party failed to comport with the state's valid procedural rule. On federalism grounds, the Supreme Court prefers not to disrupt the state's maintenance of uniform and predictable procedures. Thus, litigants cannot ignore legitimate state procedures and seek review of the federal issues in the Supreme Court.

The Supreme Court, however, maintains the power to review state court decisions if the Court deems the state procedural rule is illegitimate, inadequate, or arbitrary. In *Henry v. Mississippi,* 379 U.S. 443 (1965), the Court demonstrated the breadth of this power. The case involved a state rule regarding the doctrine of waiver and the admission of evidence. The Supreme Court determined that the state rule was procedural and did not adequately serve an important state purpose, and thus the state rule's inadequacy warranted Supreme Court review. In so doing, the Court noted the import of state substantive versus procedural rules—a substantive rule meets the adequacy threshold when reversal of the state court's federal law ruling would not change the outcome of the case; a procedural rule must serve a legitimate interest of the state to be adequate. Finding the state's procedural rule inadequate, the Court in *Henry* exercised its appellate jurisdiction and widened its ability to review state court opinions.

The factual and historical context of *Henry* may limit the reach of its holding. Although the Court did not mention Aaron Henry's race or activism, consider that Henry was an African-American male and a civil rights activist arrested and convicted in the Deep South for "offensive contact" with an eighteen-year-old hitchhiker. With this backdrop, the Supreme Court announces its power to assess the federal question of when and how a state may legitimately preclude consideration of a federal issue through a state procedural forfeiture rule.

Ultimately, the *Henry* Court vacated the conviction and remanded for the state court to determine if Henry knowingly waived his federal claim under the circumstances. Given the unique unspoken facts of *Henry* and the timing of the case (the middle of the civil rights movement), the Court's heightened interest in examining the Mississippi court's procedural behavior may cabin the import of the ruling. The Supreme Court, however, has not clarified its jurisprudence since *Henry*. Rather, it has considered such issues case by case.

The Court's "settled rule" sounds clear: "where the judgment of a state court rests upon two grounds, one of which is federal and the other nonfederal in character, our jurisdiction fails if the nonfederal ground is independent of the federal ground and adequate to support the judgment." *Fox Film Corp. v. Muller*, 296 U.S. 207, 210 (1935). A vexing issue arises, however, when a state court decision is ambiguous regarding whether its holding relies upon state versus federal law. State courts are free to base rulings exclusively on state-law grounds. Often, however, state courts cite both state and federal authority. For example, the state may be considering an issue under a state constitutional provision that is parallel to the federal Constitution. In such a case, the state supreme court may ambiguously add a string citation that includes Supreme Court opinions interpreting the federal constitutional provision. May the Supreme Court review the state court decision? Should it?

MICHIGAN v. LONG

463 U.S. 1032 (1983)

JUSTICE O'CONNOR delivered the opinion of the Court.

In *Terry v. Ohio*, 392 U.S. 1 (1968), we upheld the validity of a protective search for weapons in the absence of probable cause to arrest because it is unreasonable to deny a police officer the right "to neutralize the threat of physical harm," when he possesses an articulable suspicion that an individual is armed and dangerous. We did not, however, expressly address whether such a protective search for weapons could extend to an area beyond the person in the absence of probable cause to arrest. In the present case, respondent David Long was convicted for possession of marijuana found by police in the passenger compartment and trunk of the automobile that he was driving. The police searched the passenger compartment because they had reason to believe that the vehicle contained weapons potentially dangerous to the officers. We hold that the protective search of the passenger compartment was reasonable under the principles articulated in *Terry* and other decisions of this Court. We also examine Long's argument that the decision below rests upon an adequate and independent state ground, and we decide in favor of our jurisdiction.

I

Deputies Howell and Lewis . . . observed a car traveling erratically and at excessive speed [and] turning down a side road, where it swerved off into a shallow ditch. . . . Long, the only occupant of the automobile, met the deputies at the rear of the car. . . . The door on the driver's side of the vehicle was left open.

Long and Deputy Lewis then stood by the rear of the vehicle while Deputy Howell shined his flashlight into the interior of the vehicle, but did not actually enter it. The purpose of Howell's action was "to search for other weapons." The officer noticed that something was protruding from under the armrest on the front seat. He knelt in the vehicle and lifted the armrest. He saw an open pouch on the front seat, and upon flashing his light on the pouch, determined that it contained what appeared to be marijuana. After Deputy Howell showed the pouch and its contents to Deputy Lewis, Long was arrested for possession of marijuana. A further search of the interior of the vehicle, including the glovebox, revealed neither more contraband nor the vehicle registration. The officers decided to impound the vehicle. Deputy Howell opened the trunk, which did not have a lock, and discovered inside it approximately 75 pounds of marijuana.

The Barry County Circuit Court denied Long's motion to suppress the marijuana taken from both the interior of the car and its trunk. He was subsequently convicted of possession of marijuana. The Michigan Court of Appeals affirmed Long's conviction, holding that the search of the passenger compartment was valid as a protective search under *Terry*, and that the search of the trunk was valid as an inventory search under *South Dakota v. Opperman*, 428 U.S. 364 (1976). The Michigan Supreme Court reversed. The court held that "the sole justification of the *Terry* search, protection of the police officers and others nearby, cannot justify the search in this case." The marijuana found in Long's trunk was considered by the court below to be the "fruit" of the illegal search of the interior, and was also suppressed.

II

Before reaching the merits, we must consider Long's argument that we are without jurisdiction to decide this case because the decision below rests on an adequate and independent state ground. The court below referred twice to the state constitution in its opinion, but otherwise relied exclusively on federal law. Long argues that the Michigan courts have provided greater protection from searches and seizures under the state constitution than is afforded under the Fourth Amendment, and the references to the state constitution therefore establish an adequate and independent ground for the decision below.

It is, of course, "incumbent upon this Court . . . to ascertain for itself . . . whether the asserted non-federal ground independently and adequately supports the judgment." *Abie State Bank v. Bryan*, 282 U.S. 765, 773 (1931). Although we have announced a number of principles in order to help us determine whether various forms of references to state law constitute adequate and independent state grounds,[10] we openly admit that we have thus far not

10. [Footnote 4 in Court's opinion.] For example, we have long recognized that "where the judgment of a state court rests upon two grounds, one of which is federal and the other non-federal in character, our jurisdiction fails if the non-federal ground is independent of the federal ground and adequate to support the judgment." *Fox Film Corp. v. Muller*, 296 U.S. 207, 210 (1935). We may review a state case decided on a federal ground even if it is clear that there was an available state ground for decision on which the state court could properly have relied. *Beecher v. Alabama*, 389 U.S. 35, 37, n.3 (1967). Also, if, in our view, the state court "'felt compelled by what it understood to be federal constitutional considerations to construe . . . its own law in the manner that it did,'" then we will not treat a normally adequate state ground as independent, and there will be no question about our jurisdiction. *Delaware v. Prouse*, 440 U.S. 648, 653 (1979) (quoting *Zacchini v. Scripps-Howard Broadcasting Co.*, 433 U.S. 562, 568 (1977)). Finally, "where the non-federal ground is so interwoven with the [federal ground] as not to be an independent matter, or is not of sufficient breadth to sustain the judgment without any decision of the other, our jurisdiction is plain." *Enterprise Irrigation District v. Farmers Mutual Canal Company*, 243 U.S. 157, 164 (1917).

developed a satisfying and consistent approach for resolving this vexing issue. In some instances, we have taken the strict view that if the ground of decision was at all unclear, we would dismiss the case. *See, e.g., Lynch v. New York*, 293 U.S. 52 (1934). In other instances, we have vacated, *e.g., Minnesota v. National Tea Co.*, 309 U.S. 551 (1940), or continued a case, *see, e.g., Herb v. Pitcairn*, 324 U.S. 117 (1945), in order to obtain clarification about the nature of a state court decision. *See also California v. Krivda*, 409 U.S. 33 (1972). In more recent cases, we have ourselves examined state law to determine whether state courts have used federal law to guide their application of state law or to provide the actual basis for the decision that was reached. *See Texas v. Brown*, 460 U.S. 730, 732-33 n.1 (1983) (plurality opinion). In *Oregon v. Kennedy*, 456 U.S. 667, 670-671 (1982), we rejected an invitation to remand to the state court for clarification even when the decision rested in part on a case from the state court, because we determined that the state case itself rested upon federal grounds. We added that "[e]ven if the case admitted of more doubt as to whether federal and state grounds for decision were intermixed, the fact that the state court relied to the extent it did on federal grounds requires us to reach the merits."

This ad hoc method of dealing with cases that involve possible adequate and independent state grounds is antithetical to the doctrinal consistency that is required when sensitive issues of federal-state relations are involved. Moreover, none of the various methods of disposition that we have employed thus far recommends itself as the preferred method that we should apply to the exclusion of others, and we therefore determine that it is appropriate to reexamine our treatment of this jurisdictional issue in order to achieve the consistency that is necessary.

The process of examining state law is unsatisfactory because it requires us to interpret state laws with which we are generally unfamiliar, and which often, as in this case, have not been discussed at length by the parties. Vacation and continuance for clarification have also been unsatisfactory both because of the delay and decrease in efficiency of judicial administration, *see Dixon v. Duffy*, 344 U.S. 143 (1952),[11] and, more important, because these methods of disposition place significant burdens on state courts to demonstrate the presence or absence of our jurisdiction. Finally, outright dismissal of cases is clearly not a panacea because it cannot be doubted that there is an important need for uniformity in federal law, and that this need goes unsatisfied when we fail to review an opinion that rests primarily upon federal grounds and where the independence of an alleged state ground is not apparent from the four corners of the opinion. We have long recognized that dismissal is inappropriate "where there is strong indication . . . that the federal constitution as judicially construed controlled the decision below."

Respect for the independence of state courts, as well as avoidance of rendering advisory opinions, have been the cornerstones of this Court's refusal to decide cases where there is an adequate and independent state ground. It is precisely because of this respect for state courts, and this desire to avoid advisory opinions, that we do not wish to continue to decide issues of state law that go

11. [Footnote 5 in Court's opinion.] Indeed, Dixon v. Duffy is also illustrative of another difficulty involved in our requiring state courts to reconsider their decisions for purposes of clarification. In *Dixon*, we continued the case on two occasions in order to obtain clarification, but none was forthcoming: "[T]he California court advised petitioner's counsel informally that it doubted its jurisdiction to render such a determination." 344 U.S. at 145. We then vacated the judgment of the state court, and remanded.

beyond the opinion that we review, or to require state courts to reconsider cases to clarify the grounds of their decisions. Accordingly, when, as in this case, a state court decision fairly appears to rest primarily on federal law, or to be interwoven with the federal law, and when the adequacy and independence of any possible state law ground is not clear from the face of the opinion, we will accept as the most reasonable explanation that the state court decided the case the way it did because it believed that federal law required it to do so. If a state court chooses merely to rely on federal precedents as it would on the precedents of all other jurisdictions, then it need only make clear by a plain statement in its judgment or opinion that the federal cases are being used only for the purpose of guidance, and do not themselves compel the result that the court has reached. In this way, both justice and judicial administration will be greatly improved. If the state court decision indicates clearly and expressly that it is alternatively based on bona fide separate, adequate, and independent grounds, we, of course, will not undertake to review the decision.

This approach obviates in most instances the need to examine state law in order to decide the nature of the state court decision, and will at the same time avoid the danger of our rendering advisory opinions.[12] It also avoids the unsatisfactory and intrusive practice of requiring state courts to clarify their decisions to the satisfaction of this Court. We believe that such an approach will provide state judges with a clearer opportunity to develop state jurisprudence unimpeded by federal interference, and yet will preserve the integrity of federal law. "It is fundamental that state courts be left free and unfettered by us in interpreting their state constitutions. But it is equally important that ambiguous or obscure adjudications by state courts do not stand as barriers to a determination by this Court of the validity under the federal constitution of state action." *National Tea Co.*, *supra*, at 557.

The principle that we will not review judgments of state courts that rest on adequate and independent state grounds is based, in part, on "the limitations of our own jurisdiction." *Herb v. Pitcairn*, 324 U.S. 117, 125 (1945). The jurisdictional concern is that we not "render an advisory opinion, and if the same judgment would be rendered by the state court after we corrected its views of federal laws, our review could amount to nothing more than an advisory opinion." Our requirement of a "plain statement" that a decision rests upon adequate and independent state grounds does not in any way authorize the rendering of advisory opinions. Rather, in determining, as we must, whether we have jurisdiction to review a case that is alleged to rest on adequate and independent state grounds, we merely assume that there are no such grounds when it is not clear from the opinion itself that the state court relied upon an adequate and independent state ground and when it fairly appears that the state court rested its decision primarily on federal law.

Our review of the decision below under this framework leaves us unconvinced that it rests upon an independent state ground. Apart from its two citations to the state constitution, the court below relied exclusively on its understanding of *Terry* and other federal cases. Not a single state case was cited to support the state court's holding that the search of the passenger compartment was unconstitutional. Indeed, the court declared that the search in this case was unconstitutional because "[t]he Court of Appeals erroneously applied the principles of

12. [Footnote 6 in Court's opinion.] There may be certain circumstances in which clarification is necessary or desirable, and we will not be foreclosed from taking the appropriate action.

Terry v. Ohio . . . to the search of the interior of the vehicle in this case." The references to the state constitution in no way indicate that the decision below rested on grounds in any way independent from the state court's interpretation of federal law. Even if we accept that the Michigan constitution has been interpreted to provide independent protection for certain rights also secured under the Fourth Amendment, it fairly appears in this case that the Michigan Supreme Court rested its decision primarily on federal law.

Rather than dismissing the case, or requiring that the state court reconsider its decision on our behalf solely because of a mere possibility that an adequate and independent ground supports the judgment, we find that we have jurisdiction in the absence of a plain statement that the decision below rested on an adequate and independent state ground. It appears to us that the state court "felt compelled by what it understood to be federal constitutional considerations to construe . . . its own law in the manner it did." *Zacchini v. Scripps-Howard Broadcasting Co.*, 433 U.S. 562, 568 (1977).[13]

[In Parts III and IV, the Court held the search valid under *Terry v. Ohio* and remanded the case for the Michigan Supreme Court's consideration of an alternative federal constitutional issue that the court did not resolve in its earlier decision.]

The decision of the Michigan Supreme Court is reversed, and the case is remanded for further proceedings not inconsistent with this opinion.

It is so ordered.

JUSTICE BLACKMUN, concurring in part and concurring in the judgment.

While I am satisfied that the Court has jurisdiction in this particular case, I do not join the Court, in Part II of its opinion, in fashioning a new presumption of jurisdiction over cases coming here from state courts. Although I agree with the Court that uniformity in federal criminal law is desirable, I see little efficiency and an increased danger of advisory opinions in the Court's new approach.

[Justice Brennan's dissenting opinion, joined by Justice Marshall, is omitted.]

* * * *

JUSTICE STEVENS, dissenting.

The jurisprudential questions presented in this case are far more important than the question whether the Michigan police officer's search of respondent's car violated the Fourth Amendment. The case raises profoundly significant questions concerning the relationship between two sovereigns — the State of Michigan and the United States of America.

The Supreme Court of the State of Michigan expressly held "that the deputies' search of the vehicle was proscribed by the Fourth Amendment of the United States Constitution and art. 1, § 11 of the Michigan Constitution."

13. [Footnote 10 in Court's opinion.] There is nothing unfair about requiring a plain statement of an independent state ground in this case. Even if we were to rest our decision on an evaluation of the state law relevant to Long's claim, as we have sometimes done in the past, our understanding of Michigan law would also result in our finding that we have jurisdiction to decide this case. Under state search and seizure law, a "higher standard" is imposed under art. 1, § 11 of the 1963 Michigan Constitution. *See People v. Secrest*, 321 N.W.2d 368, 369 (Mich. 1982). If, however, the item seized is, *inter alia*, a "narcotic drug . . . seized by a peace officer outside the curtilage of any dwelling house in this state," art. 1, § 11 of the 1963 Michigan Constitution, then the seizure is governed by a standard identical to that imposed by the Fourth Amendment. . . .

The state law ground is clearly adequate to support the judgment, but the question whether it is independent of the Michigan Supreme Court's understanding of federal law is more difficult. Four possible ways of resolving that question present themselves: (1) asking the Michigan Supreme Court directly, (2) attempting to infer from all possible sources of state law what the Michigan Supreme Court meant, (3) presuming that adequate state grounds are independent unless it clearly appears otherwise, or (4) presuming that adequate state grounds are not independent unless it clearly appears otherwise. This Court has, on different occasions, employed each of the first three approaches; never until today has it even hinted at the fourth. In order to "achieve the consistency that is necessary," the Court today undertakes a reexamination of all the possibilities. It rejects the first approach as inefficient and unduly burdensome for state courts, and rejects the second approach as an inappropriate expenditure of our resources. Although I find both of those decisions defensible in themselves, I cannot accept the Court's decision to choose the fourth approach over the third — to presume that adequate state grounds are intended to be dependent on federal law unless the record plainly shows otherwise. I must therefore dissent.

If we reject the intermediate approaches, we are left with a choice between two presumptions: one in favor of our taking jurisdiction, and one against it. Historically, the latter presumption has always prevailed. *See, e.g., Durley v. Mayo,* 351 U.S. 277, 285 (1956); *Stembridge v. Georgia,* 343 U.S. 541, 547 (1952); *Lynch v. New York,* 293 U.S. 52 (1934). The rule, as succinctly stated in *Lynch,* was as follows:

> Where the judgment of the state court rests on two grounds, one involving a federal question and the other not, or if it does not appear upon which of two grounds the judgment was based, and the ground independent of a federal question is sufficient in itself to sustain it, this Court will not take jurisdiction.

The Court today points out that in several cases we have weakened the traditional presumption by using the other two intermediate approaches identified above. Since those two approaches are now to be rejected, however, I would think that *stare decisis* would call for a return to historical principle. Instead, the Court seems to conclude that because some precedents are to be rejected, we must overrule them all.

Even if I agreed with the Court that we are free to consider as a fresh proposition whether we may take presumptive jurisdiction over the decisions of sovereign states, I could not agree that an expansive attitude makes good sense. It appears to be common ground that any rule we adopt should show "respect for state courts, and [a] desire to avoid advisory opinions." And I am confident that all members of this Court agree that there is a vital interest in the sound management of scarce federal judicial resources. All of those policies counsel against the exercise of federal jurisdiction. They are fortified by my belief that a policy of judicial restraint — one that allows other decisional bodies to have the last word in legal interpretation until it is truly necessary for this Court to intervene — enables this Court to make its most effective contribution to our federal system of government.

The nature of the case before us hardly compels a departure from tradition. These are not cases in which an American citizen has been deprived of a right secured by the United States Constitution or a federal statute. Rather, they are cases in which a state court has upheld a citizen's assertion of a right, finding the citizen to be protected under both federal and state law. The complaining party is an officer of the state itself, who asks us to rule that the state court interpreted federal rights too broadly and "overprotected" the citizen.

Such cases should not be of inherent concern to this Court. . . .

In this case the State of Michigan has arrested one of its citizens and the Michigan Supreme Court has decided to turn him loose. The respondent is a United States citizen as well as a Michigan citizen, but since there is no claim that he has been mistreated by the State of Michigan, the final outcome of the state processes offended no federal interest whatever. Michigan simply provided greater protection to one of its citizens than some other State might provide or, indeed, than this Court might require throughout the country.

I believe that in reviewing the decisions of state courts, the primary role of this Court is to make sure that persons who seek to vindicate federal rights have been fairly heard. . . .

Until recently we had virtually no interest in cases of this type. . . . Some time during the past decade . . . our priorities shifted. The result is a docket swollen with requests by states to reverse judgments that their courts have rendered in favor of their citizens. I am confident that a future Court will recognize the error of this allocation of resources [and] reconsider the propriety of today's expansion of our jurisdiction.

The Court offers only one reason for asserting authority over cases such as the one presented today: "an important need for uniformity in federal law [that] goes unsatisfied when we fail to review an opinion that rests primarily upon federal grounds and where the independence of an alleged state ground is not apparent from the four corners of the opinion." Of course, the supposed need to "review an opinion" clashes directly with our oft-repeated reminder that "our power is to correct wrong judgments, not to revise opinions." *Herb v. Pitcairn*, 324 U.S. 117, 126 (1945). The clash is not merely one of form: the "need for uniformity in federal law" is truly an ungovernable engine. That same need is no less present when it is perfectly clear that a state ground is both independent and adequate. In fact, it is equally present if a state prosecutor announces that he believes a certain policy of nonenforcement is commanded by federal law. Yet we have never claimed jurisdiction to correct such errors, no matter how egregious they may be, and no matter how much they may thwart the desires of the state electorate. We do not sit to expound our understanding of the Constitution to interested listeners in the legal community; we sit to resolve disputes. If it is not apparent that our views would affect the outcome of a particular case, we cannot presume to interfere.

Finally, I am thoroughly baffled by the Court's suggestion that it must stretch its jurisdiction and reverse the judgment of the Michigan Supreme Court in order to show "[r]espect for the independence of state courts." . . .

I respectfully dissent.

DISCUSSION AND QUESTIONS

Now that you have read *Michigan v. Long*, reread the chapter's Reference Problem. Ask yourself how those facts would stand up under the Court's reasoning in *Michigan v. Long*. How should the Supreme Court proceed if it is unclear whether the state court relied independently on a state-law ground?

Prior to *Michigan v. Long,* the Court engaged in varied approaches, making application of the principle unpredictable. Now, with *Michigan v. Long,* the Court seeks to clarify the waters. For additional elucidation of *Long,* see Edward A. Purcell, Jr., *The Story of* Michigan v. Long: *Supreme Court Review and the Workings of American Federalism, in* FEDERAL COURTS STORIES 57-86 (2010). Do you agree that the Court succeeded? As you analyze the holding and reasoning of *Michigan v. Long,* consider how the exclusionary rule, if required under Michigan law, would affect the outcome.

Some view *Michigan v. Long* as fundamentally flawed. For example, Justice Ginsburg, joined by Justice Stevens, has called for the Court to overrule *Michigan v. Long.*[14] In a dissenting opinion, Justice Ginsburg reasoned that the *Michigan v. Long* presumption of jurisdiction unduly interferes with the ability of states to conduct experimentation; furthermore, the presumption wastes judicial resources and involves the Court in issuing prohibited advisory opinions. Do you agree? Even if you see merit in Justice Ginsburg's criticisms, are we better off after *Michigan v. Long* because at least the Court has clarified the law? Consider how you might resolve the conflicting interests if you could craft the Court's jurisprudence from scratch.

Despite misgivings about the *Long* presumption *in favor of* Supreme Court jurisdiction, Justice Ginsburg recently authored an opinion applying the *Long* presumption to find jurisdiction over a challenge to a *Miranda* warning, even though the Florida Supreme Court relied, at least in part, on its own Constitution to rule the warning inadequate. *Florida v. Powell,* 559 U.S. 50 (2010). The Tampa Police had warned Powell that he had "the right to talk to a lawyer before answering any of our questions." *Id.* at 54. Powell confessed to unlawful possession of a handgun. Powell sought to suppress the confession on the ground that the warning inadequately conveyed his *Miranda* rights, including the right to consult a lawyer any time during police questioning. The Florida trial court denied Powell's motion, and the jury convicted him. The interim appellate court ruled in Powell's favor that the warning failed to satisfy the Florida and U.S. Constitutions; the court also certified the question to the Florida Supreme Court, which surveyed Supreme Court and Florida precedent to find the warning constitutionally infirm. The United States Supreme Court reversed.

In *Powell,* the United States Supreme Court determined that jurisdiction was proper, despite Powell's claim of adequate and independent state grounds for the Florida Supreme Court ruling. Part II of Justice Ginsburg's majority opinion noted that "the Florida Supreme Court treated state and federal law as interchangeable and interwoven." *Id.* at 57. According to Justice Ginsburg, the Florida high court focused on *Miranda*'s requirement, rather than on Florida laws' independent requirements. The Court found jurisdiction because it could not "identify, 'from the face of the opinion,' a clear statement that the decision rested on a state ground separate from *Miranda.*" *Id.* at 58. On the merits, the Court ruled in Part III of the opinion that the warning given, although different than the standard F.B.I. "exemplary" warnings, satisfied *Miranda* as "they communicated the same essential message." *Id.* at 64.

Justice Stevens remains critical of *Long.* In *Powell,* Justice Stevens, joined by Justice Breyer as to Part II on the merits, dissented to the Court's opinion: "The Court's power to review that decision is doubtful at best; moreover, the Florida Supreme Court has the better view on the merits." *Id.* at 65. In Part I, Justice

14. *Arizona v. Evans,* 514 U.S. 1, 23 (1995) (Ginsburg, J., dissenting).

Stevens found that the Florida Supreme Court sufficiently demonstrated an independent state ground for its ruling, even though the court's state analysis was interwoven with federal law. He implored that *Long*'s "novel presumption" be applied narrowly "to truly ambiguous cases" in order to ensure proper respect for state court independence and to avoid the prohibition against advisory opinions. *Id.* at 65. On the merits (Part II), Justice Stevens concluded that the warning given violated the Fifth Amendment privilege because the warning "did not reasonably convey to Powell his right to have a lawyer with him during the interrogation." *Id.* at 72.

Assess how the Florida Supreme Court might have reacted upon reading the Supreme Court's reversal. Did the Florida Supreme Court *unintentionally* fail to provide a clear statement of its adequate and independent state grounds for its ruling? Did the Florida high court view Florida law and federal law as inextricably interwoven? Recall that states are free to provide broader constitutional protections to citizens than the U.S. Constitution provides. Is *Michigan v. Long* operating smoothly as intended? Consider whether the *Powell* Court's application of the *Long* presumption appropriately balanced federalism concerns or caused the Court to unduly encroach on state interests.

b. Review of Lower Federal Court Decisions

Remember that the bulk of the Supreme Court's docket is its appellate jurisdiction rather than its original jurisdiction. The Court's appellate jurisdiction includes the Court's power to review both state court and federal court decisions. Federalism tensions exist regarding the Court's review of state decisions but do not exist regarding review of lower federal courts. Thus, the Court's review of lower federal court decisions garners significantly less attention.

Also, the Constitution expressly grants the Supreme Court appellate jurisdiction over all cases invoking federal subject matter jurisdiction (i.e., federal question cases) for which the Court does not possess original jurisdiction. Further, Congress has expansively authorized appellate jurisdiction. Pursuant to 28 U.S.C. § 1254, the Supreme Court may grant a writ of certiorari to review a case "upon the petition of any party to any civil or criminal case before or after rendition of judgment or decree." The Supreme Court thus has extensive power to review the federal courts below it. This power includes granting certiorari "upon the petition of any party" under § 1254(1), including petitions brought by prevailing parties, as well as those who have lost, in the courts below. *See Camreta v. Greene*, 563 U.S. ____, 131 S. Ct. 2020 (2011) (finding immunized officials satisfied standing requirements and, although prudential concerns generally supported declining certiorari of cases brought by winners, the Constitution permits consideration, which will allow the Court to address standards of official conduct). For a substantive critique of *Camreta* and *Davis* (discussed in chapter 11), see Orin S. Kerr, *Fourth Amendment Remedies and Development of the Law: A Comment on* Camreta v. Greene *and* Davis v. United States, CATO S. CT. REV. 237 (2011) (arguing that the Fourth Amendment requires more robust remedies to foster cases and controversies and create incentives to litigate claims).

Note also that cases proceeding in the lower federal courts must have already asserted federal subject matter jurisdiction in order to be in the federal court system. Lower federal courts exist under the Supreme Court's review power, and the existence of this power may affect rulings because judges do not relish being overruled. Yet the infrequency of the Supreme Court's grant of certiorari petitions results in countless federal cases' ending with the ruling of a federal appellate court. Although the Court grants certiorari to resolve circuit court splits, it does not always. Thus, some splits remain with inconsistent interpretations of federal law. Does the Supreme Court abdicate its responsibility when it declines to correct circuit splits? Should Congress consider the creation of a national court of appeals to resolve such cases? Is it fair to conclude that state courts seek insulation from Supreme Court review, while lower federal courts prefer Supreme Court review and hope for vindication?

An interesting distinction arises with respect to the explicit statutory allowance for the Court to review a federal court case prior to a final judgment. Pursuant to § 1254, the Supreme Court may grant a writ of certiorari any time after a case has been docketed in the federal appellate courts.[15] Thus, the Supreme Court, in its discretion, can decide that the case warrants skipping review in the federal appellate court. Although rare, this option enables the Court to expedite matters of supreme federal importance where a timely decision is critical.

3. *Inferior Federal Courts and the Rooker-Feldman Doctrine*

May a state court litigant ever secure review in the inferior federal courts? It depends.

The answer is yes for criminal defendants who successfully seek a writ of habeas corpus to challenge confinement in violation of federal laws, treaties, or the Constitution.[16] Technically, if a federal court grants a habeas corpus petition challenging a state conviction,[17] the case arrives in federal court as a separately filed civil suit constituting collateral review of the criminal conviction rather than a direct review of the state court ruling.[18]

The answer is no for civil litigants who lose in state courts and seek appeal in federal district courts. This bar stems principally from two Supreme Court cases, which combine to create the "*Rooker-Feldman*" doctrine. The plaintiffs in *Rooker v. Fidelity Trust Co.*, 263 U.S. 413 (1923), sought a federal court declaration that a state court judgment was "null and void." The *Rooker* Court concluded that federal courts lack jurisdiction to reverse or modify a state court decision. The Supreme Court reaffirmed the lower federal court's lack of judicial review authority over state court judgments in *District of Columbia Court of Appeals v. Feldman*, 460 U.S. 462 (1983).

The Court more recently described the prohibition as barring a losing party from effectively seeking appellate review of a state court judgment in a federal

15. The federal statute further authorizes federal appellate courts to certify certain vexing, discrete questions to the Supreme Court. 28 U.S.C. § 1254(2). Accordingly, the federal appellate tribunal may certify "any question of law in any civil or criminal case as to which instructions are desired, and upon such certification the Supreme Court may give binding instructions or require the entire record to be sent up for decision of the entire matter in controversy." The federal appellate courts rarely invoke this certification mechanism, and the Supreme Court deems such jurisdiction to be discretionary. *See NLRB v. White Swan Co.*, 313 U.S. 23 (1941).

16. See Chapter 13 (exploring habeas corpus relief).

17. A federal prisoner may also seek habeas relief in federal courts pursuant to 28 U.S.C. § 2255.

18. A prisoner may seek review of the original state conviction through the state system. After exhausting all available state appeals, the prisoner may seek review of the final judgment in the United States Supreme Court.

district court on the ground that the state ruling itself violated the loser's federal rights.[19] The Supreme Court has not barred a case pursuant to *Rooker-Feldman* since 1983 (the year of *Feldman*). The inferior federal courts, however, regularly dismiss cases for lacking jurisdiction on the basis of *Rooker-Feldman.*

The *Rooker-Feldman* doctrine intersects with three areas of federal court jurisprudence: (i) civil rights suits under § 1983 (Chapter 9), (ii) *Younger* abstention (Chapter 10), and (iii) res judicata. Section 1983 provides a mechanism for federal court review of state and local violations of federal law, but it is not a grant of jurisdiction; federal jurisdiction exists pursuant to federal question jurisdiction, 28 U.S.C. § 1331.[20] According to the *Rooker-Feldman* doctrine, however, federal courts do not possess jurisdiction under § 1983 to review state court decisions. Thus, federal court review of state court decisions occurs in the United States Supreme Court. *Younger* abstention further limits lower federal courts by dictating that federal courts not interfere with pending state court proceedings. Res judicata principles require that federal courts give preclusive effect to state court decisions. As a practical matter, the conjunction of *Younger* and res judicata restrictions on federal courts calls into question the need for the *Rooker-Feldman* doctrine as a further limitation.

Consider whether the *Rooker-Feldman* doctrine serves valid, additional purposes for defining the proper scope of federal court jurisdiction and balancing federalism principles as you review the cases and related problems.

ROOKER v. FIDELITY TRUST CO.

263 U.S. 413 (1923)

JUSTICE VAN DEVANTER delivered the opinion of the Court.

This is a bill in equity to have a judgment of a circuit court in Indiana, which was affirmed by the Supreme Court of the state, declared null and void, and to obtain other relief dependent on that outcome. An effort to have the judgment reviewed by this court on writ of error had failed because the record did not disclose the presence of any question constituting a basis for such a review. The parties to the bill are the same as in the litigation in the state court, but with an addition of two defendants whose presence does not need special notice. All are citizens of the same state. The grounds advanced for resorting to the District Court are that the judgment was rendered and affirmed in contravention of the contract clause of the Constitution of the United States and the due process of law and equal protection clauses of the Fourteenth Amendment, in that it gave effect to a state statute alleged to be in conflict with those clauses and did not give effect to a prior decision in the same cause by the Supreme Court of the State which is alleged to have become the "law of the case." The District Court was of opinion that the suit was not within its jurisdiction as defined by Congress, and on that ground dismissed the bill. The plaintiffs have appealed directly to this court under section 238 of the Judicial Code.

* * * *

19. *Johnson v. DeGrandy*, 512 U.S. 997, 1005-06 (1994).
20. It also exists via 28 U.S.C. § 1343(3), which provides jurisdiction for actions claiming violations of federal laws regarding equal rights of citizens.

It affirmatively appears from the bill that the judgment was rendered in a cause wherein the circuit court had jurisdiction of both the subject-matter and the parties, that a full hearing was had therein, that the judgment was responsive to the issues, and that it was affirmed by the Supreme Court of the state on an appeal by the plaintiffs. If the constitutional questions stated in the bill actually arose in the cause, it was the province and duty of the state courts to decide them; and their decision, whether right or wrong, was an exercise of jurisdiction. If the decision was wrong, that did not make the judgment void, but merely left it open to reversal or modification in an appropriate and timely appellate proceeding. Unless and until so reversed or modified, it would be an effective and conclusive adjudication. Under the legislation of Congress, no court of the United States other than this court could entertain a proceeding to reverse or modify the judgment for errors of that character. To do so would be an exercise of appellate jurisdiction. The jurisdiction possessed by the District Courts is strictly original. Besides, the period within which a proceeding might be begun for the correction of errors such as are charged in the bill had expired before it was filed, and . . . after that period elapses an aggrieved litigant cannot be permitted to do indirectly what he no longer can do directly.

Some parts of the bill speak of the judgment as given without jurisdiction and absolutely void; but this is merely mistaken characterization. A reading of the entire bill shows indubitably that there was full jurisdiction in the state courts and that the bill at best is merely an attempt to get rid of the judgment for alleged errors of law committed in the exercise of that jurisdiction.

In what has been said we have proceeded on the assumption that the constitutional questions alleged to have arisen in the state courts respecting the validity of a state statute and the effect to be given to a prior decision in the same cause by the Supreme Court of the state were questions of substance, but we do not hold that they were such — the assumption being indulged merely for the purpose of testing the nature of the bill and the power of the District Court to entertain it.

* * * *

Decree affirmed.

PROBLEM 12-2

We Got Rooked.

Plaintiffs in a toxic tort case obtained a major punitive damages award from an Oklahoma jury. The trial judge denied remittitur and upheld the punitive award as (i) not excessive and (ii) consistent with the Fourteenth Amendment due process. The intermediate appellate court affirmed the award. Defendants appealed to the Oklahoma Supreme Court. Plaintiffs concerned about perceived pro-business composition of the court filed several motions to recuse individual justices. The Oklahoma Supreme Court, following its own procedures, denied plaintiffs' motions and subsequently ruled in favor of the defendants on the issue of punitive damages as excessive and in violation of the U.S. Constitution.

Plaintiffs then filed suit in federal district court, challenging the denial of their recusal motions. Plaintiffs contended that denial of the recusal motions constituted a federal due process violation by precluding them from having an impartial tribunal.

Does the federal court have jurisdiction over plaintiffs' challenge? What, if any, other court could review the Oklahoma Supreme Court's decision on either the recusal motions or the reversal of the punitive damages award?

Now consider the *Feldman* case and test your analysis.

DISTRICT OF COLUMBIA COURT OF APPEALS v. FELDMAN

460 U.S. 462 (1983)

JUSTICE BRENNAN delivered the opinion of the Court.

We must decide in these cases what authority the United States District Court for the District of Columbia and the United States Court of Appeals for the District of Columbia Circuit have to review decisions of the District of Columbia Court of Appeals in bar admission matters. The United States Court of Appeals for the District of Columbia Circuit, reversing the United States District Court, held that the District Court had jurisdiction to review the District of Columbia Court of Appeals' denials of the respondents' requests for waivers of a bar admission rule that requires applicants to have graduated from an approved law school. We vacate the decision of the United States Court of Appeals for the District of Columbia Circuit, and remand the case for proceedings consistent with this opinion.

I

We have discussed in detail in earlier opinions the changes in the structure of the District of Columbia court system effected by the District of Columbia Court Reform and Criminal Procedure Act of 1970. For purposes of this case, three provisions of that legislation are crucial. One provision made "final judgments and decrees of the District of Columbia Court of Appeals . . . reviewable by the Supreme Court of the United States in accordance with section 1257 of title 28, United States Code." Another provision amended 28 U.S.C. § 1257 to specify that the term "highest court of a state" as used in § 1257 includes the District of Columbia Court of Appeals. These provisions make the judgments of the District of Columbia Court of Appeals, like the judgments of state courts, directly reviewable in this Court. Cases no longer have to proceed from the local courts to the United States Court of Appeals and then to this Court under 28 U.S.C. § 1254. The third provision authorized the District of Columbia Court of Appeals to "make such rules as it deems proper respecting the examination, qualification, and admission of persons to membership in its bar, and their censure, suspension, and expulsion." This provision divested the United States District Court of its former authority to supervise admission to the District of Columbia bar.

Pursuant to its new rulemaking authority, the District of Columbia Court of Appeals adopted, as part of its general rules, Rule 46 I (1973), which governs admission to the bar. Rule 46 I(b)(3) states:

> (3) Proof of Legal Education. An applicant who has graduated from a law school that at the time of graduation was approved by the American Bar Association or

> who shall be eligible to be graduated from an approved law school within 60 days of the date of the examination will be permitted to take the bar examination. Under no circumstances shall an applicant be admitted to the bar without having first submitted to the Secretary to the Committee [on Admissions] a certificate verifying that he has graduated from an approved law school.[21]

Neither of the respondents graduated from an approved law school. Their efforts to avoid the operation of Rule 46 I(b)(3) form the foundation of this case.

A

Respondent Feldman did not attend law school. Instead, he pursued an alternative path to a legal career provided by the State of Virginia involving a highly structured program of study in the office of a practicing attorney. In addition to his work and study at a law firm in Charlottesville, Virginia, Feldman formally audited classes at the University of Virginia School of Law. For the final six months of his alternative course of study, Feldman served as a law clerk to a United States District Judge.

Having passed the Virginia bar examination, Feldman was admitted to that state's bar in April, 1976. In March of that year he had begun working as a staff attorney for the Baltimore, Maryland Legal Aid Bureau. He continued in that job until January, 1977. Like the District of Columbia, Maryland has a rule limiting access to the bar examination to graduates of ABA-approved law schools, but the Maryland Board of Law Examiners waived the rule for Feldman. Feldman passed the Maryland examination and later was admitted to that state's bar.

In November, 1976 Feldman applied to the Committee on Admissions of the District of Columbia Bar for admission to the District bar under a rule which, prior to its recent amendment, allowed a member of a bar in another jurisdiction to seek membership in the District bar without examination. In January, 1977 the Committee denied Feldman's application on the ground that he had not graduated from an approved law school. Initially, the Committee stated that waivers of Rule 46 I(b)(3), or exceptions to it, were not authorized. Following further contact with the Committee, however, Feldman was granted an informal hearing. After the hearing, the Committee reaffirmed its denial of Feldman's application and stated that only the District of Columbia Court of Appeals could waive the requirement of graduation from an approved law school.

In June, 1977 Feldman submitted to the District of Columbia Court of Appeals a petition for admission to the bar without examination. Alternatively, Feldman requested that he be allowed to sit for the bar examination. In his petition, Feldman described his legal training, work experience, and other qualifications. He suggested that his professional training and education were "equal to that received by those who have attended an A.B.A. approved law school." In view of his training, experience, and success in passing the bar examinations in other jurisdictions, Feldman stated that "the objectives of the District of Columbia's

21. [Footnote 1 in Court's opinion.] Under Rule 46 I(b)(4), a graduate of an unaccredited law school "may be permitted admission to an examination only after receiving credit for 24 semester hours of study in a law school that at the time of study was approved by the American Bar Association and with Committee approval."

procedures and requirements for admission to the Bar will not be frustrated by granting this petition."

* * * *

On March 30, 1978, the District of Columbia Court of Appeals issued a per curiam order denying Feldman's petition. The order stated simply that "[o]n consideration of the petition of Marc Feldman to waive the provisions of Rule 46 of the General Rules of this Court, it is ORDERED that applicant's petition is denied."

In May, 1978, Feldman filed a complaint in the United States District Court for the District of Columbia challenging the District of Columbia Court of Appeals' refusal to waive Rule 46 I(b)(3) on his behalf. The complaint stated that the "defendants' refusal to consider plaintiff's individual qualifications to practice law is unlawful in view of his demonstrated fitness and competence, as well as the prior admission to the D.C. bar of several other individuals who did not attend an accredited law school." Feldman sought "a declaration that defendants' actions have violated the Fifth Amendment to the Constitution and the Sherman Act, and . . . an injunction requiring defendants either to grant plaintiff immediate admission to the District of Columbia bar or to permit him to sit for the bar examination as soon as possible."

* * * *

The District Court granted the defendants' motion to dismiss on the ground that it lacked subject matter jurisdiction over the action. The court found that the District of Columbia Court of Appeals' order denying Feldman's petition was a judicial act "which fully encompassed the constitutional and statutory issues raised." The court stated that if it were "to assume jurisdiction over the subject matter of this lawsuit, it would find itself in the unsupportable position of reviewing an order of a jurisdiction's highest court."

* * * *

C

Both [plaintiffs] appealed the dismissals of their complaints to the United States Court of Appeals for the District of Columbia Circuit. The District of Columbia Circuit affirmed the dismissals of [plaintiffs'] antitrust claims on the ground that they were insubstantial.[22] The court, however, concluded that the waiver proceedings in the District of Columbia Court of Appeals "were not judicial in the federal sense, and thus did not foreclose litigation of the constitutional contentions in the District Court." The court therefore reversed the dismissals of the constitutional claims and remanded them for consideration on the merits.

Although the District of Columbia Circuit acknowledged that "review of a final judgment of the highest judicial tribunal of a state is vested solely in the Supreme Court of the United States," and that the United States District Court therefore is without authority to review determinations by the District of Columbia Court of Appeals in judicial proceedings, the court found that the District Court has jurisdiction over these cases because the proceedings in the District of Columbia Court of Appeals "were not judicial. . . ." The court based this conclusion on a finding

22. [Footnote 11 in Court's opinion.] We denied respondents' cross-petitions for certiorari from the disposition of the antitrust claims. Those claims, therefore, are not before us.

that neither [plaintiff] asserted in [his] waiver petition[] "any sort of right to be admitted to the District of Columbia bar, or even to take the examination therefor." [Plaintiffs] simply sought an exemption from the rule. . . .

* * * *

II

The District of Columbia Circuit properly acknowledged that the United States District Court is without authority to review final determinations of the District of Columbia Court of Appeals in judicial proceedings. Review of such determinations can be obtained only in this Court. A crucial question in this case, therefore, is whether the proceedings before the District of Columbia Court of Appeals were judicial in nature.[23]

A

This Court has considered the distinction between judicial and administrative or ministerial proceedings on several occasions. In Prentis v. Atlantic Coast Line, 211 U.S. 210 (1908), a railroad challenged in federal court the constitutionality of rail passenger rates set by the state corporation commission. The question presented by the case was whether the federal court was free to enjoin implementation of the rate order. In considering this question, we assumed that the state corporation commission was, at least for some purposes, a court. We held, however, that the federal court could enjoin implementation of the rate order because the commission had acted in a legislative as opposed to a judicial capacity in setting the rates. In reaching this conclusion, we stated:

> A judicial inquiry investigates, declares and enforces liabilities as they stand on present or past facts and under laws supposed already to exist. That is its purpose and end. Legislation on the other hand looks to the future and changes existing conditions by making a new rule to be applied thereafter to all or some part of those subject to its power. The establishment of a rate is the making of a rule for the future, and therefore is an act legislative not judicial in kind. . . .

We went on to suggest that the nature of a proceeding "depends not upon the character of the body but upon the character of the proceedings."

In In re Summers, 325 U.S. 561 (1945), we considered the petitioner's challenge to the constitutionality of a state Supreme Court's refusal to admit him to the practice of law. At the outset, we noted that the record was not in the "customary form" because the state court had not treated the proceeding as "judicial." In fact, the state court contested our certiorari jurisdiction on the ground that the state court proceedings had not been judicial in nature and that no case or controversy therefore existed in this Court under Article III of the Federal Constitution. In considering this contention, we conceded that the state court proceeding might not have been judicial under state law and that the denial of the petitioner's application for admission to the bar was treated "as a ministerial act which is performed by virtue of the judicial power, such as the

23. [Footnote 13 in Court's opinion.] As the District of Columbia Circuit recognized, it is a question of federal law whether "a particular proceeding before another tribunal was truly judicial" for purposes of ascertaining the jurisdiction of a federal court.

appointment of a clerk or bailiff or the specification of the requirements of eligibility or the course of study for applicants for admission to the bar, rather than a judicial proceeding." We stated, however, that in determining the nature of the proceedings "we must for ourselves appraise the circumstances of the refusal."

In conducting this appraisal, we first stated:

> A case arises, within the meaning of the Constitution, when any question respecting the Constitution, treaties or laws of the United States has assumed "such a form that the judicial power is capable of acting on it." . . . A declaration on rights as they stand must be sought, not on rights which may arise in the future, and there must be an actual controversy over an issue, not a desire for an abstract declaration of the law. The form of the proceeding is not significant. It is the nature and effect which is controlling.

Applying this standard, we noted that the state court had concluded that the report of the Committee on Character and Fitness, which refused to issue a favorable certificate, should be sustained. The state court, therefore, considered the petitioner's petition "on its merits." Although "no entry was placed by the Clerk in the file, on a docket, or in a judgment roll," we found that the state court had taken "cognizance of the petition and passed an order which [was] validated by the signature of the presiding officer." We stated:

> Where relief is thus sought in a state court against the action of a committee, appointed to advise the court, and the court takes cognizance of the complaint without requiring the appearance of the committee or its members, we think the consideration of the petition by the Supreme Court, the body which has authority itself by its own act to give the relief sought, makes the proceeding adversary in the sense of a true case or controversy. A claim of a present right to admission to the bar of a state and a denial of that right is a controversy. When the claim is made in a state court and a denial of the right is made by judicial order, it is a case which may be reviewed under Article III of the Constitution when federal questions are raised and proper steps taken to that end, in this Court.

B

These precedents clearly establish that the proceedings in the District of Columbia Court of Appeals surrounding [plaintiffs'] petitions for waiver were judicial in nature. The proceedings were not legislative, ministerial, or administrative. The District of Columbia Court of Appeals did not "loo[k] to the future and chang[e] existing conditions by making a new rule to be applied thereafter to all or some part of those subject to its power." Nor did it engage in rulemaking or specify "the requirements of eligibility or the course of study for applicants for admission to the bar. . . ." Nor did the District of Columbia Court of Appeals simply engage in ministerial action. Instead, the proceedings before the District of Columbia Court of Appeals involved a "judicial inquiry" in which the court was called upon to investigate, declare, and enforce "liabilities as they [stood] on present or past facts and under laws supposed already to exist."

* * * *

In essence, Feldman argued on policy grounds that the rule should not be applied to him because he had fulfilled the spirit, if not the letter, of Rule 46

I(b)(3). Alternatively, he argued in his letter that the rule was invalid. In short, he was seeking "a declaration on rights as they [stood] . . . not on rights which [might] arise in the future. . . ." This required the District of Columbia Court of Appeals to determine in light of existing law and in light of Feldman's qualifications and arguments whether Feldman's petition should be granted. The court also had before it legal arguments against the validity of the rule. When it issued a per curiam order denying Feldman's petition, it determined as a legal matter that Feldman was not entitled to be admitted to the bar without examination or to sit for the bar examination. The court had adjudicated Feldman's "claim of a present right to admission to the bar," and rejected it. This is the essence of a judicial proceeding.

* * * *

III

A

A determination that the proceedings . . . were judicial does not finally dispose of this case. As we have noted, a United States District Court has no authority to review final judgments of a state court in judicial proceedings. Review of such judgments may be had only in this Court. Therefore, to the extent that Hickey and Feldman sought review in District Court of the District of Columbia Court of Appeals' denial of their petitions for waiver the District Court lacked subject matter jurisdiction over their complaints. Hickey and Feldman should have sought review of the District of Columbia Court of Appeals' judgments in this Court. To the extent that Hickey and Feldman mounted a general challenge to the constitutionality of Rule 46 I(b)(3), however, the District Court did have subject matter jurisdiction over their complaints.

The difference between seeking review in a federal district court of a state court's final judgment in a bar admission matter and challenging the validity of a state bar admission rule has been recognized in the lower courts and, at least implicitly, in the opinions of this Court.

* * * *

B

Applying this standard to the respondents' complaints, it is clear that their allegations that the District of Columbia Court of Appeals acted arbitrarily and capriciously in denying their petitions for waiver and that the court acted unreasonably and discriminatorily in denying their petitions in view of its former policy of granting waivers to graduates of unaccredited law schools, required the District Court to review a final judicial decision of the highest court of a jurisdiction in a particular case. These allegations are inextricably intertwined with the District of Columbia Court of Appeals' decisions, in judicial proceedings, to deny the respondents' petitions. The District Court, therefore, does not have jurisdiction over these elements of the respondents' complaints.

The remaining allegations in the complaints, however, involve a general attack on the constitutionality of Rule 46 I(b)(3). The respondents' claims that the rule is unconstitutional because it creates an irrebuttable presumption that only graduates of accredited law schools are fit to practice law, discriminates against those who have obtained equivalent legal training by other means, and impermissibly delegates the District of Columbia Court of Appeals' power to regulate the bar to the American Bar Association, do not require review of a judicial decision in a particular case. The District Court, therefore, has subject matter jurisdiction over these elements of the respondents' complaints.

In deciding that the District Court has jurisdiction over those elements of the respondents' complaints that involve a general challenge to the constitutionality of Rule 46 I(b)(3), we expressly do not reach the question of whether the doctrine of res judicata forecloses litigation on these elements of the complaints. We leave that question to the District Court on remand.

IV

The judgment of the District of Columbia Circuit is vacated and the cases are remanded to the District Court for further proceedings consistent with this opinion.

So ordered.

JUSTICE STEVENS, dissenting.

There are many crafts in which the State performs a licensing function. That function is important, not only to those seeking access to a gainful occupation but to the members of the public served by the profession as well. State-created rules governing the grant or denial of licenses must comply with constitutional standards and must be administered in accordance with due process of law. Given these acknowledged constitutional limitations on action by the State, it should be beyond question that a federal district court has subject matter jurisdiction over an individual's lawsuit raising federal constitutional challenges either to licensing rules themselves or to their application in his own case. Curiously, however, the Court today ignores basic jurisdictional principles when it decides a jurisdictional issue affecting the licensing of members of the legal profession.

The Court holds that respondents may make a general constitutional attack on the rules governing the admission of lawyers to practice in the District of Columbia. I agree. But the Court also concludes that a United States District Court has no subject matter jurisdiction over a claim that those rules have been administered in an unconstitutional manner. According to the Court's opinion, respondents' contentions that bar admission rules have been unconstitutionally applied to them by the District of Columbia Court of Appeals somehow constitute impermissible attempts to secure appellate review of final judgments of that court. There are two basic flaws in the Court's analysis.

First, neither [plaintiff] requested the District of Columbia Court of Appeals to pass on the validity of Rule 46 I(b)(3) or to grant them admission to the bar or the bar examination as a matter of right. Rather, each of them asked the court to waive the requirements of the rule for a variety of reasons. I would not characterize the court's refusal to grant a requested waiver as an adjudication. Unlike the decision of the Supreme Court of Illinois reviewed in In re Summers, 325 U.S. 561 (1945), the order of the District of Columbia Court of Appeals did not determine a claim of right, nor did it even apply standard equitable principles to a prayer for relief. Rather, that court performed no more and no less than the administrative function of a licensing board. As the United States Court of Appeals wrote, Hickey asked the court "to make a policy decision equating his personal qualities with accredited legal education, not an adjudication requiring resort to legal principles," and Feldman "invoked the administrative discretion of that body, simply asking that it temper its rule in his favor, for personal and not legal reasons." Rejection of those petitions was not "adjudicative" and was therefore not susceptible to certiorari review in this Court.

Second, even if the refusal to grant a waiver were an adjudication, the federal statute that confers jurisdiction upon the United States District Court to entertain a constitutional challenge to the rules themselves also authorizes that court to entertain a collateral attack upon the unconstitutional application of those rules. The Court's opinion fails to distinguish between two concepts: appellate review and collateral attack. If a challenge to a state court's decision is brought in United States District Court and alleges violations of the United States Constitution, then by definition it does not seek appellate review. It is plainly within the federal-question jurisdiction of the federal court. There may be other reasons for denying relief to the plaintiff—such as failure to state a cause of action, claim or issue preclusion, or failure to prove a violation of constitutional rights.[24] But it does violence to jurisdictional concepts for this Court to hold, as it does, that the federal district court has no jurisdiction to conduct independent review of a specific claim that a licensing body's action did not comply with federal constitutional standards. The fact that the licensing function in the legal profession is controlled by the judiciary is not a sufficient reason to immunize allegedly unconstitutional conduct from review in the federal courts.

I therefore respectfully dissent.

DISCUSSION AND QUESTIONS

The combination of *Rooker* and *Feldman* block a state court losing party from effectively attempting to garner appellate review of the state court decision in a federal district court based on the losing party's assertion that the state judgment itself violates the losing party's federal rights. As discussed, in the years following *Feldman*, the Supreme Court has not dismissed a case based upon the *Rooker-Feldman* doctrine, but many lower federal courts have. Thorny issues arise regarding the timing of the collateral proceedings. Must the state court action be complete? Also keep in mind that *Younger* abstention (see Chapter 10) generally prohibits a party from using a federal court action to enjoin a pending state court proceeding.

The Court continues to narrow the scope of the *Rooker-Feldman* doctrine in response to lower courts' proclivity for dismissing cases on such grounds. The doctrine's range is unclear because the underlying rationale remains: cautioning against permitting a party who has already lost in state court to then seek review and reversal from a federal district court. How might the *Rooker-Feldman* doctrine apply to a party who lost a state administrative ruling as in *Jacobs* (Chapter 10), where plaintiff brought suit in federal district court to declare that a

24. [Footnote 2 in Justice Stevens's dissenting opinion.] Constitutional challenges to specific licensing actions may, of course, fail on the merits. But in my view, if plaintiffs challenging a bar admissions decision by a state court prove facts comparable to the allegations made by the appellants *in Yick Wo v. Hopkins*, 118 U.S. 356 (1886), they would clearly be entitled to relief in the United States District Court. If they were seeking admission to any other craft regulated by the state, they would unquestionably have such a right.

federal statute preempted a prior decision of the Iowa Utilities Board regarding intrastate access fees?

Consider the following problem and test your understanding of how the Supreme Court might interpret the modern application of the *Rooker-Feldman* doctrine.

PROBLEM 12-3

Strategic Court Jockeying

Middle East Corporation ("MEC") filed a state court suit seeking a declaratory judgment against Future Oil Company, an American-based company. In response, Future Oil Company filed suit in federal district court alleging improper overcharging via royalties. MEC counterclaimed in the federal district court suit, but also moved to dismiss the federal case pursuant to the Foreign Sovereign Immunities Act. The federal district court denied the motion, and MEC sought interlocutory review in the relevant federal court of appeals.

Meanwhile, during the pendency of the federal court appeal, the state court ruled in favor of Future Oil Company. In light of this state court decision, the federal court of appeals dismissed the case and relied upon the *Rooker-Feldman* doctrine. MEC appealed the federal appellate court decision to the Supreme Court, and the Court granted certiorari.

How should the Supreme Court rule regarding lower federal court jurisdiction? [Note: Consider the relevance, if any, of the *Younger* doctrine and res judicata, in addition to the *Rooker-Feldman* doctrine.]

D. SOME ADDITIONAL PROBLEMS

The problems that follow provide additional practice concerning the topics covered in Chapter 12.

PROBLEM 12-4

Water Water Everywhere, but Not a Court to Ink

A proposed bill in the U.S. Congress advanced by the California delegation seeks to narrow Supreme Court jurisdiction. California is unsatisfied with recent Supreme Court jurisprudence on water rights. Therefore, California plans to use its sizeable congressional delegation to pass a law restricting the Supreme Court from hearing cases involving water disputes between states.

Assuming that the law passes, how would the Supreme Court rule regarding its jurisdiction to hear a subsequent case filed in the Supreme Court by Nevada against California over a water rights dispute?

PROBLEM 12-5

Legislative Ambiguity

Voters in Florida approve a constitutional amendment that protects against unreasonable searches and seizures. The amendment alters the Constitution of Florida to read:

> This right shall be construed in conformity with the Fourth Amendment to the United States Constitution, as interpreted by the United Supreme Court. Articles or information obtained in violation of this right shall not be admissible in evidence if such articles or information would be inadmissible under the decisions of the United States Supreme Court construing the Fourth Amendment to the United States Constitution.

In Florida state court, Rita Cole is convicted of possession of methamphetamine and sentenced to jail time. Rita appeals via the state channels. Ultimately, the Florida Supreme Court reverses Rita's conviction on the ground that the state police search was unreasonable and the evidence should be suppressed in accordance with the Florida Constitution. The State of Florida appeals the reversal to the United States Supreme Court.

Should the United States Supreme Court find jurisdiction to review the Florida Supreme Court's decision?

PROBLEM 12-6

State Insulation Blanket

Nevada has a state statute providing that for certain misdemeanors, including minor traffic violations such as driving on a suspended license and failure to wear a safety belt, the police must issue a citation rather than arrest the individual. Nevada police officers pull over Virgil Nugent for failing to wear his safety belt in violation of state law. They arrest Virgil and conduct a search that uncovers significant amounts of narcotics and corresponding paraphernalia.

Virgil is convicted in Nevada state court for possession with the intent to distribute narcotics and sentenced to Nevada state prison. Virgil appeals. The intermediate appellate court reverses the conviction and relies upon Nevada's statute to conclude that the search was unreasonable. Given slim state precedent regarding the exclusionary effect, the court reasons that a violation of the state statute is a violation of the U.S. Constitution's Fourth Amendment. The court therefore suppresses the evidence supporting the conviction. Nevada appeals to the state supreme court.

The Nevada Supreme Court has read the briefs and heard oral argument. Nevada maintains that the court below misconstrued Fourth Amendment law because the United States Supreme Court has held that there is no Fourth Amendment violation in such circumstances. As a law clerk to a Nevada Supreme Court justice who believes the conviction should not stand under Nevada law, how would you advise the justice to draft the opinion?

CHAPTER 13

Habeas Corpus

A. A REFERENCE PROBLEM

In this chapter we consider the power of the federal courts to grant writs of habeas corpus to individuals claiming that their detention is in violation of federal law. The Reference Problem below introduces many of the concepts we explore.

* * * *

This Reference Problem is actually in two parts. Common to both of them is the United States Supreme Court's decision in *Crawford v. Washington,* 541 U.S.

36 (2004). In *Crawford*, the Court held that the Sixth Amendment's Confrontation Clause[1] allows a testimonial statement to be introduced at trial against an accused only if the accuser has been subject to cross-examination. In so doing, the Court overruled its decision in *Ohio v. Roberts*, 448 U.S. 56 (1980), in which it held that the Confrontation Clause was satisfied so long as the statement at issue had sufficient indicia of reliability.

Scenario #1. In the first scenario, assume you are a federal district judge in the Eastern District of Virginia. John Woodward was convicted in a Virginia state trial court of the battery of his wife, Jane. On the night of November 21, 2001, Jane called the police to report that her husband had been drinking and had hit her. When the police arrived at the Woodward house, one of the officers took Jane aside and asked her what had happened. Another officer spoke with John in a separate room. Jane told the officer with whom she was speaking that John had been drinking all day and then hit her several times for no reason. Based on Jane's statements, the police took John into custody.

Jane refused to testify against her husband at his battery trial, which took place in 2002. The prosecutor put the police officer on the stand and, through him, elicited a description of what Jane had said the night she called the police. John's attorney did not object even though there is a Virginia state court rule that requires such an objection to preserve a claim of error. John was convicted of battery and sentenced to five years in prison.

John appealed his conviction through the Virginia state courts. His claim was that the introduction of his wife's statements through the police officer violated his rights under the Confrontation Clause. The state argued in response that John had forfeited any such claim because his counsel did not object and, in the alternative, that the introduction of the testimony was constitutional because it had sufficient indicia of reliability. You may assume the state is correct that the statement would have been admissible under *Ohio v. Roberts*. The Virginia Supreme Court upheld the conviction, stating that "on the record as a whole we cannot say that there has been an error that can be remedied under the facts presented." The Virginia Supreme Court issued its decision in 2003. John did not seek review in the United States Supreme Court.

After the United States Supreme Court decided *Crawford*, John filed a petition in federal court, seeking a writ of habeas corpus because he claims the introduction of the testimony at trial violated his Sixth Amendment rights. You should also assume that the introduction of the statement at issue violates the rule *Crawford* articulates.

As the judge, should you grant the writ John seeks? You almost certainly will not be able to answer this question at this point. For now, consider these questions:

- If there has been a constitutional violation, shouldn't the federal court be required to correct it? If not, what other values might indicate that the error should go uncorrected?
- Should it matter that at the time of trial Jane's statements were admissible under *Ohio v. Roberts*?

1. The Sixth Amendment provides in relevant part, "In all criminal prosecutions, the accused shall enjoy the right . . . to be confronted with the witnesses against him."

- Should the federal court be allowed to take additional evidence if it is unsure about what happened the night the police questioned Jane?
- What is the import, if any, of John's attorney's failure to object to the testimony at trial as required by Virginia state law? Does it matter that the Virginia Supreme Court's decision upholding the conviction is not clear as to whether that Court considered the Sixth Amendment issue or instead relied solely on the state rule?
- Does it matter that John did not seek a writ of habeas corpus in federal court until three years after the Virginia Supreme Court's decision?
- Does it matter that John did not seek direct review of the Virginia Supreme Court's decision in the United States Supreme Court?
- Finally, why should John be allowed to get a "second bite at the apple" at all? After all, the Virginia state courts have to apply the Constitution as much as do the federal courts.

Scenario #2. In the second scenario assume that you are a federal judge only a few miles from Virginia in the United States District Court for the District of Columbia. You have pending before you a petition for a writ of habeas corpus by Omar Ali. Mr. Ali is a non-citizen being detained at the United States Naval Base in Guantanamo Bay, Cuba. He has been designated as an "enemy combatant" and has been told he will be tried by a military commission. In his petition, he claims that he is being held in violation of the Constitution. He also alleges that the rules that govern the admissibility of evidence in his pending military commission trial allow the introduction of testimony that violates the Sixth Amendment as interpreted in *Crawford.*

How would you rule on the petition? Again, you will likely not have the substantive knowledge to answer this question. But consider the following:

- Does the court even have jurisdiction? Mr. Ali is not in Washington. Moreover, even if the federal court does have jurisdiction, is this the type of case in which judges should be involved at all?
- Does Mr. Ali have rights under the Sixth Amendment? He is a non-citizen being held outside the United States. Does it matter that the United States exercises total control over Guantanamo Bay even though Cuba technically remains sovereign over that area?
- Assuming that Mr. Ali has rights under the Sixth Amendment, how should the court handle claims by the United States government that revealing the identity of the accuser would compromise intelligence-gathering procedures?
- Should the court simply defer to the executive branch's determination of issues involved in the War on Terror? What constitutional principles should inform this decision?

* * * *

As these two scenarios should make clear, this chapter is in some respects two chapters in one. Scenario #1 raises issues concerning the role of the federal courts in policing state court proceedings. Scenario #2 raises issues of the appropriate role of the judiciary when the political branches of the federal government are involved. We deal with these issues separately below. However, you should also see that there is a certain commonality between the role of the federal courts in these scenarios. In both, the courts are called upon to secure individual rights guaranteed by the Constitution. Moreover, in both the courts need to take heed of important constitutional principles of federalism and/or separation of powers. This material is complex, but it is also a wonderful means to review much of what we have covered so far in this course.

B. CONTEXT AND BACKGROUND

The common-law writ of habeas corpus has a storied history both in the United States as well as in England from which it was inherited. The writ is essentially a procedural device most often used to test the legality of a prisoner's detention.[2] As we will introduce in this section and explore in the balance of the chapter, the writ of habeas corpus—also known as the Great Writ—serves several purposes in our constitutional form of government. Studying the writ also raises many of the themes we have explored in the text, including those related to separation of powers, federalism, and the appropriate role of the federal courts in the United States.

1. English Historical Origins and Uses of the Writ

The history of the Great Writ is complex and not entirely clear. We cannot do justice to its richness in the space provided.[3] Our goal is to provide a brief summary of the historical origins and uses of the writ. A basic understanding of these issues is critical to appreciate many of the contemporary debates surrounding habeas corpus.

The writ of habeas corpus developed in the courts of Medieval England. In its earliest incarnation, it was used principally as a means to enforce allocations of authority between and among the various power centers in the feudally organized country. So, for example, the writ was used to ensure that the courts maintained by local lords and barons did not exceed their authority at the expense of the monarch and his or her tribunals. Thus, at the start, the writ was not primarily focused on ensuring the individual liberty of subjects. To the extent it served this function, it did so as a means to maintain or to establish structural limits on the authority of what we would today consider to be different government institutions.

Eventually, the writ of habeas corpus began to be used more directly as a device to protect individual liberty. In the early 1600s, great common-law advocates such as Sir Edward Coke (often referred to as the "father of the common law") successfully argued that the writ should be used to enforce Magna Carta's

2. Historically, there were several types of writs of habeas corpus. The Great Writ, and the writ to which we refer most commonly today, was the writ of habeas corpus ad subjiciendum, which was used to test the legality of a person's detention.

3. For students interested in learning more about the historical origins of habeas corpus we recommend the following sources: William F. Duker, A Constitutional History of Habeas Corpus (1980); Daniel J. Meador, Habeas Corpus and Magna Carta (1966); Paul D. Halliday, Habeas Corpus: From England to Empire (2010); Robert Walker, The Constitutional and Legal Development of the Habeas Corpus as the Writ of Liberty (1960).

guarantee that no person should be imprisoned "except by lawful judgment of his peers or by the law of the land."[4] This provision is the historical grandparent of what would become the right to "due process of law" enshrined in the United States Constitution.

The English courts began to use the writ of habeas corpus for this more direct liberty-protecting purpose on their own — that is, without specific statutory authorization. However, in several important statutes enacted during the mid-1600s, Parliament codified the writ, including its use explicitly to protect individual liberty.[5] The writ was used principally in connection with executive detentions. In was not generally used as it is often today in the United States to address claimed errors in a judicial proceeding. To the extent it was used in connection with a judicially ordered detention, the issue was whether the court ordering the detention had jurisdiction over the petitioner.

2. *Early American Experience with Habeas Corpus*

Habeas corpus made its way across the Atlantic with the British as they colonized what would become the United States. It is generally accepted that the writ of habeas corpus was available through the common law in the British colonies. By the time of the Constitutional Convention in 1787, four states guaranteed the availability of the writ in their state constitutions. However, one should not take from this statistic that the writ was not accepted in the relatively newly independent states. Instead, many have argued that it was so well known that there was little perceived need to either codify it in statutes or include it in state constitutions.

In any event, the Framers of the Constitution understood the importance of the writ of habeas corpus to the protection of individual rights. As the Supreme Court described:

> This history [of the writ in England] was known to the Framers. It no doubt confirmed their view that pendular swings to and away from individual liberty were endemic to undivided, uncontrolled power. The Framers' inherent distrust of government power was the driving force behind the constitutional plan that allocated powers among three independent branches. This design serves not only to make government accountable, but also to secure individual liberty.[6]

As part of this constitutional plan designed with the goal of protecting individual liberty, the Framers included in the Constitution what is known as the Suspension Clause. U.S. CONST. art. I, § 9, cl. 2. It provides: "The Privilege of the Writ of Habeas Corpus shall not be suspended, unless when in Cases of Rebellion or Invasion the public Safety may require it." We will consider the meaning of the Suspension Clause in more detail later in this chapter.[7] For now, however, it is sufficient to note that a majority of the Supreme Court has

4. This provision is found in Chapter 39 of Magna Carta.
5. *See, e.g.*, The Petition of Rights (1627), the Star Chamber Act (1641), and the Habeas Corpus Act (1679).
6. *See Boumediene v. Bush*, 553 U.S. 723, 742 (2008).
7. See *infra* section C.1.

concluded that the Suspension Clause indicates that "the Framers deemed the writ to be an essential mechanism in the separation-of-powers scheme."[8]

Whatever the Suspension Clause means for the general availability of the writ, much of the early American experience came through congressional action. In the Judiciary Act of 1789, Congress provided that federal courts had the authority to grant writs of habeas corpus for persons held in *federal* custody in violation of federal law.[9] Federal courts did not have general authority to issues writs of habeas corpus with respect to persons held in *state* custody until after the Civil War. Largely motivated by a concern that Southern states would be hostile to the rights of the newly freed slaves, Congress in 1867 extended the federal courts' authority to consider the legality of detention claimed to be in violation of federal law to those held in state as well as federal custody.[10]

Thus, beginning in the period after the Civil War, federal courts generally had the authority to use the writ of habeas corpus to consider the detention of persons allegedly held in violation of federal law by either federal or state authorities. The practical impact of this expansion of the federal courts' authority was to create what one can view as two tracks on which habeas corpus law would develop, recognizing that there are issues common to both of them.[11]

On one track was the federal courts' authority to consider detention by *federal* authorities. For our purposes, this track principally concerns detention by federal executive officials.[12] As you might expect, when considering such executive detention—whether it be in the context of immigration or the War on Terror, to name just two examples—the issues with which we have dealt throughout this book concerning separation of powers are at the forefront.

The other track concerns the authority of the federal courts to issue writs of habeas corpus for persons held pursuant to the judgment of a state court. Here, a petitioner will have had a state court trial, the ability for state court appeals, the possibility of United States Supreme Court review on direct appeal for any claimed federal law error, and even the availability of state collateral attacks on the judgment. Thus, one sees looming on this track many of the issues with which we have dealt thus far concerning federalism and, in particular, the parity debate concerning the ability of state courts to enforce federal rights.[13]

8. *See Boumediene v. Bush*, 553 U.S. at 743.

9. *See* Judiciary Act of 1789, ch. 20, 1 Stat. 73, 81-82.

10. *See* Act of Feb. 5, 1867, ch. 28, 14 Stat. 385.

11. We explore in greater detail the development of the law concerning the writ of habeas corpus on both these tracks in section C below.

12. To be sure, federal detention can also be the result of judicial action. Federal courts had the authority to consider federal judicial detention using the writ of habeas corpus as well. Today, however, habeas corpus in this context has been replaced by a statutory substitute in which the federal court that sentenced the prisoner may consider a motion to vacate, set aside, or correct the prisoner's sentence. *See* 28 U.S.C. § 2255. We will not address motions under § 2255 in this chapter. This omission does not mean that these motions are not practically important. Rather, § 2255 does not raise the significant federalism concerns implicated by a federal court's use of habeas corpus with respect to state prisoners.

13. Of course, as we will see there are also separation-of-powers concerns at play in this area as well because much of the law dealing with a federal court's power to issue writs of habeas corpus for a person held pursuant to the judgment of a state court is the result of congressional action.

3. Chapter Goals and Plan of Coverage

As the brief history above indicates, the study of habeas corpus raises a host of issues. In section C below, we have divided the discussion into two parts corresponding to the two tracks we have described above. We first consider federal courts' use of the writ of habeas corpus for those persons held in non-judicial federal custody. In particular we focus on decisions of the Supreme Court in the "War on Terror," including its exposition of the meaning of the Suspension Clause. Our principal goals in this part are to provide an overview of this area of the law and to raise the serious separation-of-powers concerns that are implicated by the use of the writ in connection with executive detention. When you consider this material, focus on what the federal courts' proper role should be given both the American structure of government as well as the importance of the writ to the protection of individual liberty.

The second part of section C turns to the use of the writ of habeas corpus for state prisoners. We will canvass the development of the law in this area and then focus principally on the current statutory structure under which the writ's availability has been greatly reduced. When you consider this material, focus on the various federalism concerns that are implicated by federal court review of state court actions. In addition, consider whether the courts have been faithful to congressional directions concerning the use to which the writ should be put as well as whether these directions undermine the appropriate role of the federal courts in American constitutional government.

C. THE LAW AND PROBLEMS

This section is divided into two parts. Section C.1 deals with the federal courts' authority to issue writs of habeas corpus for persons held in federal executive custody allegedly in violation of federal law. Section C.2 considers federal courts' authority to issue writs of habeas corpus for persons allegedly held in violation of federal law pursuant to the judgment of state courts. There are issues that are common to these two scenarios. When such commonality exists, we will make note of it.

Before turning to executive detention and then state incarceration specifically, a few additional preliminary points are worth mentioning concerning the procedural nature of habeas corpus. First, habeas corpus proceedings are technically civil actions even though in most situations the underlying issues will raise matters of criminal law and procedure. There are many special rules governing habeas corpus proceedings that distinguish them from the run-of-the-mill civil case. For example, discovery is quite limited in a habeas corpus proceeding if, indeed, it is allowed at all. However, to the extent that there is no special habeas corpus rule on a given point, general principles of civil litigation will govern.

Second, one should understand at least basically what a habeas corpus case looks like in federal court. The person seeking the writ commences the action with a petition (sometimes called an application).[14] That document resembles

14. In this chapter we use the terms "petitioner" and "applicant" interchangeably. The same is true with respect to the terms "petition" and "application."

in many respects the complaint in an ordinary civil case. The petition will recite the relevant jurisdictional prerequisites about which we will learn later (e.g., that the petitioner is in custody pursuant to the judgment of a state court) and will spell out the alleged basis on which her continued detention is in violation of federal law. *See* 28 U.S.C. § 2242.

In some cases, it will be apparent from the face of the petition that the writ should not be granted. In such cases, the court will deny the petition without the need for a response from the respondent, who is the governmental official who has custody of the petitioner (often the prison warden in the case of a state prisoner). *See* 28 U.S.C. § 2243. If the petition states a valid claim on its face, the court will order the respondent to submit a substantive response, sometimes called a return. *See id.* The petitioner often is required to respond to the return by submitting a traverse, something akin to a reply in non-habeas contexts.

What happens after the return and traverse are submitted depends on the substance of the petitioner's allegations as well as the statutory procedures in place. We will consider these details (such as whether the federal court can hold an evidentiary hearing) below. But what happens if the court determines that the petitioner's federal claims have merit? The answer to this question depends. If the petitioner's claims go to the authority of the government official to hold the petitioner, a court may order her release. However, more common, particularly in the context of state prisoners, is a situation in which there has been some error in the underlying trial that rises to a level sufficient to grant the writ. In this case, a court will often order that the petitioner be released unless the government conducts a new trial within some specified period. Finally, there are errors that do not go to the fact of conviction itself but rather to a sentence that has been imposed. In this case, the writ will direct resentencing instead of release.

It is also important as we will see to keep in mind that habeas corpus is deemed a collateral proceeding as opposed to a direct review or appeal. We will discuss specific distinctions in this regard at several places below. For now, it is sufficient for you to know that when a federal court considers a petition for a writ of habeas corpus in the context of a person held pursuant to a state court's judgment, it is not sitting as a court in the direct chain of appellate review. The state prisoner will have already had a direct appeal (or have had the opportunity to have such a review) in the state courts with possible review in the Supreme Court of the United States.

Finally, as has been implicit in much of the discussion above, habeas corpus is largely a creature of statute. As we will see, the Constitution and its Suspension Clause play a role, but by and large statutes rule the day. There are some statutory issues that are applicable to both habeas review of federal executive detention and habeas review of state prisoners' claims. We discuss some of the more important commonalities in the next few paragraphs.

The generic starting point for all habeas corpus actions is 28 U.S.C. § 2241. Section 2241(a) provides the statutory authorization for federal courts to issue writs of habeas corpus to persons based on one of the grounds set forth in § 2241(c). Subsection (c) lists five situations in which the writ may be granted. All but subsection (c)(5) concern challenges to the legality of detention. Subsection (c)(5) deals with the issuance of a writ to ensure testimony. We will return at various points in this section of the chapter to a discussion of how a court is to determine whether the allegations of illegal detention are sufficient to grant the writ.

One of the basic restrictions on a federal court's authority to grant writs of habeas corpus is the language in § 2241(a) requiring that federal courts and judges act only "within their respective jurisdiction." In most cases, this situation is straightforward. A person will be held in State X and the person whom the petitioner claims is holding them in violation of law will also be in State X. In such a situation a federal court in State X (assuming for the moment that X has only one judicial district) will be acting within its jurisdiction. However, there are situations in which this statutory requirement can be more elusive. We will consider these matters below in connection with our discussion of executive detention.[15]

With some of the underbrush cleared, we now turn to a consideration of federal executive detention and then to state prisoners.

1. *Habeas Corpus and Federal Executive Detention*

In this section we consider the use of the writ of habeas corpus in connection with detention of persons by the federal executive. Before we engage this subject in depth, consider Problem 13-1 as a means to set the stage.

PROBLEM 13-1

The Constitutional Stakes

Jane Jones was a cattle rancher in a small town in Wyoming. In a political surprise, she was recently elected to the United States Senate in a year when running as a political outsider was a particular advantage. Senator Jones is a bright person, but she recognizes that there is much about her new job that she is unprepared to face. She has addressed this problem by hiring an accomplished staff, including you.

One issue that particularly troubles Senator Jones is the role of federal habeas corpus with respect to persons held by order of the President. Like many Americans she has followed the litigation concerning enemy combatants and others in the newspapers. And she is well aware that the fight against terrorism is likely to continue well into the future. She knows that she will eventually be called upon to take a position on the issue of the scope of presidential detention authority. She also knows that she will need to understand the details of habeas corpus at some point. For now, however, she is more interested in the bigger picture.

Senator Jones has asked you to brief her about the constitutional values that are at play in the debate about the proper role of the federal courts with respect to habeas corpus and executive detention. What would you tell the Senator? Why?

15. Section 2241(c) also requires that the person seeking the writ be "in custody." This requirement is usually not a significant hurdle. There are situations, however, in which a person may no longer be in physical custody but might still have her liberty impaired sufficiently to qualify under the statute to seek a writ of habeas corpus.

As Problem 13-1 demonstrates, and recent experience underscores, the use of habeas corpus in connection with persons held by the executive branch raises profound constitutional questions. We explore some of these questions in the balance of this section. Beware, however, that this area of the law remains in flux.

Federal court review through habeas corpus of executive detention can occur in a number of situations. These include claims by those held in the immigration context, those held in connection with their service in the United States military, and those held before conviction in a federal court (such as in the context of the denial of bail). Of late, however, this area has been addressed most extensively in connection with the use of detention in the "Global War on Terror." It is on that use of habeas corpus that we focus. Using principally the cases the Supreme Court has decided in this area in the aftermath of 9/11, we explore the meaning of the Constitution's Suspension Clause, the geographic reach of the writ, the method by which the Court construes statutes to avoid answering difficult constitutional questions, and the broader issues these decisions raise about the fundamental role of the federal courts in the American constitutional system of government.

One introductory point about which you may wonder as you consider this material is the absence of state courts from the discussion. As we have said time and again, state courts have an obligation equal to that of the federal judiciary to uphold the United States Constitution. If a person were truly being held in violation of the Constitution, one might think that a state court would have an obligation to act. However, the Supreme Court has held that a state court lacks the authority to issue a writ of habeas corpus with respect to a person held in federal custody.[16] Thus, the field here must be occupied by federal courts if at all.

There are many ways in which one could organize the material we present below. We have elected to proceed chronologically and weave substantive matters into the chronology as appropriate. The starting point, of course, is the events of September 11, 2001. The terrorist attacks on that Tuesday morning in New York, Virginia, and Pennsylvania set in motion developments in many areas of American life. The law of federal courts was no exception.

Just days after the 9/11 attack, Congress passed the Authorization for the Use of Military Force (AUMF). The AUMF authorized the President "to use all necessary and appropriate force against those nations, organizations, or persons he determines planned, authorized, committed, or aided the terrorist attacks that occurred on September 11, 2001, or harbored such organizations or persons, in order to prevent any future acts of international terrorism against the United States by such nations, organizations or persons."[17] Several months later, the President unilaterally established a system of military commissions to try persons the President determined to be "enemy combatants." These two developments play important roles in the cases we discuss below.

a. The 2004 Trilogy: *Rasul*, *Padilla*, and *Hamdi*

The Supreme Court first entered the field in the war on terror with a series of three decisions in 2004. These decisions both individually and collectively tell us

16. *See, e.g., Tarble's Case*, 80 U.S. 397 (1872).
17. Pub. L. No. 107-40, 115 Stat. 224 (codified as a note following 50 U.S.C. § 1541).

much about the use of habeas corpus with respect to executive detention generally as well as provide the foundation for much that would come later in the War on Terror.

Rasul v. Bush, 542 U.S. 466 (2004). *Rasul* dealt with several non-citizens captured in Afghanistan and detained by the United States at the United States Naval Base at Guantanamo Bay, Cuba. They sought a writ of habeas corpus in the United States District Court for the District of Columbia, asserting that their continued detention by unilateral executive action was in violation of the Constitution and other law. The petitioners asserted that they were not enemy combatants, in other words that they had not fought against the United States or its allies. The lower federal courts dismissed the petitions for lack of jurisdiction. The Supreme Court reversed those decisions.

The Court held (6-3) that the federal courts had jurisdiction to consider the petitioners' habeas corpus actions on the basis of 28 U.S.C. § 2241(a). It reasoned that the language "within their respective jurisdictions" in the statute was sufficiently broad to include persons held at Guantanamo Bay. The Court acknowledged that as a general matter United States law does not apply extraterritorially. However, the Court held that Guantanamo Bay was unique. While not subject to United States sovereignty, it was subject to the exclusive control of the United States under a treaty with Cuba. Because the District Court in the District of Columbia unquestionably had jurisdiction over President Bush, it possessed the requisite statutory basis to consider the petitioners' habeas claims.

In order to reach its decision, the Court also had to distinguish *Johnson v. Eisentrager*, 339 U.S. 763 (1950), one of its precedents that appeared to doom the petitioners' cases. In *Eisentrager*, German citizens captured in China and tried by a U.S. military commission in that country sought to pursue a writ of habeas corpus in the District Court in the District of Columbia on the basis that their continued detention was unlawful. The petitioners were being held at a U.S. military prison in Germany. The Supreme Court held that the federal courts lacked jurisdiction to consider the petitioners' claims. In *Rasul*, Justice Stevens, writing for the majority, first noted that the petitioners in the two cases were different in respects the Court found significant:

> [The *Rasul* petitioners] are not nationals of countries at war with the United States, and they deny that they have engaged in or plotted acts of aggression against the United States; they have never been afforded access to any tribunal, much less charged with and convicted of wrongdoing; and for more than two years they have been imprisoned in territory over which the United States exercised exclusive jurisdiction and control.[18]

The *Rasul* Court did not explain precisely why these differences mattered to the jurisdictional question or whether any one of them was more significant than another. Moreover, the *Rasul* Court went on to limit *Eisentrager*'s holding to the petitioners' *constitutional* right to seek habeas corpus. So limited, the Court said that *Eisentrager* posed no bar to the *Rasul* petitioners. The Court would return to *Eisentrager* in a later decision discussed below.

By ruling as it did in *Rasul*, the Court was able to avoid addressing some important constitutional issues, in particular whether the Constitution's

18. *Rasul*, 542 U.S. at 476.

Suspension Clause applied to the *Rasul* petitioners and what that Clause might mean if there was no statutory authorization to seek a writ of habeas corpus.[19] We will return to a discussion of this constitutional provision below in connection with the Court's 2008 decision in *Boumediene v. Bush.*

We can see in *Rasul* an important feature of the Court's approach in this area. When at all possible it bases its decisions on an interpretation of a statute as opposed to a constitutional ground. This approach is similar to the one we discussed in Chapter 3 concerning jurisdiction-stripping cases more generally. Why might the Court take this approach? Is it faithful to constitutional values of separation of powers, or is it antithetical to such values?

Rumsfeld v. Padilla, 542 U.S. 426 (2004). Jose Padilla was an American citizen originally detained at Chicago's O'Hare airport as a "material witness" in connection with a New York federal grand jury's investigation of the September 11 attacks. He was taken from Chicago to New York City, where he moved to vacate the material witness warrant in the United States District Court for the Southern District of New York. Before the federal court ruled on that motion, the President ordered that Mr. Padilla be classified as an enemy combatant and taken into military custody. In an *ex parte* proceeding, the federal district court ordered that he be transferred based on the President's designation. Mr. Padilla was then taken to a Navy prison in South Carolina.

After finding out about his transfer, Mr. Padilla's lawyer sought a writ of habeas corpus in the Southern District of New York, asserting that the President had no authority to detain his client. He named as respondents President Bush, Secretary of Defense Rumsfeld, and the naval commander of the South Carolina brig. The government contended that the Southern District of New York was not the appropriate judicial district to adjudicate the petition. The Supreme Court eventually agreed.

The Court, in a 5-4 decision, held that the only proper respondent in Mr. Padilla's case was the commander of the South Carolina naval prison and that she was not subject to the jurisdiction of the New York federal court. The Court based this holding on what it termed the "traditional" rule that a habeas corpus petitioner must seek the writ in the federal judicial district in which his or her immediate custodian was located. In this case, that meant that the District of South Carolina was the appropriate federal court.

What one can see from *Padilla* is how factual differences between petitioners can lead to quite different results on similar questions. For example, note that in *Rasul* the petitioner was allowed to name as a respondent President Bush and bring his petition in the federal court in the District of Columbia. This result was driven by the practical reality that, having concluded that § 2241 provided an avenue for relief, the Court had to face the reality that *no* federal court covered Guantanamo Bay. For Mr. Padilla, he was held in the United States and, therefore, the "traditional" rule led to a conclusion that only the location of his immediate jailor was appropriate.[20]

19. Recall that the Suspension Clause provides: "The Privilege of the Writ of Habeas Corpus shall not be suspended, unless when in Cases of Rebellion or Invasion the public Safety may require it." U.S. CONST. art. I, § 9, cl. 2

20. Mr. Padilla again sought a writ of habeas corpus, this time in the District of South Carolina. Eventually, the United States Court of Appeals for the Fourth Circuit held against him, ruling that the President had the authority to detain him. While a petition for a writ of certiorari was pending, the government sought permission to transfer him to civilian custody for trial in Miami. The Fourth

***Hamdi v. Rumsfeld*, 542 U.S. 507 (2004).** The third 2004 decision concerned an American citizen named Yaser Hamdi. Mr. Hamdi was captured in Afghanistan and in 2002 transported to Guantanamo Bay, Cuba. Once he was identified as an American citizen, he was transferred to the Navy prison facility in South Carolina. The U.S. government designated Mr. Hamdi as an enemy combatant and took the position that he could be held indefinitely.

Through his father, Hamdi sought a writ of habeas corpus alleging that he was being unlawfully detained. After extensive lower court proceedings, the Fourth Circuit eventually ruled against Hamdi. The Supreme Court reversed but was unable to marshal a single opinion commanding a majority of the justices. Before describing the various opinions in the case — running more than 100 pages in the *U.S. Reporter* — it is significant to note that all nine justices either expressly or by implication agreed that Hamdi could use habeas corpus to test the validity of his detention.

Justice O'Connor authored the plurality opinion, which was joined by Chief Justice Rehnquist and Justices Kennedy and Breyer. It concluded that the President had the authority under the AUMF to detain Hamdi. The plurality did not reach the claim that the President had inherent authority under Article II to detain Hamdi.

However, the plurality also concluded that such detention based on Hamdi's designation as an enemy combatant was not immune from judicial review. Hamdi and those in his position were entitled to a review of the Executive's designation before a federal court. The precise contours of such review were left to the lower courts in the first instance. The plurality instructed that the lower courts should follow the balancing test from *Mathews v. Eldridge*, 424 U.S. 319 (1976), pursuant to which a court determines the procedures required by considering the government's interest, the petitioner's interest, and the ways in which increased procedural protections will make an accurate outcome more likely.

Justice Souter, along with Justice Ginsburg, contended that neither the AUMF nor the President's unilateral powers supported Hamdi's detention. However, in order to give effect to the plurality's judgment concerning the availability of judicial review, they concurred in the judgment remanding the case for further proceedings.

Justice Scalia, joined by Justice Stevens, argued in dissent that Hamdi's detention was unlawful because he was a citizen and was detained in the United States. Based on his reading of the relevant history, Justice Scalia concluded that without a valid suspension of the writ of habeas corpus under the Suspension Clause, Hamdi had to be brought before a civilian court for trial.

Finally, Justice Thomas dissented on the grounds that the President had the authority to detain Hamdi under both the AUMF and his own executive powers. In addition, Justice Thomas argued that Hamdi was owed no process beyond what he had already been provided. Thus, he argued that the flexible balancing approach of *Mathews* was inappropriate.

Circuit refused permission for the transfer. The Supreme Court reversed this determination. Mr. Padilla was eventually tried on non-terrorism charges and convicted of certain counts.

b. 2006: *Hamdan v. Rumsfeld*, 548 U.S. 557 (2006)

After the 2004 trilogy, several things were clear. First, it was confirmed that the status of detainees (e.g., citizen versus non-citizen) was important in the analysis of a federal court's power to consider habeas petitions. Second, the location at which the detainees were both captured and eventually held was also significant. Third, there was something special about Guantanamo Bay that made it in some respects at least much like an actual part of the United States. And fourth, the Court was willing to enter the debate in the War on Terror but was doing so cautiously. For example, *Hamdi* reflected deference to the political branches while incorporating a non-trivial role for the judicial branch. Similarly, *Rasul* was a statute-based decision subject to alteration by Congress.

Congress, in fact, took up the Court's invitation to consider *Rasul*. Shortly after the decision, Congress passed and the President signed into law the Detainee Treatment Act of 2005 (the "DTA").[21] The DTA did a number of things, such as impose certain limitations on interrogation techniques. For present purposes, two interrelated aspects of the statute are important. First, the DTA amended § 2241 to provide in a new subsection (e) that no federal court or judge could entertain a petition seeking a writ of habeas corpus from a detainee at Guantanamo Bay who had been classified as an enemy combatant (or any other complaint alleging a cause of action by such detainee related to his or her detention). In this way, the DTA was meant to change the result reached in *Rasul*.

The second thing the DTA did was create a system of review in the D.C. Circuit for detainees classified as enemy combatants. That system of review is discussed in greater detail in *Boumediene v. Bush* below. In brief, a detainee could challenge his classification as an enemy combatant (made by a body called a Combat Status Review Tribunal or CSRT) directly in the circuit court, which had exclusive jurisdiction over the matter. A challenge could be based only on the failure to follow the Department of Defense's rules and regulations or, if applicable, the Constitution. A detainee convicted by a military commission could also challenge his conviction and sentence in the D.C. Circuit. As we will see in *Boumediene*, the utility of these provisions was a matter of intense dispute.

It was, however, the DTA's limitation on federal courts' habeas jurisdiction that came before the Court in 2006 in *Hamdan v. Rumsfeld*. In *Hamdan*, the Court considered the dismissal for want of jurisdiction under the DTA of a petition for a writ of habeas corpus of Salim Hamdan, alleged to have been Osama Bin Laden's bodyguard and driver. Hamdan had filed his petition before the DTA was enacted. Hamdan alleged that the system of military commissions President Bush unilaterally established at Guantanamo Bay was unlawful. Once the DTA became law, the government moved to dismiss the petition and the motion was granted.

The Court reversed the dismissal in a 5-3 decision.[22] It held that the DTA's provision precluding habeas jurisdiction for detainees held at Guantanamo Bay did not apply as a matter of statutory interpretation to cases pending on the date of its enactment. The Court then declined to abstain from adjudicating the matter.

21. 119 Stat. 2739 (codified as a note at 10 U.S.C. § 801).

22. Chief Justice Roberts did not participate because he had been on the D.C. Circuit panel that had heard Hamdan's appeal.

As to the merits of Hamdan's claims, the Court concluded that the system of military commissions at Guantanamo Bay was unlawful because it did not comply with requirements Congress had set forth in the Uniform Code of Military Justice. As such, the majority concluded that any independent authority the President might have to create such tribunals had been trumped. Note that by ruling in the manner it did, the Court once again left to Congress the ability to adopt the system of military commissions the President had unlawfully unilaterally established.[23]

In the back and forth that has characterized this area, Congress again took up the Court's challenge when it enacted the Military Commissions Act of 2006 (the "MCA").[24] In addition to authorizing the military commission system at Guantanamo Bay, the MCA did a number of other things. Most importantly for our consideration, it precluded habeas corpus jurisdiction over all petitions by detainees at Guantanamo Bay whether filed before or after its enactment. The Supreme Court confronted that provision two years later in the decision excerpted below.

c. 2008: *Boumediene v. Bush*, 553 U.S. 723 (2008)

The Court returned to the War on Terror in 2008 with *Boumediene v. Bush*, 553 U.S. 723 (2008), one of the Court's most important constitutional decisions in many years.[25]

BOUMEDIENE v. BUSH

553 U.S. 723 (2008)

JUSTICE KENNEDY delivered the opinion of the Court.

Petitioners are aliens designated as enemy combatants and detained at the United States Naval Station at Guantanamo Bay, Cuba. There are others detained there, also aliens, who are not parties to this suit.

Petitioners present a question not resolved by our earlier cases relating to the detention of aliens at Guantanamo: whether they have the constitutional privilege of habeas corpus, a privilege not to be withdrawn except in conformance with the Suspension Clause, Art. I, § 9, cl. 2. We hold these petitioners do have the habeas corpus privilege. Congress has enacted a statute, the Detainee Treatment Act of 2005 (DTA), that provides certain procedures for review of the detainees' status. We hold that those procedures are not an adequate and effective substitute for habeas corpus. Therefore § 7 of the Military Commissions

23. The *Hamdan* Court also held that Common Article III of the Geneva Conventions was applicable to the detainees held at Guantanamo Bay. We do not explore that important aspect of *Hamdan* in this text.

24. Pub. L. No. 109-366, 120 Stat. 2600.

25. The Court also decided another War on Terror case in 2008, *Munaf v. Geren*, 553 U.S. 674 (2008). In *Munaf*, the Court held that federal courts have jurisdiction to adjudicate petitions for writs of habeas corpus filed by United States citizens held outside the United States by American forces operating subject to an American chain of command. In the case at bar, the petitioner was held in Iraq by American forces operating as part of a multi-national force in that country. The Court also held, however, that federal courts lacked the authority to enjoin the military from transferring petitioners who were alleged to have committed crimes in and were detained in a foreign sovereign's territory for the purposes of criminal prosecution.

Act of 2006 (MCA), 28 U.S.C.A. § 2241(e) operates as an unconstitutional suspension of the writ. We do not address whether the President has authority to detain these petitioners nor do we hold that the writ must issue. These and other questions regarding the legality of the detention are to be resolved in the first instance by the District Court.

I

Under the Authorization for Use of Military Force (AUMF) the President is authorized "to use all necessary and appropriate force against those nations, organizations, or persons he determines planned, authorized, committed, or aided the terrorist attacks that occurred on September 11, 2001, or harbored such organizations or persons, in order to prevent any future acts of international terrorism against the United States by such nations, organizations or persons."

In *Hamdi v. Rumsfeld*, five Members of the Court recognized that detention of individuals who fought against the United States in Afghanistan "for the duration of the particular conflict in which they were captured, is so fundamental and accepted an incident to war as to be an exercise of the 'necessary and appropriate force' Congress has authorized the President to use." After *Hamdi*, the Deputy Secretary of Defense established Combatant Status Review Tribunals (CSRTs) to determine whether individuals detained at Guantanamo were "enemy combatants," as the Department defines that term. A later memorandum established procedures to implement the CSRTs. The Government maintains these procedures were designed to comply with the due process requirements identified by the plurality in *Hamdi*.

Interpreting the AUMF, the Department of Defense ordered the detention of these petitioners, and they were transferred to Guantanamo. Some of these individuals were apprehended on the battlefield in Afghanistan, others in places as far away from there as Bosnia and Gambia. All are foreign nationals, but none is a citizen of a nation now at war with the United States. Each denies he is a member of the al Qaeda terrorist network that carried out the September 11 attacks or of the Taliban regime that provided sanctuary for al Qaeda. Each petitioner appeared before a separate CSRT; was determined to be an enemy combatant; and has sought a writ of habeas corpus in the United States District Court for the District of Columbia.

The first actions commenced in February 2002. The District Court ordered the cases dismissed for lack of jurisdiction because the naval station is outside the sovereign territory of the United States. The Court of Appeals for the District of Columbia Circuit affirmed. We granted certiorari and reversed, holding that 28 U.S.C. § 2241 extended statutory habeas corpus jurisdiction to Guantanamo. *See Rasul v. Bush.* The constitutional issue presented in the instant cases was not reached in *Rasul.*

After *Rasul*, petitioners' cases were consolidated and entertained in two separate proceedings. In the first set of cases, Judge Richard J. Leon granted the Government's motion to dismiss, holding that the detainees had no rights that could be vindicated in a habeas corpus action. In the second set of cases Judge Joyce Hens Green reached the opposite conclusion, holding the detainees had rights under the Due Process Clause of the Fifth Amendment.

While appeals were pending from the District Court decisions, Congress passed the DTA. Subsection (e) of § 1005 of the DTA amended 28 U.S.C. § 2241 to provide that "no court, justice, or judge shall have jurisdiction to hear or consider . . . an application for a writ of habeas corpus filed by or on behalf of an alien detained by the Department of Defense at Guantanamo Bay, Cuba." Section 1005 further provides that the Court of Appeals for the District of Columbia Circuit shall have "exclusive" jurisdiction to review decisions of the CSRTs.

In *Hamdan v. Rumsfeld*, the Court held this provision did not apply to cases (like petitioners') pending when the DTA was enacted. Congress responded by passing the MCA, which again amended § 2241. The text of the statutory amendment is discussed below. (Four Members of the *Hamdan* majority noted that "[n]othing prevent[ed] the President from returning to Congress to seek the authority he believes necessary." (Breyer, J., concurring). The authority to which the concurring opinion referred was the authority to "create military commissions of the kind at issue" in the case. Nothing in that opinion can be construed as an invitation for Congress to suspend the writ.)

* * * *

The Court of Appeals concluded that MCA § 7 must be read to strip from it, and all federal courts, jurisdiction to consider petitioners' habeas corpus applications; that petitioners are not entitled to the privilege of the writ or the protections of the Suspension Clause; and, as a result, that it was unnecessary to consider whether Congress provided an adequate and effective substitute for habeas corpus in the DTA.

We granted certiorari.

II

As a threshold matter, we must decide whether MCA § 7 denies the federal courts jurisdiction to hear habeas corpus actions pending at the time of its enactment. We hold the statute does deny that jurisdiction, so that, if the statute is valid, petitioners' cases must be dismissed. [In the remainder of this portion of the opinion, the Court rejected the contention that the statute could be construed not to apply to actions pending on the date of its enactment. The Court recounted the sequence of events leading to the disputed portion of the MCA, in particular the Court's decision in *Hamdan* relying on statutory grounds.]

If this ongoing dialogue between and among the branches of Government is to be respected, we cannot ignore that the MCA was a direct response to *Hamdan*'s holding that the DTA's jurisdiction-stripping provision had no application to pending cases. The Court of Appeals was correct to take note of the legislative history when construing the statute and we agree with its conclusion that the MCA deprives the federal courts of jurisdiction to entertain the habeas corpus actions now before us.

III

In deciding the constitutional questions now presented we must determine whether petitioners are barred from seeking the writ or invoking the protections of the Suspension Clause either because of their status, *i.e.*, petitioners' designation by the Executive Branch as enemy combatants, or their physical location, *i.e.*, their presence at Guantanamo Bay. The Government contends that noncitizens designated as enemy combatants and detained in territory located outside our Nation's borders have no constitutional rights and no privilege of habeas corpus. Petitioners contend they do have cognizable constitutional rights and that Congress, in seeking to eliminate recourse to habeas corpus as a means to assert those rights, acted in violation of the Suspension Clause.

We begin with a brief account of the history and origins of the writ. Our account proceeds from two propositions. First, protection for the privilege of habeas corpus was one of the few safeguards of liberty specified in a Constitution that, at the outset, had no Bill of Rights. In the system conceived by the Framers the writ had a centrality that must inform proper interpretation of the Suspension Clause. Second, to the extent there were settled precedents or legal commentaries in 1789 regarding the extraterritorial scope of the writ or its application to enemy aliens, those authorities can be instructive for the present cases.

A

The Framers viewed freedom from unlawful restraint as a fundamental precept of liberty, and they understood the writ of habeas corpus as a vital instrument to secure that freedom. Experience taught, however, that the common-law writ all too often had been insufficient to guard against the abuse of monarchial power. That history counseled the necessity for specific language in the Constitution to secure the writ and ensure its place in our legal system.

Magna Carta [in Article 39] decreed that no man would be imprisoned contrary to the law of the land. Important as the principle was, the Barons at Runnymede prescribed no specific legal process to enforce it. Holdsworth tells us, however, that gradually the writ of habeas corpus became the means by which the promise of Magna Carta was fulfilled.

The development was painstaking, even by the centuries-long measures of English constitutional history. The writ was known and used in some form at least as early as the reign of Edward I. Yet at the outset it was used to protect not the rights of citizens but those of the King and his courts. The early courts were considered agents of the Crown, designed to assist the King in the exercise of his power. Thus the writ, while it would become part of the foundation of liberty for the King's subjects, was in its earliest use a mechanism for securing compliance with the King's laws. Over time it became clear that by issuing the writ of habeas corpus common-law courts sought to enforce the King's prerogative to inquire into the authority of a jailer to hold a prisoner.

Even so, from an early date it was understood that the King, too, was subject to the law. As the writers said of Magna Carta, "it means this, that the king is and shall be below the law. And, by the 1600's, the writ was deemed less an instrument of the King's power and more a restraint upon it.

Still, the writ proved to be an imperfect check. Even when the importance of the writ was well understood in England, habeas relief often was denied by the courts or suspended by Parliament. Denial or suspension occurred in times of political unrest, to the anguish of the imprisoned and the outrage of those in sympathy with them.

* * * *

This history was known to the Framers. It no doubt confirmed their view that pendular swings to and away from individual liberty were endemic to undivided, uncontrolled power. The Framers' inherent distrust of governmental power was the driving force behind the constitutional plan that allocated powers among three independent branches. This design serves not only to make Government accountable but also to secure individual liberty. Because the Constitution's separation-of-powers structure, like the substantive guarantees of the Fifth and Fourteenth Amendments, protects persons as well as citizens, foreign nationals who have the privilege of litigating in our courts can seek to enforce separation-of-powers principles.

That the Framers considered the writ a vital instrument for the protection of individual liberty is evident from the care taken to specify the limited grounds for its suspension: "The Privilege of the Writ of Habeas Corpus shall not be suspended, unless when in Cases of Rebellion or Invasion the public Safety may require it." Art. I, § 9, cl. 2. The word "privilege" was used, perhaps, to avoid mentioning some rights to the exclusion of others. (Indeed, the only mention of the term "right" in the Constitution, as ratified, is in its clause giving Congress the power to protect the rights of authors and inventors. *See* Art. I, § 8, cl. 8.)

Surviving accounts of the ratification debates provide additional evidence that the Framers deemed the writ to be an essential mechanism in the separation-of-powers scheme. [The Court then discussed some of these debates.]

* * * *

In our own system the Suspension Clause is designed to protect against . . . cyclical abuses. The Clause protects the rights of the detained by a means consistent with the essential design of the Constitution. It ensures that, except during periods of formal suspension, the Judiciary will have a time-tested device, the writ, to maintain the "delicate balance of governance" that is itself the surest safeguard of liberty. The Clause protects the rights of the detained by affirming the duty and authority of the Judiciary to call the jailer to account. The separation-of-powers doctrine, and the history that influenced its design, therefore must inform the reach and purpose of the Suspension Clause.

B

The broad historical narrative of the writ and its function is central to our analysis, but we seek guidance as well from founding-era authorities addressing the specific question before us: whether foreign nationals, apprehended and detained in distant countries during a time of serious threats to our Nation's security, may assert the privilege of the writ and seek its protection. The Court has been careful not to foreclose the possibility that the protections of the Suspension Clause have expanded along with post-1789 developments that define the present scope of the writ. *See INS v. St. Cyr.* But the analysis may begin with precedents as of 1789, for the Court has said that "at the absolute minimum" the Clause protects the writ as it existed when the Constitution was drafted and ratified.

To support their arguments, the parties in these cases have examined historical sources to construct a view of the common-law writ as it existed in 1789 — as have *amici* whose expertise in legal history the Court has relied upon in the past. The Government argues the common-law writ ran only to those territories over which the Crown was sovereign. Petitioners argue that jurisdiction followed the King's officers. Diligent search by all parties reveals no certain conclusions. In none of the cases cited do we find that a common-law court would or would not have granted, or refused to hear for lack of jurisdiction, a petition for a writ of habeas corpus brought by a prisoner deemed an enemy combatant, under a standard like the one the Department of Defense has used in these cases, and when held in a territory, like Guantanamo, over which the Government has total military and civil control. [The Court then spent several pages discussing potential historical analogies from England and lands under its control concerning the use of the writ.]

* * * *

Each side in the present matter argues that the very lack of a precedent on point supports its position. The Government points out there is no evidence that a court sitting in England granted habeas relief to an enemy alien detained abroad; petitioners respond there is no evidence that a court refused to do so for lack of jurisdiction.

Both arguments are premised, however, upon the assumption that the historical record is complete and that the common law, if properly understood, yields a definite answer to the questions before us. There are reasons to doubt both assumptions. Recent scholarship points to the inherent shortcomings in the historical record. And given the unique status of Guantanamo Bay and the particular dangers of terrorism in the modern age, the common-law courts simply may not have confronted cases with close parallels to this one. We decline, therefore, to infer too much, one way or the other, from the lack of historical evidence on point.

IV

Drawing from its position that at common law the writ ran only to territories over which the Crown was sovereign, the Government says the Suspension Clause affords petitioners no rights because the United States does not claim sovereignty over the place of detention.

Guantanamo Bay is not formally part of the United States. And under the terms of the lease between the United States and Cuba, Cuba retains "ultimate sovereignty" over the territory while the United States exercises "complete jurisdiction and control." Under the terms of the 1934 Treaty, however, Cuba effectively has no rights as a sovereign until the parties agree to modification of the 1903 Lease Agreement or the United States abandons the base.

The United States contends, nevertheless, that Guantanamo is not within its sovereign control. This was the Government's position well before the events of September 11, 2001. And in other contexts the Court has held that questions of sovereignty are for the political branches to decide. Even if this were a treaty interpretation case that did not involve a political question, the President's construction of the lease agreement would be entitled to great respect.

We therefore do not question the Government's position that Cuba, not the United States, maintains sovereignty, in the legal and technical sense of the term, over Guantanamo Bay. . . . Accordingly, for purposes of our analysis, we accept the Government's position that Cuba, and not the United States, retains *de jure* sovereignty over Guantanamo Bay. As we did in *Rasul*, however, we take notice of the obvious and uncontested fact that the United States, by virtue of its complete jurisdiction and control over the base, maintains *de facto* sovereignty over this territory.

Were we to hold that the present cases turn on the political question doctrine, we would be required first to accept the Government's premise that *de jure* sovereignty is the touchstone of habeas corpus jurisdiction. This premise, however, is unfounded. For the reasons indicated above, the history of common-law habeas corpus provides scant support for this proposition; and, for the reasons indicated below, that position would be inconsistent with our precedents and contrary to fundamental separation-of-powers principles.

A

The Court has discussed the issue of the Constitution's extraterritorial application on many occasions. These decisions undermine the Government's argument that, at least as applied to noncitizens, the Constitution necessarily stops where *de jure* sovereignty ends. [The Court then went on to canvass a number of its prior decisions concerning the extraterritorial application of certain constitutional principles, eventually turning to *Johnson v. Eisentrager.*]

* * * *

Practical considerations weighed heavily as well in *Johnson v. Eisentrager*, where the Court addressed whether habeas corpus jurisdiction extended to enemy aliens who had been convicted of violating the laws of war. The prisoners were detained at Landsberg Prison in Germany during the Allied Powers' post-war occupation. The Court stressed the difficulties of ordering the Government to produce the prisoners in a habeas corpus proceeding. It "would require allocation of shipping space, guarding personnel, billeting and rations" and would damage the prestige of military commanders at a sensitive time. In considering these factors the Court sought to balance the constraints of military occupation with constitutional necessities.

True, the Court in *Eisentrager* denied access to the writ, and it noted the prisoners "at no relevant time were within any territory over which the United States is sovereign, and [that] the scenes of their offense, their capture, their trial and their punishment were all beyond the territorial jurisdiction of any court of the United States." The Government seizes upon this language as proof positive that the *Eisentrager* Court adopted a formalistic, sovereignty-based test for determining the reach of the Suspension Clause. We reject this reading for three reasons.

First, we do not accept the idea that the above-quoted passage from *Eisentrager* is the only authoritative language in the opinion and that all the rest is dicta. The Court's further determinations, based on practical considerations, were integral to Part II of its opinion and came before the decision announced its holding.

Second, because the United States lacked both *de jure* sovereignty and plenary control over Landsberg Prison, it is far from clear that the *Eisentrager* Court used the term sovereignty only in the narrow technical sense and not to connote the degree of control the military asserted over the facility. The Justices who decided *Eisentrager* would have understood sovereignty as a multifaceted concept. In its principal brief in *Eisentrager*, the Government advocated a bright-line test for determining the scope of the writ, similar to the one it advocates in these cases. Yet the Court mentioned the concept of territorial sovereignty only twice in its opinion. That the Court devoted a significant portion of Part II to a discussion of practical barriers to the running of the writ suggests that the Court was not concerned exclusively with the formal legal status of Landsberg Prison but also with the objective degree of control the United States asserted over it. Even if we assume the *Eisentrager* Court considered the United States' lack of formal legal sovereignty over Landsberg Prison as the decisive factor in that case, its holding is not inconsistent with a functional approach to questions of extraterritoriality. The formal legal status of a given territory affects, at least to some extent, the political branches' control over that territory. *De jure* sovereignty is a factor that bears upon which constitutional guarantees apply there.

Third, if the Government's reading of *Eisentrager* were correct, the opinion would have marked not only a change in, but a complete repudiation of, [some earlier cases in which the Court found a] functional approach to questions of extraterritoriality. We cannot accept the Government's view. Nothing in *Eisentrager* says that *de jure* sovereignty is or has ever been the only relevant consideration in determining the geographic reach of the Constitution or of habeas corpus. Were that the case, there would be considerable tension between *Eisentrager*, on the one hand, and the *Insular Cases* and *Reid*, on the other. Our cases need not be read to conflict in this manner. A constricted reading of *Eisentrager* overlooks what we see as a common thread uniting [the Court's precedent] . . . : the idea that questions of extraterritoriality turn on objective factors and practical concerns, not formalism.

B

The Government's formal sovereignty-based test raises troubling separation-of-powers concerns as well. The political history of Guantanamo illustrates the deficiencies of this approach. The United States has maintained complete and uninterrupted control of the bay for over 100 years. At the close of the Spanish-American War, Spain ceded control over the entire island of Cuba to the United States and specifically "relinquishe[d] all claim[s] of sovereignty . . . and title." From the date the treaty with Spain was signed until the Cuban Republic was established on May 20, 1902, the United States governed the territory "in trust" for the benefit of the Cuban people. And although it recognized, by entering into the 1903 Lease Agreement, that Cuba retained "ultimate sovereignty" over Guantanamo, the United States continued to maintain the same plenary control it had enjoyed since 1898. Yet the Government's view is that the Constitution had no effect there, at least as to noncitizens, because the United States disclaimed sovereignty in the formal sense of the term. The necessary implication of the argument is that by surrendering formal sovereignty over any unincorporated territory to a third party, while at the same time entering into a lease that grants total control over the territory back to the United States, it would be possible for the political branches to govern without legal constraint.

Our basic charter cannot be contracted away like this. The Constitution grants Congress and the President the power to acquire, dispose of, and govern territory, not the power to decide when and where its terms apply. Even when the United States acts outside its borders, its powers are not "absolute and unlimited" but are subject "to such restrictions as are expressed in the Constitution." Abstaining from questions involving formal sovereignty and territorial governance is one thing. To hold the political branches have the power to switch the Constitution on or off at will is quite another. The former position reflects this Court's recognition that certain matters requiring political judgments are best left to the political branches. The latter would permit a striking anomaly in our tripartite system of government, leading to a regime in which Congress and the President, not this Court, say "what the law is." *Marbury v. Madison.*

These concerns have particular bearing upon the Suspension Clause question in the cases now before us, for the writ of habeas corpus is itself an indispensable mechanism for monitoring the separation of powers. The test for determining the scope of this provision must not be subject to manipulation by those whose power it is designed to restrain.

C

As we recognized in *Rasul*, the outlines of a framework for determining the reach of the Suspension Clause are suggested by the factors the Court relied upon in *Eisentrager*. In addition to the practical concerns discussed above, the *Eisentrager* Court found relevant that each petitioner:

> "(a) is an enemy alien; (b) has never been or resided in the United States; (c) was captured outside of our territory and there held in military custody as a prisoner of war; (d) was tried and convicted by a Military Commission sitting outside the United States; (e) for offenses against laws of war committed outside the United States; (f) and is at all times imprisoned outside the United States."

Based on this language from *Eisentrager*, and the reasoning in our other extraterritoriality opinions, we conclude that at least three factors are relevant in determining the reach of the Suspension Clause: (1) the citizenship and status of the detainee and the adequacy of the process through which that status determination was made; (2) the nature of the sites where apprehension and then detention took place; and (3) the practical obstacles inherent in resolving the prisoner's entitlement to the writ.

Applying this framework, we note at the onset that the status of these detainees is a matter of dispute. The petitioners, like those in *Eisentrager*, are not American citizens. But the petitioners in *Eisentrager* did not contest, it seems, the Court's assertion that they were "enemy alien[s]." In the instant cases, by contrast, the detainees deny they are enemy combatants. They have been afforded some process in CSRT proceedings to determine their status; but, unlike in *Eisentrager*, there has been no trial by military commission for violations of the laws of war. The difference is not trivial. The records from the *Eisentrager* trials suggest that, well before the petitioners brought their case to this Court, there had been a rigorous adversarial process to test the legality of their detention. The *Eisentrager* petitioners were charged by a bill of particulars that made detailed factual allegations against them. To rebut the accusations, they were entitled to representation by counsel, allowed to introduce evidence on their own behalf, and permitted to cross-examine the prosecution's witnesses.

In comparison the procedural protections afforded to the detainees in the CSRT hearings are far more limited, and, we conclude, fall well short of the procedures and adversarial mechanisms that would eliminate the need for habeas corpus review. Although the detainee is assigned a "Personal Representative" to assist him during CSRT proceedings, the Secretary of the Navy's memorandum makes clear that person is not the detainee's lawyer or even his "advocate." The Government's evidence is accorded a presumption of validity. The detainee is allowed to present "reasonably available" evidence, but his ability to rebut the Government's evidence against him is limited by the circumstances of his confinement and his lack of counsel at this stage. And although the detainee can seek review of his status determination in the Court of Appeals, that review process cannot cure all defects in the earlier proceedings.

As to the second factor relevant to this analysis, the detainees here are similarly situated to the *Eisentrager* petitioners in that the sites of their apprehension and detention are technically outside the sovereign territory of the United States. As noted earlier, this is a factor that weighs against finding they have rights under the Suspension Clause. But there are critical differences between Landsberg Prison, circa 1950, and the United States Naval Station at Guantanamo Bay in 2008. Unlike its present control over the naval station, the United States' control over the prison in Germany was neither absolute nor indefinite. Like all parts of occupied Germany, the prison was under the jurisdiction of the combined Allied Forces. The United States was therefore answerable to its Allies for all activities occurring there. The Allies had not planned a long-term occupation of Germany, nor did they intend to displace all German institutions even during the period of occupation. The Court's holding in *Eisentrager* was thus consistent with the *Insular Cases,* where it had held there was no need to extend full constitutional protections to territories the United States did not intend to govern indefinitely. Guantanamo Bay, on the other hand, is no transient possession. In every practical sense Guantanamo is not abroad; it is within the constant jurisdiction of the United States.

As to the third factor, we recognize, as the Court did in *Eisentrager,* that there are costs to holding the Suspension Clause applicable in a case of military detention abroad. Habeas corpus proceedings may require expenditure of funds by the Government and may divert the attention of military personnel from other pressing tasks. While we are sensitive to these concerns, we do not find them dispositive. Compliance with any judicial process requires some incremental expenditure of resources. Yet civilian courts and the Armed Forces have functioned along side each other at various points in our history. The Government presents no credible arguments that the military mission at Guantanamo would be compromised if habeas corpus courts had jurisdiction to hear the detainees' claims. And in light of the plenary control the United States asserts over the base, none are apparent to us.

The situation in *Eisentrager* was far different, given the historical context and nature of the military's mission in post-War Germany. When hostilities in the European Theater came to an end, the United States became responsible for an occupation zone encompassing over 57,000 square miles with a population of 18 million. In addition to supervising massive reconstruction and aid efforts the American forces stationed in Germany faced potential security threats from a defeated enemy. In retrospect the post-War occupation may seem uneventful. But at the time *Eisentrager* was decided, the Court was right to be concerned about judicial interference with the military's efforts to contain "enemy elements, guerilla fighters, and 'were-wolves.'"

Similar threats are not apparent here; nor does the Government argue that they are. The United States Naval Station at Guantanamo Bay consists of 45 square miles of land and water. The base has been used, at various points, to house migrants and refugees temporarily. At present, however, other than the detainees themselves, the only long-term residents are American military personnel, their families, and a small number of workers. The detainees have been deemed enemies of the United States. At present, dangerous as they may be if released, they are contained in a secure prison facility located on an isolated and heavily fortified military base.

There is no indication, furthermore, that adjudicating a habeas corpus petition would cause friction with the host government. No Cuban court has jurisdiction over American military personnel at Guantanamo or the enemy combatants detained there. While obligated to abide by the terms of the lease, the United States is, for all practical purposes, answerable to no other sovereign for its acts on the base. Were that not the case, or if the detention facility were located in an active theater of war, arguments that issuing the writ would be "impracticable or anomalous" would have more weight. Under the facts presented here, however, there are few practical barriers to the running of the writ. To the extent barriers arise, habeas corpus procedures likely can be modified to address them.

It is true that before today the Court has never held that noncitizens detained by our Government in territory over which another country maintains *de jure* sovereignty have any rights under our Constitution. But the cases before us lack any precise historical parallel. They involve individuals detained by executive order for the duration of a conflict that, if measured from September 11, 2001, to the present, is already among the longest wars in American history. The detainees, moreover, are held in a territory that, while technically not part of the United States, is under the complete and total control of our Government. Under these circumstances the lack of a precedent on point is no barrier to our holding.

We hold that Art. I, § 9, cl. 2, of the Constitution has full effect at Guantanamo Bay. If the privilege of habeas corpus is to be denied to the detainees now before us, Congress must act in accordance with the requirements of the Suspension Clause. This Court may not impose a *de facto* suspension by abstaining from these controversies. The MCA does not purport to be a formal suspension of the writ; and the Government, in its submissions to us, has not argued that it is. Petitioners, therefore, are entitled to the privilege of habeas corpus to challenge the legality of their detention.

V

In light of this holding the question becomes whether the statute stripping jurisdiction to issue the writ avoids the Suspension Clause mandate because Congress has provided adequate substitute procedures for habeas corpus. The Government submits there has been compliance with the Suspension Clause because the DTA review process in the Court of Appeals, see DTA § 1005(e), provides an adequate substitute. Congress has granted that court jurisdiction to consider

> "(i) whether the status determination of the [CSRT] . . . was consistent with the standards and procedures specified by the Secretary of Defense . . . and (ii) to the extent the Constitution and laws of the United States are applicable, whether the use of such standards and procedures to make the determination is consistent with the Constitution and laws of the United States." § 1005(e)(2)(C).

* * * *

A

Our case law does not contain extensive discussion of standards defining suspension of the writ or of circumstances under which suspension has occurred. This simply confirms the care Congress has taken throughout our Nation's history to preserve the writ and its function. Indeed, most of the major legislative enactments pertaining to habeas corpus have acted not to contract the writ's protection but to expand it or to hasten resolution of prisoners' claims.

There are exceptions, of course. Title I of the Antiterrorism and Effective Death Penalty Act of 1996 (AEDPA) contains certain gatekeeping provisions that restrict a prisoner's ability to bring new and repetitive claims in "second or successive" habeas corpus actions. We upheld these provisions against a Suspension Clause challenge in *Felker v. Turpin.* The provisions at issue in *Felker,* however, did not constitute a substantial departure from common-law habeas procedures. The provisions, for the most part, codified the longstanding abuse-of-the-writ doctrine. AEDPA applies, moreover, to federal, postconviction review after criminal proceedings in state court have taken place. As of this point, cases discussing the implementation of that statute give little helpful instruction (save perhaps by contrast) for the instant cases, where no trial has been held.

The two leading cases addressing habeas substitutes . . . likewise provide little guidance here. The statutes at issue [in those cases] were attempts to streamline habeas corpus relief, not to cut it back.

* * * *

Unlike in [these earlier cases], here we confront statutes, the DTA and the MCA, that were intended to circumscribe habeas review. . . . When Congress has intended to replace traditional habeas corpus with habeas-like substitutes . . . it has granted to the courts broad remedial powers to secure the historic office of the writ. . . .

In contrast the DTA's jurisdictional grant is quite limited. The Court of Appeals has jurisdiction not to inquire into the legality of the detention generally but only to assess whether the CSRT complied with the "standards and procedures specified by the Secretary of Defense" and whether those standards and procedures are lawful. . . . [M]oreover, there has been no effort to preserve habeas corpus review as an avenue of last resort. No saving clause exists in either the MCA or the DTA. And MCA § 7 eliminates habeas review for these petitioners.

The differences between the DTA and the habeas statute that would govern in MCA § 7's absence, 28 U.S.C. § 2241, are likewise telling. In § 2241 Congress confirmed the authority of "any justice" or "circuit judge" to issue the writ. That statute accommodates the necessity for factfinding that will arise in some cases by allowing the appellate judge or Justice to transfer the case to a district court of competent jurisdiction, whose institutional capacity for factfinding is superior to his or her own. By granting the Court of Appeals "exclusive" jurisdiction over petitioners' cases Congress has foreclosed that option. This choice indicates Congress intended the Court of Appeals to have a more limited role in enemy combatant status determinations than a district court has in habeas corpus proceedings. The DTA should be interpreted to accord some latitude to the Court of Appeals to fashion procedures necessary to make its review function a meaningful one, but, if congressional intent is to be respected, the procedures adopted cannot be as extensive or as protective of the rights of the detainees as they would be in a § 2241 proceeding. Otherwise there would have been no, or very little, purpose for enacting the DTA.

To the extent any doubt remains about Congress' intent, the legislative history confirms what the plain text strongly suggests: In passing the DTA Congress did not intend to create a process that differs from traditional habeas corpus process in name only. It intended to create a more limited procedure.

It is against this background that we must interpret the DTA and assess its adequacy as a substitute for habeas corpus. . . .

B

We do not endeavor to offer a comprehensive summary of the requisites for an adequate substitute for habeas corpus. We do consider it uncontroversial, however, that the privilege of habeas corpus entitles the prisoner to a meaningful opportunity to demonstrate that he is being held pursuant to "the erroneous application or interpretation" of relevant law. And the habeas court must have the power to order the conditional release of an individual unlawfully detained—though release need not be the exclusive remedy and is not the appropriate one in every case in which the writ is granted. These are the easily identified attributes of any constitutionally adequate habeas corpus proceeding. But, depending on the circumstances, more may be required.

* * * *

Where a person is detained by executive order, rather than, say, after being tried and convicted in a court, the need for collateral review is most pressing. A criminal conviction in the usual course occurs after a judicial hearing before a tribunal disinterested in the outcome and committed to procedures designed to ensure its own independence. These dynamics are not inherent in executive detention orders or executive review procedures. In this context the need for habeas corpus is more urgent. The intended duration of the detention and the reasons for it bear upon the precise scope of the inquiry. Habeas corpus proceedings need not resemble a criminal trial, even when the detention is by executive order. But the writ must be effective. The habeas court must have sufficient authority to conduct a meaningful review of both the cause for detention and the Executive's power to detain.

To determine the necessary scope of habeas corpus review, therefore, we must assess the CSRT process, the mechanism through which petitioners' designation as enemy combatants became final. Whether one characterizes the CSRT process as direct review of the Executive's battlefield determination that the detainee is an enemy combatant—as the parties have and as we do—or as the first step in the collateral review of a battlefield determination makes no difference in a proper analysis of whether the procedures Congress put in place are an adequate substitute for habeas corpus. What matters is the sum total of procedural protections afforded to the detainee at all stages, direct and collateral.

Petitioners identify what they see as myriad deficiencies in the CSRTs. The most relevant for our purposes are the constraints upon the detainee's ability to rebut the factual basis for the Government's assertion that he is an enemy combatant. As already noted, at the CSRT stage the detainee has limited means to find or present evidence to challenge the Government's case against him. He does not have the assistance of counsel and may not be aware of the most critical allegations that the Government relied upon to order his detention. The detainee can confront witnesses that testify during the CSRT proceedings. But given that there are in effect no limits on the admission of hearsay evidence—the only requirement is that the tribunal deem the evidence "relevant and helpful,"—the detainee's opportunity to question witnesses is likely to be more theoretical than real.

* * * *

Even if we were to assume that the CSRTs satisfy due process standards, it would not end our inquiry. Habeas corpus is a collateral process that exists, in Justice Holmes' words, to "cu[t] through all forms and g[o] to the very tissue of the structure. It comes in from the outside, not in subordination to the proceedings, and although every form may have been preserved opens the inquiry whether they have been more than an empty shell." Even when the procedures authorizing detention are structurally sound, the Suspension Clause remains applicable and the writ relevant. This is so . . . even where the prisoner is detained after a criminal trial conducted in full accordance with the protections of the Bill of Rights. . . .

Although we make no judgment as to whether the CSRTs, as currently constituted, satisfy due process standards, we agree with petitioners that, even when all the parties involved in this process act with diligence and in good faith, there is considerable risk of error in the tribunal's findings of fact. This is a risk inherent in any process that . . . is "closed and accusatorial." And given that the consequence of error may be detention of persons for the duration of hostilities that may last a generation or more, this is a risk too significant to ignore.

For the writ of habeas corpus, or its substitute, to function as an effective and proper remedy in this context, the court that conducts the habeas proceeding must have the means to correct errors that occurred during the CSRT proceedings. This includes some authority to assess the sufficiency of the Government's evidence against the detainee. It also must have the authority to admit and consider relevant exculpatory evidence that was not introduced during the earlier proceeding. Federal habeas petitioners long have had the means to supplement the record on review, even in the postconviction habeas setting. Here that opportunity is constitutionally required.

Consistent with the historic function and province of the writ, habeas corpus review may be more circumscribed if the underlying detention proceedings are more thorough than they were here. In two habeas cases involving enemy aliens tried for war crimes, *In re Yamashita* and *Ex parte Quirin*, for example, this Court limited its review to determining whether the Executive had legal authority to try the petitioners by military commission. Military courts are not courts of record. And the procedures used to try General Yamashita have been sharply criticized by Members of this Court. We need not revisit these cases, however. For on their own terms, the proceedings in *Yamashita* and *Quirin*, like those in *Eisentrager*, had an adversarial structure that is lacking here.

The extent of the showing required of the Government in these cases is a matter to be determined. We need not explore it further at this stage. We do hold that when the judicial power to issue habeas corpus properly is invoked the judicial officer must have adequate authority to make a determination in light of the relevant law and facts and to formulate and issue appropriate orders for relief, including, if necessary, an order directing the prisoner's release.

C

We now consider whether the DTA allows the Court of Appeals to conduct a proceeding meeting these standards. [The Court concluded that it was possible to read the DTA as allowing release as a remedy and for a challenge to detention under the AUMF.]

* * * *

The absence of a release remedy and specific language allowing AUMF challenges are not the only constitutional infirmities from which the statute potentially suffers, however. The more difficult question is whether the DTA permits the Court of Appeals to make requisite findings of fact. The DTA enables petitioners to request "review" of their CSRT determination in the Court of Appeals; but the "Scope of Review" provision confines the Court of Appeals' role to reviewing whether the CSRT followed the "standards and procedures" issued by the Department of Defense and assessing whether those "standards and procedures" are lawful. Among these standards is "the requirement that the conclusion of the Tribunal be supported by a preponderance of the evidence . . . allowing a rebuttable presumption in favor of the Government's evidence."

Assuming the DTA can be construed to allow the Court of Appeals to review or correct the CSRT's factual determinations, as opposed to merely certifying that the tribunal applied the correct standard of proof, we see no way to construe the statute to allow what is also constitutionally required in this context: an opportunity for the detainee to present relevant exculpatory evidence that was not made part of the record in the earlier proceedings.

* * * *

Under the DTA the Court of Appeals has the power to review CSRT determinations by assessing the legality of standards and procedures. This implies the power to inquire into what happened at the CSRT hearing and, perhaps, to remedy certain deficiencies in that proceeding. But should the Court of Appeals determine that the CSRT followed appropriate and lawful standards and procedures, it will have reached the limits of its jurisdiction. There is no language in the DTA that can be construed to allow the Court of Appeals to admit and consider newly discovered evidence that could not have been made part of the CSRT record because it was unavailable to either the Government or the detainee when the CSRT made its findings. This evidence, however, may be critical to the detainee's argument that he is not an enemy combatant and there is no cause to detain him.

* * * *

By foreclosing consideration of evidence not presented or reasonably available to the detainee at the CSRT proceedings, the DTA disadvantages the detainee by limiting the scope of collateral review to a record that may not be accurate or complete. In other contexts, *e.g.*, in post-trial habeas cases where the prisoner already has had a full and fair opportunity to develop the factual predicate of his claims, similar limitations on the scope of habeas review may be appropriate. In this context, however, where the underlying detention proceedings lack the necessary adversarial character, the detainee cannot be held responsible for all deficiencies in the record.

* * * *

We do not imply DTA review would be a constitutionally sufficient replacement for habeas corpus but for these limitations on the detainee's ability to present exculpatory evidence. For even if it were possible, as a textual matter, to read into the statute each of the necessary procedures we have identified, we could not overlook the cumulative effect of our doing so. To hold that the detainees at Guantanamo may, under the DTA, challenge the President's legal authority to detain them, contest the CSRT's findings of fact, supplement the record on review with exculpatory evidence, and request an order of release would come close to reinstating the § 2241 habeas corpus process Congress sought to deny them. The language of the statute, read in light of Congress' reasons for enacting it, cannot bear this interpretation. Petitioners have met their burden of establishing that the DTA review process is, on its face, an inadequate substitute for habeas corpus.

Although we do not hold that an adequate substitute must duplicate § 2241 in all respects, it suffices that the Government has not established that the detainees' access to the statutory review provisions at issue is an adequate substitute for the writ of habeas corpus. MCA § 7 thus effects an unconstitutional suspension of the writ. In view of our holding we need not discuss the reach of the writ with respect to claims of unlawful conditions of treatment or confinement.

VI

A

In light of our conclusion that there is no jurisdictional bar to the District Court's entertaining petitioners' claims the question remains whether there are prudential barriers to habeas corpus review under these circumstances.

The Government argues petitioners must seek review of their CSRT determinations in the Court of Appeals before they can proceed with their habeas corpus actions in the District Court. As noted earlier, in other contexts and for prudential reasons this Court has required exhaustion of alternative remedies before a prisoner can seek federal habeas relief. Most of these cases were brought by prisoners in state custody, and thus involved federalism concerns that are not relevant here. But we have extended this rule to require defendants in courts-martial to exhaust their military appeals before proceeding with a federal habeas corpus action.

The real risks, the real threats, of terrorist attacks are constant and not likely soon to abate. The ways to disrupt our life and laws are so many and unforeseen that the Court should not attempt even some general catalogue of crises that might occur. Certain principles are apparent, however. Practical considerations and exigent circumstances inform the definition and reach of the law's writs, including habeas corpus. The cases and our tradition reflect this precept.

In cases involving foreign citizens detained abroad by the Executive, it likely would be both an impractical and unprecedented extension of judicial power to assume that habeas corpus would be available at the moment the prisoner is taken into custody. If and when habeas corpus jurisdiction applies, as it does in these cases, then proper deference can be accorded to reasonable procedures for screening and initial detention under lawful and proper conditions of confinement and treatment for a reasonable period of time. Domestic exigencies, furthermore, might also impose such onerous burdens on the Government that here, too, the Judicial Branch would be required to devise sensible rules for staying habeas corpus proceedings until the Government can comply with its requirements in a responsible way. Here, as is true with detainees apprehended abroad, a relevant consideration in determining the courts' role is whether there are suitable alternative processes in place to protect against the arbitrary exercise of governmental power.

The cases before us, however, do not involve detainees who have been held for a short period of time while awaiting their CSRT determinations. Were that the case, or were it probable that the Court of Appeals could complete a prompt review of their applications, the case for requiring temporary abstention or exhaustion of alternative remedies would be much stronger. These qualifications no longer pertain here. In some of these cases six years have elapsed without the judicial oversight that habeas corpus or an adequate substitute demands. And there has been no showing that the Executive faces such onerous burdens that it cannot respond to habeas corpus actions. To require these detainees to complete DTA review before proceeding with their habeas corpus actions would be to require additional months, if not years, of delay. The first DTA review applications were filed over a year ago, but no decisions on the merits have been issued. While some delay in fashioning new procedures is unavoidable, the costs of delay can no longer be borne by those who are held in custody. The detainees in these cases are entitled to a prompt habeas corpus hearing.

Our decision today holds only that the petitioners before us are entitled to seek the writ; that the DTA review procedures are an inadequate substitute for habeas corpus; and that the petitioners in these cases need not exhaust the review procedures in the Court of Appeals before proceeding with their habeas actions in the District Court. The only law we identify as unconstitutional is MCA § 7, 28 U.S.C.A. § 2241(e). Accordingly, both the DTA and the CSRT process remain intact. Our holding with regard to exhaustion should not be read to imply that a habeas court should intervene the moment an enemy combatant steps foot in a territory where the writ runs. The Executive is entitled to a reasonable period of time to determine a detainee's status before a court entertains that detainee's habeas corpus petition. The CSRT process is the mechanism Congress and the President set up to deal with these issues. Except in cases of undue delay, federal courts should refrain from entertaining an enemy combatant's habeas corpus petition at least until after the Department, acting via the CSRT, has had a chance to review his status.

B

Although we hold that the DTA is not an adequate and effective substitute for habeas corpus, it does not follow that a habeas corpus court may disregard the dangers the detention in these cases was intended to prevent. [The Court's precedents] stand for the proposition that the Suspension Clause does not resist innovation in the field of habeas corpus. Certain accommodations can be made to reduce the burden habeas corpus proceedings will place on the military without impermissibly diluting the protections of the writ.

In the DTA Congress sought to consolidate review of petitioners' claims in the Court of Appeals. Channeling future cases to one district court would no doubt reduce administrative burdens on the Government. This is a legitimate objective that might be advanced even without an amendment to § 2241. If, in a future case, a detainee files a habeas petition in another judicial district in which a proper respondent can be served, the Government can move for change of venue to the court that will hear these petitioners' cases, the United States District Court for the District of Columbia.

Another of Congress' reasons for vesting exclusive jurisdiction in the Court of Appeals, perhaps, was to avoid the widespread dissemination of classified information. The Government has raised similar concerns here and elsewhere. We make no attempt to anticipate all of the evidentiary and access-to-counsel issues that will arise during the course of the detainees' habeas corpus proceedings. We recognize, however, that the Government has a legitimate interest in protecting sources and methods of intelligence gathering; and we expect that the

District Court will use its discretion to accommodate this interest to the greatest extent possible.

These and the other remaining questions are within the expertise and competence of the District Court to address in the first instance.

* * * [Break in the Court's opinion.]

In considering both the procedural and substantive standards used to impose detention to prevent acts of terrorism, proper deference must be accorded to the political branches. Unlike the President and some designated Members of Congress, neither the Members of this Court nor most federal judges begin the day with briefings that may describe new and serious threats to our Nation and its people. The law must accord the Executive substantial authority to apprehend and detain those who pose a real danger to our security.

Officials charged with daily operational responsibility for our security may consider a judicial discourse on the history of the Habeas Corpus Act of 1679 and like matters to be far removed from the Nation's present, urgent concerns. Established legal doctrine, however, must be consulted for its teaching. Remote in time it may be; irrelevant to the present it is not. Security depends upon a sophisticated intelligence apparatus and the ability of our Armed Forces to act and to interdict. There are further considerations, however. Security subsists, too, in fidelity to freedom's first principles. Chief among these are freedom from arbitrary and unlawful restraint and the personal liberty that is secured by adherence to the separation of powers. It is from these principles that the judicial authority to consider petitions for habeas corpus relief derives.

Our opinion does not undermine the Executive's powers as Commander in Chief. On the contrary, the exercise of those powers is vindicated, not eroded, when confirmed by the Judicial Branch. Within the Constitution's separation-of-powers structure, few exercises of judicial power are as legitimate or as necessary as the responsibility to hear challenges to the authority of the Executive to imprison a person. Some of these petitioners have been in custody for six years with no definitive judicial determination as to the legality of their detention. Their access to the writ is a necessity to determine the lawfulness of their status, even if, in the end, they do not obtain the relief they seek.

Because our Nation's past military conflicts have been of limited duration, it has been possible to leave the outer boundaries of war powers undefined. If, as some fear, terrorism continues to pose dangerous threats to us for years to come, the Court might not have this luxury. This result is not inevitable, however. The political branches, consistent with their independent obligations to interpret and uphold the Constitution, can engage in a genuine debate about how best to preserve constitutional values while protecting the Nation from terrorism.

It bears repeating that our opinion does not address the content of the law that governs petitioners' detention. That is a matter yet to be determined. We hold that petitioners may invoke the fundamental procedural protections of habeas corpus. The laws and Constitution are designed to survive, and remain in force, in extraordinary times. Liberty and security can be reconciled; and in our system they are reconciled within the framework of the law. The Framers decided that habeas corpus, a right of first importance, must be a part of that framework, a part of that law.

The determination by the Court of Appeals that the Suspension Clause and its protections are inapplicable to petitioners was in error. The judgment of the Court of Appeals is reversed. The cases are remanded to the Court of Appeals with instructions that it remand the cases to the District Court for proceedings consistent with this opinion.

It is so ordered.

[A concurring opinion by Justice Souter is omitted.]

CHIEF JUSTICE ROBERTS, with whom JUSTICE SCALIA, JUSTICE THOMAS, and JUSTICE ALITO join, dissenting.

Today the Court strikes down as inadequate the most generous set of procedural protections ever afforded aliens detained by this country as enemy combatants. The political branches crafted these procedures amidst an ongoing military conflict, after much careful investigation and thorough debate. The Court rejects them today out of hand, without bothering to say what due process rights the detainees possess, without explaining how the statute fails to vindicate those rights, and before a single petitioner has even attempted to avail himself of the law's operation. And to what effect? The majority merely replaces a review system designed by the people's representatives with a set of shapeless procedures to be defined by federal courts at some future date. One cannot help but think, after surveying the modest practical results of the majority's ambitious opinion, that this decision is not really about the detainees at all, but about control of federal policy regarding enemy combatants.

The majority is adamant that the Guantanamo detainees are entitled to the protections of habeas corpus—its opinion begins by deciding that question. I regard the issue as a difficult one, primarily because of the unique and unusual jurisdictional status of Guantanamo Bay. I nonetheless agree with Justice Scalia's analysis of our precedents and the pertinent history of the writ, and accordingly join his dissent. The important point for me, however, is that the Court should have resolved these cases on other grounds. Habeas is most fundamentally a procedural right, a mechanism for contesting the legality of executive detention. The critical threshold question in these cases, prior to any inquiry about the writ's scope, is whether the system the political branches designed protects whatever rights the detainees may possess. If so, there is no need for any additional process, whether called "habeas" or something else.

Congress entrusted that threshold question in the first instance to the Court of Appeals for the District of Columbia Circuit, as the Constitution surely allows Congress to do. But before the D.C. Circuit has addressed the issue, the Court cashiers the statute, and without answering this critical threshold question itself. The Court does eventually get around to asking whether review under the DTA is, as the Court frames it, an "adequate substitute" for habeas, but even then its opinion fails to determine what rights the detainees possess and whether the DTA system satisfies them. The majority instead compares the undefined DTA process to an equally undefined habeas right—one that is to be given shape only in the future by district courts on a case-by-case basis. This whole approach is misguided.

It is also fruitless. How the detainees' claims will be decided now that the DTA is gone is anybody's guess. But the habeas process the Court mandates will most likely end up looking a lot like the DTA system it replaces, as the district court judges shaping it will have to reconcile review of the prisoners' detention with the undoubted need to protect the American people from the terrorist threat—precisely the challenge Congress undertook in drafting the DTA. All that today's opinion has done is shift responsibility for those sensitive foreign policy and national security decisions from the elected branches to the Federal Judiciary.

I believe the system the political branches constructed adequately protects any constitutional rights aliens captured abroad and detained as enemy combatants may enjoy. I therefore would dismiss these cases on that ground. With all respect for the contrary views of the majority, I must dissent.

I

.... Given the posture in which these cases came to us, the Court should have declined to intervene until the D.C. Circuit had assessed the nature and validity of the congressionally mandated proceedings in a given detainee's case.

The political branches created a two-part, collateral review procedure for testing the legality of the prisoners' detention: It begins with a hearing before a Combatant Status Review Tribunal (CSRT) followed by review in the D.C. Circuit. As part of that review, Congress authorized the D.C. Circuit to decide whether the CSRT proceedings are consistent with "the Constitution and laws of the United States." No petitioner, however, has invoked the D.C. Circuit review the statute specifies. As a consequence, that court has had no occasion to decide whether the CSRT hearings, followed by review in the Court of Appeals, vindicate whatever constitutional and statutory rights petitioners may possess.

Remarkably, this Court does not require petitioners to exhaust their remedies under the statute; it does not wait to see whether those remedies will prove sufficient to protect petitioners' rights. Instead, it not only denies the D.C. Circuit the opportunity to assess the statute's remedies, it refuses to do so itself: the majority expressly declines to decide whether the CSRT procedures, coupled with Article III review, satisfy due process.

It is grossly premature to pronounce on the detainees' right to habeas without first assessing whether the remedies the DTA system provides vindicate whatever rights petitioners may claim. The plurality in *Hamdi v. Rumsfeld* explained that the Constitution guaranteed an American *citizen* challenging his detention as an enemy combatant the right to "notice of the factual basis for his classification, and a fair opportunity to rebut the Government's factual assertions before a neutral decisionmaker." The plurality specifically stated that constitutionally adequate collateral process could be provided "by an appropriately authorized and properly constituted military tribunal," given the "uncommon potential to burden the Executive at a time of ongoing military conflict." This point is directly pertinent here, for surely the Due Process Clause does not afford *non*-citizens in such circumstances greater protection than citizens are due.

If the CSRT procedures meet the minimal due process requirements outlined in *Hamdi,* and if an Article III court is available to ensure that these procedures are followed in future cases, there is no need to reach the Suspension Clause question. Detainees will have received all the process the Constitution could possibly require, whether that process is called "habeas" or something else. The question of the writ's reach need not be addressed.

* * * *

The Court is ... concerned that requiring petitioners to pursue "DTA review before proceeding with their habeas corpus actions" could involve additional delay. The nature of the habeas remedy the Court instructs lower courts to craft on remand, however, is far more unsettled than the process Congress provided in the DTA. There is no reason to suppose that review according to procedures the Federal Judiciary will design, case by case, will proceed any faster than the DTA process petitioners disdained.

On the contrary, the system the Court has launched (and directs lower courts to elaborate) promises to take longer. The Court assures us that before bringing their habeas petitions, detainees must usually complete the CSRT process. Then they may seek review in federal district court. Either success or failure there will surely result in an appeal to the D.C. Circuit — exactly where judicial review *starts* under Congress' system. The effect of the Court's decision is to add additional layers of quite possibly redundant review. And because nobody knows how these new layers of "habeas" review will operate, or what new procedures they will require, their contours will undoubtedly be subject to fresh bouts of litigation. If the majority were truly concerned about delay, it would have required petitioners to use the DTA process that has been available to them for 2 1/2 years, with its Article III review in the D.C. Circuit. That system might well have provided petitioners all the relief to which they are entitled long before the Court's newly installed habeas review could hope to do so.

The Court's refusal to require petitioners to exhaust the remedies provided by Congress violates the "traditional rules governing our decision of constitutional questions." The Court's disrespect for these rules makes its decision an awkward business. It rushes to decide the fundamental question of the reach of habeas corpus when the functioning of the DTA may make that decision entirely unnecessary, and it does so with scant idea of how DTA judicial review will actually operate.

II

The majority's overreaching is particularly egregious given the weakness of its objections to the DTA. Simply put, the Court's opinion fails on its own terms. The majority strikes down the statute because it is not an "adequate substitute" for habeas review, but fails to show what rights the detainees have that cannot be vindicated by the DTA system.

Because the central purpose of habeas corpus is to test the legality of executive detention, the writ requires most fundamentally an Article III court able to hear the prisoner's claims and, when necessary, order release. Beyond that, the process a given prisoner is entitled to receive depends on the circumstances and the rights of the prisoner. [T]he majority appears to concede that the DTA provides an Article III court competent to order release. The only issue in dispute is the process the Guantanamo prisoners are entitled to use to test the legality of their detention. *Hamdi* concluded that American citizens detained as enemy combatants are entitled to only limited process, and that much of that process could be supplied by a military tribunal, with review to follow in an Article III court. That is precisely the system we have here. It is adequate to vindicate whatever due process rights petitioners may have.

A

The Court reaches the opposite conclusion partly because it misreads the statute. The majority appears not to understand how the review system it invalidates actually works — specifically, how CSRT review and review by the D.C. Circuit fit together. . . .

The Court attempts to explain its glancing treatment of the CSRTs by arguing that "[w]hether one characterizes the CSRT process as direct review of the Executive's battlefield determination . . . or as the first step in the collateral review of a battlefield determination makes no difference." First of all, the majority is quite wrong to dismiss the Executive's determination of detainee status as no more than a "battlefield" judgment, as if it were somehow provisional and made in great haste. In fact, detainees are designated "enemy combatants" only after "multiple levels of review by military officers and officials of the Department of Defense."

The majority is equally wrong to characterize the CSRTs as part of that initial determination process. They are instead a means for detainees to *challenge* the Government's determination. . . . The CSRTs operate much as habeas courts would if hearing the detainee's collateral challenge for the first time: They gather evidence, call witnesses, take testimony, and render a decision on the legality of the Government's detention. If the CSRT finds a particular detainee has been improperly held, it can order release.

The majority insists that even if "the CSRTs satisf[ied] due process standards," full habeas review would still be necessary, because habeas is a collateral remedy available even to prisoners "detained pursuant to the most rigorous proceedings imaginable." This comment makes sense only if the CSRTs are incorrectly viewed as a method used by the Executive for determining the prisoners' status, and not as themselves part of the collateral review to test the validity of that determination. The majority can deprecate the importance of the CSRTs only by treating them as something they are not.

* * * *

. . . CSRT review is just the first tier of collateral review in the DTA system. The statute provides additional review in an Article III court. Given the rationale of today's decision, it is well worth recalling exactly what the DTA provides in this respect. The statute directs the D.C. Circuit to consider whether a particular alien's status determination "was consistent with the standards and procedures specified by the Secretary of Defense" *and* "whether the use of such standards and procedures to make the determination is consistent with the Constitution and laws of the United States." That is, a *court* determines whether the CSRT procedures are constitutional, and a *court* determines whether those procedures were followed in a particular case.

In short, the *Hamdi* plurality concluded that this type of review would be enough to satisfy due process, even for citizens. Congress followed the Court's lead, only to find itself the victim of a constitutional bait and switch.

* * * *

B

Given the statutory scheme the political branches adopted, and given *Hamdi*, it simply will not do for the majority to dismiss the CSRT procedures as "far more limited" than those used in military trials, and therefore beneath the level of process "that would eliminate the need for habeas corpus review." The question is not how much process the CSRTs provide in comparison to other modes of adjudication. The question is whether the CSRT procedures—coupled with the judicial review specified by the DTA—provide the "basic process" *Hamdi* said the Constitution affords American citizens detained as enemy combatants.

By virtue of its refusal to allow the D.C. Circuit to assess petitioners' statutory remedies, and by virtue of its own refusal to consider, at the outset, the fit between those remedies and due process, the majority now finds itself in the position of evaluating whether the DTA system is an adequate substitute for habeas review without knowing what rights either habeas or the DTA is supposed to protect. The majority attempts to elide this problem by holding that petitioners have a right to habeas corpus and then comparing the DTA against the "historic office" of the writ. But habeas is, as the majority acknowledges, a flexible remedy rather than a substantive right. Its "precise application . . . change[s] depending upon the circumstances." The shape of habeas review ultimately depends on the nature of the rights a petitioner may assert.

The scope of federal habeas review is traditionally more limited in some contexts than in others, depending on the status of the detainee and the rights he may assert.

Declaring that petitioners have a right to habeas in no way excuses the Court from explaining why the DTA does not protect whatever due process or statutory rights petitioners may have. Because if the DTA provides a means for vindicating petitioners' rights, it is necessarily an adequate substitute for habeas corpus.

For my part, I will assume that any due process rights petitioners may possess are no greater than those of American citizens detained as enemy combatants. It is worth noting again that the *Hamdi* controlling opinion said the Constitution guarantees citizen detainees only "basic" procedural rights, and that the process for securing those rights can "be tailored to alleviate [the] uncommon potential to burden the Executive at a time of ongoing military conflict." The majority, however, objects that "the procedural protections afforded to the detainees in the CSRT hearings are . . . limited." But the evidentiary and other limitations the Court complains of reflect the nature of the issue in contest, namely, the status of aliens captured by our Armed Forces abroad and alleged to be enemy combatants. Contrary to the repeated suggestions of the majority, DTA review need not parallel the habeas privileges enjoyed by noncombatant American citizens, as set out in 28 U.S.C. § 2241. It need only provide process adequate for noncitizens detained as alleged combatants.

To what basic process are these detainees due as habeas petitioners? We have said that "at the absolute minimum," the Suspension Clause protects the writ "'as it existed in 1789.'" *St. Cyr.* The majority admits that a number of historical authorities suggest that at the time of the Constitution's ratification, "common-law courts abstained altogether from matters involving prisoners of war." If this is accurate, the process provided prisoners under the DTA is plainly more than sufficient — it allows alleged combatants to challenge both the factual and legal bases of their detentions.

Assuming the constitutional baseline is more robust, the DTA still provides adequate process, and by the majority's own standards. Today's Court opines that the Suspension Clause guarantees prisoners such as the detainees "a meaningful opportunity to demonstrate that [they are] being held pursuant to the erroneous application or interpretation of relevant law." Further, the Court holds that to be an adequate substitute, any tribunal reviewing the detainees' cases "must have the power to order the conditional release of an individual unlawfully detained." The DTA system — CSRT review of the Executive's determination followed by D.C. Circuit review for sufficiency of the evidence and the constitutionality of the CSRT process — meets these criteria.

C

At the CSRT stage, every petitioner has the right to present evidence that he has been wrongfully detained. This includes the right to call witnesses who are reasonably available, question witnesses called by the tribunal, introduce documentary evidence, and testify before the tribunal. [The Chief Justice then described the means under the regulations by which the petitioners could challenge the government's evidence and introduce his or her own. The majority had largely rejected these methods as illusory.]

All told, the DTA provides the prisoners held at Guantanamo Bay adequate opportunity to contest the bases of their detentions, which is all habeas corpus need allow. The DTA provides more opportunity and more process, in fact, than that afforded prisoners of war or any other alleged enemy combatants in history.

D

Despite these guarantees, the Court finds the DTA system an inadequate habeas substitute, for one central reason: Detainees are unable to introduce at the appeal stage exculpatory evidence discovered after the conclusion of their CSRT proceedings. The Court hints darkly that the DTA may suffer from other infirmities, but it does not bother to name them, making a response a bit difficult. As it stands, I can only assume the Court regards the supposed defect it did identify as the gravest of the lot.

If this is the most the Court can muster, the ice beneath its feet is thin indeed. As noted, the CSRT procedures provide ample opportunity for detainees to introduce exculpatory evidence—whether documentary in nature or from live witnesses—before the military tribunals. And if their ability to introduce such evidence is denied contrary to the Constitution or laws of the United States, the D.C. Circuit has the authority to say so on review.

Nevertheless, the Court asks us to imagine an instance in which evidence is discovered *after* the CSRT panel renders its decision, but *before* the Court of Appeals reviews the detainee's case. This scenario, which of course has not yet come to pass as no review in the D.C. Circuit has occurred, provides no basis for rejecting the DTA as a habeas substitute. While the majority is correct that the DTA does not contemplate the introduction of "newly discovered" evidence before the Court of Appeals, petitioners and the Solicitor General agree that the DTA *does* permit the D.C. Circuit to remand a detainee's case for a new CSRT determination. In the event a detainee alleges that he has obtained new and persuasive exculpatory evidence that would have been considered by the tribunal below had it only been available, the D.C. Circuit could readily remand the case to the tribunal to allow that body to consider the evidence in the first instance. The Court of Appeals could later review any new or reinstated decision in light of the supplemented record.

If that sort of procedure sounds familiar, it should. Federal appellate courts reviewing factual determinations follow just such a procedure in a variety of circumstances.

A remand is not the only relief available for detainees caught in the Court's hypothetical conundrum. The DTA expressly directs the Secretary of Defense to "provide for periodic review of any new evidence that may become available relating to the enemy combatant status of a detainee." Regulations issued by the Department of Defense provide that when a detainee puts forward new, material evidence "not previously presented to the detainee's CSRT," the Deputy

Secretary of Defense "'will direct that a CSRT convene to reconsider the basis of the detainee's . . . status in light of the new information.'" Pursuant to DTA § 1005(e)(2)(A), the resulting CSRT determination is again reviewable in full by the D.C. Circuit.

In addition, DTA § 1005(d)(1) further requires the Department of Defense to conduct a yearly review of the status of each prisoner. The Deputy Secretary of Defense has promulgated concomitant regulations establishing an Administrative Review Board to assess "annually the need to continue to detain each enemy combatant." In the words of the implementing order, the purpose of this annual review is to afford every detainee the opportunity "to explain why he is no longer a threat to the United States" and should be released. The Board's findings are forwarded to a presidentially appointed, Senate-confirmed civilian within the Department of Defense whom the Secretary of Defense has designated to administer the review process. This designated civilian official has the authority to order release upon the Board's recommendation.

The Court's hand wringing over the DTA's treatment of later-discovered exculpatory evidence is the most it has to show after a roving search for constitutionally problematic scenarios. But "[t]he delicate power of pronouncing an Act of Congress unconstitutional," we have said, "is not to be exercised with reference to hypothetical cases thus imagined." The Court today invents a sort of reverse facial challenge and applies it with gusto: If there is *any* scenario in which the statute *might* be constitutionally infirm, the law must be struck down. The Court's new method of constitutional adjudication only underscores its failure to follow our usual procedures and require petitioners to demonstrate that *they* have been harmed by the statute they challenge. In the absence of such a concrete showing, the Court is unable to imagine a plausible hypothetical in which the DTA is unconstitutional.

E

[In this section, the Chief Justice explained why the DTA should be interpreted to allow a court to order a detainee's release under certain circumstances.]

III

For all its eloquence about the detainees' right to the writ, the Court makes no effort to elaborate how exactly the remedy it prescribes will differ from the procedural protections detainees enjoy under the DTA. The Court objects to the detainees' limited access to witnesses and classified material, but proposes no alternatives of its own. Indeed, it simply ignores the many difficult questions its holding presents. What, for example, will become of the CSRT process? The majority says federal courts should *generally* refrain from entertaining detainee challenges until after the petitioner's CSRT proceeding has finished. But to what deference, if any, is that CSRT determination entitled?

There are other problems. Take witness availability. What makes the majority think witnesses will become magically available when the review procedure is labeled "habeas"? Will the location of most of these witnesses change — will they suddenly become easily susceptible to service of process? Or will subpoenas issued by American habeas courts run to Basra? And if they did, how would they be enforced? Speaking of witnesses, will detainees be able to call active-duty military officers as witnesses? If not, why not?

The majority has no answers for these difficulties. What it does say leaves open the distinct possibility that its "habeas" remedy will, when all is said and done, end up looking a great deal like the DTA review it rejects. But "[t]he role of the judiciary is limited to determining whether the procedures meet the essential standard of fairness under the Due Process Clause and does not extend to imposing procedures that merely displace congressional choices of policy."

The majority rests its decision on abstract and hypothetical concerns. Step back and consider what, in the real world, Congress and the Executive have actually granted aliens captured by our Armed Forces overseas and found to be enemy combatants:

- The right to hear the bases of the charges against them, including a summary of any classified evidence.
- The ability to challenge the bases of their detention before military tribunals modeled after Geneva Convention procedures. Some 38 detainees have been released as a result of this process.
- The right, before the CSRT, to testify, introduce evidence, call witnesses, question those the Government calls, and secure release, if and when appropriate.
- The right to the aid of a personal representative in arranging and presenting their cases before a CSRT.
- Before the D.C. Circuit, the right to employ counsel, challenge the factual record, contest the lower tribunal's legal determinations, ensure compliance with the Constitution and laws, and secure release, if any errors below establish their entitlement to such relief.

In sum, the DTA satisfies the majority's own criteria for assessing adequacy. This statutory scheme provides the combatants held at Guantanamo greater procedural protections than have ever been afforded alleged enemy detainees—whether citizens or aliens—in our national history.

* * * [Break in the Chief Justice's dissent.]

So who has won? Not the detainees. The Court's analysis leaves them with only the prospect of further litigation to determine the content of their new habeas right, followed by further litigation to resolve their particular cases, followed by further litigation before the D.C. Circuit—where they could have started had they invoked the DTA procedure. Not Congress, whose attempt to "determine—through democratic means—how best" to balance the security of the American people with the detainees' liberty interests, has been unceremoniously brushed aside. Not the Great Writ, whose majesty is hardly enhanced by its extension to a jurisdictionally quirky outpost, with no tangible benefit to anyone. Not the rule of law, unless by that is meant the rule of lawyers, who will now arguably have a greater role than military and intelligence officials in shaping policy for alien enemy combatants. And certainly not the American people, who today lose a bit more control over the conduct of this Nation's foreign policy to unelected, politically unaccountable judges.

I respectfully dissent.

JUSTICE SCALIA, with whom THE CHIEF JUSTICE, JUSTICE THOMAS, and JUSTICE ALITO join, dissenting.

Today, for the first time in our Nation's history, the Court confers a constitutional right to habeas corpus on alien enemies detained abroad by our military forces in the course of an ongoing war. The Chief Justice's dissent, which I join, shows that the procedures prescribed by Congress in the Detainee Treatment Act provide the essential protections that habeas corpus guarantees; there has thus been no suspension of the writ, and no basis exists for judicial intervention beyond what the Act allows. My problem with today's opinion is more fundamental still: The writ of habeas corpus does not, and never has, run in favor of aliens abroad; the Suspension Clause thus has no application, and the Court's intervention in this military matter is entirely *ultra vires.*

I shall devote most of what will be a lengthy opinion to the legal errors contained in the opinion of the Court. Contrary to my usual practice, however, I think it appropriate to begin with a description of the disastrous consequences of what the Court has done today.

I

America is at war with radical Islamists. The enemy began by killing Americans and American allies abroad: 241 at the Marine barracks in Lebanon, 19 at the Khobar Towers in Dhahran, 224 at our embassies in Dar es Salaam and Nairobi, and 17 on the USS Cole in Yemen. On September 11, 2001, the enemy brought the battle to American soil, killing 2,749 at the Twin Towers in New York City, 184 at the Pentagon in Washington, D.C., and 40 in Pennsylvania. It has threatened further attacks against our homeland; one need only walk about buttressed and barricaded Washington, or board a plane anywhere in the country, to know that the threat is a serious one. Our Armed Forces are now in the field against the enemy, in Afghanistan and Iraq. Last week, 13 of our countrymen in arms were killed.

The game of bait-and-switch that today's opinion plays upon the Nation's Commander in Chief will make the war harder on us. It will almost certainly cause more Americans to be killed. That consequence would be tolerable if necessary to preserve a time-honored legal principle vital to our constitutional Republic. But it is this Court's blatant *abandonment* of such a principle that produces the decision today. The President relied on our settled precedent in *Johnson v. Eisentrager* when he established the prison at Guantanamo Bay for enemy aliens. Citing that case, the President's Office of Legal Counsel advised him "that the great weight of legal authority indicates that a federal district court could not properly exercise habeas jurisdiction over an alien detained at [Guantanamo Bay]." Had the law been otherwise, the military surely would not have transported prisoners there, but would have kept them in Afghanistan, transferred them to another of our foreign military bases, or turned them over to allies for detention. Those other facilities might well have been worse for the detainees themselves.

In the long term, then, the Court's decision today accomplishes little, except perhaps to reduce the well-being of enemy combatants that the Court ostensibly seeks to protect. In the short term, however, the decision is devastating. At least 30 of those prisoners hitherto released from Guantanamo Bay have returned to the battlefield. Some have been captured or killed. But others have succeeded in carrying on their atrocities against innocent civilians. In one case, a detainee released from Guantanamo Bay masterminded the kidnapping of two Chinese dam workers, one of whom was later shot to death when used as a human shield against Pakistani commandoes. Another former detainee promptly resumed his post as a senior Taliban commander and murdered a United Nations engineer and three Afghan soldiers. Still another murdered an Afghan judge. It was reported only last month that a released detainee carried out a suicide bombing against Iraqi soldiers in Mosul, Iraq.

These, mind you, were detainees whom *the military* had concluded were not enemy combatants. Their return to the kill illustrates the incredible difficulty of assessing who is and who is not an enemy combatant in a foreign theater of operations where the environment does not lend itself to rigorous evidence collection. Astoundingly, the Court today raises the bar, requiring military officials to appear before civilian courts and defend their decisions under procedural and evidentiary rules that go beyond what Congress has specified. As The Chief Justice's dissent makes clear, we have no idea what those procedural and evidentiary rules are, but they will be determined by civil courts and (in the Court's contemplation at least) will be more detainee-friendly than those now applied, since otherwise there would no reason to hold the congressionally prescribed procedures unconstitutional. If they impose a higher standard of proof (from foreign battlefields) than the current procedures require, the number of the enemy returned to combat will obviously increase.

But even when the military has evidence that it can bring forward, it is often foolhardy to release that evidence to the attorneys representing our enemies. And one escalation of procedures that the Court *is* clear about is affording the detainees increased access to witnesses (perhaps troops serving in Afghanistan?) and to classified information. During the 1995 prosecution of Omar Abdel Rahman, federal prosecutors gave the names of 200 unindicted co-conspirators to the "Blind Sheik's" defense lawyers; that information was in the hands of Osama Bin Laden within two weeks. In another case, trial testimony revealed to the enemy that the United States had been monitoring their cellular network, whereupon they promptly stopped using it, enabling more of them to evade capture and continue their atrocities.

And today it is not just the military that the Court elbows aside. A mere two Terms ago in *Hamdan v. Rumsfeld* when the Court held (quite amazingly) that the Detainee Treatment Act of 2005 had not stripped habeas jurisdiction over Guantanamo petitioners' claims, four Members of today's five-Justice majority joined an opinion saying the following:

> "Nothing prevents the President from returning to Congress to seek the authority [for trial by military commission] he believes necessary.
>
> "Where, as here, no emergency prevents consultation with Congress, judicial insistence upon that consultation does not weaken our Nation's ability to deal with danger. To the contrary, that insistence strengthens the Nation's ability to determine—through democratic means—how best to do so. The Constitution places its faith in those democratic means." (Breyer, J., concurring).[26]

26. [Footnote 1 in Justice Scalia's dissent.] Even today, the Court cannot resist striking a pose of faux deference to Congress and the President. Citing the above quoted passage, the Court says: "The political branches, consistent with their independent obligations to interpret and uphold the Constitution, can engage in a genuine debate about how best to preserve constitutional values

Turns out they were just kidding. For in response, Congress, at the President's request, quickly enacted the Military Commissions Act, emphatically reasserting that it did not want these prisoners filing habeas petitions. It is therefore clear that Congress and the Executive — *both* political branches — have determined that limiting the role of civilian courts in adjudicating whether prisoners captured abroad are properly detained is important to success in the war that some 190,000 of our men and women are now fighting. As the Solicitor General argued, "the Military Commissions Act and the Detainee Treatment Act . . . represent an effort by the political branches to strike an appropriate balance between the need to preserve liberty and the need to accommodate the weighty and sensitive governmental interests in ensuring that those who have in fact fought with the enemy during a war do not return to battle against the United States."

But it does not matter. The Court today decrees that no good reason to accept the judgment of the other two branches is "apparent." "The Government," it declares, "presents no credible arguments that the military mission at Guantanamo would be compromised if habeas corpus courts had jurisdiction to hear the detainees' claims." What competence does the Court have to second-guess the judgment of Congress and the President on such a point? None whatever. But the Court blunders in nonetheless. Henceforth, as today's opinion makes unnervingly clear, how to handle enemy prisoners in this war will ultimately lie with the branch that knows least about the national security concerns that the subject entails.

II

A

The Suspension Clause of the Constitution provides: "The Privilege of the Writ of Habeas Corpus shall not be suspended, unless when in Cases of Rebellion or Invasion the public Safety may require it." Art. I, § 9, cl. 2. As a court of law operating under a written Constitution, our role is to determine whether there is a conflict between that Clause and the Military Commissions Act. A conflict arises only if the Suspension Clause preserves the privilege of the writ for aliens held by the United States military as enemy combatants at the base in Guantanamo Bay, located within the sovereign territory of Cuba.

We have frequently stated that we owe great deference to Congress' view that a law it has passed is constitutional. That is especially so in the area of foreign and military affairs; "perhaps in no other area has the Court accorded Congress greater deference." Indeed, we accord great deference even when the President acts alone in this area.

In light of those principles of deference, the Court's conclusion that "the common law [does not] yiel[d] a definite answer to the questions before us," leaves it no choice but to affirm the Court of Appeals. The writ as preserved in the Constitution could not possibly extend farther than the common law provided when that Clause was written. The Court admits that it cannot determine whether the writ historically extended to aliens held abroad, and it concedes (necessarily) that Guantanamo Bay lies outside the sovereign territory of

---

while protecting the Nation from terrorism." Indeed. What the Court apparently means is that the political branches can debate, after which the Third Branch will decide.

the United States. Together, these two concessions establish that it is (in the Court's view) perfectly ambiguous whether the common-law writ would have provided a remedy for these petitioners. If that is so, the Court has no basis to strike down the Military Commissions Act, and must leave undisturbed the considered judgment of the coequal branches.

How, then, does the Court weave a clear constitutional prohibition out of pure interpretive equipoise? The Court resorts to "fundamental separation-of-powers principles" to interpret the Suspension Clause. According to the Court, because "the writ of habeas corpus is itself an indispensable mechanism for monitoring the separation of powers," the test of its extraterritorial reach "must not be subject to manipulation by those whose power it is designed to restrain."

That approach distorts the nature of the separation of powers and its role in the constitutional structure. The "fundamental separation-of-powers principles" that the Constitution embodies are to be derived not from some judicially imagined matrix, but from the sum total of the individual separation-of-powers provisions that the Constitution sets forth. Only by considering them one-by-one does the full shape of the *Constitution's* separation-of-powers principles emerge. It is nonsensical to interpret those provisions themselves in light of some general "separation-of-powers principles" dreamed up by the Court. Rather, they must be interpreted to mean what they were understood to mean when the people ratified them. And if the understood scope of the writ of habeas corpus was "designed to restrain" (as the Court says) the actions of the Executive, the understood *limits* upon that scope were (as the Court seems not to grasp) just as much "designed to restrain" the incursions of the Third Branch. "Manipulation" of the territorial reach of the writ by the Judiciary poses just as much a threat to the proper separation of powers as "manipulation" by the Executive. As I will show below, manipulation is what is afoot here. The understood limits upon the writ deny our jurisdiction over the habeas petitions brought by these enemy aliens, and entrust the President with the crucial wartime determinations about their status and continued confinement.

B

The Court purports to derive from our precedents a "functional" test for the extraterritorial reach of the writ, which shows that the Military Commissions Act unconstitutionally restricts the scope of habeas. That is remarkable because the most pertinent of those precedents, *Johnson v. Eisentrager*, conclusively establishes the opposite. . . .

* * * *

Eisentrager thus held—*held* beyond any doubt—that the Constitution does not ensure habeas for aliens held by the United States in areas over which our Government is not sovereign.

The Court would have us believe that *Eisentrager* rested on "[p]ractical considerations," such as the "difficulties of ordering the Government to produce the prisoners in a habeas corpus proceeding." Formal sovereignty, says the Court, is merely one consideration "that bears upon which constitutional guarantees apply" in a given location. This is a sheer rewriting of the case. *Eisentrager* mentioned practical concerns, to be sure—but not for the purpose of determining *under what circumstances* American courts could issue writs of habeas corpus for aliens abroad. It cited them to support *its holding* that the

Constitution does not empower courts to issue writs of habeas corpus to aliens abroad *in any circumstances*. . . .

The Court also tries to change *Eisentrager* into a "functional" test by quoting a paragraph that lists the characteristics of the German petitioners: [Justice Scalia listed the six factors from the case.] But that paragraph is introduced by a sentence stating that "[t]he foregoing demonstrates *how much further we must go* if we are to invest these enemy aliens, resident, captured and imprisoned abroad, with standing to demand access to our courts." How much further than *what*? Further than the rule set forth in the prior section of the opinion, which said that "in extending constitutional protections beyond the citizenry, the Court has been at pains to point out that it was the alien's presence within its territorial jurisdiction that gave the Judiciary power to act." In other words, the characteristics of the German prisoners were set forth, not in application of some "functional" test, but to show that the case before the Court represented an *a fortiori* application of the ordinary rule. . . . *Eisentrager* nowhere mentions a "functional" test, and the notion that it is based upon such a principle is patently false.

* * * *

The Court tries to reconcile *Eisentrager* with its holding today by pointing out that in postwar Germany, the United States was "answerable to its Allies" and did not "pla[n] a long-term occupation." Those factors were not mentioned in *Eisentrager*. Worse still, it is impossible to see how they relate to the Court's asserted purpose in creating this "functional" test—namely, to ensure a judicial inquiry into detention and prevent the political branches from acting with impunity. Can it possibly be that the Court trusts the political branches more when they are beholden to foreign powers than when they act alone?

After transforming the *a fortiori* elements discussed above into a "functional" test, the Court is still left with the difficulty that most of those elements exist here as well with regard to all the detainees. To make the application of the newly crafted "functional" test produce a different result in the present cases, the Court must rely upon factors (d) and (e): The Germans had been tried by a military commission for violations of the laws of war; the present petitioners, by contrast, have been tried by a Combatant Status Review Tribunal (CSRT) whose procedural protections, according to the Court's *ipse dixit*, "fall well short of the procedures and adversarial mechanisms that would eliminate the need for habeas corpus review." But no one looking for "functional" equivalents would put *Eisentrager* and the present cases in the same category, much less place the present cases in a preferred category. The difference between them cries out for lesser procedures in the present cases. The prisoners in *Eisentrager* were *prosecuted* for crimes after the cessation of hostilities; the prisoners here are enemy combatants *detained* during an ongoing conflict.

The category of prisoner comparable to these detainees are not the *Eisentrager* criminal defendants, but the more than 400,000 prisoners of war detained in the United States alone during World War II. Not a single one was accorded the right to have his detention validated by a habeas corpus action in federal court—and that despite the fact that they were present on U.S. soil. The Court's analysis produces a crazy result: Whereas those convicted and sentenced to death for war crimes are without judicial remedy, all enemy combatants detained during a war, at least insofar as they are confined in an area away from the battlefield over which the United States exercises "absolute and indefinite" control, may seek a writ of habeas corpus in federal court. And, as an even more bizarre implication from the Court's reasoning, those prisoners whom the military plans to try by full-dress Commission at a future date may file habeas petitions and secure release before their trials take place.

There is simply no support for the Court's assertion that constitutional rights extend to aliens held outside U.S. sovereign territory, and *Eisentrager* could not be clearer that the privilege of habeas corpus does not extend to aliens abroad. By blatantly distorting *Eisentrager*, the Court avoids the difficulty of explaining why it should be overruled. The rule that aliens abroad are not constitutionally entitled to habeas corpus has not proved unworkable in practice; if anything, it is the Court's "functional" test that does not (and never will) provide clear guidance for the future. *Eisentrager* forms a coherent whole with the accepted proposition that aliens abroad have no substantive rights under our Constitution. Since it was announced, no relevant factual premises have changed. It has engendered considerable reliance on the part of our military. And, as the Court acknowledges, text and history do not clearly compel a contrary ruling. It is a sad day for the rule of law when such an important constitutional precedent is discarded without an *apologia*, much less an apology.

C

What drives today's decision is neither the meaning of the Suspension Clause, nor the principles of our precedents, but rather an inflated notion of judicial supremacy. The Court says that if the extraterritorial applicability of the Suspension Clause turned on formal notions of sovereignty, "it would be possible for the political branches to govern without legal constraint" in areas beyond the sovereign territory of the United States. That cannot be, the Court says, because it is the duty of this Court to say what the law is. It would be difficult to imagine a more question-begging analysis. "The very foundation of the power of the federal courts to declare Acts of Congress unconstitutional lies in the power and duty of those courts to decide cases and controversies *properly before them.*" Our power "to say what the law is" is circumscribed by the limits of our statutorily and constitutionally conferred jurisdiction. And that is precisely the question in these cases: whether the Constitution confers habeas jurisdiction on federal courts to decide petitioners' claims. It is both irrational and arrogant to say that the answer must be yes, because otherwise we would not be supreme.

But so long as there are *some* places to which habeas does not run — so long as the Court's new "functional" test will not be satisfied *in every case* — then there will be circumstances in which "it would be possible for the political branches to govern without legal constraint." Or, to put it more impartially, areas in which the legal determinations of the *other* branches will be (shudder!) *supreme.* In other words, judicial supremacy is not really assured by the constitutional rule that the Court creates. The gap between rationale and rule leads me to conclude that the Court's ultimate, unexpressed goal is to preserve the power to review the confinement of enemy prisoners held by the Executive anywhere in the world. The "functional" test usefully evades the precedential landmine of *Eisentrager* but is so inherently subjective that it clears a wide path for the Court to traverse in the years to come.

III

Putting aside the conclusive precedent of *Eisentrager*, it is clear that the original understanding of the Suspension Clause was that habeas corpus was not available to aliens abroad. . . . [Justice Scalia then canvassed the historical record and concluded that the writ would not have run in favor of petitioners such as those at issue in the case. He continued:]

* * * *

In sum, *all* available historical evidence points to the conclusion that the writ would not have been available at common law for aliens captured and held outside the sovereign territory of the Crown. . . . The Court finds it significant that there is no recorded case *denying* jurisdiction to such prisoners either. But a case standing for the remarkable proposition that the writ could issue to a foreign land would surely have been reported, whereas a case denying such a writ for lack of jurisdiction would likely not. At a minimum, the absence of a reported case either way leaves unrefuted the voluminous commentary stating that habeas was confined to the dominions of the Crown.

What history teaches is confirmed by the nature of the limitations that the Constitution places upon suspension of the common-law writ. It can be suspended only "in Cases of Rebellion or Invasion." Art. I, § 9, cl. 2. The latter case (invasion) is plainly limited to the territory of the United States; and while it is conceivable that a rebellion could be mounted by American citizens abroad, surely the overwhelming majority of its occurrences would be domestic. If the extraterritorial scope of habeas turned on flexible, "functional" considerations, as the Court holds, why would the Constitution limit its suspension almost entirely to instances of domestic crisis? Surely there is an even greater justification for suspension in foreign lands where the United States might hold prisoners of war during an ongoing conflict. And correspondingly, there is less threat to liberty when the Government suspends the writ's (supposed) application in foreign lands, where even on the most extreme view prisoners are entitled to fewer constitutional rights. It makes no sense, therefore, for the Constitution generally to forbid suspension of the writ abroad if indeed the writ has application there.

* * * *

In sum, because I conclude that the text and history of the Suspension Clause provide no basis for our jurisdiction, I would affirm the Court of Appeals even if *Eisentrager* did not govern these cases.

* * * [Break in Justice Scalia's dissent.]

Today the Court warps our Constitution in a way that goes beyond the narrow issue of the reach of the Suspension Clause, invoking judicially brainstormed separation-of-powers principles to establish a manipulable "functional" test for the extraterritorial reach of habeas corpus (and, no doubt, for the extraterritorial reach of other constitutional protections as well). It blatantly misdescribes important precedents, most conspicuously Justice Jackson's opinion for the Court in *Johnson v. Eisentrager*. It breaks a chain of precedent as old as the common law that prohibits judicial inquiry into detentions of aliens abroad absent statutory authorization. And, most tragically, it sets our military commanders the impossible task of proving to a civilian court, under whatever standards this Court devises in the future, that evidence supports the confinement of each and every enemy prisoner.

The Nation will live to regret what the Court has done today. I dissent.

DISCUSSION AND QUESTIONS

Boumediene answers some questions but leaves many other matters open for debate. Begin with the clearly established parts of the decision. The Court left no doubt that the writ of habeas corpus runs to those detained at Guantanamo Bay. The Court took the step left untaken in *Rasul* by holding that the Suspension Clause does not allow Congress to block access to the federal courts for those held at the Naval Base in Cuba unless it validly suspends the writ or creates an adequate substitute procedure. Thus, for purposes of at least the Suspension Clause, Guantanamo Bay can be said to be functionally as much a part of the United States as Des Moines, Iowa.[27]

Second, because of its holding concerning the applicability of the Suspension Clause to Guantanamo Bay, the Court has ensured that the federal courts will retain a meaningful role in dealing with the War on Terror. Justice Kennedy views such involvement as critical to separation-of-powers principles, while Justice Scalia views it as fundamentally inconsistent with such principles. Who has the better argument based on the constitutional principles we have discussed in the course?

Third, *Boumediene* tells us a bit more about the meaning of the Suspension Clause itself. The Court has had relatively few occasions to consider the clause in its history.[28] In recent times, the Court had made clear that the clause itself protects some form of habeas corpus. In *INS v. St. Cyr*, the Court held that the Suspension Clause "at a minimum" protects the writ as it existed in 1789.[29] We know after *Boumediene* that a failure clearly to establish that the writ in fact reached a certain situation in 1789 is not fatal to a claim that your right to seek this form of relief is constitutionally protected. After all, Justice Kennedy forthrightly admitted that the historical evidence was not clear in the case before the Court.

Fourth, we know from *Boumediene* that the procedures Congress established for review of enemy combatant determination in the DTA are not adequate substitutes for habeas corpus. Correspondingly, the Court also reaffirmed that the Suspension Clause requires that a federal court exercising habeas corpus jurisdiction must have real tools with which to perform its work, such as the ability to meaningfully test the factual underpinnings of the government's claims.

While *Boumediene* made clear that the petitioners had a constitutionally protected right to pursue a writ of habeas corpus, the Court did not provide much in the way of guidance concerning many significant details both as to the substance of the constitutional claims at issue in these cases and regarding the procedural devices to be employed to adjudicate the claims. And the Court has not seen fit to return to the field after *Boumediene*. The development of the law in this area is largely beyond the scope of this text. The key point for present purposes is that the legal developments concerning the detainees held at Guantanamo Bay in

27. It may be that Guantanamo Bay is like Des Moines, Iowa, but Bagram Air Force Base in Afghanistan is not. In May 2010, the United States Court of Appeals for the District of Columbia Circuit held that the protections of the Suspension Clause did not extend to detainees held at a military prison on an Air Force base in Bagram in Afghanistan. The court applied the factors discussed in *Boumediene* to conclude that the Constitution did not require access to the Article III courts to challenge the legality of detention. The principal reason was that the prison facility was located in the equivalent of a war zone. *Al Maqaleh v. Gates*, 605 F.3d 84 (D.C. Cir. 2010).

28. The writ itself has only been suspended four times: once in the Civil War in certain areas, once during reconstruction in certain areas, once in the Philippines in 1905, and once in Hawaii during World War II.

29. 533 U.S. 289, 301 (1996).

the United States District Court for the District of Columbia and, most importantly, the United States Court of Appeals for the District of Columbia Circuit were only possible because of the decision in *Boumediene*. Simply put, the Supreme Court kept the courts in the game.

We began this section with Problem 13-1, addressing broad constitutional questions underlying habeas review of executive detention. Return to that problem now. Would your briefing for Senator Jones differ after reading this material? If so, how? If not, why not?

2. *Habeas Corpus and State Court Detention*

This subsection considers federal courts' authority to grant writs of habeas corpus with respect to persons allegedly held in violation of federal law pursuant to the judgment of state courts. As such, values of federalism are implicated here far more than they are in connection with the material we addressed in the previous subsection. Today, the availability of habeas corpus in federal court for state prisoners is largely dictated by federal statutes. Most importantly as we will learn, Congress reshaped the landscape in this area in 1996, when it enacted the Antiterrorism and Effective Death Penalty Act (AEDPA).[30] It is on this statute, and the Supreme Court's interpretation of it, that we will principally focus. We begin, however, with a brief description of the development of the law of habeas corpus for state prisoners from 1867 (when federal courts first entered the field in a meaningful way) though 1996.

Before we begin, it is important to reiterate a point we made earlier in this chapter concerning the inherent limitations on studying habeas corpus in a Federal Courts course. Simply put, this is not a class in post-conviction relief. The law concerning habeas corpus for state prisoners is highly complex. Our goal is *not* to provide a complete detailed description of all facets of this area. Rather, we aim for two things in the context of this course dealing with the role of federal courts in the American constitutional system. First, we provide an overview—or perhaps better described, a road map—of the many hurdles a state prisoner needs to clear to obtain a writ of habeas corpus from a federal court. We consider some of these issues only superficially, while we address others in more detail. Second, for those issues into which we go in greater depth, we focus not just on the state of the law but also on the broader issues of federalism and separation of powers at the heart of the study of federal courts. What this means for you as a student is that you should always keep in mind how these broader principles are implicated in the detailed statutory environment in which we find ourselves.

a. Some Historical Background

While much of the historical background concerning federal courts' authority to grant writs of habeas corpus for persons in state custody is discussed below when considering the current state of the law, it is worthwhile to begin with at least a broad overview of that history. For all intents and purposes, the story of federal courts' power to consider habeas corpus petitions from state prisoners

30. Pub. L. No. 104-132, 110 Stat. 1214.

begins with the Act of February 5, 1867.[31] That statute extended federal courts' authority to grant writs of habeas corpus generally to those persons in state custody in violation of federal law. While it may seem odd that federal courts did not have the authority to issue the writ with respect to state prisoners before 1867, that state of affairs was consistent with the constitutional environment at the time. For example, as we discussed in Chapter 5, Congress did not confer general federal question jurisdiction on the federal courts until two decades after the Civil War. The development of federal law was left largely to the state courts, subject to some level of Supreme Court review. In addition, recall that the Bill of Rights did not apply to the states until the Fourteenth Amendment was ratified and then only as certain rights were incorporated through that provision's Due Process Clause.

In any event, there is a serious debate among federal courts scholars (as well as justices of the Supreme Court) concerning the types of errors that supported the grant of a writ of habeas corpus between the 1867 statute's enactment and the Supreme Court's seminal 1953 decision *Brown v. Allen.*[32] Some argue that the writ was used primarily to ensure that the state court had jurisdiction over the prisoner with respect to whom it entered a judgment. Under this theory, it was not used to police state court decisionmaking for constitutional errors generally.[33] The opposing historical view is that the writ reached beyond jurisdiction as a practical matter to consider a wide range of substantive constitutional claims, even if those claims were discussed in jurisdictional terms.[34]

Whatever the truth about the writ's use from 1867-1953, there is no question that the Court's decision in *Brown v. Allen* in 1953 is highly significant. Depending on one's view of history, it either changed the nature of federal habeas corpus review or brought the stated law into conformance with actual practice. In either event, however, it marked a turning point.

In *Brown,* the Supreme Court made unmistakably clear that, in the words of Professor Paul Bator, the statutory grant concerning federal habeas corpus provided federal courts with the authority to "redetermine the merits of federal constitutional questions decided in state criminal proceedings."[35] Thus, in the years after *Brown v. Allen,* the federal courts were actively involved in reviewing collateral challenges to state court constitutional decisions in the criminal procedure realm. This endeavor occurred simultaneously with, and may have been part and parcel of, the Warren Court's general development of constitutional criminal procedure doctrine during the late 1950s and 1960s.

31. *See* 14 Stat. 385. There were limited situations before 1867 in which Congress granted such authority to the federal courts. A prime example concerns the power to grant habeas corpus in connection with bankruptcy proceedings. This authority was used when states imprisoned debtors who may have had their debts discharged or otherwise abated in federal bankruptcy proceedings.

32. 344 U.S. 443 (1953).

33. Perhaps the most prominent academic advocate of this view is Professor Paul Bator. *See, e.g., Finality in Criminal Law and Federal Habeas Corpus for State Prisoners,* 76 HARV. L. REV. 441 (1963). On the Court, Justice Harlan also appeared to accept this understanding of the use of the writ from 1867-1953, *see Fay v. Noia,* 372 U.S. 391, 449 (1963) (Harlan, J., dissenting), as did Chief Justice Rehnquist writing for the Court in *Felker v. Turpin,* 518 U.S. 651 (1996).

34. *See, e.g.,* James Liebman, *Apocalypse Next Time?: The Anachronistic Attack on Habeas Corpus/Direct Review Parity,* 92 COLUM. L. REV. 1997 (1992); Ann Woolhandler, *Demodeling Habeas,* 45 STAN. L. REV. 575 (1993). Justice Brennan's majority opinion in *Faye v. Noia* also articulated this broader view of the role of habeas corpus in the period from 1867 to 1953. *See Faye v. Noia,* 372 U.S. 391 (1963).

35. Bator, *supra* note 33, at 500.

During the Burger and early Rehnquist Courts (basically from the early 1970s through the mid-1990s), the pendulum swung back from decisions broadly interpreting the federal courts' authority in this area toward a more restrictive view of that power. We will discuss many of these decisions in the context of what follows. In general, however, the Supreme Court began to interpret the statutes providing the federal courts with habeas jurisdiction over state prisoners in such a way that more deference was given to state court determinations and, correspondingly, state prisoners had a more difficult time pursuing their habeas corpus petitions in federal court.

In 1996, Congress entered the field in a dramatic way by significantly amending the statutory framework within which habeas corpus operates. These statutory revisions, as well as the Supreme Court's interpretations of them, provide the framework for the great majority of habeas corpus law today. We turn to that 1996 statute now.

b. The Law Under AEDPA

As we have learned, by 1996 the Supreme Court had begun to restrict the ability of state prisoners to obtain writs of habeas corpus from federal courts through a process of interpreting and reinterpreting federal statutes. For a host of reasons, some of which are not entirely clear, Congress decided to take matters into its own hands by enacting a set of sweeping reforms in the Antiterrorism and Effective Death Penalty Act of 1996.[36] The effect of AEDPA on the law in this area cannot be overstated. It was a sea change in the law that almost universally makes it far more difficult for a state prisoner to obtain federal habeas relief than had been the case previously. In this section, we consider the current statutory framework and how it has been interpreted. Note that although we present issues in a certain sequence, most often a federal court may consider issues in a number of different orders. We will highlight situations in which a particular order is required.[37]

EXPLORING DOCTRINE

Federalism and the Appropriate Role of Federal Courts

Whenever a federal court grants a writ of habeas corpus sought by a prisoner confined pursuant to the judgment of a state court, the federal judge must conclude that the person is held in violation of federal law. The federal error—almost always one of constitutional law—will already have been passed on by state court judges, usually including judges on state appellate courts, perhaps even the state supreme court. What

36. Congress provided for certain special procedures to be utilized in the context of state prisoners subject to death sentences. *See* 28 U.S.C. §§ 2261-2265. These provisions apply to states that adopt certain rules ensuring the appointment of counsel in state post-conviction proceedings for certain classes of prisoners. In general, habeas corpus proceedings in federal court are fast-tracked for such prisoners. We do not address these special capital sentencing procedures in this chapter.

37. You may also find it helpful to refer at times to Figure 13-8 below as you consider the material in this section. That Figure is a flowchart of various steps a federal court may consider in evaluating a state petitioner's habeas petition.

federalism issues are implicated by this state of affairs? Should the federal courts be concerned about them? If so, what is the appropriate magnitude of that concern?

When considering these matters, also think about the role of the federal courts in preserving individual rights. If there has in fact been a constitutional error, do the federal courts have an obligation to correct the error even if federalism values may be undermined? Why or why not?

i. A Statutory Overview and Preview of Coverage

As we have seen, habeas corpus is largely a creature of statute. That is particularly true in the context of petitions filed by state prisoners in federal court. Before we consider the relevant statutory provisions in detail, it is helpful to have a broad view of the landscape. Recall also that the generic matters we discussed above in the introductory portion of section C of the chapter concerning § 2241 apply in the context of state prisoners as well. For example, ensuring that the petitioner is actually "in custody" is required.[38] We will not reiterate the discussion of these concepts here.

In the balance of this subsection, we consider the following matters. You should not expect to understand the doctrines we outline here. This list is meant as a crude road map of sorts. It should be useful both as a preview of where we will go and also, at the end of this section, as a review of where we will have been.

- We begin by considering the foundational requirements for a federal court to grant a petition for a writ of habeas corpus of a person held pursuant to the judgment of a state court. These requirements are set forth in 28 U.S.C. § 2254(a). This section establishes a checklist for the basic requirements to grant the writ, although much of the details are dealt with in other sections and court opinions.
- Next, we discuss the statutorily mandated time limits (essentially statutes of limitations) within which state prisoners must file their petitions in order for a federal court to consider their claims at all. These time limits are set forth in 28 U.S.C. § 2244(d). We also consider various court-created doctrines under which these time limits may be tolled.
- The next topic concerns the requirement that a state prisoner seeking a writ of habeas corpus exhaust her state remedies to raise the alleged federal error. We explore both the statutory requirements under 28 U.S.C. §§ 2254(b) and (c) as well as the justifications for the rule in the first instance. We also consider how the rule should be applied when a state prisoner raises more than one federal error and she has exhausted her state remedies as to some but not all of the claims.

38. There tend to be few questions concerning the requirement that a federal court or judge act "within its respective jurisdiction" in the state prisoner context. One reason for this reality is § 2241(d)'s provision that in states with more than one federal judicial district a state prisoner may file her petition either in the district in which she is held in custody (i.e., the location of the prison) or in the district in which she was convicted.

- After considering exhaustion, the chapter turns to the importance of the reason the petitioner lost when she raised the error at issue in the state court system. One possibility is that the state court considered the federal issue and ruled against the petitioner. This is a decision "on the merits" of the claim. However, it is also possible that the state court might have ruled against the petitioner on a ground separate from the federal claim. For example, perhaps the petitioner did not file her appeal within the time provided by state law. If that is the case, the petitioner is said to have lost on the basis of a "procedural default" instead of on the merits. As we will see, if that is the case, it will be quite difficult for the petitioner to have the federal court reach the merits of her claim.
- Next, we consider what is, in many respects, the heart of the matter. How should a federal court go about evaluating the substantive merits of the petitioner's federal claims? It is on this topic that we will focus most attention because, among other reasons, it raises in the clearest terms the federalism and separation-of-powers concerns that have occupied us for much of the course. As we will see, the standards used to judge the merits of a petitioner's claim vary depending on whether that claim was decided on the merits (*see* 28 U.S.C. § 2254(d)) or whether the claim was decided based on a state procedural default and the petitioner has satisfied the high hurdle that would nevertheless justify a merits-based consideration in a federal court.
- After considering the standards used to judge the merits of a claim, we discuss under what circumstances a federal court may develop the factual record beyond that existing in the state court. *See, e.g.*, 28 U.S.C. § 2254(e). In many cases, if the petitioner is unable to obtain a federal court evidentiary hearing, she will be unlikely to succeed on her claims.
- We then consider the harmless error rule. As we will learn, even if a petitioner is able to navigate all the rocks in the habeas corpus sea, she will still not prevail if the court concludes that the error alleged would not have made a material difference in the outcome of the state court proceeding.
- Our final topic concerns situations in which a state prisoner seeks a writ of habeas corpus in federal court on more than one occasion. The bar to such second or successive petitions is quite high and is rarely able to be satisfied. *See* 28 U.S.C. § 2244(b). In sum, a state prisoner usually gets only one bite at the federal apple.

ii. The Foundational Requirements: 28 U.S.C. § 2254(a)

Read 28 U.S.C. § 2254(a). This provision sets the parameters of the federal courts' authority to issue writs of habeas corpus in the area we are considering. The Supreme Court has instructed that the foundational requirements of § 2254(a) should be considered before proceeding to the other matters we will discuss.[39] As an initial matter, note that the authority to grant writs with respect to state petitioners is conferred on all levels of the federal court system, from the Supreme Court through the district courts. In addition, it is important that the authority to grant the writ extends to "persons;" thus it is not limited to United States citizens. Of course, the authority is subject to limitation set forth in

39. *See Lambrix v. Singletary*, 520 U.S. 518, 524-25 (1997).

§ 2241(a) discussed above that the court (or judge) act "within [its] respective jurisdiction[]."[40]

The section applies when two basic conditions are present:

The petitioner must be "in custody pursuant to the judgment of a State court."

There is rarely a question about the latter part of this requirement concerning the presence of a state court judgment. There is also usually no issue concerning the requirement that the petitioner be "in custody." The stereotypical situation involves a person convicted of a crime and serving her sentence in a state correctional facility.

There are, however, situations in which the custodial requirement is less clear. Take, for example, the situation of a person on parole. That person may have sufficient limitations placed on her liberty, such as restrictions on her movement, that she will be deemed to be "in custody" for federal habeas corpus purposes.[41] Thus, the "in custody" requirement is at least slightly broader than it might appear at first blush.

The claim must be that the petitioner's continued detention is "in violation of the Constitution or laws or treaties of the United States."

The second foundational requirement under § 2254(a) is that the petitioner claim that she is in custody "in violation of the Constitution or law or treaties of the United States." It is not enough—even if true, and as reiterated repeatedly by the Supreme Court—that the petitioner is being held in violation of a state law.[42] The federal courts' authority to grant the writ is limited to violations of federal law. As the statute makes clear, it is possible that the illegality can flow from a federal statute[43] or a treaty. However, the overwhelming number of cases concern detention that is said to be in violation of some provision of the United States Constitution.

You should note at this point that § 2254(a) itself tells one nothing about *how* the court is to determine whether the petitioner is, in fact, being held in violation of federal law. That issue is more complicated. We consider it below when we discuss the types of claims that are cognizable in connection with a petition for a writ of habeas corpus. Before doing so, however, we consider several other hurdles a petitioner must clear even after she has satisfied the foundational requirements of § 2254(a).[44]

40. See *supra* section C.1.

41. *See, e.g., Jones v. Cunningham*, 371 U.S. 236 (1963).

42. *See, e.g., Swarthout v. Cooke*, 131 S. Ct. 859 (2011); *Wilson v. Corcoran*, 131 S. Ct. 13 (2010).

43. For example, the Supreme Court has indicated that a statutory violation could qualify a petitioner for habeas relief if the violation led to a "fundamental defect" in the state court proceeding. *See Reed v. Farley*, 512 U.S. 339 (1994).

44. Should a petitioner be denied the writ in the federal district court on any of the grounds we will discuss, she does not have an automatic right to appeal that denial. Instead she must seek a "Certificate of Appealability" from the district court, a circuit court judge, or a Supreme Court justice. *See* 28 U.S.C. § 2253(c). To obtain the certificate the petitioner must make "a substantial showing of the denial of a constitutional right." 28 U.S.C. § 2253(c)(2). The Supreme Court has indicated that the petitioner need not show that she will prevail on an appeal. Rather, the standard is whether "reasonable jurists could debate whether . . . the petition should have been resolved in a different manner or the issues presented [are] adequate to deserve encouragement to proceed further." *See Miller-El v. Cockrell*, 537 U.S. 322, 336-38 (2003) (citation and internal quotation marks omitted).

iii. *Time Limits: 28 U.S.C. § 2244(d)*

One of the issues that has always plagued the law concerning habeas corpus is the tension between the judicial system's interests in accuracy and fairness on the one hand and finality on the other. As a society we want the results of criminal trials to be the result of fair proceedings and yield accurate results. At the same time, matters must finally come to rest if the overall adjudicative system is to function. You will be able to see this tension at play in many areas of federal habeas corpus law.

Resolving the tension between the values of fairness/accuracy and finality could be done in many ways. For example, one could address the issue on a case-by-case basis in which balancing the values was left to the discretion of the federal courts. Under AEDPA, Congress has taken a different approach setting timely filing requirements on a system-wide basis. Those requirements are found in 28 U.S.C. § 2244(d).

A state petitioner must file her petition within one year of the latest of four dates. By far the most common situation is that she must file her petition within one year of "the date on which the [state court] judgment became final by conclusion of direct review or the expiration of the time for seeking such review." 28 U.S.C. § 2244(d)(1)(A).[45] By "direct review," the statute refers to the end of the chain by which a person convicted in a state court can challenge her conviction by one trip through the relevant appellate courts. For example, if a person is convicted in a state court in Pinellas County, Florida, she would be able to appeal to the state intermediate appellate court for that area of the state (the Second District Court of Appeal). She might then have the ability to appeal to the Florida Supreme Court. Thereafter, she could seek review of federal issues in the Supreme Court of the United States by writ of certiorari. The direct review chain in this situation ends with the United States Supreme Court. The one-year window within which to file a habeas corpus petition would run from the date on which the United States Supreme Court either denied certiorari if the state petitioner sought such review or the date on which the state petitioner's time to seek such review expired.[46]

AEDPA also provides three other situations that, in theory at least, could provide a later starting point for the one-year window than the expiration of the direct appeal chain. The first of these is when the state takes action in violation of federal law that impedes a petitioner from filing a petition (and the petitioner in fact was prevented from such filing). *See* 28 U.S.C. § 2244(d)(1)(B). For example, if the state prison system did not allow the petitioner to have access to the mail or an attorney, the time period would run only when those impediments to filing were removed. As you might imagine, this provision of the statute is not often successfully invoked.

The statute also provides that the one-year period could begin to run on "the date on which the constitutional right asserted was initially recognized by

45. The time limits are shorter for persons subject to a sentence of death if the state at issue has qualified for such expedited proceedings. *See* 28 U.S.C. § 2263.

46. The Supreme Court made clear that a state court's decision to allow a prisoner to file an out-of-time direct appeal makes the state court judgment non-final for purposes of the one-year limitation in § 2244(d)(1)(A). The one-year limitation ends when the petitioner's out-of-time appeal concludes the direct appellate chain. *See Jimenez v. Quarterman*, 555 U.S. 113 (2009). The Court has also held that a judgment is "final" for purposes of § 2244(d)(1)(A) when the time for seeking review in the state court expires and not when the mandate of the lower court enters. *See Gonzalez v. Thaler*, 132 S. Ct. 641, 652-56 (2012).

the Supreme Court, if the right has been newly recognized by the Supreme Court and made retroactive applicable to cases on collateral review." *See* 28 U.S.C. § 2244(d)(1)(C). We will study the question of retroactively below. As you will recognize when we do so, this subsection will not provide many petitioners with extra time within which to file petitions because it is almost impossible to satisfy the stringent test under which a newly recognized constitutional right will be retroactively applied in the context of collateral review.[47] Thus, as a practical matter, this section of the statute will almost never come into play.

Finally, the statute provides that the one-year period could run from "the date on which the factual predicate of the claim or claims presented could have been discovered through the exercise of due diligence." 28 U.S.C. § 2244(d)(1)(D). The idea embodied in this provision is really one of fairness. If the fact that underlies the petitioner's claim is one that she could not have discovered with due diligence, then it makes sense to start the one-year clock on the date when she first could have discovered the fact. We will consider what is meant by due diligence in habeas more generally when we discuss the situations in which a state prisoner may obtain an evidentiary hearing in federal court. For now, you should know that this section of the statute will also not apply to a great many claims.

Two final points are worth making. First, the Supreme Court has held that § 2244(d) is subject to equitable tolling in appropriate cases. *See Holland v. Florida*, 130 S. Ct. 2549 (2010). The Court was less clear as to what constitutes an "extraordinary circumstance" justifying the application of equitable tolling. What is clear, however, is that the Court precluded the application of rigid rules because habeas proceedings are equitable in nature. And in its 2011 Term, the Supreme Court held that a federal court does not have the discretion to raise on its own accord a timeliness issue under § 2244 when the state has made a "deliberate" waiver of such a defense. *See Wood v. Milyard*, 132 S. Ct. 1826, 1829-30 (2012).

iv. Exhaustion of State Remedies: 28 U.S.C. § 2254(b) and (c)

Assuming that a state petitioner has satisfied the general prerequisites of §§ 2241 and 2254(a) and has filed her petition within the time limits imposed under § 2244(d), she must next ensure that she has exhausted her state remedies. *See* 28 U.S.C. § 2254(b), (c). We will explore what the exhaustion requirement entails in this section. First, however, consider the following questions about the values that may underlie the requirement in the first instance and whether it is consistent with some of the other doctrines we have discussed in the course.

47. Recall that collateral review is to be contrasted with direct review. As explained above, direct review is the first movement of a person convicted of a crime through the appellate system. Collateral review refers to those situations—like habeas corpus—in which a person is going through the system a second time around. So, for example, in the example in the text above concerning the Pinellas County conviction, the direct review ended with the United States Supreme Court. If the person convicted in that case then sought a writ of habeas corpus in the federal courts (or the Florida state courts) she would be engaged in a collateral proceeding.

EXPLORING DOCTRINE

The Exhaustion Doctrine and the Values It Might Serve

The exhaustion requirement ensures that a petitioner has presented her federal claims to a state court before a federal court may consider them. Why might Congress have concluded that this requirement is so important that an otherwise valid federal claim should be precluded from adjudication in a federal court? Assuming that there is a value of sufficient importance to justify this outcome, are there other constitutional values that might weigh against the exhaustion doctrine?

When considering your responses to these questions, compare the situation in habeas with that which we encountered in connection with civil rights claims under § 1983. As we learned, there is no exhaustion requirement in that context. Are there different constitutional values at play in connection with § 1983, or are the doctrine in habeas and that in the civil rights field incurably inconsistent?

The exhaustion doctrine began as a judicially crafted limitation on the ability of state prisoners to seek a writ of habeas corpus from a federal court.[48] Congress first codified the doctrine in 1948, and it has remained a part of statutory habeas corpus law since that time. The Supreme Court has given its views about at least the first question we posed above. It has indicated that the exhaustion doctrine is important both to ensure the values of federalism as well as for the practical reason of giving a federal court the raw material with which to address a habeas petition. Specifically, the Court has held that the doctrine: "protects the state courts' role in the enforcement of federal law"; "prevent[s] disruption of state judicial proceedings"; "minimizes friction between our federal and state systems of justice"; and ensures better developed factual records.[49]

The current statutory requirements for exhaustion are found principally in 28 U.S.C. § 2254(b)(1). That section provides that a writ of habeas corpus shall not be granted in most cases unless the petitioner establishes that she "has exhausted the remedies available in the courts of the State." Under the statute, a petitioner is excused from the exhaustion requirement if the state does not provide a means of exhaustion or if the state process is ineffective. *See* 28 U.S.C. § 2254(b)(1)(B).

The Supreme Court's interpretations of § 2254(b) have provided important details for its practical application. First, the Court has held that the exhaustion requirement applies only to those state remedies that remain available to the petitioner at the time of filing. Thus, for example, if the time to appeal has expired, there is nothing to exhaust. As we will see in the next subsection, if that is the case, the petitioner will face a formidable hurdle to having her claims considered substantively in federal court. However, the difficulty will not arise from the exhaustion doctrine.[50]

48. *See Ex parte Royall*, 117 U.S. 241 (1886).
49. *See Rose v. Lundy*, 455 U.S. 509, 518 (1982).
50. *See, e.g., Fay v. Noia*, 372 U.S. 391 (1963).

Second, the Court has held that, despite the language in § 2254(c), a petitioner is generally not required to avail herself of state collateral remedies such as habeas corpus if she has already pursued her direct remedies.[51] There may be instances in which state collateral review is the only procedure available to a petitioner, such as when she claims ineffective assistance of counsel in her principal case and state law provides that such claims must be raised in a collateral proceeding instead of on direct appeal. In those situations a petitioner would be required to use the state collateral remedy in order to satisfy the exhaustion requirement.

Third, the Court has held that in order to satisfy the exhaustion requirement, a petitioner must have sought review in the highest court of a state even if such review is discretionary.[52] However, the petitioner need not have sought a writ of certiorari in the Supreme Court of the United States because such remedy is a federal one, not one provided by the state.[53]

Two other statutory details are significant with respect to the exhaustion requirement. First, the federal court may excuse a failure to exhaust available state remedies if it rules against the petitioner on the merits of her claim. *See* 28 U.S.C. § 2254(b)(2). Second, a state may not be precluded from raising the exhaustion requirement unless "the State, through counsel, expressly waives the requirement." *See* 28 U.S.C. § 2254(b)(3).

An issue that has caused difficulties concerning exhaustion deals with so-called "mixed petitions." A mixed petition is one that includes more than one claim and in which the petitioner has exhausted state remedies as to one claim but not as to others. In such a situation, the federal court has several options. One that was often used before the 1996 enactment of AEDPA was to dismiss the petition without prejudice to allow the petitioner to return to the state court to exhaust her state remedies for the relevant claims. This approach worked well but became problematic after Congress imposed the strict one-year filing requirements set forth in 28 U.S.C. § 2244(d) discussed above. In such a situation the petitioner might lose the ability to present some of her claims to a federal court because exhausting her state remedies as to the unexhausted claim might push the petitioner beyond the relevant one-year filing deadline.

Another option would be to give the petitioner the choice of what to do. In other words, she could elect to dismiss her unexhausted claims and proceed solely on the one for which she had satisfied the exhaustion requirement. This tack would allow the petitioner to avoid having her exhausted claims time barred. The difficulty with this approach is that the petitioner would effectively forfeit her ability to present the unexhausted claims to a federal court. Even if she returned to state court with respect to the unexhausted claims, the rules we discuss below making it extraordinarily difficult to file a second writ of habeas corpus would likely prevent her from returning to federal court on the previously unexhausted claims. *See* 28 U.S.C. § 2244(b).

Recognizing the difficulty with the various options of dealing with mixed petitions, federal courts began to use a procedure called "stay-and-abeyance." Under this approach, the federal court would stay consideration of the petition but not dismiss it. Instead, it would refrain from taking action so that the petitioner could

51. *See, e.g., Francisco v. Gathright*, 419 U.S. 59 (1974) (per curiam); *Brown v. Allen*, 344 U.S. 443, 447-50 (1953).

52. *See O'Sullivan v. Boerchel*, 526 U.S. 838 (1999).

53. *See Fay v. Noia*, 372 U.S. 391 (1963).

return to state court and utilize available state remedies with respect to the unexhausted claims. After completing that process, the federal court would proceed to adjudicate the habeas petition with respect to all claims remaining after the state court's actions. The Supreme Court affirmed the use of the stay-and-abeyance procedure so long as the petitioner had shown "good cause" for her failure to exhaust her state remedies.[54] The Court also cautioned, however, that when exercising its discretion to use the procedure the district court must remain cognizant of AEDPA's principal goals, such as avoiding delay.[55]

v. Implications of State Procedural Defaults

Assuming that the petitioner has met the prerequisites of §§ 2241 and 2254(a), satisfied the timely filing requirements set forth in § 2244(d), and exhausted all her available state remedies under § 2254(b), one might think that the federal court is now positioned to evaluate the substantive merits of her federal claims. However, there are still additional barriers that may preclude such a substantive consideration of her claims. This subsection discusses one of those impediments, the presence of a state procedural default.

Unlike the other barriers to relief we have considered thus far, the rules concerning state procedural defaults are judge-crafted. We can provide no statutory citation as we have before because there is none.[56] First, what does one mean by a state procedural default? Essentially, the term means that the petitioner lost in state court not based on a substantive consideration of the federal issue raised, such as a violation of the Sixth Amendment's right to confront your accuser. Rather, the petitioner lost because she failed to comply with a state procedural requirement, such as that requiring her to file her appeal within a certain period of time.

As explained in *Coleman v. Thompson*, excepted below, the Supreme Court has changed its position through the years as to the impact of a petitioner's loss on a state procedural ground. At one point, the Court took the position that such a state ground of decision essentially barred federal court consideration of the merits of the petitioner's federal claims.[57] Later, in its 1963 decision in *Fay v. Noia*, the Court adopted a far more petitioner-friendly stance under which a state procedural default would bar federal court consideration of the federal claims only if the state petitioner "deliberately bypassed" the state remedy available.[58] In other words, only if the state petitioner was said to have engaged in some sort of gamesmanship in the state court would a state procedural default bar federal review.

The pendulum began to swing back toward a more restrictive view concerning state procedural defaults with the Court's decision in *Wainwright v. Sykes*, 433 U.S. 72 (1977). In that case, the Court limited *Fay v. Noia*'s deliberate bypass standard to situations in which a petitioner had lost her right to appeal completely such as by missing the deadline to file an appeal. For other procedural

54. The Court did not define "good cause" when it blessed the use of the procedure. It may be that the Court meant to incorporate its definition of the term in connection with other areas of habeas corpus law. We consider the term in more detail below when discussing state procedural default.

55. *See Rhines v. Weber*, 544 U.S. 269 (2005).

56. Congress has enacted rules concerning state procedural defaults in connection with certain capital cases. *See, e.g.*, 28 U.S.C. § 2264.

57. *See Daniels v. Allen*, 344 U.S. 443 (1953).

58. *See Fay v. Noia*, 372 U.S. 391 (1963).

defaults, such as for example a failure to follow a state rule requiring contemporaneous objection at trial, the Court adopted a presumption that federal review was barred if the state court's decision was based on the state rule. In such a situation, a petitioner would only be excused from the default if she were able to show that she had good cause for the failure to follow the state rule and that she was actually prejudiced by the procedural default. *Coleman* below explains the meaning of these concepts.

Now read *Coleman v. Thompson,* in which the Court reviewed the history of the state procedural default rules and set forth the current state of the law. As you will see, after *Coleman* the pendulum has swung even farther toward state procedural defaults barring federal review.

COLEMAN v. THOMPSON

501 U.S. 722 (1991)

JUSTICE O'CONNOR delivered the opinion of the Court.

This is a case about federalism. It concerns the respect that federal courts owe the States and the States' procedural rules when reviewing the claims of state prisoners in federal habeas corpus.

I

A Buchanan County, Virginia, jury convicted Roger Keith Coleman of rape and capital murder and fixed the sentence at death for the murder. The trial court imposed the death sentence, and the Virginia Supreme Court affirmed both the convictions and the sentence. This Court denied certiorari.

Coleman then filed a petition for a writ of habeas corpus in the Circuit Court for Buchanan County, raising numerous federal constitutional claims that he had not raised on direct appeal. After a 2-day evidentiary hearing, the Circuit Court ruled against Coleman on all claims. The court entered its final judgment on September 4, 1986.

Coleman filed his notice of appeal with the Circuit Court on October 7, 1986, 33 days after the entry of final judgment. Coleman subsequently filed a petition for appeal in the Virginia Supreme Court. The Commonwealth of Virginia, as appellee, filed a motion to dismiss the appeal. The sole ground for dismissal urged in the motion was that Coleman's notice of appeal had been filed late. Virginia Supreme Court Rule 5:9(a) provides that no appeal shall be allowed unless a notice of appeal is filed with the trial court within 30 days of final judgment.

The Virginia Supreme Court did not act immediately on the Commonwealth's motion, and both parties filed several briefs on the subject of the motion to dismiss and on the merits of the claims in Coleman's petition. On May 19, 1987, the Virginia Supreme Court issued the following order, dismissing Coleman's appeal:

> "On December 4, 1986 came the appellant, by counsel, and filed a petition for appeal in the above-styled case.

> "Thereupon came the appellee, by the Attorney General of Virginia, and filed a motion to dismiss the petition for appeal; on December 19, 1986 the appellant filed a memorandum in opposition to the motion to dismiss; on December 19, 1986 the appellee filed a reply to the appellant's memorandum; on December 23, 1986 the appellee filed a brief in opposition to the petition for appeal; on December 23, 1986 the appellant filed a surreply in opposition to the appellee's motion to dismiss; and on January 6, 1987 the appellant filed a reply brief.
>
> "Upon consideration whereof, the motion to dismiss is granted and the petition for appeal is dismissed."

This Court again denied certiorari.

Coleman next filed a petition for writ of habeas corpus in the United States District Court for the Western District of Virginia. In his petition, Coleman presented four federal constitutional claims he had raised on direct appeal in the Virginia Supreme Court and seven claims he had raised for the first time in state habeas. The District Court concluded that, by virtue of the dismissal of his appeal by the Virginia Supreme Court in state habeas, Coleman had procedurally defaulted the seven claims. The District Court nonetheless went on to address the merits of all 11 of Coleman's claims. The court ruled against Coleman on all of the claims and denied the petition.

The United States Court of Appeals for the Fourth Circuit affirmed. . . . We granted certiorari to resolve several issues concerning the relationship between state procedural defaults and federal habeas review, and now affirm.

II

A

This Court will not review a question of federal law decided by a state court if the decision of that court rests on a state law ground that is independent of the federal question and adequate to support the judgment. This rule applies whether the state law ground is substantive or procedural. In the context of direct review of a state court judgment, the independent and adequate state ground doctrine is jurisdictional. Because this Court has no power to review a state law determination that is sufficient to support the judgment, resolution of any independent federal ground for the decision could not affect the judgment and would therefore be advisory.

We have applied the independent and adequate state ground doctrine not only in our own review of state court judgments, but in deciding whether federal district courts should address the claims of state prisoners in habeas corpus actions. The doctrine applies to bar federal habeas when a state court declined to address a prisoner's federal claims because the prisoner had failed to meet a state procedural requirement. In these cases, the state judgment rests on independent and adequate state procedural grounds.

The basis for application of the independent and adequate state ground doctrine in federal habeas is somewhat different than on direct review by this Court. When this Court reviews a state court decision on direct review pursuant to 28 U.S.C. § 1257, it is reviewing the *judgment*; if resolution of a federal question cannot affect the judgment, there is nothing for the Court to do. This is not the case in habeas. When a federal district court reviews a state prisoner's habeas corpus petition pursuant to 28 U.S.C. § 2254, it must decide whether the petitioner is "in custody in violation of the Constitution or laws or treaties of the United States." The court does not review a judgment, but the lawfulness of the petitioner's custody *simpliciter.*

Nonetheless, a state prisoner is in custody *pursuant* to a judgment. When a federal habeas court releases a prisoner held pursuant to a state court judgment that rests on an independent and adequate state ground, it renders ineffective the state rule just as completely as if this Court had reversed the state judgment on direct review. In such a case, the habeas court ignores the State's legitimate reasons for holding the prisoner.

In the habeas context, the application of the independent and adequate state ground doctrine is grounded in concerns of comity and federalism. Without the rule, a federal district court would be able to do in habeas what this Court could not do on direct review; habeas would offer state prisoners whose custody was supported by independent and adequate state grounds an end run around the limits of this Court's jurisdiction and a means to undermine the State's interest in enforcing its laws.

When the independent and adequate state ground supporting a habeas petitioner's custody is a state procedural default, an additional concern comes into play. This Court has long held that a state prisoner's federal habeas petition should be dismissed if the prisoner has not exhausted available state remedies as to any of his federal claims. This exhaustion requirement is also grounded in principles of comity; in a federal system, the States should have the first opportunity to address and correct alleged violations of state prisoner's federal rights. . . .

These same concerns apply to federal claims that have been procedurally defaulted in state court. Just as in those cases in which a state prisoner fails to exhaust state remedies, a habeas petitioner who has failed to meet the State's procedural requirements for presenting his federal claims has deprived the state courts of an opportunity to address those claims in the first instance. A habeas petitioner who has defaulted his federal claims in state court meets the technical requirements for exhaustion; there are no state remedies any longer "available" to him. In the absence of the independent and adequate state ground doctrine in federal habeas, habeas petitioners would be able to avoid the exhaustion requirement by defaulting their federal claims in state court. The independent and adequate state ground doctrine ensures that the States' interest in correcting their own mistakes is respected in all federal habeas cases.

B

It is not always easy for a federal court to apply the independent and adequate state ground doctrine. State court opinions will, at times, discuss federal questions at length and mention a state law basis for decision only briefly. In such cases, it is often difficult to determine if the state law discussion is truly an independent basis for decision or merely a passing reference. In other cases, state opinions purporting to apply state constitutional law will derive principles by reference to federal constitutional decisions from this Court. Again, it is unclear from such opinions whether the state law decision is independent of federal law.

In *Michigan v. Long* we provided a partial solution to this problem in the form of a conclusive presumption. Prior to *Long*, when faced with ambiguous state court decisions, this Court had adopted various inconsistent and unsatisfactory solutions including dismissal of the case, remand to the state court for clarification, or an independent investigation of state law. These solutions were burdensome both to this Court and to the state courts. They were also largely unnecessary in those cases where it fairly appeared that the state court decision rested primarily on federal law. The most reasonable conclusion in such cases is that there is not an independent and adequate state ground for the decision. Therefore, in order to minimize the costs associated with resolving ambiguities in state court decisions while still fulfilling our obligation to determine if there was an independent and adequate state ground for the decision, we established a conclusive presumption of jurisdiction in these cases:

> "When, as in this case, a state court decision fairly appears to rest primarily on federal law, or to be interwoven with the federal law, and when the adequacy and independence of any possible state law ground is not clear from the face of the opinion, we will accept as the most reasonable explanation that the state court decided the case the way it did because it believed that federal law required it to do so."

After *Long*, a state court that wishes to look to federal law for guidance or as an alternative holding while still relying on an independent and adequate state ground can avoid the presumption by stating "clearly and expressly that [its decision] is . . . based on bona fide separate, adequate, and independent grounds."

In *Caldwell v. Mississippi* we applied the *Long* presumption in the context of an alleged independent and adequate state procedural ground. Caldwell, a criminal defendant, challenged at trial part of the prosecutor's closing argument to the jury, but he did not raise the issue on appeal to the Mississippi Supreme Court. That court raised the issue *sua sponte*, discussing this federal question at length in its opinion and deciding it against Caldwell. The court also made reference to its general rule that issues not raised on appeal are deemed waived. The State argued to this Court that the procedural default constituted an independent and adequate state ground for the Mississippi court's decision. We rejected this argument, noting that the state decision "'fairly appears to rest primarily on federal law,'" and there was no clear and express statement that the Mississippi Supreme Court was relying on procedural default as an independent ground.

Long and *Caldwell* were direct review cases. We first considered the problem of ambiguous state court decisions in the application of the independent and adequate state ground doctrine in a federal habeas case in *Harris v. Reed.* Harris, a state prisoner, filed a petition for state postconviction relief, alleging that his trial counsel had rendered ineffective assistance. The state trial court dismissed the petition, and the Appellate Court of Illinois affirmed. In its order, the Appellate Court referred to the Illinois rule that "'those [issues] which could have been presented [on direct appeal], but were not, are considered waived.'" The court concluded that Harris could have raised his ineffective assistance claims on direct review. Nonetheless, the court considered and rejected Harris' claims on the merits. Harris then petitioned for federal habeas.

The situation presented to this Court was nearly identical to that in *Long* and *Caldwell:* a state court decision that fairly appeared to rest primarily on federal law in a context in which a federal court has an obligation to determine if the state court decision rested on an independent and adequate state ground. "Faced with a common problem, we adopted a common solution." *Harris* applied in federal habeas the presumption this Court adopted in *Long* for direct review cases. Because the Illinois Appellate Court did not "clearly and expressly" rely on waiver as a ground for rejecting Harris' ineffective assistance of counsel claims, the *Long* presumption applied and Harris was not barred from federal habeas.

After *Harris,* federal courts on habeas corpus review of state prisoner claims, like this Court on direct review of state court judgments, will presume that there is no independent and adequate state ground for a state court decision when the decision "fairly appears to rest primarily on federal law, or to be interwoven with the federal law, and when the adequacy and independence of any possible state law ground is not clear from the face of the opinion." In habeas, if the decision of the last state court to which the petitioner presented his federal claims fairly appeared to rest primarily on resolution of those claims, or to be interwoven with those claims, and did not clearly and expressly rely on an independent and adequate state ground, a federal court may address the petition.[59]

III

A

Coleman contends that the presumption of *Long* and *Harris* applies in this case and precludes a bar to habeas because the Virginia Supreme Court's order dismissing Coleman's appeal did not "clearly and expressly" state that it was based on state procedural grounds. Coleman reads *Harris* too broadly. A predicate to the application of the *Harris* presumption is that the decision of the last state court to which the petitioner presented his federal claims must fairly appear to rest primarily on federal law or to be interwoven with federal law.

Coleman relies on other language in *Harris.* That opinion announces that "a procedural default does not bar consideration of a federal claim on either direct or habeas review unless the last state court rendering a judgment in the case clearly and expressly states that its judgment rests on a state procedural bar." Coleman contends that this rule, by its terms, applies to all state court judgments, not just those that fairly appear to rest primarily on federal law.

Coleman has read the rule out of context. It is unmistakably clear that *Harris* applies the same presumption in habeas that *Long* and *Caldwell* adopted in direct review cases in this Court. Indeed, the quoted passage purports to state the rule "on either direct or habeas review." *Harris,* being a federal habeas case, could not change the rule for direct review; the reference to both direct and habeas review makes plain that *Harris* applies precisely the same rule as *Long. Harris* describes the *Long* presumption, and hence its own, as applying only in those cases in which "'it fairly appears that the state court rested its decision primarily on federal law.'" That in one particular exposition of its rule *Harris* does not mention the predicate to application of the presumption does not change the holding of the opinion.

Coleman urges a broader rule: that the presumption applies in all cases in which a habeas petitioner presented his federal claims to the state court. This rule makes little sense. In direct review cases, "it is . . . 'incumbent upon this Court . . . to ascertain for itself . . . whether the asserted non-federal ground independently and adequately supports the [state court] judgment.'" Similarly,

59. [Footnote * in the Court's opinion.] This rule does not apply if the petitioner failed to exhaust state remedies and the court to which the petitioner would be required to present his claims in order to meet the exhaustion requirement would now find the claims procedurally barred. In such a case there is a procedural default for purposes of federal habeas regardless of the decision of the last state court to which the petitioner actually presented his claims.

federal habeas courts must ascertain for themselves if the petitioner is in custody pursuant to a state court judgment that rests on independent and adequate state grounds. In cases in which the *Long* and *Harris* presumption applies, federal courts will conclude that the relevant state court judgment does not rest on an independent and adequate state ground. The presumption, like all conclusive presumptions, is designed to avoid the costs of excessive inquiry where a *per se* rule will achieve the correct result in almost all cases. . . .

Per se rules should not be applied, however, in situations where the generalization is incorrect as an empirical matter; the justification for a conclusive presumption disappears when application of the presumption will not reach the correct result most of the time. The *Long* and *Harris* presumption works because in the majority of cases in which a state court decision fairly appears to rest primarily on federal law or to be interwoven with such law, and the state court does not plainly state that it is relying on an independent and adequate state ground, the state court decision did not in fact rest on an independent and adequate state ground. We accept errors in those small number of cases where there was nonetheless an independent and adequate state ground in exchange for a significant reduction in the costs of inquiry.

The tradeoff is very different when the factual predicate does not exist. In those cases in which it does not fairly appear that the state court rested its decision primarily on federal grounds, it is simply not true that the "most reasonable explanation" is that the state judgment rested on federal grounds. Yet Coleman would have the federal courts apply a conclusive presumption of no independent and adequate state grounds in every case in which a state prisoner presented his federal claims to a state court, regardless of whether it fairly appears that the state court addressed those claims. We cannot accept such a rule, for it would greatly and unacceptably expand the risk that federal courts will review the federal claims of prisoners in custody pursuant to judgments resting on independent and adequate state grounds. Any efficiency gained by applying a conclusive presumption, and thereby avoiding inquiry into state law, is simply not worth the cost in the loss of respect for the State that such a rule would entail.

It may be argued that a broadly applicable presumption is not counterfactual after it is announced: Once state courts know that their decisions resting on independent and adequate state procedural grounds will be honored in federal habeas only if there is a clear and express statement of the default, these courts will provide such a statement in all relevant cases. This argument does not help Coleman. Even assuming that *Harris* can be read as establishing a presumption in all cases, the Virginia Supreme Court issued its order dismissing Coleman's appeal *before* this Court decided *Harris*. As to this state court order, the absence of an express statement of procedural default is not very informative.

In any event, we decline to establish such a rule here, for it would place burdens on the States and state courts in exchange for very little benefit to the federal courts. We are, as an initial matter, far from confident that the empirical assumption of the argument for such a rule is correct. It is not necessarily the case that state courts will take pains to provide a clear and express statement of procedural default in all cases, even after announcement of the rule. State courts presumably have a dignitary interest in seeing that their state law decisions are not ignored by a federal habeas court, but most of the price paid for federal review of state prisoner claims is paid by the State. When a federal habeas court considers the federal claims of a prisoner in state custody for independent and adequate state law reasons, it is the State that must respond. It is the State that pays the price in terms of the uncertainty and delay added to the enforcement of its criminal laws. It is the State that must retry the petitioner if the federal courts reverse his conviction. If a state court, in the course of disposing of cases on its overcrowded docket, neglects to provide a clear and express statement of procedural default, or is insufficiently motivated to do so, there is little the State can do about it. Yet it is primarily respect for the State's interests that underlies the application of the independent and adequate state ground doctrine in federal habeas.

A broad presumption would also put too great a burden on the state courts. It remains the duty of the federal courts, whether this Court on direct review, or lower federal courts in habeas, to determine the scope of the relevant state court judgment. We can establish a *per se* rule that eases the burden of inquiry on the federal courts in those cases where there are few costs to doing so, but we have no power to tell state courts how they must write their opinions. We encourage state courts to express plainly, in every decision potentially subject to federal review, the grounds upon which their judgments rest, but we will not impose on state courts the responsibility for using particular language in every case in which a state prisoner presents a federal claim — every state appeal, every denial of state collateral review — in order that federal courts might not be bothered with reviewing state law and the record in the case.

Nor do we believe that the federal courts will save much work by applying the *Harris* presumption in all cases. The presumption at present applies only when it fairly appears that a state court judgment rested primarily on federal law or was interwoven with federal law, that is, in those cases where a federal court has good reason to question whether there is an independent and adequate state ground for the decision. In the rest of the cases, there is little need for a conclusive presumption. In the absence of a clear indication that a state court rested its decision on federal law, a federal court's task will not be difficult.

There is, in sum, little that the federal courts will gain by applying a presumption of federal review in those cases where the relevant state court decision does not fairly appear to rest primarily on federal law or to be interwoven with such law, and much that the States and state courts will lose. We decline to so expand the *Harris* presumption.

B

The *Harris* presumption does not apply here. Coleman does not argue, nor could he, that it "fairly appears" that the Virginia Supreme Court's decision rested primarily on federal law or was interwoven with such law. The Virginia Supreme Court stated plainly that it was granting the Commonwealth's motion to dismiss the petition for appeal. That motion was based solely on Coleman's failure to meet the Supreme Court's time requirements. There is no mention of federal law in the Virginia Supreme Court's three-sentence dismissal order. It "fairly appears" to rest primarily on state law.

Coleman concedes that the Virginia Supreme Court dismissed his state habeas appeal as untimely, applying a state procedural rule. He argues instead that the court's application of this procedural rule was not independent of federal law. [The Court then rejected Coleman's argument that the Virginia Supreme Court necessarily considered federal law because, he argued, that court could waive the rule at issue in order to avoid a serious constitutional error.]

* * * *

Finally, Coleman argues that the Virginia Supreme Court's dismissal order in this case is at least ambiguous because it was issued "upon consideration" of all the filed papers, including Coleman's petition for appeal and the Commonwealth's brief in opposition, both of which discussed the merits of Coleman's federal claims. There is no doubt that the Virginia Supreme Court's "consideration" of all filed papers adds some ambiguity, but we simply cannot read it as overriding the court's explicit grant of a dismissal motion based solely on procedural grounds. Those grounds are independent of federal law.

* * * *

IV

In *Daniels v. Allen*, the companion case to *Brown v. Allen* we confronted a situation nearly identical to that here. Petitioners were convicted in a North Carolina trial court and then were one day late in filing their appeal as of right in the North Carolina Supreme Court. That court rejected the appeals as procedurally barred. We held that federal habeas was also barred unless petitioners could prove that they were "detained without opportunity to appeal because of lack of counsel, incapacity, or some interference by officials."

Fay v. Noia overruled this holding. Noia failed to appeal at all in state court his state conviction, and then sought federal habeas review of his claim that his confession had been coerced. This Court held that such a procedural default in state court does not bar federal habeas review unless the petitioner has deliberately bypassed state procedures by intentionally forgoing an opportunity for state review. *Fay* thus created a presumption in favor of federal habeas review of claims procedurally defaulted in state court. The Court based this holding on its conclusion that a State's interest in orderly procedure is sufficiently vindicated by the prisoner's forfeiture of his state remedies. "Whatever residuum of state interest there may be under such circumstances is manifestly insufficient in the face of the federal policy . . . of affording an effective remedy for restraints contrary to the Constitution."

Our cases after *Fay* that have considered the effect of state procedural default on federal habeas review have taken a markedly different view of the important interests served by state procedural rules. . . . We held that a federal court on collateral review could not hear the claim unless [the petitioner] could show "cause" for his failure to [follow the procedural rule at issue] and actual prejudice as a result of the alleged constitutional violations.

* * * *

Wainwright v. Sykes applied the cause and prejudice standard more broadly. Sykes did not object at trial to the introduction of certain inculpatory statements he had earlier made to the police. Under Florida law, this failure barred state courts from hearing the claim on either direct appeal or state collateral review. We recognized that this contemporaneous objection rule served strong state interests in the finality of its criminal litigation. To protect these interests, we adopted the same presumption against federal habeas review of claims defaulted in state court for failure to object at trial that [an earlier case] had adopted in the grand jury context: the cause and prejudice standard. . . .

In so holding, *Sykes* limited *Fay* to its facts. The cause and prejudice standard in federal habeas evinces far greater respect for state procedural rules than does the deliberate bypass standard of *Fay*. These incompatible rules are based on very different conceptions of comity and of the importance of finality in state criminal litigation. In *Sykes*, we left open the question whether the deliberate bypass standard still applied to a situation like that in *Fay*, where a petitioner has surrendered entirely his right to appeal his state conviction. We rejected explicitly, however, "the sweeping language of *Fay v. Noia*, going far beyond the facts of the case eliciting it."

* * * *

Recognizing that the writ of habeas corpus "is a bulwark against convictions that violate fundamental fairness," we also acknowledged that "the Great Writ entails significant costs." The most significant of these is the cost to finality in criminal litigation that federal collateral review of state convictions entails. . . . Moreover, "federal intrusions into state criminal trials frustrate both the States' sovereign power to punish offenders and their good-faith attempts to honor constitutional rights." These costs are particularly high, we explained, when a state prisoner, through a procedural default, prevents adjudication of his constitutional claims in state court. Because these costs do not depend on the type of claim the prisoner raised, we reaffirmed that a state procedural default of any federal claim will bar federal habeas unless the petitioner demonstrates cause and actual prejudice. . . .

* * * *

[I]n *Sykes*, we left open the question whether *Fay*'s deliberate bypass standard continued to apply under the facts of that case, where a state prisoner has defaulted his entire appeal. We are now required to answer this question. By filing late, Coleman defaulted his entire state collateral appeal. This was no doubt an inadvertent error, and respondent concedes that Coleman did not "understandingly and knowingly" forgo the privilege of state collateral appeal. Therefore, if the *Fay* deliberate bypass standard still applies, Coleman's state procedural default will not bar federal habeas.

In *Harris*, we described in broad terms the application of the cause and prejudice standard, hinting strongly that *Fay* had been superseded. . . .

We now make it explicit: In all cases in which a state prisoner has defaulted his federal claims in state court pursuant to an independent and adequate state procedural rule, federal habeas review of the claims is barred unless the prisoner can demonstrate cause for the default and actual prejudice as a result of the alleged violation of federal law, or demonstrate that failure to consider the claims will result in a fundamental miscarriage of justice. *Fay* was based on a conception of federal/state relations that undervalued the importance of state procedural rules. The several cases after *Fay* that applied the cause and prejudice standard to a variety of state procedural defaults represent a different view. We now recognize the important interest in finality served by state procedural rules, and the significant harm to the States that results from the failure of federal courts to respect them.

* * * *

We also eliminate inconsistency between the respect federal courts show for state procedural rules and the respect they show for their own. This Court has long understood the vital interest served by *federal* procedural rules, even when they serve to bar federal review of constitutional claims. . . .

* * * *

No less respect should be given to state rules of procedure.

V

A

Coleman maintains that there was cause for his default. The late filing was, he contends, the result of attorney error of sufficient magnitude to excuse the default in federal habeas.

Murray v. Carrier considered the circumstances under which attorney error constitutes cause. Carrier argued that his attorney's inadvertence in failing to raise certain claims in his state appeal constituted cause for the default sufficient to allow federal habeas review. We rejected this claim, explaining that the costs associated with an ignorant or inadvertent procedural default are no less than where the failure to raise a claim is a deliberate strategy: It deprives the state courts of the opportunity to review trial errors. When a federal habeas court hears such a claim, it undercuts the State's ability to enforce its procedural rules just as surely as when the default was deliberate. We concluded: "So long as a defendant is represented by counsel whose performance is not constitutionally ineffective under the standard we discern no inequity in requiring him to bear the risk of attorney error that results in a procedural default."

Applying the *Carrier* rule as stated, this case is at an end. There is no constitutional right to an attorney in state post-conviction proceedings. Consequently, a petitioner cannot claim constitutionally ineffective assistance of counsel in such proceedings. Coleman contends that it was his attorney's error that led to the late filing of his state habeas appeal. This error cannot be constitutionally ineffective; therefore Coleman must "bear the risk of attorney error that results in a procedural default."

* * * *

Where a petitioner defaults a claim as a result of the denial of the right to effective assistance of counsel, the State, which is responsible for the denial as a constitutional matter, must bear the cost of any resulting default and the harm to state interests that federal habeas review entails. A different allocation of costs is appropriate in those circumstances where the State has no responsibility to ensure that the petitioner was represented by competent counsel. As between the State and the petitioner, it is the petitioner who must bear the burden of a failure to follow state procedural rules. In the absence of a constitutional violation, the petitioner bears the risk in federal habeas for all attorney errors made in the course of the representation, as *Carrier* says explicitly.

B

* * * *

Because Coleman had no right to counsel to pursue his appeal in state habeas, any attorney error that led to the default of Coleman's claims in state court cannot constitute cause to excuse the default in federal habeas. As Coleman does not argue in this Court that federal review of his claims is necessary to prevent a fundamental miscarriage of justice, he is barred from bringing these claims in federal habeas. Accordingly, the judgment of the Court of Appeals is

Affirmed.

[A concurring opinion by Justice White is omitted.]

JUSTICE BLACKMUN, with whom JUSTICE MARSHALL and JUSTICE STEVENS join, dissenting.

Federalism; comity; state sovereignty; preservation of state resources; certainty: The majority methodically inventories these multifarious state interests before concluding that the plain-statement rule of *Michigan v. Long* does not apply to a summary order. One searches the majority's opinion in vain, however, for any mention of petitioner Coleman's right to a criminal proceeding free from constitutional defect or his interest in finding a forum for his constitutional challenge to his conviction and sentence of death. Nor does the majority even allude to the "important need for uniformity in federal law," which justified this Court's adoption of the plain-statement rule in the first place. Rather, displaying obvious exasperation with the breadth of substantive federal habeas doctrine and the expansive protection afforded by the Fourteenth Amendment's guarantee of fundamental fairness in state criminal proceedings, the Court today continues its crusade to erect petty procedural barriers in the path of any state prisoner seeking review of his federal constitutional claims. Because I believe that the Court is creating a Byzantine morass of arbitrary, unnecessary, and unjustifiable impediments to the vindication of federal rights, I dissent.

I

The Court cavalierly claims that "this is a case about federalism," and proceeds without explanation to assume that the purposes of federalism are advanced whenever a federal court refrains from reviewing an ambiguous state-court judgment. Federalism, however, has no inherent normative value: It does not, as the majority appears to assume, blindly protect the interests of States from any incursion by the federal courts. Rather, federalism secures to citizens the liberties that derive from the diffusion of sovereign power. "Federalism is a device for realizing the concepts of decency and fairness which are among the fundamental principles of liberty and justice lying at the base of all our civil and political institutions." In this context, it cannot lightly be assumed that the interests of federalism are fostered by a rule that impedes federal review of federal constitutional claims.

Moreover, the form of federalism embraced by today's majority bears little resemblance to that adopted by the Framers of the Constitution and ratified by the original States. The majority proceeds as if the sovereign interests of the States and the Federal Government were coequal. Ours, however, is a federal republic, conceived on the principle of a supreme federal power and constituted first and foremost of citizens, not of sovereign States. The citizens expressly declared: "This Constitution, and the Laws of the United States which shall be made in Pursuance thereof . . . shall be the supreme Law of the Land." U.S. Const., Art. VI, cl. 2. James Madison felt that a constitution without this Clause "would have been evidently and radically defective." The ratification of the Fourteenth Amendment by the citizens of the several States expanded federal powers even further, with a corresponding diminution of state sovereignty. Thus, "the sovereignty of the States is limited by the Constitution itself."

Federal habeas review of state-court judgments, respectfully employed to safeguard federal rights, is no invasion of state sovereignty. Since 1867, Congress has acted within its constitutional authority to "'interpose the federal courts between the States and the people, as guardians of the people's federal rights —

to protect the people from unconstitutional action.'" . . . Thus, the considered exercise by federal courts—in vindication of fundamental constitutional rights—of the habeas jurisdiction conferred on them by Congress exemplifies the full expression of this Nation's federalism.

That the majority has lost sight of the animating principles of federalism is well illustrated by its discussion of the duty of a federal court to determine whether a state-court judgment rests on an adequate and independent state ground. According to the majority's formulation, establishing this duty in the federal court serves to diminish the risk that a federal habeas court will review the federal claims of a prisoner in custody pursuant to a judgment that rests upon an adequate and independent state ground. In reality, however, this duty of a federal court to determine its jurisdiction originally was articulated to ensure that federal rights were not improperly denied a federal forum. Thus, the quote artfully reconstituted by the majority, originally read: "It is incumbent upon this Court, when it is urged that the decision of the state court rests upon a non-federal ground, to ascertain for itself, *in order that constitutional guarantees may appropriately be enforced,* whether the asserted nonfederal ground independently and adequately supports the judgment." Similarly, the Court has stated that the duty "cannot be disregarded without neglecting or renouncing a jurisdiction conferred by the law and designed to protect and maintain the supremacy of the Constitution and the laws made in pursuance thereof." Indeed, the duty arose out of a distinct distrust of state courts, which this Court perceived as attempting to evade federal review.

From these noble beginnings, the Court has managed to transform the duty to protect federal rights into a self-fashioned abdication. Defying the constitutional allocation of sovereign authority, the Court now requires a federal court to scrutinize the state-court judgment with an eye to denying a litigant review of his federal claims rather than enforcing those provisions of the Federal Bill of Rights that secure individual autonomy.

II

Even if one acquiesced in the majority's unjustifiable elevation of abstract federalism over fundamental precepts of liberty and fairness, the Court's conclusion that the plain-statement rule of *Michigan v. Long* does not apply to a summary order defies both settled understandings and compassionate reason.

A

As an initial matter, it cannot seriously be disputed that the Court's opinion in *Harris v. Reed,* expressly considered this issue and resolved the question quite contrary to the Court's holding today. Both *Long* and *Harris* involved a federal review of a state-court opinion that, on its face, addressed the merits of the underlying claims and resolved those claims with express reference to both state and federal law. In each case, it was not disputed that the alleged state ground had been invoked: The Court was faced with the question whether that state ground was adequate to support the judgment and independent of federal law. Accordingly, the *Long* and *Harris* Courts spoke of state-court judgments that "fairly appear to rest primarily on federal law, or to be interwoven with federal law," or that contained "ambiguous . . . references to state law."

The majority asserts that these statements establish a factual predicate for the application of the plain-statement rule. Neither opinion, however, purported to limit the application of the plain-statement rule to the narrow circumstances presented in the case under review. In fact, the several opinions in *Harris* make plain that for purposes of federal habeas, the Court was adopting the *Long* presumption for all cases where federal claims are presented to state courts.

* * * *

B

* * * *

It is well settled that the existence of a state procedural default does not divest a federal court of jurisdiction on collateral review. Rather, the important office of the federal courts in vindicating federal rights gives way to the States' enforcement of their procedural rules to protect the States' interest in being an equal partner in safeguarding federal rights. This accommodation furthers the values underlying federalism in two ways. First, encouraging a defendant to assert his federal rights in the appropriate state forum makes it possible for transgressions to be arrested sooner and before they influence an erroneous deprivation of liberty. Second, thorough examination of a prisoner's federal claims in state court permits more effective review of those claims in federal court, honing the accuracy of the writ as an implement to eradicate unlawful detention. The majority ignores these purposes in concluding that a State need not bear the burden of making clear its intent to rely on such a rule. When it is uncertain whether a state-court judgment denying relief from federal claims rests on a procedural bar, it is inconsistent with federalism principles for a federal court to exercise discretion to decline to review those federal claims.

In justifying its new rule, the majority first announces that, as a practical matter, the application of the *Long* presumption to a summary order entered in a case where a state prisoner presented federal constitutional claims to a state court is unwarranted, because "it is simply not true that the 'most reasonable explanation' is that the state judgment rested on federal grounds." The majority provides no support for this flat assertion. In fact, the assertion finds no support in reality. "Under our federal system, the federal and state 'courts [are] equally bound to guard and protect the rights secured by the Constitution.'" Accordingly, state prisoners are required to present their federal claims to state tribunals before proceeding to federal habeas, "to protect the state courts' role in the enforcement of federal law and prevent disruption of state judicial proceedings." Respect for the States' responsible assumption of this solemn trust compels the conclusion that state courts presented with federal constitutional claims actually resolve those claims unless they indicate to the contrary.

The majority claims that applying the plain-statement rule to summary orders "would place burdens on the States and state courts," suggesting that these burdens are borne independently by the States and their courts. The State, according to the majority, "pays the price" for federal review of state prisoner claims "in terms of the uncertainty and delay" as well as in the cost of a retrial. The majority is less clear about the precise contours of the burden this rule is said to place on state courts, merely asserting that it "would also put too great a burden on the state courts."

The majority's attempt to distinguish between the interests of state courts and the interests of the States in this context is inexplicable. States do not exist independent of their officers, agents, and citizens. Rather, "through the structure of its government, and the character of those who exercise government authority, a State defines itself as a sovereign." The majority's novel conception of dichotomous interests is entirely unprecedented. Moreover, it admits of no readily apparent limiting principle. For instance, should a federal habeas court decline to review claims that the state judge committed constitutional error at trial simply because the costs of a retrial will be borne by the State? After all, as the majority asserts, "there is little the State can do about" constitutional errors made by its trial judges.

Even if the majority correctly attributed the relevant state interests, they are, nonetheless, misconceived. The majority appears most concerned with the financial burden that a retrial places on the States. Of course, if the initial trial conformed to the mandate of the Federal Constitution, not even the most probing federal review would necessitate a retrial. Thus, to the extent the State must "pay the price" of retrying a state prisoner, that price is incurred as a direct result of the State's failure scrupulously to honor his federal rights, not as a consequence of unwelcome federal review.

The majority also contends without elaboration that a "broad presumption [of federal jurisdiction] would . . . put too great a burden on the state courts." This assertion not only finds no support in *Long*, where the burden of the presumption on state courts is not even mentioned, but also is premised on the misconception that the plain-statement rule serves only to relieve the federal court of the "bother" of determining the basis of the relevant state-court judgment. Viewed responsibly, the plain-statement rule provides a simple mechanism by which a state court may invoke the discretionary deference of the federal habeas court and virtually insulate its judgment from federal review. While state courts may choose to draw their orders as they wish, the right of a state prisoner, particularly one sentenced to death, to have his federal claim heard by a federal habeas court is simply too fundamental to yield to the State's incidental interest in issuing ambiguous summary orders.

C

Not only is the majority's abandonment of the plain-statement rule for purposes of summary orders unjustified, it is also misguided. In *Long*, the Court adopted the plain-statement rule because we had "announced a number of principles in order to help us determine" whether ambiguous state-court judgments rested on adequate and independent state grounds, but had "not developed a satisfying and consistent approach for resolving this vexing issue." Recognizing that "this ad hoc method of dealing with cases that involve possible adequate and independent state grounds is antithetical to the doctrinal consistency that is *required* when sensitive issues of federal-state relations are involved," the Court determined that a broad presumption of federal jurisdiction combined with a simple mechanism by which state courts could clarify their intent to rely on state grounds would best "provide state judges with a clearer opportunity to develop state jurisprudence unimpeded by federal interference, and yet will preserve the integrity of federal law." Today's decision needlessly resurrects the piecemeal approach eschewed by *Long* and, as a consequence, invites the intrusive and unsatisfactory federal inquiry into unfamiliar state law that *Long* sought to avoid.

* * * *

III

Having abandoned the plain-statement rule with respect to a summary order, the majority must consider Coleman's argument that the untimely filing of his notice of appeal was the result of attorney error of sufficient magnitude as to constitute cause for his procedural default. In a sleight of logic that would be ironic if not for its tragic consequences, the majority concludes that a state prisoner pursuing state collateral relief must bear the risk of his attorney's grave errors—even if the result of those errors is that the prisoner will be executed without having presented his federal claims to a federal court—because this attribution of risk represents the appropriate "allocation of costs." Whether unprofessional attorney conduct in a state postconviction proceeding should bar federal habeas review of a state prisoner's conviction and sentence of death is not a question of *costs* to be allocated most efficiently. It is, rather, another circumstance where this Court must determine whether federal rights should yield to state interests. In my view, the obligation of a federal habeas court to correct fundamental constitutional violations, particularly in capital cases, should not accede to the State's "discretion to develop and implement programs to aid prisoners seeking to secure postconviction review."

* * * *

I dissent.

DISCUSSION AND QUESTIONS

There is much to discuss in *Coleman* concerning the details of habeas corpus law. Before considering that doctrine, however, take a moment to think about the questions posed below.

EXPLORING DOCTRINE

The Procedural Default Rules and Constitutional Values

The positions taken by Justice O'Connor's majority opinion and Justice Blackmun's dissent could not be more divergent. Not only do these two justices reach different conclusions about the result in *Coleman,* but also they do not even really agree as to what the case is fundamentally about. Consider Justice O'Connor's opening line: "This is a case about federalism." For Justice Blackmun, the case is about "Coleman's right to a criminal proceeding free from constitutional defect. . . ." Of course, they are both correct in some sense. Who has the better argument? Why? Should it matter at all that we are considering a question of life and death? In addition, are federalism values even more important in this context because we are considering not only the state's interest in applying federal law—something the Court has indicated is important in other contexts such as the exhaustion rules—but also the state's interest in applying *state* law?

Also, consider whether the entire state procedural default doctrine itself is inconsistent with *separation-of-powers* principles. Given Congress' near occupation of the habeas corpus landscape, is it appropriate for the Court to craft such a significant non-statutory restriction on the role of federal courts in this area?

Leaving aside the reasons for adopting the doctrine, consider how one should approach a question concerning a state procedural default.

Is the state decision in fact based on a state procedural ground? The first step is to determine whether the state court's decision is in fact based on a state ground or whether the state court considered the substantive merits of the petitioner's federal claim. As *Coleman* indicates, the Court imports the concept of the "independent and adequate state ground" from *Michigan v. Long*, 463 U.S. 1032 (1983), about which we learned in Chapter 12.

As you recall, *Michigan v. Long* concerned the Supreme Court's appellate jurisdiction. If the state court decision in that context was based on a state-law ground that was independent of any federal issue and also was adequate to support the state court's judgment, there was no basis under the Constitution for the Supreme Court to exercise appellate jurisdiction. The situation is different in the habeas context. We are not here concerned with jurisdiction as in *Michigan v. Long*. In this context, the driving values are ones of comity and federalism. Should the Court have adopted a doctrine based on jurisdiction in a setting in which jurisdiction is not in reality at issue?

While the Court adopted the *Michigan v. Long* framework, it instructed that the test be applied differently in the habeas context than it is in the context of the Supreme Court's appellate jurisdiction. In the appellate jurisdiction context, a state court decision will be presumed to be based on federal law unless the state court expressly relies on state law for its decision. However, in the habeas context, the *Coleman* Court tells us that a state court decision is presumably based on federal law only if "the decision of the last state court to which the petitioner presented his federal claims . . . fairly appears to rest primarily on federal law or to be interwoven with federal law."[60] As we saw in *Coleman*, this standard tends to construe ambiguity in the state court in favor of restricting the role of federal courts. The opposite is true in connection with the Supreme Court's appellate jurisdiction.

The Supreme Court has returned to the question of what constitutes an adequate and independent state ground such that federal habeas review is precluded under *Coleman*. First, in *Beard v. Kindler*, 130 S. Ct. 612 (2009), the Court reaffirmed that a state procedural rule is adequate so long as the rule in question was "firmly established and regularly followed." *Id.* at 617 (quoting *Lee v. Kemna*, 534 U.S. 362, 376 (2002)). The Court then went on to hold that the fact that a state rule is discretionary rather than mandatory does not automatically mean that the rule is inadequate under *Coleman*. So long as the rule is one that was "firmly established and regularly followed," its application can bar federal habeas relief under *Coleman*. *Id.* at 617-19. The Court followed up on this point in its 2011 decision in *Walker v. Martin*, 131 S. Ct. 1120 (2011). *Walker* held that California's flexible requirement that a state prisoner file her state habeas corpus petition "as

60. *Coleman*, 501 U.S. at 735.

promptly as the circumstances allow" was sufficiently well-established and, therefore, could serve as an adequate and independent state ground.[61]

Taken together, these decisions establish that when a state court summarily rejects all the claims raised by a defendant or rejects some and fails to discuss others, the federal court will assume that the state court decided the federal claims on the merits. This assumption may be rebutted, but the standard is a difficult one to meet.

Once one has determined that the petitioner lost in state court on a state procedural issue, the rule is that she is presumptively barred from having her federal claims heard in federal court. In this regard, *Coleman* fully overrules *Fay v. Noia* and its deliberate bypass standard even in the context of a total loss of a petitioner's right to appeal. The petitioner can be excused of her state procedural default under only narrow circumstances.

Excuse option I: The "cause and prejudice" standard. As the Court had outlined in *Wainwright v. Sykes*, a petitioner can be excused of her state procedural default if she establishes that (1) she has "cause" for her failure not to follow the state procedural rule and (2) she has been actually prejudiced as a result of the procedural default. The Court has generally defined "cause" narrowly, making it difficult for petitioners to satisfy this prong of the test. Examples of "cause" according to the Court include (a) when the state interferes with the petitioner's ability to comply with the state procedural rule;[62] (b) when the petitioner's claim is based on a novel legal argument;[63] and (c) when the procedural default is the result of constitutionally ineffective assistance of counsel.[64]

A few additional words are important concerning the possibility that ineffective assistance of counsel might constitute "cause." This standard is a difficult one to meet in its own regard. As an initial matter, as we saw in *Coleman* itself, you must have a constitutional right to counsel in the first instance in order to demonstrate that counsel's error is "cause" for the procedural default. No matter how poor your counsel's performance might be, if you had no constitutional right to counsel, his or her failure will not constitute "cause" under this standard. Moreover, once a petitioner has satisfied that prerequisite, she must meet the stringent standard articulated in *Strickland v. Washington*, 466 U.S. 478 (1986), to establish that her counsel was ineffective. That standard is that the counsel's performance fell below the minimum level of competence *and* that she was prejudiced by counsel's failure.

In *Martinez v. Ryan*, the Supreme Court held that there is a narrow exception to *Coleman*'s rule that inadequate assistance of counsel on collateral review cannot be "cause" for excusing a procedural default. 132 S. Ct. 1309, 1316 (2012). Specifically, the Court held that "[t]his opinion qualifies *Coleman* by recognizing a narrow exception: Inadequate assistance of counsel at initial-review collateral proceedings may establish cause for a prisoner's procedural default of a claim of ineffective of assistance at trial." *Id.* What the Court meant

61. The Court reiterated these points in 2011 and 2013. *See Johnson v. Williams*, 133 S. Ct. 1088 (2013); *Harrington v. Richter*, 131 S. Ct. 770 (2011).

62. *See, e.g., Murray v. Carrier*, 477 U.S. 478 (1986).

63. *See Reed v. Ross*, 468 U.S. 1 (1984). One should rely on this type of "cause" cautiously. First, the Court has expressed some doubt about its continued viability. Second, even if this still satisfies the "cause" requirement, we will see in the next subsection of this chapter that relying on a novel legal claim will generally not assist a petitioner when a federal court addresses the substantive merits.

64. *See Coleman, supra.*

when referring to "initial review collateral proceedings" was a situation in which the first opportunity to raise the claim at issue came at the collateral review proceeding stage. Interestingly, the Court expressly left open the question whether the Constitution requires effective assistance of counsel at this stage of the proceedings. *Id.*

In its 2012 Term, the Court made clear that the exception it recognized in *Martinez v. Ryan* was not limited to situations in which state law formally required ineffective assistance claims to be raised in collateral proceedings. The Court held that if the design and operation of a state's system as a practical matter made it highly unlikely that the ineffective assistance issue would be raised in a direct appeal, the *Martinez* rule applied.[65]

The Court has also found the "cause" portion of the procedural default formula satisfied when a petitioner's lawyers effectively abandoned him and that abandonment led to the state procedural default. *See Maples v. Thomas*, 132 S. Ct. 912, 916-17 (2012).

Once a petitioner has established that she has "cause," she must show that she has been actually prejudiced as a result of the state procedural default. Although the Court has been less than clear about the specifics, it has indicated that there needs to be sufficient evidence to question the accuracy of the state court's substantive finding of the petitioner's guilt in order to show that the petitioner was harmed by the application of the state procedural rule. The Court has not provided the details by which this question is answered, but one would likely be on solid ground if one concluded that the showing would be a difficult one.

Excuse option II: The "actual innocence gateway." The second option for a petitioner to avoid the state procedural default bar is referred to as the "actual innocence gateway." As the Court explained, if a petitioner establishes that the substantive federal error made at the state court level "probably resulted in the conviction of one who is actually innocent," the federal court may proceed to consider substantively the petitioner's claim.[66] In order to satisfy this standard, the petitioner must show that there is new, reliable evidence and that based on this new evidence "it is more likely than not that no reasonable juror would have convicted him in light of the new evidence."[67] The burden is even more difficult for one challenging not a finding of guilt but only a death sentence. In this instance the petitioner must show "by clear and convincing evidence that but for the constitutional error, no reasonable juror would [have found the petitioner] eligible for the death penalty."[68]

In its most recent discussion of the actual innocence gateway, the Supreme Court held that "actual innocence, if proved, serves as a gateway through which a petitioner may pass whether the impediment is a procedural bar . . . - or . . . expiration of the statute of limitation." The Court also stressed, however, that "tenable actual innocence gateway pleas are rare."[69]

* * * *

65. *Trevino v. Thaler*, 133 S. Ct. 1911 (2013).
66. *See Murray v. Carrier*, 477 U.S. 478, 496 (1986).
67. *See Schlup v. Delo*, 513 U.S. 298 (1995).
68. *See Sawyer v. Whitley*, 505 U.S. 333 (1992).
69. *McQuiggin v. Perkins*, 133 S. Ct. 1924 (2013).

We graphically summarize in Figure 13-1 the steps to consider when addressing state procedural defaults.

FIGURE 13-1

State Procedural Defaults: A Checklist

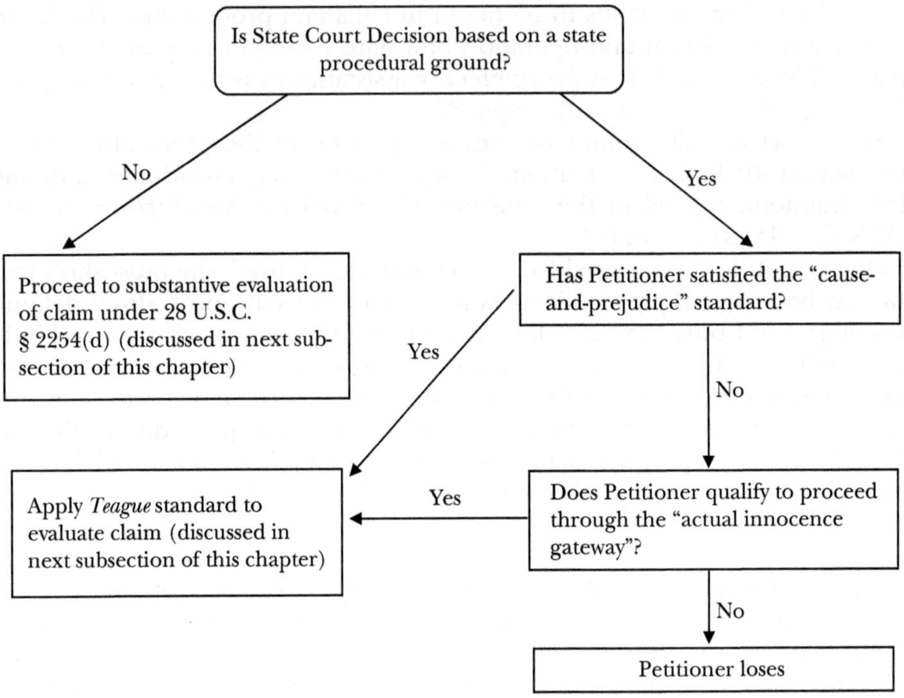

Test your understanding of state procedural default doctrine with Problem 13-2:

PROBLEM 13-2

May the Federal Court Confront the Issue?

Return to the facts in Scenario #1 from the Reference Problem in this chapter. Recall that John Woodward has been convicted of battery in a Virginia state court. He claims that his Sixth Amendment right to confront the witnesses against him was violated in his trial. Assuming for the moment that John could benefit from the constitutional rule he asserts was violated, can a federal court address the issue in a habeas action or is his claim barred based on a procedural default? If it is barred, can John qualify for any of the exceptions to the procedural default doctrine? Make sure to explain your answer.

Take a moment to consider where one is left after addressing the issue of a state procedural default. If the petitioner has not met the high burden of establishing that she is excused from the default under either the cause-and-prejudice standard or the actual innocence gateway, she loses. If, however, she is able to satisfy one or the other of these exceptions, the petitioner has succeeded only in having the federal court consider her claims substantively. In other words, clearing this hurdle does not mean that the petitioner will prevail. In the next subsection the chapter turns to the substantive consideration of a habeas corpus claim both when the petitioner avoids a state procedural default and when the state court decision is said to have been "on the merits" of the federal claim at issue.

vi. Claims Cognizable: Teague *and 28 U.S.C. § 2254(d)*

Assuming that the petitioner had satisfied all the requirements we have discussed thus far—including avoiding the bar flowing from a state procedural default if that barrier is applicable—the federal court may consider the merits of her federal claims. As an initial matter, there are some substantive claims that simply will not warrant habeas relief even if they are true. For example, Congress has exempted from habeas relief "ineffectiveness or incompetence of counsel during Federal or State collateral post-conviction proceedings." *See* 28 U.S.C. § 2254(i). Similarly, the Supreme Court has held that a state petitioner is generally not eligible for habeas relief based on a claim that state authorities violated her rights to be free from an unconstitutional search or seizure under the Fourth Amendment.[70]

Outside the narrow situations in which a claim is excluded entirely from habeas relief, the key question is: what is the state of federal law with respect to the petitioner's claims? We begin consideration of this issue with the Supreme Court's decision in *Teague v. Lane.* Note that *Teague* was decided before AEDPA. However, as we will learn, it continues to play an important role in the post-AEDPA world.

TEAGUE v. LANE

489 U.S. 288 (1989)

JUSTICE O'CONNOR announced the judgment of the Court and delivered the opinion of the Court with respect to Parts I, II, and III, and an opinion with respect to Parts IV and V, in which THE CHIEF JUSTICE, JUSTICE SCALIA, and JUSTICE KENNEDY join.

In *Taylor v. Louisiana,* this Court held that the Sixth Amendment required that the jury venire be drawn from a fair cross section of the community. The Court stated, however, that "in holding that petit juries must be drawn from a source fairly representative of the community we impose no requirement that petit juries actually chosen must mirror the community and reflect the various

70. *See Stone v. Powell,* 428 U.S. 465 (1976). The Court reasoned that the principal goal of the exclusionary rule is to deter Fourth Amendment violations. As such, the Court concluded that the time between the alleged violation and the exclusion of evidence in a federal habeas proceeding was sufficiently long that the goal of deterrence would not be served. The Court has declined to extend *Stone's* holding beyond the Fourth Amendment context. *See, e.g., Withrow v. Williams,* 507 U.S. 680 (1993) (declining to extend *Stone v. Powell* to a claim that the state violated petitioner's rights under the Fifth Amendment).

distinctive groups in the population. Defendants are not entitled to a jury of any particular composition." The principal question presented in this case is whether the Sixth Amendment's fair cross section requirement should now be extended to the petit jury. Because we adopt Justice Harlan's approach to retroactivity for cases on collateral review, we leave the resolution of that question for another day.

I

Petitioner, a black man, was convicted by an all-white Illinois jury of three counts of attempted murder, two counts of armed robbery, and one count of aggravated battery. During jury selection for petitioner's trial, the prosecutor used all 10 of his peremptory challenges to exclude blacks. Petitioner's counsel used one of his 10 peremptory challenges to exclude a black woman who was married to a police officer. After the prosecutor had struck six blacks, petitioner's counsel moved for a mistrial. The trial court denied the motion. When the prosecutor struck four more blacks, petitioner's counsel again moved for a mistrial, arguing that petitioner was "entitled to a jury of his peers." The prosecutor defended the challenges by stating that he was trying to achieve a balance of men and women on the jury. The trial court denied the motion, reasoning that the jury "appear[ed] to be a fair [one]."

On appeal, petitioner argued that the prosecutor's use of peremptory challenges denied him the right to be tried by a jury that was representative of the community. The Illinois Appellate Court rejected petitioner's fair cross section claim. The Illinois Supreme Court denied leave to appeal, and we denied certiorari.

Petitioner then filed a petition for a writ of habeas corpus in the United States District Court for the Northern District of Illinois. Petitioner repeated his fair cross section claim, and argued that the opinions of several Justices concurring in, or dissenting from, the denial of certiorari in *McCray v. New York*, had invited a reexamination of *Swain v. Alabama*, which prohibited States from purposefully and systematically denying blacks the opportunity to serve on juries. He also argued, for the first time, that under *Swain* a prosecutor could be questioned about his use of peremptory challenges once he volunteered an explanation. The District Court, though sympathetic to petitioner's arguments, held that it was bound by *Swain* and Circuit precedent.

On appeal, petitioner repeated his fair cross section claim and his *McCray* argument. A panel of the Court of Appeals agreed with petitioner that the Sixth Amendment's fair cross section requirement applied to the petit jury and held that petitioner had made out a prima facie case of discrimination. A majority of the judges on the Court of Appeals voted to rehear the case en banc, and the panel opinion was vacated. Rehearing was postponed until after our decision in *Batson v. Kentucky*, which overruled a portion of *Swain*. After *Batson* was decided, the Court of Appeals held that petitioner could not benefit from the rule in that case because *Batson* would not be applied retroactively to cases on collateral review. The Court of Appeals also held that petitioner's *Swain* claim was procedurally barred and in any event meritless. The Court of Appeals rejected petitioner's fair cross section claim, holding that the fair cross section requirement was limited to the jury venire. Judge Cudahy dissented, arguing that the fair cross section requirement should be extended to the petit jury.

II

Petitioner's first contention is that he should receive the benefit of our decision in *Batson* even though his conviction became final before *Batson* was decided. Before addressing petitioner's argument, we think it helpful to explain how *Batson* modified *Swain*. *Swain* held that a "State's purposeful or deliberate denial" to blacks of an opportunity to serve as jurors solely on account of race violates the Equal Protection Clause of the Fourteenth Amendment. In order to establish a prima facie case of discrimination under *Swain*, a defendant had to demonstrate that the peremptory challenge system had been "perverted." A defendant could raise an inference of purposeful discrimination if he showed that the prosecutor in the county where the trial was held "in case after case, whatever the circumstances, whatever the crime and whoever the defendant or the victim may be," has been responsible for the removal of qualified blacks who had survived challenges for cause, with the result that no blacks ever served on petit juries.

In *Batson*, the Court overruled that portion of *Swain* setting forth the evidentiary showing necessary to make out a prima facie case of racial discrimination under the Equal Protection Clause. The Court held that a defendant can establish a prima facie case by showing that he is a "member of a cognizable racial group," that the prosecutor exercised "peremptory challenges to remove from the venire members of the defendant's race," and that those "facts and any other relevant circumstances raise an inference that the prosecutor used that practice to exclude the veniremen from the petit jury on account of their race." Once the defendant makes out a prima facie case of discrimination, the burden shifts to the prosecutor "to come forward with a neutral explanation for challenging black jurors."

In *Allen v. Hardy*, the Court held that *Batson* constituted an "explicit and substantial break with prior precedent" because it overruled a portion of *Swain*. Employing the retroactivity standard of *Linkletter v. Walker*, the Court concluded that the rule announced in *Batson* should not be applied retroactively on collateral review of convictions that became final before *Batson* was announced. The Court defined final to mean a case "'where the judgment of conviction was rendered, the availability of appeal exhausted, and the time for petition for certiorari had elapsed before our decision in' *Batson*. . . ."

Petitioner's conviction became final 2 1/2 years prior to *Batson*, thus depriving petitioner of any benefit from the rule announced in that case. Petitioner argues, however, that *Batson* should be applied retroactively to all cases pending on direct review at the time certiorari was denied in *McCray* because the opinions filed in *McCray* destroyed the precedential effect of *Swain*. The issue in *McCray* and its companion cases was whether the Constitution prohibited the use of peremptory challenges to exclude members of a particular group from the jury, based on the prosecutor's assumption that they would be biased in favor of other members of that same group. Justices Marshall and Brennan dissented from the denial of certiorari, expressing the views that *Swain* should be reexamined and that the conduct complained of violated a defendant's Sixth Amendment right to be tried by an impartial jury drawn from a fair cross section of the community. Justices Stevens, Blackmun, and Powell concurred in the denial of certiorari. They agreed that the issue was an important one, but stated that it was a "sound exercise of discretion for the Court to allow the various States to serve as laboratories in which the issue receives further study before it is addressed."

We reject the basic premise of petitioner's argument. As we have often stated, the "denial of a writ of certiorari imports no expression of opinion upon the merits of the case. . . ." We find that *Allen v. Hardy* is dispositive, and that petitioner cannot benefit from the rule announced in *Batson.*

III

Petitioner's second contention is that he has established a violation of the Equal Protection Clause under *Swain.* [The Court then determined that Teague had failed to raise this claim in the Illinois courts and was, therefore, procedurally barred from doing so now. The Court also determined that Teague was not excused from this failure under the "cause and prejudice" standard discussed above in connection with state procedural defaults.]

IV

Petitioner's third and final contention is that the Sixth Amendment's fair cross section requirement applies to the petit jury. As we noted at the outset, *Taylor* expressly stated that the fair cross section requirement does not apply to the petit jury. Petitioner nevertheless contends that the *ratio decidendi* of *Taylor* cannot be limited to the jury venire, and he urges adoption of a new rule. Because we hold that the rule urged by petitioner should not be applied retroactively to cases on collateral review, we decline to address petitioner's contention.

A

In the past, the Court has, without discussion, often applied a new constitutional rule of criminal procedure to the defendant in the case announcing the new rule, and has confronted the question of retroactivity later when a different defendant sought the benefit of that rule. In several cases, however, the Court has addressed the retroactivity question in the very case announcing the new rule. These two lines of cases do not have a unifying theme, and we think it is time to clarify how the question of retroactivity should be resolved for cases on collateral review.

* * * *

In our view, the question "whether a decision [announcing a new rule should] be given prospective or retroactive effect should be faced at the time of [that] decision." Retroactivity is properly treated as a threshold question, for, once a new rule is applied to the defendant in the case announcing the rule, evenhanded justice requires that it be applied retroactively to all who are similarly situated. Thus, before deciding whether the fair cross section requirement should be extended to the petit jury, we should ask whether such a rule would be applied retroactively to the case at issue. This retroactivity determination would normally entail application of the *Linkletter* standard, but we believe that our approach to retroactivity for cases on collateral review requires modification.

It is admittedly often difficult to determine when a case announces a new rule, and we do not attempt to define the spectrum of what may or may not constitute a new rule for retroactivity purposes. In general, however, a case announces a new rule when it breaks new ground or imposes a new obligation on the States or the Federal Government. To put it differently, a case announces a new rule if the result was not *dictated* by precedent existing at the time the defendant's conviction became final. Given the strong language in *Taylor* and our statement in *Akins v. Texas*, that "[f]airness in [jury] selection has never been held to require proportional representation of races upon a jury," application of the fair cross section requirement to the petit jury would be a new rule.

Not all new rules have been uniformly treated for retroactivity purposes. Nearly a quarter of a century ago, in *Linkletter*, the Court attempted to set some standards by which to determine the retroactivity of new rules. The question in *Linkletter*, was whether *Mapp v. Ohio*, which made the exclusionary rule applicable to the States, should be applied retroactively to cases on collateral review. The Court determined that the retroactivity of *Mapp* should be determined by examining the purpose of the exclusionary rule, the reliance of the States on prior law, and the effect on the administration of justice of a retroactive application of the exclusionary rule. Using that standard, the Court held that *Mapp* would only apply to trials commencing after that case was decided.

The *Linkletter* retroactivity standard has not led to consistent results. Instead, it has been used to limit application of certain new rules to cases on direct review, other new rules only to the defendants in the cases announcing such rules, and still other new rules to cases in which trials have not yet commenced. . . .

* * * *

Dissatisfied with the *Linkletter* standard, Justice Harlan advocated a different approach to retroactivity. He argued that new rules should always be applied retroactively to cases on direct review, but that generally they should not be applied retroactively to criminal cases on collateral review.

In *Griffith v. Kentucky*, we rejected as unprincipled and inequitable the *Linkletter* standard for cases pending on direct review at the time a new rule is announced, and adopted the first part of the retroactivity approach advocated by Justice Harlan. We agreed with Justice Harlan that "failure to apply a newly declared constitutional rule to criminal cases pending on direct review violates basic norms of constitutional adjudication." We gave two reasons for our decision. First, because we can only promulgate new rules in specific cases and cannot possibly decide all cases in which review is sought, "the integrity of judicial review" requires the application of the new rule to "all similar cases pending on direct review. . . ."

Second, because "selective application of new rules violates the principle of treating similarly situated defendants the same," we refused to continue to tolerate the inequity that resulted from not applying new rules retroactively to defendants whose cases had not yet become final. Although new rules that constituted clear breaks with the past generally were not given retroactive effect under the *Linkletter* standard, we held that "a new rule for the conduct of criminal prosecutions is to be applied retroactively to all cases, state or federal, pending on direct review or not yet final, with no exception for cases in which the new rule constitutes a 'clear break' with the past."

The *Linkletter* standard also led to unfortunate disparity in the treatment of similarly situated defendants on collateral review. . . . This disparity in treatment was a product of two factors: our failure to treat retroactivity as a threshold question and the *Linkletter* standard's inability to account for the nature and function of collateral review. Having decided to rectify the first of those inadequacies, we now turn to the second.

B

Justice Harlan believed that new rules generally should not be applied retroactively to cases on collateral review. He argued that retroactivity for cases on collateral review could "be responsibly [determined] only by focusing, in the first instance, on the nature, function, and scope of the adjudicatory process in which such cases arise. The relevant frame of reference, in other words, is not the purpose of the new rule whose benefit the [defendant] seeks, but instead the purposes for which the writ of habeas corpus is made available." With regard to the nature of habeas corpus, Justice Harlan wrote:

> "Habeas corpus always has been a *collateral* remedy, providing an avenue for upsetting judgments that have become otherwise final. It is not designed as a substitute for direct review. The interest in leaving concluded litigation in a state of repose, that is, reducing the controversy to a final judgment not subject to further judicial revision, may quite legitimately be found by those responsible for defining the scope of the writ to outweigh in some, many, or most instances the competing interest in readjudicating convictions according to all legal standards in effect when a habeas petition is filed."

Given the "broad scope of constitutional issues cognizable on habeas," Justice Harlan argued that it is "sounder, in adjudicating habeas petitions, generally to apply the law prevailing at the time a conviction became final than it is to seek to dispose of [habeas] cases on the basis of intervening changes in constitutional interpretation." As he had explained . . . "the threat of habeas serves as a necessary additional incentive for trial and appellate courts throughout the land to conduct their proceedings in a manner consistent with established constitutional standards. In order to perform this deterrence function, . . . the habeas court need only apply the constitutional standards that prevailed at the time the original proceedings took place."

Justice Harlan identified only two exceptions to his general rule of nonretroactivity for cases on collateral review. First, a new rule should be applied retroactively if it places "certain kinds of primary, private individual conduct beyond the power of the criminal law-making authority to proscribe." Second, a new rule should be applied retroactively if it requires the observance of "those procedures that . . . are 'implicit in the concept of ordered liberty.'"

* * * *

We agree with Justice Harlan's description of the function of habeas corpus. "[T]he Court never has defined the scope of the writ simply by reference to a perceived need to assure that an individual accused of crime is afforded a trial free of constitutional error." Rather, we have recognized that interests of comity and finality must also be considered in determining the proper scope of habeas review. Thus, if a defendant fails to comply with state procedural rules and is barred from litigating a particular constitutional claim in state court, the claim can be considered on federal habeas only if the defendant shows cause for the default and actual prejudice resulting therefrom. We have declined to make the application of the procedural default rule dependent on the magnitude of the constitutional claim at issue, or on the State's interest in the enforcement of its procedural rule. [Editors' note: We discussed these issues above when considering rules concerning state procedural defaults.]

This Court has not "always followed an unwavering line in its conclusions as to the availability of the Great Writ. Our development of the law of federal habeas corpus has been attended, seemingly, with some backing and filling." Nevertheless, it has long been established that a final civil judgment entered under a given rule of law may withstand subsequent judicial change in that rule. . . .

These underlying considerations of finality find significant and compelling parallels in the criminal context. Application of constitutional rules not in existence at the time a conviction became final seriously undermines the principle of finality which is essential to the operation of our criminal justice system. Without finality, the criminal law is deprived of much of its deterrent effect. The fact that life and liberty are at stake in criminal prosecutions "shows only that 'conventional notions of finality' should not have *as much* place in criminal as in civil litigation, not that they should have *none*." "[I]f a criminal judgment is ever to be final, the notion of legality must at some point include the assignment of final competence to determine legality."

As explained by Professor Mishkin:

> "From this aspect, the *Linkletter* problem becomes not so much one of prospectivity or retroactivity of the rule but rather of the availability of collateral attack — in [that] case federal habeas corpus — to go behind the otherwise final judgment of conviction. . . . For the potential availability of collateral attack is what created the 'retroactivity' problem of *Linkletter* in the first place; there seems little doubt that without that possibility the Court would have given short shrift to any arguments for 'prospective limitation' of the *Mapp* rule."

The "costs imposed upon the State[s] by retroactive application of new rules of constitutional law on habeas corpus . . . generally far outweigh the benefits of this application." In many ways the application of new rules to cases on collateral review may be more intrusive than the enjoining of criminal prosecutions, cf. *Younger v. Harris*, for it *continually* forces the States to marshal resources in order to keep in prison defendants whose trials and appeals conformed to then-existing constitutional standards. Furthermore, . . . "[s]tate courts are understandably frustrated when they faithfully apply existing constitutional law only to have a federal court discover, during a [habeas] proceeding, new constitutional commands."

We find these criticisms to be persuasive, and we now adopt Justice Harlan's view of retroactivity for cases on collateral review. Unless they fall within an exception to the general rule, new constitutional rules of criminal procedure will not be applicable to those cases which have become final before the new rules are announced.

V

Petitioner's conviction became final in 1983. As a result, the rule petitioner urges would not be applicable to this case, which is on collateral review, unless it would fall within an exception.

The first exception suggested by Justice Harlan — that a new rule should be applied retroactively if it places "certain kinds of primary, private individual conduct beyond the power of the criminal law-making authority to proscribe" — is not relevant here. Application of the fair cross section requirement to the petit jury would not accord constitutional protection to any primary activity whatsoever.

The second exception suggested by Justice Harlan — that a new rule should be applied retroactively if it requires the observance of "those procedures that . . . are 'implicit in the concept of ordered liberty'" — we apply with a modification. The language used by Justice Harlan in *Mackey* leaves no doubt that he meant the second exception to be reserved for watershed rules of criminal procedure:

> "Typically, it should be the case that any conviction free from federal constitutional error at the time it became final, will be found, upon reflection, to have been fundamentally fair and conducted under those procedures essential to the substance of a full hearing. However, in some situations it might be that time and growth in social capacity, as well as judicial perceptions of what we can rightly demand of the adjudicatory process, will properly alter our understanding of the *bedrock procedural elements* that must be found to vitiate the fairness of a particular conviction. For example, such, in my view, is the case with the right to counsel at trial now held a necessary condition precedent to any conviction for a serious crime." (emphasis added).

. . . Justice Harlan had reasoned that one of the two principal functions of habeas corpus was "to assure that no man has been incarcerated under a procedure which creates an impermissibly large risk that the innocent will be convicted," and concluded "from this that all 'new' constitutional rules which significantly improve the pre-existing factfinding procedures are to be retroactively applied on habeas." [Later,] Justice Harlan gave three reasons for shifting to the less defined *Palko* approach. First, he observed that recent precedent . . . led "ineluctably . . . to the conclusion that it is not a principal purpose of the writ to inquire whether a criminal convict did in fact commit the deed alleged." Second, he noted that [other] cases . . . gave him reason to doubt the marginal effectiveness of claimed improvements in factfinding. Third, he found "inherently intractable the purported distinction between those new rules that are designed to improve the factfinding process and those designed principally to further other values."

We believe it desirable to combine the accuracy element of . . . the second exception with the . . . requirement that the procedure at issue must implicate the fundamental fairness of the trial. . . . Finally, we believe that Justice Harlan's concerns about the difficulty in identifying both the existence and the value of accuracy-enhancing procedural rules can be addressed by limiting the scope of the second exception to those new procedures without which the likelihood of an accurate conviction is seriously diminished.

Because we operate from the premise that such procedures would be so central to an accurate determination of innocence or guilt, we believe it unlikely that many such components of basic due process have yet to emerge. We are also of the view that such rules are "best illustrated by recalling the classic grounds for the issuance of a writ of habeas corpus — that the proceeding was dominated by mob violence; that the prosecutor knowingly made use of perjured testimony; or that the conviction was based on a confession extorted from the defendant by brutal methods."[71]

71. [Footnote 2 in the Court's opinion.] Because petitioner is not under sentence of death, we need not, and do not, express any views as to how the retroactivity approach we adopt today is to be

An examination of our decision in *Taylor* applying the fair cross section requirement to the jury venire leads inexorably to the conclusion that adoption of the rule petitioner urges would be a far cry from the kind of absolute prerequisite to fundamental fairness that is "implicit in the concept of ordered liberty." The requirement that the jury venire be composed of a fair cross section of the community is based on the role of the jury in our system. Because the purpose of the jury is to guard against arbitrary abuses of power by interposing the commonsense judgment of the community between the State and the defendant, the jury venire cannot be composed only of special segments of the population. "Community participation in the administration of the criminal law . . . is not only consistent with our democratic heritage but is also critical to public confidence in the fairness of the criminal justice system." But as we stated in *Daniel v. Louisiana*, which held that *Taylor* was not to be given retroactive effect, the fair cross section requirement "[does] not rest on the premise that every criminal trial, or any particular trial, [is] necessarily unfair because it [is] not conducted in accordance with what we determined to be the requirements of the Sixth Amendment." Because the absence of a fair cross section on the jury venire does not undermine the fundamental fairness that must underlie a conviction or seriously diminish the likelihood of obtaining an accurate conviction, we conclude that a rule requiring that petit juries be composed of a fair cross section of the community would not be a "bedrock procedural element" that would be retroactively applied under the second exception we have articulated.

Were we to recognize the new rule urged by petitioner in this case, we would have to give petitioner the benefit of that new rule even though it would not be applied retroactively to others similarly situated. In the words of Justice Brennan, such an inequitable result would be "an unavoidable consequence of the necessity that constitutional adjudications not stand as mere dictum." But the harm caused by the failure to treat similarly situated defendants alike cannot be exaggerated: such inequitable treatment "hardly comports with the ideal of 'administration of justice with an even hand.'" Our refusal to allow such disparate treatment in the direct review context led us to adopt the first part of Justice Harlan's retroactivity approach in *Griffith*. "The fact that the new rule may constitute a clear break with the past has no bearing on the 'actual inequity that results' when only one of many similarly situated defendants receives the benefit of the new rule."

If there were no other way to avoid rendering advisory opinions, we might well agree that the inequitable treatment described above is "an insignificant cost for adherence to sound principles of decision-making." But there is a more principled way of dealing with the problem. We can simply refuse to announce a new rule in a given case unless the rule would be applied retroactively to the defendant in the case and to all others similarly situated. We think this approach is a sound one. Not only does it eliminate any problems of rendering advisory opinions, it also avoids the inequity resulting from the uneven application of new rules to similarly situated defendants. We therefore hold that, implicit in the retroactivity approach we adopt today, is the principle that habeas corpus cannot

applied in the capital sentencing context. We do, however, disagree with Justice Stevens' suggestion that the finality concerns underlying Justice Harlan's approach to retroactivity are limited to "making convictions final," and are therefore "wholly inapplicable to the capital sentencing context." As we have often stated, a criminal judgment necessarily includes the sentence imposed upon the defendant. Collateral challenges to the sentence in a capital case, like collateral challenges to the sentence in a noncapital case, delay the enforcement of the judgment at issue and decrease the possibility that "there will at some point be the certainty that comes with an end to litigation."

be used as a vehicle to create new constitutional rules of criminal procedure unless those rules would be applied retroactively to *all* defendants on collateral review through one of the two exceptions we have articulated. Because a decision extending the fair cross section requirement to the petit jury would not be applied retroactively to cases on collateral review under the approach we adopt today, we do not address petitioner's claim.

For the reasons set forth above, the judgment of the Court of Appeals is affirmed.

It is so ordered.

[Concurring opinions by Justice White and Justice Blackmun have been omitted.]

JUSTICE STEVENS, with whom JUSTICE BLACKMUN joins as to Part I, concurring in part and concurring in the judgment.

I

For the reasons stated in Part III of Justice Brennan's dissent, I am persuaded this petitioner has alleged a violation of the Sixth Amendment. I also believe the Court should decide that question in his favor. I do not agree with Justice O'Connor's assumption that a ruling in petitioner's favor on the merits of the Sixth Amendment issue would require that his conviction be set aside.

When a criminal defendant claims that a procedural error tainted his conviction, an appellate court often decides whether error occurred before deciding whether that error requires reversal or should be classified as harmless. I would follow a parallel approach in cases raising novel questions of constitutional law on collateral review, first determining whether the trial process violated any of the petitioner's constitutional rights and then deciding whether the petitioner is entitled to relief. If error occurred, factors relating to retroactivity—most importantly, the magnitude of unfairness—should be examined before granting the petitioner relief. Proceeding in reverse, a plurality of the Court today declares that a new rule should not apply retroactively without ever deciding whether there is such a rule.

In general, I share Justice Harlan's views about retroactivity. Thus I joined the Court in holding that, as Justice Harlan had urged, new criminal procedural rules should be applied to all defendants whose convictions are not final when the rule is announced. I also agree with Justice Harlan that defendants seeking collateral review should not benefit from new rules unless those rules "fre[e] individuals from punishment for conduct that is constitutionally protected" or unless the original trial entailed elements of fundamental unfairness. Thus, although I question the propriety of making such an important change in the law without briefing or argument, I am persuaded that the Court should adopt Justice Harlan's analysis of retroactivity for habeas corpus cases as well for cases still on direct review.

I do not agree, however, with the plurality's dicta proposing a "modification" of Justice Harlan's fundamental fairness exception. . . .

The plurality wrongly resuscitates Justice Harlan's early view, indicating that the only procedural errors deserving correction on collateral review are those that undermine "an accurate determination of innocence or guilt. . . ."

I cannot agree that it is "unnecessarily anachronistic," to issue a writ of habeas corpus to a petitioner convicted in a manner that violates fundamental principles of liberty. Furthermore, a touchstone of factual innocence would provide little guidance in certain important types of cases, such as those challenging the constitutionality of capital sentencing hearings. Even when assessing errors at the guilt phase of a trial, factual innocence is too capricious a factor by which to determine if a procedural change is sufficiently "*bedrock*" or "watershed" to justify application of the fundamental fairness exception. In contrast, given our century-old proclamation that the Constitution does not allow exclusion of jurors because of race, a rule promoting selection of juries free from racial bias clearly implicates concerns of fundamental fairness.

As a matter of first impression, therefore, I would conclude that a guilty verdict delivered by a jury whose impartiality might have been eroded by racial prejudice is fundamentally unfair. Constraining that conclusion is the Court's holding in *Allen v. Hardy*—an opinion I did not join—that *Batson v. Kentucky* cannot be applied retroactively to permit collateral review of convictions that became final before it was decided. It is true that the *Batson* decision rested on the Equal Protection Clause of the Fourteenth Amendment and that this case raises a Sixth Amendment issue. In both cases, however, petitioners pressed their objections to the jury selection on both grounds. Both cases concern the constitutionality of allowing the use of peremptories to yield a jury that may be biased against a defendant on account of race. Identical practical ramifications will ensue from our holdings in both cases. Thus if there is no fundamental unfairness in denying retroactive relief to a petitioner denied his Fourteenth Amendment right to a fairly chosen jury, as the Court held in *Allen*, there cannot be fundamental unfairness in denying this petitioner relief for the violation of his Sixth Amendment right to an impartial jury. I therefore agree that the judgment of the Court of Appeals must be affirmed.

II

[In Part II of his opinion Justice Stevens expressed his disagreement with Justice O'Connor's opinion rejecting Teague's *Swain* argument. However, he agreed that Teague was procedurally barred from asserting that claim because he had not presented it to the state courts.]

JUSTICE BRENNAN, with whom JUSTICE MARSHALL joins, dissenting.

Today a plurality of this Court, without benefit of briefing and oral argument, adopts a novel threshold test for federal review of state criminal convictions on habeas corpus. It does so without regard for—indeed, without even mentioning—our contrary decisions over the past 35 years delineating the broad scope of habeas relief. The plurality further appears oblivious to the importance we have consistently accorded the principle of *stare decisis* in nonconstitutional cases. Out of an exaggerated concern for treating similarly situated habeas petitioners the same, the plurality would for the first time preclude the federal courts from considering on collateral review a vast range of important constitutional challenges; where those challenges have merit, it would bar the vindication of personal constitutional rights and deny society a check against further violations until the same claim is presented on direct review. In my view, the plurality's "blind adherence to the principle of treating like cases alike" amounts to "letting the tail wag the dog" when it stymies the resolution of substantial and unheralded constitutional questions. Because I cannot acquiesce in this unprecedented curtailment of the reach of the Great Writ, particularly in the absence of any discussion of these momentous changes by the parties or the lower courts, I dissent.

I

The federal habeas corpus statute provides that a federal court "shall entertain an application for a writ of habeas corpus in behalf of a person in custody pursuant to the judgment of a State court only on the ground that he is in custody in violation of the Constitution or laws or treaties of the United States." 28 U.S.C. § 2254. For well over a century, we have read this statute and its forbears to authorize federal courts to grant writs of habeas corpus whenever a person's liberty is unconstitutionally restrained. Shortly after the Habeas Corpus Act of 1867, empowered federal courts to issue writs of habeas corpus to state authorities, we noted: "This legislation is of the most comprehensive character. It brings within the *habeas corpus* jurisdiction of every court and of every judge every possible case of privation of liberty contrary to the National Constitution, treaties, or laws. It is impossible to widen this jurisdiction." Nothing has happened since to persuade us to alter that judgment. Our thorough survey in *Fay v. Noia* of the history of habeas corpus at common law and in its federal statutory embodiment led us to conclude that "conventional notions of finality in criminal litigation cannot be permitted to defeat the manifest federal policy that federal constitutional rights of personal liberty shall not be denied without the fullest opportunity for plenary federal judicial review." In *Noia* we therefore held that federal courts have the power to inquire into any constitutional defect in a state criminal trial, provided that the petitioner remains "in custody" by virtue of the judgment rendered at that trial. Our subsequent rulings have not departed from that teaching in cases where the presentation of a petitioner's claim on collateral review is not barred by a procedural default.

* * * *

Our precedents thus supply no support for the plurality's curtailment of habeas relief.[72] Just as it was "a fortuity that we overruled *Swain v. Alabama*, [which set forth an unduly strict standard for proving that a prosecutor's use of peremptory challenges was racially discriminatory in violation of the Equal

72. [Footnote 2 in Justice Brennan's dissent.] Until today, this Court has imposed but one substantive limitation on the cognizability of habeas claims. In *Stone v. Powell*, the Court held that where a State has provided a defendant with an opportunity for full and fair litigation of a claim that evidence used against him was obtained through an unlawful search or seizure in violation of the Fourth Amendment, he may not relitigate that claim on federal habeas. The Court noted, however, that "Fourth Amendment violations are different in kind from denials of Fifth or Sixth Amendment rights" and it expressly stated that its decision was "*not* concerned with the scope of the habeas corpus statute as authority for litigating constitutional claims generally," in substantial part because "the exclusionary rule is a judicially created remedy rather than a personal constitutional right." None of the Court's reasoning in *Stone v. Powell* supports the plurality's present decision not to adjudicate Teague's claim, because Teague is attempting to vindicate what he alleges is a fundamental personal right, rather than trying to invoke a prophylactic rule devised by this Court to deter violations of personal constitutional rights by law enforcement officials. In cases of this kind, our reluctance to allow federal courts to interfere with state criminal processes has never been deemed paramount. . . .

Protection Clause], in a case that came to us on direct review" when "[w]e could as easily have granted certiorari and decided the matter in a case on collateral review" so too there is no reason why we cannot decide Teague's almost identical claim under the Sixth Amendment on collateral review rather than in a case on direct review. Because there is no basis for extending the Court's rationale in *Stone v. Powell*, to preclude review of Teague's challenge to the composition of the jury that convicted him, and because I perceive no other ground consistent with our precedents for limiting the cognizability of constitutional claims on federal habeas corpus, I would reach the merits of Teague's Sixth Amendment argument and hold in his favor.

II

Unfortunately, the plurality turns its back on established case law and would erect a formidable new barrier to relief. Any time a federal habeas petitioner's claim, if successful, would result in the announcement of a new rule of law, the plurality says, it may only be adjudicated if that rule would "plac[e] 'certain kinds of primary, private individual conduct beyond the power of the criminal law-making authority to proscribe,'" or if it would mandate "new procedures without which the likelihood of an accurate conviction is seriously diminished."

A

[Section II A of Justice Brennan's dissent faults the Court for considering issues not raised by the parties.]

B

[Section II B of Justice Brennan's dissent faults the Court for, in his view, failing to adhere to *stare decisis*.]

C

The plurality does not so much as mention *stare decisis*. Indeed, from the plurality's exposition of its new rule, one might infer that its novel fabrication will work no great change in the availability of federal collateral review of state convictions. Nothing could be further from the truth. Although the plurality declines to "define the spectrum of what may or may not constitute a new rule for retroactivity purposes," it does say that generally "a case announces a new rule when it breaks new ground or imposes a new obligation on the States or the Federal Government." Otherwise phrased, "a case announces a new rule if the result was not *dictated* by precedent existing at the time the defendant's conviction became final." This account is extremely broad. Few decisions on appeal or collateral review are "*dictated*" by what came before. Most such cases involve a question of law that is at least debatable, permitting a rational judge to resolve the case in more than one way. Virtually no case that prompts a dissent on the relevant legal point, for example, could be said to be "*dictated*" by prior decisions. By the plurality's test, therefore, a great many cases could only be heard on habeas if the rule urged by the petitioner fell within one of the two exceptions the plurality has sketched. Those exceptions, however, are narrow. Rules that place "'certain kinds of primary, private individual conduct beyond the power of the criminal lawmaking authority to proscribe'" are rare. And rules that would require "new procedures without which the likelihood of an accurate conviction is seriously diminished" are not appreciably more common. The plurality admits, in fact, that it "believe[s] it unlikely that many such components of basic due process have yet to emerge." The plurality's approach today can thus be expected to contract substantially the Great Writ's sweep.

* * * *

D

These are massive changes, unsupported by precedent. They also lack a reasonable foundation. By exaggerating the importance of treating like cases alike and granting relief to all identically positioned habeas petitioners or none, "the Court acts as if it has no choice but to follow a mechanical notion of fairness without pausing to consider 'sound principles of decisionmaking.'" Certainly it is desirable, in the interest of fairness, to accord the same treatment to all habeas petitioners with the same claims. Given a choice between deciding an issue on direct or collateral review that might result in a new rule of law that would not warrant retroactive application to persons on collateral review other than the petitioner who brought the claim, we should ordinarily grant certiorari and decide the question on direct review. Following our decision in *Griffith v. Kentucky*, a new rule would apply equally to all persons whose convictions had not become final before the rule was announced, whereas habeas petitioners other than the one whose case we decided might not benefit from such a rule if we adopted it on collateral review. Taking cases on direct review ahead of those on habeas is especially attractive because the retrial of habeas petitioners usually places a heavier burden on the States than the retrial of persons on direct review. Other things being equal, our concern for fairness and finality ought to therefore lead us to render our decision in a case that comes to us on direct review.

Other things are not always equal, however. Sometimes a claim which, if successful, would create a new rule not appropriate for retroactive application on collateral review is better presented by a habeas case than by one on direct review. In fact, sometimes the claim is *only* presented on collateral review. In that case, while we could forgo deciding the issue in the hope that it would eventually be presented squarely on direct review, that hope might be misplaced, and even if it were in time fulfilled, the opportunity to check constitutional violations and to further the evolution of our thinking in some area of the law would in the meanwhile have been lost. In addition, by preserving our right and that of the lower federal courts to hear such claims on collateral review, we would not discourage their litigation on federal habeas corpus and thus not deprive ourselves and society of the benefit of decisions by the lower federal courts when we must resolve these issues ourselves.

The plurality appears oblivious to these advantages of our settled approach to collateral review. Instead, it would deny itself these benefits because adherence to precedent would occasionally result in one habeas petitioner's obtaining redress while another petitioner with an identical claim could not qualify for relief. In my view, the uniform treatment of habeas petitioners is not worth the price the plurality is willing to pay. Permitting the federal courts to decide novel habeas claims not substantially related to guilt or innocence has profited our society immensely. Congress has not seen fit to withdraw those benefits by amending the statute that provides for them. And although a favorable decision for a petitioner might not extend to another prisoner whose identical claim has become final, it is at least arguably better that the wrong done to one person be righted than that none of the injuries inflicted on those whose convictions have become final be redressed, despite the resulting inequality in treatment. . . .

Perfectly even-handed treatment of habeas petitioners can by no means justify the plurality's *sua sponte* renunciation of the ample benefits of adjudicating novel constitutional claims on habeas corpus that do not bear substantially on guilt or innocence.

III

[In Part III of his dissent Justice Brennan rejected the majority's application of the test it had adopted to Teague's claim.]

IV

A majority of this Court's Members now share the view that cases on direct and collateral review should be handled differently for retroactivity purposes. In *Griffith*, the Court adopted Justice Harlan's proposal that a new rule be applied retroactively to all convictions not yet final when the rule was announced. If we had adhered to our precedents, reached Teague's Sixth Amendment claim, and ruled in his favor, we would ultimately have had to decide whether we should continue to apply to habeas cases the three-factor approach [in earlier cases concerning retroactivity on collateral review] or whether we should embrace most of the other half of Justice Harlan's proposal and ordinarily refuse to apply new rules retroactively to cases on collateral review, except in the cases where they are announced.

In my view, that is not a question we should decide here. The better course would have been to grant certiorari in another case on collateral review raising the same issue and to resolve the question after full briefing and oral argument. Justices Blackmun and Stevens disagree. They concur in the Court's judgment on this point because they find further discussion unnecessary and because they believe that, although Teague's Sixth Amendment claim is meritorious, neither he nor other habeas petitioners may benefit from a favorable ruling. As I said in [an earlier case] according a petitioner relief when his claim prevails seems to me "an unavoidable consequence of the necessity that constitutional adjudications not stand as mere dictum." But I share the view of Justices Blackmun and Stevens that the retroactivity question is one we need not address until Teague's claim has been found meritorious. Certainly it is not one the Court need decide *before* it considers the merits of Teague's claim because, as the plurality mistakenly contends, its resolution properly determines whether the merits should be reached. By repudiating our familiar approach without regard for the doctrine of *stare decisis*, the plurality would deprive us of the manifold advantages of deciding important constitutional questions when they come to us first or most cleanly on collateral review. I dissent.

DISCUSSION AND QUESTIONS

Teague can be seen as a case about choice of law. In other words, *Teague* provides the means to determine the content of federal law at the relevant time given the petitioner's allegations. As such, it concerns principally a question of *timing*. The goal—according to the Court—is to judge whether the state court applied federal law correctly as of the time it made the relevant decision. This is why the *Teague* Court discusses "new" rules and "old" rules. A diagram is helpful in considering the Court's approach:[73]

FIGURE 13-2

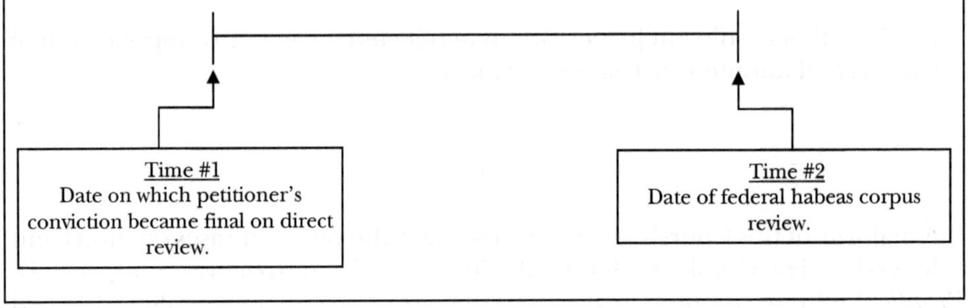

A *Teague* Timeline

Under *Teague*, if the law is the same at Time #1 and Time #2, there is no issue as to the appropriate federal rule to apply. The rules are the same and the federal habeas court should adjudicate the petitioner's federal claims under the relevant law. To make this assessment, the federal court must determine what the federal law was at Time #1 and ensure that, assuming the petitioner's allegations are true, she has stated a violation of her federal rights. There is no question of a "new rule" because federal law is the same at all relevant points.[74]

The difficulty comes when the law at Time #1 and the law at Time #2 are, or may be, different. In this situation stated most starkly, the petitioner would prevail if the law at Time #2 was applicable but would lose if the law at Time #1 stated the relevant rule. The rule adopted in *Teague* leads to the result in most cases that the petitioner will not prevail because in almost every case the federal court should apply the law as it stood at Time #1.

The result in *Teague* concerns situations in which the state prisoner is advancing a collateral habeas corpus claim. As the Court explains, the rule is different in the context of a direct appeal. In this situation, a state prisoner will be entitled to the application of a new rule (as will all persons who have not yet completed their direct appeals).[75] The Court indicated that in this context the importance of ensuring the growth of federal law, as well as fairness to similarly situated parties on direct review, outweighed the negative effects of "second-guessing" state courts that correctly applied the rule existing at the relevant time. As *Teague* demonstrates, the Court adopts a different approach for habeas corpus.

73. Justice O'Connor wrote for a plurality in *Teague*. A majority of the Court later adopted and applied the *Teague* analysis. *See, e.g., Penry v. Lynaugh*, 492 U.S. 302 (1989).

74. As Justice O'Connor recognized in *Teague*, determining whether a rule is a new one is not always an easy task. For situations in which there is a clear break from past precedent the question is straightforward. *See Teague*, 489 U.S. at 301. However, a new rule can also develop over time due to "gradual developments in the law over which reasonable jurists may disagree." *See Sawyer v. Smith*, 497 U.S. 227, 234 (1990). The Supreme Court and the lower federal courts have struggled since *Teague* to determine when a rule evolves sufficiently to be "new" for purposes of retroactivity analysis. This is particularly the case when the old rule is one that is based on a facts and circumstances type of approach.

75. *See Griffith v. Kentucky*, 479 U.S. 314 (1987).

Returning to the collateral review context, note that there are two ways in which one can face a situation in which the law at Time #1 and Time #2 are different. One possibility is that at Time #1 the rule is that a certain action is not in violation of federal law. After the petitioner's conviction becomes final on direct review, the Supreme Court decides a case in which it determines that the Constitution is violated by the act the petitioner describes. Then the petitioner files her federal habeas corpus petition. Here, we know what the relevant law actually is at Time #2 — it is the Court's decision stating that the act in question is unconstitutional. *Teague* mandates that unless the petitioner comes within one of the narrow *Teague* exceptions (discussed below), the federal court should apply the law that existed at Time #1. As a result the petitioner would not prevail.

The second situation is different in an important respect. In this case, the law at Time #1 states that a given action is not in violation of federal law. The petitioner seeks federal habeas corpus relief and argues that federal law *should be different.* In other words, there has been no intervening decision establishing that the action in question is in violation of the Constitution. In this situation, the petitioner still loses (unless she can satisfy one of the *Teague* exceptions).[76] What is important, however, is how the Court instructs the lower courts to evaluate the petitioner's argument that the law at Time #2 should recognize a constitutional violation.

Teague teaches that the federal court should only *assume* that the petitioner's assertion that there was a constitutional violation at Time #2 was correct and then analyze whether the petitioner would be entitled to have that "new rule" applied to her. In other words, the federal court is not to actually decide what the new rule should be. The effect of proceeding in this manner is that federal law generally will not be developed in the context of habeas corpus. Recognize that one could still reach the result in *Teague*— the petitioner could still lose if she sought application of a new rule — if one required the federal court to actually decide whether the asserted new rule was correct. Thus, one could provide for the growth of federal law in federal court even if one still made it difficult for petitioners to benefit from new rules. The counter-argument on which the Court relies is that proceeding in a different manner would produce advisory opinions.

Another important aspect of *Teague* concerns where one may look to determine the content of federal law at Time #1 and Time #2. As you should see at this point, a state petitioner has a strong incentive to show that the rule at Time #2 is not in fact a new one. All things being equal, the more places where one can look to establish that rule is not new, the better. Under *Teague* there is no express limitation on the sources establishing the federal rule. One could find the rule in state court decisions, federal court decisions at the district and circuit levels, as well as the Supreme Court. To be sure, there are still difficult questions to face under this approach. For example, assume that the petitioner was convicted in New York state court. She claims that a certain action was in violation of the Constitution. There is no court decision from the New York state courts on point nor are there any decisions in the United States Court of Appeals for the Second Circuit. However, there is a decision from the United States Court of Appeals for the Ninth Circuit in petitioner's favor. Does this decision establish that the law at Time #2 is such that the petitioner should prevail because she seeks the application of an "old rule"? The Supreme Court has never provided concrete guidance on this issue. As with

76. In an important decision, the Court ruled that *Teague*'s retroactivity rules are not constitutionally mandated. Thus, a state court is not bound to follow them. The result is that a state court is free to give the benefit of a "new rule" to a petitioner in the context of state collateral review proceedings. *See Danforth v. Minnesota*, 552 U.S. 264 (2008).

many other areas of the law, it appears that one would need to evaluate the specific context of the lower court decisions to decide whether the rule advocated was new or was in fact established through a combination of lower court decisions.

Finally, one should consider the two *Teague* exceptions under which a petitioner would be entitled to the application of a "new rule." The first exception is where the "new rule" precludes a state from criminalizing the conduct for which the petitioner was convicted. As you might expect, this situation does not often arise. The second exception concerns rules "without which the likelihood of an accurate conviction is seriously diminished." This later exception is often referred to as dealing with "watershed rules" of criminal procedure. An example is the constitutional rule guaranteeing a person accused of certain crimes the assistance of counsel. This second exception has been interpreted narrowly. Indeed, the Court has suggested that there are few (if any) rules not already established that would qualify as a watershed rule

The *Teague* analysis is visually depicted in Figure 13-3:

FIGURE 13-3

Teague v. Lane

Step #1: Determine the date on which petitioner's state court conviction became final on direct review. ("Time #1")

Step #2: Determine content of federal law at Time #1.

Step #3: Ask whether, if true, petitioner's allegations would establish a violation of federal law at Time #1.

If yes → Petitioner is not asserting a "new rule." Apply law.

If no → Petitioner is asserting a "new rule." Proceed to Step #4.

Step #4: Assuming that the new rule asserted by petitioner is correct, does the new rule preclude the state from criminalizing the conduct for which petitioner was convicted?

Yes → Petitioner gets benefit of "new rule." Court proceeds to actually decide whether the new rule is in fact correct.

No → Proceed to Step #5

Step #5: Assuming that the new rule asserted by petitioner is correct, is the rule one "without which the likelihood of an accurate conviction is seriously diminished"?

Yes → Petitioner gets benefit of "new rule." Court proceeds to actually decide whether the new rule is in fact correct.

No → Petitioner does not get benefit of new rule.

Test your understanding of *Teague* with the following problem:

PROBLEM 13-3

The Confusing Sentence Enhancement

Jane Chen is a 25-year-old resident of Los Angeles, California, which is within the jurisdiction of the United States Court of Appeals for the Ninth Circuit. Jane got involved with drugs when she was in high school, and her life spun out of control. On the night of June 10, 2012, Jane was partying with a group of people at the house of John Grant. Jane and John had dated in the past but had recently had a nasty breakup. There was much drinking and drug use at the party. Late in the evening John and Jane got into a heated argument. Jane took out a gun she carried for protection. No one is sure exactly what happened next, but the gun Jane took out went off and shot John in the chest. He was severely injured although he eventually recovered.

Jane was charged with aggravated assault and attempted murder under California law. The prosecutors also included in the indictment (or charging document) a sentence enhancement known under California law as "Enhancement B." Enhancement B provided that if a person was convicted of an offence in which the person "personally used a firearm" the person would have an additional ten years added to her sentence. There is also a sentence enhancement provision under California law known "Enhancement D." Enhancement D provides that if a person was convicted of an offence in which she "intentionally and personally discharged a firearm" an additional 25 years would be added to her sentence. Jane's indictment did not include a reference to Enhancement D.

Jane went to trial in December 2012. An odd thing happened at the end of the trial. The trial judge instructed the jury that it should determine whether Jane had "intentionally and personally discharged a firearm" in the course of John's shooting. In other words, the trial judge quoted the language of Enhancement D instead of Enhancement B. Jane's counsel appropriately objected at the time the instruction was given. The jury convicted Jane of the substantive offenses and found that Jane had "intentionally and personally discharged the firearm." The jury rendered its verdict on January 5, 2013.

Jane appealed the jury's verdict in the California state court system. Her claim was that her conviction was unconstitutional because she was convicted under Enhancement D when the indictment only referred to Enhancement B. Jane based her argument on a United States Supreme Court case (*Alpha v. Beta*)[77] that held that a criminal defendant has a right to know the charges against him or her as well as the punishment applicable to the violation of such laws. Jane also relied on a Ninth Circuit case (*Omega v. Theta*) that had held that a failure to specify a sentence enhancement in an indictment could not be cured by a later disclosure of an enhancement during trial. The California state courts had not ruled on the issue.

The state argued on appeal that *Alpha* did not deal with the issue of whether a failure to include an enhancement in an indictment could be cured. The state argued that the Ninth Circuit's rule in *Omega* was incorrect and that, instead, the state courts should follow the rule from the Fifth Circuit in *Delta v. Phi.* The Fifth Circuit had specifically held that a failure to include an enhancement in an

77. The substantive law cited in this question may or may not reflect actual law. You should not apply other knowledge of the actual law you might have.

indictment could be cured by disclosure of the enhancement at trial. All the cases cited above had been decided before Jane was put on trial.

The California Supreme Court denied Jane's appeal on April 30, 2013, ruling that the Fifth Circuit had reached the correct conclusion in *Delta.* Jane did not appeal the California Supreme Court's decision. She also did not pursue habeas corpus relief in the California state court system even though such an avenue was available to her. Instead, on February 1, 2014, Jane filed a petition for writ of habeas corpus in an appropriate federal court under 28 U.S.C. §§ 2241 and 2254.

You are a clerk to the United States District Judge to whom the case has been assigned. The judge has asked you to prepare a memorandum discussing how he should approach Jane's petition for a writ of habeas corpus. The judge would like you to advise him whether the writ should be granted. Please prepare the memorandum for your judge. Be as comprehensive as you can given the facts you have been provided. For present purposes you should assume that the amendments that AEDPA made to § 2254(d) discussed next had not been enacted.

When it enacted AEDPA, Congress made significant changes to the way in which a federal court determines the relevant content of federal law for purposes of adjudicating habeas corpus claims. The key statutory provision is 28 U.S.C. § 2254(d). The following case considers how that statutory provision changed the collateral review landscape.

TERRY WILLIAMS v. TAYLOR

529 U.S. 362 (2000)

JUSTICE STEVENS announced the judgment of the Court and delivered the opinion of the Court with respect to Parts I, III, and IV, and an opinion with respect to Parts II and v.[78]

The questions presented are whether Terry Williams' constitutional right to the effective assistance of counsel as defined in *Strickland v. Washington,* was violated, and whether the judgment of the Virginia Supreme Court refusing to set aside his death sentence "was contrary to, or involved an unreasonable application of, clearly established Federal law, as determined by the Supreme Court of the United States," within the meaning of 28 U.S.C. § 2254(d)(1). We answer both questions affirmatively.

I

On November 3, 1985, Harris Stone was found dead in his residence on Henry Street in Danville, Virginia. Finding no indication of a struggle, local officials determined that the cause of death was blood alcohol poisoning, and the case was considered closed. Six months after Stone's death, Terry Williams, who was

78. [Footnote * in the Court's opinion.] Justice Souter, Justice Ginsburg, and Justice Breyer join this opinion in its entirety. Justice O'Connor and Justice Kennedy join Parts I, III, and IV of this opinion.

then incarcerated in the "I" unit of the city jail for an unrelated offense, wrote a letter to the police stating that he had killed "'that man down on Henry Street'" and also stating that he "'did it'" to that "'lady down on West Green Street'" and was "'very sorry.'" The letter was unsigned, but it closed with a reference to "I cell." The police readily identified Williams as its author, and, on April 25, 1986, they obtained several statements from him. In one Williams admitted that, after Stone refused to lend him "'a couple of dollars,'" he had killed Stone with a mattock and took the money from his wallet. In September 1986, Williams was convicted of robbery and capital murder.

At Williams' sentencing hearing, the prosecution proved that Williams had been convicted of armed robbery in 1976 and burglary and grand larceny in 1982. The prosecution also introduced the written confessions that Williams had made in April. The prosecution described two auto thefts and two separate violent assaults on elderly victims perpetrated after the Stone murder. On December 4, 1985, Williams had started a fire outside one victim's residence before attacking and robbing him. On March 5, 1986, Williams had brutally assaulted an elderly woman on West Green Street—an incident he had mentioned in his letter to the police. That confession was particularly damaging because other evidence established that the woman was in a "vegetative state" and not expected to recover. Williams had also been convicted of arson for setting a fire in the jail while awaiting trial in this case. Two expert witnesses employed by the State testified that there was a "high probability" that Williams would pose a serious continuing threat to society.

The evidence offered by Williams' trial counsel at the sentencing hearing consisted of the testimony of Williams' mother, two neighbors, and a taped excerpt from a statement by a psychiatrist. One of the neighbors had not been previously interviewed by defense counsel, but was noticed by counsel in the audience during the proceedings and asked to testify on the spot. The three witnesses briefly described Williams as a "nice boy" and not a violent person. The recorded psychiatrist's testimony did little more than relate Williams' statement during an examination that in the course of one of his earlier robberies, he had removed the bullets from a gun so as not to injure anyone.

In his cross-examination of the prosecution witnesses, Williams' counsel repeatedly emphasized the fact that Williams had initiated the contact with the police that enabled them to solve the murder and to identify him as the perpetrator of the recent assaults, as well as the car thefts. In closing argument, Williams' counsel characterized Williams' confessional statements as "dumb," but asked the jury to give weight to the fact that he had "turned himself in, not on one crime but on four . . . that the [police otherwise] would not have solved." The weight of defense counsel's closing, however, was devoted to explaining that it was difficult to find a reason why the jury should spare Williams' life.[79]

The jury found a probability of future dangerousness and unanimously fixed Williams' punishment at death. The trial judge concluded that such

79. [Footnote 2 in Court's opinion.] In defense counsel's words: "I will admit too that it is very difficult to ask you to show mercy to a man who maybe has not shown much mercy himself. I doubt very seriously that he thought much about mercy when he was in Mr. Stone's bedroom that night with him. I doubt very seriously that he had mercy very highly on his mind when he was walking along West Green and the incident with Alberta Stroud. I doubt very seriously that he had mercy on his mind when he took two cars that didn't belong to him. Admittedly it is very difficult to get up and ask that you give this man mercy when he has shown so little of it himself. But I would ask that you would."

punishment was "proper" and "just" and imposed the death sentence. The Virginia Supreme Court affirmed the conviction and sentence. It rejected Williams' argument that when the trial judge imposed sentence, he failed to give mitigating weight to the fact that Williams had turned himself in.

STATE HABEAS CORPUS PROCEEDINGS

In 1988 Williams filed for state collateral relief in the Danville Circuit Court. The petition was subsequently amended, and the Circuit Court (the same judge who had presided over Williams' trial and sentencing) held an evidentiary hearing on Williams' claim that trial counsel had been ineffective. Based on the evidence adduced after two days of hearings, Judge Ingram found that Williams' conviction was valid, but that his trial attorneys had been ineffective during sentencing. Among the evidence reviewed that had not been presented at trial were documents prepared in connection with Williams' commitment when he was 11 years old that dramatically described mistreatment, abuse, and neglect during his early childhood, as well as testimony that he was "borderline mentally retarded," had suffered repeated head injuries, and might have mental impairments organic in origin. The habeas hearing also revealed that the same experts who had testified on the State's behalf at trial believed that Williams, if kept in a "structured environment," would not pose a future danger to society.

Counsel's failure to discover and present this and other significant mitigating evidence was "below the range expected of reasonable, professional competent assistance of counsel." Counsel's performance thus "did not measure up to the standard required under the holding of *Strickland v. Washington* and [if it had,] there is a reasonable probability that the result of the sentencing phase would have been different." Judge Ingram therefore recommended that Williams be granted a rehearing on the sentencing phase of his trial.

The Virginia Supreme Court did not accept that recommendation. Although it assumed, without deciding, that trial counsel had been ineffective, it disagreed with the trial judge's conclusion that Williams had suffered sufficient prejudice to warrant relief. Treating the prejudice inquiry as a mixed question of law and fact, the Virginia Supreme Court accepted the factual determination that available evidence in mitigation had not been presented at the trial, but held that the trial judge had misapplied the law in two respects. First, relying on our decision in *Lockhart v. Fretwell* the court held that it was wrong for the trial judge to rely "'on mere outcome determination'" when assessing prejudice. Second, it construed the trial judge's opinion as having "adopted a *per se* approach" that would establish prejudice whenever any mitigating evidence was omitted.

The court then reviewed the prosecution evidence supporting the "future dangerousness" aggravating circumstance, reciting Williams' criminal history, including the several most recent offenses to which he had confessed. In comparison, it found that the excluded mitigating evidence — which it characterized as merely indicating "that numerous people, mostly relatives, thought that defendant was nonviolent and could cope very well in a structured environment," — "barely would have altered the profile of this defendant that was presented to the jury," On this basis, the court concluded that there was no reasonable possibility that the omitted evidence would have affected the jury's sentencing recommendation, and that Williams had failed to demonstrate that his sentencing proceeding was fundamentally unfair.

FEDERAL HABEAS CORPUS PROCEEDINGS

Having exhausted his state remedies, Williams sought a federal writ of habeas corpus pursuant to 28 U.S.C. § 2254. After reviewing the state habeas hearing transcript and the state courts' findings of fact and conclusions of law, the federal trial judge agreed with the Virginia trial judge: The death sentence was constitutionally infirm.

* * * *

The Federal Court of Appeals reversed. It construed § 2254(d)(1) as prohibiting the grant of habeas corpus relief unless the state court "'decided the question by interpreting or applying the relevant precedent in a manner that reasonable jurists would all agree is unreasonable.'" Applying that standard, it could not say that the Virginia Supreme Court's decision on the prejudice issue was an unreasonable application of the tests developed in either *Strickland* or *Lockhart.* It explained that the evidence that Williams presented a future danger to society was "simply overwhelming," it endorsed the Virginia Supreme Court's interpretation of *Lockhart* and it characterized the state court's understanding of the facts in this case as "reasonable."

We granted certiorari, and now reverse.

II

In 1867, Congress enacted a statute providing that federal courts "shall have power to grant writs of habeas corpus in all cases where any person may be restrained of his or her liberty in violation of the constitution, or of any treaty or law of the United States. . . ." Over the years, the federal habeas corpus statute has been repeatedly amended, but the scope of that jurisdictional grant remains the same. It is, of course, well settled that the fact that constitutional error occurred in the proceedings that led to a state-court conviction may not alone be sufficient reason for concluding that a prisoner is entitled to the remedy of habeas. On the other hand, errors that undermine confidence in the fundamental fairness of the state adjudication certainly justify the issuance of the federal writ. The deprivation of the right to the effective assistance of counsel recognized in *Strickland* is such an error.

The warden here contends that federal habeas corpus relief is prohibited by the amendment to 28 U.S.C. § 2254 enacted as a part of the Antiterrorism and Effective Death Penalty Act of 1996 (AEDPA). [The court then quoted § 2254(d)(1).]

In this case, the Court of Appeals . . . read the amendment as prohibiting federal courts from issuing the writ unless:

> "'(a) the state court decision is in 'square conflict' with Supreme Court precedent that is controlling as to law and fact or (b) if no such controlling decision exists, 'the state court's resolution of a question of pure law rests upon an objectively unreasonable derivation of legal principles from the relevant Supreme Court precedents, or if its decision rests upon an objectively unreasonable application of established principles to new facts.'"

Accordingly, it held that a federal court may issue habeas relief only if "the state courts have decided the question by interpreting or applying the relevant precedent in a manner that reasonable jurists would all agree is unreasonable."

We are convinced that that interpretation of the amendment is incorrect. It would impose a test for determining when a legal rule is clearly established that simply cannot be squared with the real practice of decisional law. It would apply a standard for determining the "reasonableness" of state-court decisions that is not contained in the statute itself, and that Congress surely did not intend. And it would wrongly require the federal courts, including this Court, to defer to state judges' interpretations of federal law.

As the Fourth Circuit would have it, a state-court judgment is "unreasonable" in the face of federal law only if all reasonable jurists would agree that the state court was unreasonable. Thus, in this case, for example, even if the Virginia Supreme Court misread our opinion in *Lockhart*, we could not grant relief unless we believed that none of the judges who agreed with the state court's interpretation of that case was a "reasonable jurist." But the statute says nothing about "reasonable judges," presumably because all, or virtually all, such judges occasionally commit error; they make decisions that in retrospect may be characterized as "unreasonable." Indeed, it is most unlikely that Congress would deliberately impose such a requirement of unanimity on federal judges. As Congress is acutely aware, reasonable lawyers and lawgivers regularly disagree with one another. Congress surely did not intend that the views of one such judge who might think that relief is not warranted in a particular case should always have greater weight than the contrary, considered judgment of several other reasonable judges.

The inquiry mandated by the amendment relates to the way in which a federal habeas court exercises its duty to decide constitutional questions; the amendment does not alter the underlying grant of jurisdiction in § 2254(a). When federal judges exercise their federal-question jurisdiction under the "judicial Power" of Article III of the Constitution, it is "emphatically the province and duty" of those judges to "say what the law is." *Marbury v. Madison*. At the core of this power is the federal courts' independent responsibility—independent from its coequal branches in the Federal Government, and independent from the separate authority of the several States—to interpret federal law. A construction of AEDPA that would require the federal courts to cede this authority to the courts of the States would be inconsistent with the practice that federal judges have traditionally followed in discharging their duties under Article III of the Constitution. If Congress had intended to require such an important change in the exercise of our jurisdiction, we believe it would have spoken with much greater clarity than is found in the text of AEDPA.

This basic premise informs our interpretation of both parts of § 2254(d)(1): first, the requirement that the determinations of state courts be tested only against "clearly established Federal law, as determined by the Supreme Court of the United States," and second, the prohibition on the issuance of the writ unless the state court's decision is "contrary to, or involved an unreasonable application of," that clearly established law. We address each part in turn.

THE "CLEARLY ESTABLISHED LAW" REQUIREMENT

In *Teague v. Lane* we held that the petitioner was not entitled to federal habeas relief because he was relying on a rule of federal law that had not been announced until after his state conviction became final. The antiretroactivity rule recognized in *Teague*, which prohibits reliance on "new rules," is the functional equivalent of a statutory provision commanding exclusive reliance on "clearly established law." Because there is no reason to believe that Congress intended to require federal courts to ask both whether a rule sought on habeas is "new" under *Teague*—which remains the law—and also whether it is "clearly established" under AEDPA, it seems safe to assume that Congress had congruent concepts in mind. It is perfectly clear that AEDPA codifies *Teague* to the extent that *Teague* requires federal habeas courts to deny relief that is contingent upon a rule of law not clearly established at the time the state conviction became final.

Teague's core principles are therefore relevant to our construction of this requirement. Justice Harlan recognized the "inevitable difficulties" that come with "attempting 'to determine whether a particular decision has really announced a "new" rule at all or whether it has simply applied a well-established constitutional principle to govern a case which is closely analogous to those which have been previously considered in the prior case law.'" But *Teague* established some guidance for making this determination, explaining that a federal habeas court operates within the bounds of comity and finality if it applies a rule "dictated by precedent existing at the time the defendant's conviction became final." A rule that "breaks new ground or imposes a new obligation on the States or the Federal Government" falls outside this universe of federal law.

To this, AEDPA has added, immediately following the "clearly established law" requirement, a clause limiting the area of relevant law to that "determined by the Supreme Court of the United States." 28 U.S.C. § 2254(d)(1). If this Court has not broken sufficient legal ground to establish an asked-for constitutional principle, the lower federal courts cannot themselves establish such a principle with clarity sufficient to satisfy the AEDPA bar. In this respect, . . . this clause "extends the principle of *Teague* by limiting the source of doctrine on which a federal court may rely in addressing the application for a writ. . . ."

In the context of this case, we also note that, as our precedent interpreting *Teague* has demonstrated, rules of law may be sufficiently clear for habeas purposes even when they are expressed in terms of a generalized standard rather than as a bright-line rule. As Justice Kennedy has explained:

> "If the rule in question is one which of necessity requires a case-by-case examination of the evidence, then we can tolerate a number of specific applications without saying that those applications themselves create a new rule. . . . Where the beginning point is a rule of this general application, a rule designed for the specific purpose of evaluating a myriad of factual contexts, it will be the infrequent case that yields a result so novel that it forges a new rule, one not dictated by precedent."

Moreover, the determination whether or not a rule is clearly established at the time a state court renders its final judgment of conviction is a question as to which the "federal courts must make an independent evaluation."

It has been urged, in contrast, that we should read *Teague* and its progeny to encompass a broader principle of deference requiring federal courts to "validate 'reasonable, good-faith interpretations' of the law" by state courts. The position has been bolstered with references to our statements elucidating the 'new rule' inquiry as one turning on whether "reasonable jurists" would agree the rule was not clearly established. This presumption of deference was in essence the position taken by three Members of this Court in [an earlier case.]

Teague, however, does not extend this far. The often repeated language that *Teague* endorses "reasonable, good-faith interpretations" by state courts is an explanation of policy, not a statement of law. The *Teague* cases reflect this Court's view that habeas corpus is not to be used as a second criminal trial, and federal courts are not to run roughshod over the considered findings and judgments of the state courts that conducted the original trial and heard the initial appeals. On the contrary, we have long insisted that federal habeas courts attend closely to those considered decisions, and give them full effect when their findings and judgments are consistent with federal law. But as Justice O'Connor explained . . . :

> *"The duty of the federal court in evaluating whether a rule is 'new' is not the same as deference; . . .* *Teague* does not direct federal courts to spend less time or effort scrutinizing the existing federal law, on the ground that they can assume the state courts interpreted it properly.
>
> "The maxim that federal courts should 'give great weight to the considered conclusions of a coequal state judiciary' . . . does not mean that we have held in the past that federal courts must presume the correctness of a state court's legal conclusions on habeas, or that a state court's incorrect legal determination has ever been allowed to stand because it was reasonable. We have always held that federal courts, even on habeas, have an independent obligation to say what the law is."

We are convinced that in the phrase, "clearly established law," Congress did not intend to modify that independent obligation.

THE "CONTRARY TO, OR AN UNREASONABLE APPLICATION OF," REQUIREMENT

The message that Congress intended to convey by using the phrases, "contrary to" and "unreasonable application of" is not entirely clear. The prevailing view in the Circuits is that the former phrase requires *de novo* review of 'pure' questions of law and the latter requires some sort of "reasonability" review of so-called mixed questions of law and fact.

We are not persuaded that the phrases define two mutually exclusive categories of questions. Most constitutional questions that arise in habeas corpus proceedings — and therefore most "decisions" to be made — require the federal judge to apply a rule of law to a set of facts, some of which may be disputed and some undisputed. For example, an erroneous conclusion that particular circumstances established the voluntariness of a confession, or that there exists a conflict of interest when one attorney represents multiple defendants, may well be described either as "contrary to" or as an "unreasonable application of" the governing rule of law. In constitutional adjudication, as in the common law, rules of law often develop incrementally as earlier decisions are applied to new factual situations. But rules that depend upon such elaboration are hardly less lawlike than those that establish a bright-line test.

Indeed, our pre-AEDPA efforts to distinguish questions of fact, questions of law, and "mixed questions," and to create an appropriate standard of habeas review for each, generated some not insubstantial differences of opinion as to which issues of law fell into which category of question, and as to which standard of review applied to each. We thus think the Fourth Circuit was correct when it attributed the lack of clarity in the statute, in part, to the overlapping meanings of the phrases "contrary to" and "unreasonable application of."

The statutory text likewise does not obviously prescribe a specific, recognizable standard of review for dealing with either phrase. Significantly, it does not use any term, such as *"de novo"* or "plain error," that would easily identify a familiar standard of review. Rather, the text is fairly read simply as a command that a federal court not issue the habeas writ unless the state court was wrong as a matter of law or unreasonable in its application of law in a given case. The suggestion that a wrong state-court "decision"—a legal judgment rendered "after consideration of *facts, and . . . law,*" may no longer be redressed through habeas (because it is unreachable under the "unreasonable application" phrase) is based on a mistaken insistence that the § 2254(d)(1) phrases have not only independent, but mutually exclusive, meanings. Whether or not a federal court can issue the writ "under [the] 'unreasonable application' clause," the statute is clear that habeas may issue under § 2254(d)(1) if a state court "decision" is "contrary to . . . clearly established Federal law." We thus anticipate that there will be a variety of cases, like this one, in which both phrases may be implicated.

Even though we cannot conclude that the phrases establish "a body of rigid rules," they do express a "mood" that the federal judiciary must respect. In this respect, it seems clear that Congress intended federal judges to attend with the utmost care to state-court decisions, including all of the reasons supporting their decisions, before concluding that those proceedings were infected by constitutional error sufficiently serious to warrant the issuance of the writ. Likewise, the statute in a separate provision provides for the habeas remedy when a state-court decision "was based on an unreasonable determination of the facts *in light of the evidence presented in the State court proceeding.*" 28 U.S.C. § 2254(d)(2) (emphasis added). While this provision is not before us in this case, it provides relevant context for our interpretation of § 2254(d)(1); in this respect, it bolsters our conviction that federal habeas courts must make as the starting point of their analysis the state courts' determinations of fact, including that aspect of a "mixed question" that rests on a finding of fact. AEDPA plainly sought to ensure a level of "deference to the determinations of state courts," provided those determinations did not conflict with federal law or apply federal law in an unreasonable way. Congress wished to curb delays, to prevent "retrials" on federal habeas, and to give effect to state convictions to the extent possible under law. When federal courts are able to fulfill these goals within the bounds of the law, AEDPA instructs them to do so.

On the other hand, it is significant that the word "deference" does not appear in the text of the statute itself. Neither the legislative history, nor the statutory text suggests any difference in the so-called "deference" depending on which of the two phrases is implicated.[80] Whatever "deference" Congress had in mind with respect to both phrases, it surely is not a requirement that federal courts actually defer to a state-court application of the federal law that is, in the independent judgment of the federal court, in error. As Judge Easterbrook noted with respect to the phrase "contrary to":

80. [Footnote 13 in Justice Stevens's opinion.] As Judge Easterbrook has noted, the statute surely does not require the kind of "deference" appropriate in other contexts: "It does not tell us to 'defer' to state decisions, as if the Constitution means one thing in Wisconsin and another in Indiana. Nor does it tell us to treat state courts the way we treat federal administrative agencies. Deference after the fashion of *Chevron U.S.A. Inc. v. Natural Resources Defense Council, Inc.*, depends on delegation. Congress did not delegate interpretive or executive power to the state courts. They exercise powers under their domestic law, constrained by the Constitution of the United States. 'Deference' to the jurisdictions bound by those constraints is not sensible."

"Section 2254(d) requires us to give state courts' opinions a respectful reading, and to listen carefully to their conclusions, but when the state court addresses a legal question, it is the law 'as determined by the Supreme Court of the United States' that prevails."[81]

Our disagreement with Justice O'Connor about the precise meaning of the phrase "contrary to," and the word "unreasonable," is, of course, important, but should affect only a narrow category of cases. The simplest and first definition of "contrary to" as a phrase is "in conflict with." In this sense, we think the phrase surely capacious enough to include a finding that the state-court "decision" is simply "erroneous" or wrong. (We hasten to add that even "diametrically different" from, or "opposite" to, an established federal law would seem to include "decisions" that are wrong in light of that law.) And there is nothing in the phrase "contrary to"—as Justice O'Connor appears to agree—that implies anything less than independent review by the federal courts. Moreover, state-court decisions that do not "conflict" with federal law will rarely be "unreasonable" under either her reading of the statute or ours. We all agree that state-court judgments must be upheld unless, after the closest examination of the state-court judgment, a federal court is firmly convinced that a federal constitutional right has been violated. Our difference is as to the cases in which, at first-blush, a state-court judgment seems entirely reasonable, but thorough analysis by a federal court produces a firm conviction that that judgment is infected by constitutional error. In our view, such an erroneous judgment is "unreasonable" within the meaning of the act even though that conclusion was not immediately apparent.

In sum, the statute directs federal courts to attend to every state-court judgment with utmost care, but it does not require them to defer to the opinion of every reasonable state-court judge on the content of federal law. If, after carefully weighing all the reasons for accepting a state court's judgment, a federal

81. [Footnote 14 in Justice Stevens's opinion.] The Court advances three reasons for adopting its alternative construction of the phrase "unreasonable application of." First, the use of the word "unreasonable" in the statute suggests that Congress was directly influenced by the "patently unreasonable" standard advocated by Justice Thomas in his opinion in *Wright v. West*; second, the legislative history supports this view; and third, Congress must have intended to change the law more substantially than our reading 28 U.S.C. §2254(d)(1) permits.

None of these reasons is persuasive. First, even though, as the Court recognizes, the term "unreasonable" is "difficult to define," neither the statute itself nor the Court's explanation of it, suggests that AEDPA's "unreasonable application of" has the same meaning as Justice Thomas' "'patently unreasonable'" standard mentioned in his dictum in *Wright*. To the extent the "broader debate" in *Wright* touched upon the Court's novel distinction today between what is "wrong" and what is "unreasonable," it was in the context of a discussion not about the *standard of review* habeas courts should use for law-application questions, but about whether a rule is "new" or "old" such that *Teague*'s retroactivity rule would bar habeas relief; Justice Thomas contended that *Teague* barred habeas "whenever the state courts have interpreted old precedents *reasonably*, not [as Justice O'Connor suggested] only when they have done so 'properly.'" *Teague*, of course, as Justice O'Connor correctly pointed out, "did not establish a standard of review at all"; rather than instructing a court *how* to review a claim, it simply asks, in absolute terms, *whether* a rule was clear at the time of a state-court decision. We thus do not think *Wright* "confirms" anything about the meaning of §2254(d)(1), which is, as our division reflects, anything but "clear."

As for the other bases for Justice O'Connor's view, the only two specific citations to the legislative history upon which she relies, do no more than beg the question. One merely quotes the language of the statute without elaboration, and the other goes to slightly greater length in stating that state-court judgments must be upheld unless "unreasonable." Neither sheds any light on what the content of the hypothetical category of "decisions" that are wrong but nevertheless not "unreasonable." Finally, while we certainly agree with the Court, that AEDPA wrought substantial changes in habeas law; there is an obvious fallacy in the assumption that because the statute changed pre-existing law in some respects, it must have rendered this specific change here.

court is convinced that a prisoner's custody—or, as in this case, his sentence of death—violates the Constitution, that independent judgment should prevail. Otherwise the federal "law as determined by the Supreme Court of the United States" might be applied by the federal courts one way in Virginia and another way in California. In light of the well-recognized interest in ensuring that federal courts interpret federal law in a uniform way, we are convinced that Congress did not intend the statute to produce such a result.

III

In this case, Williams contends that he was denied his constitutionally guaranteed right to the effective assistance of counsel when his trial lawyers failed to investigate and to present substantial mitigating evidence to the sentencing jury. The threshold question under AEDPA is whether Williams seeks to apply a rule of law that was clearly established at the time his state-court conviction became final. That question is easily answered because the merits of his claim are squarely governed by our holding in *Strickland v. Washington.*

We explained in *Strickland* that a violation of the right on which Williams relies has two components:

> "First, the defendant must show that counsel's performance was deficient. This requires showing that counsel made errors so serious that counsel was not functioning as the 'counsel' guaranteed the defendant by the Sixth Amendment. Second, the defendant must show that the deficient performance prejudiced the defense. This requires showing that counsel's errors were so serious as to deprive the defendant of a fair trial, a trial whose result is reliable."

To establish ineffectiveness, a "defendant must show that counsel's representation fell below an objective standard of reasonableness." To establish prejudice he "must show that there is a reasonable probability that, but for counsel's unprofessional errors, the result of the proceeding would have been different. A reasonable probability is a probability sufficient to undermine confidence in the outcome."

It is past question that the rule set forth in *Strickland* qualifies as "clearly established Federal law, as determined by the Supreme Court of the United States." That the *Strickland* test "of necessity requires a case-by-case examination of the evidence," obviates neither the clarity of the rule nor the extent to which the rule must be seen as "established" by this Court. This Court's precedent "dictated" that the Virginia Supreme Court apply the *Strickland* test at the time that court entertained Williams' ineffective-assistance claim. And it can hardly be said that recognizing the right to effective counsel "breaks new ground or imposes a new obligation on the States." Williams is therefore entitled to relief if the Virginia Supreme Court's decision rejecting his ineffective-assistance claim was either "contrary to, or involved an unreasonable application of," that established law. It was both.

IV

The Virginia Supreme Court erred in holding that our decision in *Lockhart v. Fretwell,* modified or in some way supplanted the rule set down in *Strickland.* It is true that while the *Strickland* test provides sufficient guidance for resolving virtually all ineffective-assistance-of-counsel claims, there are situations in which the overriding focus on fundamental fairness may affect the analysis. Thus, on the one hand, as *Strickland* itself explained, there are a few situations in which prejudice may be presumed. And, on the other hand, there are also situations in which it would be unjust to characterize the likelihood of a different outcome as legitimate "prejudice." Even if a defendant's false testimony might have persuaded the jury to acquit him, it is not fundamentally unfair to conclude that he was not prejudiced by counsel's interference with his intended perjury.

Similarly, in *Lockhart*, we concluded that, given the overriding interest in fundamental fairness, the likelihood of a different outcome attributable to an incorrect interpretation of the law should be regarded as a potential "windfall" to the defendant rather than the legitimate "prejudice" contemplated by our opinion in *Strickland*. The death sentence that Arkansas had imposed on Bobby Ray Fretwell was based on an aggravating circumstance (murder committed for pecuniary gain) that duplicated an element of the underlying felony (murder in the course of a robbery). Shortly before the trial, the United States Court of Appeals for the Eighth Circuit had held that such "double counting" was impermissible, but Fretwell's lawyer (presumably because he was unaware of the . . . decision) failed to object to the use of the pecuniary gain aggravator. Before Fretwell's claim for federal habeas corpus relief reached this Court, the [Eighth Circuit] case was overruled. Accordingly, even though the Arkansas trial judge probably would have sustained a timely objection to the double counting, it had become clear that the State had a right to rely on the disputed aggravating circumstance. Because the ineffectiveness of Fretwell's counsel had not deprived him of any substantive or procedural right to which the law entitled him, we held that his claim did not satisfy the "prejudice" component of the *Strickland* test.

Cases such as . . . *Lockhart v. Fretwell* do not justify a departure from a straightforward application of *Strickland* when the ineffectiveness of counsel *does* deprive the defendant of a substantive or procedural right to which the law entitles him. In the instant case, it is undisputed that Williams had a right—indeed, a constitutionally protected right—to provide the jury with the mitigating evidence that his trial counsel either failed to discover or failed to offer.

Nevertheless, the Virginia Supreme Court read our decision in *Lockhart* to require a separate inquiry into fundamental fairness even when Williams is able to show that his lawyer was ineffective and that his ineffectiveness probably affected the outcome of the proceeding. . . .

Unlike the Virginia Supreme Court, the state trial judge omitted any reference to *Lockhart* and simply relied on our opinion in *Strickland* as stating the correct standard for judging ineffective-assistance claims. . . . The trial judge analyzed the ineffective-assistance claim under the correct standard; the Virginia Supreme Court did not.

We are likewise persuaded that the Virginia trial judge correctly applied both components of that standard to Williams' ineffectiveness claim. Although he concluded that counsel competently handled the guilt phase of the trial, he found that their representation during the sentencing phase fell short of professional standards—a judgment barely disputed by the State in its brief to this Court. The record establishes that counsel did not begin to prepare for that phase of the proceeding until a week before the trial. They failed to conduct an investigation that would have uncovered extensive records graphically describing Williams' nightmarish childhood, not because of any strategic calculation but because they incorrectly thought that state law barred access to such records. Had they done so, the jury would have learned that Williams' parents had been imprisoned for the criminal neglect of Williams and his siblings, that Williams had been severely and repeatedly beaten by his father, that he had been committed to the custody of the social services bureau for two years during his parents' incarceration (including one stint in an abusive foster home), and then, after his parents were released from prison, had been returned to his parents' custody.

Counsel failed to introduce available evidence that Williams was "borderline mentally retarded" and did not advance beyond sixth grade in school. They failed to seek prison records recording Williams' commendations for helping to crack a prison drug ring and for returning a guard's missing wallet, or the testimony of prison officials who described Williams as among the inmates "least likely to act in a violent, dangerous or provocative way." Counsel failed even to return the phone call of a certified public accountant who had offered to testify that he had visited Williams frequently when Williams was incarcerated as part of a prison ministry program, that Williams "seemed to thrive in a more regimented and structured environment," and that Williams was proud of the carpentry degree he earned while in prison.

Of course, not all of the additional evidence was favorable to Williams. The juvenile records revealed that he had been thrice committed to the juvenile system — for aiding and abetting larceny when he was 11 years old, for pulling a false fire alarm when he was 12, and for breaking and entering when he was 15. But as the Federal District Court correctly observed, the failure to introduce the comparatively voluminous amount of evidence that did speak in Williams' favor was not justified by a tactical decision to focus on Williams' voluntary confession. Whether or not those omissions were sufficiently prejudicial to have affected the outcome of sentencing, they clearly demonstrate that trial counsel did not fulfill their obligation to conduct a thorough investigation of the defendant's background.

We are also persuaded, unlike the Virginia Supreme Court, that counsel's unprofessional service prejudiced Williams within the meaning of *Strickland*. After hearing the additional evidence developed in the postconviction proceedings, the very judge who presided at Williams' trial and who once determined that the death penalty was "just" and "appropriate," concluded that there existed "a reasonable probability that the result of the sentencing phase would have been different" if the jury had heard that evidence. We do not agree with the Virginia Supreme Court that Judge Ingram's conclusion should be discounted because he apparently adopted "a *per se* approach to the prejudice element" that placed undue "emphasis on mere outcome determination." Judge Ingram did stress the importance of mitigation evidence in making his "outcome determination," but it is clear that his predictive judgment rested on his assessment of the totality of the omitted evidence rather than on the notion that a single item of omitted evidence, no matter how trivial, would require a new hearing.

The Virginia Supreme Court's own analysis of prejudice reaching the contrary conclusion was thus unreasonable in at least two respects. First, as we have already explained, the State Supreme Court mischaracterized at best the appropriate rule, made clear by this Court in *Strickland*, for determining whether counsel's assistance was effective within the meaning of the Constitution. While it may also have conducted an "outcome determinative" analysis of its own, it is evident to us that the court's decision turned on its erroneous view that a "mere" difference in outcome is not sufficient to establish constitutionally ineffective assistance of counsel. Its analysis in this respect was thus not only "contrary to," but also, inasmuch as the Virginia Supreme Court relied on the inapplicable exception recognized in *Lockhart*, an "unreasonable application of" the clear law as established by this Court.

Second, the State Supreme Court's prejudice determination was unreasonable insofar as it failed to evaluate the totality of the available mitigation evidence—both that adduced at trial, and the evidence adduced in the habeas proceeding—in reweighing it against the evidence in aggravation. This error is apparent in its consideration of the additional mitigation evidence developed in the postconviction proceedings. The court correctly found that as to "the factual part of the mixed question," there was "really . . . no . . . dispute" that available mitigation evidence was not presented at trial. As to the prejudice determination comprising the "legal part" of its analysis, it correctly emphasized the strength of the prosecution evidence supporting the future dangerousness aggravating circumstance.

But the state court failed even to mention the sole argument in mitigation that trial counsel did advance—Williams turned himself in, alerting police to a crime they otherwise would never have discovered, expressing remorse for his actions, and cooperating with the police after that. While this, coupled with the prison records and guard testimony, may not have overcome a finding of future dangerousness, the graphic description of Williams' childhood, filled with abuse and privation, or the reality that he was "borderline mentally retarded," might well have influenced the jury's appraisal of his moral culpability. The circumstances recited in his several confessions are consistent with the view that in each case his violent behavior was a compulsive reaction rather than the product of cold-blooded premeditation. Mitigating evidence unrelated to dangerousness may alter the jury's selection of penalty, even if it does not undermine or rebut the prosecution's death-eligibility case. The Virginia Supreme Court did not entertain that possibility. It thus failed to accord appropriate weight to the body of mitigation evidence available to trial counsel.

V

In our judgment, the state trial judge was correct both in his recognition of the established legal standard for determining counsel's effectiveness, and in his conclusion that the entire postconviction record, viewed as a whole and cumulative of mitigation evidence presented originally, raised "a reasonable probability that the result of the sentencing proceeding would have been different" if competent counsel had presented and explained the significance of all the available evidence. It follows that the Virginia Supreme Court rendered a "decision that was contrary to, or involved an unreasonable application of, clearly established Federal law." Williams' constitutional right to the effective assistance of counsel as defined in *Strickland v. Washington* was violated.

Accordingly, the judgment of the Court of Appeals is reversed, and the case is remanded for further proceedings consistent with this opinion.

It is so ordered.

JUSTICE O'CONNOR delivered the opinion of the Court with respect to Part II (except as to the footnote), concurred in part, and concurred in the judgment.[82]

In 1996, Congress enacted the Antiterrorism and Effective Death Penalty Act (AEDPA). In that Act, Congress placed a new restriction on the power of federal courts to grant writs of habeas corpus to state prisoners. The relevant provision, 28 U.S.C. § 2254(d)(1) prohibits a federal court from granting an application for a writ of habeas corpus with respect to a claim adjudicated on the merits in state court unless that adjudication "resulted in a decision that was contrary to, or involved an unreasonable application of, clearly established Federal law, as determined by the Supreme Court of the United States." The Court holds today that the Virginia Supreme Court's adjudication of Terry Williams' application for state habeas corpus relief resulted in just such a decision. I agree with that determination and join Parts I, III, and IV of the Court's opinion. Because I disagree, however, with the interpretation of § 2254(d)(1) set forth in Part II of Justice Stevens' opinion, I write separately to explain my views.

I

Before 1996, this Court held that a federal court entertaining a state prisoner's application for habeas relief must exercise its independent judgment when deciding both questions of constitutional law and mixed constitutional questions (*i.e.*, application of constitutional law to fact). In other words, a federal habeas court owed no deference to a state court's resolution of such questions of law or mixed questions. In 1991, in the case of *Wright v. West* we revisited our prior holdings by asking the parties to address the following question in their briefs:

> "In determining whether to grant a petition for writ of habeas corpus by a person in custody pursuant to the judgment of a state court, should a federal court give deference to the state court's application of law to the specific facts of the petitioner's case or should it review the state court's determination *de novo*?"

Although our ultimate decision did not turn on the answer to that question, our several opinions did join issue on it.

Justice Thomas, announcing the judgment of the Court, acknowledged that our precedents had "treated as settled the rule that mixed constitutional questions are 'subject to plenary federal review' on habeas." He contended, nevertheless, that those decisions did not foreclose the Court from applying a rule of deferential review for reasonableness in future cases. According to Justice Thomas, the reliance of our precedents on *Brown v. Allen* was erroneous because the Court in *Brown* never explored in detail whether a federal habeas court, to deny a state prisoner's application, must conclude that the relevant state-court adjudication was "correct" or merely that it was "reasonable." Justice Thomas suggested that the time to revisit our decisions may have been at hand, given that

82. [Footnote * in Justice O'Connor's opinion.] Justice Kennedy joins this opinion in its entirety. The Chief Justice and Justice Thomas join this opinion with respect to Part II. Justice Scalia joins this opinion with respect to Part II, except as to the footnote.

our more recent habeas jurisprudence in the nonretroactivity context, see, *e.g.*, *Teague v. Lane,* had called into question the then-settled rule of independent review of mixed constitutional questions.

I wrote separately in *Wright* because I believed Justice Thomas had "understated the certainty with which *Brown v. Allen* rejected a deferential standard of review of issues of law." I also explained that we had considered the standard of review applicable to mixed constitutional questions on numerous occasions and each time we concluded that federal habeas courts had a duty to evaluate such questions independently. With respect to Justice Thomas' suggestion that *Teague* and its progeny called into question the vitality of the independent-review rule, I noted that "*Teague* did not establish a 'deferential' standard of review" because "it did not establish a standard of review at all." While *Teague* did hold that state prisoners could not receive "the retroactive benefit of new rules of law," it "did *not* create any deferential standard of review with regard to old rules."

Finally, and perhaps most importantly for purposes of today's case, I stated my disagreement with Justice Thomas' suggestion that *de novo* review is incompatible with the maxim that federal habeas courts should "give great weight to the considered conclusions of a coequal state judiciary," Our statement . . . signified only that a state-court decision is due the same respect as any other "persuasive, well-reasoned authority." "But this does not mean that we have held in the past that federal courts must presume the correctness of a state court's legal conclusions on habeas, or that a state court's incorrect legal determination has ever been allowed to stand because it was reasonable. We have always held that federal courts, even on habeas, have an independent obligation to say what the law is." Under the federal habeas statute as it stood in 1992, then, our precedents dictated that a federal court should grant a state prisoner's petition for habeas relief if that court were to conclude in its independent judgment that the relevant state court had erred on a question of constitutional law or on a mixed constitutional question.

If today's case were governed by the federal habeas statute prior to Congress' enactment of AEDPA in 1996, I would agree with Justice Stevens that Williams' petition for habeas relief must be granted if we, in our independent judgment, were to conclude that his Sixth Amendment right to effective assistance of counsel was violated.

II

A

Williams' case is *not* governed by the pre-1996 version of the habeas statute . . . Accordingly, for Williams to obtain federal habeas relief, he must first demonstrate that his case satisfies the condition set by § 2254(d)(1). That provision modifies the role of federal habeas courts in reviewing petitions filed by state prisoners.

Justice Stevens' opinion in Part II essentially contends that § 2254(d)(1) does not alter the previously settled rule of independent review. Indeed, the opinion concludes its statutory inquiry with the somewhat empty finding that § 2254(d)(1) does no more than express a "'mood' that the federal judiciary must respect." For Justice Stevens, the congressionally enacted "mood" has two important qualities. First, "federal courts [must] attend to every state-court judgment with utmost care" by "carefully weighing all the reasons for accepting a state court's judgment." Second, if a federal court undertakes that careful review and yet remains convinced that a prisoner's custody violates the Constitution, "that independent judgment should prevail."

[Justice O'Connor concluded that Justice Stevens had interpreted 2254(d)(1) to do no more than enact pre-AEDPA law.]

* * * *

That Justice Stevens would find the new § 2254(d)(1) to have no effect on the prior law of habeas corpus is remarkable given his apparent acknowledgment that Congress wished to bring change to the field. That acknowledgment is correct and significant to this case. It cannot be disputed that Congress viewed § 2254(d)(1) as an important means by which its goals for habeas reform would be achieved.

Justice Stevens arrives at his erroneous interpretation by means of one critical misstep. He fails to give independent meaning to both the "contrary to" and "unreasonable application" clauses of the statute. By reading § 2254(d)(1) as one general restriction on the power of the federal habeas court, Justice Stevens manages to avoid confronting the specific meaning of the statute's "unreasonable application" clause and its ramifications for the independent-review rule. It is, however, a cardinal principle of statutory construction that we must "'give effect, if possible, to every clause and word of a statute.'" Section 2254(d)(1) defines two categories of cases in which a state prisoner may obtain federal habeas relief with respect to a claim adjudicated on the merits in state court. Under the statute, a federal court may grant a writ of habeas corpus if the relevant state-court decision was either (1) "*contrary to* . . . clearly established Federal law, as determined by the Supreme Court of the United States," or (2) "*involved an unreasonable application of* . . . clearly established Federal law, as determined by the Supreme Court of the United States." (Emphases added.)

The Court of Appeals for the Fourth Circuit properly accorded both the "contrary to" and "unreasonable application" clauses independent meaning. . . . With respect to the first of the two statutory clauses, the Fourth Circuit held . . . that a state-court decision can be "contrary to" this Court's clearly established precedent in two ways. First, a state-court decision is contrary to this Court's precedent if the state court arrives at a conclusion opposite to that reached by this Court on a question of law. Second, a state-court decision is also contrary to this Court's precedent if the state court confronts facts that are materially indistinguishable from a relevant Supreme Court precedent and arrives at a result opposite to ours.

The word "contrary" is commonly understood to mean "diametrically different," "opposite in character or nature," or "mutually opposed." WEBSTER'S THIRD NEW INTERNATIONAL DICTIONARY 495 (1976). The text of § 2254(d)(1) therefore suggests that the state court's decision must be substantially different from the relevant precedent of this Court. The Fourth Circuit's interpretation of the "contrary to" clause accurately reflects this textual meaning. A state-court decision will certainly be contrary to our clearly established precedent if the state court applies a rule that contradicts the governing law set forth in our cases. Take, for example, our decision in *Strickland v. Washington*. If a state court were to reject a prisoner's claim of ineffective assistance of counsel on the grounds that the prisoner had not established by a preponderance of the evidence that the result of his criminal proceeding would have been different, that decision would be "diametrically different," "opposite in character or nature," and "mutually opposed" to our clearly established precedent because we held in *Strickland* that the prisoner need only demonstrate a "reasonable probability that . . . the result of the proceeding would have been different." A state-court decision will also be contrary to this Court's clearly established precedent if the state court confronts a set of facts that are materially indistinguishable from a decision of this Court and nevertheless arrives at a result different from our precedent. Accordingly, in either of these two scenarios, a federal court will be unconstrained by § 2254(d)(1) because the state-court decision falls within that provision's "contrary to" clause.

On the other hand, a run-of-the-mill state-court decision applying the correct legal rule from our cases to the facts of a prisoner's case would not fit comfortably within § 2254(d)(1)'s "contrary to" clause. Assume, for example, that a state-court decision on a prisoner's ineffective-assistance claim correctly identifies *Strickland* as the controlling legal authority and, applying that framework, rejects the prisoner's claim. Quite clearly, the state-court decision would be in accord with our decision in *Strickland* as to the legal prerequisites for establishing an ineffective-assistance claim, even assuming the federal court considering the prisoner's habeas application might reach a different result applying the *Strickland* framework itself. It is difficult, however, to describe such a run-of-the-mill state-court decision as "diametrically different" from, "opposite in character or nature" from, or "mutually opposed" to *Strickland*, our clearly established precedent. Although the state-court decision may be contrary to the federal court's conception of how *Strickland* ought to be applied in that particular case, the decision is not "mutually opposed" to *Strickland* itself.

Justice Stevens would instead construe § 2254(d)(1)'s "contrary to" clause to encompass such a routine state-court decision. That construction, however, saps the "unreasonable application" clause of any meaning. If a federal habeas court can, under the "contrary to" clause, issue the writ whenever it concludes that the state court's *application* of clearly established federal law was incorrect, the "unreasonable application" clause becomes a nullity. We must, however, if possible, give meaning to every clause of the statute. Justice Stevens not only makes no attempt to do so, but also construes the "contrary to" clause in a manner that ensures that the "unreasonable application" clause will have no independent meaning. We reject that expansive interpretation of the statute. Reading § 2254(d)(1)'s "contrary to" clause to permit a federal court to grant relief in cases where a state court's error is limited to the manner in which it *applies* Supreme Court precedent is suspect given the logical and natural fit of the neighboring "unreasonable application" clause to such cases.

The Fourth Circuit's interpretation of the "unreasonable application" clause of § 2254(d)(1) is generally correct. That court held . . . that a state-court decision can involve an "unreasonable application" of this Court's clearly established precedent in two ways. First, a state-court decision involves an unreasonable application of this Court's precedent if the state court identifies the correct governing legal rule from this Court's cases but unreasonably applies it to the facts of the particular state prisoner's case. Second, a state-court decision also involves an unreasonable application of this Court's precedent if the state court either unreasonably extends a legal principle from our precedent to a new context where it should not apply or unreasonably refuses to extend that principle to a new context where it should apply.

A state-court decision that correctly identifies the governing legal rule but applies it unreasonably to the facts of a particular prisoner's case certainly would qualify as a decision "involving an unreasonable application of . . . clearly established Federal law." Indeed, we used the almost identical phrase "application of law" to describe a state court's application of law to fact in the certiorari question we posed to the parties in *Wright.*

The Fourth Circuit also held . . . that state-court decisions that unreasonably extend a legal principle from our precedent to a new context where it should not apply (or unreasonably refuse to extend a legal principle to a new context where it should apply) should be analyzed under § 2254(d)(1)'s "unreasonable application" clause. Although that holding may perhaps be correct, the classification does have some problems of precision. Just as it is sometimes difficult to distinguish a mixed question of law and fact from a question of fact, it will often be difficult to identify separately those state-court decisions that involve an unreasonable application of a legal principle (or an unreasonable failure to apply a legal principle) to a new context. Indeed, on the one hand, in some cases it will be hard to distinguish a decision involving an unreasonable extension of a legal principle from a decision involving an unreasonable application of law to facts. On the other hand, in many of the same cases it will also be difficult to distinguish a decision involving an unreasonable extension of a legal principle from a decision that "arrives at a conclusion opposite to that reached by this Court on a question of law." Today's case does not require us to decide how such "extension of legal principle" cases should be treated under § 2254(d)(1). For now it is sufficient to hold that when a state-court decision unreasonably applies the law of this Court to the facts of a prisoner's case, a federal court applying § 2254(d)(1) may conclude that the state-court decision falls within that provision's "unreasonable application" clause.

B

There remains the task of defining what exactly qualifies as an "unreasonable application" of law under § 2254(d)(1). The Fourth Circuit held . . . that a state-court decision involves an "unreasonable application of . . . clearly established Federal law" only if the state court has applied federal law "in a manner that reasonable jurists would all agree is unreasonable." The placement of this additional overlay on the "unreasonable application" clause was erroneous. . . .

Defining an "unreasonable application" by reference to a "reasonable jurist," however, is of little assistance to the courts that must apply § 2254(d)(1) and, in fact, may be misleading. Stated simply, a federal habeas court making the "unreasonable application" inquiry should ask whether the state court's application of clearly established federal law was objectively unreasonable. The federal habeas court should not transform the inquiry into a subjective one by resting its determination instead on the simple fact that at least one of the Nation's jurists has applied the relevant federal law in the same manner the state court did in the habeas petitioner's case. The "all reasonable jurists" standard would tend to mislead federal habeas courts by focusing their attention on a subjective inquiry rather than on an objective one. . . .

The term "unreasonable" is no doubt difficult to define. That said, it is a common term in the legal world and, accordingly, federal judges are familiar with its meaning. For purposes of today's opinion, the most important point is that an *unreasonable* application of federal law is different from an *incorrect* application of federal law. Our opinions in *Wright,* for example, make that difference clear. . . . In § 2254(d)(1), Congress specifically used the word "unreasonable," and not a term like "erroneous" or "incorrect." Under § 2254(d)(1)'s "unreasonable application" clause, then, a federal habeas court may not issue the writ simply because that court concludes in its independent judgment that the relevant state-court decision applied clearly established federal law erroneously or incorrectly. Rather, that application must also be unreasonable.

* * * *

In sum, § 2254(d)(1) places a new constraint on the power of a federal habeas court to grant a state prisoner's application for a writ of habeas corpus with respect to claims adjudicated on the merits in state court. Under § 2254(d)(1), the writ may issue only if one of the following two conditions is satisfied—the state-court adjudication resulted in a decision that (1) "was contrary to . . . clearly established Federal law, as determined by the Supreme Court of the United States," or (2) "involved an unreasonable application of . . . clearly established Federal law, as determined by the Supreme Court of the United States." Under the "contrary to" clause, a federal habeas court may grant the writ if the state court arrives at a conclusion opposite to that reached by this Court on a question of law or if the state court decides a case differently than this Court has on a set of materially indistinguishable facts. Under the "unreasonable application" clause, a federal habeas court may grant the writ if the state court identifies the correct governing legal principle from this Court's decisions but unreasonably applies that principle to the facts of the prisoner's case.

III

Although I disagree with Justice Stevens concerning the standard we must apply under § 2254(d)(1) in evaluating Terry Williams' claims on habeas, I agree with the Court that the Virginia Supreme Court's adjudication of Williams' claim of ineffective assistance of counsel resulted in a decision that was both contrary to and involved an unreasonable application of this Court's clearly established precedent. Specifically, I believe that the Court's discussion in Parts III and IV is correct and that it demonstrates the reasons that the Virginia Supreme Court's decision in Williams' case, even under the interpretation of § 2254(d)(1) I have set forth above, was both contrary to and involved an unreasonable application of our precedent.

First, I agree with the Court that our decision in *Strickland* undoubtedly qualifies as "clearly established Federal law, as determined by the Supreme Court of the United States," within the meaning of § 2254(d)(1). Second, I agree that the Virginia Supreme Court's decision was contrary to that clearly established federal law to the extent it held that our decision in *Lockhart v. Fretwell*, somehow modified or supplanted the rule set forth in *Strickland.* Specifically, the Virginia Supreme Court's decision was contrary to *Strickland* itself, where we held that a defendant demonstrates prejudice by showing "that there is a reasonable probability that, but for counsel's unprofessional errors, the result of the proceeding would have been different." The Virginia Supreme Court held, in contrast, that such a focus on outcome determination was insufficient standing alone. *Lockhart* does not support that broad proposition. . . . Accordingly, as the Court ably explains, the Virginia Supreme Court's decision was contrary to *Strickland.*

To be sure, as The Chief Justice notes, the Virginia Supreme Court did also inquire whether Williams had demonstrated a reasonable probability that, but for his trial counsel's unprofessional errors, the result of his sentencing would have been different. It is impossible to determine, however, the extent to which the Virginia Supreme Court's error with respect to its reading of *Lockhart* affected its ultimate finding that Williams suffered no prejudice. For example, at the conclusion of its discussion of whether Williams had demonstrated a reasonable probability of a different outcome at sentencing, the Virginia Supreme Court faulted the Virginia Circuit Court for its "emphasis on mere outcome determination, without proper attention to whether the result of the criminal proceeding was fundamentally unfair or unreliable." As the Court explains, however, Williams' case did not implicate the unusual circumstances present in cases like *Lockhart*. . . . Accordingly, for the very reasons I set forth in my *Lockhart* concurrence, the emphasis on outcome was entirely appropriate in Williams' case.

Third, I also agree with the Court that, to the extent the Virginia Supreme Court did apply *Strickland*, its application was unreasonable. As the Court correctly recounts, Williams' trial counsel failed to conduct investigation that would have uncovered substantial amounts of mitigation evidence. For example, speaking only of that evidence concerning Williams' "nightmarish childhood," the mitigation evidence that trial counsel failed to present to the jury showed that "Williams' parents had been imprisoned for the criminal neglect of Williams and his siblings, that Williams had been severely and repeatedly beaten by his father, that he had been committed to the custody of the social services bureau for two years during his parents' incarceration (including one stint in an abusive foster home), and then, after his parents were released from prison, had been returned to his parents' custody." The consequence of counsel's failure to conduct the requisite, diligent investigation into his client's troubling background and unique personal circumstances manifested itself during his generic, unapologetic closing argument, which provided the jury with no reasons to spare petitioner's life. More generally, the Virginia Circuit Court found that Williams' trial counsel failed to present evidence showing that Williams "had a deprived and abused upbringing; that he may have been a neglected and mistreated child; that he came from an alcoholic family; . . . that he was borderline mentally retarded;" and that "[his] conduct had been good in certain structured settings in his life (such as when he was incarcerated)." In addition, the Circuit Court noted the existence of "friends, neighbors and family of [Williams] who would have testified that he had redeeming qualities." Based on its consideration of all of this evidence, the same trial judge that originally found Williams' death sentence "justified and warranted," concluded that trial counsel's deficient performance prejudiced Williams, and accordingly recommended that Williams be granted a new sentencing hearing. The Virginia Supreme Court's decision reveals an obvious failure to consider the totality of the omitted mitigation evidence. For that reason, and the remaining factors discussed in the Court's opinion, I believe that the Virginia Supreme Court's decision "involved an unreasonable application of . . . clearly established Federal law, as determined by the Supreme Court of the United States."

Accordingly, although I disagree with the interpretation of § 2254(d)(1) set forth in Part II of Justice Stevens' opinion, I join Parts I, III, and IV of the Court's opinion and concur in the judgment of reversal.

CHIEF JUSTICE REHNQUIST, with whom JUSTICE SCALIA and JUSTICE THOMAS join, concurring in part and dissenting in part.

I agree with the Court's interpretation of 28 U.S.C. § 2254(d)(1), but disagree with its decision to grant habeas relief in this case.

There is "clearly established Federal law, as determined by [this Court]" that governs petitioner's claim of ineffective assistance of counsel: *Strickland v. Washington.* Thus, we must determine whether the Virginia Supreme Court's adjudication was "contrary to" or an "unreasonable application of" *Strickland.*

Generally, in an ineffective-assistance-of-counsel case where the state court applies *Strickland,* federal habeas courts can proceed directly to "unreasonable application" review. But, according to the substance of petitioner's argument, this could be one of the rare cases where a state court applied the wrong Supreme Court precedent, and, consequently, reached an incorrect result. Petitioner argues, and the Court agrees, that the Virginia Supreme Court improperly held that *Lockhart v. Fretwell* "modified or in some way supplanted" the rule set down in *Strickland.* I agree that such a holding would be improper. But the Virginia Supreme Court did not so hold as it did not rely on *Lockhart* to reach its decision.

* * * *

The question then becomes whether the Virginia Supreme Court's adjudication resulted from an "unreasonable application of" *Strickland.* In my view, it did not.

I, like the Virginia Supreme Court and the Federal Court of Appeals below, will assume without deciding that counsel's performance fell below an objective standard of reasonableness. As to the prejudice inquiry, I agree with the Court of Appeals that evidence showing that petitioner presented a future danger to society was overwhelming. . . .

* * * *

Here, there was strong evidence that petitioner would continue to be a danger to society, both in and out of prison. It was not, therefore, unreasonable for the Virginia Supreme Court to decide that a jury would not have been swayed by evidence demonstrating that petitioner had a terrible childhood and a low IQ. The potential mitigating evidence that may have countered the finding that petitioner was a future danger was testimony that petitioner was not dangerous while in detention. But, again, it is not unreasonable to assume that the jury would have viewed this mitigation as unconvincing upon hearing that petitioner set fire to his cell while awaiting trial for the murder at hand and has repeated visions of harming other inmates.

Accordingly, I would hold that habeas relief is barred by 28 U.S.C. § 2254(d).

DISCUSSION AND QUESTIONS

Congress' enactment of § 2254(d) and the Supreme Court's interpretations of that statute have significantly altered the landscape in this area of the law. In this subsection we explore the state of the law, the many questions still unanswered, and the broader doctrinal issues this statute raises.

Several introductory points are critical to understanding how § 2254(d) operates. First, notice that it applies on a claim-by-claim basis. An application containing more than one claim may raise more than one issue under the statute.

Second, the section applies only to claims that have been "adjudicated on the merits in State court proceedings." If a claim has not been adjudicated on the merits, most commonly when the state court decision is based on a state procedural rule, § 2254(d) has no application. In such a situation one would first need to determine whether the petitioner satisfies one of the exceptions to the state procedural default rule. If she does, the substantive merits of the claim would be adjudicated in federal court under the pre-AEDPA rules, including *Teague.*

Assuming the claim at issue has been adjudicated on the merits in the state court, § 2254(d) states the rule a federal court must follow. It provides that the federal court should *not* grant the writ unless the petitioner comes within the terms of either subsection (d)(1) or subsection (d)(2). In reality, the Supreme Court has read these two provisions to create three grounds upon which the writ can be granted, two dictated by subsection (d)(1) and one by subsection (d)(2). We explore each subsection separately below.

Before turning to the requirements of (d)(1) and (d)(2), it is worthwhile to stop to consider an overarching issue that provides the foundation for § 2254(d) as a whole. At its heart, this statutory provision reflects a determination about the appropriate level of deference a federal court should give to state court decisions. In other words, to what extent should a federal court look over the shoulder of a state court when considering a habeas corpus petition? As we discuss below, Congress has directed that federal courts defer to a fairly significant degree to state courts, although how much may be difficult to state with certainty. Before turning to the details, explore this topic by considering the following question:

EXPLORING DOCTRINE

The Appropriate Role of Deference to State Courts in Habeas Corpus

By definition, when a federal court considers an application from a state prisoner for a writ of habeas corpus it is reviewing questions considered by state courts. Also by definition, the state court prisoner is raising matters of federal law, most commonly questions concerning the individual rights guaranteed by the Constitution. Finally, recall that when considering constitutional questions, *Marbury v. Madison* provides that it is the courts' role to "say what the law is." Given these factors, what should be the appropriate role of deference to state court decisions when a federal court considers a request that it grant a writ of habeas corpus? How do you balance competing constitutional values to reach your conclusion? Does it matter what type of issue the petitioner raises (e.g., a pure question of law, a mixed question of law and fact, or a pure question of fact)? Why or why not?

We now consider subsections (d)(1) and (d)(2) separately. After doing so, we provide a synthesis of how they operate together.

28 U.S.C. § 2254(d)(1). Williams concerns the first subsection of § 2254(d). As the Court instructs in that decision, the starting point for applying this part of the statute is to determine the relevant law to be applied to the claim at issue. The statute directs that the law used to judge the claim is "clearly established Federal law, as determined by the Supreme Court of the United States." Thus, one is confined only to Supreme Court decisions and within that realm only to legal doctrines that are "clearly established."[83] Indeed, the Supreme Court has made clear that it is error for federal courts to rely on circuit court decisions even when those decisions might fairly be said to be explaining a Supreme Court precedent. The fact remains that those decisions are not decisions of the Supreme Court and, therefore, § 2254(d)(1) does not allow them to be considered.[84]

You should recognize both from the statutory text and *Williams* that this requirement seems to incorporate at least some of the Court's decision in *Teague*. The precise relationship between *Teague* and § 2254(d)(1) is not entirely clear. The Supreme Court has indicated that they are distinct, but related, doctrines. What is clear is that subsection (d)(1) alters the *Teague* analysis at least with respect to the sources of law—only the Supreme Court can state the rule to be applied. It also appears that (d)(1) does embody the same type of analysis used under *Teague* to determine when a rule is "clearly established" even if the sources of that rule are more restrictive than under *Teague*. An open question is whether § 2254(d)(1) incorporates the two *Teague* exceptions. That is, may a petitioner get the benefit of a "new rule"—one that is not "clearly established"—if she satisfies a *Teague* exception such as when the constitutional rule is a "watershed" one? The Supreme Court has acted under the assumption that the exceptions are applicable but has not directly held that this is the case.[85]

As you know from *Williams*, the Supreme Court has interpreted subsection (d)(1) to set forth two independent ways in which a state court decision can provide grounds for federal habeas relief. The first is if the state court's determination is "contrary to" the clearly established Supreme Court rule. This question is essentially a pure question of law.

Williams articulates two ways in which a state court determination can be "contrary to" relevant law. First, if the state court applies a rule that contradicts clearly established law, it is contrary to that law. Second, the state court determination is contrary to relevant federal law "if the state court confronts a set of facts materially indistinguishable from [those present in a Supreme Court] decision and nevertheless arrives at a different outcome."

As you might imagine, it will be a rare situation when a state court simply identifies and applies the incorrect rule, especially when the rule is one that has

83. There are also connections between the requirements in § 2254(d)(1) (and their incorporation of some elements from *Teague*) and other statutory habeas provisions. For example, as we noted above when considering the time limits associated with filing applications for writs of habeas corpus, a petitioner generally must do so within one year of the date on which her state court conviction became final on direct review. *See* 28 U.S.C. § 2244(d)(1)(A). One of the exceptions that allows the one-year time clock to begin on a later date is when the claim at issue is based on a constitutional right the Supreme Court has recognized "if the right has been newly recognized by the Supreme Court and made retroactively applicable to cases on collateral review." *See* 28 U.S.C. § 2244(d)(1)(C). As you should be able to tell by now, satisfying this standard is difficult. It is even more so given the Supreme Court's decision that this statutory provision requires an actual holding of the Court making the claim retroactive in a collateral review situation. *See Tyler v. Cain*, 533 U.S. 656 (2001).

84. *See, e.g., Parker v. Matthews*, 132 S. Ct. 2148 (2012); *Renico v. Lett*, 130 S. Ct. 1855, 1865 (2010).

85. *See, e.g., Whorton v. Bockting*, 127 S. Ct. 1173 (2007) (holding that the Court's Sixth Amendment Confrontation Clause decision in *Crawford v. Washington*, 541 U.S. 36 (2004), did not set forth a "watershed" rule of criminal procedure).

been clearly established by the Supreme Court. This is even more so given that the Supreme Court has held that federal courts should (1) assume that state courts know the law and follow it;[86] and (2) that there is no requirement that the state court actually cite the relevant Supreme Court decisions so long as they apply the rules for which those decisions stand.[87]

As *Williams* makes clear, it is not impossible for state court determinations to run afoul of the "contrary to" portion of subsection (d)(1). Recall that in *Williams* a majority of the Court determined that the Virginia Supreme Court had mistakenly concluded that *Strickland v. Washington* did not provide the correct legal rule by which to adjudicate the petitioner's claims. Thus, the decision was "contrary to" the relevant clearly established law.

Williams is also important in its discussion concerning subsection (d)(1)'s "contrary to" language with respect to the level of deference a federal court must show to a state court on such a pure question of law. A majority agreed that a federal court should show "respectful consideration" for a state court's determination but that no deference to such legal questions was mandated. The same result does not obtain with respect to the other avenue for relief under subsection (d)(1).

That other avenue of relief is when a state court determination is "an unreasonable application of" clearly established Supreme Court precedent. This portion of the statute concerns the application of law to fact. As you might imagine, many more cases will concern application of law to fact than simply the identification of an incorrect rule. Here, Justice O'Connor parts company with Justice Stevens in *Williams* both as to the details of application as well as the underlying question of the role of deference. Justice O'Connor's view—which states the law—is that Congress has mandated that federal courts generally defer to state courts in their application of law to facts even when that application is objectively incorrect. Only if the application is unreasonable is the deference overcome.

Justice O'Connor tells us (somewhat unhelpfully given the use of the term "unreasonable" to define "unreasonable application") that a state court determination runs afoul of this portion of subsection (d)(1) in two situations. First, a petitioner satisfies the "unreasonable application" standard when the "state court identifies the correct legal rule but unreasonably applies it to the facts of a particular case." Second, the standard is satisfied when the state court determination involves either an unreasonable extension of the Supreme Court's rule or an unreasonable refusal to extend the rule.

What is critical to understanding Justice O'Connor's interpretation of this portion of subsection (d)(1) is that there is a difference between a decision that is incorrect and one that unreasonable. A federal court must defer to a state court's erroneous application of law to facts unless that application is so erroneous that it is not only wrong but unreasonably so.[88] One can visualize the situation in Figure 13-4 below in which only decisions falling in the shaded section would be the basis for federal habeas relief even though all decisions are incorrect.

86. *See Woodford v. Visciotti*, 537 U.S. 19 (2002).

87. *See Early v. Packer*, 537 U.S. 3 (2002) (*per curiam*).

88. The Court has held that a federal court may not consider evidence developed in a federal evidentiary hearing when making its determination under § 2254(d)(1). In the words of Justice Thomas writing for a closely divided Court: "We now hold that review under § 2254(d)(1) is limited to the record that was before the state court that adjudicated the claim on the merits." *Cullen v. Pinholster*, 131 S. Ct. 1388, 1389 (2011).

FIGURE 13-4

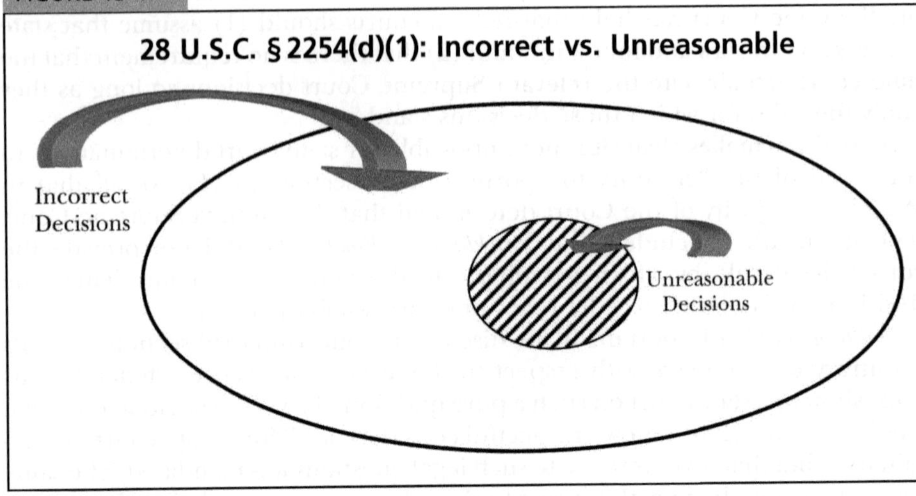

How does one determine when a given determination is so incorrect as to be unreasonable? As is often said, the devil is in the details and the Supreme Court provides precious little in that department. We know that something is not reasonable merely because a reasonable jurist could take the position at issue. Justice O'Connor rejects this approach, which the Fourth Circuit had taken in *Williams.* We also know that it is possible for a state court determination to be unreasonable even if the clearly established law at issue concerns a standard that must be applied on a case-by-case basis. *Strickland* is such a test, yet the Court concluded that it qualified as "clearly established" and that the Virginia Supreme Court's application of the test in *Williams* was unreasonable. But the Court has not been entirely consistent in how it treats these standard-based rules. For example, in a later decision the Court stated as follows: "Applying a general standard to a specific case can demand a substantial element of judgment. As a result, evaluating whether a rule application was unreasonable requires considering the rule's specificity. The more general the rule, the more leeway courts have in reaching outcomes in case by case determinations."[89] At the end of the day, one must accept, perhaps, that defining what is an unreasonable application of clearly established Supreme Court precedent cannot be done in the abstract.

89. *See Yarborough v. Alvarado,* 541 U.S. 652, 664 (2004). *Yarborough* concerned the application of the clearly established standard concerning when a suspect was "in custody" for purposes of the *Miranda* warnings. The Court made a similar point when considering a habeas corpus petition concerning whether California's three-strikes rule was "grossly disproportionate" under the Eighth Amendment's prohibition of cruel and unusual punishments. *See Lockyear v. Andrade,* 538 U.S. 63 (2003). However, after both these cases the Court once again found a state court determination to be an unreasonable application of clearly established law in the context of the Sixth Amendment's right to effective assistance of counsel. *See Rompilla v. Beard,* 545 U.S. 374 (2005). The Supreme Court has reiterated its position concerning the interaction of general rules and the deference owed to state court decisions. In *Renico v. Lett,* Chief Justice Roberts, writing for a majority of the Court, forcefully reiterated *Yarborough*'s holding that the more general a rule is, the "greater the potential for reasoned disagreement among fair-minded judges." 130 S. Ct. 1855, 1863 (2010). But it also remains possible to prevail on a federal habeas claim even when the underlying constitutional rule is a general one, such as the standard concerning ineffective assistance of counsel. *See Porter v. McCollum,* 558 U.S. 30 (2009) (*per curiam*) (holding that Florida Supreme Court's decision that counsel's performance was not deficient under *Strickland v. Washington* was objectively unreasonable).

While it is possible to point to decisions in which the Court finds a state court decision "unreasonable," there is no denying that deference to state courts is quite high for the current Court. For example, in *Harrington v. Richter*, the Court reversed the Ninth Circuit's grant of habeas to a California state prisoner who had asserted ineffective assistance of counsel claims. Along the way the Court noted that "even a strong case for relief does not mean that the state court's contrary conclusion was unreasonable."[90] The Court went on to note that "[i]f this standard [under § 2254(d)] is difficult to meet, that is because it is meant to be."[91] And, finally, the Court summarized its views as follows: "As a condition for obtaining habeas corpus from a federal court, a state prisoner must show that the state court's ruling was so lacking in justification that there was an error well understood and comprehended in existing law beyond any possibility for fair-minded disagreement."[92]

Three additional points are worthy of mention before leaving (d)(1). First, as we discussed earlier, one aspect of habeas doctrine under both § 2254(d) and *Teague v. Lane* is that the growth of federal constitutional law is constrained. A court may rule a petitioner loses because the constitutional argument he or she advances was not "clearly established" at the relevant time. A court may make this determination without actually deciding what the correct constitutional rule is. *Smith v. Spisak*, 558 U.S. 139 (2010), is a prime example. In that case, the petitioner argued, in part, that jury instructions in a capital case were deficient because they required the jury to unanimously reject a death sentence prior to considering other possible sentences. The Court held that its cases had not established that principle in the past and declined to address it in the case at bar.

Another example is *White v. Woodall*, 134 S. Ct. 1697 (2013). The issue in that case concerned whether a criminal defendant at the *penalty* phase was entitled to an instruction that the defendant's failure to testify could not be considered. The law was clearly established that a defendant was constitutionally entitled to such an instruction at the *guilt* phase.[93] The court of appeals had concluded that the writ should be granted because the state court did not give the instruction. The Supreme Court held that was error. The Court explained that whether or not the Constitution required such an instruction, the Court's holding that such an instruction was necessary at the guilt phase did not address the penalty phase. As such the state court's decision was not inconsistent with a Supreme Court holding.[94]

But it appears that the Court is also willing to reach out and decide a constitutional question for the first time, at least when the decision is one that is not in favor of the petitioner. In *Berghuis v. Thompkins*, 130 S. Ct. 2250 (2010), the Court held that a suspect must unambiguously assert his or her right to remain silent under *Miranda v. Arizona* even if that person has remained silent in the face of questions for two to three hours.[95] It seems that the Court could have decided this case without definitively resolving the issue by relying on the

90. 130 S. Ct. 770, 786 (2011).
91. *Id.*
92. *Id.* at 786-87.
93. *See Carter, Estelle v. Smith*, 451 U.S. 454 (1981).
94. 134 S. Ct. at 1702-05.
95. 130 S. Ct. at 2259-65

requirement that a law must be "clearly established" to provide a basis for habeas relief. Indeed, Justice Sotomayor forcefully made this point in dissent.[96]

The second noteworthy point concerns *In re Davis*, 557 U.S. 952 (2009). This case is noteworthy first because it concerns an original writ of habeas corpus in the Supreme Court. The Court referred the matter to a district court for evidentiary proceedings. The Court's action was simply an order referring the matter, but there were dueling concurring and dissenting opinions. Of note in these opinions was a dispute as to whether the limitations contained in § 2254(d)(1) apply to original writs of habeas corpus. Justice Scalia indicated that they did.[97] Justice Stevens, on the other hand, expressed skepticism on this point. Justice Stevens also indicated that § 2254(d)(1) might very well be unconstitutional to the extent it precluded consideration of a claim of actual innocence.[98] After the district court's evidentiary hearing, the Supreme Court ultimately denied the writ without dissent.[99]

Third, the Court has made clear that there is no need for a state court to issue an opinion in order for its decision to be one "adjudicated on the merits" for purposes of § 2254(d).[100] The Court held that "[w]hen a federal claim has been presented to a state court and the state court has denied relief, it may be presumed that the state court adjudicated the claim on the merits in the absence of any indication of state-law procedural principles to the contrary."[101] The Court noted that "[t]he presumption may be overcome when there is reason to think some other explanation for the state court's decision is more likely."[102]

Finally, the Court addressed a theory that has been advanced in the courts of appeals under § 2254(d) — the unreasonable failure to extend Supreme Court precedent. While not entirely foreclosing the possibility, the Court strongly suggested that the statutory construct suggested that "[t]he appropriate time to consider the question as a matter of first impression would be on direct review, not in a habeas case governed by § 2254(d)(1)."[103]

Figure 13-5 on page 1037 summarizes the operation of subsection (d)(1). Problem 13-4 provides an opportunity to practice applying the Court's interpretation of this statutory provision.

PROBLEM 13-4

The Confusing Sentence Enhancement Again

Return to the facts from Problem 13-3 above. Now assume that the AEDPA amendments to § 2254(d) are in place and applicable to Jane's habeas petition. How does your analysis change? Is your ultimate conclusion different? Why or why not?

96. *Id.* at 2266 (Sotomayor, J., dissenting).
97. 557 U.S. at 954-55 (Scalia, J., dissenting).
98. *Id.* at 953-54.
99. *In re Davis*, 131 S. Ct. 1808 (2011).
100. *Harrington v. Richter*, 131 S. Ct. 770, 783-85 (2011).
101. *Id.* at 784-85.
102. *Id.* at 785.
103. *White v. Woodall*, 134 S. Ct. 1697, 1706 (2014).

FIGURE 13-5

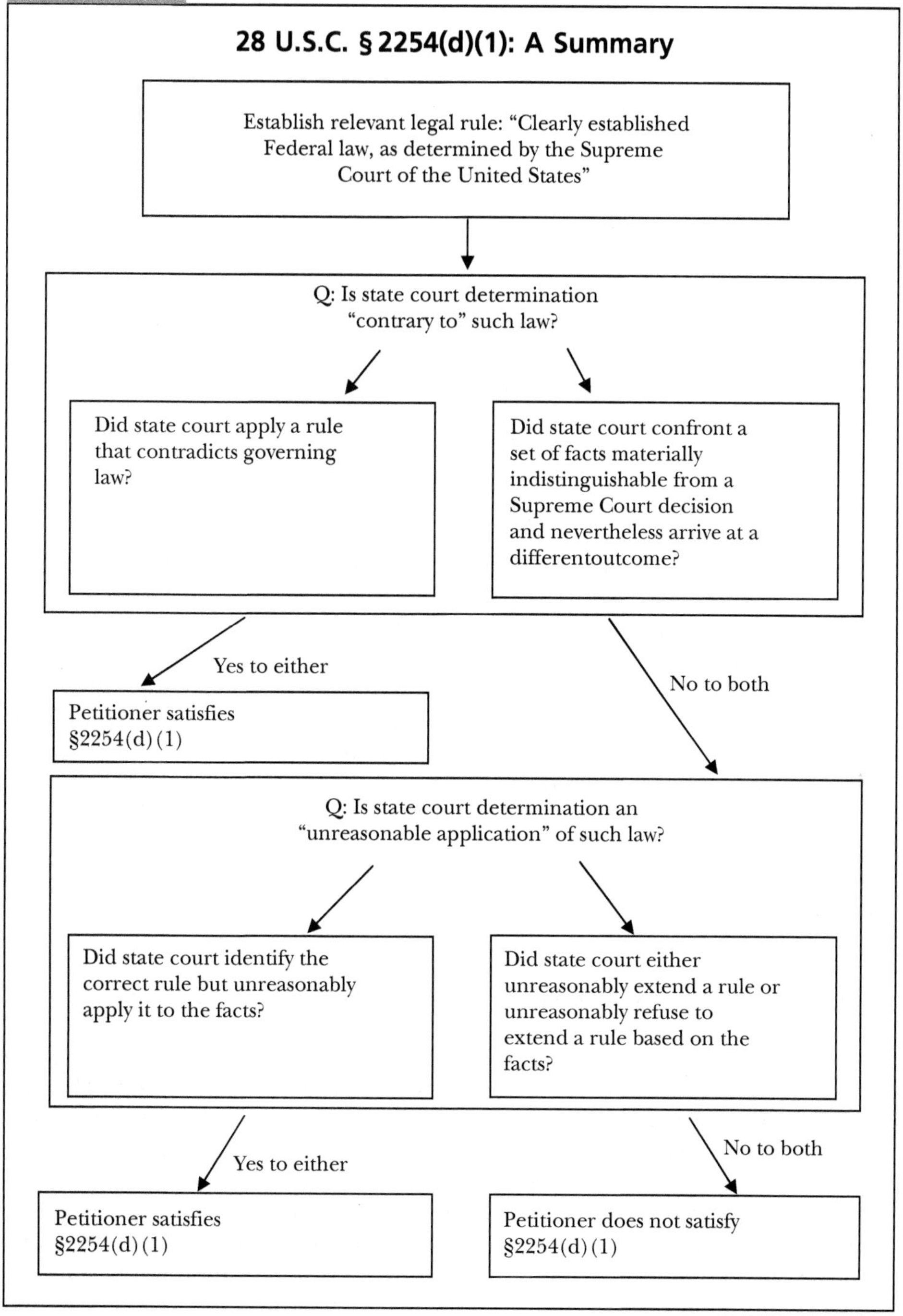

28 U.S.C. § 2254(d)(2). The third basis on which a federal court is authorized to grant a writ of habeas corpus under § 2254(d) is when the state court decision is "based on an unreasonable determination of facts in light of the evidence presented in the State court proceeding." 28 U.S.C. § 2254(d)(2). This statutory provision focuses on pure factually questions. It also embodies great deference to state court actions. Note also that subsection (d)(2) adopts the same distinction as discussed above between something that is incorrect (not a ground on which to grant habeas relief) and something that is so incorrect as to be unreasonable (what is required to grant relief).

Seen in isolation, subsection (d)(2) can be applied without any more difficulty than those issues discussed concerning the "unreasonable application" prong of subsection (d)(1). However, matters become more complicated when one considers certain portions of 28 U.S.C. §2254(e). Section 2254(e)(1) provides that "a determination of a factual issue made by a State court shall be presumed to be correct." Thus, it would seem that (e)(1) makes (d)(2) meaningless. However, that result can be avoided because (e)(1) goes on to provide that the state applicant can overcome the presumption by clear and convincing evidence. Yet difficulties still remain. The issue under subsection (e)(1) goes to the correctness of the state court factual determination, while (d)(2) concerns its reasonableness. It may be that any fact that an applicant shows to be incorrect under the clear and convincing standard is by definition unreasonable under subsection (d)(2). However, this issue has not been definitely resolved. The Supreme Court has declined to resolve these potential conflicts.[104]

The confusion is augmented by subsection (d)(2)'s proviso that the unreasonableness determination must be based on "the evidence presented in the State court proceeding." As we will see in the next portion of this chapter, in some situations the habeas statute allows a federal court to hold an evidentiary hearing in which new facts are presented. *See* 28 U.S.C. §2254(e)(2). Precisely how the availability of an evidentiary hearing in federal court operates in the context of subsection (d)(2) is unclear. The reality is that in addition to some of the other concerns we have discussed above, the interaction of subsections (d)(2) and (e) reflect extraordinarily poor drafting on the part of Congress.[105]

* * * *

We summarize the operation of both subsections of 28 U.S.C. §2254(d) in Figure 13-6 on page 1039.

vii. Factual Findings, Evidentiary Hearings, and 28 U.S.C. §2254(e)

As we discussed above concerning 28 U.S.C. §2254(d)(2), an important feature of some habeas corpus actions concerns the deference a federal court should show to factual determinations a state court has made. Subsection (d)(2) addresses that issue in the context of such determinations based on the evidence presented to the state court. 28 U.S.C. §2254(e)(1) more broadly concerns the presumptive validity of state court factual determinations. As we explored, there is a certain tension between these two statutory provisions when they both apply.

In this subsection of the chapter we consider a distinct (although potentially interrelated) issue: When may a federal court hold an evidentiary hearing on a state petitioner's claims. Prior to AEDPA, the answer to this question had been developed through court decisions. As in other areas, the Supreme Court

104. *Wood v. Allen*, 130 S. Ct. 841, 851 (2010) ("[W]e leave for another day the questions of how and when §2254(e)(1) applies to a state court's factual determinations under §2254(d)(2)."); *see also Burt v. Titlow*, 134 S. Ct. 10 (2013).

105. You should also remember that (d)(2) and (e)(1) will not always operate together. Subsection (d)(2) applies only in the context of a state court adjudication on the merits.

FIGURE 13-6

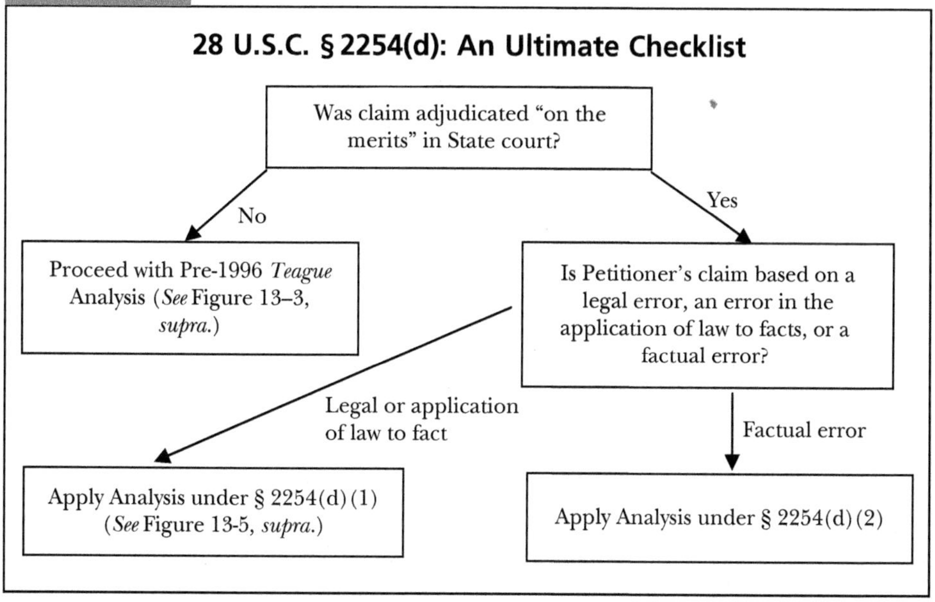

doctrine in this area ebbed and flowed in terms of the flexibility a district court had concerning whether to hold a hearing.

The standard in place when AEDPA was enacted in 1996 was largely dictated by the Supreme Court's 1992 decision in *Keeney v. Tamayo-Reyes*, 504 U.S. 1 (1992). In brief, the Court held that a federal court is *required* to hold an evidentiary hearing when a the factual record had not been developed in state court only when the petitioner was able to show (1) that (a) there was "cause" for the failure to develop the record and (b) there was prejudice flowing from that failure; *or* (2) a "fundamental miscarriage of justice" would result if a hearing were not held. These standards were meant to restrict the situations in which a federal court was required to hold a hearing. If the standards were not met, the federal court was not precluded from holding an evidentiary hearing. Rather, the failure to satisfy the standards meant only that there was no obligation to hold a hearing. The district court retained discretion to hold an evidentiary hearing.

Matters stood this way when Congress enacted AEDPA in 1996. The key provision is 28 U.S.C. § 2254(e)(2). The Court's most important interpretation of that provision came in *Michael Williams v. Taylor*, excerpted below.

MICHAEL WILLIAMS v. TAYLOR

529 U.S. 420 (2000)

JUSTICE KENNEDY delivered the opinion of the Court.

Petitioner Michael Wayne Williams received a capital sentence for the murders of Morris Keller, Jr., and Keller's wife, Mary Elizabeth. Petitioner later sought a writ of habeas corpus in federal court. Accompanying his petition was a request for an evidentiary hearing on constitutional claims which, he alleged, he had been unable to develop in state-court proceedings. The question in this case is whether 28 U.S.C. § 2254(e)(2) as amended by the Antiterrorism and Effective Death Penalty Act of 1996 (AEDPA), bars the evidentiary hearing petitioner seeks. If petitioner "has failed to develop the factual basis of [his] claims in State court proceedings," his case is subject to § 2254(e)(2), and he may not receive a hearing because he concedes his inability to satisfy the statute's further stringent conditions for excusing the deficiency.

I

On the evening of February 27, 1993, Verena Lozano James dropped off petitioner and his friend Jeffrey Alan Cruse near a local store in a rural area of Cumberland County, Virginia. The pair planned to rob the store's employees and customers using a .357 revolver petitioner had stolen in the course of a quadruple murder and robbery he had committed two months earlier. Finding the store closed, petitioner and Cruse walked to the Kellers' home. Petitioner was familiar with the couple, having grown up down the road from where they lived. He told Cruse they would have "a couple thousand dollars." Cruse, who had been holding the .357, handed the gun to petitioner and knocked on the door. When Mr. Keller opened the door, petitioner pointed the gun at him as the two intruders forced their way inside. Petitioner and Cruse forced Mr. Keller to the kitchen, where they discovered Mrs. Keller. Petitioner ordered the captives to remove their clothing. While petitioner kept guard on the Kellers, Cruse searched the house for money and other valuables. He found a .38-caliber handgun and bullets. Upon Cruse's return to the kitchen, petitioner had Cruse tie their captives with telephone cords. The Kellers were confined to separate closets while the intruders continued ransacking the house.

When they gathered all they wanted, petitioner and Cruse decided to rape Mrs. Keller. With Mrs. Keller pleading with them not to hurt her or her husband, petitioner raped her. Cruse did the same. Petitioner then ordered the Kellers to shower and dress and "take a walk" with him and Cruse. As they were leaving, petitioner told Mrs. Keller he and Cruse were going to burn down the house. Mrs. Keller begged to be allowed to retrieve her marriage license, which she did, guarded by petitioner.

As the prosecution later presented the case, details of the murders were as follows. Petitioner, now carrying the .38, and Cruse, carrying the .357, took the Kellers to a thicket down a dirt road from the house. With petitioner standing behind Mr. Keller and Cruse behind Mrs. Keller, petitioner told Cruse, "We'll shoot at the count of three." At the third count, petitioner shot Mr. Keller in the head, and Mr. Keller collapsed to the ground. Cruse did not shoot Mrs. Keller at the same moment. Saying "he didn't want to leave no witnesses," petitioner urged Cruse to shoot Mrs. Keller. Cruse fired one shot into her head. Despite his wound, Mr. Keller stood up, but petitioner shot him a second time. To ensure the Kellers were dead, petitioner shot each of them two or three more times.

After returning to the house and loading the stolen property into the Kellers' jeep, petitioner and Cruse set fire to the house and drove the jeep to Fredericksburg, Virginia, where they sold some of the property. They threw the remaining property and the .357 revolver into the Rappahannock River and set fire to the jeep.

Pursuing a lead from Verena James, the police interviewed Cruse about the fire at the Kellers' home. Petitioner had fled to Florida. Cruse provided no useful information until the police discovered the bodies of the victims, at which point Cruse consulted counsel. In a plea bargain Cruse agreed to disclose the details of the crimes in exchange for the Commonwealth's promise not to seek the death penalty against him. Cruse described the murders but made no mention of his own act of rape. When the Commonwealth discovered the omission, it revoked the plea agreement and charged Cruse with capital murder.

Petitioner was arrested and charged with robbery, abduction, rape, and the capital murders of the Kellers. At trial in January 1994, Cruse was the Commonwealth's main witness. He recounted the murders as we have just described. Cruse testified petitioner raped Mrs. Keller, shot Mr. Keller at least twice, and shot Mrs. Keller several times after she had been felled by Cruse's bullet. He also described petitioner as the mastermind of the murders. The circumstances of the first plea agreement between the Commonwealth and Cruse and its revocation were disclosed to the jury. Testifying on his own behalf, petitioner admitted he was the first to shoot Mr. Keller and it was his idea to rob the store and set fire to the house. He denied, however, raping or shooting Mrs. Keller, and claimed to have shot Mr. Keller only once. Petitioner blamed Cruse for the remaining shots and disputed some other parts of Cruse's testimony.

The jury convicted petitioner on all counts. After considering the aggravating and mitigating evidence presented during the sentencing phase, the jury found the aggravating circumstances of future dangerousness and vileness of the crimes and recommended a death sentence. The trial court imposed the recommended sentence. The Supreme Court of Virginia affirmed petitioner's convictions and sentence and we denied certiorari. In a separate proceeding, Cruse pleaded guilty to the capital murder of Mrs. Keller and the first-degree murder of Mr. Keller. After the prosecution asked the sentencing court to spare his life because of his testimony against petitioner, Cruse was sentenced to life imprisonment.

Petitioner filed a habeas petition in state court alleging, in relevant part, that the Commonwealth failed to disclose a second agreement it had reached with Cruse after the first one was revoked. The new agreement, petitioner alleged, was an informal undertaking by the prosecution to recommend a life sentence in exchange for Cruse's testimony. Finding no merit to petitioner's claims, the Virginia Supreme Court dismissed the habeas petition, and we again denied certiorari.

Petitioner filed a habeas petition in the United States District Court for the Eastern District of Virginia on November 20, 1996. In addition to his claim regarding the alleged undisclosed agreement between the Commonwealth and Cruse, the petition raised three claims relevant to questions now before us. First, petitioner claimed the prosecution had violated *Brady v. Maryland,* in failing to disclose a report of a confidential pre-trial psychiatric examination of Cruse. Second, petitioner alleged his trial was rendered unfair by the seating of a juror who at *voir dire* had not revealed possible sources of bias. Finally, petitioner alleged one of the prosecutors committed misconduct in failing to reveal his knowledge of the juror's possible bias.

The District Court granted an evidentiary hearing on the undisclosed agreement and the allegations of juror bias and prosecutorial misconduct but denied a hearing on the psychiatric report. Before the evidentiary hearing could be held, the Commonwealth filed an application for an emergency stay and a petition for a writ of mandamus and prohibition in the Court of Appeals. The Commonwealth argued that petitioner's evidentiary hearing was prohibited by 28 U.S.C. § 2254(e)(2). A divided panel of the Court of Appeals granted the emergency stay and remanded for the District Court to apply the statute to petitioner's request for an evidentiary hearing. On remand, the District Court vacated its order granting an evidentiary hearing and dismissed the petition, having determined petitioner could not satisfy § 2254(e)(2)'s requirements.

The Court of Appeals affirmed. It first considered petitioner's argument that § 2254(e)(2) did not apply to his case because he had been diligent in attempting to develop his claims in state court. . . . [T]he Court of Appeals agreed with petitioner that § 2254(e)(2) would not apply if he had exercised diligence in state court. The court held, however, that petitioner had not been diligent and so had "failed to develop" in state court the factual bases of his *Brady*, juror bias, and prosecutorial misconduct claims. The Court of Appeals concluded petitioner could not satisfy the statute's conditions for excusing his failure to develop the facts and held him barred from receiving an evidentiary hearing. The Court of Appeals ruled in the alternative that, even if § 2254(e)(2) did not apply, petitioner would be ineligible for an evidentiary hearing under the cause and prejudice standard of pre-AEDPA law.

Addressing petitioner's claim of an undisclosed informal agreement between the Commonwealth and Cruse, the Court of Appeals rejected it on the merits under 28 U.S.C. § 2254(d)(1) and, as a result, did not consider whether § 2254(e)(2) applied.

On October 18, 1999, petitioner filed an application for stay of execution and a petition for a writ of certiorari. On October 28, we stayed petitioner's execution and granted certiorari to decide whether § 2254(e)(2) precludes him from receiving an evidentiary hearing on his claims. We now affirm in part and reverse in part.

II

A

Petitioner filed his federal habeas petition after AEDPA's effective date, so the statute applies to his case. The Commonwealth argues AEDPA bars petitioner from receiving an evidentiary hearing on any claim whose factual basis was not developed in state court, absent narrow circumstances not applicable here. Petitioner did not develop, or raise, his claims of juror bias, prosecutorial misconduct, or the prosecution's alleged *Brady* violation regarding Cruse's psychiatric report until he filed his federal habeas petition. Petitioner explains he could not have developed the claims earlier because he was unaware, through no fault of his own, of the underlying facts. As a consequence, petitioner contends, AEDPA erects no barrier to an evidentiary hearing in federal court.

Section 2254(e)(2), the provision which controls whether petitioner may receive an evidentiary hearing in federal district court on the claims that were not developed in the Virginia courts, becomes the central point of our analysis. [The Court then quoted the statute.]

By the terms of its opening clause the statute applies only to prisoners who have "failed to develop the factual basis of a claim in State court proceedings." If the prisoner has failed to develop the facts, an evidentiary hearing cannot be granted unless the prisoner's case meets the other conditions of § 2254(e)(2). Here, petitioner concedes his case does not comply with § 2254(e)(2)(B), so he may receive an evidentiary hearing only if his claims fall outside the opening clause.

There was no hearing in state court on any of the claims for which petitioner now seeks an evidentiary hearing. That, says the Commonwealth, is the end of the matter. In its view petitioner, whether or not through his own fault or neglect, still "failed to develop the factual basis of a claim in State court proceedings." Petitioner, on the other hand, says the phrase "failed to develop" means lack of diligence in developing the claims, a defalcation he contends did not occur since he made adequate efforts during state-court proceedings to discover and present the underlying facts. The Court of Appeals agreed with petitioner's interpretation of § 2254(e)(2) but believed petitioner had not exercised enough diligence to avoid the statutory bar. We agree with petitioner and the Court of Appeals that "failed to develop" implies some lack of diligence; but, unlike the Court of Appeals, we find no lack of diligence on petitioner's part with regard to two of his three claims.

B

We start, as always, with the language of the statute. Section 2254(e)(2) begins with a conditional clause, "if the applicant has failed to develop the factual basis of a claim in State court proceedings," which directs attention to the prisoner's efforts in state court. We ask first whether the factual basis was indeed developed in state court, a question susceptible, in the normal course, of a simple yes or no answer. Here the answer is no.

The Commonwealth would have the analysis begin and end there. Under its no-fault reading of the statute, if there is no factual development in the state court, the federal habeas court may not inquire into the reasons for the default when determining whether the opening clause of § 2254(e)(2) applies. We do not agree with the Commonwealth's interpretation of the word "failed."

We do not deny "fail" is sometimes used in a neutral way, not importing fault or want of diligence. So the phrase "We fail to understand his argument" can mean simply "We cannot understand his argument." This is not the sense in which the word "failed" is used here, however.

We give the words of a statute their "'ordinary, contemporary, common meaning,'" absent an indication Congress intended them to bear some different import. In its customary and preferred sense, "fail" connotes some omission, fault, or negligence on the part of the person who has failed to do something. To say a person has failed in a duty implies he did not take the necessary steps to fulfill it. He is, as a consequence, at fault and bears responsibility for the failure. In this sense, a person is not at fault when his diligent efforts to perform an act are thwarted, for example, by the conduct of another or by happenstance. Fault lies, in those circumstances, either with the person who interfered with the accomplishment of the act or with no one at all. We conclude Congress used the word "failed" in the sense just described. Had Congress intended a no-fault standard, it would have had no difficulty in making its intent plain. It would have had to do no more than use, in lieu of the phrase "has failed to," the phrase "did not."

Under the opening clause of § 2254(e)(2), a failure to develop the factual basis of a claim is not established unless there is lack of diligence, or some greater fault, attributable to the prisoner or the prisoner's counsel. In this we agree with the Court of Appeals and with all other courts of appeals which have addressed the issue.

* * * *

Interpreting § 2254(e)(2) so that "failed" requires lack of diligence or some other fault avoids putting it in needless tension with § 2254(d). A prisoner who developed his claim in state court and can prove the state court's decision was "contrary to, or an unreasonable application of, clearly established federal law, as determined by the Supreme Court of the United States," is not barred from obtaining relief by § 2254(d)(1). If the opening clause of § 2254(e)(2) covers a request for an evidentiary hearing on a claim which was pursued with diligence but remained undeveloped in state court because, for instance, the prosecution concealed the facts, a prisoner lacking clear and convincing evidence of innocence could be barred from a hearing on the claim even if he could satisfy § 2254(d). *See* 28 U.S.C. § 2254(e)(2)(B). The "failed to develop" clause does not bear this harsh reading, which would attribute to Congress a purpose or design to bar evidentiary hearings for diligent prisoners with meritorious claims just because the prosecution's conduct went undetected in state court. We see no indication that Congress by this language intended to remove the distinction between a prisoner who is at fault and one who is not.

The Commonwealth argues a reading of "failed to develop" premised on fault empties § 2254(e)(2)(A)(ii) of its meaning. To treat the prisoner's lack of diligence in state court as a prerequisite for application of § 2254(e)(2), the Commonwealth contends, renders a nullity of the statute's own diligence provision requiring the prisoner to show "a factual predicate [of his claim] could not have been previously discovered through the exercise of due diligence." § 2254(e)(2)(A)(ii). We disagree.

The Commonwealth misconceives the inquiry mandated by the opening clause of § 2254(e)(2). The question is not whether the facts could have been discovered but instead whether the prisoner was diligent in his efforts. The purpose of the fault component of "failed" is to ensure the prisoner undertakes his own diligent search for evidence. Diligence for purposes of the opening clause depends upon whether the prisoner made a reasonable attempt, in light of the information available at the time, to investigate and pursue claims in state court; it does not depend, as the Commonwealth would have it, upon whether those efforts could have been successful. Though lack of diligence will not bar an evidentiary hearing if efforts to discover the facts would have been in vain, see § 2254(e)(2)(A)(ii), and there is a convincing claim of innocence, see § 2254(e)(2)(B), only a prisoner who has neglected his rights in state court need satisfy these conditions. The statute's later reference to diligence pertains to cases in which the facts could not have been discovered, whether there was diligence or not. In this important respect § 2254(e)(2)(A)(ii) bears a close resemblance to (e)(2)(A)(i), which applies to a new rule that was not available at the time of the earlier proceedings. In these two parallel provisions Congress has given prisoners who fall within § 2254(e)(2)'s opening clause an opportunity to obtain an evidentiary hearing where the legal or factual basis of the claims did not exist at the time of state-court proceedings.

We are not persuaded by the Commonwealth's further argument that anything less than a no-fault understanding of the opening clause is contrary to AEDPA's purpose to further the principles of comity, finality, and federalism.

There is no doubt Congress intended AEDPA to advance these doctrines. Federal habeas corpus principles must inform and shape the historic and still vital relation of mutual respect and common purpose existing between the States and the federal courts. In keeping this delicate balance we have been careful to limit the scope of federal intrusion into state criminal adjudications and to safeguard the States' interest in the integrity of their criminal and collateral proceedings.

It is consistent with these principles to give effect to Congress' intent to avoid unneeded evidentiary hearings in federal habeas corpus, while recognizing the statute does not equate prisoners who exercise diligence in pursuing their claims with those who do not. Principles of exhaustion are premised upon recognition by Congress and the Court that state judiciaries have the duty and competence to vindicate rights secured by the Constitution in state criminal proceedings. Diligence will require in the usual case that the prisoner, at a minimum, seek an evidentiary hearing in state court in the manner prescribed by state law. "Comity . . . dictates that when a prisoner alleges that his continued confinement for a state court conviction violates federal law, the state courts should have the first opportunity to review this claim and provide any necessary relief." For state courts to have their rightful opportunity to adjudicate federal rights, the prisoner must be diligent in developing the record and presenting, if possible, all claims of constitutional error. If the prisoner fails to do so, himself or herself contributing to the absence of a full and fair adjudication in state court, § 2254(e)(2) prohibits an evidentiary hearing to develop the relevant claims in federal court, unless the statute's other stringent requirements are met. Federal courts sitting in habeas are not an alternative forum for trying facts and issues which a prisoner made insufficient effort to pursue in state proceedings. Yet comity is not served by saying a prisoner "has failed to develop the factual basis of a claim" where he was unable to develop his claim in state court despite diligent effort. In that circumstance, an evidentiary hearing is not barred by § 2254(e)(2).

III

Now we apply the statutory test. If there has been no lack of diligence at the relevant stages in the state proceedings, the prisoner has not "failed to develop" the facts under § 2254(e)(2)'s opening clause, and he will be excused from showing compliance with the balance of the subsection's requirements. We find lack of diligence as to one of the three claims but not as to the other two.

A

Petitioner did not exercise the diligence required to preserve the claim that nondisclosure of Cruse's psychiatric report was in contravention of *Brady v. Maryland.* The report concluded Cruse "had little recollection of the [murders of the Kellers], other than vague memories, as he was intoxicated with alcohol and marijuana at the time." The report had been prepared in September 1993, before petitioner was tried; yet it was not mentioned by petitioner until he filed his federal habeas petition and attached a copy of the report. Petitioner explained that an investigator for his federal habeas counsel discovered the report in Cruse's court file but state habeas counsel had not seen it when he had reviewed the same file. State habeas counsel averred as follows:

> "Prior to filing [petitioner's] habeas corpus petition with the Virginia Supreme Court, I reviewed the Cumberland County court files of [petitioner] and of his co-defendant, Jeffrey Cruse. . . . I have reviewed the attached psychiatric evaluation of Jeffrey Cruse. . . . I have no recollection of seeing this report in Mr. Cruse's court file when I examined the file. Given the contents of the report, I am confident that I would remember it."

The trial court was not satisfied with this explanation for the late discovery. Nor are we.

There are repeated references to a "psychiatric" or "mental health" report in a transcript of Cruse's sentencing proceeding, a copy of which petitioner's own state habeas counsel attached to the state habeas petition he filed with the Virginia Supreme Court. The transcript reveals that Cruse's attorney described the report with details that should have alerted counsel to a possible *Brady* claim. As Cruse's attorney said:

> "The psychiatric report . . . points out that [Cruse] is significantly depressed. He suffered from post traumatic stress. His symptoms include nightmares, sleeplessness, sobbing, reddening of the face, severe depression, flash backs. . . . The psychological report states he is overwhelmed by feelings of guilt and shame in his actions. He is numb. He is trying to suppress his feelings, but when he has feelings, there is only pain and sadness."

The description accords with the contents of the psychiatric report, which diagnosed Cruse as suffering from post-traumatic stress disorder:

> "[Cruse] has recurrent nightmares and visualizes the face of the woman that he killed. When attempting to describe this nightmare, he breaks openly into tears and his face reddens. . . . He continues to feel worthless as a person. . . . He has no hope for his future and has been thinking of suicide constantly. . . . He does describe inability to sleep, often tossing and turning, waking up, and feeling fatigued during the day. . . . He described neurovegetative symptoms of major depression and post-traumatic nightmares, recurrent in nature, of the [murders]."

The transcript put petitioner's state habeas counsel on notice of the report's existence and possible materiality. The sole indication that counsel made some effort to investigate the report is an October 30, 1995, letter to the prosecutor in which counsel requested "all reports of physical and mental examinations, scientific tests, or experiments conducted in connection with the investigation of the offense, including but not limited to: . . . all psychological test or polygraph examinations performed upon any prosecution witness and all documents referring or relating to such tests. . . ." After the prosecution declined the requests absent a court order, it appears counsel made no further efforts to find the specific report mentioned by Cruse's attorney. Given knowledge of the report's existence and potential importance, a diligent attorney would have done more. Counsel's failure to investigate these references in anything but a cursory manner triggers the opening clause of § 2254(e)(2).

As we hold there was a failure to develop the factual basis of this *Brady* claim in state court, we must determine if the requirements in the balance of § 2254(e)(2) are satisfied so that petitioner's failure is excused. Subparagraph (B) of § 2254(e)(2) conditions a hearing upon a showing, by clear and convincing evidence, that no reasonable factfinder would have found petitioner guilty of capital murder but for the alleged constitutional error. Petitioner concedes he cannot make this showing, and the case has been presented to us on that premise. For these reasons, we affirm the Court of Appeals' judgment barring an evidentiary hearing on this claim.

B

We conclude petitioner has met the burden of showing he was diligent in efforts to develop the facts supporting his juror bias and prosecutorial misconduct claims in collateral proceedings before the Virginia Supreme Court.

Petitioner's claims are based on two of the questions posed to the jurors by the trial judge at *voir dire*. First, the judge asked prospective jurors, "Are any of you related to the following people who may be called as witnesses?" Then he read the jurors a list of names, one of which was "Deputy Sheriff Claude Meinhard." Bonnie Stinnett, who would later become the jury foreperson, had divorced Meinhard in 1979, after a 17-year marriage with four children. Stinnett remained silent, indicating the answer was "no." Meinhard, as the officer who investigated the crime scene and interrogated Cruse, would later become the prosecution's lead-off witness at trial.

After reading the names of the attorneys involved in the case, including one of the prosecutors, Robert Woodson, Jr., the judge asked, "Have you or any member of your immediate family ever been represented by any of the aforementioned attorneys?" Stinnett again said nothing, despite the fact Woodson had represented her during her divorce from Meinhard.

In an affidavit she provided in the federal habeas proceedings, Stinnett claimed "[she] did not respond to the judge's [first] question because [she] did not consider [herself] 'related' to Claude Meinhard in 1994 [at *voir dire*]. . . . Once our marriage ended in 1979, I was no longer related to him." As for Woodson's earlier representation of her, Stinnett explained as follows:

> "When Claude and I divorced in 1979, the divorce was uncontested and Mr. Woodson drew up the papers so that the divorce could be completed. Since neither Claude nor I was contesting anything, I didn't think Mr. Woodson "represented" either one of us."

Woodson provided an affidavit in which he admitted "[he] was aware that Juror Bonnie Stinnett was the ex-wife of then Deputy Sheriff Claude Meinhard and [he] was aware that they had been divorced for some time." Woodson stated, however, "to [his] mind, people who are related only by marriage are no longer 'related' once the marriage ends in divorce." Woodson also "had no recollection of having been involved as a private attorney in the divorce proceedings between Claude Meinhard and Bonnie Stinnett." He explained that "whatever [his] involvement was in the 1979 divorce, by the time of trial in 1994 [he] had completely forgotten about it."

Even if Stinnett had been correct in her technical or literal interpretation of the question relating to Meinhard, her silence after the first question was asked could suggest to the finder of fact an unwillingness to be forthcoming; this in turn could bear on the veracity of her explanation for not disclosing that Woodson had been her attorney. Stinnett's failure to divulge material information in response to the second question was misleading as a matter of fact because, under any interpretation, Woodson had acted as counsel to her and Meinhard in their divorce. Coupled with Woodson's own reticence, these omissions as a whole disclose the need for an evidentiary hearing. It may be that petitioner could establish that Stinnett was not impartial, or that Woodson's silence so infected the trial as to deny due process.

In ordering an evidentiary hearing on the juror bias and prosecutorial misconduct claims, the District Court concluded the factual basis of the claims was not reasonably available to petitioner's counsel during state habeas proceedings. After the Court of Appeals vacated this judgment, the District Court dismissed the petition and the Court of Appeals affirmed under the theory that state habeas counsel should have discovered Stinnett's relationship to Meinhard and Woodson.

We disagree with the Court of Appeals on this point. The trial record contains no evidence which would have put a reasonable attorney on notice that Stinnett's non-response was a deliberate omission of material information. State habeas counsel did attempt to investigate petitioner's jury, though prompted by concerns about a different juror. Counsel filed a motion for expert services with the Virginia Supreme Court, alleging "irregularities, improprieties and omissions existed with respect to the empaneling *[sic]* of the jury." Based on these suspicions, counsel requested funding for an investigator "to examine all circumstances relating to the empanelment of the jury and the jury's consideration of the case." The Commonwealth opposed the motion, and the Virginia Supreme Court denied it and dismissed the habeas petition, depriving petitioner of a further opportunity to investigate. The Virginia Supreme Court's denial of the motion is understandable in light of petitioner's vague allegations, but the vagueness was not the fault of petitioner. Counsel had no reason to believe Stinnett had been married to Meinhard or been represented by Woodson. The underdevelopment of these matters was attributable to Stinnett and Woodson, if anyone. We do not suggest the State has an obligation to pay for investigation of as yet undeveloped claims; but if the prisoner has made a reasonable effort to discover the claims to commence or continue state proceedings, § 2254(e)(2) will not bar him from developing them in federal court.

The Court of Appeals held state habeas counsel was not diligent because petitioner's investigator on federal habeas discovered the relationships upon interviewing two jurors who referred in passing to Stinnett as "Bonnie Meinhard." The investigator later confirmed Stinnett's prior marriage to Meinhard by checking Cumberland County's public records. We should be surprised, to say the least, if a district court familiar with the standards of trial practice were to hold that in all cases diligent counsel must check public records containing personal information pertaining to each and every juror. Because of Stinnett and Woodson's silence, there was no basis for an investigation into Stinnett's marriage history. Section 2254(e)(2) does not apply to petitioner's related claims of juror bias and prosecutorial misconduct.

* * * *

Our analysis should suffice to establish cause for any procedural default petitioner may have committed in not presenting these claims to the Virginia courts in the first instance. Questions regarding the standard for determining the prejudice that petitioner must establish to obtain relief on these claims can be addressed by the Court of Appeals or the District Court in the course of further proceedings. These courts . . . will take due account of the District Court's earlier decision to grant an evidentiary hearing based in part on its belief that "Juror Stinnett deliberately failed to tell the truth on voir dire."

IV

Petitioner alleges the Commonwealth failed to disclose an informal plea agreement with Cruse. The Court of Appeals rejected this claim on the merits under § 2254(d)(1), so it is unnecessary to reach the question whether § 2254(e)(2) would permit a hearing on the claim.

The decision of the Court of Appeals is affirmed in part and reversed in part. The case is remanded for further proceedings consistent with this opinion.

It is so ordered.

DISCUSSION AND QUESTIONS

There is no question that Congress sought through § 2254(e)(2) to further restrict the situations in which a federal court might hold an evidentiary hearing. The Court has made this point clear, noting that "[a]lthough state prisoners may sometimes submit new evidence in federal court, AEDPA's statutory scheme is designed to strongly discourage them from doing so."[106] Notice that the statute is phrased in such a way that, if it applies, a petitioner may obtain an evidentiary hearing only if she satisfies the stated conditions. This approach is different from the one in place prior to AEDPA under which a hearing was required in narrow circumstances but the district court retained discretion to hold hearings beyond those requirements.

The initial question one faces when confronted with a petitioner's request for an evidentiary hearing is whether subsection (e)(2) applies at all. The statute itself directs that the restrictions apply only to those claims for which the petitioner "failed to develop the factual basis for the claim in State court proceedings." *Michael Williams* explains that "a failure to develop the factual basis of the claim is not established unless there is a lack of diligence, or some other greater fault, attributable to the prisoner or the prisoner's counsel."[107] The Court further held that diligence "depends upon whether the prisoner made a reasonable attempt, in light of the information available at the time, to investigate and pursue claims in state court."[108] You can see how this standard works in operation by considering again how Justice Kennedy applies it to the three fact-based claims that Mr. Williams advanced.

When § 2254(e)(2) applies, a state prisoner may obtain an evidentiary hearing only if she satisfies certain stringent conditions. First, she must show either that her claim relies on a "new rule of constitutional law, made retroactive to cases on collateral review by the Supreme Court, that was previously unavailable," *see* 28 U.S.C. § 2254(e)(2)(A)(i), *or* that her claim relies on "a factual predicate that could not have been discovered through the exercise of due diligence," *see* 28 U.S.C. § 2254(e)(2)(A)(ii). Second, if she establishes one of these two things, the petitioner must show that "the facts underlying the claim would be sufficient to establish by clear and convincing evidence that but for the constitutional error, no reasonable factfinder would have found [her] guilty of the underlying offense." *See* 28 U.S.C. § 2254(e)(2)(B).

106. *Cullen v. Pinholster*, 131 S. Ct. 1388, 1401 (2011).
107. *Michael Williams*, 529 U.S. at 432.
108. *Id.* at 435.

These standards are exceedingly high. For example, as you will no doubt recognize by this point, it will be a rare case indeed in which a prisoner is able to take advantage of a new rule of constitutional law. Moreover, even if the prisoner satisfies one of the first prongs of the statutory test, she must still clear the significant hurdle imposed under § 2254(e)(2)(B). In this regard, you should note that the statute requires that the facts sought to be developed in a federal court evidentiary hearing must go to guilt or innocence. Thus, by its literal terms claims based on matters such as the appropriate sentence—including a death sentence—are not ones for which a hearing may be had. In addition, the burden imposed on the petitioner under subsection (e)(2)(B) is quite high; she must show that no reasonable factfinder would have found her guilty and that showing must be made under the clear and convincing evidence standard. The result of all of these factors is that it will be a rare petitioner who is able to obtain an evidentiary hearing in federal court when subsection (e)(2) applies.

What happens when the state prisoner's request for an evidentiary hearing is not governed by 28 U.S.C. § 2254(e)(2)? It appears that if the statute does not apply, the petitioner's request for an evidentiary hearing is governed by the standards the Court articulated before AEDPA, which we discussed in the paragraphs above before the excerpts from *Michael Williams.*[109]

We provide a graphic depiction of the rules governing requests for evidentiary hearings in Figure 13-7 on page 1051.

viii. The Harmless Error Rule

Even if the habeas petitioner has satisfied every other hurdle necessary to obtain relief, she may still fail in her quest due to the harmless error rule, yet another judicially crafted doctrine. The fundamental notion of harmless error analysis is that a constitutional error in a proceeding will not be the basis for granting relief if the error would not have made a difference in the result. In more colloquial terms: no harm; no foul. The key practical issue concerns the standards under which a court, having concluded that there has been error, determines whether the mistake indeed would have made no difference.

Once again, the difference between matters considered on direct review and those that arise in collateral proceedings becomes important. In the direct review context, the test for showing that an error is harmless is a difficult one. The state must demonstrate "beyond a reasonable doubt" that the error at issue would not have made a difference in the outcome in question.[110]

In contrast, on collateral review the burden on the state to show that an error is harmless is less demanding. In the collateral review setting, the state satisfies its burden if it shows that the error had no "substantial and injurious effect or

109. It is possible to infer this result from *Michael Williams.* At least one federal circuit court of appeals has expressly reached this conclusion. *See Bryan v. Mullin,* 335 F.3d 1207 (10th Cir. 2003).

110. *See Chapman v. California,* 386 U.S. 18 (1967). There are certain "structural" errors that cast so grave a question on the adjudicative process that they can never be harmless. Such structural errors—such as the deprivation entirely of the right to counsel—are rare.

influence" on the outcome in question.[111] The precise contours of the collateral review harmless error analysis remain uncertain. What is clear, however, is that the state has a better chance to show that an error is harmless on collateral review than it does on direct review.[112]

* * * *

FIGURE 13-7

The Availability of Evidentiary Hearings in Federal Court

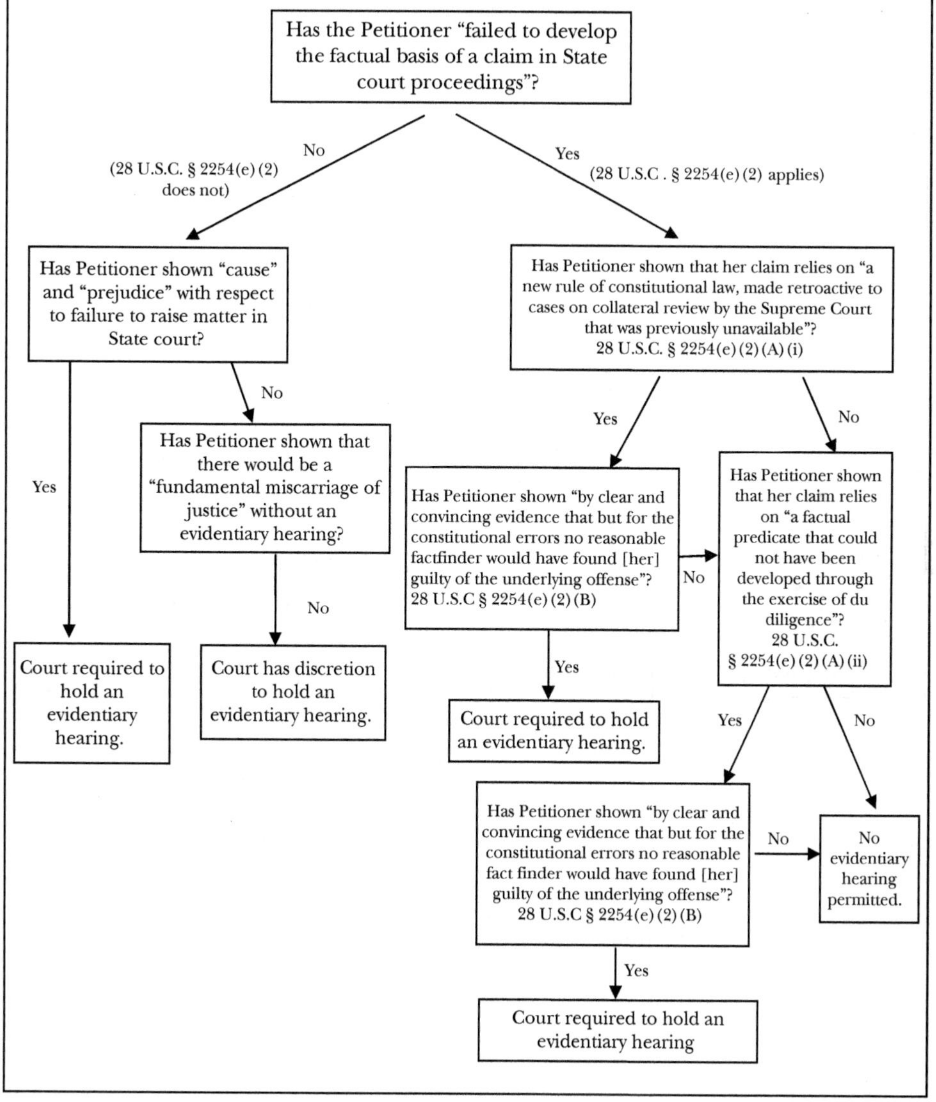

111. *See Brecht v. Abrahamson*, 507 U.S. 619, 637 (1993).

112. The Court has made clear that if the relevant evidence is in "equipoise" and the federal court has "grave doubt" about the matter, the state has not met its burden. *See O'Neal v. McAninch*, 513 U.S. 432, 444-45 (1995).

FIGURE 13-8

Non-Second or Successive Petition Habeas Corpus: *A Flowchart*

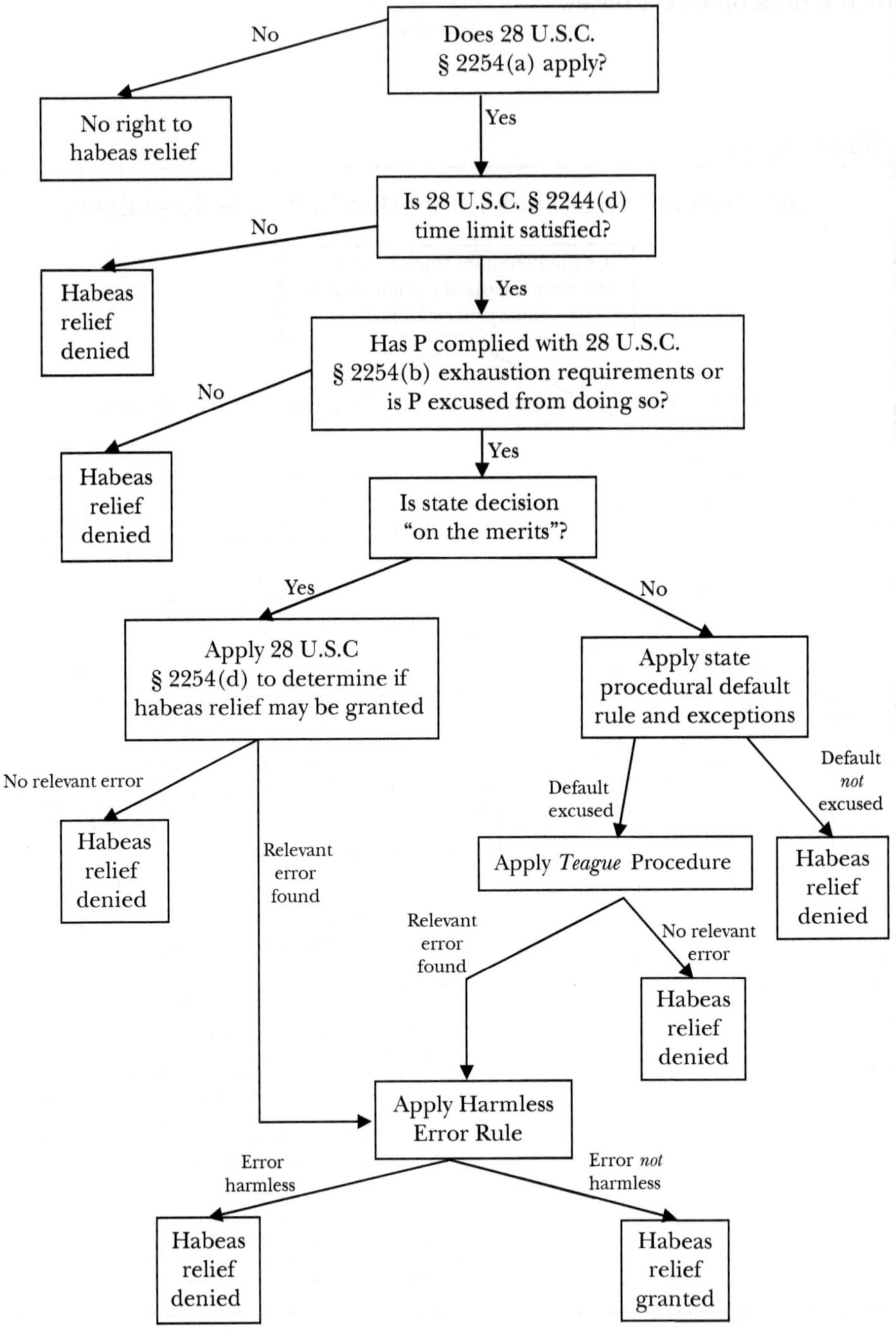

At this point, it is worthwhile to take stock of where we have been. Figure 13-8 is a flowchart depicting many of the issues we have discussed thus far. You can think of it as a road map of sorts, laying out the various obstacles a habeas petitioner needs to navigate in order to be successful. Note, however, that in many respects the order of the various hurdles is not set in stone. That is, for example, a judge might consider the harmless error rule earlier in the analysis than is depicted in the flowchart.[113] The order we present is a logical one that can be used to review most of the material covered to this point.

ix. Second or Successive Petitions: 28 U.S.C. § 2244(b)

As we have noted at several points in our discussion of federal courts' authority to grant writs of habeas corpus to state prisoners, one of the concerns that has always been present deals with the importance of finality of litigated matters. This concern is present whenever a federal court sits in collateral review under § 2254 because, by definition, another court has already been involved in the adjudication of the claim. This concern is heightened when a petitioner has not only had her day in state court but also has had a previous opportunity to present claims to a federal court. This situation concerns a second (or successive) petition, by which we mean that the petitioner has already filed at least one application seeking a writ of habeas corpus with a federal court.

In the 1960s, the Supreme Court adopted a standard that made it relatively easy for a state prisoner to file more than one writ of habeas corpus in a federal court. The limiting factor was whether the prisoner had "abused the writ," a standard similar in many respects to the deliberate bypass rule we discussed above in the context of procedural default.[114]

Beginning in the 1970s, the Supreme Court began to make it more difficult to file second petitions. This movement culminated in *McCleskey v. Zant*, 499 U.S. 467 (1991). In this decision, the Court overruled its earlier decisions in this area and adopted the "cause and prejudice" standard as the test.

Congress entered the field in 1996 with AEDPA, making it more difficult still for state prisoners to file more than one writ of habeas corpus. The relevant statutory provision is 28 U.S.C. § 2244(b). This statute first erects an absolute bar with respect to the filing of a second application concerning a claim that had been the subject of an earlier application. *See* 28 U.S.C. § 2244(b)(1). The more interesting and controversial part of the statute concerns second petitions involving claims that were *not* presented in the earlier one.

In AEDPA Congress further limited the situations in which a second petition may be used to litigate a claim that was not presented in an earlier petition. Subsection 2244(b)(2) sets forth the requirements a petitioner must satisfy to file such a petition. The statute requires that a second or successive petition be dismissed unless the petitioner is able to satisfy one of two requirements. First, a second/successive petition will be allowed if the petitioner "shows that the claim relies on a new rule of constitutional law, made retroactive to cases on collateral review by the Supreme Court, that was not previously available." 28 U.S.C. § 2244(b)(2)(A). As we have seen at numerous points in this chapter, it is exceedingly difficult for a petitioner to satisfy this type of condition.

113. The Court has, however, indicated that a court should generally address the harmless error question only after it has concluded that there has, in fact, been an error. *See Lockhart v. Fretwell*, 506 U.S. 364, 369 n.2 (1993).

114. *See, e.g., Sanders v. United States*, 373 U.S. 1 (1963). Note that *Sanders* dealt with a federal prisoner, but its description of the "abuse of the writ" standard was applied to state prisoners as well.

Second, a second/successive petition is allowed if the petitioner is able to show that "the factual predicate for the claim could not have been discovered previously through the exercise of due diligence," 28 U.S.C. § 2244(b)(2)(B)(i), *and* that "the facts underlying the claim, if proven and viewed in the light of the evidence as a whole, would be sufficient to establish by clear and convincing evidence that, but for the constitutional error, no reasonable factfinder would have found the applicant guilty of the underlying offense," 28 U.S.C. § 2244(b)(2)(A). As we have also seen, this second standard is difficult to meet. It also raises concerns as to whether a claim in a second petition that goes only to a sentence could ever qualify.

The Supreme Court has dealt with several issues concerning the scope of § 2244(b)(2) that are worth considering. The first question relates to a situation in which a petitioner files her first petition and does not include in it a claim that is not yet ripe. For example, assume that the petitioner had been convicted of a capital crime and sought a writ with respect to some alleged constitutional error in her state court trial and also claimed that she could not be executed because she was incompetent. The writ is not granted as to the trial error and is dismissed as premature with respect to the incompetency claim. Thereafter, she is scheduled to be executed and then reasserts the incompetency claim in federal court. Is this second filing governed by § 2244(b)(2)? No, said the Supreme Court in *Stewart v. Martinez-Villareal*, 523 U.S. 637 (1998), at least when the claim had been included—even if premature—in the first petition. The Court left open whether the result would have been different had the petitioner not included the unripe incompetency claim in the first petition. Recently, however, the Court ruled that § 2244(b) does not bar a second petition when the facts underlying the claim asserted did not exist at the time of the first filing. *See Panetti v. Quarterman*, 127 S. Ct. 2842 (2007). *Panetti* also concerned a claim of mental competency in connection with a pending execution.

Now consider this scenario: A person in state custody prevails on her federal habeas corpus petition with respect to a challenge to her sentence (not her conviction). The state court conducts a new sentencing hearing. Thereafter, the person files a writ of habeas corpus with respect to her new sentence. Among her claims of error are arguments that she could have made, but did not, when she challenged her original sentence. Is the current habeas corpus petition subject to the requirements in § 2244(b) concerning second or successive petitions? The Supreme Court held that § 2244(b) does not apply to the new petition because the petition in this case is challenging a new state court "judgment."[115] The Court declined to address whether in this situation the person would also be able to assert additional claims concerning the underlying conviction, which also would technically be a part of the new judgment.[116]

The second issue arises from the Court's holding that when a petitioner has certain claims in a first-filed petition dismissed for failure to exhaust state remedies, she does not run afoul of the rules against second petitions by returning to federal court after satisfying the exhaustion requirement.[117] Of course, the

115. *Magwood v. Patterson*, 130 S. Ct. 2788 (2010).

116. *Id.* at 2802.

117. *See Slack v. McDaniel*, 529 U.S. 473 (2000). *Slack* technically concerned pre-AEDPA law, but the Court indicated that the result would be the same under the current version of § 2244(b)(2). *Id.* at 486.

petitioner may still be precluded from proceeding based on the time limits on filing habeas claims. *See* 28 U.S.C. § 2244(d).

Finally, one can also have an issue as to whether a second filing is in reality a petition for a writ of habeas corpus if not so denominated. A classic example of such a situation is when the second filing is made under 42 U.S.C. § 1983. As we learned in Chapter 9, this statute allows a person to sue a state official for a violation of her federal rights. As you should see, there is an overlap of coverage between the habeas statutes and § 1983. This overlap allows state petitioners a means to avoid restrictions on habeas.

In a series of cases the Supreme Court has attempted to articulate a standard by which one can classify such § 1983 claims as the functional equivalent of habeas on the one hand or "true" § 1983 claims on the other. Essentially, if a state prisoner is "challenging the very fact or duration of his physical imprisonment," the only avenue open to him is habeas. If, on the other hand, he is challenging the conditions of confinement, then § 1983 is legitimately available.[118] Recently, the Court has dealt with this issue in the context of claims that a certain method of execution is unconstitutional under the Eighth Amendment. In these cases, the prisoner had earlier filed a habeas petition and then, closer to the prisoner's execution date, filed a § 1983 action. The Court allowed the § 1983 claims to proceed although it recognized the difficulties inherent in its test when one confronts claims concerning death sentences.[119] The Court has also held that a prisoner seeking access to DNA evidence may proceed by way of § 1983 and is, therefore, not required to utilize a habeas corpus petition for that particular claim.[120] The lesson to take from these cases is that any second filing will be subject to a claim that a prisoner is merely trying to avoid the bar on successive habeas petitions.[121] Like the death row inmates who filed § 1983 actions, a state petitioner may successfully ward off the challenge, but it is a battle that will be fought.

The final point concerning filing second petitions deals with the procedure by which a state prisoner may do so. A person wishing to file a second or successive petition must obtain permission from the relevant court of appeals. *See* 28 U.S.C. § 2244(b)(3). The court of appeals should grant permission to file the petition if the prisoner "makes a prima facie showing" that she satisfies the conditions for filing a second petition. *See* 28 U.S.C. § 2244(b)(3)(C). The district court may still decline to issue the writ on the grounds that the petitioner does not actually establish that she has satisfied the standards for filing more than one petition. *See* 28 U.S.C. § 2244(b)(4).

A controversial issue in this area concerns the restrictions Congress placed on the appealability of a court of appeal's decision under § 2244(b)(3). Such decision "shall not be appealable and shall not be the subject of a petition for rehearing or for a writ of certiorari." *See* 28 U.S.C. § 2244(b)(3)(E). As you may recall from Chapter 3, such a restriction on the appellate jurisdiction of

118. *See Preiser v. Rodriguez*, 411 U.S. 475 (1973).

119. *See Hill v. McDonough*, 547 U.S. 573 (2006); *Nelson v. Campbell*, 541 U.S. 637 (1994).

120. *Skinner v. Switzer*, 131 S. Ct. 1289 (2011).

121. Another example the Court has confronted concerns a prisoner's use of Federal Rule of Civil Procedure 60(b) to attempt to obtain "relief from judgment" with respect to a federal court's earlier denial of a habeas corpus petition. The Court held that the Rule 60(b) motion was not the equivalent of a habeas corpus petition and, therefore, not subject to the § 2244(b) requirements. *See Gonzalez v. Crosby*, 545 U.S. 524 (2005). The petitioner in such a situation is still unlikely to prevail given the high standards set under Rule 60(b), but the failure will not be due to AEDPA's prohibitions on second habeas corpus petitions.

the Supreme Court raises important constitutional issues.[122] The Court avoided those issues by holding that Congress had not foreclosed all routes by which a petitioner could reach the Supreme Court. For example, such a petitioner could file an original petition in the Supreme Court directly, even though this route is seldom used and seldom successful.[123] Thus, in reality the courts of appeals largely have the last word in terms of a person's ability to file a second or successive writ of habeas corpus in federal court.

D. SOME ADDITIONAL PROBLEMS

The problems that follow provide additional practice concerning the topics covered in Chapter 13.

PROBLEM 13-5

The Nightclub Shooting and a Dishonest District Attorney

Jean Valjean was convicted in Florida state court of murder of Mr. Javer. Valjean's defense was that he killed Javer in self-defense. The prosecutor argued instead that Valjean acted out of a jealous rage because Javer was having an affair with Valjean's wife, Fantine. At trial, the prosecutor put on three witnesses who testified that Javer had been drinking heavily on the night he was killed. Each of those witnesses testified that Javer passed out around 11:00 P.M. on the night in question. He was last seen slumped on a table in the corner. In addition, the prosecution had the medical examiner testify concerning the cause of Javer's death. She testified that Javer's wounds were consistent with being stabbed in the back while slumped over a surface such as a table. The medical examiner also testified that Javer's blood alcohol level was nearly three times the legal limit and was such that it was highly unlikely that he could function.

Valjean took the stand in his own defense. He testified that Javer had attacked him with a knife that evening and that, after a heated fight, Valjean had stabbed Javer. Valjean did have some bruises on his face, but he admitted on cross-examination that he was a semi-professional boxer and often had bruises. In addition, Valjean admitted during cross-examination that he knew that his wife Fantine was having an affair with Javer. He refused to admit, however, that the affair bothered him. He said that he and Fantine had "an arrangement" in which each of them could "go with" other people.

The jury convicted Valjean of murder in January 2012. He was ultimately sentenced to life in prison. Valjean's conviction was affirmed by the intermediate appellate court, and both the Florida Supreme Court and the United States Supreme Court denied review. Valjean's conviction became final on direct review on June 30, 2013.

In January 2015, a local newspaper broke a story concerning corruption in the local state attorney's office. In particular, the paper alleged that the state attorney had a policy of withholding relevant evidence from criminal defendants in

122. Indeed, this portion of AEDPA served as the model for Problem 3-1.
123. *See Felker v. Turpin*, 518 U.S. 651 (1996).

high-profile murder cases. In response to the article, the Florida Attorney General conducted an investigation and concluded that, while there was no policy to withhold evidence, there were some instances in which the state attorney did not comply with "*Brady* requests" by defense counsel.

At this point, you may wish to know what the Attorney General meant by a *Brady* request. In 1963, the United States Supreme Court decided *Brady v. Maryland*, 373 U.S. 83 (1963). In *Brady*, the defendant had been convicted of murder and sentenced to death. The prosecutor in that case had withheld from the defendant the fact that one of the defendant's co-conspirators in the crime had admitted doing the actual killing. The Court held that "the suppression by the prosecutor of evidence favorable to an accused upon request violates due process where the evidence is material either to guilt or punishment." *Brady*, 373 U.S. at 87. For purposes of this problem, you should assume that the Court has not returned to the *Brady* issue since it issued the opinion.

Valjean's lawyer had made a proper *Brady* request. In particular, the lawyer requested any information in the prosecutor's possession concerning Javer's violent tendencies. Valjean's counsel wanted the information to buttress his argument that Valjean acted in self-defense, the idea being that Javer was a violent person. The prosecutor did not disclose anything in response to the *Brady* request. In turns out, however, that the prosecutor had three witness statements from people who said that Javer had an incredibly violent temper and would often pick fights with people.

Valjean first found out about these statements in February 2015 when they were made available as a result of the Attorney General's investigation. He filed a state post-conviction motion immediately after learning about the statements. The state courts rejected the motion, explaining that the situation did not constitute a violation of the *Brady* rule because the facts of *Brady* and Valjean's case are different.

His lawyer has now filed a petition for a writ of habeas corpus in the appropriate United States District Court. He claims the state violated its *Brady* duty in not disclosing the witness statements. You should assume that Valjean has properly exhausted all available state-law remedies and that there is no issue with a state procedural default. The state has opposed Valjean's petition, arguing that Valjean's petition was filed too late, that he does not otherwise satisfy the standards for granting the writ, and that in any event any error that might have occurred, even if cognizable under the habeas statute, is not sufficient to grant the writ given the evidence submitted at trial.

You are the United States District Judge to whom Valjean's case has been assigned. How do you rule on Valjean's petition for a writ of habeas corpus? Be sure to refer to relevant statutory provisions as part of your opinion.

PROBLEM 13-6

The Case of the Savvy, Yet Incompetent (?), Defendant

You may wish to know the following about constitutional law: In 1986, the United States Supreme Court decided *Wainwright v. Greenfield*, 474 U.S. 284 (1986). *Wainwright* held that it is constitutional error under the Fourteenth Amendment's Due Process Clause for a prosecutor to offer evidence during a trial that a defendant, after being read his *Miranda* warnings, invoked his right to counsel when the purpose of presenting such evidence is to rebut a defendant's claim that he is not responsible for the underlying crime as a result of insanity. The Court has never overruled *Wainwright.*

John Marshall is a citizen of the State of Marbury, one of the United States. On the morning of March 14, 2010, Marshall was drinking in a bar in Jefferson City, the capital of Marbury. A fight broke out between Marshall and another patron in the bar. During that fight, Marshall pulled a gun and shot several times at his opponent in the fight. Marshall missed. By that time, the Jefferson City Police had arrived on the scene. They immediately placed Marshall under arrest.

Pursuant to police policy, as soon as Marshall was placed under arrest the arresting officers read Marshall his *Miranda* rights (i.e., the right to remain silent and the right to have a lawyer, etc.). After listening to his rights, Marshall immediately requested that he be allowed to speak with a lawyer. The police complied with this request. At all times thereafter, Marshall was represented by a Marbury public defender.

The State Attorney for Jefferson City timely charged Marshall with attempted murder under relevant Marbury law. After considering the situation and speaking with Marshall, Marshall's public defender decided Marshall might not be competent to stand trial. Marbury law provided that "a person cannot be tried for any offense while he or she is mentally incompetent. A person is mentally incompetent if, as a result of a mental disorder or developmental disability, the person is unable to understand the nature of the criminal proceedings or to assist counsel in the conduct of a defense in a rational manner."

In order to judge competency, Marbury requires that a jury be assembled to hear evidence and enter a finding of competent or not competent. The jury that makes this determination is different from the jury that decides guilt or innocence at a trial (assuming that the defendant is found competent to stand trial). You should assume that no appeal is allowed from the competency determination until a defendant has been found guilty.

A jury was empanelled to determine Marshall's competency to stand trial. During that trial, Marshall introduced testimony from a psychiatrist who concluded based on his observations that Marshall was not competent to stand trial and indeed had not been competent at the time of the offense. During cross-examination, the State Attorney asked the defense witness whether he knew that Marshall had requested an attorney immediately after being arrested. The witness said he did not know that was the case. The State Attorney then asked whether this information would have changed the testimony given. The witness said no. Marshall's lawyer did not object during this series of questions and did not move to strike any answers given.

The state called its own psychiatric witness. The state's witness testified that Marshall was competent. A significant basis of the state's expert's opinion was that Marshall had requested a lawyer immediately after being informed of his *Miranda* warnings. Marshall's lawyer did not object to this line of questioning.

During closing arguments, the State Attorney made repeated references to Marshall's invocation of his right to counsel as a reason to reject the incompetency argument. Marshall's lawyer did no object. The jury returned a verdict of "competent" after deliberating for about an hour.

After the competency hearing, Marshall entered a conditional plea of guilty. The conditional nature of the plea allowed Marshall to appeal the finding of competency. He was sentenced to ten years in prison. He remains incarcerated at the Marbury State prison.

On appeal, Marshall argued only one point: the State's reference to Marshall's invocation of the right to counsel at the competency hearing was a violation of the Fourteenth Amendment's Due Process Clause. Marshall's attorney felt he was on solid ground because the Marbury First District Court of Appeal (the intermediate appellate court covering Jefferson City) had ruled the previous year in *Hamilton v. Burr* that the *Wainwright* rule was applicable at competency hearings as well as at the guilt or penalty phase. Neither the Marbury Supreme Court nor the United States Supreme Court has ruled that *Wainwright* applies in a competency proceeding. You may also assume that the United States Court of Appeals for the Thirteenth Circuit (which covered the State of Marbury) had ruled in accord with *Hamilton v. Burr* that the *Wainwright* rule *was* applicable at competency hearings.

Before the intermediate appellate court ruled — indeed before the state even responded — the Marbury Supreme Court utilized a procedure to take the case on direct appeal. It ordered that the state respond to Marshall's brief.

The state responded with two arguments. First, the state argued that Marshall had forfeited his argument concerning the reference to the invocation of the right to counsel by not objecting at trial. Marbury has a rule requiring such objections. Second, the state argued that *Wainwright* should not apply to a competency hearing and that the intermediate appellate court's decision in *Hamilton v. Burr* was incorrect.

On February 15, 2011, the Supreme Court of Marbury issued the following order after the briefs had been filed:

"The Court has determined that this case is appropriate for resolution without oral argument. Based on the parties' briefs it is ordered that the appeal is dismissed. IT IS SO ORDERED."

Marshall sought a writ of certiorari from the United States Supreme Court. The writ was denied on June 18, 2011.

After the U.S. Supreme Court refused to grant certiorari, Marshall petitioned for a writ of habeas corpus (under 28 U.S.C. § 2254) in the United States District Court for the District of Marbury. He specifically did not pursue post-conviction proceedings that were available to him in the State of Marbury's courts. His sole claim in his federal habeas corpus petition is that the Marbury State Attorney's repeated references at the competency hearing to Marshall's invocation of his right to counsel after being read his *Miranda* warnings violated the Fourteenth Amendment's Due Process Clause.[124] Marshall has not requested that the federal court conduct an evidentiary hearing.

You are a law clerk to the United States District Court Judge to whom Marshall's habeas corpus petition has been assigned. The Judge has asked you to prepare a memorandum on Marshall's habeas corpus petition. If there is a realistic possibility that one of two possible paths might be taken, explain why that is the case, which one is most likely to be correct, and how the analysis on each path would proceed. You may assume that today's date is March 1, 2012.

124. You should assume that Marshall had *not* alleged ineffective assistance of counsel. However, you should also assume that Marshall was constitutionally entitled to counsel at the competency hearing and that such counsel was required to be effective within the meaning of *Strickland v. Washington*. You should assume that under *Strickland* counsel is constitutionally ineffective if his or her performance falls below the minimum standard of performance of a lawyer and prejudice results from this deficient performance.

APPENDIX A

Transcript of Articles of Confederation

To all to whom these Presents shall come, we the undersigned Delegates of the States affixed to our Names send greeting.

Articles of Confederation and perpetual Union between the states of New Hampshire, Massachusetts-bay Rhode Island and Providence Plantations, Connecticut, New York, New Jersey, Pennsylvania, Delaware, Maryland, Virginia, North Carolina, South Carolina and Georgia.

I.

The Stile of this Confederacy shall be **"The United States of America".**

II.

Each state retains its sovereignty, freedom, and independence, and every power, jurisdiction, and right, which is not by this Confederation expressly delegated to the United States, in Congress assembled.

III.

The said States hereby severally enter into a firm league of friendship with each other, for their common defense, the security of their liberties, and their mutual and general welfare, binding themselves to assist each other, against all force offered to, or attacks made upon them, or any of them, on account of religion, sovereignty, trade, or any other pretense whatever.

IV.

The better to secure and perpetuate mutual friendship and intercourse among the people of the different States in this Union, the free inhabitants of each of these States, paupers, vagabonds, and fugitives from justice excepted, shall be entitled to all privileges and immunities of free citizens in the several States; and the people of each State shall free ingress and regress to and from any other State, and shall enjoy therein all the privileges of trade and commerce, subject to the same duties, impositions, and restrictions as the inhabitants thereof respectively, provided that such restrictions shall not extend so far as to prevent the removal of property imported into any State, to any other State, of which the owner is an inhabitant; provided also that no imposition, duties or restriction shall be laid by any State, on the property of the United States, or either of them.

If any person guilty of, or charged with, treason, felony, or other high misdemeanor in any State, shall flee from justice, and be found in any of the United States, he shall, upon demand of the Governor or executive power of the State from which he fled, be delivered up and removed to the State having jurisdiction of his offense.

Full faith and credit shall be given in each of these States to the records, acts, and judicial proceedings of the courts and magistrates of every other State.

V.

For the most convenient management of the general interests of the United States, delegates shall be annually appointed in such manner as the legislatures of each State shall direct, to meet in Congress on the first Monday in November, in every year, with a power reserved to each State to recall its delegates, or any of them, at any time within the year, and to send others in their stead for the remainder of the year.

No State shall be represented in Congress by less than two, nor more than seven members; and no person shall be capable of being a delegate for more than three years in any term of six years; nor shall any person, being a delegate, be capable of holding any office under the United States, for which he, or another for his benefit, receives any salary, fees or emolument of any kind.

Each State shall maintain its own delegates in a meeting of the States, and while they act as members of the committee of the States.

In determining questions in the United States in Congress assembled, each State shall have one vote.

Freedom of speech and debate in Congress shall not be impeached or questioned in any court or place out of Congress, and the members of Congress shall be protected in their persons from arrests or imprisonments, during the time of their going to and from, and attendence on Congress, except for treason, felony, or breach of the peace.

VI.

No State, without the consent of the United States in Congress assembled, shall send any embassy to, or receive any embassy from, or enter into any conference, agreement, alliance or treaty with any King, Prince or State; nor shall any person holding any office of profit or trust under the United States, or any of them, accept any present, emolument, office or title of any kind whatever from any King, Prince or foreign State; nor shall the United States in Congress assembled, or any of them, grant any title of nobility.

No two or more States shall enter into any treaty, confederation or alliance whatever between them, without the consent of the United States in Congress assembled, specifying accurately the purposes for which the same is to be entered into, and how long it shall continue.

No State shall lay any imposts or duties, which may interfere with any stipulations in treaties, entered into by the United States in Congress assembled, with any King, Prince or State, in pursuance of any treaties already proposed by Congress, to the courts of France and Spain.

No vessel of war shall be kept up in time of peace by any State, except such number only, as shall be deemed necessary by the United States in Congress assembled, for the defense of such State, or its trade; nor shall any body of forces be kept up by any State in time of peace, except such number only, as in the judgement of the United States in Congress assembled, shall be deemed requisite to garrison the forts necessary for the defense of such State; but every State shall always keep up a well-regulated and disciplined militia, sufficiently armed and accoutered, and shall provide and constantly have ready for use, in public stores, a due number of filed pieces and tents, and a proper quantity of arms, ammunition and camp equipage.

No State shall engage in any war without the consent of the United States in Congress assembled, unless such State be actually invaded by enemies, or shall have received certain advice of a resolution being formed by some nation of Indians to invade such State, and the danger is so imminent as not to admit of a delay till the United States in Congress assembled can be consulted; nor shall any State grant commissions to any ships or vessels of war, nor letters of marque or reprisal, except it be after a declaration of war by the United States in Congress assembled, and then only against the Kingdom or State and the subjects thereof, against which war has been so declared, and under such regulations as shall be established by the United States in Congress assembled, unless such State be infested by pirates, in which case vessels of war may be fitted out for that occasion, and kept so long as the danger shall continue, or until the United States in Congress assembled shall determine otherwise.

VII.

When land forces are raised by any State for the common defense, all officers of or under the rank of colonel, shall be appointed by the legislature of each State respectively, by whom such forces shall be raised, or in such manner as such State shall direct, and all vacancies shall be filled up by the State which first made the appointment.

VIII.

All charges of war, and all other expenses that shall be incurred for the common defense or general welfare, and allowed by the United States in Congress assembled, shall be defrayed out of a common treasury, which shall be supplied by the several States in proportion to the value of all land within each State, granted or surveyed for any person, as such land and the buildings and improvements thereon shall be estimated according to such mode as the United States in Congress assembled, shall from time to time direct and appoint.

The taxes for paying that proportion shall be laid and levied by the authority and direction of the legislatures of the several States within the time agreed upon by the United States in Congress assembled.

IX.

The United States in Congress assembled, shall have the sole and exclusive right and power of determining on peace and war, except in the cases mentioned in the sixth article—of sending and receiving ambassadors—entering into treaties and alliances, provided that no treaty of commerce shall be made whereby the legislative power of the respective States shall be restrained from imposing such imposts and duties on foreigners, as their own people are subjected to, or from prohibiting the exportation or importation of any species of goods or commodities whatsoever—of establishing rules for deciding in all cases, what captures on land or water shall be legal, and in what manner prizes taken by land or naval forces in the service of the United States shall be divided or appropriated—of granting letters of marque and reprisal in times of peace—appointing courts for the trial of piracies and felonies committed on the high seas and establishing courts for receiving and determining finally appeals in all cases of captures, provided that no member of Congress shall be appointed a judge of any of the said courts.

The United States in Congress assembled shall also be the last resort on appeal in all disputes and differences now subsisting or that hereafter may arise between two or more States concerning boundary, jurisdiction or any other causes whatever; which authority shall always be exercised in the manner following. Whenever the legislative or executive authority or lawful agent of any State in controversy with another shall present a petition to Congress stating the matter in question and praying for a hearing, notice thereof shall be given by order of Congress to the legislative or executive authority of the other State in controversy, and a day assigned for the appearance of the parties by their lawful agents, who shall then be directed to appoint by joint consent, commissioners or judges to constitute a court for hearing and determining the matter in question: but if they cannot agree, Congress shall name three persons out of each of the United States, and from the list of such persons each party shall alternately strike out one, the petitioners beginning, until the number shall be reduced to thirteen; and from that number not less than seven, nor more than nine names as Congress shall direct, shall in the presence of Congress be drawn out by lot, and the persons whose names shall be so drawn or any five of them, shall be commissioners or judges, to hear and finally determine the controversy, so always as a major part of the judges who shall hear the cause shall agree in the determination: and if either party shall neglect to attend at the day appointed, without showing reasons, which Congress shall judge sufficient, or being present shall refuse to strike, the Congress shall proceed to nominate three persons out of each State, and the secretary of Congress shall strike in behalf of such party absent or refusing; and the judgement and sentence of the court to be appointed, in the manner before prescribed, shall be final and conclusive; and if any of the parties shall refuse to submit to the authority of such court, or to appear or defend their claim or cause, the court shall nevertheless proceed to pronounce sentence, or judgement, which shall in like manner be final and decisive, the judgement or sentence and other proceedings being in either case transmitted to Congress, and lodged among the acts of Congress for the security of the parties concerned: provided that every commissioner, before he sits in judgement, shall take an oath to be administered by one of the judges of the supreme or superior court of the State, where the cause shall be tried, 'well and truly to hear and determine the matter in question, according to the best of his judgement, without favor, affection or hope of reward': provided also, that no State shall be deprived of territory for the benefit of the United States.

All controversies concerning the private right of soil claimed under different grants of two or more States, whose jurisdictions as they may respect such lands, and the States which passed such grants are adjusted, the said grants or either of them being at the same time claimed to have originated antecedent to such settlement of jurisdiction, shall on the petition of either party to the Congress of the United States, be finally determined as near as may be in the same manner as is before prescribed for deciding disputes respecting territorial jurisdiction between different States.

The United States in Congress assembled shall also have the sole and exclusive right and power of regulating the alloy and value of coin struck by their own authority, or by that of the respective States—fixing the standards of weights and measures throughout the United States—regulating the trade and managing all affairs with the Indians, not members of any of the States, provided that the legislative right of any State within its own limits be not infringed or violated—establishing or regulating post offices from one State to another, throughout all the United States, and exacting such postage on the papers passing through the same as may be requisite to defray the expenses of the said office—appointing all officers of the land forces, in the service of the United States, excepting regimental officers—appointing all the officers of the naval forces, and commissioning all officers whatever in the service of the United States—making rules for the government and regulation of the said land and naval forces, and directing their operations.

The United States in Congress assembled shall have authority to appoint a committee, to sit in the recess of Congress, to be denominated 'A Committee of the States', and to consist of one delegate from each State; and to appoint such other committees and civil officers as may be necessary for managing the general affairs of the United States under their direction—to appoint one of their members to preside, provided that no person be allowed to serve in the office of president more than one year in any term of three years; to ascertain the necessary sums of money to be raised for the service of the United States, and to appropriate and apply the same for defraying the public expenses—to borrow money, or emit bills on the credit of the United States, transmitting every half-year to the respective States an account of the sums of money so borrowed or emitted—to build and equip a navy—to agree upon the number of land forces, and to make requisitions from each State for its quota, in proportion to the number of white inhabitants in such State; which requisition shall be binding, and thereupon the legislature of each State shall appoint the regimental officers, raise the men and cloath, arm and equip them in a solid-like manner, at the expense of the United States; and the officers and men so cloathed, armed and equipped shall march to the place appointed, and within the time agreed on by the United States in Congress assembled. But if the United States in Congress assembled shall, on consideration of circumstances judge proper that any State should not raise men, or should raise a smaller number of men than the quota thereof, such extra number shall be raised, officered, cloathed, armed and equipped in the same manner as the quota of each State, unless the legislature of such State shall judge that such extra number cannot be safely spread out in the same, in which case they shall raise, officer, cloath, arm and equip as many of such extra number as they judge can be safely spared. And the officers and men so cloathed, armed, and equipped, shall march to the place appointed, and within the time agreed on by the United States in Congress assembled.

The United States in Congress assembled shall never engage in a war, nor grant letters of marque or reprisal in time of peace, nor enter into any treaties or alliances, nor coin money, nor regulate the value thereof, nor ascertain the sums and expenses necessary for the defense and welfare of the United States, or any of them, nor emit bills, nor borrow money on the credit of the United States, nor appropriate money, nor agree upon the number of vessels of war, to be built or purchased, or the number of land or sea forces to be raised, nor appoint a commander in chief of the army or navy, unless nine States assent to the same: nor shall a question on any other point, except for adjourning from day to day be determined, unless by the votes of the majority of the United States in Congress assembled.

The Congress of the United States shall have power to adjourn to any time within the year, and to any place within the United States, so that no period of adjournment be for a longer duration than the space of six months, and shall publish the journal of their proceedings monthly, except such parts thereof relating to treaties, alliances or military operations, as in their judgement require secrecy; and the yeas and nays of the delegates of each State on any question shall be entered on the journal, when it is desired by any delegates of a State, or any of them, at his or their request shall be furnished with a transcript of the said journal, except such parts as are above excepted, to lay before the legislatures of the several States.

X.

The Committee of the States, or any nine of them, shall be authorized to execute, in the recess of Congress, such of the powers of Congress as the United States in Congress assembled, by the consent of the nine States, shall from time to time think expedient to vest them with; provided that no power be delegated to the said Committee, for the exercise of which, by the Articles of Confederation, the voice of nine States in the Congress of the United States assembled be requisite.

XI.

Canada acceding to this confederation, and adjoining in the measures of the United States, shall be admitted into, and entitled to all the advantages of this Union; but no other colony shall be admitted into the same, unless such admission be agreed to by nine States.

XII.

All bills of credit emitted, monies borrowed, and debts contracted by, or under the authority of Congress, before the assembling of the United States, in pursuance of the present confederation, shall be deemed and considered as a charge against the United States, for payment and satisfaction whereof the said United States, and the public faith are hereby solemnly pledged.

XIII.

Every State shall abide by the determination of the United States in Congress assembled, on all questions which by this confederation are submitted to them. And the Articles of this Confederation shall be inviolably observed by every State, and the Union shall be perpetual; nor shall any alteration at any time hereafter be made in any of them; unless such alteration be agreed to in a Congress of the United States, and be afterwards confirmed by the legislatures of every State.

And Whereas it hath pleased the Great Governor of the World to incline the hearts of the legislatures we respectively represent in Congress, to approve of, and to authorize us to ratify the said Articles of Confederation and perpetual Union. Know Ye that we the undersigned delegates, by virtue of the power and authority to us given for that purpose, do by these presents, in the name and in behalf of our respective constituents, fully and entirely ratify and confirm each and every of the said Articles of Confederation and perpetual Union, and all and singular the matters and things therein contained: And we do further solemnly plight and engage the faith of our respective constituents, that they shall abide by the determinations of the United States in Congress assembled, on all questions, which by the said Confederation are submitted to them. And that the Articles thereof shall be inviolably observed by the States we respectively represent, and that the Union shall be perpetual.

In Witness whereof we have hereunto set our hands in Congress. Done at Philadelphia in the State of Pennsylvania the ninth day of July in the Year of our Lord One Thousand Seven Hundred and Seventy-Eight, and in the Third Year of the independence of America.

Agreed to by Congress 15 November 1777. In force after ratification by Maryland, 1 March 1781.

APPENDIX
B

Constitution for the United States of America

We the People of the United States, in Order to form a more perfect Union, establish Justice, insure domestic Tranquility, provide for the common defence, promote the general Welfare, and secure the Blessings of Liberty to ourselves and our Posterity, do ordain and establish this Constitution for the United States of America.

Article. I.

Section. 1. All legislative Powers herein granted shall be vested in a Congress of the United States, which shall consist of a Senate and House of Representatives.

Section. 2. The House of Representatives shall be composed of Members chosen every second Year by the People of the several States, and the Electors in each State shall have the Qualifications requisite for Electors of the most numerous Branch of the State Legislature.

No Person shall be a Representative who shall not have attained to the Age of twenty five Years, and been seven Years a Citizen of the United States, and who shall not, when elected, be an Inhabitant of that State in which he shall be chosen.

Representatives and direct Taxes shall be apportioned among the several States which may be included within this Union, according to their respective Numbers, which shall be determined by adding to the whole Number of free Persons, including those bound to Service for a Term of Years, and excluding Indians not taxed, three fifths of all other Persons. The actual Enumeration shall be made within three Years after the first Meeting of the Congress of the United States, and within every subsequent Term of ten Years, in such Manner as they shall by Law direct. The Number of Representatives shall not exceed one for every thirty Thousand, but each State shall have at Least one Representative; and until such enumeration shall be made, the State of New Hampshire shall be entitled to chuse three, Massachusetts eight, Rhode-Island and Providence Plantations one, Connecticut five, New-York six, New Jersey four, Pennsylvania eight, Delaware one, Maryland six, Virginia ten, North Carolina five, South Carolina five, and Georgia three.

When vacancies happen in the Representation from any State, the Executive Authority thereof shall issue Writs of Election to fill such Vacancies.

The House of Representatives shall chuse their Speaker and other Officers; and shall have the sole Power of Impeachment.

Section. 3. The Senate of the United States shall be composed of two Senators from each State, chosen by the Legislature thereof, for six Years; and each Senator shall have one Vote.

Immediately after they shall be assembled in Consequence of the first Election, they shall be divided as equally as may be into three Classes. The Seats of the Senators of the first Class shall be vacated at the Expiration of the second Year, of the second Class at the Expiration of the fourth Year, and of the third Class at the Expiration of the sixth Year, so that one third may be chosen every second Year; and if Vacancies happen by Resignation, or otherwise, during the Recess of the Legislature of any State, the Executive thereof may make temporary Appointments until the next Meeting of the Legislature, which shall then fill such Vacancies.

No Person shall be a Senator who shall not have attained to the Age of thirty Years, and been nine Years a Citizen of the United States, and who shall not, when elected, be an Inhabitant of that State for which he shall be chosen.

The Vice President of the United States shall be President of the Senate, but shall have no Vote, unless they be equally divided.

The Senate shall chuse their other Officers, and also a President pro tempore, in the Absence of the Vice President, or when he shall exercise the Office of President of the United States.

The Senate shall have the sole Power to try all Impeachments. When sitting for that Purpose, they shall be on Oath or Affirmation. When the President of the United States is tried, the Chief Justice shall preside: And no Person shall be convicted without the Concurrence of two thirds of the Members present.

Judgment in Cases of Impeachment shall not extend further than to removal from Office, and disqualification to hold and enjoy any Office of honor, Trust or Profit under the United States: but the Party convicted shall nevertheless be liable and subject to Indictment, Trial, Judgment and Punishment, according to Law.

Section. 4. The Times, Places and Manner of holding Elections for Senators and Representatives, shall be prescribed in each State by the Legislature thereof; but the Congress may at any time by Law make or alter such Regulations, except as to the Places of chusing Senators.

The Congress shall assemble at least once in every Year, and such Meeting shall be on the first Monday in December [Modified by Amendment XX], unless they shall by Law appoint a different Day.

Section. 5. Each House shall be the Judge of the Elections, Returns and Qualifications of its own Members, and a Majority of each shall constitute a Quorum to do Business; but a smaller Number may adjourn from day to day, and may be authorized to compel the Attendance of absent Members, in such Manner, and under such Penalties as each House may provide.

Each House may determine the Rules of its Proceedings, punish its Members for disorderly Behaviour, and, with the Concurrence of two thirds, expel a Member.

Each House shall keep a Journal of its Proceedings, and from time to time publish the same, excepting such Parts as may in their Judgment require Secrecy; and the Yeas and Nays of the Members of either House on any question shall, at the Desire of one fifth of those Present, be entered on the Journal.

Neither House, during the Session of Congress, shall, without the Consent of the other, adjourn for more than three days, nor to any other Place than that in which the two Houses shall be sitting.

Section. 6. The Senators and Representatives shall receive a Compensation for their Services, to be ascertained by Law, and paid out of the Treasury of the United States. They shall in all Cases, except Treason, Felony and Breach of the Peace, be privileged from Arrest during their Attendance at the Session of their respective Houses, and in going to and returning from the same; and for any Speech or Debate in either House, they shall not be questioned in any other Place.

No Senator or Representative shall, during the Time for which he was elected, be appointed to any civil Office under the Authority of the United States, which shall have been created, or the Emoluments whereof shall have been encreased during such time; and no Person holding any Office under the United States, shall be a Member of either House during his Continuance in Office.

Section. 7. All Bills for raising Revenue shall originate in the House of Representatives; but the Senate may propose or concur with Amendments as on other Bills.

Every Bill which shall have passed the House of Representatives and the Senate, shall, before it become a Law, be presented to the President of the United States; If he approve he shall sign it, but if not he shall return it, with his Objections to that House in which it shall have originated, who shall enter the Objections at large on their Journal, and proceed to reconsider it. If after such Reconsideration two thirds of that House shall agree to pass the Bill, it shall be sent, together with the Objections, to the other House, by which it shall likewise be reconsidered, and if approved by two thirds of that House, it shall become a Law. But in all such Cases the Votes of both Houses shall be determined by yeas and Nays, and the Names of the Persons voting for and against the Bill shall be entered on the Journal of each House respectively. If any Bill shall not be returned by the President within ten Days (Sundays excepted) after it shall have been presented to him, the Same shall be a Law, in like Manner as if he had signed it, unless the Congress by their Adjournment prevent its Return, in which Case it shall not be a Law.

Every Order, Resolution, or Vote to which the Concurrence of the Senate and House of Representatives may be necessary (except on a question of Adjournment) shall be presented to the President of the United States; and before the Same shall take Effect, shall be approved by him, or being disapproved by him, shall be repassed by two thirds of the Senate and House of Representatives, according to the Rules and Limitations prescribed in the Case of a Bill.

Section. 8. The Congress shall have Power To lay and collect Taxes, Duties, Imposts and Excises, to pay the Debts and provide for the common Defence and general Welfare of the United States; but all Duties, Imposts and Excises shall be uniform throughout the United States;

To borrow Money on the credit of the United States;

To regulate Commerce with foreign Nations, and among the several States, and with the Indian Tribes;

To establish an uniform Rule of Naturalization, and uniform Laws on the subject of Bankruptcies throughout the United States;

To coin Money, regulate the Value thereof, and of foreign Coin, and fix the Standard of Weights and Measures;

To provide for the Punishment of counterfeiting the Securities and current Coin of the United States;

To establish Post Offices and post Roads;

To promote the Progress of Science and useful Arts, by securing for limited Times to Authors and Inventors the exclusive Right to their respective Writings and Discoveries;

To constitute Tribunals inferior to the supreme Court;

To define and punish Piracies and Felonies committed on the high Seas, and Offences against the Law of Nations;

To declare War, grant Letters of Marque and Reprisal, and make Rules concerning Captures on Land and Water;

To raise and support Armies, but no Appropriation of Money to that Use shall be for a longer Term than two Years;

To provide and maintain a Navy;

To make Rules for the Government and Regulation of the land and naval Forces;

To provide for calling forth the Militia to execute the Laws of the Union, suppress Insurrections and repel Invasions;

To provide for organizing, arming, and disciplining, the Militia, and for governing such Part of them as may be employed in the Service of the United States, reserving to the States respectively, the Appointment of the Officers, and the Authority of training the Militia according to the discipline prescribed by Congress;

To exercise exclusive Legislation in all Cases whatsoever, over such District (not exceeding ten Miles square) as may, by Cession of particular States, and the Acceptance of Congress, become the Seat of the Government of the United States, and to exercise like Authority over all Places purchased by the Consent of the Legislature of the State in which the Same shall be, for the Erection of Forts, Magazines, Arsenals, dock-Yards, and other needful Buildings;—And

To make all Laws which shall be necessary and proper for carrying into Execution the foregoing Powers, and all other Powers vested by this Constitution in the Government of the United States, or in any Department or Officer thereof.

Section. 9. The Migration or Importation of such Persons as any of the States now existing shall think proper to admit, shall not be prohibited by the Congress prior to the Year one thousand eight hundred and eight, but a Tax or duty may be imposed on such Importation, not exceeding ten dollars for each Person.

The Privilege of the Writ of Habeas Corpus shall not be suspended, unless when in Cases of Rebellion or Invasion the public Safety may require it.

No Bill of Attainder or ex post facto Law shall be passed.

No Capitation, or other direct, Tax shall be laid, unless in Proportion to the Census or Enumeration herein before directed to be taken.

No Tax or Duty shall be laid on Articles exported from any State.

No Preference shall be given by any Regulation of Commerce or Revenue to the Ports of one State over those of another; nor shall Vessels bound to, or from, one State, be obliged to enter, clear, or pay Duties in another.

No Money shall be drawn from the Treasury, but in Consequence of Appropriations made by Law; and a regular Statement and Account of the Receipts and Expenditures of all public Money shall be published from time to time.

No Title of Nobility shall be granted by the United States: And no Person holding any Office of Profit or Trust under them, shall, without the Consent of the Congress, accept of any present, Emolument, Office, or Title, of any kind whatever, from any King, Prince, or foreign State.

Section. 10. No State shall enter into any Treaty, Alliance, or Confederation; grant Letters of Marque and Reprisal; coin Money; emit Bills of Credit; make any Thing but gold and silver Coin a Tender in Payment of Debts; pass any Bill of Attainder, ex post facto Law, or Law impairing the Obligation of Contracts, or grant any Title of Nobility.

No State shall, without the Consent of the Congress, lay any Imposts or Duties on Imports or Exports, except what may be absolutely necessary for executing it's inspection Laws; and the net Produce of all Duties and Imposts, laid by any State on Imports or Exports, shall be for the Use of the Treasury of the United States; and all such Laws shall be subject to the Revision and Controul of the Congress.

No State shall, without the Consent of Congress, lay any Duty of Tonnage, keep Troops, or Ships of War in time of Peace, enter into any Agreement or Compact with another State, or with a foreign Power, or engage in War, unless actually invaded, or in such imminent Danger as will not admit of delay.

Article. II.

Section. 1. The executive Power shall be vested in a President of the United States of America. He shall hold his Office during the Term of four Years, and, together with the Vice President, chosen for the same Term, be elected, as follows:

Each State shall appoint, in such Manner as the Legislature thereof may direct, a Number of Electors, equal to the whole Number of Senators and Representatives to which the State may be entitled in the Congress: but no Senator or Representative, or Person holding an Office of Trust or Profit under the United States, shall be appointed an Elector.

The Electors shall meet in their respective States, and vote by Ballot for two Persons, of whom one at least shall not be an Inhabitant of the same State with themselves. And they shall make a List of all the Persons voted for, and of the Number of Votes for each; which List they shall sign and certify, and transmit sealed to the Seat of the Government of the United States, directed to the President of the Senate. The President of the Senate shall, in the Presence of the Senate and House of Representatives, open all the Certificates, and the Votes shall then be counted. The Person having the greatest Number of Votes shall be the President, if such Number be a Majority of the whole Number of Electors appointed; and if there be more than one who have such Majority, and have an equal Number of Votes, then the House of Representatives shall immediately chuse by Ballot one of them for President; and if no Person have a Majority, then from the five highest on the List the said House shall in like Manner chuse the President. But in chusing the President, the Votes shall be taken by States, the Representation from each State having one Vote; a quorum for this Purpose shall consist of a Member or Members from two thirds of the States, and a Majority of all the States shall be necessary to a Choice. In every Case, after the Choice of the President, the Person having the greatest Number of Votes of the Electors shall be the Vice President. But if there should remain two or more who have equal Votes, the Senate shall chuse from them by Ballot the Vice President.

The Congress may determine the Time of chusing the Electors, and the Day on which they shall give their Votes; which Day shall be the same throughout the United States.

No Person except a natural born Citizen, or a Citizen of the United States, at the time of the Adoption of this Constitution, shall be eligible to the Office of President; neither shall any Person be eligible to that Office who shall not have attained to the Age of thirty five Years, and been fourteen Years a Resident within the United States.

In Case of the Removal of the President from Office, or of his Death, Resignation, or Inability to discharge the Powers and Duties of the said Office, the Same shall devolve on the Vice President, and the Congress may by Law provide for the Case of Removal, Death, Resignation or Inability, both of the President and Vice President, declaring what Officer shall then act as President, and such Officer shall act accordingly, until the Disability be removed, or a President shall be elected.

The President shall, at stated Times, receive for his Services, a Compensation, which shall neither be increased nor diminished during the Period for which he shall have been elected, and he shall not receive within that Period any other Emolument from the United States, or any of them.

Before he enter on the Execution of his Office, he shall take the following Oath or Affirmation: — "I do solemnly swear (or affirm) that I will faithfully execute the Office of President of the United States, and will to the best of my Ability, preserve, protect and defend the Constitution of the United States."

Section. 2. The President shall be Commander in Chief of the Army and Navy of the United States, and of the Militia of the several States, when called into the actual Service of the United States; he may require the Opinion, in writing, of the principal Officer in each of the executive Departments, upon any Subject relating to the Duties of their respective Offices, and he shall have Power to grant Reprieves and Pardons for Offences against the United States, except in Cases of Impeachment.

He shall have Power, by and with the Advice and Consent of the Senate, to make Treaties, provided two thirds of the Senators present concur; and he shall nominate, and by and with the Advice and Consent of the Senate, shall appoint Ambassadors, other public Ministers and Consuls, Judges of the supreme Court, and all other Officers of the United States, whose Appointments are not herein otherwise provided for, and which shall be established by Law: but the Congress may by Law vest the Appointment of such inferior Officers, as they think proper, in the President alone, in the Courts of Law, or in the Heads of Departments.

The President shall have Power to fill up all Vacancies that may happen during the Recess of the Senate, by granting Commissions which shall expire at the End of their next Session.

Section. 3. He shall from time to time give to the Congress Information of the State of the Union, and recommend to their Consideration such Measures as he shall judge necessary and expedient; he may, on extraordinary Occasions, convene both Houses, or either of them, and in Case of Disagreement between them, with Respect to the Time of Adjournment, he may adjourn them to such Time as he shall think proper; he shall receive Ambassadors and other public Ministers; he shall take Care that the Laws be faithfully executed, and shall Commission all the Officers of the United States.

Section. 4. The President, Vice President and all civil Officers of the United States, shall be removed from Office on Impeachment for, and Conviction of, Treason, Bribery, or other high Crimes and Misdemeanors.

Article. III.

Section. 1. The judicial Power of the United States shall be vested in one supreme Court, and in such inferior Courts as the Congress may from time to time ordain and establish. The Judges, both of the supreme and inferior Courts, shall hold their Offices during good Behaviour, and shall, at stated Times, receive for their Services a Compensation, which shall not be diminished during their Continuance in Office.

Section. 2. The judicial Power shall extend to all Cases, in Law and Equity, arising under this Constitution, the Laws of the United States, and Treaties made, or which shall be made, under their Authority;—to all Cases affecting Ambassadors, other public Ministers and Consuls;—to all Cases of admiralty and maritime Jurisdiction;—to Controversies to which the United States shall be a Party;—to Controversies between two or more States;—between a State and Citizens of another State;—between Citizens of different States;—between Citizens of the same State claiming Lands under Grants of different States, and between a State, or the Citizens thereof, and foreign States, Citizens or Subjects.

In all Cases affecting Ambassadors, other public Ministers and Consuls, and those in which a State shall be Party, the supreme Court shall have original Jurisdiction. In all the other Cases before mentioned, the supreme Court shall have appellate Jurisdiction, both as to Law and Fact, with such Exceptions, and under such Regulations as the Congress shall make.

The Trial of all Crimes, except in Cases of Impeachment, shall be by Jury; and such Trial shall be held in the State where the said Crimes shall have been committed; but when not committed within any State, the Trial shall be at such Place or Places as the Congress may by Law have directed.

Section. 3. Treason against the United States shall consist only in levying War against them, or in adhering to their Enemies, giving them Aid and Comfort. No Person shall be convicted of Treason unless on the Testimony of two Witnesses to the same overt Act, or on Confession in open Court.

The Congress shall have Power to declare the Punishment of Treason, but no Attainder of Treason shall work Corruption of Blood, or Forfeiture except during the Life of the Person attainted.

Article. IV.

Section. 1. Full Faith and Credit shall be given in each State to the public Acts, Records, and judicial Proceedings of every other State. And the Congress may by general Laws prescribe the Manner in which such Acts, Records and Proceedings shall be proved, and the Effect thereof.

Section. 2. The Citizens of each State shall be entitled to all Privileges and Immunities of Citizens in the several States.

A Person charged in any State with Treason, Felony, or other Crime, who shall flee from Justice, and be found in another State, shall on Demand of the executive Authority of the State from which he fled, be delivered up, to be removed to the State having Jurisdiction of the Crime.

No Person held to Service or Labour in one State, under the Laws thereof, escaping into another, shall, in Consequence of any Law or Regulation therein, be discharged from such Service or Labour, but shall be delivered up on Claim of the Party to whom such Service or Labour may be due.

Section. 3. New States may be admitted by the Congress into this Union; but no new State shall be formed or erected within the Jurisdiction of any other State; nor any State be formed by the Junction of two or more States, or Parts of States, without the Consent of the Legislatures of the States concerned as well as of the Congress.

The Congress shall have Power to dispose of and make all needful Rules and Regulations respecting the Territory or other Property belonging to the United States; and nothing in this Constitution shall be so construed as to Prejudice any Claims of the United States, or of any particular State.

Section. 4. The United States shall guarantee to every State in this Union a Republican Form of Government, and shall protect each of them against Invasion; and on Application of the Legislature, or of the Executive (when the Legislature cannot be convened), against domestic Violence.

Article. V.

The Congress, whenever two thirds of both Houses shall deem it necessary, shall propose Amendments to this Constitution, or, on the Application of the Legislatures of two thirds of the several States, shall call a Convention for proposing Amendments, which, in either Case, shall be valid to all Intents and Purposes, as Part of this Constitution, when ratified by the Legislatures of three fourths of the several States, or by Conventions in three fourths thereof, as the one or the other Mode of Ratification may be proposed by the Congress; Provided that no Amendment which may be made prior to the Year One thousand eight hundred and eight shall in any Manner affect the first and fourth Clauses in the Ninth Section of the first Article; and that no State, without its Consent, shall be deprived of its equal Suffrage in the Senate.

Article. VI.

All Debts contracted and Engagements entered into, before the Adoption of this Constitution, shall be as valid against the United States under this Constitution, as under the Confederation.

This Constitution, and the Laws of the United States which shall be made in Pursuance thereof; and all Treaties made, or which shall be made, under the Authority of the United States, shall be the supreme Law of the Land; and the Judges in every State shall be bound thereby, any Thing in the Constitution or Laws of any State to the Contrary notwithstanding.

The Senators and Representatives before mentioned, and the Members of the several State Legislatures, and all executive and judicial Officers, both of the United States and of the several States, shall be bound by Oath or Affirmation, to support this Constitution; but no religious Test shall ever be required as a Qualification to any Office or public Trust under the United States.

Article. VII.

The Ratification of the Conventions of nine States, shall be sufficient for the Establishment of this Constitution between the States so ratifying the Same.

[BILL OF RIGHTS]

Article the Third [Amendment I]

Congress shall make no law respecting an establishment of religion, or prohibiting the free exercise thereof; or abridging the freedom of speech, or of the press; or the right of the people peaceably to assemble, and to petition the Government for a redress of grievances.

Article the Fourth [Amendment II]

A well regulated Militia, being necessary to the security of a free State, the right of the people to keep and bear Arms, shall not be infringed.

Article the Fifth [Amendment III]

No Soldier shall, in time of peace be quartered in any house, without the consent of the Owner, nor in time of war, but in a manner to be prescribed by law.

Article the Sixth [Amendment IV]

The right of the people to be secure in their persons, houses, papers, and effects, against unreasonable searches and seizures, shall not be violated, and no Warrants shall issue, but upon probable cause, supported by Oath or affirmation, and particularly describing the place to be searched, and the persons or things to be seized.

Article the Seventh [Amendment V]

No person shall be held to answer for a capital, or otherwise infamous crime, unless on a presentment or indictment of a Grand Jury, except in cases arising in the land or naval forces, or in the Militia, when in actual service in time of War or public danger; nor shall any person be subject for the same offence to be twice put in jeopardy of life or limb; nor shall be compelled in any criminal case to be a witness against himself, nor be deprived of life, liberty, or property, without due process of law; nor shall private property be taken for public use, without just compensation.

Article the Eighth [Amendment VI]

In all criminal prosecutions, the accused shall enjoy the right to a speedy and public trial, by an impartial jury of the State and district wherein the crime shall have been committed, which district shall have been previously ascertained by law, and to be informed of the nature and cause of the accusation; to be confronted with the witnesses against him; to have compulsory process for obtaining witnesses in his favor, and to have the Assistance of Counsel for his defence.

Article the Ninth [Amendment VII]

In Suits at common law, where the value in controversy shall exceed twenty dollars, the right of trial by jury shall be preserved, and no fact tried by a jury, shall be otherwise re-examined in any Court of the United States, than according to the rules of the common law.

Article the Tenth [Amendment VIII]

Excessive bail shall not be required, nor excessive fines imposed, nor cruel and unusual punishments inflicted.

Article the Eleventh [Amendment IX]

The enumeration in the Constitution, of certain rights, shall not be construed to deny or disparage others retained by the people.

Article the Twelfth [Amendment X]

The powers not delegated to the United States by the Constitution, nor prohibited by it to the States, are reserved to the States respectively, or to the people.

[ADDITIONAL AMENDMENTS TO THE CONSTITUTION]

[Article. XI.][Proposed 1794; Ratified 1798]

The Judicial power of the United States shall not be construed to extend to any suit in law or equity, commenced or prosecuted against one of the United States by Citizens of another State, or by Citizens or Subjects of any Foreign State.

[Article. XII.][Proposed 1803; Ratified 1804]

The Electors shall meet in their respective states, and vote by ballot for President and Vice-President, one of whom, at least, shall not be an inhabitant of the same state with themselves; they shall name in their ballots the person voted for as President, and in distinct ballots the person voted for as Vice-President, and they shall make distinct lists of all persons voted for as President, and of all persons voted for as Vice-President, and of the number of votes for each, which lists they shall sign and certify, and transmit sealed to the seat of the government of the United States, directed to the President of the Senate; — The President of the Senate shall, in the presence of the Senate and House of Representatives, open all the certificates and the votes shall then be counted; — The person having the greatest number of votes for President, shall be the President, if such number be a majority of the whole number of Electors appointed; and if no person have such majority, then from the persons having the highest numbers not exceeding three on the list of those voted for as President, the House of Representatives shall choose immediately, by ballot, the President. But in choosing the President, the votes shall be taken by states, the representation from each state having one vote; a quorum for this purpose shall consist of a member or members from two-thirds of the states, and a majority of all the states shall be necessary to a choice. And if the House of Representatives shall not choose a President whenever the right of choice shall devolve upon them, before the fourth day of March next following, then the Vice-President shall act as President, as in the case of the death or other constitutional disability of the President. — The person having the greatest number of votes as Vice-President, shall be the Vice-President, if such number be a majority of the whole number of Electors appointed, and if no person have a majority, then from the two highest numbers on the list, the Senate shall choose the Vice-President; a quorum for the purpose shall consist of two-thirds of the whole number of Senators, and a majority of the whole number shall be necessary to a choice. But no person constitutionally ineligible to the office of President shall be eligible to that of Vice-President of the United States.

[Article. XIII.] [Proposed 1865; Ratified 1865]

Section. 1. Neither slavery nor involuntary servitude, except as a punishment for crime whereof the party shall have been duly convicted, shall exist within the United States, or any place subject to their jurisdiction.

Section. 2. Congress shall have power to enforce this article by appropriate legislation.

[Article. XIV.] [Proposed 1866; Ratified 1868]

Section. 1. All persons born or naturalized in the United States, and subject to the jurisdiction thereof, are citizens of the United States and of the State wherein they reside. No State shall make or enforce any law which shall abridge the privileges or immunities of citizens of the United States; nor shall any State deprive any person of life, liberty, or property, without due process of law; nor deny to any person within its jurisdiction the equal protection of the laws.

Section. 2. Representatives shall be apportioned among the several States according to their respective numbers, counting the whole number of persons in each State, excluding Indians not taxed. But when the right to vote at any election for the choice of electors for President and Vice President of the

United States, Representatives in Congress, the Executive and Judicial officers of a State, or the members of the Legislature thereof, is denied to any of the male inhabitants of such State, being twenty-one years of age, and citizens of the United States, or in any way abridged, except for participation in rebellion, or other crime, the basis of representation therein shall be reduced in the proportion which the number of such male citizens shall bear to the whole number of male citizens twenty-one years of age in such State.

Section. 3. No person shall be a Senator or Representative in Congress, or elector of President and Vice President, or hold any office, civil or military, under the United States, or under any State, who, having previously taken an oath, as a member of Congress, or as an officer of the United States, or as a member of any State legislature, or as an executive or judicial officer of any State, to support the Constitution of the United States, shall have engaged in insurrection or rebellion against the same, or given aid or comfort to the enemies thereof. But Congress may by a vote of two-thirds of each House, remove such disability.

Section. 4. The validity of the public debt of the United States, authorized by law, including debts incurred for payment of pensions and bounties for services in suppressing insurrection or rebellion, shall not be questioned. But neither the United States nor any State shall assume or pay any debt or obligation incurred in aid of insurrection or rebellion against the United States, or any claim for the loss or emancipation of any slave; but all such debts, obligations and claims shall be held illegal and void.

Section. 5. The Congress shall have power to enforce, by appropriate legislation, the provisions of this article.

[Article. XV.] [Proposed 1869; Ratified 1870]

Section. 1. The right of citizens of the United States to vote shall not be denied or abridged by the United States or by any State on account of race, color, or previous condition of servitude.

Section. 2. The Congress shall have power to enforce this article by appropriate legislation.

Article. XVI. [Proposed 1909; Questionably Ratified 1913]

The Congress shall have power to lay and collect taxes on incomes, from whatever source derived, without apportionment among the several States, and without regard to any census or enumeration.

Article. [XVII.] [Proposed 1912; Ratified 1913]

The Senate of the United States shall be composed of two Senators from each State, elected by the people thereof, for six years; and each Senator shall have one vote. The electors in each State shall have the qualifications requisite for electors of the most numerous branch of the State legislatures.

When vacancies happen in the representation of any State in the Senate, the executive authority of such State shall issue writs of election to fill such vacancies: Provided, That the legislature of any State may empower the executive thereof to make temporary appointments until the people fill the vacancies by election as the legislature may direct.

This amendment shall not be so construed as to affect the election or term of any Senator chosen before it becomes valid as part of the Constitution.

Article. [XVIII.] [Proposed 1917; Ratified 1919; Repealed 1933 (See Amendment XXI, Section 1)]

Section. 1. After one year from the ratification of this article the manufacture, sale, or transportation of intoxicating liquors within, the importation thereof into, or the exportation thereof from the United States and all territory subject to the jurisdiction thereof for beverage purposes is hereby prohibited.

Section. 2. The Congress and the several States shall have concurrent power to enforce this article by appropriate legislation.

Section. 3. This article shall be inoperative unless it shall have been ratified as an amendment to the Constitution by the legislatures of the several States, as provided in the Constitution, within seven years from the date of the submission hereof to the States by the Congress.

Article. [XIX.] [Proposed 1919; Ratified 1920]

The right of citizens of the United States to vote shall not be denied or abridged by the United States or by any State on account of sex.

Congress shall have power to enforce this article by appropriate legislation.

Article. [XX.] [Proposed 1932; Ratified 1933]

Section. 1. The terms of the President and Vice President shall end at noon on the 20th day of January, and the terms of Senators and Representatives at noon on the 3d day of January, of the years in which such terms would have ended if this article had not been ratified; and the terms of their successors shall then begin.

Section. 2. The Congress shall assemble at least once in every year, and such meeting shall begin at noon on the 3d day of January, unless they shall by law appoint a different day.

Section. 3. If, at the time fixed for the beginning of the term of the President, the President elect shall have died, the Vice President elect shall become President. If a President shall not have been chosen before the time fixed for the beginning of his term, or if the President elect shall have failed to qualify, then the Vice President elect shall act as President until a President shall have qualified; and the Congress may by law provide for the case wherein neither a President elect nor a Vice President elect shall have qualified, declaring who shall then act as President, or the manner in which one who is to act shall be selected, and such person shall act accordingly until a President or Vice President shall have qualified.

Section. 4. The Congress may by law provide for the case of the death of any of the persons from whom the House of Representatives may choose a President whenever the right of choice shall have devolved upon them, and for the case of the death of any of the persons from whom the Senate may choose a Vice President whenever the right of choice shall have devolved upon them.

Section. 5. Sections 1 and 2 shall take effect on the 15th day of October following the ratification of this article.

Section. 6. This article shall be inoperative unless it shall have been ratified as an amendment to the Constitution by the legislatures of three-fourths of the several States within seven years from the date of its submission.

Article. [XXI.] [Proposed 1933; Ratified 1933]

Section. 1. The eighteenth article of amendment to the Constitution of the United States is hereby repealed.

Section. 2. The transportation or importation into any State, Territory, or possession of the United States for delivery or use therein of intoxicating liquors, in violation of the laws thereof, is hereby prohibited.

Section. 3. This article shall be inoperative unless it shall have been ratified as an amendment to the Constitution by conventions in the several States, as provided in the Constitution, within seven years from the date of the submission hereof to the States by the Congress.

Article. [XXII.] [Proposed 1947; Ratified 1951]

Section. 1. No person shall be elected to the office of the President more than twice, and no person who has held the office of President, or acted as President, for more than two years of a term to which some other person was elected President shall be elected to the office of the President more than once. But this Article shall not apply to any person holding the office of President when this Article was proposed by the Congress, and shall not prevent any person who may be holding the office of President, or acting as President, during the term within which this Article becomes operative from holding the office of President or acting as President during the remainder of such term.

Section. 2. This article shall be inoperative unless it shall have been ratified as an amendment to the Constitution by the legislatures of three-fourths of the several States within seven years from the date of its submission to the States by the Congress.

Article. [XXIII.] [Proposed 1960; Ratified 1961]

Section. 1. The District constituting the seat of Government of the United States shall appoint in such manner as the Congress may direct:

A number of electors of President and Vice President equal to the whole number of Senators and Representatives in Congress to which the District would be entitled if it were a State, but in no event more than the least populous State; they shall be in addition to those appointed by the States, but they shall be considered, for the purposes of the election of President and Vice President, to be electors appointed by a State; and they shall meet in the District and perform such duties as provided by the twelfth article of amendment.

Section. 2. The Congress shall have power to enforce this article by appropriate legislation.

Article. [XXIV.] [Proposed 1962; Ratified 1964]

Section. 1. The right of citizens of the United States to vote in any primary or other election for President or Vice President, for electors for President or Vice President, or for Senator or Representative in Congress, shall not be denied or abridged by the United States or any State by reason of failure to pay any poll tax or other tax.

Section. 2. The Congress shall have power to enforce this article by appropriate legislation.

Article. [XXV.] [Proposed 1965; Ratified 1967]

Section. 1. In case of the removal of the President from office or of his death or resignation, the Vice President shall become President.

Section. 2. Whenever there is a vacancy in the office of the Vice President, the President shall nominate a Vice President who shall take office upon confirmation by a majority vote of both Houses of Congress.

Section. 3. Whenever the President transmits to the President pro tempore of the Senate and the Speaker of the House of Representatives his written declaration that he is unable to discharge the powers and duties of his office, and until he transmits to them a written declaration to the contrary, such powers and duties shall be discharged by the Vice President as Acting President.

Section. 4. Whenever the Vice President and a majority of either the principal officers of the executive departments or of such other body as Congress may by law provide, transmit to the President pro tempore of the Senate and the Speaker of the House of Representatives their written declaration that the President is unable to discharge the powers and duties of his office, the Vice President shall immediately assume the powers and duties of the office as Acting President.

Thereafter, when the President transmits to the President pro tempore of the Senate and the Speaker of the House of Representatives his written declaration that no inability exists, he shall resume the powers and duties of his office unless the Vice President and a majority of either the principal officers of the executive department or of such other body as Congress may by law provide, transmit within four days to the President pro tempore of the Senate and the Speaker of the House of Representatives their written declaration that the President is unable to discharge the powers and duties of his office. Thereupon Congress shall decide the issue, assembling within forty-eight hours for that purpose if not in session. If the Congress, within twenty-one days after receipt of the latter written declaration, or, if Congress is not in session, within twenty-one days after Congress is required to assemble, determines by two-thirds vote of both Houses that the President is unable to discharge the powers and duties of his office, the Vice President shall continue to discharge the same as Acting President; otherwise, the President shall resume the powers and duties of his office.

Article. [XXVI.] [Proposed 1971; Ratified 1971]

Section. 1. The right of citizens of the United States, who are eighteen years of age or older, to vote shall not be denied or abridged by the United States or by any State on account of age.

Section. 2. The Congress shall have power to enforce this article by appropriate legislation.

Article. [XXVII.] [Proposed 1789; Ratified 1992; Second of twelve Articles comprising the Bill of Rights]

No law, varying the compensation for the services of the Senators and Representatives, shall take effect, until an election of Representatives shall have intervened.

APPENDIX C

Selected Statutes

SELECTED PROVISIONS OF TITLE 28 OF THE UNITED STATES CODE

Chapter 51 — Supreme Court

28 U.S.C. § 1251. Original jurisdiction

(a) The Supreme Court shall have original and exclusive jurisdiction of all controversies between two or more States.

(b) The Supreme Court shall have original but not exclusive jurisdiction of:

(1) All actions or proceedings to which ambassadors, other public ministers, consuls, or vice consuls of foreign states are parties;

(2) All controversies between the United States and a State;

(3) All actions or proceedings by a State against the citizens of another State or against aliens.

28 U.S.C. § 1253. Direct appeals from decisions of three-judge courts

Except as otherwise provided by law, any party may appeal to the Supreme Court from an order granting or denying, after notice and hearing, an interlocutory or permanent injunction in any civil action, suit or proceeding required by any Act of Congress to be heard and determined by a district court of three judges.

28 U.S.C. § 1254. Courts of appeals; certiorari; certified questions

Cases in the courts of appeals may be reviewed by the Supreme Court by the following methods:

(1) By writ of certiorari granted upon the petition of any party to any civil or criminal case, before or after rendition of judgment or decree;

(2) By certification at any time by a court of appeals of any question of law in any civil or criminal case as to which instructions are desired, and upon such certification the Supreme Court may give binding instructions or require the entire record to be sent up for decision of the entire matter in controversy.

28 U.S.C. § 1257. State courts; certiorari

(a) Final judgments or decrees rendered by the highest court of a State in which a decision could be had, may be reviewed by the Supreme Court by writ of certiorari where the validity of a treaty or statute of the United States is drawn in question or where the validity of a statute of any State is drawn in question on the ground of its being repugnant to the Constitution, treaties, or laws of the United States, or where any title, right, privilege, or immunity is specially set up or claimed under the Constitution or the treaties or statutes of, or any commission held or authority exercised under, the United States.

(b) For the purposes of this section, the term "highest court of a State" includes the District of Columbia Court of Appeals.

Chapter 83 — Courts of Appeals

28 U.S.C. § 1291. Final decisions of district courts

The courts of appeals (other than the United States Court of Appeals for the Federal Circuit) shall have jurisdiction of appeals from all final decisions of the district courts of the United States, the United States District Court for the District of the Canal Zone, the District Court of Guam, and the District Court of the Virgin Islands, except where a direct review may be had in the Supreme Court. The jurisdiction of the United States Court of Appeals for the Federal Circuit shall be limited to the jurisdiction described in sections 1292(c) and (d) and 1295 of this title.

28 U.S.C. § 1292. Interlocutory decisions

(a) Except as provided in subsections (c) and (d) of this section, the courts of appeals shall have jurisdiction of appeals from:

(1) Interlocutory orders of the district courts of the United States, the United States District Court for the District of the Canal Zone, the District Court of Guam, and the District Court of the Virgin Islands, or of the judges thereof, granting, continuing, modifying, refusing or dissolving injunctions, or refusing to dissolve or modify injunctions, except where a direct review may be had in the Supreme Court;

(2) Interlocutory orders appointing receivers, or refusing orders to wind up receiverships or to take steps to accomplish the purposes thereof, such as directing sales or other disposals of property;

(3) Interlocutory decrees of such district courts or the judges thereof determining the rights and liabilities of the parties to admiralty cases in which appeals from final decrees are allowed.

(b) When a district judge, in making in a civil action an order not otherwise appealable under this section, shall be of the opinion that such order involves a controlling question of law as to which there is substantial ground for difference of opinion and that an immediate appeal from the order may materially advance the ultimate termination of the litigation, he shall so state in writing in such order. The Court of Appeals which would have jurisdiction of an appeal of such action may thereupon, in its discretion, permit an appeal to be taken from such order, if application is made to it within ten days after the entry of the order: Provided, however, That application for an appeal hereunder shall not stay proceedings in the district court unless the district judge or the Court of Appeals or a judge thereof shall so order.

(c) The United States Court of Appeals for the Federal Circuit shall have exclusive jurisdiction —

(1) of an appeal from an interlocutory order or decree described in subsection (a) or (b) of this section in any case over which the court would have jurisdiction of an appeal under section 1295 of this title; and

(2) of an appeal from a judgment in a civil action for patent infringement which would otherwise be appealable to the United States Court of Appeals for the Federal Circuit and is final except for an accounting.

(d)(1) When the chief judge of the Court of International Trade issues an order under the provisions of section 256(b) of this title, or when any judge of the Court of International Trade, in issuing any other interlocutory order, includes in the order a statement that a controlling question of law is involved with respect to which there is a substantial ground for difference of opinion and that an immediate appeal from that order may materially advance the ultimate termination of the litigation, the United States Court of Appeals for the Federal Circuit may, in its discretion, permit an appeal to be taken from such order, if application is made to that Court within ten days after the entry of such order.

(2) When the chief judge of the United States Court of Federal Claims issues an order under section 798(b) of this title, or when any judge of the United States Court of Federal Claims, in issuing an interlocutory order, includes in the order a statement that a controlling question of law is involved with respect to which there is a substantial ground for difference of opinion and that an immediate appeal from that order may materially advance the ultimate termination of the litigation, the United States Court of Appeals for the Federal Circuit may, in its discretion, permit an appeal to be taken from such order, if application is made to that Court within ten days after the entry of such order.

(3) Neither the application for nor the granting of an appeal under this subsection shall stay proceedings in the Court of International Trade or in the Court of Federal Claims, as the case may be, unless a stay is ordered by a judge of the Court of International Trade or of the Court of Federal Claims or by the United States Court of Appeals for the Federal Circuit or a judge of that court.

(4)(A) The United States Court of Appeals for the Federal Circuit shall have exclusive jurisdiction of an appeal from an interlocutory order of a district court of the United States, the District Court of Guam, the District Court of the Virgin Islands, or the District Court for the Northern Mariana Islands, granting or denying, in whole or in part, a motion to transfer an action to the United States Court of Federal Claims under section 1631 of this title.

(B) When a motion to transfer an action to the Court of Federal Claims is filed in a district court, no further proceedings shall be taken in the district court until 60 days after the court has ruled upon the motion. If an appeal is taken from the district court's grant or denial of the motion, proceedings shall be further stayed until the appeal has been decided by the Court of Appeals for the Federal Circuit. The stay of proceedings in the district court shall not bar the granting of preliminary or injunctive relief, where appropriate and where expedition is reasonably necessary. However, during the period in which proceedings are stayed as provided in this subparagraph, no transfer to the Court of Federal Claims pursuant to the motion shall be carried out.

(e) The Supreme Court may prescribe rules, in accordance with section 2072 of this title, to provide for an appeal of an interlocutory decision to the courts of appeals that is not otherwise provided for under subsection (a), (b), (c), or (d).

Chapter 85 — District Courts; Jurisdiction

28 U.S.C. § 1331. Federal question

The district courts shall have original jurisdiction of all civil actions arising under the Constitution, laws, or treaties of the United States.

28 U.S.C. § 1332. Diversity of Citizenship; amount in controversy; costs

(a) The district courts shall have original jurisdiction of all civil actions where the matter in controversy exceeds the sum or value of $75,000, exclusive of interest and costs, and is between —

(1) citizens of different States;

(2) citizens of a State and citizens or subjects of a foreign state;

(3) citizens of different States and in which citizens or subjects of a foreign state are additional parties; and

(4) a foreign state, defined in section 1603(a) of this title, as plaintiff and citizens of a State or of different States.

For the purposes of this section, section 1335, and section 1441, an alien admitted to the United States for permanent residence shall be deemed a citizen of the State in which such alien is domiciled.

(b) Except when express provision therefor is otherwise made in a statute of the United States, where the plaintiff who files the case originally in the Federal courts is finally adjudged to be entitled to recover less than the sum or value of $75,000, computed without regard to any setoff or counterclaim to which the defendant may be adjudged to be entitled, and exclusive of interest and costs, the district court may deny costs to the plaintiff and, in addition, may impose costs on the plaintiff.

(c) For the purposes of this section and section 1441 of this title —

(1) a corporation shall be deemed to be a citizen of any State by which it has been incorporated and of the State where it has its principal place of business, except that in any direct action against the insurer of a policy or contract of liability insurance, whether incorporated or unincorporated, to which action

the insured is not joined as a party-defendant, such insurer shall be deemed a citizen of the State of which the insured is a citizen, as well as of any State by which the insurer has been incorporated and of the State where it has its principal place of business; and

(2) the legal representative of the estate of a decedent shall be deemed to be a citizen only of the same State as the decedent, and the legal representative of an infant or incompetent shall be deemed to be a citizen only of the same State as the infant or incompetent.

(d)(1) In this subsection —

(A) the term "class" means all of the class members in a class action;

(B) the term "class action" means any civil action filed under rule 23 of the Federal Rules of Civil Procedure or similar State statute or rule of judicial procedure authorizing an action to be brought by 1 or more representative persons as a class action;

(C) the term "class certification order" means an order issued by a court approving the treatment of some or all aspects of a civil action as a class action; and

(D) the term "class members" means the persons (named or unnamed) who fall within the definition of the proposed or certified class in a class action.

(2) The district courts shall have original jurisdiction of any civil action in which the matter in controversy exceeds the sum or value of $5,000,000, exclusive of interest and costs, and is a class action in which —

(A) any member of a class of plaintiffs is a citizen of a State different from any defendant;

(B) any member of a class of plaintiffs is a foreign state or a citizen or subject of a foreign state and any defendant is a citizen of a State; or

(C) any member of a class of plaintiffs is a citizen of a State and any defendant is a foreign state or a citizen or subject of a foreign state.

(3) A district court may, in the interests of justice and looking at the totality of the circumstances, decline to exercise jurisdiction under paragraph (2) over a class action in which greater than one-third but less than two-thirds of the members of all proposed plaintiff classes in the aggregate and the primary defendants are citizens of the State in which the action was originally filed based on consideration of —

(A) whether the claims asserted involve matters of national or interstate interest;

(B) whether the claims asserted will be governed by laws of the State in which the action was originally filed or by the laws of other States;

(C) whether the class action has been pleaded in a manner that seeks to avoid Federal jurisdiction;

(D) whether the action was brought in a forum with a distinct nexus with the class members, the alleged harm, or the defendants;

(E) whether the number of citizens of the State in which the action was originally filed in all proposed plaintiff classes in the aggregate is substantially larger than the number of citizens from any other State, and the citizenship of the other members of the proposed class is dispersed among a substantial number of States; and

(F) whether, during the 3-year period preceding the filing of that class action, 1 or more other class actions asserting the same or similar claims on behalf of the same or other persons have been filed.

(4) A district court shall decline to exercise jurisdiction under paragraph (2) —

(A) (i) over a class action in which —

(I) greater than two-thirds of the members of all proposed plaintiff classes in the aggregate are citizens of the State in which the action was originally filed;

(II) at least 1 defendant is a defendant —

(aa) from whom significant relief is sought by members of the plaintiff class;

(bb) whose alleged conduct forms a significant basis for the claims asserted by the proposed plaintiff class; and

(cc) who is a citizen of the State in which the action was originally filed; and

(III) principal injuries resulting from the alleged conduct or any related conduct of each defendant were incurred in the State in which the action was originally filed; and

(ii) during the 3-year period preceding the filing of that class action, no other class action has been filed asserting the same or similar factual allegations against any of the defendants on behalf of the same or other persons; or

(B) two-thirds or more of the members of all proposed plaintiff classes in the aggregate, and the primary defendants, are citizens of the State in which the action was originally filed.

(5) Paragraphs (2) through (4) shall not apply to any class action in which —

(A) the primary defendants are States, State officials, or other governmental entities against whom the district court may be foreclosed from ordering relief; or

(B) the number of members of all proposed plaintiff classes in the aggregate is less than 100.

(6) In any class action, the claims of the individual class members shall be aggregated to determine whether the matter in controversy exceeds the sum or value of $5,000,000, exclusive of interest and costs.

(7) Citizenship of the members of the proposed plaintiff classes shall be determined for purposes of paragraphs (2) through (6) as of the date of filing of the complaint or amended complaint, or, if the case stated by the initial pleading is not subject to Federal jurisdiction, as of the date of service by plaintiffs of an amended pleading, motion, or other paper, indicating the existence of Federal jurisdiction.

(8) This subsection shall apply to any class action before or after the entry of a class certification order by the court with respect to that action.

(9) Paragraph (2) shall not apply to any class action that solely involves a claim —

(A) concerning a covered security as defined under 16(f)(3)(1) of the Securities Act of 1933 (15 U.S.C. 78p(f)(3)(2)) and section 28(f)(5)(E) of the Securities Exchange Act of 1934 (15 U.S.C. 78bb(f)(5)(E));

(B) that relates to the internal affairs or governance of a corporation or other form of business enterprise and that arises under or by virtue of the laws of the State in which such corporation or business enterprise is incorporated or organized; or

(C) that relates to the rights, duties (including fiduciary duties), and obligations relating to or created by or pursuant to any security (as defined under section 2(a)(1) of the Securities Act of 1933 (15 U.S.C. 77b(a)(1)) and the regulations issued thereunder).

(10) For purposes of this subsection and section 1453, an unincorporated association shall be deemed to be a citizen of the State where it has its principal place of business and the State under whose laws it is organized.

(11)(A) For purposes of this subsection and section 1453, a mass action shall be deemed to be a class action removable under paragraphs (2) through (10) if it otherwise meets the provisions of those paragraphs.

(B)(i) As used in subparagraph (A), the term "mass action" means any civil action (except a civil action within the scope of section 1711(2)) in which monetary relief claims of 100 or more persons are proposed to be tried jointly on the ground that the plaintiffs' claims involve common questions of law or fact, except that jurisdiction shall exist only over those plaintiffs whose claims in a mass action satisfy the jurisdictional amount requirements under subsection (a).

(ii) As used in subparagraph (A), the term "mass action" shall not include any civil action in which —

(I) all of the claims in the action arise from an event or occurrence in the State in which the action was filed, and that allegedly resulted in injuries in that State or in States contiguous to that State;

(II) the claims are joined upon motion of a defendant;

(III) all of the claims in the action are asserted on behalf of the general public (and not on behalf of individual claimants or members of a purported class) pursuant to a State statute specifically authorizing such action; or

(IV) the claims have been consolidated or coordinated solely for pretrial proceedings.

(C)(i) Any action(s) removed to Federal court pursuant to this subsection shall not thereafter be transferred to any other court pursuant to section 1407, or the rules promulgated thereunder, unless a majority of the plaintiffs in the action request transfer pursuant to section 1407.

(ii) This subparagraph will not apply —

(I) to cases certified pursuant to rule 23 of the Federal Rules of Civil Procedure; or

(II) if plaintiffs propose that the action proceed as a class action pursuant to rule 23 of the Federal Rules of Civil Procedure.

(D) The limitations periods on any claims asserted in a mass action that is removed to Federal court pursuant to this subsection shall be deemed tolled during the period that the action is pending in Federal court.

(e) The word "States", as used in this section, includes the Territories, the District of Columbia, and the Commonwealth of Puerto Rico.

28 U.S.C. § 1333. Admiralty, maritime and prize cases

The district courts shall have original jurisdiction, exclusive of the courts of the States, of:

(1) Any civil case of admiralty or maritime jurisdiction, saving to suitors in all cases all other remedies to which they are otherwise entitled.

(2) Any prize brought into the United States and all proceedings for the condemnation of property taken as prize.

28 U.S.C. § 1338. Patents, plant variety protections, copyrights, mask works, designs, trademarks, and unfair competition

(a) The district courts shall have original jurisdiction of any civil action arising under any Act of Congress relating to patents, plant variety protection, copyrights and trademarks. Such jurisdiction shall be exclusive of the courts of the states in patent, plant variety protection and copyright cases.

(b) The district courts shall have original jurisdiction of any civil action asserting a claim of unfair competition when joined with a substantial and related claim under the copyright, patent, plant variety protection or trademark laws.

(c) Subsections (a) and (b) apply to exclusive rights in mask works under chapter 9 of title 17, and to exclusive rights in designs under chapter 13 of title 17, to the same extent as such subsections apply to copyrights.

28 U.S.C. § 1341. Taxes by States

The district courts shall not enjoin, suspend or restrain the assessment, levy or collection of any tax under State law where a plain, speedy and efficient remedy may be had in the courts of such State.

28 U.S.C. § 1342. Rate orders of State agencies

The district courts shall not enjoin, suspend or restrain the operation of, or compliance with, any order affecting rates chargeable by a public utility and made by a State administrative agency or a rate-making body of a State political subdivision, where:

(1) Jurisdiction is based solely on diversity of citizenship or repugnance of the order to the Federal Constitution; and,

(2) The order does not interfere with interstate commerce; and,

(3) The order has been made after reasonable notice and hearing; and,

(4) A plain, speedy and efficient remedy may be had in the courts of such State.

28 U.S.C. § 1343. Civil rights and elective franchise

(a) The district courts shall have original jurisdiction of any civil action authorized by law to be commenced by any person:

(1) To recover damages for injury to his person or property, or because of the deprivation of any right or privilege of a citizen of the United States, by any act done in furtherance of any conspiracy mentioned in section 1985 of Title 42;

(2) To recover damages from any person who fails to prevent or to aid in preventing any wrongs mentioned in section 1985 of Title 42 which he had knowledge were about to occur and power to prevent;

(3) To redress the deprivation, under color of any State law, statute, ordinance, regulation, custom or usage, of any right, privilege or immunity secured by the Constitution of the United States or by any Act of Congress providing for equal rights of citizens or of all persons within the jurisdiction of the United States;

(4) To recover damages or to secure equitable or other relief under any Act of Congress providing for the protection of civil rights, including the right to vote.

(b) For purposes of this section —

(1) the District of Columbia shall be considered to be a State; and

(2) any Act of Congress applicable exclusively to the District of Columbia shall be considered to be a statute of the District of Columbia.

28 U.S.C. § 1345. United States as plaintiff

Except as otherwise provided by Act of Congress, the district courts shall have original jurisdiction of all civil actions, suits or proceedings commenced by the United States, or by any agency or officer thereof expressly authorized to sue by Act of Congress.

28 U.S.C. § 1346. United States as defendant

(a) The district courts shall have original jurisdiction, concurrent with the United States Court of Federal Claims, of:

(1) Any civil action against the United States for the recovery of any internal-revenue tax alleged to have been erroneously or illegally assessed or collected, or any penalty claimed to have been collected without authority or any sum alleged to have been excessive or in any manner wrongfully collected under the internal-revenue laws;

(2) Any other civil action or claim against the United States, not exceeding $10,000 in amount, founded either upon the Constitution, or any Act of Congress, or any regulation of an executive department, or upon any express or implied contract with the United States, or for liquidated or unliquidated damages in cases not sounding in tort, except that the district courts shall not have jurisdiction of any civil action or claim against the United States founded upon any express or implied contract with the United States or for liquidated or unliquidated damages in cases not sounding in tort which are subject to sections 8(g)(1) and 10(a)(1) of the Contract Disputes Act of 1978. For the purpose of this paragraph, an express or implied contract with the Army and Air Force Exchange Service, Navy Exchanges, Marine Corps Exchanges, Coast Guard Exchanges, or Exchange Councils of the National Aeronautics and Space Administration shall be considered an express or implied contract with the United States.

(b)(1) Subject to the provisions of chapter 171 of this title, the district courts, together with the United States District Court for the District of the Canal Zone and the District Court of the Virgin Islands, shall have exclusive jurisdiction of civil actions on claims against the United States, for money damages, accruing on and after January 1, 1945, for injury or loss of property, or personal injury or death caused by the negligent or wrongful act or omission of any employee of the Government while acting within the scope of his office or employment, under circumstances where the United States, if a private person, would be liable to the claimant in accordance with the law of the place where the act or omission occurred.

(2) No person convicted of a felony who is incarcerated while awaiting sentencing or while serving a sentence may bring a civil action against the United States or an agency, officer, or employee of the Government, for mental or emotional injury suffered while in custody without a prior showing of physical injury.

(c) The jurisdiction conferred by this section includes jurisdiction of any set-off, counterclaim, or other claim or demand whatever on the part of the United States against any plaintiff commencing an action under this section.

(d) The district courts shall not have jurisdiction under this section of any civil action or claim for a pension.

(e) The district courts shall have original jurisdiction of any civil action against the United States provided in section 6226, 6228(a), 7426, or 7428 (in the case of the United States district court for the District of Columbia) or section 7429 of the Internal Revenue Code of 1986.

(f) The district courts shall have exclusive original jurisdiction of civil actions under section 2409a to quiet title to an estate or interest in real property in which an interest is claimed by the United States.

(g) Subject to the provisions of chapter 179, the district courts of the United States shall have exclusive jurisdiction over any civil action commenced under section 453(2) of title 3, by a covered employee under chapter 5 of such title.

28 U.S.C. § 1359. Parties collusively joined or made

A district court shall not have jurisdiction of a civil action in which any party, by assignment or otherwise, has been improperly or collusively made or joined to invoke the jurisdiction of such court.

28 U.S.C. § 1367. Supplemental Jurisdiction

(a) Except as provided in subsections (b) and (c) or as expressly provided otherwise by Federal statute, in any civil action of which the district courts have original jurisdiction, the district courts shall have supplemental jurisdiction over all other claims that are so related to claims in the action within such original jurisdiction that they form part of the same case or controversy under Article III of the United States Constitution. Such supplemental jurisdiction shall include claims that involve the joinder or intervention of additional parties.

(b) In any civil action of which the district courts have original jurisdiction founded solely on section 1332 of this title, the district courts shall not have supplemental jurisdiction under subsection (a) over claims by plaintiffs against persons made parties under Rule 14, 19, 20, or 24 of the Federal Rules of Civil Procedure, or over claims by persons proposed to be joined as plaintiffs under Rule 19 of such rules, or seeking to intervene as plaintiffs under Rule 24 of such rules, when exercising supplemental jurisdiction over such claims would be inconsistent with the jurisdictional requirements of section 1332.

(c) The district courts may decline to exercise supplemental jurisdiction over a claim under subsection (a) if —

(1) the claim raises a novel or complex issue of State law,

(2) the claim substantially predominates over the claim or claims over which the district court has original jurisdiction,

(3) the district court has dismissed all claims over which it has original jurisdiction, or

(4) in exceptional circumstances, there are other compelling reasons for declining jurisdiction.

(d) The period of limitations for any claim asserted under subsection (a), and for any other claim in the same action that is voluntarily dismissed at the same time as or after the dismissal of the claim under subsection (a), shall be tolled while the claim is pending and for a period of 30 days after it is dismissed unless State law provides for a longer tolling period.

(e) As used in this section, the term "State" includes the District of Columbia, the Commonwealth of Puerto Rico, and any territory or possession of the United States.

28 U.S.C. § 1369. Multiparty, multiforum jurisdiction

(a) In General. — The district courts shall have original jurisdiction of any civil action involving minimal diversity between adverse parties that arises from a single accident, where at least 75 natural persons have died in the accident at a discrete location, if —

(1) a defendant resides in a State and a substantial part of the accident took place in another State or other location, regardless of whether that defendant is also a resident of the State where a substantial part of the accident took place;

(2) any two defendants reside in different States, regardless of whether such defendants are also residents of the same State or States; or

(3) substantial parts of the accident took place in different States.

(b) Limitation of Jurisdiction of District Courts. — The district court shall abstain from hearing any civil action described in subsection (a) in which —

(1) the substantial majority of all plaintiffs are citizens of a single State of which the primary defendants are also citizens; and

(2) the claims asserted will be governed primarily by the laws of that State.

(c) Special Rules and Definitions. — For purposes of this section —

(1) minimal diversity exists between adverse parties if any party is a citizen of a State and any adverse party is a citizen of another State, a citizen or subject of a foreign state, or a foreign state as defined in section 1603(a) of this title;

(2) a corporation is deemed to be a citizen of any State, and a citizen or subject of any foreign state, in which it is incorporated or has its principal place of business, and is deemed to be a resident of any State in which it is incorporated or licensed to do business or is doing business;

(3) the term "injury" means —

(A) physical harm to a natural person; and

(B) physical damage to or destruction of tangible property, but only if physical harm described in subparagraph (A) exists;

(4) the term "accident" means a sudden accident, or a natural event culminating in an accident, that results in death incurred at a discrete location by at least 75 natural persons; and

(5) the term "State" includes the District of Columbia, the Commonwealth of Puerto Rico, and any territory or possession of the United States.

(d) Intervening Parties. — In any action in a district court which is or could have been brought, in whole or in part, under this section, any person with a claim arising from the accident described in subsection (a) shall be permitted to intervene as a party plaintiff in the action, even if that person could not have brought an action in a district court as an original matter.

(e) Notification of Judicial Panel on Multidistrict Litigation. — A district court in which an action under this section is pending shall promptly notify the judicial panel on multidistrict litigation of the pendency of the action.

Chapter 89 — District Courts; Removal of Cases from State Courts

28 U.S.C. § 1441. Removal of civil actions

(a) Generally. — Except as otherwise expressly provided by Act of Congress, any civil action brought in a State court of which the district courts of the United States have original jurisdiction, may be removed by the defendant or the defendants, to the district court of the United States for the district and division embracing the place where such action is pending.

(b) Removal based on diversity of citizenship. — (1) In determining whether a civil action is removable on the basis of the jurisdiction under section 1332(a) of this title, the citizenship of defendants sued under fictitious names shall be disregarded.

(2) A civil action otherwise removable solely on the basis of the jurisdiction under section 1332(a) of this title may not be removed if any of the parties in interest properly joined and served as defendants is a citizen of the State in which such action is brought.

(c) Joinder of Federal law claims and State law claims. — (1) If a civil action includes —

(A) a claim arising under the Constitution, laws, or treaties of the United States (within the meaning of section 1331of this title), and

(B) a claim not within the original or supplemental jurisdiction of the district court or a claim that has been made nonremovable by statute, the entire action may be removed if the action would be removable without the inclusion of the claim described in subparagraph (B).

(2) Upon removal of an action described in paragraph (1), the district court shall sever from the action all claims described in paragraph (1)(B) and shall remand the severed claims to the State court from which the action was removed. Only defendants against whom a claim described in paragraph (1)(A) has been asserted are required to join in or consent to the removal under paragraph (1).

(d) Actions against foreign States. — Any civil action brought in a State court against a foreign state as defined in section 1603(a) of this title may be removed by the foreign state to the district court of the United States for the district and division embracing the place where such action is pending. Upon removal the action shall be tried by the court without jury. Where removal is based upon this subsection, the time limitations of section 1446(b) of this chapter may be enlarged at any time for cause shown.

(e) Multiparty, multiforum jurisdiction.—(1) Notwithstanding the provisions of subsection (b) of this section, a defendant in a civil action in a State court may remove the action to the district court of the United States for the district and division embracing the place where the action is pending if—

(A) the action could have been brought in a United States district court under section 1369 of this title; or

(B) the defendant is a party to an action which is or could have been brought, in whole or in part, under section 1369 in a United States district court and arises from the same accident as the action in State court, even if the action to be removed could not have been brought in a district court as an original matter.

The removal of an action under this subsection shall be made in accordance with section 1446 of this title, except that a notice of removal may also be filed before trial of the action in State court within 30 days after the date on which the defendant first becomes a party to an action under section 1369 in a United States district court that arises from the same accident as the action in State court, or at a later time with leave of the district court.

(2) Whenever an action is removed under this subsection and the district court to which it is removed or transferred under section 1407(j) has made a liability determination requiring further proceedings as to damages, the district court shall remand the action to the State court from which it had been removed for the determination of damages, unless the court finds that, for the convenience of parties and witnesses and in the interest of justice, the action should be retained for the determination of damages.

(3) Any remand under paragraph (2) shall not be effective until 60 days after the district court has issued an order determining liability and has certified its intention to remand the removed action for the determination of damages. An appeal with respect to the liability determination of the district court may be taken during that 60-day period to the court of appeals with appellate jurisdiction over the district court. In the event a party files such an appeal, the remand shall not be effective until the appeal has been finally disposed of. Once the remand has become effective, the liability determination shall not be subject to further review by appeal or otherwise.

(4) Any decision under this subsection concerning remand for the determination of damages shall not be reviewable by appeal or otherwise.

(5) An action removed under this subsection shall be deemed to be an action under section 1369 and an action in which jurisdiction is based on section 1369 of this title for purposes of this section and sections 1407, 1697, and 1785 of this title.

(6) Nothing in this subsection shall restrict the authority of the district court to transfer or dismiss an action on the ground of inconvenient forum.

(f) Derivative removal jurisdiction.—The court to which a civil action is removed under this section is not precluded from hearing and determining any claim in such civil action because the State court from which such civil action is removed did not have jurisdiction over that claim.

28 U.S.C. § 1442. Federal officers or agencies sued or prosecuted

(a) A civil action or criminal prosecution commenced in a State court against any of the following may be removed by them to the district court of the United States for the district and division embracing the place wherein it is pending:

(1) The United States or any agency thereof or any officer (or any person acting under that officer) of the United States or of any agency thereof, sued in an official or individual capacity for any act under color of such office or on account of any right, title or authority claimed under any Act of Congress for the apprehension or punishment of criminals or the collection of the revenue.

(2) A property holder whose title is derived from any such officer, where such action or prosecution affects the validity of any law of the United States.

(3) Any officer of the courts of the United States, for any act under color of office or in the performance of his duties;

(4) Any officer of either House of Congress, for any act in the discharge of his official duty under an order of such House.

(b) A personal action commenced in any State court by an alien against any citizen of a State who is, or at the time the alleged action accrued was, a civil officer of the United States and is a nonresident of such State, wherein jurisdiction is obtained by the State court by personal service of process, may be removed by the defendant to the district court of the United States for the district and division in which the defendant was served with process.

28 U.S.C. § 1443. Civil rights cases

Any of the following civil actions or criminal prosecutions, commenced in a State court may be removed by the defendant to the district court of the United States for the district and division embracing the place wherein it is pending:

(1) Against any person who is denied or cannot enforce in the courts of such State a right under any law providing for the equal civil rights of citizens of the United States, or of all persons within the jurisdiction thereof;

(2) For any act under color of authority derived from any law providing for equal rights, or for refusing to do any act on the ground that it would be inconsistent with such law.

28 U.S.C. § 1445. Nonremovable actions

(a) A civil action in any State court against a railroad or its receivers or trustees, arising under sections 1-4 and 5-10 of the Act of April 22, 1908 (45 U.S.C. 51-54, 55-60), may not be removed to any district court of the United States.

(b) A civil action in any State court against a carrier or its receivers or trustees to recover damages for delay, loss, or injury of shipments, arising under section 11706 or 14706 of title 49, may not be removed to any district court of the United States unless the matter in controversy exceeds $10,000, exclusive of interest and costs.

(c) A civil action in any State court arising under the workmen's compensation laws of such State may not be removed to any district court of the United States.

(d) A civil action in any State court arising under section 40302 of the Violence Against Women Act of 1994 may not be removed to any district court of the United States.

28 U.S.C. § 1446. Procedure for removal of civil actions

(a) Generally.—A defendant or defendants desiring to remove any civil action from a State court shall file in the district court of the United States for the district and division within which such action is pending a notice of removal signed pursuant to Rule 11 of the Federal Rules of Civil Procedure and containing a short and plain statement of the grounds for removal, together with a copy of all process, pleadings, and orders served upon such defendant or defendants in such action.

(b) Requirements; generally.— (1) The notice of removal of a civil action or proceeding shall be filed within 30 days after the receipt by the defendant, through service or otherwise, of a copy of the initial pleading setting forth the claim for relief upon which such action or proceeding is based, or within 30 days after the service of summons upon the defendant if such initial pleading has then been filed in court and is not required to be served on the defendant, whichever period is shorter.

(2)(A) When a civil action is removed solely under section 1441(a), all defendants who have been properly joined and served must join in or consent to the removal of the action.

(B) Each defendant shall have 30 days after receipt by or service on that defendant of the initial pleading or summons described in paragraph (1) to file the notice of removal.

(C) If defendants are served at different times, and a later-served defendant files a notice of removal, any earlier-served defendant may consent to the removal even though that earlier-served defendant did not previously initiate or consent to removal.

(3) Except as provided in subsection (c), if the case stated by the initial pleading is not removable, a notice of removal may be filed within 30 days after receipt by the defendant, through service or otherwise, of a copy of an amended pleading, motion, order or other paper from which it may first be ascertained that the case is one which is or has become removable.

(c) Requirements; removal based on diversity of citizenship.— (1) A case may not be removed under subsection (b)(3) on the basis of jurisdiction conferred by section 1332 more than 1 year after commencement of the action, unless the district court finds that the plaintiff has acted in bad faith in order to prevent a defendant from removing the action.

(2) If removal of a civil action is sought on the basis of the jurisdiction conferred by section 1332(a), the sum demanded in good faith in the initial pleading shall be deemed to be the amount in controversy, except that—

(A) the notice of removal may assert the amount in controversy if the initial pleading seeks—

(i) nonmonetary relief; or

(ii) a money judgment, but the State practice either does not permit demand for a specific sum or permits recovery of damages in excess of the amount demanded; and

(B) removal of the action is proper on the basis of an amount in controversy asserted under subparagraph (A) if the district court finds, by the preponderance of the evidence, that the amount in controversy exceeds the amount specified in section 1332(a).

(3)(A) If the case stated by the initial pleading is not removable solely because the amount in controversy does not exceed the amount specified in section 1332(a), information relating to the amount in controversy in the record of the State proceeding, or in responses to discovery, shall be treated as an "other paper" under subsection (b)(3).

(B) If the notice of removal is filed more than 1 year after commencement of the action and the district court finds that the plaintiff deliberately failed to disclose the actual amount in controversy to prevent removal, that finding shall be deemed bad faith under paragraph (1).

(d) Notice to adverse parties and State court.—Promptly after the filing of such notice of removal of a civil action the defendant or defendants shall give written notice thereof to all adverse parties and shall file a copy of the notice with the clerk of such State court, which shall effect the removal and the State court shall proceed no further unless and until the case is remanded.

(e) Counterclaim in 337 proceeding.—With respect to any counterclaim removed to a district court pursuant to section 337(c) of the Tariff Act of 1930, the district court shall resolve such counterclaim in the same manner as an original complaint under the Federal Rules of Civil Procedure, except that the payment of a filing fee shall not be required in such cases and the counterclaim shall relate back to the date of the original complaint in the proceeding before the International Trade Commission under section 337 of that Act.

[(f) Redesignated (e)]

(g) Where the civil action or criminal prosecution that is removable under section 1442(a) is a proceeding in which a judicial order for testimony or documents is sought or issued or sought to be enforced, the 30-day requirement of subsection (b) of this section and paragraph (1) of section 1455(b) is satisfied if the person or entity desiring to remove the proceeding files the notice of removal not later than 30 days after receiving, through service, notice of any such proceeding.

28 U.S.C. § 1447. Procedure after removal generally

(a) In any case removed from a State court, the district court may issue all necessary orders and process to bring before it all proper parties whether served by process issued by the State court or otherwise.

(b) It may require the removing party to file with its clerk copies of all records and proceedings in such State court or may cause the same to be brought before it by writ of certiorari issued to such State court.

(c) A motion to remand the case on the basis of any defect other than lack of subject matter jurisdiction must be made within 30 days after the filing of the notice of removal under section 1446(a). If at any time before final judgment it appears that the district court lacks subject matter jurisdiction, the case shall be remanded. An order remanding the case may require payment of just costs and any actual expenses, including attorney fees, incurred as a result of the removal. A certified copy of the order of remand shall be mailed by the clerk to the clerk of the State court. The State court may thereupon proceed with such case.

(d) An order remanding a case to the State court from which it was removed is not reviewable on appeal or otherwise, except that an order remanding a case to the State court from which it was removed pursuant to section 1442 or 1443 of this title shall be reviewable by appeal or otherwise.

(e) If after removal the plaintiff seeks to join additional defendants whose joinder would destroy subject matter jurisdiction, the court may deny joinder, or permit joinder and remand the action to the State court.

28 U.S.C. § 1453. Removal of class actions

(a) Definitions.—In this section, the terms "class", "class action", "class certification order", and "class member" shall have the meanings given such terms under section 1332(d)(1).

(b) In General.—A class action may be removed to a district court of the United States in accordance with section 1446 (except that the 1-year limitation under section 1446(b) shall not apply), without regard to whether any defendant is a citizen of the State in which the action is brought, except that such action may be removed by any defendant without the consent of all defendants.

(c) Review of Remand Orders.—

(1) In general.—Section 1447 shall apply to any removal of a case under this section, except that notwithstanding section 1447(d), a court of appeals may accept an appeal from an order of a district court granting or denying a motion to remand a class action to the State court from which it was removed if application is made to the court of appeals not less than 7 days after entry of the order.

(2) Time period for judgment.—If the court of appeals accepts an appeal under paragraph (1), the court shall complete all action on such appeal, including rendering judgment, not later than 60 days after the date on which such appeal was filed, unless an extension is granted under paragraph (3).

(3) Extension of time period.—The court of appeals may grant an extension of the 60-day period described in paragraph (2) if—

(A) all parties to the proceeding agree to such extension, for any period of time; or

(B) such extension is for good cause shown and in the interests of justice, for a period not to exceed 10 days.

(4) Denial of appeal.—If a final judgment on the appeal under paragraph (1) is not issued before the end of the period described in paragraph (2), including any extension under paragraph (3), the appeal shall be denied.

(d) Exception.—This section shall not apply to any class action that solely involves—

(1) a claim concerning a covered security as defined under section 16(f)(3) of the Securities Act of 1933 (15 U.S.C. 78p(f)(3)) and section 28(f)(5)(E) of the Securities Exchange Act of 1934 (15 U.S.C. 78bb(f)(5)(E));

(2) a claim that relates to the internal affairs or governance of a corporation or other form of business enterprise and arises under or by virtue of the laws of the State in which such corporation or business enterprise is incorporated or organized; or

(3) a claim that relates to the rights, duties (including fiduciary duties), and obligations relating to or created by or pursuant to any security (as defined

under section 2(a)(1) of the Securities Act of 1933 (15 U.S.C. 77b(a)(1)) and the regulations issued thereunder).

Chapter 111 — General Provisions

28 U.S.C. § 1651. Writs

(a) The Supreme Court and all courts established by Act of Congress may issue all writs necessary or appropriate in aid of their respective jurisdictions and agreeable to the usages and principles of law.

(b) An alternative writ or rule nisi may be issued by a justice or judge of a court which has jurisdiction.

28 U.S.C. § 1652. State laws as rules of decision

The laws of the several states, except where the Constitution or treaties of the United States or Acts of Congress otherwise require or provide, shall be regarded as rules of decision in civil actions in the courts of the United States, in cases where they apply.

Chapter 115 — Evidence; Documentary

28 U.S.C. § 1738. State and Territorial statutes and judicial proceedings; full faith and credit

The Acts of the legislature of any State, Territory, or Possession of the United States, or copies thereof, shall be authenticated by affixing the seal of such State, Territory or Possession thereto.

The records and judicial proceedings of any court of any such State, Territory or Possession, or copies thereof, shall be proved or admitted in other courts within the United States and its Territories and Possessions by the attestation of the clerk and seal of the court annexed, if a seal exists, together with a certificate of a judge of the court that the said attestation is in proper form.

Such Acts, records and judicial proceedings or copies thereof, so authenticated, shall have the same full faith and credit in every court within the United States and its Territories and Possessions as they have by law or usage in the courts of such State, Territory or Possession from which they are taken.

Chapter 131 — Rules of Courts

28 U.S.C. § 2101. Rule-making power generally

(a) The Supreme Court and all courts established by Act of Congress may from time to time prescribe rules for the conduct of their business. Such rules shall be consistent with Acts of Congress and rules of practice and procedure prescribed under section 2072 of this title.

(b) Any rule prescribed by a court, other than the Supreme Court, under subsection (a) shall be prescribed only after giving appropriate public notice and an opportunity for comment. Such rule shall take effect upon the date specified by the prescribing court and shall have such effect on pending proceedings as the prescribing court may order.

(c)(1) A rule of a district court prescribed under subsection (a) shall remain in effect unless modified or abrogated by the judicial council of the relevant circuit.

(2) Any other rule prescribed by a court other than the Supreme Court under subsection (a) shall remain in effect unless modified or abrogated by the Judicial Conference.

(d) Copies of rules prescribed under subsection (a) by a district court shall be furnished to the judicial council, and copies of all rules prescribed by a court other than the Supreme Court under subsection (a) shall be furnished to the Director of the Administrative Office of the United States Courts and made available to the public.

(e) If the prescribing court determines that there is an immediate need for a rule, such court may proceed under this section without public notice and opportunity for comment, but such court shall promptly thereafter afford such notice and opportunity for comment.

(f) No rule may be prescribed by a district court other than under this section.

28 U.S.C. § 2072. Rules of procedure and evidence; power to prescribe

(a) The Supreme Court shall have the power to prescribe general rules of practice and procedure and rules of evidence for cases in the United States district courts (including proceedings before magistrate judges thereof) and courts of appeals.

(b) Such rules shall not abridge, enlarge or modify any substantive right. All laws in conflict with such rules shall be of no further force or effect after such rules have taken effect.

(c) Such rules may define when *a* ruling of a district court is final for the purposes of appeal under section 1291 of this title.

28 U.S.C. § 2073. Rule of procedure and evidence; method of prescribing

(a)(1) The Judicial Conference shall prescribe and publish the procedures for the consideration of proposed rules under this section.

(2) The Judicial Conference may authorize the appointment of committees to assist the Conference by recommending rules to be prescribed under sections 2072 and 2075 of this title. Each such committee shall consist of members of the bench and the professional bar, and trial and appellate judges.

(b) The Judicial Conference shall authorize the appointment of a standing committee on rules of practice, procedure, and evidence under subsection (a) of this section. Such standing committee shall review each recommendation of any other committees so appointed and recommend to the Judicial Conference rules of practice, procedure, and evidence and such changes in rules proposed by a committee appointed under subsection (a)(2) of this section as may be necessary to maintain consistency and otherwise promote the interest of justice.

(c)(1) Each meeting for the transaction of business under this chapter by any committee appointed under this section shall be open to the public, except when the committee so meeting, in open session and with a majority present, determines that it is in the public interest that all or part of the remainder of the meeting on that day shall be closed to the public, and states the reason for so closing the meeting. Minutes of each meeting for the transaction of business under this chapter shall be maintained by the committee and made available to the public, except that any portion of such minutes, relating to a closed meeting and made available to the public, may contain such deletions as may be necessary to avoid frustrating the purposes of closing the meeting.

(2) Any meeting for the transaction of business under this chapter, by a committee appointed under this section, shall be preceded by sufficient notice to enable all interested persons to attend.

(d) In making a recommendation under this section or under section 2072 or 2075, the body making that recommendation shall provide a proposed rule, an explanatory note on the rule, and a written report explaining the body's action, including any minority or other separate views.

(e) Failure to comply with this section does not invalidate a rule prescribed under section 2072 or 2075 of this title.

28 U.S.C. § 2074. Rules of procedure and evidence; submission to Congress; effective date

(a) The Supreme Court shall transmit to the Congress not later than May 1 of the year in which a rule prescribed under section 2072 is to become effective a copy of the proposed rule. Such rule shall take effect no earlier than December 1 of the year in which such rule is so transmitted unless otherwise provided by law. The Supreme Court may fix the extent such rule shall apply to proceedings then pending, except that the Supreme Court shall not require the application of such rule to further proceedings then pending to the extent that, in the opinion of the court in which such proceedings are pending, the application of such rule in such proceedings would not be feasible or would work injustice, in which event the former rule applies.

(b) Any such rule creating, abolishing, or modifying an evidentiary privilege shall have no force or effect unless approved by Act of Congress.

Chapter 133 — Review — Miscellaneous Provisions

28 U.S.C. § 2101. Supreme Court; time for appeal or certiorari; docketing; stay

(a) A direct appeal to the Supreme Court from any decision under section 1253 of this title, holding unconstitutional in whole or in part, any Act of Congress, shall be taken within thirty days after the entry of the interlocutory or final order, judgment or decree. The record shall be made up and the case docketed within sixty days from the time such appeal is taken under rules prescribed by the Supreme Court.

(b) Any other direct appeal to the Supreme Court which is authorized by law, from a decision of a district court in any civil action, suit or proceeding, shall be taken within thirty days from the judgment, order or decree, appealed from, if interlocutory, and within sixty days if final.

(c) Any other appeal or any writ of certiorari intended to bring any judgment or decree in a civil action, suit or proceeding before the Supreme Court for review shall be taken or applied for within ninety days after the entry of such judgment or decree. A justice of the Supreme Court, for good cause shown, may extend the time for applying for a writ of certiorari for a period not exceeding sixty days.

(d) The time for appeal or application for a writ of certiorari to review the judgment of a State court in a criminal case shall be as prescribed by rules of the Supreme Court.

(e) An application to the Supreme Court for a writ of certiorari to review a case before judgment has been rendered in the court of appeals may be made at any time before judgment.

(f) In any case in which the final judgment or decree of any court is subject to review by the Supreme Court on writ of certiorari, the execution and enforcement of such judgment or decree may be stayed for a reasonable time to enable the party aggrieved to obtain a writ of certiorari from the Supreme Court. The stay may be granted by a judge of the court rendering the judgment or decree or by a justice of the Supreme Court, and may be conditioned on the giving of security, approved by such judge or justice, that if the aggrieved party fails to make application for such writ within the period allotted therefore, or fails to obtain an order granting his application, or fails to make his plea good in the Supreme Court, he shall answer for all damages and costs which the other party may sustain by reason of the stay.

(g) The time for application for a writ of certiorari to review a decision of the United States Court of Appeals for the Armed Forces shall be as prescribed by rules of the Supreme Court.

Chapter 151 — Declaratory Judgments

28 U.S.C. § 2201. Creation of remedy

(a) In a case of actual controversy within its jurisdiction, except with respect to Federal taxes other than actions brought under section 7428 of the Internal Revenue Code of 1986, a proceeding under section 505 or 1146 of title 11, or in any civil action involving an antidumping or countervailing duty proceeding regarding a class or kind of merchandise of a free trade area country (as defined in section 516A(f)(10) of the Tariff Act of 1930), as determined by the administering authority, any court of the United States, upon the filing of an appropriate pleading, may declare the rights and other legal relations of any interested party seeking such declaration, whether or not further relief is or could be sought. Any such declaration shall have the force and effect of a final judgment or decree and shall be reviewable as such.

(b) For limitations on actions brought with respect to drug patents see section 505 or 512 of the Federal Food, Drug, and Cosmetic Act.

Chapter 153 — Habeas Corpus

28 U.S.C. § 2241. Power to grant writ

(a) Writs of habeas corpus may be granted by the Supreme Court, any justice thereof, the district courts and any circuit judge within their respective jurisdictions. The order of a circuit judge shall be entered in the records of the district court of the district wherein the restraint complained of is had.

(b) The Supreme Court, any justice thereof, and any circuit judge may decline to entertain an application for a writ of habeas corpus and may transfer the application for hearing and determination to the district court having jurisdiction to entertain it.

(c) The writ of habeas corpus shall not extend to a prisoner unless—

(1) He is in custody under or by color of the authority of the United States or is committed for trial before some court thereof; or

(2) He is in custody for an act done or omitted in pursuance of an Act of Congress, or an order, process, judgment or decree of a court or judge of the United States; or

(3) He is in custody in violation of the Constitution or laws or treaties of the United States; or

(4) He, being a citizen of a foreign state and domiciled therein is in custody for an act done or omitted under any alleged right, title, authority, privilege, protection, or exemption claimed under the commission, order or sanction of any foreign state, or under color thereof, the validity and effect of which depend upon the law of nations; or

(5) It is necessary to bring him into court to testify or for trial.

(d) Where an application for a writ of habeas corpus is made by a person in custody under the judgment and sentence of a State court of a State which contains two or more Federal judicial districts, the application may be filed in the district court for the district wherein such person is in custody or in the district court for the district within which the State court was held which convicted and sentenced him and each of such district courts shall have concurrent jurisdiction to entertain the application. The district court for the district wherein such an application is filed in the exercise of its discretion and in furtherance of justice may transfer the application to the other district court for hearing and determination.

(e)(1) No court, justice, or judge shall have jurisdiction to hear or consider an application for a writ of habeas corpus filed by or on behalf of an alien detained by the United States who has been determined by the United States to have been properly detained as an enemy combatant or is awaiting such determination.

(2) Except as provided in paragraphs (2) and (3) of section 1005(e) of the Detainee Treatment Act of 2005 (10 U.S.C. 801 note), no court, justice, or judge shall have jurisdiction to hear or consider any other action against the United States or its agents relating to any aspect of the detention, transfer, treatment, trial, or conditions of confinement of an alien who is or was detained by the United States and has been determined by the United States to have been properly detained as an enemy combatant or is awaiting such determination.

28 U.S.C. § 2242. Application

Application for a writ of habeas corpus shall be in writing signed and verified by the person for whose relief it is intended or by someone acting in his behalf.

It shall allege the facts concerning the applicant's commitment or detention, the name of the person who has custody over him and by virtue of what claim or authority, if known.

It may be amended or supplemented as provided in the rules of procedure applicable to civil actions.

If addressed to the Supreme Court, a justice thereof or a circuit judge it shall state the reasons for not making application to the district court of the district in which the applicant is held.

28 U.S.C. § 2243. Issuance of writ; return; hearing; decision

A court, justice or judge entertaining an application for a writ of habeas corpus shall forthwith award the writ or issue an order directing the respondent to show cause why the writ should not be granted, unless it appears from the application that the applicant or person detained is not entitled thereto.

The writ, or order to show cause shall be directed to the person having custody of the person detained. It shall be returned within three days unless for good cause additional time, not exceeding twenty days, is allowed.

The person to whom the writ or order is directed shall make a return certifying the true cause of the detention.

When the writ or order is returned a day shall be set for hearing, not more than five days after the return unless for good cause additional time is allowed.

Unless the application for the writ and the return present only issues of law the person to whom the writ is directed shall be required to produce at the hearing the body of the person detained.

The applicant or the person detained may, under oath, deny any of the facts set forth in the return or allege any other material facts.

The return and all suggestions made against it may be amended, by leave of court, before or after being filed.

The court shall summarily hear and determine the facts, and dispose of the matter as law and justice require.

28 U.S.C. § 2244. Finality of determination

(a) No circuit or district judge shall be required to entertain an application for *a* writ of habeas corpus to inquire into the detention of a person pursuant to a judgment of a court of the United States if it appears that the legality of such detention has been determined by a judge or court of the United States on a prior application for a writ of habeas corpus, except as provided in section 2255.

(b)(1) A claim presented in a second or successive habeas corpus application under section 2254 that was presented in a prior application shall be dismissed.

(2) A claim presented in a second or successive habeas corpus application under section 2254 that was not presented in a prior application shall be dismissed unless—

(A) the applicant shows that the claim relies on a new rule of constitutional law, made retroactive to cases on collateral review by the Supreme Court, that was previously unavailable; or

(B)(i) the factual predicate for the claim could not have been discovered previously through the exercise of due diligence; and

(ii) the facts underlying the claim, if proven and viewed in light of the evidence as a whole, would be sufficient to establish by clear and convincing evidence that, but for constitutional error, no reasonable factfinder would have found the applicant guilty of the underlying offense.

(3) (A) Before a second or successive application permitted by this section is filed in the district court, the applicant shall move in the appropriate court of appeals for an order authorizing the district court to consider the application.

(B) A motion in the court of appeals for an order authorizing the district court to consider a second or successive application shall be determined by a three-judge panel of the court of appeals.

(C) The court of appeals may authorize the filing of a second or successive application only if it determines that the application makes a prima facie showing that the application satisfies the requirements of this subsection.

(D) The court of appeals shall grant or deny the authorization to file a second or successive application not later than 30 days after the filing of the motion.

(E) The grant or denial of an authorization by a court of appeals to file a second or successive application shall not be appealable and shall not be the subject of a petition for rehearing or for a writ of certiorari.

(4) A district court shall dismiss any claim presented in a second or successive application that the court of appeals has authorized to be filed unless the applicant shows that the claim satisfies the requirements of this section.

(c) In a habeas corpus proceeding brought in behalf of a person in custody pursuant to the judgment of a State court, a prior judgment of the Supreme Court of the United States on an appeal or review by a writ of certiorari at the instance of the prisoner of the decision of such State court, shall be conclusive as to all issues of fact or law with respect to an asserted denial of a Federal right which constitutes ground for discharge in a habeas corpus proceeding, actually adjudicated by the Supreme Court therein, unless the applicant for the writ of habeas corpus shall plead and the court shall find the existence of a material and controlling fact which did not appear in the record of the proceeding in the Supreme Court and the court shall further find that the applicant for the writ of habeas corpus could not have caused such fact to appear in such record by the exercise of reasonable diligence.

(d) (1) A 1-year period of limitation shall apply to an application for a writ of habeas corpus by a person in custody pursuant to the judgment of a State court. The limitation period shall run from the latest of—

(A) the date on which the judgment became final by the conclusion of direct review or the expiration of the time for seeking such review;

(B) the date on which the impediment to filing an application created by State action in violation of the Constitution or laws of the United States is removed, if the applicant was prevented from filing by such State action;

(C) the date on which the constitutional right asserted was initially recognized by the Supreme Court, if the right has been newly recognized by the Supreme Court and made retroactively applicable to cases on collateral review; or

(D) the date on which the factual predicate of the claim or claims presented could have been discovered through the exercise of due diligence.

(2) The time during which a properly filed application for State post-conviction or other collateral review with respect to the pertinent judgment or claim is pending shall not be counted toward any period of limitation under this subsection.

28 U.S.C. § 2248. Return or answer; conclusiveness

The allegations of a return to the writ of habeas corpus or of an answer to an order to show cause in a habeas corpus proceeding, if not traversed, shall be accepted as true except to the extent that the judge finds from the evidence that they are not true.

28 U.S.C. § 2253. Appeals

(a) In a habeas corpus proceeding or a proceeding under section 2255 before a district judge, the final order shall be subject to review, on appeal, by the court of appeals for the circuit in which the proceeding is held.

(b) There shall be no right of appeal from a final order in a proceeding to test the validity of a warrant to remove to another district or place for commitment or trial a person charged with a criminal offense against the United States, or to test the validity of such person's detention pending removal proceedings.

(c) (1) Unless a circuit justice or judge issues a certificate of appealability, an appeal may not be taken to the court of appeals from—

(A) the final order in a habeas corpus proceeding in which the detention complained of arises out of process issued by a State court; or

(B) the final order in a proceeding under section 2255.

(2) A certificate of appealability may issue under paragraph (1) only if the applicant has made a substantial showing of the denial of a constitutional right.

(3) The certificate of appealability under paragraph (1) shall indicate which specific issue or issues satisfy the showing required by paragraph (2).

28 U.S.C. § 2254. State custody; remedies in State courts

(a) The Supreme Court, a Justice thereof, a circuit judge, or a district court shall entertain an application for a writ of habeas corpus in behalf of a person in custody pursuant to the judgment of a State court only on the ground that he is in custody in violation of the Constitution or laws or treaties of the United States.

(b) (1) An application for a writ of habeas corpus on behalf of a person in custody pursuant to the judgment of a State court shall not be granted unless it appears that—

(A) the applicant has exhausted the remedies available in the courts of the State; or

(B) (i) there is an absence of available State corrective process; or

(ii) circumstances exist that render such process ineffective to protect the rights of the applicant.

(2) An application for a writ of habeas corpus may be denied on the merits, notwithstanding the failure of the applicant to exhaust the remedies available in the courts of the State.

(3) A State shall not be deemed to have waived the exhaustion requirement or be estopped from reliance upon the requirement unless the State, through counsel, expressly waives the requirement.

(c) An applicant shall not be deemed to have exhausted the remedies available in the courts of the State, within the meaning of this section, if he has the right under the law of the State to raise, by any available procedure, the question presented.

(d) An application for a writ of habeas corpus on behalf of a person in custody pursuant to the judgment of a State court shall not be granted with respect to any claim that was adjudicated on the merits in State court proceedings unless the adjudication of the claim—

(1) resulted in a decision that was contrary to, or involved an unreasonable application of, clearly established Federal law, as determined by the Supreme Court of the United States; or

(2) resulted in a decision that was based on an unreasonable determination of the facts in light of the evidence presented in the State court proceeding.

(e)(1) In a proceeding instituted by an application for a writ of habeas corpus by a person in custody pursuant to the judgment of a State court, a determination of a factual issue made by a State court shall be presumed to be correct. The applicant shall have the burden of rebutting the presumption of correctness by clear and convincing evidence.

(2) If the applicant has failed to develop the factual basis of a claim in State court proceedings, the court shall not hold an evidentiary hearing on the claim unless the applicant shows that—

(A) the claim relies on—

(i) a new rule of constitutional law, made retroactive to cases on collateral review by the Supreme Court, that was previously unavailable; or

(ii) a factual predicate that could not have been previously discovered through the exercise of due diligence; and

(B) the facts underlying the claim would be sufficient to establish by clear and convincing evidence that but for constitutional error, no reasonable factfinder would have found the applicant guilty of the underlying offense.

(f) If the applicant challenges the sufficiency of the evidence adduced in such State court proceeding to support the State court's determination of a factual issue made therein, the applicant, if able, shall produce that part of the record pertinent to a determination of the sufficiency of the evidence to support such determination. If the applicant, because of indigency or other reason is unable to produce such part of the record, then the State shall produce such part of the record and the Federal court shall direct the State to do so by order directed to an appropriate State official. If the State cannot provide such pertinent part of the record, then the court shall determine under the existing facts and circumstances what weight shall be given to the State court's factual determination.

(g) A copy of the official records of the State court, duly certified by the clerk of such court to be a true and correct copy of a finding, judicial opinion, or other reliable written indicia showing such a factual determination by the State court shall be admissible in the Federal court proceeding.

(h) Except as provided in section 408 of the Controlled Substances Act, in all proceedings brought under this section, and any subsequent proceedings on review, the court may appoint counsel for an applicant who is or becomes financially unable to afford counsel, except as provided by ***a*** rule promulgated by the Supreme Court pursuant to statutory authority. Appointment of counsel under this section shall be governed by section 3006A of title 18.

(i) The ineffectiveness or incompetence of counsel during Federal or State collateral post-conviction proceedings shall not be a ground for relief in a proceeding arising under section 2254.

Chapter 155 — Injunctions; Three-Judge Courts

28 U.S.C. § 2283. Stay of State court proceedings

A court of the United States may not grant an injunction to stay proceedings in a State court except as expressly authorized by Act of Congress, or where necessary in aid of its jurisdiction, or to protect or effectuate its judgments.

Chapter 171 — Torts Claims Procedure

28 U.S.C. § 2674. Liability of United States

The United States shall be liable, respecting the provisions of this title relating to tort claims, in the same manner and to the same extent as a private individual under like circumstances, but shall not be liable for interest prior to judgment or for punitive damages.

If, however, in any case wherein death was caused, the law of the place where the act or omission complained of occurred provides, or has been construed to provide, for damages only punitive in nature, the United States shall be liable for actual or compensatory damages, measured by the pecuniary injuries resulting from such death to the persons respectively, for whose benefit the action was brought, in lieu thereof.

With respect to any claim under this chapter, the United States shall be entitled to assert any defense based upon judicial or legislative immunity which otherwise would have been available to the employee of the United States whose act or omission gave rise to the claim, as well as any other defenses to which the United States is entitled.

With respect to any claim to which this section applies, the Tennessee Valley Authority shall be entitled to assert any defense which otherwise would have been available to the employee based upon judicial or legislative immunity, which otherwise would have been available to the employee of the Tennessee Valley Authority whose act or omission gave rise to the claim as well as any other defenses to which the Tennessee Valley Authority is entitled under this chapter.

28 U.S.C. § 2679. Exclusiveness of remedy

(a) The authority of any federal agency to sue and be sued in its own name shall not be construed to authorize suits against such federal agency on claims which are cognizable under section 1346(b) of this title, and the remedies provided by this title in such cases shall be exclusive.

(b)(1) The remedy against the United States provided by sections 1346(b) and 2672 of this title for injury or loss of property, or personal injury or death arising or resulting from the negligent or wrongful act or omission of any employee of the Government while acting within the scope of his office or employment is exclusive of any other civil action or proceeding for money damages by reason of the same subject matter against the employee whose act or omission gave rise to the claim or against the estate of such employee. Any other civil action or proceeding for money damages arising out of or relating to the same subject matter against the employee or the employee's estate is precluded without regard to when the act or omission occurred.

(2) Paragraph (1) does not extend or apply to a civil action against an employee of the Government—

(A) which is brought for a violation of the Constitution of the United States, or

(B) which is brought for a violation of a statute of the United States under which such action against an individual is otherwise authorized.

(c) The Attorney General shall defend any civil action or proceeding brought in any court against any employee of the Government or his estate for any such damage or injury. The employee against whom such civil action or proceeding is brought shall deliver within such time after date of service or knowledge of service as determined by the Attorney General, all process served upon him or an attested true copy thereof to his immediate superior or to whomever was designated by the head of his department to receive such papers and such person shall promptly furnish copies of the pleadings and process therein to the United States attorney for the district embracing the place wherein the proceeding is brought, to the Attorney General, and to the head of his employing Federal agency.

(d)(1) Upon certification by the Attorney General that the defendant employee was acting within the scope of his office or employment at the time of the incident out of which the claim arose, any civil action or proceeding commenced upon such claim in a United States district court shall be deemed an action against the United States under the provisions of this title and all references thereto, and the United States shall be substituted as the party defendant.

(2) Upon certification by the Attorney General that the defendant employee was acting within the scope of his office or employment at the time of the incident out of which the claim arose, any civil action or proceeding commenced upon such claim in a State court shall be removed without bond at any time before trial by the Attorney General to the district court of the United States for the district and division embracing the place in which the action or proceeding is pending. Such action or proceeding shall be deemed to be an action or proceeding brought against the United States under the provisions of this title and all references thereto, and the United States shall be substituted as the party defendant. This certification of the Attorney General shall conclusively establish scope of office or employment for purposes of removal.

(3) In the event that the Attorney General has refused to certify scope of office or employment under this section, the employee may at any time before trial petition the court to find and certify that the employee was acting within the scope of his office or employment. Upon such certification by the court, such action or proceeding shall be deemed to be an action or proceeding brought against the United States under the provisions of this title and all references thereto, and the United States shall be substituted as the party defendant. A copy of the petition shall be served upon the United States in accordance with the provisions of Rule 4(d)(4) of the Federal Rules of Civil Procedure. In the event the petition is filed in a civil action or proceeding pending in a State court, the action or proceeding may be removed without bond by the Attorney General to the district court of the United States for the district and division embracing the place in which it is pending. If, in considering the petition, the district court determines that the employee was not acting within the scope of his office or employment, the action or proceeding shall be remanded to the State court.

(4) Upon certification, any action or proceeding subject to paragraph (1), (2), or (3) shall proceed in the same manner as any action against the United States filed pursuant to section 1346(b) of this title and shall be subject to the limitations and exceptions applicable to those actions.

(5) Whenever an action or proceeding in which the United States is substituted as the party defendant under this subsection is dismissed for failure first to present a claim pursuant to section 2675(a) of this title, such a claim shall be deemed to be timely presented under section 2401(b) of this title if—

(A) the claim would have been timely had it been filed on the date the underlying civil action was commenced, and

(B) the claim is presented to the appropriate Federal agency within 60 days after dismissal of the civil action.

(e) The Attorney General may compromise or settle any claim asserted in such civil action or proceeding in the manner provided in section 2677, and with the same effect.

SELECTED PROVISIONS OF TITLE 42 OF THE UNITED STATES CODE

Chapter 21 — Civil Rights

42 U.S.C. § 1981. Equal rights under law

(a) Statement of equal rights: All persons within the jurisdiction of the United States shall have the same right in every State and Territory to make and enforce contracts, to sue, be parties, give evidence, and to the full and equal benefit of all laws and proceedings for the security of persons and property as is enjoyed by white citizens, and shall be subject to like punishment, pains, penalties, taxes, licenses, and exactions of every kind, and to no other.

(b) "Make and enforce contracts" defined: For purposes of this section, the term "make and enforce contracts" includes the making, performance, modification, and termination of contracts, and the enjoyment of all benefits, privileges, terms, and conditions of the contractual relationship.

(c) Protection against impairment: The rights protected by this section are protected against impairment by nongovernmental discrimination and impairment under color of State law.

42 U.S.C. § 1982. Property rights of citizens

All citizens of the United States shall have the same right, in every State and Territory, as is enjoyed by white citizens thereof to inherit, purchase, lease, sell, hold, and convey real and personal property.

42 U.S.C. § 1983. Civil action for deprivation of rights

Every person who, under color of any statute, ordinance, regulation, custom, or usage, of any State or Territory or the District of Columbia, subjects, or causes to be subjected, any citizen of the United States or other person within the jurisdiction thereof to the deprivation of any rights, privileges, or immunities secured by the Constitution and laws, shall be liable to the party injured in an action at law, suit in equity, or other proper proceeding for redress, except that in any action brought against a judicial officer for an act or omission taken in such officer's judicial capacity, injunctive relief shall not be granted unless a declaratory decree was violated or declaratory relief was unavailable. For the purposes of this section, any Act of Congress applicable exclusively to the District of Columbia shall be considered to be a statute of the District of Columbia.

42 U.S.C. § 1985. Conspiracy to interfere with civil rights

(1) Preventing officer from performing duties: If two or more persons in any State or Territory conspire to prevent, by force, intimidation, or threat, any person from accepting or holding any office, trust, or place of confidence under the United States, or from discharging any duties thereof; or to induce by like means any officer of the United States to leave any State, district, or place, where his duties as an officer are required to be performed, or to injure him in his person or property on account of his lawful discharge of the duties of his office, or while engaged in the lawful discharge thereof, or to injure his property so as to molest, interrupt, hinder, or impede him in the discharge of his official duties;

(2) Obstructing justice; intimidating party, witness, or juror: If two or more persons in any State or Territory conspire to deter, by force, intimidation, or threat, any party or witness in any court of the United States from attending such court, or from testifying to any matter pending therein, freely, fully, and truthfully, or to injure such party or witness in his person or property on account of his having so attended or testified, or to influence the verdict, presentment, or indictment of any grand or petit juror in any such court, or to injure such juror in his person or property on account of any verdict, presentment, or indictment lawfully assented to by him, or of his being or having been such juror; or if two or more persons conspire for the purpose of impeding, hindering, obstructing, or defeating, in any manner, the due course of justice in any State or Territory, with intent to deny to any citizen the equal protection of the laws, or to injure him or his property for lawfully enforcing, or attempting to enforce, the right of any person, or class of persons, to the equal protection of the laws;

(3) Depriving persons of rights or privileges: If two or more persons in any State or Territory conspire or go in disguise on the highway or on the premises of another, for the purpose of depriving, either directly or indirectly, any person or class of persons of the equal protection of the laws, or of equal privileges and immunities under the laws; or for the purpose of preventing or hindering the constituted authorities of any State or Territory from giving or securing to all persons within such State or Territory the equal protection of the laws; or if two or more persons conspire to prevent by force, intimidation, or threat, any citizen who is lawfully entitled to vote, from giving his support or advocacy in a legal manner, toward or in favor of the election of any lawfully qualified person as an elector for President or Vice President, or as a Member of Congress of the United States; or to injure any citizen in person or property on account of such support or advocacy; in any case of conspiracy set forth in this section, if one or more persons engaged therein do, or cause to be done, any act in furtherance of the object of such conspiracy, whereby another is injured in his person or property, or deprived of having and exercising any right or privilege

of a citizen of the United States, the party so injured or deprived may have an action for the recovery of damages occasioned by such injury or deprivation, against any one or more of the conspirators.

42 U.S.C. § 1988. Proceedings in vindication of civil rights

(a) Applicability of statutory and common law

The jurisdiction in civil and criminal matters conferred on the district courts by the provisions of titles 13, 24, and 70 of the Revised Statutes for the protection of all persons in the United States in their civil rights, and for their vindication, shall be exercised and enforced in conformity with the laws of the United States, so far as such laws are suitable to carry the same into effect; but in all cases where they are not adapted to the object, or are deficient in the provisions necessary to furnish suitable remedies and punish offenses against law, the common law, as modified and changed by the constitution and statutes of the State wherein the court having jurisdiction of such civil or criminal cause is held, so far as the same is not inconsistent with the Constitution and laws of the United States, shall be extended to and govern the said courts in the trial and disposition of the cause, and, if it is of a criminal nature, in the infliction of punishment on the party found guilty.

(b) Attorney's fees

In any action or proceeding to enforce a provision of sections 1981, 1981a, 1982, 1983, 1985, and 1986 of this title, title IX of Public Law 92-318 [20 U.S.C. 1681 et seq.], the Religious Freedom Restoration Act of 1993 [42 U.S.C. 2000bb et seq.], the Religious Land Use and Institutionalized Persons Act of 2000 [42 U.S.C.2000cc et seq.], title VI of the Civil Rights Act of 1964 [42 U.S.C. 2000d et seq.], or section 13981 of this title, the court, in its discretion, may allow the prevailing party, other than the United States, a reasonable attorney's fee as part of the costs, except that in any action brought against a judicial officer for an act or omission taken in such officer's judicial capacity such officer shall not be held liable for any costs, including attorney's fees, unless such action was clearly in excess of such officer's jurisdiction.

(c) Expert fees

In awarding an attorney's fee under subsection (b) of this section in any action or proceeding to enforce a provision of section 1981 or 1981a of this title, the court, in its discretion, may include expert fees as part of the attorney's fee.

TABLE OF CASES

Principal cases appear in italics.

INDEX